ANANYA

A PORTRAIT OF INDIA

Natyasaraswati, Belur (Hoysala)

The Association of Indians in America | New York

ANANYA

A PORTRAIT OF INDIA

Edited by

S. N. Sridhar
Professor of Linguistics
Director, Center for India Studies
State University of New York at Stony Brook

Nirmal K. Mattoo
National President,
The Association of Indians in America

The text of this book is composed in Garamond.
Composition by Ashu M. Patel.
Book Design by Ashu M. Patel.

First Edition

Library of Congress Cataloging-in-Publication Data
Sridhar, S. N. and Nirmal K. Mattoo
Ananya: A Portrait of India / by S. N. Sridhar and Nirmal K. Mattoo—1st. ed.

ISBN 0-9659771-1-0

The Association of Indians in America, 385 Seneca Avenue, Ridgewood, Queens, NY 11385
Phone: (718) 545-3617 / Fax: (516) 671-3601

In Celebration of the
50th Anniversary of India's Independence.
August 15, 1997.

अनन्य

a·na·nya (a′na nya), adj.

1. like no other 2. incomparable 3. unique

Contents

Figures

Diagrams

Tables

Plates

Plate 29. Female bust, Gupta Period, 6th Century C.E., Gwalior.
Plate 30. Karttikeya, Gupta Period.
Plate 31. Buddha, Gupta Period, Sarnath Stlye, 4th Century C.E.
Plate 32. Charminar, Hyderabad, 16th Century C.E.
Plate 33. Taj Mahal, Agra, 17th Century C.E.
Plate 34. Golgumbaz Mausoleum, Bijapur, 17th Century C.E.
Plate 35. Aiyanar on an Elephant, Thogur, 16th Century C.E.

Illustration Credits

The publishers gratefully acknowledge the help of many individuals and institutions for their assistance in collecting the illustrations for this volume. In particular, thanks to R.C. Sharma, Nalini Rao, and Robert Arnette for his generosity in permitting us to use photographs from his India Unveiled (Atman Press, Columbia, GA, 1996).

Every effort has been made to obtain permission to use copyright materials; the publishers apologize for any errors and omissions and would welcome these being brought to their attention.

Government of India, 14, 16, 17, 20, 21, 35, 45,
Bharat Kala Bhavan, Varanasi, 46,
Cleveland Museum of Art, 45,
Kishangarh Darbar, Rajasthan, plate, Radha
Robert Arnett, 19, 32, 33, 50,
APA Productions (HK), Ltd., 32, 34,
National Museum, New Delhi, 30,
Patna Museum, Plate 9
Bharat Ramamrutham, 22
George Michell, 23

Pronunciation

We have tried to walk a middle line between convenience and accuracy in indicating the pronunciation of Indian words. We have used diacritics where pronunciation is important for the subject matter, and used regular Romanization where exact pronunciation is not crucial. Wherever titles of books are given in italics, diacritics are not used.

The following conventions are used: A dot under a letter suggests that it is a retroflex consonant, as in ṭ, ḍ, ḷ, ṣ, except in the case of [ṃ], where it stands for a syllabic nasal, and [ṛ] which indicates the Sanskrit sound as in the first sound of words like the Rig Veda. [ś] stands for the first sound in "shirt" and [č] is the first sound in "choose." A line above a vowel letter [ā, ē, ī, ō] indicates a long vowel, as in Italian.

In Tamil, [ṟ] stands for a trilled alveolar sound as in "borrow;" when it follows the n sound, it is pronounced [ndr] as in "kindred;" and it occurs as [ṟṟ] it is pronounced [tr] as in "metro.

A single [ṭ] is pronounced as a [ē] between two vowels, and a double {22] is pronounced as in "letter."

[ṉ] is an alveolar sound as in the last sound of "man."

ACKNOWLEDGMENTS

Grateful acknowledgements are made to the following for permission to reproduce copyrighted material: Robert Arnett for color illustrations from Robert Arnett's *India Unveiled* (Atman Press, Columbus, Georgia, 1996); Kavyalaya Publishers, Mysore, for M. Hiriyanna's "The Upanishads" and "Bhagavadgita" from his book, *Outlines of Indian Philosophy,* 48-83, and 116-132); Johns Hopkins University Press for an earlier version of Robert Hardgrave, Jr.'s "India: The Dilemmas of Diversity" in *The Journal of Democracy*, Vol. 4 (Oct 1993), pp. 54-68; Princeton University Press for Alan Roland's "The Spiritual Self in Indian Psychology," from *In Search of Self in India and Japan* (1989); *Daedalus*, journal of The American Academy of Arts and Sciences for Girish Karnad's "Theater in India," from the issue entitled "Another India," ; Sangeet Natak Akademi, New Delhi, for an earlier version of R. Satyanarayana's "Karnataka Music: A Synoptic Survey" from *Aspects of Indian Music* ed. By Sumati Murtatkar, (1987); and *The Hindu* for V.S. Arunachalam's "This Time, A Tryst with Technology," from The Hindu, August 15, 1997.

This project has been a community effort. So many individuals have helped us with ideas, encouragement, and assistance that we are overwhelmed by it. Our words of thanks can only suggest our gratitude, to: Premila Bhat, Sumit Choudhury, Aditya Mattoo, Meenakshi Mattoo, and Vijay Mattoo, for help with production; to the dedicated volunteers at the Center for India Studies, Stony Brook, including, especially, Sephali Gandhi, Mandip Jassal, and Shimona Quazi, for various types of help; to Rita Bhandari, Jennifer Hanson, Michelle Irigashi, Ramin Jaleshgari, Amita Kachru, Sean Matthews, Peter Warden, for editorial assistance; to Shalin Bhatt, Supriya Chakravarthy, Keny Patel, also of the Center for their indefatigable hard work, dedication, and sacrifice beyond the call of duty or reason; to Braj and Yamuna Kachru, Pradeep Mehendiratta C.D. Narasimhaiah, Vishwanath Prasad, and S.R. Rao, for valuable advice and logistical support; to Narinder Kukar, and the members of the National Executive Council of the Association of Indians in America, as well as the many supporters and well-wishers; to Augustina Mattoo for indispensable support; to Meena Sridhar who has been a practically the third editor of the volume; to Ganesh Bhat and colleagues for minding the store so Nirmal could attend to the volume; and above all, to Ashu M. Patel, technical director of the project, whose incredible talent, energy, and effort are only matched by his loyalty and dedication.

I | Introduction

Chapter 1 | Ananya: Like No Other

S. N. Sridhar and Nirmal K. Mattoo

The 50th anniversary of India's independence from British colonial rule is an occasion for celebration. Half a century ago, the non-violent revolution led by Mahatma Gandhi forced the mightiest empire in history to grant India freedom. Given the impossible odds facing the country, many experts predicted doom. However, under the leadership of Jawaharlal Nehru, India not only survived the "dangerous decades," it went on to lay a solid foundation for a more integrated, equitable, and above all, free polity. The nation's investments in democratic institutions, land reforms, irrigation and food production, industrial infrastructure, higher education, public health, empowerment of minorities and historically underprivileged classes, and so forth have made today's India a stronger, better integrated, more equitable, and progressive nation, confident of realizing its potential as a major, constructive force in the world.

This is also an occasion for remembrance and reflection. Independence did not come easy. Although the *satyagraha* (civil disobedience) movement was non-violent, hundreds of thousands sacrificed their careers, families, and some even their lives, as they suffered police beatings without resistance, courted arrest, spent long years in British India's jails, and came out to repeat the cycle, until the colonizer ran out of prison space and tired of his own injustice and brutality. India set an example for the world, which was adopted most notably in the Civil Rights movement of the 1960s in the United States by Martin Luther King, Jr., and even now used around the world.

That wasn't the first time that the world had looked to India for inspiration. Gandhi's commitment to Truth, non-violence, and pluralism represent a world-view that has come down in an unbroken tradition since the Vedas called the entire earth a family (*vasudhaiva kutumbaka*), welcomed ideas from all corners of the universe (*a no bhadrah rtavo yan tu vishwatah*) and refused to claim exclusive status for their vision. The ideals of the pursuit of knowledge, unselfish performance of duty, detachment, self-control and non-violence, so eloquently expressed in the Upanishads, the Bhagavadgita, the tenets of the Buddha and Mahavira, the edicts of Ashoka, and the songs of the Bhakti poets have defined the Indian ethos for millennia. Gandhi integrated these with the example of Jesus Christ, and others. In this sense, Gandhi's message is both quintessentially Indian, and therefore, universal.

It has probably never been more important for the world to know about India than now. What was the vision of India that inspired Gandhi and Nehru, and the countless freedom fighters? Is that vision still valid? And, in a broader sense, what does India stand for? What values, forces and events shaped this rich and ancient civilization? What are its accomplishments and shortcomings? How did it come to be so varied and what gives it cohesion? What is its contribution to the enrichment of humanity? Why, and what, should one know about India?

India, with its 920 million people, is the second most populous nation on earth; the fifth largest economy; a Big Emerging Market with a middle class consumer base of 200 million people; and the world's largest democracy. India has recently opened its doors to global competition, and international corporations are entering the market rapidly. Above all, India represents a grand experiment crucial to humanity's future in participatory democracy, secularism, multiculturalism, affirmative action, and ecologically viable development, to name only a few.

Knowledge of India is also increasingly important to Indians themselves. As India enters the next millennium, the nation is undergoing a radical transformation in its social structure, which calls for a new integration, and a new alignment, both with its own past and with the outside world. There is a heightened sense of nationalism, and a desire to recover, understand, and interpret its heritage; freed from the lingering distortions of colonialism and Orientalism. There is also a new internationalism and pragmatism which is skeptical of essentialist rhetoric.

Knowledge of India is also important to the large Indian Diaspora—now about 20 million strong and settled in all parts of the globe. Indians abroad find themselves called upon everyday to view their land of birth or ancestry through others' eyes, and to explain their customs, attitudes and values. Their intuitive knowledge of India helps, but India is so vast and varied that, as in the fable of the blind men and the elephant, most of us know only some aspects of it. The Indian educational system, still recovering from colonial amnesia, teaches them more about British and European history and culture than their own.

As the younger generations of expatriates, now in high schools, colleges, and beginning their careers, try to construct their identity in relation to the their family and world beyond, they also seek answers to these same questions.

Most of us have often wished we could read, and recommend to our relatives, friends, neighbors, and business associates, a reliable and readable book which would be a broad introduction to India for the general reader, one that would convey the richness of Indian civilization without getting tangled in technicalities or irritating overgeneralization. A book that would be authentic without being pedantic; lively, but not superficial; comprehensive, yet not overly detailed, and up to date, yet true to the historical context. Although a lot has been written on India, no single book seems to fit the bill. Most of the available books tend to be aimed at the academic specialist, narrowly focused on a specific aspect, or at the other extreme, rather simplistic, or opinionated. Works such as A. L. Basham's *The Wonder That Was India,* continue to inspire generations of readers, but even they either cover only a part of the story and need to be complemented with other works or, need to be updated, or both.

The Association of Indians in America (AIA) is the oldest and largest organization of Indians in the United States, with chapters in many parts of the country. Over two years ago, when its National Executive Council began to ponder plans for celebrating the 50th anniversary of India's Independence, the idea of a book that would further understanding of India suggested itself. The establishment of the Center for India Studies at the State University of New York, Stony Brook, the youngest academic institution dedicated to the study of India and Indians in America, created the conditions for a fruitful collaboration. We knew we were attempting the impossible: Under the best of circumstances, putting together a book on India is a daunting proposition. It becomes even more so when one has to function under what many friends told us was an impossible time frame—we had literally just under a year from design until its scheduled release on August 15, 1997. This is an important constraint which has shaped the nature and limitations of this volume in quite a few ways, and we urge the readers to keep it constantly in mind in evaluating this work. Nevertheless, if we have been able to put together what we believe is an important contribution to the available range of resources on India, the credit goes to the cooperation of our distinguished authors and the faith, dedication and incredible hard work of the members of the

Association of Indians in America and of the Center for India Studies, Stony Brook. Without their sacrifices, there simply would be no volume.

In planning the volume, we have attempted to achieve the following objectives:

> The book should be a reliable guide for understanding and appreciating the highlights of Indian civilization—its history, evolution, accomplishments, challenges, contributions, formative forces, and structural principles. It should focus on the most salient aspects, not the minutiae. It should also include, in addition to the traditional areas of arts, religion, philosophy, and literature, areas such as, society, politics, science and technology, business, economy, and the Diaspora. However, the volume should not attempt an exhaustive, encyclopedic treatment, but be extremely selective in presenting significant, and interesting aspects of Indian culture. The book should be, above all, a pleasure to read rather than a duty. The intended audience is the educated general reader or a beginning student, and not the specialist. It should therefore be written in a simple, lively style, with a minimum of scholarly apparatus. However, plenty of references for further reading should be included and a detailed index provided to help to locate topics. Although the book celebrates India, it should not ignore the problems and short comings. Constructive, critical perspectives on social, political, economic and cultural issues enhance the value of any book. Broad, authoritative overviews and interpretations should be emphasized, but controversial topics, opinions and theories should also be represented, especially in areas where scholarly opinion is itself divided. The scope of the volume should include current issues. Topics should be treated as substantively as possible, even if that means reduction in the range of areas covered. Lastly, given the complexities of the issues, multiple perspectives on the same topics should be presented wherever necessary.

Once we defined the type of book we wanted, the question of what areas to cover remained. After all, as the cliché goes, India is not a country but a continent; not just a nation but a civilization. How does one do justice to 5,000 years of history, especially one so varied and rich in cross-currents as that of India, in a single volume? India is a country where major religions were born and spread to nearly half of humanity; where, from the beginning of time, wise men questioned the purpose of existence and our role in the universe; where learning and the learned were valued higher than kings; where philosophy blossomed centuries before it did in Greece; where the study of language was so developed in 5th century BCE that the founder of American linguistics, Leonard Bloomfield, called Panini's Sanskrit grammar, "one of the greatest monuments of human intelligence," and based his own model on its descriptive techniques; where the Pythagorean theorem was formulated a thousand years prior; the value of *pi* was calculated "approximately" as 3.1416 in 499 CE by Aryabhatta (The modern value is 3.1415926); and where the value of zero (*shunya*) and infinity were discovered; and of which the Syrian astronomer-monk Severus Sebokht wrote in 662 CE (Cited in Basham 1963:vi):

> I shall not now speak of the knowledge of the Hindus,...of their subtle discoveries in the sciences of astronomy—discoveries even more ingenious than those of the Greeks and Babylonians—of their rational system of Mathematics, of their method of calculation which no words can praise strongly enough—I mean the system of using nine symbols. If these things were known by the people who think that they alone have mastered the sciences because they speak Greek they would perhaps be convinced, though a little late in the day, that other folk, not only Greek, but men of different tongue, know something as well as they.

India is a country where medicine reached a level of sophistication comparable to that of Greece quite early on (as described in the compendiums of Charaka in 1st-2nd century CE and Sushruta in 6th century BCE); and Caesarian section, plastic surgery, bone-setting, and other medical techniques were so advanced that Indian physicians were brought by Caliph Haroun-al-Rashid (8th century CE) and others to establish hospitals, and doctors of the East India Company found the Indians more advanced in certain aspects of medicine.

India is a country so dedicated to non-violence that, as Lin Yu-Tang said, "turning the other cheek" became a national movement capable of breaking the stronghold of British Colonialism; a country which denied neither the flesh nor the spirit among the goals of life, and evolved an elaborate science of sexuality and depicted it exuberantly in art; where intellectual life has thrived on free and fearless debate, and the most sacrosanct of orthodoxies are routinely challenged; a country where diversity is celebrated; where followers of faiths as different as Hinduism, Christianity, Islam, Judaism, Zoroastrianism, Jainism, Buddhism, Sikhism, and countless others found safe haven from persecution and open scope to practice their faith; where difference of every other sort is expected and accepted as naturally as sun and rain—this list is already too long, but it is only a crude suggestion of the enormity of India's legacy.

With such a cornucopia of material, it is inevitable that our book would end up with gaps, despite our best intentions and efforts. We are acutely aware of the many limitations and shortcomings of this volume. Our original plan included chapters on the contributions of various religious groups and their contributions to the colorful mosaic of pluralistic India. We also wanted to have chapters on dance, cuisine, medicine, textiles, and regional cultures. Indeed, we invited chapters on many of these topics, but a variety of reasons, including delays in receipt of the chapters, need for extensive revision, and most of all the time constraint have forced us to go to print without them. We hope to publish a companion volume which will fill these gaps and together with this, present a more comprehensive portrait of India. The tyranny of time has also obliged us to forego more extensive editorial treatment, such as section introductions, and to live with a less than perfect representation of the pronunciation of Indian words.

Despite these limitations, we do hope readers will find this compilation *ananya* (unique) in some small reflection of the *ananyata* (uniqueness) of its subject and that it will contribute to a more meaningful understanding and appreciation of India.

The forty chapters in this volume are organized into twelve sections. Following the Introduction, Section II gives the historical background: The chapter on Ancient Indian History (S.R. Rao) covers the Indus Civilization through Harsha; Lallanji Gopal treats the period between Harsha through the Mughals, which he calls the crucible Indian history; Irfan Habib describes India in the Mughal period, while Sabyasachi Bhattacharya anayzes the impact of British colonialism on India. The authors treat not only political history but also social, cultural, and economic aspects. Fresh perspectives are presented on topics such as the Indus script, Aryan Invasion, historicity of the Mahabharata, and the Puranas, as well as the nature of Islamic and British colonial impact and the significance of medieval Indian kingdoms.

The Indian ethos is rooted in a grand embrace of pluralism based on the Vedic proclamation of non-exclusivity of revelation, *ekam sat viprah bahudha vadanti*: "Truth is one; the wise call it by many names." Section III, on Indic religions and philosophy, describes the essentials of Classical Indic thought and world-view. India has always placed a high premium on knowledge, secular as well as spiritual. As the Bhagavadgita says, *na hi jnanena sadrsham pavitram iha vidyate*: "Nothing purifies like knowledge." India's intellectual tradition, one of the richest in the world, has yet to be fully discovered, readably translated, and evaluated. Nevertheless, as Jose Pareira's chapter makes clear, Indian thought has many analogs in Western thought and in fact has played an important role, sometimes acknowledged and often not, in the evolution of key areas of inquiry in Western philosophy.

The classical Indian world-view is expounded in the Vedas, the Upanishads, the Ramayana, the Mahabharata, the Puranas, and the Dharma Shastras. An understanding of this vision is crucial to the appreciation of Indian culture. H. K. Kesavan gives a clear exposition of the contents and scope of the Vedas and ancillary disciplines. This is followed by masterly interpretations of the Upanishads and the Bhagavadgita by one of the foremost exponents of Indian philosophy, the late M. Hiriyanna. The chapter on Buddhism and Jainism by Christopher Key Chapple describes the tenets of these religions and their enormous impact. The essence and evolution of Yoga, one of India's best known contributions to the world, is described in Georg Feuerstein's chapter. Rajeshwari Pandharipande brings out its religious, philosophical, social, and ethical dimensions of Hinduism. She traces the dynamic character of Hinduism and shows how it has adapted itself to different time through "contextualizations." Arvind Sharma's chapter deals with the challenges faced by Hinduism in post-Independence India, as it attempts to reconcile tenets of Hinduism with issues of women's equality, human rights, evolving a less-stratified society and the abolition of the dowry system.

As the world's largest democracy, India has accomplished the transition from colonialism to representative government and can now legitimately claim to have placed power in the hands of the people. Democracy, which has ancient roots in India, has come to stay as seen in the periodic and peaceful transfer of power following the largest elections in history. The tension between demands for regional autonomy and a strong Central government is an inevitable expression of the democratic process in action rather than a negation of it. The social aspect of Mahatma Gandhi's revolution proceeds apace as the traditionally disadvantaged castes and classes are empowered, as seen in the recent election of a member of the Dalit (former untouchable) community to India's highest office. The section IV on Society & Politics raises some of the most hotly debated issues in today's India, including the competing, and often conflicting, demands of affirmative action and meritocracy (H.K. Kesavan), the revolutionary change of the over two-thousand year old institution of caste (M.N. Srinivas), and the dilemmas of Indian democracy as it tries to keep its commitment to pluralism, secularism, and minority rights without downgrading majority interests as represented in election results (Robert Hardgrave, Jr.). Sita Anantha Raman's chapter discusses the state of women's education in South India and the impact of Christian missionaries and Indian princely states and philanthropists in creating educational opportunities. Alan Roland's chapter analyzes the need to recognize the role of a culture-specific world-view (what he terms "the spiritual self") in the psychological mak up of Indians.

In section V, Subhask Kak demonstrates the advanced state of scientific thinking in ancient India, in astronomy, geometry, algebra, cognitive science, and other areas, while M. A. Pai discusses science in modern India, which has emerged as the country with the third largest manpower in science and technology. It is also the eigthth most industrialized country, with impressive advances in food production, space technology, communications, and software, to name a few. Pai discusses pre and post-Independence science policy and the problems and prospects in developing a science and technology infrastructure in India. This theme is developed further in the Epilogue by V.S. Arunachalam.

The two chapters comprising section VI, Business and Economics, give an overview of India's trade, finance, and economy from five thousand years ago to the present. (This topic is also discussed in the chapter on India in the Moghul period.) Both T.N. Srinivasan's and Prakash Tandon's chapters outline India's trade relations with Europe and Asia. Tandon also traces the history of banking and finance in India, while Srinivasan analyzes post-Independence economic policy and performance and evaluates the new economic liberalization policies.

Art & Architecture are customarily regarded as among India's glorious accomplishments. India probably has one of the world's greatest concentrations of historical monuments per square mile. Indian art is a reflection of Indian ways and ideals of life and not merely an elite decorative indulgence. India's sophisticated tradition of aesthetics goes back to Bharata (c. first century CE) and includes such brilliant theorists as Anandavardhana (author of the Dhvani theory). It is necessary to view the arts of India in relation to these integrated theories of art experience, spanning different art forms, such as music, literature, sculpture, and painting. Indian art, encompassing from all religions themes, also celebrates India's pluralistic vision. In the section on Art and Architecture (VII) , R.C. Sharma and Nalini Rao contextualize the Salient features of North and South Indian art, respectively. The chapter on architecture by Satish Grover focuses on the trends in contemporary Indian architecture as it evolves a distinctive idiom, combining modernity with traditional motifs and to achieve harmony with the ecology. He also points out that there are radical departures from tradition as well, as Indian architects try to represent notions of open government and secularism and egalitarianism, as opposed to colonial exclusivity and dichotomy between the elite and the public.

Section VIII focuses on creativity and communication in India's languages and literatures. The diversity of languages in India has often been discussed as a problem. Braj B. Kachru, analyzing the situation in a historical as well as functional perspective, explains that multi-lingualism enables the individuals and groups to fulfill specific social and cultural functions, including expression of diverse identities, upward mobility, and intergroup communication. He shows how this diversity came about, why it continues, and what role it plays. He argues that Indian multilingualism is an integral expression of the pluralism of Indian society. He also shows that the grammatical and lexical "convergence," of Indian languages resulting from prolonged contact contributes to the underlying unity or "Indianness" of the culture. The chapter by Yamuna Kachru on language and culture in this section brings out the way in which the languages embody common cultural values and patterns in such crucial aspects as the use of greetings, thanking, respect levels in interpersonal relationships, as well as in organization of ideas in argumentation and discourse.

India speaks in a multiplicity of literary idioms. Sanskrit, which, as William Jones noted, has a literature rivaling that of Greek and Latin in richness, is discussed in detail in the chapter by K. Krishnamoorthy. R. Parthasarathy gives a tantalizing taste of the range and beauty of Indian literature through original translations from several languages and discusses the problems and possibilities in his chapter on "translation as afterlife." Indian literatures in the regional languages such as Marathi, Kannada, and Bengali contain some of the most sensitive and powerful expressions of Indian creativity and social transformation and their engagement with complex issues of culture, society, and modernization is treated in detail in the chapter by U.R. Anantha Murthy.

Although there was an illustrious tradition of drama in Sanskrit 2,000 years ago, and folk traditions of theatre flourished in many parts of the country, there was a long hiatus in Indian theatre until the early 20th century. The two chapters on Indian theatre by Girish Karnad and Shanta Gokhale which open the section on Film, Music & Theatre (Section IX) discuss the evolution of modern Indian drama and the variety and vitality of the theatrical tradition that has grown in various regional centers. Of interest is the way in which modern dramatists combine the music, and mythology that is so crucial a part of Indian performance, even in their realistic plays.

India is the most prolific producer of films in the world. The two streams of Indian cinema—the popular, commercial movies with their famous song and dance routines and the "art films" of Satyajit Ray, A. Gopalakrishnan and others—are discussed in terms of their themes, sources, technique, and social relevance in Wimal Dissanayake's chapter on the distinctiveness of Indian cinema.

India has an ancient and exquisitely articulated tradition of music, which also exemplifies the twin axes of diversity and unity. R. Satyanarayana, in the chapter on Karnataka music (often written as Carnatic or Carnatak music) analyzes the salient features of this school and its historical evolution. In the process he also draws our attention to the distinguishing characteristics of Hindustani music as well.

India's freedom from British Colonial rule through non-violent means represents a unique chapter in world history. This feat would not have been possible without the extraordinary moral and political leadership of Mahatma Gandhi who is rightly revered as the father of the Indian nation. Modern India owes many of its characteristics to the unique blend of historical sensitivity, cosmopolitan vision, and passionate nationalism of Jawaharlal Nehru. The making of these makers of modern India (Section X, the fusion of the men, and the mileu, with the influences, is discussed with reference to Gandhi by K.L.S. Rao and C.D. Narasimhaiah and Nehru by the latter .

The generation of immigrants from India to the United States since the mid 1960s are a distinct group from earlier generations of emigrants to other parts in that they are for the most part highly educated professionals. It is as much a tribute to their individual talents as to the openness of their adoptive countries that, by and large, within one generation, they have become successful, respected, and often influential citizens. In his chapter on Indians in the Untied States, Arthur Helweg (Section XI), presents a socio-cultural (and economic) profile of the Indian-American community. A major aspect of the immigrant experience is maintenance and transmission of cultural heritage, of which language is an essential part. Language is a prime symbol of a culture, and the maintenance of language across generations is characteristic of Indian migrant communities within India. The chapter by Kamal K. Sridhar is an empirical study of the institutional and family practices for cultural maintenance among Indian Americans.

The volume ends with a brief reflection by V.S. Arunachalam on a wide range of issues including the notion of progress and adequacy of the criteria for measuring it, especially the relevance of time, context, culture, and history. Echoing Nehru's famous words on the eve of India's independence, Arunachalam sets a new agenda before the country, "a tryst with technology."

Every country is *ananya* (unique) in its own way. Our goal has been to convey in some measure, the ways in which India is *ananya* by providing a clear, stimulating, and objective bird's eye view of the Indian panorama. If this book makes India more accessible to the readers and inspires them to pursue this interest, our efforts will have been amply rewarded.

II Historical Background

Chapter 2

From the Indus Civilization to the Golden Age

S. R. Rao

The Florentine merchant Fillipo Sassetti was the first Western scholar to remark on the great resemblance between Sanskrit and some of the principal European languages. This brought about a great change in the attitudes of Western scholars towards India. Wilkins' translation of the Bhagavadgītā created interest in Indian thought and philosophy. The philosophers Hegel and Schelling hailed India as the home of Universal Religion and of all literature and philosophy (Bopp 1845). But the European missionaries, who could not accept the high place given to Sanskrit, belittled the value of Indian literature and philosophy. Even Hegel, while conceding Sanskrit to be the foundation of European languages, called its cultural expansion a dumb, needless expansion. William Jones in his address at the Asiatic Society of Bengal in 1796 observed that the said affinity between Sanskrit and European languages was due to a common source that perhaps no longer existed. This gave room to philologists to assume a mother language which they labeled "Indo-European." The mention of Ārya in the Ṛgveda was considered as referring to the Āryan language and an ethnic race speaking Indo-European. The mention of the destruction of the *pur* (fort) of the Dasyu in the Ṛgveda was construed as an invasion of India by the Āryans and the destruction of non-Āryan fortified towns. The date of the assumed invasion was placed around 1500 B.C.E. on the basis of the fact that the Anatolian inscriptions of the Āryan speaking Hittites and Mitanni rulers (1380 B.C.E.) mention the Vedic gods Indra, Mitra, Varuṇa, and the Nāsatyas (Sethna 1992: 212-13).

Even as the controversy over the original home of the Āryans was being hotly debated, the discovery of a very ancient civilization in India was announced by John Marshall in 1924 (*The Illustrated London News*). He wrote that the civilization of the Indus valley was as great as the Mesopotamian civilization. In view of this discovery, Western scholars, who were of the opinion that India had no history before the invasion of Alexander in 327 B.C.E., had to concede that it might begin from 3000 B.C.E., the date given by Marshall in his report on the Mohenjo-daro excavation (Marshall: 1931).

The Beginning

The Indus valley, with its bounteous supply of water and fertile flood loam, was ideal for building a society which could ensure abundant food, material comforts, and spiritual progress. The Indus Civilization had a distinct personality in every field of human activity: arts and crafts, trade and commerce, religion and philosophy, and writing and language. A peace-loving people, they administered their vast territory efficiently. Until recently, it was believed that the origin and end of the Indus civilization were unknown. However, much light is shed on the beginning and decline of the civilization as a result of the excavation of several Indus civilization sites discovered in India after the political bifurcation of the subcontinent in 1947. The first site of the mature phase, discovered by the author in 1954, was Lothal (Rao 1973: 49), a port-town at the head of the Gulf of Cambay in Gujarat (Fig. 1). A. Ghosh discovered Kalibangan in Rajasthan. Subsequent explorations have yielded as many as 277 sites in Gujarat, 65 in Haryana, 100 in Punjab (India), 83 in Rajasthan, and 81 in the Uttar Pradesh-Delhi area. For the study of the beginning of the Indus civilization, Kalibangan in Rajasthan, Dholavira and Surkotada in Kutch, Banawali and Kunal in Haryana, and Kot Diji and Mehrgarh in Pakistan are significant (Rao 1991, appendix I).

A word about the terminology used by various archaeologists for the Indus civilization is necessary. It is called the "Harappa civilization" after the first site discovered, namely Harappa, and also because of the spread of this civilization in all its phases namely, Early, Mature, and Late, far beyond the Indus valley. It extends on the east over the ancient Sarasvatī valley (Hakra and Ghaggar) up to Delhi, and on the west up to the borders of Iran. In the south, it covers the whole of Gujarat and parts of Maharashtra up to the Pravara, a tributary of the Gōdāvarī, and in the north, up to Kashmir and South Russia. It would be more appropriate to name this civilization

"Sindhu" (Indus)-Sarasvatī civilization. However, for the purpose of distinguishing its origin, growth, and decline, the term "Harappa culture" is retained here.

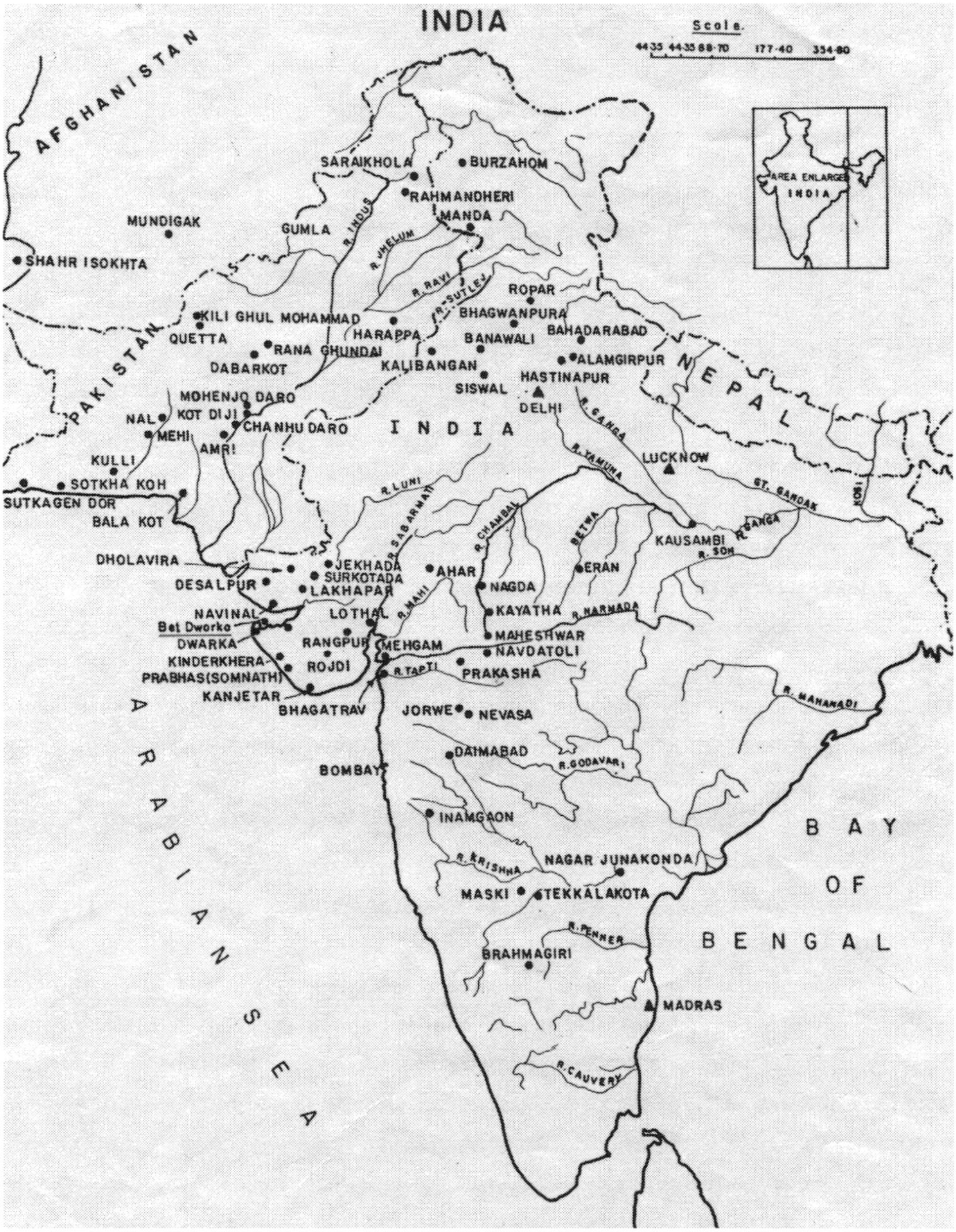

Figure 1: Harappan, Late Harappan, and other Chalcolithic Sites in India.

The Early or pre-Harappa phase made a substantial contribution to the maturity of Harappa culture in the use of kiln-fired bricks, construction of houses in a planned way on artificial terraces, introduction of terracotta cakes for ritualistic purpose, inculcation of a high sense of public hygiene, and introduction of distinct Harappan ceramic forms with attractive painted motifs such as the pīpal leaf and a horned deity. Most of these features can be seen at Kalibangan, Dholavira, and Surkotada in Period I. The use of rice was already known in 4000 B.C.E. at Koldihawa in Uttar Pradesh and cotton was domesticated, still earlier, in the pre-Harappan chalcolithic (copper/stone-using) phase at Mehragarh in Baluchistan.

Harappa culture attained maturity by 2800 B.C.E. This date is arrived at by the Carbon-14 method and duly calibrated by MASCA correction. The culture's decline started in 1900 B.C.E. and continued up to 1700-1600 B.C.E. in the Indus and Ghaggar valleys and more conspicuously further beyond in Gujarat and the Yamuna valley.

Contribution to the Progress of Humanity

The Mature Harappa culture's major contributions to the progress of humanity are: town-planning, a sense of public hygiene, standardization of goods and services, efficient central and local administration, advanced technology in metal working and dockyard construction, and introduction of a simple cursive alphabetic system of writing for easy and quick communication. Other contributions are the development of the psychophysical science of yoga and the cultural integration of forest-dwellers and pastoral folk with the politically-conscious and culturally advanced urbanites by peaceful means.

Town Planning

Harappan towns and cities were planned according to a blueprint, keeping in view the need for saving them from recurring floods of rivers. Harappa, Mohenjo-daro, Lothal, Kalibangan, Dholavira, Banawali, and Surkotada were protected by peripheral walls, while the houses within were raised on artificial terraces of mud bricks to save them from inundation. These platforms also served as common plinths for groups of houses. They were divided into a number of blocks connected by intersecting roads running in cardinal directions. Underground and surface drains connected to private drains and paved baths in houses carried the sewage into the sea through the dock at high tide. Municipal administration was so strict that inspection chambers collecting solid waste had to be provided by the house-owner to prevent the choking of underground sewers. No encroachment on public roads while rebuilding houses after floods had taken place, indicating the high civic sense of citizens. The city was divided into two main parts, namely, the Citadel or Acropolis which was occupied by the ruler, and "Lower Town" which was occupied by the ruled (Fig. 2). Both parts enjoyed all civic amenities, such as roads, drains, cesspools, and manholes to keep the city clean. The Lower Town was divided into four or five sectors. At Lothal, the bazaar was in the central sector where the rich merchants and poor craftsmen had their shops and houses. There was no stratification of society. The industrial sector, where the blacksmiths worked, was kept separate and so also the Bead Factory. For the preservation of grains, granaries with proper air-vents were built at Harappa and Mohenjo-daro. Lothal, being the major port, had a unique tidal dock with a large warehouse at one end near the Acropolis and the workers' quarters at the other. Mohenjo-daro had a public bath with provision for changing clothes in rooms built for that purpose. Dholavira had an additional sector designated by the excavator as "Middle Town." There were wells for potable water at Lothal and Mohenjo-daro, while Dholavira had an underground storage tank. Polished limestone blocks were used in Dholavira for constructing pillars flanking the gateway leading to ruler's mansion.

The Dock at Lothal

The first ever tidal dock for shipping was built at Lothal (Plate 1) in 2300 B.C.E. by erecting brick walls in the four arms of an excavated basin which measures 210 by 35 meters with a depth of 4 meters. The inlet channel, in its northern embankment, permitted entry and exit of ships at high tide. They could sail up the Bhogavo or Sabarmati river from the Gulf of Cambay. Automatic desiltation of the basin was ensured by opening the lock-gate at high tide. N.K. Panikkar and T.N. Srinivasan (1971: 36-57) observe:

> The Lothal dock being a purely tidal one, the Lothal engineers must have possessed adequate knowledge of tidal effects, the amplitude, erosion and thrust. From this knowledge they developed competence at Lothal for receiving ships at high tide and ensuring floatation of ships at low tide. This is perhaps the earliest example of knowledge of tidal phenomenon being put to a highly practical purpose both in the selection of site having the highest tidal amplitude and in adopting operation of entry and exit of ships.

R. Nigam who analyzed the sample of sediment from the floor of the Lothal dock adds, "[t]he profuse presence of gypsum and the micro organisms *foraminifera* indicate that the tidal sea water used to enter the basin" (1988: 20-21). A terracotta model of a boat gives an idea of the sail-ships of Lothal, and their size is suggested by stone anchors found in the dock. The Lothal dock is bigger than the Visakhapatnam dock (111.56 by18.29 meters) and the Bombay Merewether dock (115. 4 by 19 meters). The Lothal dock is better designed than the Phoenician dock at Biblos in Lebanon, which was built a thousand years later.

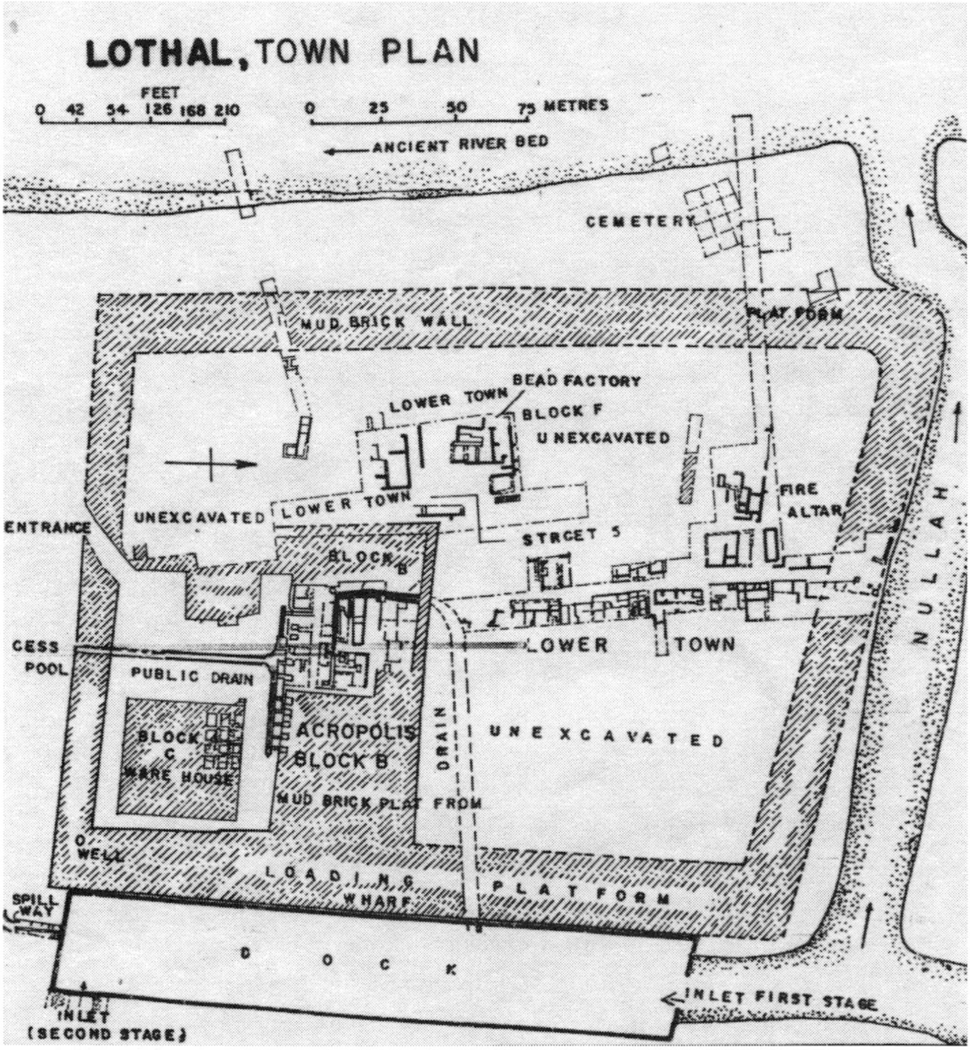

Figure 2: Lothal Town Plan.

Warehouse

While planning the town in 2300 B.C.E., the Lothal engineers constructed a warehouse on a massive platform of bricks overlooking the dock, and at the same time, easily approachable from the Acropolis where the ruler could keep an eye on the movement of ships and the handling of cargo. The warehouse where cargo was examined, sealed, and stocked originally consisted of 64 cubical blocks (Fig. 3) over which a canopy of wood protected the goods. It is here that 64 terra-cotta sealings (burnt clay labels) bearing impressions of packing material and seals were found. An accidental fire must have destroyed the canopy and goods but preserved, for posterity, the valuable evidence of the commercial use of Indus seals.

Figure 3: Lothal: Warehouse with Intersecting Air Vents and Passages Between Cubicle Platforms..

Floods

The dock as well as the warehouse were heavily damaged by the third flood in 2000 B.C.E. The river changed its course leaving the dock high and dry, but a new channel dug up by residents provided access only to small boats from the sea. The houses subsequently built on flood debris in Lower Town were leveled by a deluge in 1900 B.C.E., bringing an end to the prosperity of Lothal, the only major port town of the Harappa civilization. Most residents left for safer places, and the few who returned, lived in Jerry-built houses which were also reduced to heaps of debris by a massive flood in 1600 B.C.E. This phase of decline (Lothal Period B), dated 1900-1600 B.C.E., witnessed an attempt on the part of the Late Harappans at Lothal and elsewhere to retain the basic elements of mature Harappa culture namely, writing, metallurgy, fire-worship, and ceramics. The new ceramic form with a luster had evolved and has been designated as "Lustrous Red Ware." It survived up to 1300 B.C.E. in the Gujarat, Narmadā, and Gōdāvarī valleys.

Weights and Measures

Accuracy in measuring mass, lengths, and time is an index to the progress of science and technology. The Harappans had developed a high degree of skill in computational technique which is reflected in the planning of towns, building of warehouses, docks, baths, and granaries. They had two series of cubical stone weights. In the first series, the unit weight was 27.584 g which is higher by 50 percent than the second series unit weight of 18.1650 g. Both were in decimal graduation. It is necessary to note that the Lothal weight of 27.584 g is almost equal to the uncia of the Greeks and the ounce of the British (Mainkar 1984: 141-151). The smaller denominations are decimal graduations of the lower unit weight, the ratio being 1, 2, 5, 10, 20 and so on up to 1000. Another series of small weights occurs at Lothal in the form of gold discs weighing 50 mg, 100 mg, 250 mg, 500 mg etc., up to 3250 mg. The smallest weight is equal to half gunja or masaka or dhānya of the Arthaśāstra and five gunjas are equal to the 500 mg disc of Lothal. Thus the Harappan metrology became the basis of subsequent measurement standards. This is true of length measures also. For instance, the measurements on the ivory scale of Lothal and the shell scale of Mohenjo-daro are integrated. The smallest division on the Lothal scale is 1.704 mm and ten such divisions together equal to one angula of the Arthaśāstra.

Harappan bricks were manufactured in dimensions which were integral multiples of large Lothal graduations. The width of the foundation of the brick wall of the dock is 1.78 meters which is equal to 1000 times the small graduation on Lothal scale (Rao 1996: 208-211).

Mathematics and Astrology

The very fact that the Harappans at Lothal and Kalibangan built altars for fire-worship and offering sacrifices by using bricks of standard size and suitable shapes suggests that they had some knowledge of altar geometry, which is better established from the Sulba Sūtras of the Vedas, which give geometrical rules and procedures for constructing altars (Bag 1996: 186; for further details see Kak in this volume).

Two circular ring-like shell objects, one each from Lothal and Dholavira, have slits marked on both margins: eight in the case of the Lothal ring and twelve in the case of the Dholavira ring (Rao 1996: 211-12). The lines passing through opposite slits cut at 45 degrees in the Lothal ring of 8 slits and at 30 degrees in the Dholavira ring of 12 slits. The instrument can be used as a compass in plane table survey and also as a sextant for measuring eight or twelve whole sections of the horizon or the sky when viewed simultaneously through upper and opposite lower slits (Rao 1996: 211-12).

The Indus (Harappan) Writing

The Harappans, who were highly literate, left for posterity as many as 3100 seals and sealings (positive impressions of seals in the negative) on which inscriptions or an animal motif, or both appear (Fig. 4-5). Until recently, the Indus script was considered as undecipherable.

Figure 4: Lothal: Indus Seal (Front and Back) with a Mirror Impression of Inscription.

Figure 5: Lothal Sealings Found in the Warehouse.

However, the Indus script is no longer the closed book which it has been for some decades. This author's Sanskrit-related decipherment and interpretation of the Indus script has received important endorsements by epigraphists and linguists, including that of the renowned authority on writing, David Diringer, who considers it to be convincing. In the opinion of philologist Konrad Elst, this decipherment is free from all suspicion of distortive chauvinism or wishful theorizing. Elst observes that this decipherment is convincing because it passes several tests which other proposed decipherments have not only not passed, but which they had implied to be impossible (Elst 1994: 73).

The Dravidian hypotheses of Asko Parpola, Iravatham Mahadevan, and others assume that the Indus script is totally isolated. The Dravadian reading of Indus script had not helped in establishing a relation with the Elamite script which looks somewhat similar to the Indus signs (McAlpine 1974, 50). Paraphrasing Elst's observations, it may be pointed out that the Sanskrit-based hypothesis seems to provide a double check. On the one hand, the language written on the Indus seals is a language roughly known to us, and on the other, it uses signs of which many are known from another place and another time. The language is a dialect of Sanskrit, the script largely similar to the Semitic alphabets that appear around 1600 B.C.E. and to the Brāhmī script attested since about 400 B.C.E. (Fig. 6). Relations with Semitic and Brāhmī scripts are not assumed beforehand. The proposed reading, however, provides a good reason for postulating such relations. This also allows for outside verification of the decipherment. As the Indus civilization matures, strictly figurative signs tend to disappear, leaving a much more uniform set of fewer cursive signs (Fig. 7). These were characterized by the ligature of individual signs into compound signs (some of which look deceptively like figures) (Fig. 8) and by accenting (the adding of small diacritic

	1900-1500 B.C. LATE HARAPPAN SIGNS (BASIC)	1500-1000 B.C NORTH SEMITIC & SOUTH SEMITIC SIGNS	PHONETIC VALUE	1300-B.C. BET DWK	1300-800 B.C MEGALITHIC SANUR ETC.	3rd CENT BC ASOKAN BRAHMI GIRNAR
1	☐		b			☐ ba
2			g	g		ga
3			d			dha
4	E		h		E E	E la
5			w	h		va
6			h (breve)			
7			th			⊙ tha
8			k			+ ka
9			n			na
10			s			sa
11	○	○	c (ay)			
12			p	pā		pa
13			r			ra
14	w	w w	s	ṣ	w	sa
15		+ X	t		X	ta
16	↑		s'		↑	s'a
17			h (dot)			gha
18			m			ma
19			a	m		a
20			r (dot)			
21			s'			
22				ca		dca
23			z			
24			y			ya

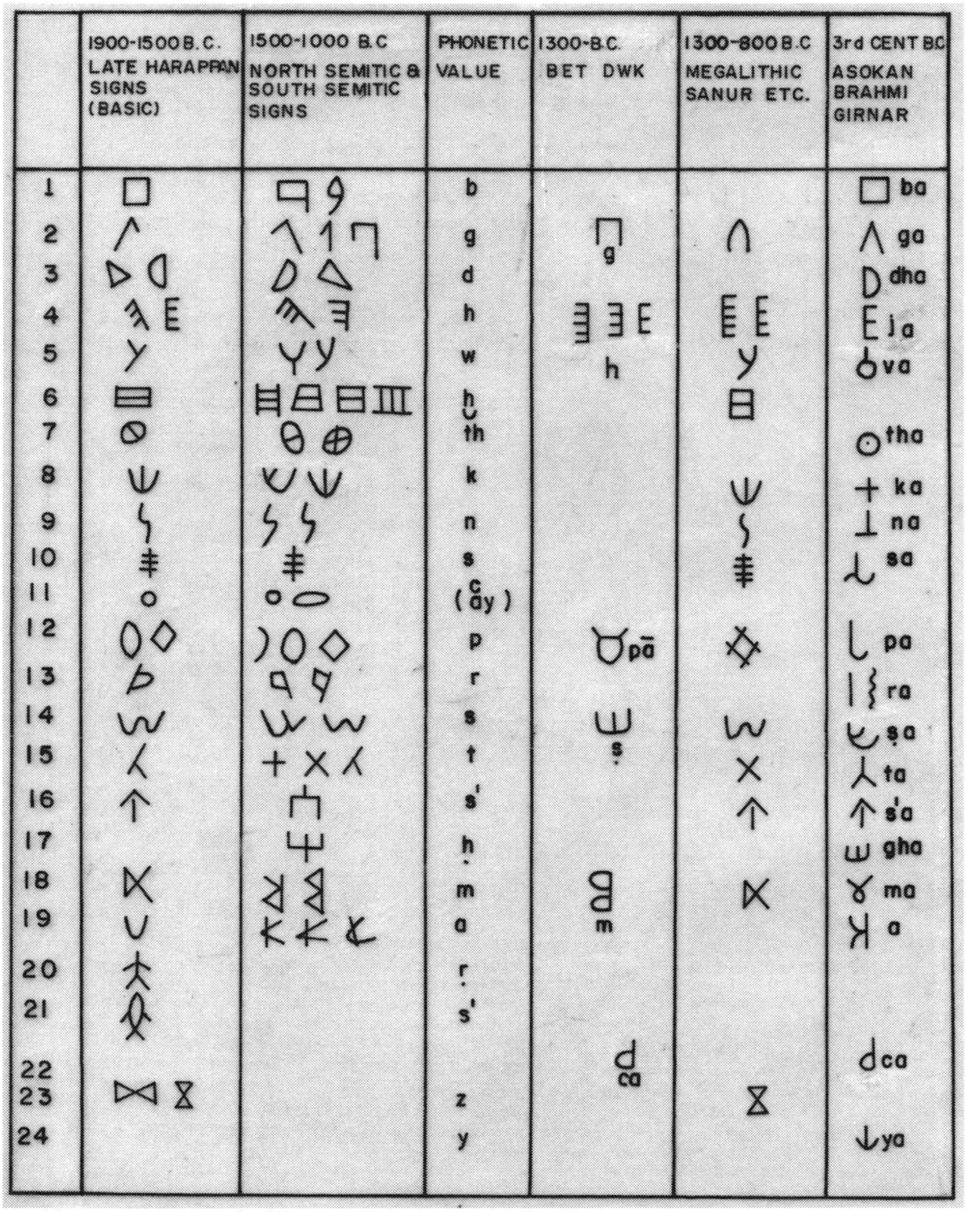

Figure 6: Phonetic Values of Comparable Bet Dwarka, Indus, and Brahmi Signs.

signs to the compounds, like the vowel signs and signs for consonant clusters in Devanāgarī script used for Sanskrit). It shares these characteristics with the later Brāhmī script, out of which modern Indian alphabets were developed, and with the

Semitic alphabet in their advanced stage (when vowel marks were added, in contexts where exact pronunciation was necessary, e.g., in the Bible and later in the Qurān). The characters indicate that the mature Indus script was phonological, and, in fact, alphabetic (rather than picto-logographic). (Note that although the Devanāgarī and related scripts are, in a sense syllabic, syllabic signs for *ka*, *ke*, *ko*, etc. have the *k* sign in common which is a typical feature of alphabetic scripts). On this analysis, there were twenty-four basic phonetic signs (some of which had alternate forms), but twenty-eight ideographs continued to be used --just as Japanese writing combines Chinese ideographs with alphabetic writing. The diacritic marks have an identifiable vowel value.

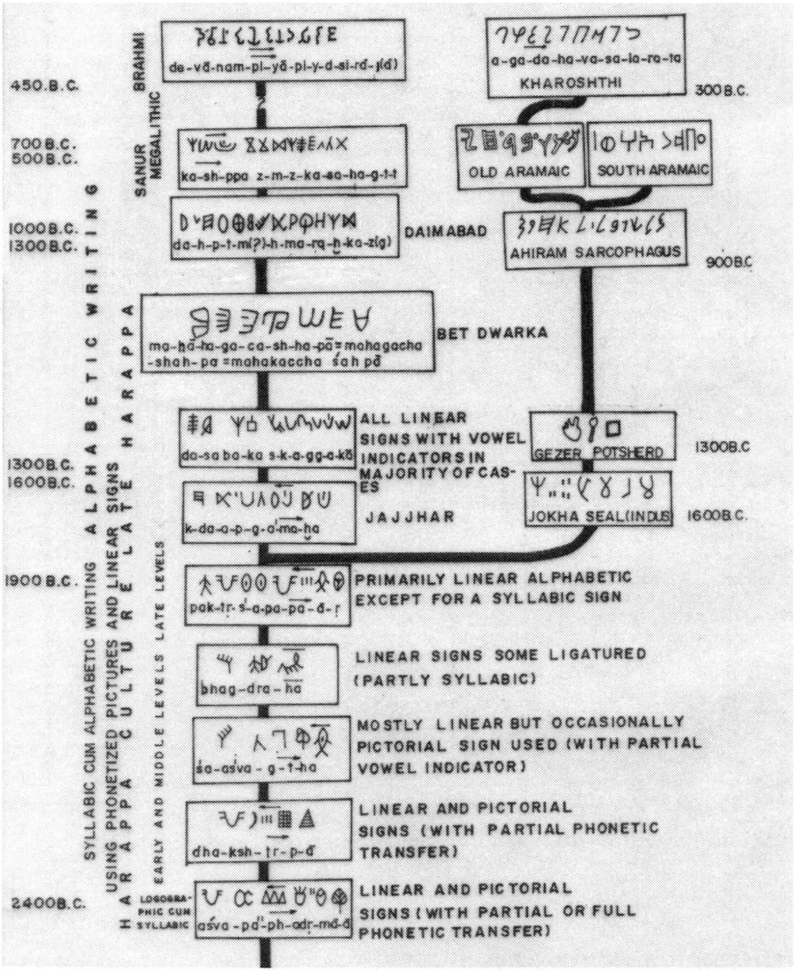

Figure 7: Evolution of Indus Script and Origin of Early Alphabets

SEMITIC ALPHABET	BASIC INDUS SIGNS	COMMON PHONETIC VALUE
⊐, 9	⊐, 9	b
∧	∧	g
◁△	▷, ̇▷	d
∧, ⨅	E, ⋩	h
Y	Y	w
⊟ ⊟	⊟ ⊞	ḥ
Ѡ	V, Ѡ	k
ら, ら	ら, ら	n
‡	‡	s
०, ०	०	ay
), ०, ◇	), ०◇	p
ᑫ, ᑫ	P	r
ш.	ш	sh
X, ⋏	X, ⋏, ⨰	t
̇⊓	̇⊓, ↑	s/ś
ⵞ	ⵞ	ḥ
Ƴ	୪, X, ⨯	m
K ⫥	U	?, a

INITIAL VOWELS } a ā ae ao r
U, ꭟ, ꭟ, ꭟ 大

a m
E.g. U + X = X' = am. 大 = ar
0 + V = 0 = pa etc.
Also 0 = pa. ꝓ = ra. ꝓꝓ = rā.
D +' = ꝏ = da ‡ = sa etc.

COMPOUND SIGNS ANALYSED

0 + I + 0 + 大 = ⊙大 = papṛ
0 + ꭟ + 0 + 大 = ⊙大 = pāpṛ
0 + 大 = 大0 = pṛ ; X = ṛk
ꝏ + 大 = 大ꝏ = dra

b ha g
9 + E + ∧ = = bhag
0 + I + ꓸ = ⊚ = pah
V + I = Y = ka

← READING

HP 307 ꭟX = bhag-rk-ā = bhaga-arka
HP ⊟X"大ꝏ⊟ = ba-dra"-ma-hā
KBG X ꭟ = ao-ma = oma
LOT ら X = ma-nā = manā
LOT Y‴ ꝓ◇ = pa-rā-ttr-ka = parā-trka

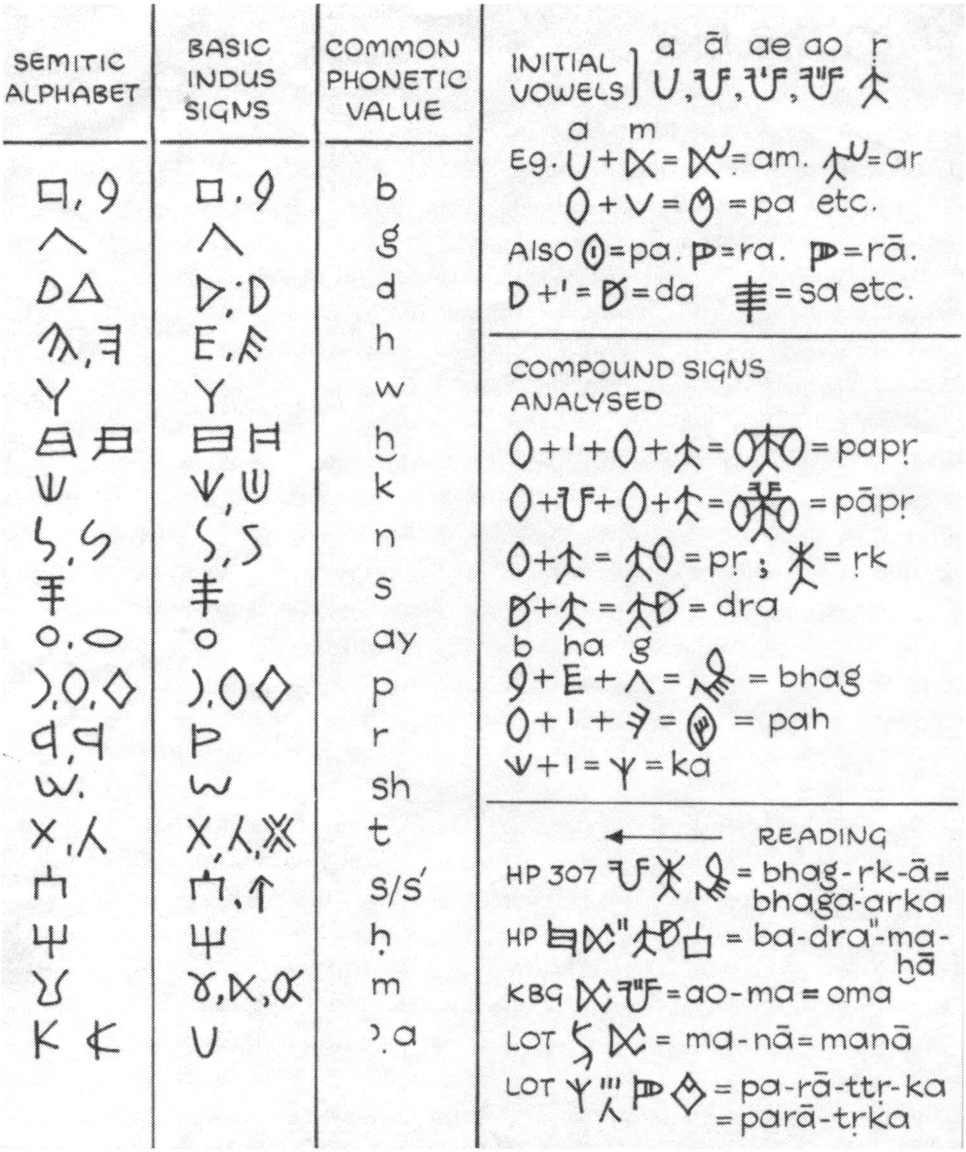

Figure 8: Vowels and Compound Signs Formed by Accenting and Ligaturing.

As many as seventeen of the twenty-four cursive signs are in common with Semitic alphabets (Hebrew, Arabic, and first of all, Phoenician) which are attested since the third-second millennium B.C.E. It is therefore quite logical to start by trying out the same sound values for the Indus signs. This yields a reading that makes sense. The script does not seem to contain retroflex consonants like the Avestan, but the reason could be that the Harappans' perception of phonetic distinctions was not yet mature or that these consonants in Sanskrit were a later development (retroactively applied to Vedic hymns), perhaps under Dravidian influence. Then again, some of the words found seem to show a development in the direction of Avestan (*hapta* instead of *sapta*), and some terminology also points to an Avestan element (*atan* rather than *agni* for "fire," *asha* rather than *satya* for "truth").

At any rate, the language is clearly akin to Sanskrit and is definitely not Dravidian. The Brahmī script evolved straight from Harappan script, and thus, would be a sister rather than a daughter of the Phoenician alphabet.

The words *eka*, *hapta*, *daśa*, and *śata* occurring in Harappan seal inscriptions stand for one, seven, ten, and one hundred respectively. In the next stage, figurative signs for words such as bird, pipal leaf, and scorpion were given syllabic value from words for birds, pipal, and insects in the language (Sanskrit) already known from cursive inscriptions, for example, vṛś from vṛščika for scorpion, aśv from aśvattha for pipal leaf, and the words *Asvaka*, *Vrsan*,□*Śakra* stand for names of persons or gods. The hierarchy of rulers was indicated by the words pati, sasa, and sasamaha which stand for lord, ruler, and great ruler respectively. The inscription on a seal with a fire altar motif reads *bag-bhaga- arkaha* meaning "(seal) of mighty or bountiful God Arka" (Fire God). In another seal, the deity under an arch of flame representing *Arka* stands for "God of Fire." The inscription below it reads *bhag-rka* (Fig. 9).

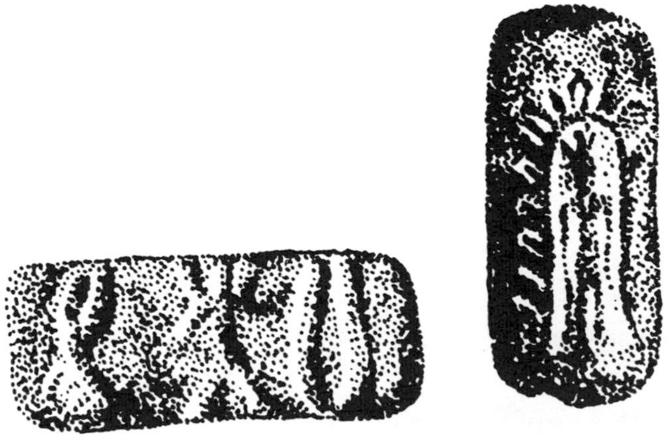

Figure 9: Indus Seal Depicting God of Fire

Religion

At Kalibangan, sacrificial altars containing terracotta cakes and bovine bones are found. An inscription on a seal from Kalibangan reads *bhadrama dvipa* conveying the sense that it is the most auspicious (bhadra-ma) land. In addition to seven fire-altars, there is a procession path laid out in the Citadel of Kalibangan for religious functions. Lothal too has yielded similar fire altars built in houses and in a public place. A gold ornament similar to the one depicted on the forehead of a statue of the "priest" (from Mohenjo-daro) and comparable to the rukma of the Vedic priest has been found in the sacrificial altar at Lothal. The Harappans practiced both burial and cremation in disposing of the dead. M.S. Vats (1974-75) reported post-cremation burials at Harappa. In short, it can be said that the religion, language, and customs followed by the Harappans are similar to those of Aryan-speaking people.

Aryan Invasion a Myth

The protagonists of the Āryan invasion theory were pleased when Wheeler (1968) declared that excavations of Harappa and Mohenjo-daro indicate the massacre of the non-Āryan population at Mohenjo-daro and the destruction of the twin cities by the invading Āryan barbarians unsympathetic to civilization. Fortunately, the renewed excavations at Harappa in 1986, and at Mohenjo-daro in 1964-66 by Dales have proved that there was evidence of neither an invasion nor any massacre at Mohenjo-daro. The very few skeletons with cut marks did not belong to a single time frame (Dales 1964: 37-43). Even if an invasion is assumed at Harappa, the so-called invaded were not present when the invaders (Cemetery H people) arrived. There is a big time-lag between the habitation deposits of the two groups (Lal 1975: 19). In fact racially, too, no distinction can be made on anthropological grounds. The Harappans were themselves an Āryan-speaking people who followed religion and customs normally attributed to Āryans. Even the negative evidence, namely the absence of the horse and rice in Indus sites, does not hold now, because rice was already in use at Lothal and Rangpur, and horse bones were found in Harappan sites of Rangpur and Lothal. In fact, rice was cultivated at Koldiwaha as early as 4000 B.C.E.

The Decline

It is now clear that the main cause for the decline of Harappa culture and the abandonment of most of the sites in the flood plains of the Indus, Sarasvatī, and Sabarmati rivers was not any invasion but the frequent inundation of the Harappan settlements which force residents to migrate to safer places. At Kalibangan and Dholavira, earthquakes too may have added to the difficulties. Recently scientists have adduced a long draught in the second millennium B.C.E. as one of the causes for the abandonment of the Indus and Sarasvatī valleys. In fact, the Sarasvatī lost the Satluj and Yamuna to the Indus and Ganga respectively, owing to tectonic activity. The paleochannels of the Sarasvatī (Hakra-Ghaggar) have been traced under the deserts of Rajasthan and in Haryana. To some extent, the Harappans themselves were responsible for the ecological deterioration resulting from denudation of forest cover and over-cultivation, thereby causing soil erosion.

Migration of the Harappan Population

The flood and quake-stricken Late Harappans from the Indus and Sarasvatī valleys moved eastward into the Yamuna valley on the one hand, and from the Indus estuary southward into Saurashtra, on the other (Rao 1973, 180-182). Later on, they moved into the Narmadā and Taptī valleys and mingled with indigeneous chalcolithics (copper-bronze and stone using people). The Late Harappans made settlements as far south as Daimabad on the Pravara, a tributary of the Gōdavarī river. They lived in small villages which lacked civic amenities but still retained the Harappan technical knowledge in metallurgy and writing as attested by the Daimabad bronze figures of a chariot, and the late Harappan script on a seal. Similarly, Harappan-type warehouses at Prabhasa, a Late Harappan site in Saurashtra, and the granary at Gilund in Central India are examples of the survival of Harappan architecture alongside ceramic wares. At Kunal in Haryana and Rangpur in Saurashtra, there is a continuity of Harappan technology and religious rites in the Late Harappan (1900-1700 B.C.E.) and post-Harappan (1700-1500 B.C.E.) periods. This rural life has been misconstrued by some historians and archaeologists as the "dark age" of India. It is inconceivable that the age which produced the Vedas and the epics Rāmāyaṇa and Mahābhārata should be considered as a dark age.

The four Vedas are a collection of samhitās made by Veda Vyāsa. Joshi (1996: 158) observes:

> There was evidently a larger body of compositions and since they spoke of the old and new ṛṣis (sages) and of pitarah (fathers) it may safely be inferred that there was at that time a tradition too, since the Vedic compositions included in the four Vedas indicate a high level of development of poetic

quality and spiritual experience which can come about only through a long period of growth.

Apart from the achievements of the Vedic people in the fields of science, mathematics, astronomy, astrology, medicine, maritime activity, religion, and philosophy (see chapters by Kesavan, Kak, Srinivasan, Tandon, and others), particular attention may be drawn to the "creation mystery" embodied in their Nāsadīya Sūtras.

During the transition from the Harappan-Vedic period to the Epic period of Indian history, the political scenario was gradually changing. There were small republics with elected rulers and large kingdoms, formed by gradually swallowing up smaller ones. From the Rāmāyaṇa and Mahābhārata, and Pāṇinī's grammar, Aṣtadhyāyī, the names of gaṇarājyas (republics), janapadas, and mahājanapadas can be ascertained. An important change in social and religious institutions was taking place, perhaps because of the gradual absorption of less sophisticated agriculturists, cattle rearers, and forest-dwellers, who Western historians have labeled as "tribal" people. The Mahābhārata gives a graphic description of the struggle for political power, and laxity in the observance of ethical standards in political and social life. The kings and kingdoms, the gaṇarājyas and the janapadas, the commoners, and heroes mentioned in the epic are not fictitious.

The Epic Age

The Mahābhārata is considered by some historians as a myth. It must be remembered that the historian is not merely a collector of facts, but also a scientist in search of laws governing social growth. Thus, it is the historian's job to study myths and symbols along with hard archaeological evidence. Legends are woven around a unique religious or political leader or social reformer of extraordinary ability who came to the rescue of a community in danger, especially when moral degradation of rulers was likely to break up the social structure. A historian has to separate the chaff from the grain and unravel the mystery surrounding the central figure without destroying the common man's belief in the divinity of his exemplary model. One such model was Kṛṣ̌ẖa, the hero of the Mahābhārata. His sole aim was to uphold the *dharma* by giving exemplary punishment to the evil-doer and his henchmen.

The importance of the Mahābhārata as a source of history of the second millennium B.C.E., after the decline of Harappa civilization and before the Buddha, cannot be overemphasized. The earlier excavations at ancient sites of the Mahābhārata tradition have not yielded convincing evidence because of the extremely limited excavations carried out at Hastinapura and Mathura. Dwarka held out some hope for the historian and archaeologist after the excavation in the forecourt of the fifteenth-fourteenth-century temple of Dwarkādhiṣ (Krishna) brought to light in 1979-80 three earlier temples, one below the other. The topmost temple of Viṣṇu can be dated to the ninth century C.E. (Plate 3, Figure 10) and the earliest temple to the first century C.E.. Further digging yielded habitation debris in which wave-rolled pottery of the fifteenth century B.C.E., and sediment brought in by a storm wave confirmed the destruction of a town by the sea. This evidence spurred a seabed excavation to locate the submerged town of ancient Dwarka.

The National Institute of Oceanography, Goa, established a Marine Archaeology Center in 1981 for the dual purpose of exploring submerged ports and shipwrecks, and for generating scientific data needed for studying the cause of submergence of ports. Young archaeologists, technicians, and scientists have braved the rough sea and conducted manual, visual, geophysical, magnetic, and related surveys during the last twelve years in the Gulf of Kutch off Bet Dwarka island and in the Arabian Sea near Dwarka. Bet Dwarka is identified with Kuśasthalī where the first town, named Dvārakā, was built under Kṛṣṇa's leadership according to the Mahābhārata. The present town of Dwarka, on the mainland at the mouth of Gomati, stands where the town of Dwarka or Dvarāvati was built, by Kṛṣṇa, after realizing that there was not enough land on Bet Dwarka to settle the increasing number of immigrant Yadavas from Mathura.

The first concrete evidence of a township of the sixteenth century B.C.E. in Bet Dwarka is provided by a fortification wall of rubble in the cliff section (terrace) near Siddi Bawa Pir on the southeastern part of the shore (Plate 2). It runs over a length of 500 meters but is greatly damaged by the sea and earth quarrying in the lower terrace. The fortification is built in box technique with long and cross walls. The pottery from the section was tested by the Thermoluminescence dating method and the date arrived at is 3528 years before the present. The intertidal zone here is full of pottery and rubble from houses destroyed by the sea. A blacksmith's stone mold and an inscribed votive jar are other important finds here. The seabed excavation yielded a unique conch shell seal engraved with a motif of a three-headed animal and also an iron stake, reminiscent of the one described in the epic. Such stakes were fixed in the moat to prevent the enemy from entering Dwarka. Another stone wall, 550 meters long forming a hexagonal enclosure in the central sector of the eastern shore of Bet Dwarka, lies submerged except in lowest tide. In this sector, there are six rock-cut wells and a Late Harappan site in the upper terrace near the Nīlakaṇṭha Mahādev temple. Further north, near the old custom house too, there are vestiges of small Late Harappan and early historical settlements. Down below in the sea is a submerged wall of massive dressed stones. From these details it becomes evident that there was a city, about 4 kilometers long, built at least in two terraces, the lower one having been swallowed by the sea. The topography of Bet Dwarka island is very similar to that of Kuśasthali with a hill on one side and the sea on other sides as described in the epic. It is here that the first Dwarka was built, but finding that enough land was not available for settling more Yadavas, Kṛṣṇa is said to have reclaimed land from the sea at the mouth of Gomati river on the mainland to build a port town. Thus the second Dwarka came into existence a few years later.

Figure 10: Vishnu Temple of 9th Century C.E. laid bare in excavation at Dwarka.

Although swells, currents, and storm waves have destroyed much of the ancient buildings now lying at the depth of 7 to 10 meters, enough remains of the plan of the city. The protection walls and bastions of massive dressed sandstone blocks built over boulder foundation (Plate 2, Plate 4) are traceable up to 1 or 2 meters wherever they are still *in situ*. In all, six enclosures (antahpuras), two on the right bank of the submerged Gomati channel, and four on its left bank, have been traced. One of them, on the right bank, seems to have housed important administrative buildings in view of the fact that its entry is an indirect one through an outer enclosure. In another sector, the massive stone pillars and beams suggest that a public building of a religious character was built here. Among the antiquities are brass arches, bars, and nails which might have formed part of a rudder or a boat. The arches, together with an inverted omega-shaped object, could have been parts of a chariot. It may be noted that the bronze chariot of Daimabad, datable to the fifteenth century B.C.E. (Rao 1991), is of the same type. A copper bell, a stone seat, and part of a marble figure, perhaps a deity, are other finds from the seabed. The large number of three-holed triangular anchors of stone found in the submerged river channel and near the harbor of ancient Dwarka can be relied upon for dating purposes. Similar anchors were in use at Kition in Syria and in Cyprus during the fourteenth century B.C.E. (Frost 1985). The Dwarka engineers are found to have modified a rocky ridge near the ancient sea shore into a berthing place and wharf by dressing the outer face and top of the rock. The large manmade holes in the modified ridge and large prismatic and triangular anchors lying at the foot of ridge indicate that sea-going vessels were anchored here while smaller boats ferried between the harbor and warehouses on the river bank.

Two inscriptions found in Bet Dwarka are of great importance. One of them reads *mahahagacha shah pa* conveying the sense "Sea god, Protect." The second inscription reads *baga* meaning "God." The two inscriptions of Bet Dwarka are read on the basis of the identical signs of the already known Semitic alphabets (Fig. 6). The inscriptions clearly indicate that the residents of ancient Dwarka spoke Sanskrit and were literate too. The inscription on the votive jar provides a link between the Harappan and Brahmi scripts and corroborates that Brāhmī was derived from the Harappan script. Both have many common features, such as, common signs, common ligature and accenting techniques, and language too. It is from Brāhmī that all the modern Indian scripts are derived.

Figure 11: Late Indus Type Seal with a Three-Headed Animal Motif (Bull, Unicorn and Goat) from Bet Dwarka Excavation.

The seal of conch shell, measuring 18 by 20 millimeters, found in the seabed excavation at Bet Dwarka, is engraved with a three-headed animal motif representing a short-horned bull, a unicorn and a goat (Fig. 11) which resembles similar motifs on the Bahrain seals of second millennium B.C.E. It is evident from the Bahrain seal found at Lothal, and the Harappan and Late Harappan pottery found in Bahrain, that Dwarka had trade and cultural contacts with Bahrain. The use of mudra (seal) for purposes of identification of persons in war time, as ordered by Kṛṣṇa, is referred to in the Harivaṃśa (Viṣṇu Parva, Dvarakā mahātmya). When Dwarka was attacked by Salva, King of Saubha, the guards of the city were asked to make sure that no unauthorized person entered the city. Another measure for defending the city was to fix iron or wooden stakes in the moat to prevent the enemy from crossing it. One such iron stake has been recovered from the Bet Dwarka excavation in the nearshore zone.

The fact that metal spearheads were attached to spears is also proved by the blacksmith's stone mold found here. Metallurgy had made great advance, as can be gauged from the brass, copper, and bronze objects recovered from Dwarka. Shell-working and pearl-fishing were important industries which, together with overseas trade, contributed to the prosperity of ancient Dwarka. In short, the finds attest to the high level of civilization described in the Mahābhārata.

Dwarka was a city-state consisting of Kuśasthali (Bet Dwarka), mainland Dwarka which was a port, and Nageswar and Pindara (Late Harappan towns) all mentioned in the epic. According to the inscription at Aihole in the Bijapur district of Karnataka, the date of the Bharata War (Mahābhārata) works out to 3102 B.C.E, but it is difficult to sustain this date on archaeological grounds. For instance, the mention of the use of iron weapons in the Bharata War is proof of a later date because iron technology was developed in India between 1600 and 1500 B.C.E.. However, the presently assigned date,1800-1700 B.C.E., to Kusasthali-Dwarka is provisional and subject to any earlier archaeological evidence that may be found in deep sea excavation. So the terminal date of the post-Mahābhārata period, represented by copper-stone and iron-using Chalcolithic and Megalithic folk of eastern, central, and southern India, can be stretched up to 500 B.C.E, when the two major religious movements were ushered in.

Classical Period

The literary, philosophic, and religious movements gained fresh impetus and made substantial contributions to the conceptual thinking of humans during the Mauryan, Gupta, and Late Gupta periods (500 B.C.E.-600 C.E.). The historian has to depend on Purāṇic genealogy of kings, and on foreign visitors to reconstruct the political, social and economic history of the second half of the first millennium B.C.E.. The Purāṇas list twenty-two Brihadratha, ten Saisunaga, and nine Nanda kings who ruled the great Empire of Magadha (Bihar) after the Bharata War. Before going into the political events that led to the reunification of India under the Mauryan rulers, Chandragupta and Aśoka, in the fourth-third centuries B.C.E., after the invasion of Darius and Alexander, the two religious movements which swept over India need to be mentioned.

Jainism and Buddhism

The twenty-fourth Tirthānkara Vardhamāna Mahāvīra of Vaiśāli (Bihar), a contemporary of Gautama Buddha, gave fresh impetus to Jainism. He was known as

"Jinā" as he had conquered his senses. In addition to the chastity and nonviolence which he practiced, he laid emphasis on three jewels (triratna), namely, right knowledge, right vision, and right conduct, which appealed to commoners thus making Jainism popular. (See Chapple, this volume, for detailed discussion on Jainism and Buddhism.)

Siddhārtha, born in 500 B.C.E., was the son of the Sākya chief Śuddhōdhana of Kapilavastu. Siddhārtha developed spiritual aspirations even though he had a good education, a wife, and a son. After practicing penance for six years, he realized that physical torture did not lead to higher spiritual attainment. He then meditated and finally gained enlightenment. He was therefore known as the "Buddha" (enlightened). He preached an eight-fold path for the control of desire, which is the cause of all unhappiness. He pointed out that character (śīla), concentration (samādhī), and insight (prajñā) were necessary for a spiritual life. Non-injury to all living creatures, (ahimsā) was one of his main tenets. He revived the Vedic Sangha (assembly) with highly disciplined Buddhist monks making it the center of education and social service. Buddha's teachings had a greater appeal to the common man, than the Upaniṣadic philosophy. It is however, Aśoka, the great Mauryan Emperor, who spread Buddhism in and outside India. Before Aśoka came to power, his grandfather, Chandra Gupta Maurya, had reconquered provinces of India ruled by the Persians and built up a coherent empire in the north. For understanding the political and economic condition of India in the fourth century B.C.E., a review of foreign invasions is necessary.

Foreign Invasions

Cyrus, the king of the Achaemenian Empire (558-530 B.C.E.) of Persia (Iran) invaded India. His successor, Darius, conquered and annexed the Indus valley and part of what is now called Rajasthan. They formed the largest provinces (satrapies) of the Persian Empire, but soon they became independent under the Sibis and Malavas who ruled over them. When Alexander invaded India, the Ambi ruler of Taxila surrendered to him in 327 B.C.E., but king Porus who fought bravely was defeated in the battle. When asked how he should be treated, Porus replied to Alexander, "treat me as a king," whereupon Alexander returned the kingdom to him. An important result of Alexander's conquest was that India came into closer contact with the Western world. Greek scholars learnt Indian philosophy (see the chapter by Pereira, this volume), and Indian rulers learnt Greek coinage. Greeks appreciated the organization of the four forces of the Indian military system and the syncretism of Greek and Indian art found its best expression in Gāndhara art. (See the chapter by R.C. Sharma, this volume.)

Ashoka

Chandragupta Maurya succeeded to the throne of Pātalīputra after overthrowing the last of the Nanda kings, with the help of the great scholar-statesman Chāṇakya, also known as Kauṭilya. His work Arthaśāstra is an authoritative document on political principles and practice, covering a very wide range of topics on administration, including selection and qualification of ministers, and duties and responsibilities of the king and his officers, both civil and military. It also deals with spy systems, the security of the ruler, trade, weights and measures, taxation, military, and navy. Bindusāra, who inherited the vast empire built by Chandragupta Maurya, after defeating Seleucus Nikator and annexing the Greek Provinces of the northwest, appointed his son Aśoka as the Governor of Taxila and Ujjain. He quelled the rebellion in the north and south.

After succeeding his father, Aśoka waged war with Kalinga which caused heavy loss of human life and brought Aśoka great remorse. Having realized that war meant greatest misery, he shunned violence and took steps to stop killing of humans and animals and causing them injury. He also established hospitals for their humane treatment. He made the conquest of dharma the sole aim of his rule and engraved on rocks his concept of dharma to make it known to everyone, ordering his officers to follow it as much as he himself did.

In his Rock Edict XIII, Aśoka says "My sons and grandsons who will hear about my conquests should not consider that further conquest should be undertaken. They should consider that the only true conquest is the conquest of dharma." He was keen on guiding the people in the proper way of life. He announced a simple code of conduct to be followed, which he called the Law of Piety. It recommended obedience to parents and teachers, the proper treatment of Brāhmaṇas and Śramaṇas, sympathy for the poor and distressed, charity, refraining from causing injury to animals, truthfulness, and purity of conduct. For implementing this noble precept, he appointed the Dharma Mahāmatyas whose duty it was to preach and practice dharma, administer monasteries and punish those who did not follow the Law of Piety (Sircar 1942: 24-26). Aśoka's noble character, love of his subjects whom he considered as his own children, his regard for truth, and his abjurance of violence in all forms make him one of the greatest emperors of the world. He ruled for 40 years, upholding dharma over the largest Empire of India which extended from Taxila and Baluchistan in the west, to Bihar in the east, and from Dehradun in the north to Karnataka in the south.

The provinces were administrated by Uparājas. As laid down in Arthaśāstra, spies were the eyes and ears of the king. Rigid tests were applied in the selection of governors, officers, ministers, and spies. Joint families were the order of the day. Megasthenes, the Greek Ambassador in the Court of Chandra Gupta, says in his *Indica* that people were honest and crimes few. Music, dance, and games provided entertainment. Education was given to all. There were universities at Taxila and Nalanda. Mauryan art had its own individuality as attested to by the famous polished stone pillars decorated with beautiful animal and other motifs. Organized guilds imparted training to artisans. Though Sanskrit was the literary language, Prakrit was used in the edicts. The sūtras (aphorisms) of Gautama and Baudhayana are assigned to this period. After Aśoka, his successors and their armies were weak, resulting in Bihar, Kalinga, and Karnataka becoming independent within 50 years.

Aśoka's Rock Edict XIII (Sircar 1957) mentions five Greek kings (yōna rājā) outside his kingdom, namely Antiyaka (Antiochus II Theos of Syria), Tulamaya (Ptolemy II Philadelphus of Egypt), Antikini (Antigonus Gomatas of Macedonia), Maga (Magas of Cyrene) and Alikasandara (Alexander of Epirus or Corinth). Aśoka sent emissaries to these kings and also Buddhist monks to Ceylon, Burma, and other countries to spread Buddhism. A branch of the Holy Bodhi Tree under which the Buddha had meditated was dispatched to Ceylon, and the relics of the Buddha were preserved in the stupas built by Aśoka.

The Golden Age of the Guptas

The last ruler of the fast declining empire of Aśoka was Brihadratha who was overthrown by his commander Puṣyamitra. Brihadratha established the Sunga dynasty and inherited a truncated kingdom. The settlements of Greeks, Parthians, and Kuśāṇas in various parts of India brought unprecedented change in Indian culture as a result of foreign contacts. Attacks on the kingdom of Puṣyamitra were made by Kharavela, King of Kalinga, and the Yavana Menander. The Andhra-śatavāhanas, who occupied the south up to the Godavari river, were a great seafaring people and issued coins bearing ship motifs. The Greek rule in India, under Demetrius, and Menander, lasted from 183 B.C.E. to 102 C.E.. Kāniṣka, who was the greatest of Kushan kings, had both military ability and religious zeal. He was a great patron of Buddhism. He built a wooden tower 400 feet high and a monastery at Peshawar which were destroyed by

Mahmud of Ghazna. Kaniṣka's empire extended over north India and beyond up to Central Asia. The Buddha, as Avalōkiteśvara, came to be considered God during this period. The foreign rulers, namely the Kuṣāṇas, Śakas and Satrapas identified themselves with Indian Culture, religion, language, and customs. It is interesting to find that the Greek Ambassador Heliodorus at the court of the king Bhagabhadra of Ujjain (Madhya Pradesh) became a Bhagavata (devotee of the Krishna cult known as Bhāgavatism) and erected a pillar at Vidiśā near Bhopal in honor of Vasudeva (Krishna), the devadeva (God of gods) whose shrine existed there.

King Chandragupta I settled in Ayodhya and ruled the Magadha (Bihar) and Tirhut regions and ushered in the Gupta era in 320 C.E. Samudragupta, his son, built up a large empire extending from the Hoogly to the Chambal rivers. His pillar inscription at Allahabad, composed by the poet Harisena, gives details of his conquests. Chandragupta II, who bore the title Vikramāditya, and ruled from 375 to 415 C.E., was not only the ablest administrator and military leader but also a great patron of art and literature. He conquered Gujarat and Malwa and entered into matrimonial alliances with the powerful Vākāṭaka rulers. Almost the whole of India was united under him and an era of great prosperity was ushered in. The nine gems of his court (poets and dramatists) included Kālidāsa, the author of *Shakuntala*, *Kumarasambhava,* and other works. Among other poets, Dandin, Magha and Bharavi are famous. The cultural renaissance begun by the Vākāṭakas is witnessed in the famous rock-cut temples and paintings of Ajanta(See Nalini Rao this volume.); it reached its zenith under the Gupta Kings. In administration, the guidelines laid down by the Arthaśāstra were followed, which kept the welfare of the people as the foremost aim. The king, and in his absence, the Supreme Court, administered justice. The Minister for Foreign Affairs, in cooperation with the military department, advised the king on treaties and foreign trade. The district councils were presided over by an officer of the central government. The Chinese traveller Fa-hsien's account gives a glimpse of administration. Vincent Smith (1958) says, "India was never ruled better than during the reign of Chandragupta Vikramāditya."

The Gupta rulers were well educated, disciplined and liberal. Experimentation in constructing temples began in their rule. However, but for a few small ones at Sanchi, nothing has survived the onslaught of vandals. The Vishnu (Viṣṇu temple, built during the post-Gupta period, at Deogarh in Jhansi district of Madhya Pradesh, is an excellent example of Gupta temple architecture and art.

For the first time, we find here the concept of Nara (man) and Nārāyana (Superman or God) symbolizing Arjuna and Kṛṣṇa of the Bhagavadgīta and Bhāgavata Purāṇa, the sacred texts of Vaiṣṇavites. The Gupta rulers were themselves devotees of Viṣṇu but they patronized all religions and sects.

Simultaneously in the south, the Chalukyan rulers of Badami in Karnataka carried out great experiments in temple building, culminating in the evolution of two major temple styles of India, namely the northern curvilinear roofed type (rekhānagara) and the southern stepped pyramidal type (vimāna) temples. The stages of this unique experiment can be followed in the seventy monuments built at Aihole, Mahakuta, Badami, and Pattadakal in the Bijapur district of Karnataka.

Works Cited

Bag, A.K. 1996. Mathematical and Astronomical Heritage of India. In Chattopadhyaya D.P. and Ravindrakumar. (eds.)

Bopp, F. 1945. *A Comparative Grammar of the Sanskrit, Zend, Greek, Latin, Lithuanian, Gothic, German and Slavonic Language*, translated by Eastwick B. Eng. Leipzig

Chattopadhyaya, D.P. and Ravindrakumar (eds.) 1996. *Science, Philosophy and Culture I*. Delhi: Project in the History of Indian Science, Philosophy, and Culture.

Dales, G.F. 1964. The Mythical Massacre of Mohenjodaro. *Expedition* X 13:36-43.

Elst, K. 1994. *Indigenous Indians*. Delhi: Aditya Prakashan

Frost, H. 1985. The Kition Anchors. In *Excavations at Kition*, edited by Karageorghis and M. Demas. Nicosia

Joshi, K. 1996. Significance of the Vedas in the Context of Indian Religion and Spirituality. In Chattopadhyaya D.P. and Ravindrakumar (eds.).

Lal, B.B. 1975. *Archaeology Since Independence*. Delhi: Motilal Banarsidas.

Mainkar, V.B. 1984. Metrology in the Indus Civilization. In *Frontiers of Indus Civilization*, edited by Lal B.B. and S.P. Gupta. Delhi: Books and Books.

Marshall, John. 1931. *Mohenjo-daro and the Indus Civilization I*. Delhi: Archaeological Survey of India.

Nigam, R. 1988. Was the Large Rectangular Structure at Lothal (A Harappan Settlement) a Dockyard or an Irrigation Tank? In *Marine Archaeology of Indian Ocean Countries*, edited by S.R. Rao. Goa: National Institute of Oceanography.

Panikkar, N.K. & T.N. Srinivasan. 1971. The Concept of Tides. *Ancient India: Journal of History of Science* 6.1.

Rao, S.R. 1973. *Lothal and the Indus Civilization.* Bombay: Asia Publishing House.

______. 1991. *Dawn and Devolution of the Indus Civilization.* Delhi: Aditya Prakashan.

______. 1993. The Aryans in Indus Civilization In *The Aryan Problem*, edited by S.B. Deo and Suryanath Kamath. Pune: Bharatiya Ithihasa Sankalana Samiti.

______. 1996. Scientific Tradition in India (3400-1500 B.C.). In D.P. Chattopadhyaya and Ravindrakumar. (eds.).

Sethna, K.D. 1992. *The Problem of Aryan Origins* (2nd edn.). Delhi: Aditya Prakashan.

Sircar, D.C. 1942. *Select Inscriptions bearing on Indian History and Civilization.* Delhi: Motilal Banarsidas.

Smith, V. A. 1958. *The Oxford History of India.* London: Oxford University Press.

Vats, M. S. 1974-1975. *Excavations at Harappa, being an account of archaeological excavations at Harappa carried out between the years 1920-21 and 1933-34.* 2 vols. Varanasi: Bharatiya.

Wheeler, R. E. M. 1968. *Early India and Pakistan: to Asoka.* (rev. edn.). New York: Praeger.

Chapter 3 | The Crucible of Indian History

Lallanji Gopal

The political stability and cultural effulgence which characterized India in the Vakataka-Gupta period were rudely disturbed in the sixth century. A high drama involving ambitious rulers, long drawn struggles, political manipulations, and the grouping of powers lasted for a century. It ended with the emergence of the imperial figure of Harsha (606-64 C.E.).

Harsha

Harsha ascended the throne of his paternal kingdom, Thaneshwar (Haryana), after his elder brother was treacherously murdered. To this was joined the neighboring kingdom of Maukharis with their capital at Kanyakubja (Kanauj, Uttar Pradesh). With the resources of the two kingdoms, Harsha extended his empire in northern India, with Assam, Nepal, Kashmir, Panjab, Sind and Gujarat under the sphere of his influence. But his progress to the south of the Vindhyas was checked by Pulakesin II, the Chalukya king of the Deccan. Harsha is sometimes mentioned as the last great Hindu king of north India. This evaluation arose from an ignorance of the achievements of many other kings of later periods who were by no means less glorious. Harsha was fortunate in having in Bana, the great prose-writer, a court-poet to eulogize his deeds and in Hsuan Tsang, the Chinese traveler, a friendly reporter to provide a fullness of detail which is the despair of historians for other ancient personalities and periods. But Harsha remains a remarkable personality. A valiant fighter and commander, he was also an astute administrator and a successful statesman. The author of three small plays and a patron of writers and scholars, he possessed fine sensibilities and a pronounced liberality and catholicity.

The five centuries after Harsha have been ignored by the historians of ancient India as poor appendages to the glories of the classical period. The experts of the medieval period give them a casual treatment as a backdrop to their main concern.

A mist of uncertainty hangs over the history following the death of Harsha. It is partially dispelled when Ysovarman (700-740), the king of Kanauj, carried his victorious army to Gauda (Bengal), the death of the Gauda King forming the subject of a poetic composition. Shortly after this, Lalitaditya Muktapida (724-760), a king of Kashmir, came out of the valley and ran across the Gangetic plain, a feat unparalleled in the history of Kashmir.

Kanauj seems to have acquired a halo around its name. It replaced Pataliputra (Patna, Bihar) as the center of imperial authority, and contenders to imperial supremacy tried to conquer it. In the course of time, it gained prestige as the main center of literature and culture. The Brahmins of the Kanauj region were recognized as supreme in terms of their scholarship and ritualistic purity; they were invited to different parts of the country to receive land-grants and to settle down.

The Chalukyas

In this period, the pattern of political history in the south was of a different nature. There were two main powers. The Chalukyas had their seat at Vatapi (Badami, Bijapur, Karnataka) in the western part of the Deccan, whereas the Pallavas had their capital at Kanchi (Kanchipuram near Madras, Tamilnadu) on the eastern coast. The two powers, after consolidating their authority, went beyond their respective regions, to enhance their imperial aura. The bone of contention between the two was the land between the Krishna and the Tungabhadra rivers. Pulakesin II (609-642) of the Chalukya family almost reached Kanchi and succeeded in annexing the northern territory between the Krishna and the Godavari. Narasimhavarman (630-668) of the Pallavas had his revenge when he occupied Vatapi after Pulakesin met his death in battle. The conflict was resumed after a lull. Vikramaditya II (733-745) of the Chalukya family overran Kanchi three times. The Pallavas were completely defeated in 740. But the Chalukya themselves could not survive long. Their feudatories, the Rashtrakutas, ousted them in 757.

The Arab Invasion of Sind: Attack and Defense

The early attempts of the Arabs under the Caliphate to extend their political authority over India receives a passing reference as a minor episode. Its significance is to be evaluated against the wider context of contemporary world history. The Arab invasion of Sind (712) under Muhammad-ibn-Qasim was not an isolated event to punish pirates for seizing Arab women. It was the final attempt after earlier ones had failed. The account reads like a tale in the *Arabian Nights* with gripping details of vigorous attack and stout defense, treachery and faithfulness, success and failure, and the dramatic turn of events. But further advance towards the east and north was effectively checked. Mansurah, a new city founded on the ruins of the earlier capital Brahmanabad, and Multan survived for some three hundred years as the seats of Muslims. In the northwest, the thrust was contained for two hundred years by the tiny principalities of Zabul and Kabul. Later, the Shahi rulers of Kabul continued the resistance. This failure of the mighty Arab power, with remarkable success in the West up to Egypt and in the east up to Central Asia through Persia, redounds to the glory of these native states; but they failed to appreciate the developments beyond the frontiers and deal with the situation in a realistic manner.

Three Empires: Struggle for Supremacy

Toward the close of the eighth century a long drawn struggle for supremacy in the north began, which lasted 150 years. The two main contestants were the Gurjara-Pratiharas, who came from Rajasthan, and the Palas of Bengal. From time to time, the Rashtrakutas of Manyakheta (Malkhed, near Sholapur) joined the fray, thus converting it into a tripartite struggle. The Gurjara-Pratiharas came to occupy Kanauj. In this struggle, the conquest of Kanauj symbolized imperial supremacy. There were several stages in the struggle, with success alternating between the Gurjara-Pratiharas and the Palas. The Gurjara-Pratiharas had a long line of remarkable kings, including Vatsaraja and Nagabhata II. Of these, the power and personality of Mihira-Bhoja (836-885) were praised by the Arab travelers. The Palas were served well by Dharmapala (770-810) and Devapala (810-850), who are eulogized as extending their empire from the extreme north to the extreme south. The Palas do not seem to have controlled the regions to the east of Bihar for long. From time to time, the Rashtrakutas invaded the north. Dhruva II (780-793), Govinda III (793-814), Indra III (914-922), and Krishna III (939-967), scored victories. But they never attempted a lasting control over the Gangetic plain. In due time, the three powers exhausted themselves and the struggle petered out. This struggle interested the contemporary Arab geographers and travelers who describe the power and empire of the three contestants. They praise the Rashtrakutas, but recognize the superior might of the Pratiharas. The Chinchani Plates (Thana, Maharashtra middle of the tenth century) record land-grants for the support of mosques. The keenness to attract Arab traders was associated with a tolerance of new religious views and practices.

The disintegration of the three empires created a void in the tenth century which was partially filled by their feudatories who fought for supremacy. Among the successors of the Pratiharas, five outstanding feudatories were the Gahadavalas, Chandellas, Paramaras, Chahamanas (Chauhans), and the Chalukyas (Solankis), who ruled in different parts of the empire from Gujarat to Bihar. According to a later tradition, all arose from the sacrificial pit of Vasishtha. A wrongful interpretation of this legend takes it to suggest an Agnikuta origin of the five families of foreigners purified by the sacrificial fire. In this period, there were other families in the region, the Kalachuris, the Chedis, and the Tomaras. The five families were possibly singled out on account of their resistance to Muslim invasions. The various kingdoms were involved in a long struggle for establishing their empire, but without any lasting success. There were decades of glory for all of them separately when they could make the neighboring kingdoms respect their superior power. They all claim some remarkable rulers, who extended political power and influence and also contributed to the cultural spheres. Bhoja (1000-1055) of the Paramara dynasty was the most outstanding king whose versatility as a man and scholar has left a deep impression on the collective memory of the country. The Chandella dynasty has a line of distinguished rulers, Dhanga (954-1008), Ganda, Vidyadhara (1017-1019), and Yasovarman. Jayasimha Siddharaja (1094-1143) and Kumarapala (1143-1171) of the Chalukya dynasty of Gujarat were also great kings. The Gahadavalas, with Kasi as their second capital, maintained the glorious traditions of Kanyakubja. Govindahcandra and Jayachandra were the two important kings of the family, though the second one earned a bad name for his enmity with Prithviraja III (1177-1192) of the Chahamana (Chauhan) dynasty, making the task of Muhammad Ghori easier. Prithviraja is honored as a hero for his valor, chivalry, and indomitable will. But, it was on account of his mistakes as a statesman and general, his failure to understand the reality of the situation, and his misplaced leniency, that Muhammad Ghori defeated him and conquered north India.

Muslim Invasions in the North

A second theme for the political history of north India in the post-Pratihara period is the entry of Muslim political power through the north-west. It covers the period up to the end of the Mughal empire and the establishment of British colonial rule. The eleventh and the twelfth centuries are treated as a prelude to the main period, divided into two phases. But the story remains incomplete and one-sided, because we do not have evidence to record the resistance offered by the vanquished and their reaction to the new arrivals.

The story begins in 1000 when Mahmud of Ghazni first invaded India. In resisting Mahmud, Anandapala, the Shahi ruler, received support from some kings of north India, but to no avail. Mahmud invaded different regions on seventeen occasions. He could not gain any permanent conquest beyond Panjab. The Yaminis succeeded him as rulers of Panjab. After a century and a half, Muizz-ud-din Muhammad, the Turkish chief of Ghur, invaded India in 1175. He was repulsed by Mularaja, the Chalukya ruler of Gujarat, in 1178, and was defeated by Prithviraja at Tarain in 1192. He later vanquished Jayachandra, the Gahadevala king and overran the Gangetic plains. Muhammad's trusted slave, Qutub-ud-din-Aibek, extended his conquests. Bakhtyar Khalji carried Turkish power in the east, capturing Gaur, the capital of Bengal, in a dramatic manner, which shows the weakness of the Indian polity at that time.

The Sultanates

Muhammad was assassinated in 1206, having established a Turkish state from Panjab to Bengal. Delhi was the capital of this state which was known as the Sultanate of Delhi (1206-1526). It included a number of dynasties, the Mameluk, the Khaljis, the Tughlaqs, the Saiyids, and the Lodis.

The Sultanate was founded by Qutub-ud-din-Aibek (1206-1210). The Sultans of the thirteenth century are referred to as the Mameluk or Slave dynasty. But this is a misnomer, because only three of the eleven sultans in this group were originally slaves. Of the three, it was only Qutub-ud-din who was a slave, the other two, Iltutmish and Balban, had been manumitted before they acquired rulership. The eleven sultans belonged to three families (Qutubi, Shamsi, and Balban) and not to one.

Iltumish (1210-1236) consolidated the conquests of Mahmud and tried to introduce political cohesion through administration. The Sultanate was saved the fury of the Mongol menace, when Changiz Khan chose to retreat. Iltutmish was succeeded by his daughter Razia (1236-1240), the only woman to become ruler of Delhi.

She exhibited rare courage and strength suppressing the initial opposition, but ultimately, the manipulations of the Turkish nobles brought about her end. Balban, who had a checkered career in many capacities before he became Sultan, broke the power of the nobility and exalted the kingly office by introducing befitting court ceremonials and etiquette. He was also able to contain the threat of Mongol invasions. In the confusion following his death (1287), Jalaluddin Khalji (1290-1296) established the Khalji dynasty.

The Chalukya and Chola Empires in the South

The political vicissitudes in North India in the eleventh to thirteenth centuries did not ruffle the Deccan and the South. They were dominated by the imperial glories of the Western Chalukyas of Kalyana and the Cholas of Tanjavur and their feudatories in the later part of their rule. The political fortunes of these families present a history which is by no means less gripping and less significant. They are, however, overshadowed by the central importance assigned to Delhi. The extent of their empire, the peace resulting from their efficient administration, and the development of art and culture under them entitle them to more importance than hitherto apportioned to them.

The Chalukyas emerged out of the ruins of the Rashtrakuta empire. Taila II (973-997) founder of the dynasty, measured swords with his northern neighbors, the Paramaras of Malwa. The Chalukya supremacy over the Deccan was complete. A branch of the family was established in eastern Deccan, with the capital at Vengi. Vikramaditya VI (1076-1126) of the main branch would rank among the greatest rulers by virtue of his achievements in peace and war. He is the hero of the Sanskrit poem, *Vikramankadevacharita*. Vijnanesvara wrote the *Mitakshara*, a commentary on the *Yajnavalkyasmrti* in his times.

The Chola empire had no lineal connection with the Cholas of the early Tamil literature. Its imperial glory begins with Rajaraja (985-1014). The whole of South India, the Maldives, and a part of Sri Lanka formed his empire. The foundations of the great Chola empire were laid by Rajaraja's organization of an efficient administration and establishment of a very effective military power, including a strong navy. Peace and happiness of the people served as the basis for their cultural developments of excellence. The Brihadisvara temple at Tanjavur remains a lasting testimony to Chola greatness. On the strong foundation of the empire, laid by Rajaraja, his son Rajendra Chola (1012-1044) raised a solid and magnificent edifice. The administrative machinery was consolidated and expanded.

The democratic functioning of the village assemblies, having real and wide powers, was harmonized with a very efficient bureaucracy, having an elaborate and well-knit system of order, scrutiny and audit. Rajendra Chola harnessed the military might of his empire for remarkable victories. He earned the distinctive appellation of "Gangaikondachola" for extending his conquest to Bengal and Bihar, reaching the Ganga river itself. He is the first Indian king whose navy crossed the Bay of Bengal to defeat the Sailendras of Malaya and Indonesia. This was not motivated by a vainglorious desire for show of power. India was directly concerned with the international sea-trade through south-east Asia and Rajendra asserted his might to protect its interest.

Taking advantage of the weaknesses of the Chalukyas and the Cholas under subsequent rulers, several feudatory families tried to assert their independent power and embark on a career of imperial glory. In the extreme south, the Pandyas, who had often fought against the hegemony of the Cholas, had a major breakthrough under Jatavarman Kulasekhara (1190-1216). Later, Maravarman Sundara Pandya I (1216-1238) carried fire and sword to the Chola capital Tanjavur.

The Hoyasalas, who started their career from Velapura (Belur, Karnataka), made their mark under Vishnuvardhana (1106-1147), who transferred his capital to Dvarasamudra (Halebid, Karnataka). The peace and prosperity of the kingdom are reflected in the high artistic merit of its temples, some of which are still extant to proclaim it.

The Yadavas, who replaced the Hoyasalas, started from the northern part of Karnataka, but are famous as the rulers of Deogori. The Kakatiyas of Warangal (Andhra Pradesh) were among the important powers of eastern Deccan.

The history of the kingdoms in the Deccan and South has its own charms, thrills, and achievements not only in war but also in peace. They have many a hero and many a towering personality in the domains of art, literature, philosophy, and religion. Their continuous fighting and internal conspiracies rendered them easy prey to the attacks of Malik Kafur and his master Ala-ud-din Khalji.

The First All India Muslim Empire

The Khaljis (1290-1320) had a very short history, but in some respects, they represent a turning point in the history of India. Ala-ud-din Khalji (1296-1316) established the first all-India Muslim empire. Some fifteen hundred years after Asoka, political unity was effected, which dominated the history of subsequent times. Henceforth, the regions in the south could not remain unaffected by the changes taking place in Delhi. For four hundred years, the enjoyment of authority by Muslim sultans and emperors was the dominant feature of India's political history. Ala-ud-din brought under his subjugation all the kingdoms down to the extreme south. Some of these dragged on for a short period before they were finally wiped out. Ala-ud-din is famous for boldly asserting his authority and rejecting the control of religious leadership. His market regulations and attempts to regulate prices were bold steps for his times.

The short duration of Khalji rule could not make any deep impact on the polity and social life. The Khaljis were followed by the Tughluqs (1320-1412), referred to as "Qaraunah Turks." Muhammad bin Tughluq (1324-1351), the son and successor of Ghiyas-ud-din Tughluq, had an innovative mind, and planned administrative changes, including the introduction of a copper currency and the shifting of the capital from Delhi to the safer and more centrally situated Daultabad. Impatient and haughty by nature, he could not plan to meet any eventuality in the actual implementation of the scheme and hence did not succeed. Firuz Tughluq (1351-1387), though bigoted in some respects, initiated several works of public welfare, such as digging canals and establishing schools and hospitals. In 1398, Timur, a Turk from Transoxiana, generally known under his nickname of "Timur-i-lang" (Timur the lame), who had annexed Afghanistan, Persia, Syria, Qurdistan, and most of Asia Minor, chose to invade India. Motivated by the lust for loot and a fanatic zeal to wipe out infidels, he perpetrated wanton destruction and the massacre of whole populations, the like of which is not recorded for any other country in history. In the resulting chaos and confusion, the empire perished.

Not only Gujarat, Malwa, and Jaunpur, but a number of smaller principalities were founded. Khizr Khan, who was appointed governor of Multan, Lahore, and Dipalpur by Timur, founded the Saiyid dynasty.

The Saiyid dynasty (1414-1451) had an ephemeral existence for thirty-seven years over a vastly reduced territory. The Lodi dynasty (1451-1526) restored a semblance of order and authority for three quarters of a century. However the attempts to reestablish authority undertaken by Ibrahim Lodi could not succeed. The rivalries and jealousies of powers in North India then offered Babur a favorable opportunity.

Thus, to term the period ending in 1526 the age of the Delhi Sultanate is to overemphasize the central importance of Delhi, not in conformity with its chronological and geographical expansion. It would be equally wrong to refer to the period as the age of Muslim India, because, besides the north Indian Sultanate and its successor states of Gujarat, Khandesh, Malwa, Jaunpur, Bengal, Sind, and Multan, the Bahmani Kingdom alone had Muslim rulers, leaving the larger principalities of Vijayanagara, Mewar, Marwar, Orissa, Assam, and Mithila beyond the label.

The Bahmani Kingdom was founded in 1347 by Gangu, who assumed the title of "Alauddin Hasan Bahman Shah." The long drawn struggle of the Bahmanis with the Vijayanagara Kingdom began during the reign of Muhammad Shah (1358-1375). Ahmad Shah I (1422-1436) shifted the capital from Gulbarga to Bidar, Karnataka. Prime minister Mahmud Gawan, one of the greatest figures in medieval India, extended the territorial limits of the kingdom and enhanced its political prestige. He overran the western coastal areas, he introduced many reforms in administration, patronized the arts, and promoted education. But, he could not win the confidence of the local factions, who had him executed by Sultan Muhammad Shah III in 1481. The glories of the kingdom dimmed. With the death of Kalimullah in 1538, the kingdom was divided into five principalities—Golconda, Bijapur, Ahmadnagar, Berar, and Bidar.

Age of Glory: The Vijayanagara Empire

Considering its political prestige and cultural achievements, resulting from the peace and tranquillity created by its administrative set-up, the Vijayanagara Kingdom (1336-1565) deserves a place among the most glorious kingdoms in the history of India. It was ruled by a succession of three dynasties, Sangama, Suluva, and Taluva. The kingdom was founded by two brothers, Harihara and Bukka, who soon came to occupy the territories in the Hoyasala kingdom. The regular clashes of the Vijayanagara kingdom with the Bahmani Sultans in their three contiguous areas could not lead to any definite result besides exhausting them.

Harihara II (1377-1406) attempted expansion of his kingdom towards the eastern coast and Sri Lanka. The testimonies of Nicolo Conti, an Italian traveler, and Abdur Razzaq, a Persian traveler, confirm the prestige of the Vijayanagara kingdom as the most prosperous and powerful state in South India under Deva Raya I (1406-1422) and Deva Raya II (1422-1446). Deva Raya I constructed a dam across the Tungabhadra, and through canals relieved the scarcity of water in the capital. After the death of Deva Raya II, the throne was usurped by the minister Suluva. This dynasty had a short life.

The third, the Taluva dynasty, is famous for Krishna Deva Raya (1509-1530), the greatest ruler of Vijayanagara, who ranks among the greatest in the annals of Indian history. In South India, the military prestige of the kingdom was at its highest. Krishna Deva Raya contained the Portuguese, but did not create a navy for completely eradicating their menace. His rule was characterized by tolerance and harmony. The peace and prosperity, created by efficient administration, were noticed by the foreign travelers Barbosa, Paes, and Nuniz. Krishna Deva Raya was himself a great scholar of Telugu and Sanskrit. The period witnessed a rich development of architecture and the flowering of Telugu literature.

The instability after the death of Krishna Deva Raya ended with Sadashiva Raya (1543-1567) coming to power. Under him, Rama Raja demonstrated high diplomatic skill, playing off one neighboring state against the other. But, all these combined to defeat the Vijayanagara Kingdom in the battle of Talikota (1565) which marks the end of the kingdom's glory.

In 1492, Vasco de Gama came to Goa on the west coast of India, which led to the establishment of a Portuguese principality. The impact of this episode was not immediately perceptible in other parts of the country. But it proved to be of abiding importance in the long run. It opened India to trade, which led to the creation of European colonies, ultimately resulting in the foundation of British rule. Thus, crossing the chronological limits of the medieval period, it is connected remotely with the ushering in of the modern period of Indian history.

The Mughal Empire

Zahir-ud-din Muhammad Babur, failing to retain his parental state of Farghana in Trans-Oxiana and the city of Samarqand, occupied Kabul in 1504. His ambition drew him to India. He invaded India and defeated Ibrahim Lodi at the Battle of Panipat (near Delhi) in 1526. Through his desperate tenacity, committed sincerity, skill as a general, and use of artillery, he overcame the strong military opposition of Rana Sanga and the Afghans in a quick series of wars. Within the short span of four years, he could not take effective steps to consolidate his gains. His son, Humayun, "tumbled" throughout his life, and weakened by the strife among his brothers failed to curb the revived Afghan challenge. He was defeated by Sher Khan, famous under his later name "Sher Shah Suri," at Bilgram (near Kanauj, U.P.) in 1540, and had to leave India.

The interlude of Afghan rule under Sher Shah (1540-1545) is one of the bright spots in Indian history. Enjoying popular regard for his just and considerate rule, Sher Shah standardized revenue administration. After a proper land survey, one-third of the gross produce, determined according to the classification of land, was fixed as land revenue. The system implemented by Todarmal and continued under Akbar was not much different from this. Sher Shah made improvements in the military system as well. He built trunk roads, one connecting Sonargaon (Bangledesh) with the Indus and another running from Agra to Burhanpur, with proper facilities for travelers. The silver rupee, which he minted, was the currency until 1835 and was adopted by the British.

The Suri dynasty survived for nine years. After the death of Islam Shah in 1554 Humayun got his chance. He entered Delhi in 1555, but "tumbled" out of life in 1556.

Akbar (1556-1605) was in his twelfth year when he became emperor. His guardian Bairam Khan helped him score a signal victory over Himu in the second battle of Panipat (1556) which sealed the Afghan cause. In the initial stages, Bairam Khan accomplished many significant conquests. In 1560, Akbar assumed charge of the government. A series of brilliant victories, achieved through superior military power, skill of generalship and astute statesmanship, brought the whole of North India under his control. Akbar was an imperialist. His conquests were purely political matters, not disfigured by religious considerations. He realized that to achieve his goal and stabilize his empire, he needed the valiant Rajputs as allies and not enemies. The earlier rulers of Delhi had failed against the indomitable will, courage, and valor of the Rajput chiefs. The new policy was the cornerstone of the strength of the Mughal empire. Akbar conquered some Rajput states, others he befriended through matrimonial and peaceful relations. It was his constant endeavor to enlist the remaining states as supporters of the Mughal empire. Akbar's success in expanding and stabilizing his empire was largely due to the active cooperation of his Rajput allies. After his success in the north, he directed his attention towards the Deccan and formulated a well-planned policy of expansion and control.

Akbar appreciated the need for building his empire based on the good will and support of all sections of people. He made a conscious effort to bring them together and to provide for their welfare. His promulgation of the Din-I-Ilahi is criticized as an ill-advised folly of attempt to found a new religion. Misplaced doubts have been cast by some about his sincerity in searching for the truth in the different religions and forging a synthesis. But, in any case, it is obvious that he had a genuine concern for harmony in his empire.

The political, social, and religious views of Akbar gave a new orientation to state policy. They worked for the peace and happiness of the people and for the stability of the empire. A deviation from them weakened the fabric of the empire and brought about its disintegration.

The fruits of Akbar's policies were enjoyed by his successor, Jahangir (1605-1627) and Shahjahan (1627-1668). They ushered in an era of peace and tranquillity which fostered the growth of art and culture, sometimes described as the "golden age."

Disintegration of the Mughal Empire

In the struggle for succession among the four sons of Shahjahan, the failure of Dara Shikoh, of liberal views and a genuine interest in Hindu philosophy and religious texts, gave a new turn to the course of Indian history. Aurangzeb (1658-1707) carried the Deccan policy to its successful end and conquered the southern states to establish an all-India empire. But the success was short-lived and contained the germs of its own disintegration. In those times of movement and transport, the effective control over a vast empire could not survive for long. It was a natural process for centrifugal forces to assert themselves in outlying areas. They were supported by the defects in the policies and actions of Aurangzeb. The economic strains of long years of war in the Deccan weakened the resources of the empire and Aurangzeb's absence from Delhi loosened his grip over the central structure.

Aurangzeb alienated the Rajputs, who no longer remained faithful supporters of the Empire. In the Deccan, he introduced the element of religion in his policy which accounted for the rise and rapid expansion of Maratha power. Aurangzeb was also actuated by imperialist considerations, but, it is not without significance that many communities, raised the banner of rebellion which highlighted issues of religious persecution. These include the Sikhs, Marathas, Jats, and Satnamis. They mustered strength and increased their striking capacity with the passage of time.

The Mughal empire lasted for a century and a half more. The authority of the emperor was curtailed by provincial governors and local chiefs. The warring factions at the court reduced the emperor to the position of a mere puppet in the hands of the King-makers. The expansion of the Maratha power and foreign invasions further diminished the authority of the empire. The increasing territorial ambition of the European trading companies first nibbled at and later swallowed several parts of the erstwhile empire. The mockery of the empire, resulting from the shrinkage of its territory and the reduction of its authority, left the last Mughal emperor master of only a small part of his imperial capital.

Not a Feudal System

The nature of the political authority of the sultans and the political instability of the period did not offer much opportunity for introducing an efficient administrative set up. The Mughal kings had the advantage of having effective power over a larger territory and for a longer duration, allowing them to pay more attention to the details of administration. The change is reflected in Babur and his successors assuming the title "Padshah" which cast off even the semblance of the overlordship of Khalifa. There were various officers in the set up to cover all aspects of administration at different levels. Many details of the system were retained by British rule. But, at the lowest level of the village, the role of the Panchayats became more pervasive and effective, eliciting from nineteenth century British officers the designation of "tiny republics" which sustained the continuity of Indian life and institutions.

The emergence of feudalism is often mentioned as the most distinguishing feature of the post-Harsha period. Though doubts have been raised about its nature, some scholars challenge the applicability of the term itself. It has been studied mostly for the closing phase of the ancient period, which is sometimes designated as the early medieval period, to distinguish it from the medieval period proper beginning with the Mameluks to the establishment of British rule.

The term "feudalism" is not restricted to the political system, but is interpreted as a socio-economic phenomenon, all-pervading and influencing all aspects of life and society including art, literature, and religion. This is criticized by some as being too sweeping a term. Feudalism in India does not have all the features found in the European context. It was more characteristic of the political structure, consisting of chiefs, lords, and overlords, and their hierarchy. In India, features of a feudal economy are evidenced, but not in full. The Central structure did not collapse totally and "fiefs" could not emerge as the basis of socio-political reality and relationship. The economy did not become completely localized and agricultural. Coins in use were by no means scarce, though their quality and artistic merit had suffered. Foreign trade also continued, albeit other competitors had joined in, and its nature and direction had changed. Feudal obligations had not acquired a set and formal nature. The peasantry were not reduced to the position of serfs. To explain all the changes in life and culture as symptomatic of a feudal economy is stretching the point. The elements of feudal polity and economy were accentuated in the medieval period by the compulsions of administration. The seats of nobles and chiefs suited feudal economy and culture.

Contemporary Social System

The Indian social system, which was based on a balanced view of life and sound sociological principles, underwent changes. Some features of Indian social life, which disfigured it and are the subject of criticism, surfaced in this period. The unrealistic orthodoxy, the rigidity of the social system, the alienation of the lower classes, and the subjugation and seclusion of the women were the major defects which weakened the Indian social system.

In the earlier phases of the period, the social system did not suffer from rigidity and orthodoxy, which came to characterize it later. The *Devalasmriti*, a text composed around 730 C.E., breathes a spirit of liberality, which may serve as a manifesto for social redress to wronged women. It provides that a woman, who has been forcibly taken by a *mlechchha* (a term for an outlandish barbaric people), can go back to her original socio-cultural group, even after long years of stay resulting in pregnancy. This liberal provision was applicable also to men, who lived with a *mlechchha* and took his food.

Al-Biruni, towards the beginning of the eleventh century, points out some important features of the Indian people. These observations are not to be dismissed as emanating from ignorance or prejudice. They are a critical analysis of the contemporary Indian mind by an outsider and may help us understand better the realities and the thoughts and attitudes affecting the social system. Al-Biruni says that the Hindus call foreigners *mlechcha*, i.e. impure, and forbid having any connection with them, be it by intermarriage or any other kind of relationship, or by sitting, eating, and drinking with them, because thereby they think they would be polluted. They consider impure anything which touches the fire and water of a foreigner. Besides they never desire that a thing which once has become polluted should be purified and thus recovered. They are not allowed to receive anybody, who does not belong to them, even if he wished it, or was inclined to their religion. He adds,

> According to their own belief, there is no other country on earth but theirs, no other race of man but theirs and no created beings besides them have any

> knowledge or science whatsoever. . . . If they traveled and mixed with other nations they would soon change their mind, for their ancestors were not as narrow minded as the present generation is.

The process of the transformation of *Varnas* (classes) into *Jatis* (castes) commenced earlier, but the caste system acquired the basic elements of its form and features in the early medieval period. There was a proliferation of castes. The traditional system explained them theoretically as originating from the inter-mixing of castes and subcastes. But actually they had different origins. The craft guilds fossilized into castes. Some social and occupational groups were also recognized as castes. The foreign population and tribal communities were also accommodated in the system. The period witnessed the emergence of the occupational group of the Kayasthas as a new caste. Among the Kshatriyas, the Rajputs came to be recognized as a distinct group. We have records of some Brahmin families transforming into Kshatriya ruling dynasties. Some castes developed subgroups based on geographical divisions. There was a tendency to demarcate hierarchical status within a caste. Thus, we hear of Kshatriyas and Sudras being divided into high and low groups. Hereditary occupational requirements and strict rules about dining and marriage within the caste contributed to the strictness of caste distinctions. Notions of sacramental purity and occupational impurity led to the attribution of grades of "untouchability" to some caste groups.

Islam and India: Perceptions and Perspectives

The period has been much wronged. When presented in dark colors of persecution and intolerance, it made the excesses of colonial rule appear comparatively mild. It suited the interests of the foreign ruling power to project the image of the two major communities in India as perpetually fighting. The narrow political interests of some people, including historians, did not help redress this perversion and instead created a jaundiced view. The basic difficulty arises from the inability to appreciate the true significance of the evidence supplied by contemporary writers who sometimes gave exaggerated figures and hyperbolic accounts to glorify the all-conquering destiny of Islam.

It is interesting that whereas the Pakistani historians often accept credulously such statements, some Indian historians treat them as recording representative scars, which, in reality, were deeper wounds. Any attempt to reject the historicity of the central facts carries conviction with none. Some historians advance economic motives to explain the cases of loot and destruction; others transfer the blame to the bigoted religious leadership for fueling the fire of enmity. The events under reference are associated with widely separated individuals and groups, but they are made to form a single unit, through their personal religion. It is not duly appreciated that the dynasties of Delhi sultans and provincial principalities were not theocratic states. It is not religion which was to blame. The events of looting, destruction, and persecution can never be justified, but are to be explained against the background of those times, when in many communities and countries, we find instances of similar actions.

Tarachand attempted a pioneering study of the impact of Islam on Indian culture(Chand 1936). His lead has not been followed by in-depth studies of all spheres of life and society. The process of cultural change worked both ways. Islamic thought and way of life brought about changes in Indian society. In the process, Islamic society also underwent significant changes not to be found in its counterparts in other countries.

What is more important is the cultural fusion which slowly and gradually proceeded. Not much ruffled by the bitterness of politics, the social relationship between various communities and classes in its natural course gave birth to the thoughts and way of life specifically Indian. The mixing of two people involves both confrontation and assimilation. Hitherto strife and misunderstanding had been over emphasized, keeping mutual adjustment and influence low key.

This was the beginning of a new India. On the foundations of the fundamental unity, based on a cultural system and values, a colorful edifice was raised. The process of change, assimilation, and adjustment is to be noticed in the lives of people and in cultural spheres. Dress, food-habits, social customs, festivities, and festivals bear its impression. Language and literature, which are the medium of expression and communication, provide powerful indications of the mutual interaction. Fields of cultural activities, art, and music bear indelible marks of the graceful steps taken by the social ethos.

A New India: Assimilation and Adjustment

This period experienced an expansion of urban life and an increase in the number of cities. In the ancient period, there were, no doubt, cities, which, in some cases, show knowledge of the principles of town-planning laid down in the texts. But, generally towns were not established; small settlements grew into towns. The tendency for the establishment of towns, accentuated under the impact of feudal polity, was developed further due to the exigencies of administration in the medieval period. The chiefs wished to imitate the emperor and the governors and, thus, promoted town-like settlements. There is evidence for the rise of many such towns, sometimes named after their founders. These towns often had definite planning with distinctive characteristics in the form of gates, surrounding walls, division of settlements, and pattern of houses. In the predominantly rural pattern of Indian life and settlements, the new dimension of towns came to be highlighted.

In India, fortification is evidenced certainly from the times of the Indus Valley civilization. In the context of feudal polity and warfare, forts and fortification received an added importance. In the Deccan and Rajasthan particularly, forts played a decisive role. The mode of warfare, the weapons used, and the location and form of forts rendered them virtually impregnable. The Mughal emperors took special interest in building strong and imposing forts at strategic places. Even after centuries, they impress with their majestic form.

Likewise, though in the ancient period gardens were maintained and horticulture was cultivated as a discipline, under the Mughals, the maintenance of gardens was developed as a distinct trait of cultured life. Gardens, orchards, and parks were laid around palaces, administrative headquarters, and public places, on river banks, and in valleys. At Agra, Lahore, Srinagar, and many other places, beautiful gardens survive to confirm this. Besides the use of new varieties of fruits and flowers and improved techniques, the gardens were characterized by a design and lay-out, an intricate lace-work of waterways, channels, fountains, waterfalls, and pavilions, which created a veritable fairy land for rest and recreation.

The classical tradition of art efflorescent in the Vakataka-Gupta age grew in the post-Harsha period. There was an outburst of architectural activity. The north Indian temples, having several regional varieties, are imposing with their majestic proportions, harmoniously blended members, tapering pinnacles, captivating figures, and decorative motifs. The south Indian temples have a different form and arrangement of members and a distinctive gateway. A third style, a mixture of these two, is also found. Later, the architectural tradition languished in North India and Central India but survived in Rajasthan. In the south, the traditions of the Chalukyas and the Rashtrakutas, on one hand, and the Pallavas and Cholas on the other, were not only maintained but also developed under the Hoysalas and the Vijayanagara Kingdom in terms of forms, artistic excellence, and ornamentation.

The sculptures in different regional schools from the early medieval period are graceful in their majestic proportions, body shapes and movements, ornamentation, and elaboration. They have a standardization and uniformity which reveal the controlling hands of traditional injunctions. But, the creativity and freshness, vivid on the specimens of the Gupta period, are not so clearly perceptible.

This period witnessed remarkable developments in the field of bronze sculpture. There were two main centers of this art, Bengal under the Palas and the Chola empire. They exhibit a high technical skill in modeling. The specimens have well proportioned figures in graceful poses, evoking admiration for their artistic excellence and harmony. The art form traveled from Bengal to Nepal and Tibet and from the Cholamandalam to Sri Lanka.

The early sultans of Delhi did not have the time to indulge in much purposeful art activity. The Indo-Persian or Indo-Sarscenic style of architecture was essentially a continuation of Indian art techniques applied by Indian artists to the requirements of their masters. Under the Tughluqs, there was a new shift from ornamentation and elaboration to puritanical simplicity and chaste sobriety. Free from the dominating influence of Delhi, the provincial dynasties gave more support to architectural creations, developing distinctive traits of their own.

Babur, with his admiration for the architecture of the Timurids, did not have one word of praise for the Turko-Afghan monuments of Delhi. Mughal architecture began with Akbar constructing forts, palaces, mosques, and mausoleums. They represent a happy synthesis of Hindu and Muslim art traditions, evolving a homogenous shape, component parts including domes, arches, portals and gateways, and decorative designs. The magnificent constructions by Shahjahan easily established his reign as that paradigmatic of the Golden Age. The Taj Mahal, ranked as one of the seven wonders of the ancient world, is the crowning glory of his reign. It translates the poetic dream of the emperor to commemorate his love for his queen Mumtaz Mahal into white marble.

The illustrious tradition of painting noticed in the temples at Ellora was continued first in the Chola and later in the Vijayanagara temples. In western India, miniature painting developed in association with the Jain. It began in Gujarat, but spread to the adjoining territories of Malwa and Rajasthan. Earlier, it was done on palm leaves. Later, paper replaced palm leaf giving the artist a better scope in matters of subject, style, and color. There was a different tradition of miniature painting in eastern India, under the Palas of Bengal, and later in Orissa.

The sultans of Delhi were hostile to painting as it is reminiscent of idolatry. But migrating Muslim scholars, theologians, and artisans brought with them the Persian style of painting. In the closing years of the Sultanate period, it influenced the classical Indian style to give birth to what is termed the "Sultanate school of painting." Under the sultans of Bijapur and Golconda, an independent style of painting developed. These kingdoms employed many Persian and Turkish artists who introduced Persian traditions of painting, especially in landscape, decorative figures, and designs. Artists coming to these courts from the Vijayanagara Kingdom synthesized these traditions with the indigenous style to originate a style of Deccan, or more properly, Bijapur, painting.

A new synthesis in painting began with two Persian painters whom Humayun brought from Iran. Under Akbar, there was a separate imperial establishment for painting in which painters from different parts of the country, both Hindus and Muslims, worked together to originate a new style, applied alike to Persian and Indian books. It created a three dimensional effect in place of the flat one of the Persian style and used Indian colors. Portuguese influence inspired the adoption of the principles of perspective. Painting reached unprecedented heights under Jahangir, especially in portraits and animal painting. The dispersal of painters from Delhi led to the growth of Rajasthani and Pahari schools of painting, emphasizing mythological scenes, cycles of seasons, and melodies.

The process of integration surfaces prominently in music and dance. The religious prohibition was not strictly followed by Muslims. Many rulers patronized musicians and practiced music. Sufi saints believed in the efficacy of music as an aid to spiritual progress. Amir Khusrau made a judicious combination of Persian melodies with Indian music. His poems were composed in Indian tunes. He introduced the Khayal style of singing, and evolved Qawwali mode of light music and his contribution to the evolution of sitar is also noteworthy.

The provincial rulers gave liberal patronage to music. Raja Mansingh Tomar of Gwalior (1486-1519) encouraged his musicians to evolve new melodies and popularized *Dhrupad* singing. His work, the *Manakutuhala*, records the distinguishing features of North Indian music. Ibrhim Adil Shah II (1580-1626), the Sultan of Bijapur, begins his *Kitab-i-Nauras* ("Book on the Nine Sentiments") with prayers to Hindu gods and goddesses and explains the melodies with his own songs. In the later half of the fourteenth century, a bifurcation of the two systems of music, Hindustani and Karnatak (Carnatic) took place, the former resulting from a mixture of the Indian and

Persian systems, the latter being the single unitary system of south India (see chapter by Satyanarayana in this volume).

Among dance styles, the Kathak shows unmistakable traits of cultural fusion. This dance style, current in North India, particularly in Uttar Pradesh, was developed by Vaisnava mystics. With the Muslim rule patronizing court dances, the Kathak style underwent major changes. Women began participating in this dance. The dancers adopted Persian dress, and themes included secular subjects. Kathak became a decorative, expressive, sensuous, and elegant art, having two centers, one in Rajasthan and the other in the Agra, Delhi, and Lucknow area.

Persian, Urdu, and the Regional Languages

In India, the state has always promoted education. The sultans of Delhi established and patronized schools based on orthodox Islamic concepts. In line with his state policy, Akbar introduced a system of education which emphasized secular elements in the curriculum. Along with Arabic studies, concerned mostly with Islamic scriptures and theology, Persian studies were popularized, which were broad-based and included many secular subjects. At higher levels, the study of rational sciences was introduced. The state run workshops provided industrial and technical education.

Sanskrit, the classical language, continued to serve its role, considerably curtailed, as the medium of exchange among people from different parts of the country. It had become the language of the cultured, and the orthodox sections. This does not mean that Sanskrit had ceased to be productive. Notable contributions were made in different branches of literature, philosophy, socio-religious codes, astrology, and many technical subjects. But this had little relevance for the common man.

Sanskrit was replaced by Persian for many purposes. Persian became the court language. Some kingdoms, which used regional languages for official work, gradually switched over to Persian. Persian acquired an all-India character. All people, who sought a career in the government, took up its study. Many Hindus acquired proficiency in the language and produced original masterpieces in it. Important Persian texts were translated into Sanskrit. Likewise, philosophical and religious texts and technical writings in Sanskrit were rendered into Persian. The wide-spread use of Persian in administrative and social life was bound to influence regional languages, which adopted both technical terms and common words of Persian.

The most remarkable development, frought with happy consequences, was the origin and growth of regional languages. We can delineate a direct line of evolution from Sanskrit, Prakrit, and Apabhramsa to regional languages from the north. In the early medieval period, there is a demonstrable transition from Apabhramsa to the provincial languages, which seem to have acquired their distinctive character in the medieval period. Among the south Indian languages, Tamil has a rich history. Kannada and Telugu, followed by Malayalam, surfaced as separate languages in the early medieval period.

The regional languages were nearer to the common people. Their effectiveness for reaching out to the general public was forcefully asserted by Eknath, who, in support of opting for Marathi, his mother tongue, in preference to Sanskrit and Prakrit, said "My language Marathi is worthy of expressing the highest sentiments and is rich, laden with the fruits of divine knowledge."

Regional languages attained a maturity which enabled them to promote independent literary writings of diverse forms and types and also serious works on technical subjects. They received great usage by poets and saints of the Bhakti movement, who realized that, for communicating with the common man directly and effectively, these languages were the most potent medium. This view was held also by the Sufi saints, who cultivated the knowledge of the vernacular languages and approached the people through them. Many Muslim scholars and religious leaders made notable contributions to the enrichment of these languages. Amir Khusrau, very early, proclaimed the Hindi language as his own. Malik Muhammad Jayasi composed the *Padmawat*, one of the earliest epic poems in *Awadhi*, a dialect of Hindi. Rahim recorded his wise maxims in Hindi. Raskhan composed his enchanting poems in praise of Krishna in Brij Bhasha. There are similar shining examples of Muslim scholars and saints using their respective regional languages.

The emblematic development of the period was the emergence of a new language, Urdu. It arose out of the requirements of the times. It has been variously termed as *Lashkari* or *Hindavi*. The soldiers, who came from outside, had to converse with the local population in the daily routine of life. Urdu originated because of the mixing of Persian with the existing form of Hindi. It is sometimes equated with the *Khariboli* form of Hindi prevalent in western Uttar Pradesh. It spread to other parts of the country. Besides Delhi and neighboring areas, Lucknow and Hyderabad established themselves as its foremost centers. Urdu is totally Indian. It is used in India and some other countries to which people of Indian origin migrated. The language has no religious connotation. Its grammar, words, style, and cultural milieu are predominantly Indian, with a coating of the Persian language. Hindus and Muslims alike have contributed to its richness. Some of the best writers, poets, and scholars of Urdu have been Hindus. It has developed some new forms of literary composition and has effectively communicated the social consciousness and national ethos. Urdu is among the finest expressions of the cultural synthesis originating in the medieval period.

The Silver Lining: The Bhakti Movement

The dark clouds of degeneration, difference, strife, and obscurantism, overhanging the social life of the medieval period have, in the early phase, the silver lining of the life and teaching of saints. These include Ramanand, Kabir, Nanak, Chaitanya, Ravidas, and Namdev. Interestingly, all the saints did not belong to higher castes. Kabir was brought up in a Muslim weaver's family. Ravidas was a cobbler. Though there were differences in some points of detail, their social and religious messages had a remarkable similarity. They believed in the unity of Godhood, advocated the path of direct communion with the God through Bhakti or love and devotion for Him, denounced mechanical rituals, external paraphernalia and intermediary of other agencies, and emphasized purity of life and thought. They believed in the brotherhood of man and challenged differentiation on the basis of birth and the condemning of others as low or untouchables.

In the ancient period, the Bhakti movement was evidenced mostly in south India. In the medieval period, it became strong in the north. It had a special significance for the new social situations and problems. The saints denounced the defects of both Hinduism and Islam and thus paved the way for bringing them closer. This liberal tradition was continued in later times. Tukaram in Maharashtra, Tukaram and Dadu in Gujarat are notable saints of the period.

The medieval period is rich in poet saints who were committed to the devotional path of theism. They sang the glories of Vishnu, mainly in his two incarnations of Rama and Krishna. They were not rigid sectarians. They augmented the ennoblement of the individual and preached social values and ideal social relationships. They offered solace to the tormented individual in the frustrating social realities, which worked for peace and harmony.

The Sufis, by the example of their personal lives and precepts, encouraged a high standard of moral life, emphasized service to humanity, the poor and the indigent, and preached inward light against dogmatic formalism. They freely conversed in Hindi, often referring to Hindu gods and sects. By their broad-minded toleration of other sects and emphasis on the unity of Godhead and the path of devotion, they prepared a common platform for intellectuals and the devout. The lower classes of the population were attracted by their precepts and practice of equality and brotherhood of man. The Sufi saints helped the spread of Islam and Muslim culture among the masses. They thus brought the two communities closer, but their impact could not ultimately be made deeper and more widespread to bring about a happier synthesis and integration.

The process of adjustment and assimilation was thwarted by orthodox elements, both among Hindus and Muslims. They opposed liberal trends and views and reiterated orthodox practices and principles. They feared the erosion of their entrenched privileges. The unholy alliance of institutional orthodoxy with political authority prevented the peaceful process of the emergence of a new India based on understanding, sympathy, and assimilation. The colonial rule tried to exploit this. A realization of this basic fact of co-existence is the lesson of medieval history.

Works Cited

Ashraf, K.M. 1955. Life and condition of the people of Hindustan. *JASB* I.

Chand, Tara. 1936. *Influence of Islam on Indian culture.* Allahabad: Indian Press.

Chandra, Satish. 1978. *Medieval India*, Part I, Part II. New Delhi: National Council of Educational Research and Training.

Elliot, H.M., and J. Dawson. [1867] 1953. *History of India as told by its own historians.* 8 vols. Calcutta: Susil Gupta.

Gokhale, B.G. 1960. *The making of the Indian nation.* Bombay: Asia Publishing House.

Gopal, L. 1964. *The Economic life of northern India (c. A.D. 700-1200).* Delhi: Motilal Banarsidas.

Habib, M. 1927. *Hazarat Amir Khusrau of Delhi.* Bombay: Asia Publishing House.

Haig, W. 1922. *Cambridge history of India*, vol. 3. Cambridge: Cambridge Univ. Press.

Husain, Y. 1957. *Glimpses of medieval Indian culture.* Bombay: Asia Publishing House.

Kramrisch, S. 1965. *The Art of India: Traditions of Indian sculpture, painting, and architecture.* London: Phaidon Press.

Lal, K.S. 1966. *Studies in medieval Indian history.* Delhi: Ranjit Printers and Publishers.

Luniya, B.N. 1978. *Life and culture in medieval India.* Indore: Kamal Prakashan.

Mahalingam, T.V. 1951. *Administration and social life under Vijayanagara empire.* Madras: University of Madras.

Majumdar, R.C., H.C. Chaudhuri, and K.K. Dutta. 1958. *An advanced history of India.* London: Macmillan.

Majumdar, R.C. (ed.) 1958. *The history and culture of the Indian people*, vols. 4-7. Bombay: Bharatiya Vidya Bhavan.

Panikkar, K.M. 1964. *A survey of Indian history.* New York: Asia Publishing House.

Ranade, M.G. 1961. *The rise of Maratha power.* New Delhi: The Publication Division.

Saran, P. 1952. *Studies in medieval Indian history.* Delhi: Vikas.

Sastri, K.A.N. 1955. *A history of South India.* Delhi: Oxford University Press.

Sivaramamurti, C. 1970. *Indian painting.* Bombay: India Book House.

Srivastava, A.L. 1953. *The Sultanate of Delhi.* Agra: S.L. Agarwala.

Tripathi, R.P. 1960. *Rise and fall of the Mughal empire.* Allahabad: Central Book Depot.

Vaidya, C.V. 1921-26. *The rise of medieval Hindu India.* 3 vols. Poona: Aryabhushan Press.

Chapter 4 | India During the Mughal Period

Irfan Habib

Traditional political history treats the Mughal period as spanning the years from 1526, when its founder Babur defeated Ibrahim Lodi at Panipat, to 1739, when Nadir Shah of Iran sacked Delhi and shattered irretrievably the prestige and authority of the Mughal emperor. Interest is attached to this period for reasons beyond dynastic or imperial history. Besides its brilliance in culture, literature and art, it is the period when, for the first time, we have quantitative, as well as qualitative, information in great detail about economic and social conditions. For much of this we are obliged to one man, Abu'l Fazl, the minister of the great Akbar (reigned, 1556-1605) and author of the remarkable *Ain-i Akbari*. But there are other historical works, administrative texts, European travellers' accounts and indigenous primary documentation, which we can also draw upon.

Economy

We can now, for example, say with some confidence that about 1601, there were some 145 million people living within the pre-Partition limits of India, that is, about 88.5 persons per square mile, as against some 240 inhabitants per square mile in 1941 (the last census year before Independence). Both the forest cover and uncultivated wastes must, therefore, have been far more extensive in 1601 than in 1941. The forests provided sustenance to a large 'gathering' sector, which furnished timber, firewood, charcoal, sandal-wood, lac, wild silks, honey, wild herbs, medicines, *bezoar* and musk, and animal skins, to swell India's gross product.

The favorable land-man ratio also shaped agricultural conditions. The individual village settlements were much smaller; the gross sown area in 1601 was 50% or less of what it was around 1910. The fields were often shifting, and there were correspondingly extensive fallows. The soil had, therefore, a greater chance of recuperation than in the last phase of British rule when land-pressure was acute and fertilizer use was minimal.

Cultivation was mainly rain-based, supported by well and pond irrigation as well as water drawn from natural flood channels. These flood channels were sometimes re-excavated as canals ('anicuts' in South India); but, there were fully man-made canals as well. The greatest work of the latter sort was Shahjahan's West Yamuna Canal (*Nahr-i Bihisht*), C.E. 1650. Owing to moderate use of underground water, the water-table was much closer to the surface than now, and elementary methods of waterlift based on the lever or pulley and cattle-power could suffice: the more complex Persian wheel, with geared wheels and pot-chain, was in use only in the North-West.

The Indian peasant cultivated a very large number of crops. The *A'in-i Akbari* lists 19 taxed crops cultivated for the *rabi* (spring) harvest in all the revenue circles of the Agra province, and 25 crops for the *kharif* (autumn) harvest. One misses here the New World crops, for example, maize, tobacco, chilli, potato, and groundnuts, of which the first two were acclimatized in the seventeenth century, while the others were acclimatized afterwards. On the other hand, the dye crops, notably indigo and *al* (red), have disappeared due to chemical competitors in the first half of this century.

The large extent of waste and fallows was favorable to the existence of a large cattle population: the relative plenitude of milk-products was reflected in the cheapness of ghee, in terms of wheat, when compared to conditions in the early part of this century.

Agriculture was carried on by individual peasants, though there was some large farming undertaken by the 'big men', through use of hired (and, in some areas, semi-servile) laborers, men, and women. The distance between such superior farmers and the petty peasants could be very great. There was, then, a whole class of 'menial' laborers, the outcastes or untouchables, today's *dalits*, who were forced or by custom prevented from occupying land and thus turned into peasants. Our documentation unfortunately only allows us fleeting glimpses of this repressed section of the rural population.

To outsiders, the villages presented a picture of unrelieved poverty -- "a poverty so great and miserable" as to be described as "dark want and bitter woe" (Pelsaert in 1626). Famines struck periodically, the most devastating ones being those of 1556 (North India), Gujarat and the Deccan (1630-32), Bihar (1670), and Deccan (1630-32). But the main factor for poverty was undoubtedly man-made, notably the heavy burden of land-tax, inherited by the Mughals from their predecessers and greatly increased by their successor, the English East India Company. The land-tax was supposed to cover the peasant's entire surplus, and, therefore, seemed to those familiar with the tenant systems of Western Europe, equivalent to rent, which made the King appear as the owner of the soil. Naturally, then, how the land-tax was assessed and collected became of crucial significance for both the agrarian economy and the finances of the state.

Much administrative ingenuity was devoted to this task. Sher Shah (1540-45) fashioned a system of measurement (*zabt*), where the area was multiplied by an assumed crop-yield, to fix the tax at a third of the yield. Akbar carried out a much more ambitious survey to enable him to fix (1579-80) revenue rates in cash, which varied according to the crops sown. In the seventeenth century, both simple crop-sharing and measurement systems remained in vogue with a tax that took half the produce. This was accounted as a fair burden in the eyes of the government. In actual fact, the control over the *jagirdars*, or holders of revenue-assignments, was seldom rigorous enough to put effective restraints upon revenue extraction; and, there were additional burdens on peasants which were imposed by the hereditary intermediaries with various customary rights enjoyed by persons known as the *zamindars*.

Though India under the Mughals was principally an agricultural country, it possessed a large non-agricultural sector in terms of persons employed. Salt-making and iron-mining were widespread; there were copper mines in Rajasthan and diamond mines in Andhra, the latter employing a large labor force. The textile industry, based on the large production of cotton, and the manufacture of all kinds of plain and dyed cloth (coarse cloth, calico, chintz, muslin, etc.), was carried on in villages and towns everywhere. Sericulture and silk-weaving became particularly widespread in Bengal, which emerged in the seventeenth century as one of the major silk-producing regions of the world. Most production was carried on by artisans in their huts, as individual producers, but merchants' workshops (*karkhanas*) were also to be found wherever the material was so expensive as to require larger capital.

India did not have roads as we know them today: a broad path cleared, dotted with inns or *sarais* at day's- journey distances, often marked by avenues of trees and distance (*kos*) minarets with bridges on smaller streams, accorded best with the concept of a good kings' road (*shah rah*) in the Mughal period. Most roads were, however, no better than cart tracks. Much bulk traffic (eg. grain, sugar, salt) was moved by the *banjaras* on backs of oxen, or carried by barges on rivers. Travellers had varying experiences of security, or the lack of it; but, the insurance rates for goods-on-transit quoted in the seventeenth century does not suggest a very high level of risk.

Trade was assisted by a trimetallic currency system of great uniformity and purity, based on the silver rupee which was first minted by Sher Shah (1540-45). A fairly developed system of commercial credit existed, with extensive deposit-banking, and brisk dealing in bills of exchange (*hundis*), which lead to the circulation of bill-money (*anth*) in the major markets. Insurance (*bima*), including marine insurance, completed the picture of a fairly advanced financial system: those who served as money-changers, bankers, and insurers were generally known as *sarrafs*, and were found practically everywhere. The universal prevalence of brokerage was a special feature of Indian markets, and the *banyas* were being particularly involved in it. The major bankers and merchants, often known as *sahs*, used to have their factors or correspondents in several towns. In the 17th century, Virji Vora, a merchant banker of Surat with an estimated capital of Rs. 8 million and a whole network of agents in India and abroad, was perhaps the most successful known representative of this class.

India's overseas trade had fluctuating fortunes. The initial Portuguese traders, following Vasco da Gama's voyage (1498), created havoc with Indian overseas shipping and trade. But by Akbar's reign, a compromise had been achieved with heavy Indian ships ('junks') plying to Red Sea, Gulf, and South-east Asian ports, on payment of tribute to the Portuguese. With the entry of the English and Dutch East India Companies, early in the next century, this arrangement broke down; but ultimately, the attractions of trade with the Mughal Empire forced the intruders to respect the safety of Indian shipping. A revived ship-building industry (mainly making ships after European design) greatly enlarged India's oversea trade, and the Indian share in it. This again broke down in the eighteenth century, as the Mughal Empire declined, and the English predominance began to be established from the 1750s onwards.

There is no doubt that Mughal India was a country of large towns; its urban population has been estimated at 15% of the total, which was about a half higher than the percentage in the closing decades of the nineteenth century. The towns contained large establishments of the nobles and officials, with a very expanded service sector (servants, retainers, soldiers, ministerial staff, other dependents) supplementing the artisanal sector. The splendor of the life of the nobility, living off revenues of the land, dazzled contemporaries; but, the middle class, comprised of merchants and professional people, was also large enough, though caste and community barriers prevented an integration of it like what was proceeding in contemporary Europe.

Society

Indian rural society was marked by the twin institutions of caste and the village community. We have seen that caste society was an important factor behind creating a large landless proletariat. In a sense the Indian village community, too, was an institution that was made necessary by the caste system. Each village needed to be served by persons of different castes to carry out certain essential functions: those of the watchman, sweeper, leather worker, barber, carpenter, blacksmith, and so on.

The peasants themselves might belong to several castes, so custom had to place the responsibility (and benefit) of managing the village on a body of headmen (*panch, muqaddams*, etc.). Custom was reinforced by the tax-authorities' need for intermediaries which could fulfill, with the assistance of another village official, the literate accountant (*patwari, kulkarni*). Such village administration was by no means democratic, and the elders' position was clearly one of hereditary right and wealth since the office of headman was not only hereditary, but could also be purchased.

The hierarchy of Indian rural society was underlined by the universal presence of a class of non-peasant superior right-holders who ranged from village headmen to chiefs, which the Mughal chancery invariably designated *zamindars*, though various local designations were current. The Mughal administration tried to systematize their rights (e.g. 10 percent of land-tax payable to them as *nankar*, and an equal amount estimated for their extra-revenue income, known as *malikana*); but whether the *zamindars* could evict peasants on failure of payment of their perquisites is not clear, and custom in this respect probably varied from locality to locality. They, however, neither fit the role of landlords, as they had become in most of India by 1900, nor of mere tax-gatherers, as the critics of the Permanent Settlement tended to see them. They formed an important class, with considerable numbers of armed retainers: Akbar's census counted 4 million infantry and nearly 400,000 horsemen serving the *zamindars* throughout the Empire. Though divided by caste and local ties, they were important to the Mughals, both as junior collaborators and as possible enemies. From the latter half of the seventeenth century, the second role began to be increasingly assumed by the zamindars, and, this undoubtedly was a factor undermining the Mughal Empire. Today, we can see the three layers of the Mughal Indian rural order, for example the "menial" landless laborers, the peasants, and the zamindars, reflected in the three great social divisions of Scheduled Castes, Other Backward Castes, and the Upper Castes that have now practically received a legal recognition in Free India.

Very different from the *zamindars* was the Mughal ruling class, town-based, bureaucratic in form, at the head of a highly professional army of some 200,000 cavalry in Shahjahan's time (1647-48). All members of the Mughal nobility were servants of the Emperor, holding ranks (*mansab*) granted by him, each rank indicating, through detailed schedules, his pay-claim (*talab*) to be satisfied either by grant of revenue-assignment (*jagir*) or cash allowance (*naqd*). Each holder of *mansab* could be posted anywhere or entrusted with any office (which might not carry any pay attached to it), and his *jagir* could be, and was, indeed, normally transferred from one locality to another after short periods. The *mansabs* were not inheritable, although the claims of those whose fathers had been in service (*khanazadan*) were usually given special consideration in appointments and promotions.

The nobility (of some 8,000 members in 1647-48) had a very large proportion (about half) drawn from Turnanis (of Central-Asian extraction) and Iranis; the other half was comprised of Afghans (much of Afghanistan was within the Mughal Empire), Indian Muslims, Rajputs, and Marathas. Its multi-racial and multi-religious character made it possibly unique among the ruling classes of the contemporary world. Bernier saw the Mughal nobility as rapacious in the extreme, devastating the countryside by trying to make their short-term *jagir* assignments yield the maximum income. On the other hand, a more favorable opinion may be formed of them when one sees their buildings, and their patronage of literature and the arts, or considers the simple fact that the large urban economy of the time depended upon the vast income they transferred from the villages to the towns.

As in villages, so in towns, caste was all-pervasive, despite the market being the dominant factor here. Although the Mughal government, unlike the Peshwas, is not known to have enforced caste restrictions on the pursuit of professions, and Muslims could theoretically follow any occupation, social constraints upon occupational mobility were very great. Caste elders (*mahajan*), at least among the mercantile classes, performed some of the functions of guilds; and artisanal communities too often had their headmen (*chaudhuris*), although they appear to have usually exercised customary influence, rather than legally valid powers.

Slaves constituted a small and varied constituent of the population, comprising imported slaves (mainly Central Asians and Africans), captives from raids on villages unable to pay tax, and children sold into slavery by impecunious parents. Agrestic slavery existed in Bihar and Kerala, but most slaves were employed as domestic servants. While slaves were subject to sale, open slave markets appear no longer to have existed, unlike in the earlier periods. In fact, in 1562-3 Akbar prohibited, under threat of condign punishments, the enslaving of women and children as well as open sale of slaves, and in 1582, he liberated his own numerous retinue of slaves. His successor Jahangir (1605-27) prohibited the traffic in eunuchs from Eastern Bengal.

Women bore varying degrees of repression at almost all levels of society. They bore their share, or more than it, of work under the customary gender division of labor. Widows in lower castes were subject to almost compulsory levirate, and, in upper castes, where widow remarriage was not permissible, were badly treated. Among families with high caste pretensions widow-burning or *sati* seemed to be spreading, despite bans and discouragement by the Mughal administration and the Peshwas. Among Muslims, rigorous seclusion was the norm for women of the upper strata, although inheritance rules were more liberal. Akbar was unique in prohibiting child marriage, propagating the virtues of monogamy, and upholding larger shares in inheritance for women. He also severely condemned *sati*.

Political Structure

It was not so much Babur's victory at Panipat (1526), or Humayun's recovery of his Indian dominions (1555-6), but the conquests of Akbar (1556-1605) that created the Mughal Empire. It was also he who built up, through a brilliant series of measures, the centralized and highly systematized structure of the Empire.

In 1574, he fused the Mughal nobility into a single service by instituting the system of *mansab* or rank that we have already mentioned. Simultaneously, he undertook a major enterprise to establish more accurate revenue rates and more realistic estimates of actual tax realization. Already in the 1560's, he had begun to transfer *jagirs*, and by now he had large areas under the direct control of his Finance Ministry. As a crowning step, he decreed in 1580 a new division of the Empire into provinces, called *subas*, and the establishment in each of them a totally new, uniform structure. The Governor of the province lost his despotic control over the province; the revenues, army, and judicial administration were now put under officers (*diwan*, *bakhshi*, *sadr*) who were not answerable to the Governor, but to corresponding central ministers who then directly reported to the Emperor.

Changes continued to be made in this system. By Akbar's later years (1595), two *mansab* ranks began to be distinguished: one (*zat*) determining the holder's personal salary and the other (*sawar*) indicating the size of the contingent and pay sanctioned for it. Under Shahjahan (1628-58), a sharp reduction of salary paid against *mansab* ranks, both *zat* and *sawar*, was put into effect, a step made inevitable, perhaps, by the generous way in which the ranks had begun to be awarded. But, essentially, the structure that Akbar had built remained intact till well into the eighteenth century.

The Emperor, as head of this vast, centralized fabric had a crucial position involving immense power as well as responsibility. Two very interesting developments took place within Mughal polity to modify this seemingly classic form of "oriental" despotism. First, there evolved under Akbar a sanctification of sovereignty as "a light emanating from God." His special link with divinity required obedience to be rendered to the Sovereign by all men; but at the same time this imposed on the Sovereign himself the duty of pursuing the path of *Sulk-i Kul* (Absolute Peace) or of tolerance of people of all groups and faiths. Even Aurangzeb (1659-1709), when it so suited him, set the King the task of modelling himself after God, who lets the bounties of nature fall on everyone irrespective of creed. Undoubtedly, this concept was modified under Aurangzeb, with his heavy emphasis on Islam, but it still survived. People in the eighteenth century often tended to assume that the only legitimate sovereign in India was the Mughal *badshah*, and unless a diploma or *farman* of recognition was obtained from him, no ruler's position could be deemed fully legitimate.

Secondly, a code simultaneously evolved to set conventions for the conduct of the ruler. Perhaps, again, following upon Akbar's great self-restraint in this regard, punishments of nobles were kept to a minimum, and executions, even in the most serious cases, were avoided as far as possible. There was a surprising degree to which the freedom of expressing one's opinion was allowed to nobles and officers. The very few exceptions (e.g., the finance minister Shah Mansur's execution, 1581), indeed, prove the rule; the first great departure from the practice came only in 1713, with Farrukhsiyar's accession. The code also prescribed an accessibility to common people, typified by the daily practice of *jharoka darshan*, which is now sometimes followed by our own politicians! Such a set of conventions was designed to give the Mughal monarchy an aura of moderation and benevolence, so much so that a historian has argued that the Empire appears more as a modern state than an old-style despotism.

The prestige accorded to the Mughal monarchy could not paper over the cracks developing within Indian polity. The taxation pressure led to peasant resistance, while *zamindars* also began to take increasingly to defiance. Shivaji (d.1680) undoubtedly gained from these ruptures to form his *swarajya*, which, after a long and severe conflict with the Mughals, led to the Maratha confederacy in the eighteenth century under the headship of the Peshwas. Other notable principalities that emerged out of similar conflicts were those of the Jats (eastern Rajasthan and Western U.P.) and the Sikhs (Punjab).

Religion

Mughal India saw rich developments in the sphere of religious thought, a richness difficult to present in a summary form. Orthodox Hinduism continued to benefit from compilations of legal texts, such as the encyclopedic *Viramitrodaya* by Mitra Mishra, written under the patronage of Jahangir's favourite noble Bir Singh Bundela. The most important change seemed, however, to occur in the area of belief, where the non-dualistic doctrines of Shankaracharya's version of Vedanta began to take a commanding position among the recognized schools of Hinduism. Practically ignored by Abu'l Fazl in his detailed account of Hindusim (1595), it is presented as currently the most important trend of Hinduism by the great text on religions, the *Dabistan-i Mazahib* (c.1655). Dara Shukoh's Persian translation of the *Upanishads* (1657) is also much influenced by Shankaracharya's interpretations. A monotheistic trend in Rama *bhakti* is represented by Tulsidas's celebrated *Ramcharitmanas* composed in Akbar's reign. Important religious currents affected Maharashtra. Tukaram (d.1649), a Sudra peasant, was influenced by both Chaitanya and Kabir (see below), while Ramdas (d.1681) combined the worship of Rama with emphasis on traditional duty towards the Brahmans and deities ('*Maharasthra dharma*').

Popular religion was now greatly affected by a much more rigorous monotheistic movement, of which the dominant figure in the Hindi/Hindustani region was Kabir (fl.1510). This weaver of Banaras rejected both Hinduism and Islam, though understandably he used terms (and even concepts) derived from various elements of both religions. His Hindi verses call for obedience to God through ethical conduct, not ritual; and he scornfully refuses to seek heaven as a reward for such obedience. Caste and untouchability have no meaning for him, and he is proud of his own humble vocation. Kabir obtained much repute, and had like his successors such firm monotheists, as Raidas the sweeper, and Sain the barber. The verses of all these three teachers were included in the *Guru Granth* collected together in 1603 by the fifth *Guru* of the Sikhs, Arjan (martyred, 1606), which shows that originally Sikhism was also seen as part of the same movement to which Kabir and other popular monotheists belonged.

Nanak (1469-1538), the first *guru* of the Sikhs, strongly believed in One God, condemned image worship, and the cult of pollution. The community (*panth*) of his followers were drawn increasingly from the Punjab peasantry, and received a militant form under the tenth and last guru, Gobind Singh (1666-1708), who prescribed the bearing of a soldier for the Sikh. Today, Sikhism has won recognition as one of the established religions of the world.

Islam in India had, by the fifteenth century, received the pantheistic ideas of Ibn al-Arabi (d.1240); and there was almost simultaneously the millenary movement led by Sayyid Muhammad of Jaunpur (d.1505), who claimed to be the promised Redeemer (*mahdi*). Both these movements, especially Ibn al-Arabi's pantheism, played their part in shaping Akbar's ideas from the mid-1570's onwards. If the world of senses was unreal and the separation from God, an illusion, as Ibn al 'Arabi had argued, then all religious differences too — indeed all religions themselves — were also illusory. These notions led Akbar to emphasize the concept of *sulh-i kul* ('absolute peace') in justification for his tolerating all religions. But at the same time he tried to form an elite group to promote absolute monotheism, respect for the sun as the greatest of God's creations, and abstinence from animal-killing, all leading up to a very uncompromising pantheism. But with all this, there always remained in him a heavy strain of commitment to reason.

Akbar's religious interests were pursued leisurely by Jahangir, who made the notable identification of Muslim Sufism (of the Ibn al-Arabi trend, presumably) with Vedanta (the pantheistic version). It was, however, Dara Shukoh (1615-59) who elaborated on this unity of beliefs in his *Majmu'al-Bahrain* (1645-5) and in 1657 produced his fundamental Persian translation of the Upanishads. In c.1655 an anonymous author wrote the *Dabistan-i Mazahib*, a detailed work on all the important religions of the world and a product of much reading and personal enquiry, with a remarkable insistence on strict impartiality and lack of bias. All the sects of Hinduism obtain detailed descriptions here, as do those of Islam; and there are chapters on Zoroastrianism, Judaism and Christianity as well.

This tolerant, though essentially monotheistic, outlook became part of the mental make-up of a large number of people belonging to what may be loosely termed Mughal culture; and it is surely worth nothing that Ram Mohan Roy's first work the *Tuhfatu'l Mwahhidin*, 'Gift for Monotheists' (1803), belongs quite firmly to this tradition.

Islamic orthodoxy and Sufism flourished as well. Shaikh Ahmad Sirhindi (1564-1624), the Naqshbandi mystic, represented the more intolerant trend in Sufism, while Shah Waliullah (1702-62) was, in many ways, the most learned and thoughtful jurist of Mughal times. Shah Waliullah is also important in that his insistence on the application of the Shari'a to reform customary practices was energetically taken up by the 'Wahhabis' in the nineteenth century.

Science and Technology

It would be superfluous to inform the reader that Mughal India did not undergo any scientific or technological revolution, and that, as a result, the distance between India and Europe in this realm was much greater in, say, 1700, than it was in 1500. But, still the period is not without its own annals of invocation of reason and innovation in technology.

The atmosphere of Akbar's court was certainly favorable to science and technological improvement. His minister Abu'l Fazl writes that a king should not, in order to gain popular applause, do anything to oppose reason. Akbar not only sought to make scientific subjects a part of the approved scholarly syllabus, but was himself involved in a series of varied technological innovations, such as prefabricated movable wooden structures; calico-dyeing; air-cooling; water-cooling by saltpetre; geared waterlift; cart-milling and gun-barrel boring; musket barrels made by winding iron-sheets; wheel-lock guns; ships' camels, and so on.

Unfortunately, these interests were not pursued by Akbar's successors. In science there was almost no attempt to enquire into European achievements; and even Jai Singh Sawai's (d.1743) astronomical endeavours were based essentially on constructing instruments of the traditional 'Islamic' design, which were by now largely obsolete. In technology, we may note the diffusion of the sand-clock, the screw, and the manually driven belt-drill as important imports. If these came overland *via* Iran, the successful copying of European ships, which began from the 1630's onwards, involved the incorporation of many features designed by European shipwrights in Indian built vessels.

Literature

Mughal India made rich contributions to Persian literature, it being probable that there were then more people reading and writing Persian in India than even in Iran. To begin with Persian lexicography, a series of dictionaries compiled in India was crowned by, perhaps the greatest of pre-modern Persian dictionaries, the *Bahar-i 'Ajam* of Tek Chand 'Bahar' (1749). Here the meaning of each word is usually justified by quotations chronologically arranged.

Historical works include such outstanding autobiographies as Babur's memoirs (originally in Turki but rendered into Persian in 1588-89) and those of his great grandson Jahangir. Abu'l Fazl in his *Akbarnama* produced a work based on much research and reflection, and in his *A'in-i Akbari*, he gives us a unique discriptive and statistical record of Akbar's empire and the culture of India. The notion of India as a country whose history ought to be written was first espoused by Nizamuddin Ahmad in his *Tabaqat-i Akbari* (1592-93), and then by Firishta in *Gulshan-i Ibrahimi* (1609-10). Mughal-Indian historiography, though oriented towards political history, remained fairly well-wedded to accuracy; and much criticism of official, even the emperor's actions could be expressed by private historians.

In poetry, Akbar's reign saw two poets of different stamps making their mark, 'Urfi (d.1590) with his reflective and lively verse, and Faizi (d.1595) with his difficult constructions and florid style. In the seventeenth century, Sa'ib (d.1677-78) obtained the recognition as a great master: He ended his days in Iran, so he must be shared between the two countries.

An intercourse between Persian and Sanskrit developed as major works in the latter language were translated into Persian. Akbar had the translation of the *Mahabharata* made under the title *Razmnama*; and, among other Sanskrit works, the *Panchatantra* too was translated. As already noted, Dara Shukoh's translation of the *Upanishads* came in the next century.

Sanskrit scholars were patronized at Mughal court. Shahjahan's court poet (*kavi-ray*), Jagannath, wrote a monumental work on poetics, the *Rasagangadhara*. A new composition of fables came in the form of Ballalasena's *Bhojaprabandha* (16th century).

It is not possible in the short compass of this essay to survey the literatures of the regional languages, particularly because the sixteenth and seventeenth centuries saw much production in these languages from Pushtu to Tamil, and Bengali and Assamese to Marathi. Much of this was devotional or religious in character, but there was much secular literature as well. In the later days of the Mughals, the common speech of North Indian camps and bazars began to acquire a standard idiom, not entirely based on any single dialect; and this became the spoken base (Hindustani) of the two literary languages, Hindi and Urdu. Poetry in Urdu began at Delhi, according to later tradition, with the arrival of the poet Wali in 1723.

Fine Arts

The grandeur of the Mughals lives on most visibly in their great monumental buildings, and in the miniature paintings of their ateliers. The Mughal architectural style has features which, separately, the expert can assign to the 'Hindu' trabeate style, to the preceding Afghan and provincial schools, and to Central Asian and Iranian styles. But there is no doubt that under the Mughals we do not simply have an orderly mix of these: Everything is subjected, in the nobler Mughal buildings at least, to a large vision, an eye for detail and an impeccable taste.

The standard for Mughal tombs is set by Humayun's tomb at Delhi (completed c.1564): it has a rectangular walled garden, served by straight criss-crossing water courses, the main building set on a platform, and crowned by a high dome just failing to be bulbous. It could be contrasted with the two great Sur tombs at Sahahasram, each surrounded by a sheet of water. In 1560s, Akbar built the great fort at Agra. In scale, as well as the delicateness of its internal buildings, it can be seen to be markedly different from the Purana Qila of Delhi, built by Humayun and completed by his adversary Sher Shah (1540-45) in the older 'Afghan' style.

Akbar's genius soon shifted to Fatehpur Sikri where he built the first monumental Mughal mosque, with its towering Buland Darwaza, showing a successful application of the recessed doorway. If the mosque is basically arcuate in construction, Akbar went out of his way to play with the trabeate device in his adjacent palace complex. The trabeate is used, however, without any impression of heaviness, displaying thereby a brilliant mastery of building techniques. Such mastery is also present in the construction of the large tanks and the aqueducts that brought water into the palace.

In his own mausoleum, Akbar applied a totally novel design for the main building: steps leading up stories of colonnades of red sandstone to reach an undomed top storey of marble. The same absence of the dome marks Jahangir's mausoleum at Lahore, smaller, but chaste.

The use of marble now became more and more wide-spread, with sandstone confined to the lower structures or to the periphery of buildings. I'timaduddala's tomb (1620s) at Agra is an exquisite building of marble, with pietra dura work of Iranian origin. In a sense it is a precursor of the Taj Mahal.

Shahjahan was, after Akbar, certainly the greatest builder among the Mughals. When his queen Mumtaz Mahal died in 1631, he decided to build the famous Taj Mahal as her mausoleum. Set on the bank of the Yamuna, the marble structure, topped with a bulbous dome, is flanked by four free standing minarets on a large platform all of marble. The building is balanced by two important sandstone buildings, one a mosque, the other a false mosque. A canal, with avenues on both sides leads through a classical Mughal garden to a majestic gateway.

His other notable buildings include the Red Fort at Delhi, and the Jami Masjid in front of it; both are part of the planned city of Shahjahanabad. The Jami Masjid is generally held to be the greatest of Mughal mosques, with marble set off tastefully against red sandstone, and domes and minarets built in wonderful proportion. The Mughal school influenced much of the architecture of the Amber rulers from the Govind-dev temple at Virendavan to Sawai Jai Singh's Jaipur (18th century): These too have a grandeur that is all their own.

In the Deccan, the only monumental Mughal building is the tomb of Rabi'a Daurani, a copy of the Taj Mahal, built by Aurangzeb at Aurangabad. The Deccan Sultanates pursued their own lively styles: two famous buildings are the gate-tower of Char Minar (at Hyderabad, 1591), and the Gol Gumbad, the tomb of Muhammad 'Adil Shah (d.1656) at Bijapur, the latter contains the largest true dome in India.

As with architecture, the Mughal school in painting really begins with Akbar, though he inherited Persian artists of the calibre of 'Abdu's Samad and Mir Sayyid Ali from his father Humayun's service. The Mughal school began with most of the features of the Persian school, notably its emphasis on line, precision of detail and eschewing of perspective. Akbar organized his atelier, drawing freely upon Indian artists, mainly for illustrating manuscript copies of books, and soon his insistence on realism began to make its mark on the painting. It says something for the scale of Akbar's enterprise that, according to one count, out of 327 known Mughal painters, no less than 260 belonged to Akbar's reign.

Jahangir's reign (1605-27) marked in some ways the apex of Mughal painting: There is a new emphasis on portraiture, and on figures of animals and flowers, in which latter sphere Mansur was the master. European techniques now began to influence Mughal painting, especially imparting to it a greater regard for perspective. Under Shahjahan the precision and grandeur continued, though some of the earlier liveliness was now missing. Bichitr is, perhaps, one of his court painters whose work makes the greatest appeal to modern eyes.

Mughal art was essentially secular and aristocratic in its choice of themes, though scenes of ordinary life as well as ordinary people are also carefully depicted. In Rajasthan and Himachal Pradesh, during the eighteenth century, Mughal techniques were used for producing religious painting, especially for depicting Krishna *lilas*.

Conclusion

The Mughals have thus left an indelible imprint on India's cultural heritage. They loved India's culture, and in their own way wished her to stand out in the world — for practising tolerance of all religions, according to Jahangir; or for a humane treatment of subjects, as Shahjahan would say. Such sentiments may, perhaps, help us to understand why despite their numerous failings, the Mughals have carved so important a niche of their own in our history.

Works Cited

Abu'l-Fazl. 1927, 1949 & 1948. *A'in-i Akbari*, 3 vols.[vol.I, trans. H. Blochmann, rev. D.C. Phillott; vols. II & III, trans. H.S. Jarrett, rev. J.Sarkar]. Calcutta: Asiatic Society of Bengal.

Ali, M. Athar. 1997. *The Mughal Nobility under Aurangzeb*. 2nd ed., Delhi: Oxford University Press.

Asher, Catherine B. 1992. *Architecture of Mughal India*. Cambridge: Cambridge University Press.

Aziz, Abdul. 1945. *Mansabdari System of the Mughal Army*. Lahore: author.

Beach, Milo Cleveland. 1992. *Mughal and Rajput Painting*. Cambridge: Cambridge University Press.

Bernier, Francois. 1916. *Travels in the Mogul Empire, A.D. 1656-1668* [trans. A. Constable, rev. V.A. Smith]. London: Oxford University Press.

Dasgupta A., and M.N. Pearson (eds.). 1987. *India and the Indian Ocean, 1500-1800*. Calcutta: Oxford University Press.

Farooque, A.K. Mohammad. 1977. *Roads and Communications in Mughal India*. Delhi: Idarah-i Adbiyat.

Habib, Irfan. 1963. *Agrarian System of Mughal India(1556-1707)*. Bombay: Asia Publishing House.

__________. 1982. *An Atlas of the Mughal Empire*. Delhi: Oxford University Press.

__________. (ed.) 1997. *Akbar and his India.* Delhi: Oxford University Press.

Hasan, Ibn. 1936. *Central Structure of the Mughal Empire.* Oxford: Oxford University Press.

Moosvi, Shireen. 1987. *Economy of the Mughal Empire,c.1595: a Statistical Study*, Delhi: Oxford University Press.

____________. 1994. *Episodes in the Life of Akbar: Contemporary Records and Reminiscences.* Delhi: National Book Trust.

Pelsaert, Francisco. 1925, *Jahangir's India* [trans. W.H. Moreland and P. Geyl]. Cambridge: Cambridge University Press.

Raychaudhuri, T., and Irfan Habib (eds.). 1982. *The Cambridge Economic History of India*, Vol.I, Cambridge: Cambridge University Press.

Richards, John F. 1993. *The Mughal Empire.* Cambridge: Cambridge University Press.

Rizvi, S. Athar Abbas. 1965. *Muslim Revivalist Movement in the Sixteenth and Seventeenth Centuries.* Lucknow: Balkrishna & Co.

Saran, P. 1941. *The Provincial Government of the Mughals(1526-1658).* Allahabad: Kitabistan.

Sharma, Sri Ram. 1972. *The Religious Policy of the Mughal Emperors.* 3rd ed. Bombay: Asia Publishing House.

Vaudville, Charlotte, 1974. *Kabir*, I, Oxford: Oxford University Press.

Chapter 5

The Colonial Impact on India

Sabyasachi Bhattacharya

It is a paradox of modern Indian history that, while on the one hand, British colonial impact left its signature on modernity in India, on the other hand, during British rule, India asserted herself by contesting that hegemony. In the economic sphere, the destruction of traditional artisanal industries, the increased burden of taxation on agriculture, the drain of wealth to England, and the denial of tariff protection to home industry, were some of the negative features of colonization. However, the unification of the national market, through the imported technology of the railways, modern factories such as cotton and steel mills, and the growth of an industrial capitalist class despite the discouragement offered by British policies, laid the basis of the modern economy. In the political sphere, the subjection of the Indian people to a colonial state controlled by the East India Company and, later, the British government was accompanied by the growth of a political space for the new Indian elite to fight for independence from British rule. India's society and culture were affected by social legislation, the spread of Western ideas, and the rise of a new middle class. At the same time, this middle class intelligentsia, far from being assimilated to Western culture, subjected it to intense critical evaluation; and the vast mass of Indians remained untouched by that culture. On the whole, Indian economy, polity, and culture underwent radical changes in the period of British colonial hegemony, but India retained her individuality and effectively challenged that hegemony, ultimately to attain independence and a substantial measure of decolonization.

Within the brief space available here, it is not easy to survey this vast panorama. I will, therefore, focus on the big picture, the most important facets of the many dimensions of India's colonial past, with an occasional look at some of the details. The crucial question is, what are the aspects of this past which appear most relevant for understanding the economy, polity, and society of India at the end of the twentieth century, in the fiftieth year of the Indian Republic? The economic underdevelopment of the Indian subcontinent is perhaps the central thing that attracts attention today in India and abroad. To what aspects of colonial rule can we trace this underdevelopment?

Rural India and the Agricultural Sector

To answer that question we first have to look at certain trends in colonial policies in the agricultural sector and developments independent of those policies. The colonial impact in the sphere of industry and commerce is more familiar to the lay public than the impact on agriculture. The destruction of the famous cottage industries (particularly textiles) during British rule, the rapacious trading activities of the Free Traders and the East India Company, and the denial of tariff protection to infant industries in India are some well-known features of our pre-independence history. Spokesmen and intellectuals of the urban bourgeoisie paid more attention to these aspects than to the changes in the agrarian scene. Thus our knowledge of changes in rural society is still rather patchy. We know a good deal about what British land revenue policies were. We also have a number of ready-made generalizations about, for instance, improvident expenditure on social occasions leading to peasant indebtedness, or the dramatic effect of railway development on marketing of crops. But the effect of British tenurial arrangements on class composition in rural society, the role of the middlemen and moneylenders in the commercialization of agriculture, the growth of the landless laborer class, and the trends in agricultural output are questions which historians have started answering quite recently.

As for the land revenue arrangements made by the British in different parts of this empire, a brief resume will suffice. In their early experiments in Bengal, from 1765 to 1793, the British tried to maximize and stabilize land revenue and to minimize the cost of revenue collection. Experiments with middlemen or revenue farmers proved them to be unstable and direct collection proved to be costly and unwieldy. The Permanent Settlement of 1793 was a compromise between the objectives of low-cost collection and the stabilization of revenue at as high a level as possible. The income from revenue was stable because it was fixed permanently. The collection costs were minimal since it was the landlord or zamindar's job to collect rent from cultivators and submit a major portion of it (about ten-elevenths in 1793) to the government; if the zamindar failed to do so, his land was auctioned away and the highest bidder obtained the right to collect rent and retain the surplus after paying revenue to the government. In the present states of West Bengal, Bihar, and parts of Uttar Pradesh, this was the system introduced. The two other major systems of land tenure were known as ryotwari and mahalwari. The former system was operative in southern and western India and the latter in northern and central India. Under ryotwari, the *ryot* was the person paying revenue to the government. Often the ryot was, to start with, the actual cultivator. The intention was to do away with an intermediary between him and the government. To decide how much revenue was to be demanded, the government's officers would have to assess the produce of land and determine what proportion of it was to be claimed as revenue. This process was known as "revenue settlement." Under this system, unlike Permanent Settlement, there was a periodical reassessment of revenue demand: thus it was a system of temporary settlement subject to revision every twenty or thirty years. The mahalwari settlements were equally temporary. A crucial distinction, however, was that it was not the individual ryot who undertook to pay revenue, but a group of landlords or village headmen in a mahal or estate. In both systems, the periodical review of what the produce was and what revenue demand should be was a costly affair. But it took care of one problem: the government could continue to increase revenue demand, i.e., the land tax, whereas under the Permanent Settlement the amount of revenue was fixed in perpetuity.

It would be misleading to think that these three systems, and their variants, were devised simply to maximize or stabilize revenue and to reduce collection costs to the extent possible. There was more to it than book-keeping arithmetic. Some historians in the olden days, when the eighteenth-century biographic tradition was strong in historiography, believed that the personal predilections of people like Lord Cornwallis or Sir Thomas Munro mattered a lot. The former was supposedly swayed by his aristocratic bias to favor the landlord class with a Permanent Settlement, and the latter by his sympathy with the ryots to introduce ryotwari. The more important elements in the social philosophy behind the revenue policies lay elsewhere. One of these elements was the desire to create or nurture a privileged class of people (above the peasantry) who owed their privileges to the British. Such a semi-feudal class did indeed constitute the most important political ally of the British. In fact, even in areas where the revenue arrangement was initially intended to be a deal directly with the ryot, there developed a class of privileged intermediaries between the actual cultivator and the government.

Moreover, the British revenue system, in conjunction with their legal system, was based on an alien notion of private property in land. Some historians contend that neither the private ownership of land in some form or other nor the sale of land was uncommon in the pre-British period. But there was a qualitative difference between the situation then and the situation brought about by British policies. The British system necessitated the mortgage or sale of land if the cultivator found it difficult to meet the demands of the landlord or the government; it also necessitated the replacement of a revenue payer by another if revenue payment fell short of government demand. The system saw to it that land was transferred to such people as were able to pay revenue: thus the defaulting peasant was compelled to sell out and so also the defaulting landlord or zamindar. It was, of course, the peasant who was most likely to default, to borrow on the security of his land, and to sell his land as a last resort and join the ranks of the landless. Up to the last quarter of the nineteenth century, the trend of revenue legislation was to strengthen the hands of the rent-receiving landlord against the rent-paying peasant and to enable the moneylender to recover loans from the peasant borrower. In the last five or six decades of British rule, an attempt was made to reverse this tendency. In particular, an attempt was made to prevent moneylenders from acquiring land from peasants. To understand this problem, one has to look at the role of moneylenders and merchants in rural society as a whole.

The predominance of the moneylender was in part due to the revenue system and, in part, to the result of the enforced commercialization of agriculture. The revenue system enabled the government gradually to jack up the revenue demand in temporary settlement areas; in permanent settlement areas, the landlords increased the rent demanded of the cultivator. This pressure on the cultivating class increased their dependence on the moneylender. Furthermore, cash was demanded of the peasant—not payment in kind. Cash could be obtained by converting crops into cash by selling it to the local merchant; or else cash could be borrowed from the moneylender at high rates of interest. At the village level, often the same person performed the role of merchant middleman and moneylender. Once the peasant fell into his grip, the peasant was forced to sell his produce to service his debts, and ultimately the process usually led to the sale of the peasant's land. The marketing of the peasant's crops was a result of this compulsion. Perhaps the growth of railways and roads and the demand for Indian agricultural goods abroad played a secondary role, though these developments were necessary preconditions for the commercialization of agriculture. We must also remember that the village moneylender and merchant was involved in the colonial agrarian system not only as the supplier of credit for meeting revenue obligations and consumption needs, or as the buyer of agricultural goods, but also as the channel for the sale of imported foreign manufactures to village consumers, and as an agents of British trade houses and Indian wholesale dealers in the cities.

In these circumstances, there was no possibility of capitalist relations developing in agriculture, although the growth of a rural proletariat, a landless agricultural laborer class, went ahead. The loans the moneylenders gave to the peasant were for non-productive purposes; and if he acquired land, he was not a capitalist landlord investing in land improvement and productivity. Merchant and usury capital, in fact, perpetuated semi-feudal relations in agrarian society. Productivity went up marginally in the case of non-food commercial crops and remained stagnant in the case of food crops; the per capita availability of food grains diminished in the last fifty years of British rule. During the same period, the number of landless agricultural laborers increased sharply. In the last decades of the nineteenth century, less than one-fifth of the agricultural population was landless. In the first three censuses of the twentieth century, the proportion became one-fourth. And by 1931, 38 percent were said to be landless. The lot of the sharecroppers and owners of dwarf-size holdings was not much better.

Such an agricultural proletariat emerged in Western countries too, but there this process was accompanied by the creation of jobs in the industrial sector. In contrast, colonial constraints on the growth of industries in India provided little opportunity for the rural proletariat to escape. Moreover, there was not the level of income sufficient in agriculture to generate demand for industrial goods. The path of industrial growth along which Western countries had traveled could not be colonial India's path.

Colonialism and India's Industrial Prospects

In the industrial sector, the governing fact was that from the 1740s England was undergoing the Industrial Revolution, and this determined England's policies in India. Until then, England was happy to trade with India to obtain not only agricultural commodities like spices and the vegetable dye indigo, but also products of artisanal industries, most prominently, cotton and silk textiles. Once the Industrial Revolution was under way in England, her trade interests naturally altered; new industries demanded raw material such as raw cotton, and a market for manufactured goods. Thus there are at least two distinct phases, the dividing line being the English Industrial Revolution.

In the first phase, when the object of the East India Company was to procure goods for export from India, the strategy of merchant capital was the obvious one: to buy these goods as cheaply as possible. It is always good to have a monopoly to allow one to do that. It is even better to have state power in one's hands for same purpose. This was the beauty of the position of the English East India Company as a government in India from 1765 in Bengal and in the following decades in other parts of India. On the one hand, the Company (and its servants engaged in private trade) developed a near monopoly with respect to some commodities like cotton cloth in Bengal. On the other hand, the Company as a government used its power to further strengthen its semi-monopolist position vis-a-vis the artisans who produced the export goods. Adam Smith underlined this feature of the English Company's role in India in the late eighteenth century: "The government of an exclusive company of merchants is perhaps the worst of all governments for any country whatever" (Smith1904:137).

Therefore, export of industrial goods from India did not bring any industrial progress. The English East India Company procured these goods at the cheapest price by curtailing free access to the market; producers were kept out of the market either by the use of informal coercion or by formal laws and regulations made by the Company's government. Such an artificial monopoly operated not only in the case of artisanal industrial goods like cotton or silk textiles, but also in the production of indigo and opium by farmers. What were the results?

First, in such an economic regime, as one would expect, a buyer's market was created as far as export goods were concerned. Thus the artisan's or indigo grower's produce did not fetch a price that allowed more than subsistence to the producer while the trading profits were substantial. This caused immense misery in India.

A second consequence that followed was that the logic of the system thus developed discouraged investment in technological advancement and increase in productivity. Why?

> Consider the situation where trading capital gets a nice profit margin with out having to make any capital investment in the production of goods. If the trader makes a good profit by buying products at a low price, why should he invest his money in the production process? At the same time, consider the producer who obtains such a low price that he cannot add to his capital stock, because he has scarcely any surplus after feeding himself and his family. How can the artisan add to his capital stock, buy more or better tools and implements, if he is forced to sell his products at a price so low as to make accumulation of funds in his hands impossible? Then who will invest in industry to increase stock or to upgrade the technology to increase productivity? The answer is, no one, because trading capital need not and the producer cannot make investments. This scheme of things contains one of the explanations of the longstanding stagnation in technology and productivity characterizing colonial India (Bhattacharya 1991: 46).

The third feature of this system was a limited space provided to indigenous capital under the over-arching domination of the trading capital of the British East India Company and later that of the foreign business houses. Foreign traders in the English Agency House in the early nineteenth century needed "native" intermediaries for the procurement of export goods and occasionally as a source of ready cash in the form of loans. The traditional Indian business communities were well acquainted with the market and centers of production; they also had liquid cash accumulated in business for generations in the past. Such Indian business communities included the Hindu, Jain, and Bohra merchants of the Gujarat coast; the Khatris and Lohnas of Punjab and Sind; the Marwari Banias of Rajasthan; the Moplas and Syrian Christians of Kerala; the Chettis and Komatis of Tamil and Andhra region; and the Vaniks of Bengal. These business communities did obtain opportunities for profitable business in the regimes established by the East India Company but always in a position subordinate to English trading capital. Petty money lending, internal trade in agricultural and artisanal products, procurement of export goods, and distribution of imported goods on behalf of English business houses were the roles assigned to native capital. At the same time, though such business opportunities were limited, it did lead to capital accumulation and independent business activities and industrial investments eventually, e.g., the growth of the Indian textile industry in Bombay and Ahmedabad by the last decades of the nineteenth century. Indian capital, having begun in the colonial regime subordinated to foreign trading capital, did carve out an independent space of its own in the long run. But it was a very long run. Such a development was impeded by many factors in the second phase of colonialism, i.e., the phase following the Industrial Revolution in England.

In this second phase, England's economic relationship with the colony altered substantially. To begin with, priorities changed. The export of raw cotton to England, rather than cotton or silk textiles and indigo dye, acquired priority. Likewise, English factories, especially the cotton mills, wanted to market their goods in India. This new pattern of trade was firmly established by the middle of the nineteenth century. In 1850-51, the share of cotton textiles was only 3.7 percent in value in India's export trade, while raw cotton accounted for 19 percent and opium 30 percent. In contrast, about a hundred years prior to that, in 1758-61, 81 percent of the total value of exports was due to export of cotton textiles. As regards imports into India, by 1850-51 English factory-made cotton textiles accounted for 31.5 percent, cotton yarn 9 percent, woolen cloth 5 percent, metals 16 percent, and so on, whereas in 1758-61, virtually no industrial goods from England were imported by India. This reversal between the 1750s and 1850s was the consequence of the growth of modern industries in England and the de-industrialization of India.

The term "de-industrialization" is used today to denote the destruction of the artisanal industries, thus reducing the share of industry in the gross national product and in the distribution of the work force. As the share of industry decreased, the share of agriculture increased, i.e., there was greater dependence on agriculture for employment and income generation. We do not have exact estimates of this process but there is no doubt that it was the opposite of the process at work in England during the Industrial Revolution. In England, the share of agriculture in national income was between 40 and 45 percent in 1750, 20 percent in 1851, and 10 percent in 1881—showing a rapid pace of industrial growth. Likewise, the contribution of foreign trade to England's national income increased from 14 percent in 1790 to 36 percent by 1880. Thus we have a striking contrast between England industrializing herself and her colony, India, undergoing the opposite process.

Such a pattern—destruction of traditional artisanal industries before the onslaught of the machines, factories, and superior organization of the Industrial Revolution—was witnessed in all countries, including England. In India, however, the destruction of artisanal industries was not counterbalanced by the growth of modern factories and new technologies. Had India been politically independent, she might have protected her indigenous industries by an appropriate tariff policy, that is to say, by charging a high duty on foreign imports. This was, in fact, the policy pursued by almost every European country in the early stages of their industrial development. India under British rule, however, could not protect her industries, new and old, because that would restrict the Indian market for British manufactures. There was a conflict between the interest of the rulers and the interests of the subjects. This was one of the main points made by Indian Nationalist thinkers and spokesmen in their analysis of the exploitative nature of the British Indian government's policies. From this perception stemmed the major Nationalist action programs like the call to boycott foreign goods during the Swadeshi agitation in Bengal in the first decade of the twentieth century, and the charkha and khadi program of Mahatma Gandhi in the second and third decades.

To push forward the objective of opening up the Indian market for British manufactures and the export of raw materials from India, Britain needed a more efficient internal transportation system. As in many other parts of the world, opening up a country meant building railways. The railways remain a lasting memorial to the nineteenth-century British empire builders. The way in which this project was carried out, however, was somewhat peculiar. The British Government in India guaranteed an interest rate of 5 percent to investors in the Indian railway companies, irrespective of profit or loss of the railways—a burden on the Indian taxpayers and an arrangement that encouraged over-expenditure rather than cost-effectiveness in railway construction and management. Further, the railway companies were sterling companies set up in England, and only investors in that country received their guaranteed interest in sterling. These companies' schemes ensured a huge export of British steel and machinery. I in most other countries, railway construction had backward linkage effects, i.e., encouraged auxiliary industries like the engineering industry and iron and steel production; not so in India. Moreover, the layout of the railway lines and the freight rate policy were designed to encourage the distribution of manufactured goods from the port cities into the interior, i.e., the sale of imported manufactures; similarly, raw material export from the interior was indirectly subsidized. Despite all this, a contemporary observer, Karl Marx, writing in the *New York Daily Tribune*, was right in thinking that the railways were the forerunners of modernization in some ways. They served to spatially integrate a far-flung empire, brought into existence a national market, and brought in new machines and technical skills. Sometimes, unintended consequences play a great role, most unexpectedly, in the history of empires. On the whole, in

British policy-level thinking, India was assigned the role of an agricultural country which need not industrialize itself, because efficient specialization dictated otherwise. As late as the 1930s, such was the judgment of no less an authority than Lord John Meynard Keynes. In the first decade of the twentieth century, about 13 percent of India's Net Domestic Product was derived from the industrial sector, and at the time of independence, 1941-45, it was only 16.7 percent.

Indian Society and Colonial Policies

The consequences of the processes discussed so far must be borne in mind in considering the societal perspective on colonial India. The poverty of the Indian people under British rule was highlighted by Nationalist thinkers like Dadabhai Naoroji. Many British historians, like W.H. Moreland, raised the question whether India was better off under the pre-British regimes. The answer to that question was arguable, indeed never established in quantifiable terms. But the point of the Nationalist critique was the impoverishment of the country during British rule and the growing economic distance between underdeveloped India and the advanced industrial countries of the West. We need not go into that debate here, but plain facts loomed large in the Indian people's perception of their welfare under British rule; for instance, the frequency of famines was often a measure in their perception. Indeed the number of famines in British India during the nineteenth century was remarkable: in northern India in 1800-04, 1837-38, 1860-61, 1868-70, 1877-78, 1896-97, and 1899-1900; in western India in 1800-04, 1812-13, 1824-25, 1833-34, 1866-67, and 1876-78; in eastern India in 1873-74, 1888-89, and 1896-97; and in Southern India in 1806-07, 1824-25, 1833-34, 1866-67, and 1876-78. These are identified in official famine reports as major famines. From the middle of the nineteenth century, we have official estimates of famine mortality that indicate that some of the famines were devastating, e.g., those of 1876-78 and 1896-97, which cost 4.3 million and 5.15 million lives, respectively. The Government of India's response to these catastrophes was to construct an elaborate system of monitoring and relief work according to a "Famine Code" for administrative action. As a result, the famine mortality rate was reduced in the twentieth century; an exception to this was the Bengal Famine of 1943, when relief work was virtually suspended due to the supply situation in the eastern theater of the Second World War. Amartya K. Sen has argued that the Bengal famine was caused mainly by alterations in "exchange entitlements" under the impact of the War economy, while food supply available in 1943 in Bengal was only 5 percent less than the average of the previous five years.

Famines throughout the nineteenth and early twentieth centuries affected mainly the poor artisans, the landless agricultural laborers, and the small farmers who lived on the margin of subsistence.

Perhaps more significant than the occasional famines was the decline in food grain available per capita in the first half of the twentieth century. Separate estimates made by George Blyn, Shivasubramanian, and A. Heston suggest the same downward trend, although the extent of this decline is estimated variously by them for the period 1901 to 1946. In the twentieth century, famines, i.e., intense subsistence crises, became less frequent than in earlier periods because localized crises could be diffused by the import of food grains by railways and steamboats, but people had less to eat in "normal" times. Another significant piece of data is the finding of the Chief of the Medical Services, a British officer who conducted a path-breaking survey in 1933: about 26 percent of the Indian rural population suffered from malnutrition. Finally, was life expectancy a good index of the state of health? According to official British Indian Census statistics, life expectancy was 25.1 years in 1881-91, 23 years in 1901-11, 26.7 years in 1921-31, and 31.7 years in 1931-41. In the fifty years since Independence, life expectancy has doubled compared to what was reported in the last census in British India in 1941.

Another commonly used index is the level of literacy. This was abysmally low, less than 10 percent in any language until Independence. Mahatma Gandhi engaged in a famous debate with Hartog during the Round Table Conference arguing that the literacy rate in India had declined under British rule. Neither side in this debate could establish its case since quantifying the pre-British literacy rate was impossible. But there was no denying the fact that there was no marked increase in literacy during the colonial period and that the indigenous system of teaching of reading, writing, and arithmetic had collapsed due to the lack of patronage which the state and the local elite provided earlier.

These are some basic facts of nineteenth- and early twentieth-century Indian society—a low level of life expectancy, subjection to cyclical famines, low nutritional levels affecting the health of a substantial section of the population, and a low level of literacy. Add to this past: the hierarchization of society into *varnas* or orders and *jatis* or castes; the low status and "untouchability" ascribed in the *dharmashastras* to certain castes; the subjection of women in a patriarchal system under *shastric* injunctions which were supposed to sanction gender discrimination and worse; the exploitation of tribal peoples who were kept beyond the pale of Hindu society; and various social practices which kept Hindu and Muslim communities far apart in their quotidian life and private spaces, although they worked together in public life.

Unlike economic policy, which was directly fashioned in British hands, colonialist thinking and action in respect of the social domain was, by and large, mediated by a "native" intelligentsia. This stratum was, of course, far removed from the vast substratum, the poorly nourished and famine stricken and socially unprivileged masses we have been talking about. This thin top layer would be called by various names in those days. There is a delightful variety of nomenclature. "Elite" is probably the reigning favorite; our old friend "Western educated" still finds employment, to one's surprise; "modern intellectuals" has distinguished adherents; "middle class" is no longer considered quite classy; and "neo-bourgeois" is a bit of an upstart and not seen in the best circles. This colonial intelligentsia, by whatever name they are called, are recognized as playing a crucial role in many Third World societies today, and this was the case in colonial times. In nineteenth-century India, they faced, Janus fashion, the West and the East, and not only mediated the British interventions in the social sphere, but also generated their own initiatives towards social reform.

Perhaps the growth of such a stratum in colonial Indian society and the unintended consequences which followed were of greater importance than the infrequent and rather ineffective social interventions made by the colonial state by way of "reforming" Hindu society. Shils (1960:269) ascribes to this "intellectual class" in Asian and African countries a salient role unparalleled "in all human history." Broomfield, in a well-known work on the role of this elite in Bengal, defines it as not so much a class but a status group "economically dependent upon land rents and professional and clerical employment, keeping its distance from the masses by its acceptance of high caste prescriptions and its command over education" (1968:12-13).

Access to education was the crucial factor in the growth of this intelligentsia. Opportunity for that was created by the British Indian government. Initially, the East India Company was motivated mainly by a desire to train its servants in Indian languages and laws. Hence the foundation of the Calcutta Fort William College, the Calcutta Madrasah, and the Sanskrit College in Varanasi in the last decades of the eighteenth century. From this beginning, there developed a deeper interest in Indian classical literature, and generally Oriental cultures, first institutionalized in the Asiatic Society of Calcutta in 1784. In the second phase, roughly in the first three decades of the 1800's, the East Indian Company's responsibility to encourage education was, in principle, admitted (1813). By 1835, it was decided, as recommended by Lord Macaulay, as well as many Indian opinion-leaders of the day, to promote the spread of "Western" education rather than spend money on Indian language and literature and other traditional forms of learning. Twenty years later, a more active involvement of the government in educating the Indian people through government-sponsored institutions was declared to be policy (1854), and in 1857-58, three universities were founded in Calcutta, Bombay, and Madras. The overall result of this trend was a great concentration of resources in higher education in the English language and English literary tradition. The beneficiary of this education policy were members of the new intelligentsia, who derived their intellectual predilections from the limited exposure they had to Western culture and systems of knowledge. However limited this exposure was and however derivative their ideas might have been, this intelligentsia developed a powerful critique of the colonial state, on the one hand, and of the evils inherent in the traditional social order, on the other. At the same time, to translate this critique into an agenda of action was beyond the colonial intelligentsia's limited capacity. It remained an incomplete endeavor, for the masses had no active and sustained part. Moreover, the situation in India was substantially different from that of Europe where the humanist, scientific, and liberal democratic intelligentsia were operating within the context of a socioeconomic transition to modern industrial capitalism over the centuries, from the Renaissance to the Industrial Revolution. Thus the role of the Indian intelligentsia was bound to be limited.

They also did not receive much support from the colonial state in the area of "social reform," except for a brief period. While James Mill and other English intellectuals were, with good reasons, highly critical of many aspects of Indian society, the policy pursued by the British government in India was in favor of the status quo till the 1830s and again reverted to non-interventionism in the social arena after 1857. In the 1830s, the administration of Governor-General William Bentinck, with the support of Raja Rammohun Roy, achieved the abolition of the heinous custom of *sati* (1829), and the strengthening of legal and administrative measures against female infanticide; another landmark was the support given by the government to Pandit Ishwar Chandra Vidyasagar's effort to make a law allowing the remarriage of Hindu widows (1856).

The revolt of 1857 created an impression in England that interference by the government in Indian social practices, often supposedly based on religious beliefs, was to be avoided in the interest of political stability. This reversion to non-interventionism was modified now and again when Indian social reformers brought about strong pressure of public opinion on issues such as legislation on minimum age of marriage, but no further initiative was taken by the government between 1829 and 1856. Promotion of modern education in the Muslim community, an initiative taken by Sir Syed Ahmed, received marginal support; but later the leaders of the community obtained the fullest support while pursuing communal political objectives. The government would neither address social problems like casteism and untouchability, despite efforts by pioneering reformers like Jotiba Phule, nor help prepare a base for social reform through the spread of literacy and primary education. A social laissez-faire policy was considered to be a means of securing loyalty to the British Raj. To do the least was considered most politic most of the time.

Colonialism and the Indian Polity

The agenda of the colonial state included an attempt to restructure the Indian polity. The direction and pace of this project was determined in the late eighteenth and early nineteenth centuries by initiatives from England; from the beginning of the twentieth century, the agenda was the outcome of an interaction between policy-makers in England and the nationalist leadership in India. At the core of the project, in the first phase, were three objectives: to develop a strong army and police force as instruments of expanding and protecting the empire, to bring into existence a sound civil service from out of the rudimentary and corrupt system of the East India Company's servants, and to erect a judicial system to dispense justice.

The first objective was achieved in the last decades of the eighteenth century by recruiting Indians to the East India Company's army and by obtaining the services of the King's Army in England whenever such a need arose. The Indians so recruited were called "sepoys," a good number of whom joined the Mutiny in 1857: at all other times, they were loyal soldiers and helped the English conquer India as well as fight England's imperialist wars from Abyssinia to China. The police system, the other instrument for the subordination of India, was begun in a rudimentary fashion by Lord Cornwallis; incidentally, he had been in command in Yorktown and surrendered in October 1781, signaling the end of England's forlorn hopes in the American War of Independence. As Governor-General of India from 1786 to 1793, Cornwallis restructured the police and civil services. An elaborate structure from the level of the village watchmen to the district superintendents of police, as well as an effective system of surveillance and intelligence gathering, was gradually developed. In the beginning, both the police system and the army were officered by Englishmen; Indians were admitted to the higher ranks by slow degrees.

The civil service was created on the foundations laid by the East India Company, with Englishmen employed as factors or agents to take care of the Company's business in India. As the Company began to acquire territories and political power, the founders of the empire like Warren Hastings or Lord Cornwallis felt the need for a body of civil servants who would be something more than clerks in counting houses. Their job would be to maintain law and order as Magistrates, to collect taxes as Collectors, and as Judges to administer justice in courts of law. The Indian Civil Service, thus created, enjoyed a reputation of being the highest paid service cadre and the least corruptible in the British Empire. From 1853, recruitment to the I.C.S. was made through public examination in English, a system in advance of England or any other country at that time, with the exception of the old system of recruiting mandarins in China. For about eighty years since its inception, Indians were not recruited to the I.C.S. until Satyendranath Tagore qualified in the examination in 1863. Indians who began to enter this service as well as subordinate services in administration were, by and large, competent men who disproved the notion that Englishmen alone were fit for responsible positions. One of the demands of the Indian political leaders in the late nineteenth century was that entry of Indians into the civil services should be facilitated.

Perhaps, more than anything else, the system of laws and the administration of justice was the proud achievement of the empire builders. Of the elements of the imperial system which proved to be lasting in the post-independence days, the legal and judicial legacy proved to be the most lasting. It can also be said to be most important in that the constitutional basis of the Republic was built upon it. Here was a society where the imperfectly understood laws of an ancient stage of social evolution, laws inappropriate to modern times, were arbitrarily applied under supposedly religious injunctions. What this caricature of an old system lacked, the British legal ideas and institutions offered: the concept of equality before law, irrespective of caste and social status; codification of laws, making them accessible and uniform in application; the growth of a profession specialized in law; and a hierarchized chain of courts of law with well-defined jurisdiction. At the same time, the British Indian legal system had some major limitations. Equality before the law was a great principle, but it was not often observed in practice when Europeans and natives were contestants in the court of law; indeed, the right of Europeans to be tried in special courts by white juries was recognized in law till the last few decades of British rule. The effect of social pressures on the course of law has been sensitively portrayed by E.M. Forster in *A Passage to India.* Moreover, as in other countries with similar legal systems, not all had equal access to law. For the poor, justice was expensive, the court of law remote and formidable, the laws codified in English, incomprehensible. For the rich, the arms of the law were occasionally pliable—particularly in the lower ranks of the police; lawyers were easily available to harass one's enemies, and justice could be denied to the opposite party by the deft use of delays.

The basic design of the system, consisting of the army and the police, the civil service, and judicial organization, was complete by the end of the nineteenth century. About this time there began an interaction between the imperial system thus erected and the Indian National Congress (founded in 1885), initially representing mainly the new Indian intelligentsia. It is neither possible nor necessary to give here a blow-by-blow account of this process of interaction. One common scenario framed by the imperial policy-makers presents this process as the pupil's progress: India being made fit to govern herself and being allowed, by the British, to participate in government by slow degrees. The other view of the process was to look upon it as a struggle, tempered by occasional compromises, by the nationalist leadership to extract concessions. The first scenario has few proponents among historians today, and the second is criticized on the ground that it focuses on elite politics and ignores the subaltern perspective, the historical role of those below the level of the participants of the dialogue and negotiations with imperialism. The contestation on these interpretative postures is related with varying evaluations of the post-colonial polity in India, an issue addressed in another chapter in this book. For the present we only need to look at the outcome of the interaction between the imperial system and its adversaries and allies.

One outcome was a series of legislations on the composition and powers of the legislative bodies of the Indian Government—then called the Imperial Government—and of the Provincial Governments. These laws, made in 1861, 1892, 1919, and 1935, illustrate the basic policy trends. At the time the Crown took over governance from the East India Company in 1858, tremendous concentration of power had been effected—in the hands of the Secretary of State for India and his Council in England, and in India, the Governor-General and his Council and civil servants in decision-making positions. The powers of the Secretary of State, a member of the British Cabinet, remained paramount, but the concentration of power, particularly legislative power, within the government in India was modified by these laws made between 1861 and 1935 through three kinds of changes. First, the enlargement of the legislative Councils, Imperial and Provincial, to include more non-official Indian members reduced the proportion of members who were British officials and government nominees. Second, the principle of election was recognized, and both the size of the electorate and the numbers elected to the legislatures increased. This was a response to the Indian nationalists' slogan, "No taxation without representation"—a slogan borrowed from the America of 1776. The franchise in India, however, despite expansion, remained very limited due to property qualifications; less than 15 percent of the Indian people voted in the last days of British rule, under the Act of 1935. Thirdly, there was a gradual increase in the powers of elected members of legislatures over subjects which had been previously "reserved," i.e., excluded from their purview. But in important matters like finance, defence, or law and order, the ultimate decision-making powers were retained by the Governor-General and the provincial Governors.

These responses to their demands were never considered adequate by the nationalist leadership. Also, no one should forget another trend of legislation typified by the Arms Act of 1878 to disarm Indians, the Vernacular Press Act of 1878 to suppress seditious writings, the provisions in the Penal Code curtailing civil liberties to protect the government against sedition, or the Rowlatt Act of 1919 allowing imprisonment without trial and conviction in a court of law.

Moreover, issues of composition and functions of legislatures and legislative politics were pushed aside in the course of the nationalist movement by more basic issues from the beginning of the Gandhian era in 1919. Some of these issues arose out of particular events which did not necessarily reflect the government's long-term policies and legislation. An instance was the Jallianwallah Bagh massacre on the occasion of a mass meeting in that garden in response to Gandhi's call for a national strike in April 1919. That massacre caused Rabindranath Tagore to write to the Viceroy, renouncing his knighthood: "The time has come when badges of honour make our shame glaring in their incongruous context of humiliation." Such events went into the making of patriotic consciousness. Some moments of naked confrontation appeared more real than moments of dialogue and negotiations. There was also a quotidian aspect to imperial power, an aspect often out of sight in the academic historians' treatment of the heroic struggles and statesmanlike concessions. In daily life, the ugly face of racism was encountered by Indians. It was met sometimes with the servility of favor-seekers, sometimes with the stoic fatalism of an ancient people inured to misfortunes, sometimes with the loyalists' self-deceiving rationalization of iniquities, and sometimes with patriotic fervor. All these moments of reaction, simultaneous and imbricated, could be seen and are still remembered as part of everyday experience in private and public spaces, in *durbars* and meetings, in the railways and public parks, in courts of law and in clubs. When G.D. Birla, one of the richest industrialists, complained in 1930 that the English manager of the Imperial Bank of India would not offer him a chair when Birla called on him, he was giving expression to a feeling that was shared by the *babu* who had to take off his shoes before meeting his sahib, or the peasant accustomed to render unacknowledged obeisance, or the Indian hanger-on on the fringes of English society who would be shown his place at the club if he was at all admitted to one or in the Governor's garden party to which an invitation was a prized thing. These manifestations of the white man's power and authority in daily life were as much a part of the imperial polity as the laws and legislatures and political movements on which historians focus all attention.

And yet the British Raj seemed stable. From the vantage point of the 1990s, the question that seems interesting is why did the Raj last as long as it did? Perhaps a major source of the Raj's stability from the revolt of 1857 onwards was that it did not radically disturb the traditional order in India, the social hierarchy, the distribution of authority and influence in civil society. From the time the Crown took over the reigns of administration from the East India Company, there was a settled policy of letting alone the Princes in the Native States so long as they did not cause any trouble by making a public spectacle of their private vices or exhibit any tendency to reclaim the power they had lost to the Paramount Power, i.e., the Queen's government represented by the Viceroy. The upper stratum of the rural elite and the landlord class in British India was likewise to remain undisturbed, a class of loyal supporters of the Raj rewarded now and then with titles specially devised for Indian subjects, invitation to the Viceroy or the Governor's durbar, or nomination to advisory position in the Councils. They had long since lost their magisterial power, and they were subject to British laws; informal power over the peasants and tenants and access to government officials and the police allowed them to retain a good deal of their dominance in rural society. The same kind of reward system and influence kept a large section of the urban elite happy and loyal to the Raj. Among them, the businessmen had grievances in respect of taxation policies and lack of governmental support; but which business class does not have these problems, and what could businessmen do without the protection to propertied classes that the Raj ensured? At the other end of the social scale, the lower castes and the untouchables, the subsistence farmers, and the landless and bonded laborers, the tribal groups at the fringes of Hindu society, and such others who belonged traditionally to the bottom of the pile were kept in their place under the Raj. Thus the traditional social and power hierarchy essentially remained intact at the top and down below. It was only in the middle order that the British Raj saw some repositioning and reshuffling and turbulence. There arose, in this segment of society, new claimants to status and power and also a critique of the traditional order and of the British Raj. To the extent this critique was merely an intellectual exercise, the Raj could ignore it. The colonial State's strategy of maintaining status quo in civil society helped secure the compliance of the subjects. The colonial state dominated a vast subcontinent without frequent resort to physical coercion on a large scale since 1857 for many decades. It was only through the withdrawal of compliance by the subject race that the coercive basis of the colonial state could be revealed, *the ultima ratio regum.* It may be, therefore, no accident that the key concepts in Mahatma Gandhi's action strategy were non-cooperation and civil disobedience, his means of building a countervailing power within civil society challenging the colonial state. The other aspect of the colonial era was the encounter of different civilizations. As we have seen earlier, many unintended consequences mar well-laid plans in imperial history, and one of the best examples was the role of the intelligentsia educated under colonial dispensation. Not only was it possible for them to create a political space for themselves to challenge colonial power, but also to resist cultural assimilation and to question the West's cultural hegemony. The struggle in terms of power and politics was over by 1947, but the encounter between the enduring civilization of India and the West remains one of the major themes of the history of this day and age.

Works Cited

Ahmed, Aziz. 1967. *Islamic modernism in India and Pakistan, 1857-1964.* London:

Bayly, C.A. 1988. *Indian society and the making of the British empire.* Cambridge: Cambridge University Press.

Bhattacharya, Sabyasachi. 1991. Political development in the New States. In *The colonial economy of India.* Delhi: Indira Gandhi Open University Press.

Blyn, Georg. 1966. *Agricultural trends in India 1891-1946.* Philadelphia: University of Pennsylvania Press

Broomfield, J.H. 1968. *Elite conflict in a plural society.* Berkeley: University of California Press.

Chandra, Bipan. 1985. *Communalism in Modern India.* Delhi: Vikas, 1984

Chaudhuri, B., T. Kessinger, S. Bhattacharya in Dharma Kumar, eds. 1983. *Cambridge Economic History of India.* vol. II Cambridge: Cambridge University Press.

Cohn, Bernard S. 1988. *An anthropologist among the historians and other essays.* Delhi:

Desai, A.R. 1959. *The social background of Indian nationalism.* Bombay: Popular

Dewey,Clive and Hopkins, eds. 1978. *The Imperial Impact.* London: Athlone Press, 1978

Frykenberg, R.E. ed. 1969. *Land control and social structure in Indian history.* Madison: University of Wisconsin Press.

Gopal, Sarvepalli. 1965. *British Policy in India, 1858-1905.* Cambridge: Cambridge University Press.

Guha, Ranajit, ed. 1982. Introduction in *Subaltern Studies 1.* Delhi: New York: Oxford University.

Jalal, Ayesha. 1995. *Democracy and Authoritarianism in South Asia: a comparative historical perspective.* Cambridge: Cambridge University Press.

Jones, Kenneth W. 1990. *Socio-religious reform movements in British India.* Cambridge: Cambridge University Press.

Marshall, P.J. 1988. *Bengal: the British bridgehead, eastern India 1740-1828.* Cambridge: Cambridge University Press.

Rothermund, D. 1978. *Government, Landlord and Peasant in India, 1865-1935.* Wiesbaden.

Sarkar, Sumit. 1983. *Modern India 1858-1947.* New Delhi.

Shils, E.A. 1961. *The intellectual between tradition and modernity.* The Hague: Mouton:

Sisson, R. and S.A. Wolpert, eds. 1988. *Congress and Indian Nationalism: the pre-independence phase.* Berkeley: University of California Press.

Srinivas, M.N. 1966. *Social change in modern India.* Berkley: University of California Press.

Stokes, Eric. 1978. *The peasants and the Raj.* Cambridge: Cambridge University Press.

Thorner, Daniel and Alice Thorner.1972. *Land and Labour in India.* Bombay.

Bagchi , A. K. 1962. *Private Investment in India 1900-39.* Cambridge: Cambridge University Press.

Tomlinson, B.R. 1993. *The economy of modern India 1860-1970.* Cambridge: Cambridge University Press.

Visaria, L & P in Dharma Kumar, ed. 1983. *Cambridge Economic History of India.* vol. II. Cambridge: Cambridge University Press.

III | Indic Religions & Philosophy

Chapter 6 The Significance of the Indic Religions for the West

José Pereira

What interest can Hindu theology have for Western readers? Can it only be that of the heirs of one great tradition of thought for the works of another in some ways more ancient than their own?

In attempting to answer this question one must remember that the West has a special relationship to the world's other cultures, in that it has concerned itself with their ideas more than they have with its own. It is the analytical and historical techniques developed by its scholars that have made an exact and profound study of non-Western cultures possible. Also, these cultures, when not secluded from one another, were only partially linked, until they were drawn together into one world scheme by the West, which is thus more ecumenical than they.

However, like other more parochial civilizations--whose complacency about their own achievement was fostered by their ignorance of that of the others--this most universal of civilizations has also tended to exalt its own achievements excessively (as students of comparative culture have observed), though less so now than before. Its historians of thought give one the feeling that the writings of its thinkers are the only fit expression of human ideas. If (they seem to imply) these ideas, as they grant is possible, take birth in a non-Western brain, it is only through their Western interpretation that their integral nature comes to be revealed: So to their first outstanding Western interpreter rightly falls the honor of being their real discoverer. In other words, the archetypes of human thought are in their plenitude Western: Their Western interpretation is thus to be taken as the "model" by which all the others are to be judged.

But we cannot permit the most ecumenical of civilizations both to enjoy the benefits of an informed extensive curiosity in other cultures, and to indulge in a flattering but parochial complacency about its own uniqueness. One main reason for this contradiction--at least in theology--is that the informed curiosity is mainly confined to the specialists in the other cultures, and the parochial complacency to (shall we say?) mere theologians, few of whom have the time and the patience to study Chinese or Sanskrit. Few great non-Western works have been readably translated and most not at all.

To come back to our question, and to frame a possible answer: The interest that Hindu theology can have for Western readers is chiefly an interest in religious insights which today, as never before, confront, and even challenge, those long traditional in the West. It is arguable that these insights first arose in the Indic world. It is, moreover, possible that the expression they received at the hands of Indic theologians, after centuries of brllliant and unflagging speculation, and in a linguistic medium unequaled for its philosophical finesse, is the model by which all their other expressions are to be judged.

If these assertions are valid, the originality of some of Western thought is diminished to the merely parochial level. Western thinkers may indeed have acquired some of these insights independently of Indic or other influence, but what they gained was previously unknown only to themselves, not to the human race as a whole--much as America was discovered for Europeans only, not for its inhabitants, hence not for mankind.

A knowledge of Hindu theology is particularly relevant to the theology of our times, for the Indic works contain so many of the ideas that modern Western theologians seem to believe are their discoveries: one is led to assume that a closer inspection of the same works will bring to light the other "discoveries" as well. Indeed, they are sure to contain the insights that future theologians will no doubt claim originality for, and which we can now avail ourselves of by merely learning Sanskrit. We can thus, with some malice, rob our successors of the pleasure of believing that the world would have wanted much invaluable wisdom, had it not been revealed to them for the first time in human history.

One of the several ways of envisaging the evolution of Western thought is that of a progressive Indicization. From a knowledge of the Western and Indic traditions a different picture of religious speculation emerges than was projected, say, by the secularist Western historians of the nineteenth century. According to their neat scheme, philosophy shone forth to the world in Greece, and from splendor to splendor until it encountered the world of Semitic religion--the source of its obscuration, triumphant in the Dark Ages, when philosophy was supplanted by theology. After a long eclipse Descartes restored its brightness, which from that moment ever increased in strength, attaining to its noonday dazzle in our own times. On the periphery of the focus of light and the mass of darkness was the outer "Oriental" world, a sort of penumbra, of little interest--except perhaps to intellectual adventurers and to lovers of the exotic. Thus there were two main bodies of speculative thought--the "enlightened" (comprising the Greek and modern Western philosophy) and the "obscurantist" (including the "medieval" and the "Oriental," both a jumble of superstition and ingenious reasoning).

In consequence of research into Scholastic, Indian and Chinese thought, this scheme passed from history into mythology--in other words, acquired a more tenacious life. A great number of Westerners still behave as though they wished the nineteenth-century scheme were true, witness their comparative neglect of the two "obscurantist" traditions. Of course there is a vogue in Oriental religions, but its stimulant is less the erudition of scholars than the unctuousness of gurus. But the great Indic theologians combine knowledge and unction--another reason why their thoughts must be made easily available in translation, if only to correct the distortion present in the minds of the aficionados of Oriental teachings. This can be realized by the simple expedient (which, alas, few have had the ability or desire to employ) of presenting the theologians' thought in a comprehensible English guise.

To revert to the nineteenth-century scheme: From the Indic standpoint, as I said, an altogether different picture emerges. In outlining it we must recall to mind the two great bodies of world religion, the Indic (comprising Hinduism, Jainism and Buddhism) and the Semitic (consisting of Judaism, Christianity and Islam). Indic religion was speculative from its inception. But the Semitic, born among non-intellectual peoples, needed the Greek to teach them philosophical habits. Thus one cultural background supplied the credere and another the intelligere, a fact also largely true of East Asian religions. In the Indic religions, however, both reason and faith existed in symbiosis, or formed their unique amalgam that is theology. Not for these religions, the conflict between the Church and the Academy that was so long in resolving (if it ever fully was) in the world of the Semitic faiths.

There were of course religious beliefs long before there was any Indic civilization, but their very first philosophic epiphanies were undoubtedly radiated by the Indic genius. One of the few archetypes that India, the *terre natale de la pluz haute philosophie*, seems definitely to have lacked was the unambiguously transcendent God who creates out of nothing--a Semitic concept that itself had long to await its theological efformation. As to the other archetypes, they were sometimes disseminated through contact, as to East Asia. Sometimes they were born anew, without apparent filiation to their matrix, as, centuries after their first Indic epiphany, in Greece. It is as if, following the law of transmigration, they had passed from one avatar to another without contact between avatars. But they were first assembled into an elaborate architectonic framework by Greek, not Indian, thinkers. Indeed, again apparently without contact, the Indian phase of elaboration began just as the Greek was about to end.

Prominent among the rare Greek archetypes that lack equivalence in India is the analogical metaphysics of Aristotle, later used as the chief basis for the "metaphysics of the Exodus," that is, of monotheistic creationism. This metaphysics was developed to its full speculative petential by the three Scholasticisms--Muslim, Jewish and Christian--attaining its model expression in the work of Aquinas and Suarez. Contemporary with the Scholasticisms was the definitive formulation of the "Indic" archetypes by Indic theologians--like Nāntirakṣita, Abhinava Gupta and Madhva--excelling the Greek achievement (and sometimes even the Christian Scholastic) in subtlety, depth and comprehensiveness. This age, in the West, extends roughly from Origen to Suarez; during its course, the avatars of the Indic archetypes invade the West less frequently than before or after. We may thus call it the Christian Interlude to the Indicization of the West, and it is perhaps the climax of the West's speculative creativity.

Scholasticism was superseded in the West by two antithetical trends--rationalism and empiricism--that Aquinas and Suarez had sought to balance, and that had also existed contentiously in India. From Descartes began an age during which the West's speculative power is supposed by many to have been at its highest. But this is just the age when the irruption of Indic ideas into Western thought is resumed, and nearly overwhelms it. It is as though the archetypal energy of religious and philosophic thought had worn out its original container and had been transmitted by an invisible conductor to a newer receptacle. I say "invisible" conductor because there was no significant contact between the two civilizations before the mid-eighteenth century. The only Oriental literature that Westerners of the preceding age knew was the Confucian, and in the translations of the Chinese texts available to them the Indic archetypes then active in the West are not in vivid focus.

At all events, most of these archetypes did not first enter world thought through the creative labors of the West. Now even those long traditional in it became imbued with more distinctively Indic nuances. Furthermore, notwithstanding the brilllance of the new interpretation, the character of model expression eluded the writings of this emerging tradition, so preoccupied with innovation and so convinced of its singularity. This was because it now seethed with the two contrasting groups of archetypes efformed by the Indic and the Scholastic traditions. At least on the surface, they were rife with areas of discord. The archetypes that Scholasticism had so consummately expressed and which had now become somewhat coarsened, tended to obfuscate those which had earlier and perhaps with greater purity been embodied in Indic thought, and so prevented them from shining in full strength. Or to use another, and somewhat contradictory metaphor, it was as though the compact substance of one group of ideas, worn to gravel, had become embedded as so much grit in the crystalline mass of the other, thus marring its transparency.

However, through the impact of Orientalism, developed from the mid-eighteenth century, there was a gradual approximation to the purity of the Indic model. In the nineteenth and twentieth centuries, as never before, prominent Western (especially Germanic) thinkers advanced theories and constructed systems directly inspired by the Indic model: among them were Hegel, Schopenhauer, Nietzsche, Engels and Jung. This process of approximation can logically have no other end but the full possession of the model itself--not only in its earlier and scriptural facets (now generally accessible), but also in its later and theological ones. This cannot be achieved through Sanskrit, but through the modern Western tongues, chiefly the best known of them, English. The inaccessibility of the theological facets, as I said, is due to their difficult language and complex thought patterns, but an attempt must be made to render them comprehensible.

From the viewpoint just described it appears that the creative heights of human thought were in the two "obscurantist" traditions, with the most "enlightened" one, the modern Western, attaining (for all its mighty upsurge) to a comparatively lower level of originality. Like all good theories, this one is an oversimplification, but I think that it has at least two merits--of being less parochial than the theory it challenges, comprehending as it does the two great bodies of world speculation, the Indic and the Western; and of being less naive, though, alas, as liable to be turned into a mythology.

Indic Archetypes

To come to these archetypes: I shall take a random thirteen. All these exist anteriorly in the Indic world, and later elsewhere. Some of them reappear in the Greek world, and few in the modern West without Greek mediation.

1. The West's "modern" age begins with the Copernican Revolution, that is, the supplanting of the Greek ideas of the universe by the Indic. As imagined by the Greeks, the universe had a fixed center, the earth, over which was a succession of astral spheres, topped by the empyrean. But Copernicus and Galileo, as the latter claimed, "by marvellous discoveries and clear demonstrations .... enlarged [this universe] a hundred thousand times beyond the belief of the wise men of bygone ages." "The Europeans of the 17th century were quite unaware that 'the wise men of bygone ages' in India had for a long time already done justice to the immensity of time and space, not, however, through marvellous discoveries and clear demonstrations, but through the intuitions of their cosmic imagination." Space, constituted of numberless world systems, is what the Buddhists call the "Saha world." (see also Kak, this volume.)

2. Idealism, the belief that physical objects exist only in relation to an experiencing subject--a major philosophical concept without clear Greek precedent-was developed by the Buddhists and consummately formulated in the third or fourth centuries C.E. by Asanga and Vasubandhu (See Chapple this volume). It appeared in the West with Berkeley, reached its zenith with Hegel in Germany in the early nineteenth century, and was later revived in the English-speaking world, there to be supplanted by realist and nominalist philosophies.

3. Materialism. From these nominalist, particularly the neopositivist, philosophies developed the belief that all knowkledge of supersensible things is void of meaning, that sensation is the sole norm of knowledge; and that inference is valid only if used for clarifying the data of experience, and not for going beyond them. Some have traced these views to Udalāka in the ninth century B.C.E., but they are clearly articulated in the doctrines of some Śramaṇa, or Wanderer sects, three centuries afterwards,

as far as the denial of the supersensible is concerned; the epistemology was formulated later, a century afterwards. Materialism appeared in Greece with Democritus.

4. Skepticism, perhaps the only direct borrowing of Greek thought from the Indic, was introduced into the West by a soldier from Alexander's Indian campaign, Pyrrho (fourth-third century B.C.E.). Pyrrho's theories are a Greek version of some early Buddhist and Jain dialectical ideas, ambiguously developed in Greece by the Skeptic Carneades (third-second century B.C.E.) and unconfusedly in India by the Buddhist Nāgārjuna (mid-second century C.E.). Among its procedures is the undermining of the foundations of theology and metaphysics through the disclosure of their supposed antinomies, formulated with expertise, by the great Nāgārjuna and (in the West) proudly attributed to Kant.

5. The "non-soul" doctrine of the self as no more than a bundle of perceptions and void of substance--claimed by the Buddhists as belonging to the very essence of their founder's docrine, and by modern Western philosophers as one of Hume's chief contributions to world thought.

6. The elimination of the thing-in-itself as a knowable, common in Buddhist doctrine, also (in the West) one of Kant's great discoveries.

7. Reality as flux. The Buddha's conviction (echoed by his Greek contemporary Heraclitus) that becoming is the universal form of reality, was magnificently elaborated by his disciple Kamalaśīla in the seventh century C.E. It almost overwhelmed Rousseau during a reverie in 1765, and with an ecstasy that was more Buddhist than Heraclitean, since it was accompanied by the experience of a state comparable to that of nirvāṇa, or of undifferentiated awareness. Conspicuous among the innumerable contemporary avatars of this doctrine of flux are the Process Theology of the bourgeois world and the dialectical metaphysics of the Communist.

8. Non-violence. This is a Jain archetype, stemming from its fundamental doctrine of life as constituting the primary essence of all things, in consequence of which the attempt to destroy it is the greatest of sins, and non-violence the greatest of virtues. Gandhi, who grew up in a Jain environment, fashioned this doctrine into a political ideology that soon became popular in the West. And today, in so far as our political

world may be said to have an ideal, it is surely non-violence. (See K.L.S. Rao, this volume.)

The above archetypes are mostly non-Hindu in origin or development. The remaining archetypes are all Hindu.

9. Reality as bipolar. This is first stated in the Upaniṣads around the ninth century B.C.E. "There are two forms of the Brahman, the formed and the unformed, the mortal and the immortal, the static and the moving, the actual and the beyond." This doctrine has two modes, which may be called the substantialist and the evolutionary.

In the former--the traditional model of Hindu theology, sponsored in the West chiefly by Spinoza--the changes are but the modal aspects of an immutable substance. In the latter, the changes (or process of becoming) constitute the concrete or moving aspect, while the immutable aspect remains abstract or ineffable. First systematized by Asanga and Vasubandhu, this variant has two major contemporary versions, the Process Theology and dialectical metaphysics already referred to. Reality, for the bourgeois system, is "God"; for the Communist, Matter or Nature. Its abstract and immutable aspect, for the former; is the eminently relative One, considered as "the absolute ground of any and all real relationships"; for the latter, it is Law, "the eternal laws of Nature." Its concrete or mutable aspect, for both, is the world of change, or process, described by the theist system as "the sum total of all real relationships," and by the Communist as "the modes of existence of matter." For the latter the process is a necessary one, a view which the former does not seem to share.

10. The "conditioning" of man's being, the inquiry into which led the Buddhists to create the world's first empirical psychology, and led both them and the Hindus to the related quest (of which the West is only now becoming aware) of its "de-conditioning" through yogic discipline.

11. Matter as energy, not inert "stuff" as classical Western physics held it to be: hence more like "mind" (one way of translating the Sāṅkhya buddhi, one of Matter's evolutes) and "life" (whose principle, say the Sāṅkhya, is Egoism, or ahaṃkāra). By an inner tension this Matter proliferates into evolutes--doctrine reincarnate in the thought of Marx and Darwin. Combined with the Taoist dialectic of Yang-Yin-Tao (re-em-

bodied in the Hegelian thesis-antithesis-synthesis) it forms part of the metaphysical foundation of Communist dogma.

12. Energy as pervading the universe, subject to human control through correct knowledge. This conviction, basic to the earliest Vedas, was partially formulated in the Hindu system of Ritualism (Mīmāmsa). But there is an important difference between the ancient and modern views. For the former, the "correct knowledge", is the ritual formulation of the hidden sound structure of physical reality through incantations, or mantras; for the latter, the " correct knowledge" is (or was) a scientific formulation of nature's immutable laws.

13. Yogic interiority. This is a new archetype, unknown to the West before our times-a conviction that the self can be experienced immediately, and not just as reflected in the experiences of the external world, and that this intuitive awareness can be arrived at through gradually eliminating our multiple concepts of phenomena by means of a systematic (yogic) control of mind and body. This direct contact confronts us with the unimaginable magnitude of power latent in the self, which we can use to control even the limitations of the body. The transplanting of this archetype into the mentality of the West was to a large degree the work of Jung, who "through the practice of depth psychology... has done in the twentieth century C.E. what the Hindus did in perhaps the eighth century B.C.E.; he has discovered empirically the existence of an immortal soul in man, dwelling outside time and space, which can actually be experienced."

Consonant with the experience of yogic interiority is the Christian belief, vehemently stressed from the eighteenth century, of the supreme value of the human individual and of his free decision. A great force in Western religion today, this belief explains contemporary unwillingness to countenance any religious values not open to personal experience or imposed regardless of individual choice. This conviction draws strength from the Indic archetype of yogic awareness, whereby we are assured immediate and intuitive contact with the source itself of this personal autonomy.

The Contemporary Vogue In Eastern Faiths

Eastern philosophies have always intrigued the Western mind, mostly because their archetypes sometimes complement, sometimes challenge, but always enrich, the religious vision of the universe projected by the archetypes of traditional Western faiths. Their popularity today is intensified by yet other reasons, for their archetype are of particular significance in the religious context of the modern West--as we see in the following four of its many situations: (1) The fact that religious feeling has been corroded by Skepticism, which has itself decayed, unable to provide an alternative for traditional belief or to smother the yearning for faith. (2) That the religious intolerance traditional in the Semitic faiths, with which the West was once bedeviled, has also abated, being replaced by a desire for mutual tolerance. (3) That the style of the traditional Western religions, perhaps through long familarity, has lost some of its stimulus, giving rise to a craving for new symbols and imagery. (4) That Christianity is no longer seen as a body of wholly singular doctrines, but as having beliefs reflected in the world's other faiths, even the beliefs that are in a fashion specific to itself. Theologians are thus challenged to re-examine the question of whether Revelation was communicated to one or more peoples.

From the eighteenth century a mode of thought skeptical of the supernatural has grown roots in the West. In latter times its force has somewhat waned, but the habits of thinking it fostered still persist-of explaning phenomena mechanically, wholly within a naturalistic framework, and without reference to supernatural or to final causes. So while a yearning for faith has grown with Skepticism's enfeeblement, an ingrained deference to its prejudices prevents an immediate return to Semitic-style religions, with their unambiguous certainties and their total commitment to a wholly transcendent God. Only the faiths of the Orient seem to be accordant with Skepticism's postulates, some of which are the following:

a. That words or propositions are inadequate to describe the Absolute. Religions with clearly defined dogmas are suspect; not so the non-dogmatic faiths, of which Buddhism is believed to be a prototype.

b. That experience is the most important kind of knowledge, and that the intuition of the divine is of primary value, while doctrinal and theological knowledge of it is secondary. There is a search for first-hand experience of the divine without commitment to any conceptual definition of it.

c. That no one body of doctrine can possess all the truth, and that all doctrinal teaching contains valid insights-which brings us to the problem of pluralism.

"The one reality is described variously by the wise." This conviction is stated early in the Vedas, the scriptures of Hinduism. From it the Jain thinkers developed the theory that every religious teaching has its true and proper extent of meaning--which, overextended, becomes erroneous. The true religion is therefore the coalescence of all these doctrines restored to their proper dimensions, thus rendered capable of existing in mutual harmony. This conception was later embodied in Christian thought, chiefly by Nicholas of Cusa, who held that there is only one faith in a variety of customs [*non est nisi religio una in rituum diversitate.* Nicholas also suggested that the method just described be employed to reduce "the great diversity of religions: to one concordant peace *ut in unam concordantem pacem tanta religionum diversitas conducatur*]."

This pluralism permits many religious and cultural modes to coexist, even in one communion. It is the ideal of many contemporary Catholic thinkers, as their Church, in her present state of renewal, and for all her bimillennial experience, has found it hard to come to terms with the contemporary world without jettisoning not a little of her cultural heritage. But in the pluralism traditional in the more sophisticated Indic world, it is possible for Scholasticism to coexist with post-liberal theology, and for plainsong to coexist with the Baluba mass. In such a pluralistic environment, newness and modernity have limited value, since the archetypes of thought are believed to have always coexisted. The acceptance of a mode of thought felt to be new does not mean the supersession of another imagined to be obsolete. Those convinced of the validity of the latter do not have to wait in patience until (as so often happens in today's West) fashion capriciously restores respectability to it.

The aesthetic character or style of religions in presenting their messages has tranquil and dramatic elements, some stressed more than others, and further distinguished by particular symbols and imagery. Hinduism seems to maintain a balance of emphasis on the tranquil and dramatic; Buddhism, Jainism, Confucianism and Taoism accent the tranquil; and Christianity, decidedly the dramatic. In turbulent times such as ours, the tranquil exerts a greater allure--one more reason for the fascination for Oriental faiths.

Hinduism was the first, if not the only, religion before Christianity to tell us that our happiness lies in the possession of God, chiefly the possession through love (mystery of the Beatific Vision) of the primacy of love in attaining to this possession (the mystery of Charity); but of its unattainability without God's gratuitous help (the mystery of Grace). It also postulates a mediatorship between God and men, especially as embodied in a feminine form (like Lakṣmī or Śakti, the counterparts of the

Madonna). Lastly, Hinduism (in its Triadic School) affirms the doctrine of kenosis, that the divine has in some fashion to empty itself in order to realize its supreme grandeur. For the most part Hinduism had these and other Christian beliefs before the birth of Christianity, which goes to support the contention of Christian universalists like Clement of Alexandria that Revelation was not given only to the Jews.

Chapter 7 | The Vedas and Vedic Philosophy

H.K. Kesavan

The Vedas are the holy scriptures of the Hindu religion and are considered to be revealed knowledge. Their scope is quite extensive, ranging from secular to spiritual matters. The central theme, however, is to declare the existence of the one single eternal transcendental reality that is the 'Divine Ground' of both humans and the universe, and to beckon human beings to aspire to its realization in order to lead a fully integrated life.

Origin, Compilation, and Scope

Vedas are referred to in the Sanskrit language as śrutis (heard or "revealed"). They are called apouruṣeyam which means not authored by any human being (puruṣa). This is in stark contrast to the holy books of other great religions where there is historical evidence of their sources. For Buddhists it is *Dhammapada*; for Christians, the *Bible*; for Muslims, the *Koran*; for Parsees, the *Zend Avesta*; for Sikhs, the *Grantha Sahib*; and so on. Hinduism is different in this respect since it does not have a single prophet or an organized church. The primary focus of the Vedas is to bring the declaration of the ultimate truth concerning man and the universe to the attention of those who are interested in treading the spiritual path and also to prescribe the ways of life that are necessary for making progress in the direction of its realization. In practice, it encourages respect for all religious faiths because, in the final analysis, they are also interested in fathoming the ultimate truths concerning man and the universe. It is precisely this viewpoint that paves the way for the universality of the message, in the sense that a person belonging to any religion can examine the value of the Vedas to him without prejudice to his own faith.

Hindu Concept of Time: Hindus consider the Vedas as anādi, that is, without a beginning. They subscribe to the concept of a pulsating universe with a continuous rhythm of creation, sustenance and destruction. It is not only cyclic, but each cycle has subcycles within it. The duration of the universe can be inferred from the scriptures on the basis of Hindu astrology (Jyōtiṣa) which is a sub-discipline within the Vedas. The astrological prediction of the duration of the universe is based on the length of the subcycles, the four yugas, which also deterrnine the length of the pulsating cycle. Our present yuga, Kaliyuga, is supposed to be 432,000 years in duration, Dvāpara-yuga twice that duration, Trēta-yuga thrice that duration, and, finally, Kṛta-yuga (Satya yuga) four times Kali-yuga's duration which is equal to 1,728,000 years. The four yugas put together are called a mahāyuga, the duration of one cycle. One thousand such mahāyugas make the period of reign of the fourteen Manus who have dominion over this universe. The same period constitutes a day for Brahma. The night of Brahma is also equal in length to his day. Brahma's day and night, put together, will extend to 8640 million years. Brahma's life-span is for 100 years, each year consisting of 365 of his days and nights. These calculations will give the total duration of the universe. It is interesting to note that the Hindus never believed in the idea of a static universe which was the prevailing scientific view before Hubble's discovery of an expanding universe. Since, according to the Hindu cosmological theory, creation, sustenance, and destruction of the universe goes on in an endless cycle, the origin of the Vedas is believed to transcend these limitations. This means that their origin is beyond the concept of time and hence belongs to the realm of eternity.

Quite apart from the investigation into the question of historicity, Indians feel grateful to the Western scholars for their painstaking efforts in bringing the message of the Vedas to the attention of the rest of the world. This feeling of gratitude has, however, a rider attached to it. The reservation arises from an acknowledgment of intrinsic difficulties that a scholar belonging to a particular religion faces while researching another religion. The uneasiness arises from the sensibilities most modern-day scholars have concerning inter-religious studies. It stems from the observation that a person belonging to one faith must live the other's tradition, at least for awhile, in order to gain the kind of empathy that is required for its true appreciation. This requirement is known as phenomenology in inter-religious studies. Unfortunately,

Indians believe that the scholarly work done by most foreigners, with, of course, notable exceptions to the general statement, has not completely captured the essence of the Vedic message.

Veda Vyāsa, the Compiler of the Vedas: Although the Vedas are considered eternal, Hindus believe that major portions of the scriptures have been lost with the passage of time. In this connection, it is interesting to note the Hindu belief that there has been a gradual decadence of spiritual consciousness with the progress of the four yugas. It is believed that our present Kali-yuga marks the lowest level of spiritual consciousness, while in Kṛta-yuga (Satya yuga) it was at its peak. This steady decay in spiritual consciousness with the passage of time over the four yugas contrasts with our own view of the opposite trend of the rapid rise in secular knowledge in our current yuga; we even talk about a knowledge explosion. In this context of providing spiritual knowledge for the people of Kali-yuga, the monumental work of sage Veda Vyāsa is singled out for its importance. He is believed to have neatly compiled, around 5000 B.C.E., the Vedic hymns that were then extant into four Vedas, namely, Ṛgveda, Yajur Veda, Sāma Veda and Atharva Veda. (See Krishnamoorthy, this volume, for a brief discussion of the contents of the four Vedas.) The sage is also considered to be author of the great epic Mahābhārata, the Gītā, the Brahma Sūtras and the eighteen purāṇas. The quintessence of the Vedic message is given in the Gītā which is the popular sacred text of the Hindus. If one text has to be singled out for its pervasive influence on the Hindus, it is the Bhagavadgītā, the 'Song of the Divine'. It is difficult to imagine the scope and contents of the writings attributed to Veda Vyāsa, or Bādarāyaṇa as he is sometimes referred to. India commemorates the memory of this incredibly prodigious scholar of the Hindu scriptures by declaring a national holiday called Gurupūrṇimā in his honor.

The Scope of the Vedas

The Vedas not only deal with matters concerning spiritual practice, but also provide guidance on the conduct of several aspects of life in a comprehensive manner. Several disciplines and sub-disciplines are spelled out in this regard within each of the four Vedas. Their characteristic feature is that each one of these disciplines and sub-disciplines when pursued to their farthest limits has the potential for helping a person towards the source of all spiritual knowledge which does not have any divisions. For example, Āyurveda, which is a discipline devoted to the science of medicine and the art of healing, derives its authority from its inextricable link to the primordial source of human consciousness. The discipline does not deal with just herbal medicine or naturopathy, but also is linked to the appropriate spiritual disciplines which bring about a harmony of body and mind. Similar emphasis is evident in every other discipline whether it is science, music, or literature. The exposition of each discipline should be such that it can retrace the steps from diversity to unity.

VEDĀNGAS: THE AUXILLIARY DISCIPLINES

There are six auxiliaries to these four Vedas called Vedāngas.

Śikṣā: Knowledge of the Vedas spread through oral transmission and as such the discipline of Śikṣā, the Vedic phonetics, is of prime importance to preserve tonal purity. It describes in detail how each syllable has to be pronounced. Its importance stems from the belief that even small changes in pronunciation can produce different results.

Vyākaraṇa: This next limb of the Vedas, is due to sage Pāṇini. There are other grammars of Sanskrit attributed to different sages, but Pāṇini's grammar supersedes them all in importance. The text is in the form of aphorisms (sūtras), which describe the structure of Sanskrit in an extremely precise, concise, and comprehensive manner. Over the centuries, many distinguished scholars have written detailed commentaries on this text. It is believed that linguistics (science of language) , which is the greatest gift of man, was born at the end of the cosmic dance of Lord Śiva (Lord Nataraja*)* when he sounded his percussion instrument called ḍhakka or ḍamaru. There were supposed to have been fourteen beats, the same number as the total number of subdivisions of the Vedas. It is also believed that the fourteen aphorisms that were given out at the end of the cosmic dance were committed to memory by sage Paṇini, and on that basis he wrote his text called Aṣṭādhyāyī*,* so called because it contains eight chapters.

Chandas: Chandas refers to the metrical composition of the Vedas which is an important consideration. The divisional unit of a hymn is called a pāda*,* meaning foot. The metre stipulates the number of letters in a pāda. It is possible for the pādas to be unequal in size although most commonly they will be equal. The anuṣṭup chandas, which has four pādas to a stanza and eight syllables to a pāda*,* is singled out for consideration because that is the metre used by sage Vālmīki for the composition of the great epic Rāmāyana.

Nirukta: It refers to etymology whereby each word is broken into its constituent syllables, and the meaning of each syllable is explained. There are several Vedic dictionaries in existence, the best known being Amara Kośa. It is believed by scholars that the discipline of linguistics (formerly known as philology) owes quite a bit to the grammar and etymology of the Sanskrit language. Of late, interest in Vedic grammar has been evinced by researchers in artificial intelligence, which is a discipline within computer sciences.

Jōytiṣa: This discipline was developed mainly to prescribe the auspicious times for performing Vedic rituals. The primary motivation for developing the discipline of mathematics was to render such detailed calculations possible. The Sanskrit word gaṇita means arithmetic, avyakta gaṇita means algebra, kṣētra gaṇita means geometry, and samīkaraṇa means equations. We read that Indians knew about the force of gravity (apana śakti), which is an inference made on the basis of a statement that appears in one of the Upaniṣads, the Praśnōpaniṣad. The theory of lightness, (lāghava-gaurava nyāya), due to the mathematician Āryabhatta, is supposed to be an allegorical reference to the rotation of planet earth round the sun. Bhūgoḷa-Śāstra means geography; the word bhū stands for earth and gōḷa stands for sphere. The word aṇḍa in Brahmāṇḍa means an egg, which suggests that the fact that the world is oval was known. The credit for discovering "Arabic" numerals that are customarily in use is attributed to Indians. The concept of 'zero' is beyond doubt an early Indian contribution. There are several such examples which are cited in support of the intellectual dynamism that existed in the past in the Indian scientific disciplines, all arising from the concern to maintain the integrity of the Vedas (See Kak, this volume, for further details).

Kalpa: We shall now comment briefly about the sixth and the last Vēdānga. After a spiritual aspirant gains knowledge in the preceding five disciplines, he is considered to be ready for action. Accordingly, this limb of the Vedas spells out in detail the practical know-how of the various rituals.

Upangas: The Subsidiary Limbs

The remaining four sub-disciplines are called upāngas, which mean subsidiary limbs. These are Mīmāṃsa, Nyāya, Purāṇa and Dharma Śāstra. The Vedas are broadly classified into two groups: Karma Kāṇḍa, which is an extensive treatment on various types of rituals, and Jñāna Kāṇḍa, whose focus is solely on aspects of knowledge, about the Absolute Truth. The orthodox Hindu view, however, is that the two portions of the Vedas are meant as complementary aspects to assist the spiritual journey.

Mīmāṃsa: The name of Sage Jaimini is associated with the first portion of Karma Kāṇḍa and is called Pūrva Mīmāṃsa. The second portion is called Uttara Mīmāṃsa, or better known as Vedānta, which means the end of the Vedas. This being the case, the prefix Pūrva is dropped from Jaimini's thesis, and it is simply referred to as Mīmāṃsa. Sage Jaimini has written the aphorisms (sūtras) for Mīmāṃsa, and the detailed commentary is by Kumārila Bhaṭṭa. There is also a second commentary by Prabhakara, and accordingly, there are two philosophical schools in Mīmāṃsa. The following quotation from Deadwyler (p. 42) presents a good summary of the scope of Karma Kāṇḍa:

> Central to this enterprise was an extremely highly developed activity of the sort now referred to as 'ritual'—in particular, the yajña, or sacrifice. The Vedic yajña was an elaborate and painstaking endeavor, in which the learned and expert performers (rtvi), working according to the Vedic paradigm (tantra), had to arrange correctly the detailed paraphernalia (pṛthak-dravya) at precisely the proper place (dēśa) and at the right time (kāla), carrying out all the prescribed procedures (dharma) and reciting the correct verbal formulae (mantra) with perfect precision. If—and only if—everything was flawlessly executed according to the most exacting standards of correctness, then the benefits for which the sacrifice was performed would accrue to the patron—the sponsor—of the sacrifice (yajamāna).

It is easy to see how the form of life that centered itself upon the Vedic yajña became a cult of technique, for mastery of technique was the key to power. By constructing a microcosmic image of the cosmos, and duplicating in fine the act of creation, the properly performed yajña gathered, condensed, and localized the power of the cosmos itself and so put this power into the hands of those adept at technique. Those who mastered yajña mastered the cosmos. The ethos of mastery through technique attained explicit expression in the writings of Karma-Mīmāṃsa, the philosophical school which took yajña as the prime Vedic dharma.

The principal texts of Vedānta are the widely known Upaniṣads. Vedānta consists of the true summary or the culmination of the teaching of the Vedas. The main concern of the Upaniṣads is to establish Brahman as the ultimate principle of the physical universe, Ātman as the innate sentient principle of a human being, and an identity between the two principles. The relation between Brahman and Ātman is crisply stated in various places in the Upaniṣads and together they are known as the Mahāvākyas or great sayings. The saying, "That thou art" appears in Sāmaveda, "I am Brahman" appears in Yajurveda, "Consciousness is Brahman" appears in Ṛgveda, and "This Ātman is Brahman" appears in Atharvaveda. However, their interpreters, who show complete unanimity of opinion in accepting the truths about Brahman and Ātman, arrive at different conclusions when it comes to the interpretation of the mahāvākyas. Sage Veda Vyāsa wrote his famous *Brahma Sutras* in an attempt to remove all these ambiguities of interpretation. But even the Brahma Sūtras, for all their grandeur, are written in a very concise style consisting of 192 sections and the original controversies arising from the differing interpretations of the mahāvākyas have remained unresolved. However, one should not lose perspective on the nature of these controversies and thereby miss the substantial amount of agreement between the various schools of thought.

Nyāya: The next upānga is called Nyāya which is the science of reasoning and is attributed to sage Gautama. It is interesting to note that Nyāya Śāstra, the logical foundations for reasoning, was a well-established discipline in India, although scientists are accustomed to giving exclusive credit for their origins to ancient Greece.

Purāṇas: We commented earlier on the importance of purāṇas in connection with the colossal contributions made by sage Veda Vyāsa. Vedic aphorisms lend themselves to interpretation in the form of stories making artful use of myths and symbols. There are eighteen purāṇas which deal with several aspects of the Vedic message. Vedic scholars claim historicity of the stories that are told, but irrespective of the veracity of this claim, no one can deny the sheer grandeur of this style of popularizing ideas connected with ethics and the essence of spiritual knowledge.

Dharma Śāstras: The fourth and the last upānga is Dharma Śāstra which gives a detailed set of moral injunctions combined with actual procedures that a spiritual aspirant should follow during the course of one's life. Thus, the discipline deals with the subject of ethics, not as an end in itself but as a means for advancing on the path of spiritual fulfillment. The modern-day world provides plenty of examples of acute conflict of all types in all spheres of life. Furthermore, since moral and ethical cleansing is considered absolutely essential for making spiritual progress, detailed guidelines become necessary as to how one should mold the course of one's life in order to achieve these aims. Philosophically speaking, we can say that the overall constraints should be such as to ensure that one's actions are always in consonance with the cosmic law governing the universe. It is here that the Dharma Śāstras come to our rescue. They are formulated by sages who have had experience of the ultimate truth, which is what gives the discipline its authority. The Dharma Śāstras are very extensive in scope embracing aspects of both secular and religious life.

In addition to the above list of fourteen, we may also include four other upāngas which are appendices to the main Vedic texts. These are Āyurveda, the science of life, Artha Śāstra, which in modem terminology is called Economics, Dhanurveda, which deals with weaponry, and Gandharva veda, which includes all the fine arts such as music, drama, and dance.

The Five Stages of Spiritual Journey

Ultimate reality is beyond the reach of intellectual operations, which in turn, depend upon language whose vocabulary is limited only to worldly matters. That is why ultimate reality is ineffable in nature. However, there are various verbal models that can, even with all their imperfections, assist us in orienting our thinking towards that one supreme reality. One such descriptive model deals with the five sheaths that exist between the state of spiritual ignorance and the state of spiritual englightenment. The discussion of this appears in the *Taittariya Upaniṣad.* The five sheaths in ascending order from the least to the most subtle levels of existence are Annamaya, Prāṇamaya, Manonmaya, Vijñānamaya, and Ānandamaya. These are the physical, vital, psychical, rational and blissful sheaths, respectively. The spiritual journey consists of penetrating these successive layers.

Annamaya refers to the physical body, and its main characteristic is the requirement of food in order to survive. This sheath is perceived only in the waking state of consciousness. Prāṇamaya is the vital sheath where life and its vital forces are experienced. This is the first subtle state. Manonmaya is the sheath provided by the mind. Experiences such as thinking, remembering, being uncertain and the like are characteristic of this layer which constitutes the second subtle state. Vijñānamaya is the sheath of the intellect. The experience of knowing is very characteristic of this layer. The three subtle states of prāṇamāyā, manonmāyā and vijñānamaya are included in the dream state. Together they are called the subtle body (sūkṣma śarīra). Ānandamaya is the sheath of bliss. The experience of being happy is characteristic of this layer. Since this universal experience comes after deep sleep, it is correlated with that state of consciousness. This is called the causal body (kāraṇa śarīra). The essential characteristics of jīva are existence and consciousness, except that they are severely constrained by the five sheaths. The suggestion, therefore, is that when the constraints are removed, that is, when spiritual ignorance is destroyed, the identity will become self-evident. Consequently, removal of these five sheaths is the main purpose of spiritual practice.

Spiritual Discipline and Practice

Metaphysical theory points out that the real basis for thinking is in the Being. Since thinking is necessary for speaking, there is also a more fundamental relationship that exists between Being and Speaking. What we normally mean by speech is the *vaikharī* stage, whereas there are, in fact, three stages preceding it. The four stages, from the most to the least subtle, are parā, paśyanti, madhyamā, and vaikharī.

Direct instruction for the realization of ātman is impossible because it is beyond the reach of the pramāṇas (valid means of inquiry) of rational knowledge. It can only be accomplished by indirect means through the exercise of skill coupled with a knowledge of the level of spiritual preparation of the seeker. Spiritual practice is meant to gradually lessen the veiling influence of the constraints and weaken the hold of the limiting adjuncts (upādhis), which mask the Self from direct experience.

The two subtlest candidates singled out for spiritual practice are the mind (prajñā) and the vital airs (prāṇa) as exemplified by breathing. Thus, mind, which is responsible for cognition, serves as an important gateway for the realization of the Self. Just as it has the capacity to identify itself with the physical body, it is equally capable of shifting its focus to the Self, and hence its importance.

The mind can undergo four types of transformations, called vṛttis. The first one is manas which is the transformation responsible for weighing the pros and cons of a thing. Second is buddhi which is the mental faculty required for determining the true nature of objects, the jñānaśakti. The third type of transformation of the mind is ahaṃkāra which is the Ego factor responsible for identifying the body with the Self. Lastly, čitta is the faculty responsible for remembering things of interest.

The subtle body is also called linga-śarīra, and it consists of all our latent impressions acquired as a result of our actions over the long history of the soul. One could say that this is the cognitive burden that a man carries when he perceives the world around him, since his perception is always colored by the traces that are left behind by his past experiences over many lives. Consequently, linga-śarīra acts as a constraint, a limiting adjunct (upādhi), on the Self.

The initial conditions for spiritual advancement vary from one person to another. The equality of man, on the other hand, is assured in terms of the realization that everyone is endowed with the element of infinite consciousness, which, in turn, ensures that every one is entitled to gain spiritual realization, albeit with varying degrees of preparation (adhikārabheda).

Three Stages of Understanding

Śravana refers to the study of the scriptures that is concerned with the aspect of hearing about the Truth from qualified spiritual guides. This is the first phase. The Truth is about the two principles of Ātman and Brahman, and according to the nondualistic interpretation of the scriptures, they are identical.

After śravana comes manana which is the stage for intellectual understanding of the truth that we have repeatedly heard from various angles. Since Vedas constitute the pramāṇa, the testimony of the existence of the supreme reality, the line of reasoning is expected to follow within the confines of this testimony. It is the stage where one acquires the indirect knowledge about the Truth, beyond a shadow of doubt.

Nididhyāsana is the final stage of direct contemplation about the Truth itself. This is the stage of spiritual practice which includes deep meditation. The chief characteristic of this stage is that it is marked by a steady progression at the experiential level. The spiritual aspirant would by then have progressed in reducing the opacity of his ignorance and gained purity of mind (čittaśuddhi) and one-pointedness (ekāgratā) in the pursuit of his goal.

Dhyana: Meditation

Meditation (dhyāna) is the principal means employed for achieving purification of the mind so that it can progressively acquire the capacity to dissolve the effects of spiritual ignorance (avidyā) enveloping knowledge of the Self.

The technique of meditation is best learnt from a preceptor because it belongs to the realm of practice; however, a brief description of the theory behind it is useful. First of all, meditation requires something to focus the practitioner's attention. This is usually the name of a holy sound, a mantra, which could be in one or more syllables.

A mantra is chanted mentally in total silence after assuming a special sitting posture with eyes closed. The idea behind repetition is that it will have the effect of slowing down the activity of a meandering mind which goes from one thought to another in an uncontrolled manner. Since the mind is nothing but a stream of thoughts, the silence that resides between two thoughts is missed by a restless mind (See Feuerstein, this volume).

The mechanism for keeping the unbridled mind under control consists of breaking the relation that exists between two successive thoughts. With some practice, the thoughts get progressively feeble until they vanish altogether resulting in experiences of total silence for longer intervals of time. The experience of 'flow of time' during meditation is altogether different than when one is fully in the waking state. With constant practice, it is possible to attain a stage where one gets firmly entrenched in the higher state of consciousness (samādhi).

Om: The Sacred Syllable

Modern day linguists also inform us that there are deeper levels of structure associated with language. But the Being is beyond the realm of name and form, and it is inconceivable at first to think that any sound could invoke correlations with that mystical entity. It is here that the scriptures come to our assistance and point towards the existence of precisely such a primal sound of the universe. The most sacred sound in the Vedic literature is the sound produced by three syllable word AUM. In the Sanskrit alphabet, 'A' is the first vowel and letter and so is the very first sound one can utter. The pronunciation of 'M' involves the closing of the lips and is the last sound one can utter. 'U' is the sound produced by rolling the breath over the whole of the tongue. Consequently, AUM pronounced as ŌM is a combination of all sounds that one can utter and so it has a universality about it. To quote Swami Ranganathananda from his book on *The Message Of The Upanisads* [36]:

> Ōm in its uttered form finally merges into its unuttered form; all uttered sound merges into the silence of the soundless. This soundless or amātra aspect of Ōm is the symbol of Brahman in Its transcendental aspect, beyond time, space and causality. This amātra aspect is indicated by the bindu or dot in the crescent over the syllable Ōm as written in Sanskrit. This Ōm, as the unity of all sound to which all matter and energy are reduced in their primordial form, is a fit symbol for Ātman or Brahman, which is the unity of all existence.

These, and possibly other, considerations led the Vedic sages to accord to Ōm the highest divine reverence and worship, and treat it as the holiest pratīka, symbol, of divinity; they called it nāda Brahman or śabda Brahman, Brahman in the form of sound. It is the holiest word for all the religions emanating from India—Hinduism, Buddhism, Jainism, and Sikhism. It is considered to be the primal sound of the universe and is called the vedavākya. It is also called the praṇava.

Four States of Consciousness

The psychic principle, which is the immanent reality that is identical to the transcendental reality, is also known by several other names in the philosophical literature. Pure consciousness (turīya), plenary consciousness, fourth state of consciousness, Self with a capital S, and eternal witness are some of the other terms that are used very frequently.

Since Hindu metaphysics proceeds with the investigation of the ultimate reality from the level of the individual self, analysis of the three states of consciousness, namely the waking, the dreaming and the sleeping states, assumes paramount importance.

The origin of such analysis goes back to antiquity, to the Upaniṣadic era. The analysis of the subject and object relationships in the three states of consciousness comprehends the totality of experience, unlike scientific analysis which is confined to the data of the waking state (jāgṛati). The search for the core meaning of existence when directed towards our inner universe instead of the external world necessitates taking the totality of human existence into its domain of investigation. The Māṇḍūkya Upaniṣad deals with a detailed study of the triad of states and points to the existence of yet another state of consciousness called turīya, the pure consciousness, which is at once eternal and non-dual in nature. The conclusion is that this fourth state of consciousness coexists with all the other three states and is therefore the real 'I' which is the constant factor in the paradoxical conjunction of being and becoming.

In the state of deep sleep (suṣupti), there is absolutely no experience of duality, and hence it is not a state in the ordinary sense of the word. There is no experience of either the subject or the object. One thing that is characteristic of this state while in it, is that one does note experience the passage of time, unlike being in the other two states. It is indeed a nondual experience that is characterized by total bliss which can be recalled only when one wakes up. The absence of cognition in deep sleep is attributed to the absence of any object of perception and is not due to the absence of consciousness since the eternal witness is always present and coexists with the sleeping state also.

The fourth state of consciousness, which is pure consciousness, is something that is ever present and beyond the requisites of space, time and causality. Pure consciousness coexists with the other three states and is therefore referred to as the eternal witness, sakṣī. Since pure consciousness is a non-manifest reality, even those who have experienced it find it extremely difficult to communicate the exact nature of the experience.

SAMKARA'S NONDUALISM: (ADVAITA)

This Upaniṣadic school of philosophy is called *Absolutistic* in contrast to the theistic schools which are also based on the Upaniṣads. Since these latter texts appear at the end of the Vedas, they are also called Vedantic schools.

It would be useful to recount some of the main philosophical issues that were subjects of considerable controversy, as well as the seminal contribution of Badarayana (also called Veda Vyāsa) that provided the much-needed intellectual clarity and coherence to spiritual thought.

Vyāsa is believed to have successfully refuted the dualistic interpretation of the Sānkhya school which also claims its authenticity on the basis of the Upaniṣadic texts. Vyāsa also disproved the claim of the Mimāṃsa school that the Karma Kaṇḍa should be accorded more prominence than the message of the Upaniṣads.

During the time of Vyāsa, even amongst those who considered Brahman as the absolute, the prevailing view was that the universe arose from Brahma, which is called Brahma pariṇāmavāda. This was in contrast to the philosophy of Sānkhya which considers Prakṛti as the first cause for the creation of the universe and, as such, called it Prakṛti pariṇāmavāda. Vyāsa is believed to have differed from the Brahma pariṇāmavāda school and instead upheld the view that the universe is only a phenomenal appearance of Brahman, in the same sense that the dream state of consciousness is only so when viewed from the vantage point of the ordinary waking state of consciousness. This latter doctrine, which was later attested by Śaṃkara, is called vivarta vāda and differs from the law of causality called satkārya vāda. We will confine our discussion to Śaṃkara's philosophy of advaita not only because of its great popularity, but also because its sheer majesty in philosophical thinking provides ample scope for drawing on the insights from scientific thinking.

Śaṃkara was a man of titanic intelligence, a spiritual giant, and perhaps the greatest missionary of Hinduism. His is said to have been born in 788 C.E. in the village of Kaladi on the banks of the river Periyar in the state of Kerala, which is at the southernmost tip of India. What is truly amazing is that he completed his most productive mission in the cause of restoring the true vision of Hinduism within a very short life span of 32 years.

Śaṃkara made his appearance at a time of total spiritual decadence of the country. The great spiritual message of Buddha that had provided a true insight into the nature of the ultimate Reality had in course of time been totally distorted by his followers, which is not an uncommon occurrence in the history of great religions. All manner of teachers had sprung up in different parts of the country, resulting in a dissonance of views on the real purport of the Vedas. Thus, the time was ripe for Śaṃkara to restore the true vision of the Vedic philosophy by removing the cobwebs of misunderstanding surrounding it. This he did with supreme success from the lofty platform of his own Self-realization. It is often said that Śaṃkara drove Buddhism out of India. This statement, suggesting a sense of triumph, however, should be understood in its proper perspective. The Hindus have always held Buddha in the highest regard, and so there could never have been any question of hostility toward Buddhism.

During a period when transportation was primitive, Śaṃkara travelled tirelessly throughout the country to spread his ageless spiritual message which is called Sanātana Dharma. This is not an organized religion, rather it is a message addressed to every individual reminding him of his spiritual heritage on the basis of which he could lead a purposeful life with robust optimism. In course of time, the message took firm roots in the country. Also, it provided the real solidifying force for a country of such vast cultural diversity. Śaṃkara established centers of learning, four monasteries (maṭhas) in the four corners of the country to ensure the propagation of his philosophy. One special feature of these maṭhas is their tradition of maintaining an uninterrupted lineage of teachers and disciples, called guru-śiṣya paramparā. It is truly astonishing to note that such lineages have been preserved from the eighth century onwards to this day. We end this short biographical note on Śaṃkara with a quotation from Sister Nivedita, who was a western disciple of Swami Vivekānanda:

> In devotion he was like St. Francis of Assissi; in intellect he was like Abelard; in dynamism and freedom, he was like Martin Luther; in imagination and efficiency he was like Ignatius Loyola. In fact, he was all these, united and exemplified in one person.

Śaṃkara wrote his own commentary on the Vēdānta Sūtras, which was almost mandatory for any philosopher of repute for establishing his bona fides amongst the Vēdāntic schools. By doing so, he clearly established his own school of philosophy called advaita, which means nondualism. His thesis is called Absolutistic since he views Brahman as the Absolute.

Śaṃkara considers the universe as a phenomenal appearance of Brahman which is called vivarta vāda. This is in contrast to the prevailing idea of Brahma pariṇāmavāda which includes the assertion that the universe is a manifestation of Brahman. Śaṃkara also proposed the Māyā doctrine in order to explain the relationship between Brahman and the universe. Consistent with this doctrine, he also enunciated his view about the relationship between Brahman and the empirical self (jīva). His conception of spiritual liberation (mokṣa) was based on the merging of jīva with Brahman after jīva divests itself of the constraint of spiritual ignorance (avidyā) imposed on it. He was very firm in his pronouncement that spiritual ignorance can only be overcome through its contrary knowledge called jñāna. The religious dimension of the advaita doctrine is contained in the concept of Saguṇa Brahman ("qualified Brahman") which ensures the theistic ideal of the Upaniṣadic God. And lastly, he was meticulous in his exposition of the concept of Brahman, also referred to as Nirguṇa Brahman (Brahman without qualifications) in order to highlight the differences in its concept from both Saguṇa Brahman and the Buddhist concept of void (śūnya).

In advaita, the psychical component is called sākṣīn, the eternal witness, and it can be equated to the concept of puruṣa of Sānkhya. Similarly, at the level of the cosmos as a whole, there is a conceptual similarity in details between Prakṛti of Sānkhya and Māyā of Advaita, although there is a basic difference in their conceptualization. Śaṃkara recognizes Brahman as the only reality. Śaṃkara's thesis emphatically asserts that Brahman is the only unsublatable reality and that all philosophical discussion should proceed from that premise, which is why his philosophy is called Absolutistic. All his deliberations pertaining to the interrelationships between spirit and matter on one hand, and spirit and the empirical self on the other, proceed from this lofty platform of the Absolute.

It is interesting to grasp the force of this philosophical argument in light of the insights provided by Godel's theorem in mathematics. The philosophical implication of that theorem is that we can never successfully explore the infinite from the realm of the finite. Śaṃkara's emphatic assertion that the philosophical investigation should proceed from the Absolute rather than from considerations of the relative field of existence can be viewed as qualitative assertion of the famous mathematical theorem which has implications for disciplines other than mathematics. If it did not proceed in this manner, it would result in the hopeless situation of first investing the unknown universe with an ultimate reality and then proceeding to investigate the existence of this reality while placing oneself in the realm of the unknown.

Accordingly, Śaṃkara's philosophy differs from the premises of Sānkhya's Prakṛti pariṇāmavāda and the then-prevailing absolutistic version called Brahma pariṇāmavāda, which are both dependent on the notion of cause-and-effect relationships, though of different kinds. In the former it refers to the cause-and-effect relations arising from Prakṛti and its evolutes with no internal contradiction, since they all refer to the relative field of existence. However, Śaṃkara argued that the Brahma pariṇāmavāda philosophy has a serious conceptual error: while it correctly recognizes Brahman as the Absolute, as in advaita, it commits the mistake of invoking a cause-and-effect relationship between Brahman and the universe by declaring that the universe is a manifestation of Brahman. It is inconceivable to think of a cause-and-effect relationship between the eternity of the Absolute and the concept of time, which gets embedded from the moment of creation of the universe. Consequently, one can expect that Śaṃkara's advaita steers clear of cause-and-effect relations in establishing the relation between Brahman and the physical world.

The Māyā doctrine is proposed to serve as the link between the Absolute and the physical universe, between eternity and time. The doctrine is careful to preserve the integrity of the two domains of the Absolute and the Relative with reference to notions of space, time and causality. This is achieved by declaring the universe as only a phenomenal appearance of Brahman rather than its manifestation. The identity between the Absolute and the empirical self (jīva) comes into play when the limiting adjuncts on jīva are not operative. The union of jīva with Brahman is the ultimate spiritual release, a state called mokṣa. Of immense significance is the optimistic assertion that mokṣa, which is the state of liberation, can be achieved in one's present life. The limiting adjunct on jīva is one's own spiritual ignorance which is called avidyā. The way to nullify the effects of avidyā is by gaining the contrary knowledge called jñāna.

The emphasis here is that spiritual knowledge alone is the ultimate liberating factor. The concept of Saguṇa Brahman which appears in the thesis is the exact philosophical counterpart of Iśvara which is the personal God of religion. In order to understand the necessity for this concept of Brahman with a prefix, one should recognize that God and devotion that are essential parts of religion, are in the field of relativity, and as such the corresponding infinite consciousness operating in that field should be distinguished from the pure consciousness of the Absolute. In order to clearly maintain the difference, the latter is called Nirguṇa Brahman which means Brahman without attributes. The Saguṇa Brahman acquires all the divinely opulent attributes of Iśvara. This interpretation is essential for the practice of religion within Śaṃkara's Absolutistic doctrine. Also, Śaṃkara found it necessary to point out the dissimilarities between his concept of Nirguṇa Brahman and the Buddhist concept of Śūnya, meaning 'void'. The latter concept has connotations of being negativistic and nihilistic, whereas the former does not even remotely suggest that description.

The concept of illusion (mithya) takes a center stage in the discussion. This prominence becomes necessary in order to explain the two-fold relationships between Brahman and the universe, and Brahman and jīva. These two relationships are explained on the basis of two types of illusions. We shall first comment on the illusion associated with the relationship between Brahman and the universe. One classical example that is often cited is the case where one mistakes a rope for a snake. This illusion will last as long as the misperception lasts. As soon as the correct knowledge of the rope dawns, the illusion of seeing a snake in place of a rope will suddenly vanish. This example provides useful analogy for considering the superposition of the world of diversity on the unchanging Brahman. As soon as the correct knowledge of Brahman is realized, the illusion of the reality of the universe will suddenly disappear.

It is the concept of cosmic illusion (Māyā) that provides the linkage between the Absolute and the physical world. We have repeatedly emphasized that the transcendental field of the Absolute is beyond the reach of space, time and causality, while the universe is very much described by those three prerequisites. The concept of illusion completely obviates the need for an appeal to the law of causality based on cause-and-effect relationships, as in satkārya vāda. The phenomenal relationship is instead based in vivarta vāda. It has to be emphasized that due to spiritual ignorance, the illusion is experienced only in the relativistic field of our worldly realities. The illusion is suddenly eradicated once the contrary knowledge to overcome the ignorance dawns on us.

Next, we discuss the relationship between Brahman and the empirical self (jīva) which is explained on the basis of a second type of illusion. The classical example that is given to reinforce the idea of this second type of illusion is the case of a white conch viewed through the medium of a yellow glass. It is assumed that the viewer is blissfully unaware of the presence of the interposing yellow glass. Under those conditions, one mistakes the white conch to be yellow. When knowledge of this distortion dawns on the viewer, he immediately recognizes that the yellow color of the conch is due to the obstructing medium, and hence a property of the conch is immediately correctly perceived. The presence of the conch is not denied; only its yellowness, which was perceived as an aspect of it, is denied. The sheet of glass is called an adjunct (upādhi), which is externally imposed on the white conch.

Based on the above analogy, the relation between Brahman and Jīva can be explained. Jīva is really Brahman itself but for the constraints imposed on it. The Brahman is untouched by either the cause of the illusion or its eventual dissolution.

We can now conclude on the basis of the two illusions, one operating at the level of the universe at large and the other at the level of the individual, that Brahman, which is one without a second, appears both as the physical world and as the empirical self. In the first case, the ultimate reality of the physical world is totally denied. And in the second, only the physical adjuncts associated with Jīva are denied. With the removal of these adjuncts, the spiritual element present in Jīva is identified as Brahman itself.

We shall further elaborate on the four central concepts of Śaṃkara's philosophy of advaita. These are 1) Māyā 2) Brahman 3) Saguṇa-Brahman, and 4) Jīva. In this list of four concepts, it is only Māya that is a physical entity while the other three are spiritual entities.

Māyā is identical in conception to Prakṛti of Sānkhya with respect to its description of nature and its evolutes. The Sānkhya schematic could very well be called the schematic of Māyā as far as the portrayal of nature's diversity is concerned. The major differences between the two concepts arise only when their respective relationships with Puruṣa and Brahman are considered. Advaita vehemently denies that there could be any such direct relationship between spirit and matter and invokes the concept of illusion to explain that relationship. Māyā has two aspects to it. The first is the veiling influence (āvaraṇa śakti), by virtue of which it effectively screens out the knowledge of Brahman. The second is the diversifying power (vikṣepa śakti) which is responsible for the phenomenal world of names and forms. It is this which characterizes the rich diversity of the universe.

As for the concept of Brahman, it is the substratum, the divine Ground of both the physical world and the empirical self. When we say that Brahman is the substratum of the physical world, we are also asserting that the cosmic principle underlying the universe is spiritual in nature because of its identity with the psychic principle of Ātman. The primary and secondary evolutes of Māyā represent actual changes in Māyā in the process of its manifestation. The changes, however, are only virtual with respect to Brahman. They are merely appearances because of the cosmic illusion implied by the superposition of the physical world on the Absolute. Brahman remains changeless for ever.

Next we discuss the concept of saguṇa Brahman (qualified Brahman) whose justification is based on an intricate philosophical argument. The purpose for evoking this concept is, however, to recognize a level of consciousness that exactly corresponds to the God of our universe which is called Iśvara. We can expect to reach out to the Lord only in the world that we are living in. Consequently, the corresponding consciousness cannot be Brahman, which is pure consciousness in the transcendental field. In order to arrive at the concept of saguṇa Brahman, we note that both Brahman and Māyā are causative factors for the universe although in very different senses. In the former, the cause is apparent while in the latter the cause is actual; the evolutes of Māyā are definitely based on cause-and-effect relationships defined by satkaryavāda. It is a combination of these two principles of causation, one that is apparent and another which is actual, that gives rise to the notion of Saguṇa Brahman. The easiest way to regard Saguṇa Brahman is that it is the philosophical counterpart of the theistic ideal of Īśvara.

Saguṇa Brahman is, therefore, the philosophical concept arising out of the combined considerations of Brahman and Māyā. The act of such supreme devotion to the Lord through which one loses one's personal identity is indeed equivalent to gaining the knowledge that is necessary to overcome spiritual ignorance in order to achieve the merger of Jīva with Brahman.

Jīva is a hybrid entity consisting of both the spiritual element, namely the Self, and an insentient element due to the internal senses; it describes the coexistence of being and becoming. The characteristic feature of Jīva is that it wrongly identifies itself with the gross body because of the influence of the internal senses. Spiritual liberation consists of overcoming the primary ignorance of wrong identification. What remains when the avidyā aspect is completely obliterated is the pure sentient element which is called sakṣi, the eternal witness.

Śaṃkara takes an unequivocal stand on what constitutes knowledge and avoids all such incongruities. According to him, all knowledge is predicated upon not only the existence of a corresponding object but also a perceiving subject. It is impossible to conceive of a knowledge which does not have the twin implication of a subject and an object. Conversely, if an object does not exist, there can be no question of its corresponding knowledge. The classical example that is cited in support of this observation is a barren woman's son. (We will assume for purposes of discussion that the impossibility suggested in this ancient example is still valid regardless of the tremendous possibilities of modern day genetic technology) The son of a barren woman exists only in verbal jargon. Since he is entirely fictitious, there can be no knowledge corresponding to this entity.

We again emphasize that advaita holds worldly realities as an illusion only when they are viewed from the realm of the transcendental field. This viewpoint is sadly mistaken to mean that the worldly realities are an illusion, thus stripping the statement of its real meaning. But Śaṃkara's critique, in which even illusory experiences are explained on the basis of objective knowledge, should put an end to all such ill-considered criticism.

Chapter 8

The Upanishads

M. Hiriyanna

The Upanishads (Upaniṣads) stand by themselves although tradition associates them closely with the Brāhmaṇas. Primarily they represent a spirit different from and even hostile to ritual and embody a theory of the universe quite distinct from the one that underlies the sacrificial teaching of the Brāhmaṇas. All the earlier Upaniṣads in some form or other indicate this antagonism while in a few it becomes quite explicit (see Deussen 1905: 61-2, 396; Macdonell 1927:46). Thus in the Muṇḍaka Upaniṣad (I. ii. 7) we have one of the clearest onslaughts against the sacrificial ceremonial, in the course of which it is stated that whosoever hopes for real good to accrue from these rites is a fool and is sure to be overtaken again and again by death and decrepitude. This opposition more often appears indirectly in the substitution of an allegorical for a literal interpretation of the rites. An illustration will show how this is done. The aśva-medha is a well-known sacrifice whose celebration signifies overlordship of the world. It is to be performed by a Kshatriya and the chief animal to be sacrificed in it is a horse. The Bṛhadāraṇyaka Upaniṣad (I. i. and ii.) gives a subjective turn to this sacrifice, and transforms it into a meditative act in which the contemplative is to offer up the whole universe in place of the horse and by thus renouncing everything attain to true autonomy—a result analogous to the overlordship associated with the performance of the regular aśva-medha (see Deussen 1912:8). The antagonism between the two teachings gradually disappears or at least is considerably softened, indicating that as the Upaniṣadic doctrine more and more triumphed, an attempt was made to reconcile them. The reconciliation is clearly traceable in the later Upaniṣads. The Śvetāśvatara Upaniṣad (ii. 6 and 7) for example alludes approvingly to Agni and Soma, the chief sacrificial deities, and commends a return to the old ritualistic worship (see Deussen 1905: 64-5).

Origin, Development, and Structure

The divergence between the two views as embodied in the Brāhmaṇas and the Upaniṣads respectively is now explained by some scholars as due to the divergence in ideals between the Brahmins and the Kshattriyas—the priests and princes of ancient India. There is indeed some ground for such a view, because the Upaniṣads ascribe more than one of their characteristic doctrines to royal personages and represent Brahmins as seeking instruction of them in respect to those doctrines. But it does not afford, as some modern scholars themselves recognize, sufficient warrant for connecting this difference in ideals with a social distinction. The prominence given to the Kṣatriyas in the Upaniṣads may after all mean nothing more than that kings were patrons of Brahmins and that the doctrines, though originating among the latter, were first welcomed by the former rather than by the ritual-ridden section of the Brahmins themselves (see Deussen 1905: 396; Bloomfield: 1908:220ff). It also implies that Brahma-knowledge (Brahma-vidyā) was not confined to the priests as the knowledge of the sacrifice for the most part, was. But we need not farther consider this question for, being a purely historical one, it does not directly concern us.

The Word Upanishad and its Meaning

The word "Upaniṣad" has been variously explained by old Indian commentators, but their explanations cannot be regarded as historically or philologically accurate, for what the commentators have done is merely to read into the word the meaning which, as the result of long use, it had come to possess by their time. Moreover, the same commentator often derives the word in alternative ways showing thereby that he was speaking not of a certainty, but only of what he considered a mere possibility (cf. Samkara on Kaṭha Upaniṣad). While thus the commentators give us no help, we fortunately find the word used in the Upaniṣads themselves, and there it generally appears as synonymous with *rahasya* or secret. That should accordingly have been its original meaning. Etymologically the word is equivalent to "sitting" (*sad*) near by (*upa*) devotedly (*ni*), and in course of time it came to signify the secret instruction imparted at such private sittings (Deussen 1905:10-15). That the teaching of these works was regarded as a mystery and that much care and anxiety were bestowed upon keeping it from the unworthy lest it should be misunderstood or misapplied, come out clearly in several Upaniṣads. According to the Praśna Upaniṣad, for example, six pupils go to a great teacher seeking instruction of him in respect to the highest reality; but he asks them to live with him for a year before instructing them, obviously with the purpose of watching them and satisfying himself of their fitness to be taught by him. Again, when Načiketas, according to the Kaṭha Upaniṣad, desires to know whether or not the soul survives after death, Yama does not reply until he has tested the sincerity and strength of mind of the young inquirer. The reluctance to impart the highest truth to every one without discrimination, we may observe in passing, was not peculiar to India, but was common to all ancient peoples. Heraclitus in early Greece, for example, is reported to have stated, "If men care for gold, they must dig for it; otherwise they must be content with straw."

The origin, development, and structure of Upaniṣadic literature as it has been handed down to us is somewhat hard to trace. Hindu tradition places it on the same footing as the other species of Vedic literature—the Mantras and the Brāhmaṇas—regarding them all alike as śruti (revelation), i.e., as works not ascribable to human authors. In the absence of any help from this source, we are left to mere conjecture. In the Upaniṣads we now and then come across short and pithy statements which bear the impress of set formulas, and the literary material in which they are found imbedded seems merely to amplify and illustrate the truth enshrined in them. Further these sayings are not infrequently styled there as "Upaniṣad." From this it has been concluded, with much probability, that the term was in the beginning applied only to these formulas which contain in a nutshell some important truth of Upaniṣadic philosophy (Deussen 1905:20). As an example of them we may instance *Tat tvam asi,* "That thou art," which teaches the ultimate identity of the individual and the cosmic souls (Chandogya Upaniṣad VI. viii. 7). It was these philosophic formulas alone that were once communicated by teacher to pupil, the communication being preceded or followed by expository discourses. The discourses, it is surmised, assumed in course of time a definite shape though not committed to writing yet, giving rise to the Upaniṣads as we now have them. To judge from the way in which these texts have grown, they contain not the thoughts of a single teacher, but of a series of teachers, and thus represent a growth in which new ideas have mingled with the old. Such a view explains the heterogeneity sometimes seen in the teaching of even one and the same Upaniṣad. At a later time, when all the ancient lore of the Hindus was brought together and arranged, the Upaniṣads in this form were appended to the Brāhmaṇas. The significance of such close association of the Upaniṣads with the Brāhmaṇas is that when this grouping was effected the two were regarded as equally old— so old that neither of them could be referred to any specific authors. Standing thus at the end of the Veda, the Upaniṣads came to be known as Vedānta or "end of the Veda"— much as the *Metaphysics* of Aristotle owed its designation to its being placed after Physics in his writings. A word which at first only indicated the position of the Upaniṣads in the collection developed later the significance of the aim or fulfilment of Vedic teaching, it being permissible to use *anta* in Sanskrit, like its equivalent "end" in English, in both these senses.

The number of Upaniṣads that have come down to us is very large — over two hundred being reckoned, but all are not equally old. The great majority of them in fact belong to comparatively recent times. Hardly more than a dozen belong to the period before the beginning of the Common Era. Even among these classical Upaniṣads, chronological differences are traceable; but generally speaking they all exhibit a family likeness both in their thoughts and in the language in which those thoughts are clothed. Hence all of them may be referred to practically the same stage in the evolution of Indian thought. We shall take into account here only the older or canonical Upaniṣads. Their date cannot be exactly determined, but they may all be regarded as pre-Buddhistic. They represent the earliest efforts of man at giving a philosophic explanation of the world, and are as such invaluable in the history of human thought. They are the admitted basis of at least one of the most important systems of Indian philosophy, namely the Vedānta, "which controls at the present time nearly all the higher thought of Brahminical India." Their importance is much more than historical, for their unique spiritual power and the elements of universal appeal which they contain may exercise a considerable influence on the re-construction of thought and realignment of life in the future.

A word may now be added as regards the form of these works. They are generally in the form of dialogues, especially the larger ones among them. Their method is more poetic than philosophic. They have been described as philosophical poems and indicate truths generally through metaphor and allegory. The language, although never bereft of the charm peculiar to the Upaniṣads, is sometimes symbolic. The style is highly elliptical and shows that the works were intended to be expounded orally by one that could readily supply whatever was lacking in their presentation of the subject. These peculiarities render the interpretation of many passages considerably difficult and account for the varied explanations given of them in the past as well as in the present. But the indefiniteness is only in regard to details, the general tenor of the teaching being quite unmistakable. Among the works comprising Vedic literature, the Upaniṣads were the first to attract the attention of foreigners. Several of these works were translated into Persian in Moghul times [See Gopal, and Habib, this volume.] and were thence rendered into Latin about the beginning of the last century. It was through this Latin translation that they came to be known for the first time in Europe; and it was through it that Schopenhauer, for instance, learnt to admire them. In recent times, numerous translations of them, direct from the Sanskrit, have appeared in Western languages. The subject-matter of Upaniṣadic teaching also has repeatedly engaged the attention of foreign scholars; and, among the many works published, should be mentioned Deussen's masterly work on the philosophy of the Upaniṣads (Deussen 1905), particularly for the wealth of information it contains and for the care and thoroughness of its analysis.

Issues in Interpretation

The first point that has to be considered is whether all the Upaniṣads— even the genuine ones— teach the same doctrine or not. Indian commentators, have all along held the view that they do (cf. Vedānta Sūtra I. i. 4); and it is inconceivable that they should have thought otherwise, for they believed that these works were revealed in the literal sense of that word. The agreement of the commentators, however, does not extend beyond the general recognition of the unity of Upaniṣadic teaching. As to what the exact nature of that teaching is, they differ widely from one another. This diversity of opinion should be a long-standing one, for we have references to it even in the earliest extant work systematizing the teaching of the Upaniṣads, viz. the Vedānta Sūtra of Bādarāyaṇa (see for example I.ii.28-31). Such wide divergence in interpretation naturally suggests a doubt that, in spite of the traditional insistence to the contrary, the Upaniṣads do not embody a single doctrine; and the doubt is confirmed by an independent study of these ancient works. A modern student, not committed beforehand to follow any particular school of Vedantic thought, will be forced to think that there are not two or three discordant views in the Upaniṣads, but several. Nor is there anything surprising in this, for the problem dealt with in them lends itself to such a variety of solutions and these works were molded into their present form in a more or less casual way. All the doctrines presented in them do not, however, stand out equally prominent. Some are merely flashes of thought, others are only slightly developed and still others are but survivals from the older period. The most prominent and the best developed teaching may, if we overlook for the moment minor details, be described as monistic and idealistic. Statements like "There is no variety here," "All this is Brahman," which insist on the unity of everything that exists, are neither few nor far between in the Upaniṣads. This monistic view may be described as idealistic for, according to an equally striking number of Upaniṣadic sayings, there is nothing in the universe which, if it is not itself mental, does not presuppose mind. "Not there the sun shines, nor the moon or the stars, not these lightnings either. Where then could this fire be? Everything shines only after the shining spirit; through its light all this shines" (Kaṭha Upaniṣad II. ii. 15).

Before giving an account of this doctrine we should explain the Upaniṣadic terms for the ultimate reality. These terms are two—"Brahman" and "ātman," which have been described as "the two pillars on which rests nearly the whole edifice of Indian philosophy." Their origin is somewhat obscure. The word "Brahman" seems at first to have meant "prayer," being derived from a root bṛh meaning "to grow" or "to burst forth." Brahman as prayer is what manifests itself in audible speech. From this should have been derived later the philosophic significance which it bears in the Upaniṣads, viz. the primary cause of the universe— what *bursts forth* spontaneously in the form of nature as a whole and not as mere speech only. The explanation of the other word is more uncertain. In all probability "atman" originally meant "breath" and then came to be applied to whatever constitutes the essential part of anything, more particularly of man, i.e. his self or soul (Muller 1928:70-72). Thus each of these terms has its own independent significance: The distinctive meaning of "Brahman" is the ultimate source of the outer world while that of "ātman" is the inner self of man. What is remarkable about these terms is that, although entirely different in their original connotation and although occasionally bearing it still in Upaniṣadic passages, they come to be prevailingly used as synonymous— each signifying alike the eternal source of the universe including nature as well as man. The development of the same significance by these two distinct terms means that the Indian, in the course of his speculation, identified the outer reality with the inner; and by such a happy identification at last reached the goal of his long quest after unity— a goal which left all mythology far behind and was truly philosophical.

Quest for Unity: Brahman and Atman

It is necessary to dwell at some length on how this identification was brought about and what its full significance is. We have stated that the word ātman developed in course of time the meaning of soul or self. That was the result of a search for the central essence of the individual as distinguished from the physical frame with which he is associated. The method here was subjective and the result was arrived at through introspection. In place of the body, breath, etc., which may easily be mistaken for the individual, we find here a deeper principle, which is Psychical, finally regarded as the essence of man. Now there was from the time of the later Mantras and Brāhmaṇas the habit of seeking for a correspondence between the individual and the world and trying to discover for every important feature of the one, an appropriate counterpart in the other. It represented an effort to express the world in terms of the individual. Such an attempt at rising from the known particular to a knowledge of the unknown universal is clearly seen in the Puruṣa-sūkta for example, where parts of the universe are described as parts of Puruṣa or a giant man. It is equally clear from one of the funeral hymns which, addressing the departed, says: "Let thine eye go to the sun; thy breath, to the wind, etc." (Ṛgveda X. 16). And we have it again when prāṇa, which as vital breath stands for an important aspect of the individual, is universalized and, as cosmic Prāṇa, is represented as the life of the world. This notion of parallelism between the individual and the world runs throughout the literature of the later Vedic period and is found in the Upaniṣads as well (see, for example, Aitareya Upaniṣad i). The practice of viewing the whole world as a cosmic individual naturally had its influence on the conception of ātman and transformed what was but a Psychical principle into a world-principle. Ātman, which as the soul or self is the inmost truth of man, became as the cosmic soul or self the inmost truth of the world. When the universe came once to be conceived in this manner, its self became the only self, the other selves being regarded as in some way identical with it.

Although this process secures the unity of the self, it does not take us as far as the unity of all Being. For the self in the case of the individual is distinguishable from the not-self such as the body; and the world-self similarly has to be distinguished from its physical embodiment, viz. the material universe. Now there was all along another movement of thought just complementary to the one we have so far sketched. It traced the visible universe to a single source named *Brahman*. The method there was objective, for it proceeded by analyzing the outer world and not by looking inward as in the line of speculation of which ātman was the goal. In accordance with the general spirit of Indian speculation, several conceptions were evolved here also (cf. Taittirīya Upaniṣad iii)— each more satisfying than the previous one to account for the universe, and Brahman was the last of the series of solutions. At some stage in the evolution of thought, this primal source of the universe, viz. Brahman, was identified with its inmost essence, viz. ātman. Thus two independent currents of thought— one resulting from the desire to understand the true nature of man and the other, that of the objective world— became blended and the blending led at once to the discovery of the unity for which there had been such a prolonged search. The physical world, which according to the ātman doctrine is only the not-self, now becomes reducible to the self. The fusing of two such outwardly different but inwardly similar conceptions into one is the chief point of Upaniṣadic teaching and is expressed in the "great-sayings" (mahāvākya) like "That thou art," "I am Brahman" or by the equation Brahman = ātman. The individual as well as the world is the manifestation of the same Reality and both are therefore essentially, one. There is, in other words, no break between nature and man or between either of them and God.

Such a synthesis, besides showing that Reality is one, carries with it an important implication. The conception of Brahman, being objective, can at best stand only for a hypothetical something— carrying no certainty necessarily with it. It is also likely for that very reason to be taken as non-spiritual in its nature. The conception of ātman on the other hand has neither of these defects; but in the sense in which we commonly understand it, it is finite and cannot represent the whole of Reality. Even as the cosmic self, it is set over against the physical world and is therefore limited by it. When, however, the two conceptions of Brahman and ātman are combined, then by a process of dialectic a third is reached which is without the flaws of either taken by itself. Like ātman it is spiritual and at the same time it is infinite unlike it. It is also indubitable, since it is conceived as fundamentally one with our own immediate self. So long as we look upon the ultimate as something not ourselves— as mere Brahman— it remains more or less an assumption and a dogma; but the moment we recognize it as one with our own self, it becomes transformed into a positive certainty, we being under an intuitive obligation to admit the reality of our own existence, however much we may be in the dark in regard to its precise nature. It is this higher reality that is described for instance as satyam jñānam anantam (cf. Taittirīya Upanishad ii. 1), where "satyam" points to its immediate certainty, "jñānam" to its spiritual nature and "anantam" to its all-inclusive or infinite character. That is the Upaniṣadic Absolute— neither Brahman nor ātman in one sense, but both in another. It manifests itself better in the human self— though not fully even there— than in the outer world which inhibits still more of its nature, because it appears there as mere insentient matter (see Aitareya Āraṇyaka II. iii. 2). The enunciation of this doctrine marked the most important advance in the whole history of India's thought. It introduced almost a revolution in the point of view from which speculation had proceeded till then. The following illustration may perhaps be of use in comprehending the nature of this change. Let us suppose that some people know Venus as only appearing in the East, and others know it as appearing only in the West — each set of people regarding the planet they observe as distinct from what the others do. If then the discovery is made by some one that the two are but the same and that the Eastern star is the Western star, the resulting transformation in the view of Venus would correspond to the change in the present case. The true conception of unity was reached in India only at this stage.

All this is very beautifully brought out in a celebrated section of the Chāndogya Upaniṣad (section VI). It is in the form of a dialogue between a father and his son. The name of the father is Uddālaka and that of his son, Śvetaketu. Śvetaketu has been to a guru and has just returned home after completing his education in the conventional sense. The father, who notices a lack of humility in Śvetaketu, fears that he might not after all have learnt from his teacher the true meaning of life. Inquiry only confirms him in this view; and he himself therefore undertakes to instruct his son. The teaching that is imparted, as is clear from these preliminaries, should be of the highest value. Uddālaka begins by postulating an ultimate entity which is to be regarded as mental or spiritual because it is stated to have thought (aikṣata) and which he terms *Sat* or Being. He then proceeds to describe how the whole universe is a manifestation of it. "In the beginning Sat alone was, without a second. It thought "May I be many." "Its diversification— first into the three elements, viz. *tejas* or "fire," ap or "water" and pṛthivī or "earth" and then into others until organic bodies, including those of human beings, have emerged— is afterwards explained. What is made out by this is that the spiritual entity postulated in the beginning is all-comprehensive and that whatever is, has sprung from it. Then "suddenly and with dramatic swiftness" the original *Sat* is identified with the self of Śvetaketu: Tat tvam asi, Śvetaketo. The purpose of the identification is obviously to bring home to the mind of Śvetaketu the undoubted reality of the postulated source of the universe. However splendid the account of *Sat* and its transformations which Uddālaka gives at first, it is objective and therefore lacks a most essential feature, viz. certitude. It is merely to be taken for granted. Uddālaka puts it forward as a hypothesis and, though convincing to Uddālaka himself because he has realized the truth, it can be nothing more than a probability for Śvetaketu. But this probable source of the universe becomes a positive certainty to him the moment he realizes that it is identical with his own self, which he knows to be real even without being taught. This teaching of course does not leave Śvetaketu's view of his own self unchanged, for it is not his individual self that he can regard as the source of the world, but rather the universal self that is immanent in it. It is true that the world has emerged from the one and that that one is Śvetaketu's self; yet it is not his private self that can explain the universe, but his self only in so far as it is one with *Sat* or the universal self. "I live; yet not I, but God liveth in me."

Idealistic Monism

When we come to consider in detail this doctrine of idealistic monism, we find that it appears in two forms between which there is rather an important difference. In some passages the Absolute is presented as cosmic or all-comprehensive in its nature (saprapañča); in some others again, as acosmic or all-exclusive (niśprapañča). There are many passages and even whole sections in the Upaniṣads treating of either. To illustrate their character, we shall refer here to one of each type:

Cosmic Ideal *(*saprapañca*)*: One of the best-known descriptions of this ideal is found in a section of the Chāndogya Upaniṣad designated Śāṇḍilya-vidyā (III. xiv). After defining Brahman cryptically as tajjalān— as that (*tat*) which gives rise (*ja*) to the world, reabsorbs (*li*) it, and supports (*an*) it— the section proceeds to describe it as "comprehending all activities, all desires, all odors, all tastes, reaching all, and so self-complete as ever to be speechless and calm." Then follows its identification with the individual self: "This is my self within the heart, smaller than rice, or barley corn, or mustard seed or grain of millet or the kernel of a grain of millet; this is my self within the heart, greater than the earth, greater than the mid-region, greater than heaven, greater than all these worlds. This is Brahman. May I become it when I depart hence."

Acosmic Ideal (niśprapanča): For this we shall select a passage from another Upaniṣad (Bṛhadāraṇyaka Upaniṣad III. viii): Here a learned lady, Gārgī by name, asks Yājñavalkya, the greatest thinker of the age and probably the first idealist of the world, to tell her what the basis of the universe is. Yājñavalkya, tracing it to its penultimate source, answers that it is space (ākāśa). Further asked to explain what constitutes the basis of space itself, Yājñavalkya mentions a principle which he describes only in a negative way, implying thereby that the ultimate reality is beyond the grasp of human experience. The negative description given is as follows: "This is the imperishable, O Gārgī, which wise people adore— not gross, not subtle, not short, not long, not red, not adhesive, without shadow, without darkness; without air, without space; unattached, without taste, without smell, without sight, without ears, without speech, without mind, without light, without breath, without mouth, without form, and without either inside or outside. Not that does anything eat; nor that does eat anything." Lest the description should be taken to mean "pure nothing," Yājñavalkya adds immediately after it that whatever is, owes its being to this transcendental reality, suggesting that if the Ultimate was a sheer blank or non-entity, it could not have given rise to the world of appearance.

It is not difficult to discover the basis for this two-fold teaching in pre-Upaniṣadic tradition. The first or saprapañča ideal resembles the doctrine underlying the "Song of Creation." Only the First Principle here, unlike *Tad Ekam* there, is not conceived objectively, but as Brahman-- ātman in the sense explained at the beginning of this section. As regards the second or niśprapañča ideal, the prevalence of the pantheistic tendency, in the later Mantras and the Brāhmaṇas describes it as somewhat inconsistent, since it aims at unity and yet clings to the double notion of God and nature. To arrive at true unity, one only of these two should be retained. If it is the notion of nature that is retained, there will be no God apart from the world. This outcome of the pantheistic tendency, viz. viewing the unity of the world as itself the Absolute, does not figure very much in the Upaniṣads, probably because it tends towards naturalism, which, though not wholly unfamiliar to them, is widely removed from their prevailing spirit (see for example, Chāndogya Upaniṣad V. xi-xviii). If, on the other hand, it is the notion of God that is selected for retention in preference to that of nature, the world of common experience with all its variety will cease to exist apart from God. That is precisely the acosmic conception; only the theistic term is here replaced by the philosophic one of Brahman.

The determination of the relative position and importance of these two conceptions is one of the most difficult problems connected with the Upaniṣads and has occupied the attention of thinkers for a very long time. According to Śaṃkara, this problem is discussed by Bādarāyaṇa in the Vedānta Sūtra (III. ii. 11 ff); and it is not improbable that at one stage it engaged the attention of the Upaniṣadic sages themselves (see, for example, Praśna Upaniṣhad i.1; v. 2). The two views as they appear here have been explained by Śaṃkara as really the same, and the apparent distinction between them as due to a difference in the standpoint from which the Absolute is looked at— cosmic from the empirical standpoint, but acosmic from the transcendental. This view is supported by the juxtaposition sometimes of the two conceptions in one and the same passage, as for example in the Muṇḍaka Upaniṣad (I. i. 6), where we have "What is invisible, intangible, colorless, nameless, eyeless and earless, devoid of hands and of feet-that is what is coeval with time and space, is all-pervading, subtle and changeless, which the wise know to be the source of beings." The saprapañča conception must in that case be understood negatively as signifying that the world is not outside Brahman and the niśprapañča conception positively as signifying that Brahman is more than the world. There is no world apart from Brahman, but it is not therefore unreal for it has its basis in Brahman. Brahman again is not nothing for it furnishes the explanation of the world, though it is not identical with it or exhausted in it. The former view would emphasize the immanence of Brahman and the latter, its transcendence, the Upaniṣadic view being that it is both immanent and transcendent. Or probably we have here two different views as the result of a difference in interpreting the result of the synthesis of the conceptions of Brahman and ātman alluded to above. The Upaniṣadic Absolute which represents this result is not, as we have seen, something objective; nor is it the subject as such, though neither is unrelated to it. Such an Absolute may be understood as being both. That would be saprapañča Brahman. In this view, the manifold things of experience have a real place in the Absolute. They actually emerge from it and are re-absorbed into it. It is Brahma-pariṇāma-vāda or the doctrine which maintains that Brahman evolves into the world. Or the Absolute may be regarded as the mere ground of both the subject and the object, in which case we would have the niśprapañča ideal. The things of common experience are then to be regarded as only phenomena, Brahman being the noumenon. That would be Brahma-vivarta-vāda or the doctrine which maintains that Brahman does not change into, but merely appears as, the world. Whatever the truth may be, the distinction has given rise to a good deal of controversy. We shall have to consider this question when treating of the Vedānta system. Meanwhile we shall proceed on the basis that, though idealistic monism is the prevalent teaching of the Upaniṣads, that doctrine is presented in them in two somewhat distinct forms.

The second of these forms necessarily involves the notion of Māyā, it being understood as the principle which shows the niśprapañča Brahman as saprapañča. It is not, therefore, right to maintain, as some have tried to do, that the doctrine of Māyā is unknown to the Upaniṣads. It is already there, but naturally it does not yet exhibit all the various features which, as the result of later elaboration and development, are associated with it in Śaṃkara's Advaita. The word "Māyā" again, it is true, occurs only rarely in the earlier Upaniṣads; but it is found in literature still older though its meaning there may not always be clearly determinable, and also in the Upaniṣads which are not very late (see Śvetaśvatara Upaniṣad iv. 10). Even in the earliest Upaniṣads where we do not find "Māyā" we have its equivalent "avidyā" (cf. Kaṭha Upaniṣad I. ii. 5). There are also statements in them like the following: "Where there is duality *as it were* (*iva*) one sees another" (Bṛhadāraṇyaka Upaniṣad IV. v. 15) which, as recognized by scholars like Deussen, clearly point to the existence in the Upaniṣads of the idea that the world is an appearance (Deussen 1905:228 ff; see also Macdonell 1927: 47).

In whichever of these two forms they may present Brahman, the Upaniṣads distinguish from it the common things constituting the universe as known to us by pointing out that they are merely nāmā and rūpa. By rūpa is here meant the specific form or nature of a thing; and by nāmā, the name or word that serves as its sign. By the two terms together we have to understand, in the case of any object, its particularity or determinate character; and the emergence of the world from Brahman is conceived as the differentiation of names and forms. Whether we regard these particular things as actual modes or as only appearances of Brahman, they are not real apart from it, which according to the monism of the Upaniṣads is the sole reality. It is not easy to discover the necessity for nāmā in this characterization, as rūpa by itself seems sufficient for particularization. It probably has reference to a belief, current at the time, in the existence of a speech-world answering to the world of things and to the need there generally is for names as much as for things in practical life. Sometimes the description of empirical objects is made more complete by introducing a third term, karma or "movement," (Bṛhadāraṇyaka Upaniṣad I. vi. 1) and thus explicitly referring to the dynamic factor, an important aspect of the world of experience.

As regards the details of the things derived from Brahman which are characterized by nāmā and rūpa, there is to be made at the outset a distinction between the inorganic and the organic. While the latter are the abode of transmigrating souls or jivas, the former are not. They serve only as "the stage erected by Brahman on which the souls have to play their part." In the inorganic realm, the Upaniṣads recognize five fundamental elements (*bhūtas*) termed pṛthivī (earth), āp (water), tejas (fire), vāyu (air), and ākāśa (ether). All the five were not known from the beginning. "Water" seems to have been the sole element thought of at first . The next stage of advance is marked by the recognition of three elements, earth, water and fire, as in the Chāndogya Upaniṣad, which are stated to emerge from Brahman in the reverse order. They correspond roughly to the solid, fluid and gaseous phases of the material universe. The last stage in the evolution of this thought, which was final and was accepted by practically all the later philosophers of India, was reached when the number of the so-called elements was raised to five by the addition of air and ether (Taittirīya Upanishad II. i). It is clear that in this its last form the classification is connected with the five-fold character of the sensory organs, whose distinctive objects, viz. odor, flavor, color, temperature and sound, are respectively the distinctive features of earth, water, fire, air and ether. But these elements, it should be remembered, are subtle or rudimentary (sūkṣma-bhūta). Out of these are made the gross ones (sthūla-bhūta), each of which contains an admixture of the other four, but gets its name as a compound from the element predominating in it. The gross elements are what we find in nature; and strictly it is they that are to be understood by the terms pṛthivī, ap, etc., the corresponding subtle elements being known as pṛthvī-matra, āpo-mātra, etc.(Praśna Upaniṣad iv. 8) The organic bodies are divided into three classes "born from the egg" (aṇḍa-ja), "born from the germ" (jīva-ja) and "bursting through the soil" (udbhijia) (Chāndogya Upaniṣad VI. iii. 1) To these is afterwards added (Aitareya Upaniṣad v. 3) a fourth variety "born from sweat" (śveda-jja), thus making four classes altogether. When organic bodies disintegrate, they are reduced to the form of the five gross elements out of which other similar bodies may be built up. Their dissolution into their constituent subtle elements does not take place until the whole universe breaks up. Regarding the time when such breaking up takes place, there is some vagueness. As in the earlier literature, the theory of *kalpa* or the eternal recurrence of creation and dissolution is not explicit in the Upaniṣads. We have not, however, to wait long for its appearance. The Śvetaśvatara Upaniṣad, which, though one of the classical Upaniṣads, is among the latest of them and is so rich in suggestions helpful in tracing the history of early Indian thought, points to it in more than one place. Thus the Highest is there stated to have "got angry at the end of time and retracted all the worlds" and to repeat that act many a time (iii. 2; v. 3). The theory is closely connected with the doctrine of karma to which we shall refer in a subsequent section.

Psychology in Indian Philosophy

When the word "psychology" is used in Indian philosophy, it should be understood in its original sense as the science or doctrine of the soul (psyche), for its teaching, except in one or two cases, is based upon the supposition that the soul exists. This study in India never branched off from philosophy and every system has therefore its own psychology. The various psychologies have, of course, a common body of doctrine; but each has its own special features as well, which are adapted to the particular school of thought to which it is affiliated. To the Upaniṣadic seers the existence of the soul is a necessary presupposition of all experience. It is the basis of all proof and itself therefore stands in need of none. "By which, one knows all this — whereby could one know that? Lo, by what means could the knower be known?" (Bṛhadāraṇyaka Upaniṣad II. iv. 14). Although for this reason the Upaniṣads do not attempt to adduce any direct proof of the existence of the soul, they contain various suggestions touching the point. For example, the soul or jīva is often described as puruśa, which is explained as puri-śaya or "what lies in the citadel of the body." It means that the existence of the physical body, with its diverse but co-operating parts, implies the existence of something whose end it serves. That something, apart from which the mechanism of the body would be meaningless, (Kaṭha Upaniṣad II. ii. 1, 3, and 5) is the soul. Another suggestion, which is based upon the karma theory, is sometimes found. In the narrow span of a single life, we cannot possibly reap the fruits of all that we do. Nor can we, so long as we confine our attention to this life alone, fully account for all the good or evil that may come to us. A single birth being thus inadequate to render intelligible all the observed facts of life, we must, if the common belief in moral requital be well founded, admit a transmigrating soul to whose actions in past lives we must look for an explanation of whatever is inexplicable in its present condition and in whose continuance after death we must find redress of any seeming injustice in this life (Kaṭha Upaniṣad II. ii. 7).

The relation of the soul to the ultimate reality or of the jīva to Brahman is somewhat differently conceived in the two views of the Absolute found in the Upaniṣads. According to the cosmic view it is an actual, though only a provisional, transformation of Brahman and is as such both identical with and different from it. According to the acosmic view, it is Brahman itself appearing as the jiva and therefore not at all different from it. Whether the jīva is an actual transformation or not, its "jīva-hood" consists in the forgetting of its essential identity with Brahman. Though ordinarily believing that it is finite and therefore distinct from the Absolute, the soul sometimes —whenever, for any reason, desire is absent — rises above such belief and ceases to be conscious of its individuality. Such self-transcendence suggests, according to the Upaniṣads, that the jīva is not in reality the limited entity it generally takes itself to be. The question is dealt with in what is known as "the doctrine of kośas" in the Taittirīya Upaniṣad (ii.1-5). The unique experience characterizing this self-transcendent state is represented there as higher than the experience of the conscious (manomaya) and the self-conscious (vijñānamaya) levels of life, because the conflicts and confusions typical of them are overcome in it; and it is described as ānandamaya to indicate that its essential mark is peace. Yet it is not identifiable with mokṣa (cf. Brahma puccham pratiśṭhā) for it is only a passing phase and those who rise to it quickly fall away from it. The peace and self-forgetfulness that distinguish it show that the attitude induced by the contemplation of Art is its best illustrations. It stands midway between common experience and moksa, where the soul's true nature is fully revealed; and if it points in one direction to the empirical self with its many struggles and imperfections, it does so equally definitely in the other to its oneness with Brahman, which is beyond all strife and contradiction.

The word "jīva" is derived from the root jīv, which means "to continue breathing." The name gives prominence to one of the two aspects of life's activity, viz. the biological or unconscious such as breathing, which goes on even when the mind is quiescent as in deep sleep. The Upaniṣads use two other terms for the soul, viz. bhoktā, "experient" and kartā, "agent" (cf. Praśna Upaniṣad iv. 9; Kaṭha Upaniṣad I. iii. 4), which together emphasize the other, viz. the psychological or conscious aspect of the activity. The principle of unconscious activity is termed prāṇa; and that of conscious activity, manas. Every soul is conditioned by these two principles throughout its empirical existence. To these comparatively permanent adjuncts of it should be added the material body, which alone is replaced at every birth. These three together — the body, prāṇa and manas, form a sort of "empirical home" for the soul. The conscious side of the soul's activity is carried on by manas with the aid of the ten *indriyas*—five of knowledge, viz. cakṣus, śrotra, tvak, ghrāṇa, and rasanā, which are respectively the organs of sight, hearing, touch, smell and flavor; and five of action, viz. vāk, pāni, pāda, pāyu, and upastha, which are respectively the organs of speech, holding, moving, excretion and generation. Various faculties of manas like vijñāna and ahaṃ-kāra are mentioned; but the Upaniṣads, at the same time, are careful to emphasize its unity. The Bṛhadāraṇyaka Upaniṣad (I. v. 3), after giving a list of several such faculties, avers "All these are manas only." As the central organ of consciousness, it is one, however widely its functions may differ. It controls both the sensory and motor organs. It co-ordinates the impressions received from outside through the former and also resolves, when necessary, upon acting with the aid of one or other of the five organs of action. The relation of manas to these two sets of organs has been compared (Deussen 1905:263) to the relation of brain to the sensory and motor nerves.

The Theory of Cognition according to the Upaniṣads is not easy to find out. Yet there are a few hints which we may put together here: The usual Upaniṣadic expression for the things of experience, we know, is nāmā-rūpa, which signifies that whatever is thought of or spoken about is the particular. The mind and the organs of sense function only within the realm of names and forms. That is, empirical knowledge is inevitably of the finite. But this does not mean that Brahman, the infinite, is unknowable. The very purpose of the Upaniṣads is to make it known. So Brahman also is knowable; only its knowledge is of a higher type than empirical knowledge. The Muṇḍaka Upaniṣad (I.I. 4-5) classifies all knowledge into two-the higher (parā vidyā) and the lower (aparā vidyā), which are respectively the knowledge of Brahman and of empirical things. The higher knowledge may not enlighten us about the details concerning particular things, but it gives us an insight into the principle of their being, as the knowledge of a lump of ,for example, may be said to do in regard to everything made of clay (cf. Chāndogya Upaniṣads VI. i. 3-4). In this sense it may be described as complete knowledge, and, as such, different from the lower knowledge, which even at its best is fragmentary. But there is no conflict between them. That is, however, only according to the cosmic conception of Brahman. There is another view equally prominent in the Upaniṣads, which harmonizes with the acosmic conception. Brahman, according to it, transcends the very conditions of knowledge and consequently cannot be known. "Speech and thought recoil from it, failing to find it"(Taittīriya Upaniṣad ii. 4). The Upaniṣads bring out this unknowability of Brahman in itself in various ways. The Iśa Upaniṣad, for example, does so by predicating contradictory features of Brahman: "It moves; it moves not. It is far; it is near. It is within all this and also without all this" (Mantra 5). But the best instance of it seems to have been found in an Upaniṣad., no longer extant, to which Samkara refers in his commentary on the Vedānta Sūtra (III. ii.17). Bādhva, asked by Bāṣkali to expound the nature of Brahman, did so, it is stated, by keeping silent. He prayed: "Teach me, sir." The other was silent, and, when addressed a second and a third time, he replied: "I am teaching, but you do not follow. The self is silence: Upaśāntoyam ātmā." This view denies the name of vidyā to empirical knowledge, which, from the ultimate standpoint, is not knowledge at all, but only a sort of ignorance or avidyā. It may be asked whether such a view, by denying the possibility of knowing Brahman, does not make the teaching agnostic. The answer is that though we cannot *know* Brahman, we can *be* it. "He who 'knows' Brahman will be Brahman" (Muṇḍaka Upaniṣad III. ii. 9). It is to the means leading to such a consummation that the name vidyā is confined here. Even before this result is reached we may realize *that* Brahman is though not *what* it is, for Brahman being fundamentally the same as our self, its existence, as already pointed out, is an immediate certainty. We cannot think of the Absolute, but all the same we are always in immediate contact with it in our own selves. Indeed we can never miss it.

States of Consciousness

We have so far had in view only the waking state. The Upaniṣads take a wider view of life and study the self under three other heads, viz. dream, dreamless sleep and what is termed the turīya state. Of these, dreaming like waking falls under psychology proper, for in it the mind functions; but the other two are supra-mental and are considered with a view to discover the real nature of the soul. It is noteworthy that at so early a period Indian thinkers should have thought of studying phenomena under varying conditions, which by eliminating or introducing one or more factors aid the discovery of their true character. Out of these four states only two seem to have been known at first, viz. waking and dream (Deussen 1905:298). Later, not only is a distinction made between dream and dreamless sleep, but a *fourth* or the turīya state is added whose very name implies a precedent stage when only three states were recognized. We shall now briefly characterize these three states:

Dreams: The references to dreams in the Upaniṣads are frequent, implying that they attracted a good deal of attention at the time. The dream-state is intermediate between waking and deep sleep. Its physical condition is that the organs of sense should become wholly quiescent; and the senses then are stated to unite with the *manas*. The essential difference therefore between waking and dreams is that while the *manas* in the former receives from outside impressions which it builds up into ideas, in the latter it fashions a world of forms unaided and by itself. For this purpose it uses the material of waking hours — generally visual and auditory. Although the stuff of which dreams are made is thus revived impressions, the experience of a dream is quite unlike reminiscence. It is felt as real for the time being—as real as perceptual experience, for as everybody knows the things dreamt of are apprehended as present and not as belonging to the past. For this reason, dreams have been described as "perception without sensation."

Dreamless sleep: In this state, described as suṣupti, the manas as well as the senses is quiescent and there is consequently a cessation of normal or empirical consciousness. There is no longer any contrasting of one object with another or even of the subject with the object, and the embodied self is then said to attain a temporary union with the Absolute. As however suṣupti is not identified with the state of release, this statement has to be understood negatively — as only signifying that the consciousness of individuality is absent at the time though the individual himself continues to be, as shown by the sense of personal identity connecting the states before and after sleep. It is not a state of consciousness in the ordinary sense; but it is not a state of blank or absolute unconsciousness either, for some sort of awareness is associated with it. It is not, however, the "objectless knowing subject" that endures in it, as it is sometimes stated (see Deussen 1905:306); for along with the object, the subject also as such disappears then. It is rather a state of non-reflective awareness, if we may so term it. This state is above all desire and is therefore described as one of unalloyed bliss. "Sleep makes us all *pashas*." In a dream-state the interests of the waking state may be absent, but it can by no means be called disinterested. It has its own pains and pleasures and lacks that complete calm which characterizes deep sleep. The perfect peace or happiness of sleep we even recollect after waking, for then our feeling is not merely that we have slept but that we have slept soundly.

Turiya state: This is a state which, as its improvised name suggests, is not within the experience of ordinary man. It may therefore be regarded as lying outside the strict limits of any empirical investigation. It is brought about voluntarily by the elimination of discursive thought, and resembles dreamless sleep in all respects but one. There is in it the same withdrawal of normal consciousness, the same absence of desires and the manifestation of almost the same bliss. But while the self fully reveals itself in the fourth state, the experience of dreamless sleep is extremely dim. The turīya is a mystic state to be testified to only by the person that is gifted with yogic power. But the truth he vouches for is not wholly beyond us. For we have on the one hand the negative evidence of suśupti and on the other the positive one of the ānandamaya phase of experience, which together enable us to get a "conjectural insight" into the nature of the knower's experience. The attainment of this state is regarded as the culmination of spiritual training.

Practical Teachings

The diversity of views noticed in connection with the theoretical teaching of the Upaniṣads has its reflex in their practical teaching — both in regard to the ideal to be achieved and the means of achieving it. To take the latter as an example: We find one Upaniṣad (Taittīriya Upaniṣads i. 9) mentioning three such different means for the attainment of immortality – devotion to truth, penance and Vedic study – and ascribing them to three specific teachers. There is sometimes also an attempt made to reconcile two opposing views current at the time, each of which was probably pursued independently. The Iśa Upaniṣad, whose main feature seems to be this spirit of synthesis, tries to harmonize two such views in regard to attaining salvation. In the first of its eighteen verses it inculcates renunciation, but in the next verse qualifies it by adding that incessant exertion also is necessary. The Upaniṣad means thereby that one should not renounce activity and withdraw from the world, but give up only all thought of reaping any personal benefit from it-thus anticipating the well-known teaching of the Bhagavadgītā. We cannot consider all this diversity of views here, but shall refer only to the more prevalent among them.

Ethics: The basis of Upaniṣadic ethics is to be found in the conception of evil, not as offending against the will of the gods or swerving from sacrificial rectitude as in the earlier period, but as the result of a metaphysical error which sees variety alone where there is also the unity of Brahman. Empirical thought, failing to grasp the ultimate reality, distorts it or cuts it up into parts and presents them as distinct from one another. Evil is due on the practical side to this mistaken view of Reality as finiteness is on the theoretical side. It is thus contingent and has no place in the Absolute rightly understood. This misleading presentation of Reality is seen in the case not only of the objective world, but also of the self. It is because each of us regards himself as distinct from others that he strives to guard or aggrandize himself. "When unity is realized and every being becomes our very self — how can there be any delusion or sorrow then?" (Iśa Up. 7). In other words, all evil is traceable to ahaṃ-kāra, the affirmation of the finite self, and the consequent tendency to live not in harmony with the rest of the world, but in opposition or at best in indifference to it. The impulse behind this ahaṃ-kāra is not in itself bad and does not need to be wholly suppressed.

The instinct to live or to strive to be, which is what ahaṃ-kāra signifies, is a common feature of all animate existence and is only a manifestation of the desire for self-realization. But, being really a desire to transcend finite being, it will remain unsatisfied until it is rationalized through a knowledge of the ultimate truth and the wider self is averred in place of the narrower one. That is the meaning of Aham Brahma asmi (Bṛhadāraṇyaka Upaniṣad I. iv. 10) which represents the realization of Brahman in one's own self as the highest ideal of life.

Ideal: There are two well-defined descriptions of the ideal in the Upaniṣads. What is sought after in the Mantras and the Brāhmaṇas is the continuance after death of individual existence in some exalted form. This ideal of reaching life's goal after death survives in the Upaniṣads; and Brahma-realization is represented as taking place after dissociation from the physical body, as for instance in the passage quoted in a previous section to illustrate the cosmic ideal. This eschatological ideal, however, appears here very much modified for, in accordance with the prevalent view of the Upanishads, what is to be reached is represented not as other than but as identical with what reaches it. "This is Brahman. May I become it when I depart hence." The significance of such a view is that mokṣa is a state of eternal bliss (ānanda), for it transcends duality which is the source of all strife. Along with this is found another ideal which regards mokṣa as a condition, not to be attained after death, but to be realized here and now, if one so wills. A person that has reached this state continues to see variety, but he is not deluded by it because he has realized in his own experience the unity of all. We have already drawn attention to the significance of this ideal in the history of Indian thought. What is most noteworthy about it is its recognition of the adequacy of the present life to perfect oneself. Unlike the former, it signifies that mokṣa or release does not consist in a *becoming* something. It only means the discovery of what has always been a fact, and is compared to the discovery of a treasure which was all along lying hidden under the floor of one's house, but which one had so far failed to find, though passing to and from over it constantly (Chāndogya Upaniṣad VIII. iii. 2). It is the view that accords with the acosmic conception of Brahman with its implication of the phenomenality of the universe.

The practical teaching of the Upaniṣads is devised to bring about Brahma-realization in the above sense. It aims, as all such teaching should do, at the rectification of our thoughts and of our deeds. Broadly speaking, the course of discipline prescribed comprises two states:

Cultivation of detachment (vairāgya): The prime object of Upaniṣadic discipline is the removal of ahaṃ-kāra, which is the basis of all evil; and vairāgya is the name given to that attitude towards the world which results from the successful eradication of the narrow selfish impulses for which it stands. Its accomplishment necessarily presupposes a long course of training through the three āśramas or disciplinary stages — those of brahma-čarya (religious student), gārhasthya (householder), and vānaprastha (anchorite) — so far as they were understood at the time. As the very word āśasrama (toil) means, they are stages of strife when selfishness is slowly but steadily rooted out. "The good is one thing, the pleasant, another; and he that wishes to live the life of the spirit must leave the sensual life far behind" (Kaṭha Upaniṣad I. ii 1 and 2). This training leads to saṃnyāsa; but we should remember that the term does not yet bear in the Upaniṣads its present significance of a formal stage in the spiritual ascent of man. There it means only the transcending of the triple mode of āśrama life, and is regarded as a consequence of Brahma-knowledge rather than a means of attaining it. In the latter sense, saṃyasa appears comparatively late (see Deussen 1905:374). The Upaniṣads, while fully recognizing the value of this preparatory training, do not ordinarily dwell at length upon it. They rather take it for granted and addres themselves to such as have already successfully undergone that training and have acquired vairāgya. That is the implication, for example, of the efforts made to keep the Upaniṣadic truth as a secret which we have already mentioned. The preliminary discipline, however, should not be viewed as wholly implicit in the Upaniṣads, for occasionally direct references to it in one or other of its various aspects are found, as for instance in a very short but most interesting section of the Bṛhadāraṇyaka Upaniṣad (V. ii). Here the inmates of the world are classified as gods (deva), men (manuṣya), and demons (asura), and are all described as the children of Prajāpati. They approach their father seeking instruction from him as to how they should conduct themselves. The answer is brief, but it clearly indicates the necessity for grades in moral discipline according to the capacity and temperament of the persons in question. To the *asuras*, the commandment given is "Have compassion on man" (dayadhvam); to the manuṣyas, "Be generous" (datta); and to the devas, "Learn self-control" (damyata). The first two of these prescribe regard for others as the chief principle of action. The third is unlike them and may appear to be purely individualistic; but, being addressed to the best, it should be taken to presuppose the training of the other two stages. The same Upaniṣad in another of its sections represents the gods as unwilling to allow man to withdraw from the sphere of social or relative morality, which is merely a rhetorical way of expressing that man ought not to break away from society until he has discharged his duty towards it and gained its goodwill, so to speak (I. iv.10. cf. Śaṃkara's commentary).

Acquisition of knowledge (jñāna): Evil being due to a misconception of the nature of Reality, its removal can be only through right knowledge; and if the cultivation of detachment is also laid down as necessary, it is only to render the acquisition of such knowledge possible. Detachment is a pre-condition of right knowledge. "Having become calm, subdued, quiet, patiently enduring and collected, one should see the self in the self" says the Bṛhadāraṇyaka Upaniṣad (IV. iv. 23). The training of this second stage is threefold: *śravaṇa, manana, and nididhyāsana* (*Id* II. iv. 5). The first stands for the study of the Upaniṣads under a proper guru: "He that has a teacher knows." (Āčāryavān puruṣo veda: Chāndogya Upaniṣad Vi. xiv. 2). It defines the place of precept and tradition in the training. It also means that the influence of an ideal is never so great on us as when we are brought into personal contact with one who is a living embodiment of that ideal. Though necessary, śravaṇa is not enough; so it is supplemented by manana or continued reflection upon what has thus been learnt with a view to get an intellectual conviction regarding it. This training is to be further supplemented by nididhyāsana or meditation, which assists directly in the realization within oneself of the unity underlying the multiplicity of the universe. The necessity for this part of the training arises as follows: Our belief in the reality of diversity as such is the result of perception and is therefore immediate. So nothing but an equally immediate apprehension of unity can effectively remove it. If variety, in the reality of which we almost instinctively believe, is not to delude us, we must *see* the unity underlying it, not merely know it. Seeing is believing. That is why the Upaniṣads speak of darśana or "spiritual perception" in respect of the ātman or Brahman (cf. Ātmā vā are draṣṭavyah: Bṛhadāraṇyaka Upaniṣad II. iv. 5). A mere reasoned conviction is not enough, though it is necessary to give us the mark, as it were, at which to shoot (cf. Muṇḍaka Upaniṣad II. ii. 2-4). A successful pursuit of this course of training will result in right knowledge, which, according to the eschatological view, will lead to mokṣa later, but which, according to the other, secures it at once.

Nididhyāsana in this sense is the highest form of meditation and is possible only after considerable practice in concentration of thought. Hence the Upaniṣads prescribe several meditative exercises of a preliminary character. They are usually called upāsanas, and the prominence given to them in the Upaniṣads is comparable to that given to rites in the Brāhmaṇas. We need notice only one or two points about them. In upāsanas, the thought may be directed wholly outwards and two selected objects, both external, may be mentally identified (as in the meditation of the universe as a "horse" alluded to above) or only one external object may be chosen and it may be thought of as identical with the contemplative's own self. There is an important difference between the two forms of meditation. While the former affords exercise only in concentration, the latter gives scope, in addition, to the cultivation of sympathetic imagination—the power to place oneself in the position of another. It accordingly serves as a more direct aid to Brahma-realization, wherein also what is contemplated, viz. Brahman, is to be identified with the contemplative's self. Again the objects of contemplation may be real objects or only symbols. Among real objects which the disciple is asked to think of as one with Brahman, we often find conceptions which were once taken for ultimate reality itself, but which in course of time, as philosophic thought progressed, were superseded by higher conceptions. Such for instance is the case with Prāṇa (see, for example, Bṛhadāraṇyaka Upaniṣad I. iii) which marked an actual stage in the evolution of the conception of the Absolute. Among the symbols used for Brahman may be mentioned the famous "Om," the mystic syllable, which finds a very important place in the Upaniṣads (cf. Praśna Upaniṣad v). Whatever form these meditations may take, they prepare the disciple for the final mode of contemplation as *Aham Brahma asmi.* When a person that has morally purified himself and has after formal study and reflection convinced himself intellectually of the truth of unity, succeeds through nididhyasāna in transforming what was heretofore known only mediately into an immediate certainty, he attains the spiritual goal. It is, however, only a very few that can achieve this goal.

The Upaniṣads themselves refer to a knower of Brahmanasa rarity. "What is hard for many--even to hear, what many fail to understand even though they hear: a marvel is he that can teach it and lucky is its obtainer--a marvel is he that knows it, when taught by the wise" (Kaṭha Upaniṣad I. ii. 7). The many fail, the one succeeds. The majority, according to the Upaniṣads, are born again after death (see Chāndogya Upaniṣad V. x. 8). The constant stream of births and deaths until mokṣa is attained is what is known as saṃsāra or transmigration. It is the lot not only of those that are not virtuous, but also of those that restrict their activity to works of piety and lack right knowledge. The law which governs the kind of birth which such a jīva gets every time it dies, is known as the law of karma, It signifies that nothing can happen without a sufficient cause in the moral as in the physical world—that each life with all its pains and pleasures is the necessary result of the actions of past lives and becomes in its turn the cause, through its own activities, of future births. It traces all suffering eventually to ourselves and thus removes bitterness against God or our neighbor. What we have been makes us what we are. According to it the future, as we shall see in a later chapter, lies entirely in our own hands so that belief in this law serves as a perpetual incentive to right conduct. The principle underlying it is thus essentially different from the notion of good as a gift of the gods which we found prevailing in an earlier period. It may appear to substitute fate for the gods of old, but it is a fate of which man himself is the master. The doctrine, however, cannot be regarded as embodying a demonstrable truth. Nevertheless, its value as a hypothesis for rationally explaining the observed iniquities of life is clear.

There is some difference of opinion as regards the origin of this doctrine. Some have stated that it was borrowed by the Aryans from the indigenous people of their new home, among whom a belief in the passing of the soul after death into trees, etc., was found. But the view ignores that that belief was a superstition and therefore essentially irrational, while the doctrine of transmigration aims at satisfying man's logical as well as his moral consciousness. On account of this important difference, the doctrine should be regarded as not connected with any primitive belief, but as gradually evolved by the Indians themselves. It is true that it is not distinctly mentioned before the age of the Upaniṣads and, even among them, not all lay equal emphasis on it. All that can be said with certainty is that it had fully developed and belief in it had widely spread by the time of Buddha. But it is not difficult to trace its gradual development from earlier times (see Deussen 1905:313ff). The Mantras indicate a belief in the immortality of the soul; and there is also prevalent in them the idea of ṛta or moral order. But these notions, though underlying the doctrine of transmigration,, do not constitute its distinctive features. The survival of the soul after death and the determination of its condition then by the moral worth of its deeds in this life are assumed by practically all religions. A true link with the doctrine is found in the notion of iṣṭāpūrta, which indeed has been described as a "distant precursor" of karma (see Keith 1925:250, 478); and it already occurs in the Ṛgveda. Iṣṭā stands for the sacrifice offered to the gods and the word pūrta means the gifts given to the priests. The main point about it for us to note is that the merit resulting from these acts cannot strictly be termed ethical and that it was yet believed to precede the person to the other world and there to await his arrival like a guardian angel, to secure bliss for him. In a funeral hymn the dead man is asked to join his iṣṭāpūrta. If we dissociate this belief from its exclusively sacrificial reference and widen it so as to include all deeds— good and bad, religious and secular— we see its closeness to the belief in karma. Again a gradation of rewards and punishments corresponding to the good and evil deeds of this life appears in the Brahmanas and among the serious punishments meted out to the sinful is "repeated dying" (punar-mṛtyu), which is represented as taking place in another world. The notion of repeated birth is not mentioned; but it is clear that it is implicit in that of repeated death. What the Upaniṣads did was to render this idea explicit and transfer the whole circle of births and deaths to this world from a hypothetical region. The soul according to this belief passes at death into another body whose character is determined by its former deeds. In its initial form, as enunciated by Yājñavalkya (Bṛhadāraṇyaka Upaniṣad III. ii. 13), there is no interval between the end of one life and the beginning of the next. The belief did not, however, long remain unmodified, because it got mixed up with the earlier belief in recompense in another world. In this modified form the doctrine teaches a two-fold reward or punishment, first in the world beyond and then in a life here (see Bṛhadāraṇyaka Upaniṣad VI. ii; Chāndogya Upaniṣad V. iii-x). But that is a detail of Hindu faith which need not be further dwelt upon here.

The Idea of God

We have described how the theism of the Mantras decayed in later times under the ritualistic preoccupation of the priests. So far as it survived, it was transformed by the general philosophic bias of Indian thinking and resulted in the monotheistic conception of Prajā-pati— a god who does not represent any of the old Vedic deities, but is one above and beyond. The old nature-gods do not regain their position in the Upaniṣads. They are not indeed abandoned, but find mention in one connection or another. Some of them even continue to be cosmic powers which is not different from their original character; but they pale before the single reality that has now been discovered and are invariably represented as subordinate to it. Asked how many gods there are, Yājñavalkya makes light of the number thirty-three fixed in an earlier period and replies that there is but one, viz. Brahman (see Bṛhadāraṇyaka Upaniṣad III. ix. 1). All the other gods, being only its manifestations, are necessarily dependent upon it. The Kena Upaniṣad speaks of Agni, Vayu, and even Indra as worsted by the might of Brahman and represents them as unable to meddle even with a blade of grass without its aid (iii; iv. 1-3). Elsewhere the sun and the other gods are described as discharging their functions through its fear (Kaṭha Upaniṣad II. iii. 3). This is the case not merely with the ancient gods of the Mantras; even Prajā-pati, the supreme god of the Brāhmaṇas, becomes thus subordinated. The Kauṣitaki Upaniṣad (i. 5) portrays him and Indra as the door-keepers of the abode of the Highest; and in the Chāndogya Upaniṣad (VII. vii-xii) he figures as but a preceptor. The fact is that we cannot properly look for any theistic view in the Upaniṣads whose main concern is with the philosophic Absolute, except where that Absolute itself is personified and spoken of as God. Such a theistic rendering of the doctrine of the Absolute is sometimes found. Of the two forms of this doctrine, it is the cosmic that lends itself easily to such transformation. But a God so derived, being identical with the ātman, cannot ultimately be differentiated from the jīva. He can stand only for an inner principle and not for an object of adoration distinct from the adorer. The Upaniṣads explicitly repudiate such an objective conception of God. "Whoever worships a deity thinking that to be one and himself another--he does not know" (Bṛhadāraṇyaka Upaniṣad I. iv. 10. Cf. Kena Upaniṣad i. 4-8). The idea of God in the Upaniṣads therefore differs fundamental from the old Vedic view of deva—a luminous something presented as external to us—or even from that of the later Prajā-pati and can be described as theistic only by courtesy. The Upaniṣadic God is described as the "inner ruler immortal" (antaryāmyamṛtah) or the "thread" (sūtra) that runs through all things and holds them together (see Bṛhadāraṇyaka Upaniṣad III. vii). He is the central truth of both animate and inanimate existence and is accordingly not merely a transcendent but also an immanent principle, He is the creator of the universe, but he brings it into being out of himself as "the spider does its web" and retracts it again into himself, so that creation really becomes another word for evolution here. In the terminology of the later Vedānta he is the efficient and, at the same time, the material cause of the universe (abhinna-nimittopādāna).

Though theism in the ordinary sense thus really is incompatible with the general spirit of the Upaniṣads, we occasionally come across it in them. In the Kaṭha Upaniṣad (I. ii. 23) references are made to a God who appears to be differentiated from the individual soul. A clearer indication of it is seen in the Śvetāśvatara Upaniṣad, where we find all the requirements of theism—belief in God, soul and the world and the conviction that devotion to the Lord is the true means of salvation (i. 10 and 12). But even here the personal conception more than once gets assimilated to the impersonal or all-comprehensive. Absolute, and it is difficult to believe that we have here anything more than monotheism in the making, though some scholars like Bhandarkar

(Vaiṣṇavism, Śaivism, etc.: 110) are of a different opinion and take it as distinctly personal.

Works Cited

Bloomfield, M. 1908. *The religion of the Vedas.* New York: G.B. Putnam

Deussen. P. 1905. [1966] *Philosophy of the Upaniṣads.* Translated from the German by A.S. Geden. New York: Dover

__________1912. *The system of the Vedanta according to Badarayana's Brahma-śutras and Cankara's Commentary theorem.* Chicago: Open Court. [1st German edn. 1883]

Keith, A.B. 1925. *The religion and philosophy of the Vedas and the Upanishads.* Cambridge, M.A.: Harvard University Press.

Mcdonnel. A.A. 1927. *India's past: A survey of her literature, religions, languages, and antiquities.* Oxford : Oxford University Press.

Muller, F.M. 1928. *The six systems of Indian Philosophy* (Collected Works, Vol. XIX) [Reprint Banaras: Chowkhamba, 1962] London: Longmans

Chapter 9

Bhagavadgītā

M. Hiriyanna

In point of popularity the Gītā is second to no work in the world of Indian thought. It has always commanded great admiration and its popularity now, if anything, is on the increase. This unique position it owes to a variety of causes. It forms a portion of an epic whose study has enraptured generations of men and women. The two characters that figure in it are most fascinating; and the occasion which calls forth its teaching is one of extreme seriousness when the fate not only of the country but of righteousness (dharma) itself is at stake. The work is written in a simple and charming style, and is in the form of a dialogue which imparts to it a dramatic interest. But such formal excellences alone are not adequate to account for its great attractiveness. It has, as we shall see, a specific message to give. For the present, it will suffice to refer to one or two other points in its teaching which invest it with special value. The work breathes throughout a spirit of toleration which is an outstanding characteristic of Hindu thought. 'Whoever with true devotion worships any deity, in him I deepen that devotion; and through it he fulfils his desire.' 'Those that devotedly worship other gods, they also worship me though only imperfectly'(vii. 21-22; ix. 23; See also iv. II). The thought here is not, as it sometimes unfortunately is, that 'one man's God is another's devil,' but that every conception of God, however crude or defective in itself, still has its own divine side and that it is not so much the nature of the object worshipped as the spirit in which the worshipper turns to it that counts. To this feature, which entitles the poem to the first place in Hindu scriptures as bringing out best their governing spirit, it adds another which explains why it has been reckoned as part of the world's literature ever since it came to be known outside India. Its author, as may be expected from one whom tradition reckons as the inspirer of practically all the Sanskrit poets, does not discuss here the subtle and recondite details of ethics or metaphysics, but deals only with the broad principles underlying them, relating them at the same time to the most fundamental aspirations of man. And this he does not by means of any abstract disquisition, but by selecting a specific situation involving a moral dilemma and pointing out how it is overcome. This concrete mode of treatment, with the suggestiveness natural to it, very much widens the scope of the teaching and makes its appeal almost universal.

Scope and Context

All this, however, does not mean that the work is easy of understanding. Far from it. It is one of the hardest books to interpret, which accounts for the numerous commentaries on it--each differing from the rest in some essential point or other. Part of this diversity in interpretation is due to the assumption that the Gītā not only concerns itself with the problem of conduct whose solution is a pressing need for man if he is to live without that inner discord which arises from consciousness of the ideal unaccompanied by mastery over self, but also is a treatise on metaphysics. Dealing as it does with a moral problem, the work necessarily touches upon metaphysical questions now and again; but they form only the background to the ethical teaching. To regard a consideration of ultimate philosophical questions as falling within the main aim of the Gītā appears to us to misjudge its character. Though the features characteristic of the background are only vaguely seen and explain the divergent accounts given of them by interpreters, what is in the focus of the picture, namely, its practical teaching, is quite distinct. Another cause of difference among the interpreters of the work is the forgetting of the occasion that evoked the teaching and expecting to find in it a complete theory of morals. The occasion is a particular one and Śri Kṛṣṇa in enunciating a course of conduct suited to it, naturally draws attention only to some of the principles on which right living should be based. The theme of the work is not accordingly the whole of moral philosophy; and there are, as will become clear later, omissions of importance in it. Our aim will be to explain the nature of the central moral truth inculcated in the work and point out its importance in the history of Indian thought. We shall also try to indicate the general features of the theory which underlies that teaching, but we shall not attempt a complete exposition of the work, by taking into account all the other teachings that may be found interspersed here and there in it. The Gītā in that respect resembles the Mahābhārata in its heterogeneous character. Since the motif of the poem is in its practical teaching, we shall take it up first. As regards the age to which the work belongs, there has been a great deal of controversy; but scholars are now mostly agreed that in its essential portions at least, it is not later than 200 B.C.E.

The Message Of The Gita: Karma Yoga

We have stated that so far as the practical teaching is concerned, there is no ambiguity. The reason for this is the setting of the poem. In the beginning, we find Arjuna despondent and declining to fight; but, as a result of Śri Kṛṣṇa's persuasion, he makes up his mind to take part in the contest. This important element in the conception of the poem would lose its entire significance if we did not regard action as its essential lesson. We may accordingly conclude that the central point of the teaching is activism, or, to use the expression of the Gītā, karma-yoga. To understand what exactly is meant by this expression, it is necessary to consider separately the two terms constituting it. *Karma* literally means 'what is done,' 'a deed'; and the word of course appears with this general meaning sometimes in the work (cf. iii. 5; v. 8-9). But by the time of the Gītā it had also come to signify that particular form of activity which is taught in the liturgical portion of Vedic literature, namely, sacrifice. Though we cannot say that the word does not at all bear this special sense in the poem (see iii.14-15; xviii.3), it by no means represents its prevailing use. What it usually signifies here is duties that, in accordance with custom and tradition, were found associated at the time with particular sections or classes of the people[1], the varṇa-dharmas as they are described[2]. The word is also sometimes used in a fourth sense in the work, namely, divine worship and devotional acts connected with it such as prayer (cf. xii.10). Of these several meanings, we should, when thinking of karma-yoga as taught in the Gītā, ordinarily take the third, namely, social obligations which in one form or another are acknowledged in all organized society. The word *yoga* means 'harnessing' or 'applying oneself to' so that karma-yoga may be rendered as 'devotion to the discharge of social obligations.' A characteristic of all voluntary deeds is that they are preceded by a desire for something, which is described as their motive or *phala*. Whenever we knowingly act, we aim at achieving some end or other. In the present case, for instance, Arjuna is actuated by a desire for sovereignty over his ancestral kingdom; and he has undertaken to fight for regaining, if possible, that sovereignty which through the force of circumstances has passed on to his wily cousins. Such an undertaking, however, would not be devotion to karma. It is devotion to its *phala*, because the karma here, namely, fighting, but serves as a means to bring about a preconceived end. For karma-yoga, the act should be viewed not as a means but as an end in itself. That is, the idea of the result, which is to ensue from the action, must be dismissed altogether from the mind before as well as during the act. The term signifies, as Śri Kṛṣṇa is never tired of repeating, the doing of a deed without the least thought of reaping its fruit. 'Your concern is solely with action— never with its fruit (ii.47). There follows, no doubt, a result from the deed that is done, but in the case of the karma-yogin, it ceases to be his end for this simple reason that it is not desired and that there can be no end conceivable apart from relation to desire. An important consequence of following this principle of action is that one can act with complete equanimity. Desire or self-interest when allowed to have its sway over us may blind us to what is right; and even when we succeed in choosing to do the right deed, undue eagerness to secure its fruit may induce us to swerve from the path of rectitude. The term yoga is in one place, explained as signifying just such equanimity or 'balance of mind' (samatvam)(ii.48). This teaching that we ought to engage ourselves in our work as members of a social order in the usual way and yet banish from our mind all thought of deriving any personal benefit therefrom is the meaning of karma-yoga and constitutes the specific message of the Gītā.

The Golden Mean

The importance of this teaching will become clear if we refer to the two ideals of life that were prevalent at the time among the orthodox--the negative ideal of renunciation and the positive one of active life. The first ideal of nivṛtti, as it is called, advocated the giving up of all karma and withdrawing from the work-a-day world entirely. The second one of pravṛtti, no doubt, recommended living in the midst of society undertaking all the obligations implied thereby; but it did not exclude the element of selfishness altogether. This is clear in the case of ritualistic activities. Those that engaged themselves in such activities, because they realized the enduring character of the self, did not, it is true, yield to the impulse of the moment, but strove for a good which was attainable in another life. Yet it was their own good they sought. Though their belief in a future life saved them from rating too high the value of worldly good, what they worked for was similar in character and their efforts cannot therefore escape being characterized as, at bottom, selfish. And in the case of activities which are not otherworldly, they directed their thoughts as much towards rights as towards duties. They regarded themselves as not only bound to discharge their indebtedness to others, but also as having a claim upon those others for what was due to themselves; and so far they fell short of a truly spiritual conception of life. The object of the Gītā is to discover the golden mean between the two ideals of pravṛtti and nivṛtti or of action and contemplation, as we might term them, preserving the excellence of both. Karma-yoga is such a mean. While it does not abandon activity, it preserves the spirit of renunciation. It commends a strenuous life, and yet gives no room for the play of selfish impulses. Thus it discards neither ideal, but by combining them refines and ennobles both. That particular attitude of the soul which renunciation signifies still remains; only it ceases to look askance at action. In other words the Gītā teaching stands not for renunciation *of* action, but for renunciation *in* action.

Arjuna's Vairagya

Arjuna who at the outset undertook to fight under the influence of one of these old ideals has, as we see him portrayed at the beginning of the work, come to be influenced by the other. He has resolved on a sudden to renounce the world and withdraw from the contest. But he forgets that the advocates of that ideal require, as a condition of adopting it, real detachment in the would-be disciple. Arjuna is but slenderly equipped for it, and yet he thinks of giving up the world. That he has not really risen above the common level in this respect is clear from the fact that his vairāgya does not spring from true enlightenment, but from narrow-mindedness, namely, the love of kith and kin (cf. i.31; ii. 6). He continues to make a distinction between his own people and others; and his excuse for inaction, as set forth in the beginning of the poem, leaves the impression that his interest even in his subjects, as distinguished from his kinsmen, is after all secondary (cf. i.33). His detachment, or rather his disinclination to fight, is in a large measure due to the uncommon situation in which he finds himself somewhat suddenly. It is not, therefore, his considered view of the universe or of the life that he has to lead in it which prompts him to this indifference. It is the result of weakness--surrendering to the power of the moment. Arjuna's vairāgya is also in a subtle and unconscious manner due to the diffidence and fear that he might not after all win the battle, so that it is at bottom faintheartedness (hṛdaya-daurbalyam) as Śri Kṛṣṇa characterizes it and eventually rāga, not virāga (ii. 3). He is still worldly-minded; and it is on empirical, not on ultimate, grounds that he adopts an attitude of inaction. He fails to realize that he is not fighting for himself or for his family or clan (kula), but for king and country-- that the interests of righteousness are in jeopardy and that, like every right-minded person, he is bound to do his best to set the situation right. The final test that Arjuna is not actuated by genuine detachment is the sadness and despondency (viṣāda) that pervade his speech. Not only is he sad, he is also in doubt (ii.1. and 7). Neither doubt nor sadness is a sign of true spirituality which would result in a feeling of triumphant freedom. Śri Kṛṣṇa's teaching is that the narrow selfish impulses of which sadness and doubt are the sign should first be overcome; and the way to do it is not to resort to the loneliness of the forest, but to live in the midst of the storm and stress of social life, doing one's duty without any thought of recompense.

Gita's Contribution To Hindu Thought

This teaching has been traced by some to earlier sources (Bhandarkar 1913:27). It is no doubt mentioned in the Iśa Upaniṣad, but without any elaboration whatsoever. Even granting that the ideal of karma-yoga is not altogether new, there is no doubt that its general acceptance is due to its impressive enunciation in the Gītā. None of the orthodox creeds or systems of thought that were evolved afterwards discarded it. Detached action became the starting-point of life's discipline according to all, superseding virtually the earlier view of activity pursued for its fruit. In this transformation of the ideal of pravṛtti consists one of the chief contributions of the Gītā to Hindu thought. We may add that though the particular circumstances that called forth the teaching have changed, it has not been rendered obsolete. For good or ill, the monastic ideal has all but disappeared now. Ours is an age of self-assertion, not of self-suppression. Men are not now likely to give up their duty to become recluses, as Arjuna wanted to do. The danger comes from the other side. In our eagerness to claim our rights and exercise them, we may ignore our duties. Hence the need for the teaching of the Gītā now is as great as ever. Its value has not lessened through lapse of time; and that is a mark of its greatness.

The Battlefield: Apt Symbol

The propriety of selecting the battle-field for imparting the teaching is that nowhere else is the subordination of individual aim to the general good so complete. The soldier may know the cause for which he is fighting, but he can hardly say how that fight is going to end. Even supposing that it is to end favorably to his cause, he, for ought he knows, will not be there at the time to share its beneficial results. Yet this uncertainty does not in the least reduce his responsibility as a fighter. He has to do his best and should therefore realize to the utmost his value and importance as an agent, but at the same time forget altogether that he is to participate in whatever good may accrue from the discharge of his duty[3]. It is the cause of a wider entity than himself that he is serving; and his thought should not go beyond realizing that his individual responsibility as an actor in the scene remains at the maximum. That represents the highest form of self-sacrifice— to work for no profit to oneself, but yet to exert oneself to the utmost; and the finest exhibition of this spirit in the world is to be seen on a battle-field. We should, however, remember that Śri Kṛṣṇa is really addressing all men through his devotee, Arjuna; and the teaching, as already observed, is not restricted in its application to the particular situation that gave rise to it. Its appeal is to all men that find themselves placed in a similar dilemma in life. In this wider sense, it takes as its essential basis the principle that activity is natural to man and that no view of life which overlooks that feature or minimizes its importance can be right. More than once is it stated in the course of the work that no man can abjure activity altogether (cf. iii. 5; xviii. 11); but this natural activity needs to be properly directed, for otherwise it is apt to be utilized for selfish or material ends and thus become the means of obscuring from man the higher end for which he exists.

Concept Of Duty

What is the direction in which the activity should be exercised? In answer to this question, the Gītā enjoins on all the performance of their respective duties. 'One should never abandon one's specific work, whether it be high or low.' It attaches little or no value to the intrinsic worth of the deed that is done by any person, so long as it is his own dharma (sva-dharma) (xviii. 47-8). The word sva-dharma may bear a wide significance but, as required by the particular context and as specified more than once in the course of the book, it means chiefly, though not solely, the duties incumbent upon the main classes into which society is divided. In other words, it is social obligations mainly that are asked here to be discharged--such as are calculated to secure and preserve the solidarity of society. It is a proof of the severely practical character of the teaching contained in the book that it does not attempt to describe these duties any further. It realizes the impossibility of detailing the acts appropriate to every station in life, and leaves their determination to the good sense or immediate judgment of the individual. There is an attempt made in one or two places to indicate what these obligations are, but only in a general way (ii. 31-8; xviii. 41-4). It may be thought that the mere injunction that one should do one's dharma leaves the matter vague. But we must remember that in the relatively simple organization of the society when the teaching was formulated, the duties of the several classes were known fairly clearly. In the present case at any rate, there is no doubt as to what the sva-dharma of Arjuna is. The prominence given to relative duties, such as depend upon the position in society of the individual, shows by the way that the treatment which the problem of conduct receives here is, as we remarked before, only partial. There is, for example, no allusion to what may be described as 'right in itself' except incidentally, as in distinguishing the worthy from the wicked--the two broad classes into which the book in one of its sections divides the whole of mankind (Ch. xvi). It emphasizes the social character of man, and, generally speaking, declines to look upon him apart from the community of which he is a member.

Motivation For Action

From what we have stated so far, it appears that a karmayōgin works without a purpose in view. No voluntary activity, however, seems conceivable without some motive or other. Will without desire, it has been said, is a fiction. What then is the motive for exertion here? There are two answers to this question: (1) ātmaśuddhi, which means 'purifying the self' or 'cleansing the heart,' (v. 11) and (2) subserving the purposes of God (Iśvara)—a fact which, by the way, implies a mixture of teaching here (iii. 30; ix. 27). The spirit in which one engages oneself in activity is different according to the two aims. What is done is done in the one case for the sake of the social whole of which the doer is a member; but in the other it is done for the sake of God, resigning its fruit to Him. What in the one appears as duty to others appears in the other as service to God. The former type of agent is directly conscious of his relation to his environment and realizes it as a factor demanding his fealty; the latter is conscious only of God conceived as a personality in constant touch with the world, and whatever he does he regards as God's work, which has therefore to be done. But whether we look upon the work done as duty or as divine service, it is not 'disinterested' in every sense of the term. The first keeps self-conquest or subjective purification as the aim; the second looks forward to the security that has been guaranteed by God-that no godly man will perish: Na me bhaktah praṇaśyati (ix. 31). But if karma-yoga is thus motivated by desire, it may be asked, in what sense it has been described as detached. In replying to this question, we should recall what we have stated before that the activity which is natural to man if not properly guided, will become the means of obscuring from him the higher end for which he exists. By such an end the Gītā understands something more than moral rectitude. It aims at the elimination of worldly desire-- even of the type commonly regarded as legitimate. Or as we might otherwise put it, it does not rest satisfied with rationalizing our impulses; it means to spiritualize them. It teaches that an active life led without any thought of securing the worldly results it may yield, sets free the springs of that inner life whose development is the one aim of man. And karma-yoga is disinterested only so far as it turns our mind from these results and sets it on the path leading to the true goal--not that it has no end at all. It does not thus do away with motives altogether; only it furnishes one and the same motive for whatever we may do,[4] namely, the betterment of our spiritual nature. Thus though the teaching, by insisting upon the discharge of social obligations at all costs, seems to ignore the individual, it does not really do so since it provides at the same time for his advancement on a higher plane of life.

The Goal: The Perfected State

The goal to be reached on this plane is conceived in two ways, according to the double motive that is set before the karma-yogin. If the motive is 'cleansing the heart,' the goal is self-realization; if, on the other hand, it is subserving the purposes of God, the end is God-realization. Of these, the first is to be understood here much as in the Upaniṣads. It is becoming Brahman (brahma-bhūyam) or absorption in the Absolute (xviii. 53). The second is reaching the presence of God (iv. 9; ix.25), though it sometimes appears, evidently under the influence of the first, as merging in him: 'He who departs from here, thinking of me alone, will enter my being.' (viii. 5). The important point here is whether individuality persists in the final condition—whether the finite as finite can attain perfection. The absolutist view decides against persistence; the purely theistic view, in favor of it. Even though the latter does not recognize the union of the individual with God, it admits the merging of the individual's will in the divine will. Whichever be the goal--becoming Brahman or attaining God's presence— saṃsāra or the realm of good and evil is transcended. Although there are statements in the work which indicate that the goal--particularly the second one--is to be reached after death (viii. 5), the prevalent idea is that it is realizable within the limits of this life (cf. v.19 and 26). There is more than one beautiful description of the man (ii. 55-58; xiv. 22-25) that has perfected himself; and we find a thrilling account of a direct perception of God by the devotees[5]. The distinctive feature of the perfected state, which is variously termed as 'the life absolute' and 'dwelling in God' (cf. ii. 72; xii. 8) is peace. Only the attitude is predominantly one of jñāna in the case of a person that sets before himself the ideal of self-realization, and one of bhakti (passionate devotion to God) in the case of the other. Karma-yoga in the former fulfils itself in enlightenment which enables one 'to see oneself in all beings and all beings in oneself' (vi. 29. Cf. iv. 33); in the latter, it finds its consummation when a loving communion is established with God. If we describe the one as the ideal of enlightenment, the other represents the ideal of love; only it is love of God, and through him, of his creatures. But whether we look upon the Gītā as the gospel of enlightenment or of love, it is equally the gospel of action.

The point to which it is necessary to draw special attention in this connection is that the Gītā requires man to continue to work even in this perfected state, there being nothing in outer activity which is incompatible with inner peace. Here we see the exalted position assigned to work by the Gītā. It contemplates no period, when activity may be wholly renounced. Passivity, in its view, is almost as reprehensible as wrong activity. Janaka, king of Videha, renowned in the Upaniṣads, and Śri Kṛṣṇa are our examples here. The one has become perfect and the other has always been so; and both alike are active (iii. 20-28). Such a view totally transforms the notion of sanyāsa by dissociating it from all inaction; and in this transformation of the ideal of nivṛtti consists another important contribution of the Gītā to Hindu thought. Karma-yoga is accordingly to be understood in a double sense— one having reference to an earlier stage of strife when the disciple, with a steady resolve is continually weaning himself from selfish activity; and the other, to a later stage when, at the dawn of truth, the strife is over and right conduct becomes quite spontaneous— the outward expression of an inner conviction that has been attained. It is karma-yoga in the first sense, which is ancillary (cf. v. 6; vi. 3), that forms the essential theme of the Gītā; the second appears now and then as but a characteristic of the goal to be kept in view by the spiritual aspirant.

Freedom And Necessity

Before leaving this topic we must refer to an important question discussed, though but briefly, in the work (see iii. 33-43). The teaching so far set forth presupposes that man is free to choose the path he likes in the conduct of life. But it appears that he can only follow the bent of his nature (prakṛti); and when that is predominantly evil, it may be said, persuasion to adopt the right path will be of little avail. In meeting this objection the Gītā first points out how the disposition to act in an evil way operates. 'In respect of every object of sense, there is always love or hatred. One should not come under the sway of either, for they are one's foes.' That is, an evil disposition operates not automatically, but invariably by appealing to our lower or what, in the light of the description given in this connection, may be styled the sensuous self. 'The senses and the mind are its habitation; and through them it deludes man. Do thou subjugate them first in order that you may bring down the ruinous foe.' We are not accordingly driven to do evil against our desire, as Arjuna wrongly assumes (aniččhan). No responsibility attaches to man for mere impulsive reaction, except in so far as he is accountable for that impulse itself. In the case of actions on the other hand, which evoke moral judgment, they are always 'willed' by the doer, so that the opportunity to have acted differently after appropriate reflection was presented to him. He should not let go the opportunity by thoughtlessly yielding to the promptings of the sensuous self. But the question still remains whether we can ignore that self. The reply is that we can, if we only will; for we are conscious of the presence in us of a self higher than it. It may remain half-concealed, 'as fire does when enveloped in smoke'; but it is still there giving rise to that inner conflict between wish and will with which we, as human beings, are necessarily familiar. It is in the consciousness of this conflict that the possibility of a right choice lies. For the nature of the higher self is such that it will not allow itself to be subordinated to the other unless we have once for all sunk back into the life of the mere animal. The Gītā takes its stand upon this fact, that man cannot ignore the still small voice within, when it asks us to 'steady the self by the self', and commends activity without any reference to the ends which the lower of the two selves may like to pursue (iii. 43). The replacement of the lower aim by the higher, we must remember, is not to be made when or as often as a selfish motive presents itself. That might prove impracticable. We are asked to be forearmed by accepting the true ideal once for all, and to see that our actions become the expression of a single coherent purpose as implied by its acceptance. That is the meaning of telling us to substitute a uniform aim, namely, the betterment of our spiritual nature, for the necessarily divergent ends of the many actions which we have to do in life. Progress in this course may be difficult and protracted, requiring continual self-training. But the Gītā heartens us to put forth our best effort by assuring us that nothing of what we do for self-development really runs to waste. 'No such effort is lost; nor is there any obstacle in the way of its coming to fruition. Even the little that we may do will help to take us nearer the goal'(ii. 40); and again, 'The doer of good, O dear one, never comes to grief' (vi. 40). It is here that precept is of service. It clarifies our notion of the true self and encourages us to persevere in our course. The question discussed here is the familiar one of freedom of will; only the Gītā, as in other matters, restricts the scope of the discussion to the point arising from the context, namely, whether a man can choose the path to the higher life.

As belief in the karma doctrine characterizes the teaching of the Gītā, we may also briefly refer here to the allied question: how freedom is consistent with the necessity implied in this doctrine. If everything we do is the inevitable consequence of what we have done in the past, all moral responsibility should cease and self-effort should become meaningless. In considering this point, it is necessary to remember that every deed that we do leads to a double result. It not only produces what may be termed its direct result—the pain or pleasure following from it according to the karma theory, but it also establishes in us a tendency to repeat the same deed in the future. This tendency is termed saṃskāra; and the direct fruit of the karma is known as its *phala*. Every deed is bound to yield its *phala*; even the gods cannot prevent it from doing so. But that is all the necessity involved in the karma theory. As regards the saṃskāra, on the other hand, we have within us the full power of control, so that we may regulate them as they tend to express themselves in action. There is thus nothing in the doctrine which either eliminates responsibility or invalidates self-effort. The necessity that governs the incidence of the direct fruit or *phala* and renders escape from it impossible, so far from unnerving us, should stimulate us to exertion. It must enable us to work for the future with confidence, unmindful of what may happen in the present as the result of our past actions over which we have no longer any control. The important point about the karma doctrine then is that, paradoxical though it may seem, it inspires us both with hope and resignation at once— hope for the future and resignation towards what may occur in the present. That is not fatalism, but the very reverse of it.

End Notes

[1]Cf. iv. 15 (pūrvaih pūrva-taram kṛtam)and xviii. 41, where the four castes are mentioned.

[2]There is not much reference in the work to the āśrama-dharma, the twin companion of varṇa-dharma.

[3]To use Sanskrit words, this means that while one should realize to the full that he is a kartā, he should altogether forget that he is a bhoktā.

[4]Cf. Samkara on Bṛhadāraṇyaka Upaniṣad (Ānandāśrama Edition) pp. 55-58.
[5]Note the expression, 'I give you the eye divine' — divyam dadāmi te čakṣuh – in xi.8.

Works Cited

Bhandakar, R.G. 1913 (1965). *Vaisnavism, Saivism and minor religious systems.* Varanasi: India Book House.

Chapter 10

Renouncer Traditions of India: Jainism and Buddhism

Christopher Key Chapple

The renouncer or Śramaṇa traditions of India include Jainism, Buddhism, and Yoga. In this chapter, we will explore the history and primary teachings of Jainism and Buddhism and discuss how their teachings have influenced the development of world culture. The documented history of India extends backward for approximately 5,000 years. In the basin of the Indus River, in modern day India and Pakistan, artifacts have been found that attest to a distinct civilization. Features of this culture include agriculture, trade with Egypt and Mesopotamia, a written language, and a sophisticated knowledge of the principles of water displacement and flow. The impressive urban ruins of this culture extend from the cities of Mohenjadaro and Harappa in Pakistan to Lothal in southern Gujarat and beyond (see McEvilley 1980 and Feuerstein & Kak 1995 for a summary of research conducted on the early phases of Indian civilization).

Although the language of these early peoples has not yet been satisfactorily deciphered (See, however, S.R.Rao, this volume) both the architecture and several small seals used for record keeping provide clues about their values and their daily life. Judging from the orderly streets, the sturdy walls, and the extensive network of pipes and drains, city life for them must have been relatively comfortable, secure, clean, and stable. These cities were continuously inhabited for over 1,000 years, far longer than New York or Toronto or Bombay, and far, far longer than Los Angeles or San Francisco.

The seals display multiple images and motifs. Animal depictions, rendered in careful detail, reveal a care for the feeding, adornment, and safety of both domesticated and wild beasts. Details of animal anatomy are rendered with utmost precision, and, particularly in the Paśupati (Lord of Beasts) seals, as they have come to be known, religious, meditative power seems to generate from or in some other way entailing a close relationship with the animal realm. These early seals, with a meditating figure surrounded by cattle, antelope, and other animals, speak of a shamanic, totemic proto-religious form. Additionally, the seals often seem to depict women with a special reverence, and numerous fertility figurines have also been found throughout India's earliest archaeological sites.

In summary, four major features characterize the civilization of early India: knowledge of and respect for water, intimacy with and reverence for animals, mastery of meditation and yogic postures, and respect for the reproductive powers of women.

Each of these early themes finds expression in later forms of Indian civilization and culture, up to the present day: Water tanks flank Hindu temples; cows continue to be adorned and worshipped; the Yoga tradition itemizes scores of yogic postures, many in imitation of animals; meditation is widely practiced; and the Goddess or devi plays a prominent role in the Hindu pantheon through her power or śakti.

In the centuries following the decline of the Indus Valley civilization, two distinct traditions of religious sensibilities arise. The first has been referred to as *Brahmanical Hinduism*, with emphasis on the Vedas, the caste system, dharma, and such texts as the Upaniṣads, the Mahābhārata, the Rāmāyāna, and the Purāṇas. This aspect of Indian religiosity has been discussed extensively in the essays by Pandharipande and A. Sharma in this volume. Parallel to Brahmanical Hinduism, a tradition arose in India closely associated with the warrior and merchant classes known as *Sramanism.* Some scholars speculated that the Śramaṇical tradition can be linked with the proto-yoga tradition hinted at in the Indus Valley seals. Śramaṇical influence on mainstream Hinduism can be found in the Upaniṣads and in the later classical Yoga tradition as described in the chapter by Georg Feuerstein. However, independent of the Vedic tradition, Śramaṇism found its own voice around the year 800 B.C.E. Śramaṇism eventually developed into several distinct traditions, including Ājivakism (Ājivaka), Jainism (Jaina), and Buddhism (Bouddha). In this chapter we will explore the two forms of Śramaṇic religion that survive into the present: Jainism and Buddhism.

Śramaṇism may broadly be defined as a philosophical and religious orientation that does not posit a creator God, emphasizes the efficacy of human action or karma, teaches a doctrine of reincarnation, and seeks to guide its followers to a state of liberation through a process of world renunciation. In general, these renouncer traditions tend to reject notions of caste (though adherents to particular Śramaṇical groups may form de facto castes), emphasize the importance of self-effort, criticize Vedic ritual, and seek to put an end to animal sacrifice. These traditions tend also to include women within their orders as meditators and accomplished renouncers.

The earliest Śramaṇical school for which record remains is Jainism. Ajivakism, which emphasizes renunciation combined with fatalism, existed in competition with Jainism for several centuries before disappearing in the thirteenth century (Dundas 1992:26). Buddhism arose a few centuries after Jainism. Although it gained many converts from Jainism and rose to prominence throughout all of Asia within a few hundred years, Buddhism effectively disappeared from India with the advent of Islam around 1000 C.E. Through Buddhism, key facets of Indian philosophy continue to play a formative role in the life and culture of Southeast Asia, China, Japan, Korea, and Tibet. In this essay, we will first examine the Jaina tradition, and then discuss the tradition of early Buddhism in India.

Jainism

Several significant historical figures and occurrences mark the contours of Jainism. Initially, the Jaina teachers Pārśvanatha and Mahāvīra provided foundational teachings to a community of followers in northeast India. The second major event involves the emergence of two distinct styles of Jainism, the Śvetāmbara or White Clad and the Digambara or Sky Clad (Naked). Each of these groups hold distinct views on the requirements of renunciation and the status of women. The third phase of Jainism involves its philosophical articulation by Umasvati in the *Tattvartha Sutra* in the second century C.E. The fourth phase entails Jainism's interaction with Indian society while maintaining its own distinct identity. In the material that follows, we will explore each of these four areas of Jainism.

Early Jaina Teachers

The historical figure first associated with Jainism, Pārśvanātha, most likely lived around 850 B.C.E. According to Jaina tradition, he was the twenty-third of twenty-four great teachers known as Tīrthānkaras. Hence, Jainas consider their tradition to be much older than even the Vedas, though no literary or archaeological evidence can corroborate this theory. Furthermore, because the first written Jaina texts do not appear for several hundred years, scholars can only surmise about the actual teachings of Pārśvanatha. Based on its centrality in later Jainism, it is assumed that Parsvanatha taught a doctrine of harmlessness or ahiṃsā. According to the *Kalpa Sutra* (Kalpa Sūtra), a Svētāmbara Jaina text dating from approximately 200 B.C.E., Pārśvanatha lived thirty years as a householder, attained *kevala* or liberation eighty-three days after renouncing the world, and taught for seventy years as a *Kevalin*, an enlightened being, gathering 16,000 male monastic followers, 38,000 nuns, and thousands of lay disciples. He conducted his work in Northeast India, primarily around the city of Varanasi (Banaras). During his lifetime, thousands reportedly attained perfection. In his one hundredth year, he ascended Mount Sammeta and fasted for one month; finally "stretching out his hands, he died, freed from all pains" (Jacobi 1894:275).

Although these stories of Pārśvanātha are somewhat shrouded in hagiography, several features indicated in these tales persist in contemporary Jainism: the predominance of women in religious orders, the keen adherence to vows of nonviolence, and the practice of fasting to death when the end is near.

The most recent of Jainism's great teachers, Mahāvīra Vardhamanā, lived approximately from 540 to 468 B.C.E. according to modern scholars; the traditional dates given by Jainas are 599 to 527 B.C.E. Like Pārśvanatha, Mahāvīra renounced the world and took up the life of a wandering meditator at the age of thirty. After nearly thirteen years of rigorous asceticsim, he achieved liberation at the age of forty-two and gained the title of Jina (Victor). During the next thirty years, he taught adherence to five vows: nonviolence (ahiṃsā), truthfulness (satya), not stealing (asteya), sexual restraint (brahmačarya), and nonpossession (aparigraha). The purpose of observing these vows was to avoid harm to all forms of living beings, including the life forms in animals, plants, and the elements. Like his predecessor, he gathered several thousand followers, including, according to the *Kalpa Sutra*, 14,000 monks, 36,000 nuns, 159,000 laymen, and 318,000 laywomen. This text also declares that 700 of his followers achieved the Jaina state of liberation, *kevala*. At the age of 72, the Jina died, leaving behind numerous followers to continue his teachings.

The earliest textual material we have for the Jaina tradition is the first part of the *Acharanga Sutra*, recorded within several decades of the death of Mahāvīra Vardhāmanā. Several passages from this Śvētāmbara Jaina text attest to the Jaina commitment to nonviolence:

All breathing, existing, living, sentient creatures should not be slain,
nor treated with violence, nor abused, nor tormented, nor driven away.
This is the pure, unchangeable, eternal law (I.4.1).

To do harm to others is to do harm to oneself.
"You are the one whom you intend to kill!
You are the one you intend to tyrannize over!"
We corrupt ourselves as soon as we intend to corrupt others.
We kill ourselves as soon as we intend to kill others. (I.5.5)

With due consideration preaching the law of the mendicants,
one should do no injury to one's self,
nor to anybody else,
nor to any of the four kinds of living beings.
A great sage, neither injuring nor injured,
becomes a shelter for all sorts of afflicted creatures,
even as an island, which is never covered with water. (I.6.5.4)

Knowing and renouncing severally and singly
actions against living beings in the regions
above, below, and on the surface,
everywhere and in all ways—
the wise one neither gives pain to these bodies,
nor orders others to do so, nor assents to their doing so.
We abhor those who give pain to these bodies (of the earth, of water, of fire, of air, of plants, of insects, of animals, of humans).
Knowing this, a wise person should not cause
any pain to any creatures. (Jacobi 1894: I.7.1.5)

Each of these quotes attests to the centrality of avoidance of harm to any life form in the Jaina religion.

Digambaras and Svetambaras

Early in the history of Jainism, differences within the community prompted the development of two distinct groups. According to some sources, differences in interpretation arose during the lifetime of Mahāvirā; other sources attribute the distinctions to a time of famine in North West India that prompted a group of Jainas to move south to Karnataka, where they developed their own religious customs and literary tradition (see Dundas 1992:40-52; Jaini 1979:5-6). The distinctions between the Śvētāmbaras and Digambaras focus primarily on details of the life of the Jina, on issues of nakedness and the status of women. Digambaras do not agree with the Śvētāmbara view that Mahāvīra's embryo was moved from the womb of a Brahman woman to that of a Ksatriya woman and that Mahāvīra was married and had a daughter. Though both groups acknowledge that Mahāvīra was naked during the period of his ascetism and throughout his teaching years until his death, the Śvētāmbaras require their monks and nuns to remain draped with white cloth throughout their lives. The Śvētāmabras also allow their mendicants to possess a begging bowl. The Digambaras, by contrast, insist that their monks eventually take the vow of total nudity and require that they eat using their hands.

The second major distinction pertains to attitudes toward women. The Digambaras mandate that in order for one to achieve liberation, one must emulate Mahāvirā and become naked. The Digambaras do not allow nuns to take the vow of nudity, and hence state that women cannot reach final *kevala*. By contrast, the Śvētāmabras allow for the possibility of women's liberation and in fact state that Malli, the ninteenth great teacher, was a woman, whereas the Digambaras claim that this teacher was a man (see Jaini 1991).

Today, the Digamabara Jainas are located primarily in Karnataka and southern Maharashtra and the Śvētāmbara Jainas are found primarily in Northern India, with greatest concentrations in Gujarat, Maharashtra, Madhya Pradesh, and Rajasthan. According to the 1991 census, less than half of one percent of India's population is Jaina (Sangave 1997:vii), though this number does not take into account the Jainas who identify themselves as Hindu when responding to the census. Additionally, several tens of thousands of Jainas have migrated from India to North America and Europe within the past decade. Despite their seemingly small numbers, Jainas have made significant contributions to Indian life and culture through their unique philosophy, their stringent ascetic practices, and their social activism on behalf of vegetarianism and nonviolence.

Umasvati and Jaina Philosophy

Umasvati, a second century Jaina thinker accepted by both Śvētāmbaras and Digāmbaras, developed a theory of karma and rebirth that provided both a physical and metaphysical underpinning to support the practice of nonviolence. He systematized the rationale for the many practices of nonviolence, which for the Jainas might include the sweeping of the ground in front of one's feet and the wearing of masks to protect insects from the force of one's breath. According to his *Tattvartha Sutra*, countless beings (jīvas) inhabit the universe, constantly changing and taking new shape due to the fettering presence of karma, described as sticky and colorful. The presence of karma impedes the soul on its quest for perfect solitude and liberation. By first accepting this view of reality and then carefully abiding by the five major vows as taught by Mahāvirā (nonviolence, truthfulness, not stealing, sexual restraint, and nonpossession), the aspirant moves toward the ultimate goal of spirituality. At the pinnacle of this achievement, all karmas disperse and the perfected one (siddha) dwells eternally in omniscient (sarvajña) solitude (kevala).

This framework outlined by Umasvati grows to include the articulation of 148 distinct karmic configurations or prakṛtis, to be overcome through a successive progression through fourteen stages of spiritual ascent or guṇāsthānas (see Tatia 1994: 279-85). Success in this process rests in the careful observance of nonviolence (ahiṃsā), through which one gradually dispels all karmas. Although no Jaina reportedly has achieved this state of *ayogi kevala* for several hundred years, thousands of Jaina monks and nuns in India practice a lifestyle that seeks to restrict and eliminate karma through the observance of monastic vows.

Everything from a rock to a drop of water up to human beings are said to be imbued with an inidividual life force (jīva). Each life form, including mountains, lakes, and trees, is said to have consciousness, bliss and energy. Living beings are classified in a hierarchical fashion according to the number of senses they possess. Earth, water, fire, air, and vegetables, the simplest forms of life, are said to possess only the sense of touch. Worms have both touch and taste. Bugs, lice, and ants have touch, taste, and smell; moths, bees, and flies add the sense of seeing. Beasts, birds, fish, and humans are said to have, in addition, both hearing and thought, bringing their total number of faculties to six. In each instance, one's status depends on the nature and quality of karma that has adhered to one's jīva.

To illustrate the nature of karma, a traditional story narrates how the personality types associated with each of the five primary colors (leśya) of karma:

> A hungry person with the most negative black karma uproots and kills an entire tree to obtain a few mangoes. The person of blue karma fells the tree by chopping the trunk, again merely to gain a handful of fruits. Fraught with gray karma, a third person spares the trunk but cuts off the major limbs of the tree. The one with orangish-red karma carelessly and needlessly lops off several branches to reach the mangoes. The fifth, exhibiting white or virtuous karma, "merely picks up ripe fruit that has dropped to the foot of the tree" (Jaini 1916:47).

This didactic tale emphasizes the need to be careful in how one procures even the necessities in order to avoid accumulating additional karmas that obscure the reality of one's innate energy, consciousness, and bliss.

The concern for avoiding harm to living beings extends beyond the theoretical to the immediately practical. During the standard Jaina temple service observed world wide today, a beginning prayer urges the Jaina practitioner to be thoughtful regarding all the many life forms that may cross one's path. All, according to Jainism, merit protection, and such protection serves to minimize and hopefully eliminate the host of negative karmas that accrue because of the failure to recognize the pervasiveness and sanctity of all life forms. The prayer begs forgiveness:

> for injury in the course of walking, in going and
> coming, in treading on living things, in treading on
> seeds, in treading on green plants, in treading on dew, insects, mould, mud, clay, spiders, and cobwebs... (Lopez 1995:238).

The prayer goes on to ask that no karma be added for these or any other actions, concluding with the Jaina practitioner taking a perfectly still standing pose (kāyōtsarga) to destroy any remaining karmas and prevent taking on new ones for the duration of the pose.

This systemization of Jaina practice led to the refinement of ritual governing the end of one's life. As mentioned earlier, the Jaina community holds in high regard the model provided by the conscious death of Pārśvanātha. By the time of Samantabhadra, a contemporary of Umasvati, a formula for moving into death became established. His text, the Ratnakaraṇḍaka Śrāvakācāra, specifies that one first give up solid food, then milk, then water, leading to one's passing from this world after several days or weeks. It must be noted that this required approval from the community, and would only be permitted when death seemed imminent (Chapple 1993:99-109). The tradition of fasting to death, referred to by the Jainas as Sallekhana or Santhara, has been quietly observed by Jainas for millenia, with many ancient inscriptions in Karnataka documenting the completion of the final fast (Settar 1989).

Jainism in Indian Culture and Society

With the codification of Jaina philosophy by Umasvati and the clear practical expectations laid out by Samantabhadra, Kundakunda, and other Jaina figures, Jainism has experienced a somewhat stable existence since the second century C.E. Jaina kings rose to prominence in Karnataka from the second century to the thirteenth century. In Gujarat, the reign of Kumārāpala (ca. 1150) saw Jainism generously supported.

The Jaina intellectual tradition initiated by Umasvati continued to flourish throughout the medieval period, particularly in the Śvetāmbara works of Haribhadra (eighth century), Hemačandra (twelfth century), and Yashōvijaya (seventeenth century). Haribhadra, a Brahman convert to the Jaina faith, wrote copiously on a wide range of topics. He attempted to catalogue a wide range of philosophical systems within the framework of the Jaina philosophy of multiple perspectivism (anekānta-vāda) in his Anekāntajayapatākā, Saḍarśanasamuccaya, and other texts. Haribhadra demonstrates intriguing links between the Yoga system of Patāñjali, Jainism, and his own intrepretations of Tantra in the Yogadṛṣṭisamuccaya. Hemačandra wrote extensively on poetics, grammar, and Jaina Yoga. Yashovijaya commented on the texts of his predecessors, and even composed a Jaina commentary on the Bhagavad Gītā (Dundas 1992:204).

Prominent Digambara thinkers and writers include Kundakunda (third century), Jinasena (ninth century), and Amritačandra (twelfth century). Kundakunda wrote several volumes on meditation emphasizing the ultimate nature of the soul. Jinasena wrote the Ādipurāṇa, which provides an account of the origin of the universe. This massive work tells the story of Rishbha, the first Tīrthankara, and his two sons. One son, Bharata, is credited with writing the Vedas. His conflict with his brother Bāhubali is memorialized in the giant statue at Śravaṇabeḷāgoḷa in Karnataka, which depicts the expiatory pose that Bāhubali assumed in remorse for challenging his older brother for the throne. Amritačandra composed many works, including the Puruṣārthasiddhyupāya, a survey of Jaina thought and practice.

Although Jainism cannot claim direct political influence since the medieval period, Jainas played an important role in influencing day to day life in India. During the time of the Buddha, they encouraged the Buddhist monks not to travel during the rainy season, to avoid harm to the many plants and animals that flourish in the roadways at that time of year (Rhys-Davids & Oldenberg 1882, III.1.1). In countless Hindu kingdoms, they advocated for prohibitions against animal sacrifice, and most likely convinced the Brahmans to adopt vegetarianism (Dumont 1970:149). During the Mughal period, the Jainas experienced great success with convincing Emperor Akbar to restrict the hunting of certain animals and to declare Jaina districts off limits to human predators (Beveridge 1897:333-34; Srivastava 1962:264). During the last years of British colonialism in India, Jaina teachers and the broader Jaina ethos shaped the life and work of Mahatma Gandhi. The Jaina monk Becharji asked Gandhi to vow to resist wine, women, and meat while studying law in England (Fischer 1950:23). The spirituality and insight of Raychandbhai, a lay jewel merchant, deeply inspired Gandhi (see Gandhi 1957:88-90), and many features of Gandhianism can be linked with the Jaina vows, including his emphasis on truth (satya) and nonviolence (ahiṃsā).

Jainas continue to play an important role in shaping the conscience of modern India. As industrialists, manufacturers, lawyers, publishers, merchants, and members of Parliament, lay Jainas strive to integrate their ethical commitment to nonviolence into the day to day operations of their respective occupations. For instance, Dr. L.M. Singhvi, a prominent jurist and current Indian High Commissioner in Great Britain, drafted the Jain Declaration on Nature and presented it to Prince Philip in 1990. This document seeks to apply Jaina teachings, cosmology, and code of conduct to the issue of environmental protection (Sangave 1994:349-54). It demonstrates not only the core Jaina principle of respect for life, but also shows contemporary Jainism's willingness to engage in social and global issues.

In summary, Jainism contributed to Indian society a fully developed nonviolent ethic that helped shape Buddhism and the societal rules of Hinduism. Its unique philosophy of multiple eternal life forms (jīva) seeking to free themselves from the snares of karma spawned a lifestyle meticulous in its avoidance of injury. For lay Jainas, this has meant lifelong vegetarianism and taking up occupations such as commerce, artistry, and publishing through which one can minimize violence done to living beings. For Jaina monks and nuns, this entails a life of minimal possessions, few comforts, and near constant wandering. I know of no religious order with as stringent vows as the Jainas. Furthermore, from this concern not to harm others, the Jainas developed a pluralistic philosophy that seeks to acknowledge the tenability of multiple points of view, but emphasizes that ultimate value can only be found in following an abstemious, nonviolent course of action. This concern with abstemiousness, parsimony, and control of the senses finds support in numerous rituals and periodic fasts. Though small in numbers, the Jainas continue to serve as a conscience to the world on the issue of concern for the welfare of all living beings.

Buddhism

The path of renunciation also found another form of expression in the life and work of the Buddha (563-483 B.C.E.). Buddhism arose from the same Śramaṇic context that gave rise to Jainism and Yoga, but with its own distinct philosophy. Unlike Jainism, it spread far from its Indian birthplace and profoundly influenced the history and culture of Central, East, and Southeast Asia. In this section of the chapter, we will explore the life of the Buddha, the importance of nonviolence in the Buddhist tradition, early Buddhist teachings, the rise of the Mahāyāna school, and the decline of Buddhism in India.

The Buddha

The Buddha himself serves as the paradigmatic renouncer to be emulated by all aspiring Buddhists. He was born into a prominent Kṣatriya or warrior family of northern India or southern Nepal, and given the name Siddhārtha Gautama, which means "one whose goal has been accomplished." According to the Pāli texts (Warren 1896:1-110), at his birth, a panel of eight Brāhmaṇā priests declared that he would mature to become either a great world leader or would renounce the world to become a monk. His father worked hard to insure that his son would have no occasion to leave worldliness behind, and shielded him from all forms of despair. However, in his twenty-ninth year, his charioteer took him out beyond the sanitized castle confines. In sequence he encountered an old man, a diseased man, a corpse, and finally a Śramaṇic renouncer. His first encounters with mortality, discomfort, and death left him pensive and distraught; the sight of the religious mendicant offered the possibility of transcendence and unconditioned bliss. He resolved that night to pursue the path of the monk and left behind a sleeping wife and infant son. He wandered for six years. He studied with two prominent teachers of meditation and nearly starved himself to death through rigorous ascetism. He eventually rejected the extreme path of bodily denial, regaining his health and luster. He eventually overcame all obstacles to his liberation through an extended period of meditation during which he battled Māra, the personification of evil and worldly attachment. This occurred under the Bōdhi Tree in Bōdh Gayā, a city in Northeast India which has become an important pilgrimage destination for Buddhists from all over the world.

The enlightenment or nirvāṇa of the Buddha consisted of a series of trances wherein he first detached himself from sense objects and calmed the passions, then entered into a state where discursive thought ceases, then entered a state of bliss, and finally became free from all opposites, a state characterized by pure awareness and equanimity. From this place of repose, he discerned the causes of human suffering as being rooted in desire and ignorance leading to an impure identity, sense attachment, acquisitiveness, existence, birth, old age, dying and rebirth. After forty-nine days of reflection, he decided to share his insight with others and at the town of Sarnath, just north of Banaras, he conducted his first public sermon, laying the foundation for the Buddhist religion. There he proclaimed the Four Noble Truths: 1) all things suffer 2) the cause of suffering is desire 3) the cessation of desire is the cessation of suffering 4) release is to be found through the Eightfold Path, which involves the cultivation of right views, intention, speech, action, livelihood, effort, mindfulness, and concentration. He soon gathered numerous disciples and taught for forty-five years, spreading his teachings or dharma throughout India.

For the first three hundred years after his death, the sermons of the Buddha were preserved and transmitted in an unbroken oral tradition. Eventually they were written down in the Pāli language (which is closely related to Sanskrit) and supplemented with additional texts. The Buddhist canon eventually grew to include an extensive collection of sermons delivered by the Buddha (the *Sutra Pitaka*), several volumes listing the numerous rules to be observed by monks and nuns (the *Vinaya Piṃaka*), and a later collection of philosophical materials that elaborate on Buddhist teachings (the Abhidharma).

Nonviolence in Buddhist Tradition

Like its sister renouncer traditions of Jainism and Yoga, Buddhism embraced the practice of nonviolence. The first Buddhist precept requires that one not harm or injure living beings. In the Mahāvagga portion of the *Vinaya*, the Buddha proclaims "A monk who has received ordination ought not intentionally destroy the life of any living being down to a worm or an ant" (Rhys-Davids & Oldenberg 1882, I.78.4) During the course of his teaching, the Buddha often used animal parables to convey key ideas, and told tales of his own past births as a rabbit, a swan, a fish, a quail, an ape, a woodpecker, an elephant, and a deer. Buddha conveys the depth of his concern for animals in the following Jātaka or past life tale:

> Once upon a time, a goat was led to a temple and was about to be sacrificed by the presiding Brāhman. Suddenly, the goat let out a laugh then uttered a moaning cry. The Brāhman, startled by this odd behavior, asked the goat what was hap pening. The goat responded as follows: "Sir, I have just remembered the history of what led up to this event. The reason I have laughed is that I realized that in the last of 500 births I have suffered as a goat; in my next life I will return as a human. The reason I have cried is out of compassion for you. You see, 500 births ago I was a Brāhman, leading a goat to the sacrifice. After killing the goat, I was con demned to 500 births as a goat. If you kill me, you will suffer the same fate." The Brāhman, visibly shaken, immediately freed the goat, who trotted away. A few minutes later, lightning struck the goat and he was freed to again become human. The Brāhman likewise was spared, due to the goat's compassionate intervention. (Jātaka tale 18 in Francis & Thomas 1916:20-22)

Several themes reflect the Buddhist approach to nonviolence in this tale, including karma and rebirth theory and compassion and the notion that animals hold the capacity for compassion.

This Buddhist commitment to nonviolence and compassion toward animals influenced the broader society under the reign of Buddhist kings. In 260 B.C.E., Aśoka (274-232 B.C.E.), the third Emperor of the Maurya dynasty of India, converted to Buddhism and proclaimed the religion throughout his empire, engraving rocks and pillars with Buddhist teachings that can be seen throughout the country even today. He enacted legislation for the protection of animals, in an attempt to make nonviolence and harmlessness to animals part of public policy (see S. R.. Rao, this volume.)

Early Buddhist Teachings

During this early phase of Buddhist history, eighteen distinct sects arose. Early missionaries brought Buddhism to Sri Lanka and Southeast Asia, where these early teachings survive in the form of *Theravada*, or the Way of the Elders. Buddhaghōṣa, the most well known and prolific of the Theravada scholars, lived in Sri Lanka during the fourth century. His massive work, the *Path of Purification* (*Visuddimagga*) remains a standard manual for the practice of Theravada Buddhism (Buddhaghosa 1976).

One foundational teaching sets Buddhism apart from its Hindu and Jaina counterparts: The doctrine of no-self. According to the teachings of the Buddha, human experience can be grouped into five aggregates (skandhas): form or body (rūpa), feeling (vedanā), perception (saṃjñā), conditioning due to past karma (saṃskāra), and consciousness (vijñāna). Unlike other systems of Indian thought, all of these are said to be impermanent, including consciousness. The task of the practicing Buddhist is to clearly comprehend the pervasiveness of these aggregates and systematically deconstruct attachment to or identity with any of them. Liberation or nirvāṇa lies in the nonidentification with any of these:

> It is by the destruction of these, the not lusting for these, it is by the cessation of, the giving up, the utter surrender of these things that the heart is called "fully freed" (Woodward 1925:14).

The Buddha proclaimed that "by thoroughly knowing, by understanding, by being detached from, by renouncing (the five aggregates) one is fit for destruction of suffering" (see Woodward 1925:26). In other words, by not being attached to one's body or the bodies of others, by not craving feelings or sense perceptions, by not falling under the sway of past actions, and by not identifying oneself with the contents of one's awareness, liberation can be gained. To illustrate the point, the Buddha asks his students the following:

> ... if, brethren, a man should gather, burn, or do what he please with all the grass, all the sticks, branches and stalks in his *Jeta Grove*— pray, would ye say 'this man is gathering, burning *us*, doing what he please with *us?*'
> 'Surely not, lord.'
> 'Why so?'
> 'Because, lord, this is not our self, nor of the nature of the self.'
> 'Even so, brethren, body (rūpa) is not of you. Put it away. Putting it away will be for your profit and welfare. Feeling is not of you. Perception, the activities (sasṃkāra) are not of you, nor consciousness. Put it away. Putting it away will be for your profit and welfare (Woodward 1925:31-32).

To further emphasize the need for nonattachment to achieve liberation, Buddha states that one must regard to things, past, present, or future, as follows: "This is not mine; this am not I; this is not the Self of me—so seeing things as they really are, by right insight, one is liberated, without grasping" (Woodward 1925:67-68). During the lifetime of the Buddha, 500 persons, referred to as *arhants*, achieved this goal through his teachings. (For recent studies on early Buddhism, see Hoffman & Mahinda 1996.)

The Rise of the Mahayana

Around the first century B.C.E., new Buddhist texts were being composed in northern India that de-emphasize one's personal quest for liberation and urge the cultivation of compassion toward all sentient beings. This new form of Buddhism, which took root in China, Japan, Korea, and Tibet, is known as the *Mahayana* or Great Vehicle. Its leading Indian theorist, Nāgārjuna, developed the Middle Way (mādhyamika), a philosophy that emphasizes the emptiness of both self and other, with the purpose of bringing its adherents to an appreciation of the immediacy of experience. In a famous phrase, he asserts that saṃsāra does not differ from nirvāṇa, that, for the enlightened, all beings are seen as enlightened beings.

A companion philosophy arose referred to as the Yogāčāra, developed by Asanga. This school of thought emphasizes the importance of meditation as the means through which the mind can be purified to reveal its true Buddha nature (tathāgatagarbha). The primary text associated with this tradition is the Laṇkāvatāra Sūtra. Other significant Sanskrit Mahayana texts include the *Lotus Sutra* (Saddharmapuṇḍarīka Sūtra), the Vimalakīrti Sūtra, and the Perfection of Wisdom Heart Sūtra (Prajñāpāramita Hṛdaya Sūtra).

The Decline of Buddhism in India

For a variety of reasons other religious traditions eclipsed Buddhism within India. After 600 C.E., the devotional movements of the Tamil saints gained popularity over Buddhism in the south, though Kāñcīpuram still included a Theravāda community until the fifteenth century (Robinson 1970:77). In central India, the philosophy of Sankara adopted the Buddhist via negativa by emphasizing the Upaniṣadic maxim "not this, not this." Around the same time, the Buddha became listed within the Vaishnavite list of Avatāras, essentially enfolding Buddhism within the broad Hindu pantheon. In northern India, Buddhism and Śaivism became intermingled, and Muslim invaders stamped out this hybrid form of Buddhism by the fifteenth century. As historian Richard Robinson has noted,

> "Buddhism flourished in Sindh, the Ganges Valley, and Orissa until Muslim invaders sacked the monasteries and butchered the monks. [The university at] Nalanda was pillaged and burned in 1198" (Robinson 1970: 77).

In addition to these outward pressures, however, the emphasis on monastic life, the absence of a strong lay community, and a gradual absorption of Buddhist teachings into Hinduism certainly helped facilitate the diminishment of Buddhism in India (Jaini 1980:81-91). Today Buddhists are found in the Chittagong Hills near India's border with Burma, and among the followers of Ambedkar who converted to Buddhism after India's independence.

While the presence of Buddhism waned in its homeland, Buddhism became a great transporter of Indian culture, language, and ideas. Traders and missionaries took Buddhism to Southeast Asia, Indonesia, Philippines, China, Tibet, Central Asia, and the Middle East. Sanskrit texts were translated into Persian and Arabic. Buddhism was extensively practiced in Iran, and helped shape the Manichean religion that proved so influential in the life of Christianity's St. Augustine of Hippo. The imprint of Buddhism can still be seen in virtually all corners of Asia.

Conclusion

During their early history, Jainism and Buddhism existed in competition with one another. Jainism predates Buddhism by several centuries. Many early Buddhists converted from the Jaina faith (Murcott 1991). The Buddha often criticized the Jainas for their extreme penance. The Jainas in later years developed elaborate arguments against the Buddhist theory of no-self, declaring that if the world is nothing more than a sequence of moments, as the Sarvāstivādin Buddhists assert, then there would be no continuity or meaning to life. Furthermore, they criticize the emptiness doctrine, stating that it diminishes the importance of suffering, the great impetus for spiritual questing, because it fundamentally denies its reality (see Chapple 1997). However, despite these philosophical differences, both traditions share a number of features, such as: nonassent to the premise of a creator God; emphasis on the process of meditation as the means to overcome the effects of past karma; inclusion of a sophisticated cosmological model; support of monastic communities; and emphasis on nonviolence and other ethical precepts.

The Jaina strives to rise above the effects of karma, eventually reaching the pinnacle of purity and sublime detachment. For the Buddhist, the world of saṃsāra or endless rebirth driven by ignorance is overcome by the cessation of desire, leading to nirvāṇa. Jainism's definition of life, although radically different from that found in the Western world and distinct from views held by Buddhists and Hindus, challenges us to more carefully consider the impact and implications of our daily actions on other life forms. The Buddhist emphasis on the transitory nature of the apparent world serves as a reminder to all people not to search for absolutes in the realm of change. Through these teachings, the renouncer traditions of India have shaped the history and culture of Asia. In the present and future, their insights into the interrelationship of life forms may be helpful for developing an indigenous Asian environmental ethic. Their emphasis on purification and meditation will continue to be useful for the process of self-exploration. Furthermore, as seen in the lives of Aśoka and Mahatma Gandhi, the renouncer commitment to nonviolence can hold promise for the world's political future and civic well being.

The contemporary world presents new challenges to the renouncer nonviolent ethic as traditionally construed. The effects of modernization, development, and industrialization complicate the observance of ahiṃsā. In terms of interpersonal relations, might not the Laṇkāvatāra Sūtra be helpful in its reminder that at one point in history, all of us have been brother or sister or father or mother to one another? In a culture moving rapidly toward the depletion of its natural resources, driven to take the stuff of trees and petroleum and turn it into garbage and deadly exhaust, might it not be helpful to marshall the ideas on nonviolence and minimal consumption to ensure a future for both our endangered species and ourselves?

Nonviolence, whether expressed through Jainism, Yoga, Buddhism, or the teachings of Mahatma Gandhi, invites the people of the earth to live sparingly and compassionately. It began with brave naked ascetics in India, and spread throughout Asia, altering human attitudes toward food and the very purpose of human life. In the *Acaranga Sutra*, Mahāvīra advises his nuns and monks to "change their minds" about things; rather than seeing big trees as "fit for palaces, gates, houses, benches..., boats, buckets, stools, trays, ploughs, machines, wheels, seats, beds, cars, and sheds" they should speak of the trees as "noble, high and round, with many branches, beautiful and magnificent" (II.4.2.11-12). So also, with a different view, with a different eye, people might likewise change the way they see the world and construe the world and others if educated in the nonviolent perspective of India's great renouncers.

Works Cited

Beveridge, H. 1897. *Akbar Nama* by Abu Fazl. Calcutta: Asiatic Society of Bengal.

Buddhaghosha, Bhandantacariya. 1976. *The path of purification (Visuddhimagga),* trans lated by Bhikkhu Nyanamoli. Boulder, CO: Shambhala.

Chapple, Christopher Key. 1993. The jaina path of nonresistant death. In *Nonviolence to animals, earth, and self in Asian traditions.* Albany: SUNY Press

_______. 1997. The centrality of the Real in Haribhadra's yoga texts. In *Approaches to Jaina studies*, edited by N. K. Wagle and Olle Quanstrom. Toronto: University of Toronto Press.

Dumont, Louis. 1970. *Homo hierarchicus: The caste system and its implications.* Chicago: University of Chicago Press.

Dundas, Paul. 1992. *The Jains.* London: Routledge.

Feuerstein, Georg and Subash Kak. 1995. *In search of the cradle of civilization: New light on Ancient India.* Wheaton: Theosophical Publishing House.

Fischer, Louis. 1950. *The life of Mahatma Gandhi.* New York: Harper and Row.

Francis, H.T. and E.J. Thomas.1916. *Jataka Tales.* Cambridge: Cambridge University Press.

Gandhi, Mohandas Karamchand. 1957. *An autobiography: My experiments with truth.* Boston: Beacon Press.

Hoffman, F. J. and Deegalle Mahinda. 1996. Pali Buddhism. Surrey: Curzon Press.

Jacobi, Hermann. 1894. *Jaina sutras translated from Prakrit.* Oxford: Clarendon Press.

Jaini, Jagmanderlal. 1916. *The outlines of Jainism.* Cambridge University Press.

Jaini, Padmanabh S. 1979. *The Jaina path of purification.* Berkeley: University of California Press.

______. 1980. The disappearance of Buddhism and survival of Jainism in India. In *Studies in the History of Buddhism*, edited by A. K. Narain. Delhi: Motilal Banarasi Das.

______. 1991. *Gender and salvation.* Berkeley: University of California Press.

Lopez, Donald S. 1995. *Religions of India in practice*, translated by John Cort. Princeton: Princeton University Press.

McEvilley, Thomas. 1980. *The archeology of Yoga.*

Murcott, Susan. 1991. *The first Buddhist women: Translations and commentary on the Terigatha.* Berkeley: Parallax Press.

Robinson, Richard. 1970. *The Buddhist religion: A historical introduction.* Belmont: Dickenson.

Rhys Davids, T. W. and Hermann Oldenberg (trans.)1882. *Mahavagga in Vinaya texts.* Oxford: Oxford University Press.

Sangave, Cilas. 1994. The Jain declaration on nature: A historical document. In *Jainism and Prakrit in Ancient and Medieval India*, edited by N. N. Bhattacharya. New Delhi: Manohar.

______. 1997. *Jaina religion and community*. Long Beach, CA:

Settar, S. 1989. *Inviting death: An Indian attitude toward the ritual death.* Leiden: E. J. Brill.

Srivastava, Ashirbadi Lal. 1962. *Akbar the Great, vol. 1: Political History, 1542-1605 A.D.* Agra: Siva Lal Agarwal.

Tatia, Nathmal (trans.) 1994. *Tattvartha sutra of Umasvati [That which is]*. San Francisco: Harper Collins.

Tobias, Michael. 1991. *Life force: The world of Jainism.* Berkeley: Asian Humanities Press.

Warren, Henry Clarke. 1896. *Buddhism in translations.* Cambridge, MA: Harvard University Press.

Woodward, F. L. (trans.) 1925. *The book of kindred sayings (Samyutta-Nikaya) or grouped suttas, part III: The Khandha book.* London: Luzac.

Chapter 11

Yoga: The Art and Science of Self-Transcendence

Georg Feuerstein

The earliest beginnings of Yoga can be dated back at least five thousand years. Its scholarly exploration was begun a little over two centuries ago, when Sir Charles Wilkins undertook the very first translation of the Bhagavadgītā (Lord's Song) into a non-Indian language, namely English. Perhaps it is no accident that this happens to be the oldest available full-fledged Yoga scripture and one that according to the Gita Press in Gorakhpur now exists in well over one thousand editions. In 1837, Sir Henry Thomas Colebrooke published the first treatment of Yoga by a Western scholar. Half a decade later, the German-born British scholar Max Müller, who was and continues to be much loved in India for championing its spiritual heritage, wrote: " . . . the Yoga philosophy deserves some attention on the part of philosophers, more particularly of the physical school of psychologists."

Western intellectuals have indeed been slow in discovering the tremendous wealth of experience and thought crystallized in the ramifying Yoga tradition. Müller's observation still stands, even though here and there a few pioneers have forged ahead to contribute to a better understanding of the yogic heritage.

The scientific study of Yoga commenced only as recently as the mid-1920's and was pioneered by Swami Kuvalayananda, founder of the Kaivalyadhama Institute in Lonavla, South India. A decade later, Shri Yogendra of the Yoga Institute of Bombay started research into the medical aspect of yogic techniques. European research of this kind was not initiated until the 1950's but gained considerable momentum in the 1970's.

This was largely due to the immense popularity of Maharshi Mahesh Yogi's Transcendental Meditation (TM), which reportedly at one time was practiced by some 500,000 Americans.

Once the property of a single culture, Yoga was introduced into the Western hemisphere by great teachers like Swami Vivekananda (chief disciple of the world-famous Paramahamsa Ramakrishna) and Swami Rama Tirtha (a former mathematics professor who came to California in 1902). This first wave of Hindu teachers was followed by Swami Yogendra (a disciple of Paramahamsa Madhavadasa), who visited the United States in 1919. A year later, the vastly popular Paramahamsa Yogananda arrived in Boston to address the International Congress of Religious Liberals and in 1925 founded the Self-Realization Fellowship in Los Angeles. These Yoga masters opened the floodgate to the West. In the intervening decades, we have seen a steady stream of yogins and swamis leaving their homeland to spread Hindu teachings on the other side of the ocean they once were forbidden to traverse.

In the 1930's and 1940's, the numerous works by Paul Brunton introduced thousands of Western seekers to Jnāna-Yoga through the person and teachings of Ramana Maharshi, the gentle sage from Tiruvannamalai, South India. Brunton was one of the first Europeans to dedicate his life to Yoga practice, and his posthumously published *Notebooks* are a testimony to his mastery of the Yoga of wise discrimination between the real and the unreal. There were a few other, less well known spiritual seekers who took Yoga seriously enough to make it their life path and become the first Western Yoga adepts and teachers. Today, there is no dearth of Yoga teachers, although Yoga masters remain a rarity. As the *Kula-Arnava-Tantra* (13.104; 108) noted a thousand or so years ago: Gurus are as numerous as lamps in every house. But, O Goddess, difficult to find is a guru who lights up everything like the Sun. Gurus who rob their disciples of their wealth are numerous. But, O Goddess, difficult to find is a guru who removes the disciples' suffering.

Contemporary Yoga has millions of adherents in Europe and the two Americas. While it is true that most Westerners practice Yoga primarily in order to repair or maintain their health and fitness, there is a growing number of people who treasure it for its timeless wisdom. Some practice it in addition to their own religious faith (thus there is now a Christian Yoga), while others seek to adopt it as a spiritual path without the trimmings of conventional religiosity. In whichever fashion these seekers may relate to Yoga, they all derive meaning from it—a meaning that they feel cannot be found within our highly secularized Western society.

Yoga has become a significant factor in the West's ongoing struggle for self-definition at a time when the old Judeo-Christian value system is crumbling under the onslaught of scientific materialism and rampant consumerism. There are those who envision an emergent new form of Yoga tailored to the needs of the global civilization of the twenty-first century. An early harbinger of this vision was Sri Aurobindo, who, starting in the opening years of the twentieth century, talked about an "Integral Yoga," which found appeal within some intellectual circles of Europe and the United States.

The Meaning and Essence of Yoga

In order to understand today's vital phase of the encounter between Yoga and the West, we need to get a clear picture of the nature and scope of Yoga within its original Indian setting. This is the main purpose of the present essay.

The Sanskrit word yoga is derived from the verbal root *yuj*, meaning literally "to yoke." Traditionally, it is explained as having the dual denotation "union" and "discipline." The term has numerous connotations and is widely used in the Sanskrit language. Its spectrum of meanings ranges from "conjunction" to "occupation" to "equipment."

In the narrow sense of the term, yoga refers to the philosophical system expounded by Patañjali, who probably lived between 200 B.C.E. and 200 C.E. However, his school of thought, as epitomized in the Yoga-Sūtra, represents only one phase in the long and intricate evolution of the yogic heritage. As we shall see, it is but the tip of a vast iceberg, the bulk of which is submerged (that is, unknown to most people).

In the broader sense of the term, yoga denotes "spirituality" or "spiritual/unitive discipline" as it has originated and evolved on the Indian subcontinent. Yoga in this sense can be found in India's three great cultural traditions—Hinduism, Buddhism, and Jainism. The focus of the present essay is on Hindu Yoga.

Often Yoga is said to comprise the following six types: Rāja-Yoga (Patanjali's Classical Yoga), Haṭha-Yoga (the forceful Yoga of bodily control), Karma-Yoga (Yoga of self-transcending action), Bhakti-Yoga (Yoga of devotion), Jnāna-Yoga (Yoga of discriminative wisdom), and Mantra-Yoga (Yoga of the recitation of sacred sounds). But the Sanskrit literature refers to or describes dozens of other approaches. To mention only a few: Tantra-Yoga (Yoga of esoteric ritual), Kuṇḍalinī-Yoga (Yoga of the serpent power), Laya-Yoga (Yoga of dissolution of the elements and the mind), Tāraka-Yoga (Yoga of light phenomena), Nāda-Yoga (Yoga of the subtle inner sound),

Shabda-Yoga (Yoga of sound). Some of these names stand for full-fledged paths; others denote merely aspects of the yogic path. In compounds like dhyāna-yoga, samādhi-yoga, or abhyāsa-yoga the word yoga simply means "practice," "discipline," or "application," namely the discipline of meditation, the practice of ecstasy, the application to practice.

Yoga and Comparative Research

Over the past several decades, our understanding and appreciation of Hindu, Buddhist, and Jaina Yoga have deepened considerably. There are many commonalities between these traditions, but also significant differences not only on the doctrinal but also the practical level. Here is a whole area of comparative research that awaits its pioneers. Even within each of the three cultural traditions, we find a broad spectrum of yogic teachings, some of which stand in contradiction to each other. Notably, there are dualistic and nondualistic schools, as well as mainstream and highly marginal schools (such as the vāma-marga or "left-hand path" in Tantrism).

Yoga is easily the single most complex and diversified spiritual tradition in the world. This alone should make us pay attention to it. Comparative research, through the method of amplification, can help us better understand the various manifestations of Yoga but also our own spiritual tradition (whatever that may be) and our present-day cultural situation. Yoga will not yield its secrets, of course, without attention to practice. The scriptures have always pointed beyond themselves, and there are countless statements to the effect that book knowledge is of no ultimate usefulness. It is good to bear this in mind when approaching Yoga as scholars. This is indeed the researcher's paradox: the very method of scholarship contradicts an essential doctrine of Yoga, namely that it can only be fully grasped in the act of perfect transcendence of the mind itself.

In order to analyze and compare, we must inevitably freeze Yoga in time and treat it like a museum piece, and yet, as Mircea Eliade observed, it is a "living fossil." That is to say, even as we seek to comprehend Yoga through the abstract categories of our research, it continues to evolve and change. But more than that, its very essence lies in the transcendence of all mental (and thus also scholarly) categories.

This insight gives us cause for humility. At the same time, however, producers of knowledge can take justified pride in their work to the degree that it helps shed light on reality and thereby, in whatever modest way, points the way to truth. But, as the Yoga tradition emphasizes, it is never thought that will set one free.

The Yoga tradition itself has had its share of great scholars, such as Śaṃkara, Rāmānuja, and Abhinava Gupta for Hindu Yoga; Nāgārjuna, Atīsha, and Tsongkhapa for Buddhist Yoga; Haribhadra, Hemačandra, and Śubhačandra for Jaina Yoga. Yet, more than scholars, these renowned individuals were first and foremost adepts of the yogic path. They knew whereof they were speaking. We can judge their philosophical or theological work by the same critical standards that we would apply to any other thinker. Yet we ought not to forget that behind all their philosophical or theological endeavors lies their immersion into yogic practice and spiritual experience. Thus while we may find fault with their reasoning, we must not offhandedly dismiss their knowledge base, which is wider than the knowledge base of typical academic philosophy or theology. The only time we can challenge the knowledge base of Yoga thinkers is when we have undertaken the same in-depth exploration of yogic experience. To put it differently, in order to criticize Yoga adepts as philosophers, we ourselves must be philosophers. In order to criticize them as adepts, we ourselves must be adepts. This seems fair and reasonable.

Yoga, Shamanism, and the Magical Realm

In its five thousand or more years of evolution, Yoga has undergone many changes, both in the realm of ideas and even more so in its technology. Its origin lies so far back that it is barely discernible, and perhaps it can be found in paleolithic shamanism. As the German psychiatrist Dietrich Langen has shown, Yoga and archaic shamanism have much in common. The quest for ecstatic transcendence of the human condition appears to be as old as humanity itself and could be called one of its defining characteristics. In our own highly secularized civilization, which largely denies the reality of and access to the ecstatic experience, the same need expresses itself in negative ways through the widespread abuse of alcohol and drugs.

Of course, Yoga represents an intellectually and technologically more sophisticated form of the same impulse that in an earlier age had led to the creation of shamanism. The most significant distinction between shamanism and Yoga is that shamans are specialists in out-of-body experiences and mediumship, whereas the primary objective of yogins is to transcend phenomenal existence as a whole and to recover their essential nature as pure consciousness.

Moreover, in contrast to the shamans, who employ their skills to serve the community as healers and religious mediators, the yogins seek above all their own salvation. In pursuing this goal, however, they may well—as in the case of the Buddhist *bodhisattva*—keep the welfare of others in mind. Still, they typically focus their energy and attention on the supreme good, which is enlightenment or Self-realization. Even Karma-Yoga (Yoga of self-transcending action) and Bhakti-Yoga (Yoga of devotion) must not be misunderstood as social activism. The former seeks to avoid negative karma by abstaining from action that is "tainted" by egoic motives; the latter involves primarily devotion to the Divine, which then spills over into the devotee's social relationships (since everyone is seen as a manifestation of the same Divine).

"Yoga," emphasizes Mircea Eliade in his classic work on the subject, "cannot possibly be confused with shamanism or classed among the techniques of ecstasy. The goal of classic Yoga remains perfect autonomy, enstasis, while shamanism is characterized by its desperate effort to attain the 'condition of a spirit', to accomplish ecstatic flight." However, especially in its Tantric form, the Yoga tradition includes many secondary features that belong to the realm of paranormal competence, which have their parallels and possibly their historical roots in shamanism.

Since time immemorial, the accomplished Yoga adepts have popularly been viewed not only as masters of gnosis (jnāna-vid) but also as possessors of extraordinary powers and abilities called *siddhis*. The Sanskrit literature is replete with stories of yogins exercising, for better or for worse, their thaumaturgical talents. Yet, the ultimate yogic siddhi has always been considered to be perfect self-transcendence through the dawning of wisdom. In fact, the great God-like powers are thought to come with liberation itself. In this sense, the Kashmiri sage Utpaladeva can declare in his celebrated *Shiva-Stotra-Avalī* (1.25) that the powers "beginning with miniaturization (aṇimā) and ending in liberation are inherent in the creeper of Your love that has ripened."

Some modern authorities favoring a thoroughly demythologized world view have expressed their regret at the presence of magical elements in Yoga. However, in light of the solid findings of parapsychology, such an attitude is neither reasonable nor helpful in understanding Yoga. If yogins continue to speak of paranormal abilities, it is undoubtedly because these are very much part of their life experience. At the same time, we need not accept each and every claim uncritically. Nor should we blindly accept the explanations offered by the authorities of Yoga for these unusual abilities. If the concern with paranormal skills is a "survival" from an earlier age, we must remember that the magical consciousness of early humanity is still very much present in all of us. To deny its presence in us is to deny part of ourselves. Thus rather than dismiss this side of Yoga as atavistic, students and researchers of Yoga would do better to avail themselves of the yogic techniques that create access to the magical dimension of consciousness and test the claims in the crucible of personal practice.

Archaic Yoga

When reflecting on the long history of Yoga, it is useful to divide what in actuality is a continuity of developments into the following five phases: 1) Archaic Yoga; 2) Preclassical Yoga; 3) Classical Yoga; 4) Postclassical Yoga; 5) Modern Yoga. These phases, which are merely convenient constructs, can of course be further subdivided. As we ascend the ladder of history, the materials for each phase become increasingly voluminous, diversified, and complex and thus ever more difficult to oversee. The heritage of Yoga extends not only over Hinduism, Buddhism, and Jainism, but also over many languages (including Sanskrit, Tamil, Pali, Prakrit, Tibetan, Marathi, Bengali, Urdu, and Hindi). There is no one Yoga researcher who has mastered all these languages, let alone the information (and wisdom) contained in the thousands of scriptures composed in them. Our knowledge of Yoga, therefore, is still rather fragmentary. It is impossible to provide here more than the barest thumbnail sketch of the evolution of Yoga as we understand it today.

The developmental phase of Archaic Yoga extends from the unknown (conjectural) origin in the spirituality of the Stone Age to the ruminations of the Vedas, notably the Ṛgveda and the Atharva-Veda, and to some extent the Brāhmaṇas and Āraṇyakas. Thus we can usefully distinguish three sub-types or sub-phases:

1. Shamanic Proto-Yoga of the pre-Vedic era
2. Vedic Yoga proper, as found in the four Vedic Samhitās
3. Late Vedic Yoga of the Brāhmaṇas and Āranyakas

The yogic teachings found in the early Vedic literature are strikingly different from those of later Yoga and are not even propounded under that name, which has prompted most scholars to reject the label "Yoga" for them. Yet, in so doing they inadvertently overemphasize difference where we also find a strong underlying continuity of essential ideas and practices. Now that the Vedic scriptures have been plausibly linked with the Indus-Sarasvati civilization and its artifacts, this fundamental continuity within India's protracted cultural history has become more evident and needs to be fully appreciated also in the context of the history of Yoga.

When we study the 1028 hymns of the Ṛgveda (Knowledge of Praise) carefully, we find that the early Vedic spirituality revolved around the ideal of harmony (rta). The Vedic people looked to their seer-bards (ṛshi) for the wisdom that would allow them to conduct their lives in flawless resonance with the cosmic order. The seers aspired to illumined vision (dhī), or higher understanding deriving from meditative absorption and ecstatic transcendence of the limiting rational mind. They accomplished this through prayerful meditation combined with ritual (karman), recitation of sacred words (mantra), and breath control, producing in themselves a state of incandescence (tapas). This old Sanskrit word means "heat" but also "ardor," and it is employed to denote the scorching heat of the sun as well as the inner heat created by intense spiritual practice and asceticism. The Vedic tapas is Yoga.

In early Vedic times, the technical term for "prayer" or "prayerful contemplation" was brahman, which much later came to stand for the ultimate Reality it was designed to reveal. Prayerful contemplation was thought to rise to the level of the deities—Gods like Indra, Agni, and Sūrya—and from there to return again like wagons loaded with precious goods for the benefit of the seer and his community. The seers asked that their meditations yield the "treasure of vigor," by which they meant the well-being and abundance of energy accruing from contact with the invisible world of higher beings. Some hymn composers compared prayerful meditation to God Indra's swift steed, while others likened it to a chariot.

Yet, even though prayerful meditation was generated by the seer's mental focusing, it was also understood to be "God-given" (deva-datta). Because of this, the Vedas came to be considered as divine revelation. As one seer-bard put it: "Let prayerful meditation spring forth from the abode of Truth" (Ṛgveda 7.36.1). All higher wisdom can be said to be revelatory, since it originates in a dimension that transcends the mind. This is captured, for instance, in the name of Hiraṇyagarbha, who is traditionally put forward as the first teacher of Yoga. The name means "Golden Womb," which in Vedāntic cosmogony refers to the point of origin of both world and mind.

Contrary to widespread opinion, the word yoga is used in the Ṛgveda in ways suggesting its subsequent technical connotation. Thus the term yoga and its verbal forms are used in the sense of "yoking" horses to a chariot, and, as a deeper reading of the Vedic hymns uncovers, this is to be understood symbolically rather than literally. Indeed, the seers were master craftsmen, whose sacred poetry is still only inadequately understood, because until recently scholars have by and large failed to appreciate its metaphorical sophistication. The more we abandon the idea that the Vedas are merely primitive poetry, the more we will be able to glimpse the rich spirituality of the early Vedic people and its astounding continuity with later Hinduism.

The Archaic Yoga of the Vedas contains all the basic psychocosmological and psychotechnological elements of subsequent Yoga. Thus the history of Yoga is one of refinement and elaboration of core ideas and practices that were created by the Vedic seers and have apparently stood the test of time. Even the Tantras, which portray the Vedic teachings as inefficient for the dark age (kali-yuga), are upon closer inspection not as thoroughly innovative as they claim to be. Rather, the Tantric heritage is firmly built upon the foundations laid thousands of years before by the Vedic seers and the composers of the ritual texts of the Brāhmaṇas and Āraṇyakas. This is a sobering realization.

Preclassical Yoga

The developmental phase of Preclassical Yoga covers a wide range of schools and teachings, starting with the early Upaniṣads (now placeable between 1800-1500 B.C.E.) and proceeding to the Mahâbhârata (especially the Bhagavadgītā and the Mokṣa-Dharma sections), the Rāmāyana, the early Purāṇas, the second generation of Upaniṣads (particularly the Katha-, the Maitrāyanīya-, and the Śvetāṣvatara-Upaniṣad), the law books (especially the Manu-Sṃriti), the medical books (notably the Charaka- and the Suṣruta-Saṃhitā), and other similar nonreligious works. This literature covers a period of roughly two thousand years, from the late Vedic era to the beginning of the Common Era. A study of these works quickly reveals the richness and remarkable variety of the early yogic heritage, a clear indication of the creative force unleashed by personal experimentation and direct experience. When we examine the earliest Upaniṣads—Bṛhad-Āraṇyaka-, Chāndogya-, and Taittirīya-Upaniṣad—we find that they continue the age-old Vedic teachings, articulating them in greater detail and here and there adding new features. For instance, most but not all scholars regard the karma doctrine and the teachings about the transcendental Self (ātman, puruṣa) as Upaniṣadic innovations. What is certain is that these texts for the first time speak openly about these ideas. In particular, the Upaniṣads wax eloquent about the Self and its identity with the ultimate Reality (often called brahman). They also furnish teachings about the subtle (sūkśma) aspects of the human being, paving the way for the elaborate notions of later Tantrism.

It is in the Taittirīya-Upaniṣad (2.4.1) that the word yoga is mentioned, still obliquely, in connection with the attainment of gnosis. However, this does not mean, as some authorities have maintained, that this is the birthplace of Yoga. History existed long before the term "history" was invented. The same holds true of Yoga. Leaning on Vedic imagery, the Kaṭha-Upaniṣad (3.3ff.) expressly states that the senses are like unruly horses that must be firmly controlled by the charioteer, which is the mind. The sage must become undistracted (apramatta), for as the text (6.11) tells us, "Yoga can be acquired and lost." This phrase—yoga-kśema in Sanskrit—clearly harks back to the Ṛgveda, again a sign of the continuity of these teachings. After the Kaṭha-Upaniṣad, references to the yogic path become increasingly explicit and elaborated. The first systematization is attempted in the Maitrāyanīya-Upaniṣad (6.18), which outlines a six-limbed (shad-anga) path comprising breath control (prāṇāyāma), sensory inhibition (pratyāhāra), meditation (dhyāna), concentration (dhāranā), examination (tarka), and ecstasy (samādhi).

The first full-fledged Yoga scripture is the Bhagavadgītā, which is an integral part of the Mahābhārata epic. This text, which understands itself (according to the colophon) as an Upaniṣad and has been accorded the honorific status of one, was probably composed in its present version before or at the time of the Buddha. The Gītā is essentially a didactic conversation between the God-man Kṛṣṇa and Prince Arjuna, who is in a quandary over his duties as a warrior—a convincing metaphor for human life itself. The occasion for the initiatic teachings is the imminent war between the Kauravas and the Pāndavas (who sought to regain their kingdom, which was being unlawfully and poorly governed by their cousins).

The Gītā mentions that by its time Yoga was already very ancient, and Lord Kṛṣṇa is presented as merely recapitulating an earlier revelation. This scripture represents a first effort to synthesize the various strands of the yogic tradition. Thus it seeks to blend Karma-Yoga, Bhakti-Yoga, and Jnāna-Yoga. The Gītā has had an enormous influence on subsequent Hindu thought and culture, as is apparent, for instance, from the many "imitation" Gītā's modeled after the original.

Scholars are uncertain about the age of the Mahābhārata but tend to place its didactic portions (notably the Mokṣa-Dharma) between 200 B.C.E. and 200 C.E., which may be too late. Some of the materials—especially those that speak of the spiritual work as tapas (asceticism) rather than yoga—may belong to the pre-Buddhist period. It is likely that the core of the epic reaches back to the time of the Bhārata war, which is described in it in great detail. It is equally likely that some of the spiritual teachings originated at that time as well, which may have been about 1500 B.C.E. or, according to some researchers, prior to the cataclysmic event that shook the north of

India about 1900 B.C.E. Be that as it may, the teachings present in the epic clearly show the great diversification of Yoga in the time preceding the emergence of Classical Yoga. Preclassical Yoga is Sāmkhya-Yoga, a tradition in which pan-en-theistic Vedānta is still organically merged with Sāmkhya-style ontology and yogic meditation technology.

Only later did this tradition crystallize into the separate streams of philosophical Sāmkhya and Yoga. The former, as articulated in the Sāmkhya-Kārikā of Īshvara Kṛṣṇa (fourth century C.E.), proceeds on the basis of discrimination and renunciation, while the latter's modus operandi is meditation. The Sāmkhya school of thought specialized in analyzing the categories of existence (called tattvas) as a prelude to the spiritual work of distinguishing between Self and non-self, that is, between the two mutually exclusive principles of pure Consciousness and materiality, or puruṣa and prakṛiti.

Classical Yoga

The luxuriant proliferation of Preclassical Yoga schools created a need for systematization. It was Patāñjali who—perhaps in response to the growing influence of Buddhism—rose to the challenge by composing his well-known Yoga-Sūtra. Nothing definite is known about him, although native Indian tradition identifies him with his namesake, the famous grammarian who lived about 200 B.C.E. This identification is unconvincing, however, and judging from the technical vocabulary of the Yoga-Sūtra, its creator more likely lived in the first or second century C.E. and appears to have been familiar with Buddhism. This relatively late date for the Yoga-Sūtra says nothing about the age of the ideas presented in it, which are clearly similar to the Sāmkhya-Yoga teachings of the preclassical period.

Consisting of 195 aphorisms (sūtra), this work is the source text of the yoga-darśana (Yoga view), which came to be regarded as one of the six principal philosophical systems of Hinduism. The other five are Sāmkhya, Nyāya, Vaiśeṣhika, Mīmāmsā, and Vedānta. By yoga-darśana, or Classical Yoga, is meant the body of teachings given by Patāñjali and explained, expanded, and to some degree modified by subsequent authorities. The most important commentaries on Patāñjali's text are the Yoga-Bhāṣhya of Vyāsa, the Tattva-Vaishāradī of Vāčaspati Mishra, the Yoga-Vārttika of Vijñāna Bhikshu, and the Yoga-Bhāṣhya-Vivaraṇa of Shankara Bhagavatpāda (who in all probability is identical to the famous Vedānta preceptor).

Classical Yoga is best known for its delineation of the eight-limbed (aṣṭa-anga) path consisting of moral observance (yama), self-discipline (niyama), posture (āsana), breath control (prāṇāyāma), sensory inhibition (pratyāhāra), concentration (dhāranā), meditation (dhyāna), and ecstasy (samādhi). Moral observance comprises nonharming (ahiṃsā), truthfulness (satya), nonstealing (asteya), chastity (brahmačarya), and greedlessness (aparigraha), which constitute the "great vow" that is applicable in all situations. Self-discipline consists of purity (śauča), contentment (saṃtoṣa), asceticism (tapas), self-study (svādhyāya), and devotion to the Lord (īshvara-pranidhāna). All these practices are designed to regulate the yogin's social and personal life in an effort to reduce the production of unwholesome volition and thus of negative karma.

Patāñjali does not mention any specific postures but simply states that āsana should be steady and comfortable. Its function is to immobilize the body in order to facilitate the meditative process. Later on, Haṭha-Yoga introduced the idea of postural practice as a means to flexibility and health, and the adepts of this form of Yoga have demonstrated tremendous inventiveness in developing a large arsenal of postures for that purpose.

Prāṇāyāma, the fourth limb of the eightfold path, means literally "extension of the breath." It is understood that prāṇa denotes both "breath" and the life energy behind it. The regulation of breathing belongs to the oldest elements of yogic practice. Already the Vedic yogins—the ṛshis and munis—and probably also their shamanic forerunners had a clear understanding of the vital connection between the breath and the mind. By regulating (harmonizing) the breath, they sought to balance the mind and tap its hidden potential. In medieval times, the masters of Hatha-Yoga also explored the health benefits of controlled breathing. Patāñjali explains breath control as "interrupting the flow of inhalation and exhalation," that is, the forced suspension of breathing. He also speaks of a fourth state in this process, which is the spontaneous suspension that occurs in deep meditation.

Patāñjali defines sensory inhibition as the disjunction of the senses from the objective environment and their imitation of the nature of the mind. As the senses become subdued, concentration takes place, which is focusing the mind upon a single locus (deṣha), be it an abstract idea, a sound vibration, or some part of the body (such as the heart or the spot between the eyebrows). Meditation is a deepening of the unified consciousness created through the preceding steps. In due course, this leads to the state of ecstasy, which is of two broad types: samprajnāta-samādhi or "conscious ecstasy" and asamprajnāta-samādhi or "supraconscious ecstasy."

In the former state, the yogin merges with the object of his contemplation—be it a tree or the universe as a whole. This experience of ontic identification can occur at various levels (from coarse to very subtle) and is accompanied by instantaneous intuitions (rather than discursive thought). In the latter state, ecstatic identification is free from such intuitions. But far from being an unconscious condition, as Carl Gustav Jung and others have maintained, it is by the testimony of those who have actually experienced it a state of superlative consciousness without an object.

The entire process, from the moral observances to the highest ecstatic state, is one of progressive restriction (nirodha). All the yogin's energies are pulled away from the outside world and focused, like a laser beam, upon the transcendental Self. If the ordinary mind can be described as being centrifugal, the yogin's mind is centripetal or, as Patāñjali states, "back-facing" (pratyanč). Reversal of all normal activities and tendencies is indeed the hallmark of Yoga.

Apart from his formulation of the eight limbs (anga) of Yoga, Patāñjali also made a significant contribution to yogic metaphysics and metapsychology. Of special merit is his systematic discussion of the causes of affliction (kleṣa)—ignorance, "I-am-ness" (asmitā), attachment, aversion, and the will to live—which drive the unenlightened mind. The task of Yoga is to eliminate the causes of suffering at the level of the subconscious karmic deposits (āśaya). These are the concatenations (vāsanā) of subconscious activators (saṃskāra) left behind in the depth of the mind as a result of all our volitional activity.

The purpose of the eightfold Yoga is to purify the conditional personality to a point where it can faithfully reflect the "light" of the transcendental Self (puruṣa). In fact, the Yoga-Sūtra (3.55) defines liberation as the state in which the mind's lucidity factor (called sattva) is equal in purity to the Self.

Patāñjali presents the entire spiritual process as the Self's gradual disentanglement from all levels of Nature (prakṛiti). His statements have traditionally been interpreted as implying a radical dualism between the principle of consciousness and the principle of materiality, or Self and non-self. However, nowhere does the Yoga-Sūtra explicitly proclaim a dualistic metaphysics, and Patāñjali's aphorisms could all be accommodated within the kind of qualified nondualism (or pan-en-theism) that characterizes the schools of Preclassical Yoga. Whatever the correct interpretation may be, it is a historical fact that Classical Yoga has not been successful as a philosophical darśana. Although the eight-limbed model of the path has been adopted by many other schools and traditions, they have typically found fault with Patāñjali's alleged dualistic metaphysics. In the sixteenth century, Vijnāna Bhikṣu endeavored to bring Classical Yoga into the mainstream of Hindu philosophy by reinterpreting Patāñjali's work in Vedāntic terms. This brings us to Postclassical Yoga.

Postclassical Yoga

Except for the interlude of Classical Yoga, which, if we can believe consensus opinion, is strictly dualistic, the Hindu Yoga authorities have always subscribed to one or the other variety of nondualism. Preclassical Yoga, as we have seen, was nondualistic Sāṃkhya-Yoga. In the era following Patāñjali, Yoga came increasingly under the influence of the more successful metaphysics of Vedânta and also Tantra.

The Sanskrit literature of Postclassical Yoga is vast and includes, inter alia, the Āgamas, the Tantras, the Pančataṇtra Samhitās, the Purāṇas, the Yoga-Upaniṣads, the voluminous Yoga-Vāsiṣṭtha, the Haṭha-Yoga manuals, and the numerous textbooks (śāstra) of the various religious communities (notably the Shaivas and Vaishnavas), as well as their respective commentaries and subcommentaries. There also is a huge literature in Tamil and other vernacular languages that has been little studied thus far.

In the postclassical era we witness a continuing effort to refine both philosophical comprehension and spiritual practice. A good example of the possibility of creative innovation even after several thousand years is the Kashmiri Śaiva tradition, as exemplified in the ingenious work of the tenth-century adept and scholar Abhinava Gupta.

The greatest breakthrough in the domain of yogic practice was made in the Tantric schools of kaya-sādhanā (body discipline), especially Hatha-Yoga. This branch of Yoga was created by Goraksha Nātha, who probably lived in the tenth century C.E. This yogic approach, which was vigorously pursued by the nāthas and siddhas of North India and the sittars of South India, grew out of the new Tantric appreciation of the world and thus also of the human body as a manifestation of the Goddess Power (Śakti). Instead of dismissing the body as a "bag of filth," as did some of the earlier Upaniṣads, the Tantric masters looked upon it as a "temple of the Divine," that is, a suitable platform for realizing the Self. This represented a significant shift in perception, which was the necessary prelude for Hatha-Yoga with its interest in health restoration and maintenance, longevity, and even immortality in a transubstantiated body.

The haṭha-yogin seeks to create a transmuted body that not only can withstand the fire of ecstasy but also serve as a vehicle for the paranormal powers (siddhi) generated through Self-realization and the yogic processes leading up to it. In order to attain both Self-realization, or liberation, and immortality in the realm of forms, the haṭha-yogin must purify the elements of the body and create a "divine body" (divya-śharīra) that is independent of the laws of Nature. Like the Tantric practitioners at large, the hatha-yogins pay utmost attention to the intermediate realm, which is wedged between the physical body and the ultimate Being-Consciousness-Bliss: the domain of the subtle body and its multilevel environment.

The agent of this process of transubstantiation in Tantra and haṭha-yoga is the microcosmic counterpart of the divine Power itself, which is called kuṇḍalinī-śakti (serpent power). It is typically awakened in the lowest psychoenergetic focal point at the base of the spinal column and then, primarily through concentration and breath control, guided upward along the bodily axis to the topmost focal point at the crown of the head. There the kundalinī-śakti reenters infinity. This process is mystically referred to as the union between Śakti and her divine spouse Śiva. It coincides with the attainment of the ecstatic state, which is said to be more complete than the ecstatic state reached by non-Tantric means.

Tantrism and other more holistic schools of Yoga in the postclassical period understand liberation not as an otherworldly state of existence but as the realization of the true condition of the present moment. This realization is referred to as "spontaneous ecstasy" (sahaja-samādhi) or "living liberation" (jīvan-mukti), which is permanent and irrevocable. In Tantric terms, this epitomizes the intrinsic co-essentiality of immanence (samsāra) and transcendence (nirvāṇa).

Modern Yoga

The label "Modern Yoga" can conveniently be applied to Yoga as it has unfolded in our present century ever since the apostolic work of Swami Vivekananda. In teaching Westerners, he and subsequent Hindu adepts to varying degrees have adapted the yogic heritage to the needs of the new cultural environment. More recently, Western-born Yoga teachers without particular allegiance to either Hinduism or the spiritual content of Yoga have created their own secularized versions. Thus Modern Yoga is a colorful tapestry of traditional and decidedly untraditional yogic schools and teachings. In some cases, what goes by the name of "Yoga" bears little resemblance to this age-old tradition. Yet, there is a solid core of genuine teachings and teachers who, it is hoped, will preserve the yogic heritage for the twenty-first century. This is a vital desideratum considering the numerous serious challenges we are facing.

What these challenges are has been spelled out by many foresightful thinkers. It is becoming more and more clear that our increasingly global civilization cannot succeed without a radical psychological reform of its members. We must learn to think and feel globally as members of the human family rather than a particular culture, creed, or race. To be able to do so, however, calls for a significant shift in our perception of the world and our intention toward it. This shift, moreover, must be made by each individual, as it cannot be forced upon anyone. We are challenged to become mature human beings by free choice. This entails tapping into our spiritual potential, and here the Yoga tradition has a vast store of information, wisdom, and technology to offer.

While the Yoga masters of yore could not have foreseen the details of our present-day circumstance, they addressed themselves to the human condition, which has basically remained the same. To put it succinctly: We, as physical organisms, are all destined to die. This places a firm ceiling on our experience, which inevitably impacts our life. We can turn a blind eye to this irrevocable fact, as do many people, or we can use it as a starting point for considering the gift of life and how we might use it wisely. If we choose the latter option, we are bound to arrive at a consideration of the spiritual capacity innate in the human species. Here Yoga has much to teach us. Its experiential wisdom is enormous, though we must be prepared to explore it in the same fashion in which it was gathered: through personal experimentation.

To summarize, broadly understood, Yoga is both an art and a science. It is an art because it addresses our innermost concerns and hopes, seeking to wrest from us a response of heart and will. Yoga is also a science because its psychotechnology is most exacting, distilled from millennia of experimentation and experience. It prescribes very precise means to accomplish definite ends, but allows for the fact that the same human potential manifests in very individual ways. Thus Yoga has great practical relevance for our contemporary quest for meaning, wholeness, harmony, and transcendence.

End Notes

1. The Yoga-Sutra offers another definition in aphorism 4.34, according to which liberation (kaivalya) results when the primary constituents (guṇa) of Nature resolve back into the transcendental core of Nature, thus ending the Self's entanglement with all levels of material existence.

Works Cited

Aurobindo, Sri. 1957. *The Synthesis of Yoga.* Pondicherry, India: Sri Aurobindo Ashram

Avalon, A. (Sir John Woodroffe). 1974. *The Serpent Power.* New York: Dover Publication. First published 1919.

Brunton, P. 1984-1988. *The Notebooks of Paul Brunton*, 16 vols. Burdett, NY: Larson Publications

Criswell, Eleanor. 1989. *How Yoga works: An Introduction to Somatic Yoga.* Novato, CA: Freeperson Press.

Eliade, Mircea. 1973. *Yoga: Immortality and Freedom.* Princeton: Princeton University Press.

__________. 1964, 1972. *Shamanism: Archaic Techniques of Ecstasy.* Princeton: Princeton University Press,

Feuerstein, Georg. 1997. *Shambhala Encyclopedia of Yoga.* Boston, MA: Shambhala Publications.

____________. 1996. *Shambhala Guide to Yoga.* Boston, MA: Shambhala Publication.

____________. 1992. *Wholeness or Transcendence? Ancient Lessons for the Emerging Global Civilization.* Burdett, NY: Larson Publications.

____________.1990. *The Yoga-Sutra of Patanjali: A New Translation and Commentary.* Rochester, VT: Inner Traditions.

Feuerstein, G., S. Kak, and D. Frawley. 1995. *In Search of the Cradle of Civilization* Wheaton, IL: Quest Books.

Muller, M. 1899. *The Six Systems of Indian Philosophy.* London: Longman, Green and Co.

Sannella, Lee. 1987. *The Kundalini Experience.* Lower Lake, CA: Integral Publishing.

Varenne, Jean. 1976. *Yoga and the Hindu Tradition.* Chicago, IL: University of Chicago Press.

Vivekananda, Swami. 1970. *The Complete Works of Swami Vivekananda.* Calcutta: Advaita Ashrama.

Chapter 12

Hinduism: The Quest for One In Many

Rajeshwari V. Pandharipande

"Fetch me a fruit of the banyan tree."
"Here is one, Sir."
"Break it."
"I have broken it, Sir."
"What do you see?"
"Very tiny seeds, Sir."
"Break one."
"I have broken it, Sir."
"Now what do you see?"
"Nothing, Sir."
"My son," the father said,
"What you do not see is the essence; and in that essence the mighty banyan tree exists. Believe me, my son, in that essence is the Self of all that is. That is the True, that is the Self. And you are that Śvetaketu!"

—Chāndogya Upaniṣad (5:13)

The above conversation between a learned father and his son Śvetaketu in one of the major Hindu scriptures succinctly summarizes the essence of Hindu philosophy, theology, rituals, and social and individual ethics. It reveals the foundational belief of

Hinduism, that there is one eternal base of this multifaceted universe and that True Reality (the Divine) is beyond the observable (the tree, the fruit, or the seeds). The goal is to realize the essential divinity within oneself and within all forms of existence. The method (path) for gaining this knowledge consists in going beyond the observable (diversity) and finding a unified underlying principle. Thus Hinduism, from its inception, remains a system which finds unity within diversity and cohesiveness within contradictions at the physical as well as conceptual levels.

Hinduism can be described as a philosophy of Viśva Darşana, 'Universal Vision' a vision of unity in the diversity of concrete and conceptual forms. The one theme which runs through Hindu philosophy, mythology, and ritual— the three major aspects of religion— is this: There is diversity at all observable levels, but this diversity is the manifestation of a single underlying principle. To deny the unity of all is a denial of transcendence and the eternity of the Divine; to deny diversity is to deny human experience; to deny the connection between the One and the many is ignorance. This is succintly presented in the Bhagavadgītā, one of the most highly venerated scriptures of Hinduism (10.32), where Kṛṣṇa, an incarnation of God, tells Arjuna, his friend and disciple, "I am the beginning, the middle, and the end of creations, Arjuna. Of sciences, I am the science of the Self; I am the dispute of the orators."

In this chapter, I will discribe various facets of Hinduism (scriptures, beliefs, rituals, and history) and point out how Hinduism has resolved the ever-emerging tension between diversity and unity. It has done this through its vision of reality as the "third eye" of knowledge (BhagavadGītā 11.8), which takes in the vision of diversity experienced by the two eyes and provides a vision of the unity of them all.

Hinduism: Preliminaries

Hinduism is the religion of Hindus, who trace their heritage in India for at least 3000 years. They constitute 83 percent of India's current population. However, there are also Hindus who have migrated to the United Kingdom, the United States, Canada, Guyana, Fiji, and other countries. Today, the total population of Hindus worldwide is about 800 million.

The Hindu system of beliefs in its earliest form (about 2000 C.E.) belonged to the Āryans, a branch of the Indo-European people who came to India from Central Europe/Asia. The Vedas, the earliest scriptures of Hinduism, were composed in Sanskrit, an Indo-European language, which is structurally similar to Latin. Over a period of 3000 years, the Āryan system of beliefs blended with the beliefs of the

Indus Valley Civilization as well as that of the Dravidians who lived in India prior to the arrival of the Āryans. Thus, what we call Hinduism today is a blend of the beliefs of the indigenous people and the Āryans who came to India. Hinduism has also come in contact with Buddhism (from the time of its inception in the 6th century C.E.), Islam (12th century C.E. to 17th century C.E.), and Christianity (from the 18th to the 20th century C.E.), and these have also influenced its identity .

In order to understand the complexity of the markers of Hindu identity some facts about Hinduism need to be taken into account. Hinduism has never been an organized institutionalized religion; there is no one founder of Hinduism; there are no Hindu counterparts of organized Christian churches which officially or semi-officially determine religious behavior. Instead, what we see today as the Hindu identity is the culmination of diverse patterns of beliefs and behaviors which have emerged over a long period of time as responses to the demands of socio-political realities. Hinduism is a river, constantly changing its course, adapting to different landscapes, constantly expanding its territory yet maintaining its continuity; it absorbs the new into the old underlying conceptual framework. Hinduism is what Yadav (1980:45) correctly calls, "a rolling conference of conceptual spaces, all of them facing all and all of them requiring all."

The problem of defining Hinduism has perplexed scholars because mutually contradictory (or apparently contradictory) beliefs can be claimed by Hindus to be legitimate beliefs. Thus, belief in the Vedas (the earliest scriptures of the Āryans) co-exists with belief in other scriptures such as the Bhagavadgītā, the Purāṇas (collections of stories of ancient gods), the epics, or no scriptures at all. Belief in one abstract divine power is as much a marker of Hinduism as the belief in multitudes of gods in various shapes, colors, and forms. A ritualist would insist that the performance of religious rituals (e.g., reciting prayers, celebrating religious festivals, etc.) is the single most important differentia of a Hindu, while some other Hindus would argue that rituals are unnecessary, and instead, performance of social/family duties or professional duties is the most religious act. It should be remembered that heterogeneity of languages, scriptures, and practices has always been deeply ingrained in Hinduism. Moreover, its contact with other systems has only accentuated this further. As a result, the search for a set of specific Hindu beliefs with the exclusion of their respective opposites is as futile as the search for śaśasṛnga ('rabbit horns,' i.e. that which is non-existent). More importantly, such a search is misguided, and it misses what is most crucial to Hindu identity; namely, unity in diversity. Rather, in order to understand the nature of Hindu ism, it is necessary to understand its underlying conceptual framework, which sanctions the above-mentioned inconsistencies by treating apparent opposites and contradictions as co-existing possibilities and perspectives rather than mutually exclusive realities.

It is interesting to note that the term "Hindu" is not used by Hindus to identify themselves. Rather, it is an alien term used by the Muslims who invaded India in the 12th-13th century C.E. and who called the land and the people around the river Sindhu, "Hindu." Through this usage, the people's belief-system came to be known as "Hinduism." Hindus themselves call their system of beliefs *Sanatana Dharma*, 'the system of Eternal laws,'— a system which involves a two-fold quest: the quest for the eternal laws which underlie this universe of phenomenal reality, as well as the quest for that which lies beyond phenomenal reality. The term dharma, which means 'that which holds together' (from the Sanskrit root dhṛ, 'to hold') is interpreted within Hinduism as a set of universal laws which hold the universe together. According to Hinduism, these laws govern the inner (spiritual) and outer (phenomenal) dimensions of the human world. To be a Hindu is to be involved in this search—to accept that religion is to accept a cosmic science. To be a Hindu is to be a seeker of knowledge. This is the reason why there has never existed a dichotomy between science and religion in the history of Hinduism. Since all branches of knowledge are viewed as religious, no knowledge is viewed as profane because it is believed to reveal one of the dimensions of the underlying system of laws (Ṛta, 'the way things exist and function'). A scientist who does not accept the gods and goddesses of the system is as much a Hindu as a priest who does. Sciences such as astronomy and mathematics were included in the Vedic studies and this view of Hinduism underlies the nature and function of the scriptures in Hinduism. (See Kesavan, this volume.)

Hindu Scriptures: Revelation as Authority

As mentioned earlier, Hinduism admits several texts as legitimate scriptures. The major scriptures are of two types: the Śruti ('those which are heard/revealed'), which include the Vedas (the four sacred books of the Āryans), the Upaniṣads (philosophical treatises on the Vedas), and the Brāhmaṇas (the manuals of the Vedic rituals); and the Smṛti ('those which are remembered'), which include the Vedāngās (the accessories of the Vedas, literally the limbs of the Vedas), the Dharma Śāstras ('the law books'), the Nibandhas ('the books of the domestic rituals and rites'), the Purāṇas ('collections of the stories of ancient gods'), and the Rāmāyaṇa and the Mahābhārata (the two great epics of Hinduism). The Smṛti texts are separated from the Śrutis by at least 700 to 800 years. Additionally, the teachings of the mystics and saints from various times are admitted as legitimate scriptures by the Hindus. Basavaṇṇa's religious songs (12th century C.E.) in Karnataka , Jñāneśvara's writings (12th century C.E.) in Maharashtra, Tulsīdāsa's Rāmačaritmānas (16th century C.E.) in the North, Ramakrishna's sayings in Bengal (19th century C.E.), and Satya Saibābā's words in the 20th century are all "scriptures" for Hindus.

The question may be asked, what authenticates these texts as scriptures? The answer is that they are the records of the "ultimate truths" (*sat*) revealed to the 'visionaries'. Embedded in the belief of the eternal laws, discussed above, is the assumption that those laws were not made by human beings (apauruṣeya); they can only be *revealed* to human beings. Those who understood, realized, or experienced those laws are called ṛṣis ('seers', 'visionaries'), not the makers of the laws. Saints and mystics experienced the eternal laws and the ultimate reality. These experiences are documented in different languages as teachings, biographies or epics composed by or about them. This view of scriptures explains why there are so many Hindu scriptures. The difference between the two types of scriptures—Śruti (that which is heard or directly experienced) and Smrti (that which is remembered)—is that the former are the records of the "truths" as they were *experienced* by the visionaries while the latter are the records of the "truths" as they were *remembered* at a later period in time.

To be a Hindu is to accept that the eternal laws do not change (nor does their experience), but the expression of the experience is bound to change along with the linguistic and sociocultural context; hence there are bound to be many Hindu scriptures. It is the experience of the Truth which authenticates a scripture. So vital is the experience of authenticity that when Gandhi was asked, "And where do you find the seal of authority?" he said, pointing to his breast, "I exercise my judgement about every scripture including the Gītā. I cannot let a scriptural text supercede my reason." (Harijan December 12, 1936, cited in Shaurie 1979:378).

Hindu Beliefs

In the following sections, I will present some of the basic beliefs of Hinduism. The discussion in these sections focuses on how Hinduism maintains and justifies its basic postulate of unity in diversity within the context of its notions of God, the world, the goal of life, the paths to attain that goal, and the structure of social classes.

God in Hinduism: One or Many

When asked, "Who is your God?," Hindus may provide countless names, including Śiva,the god of destruction; Viṣṇu, the god of sustenance; Gaṇeśa, the elephant headed god; or Kālī, the goddess, wife of Śiva. Some may declare, "Our God is nameless, and formless—how can I describe him?" If one asks, in order to better understand the above answers, "What is *not* God in Hinduism?" the answer one is most likely to get is "There is not even a particle of dust in the world that is not divine!" What is one to make of this? The fact is that in Hinduism, God is believed to be the One, omniscient, omnipotent Reality which transcends the phenomenal reality of multiple forms and yet pervades them. In spite of this, there has been no time in the history of Hinduism when there were not many gods. Their nature, character and forms, and their relationship to God have changed at different times, but they nevertheless did exist.

The relationship between One and many gods was interpreted variously at different points in time. The following discussion shows how this apparent dichotomy between One God and many gods is resolved in Hinduism.

Although the all-pervasiveness of God was fully developed in the Upaniṣads, which chronologically followed the Vedas, the concept of the oneness of God, and its all-pervasive power is quite visible in the Vedas. In the Vedas, nature gods such as Sūrya (the sun), Agni (fire), Uṣas (dawn), and Indra (the raingod) are worshipped in sacrificial rituals for worldly prosperity. Although these gods appear to be purely anthropomorphic, as Dandekar (1967), Bose (1966), and others have correctly pointed out, these many gods (*devas*) indeed are depicted as many powers of the same underlying power. The overlapping descriptions of these gods, and the recognition of each as the highest power support the assumption that in the Vedas, many gods were perceived as manifestations or powers of the highest, one, eternal, all-pervasive Reality. So similar are the descriptions that in one hymn the sacrificer asks, 'Which god should I worship with the offerings?' (kasmai devāya haviṣā vidhema?) It is clearly mentioned in the Ṛgveda (1.164.46), "God is one, the learned call it variously." Atharva Veda (13.4) also illustrates the oneness of devas. "He is the one and one alone, and in him all Devas become the One alone." These gods are created from that one self-existing energy, says one of the hymns of the Ṛgveda (10.190).

The Upaniṣads fully develop the nature of God as one all-pervasive, eternal Reality which is called Brahman (sarvaṃ khalu idam Brahma--Chāndogya Upaniṣad 3.14.1). The blissful Brahman is both the creator and sustainer, and in Brahman the created universe dissolves (ānandād imāni bhūtāni hyeva khalu jāyanti, ānandena jātāni jīvantī, ānandaṃ prayantyabhiniviśantī--Taittirīya Upaniśad 3.6.1). The later emergence of millions of gods finds its base here. Since all forms of existence (abstract and concrete) are divine, any form can be viewed as a manifestation of a power of God, or as a symbol of God.

In the Purāṇas, in the post-Upaniṣadic period, the term Iśvara "Lord," refers to the all-pervasive reality. Here, the relationship between One God and many gods is resolved differently. The three basic powers of the ultimate reality are personified as three major gods in the Purāṇic theistic traditions of Hinduism. These are Brahmā (god of creation), Viṣṇu (god of sustenance), and Śiva (god of destruction). The three form a triad—a three-headed godhead or the trinity ('Trimūrti'). All three are viewed as equally powerful, equally important, and inseparable from one another. More significantly, they symbolize the essential unity of these powers in the universe. Idol-worship of these three gods thus does not deny their basic unity. Various other gods and goddesses are viewed as manifestations of the three basic powers (creation, sustenance, and destruction) of the Divine. For example, ambādevī (goddess Ambā) is viewed as the incarnation of Pārvatī (Śiva's wife or Śiva's power of sustenance), while Bālājī is viewed as the incarnation of Viṣṇu, and Viśvanāth is one of Śiva's forms.

The Purāṇic concept which has been crucial in bringing about the intergration of different gods (and thereby the integration of diverse Hindu traditions) is the concept of Avatāra (the incarnation of God). In this belief, God incarnates in various forms in order to uphold dharma and to protect the people (Bhagavadgītā 4.7). The relationship between God and the gods is anchored in this belief. Faith in the Avatāra does not deny the basic divinity of all existence. However, it is believed that although God exists in all forms, human beings recognize certain forms as divine when they observe their god-like function of these forms at a particular time, space, and situation. An old tree which provides shade for travelers, a river which provides water for the village, an ox who ploughs the farm all day, a human being who sacrifices his or her life to protect the village—these are all recognized as divine.

Acceptance of the infinite forms of the divine justify the Hindu belief that God is infinite and all-pervasive. In the Purāṇas, the Avatāras of the divine are shown to include all forms, starting from a fish, a tortoise, and a boar to a full grown human being, clearly pointing out that divinity is not restricted only to certain forms. While Rāma and Kṛṣṇa are some of the most widely recognized incarnations of Viśṇu (the sustainer), it is not surprising then that Hindus also worship rocks and plants, as well as human beings, as symbols of the divine. That this vision of one god through diverse expressions is not merely an intellectual abstraction for the Hindus is amply demonstrated in the following: When asked by some researchers why they created clay idols/images of their gods every year and at the end of the ritual, threw them away in the river some illiterate villagers replied:

"You do not understand, our god does not abide in these images. He is everywhere; he is neither created, nor is he destroyed. This clay image is merely a symbol of the god, so we can visibly relate to Him, worship Him, once the ritual is over, we let the symbol dissolve in water. Our god can be symbolically created anew every year." (Long search (2) : 330 Million gods, C.E.)

In the sectarian Purāṇas and other texts (of the Śaiva and Vaiṣṇava sects), Śiva or Viṣṇu is elevated to the position of the one all-pervasive Iśvara with all three powers. The Śaivites and Vaiṣṇavites anchor their sects in the Śvetāśvatara Upaniṣad and the Bhagavadgītā respectively. However, a non-sectarian Hindu continues to maintain that Brahmā, Śiva, and Viṣṇu are three powers of the one Iśvara—the Supreme being. The goddesses (such as Lakṣmī, Pārvatī, Durgā, and Kāẖī, among others) are viewed as various manifestations of one Śakti ("power"), which is also variously described as the one, ultimate Divine with various powers, or as a specific power of a male god (for further discussion, see Gatewood 1985, Kinsley 1986, Pandharipande 1990, Wadley 1992).

The notion of the Divine feminine presents another axis of integration of One and many gods and goddesses. In Mahādevī or Devī ("the great goddess"), we find a fusion of goddesses of diverse geographic, historical, and philosophical origin. The sixth century C.E. text, Devī-bhāgavata purāṇa, celebrates the "Divine feminine" or the feminine vision of God, where Mahādevī is viewed as both One and many. As One God, she is identified as nameless, formless, Brahman. In *Lalita□sahasra nama* , a text which lists the one thousand names of Devī, she is described as the one who holds the universe (viśvagarbhā:637), immeasurable (aparimeyā:413), and omnipresent (sarvagā:702). These epithets clearly portray her as the ultimate reality. *Markandeya Purana* (81) unambiguously describes Devī as the One in whom there exist no dualities of any form or shape. This depiction of Devī strongly reflects the Hindu belief that God can be embodied in male (Brahmā,Viṣṇu, and Śiva) or female forms.

The vision of Devī as Divine provides another all-inclusive framework which goes beyond sectarian distinctions between Śiva and Viśṇu and unites diverse images of female goddesses of Hindu and non-Hindu origin. She is viewed as the mother of Śiva and Viśṇu (Devī Mahātmya: 1.75). She is also identified as Śakti, 'the power or energy'—the divine energy which creates the world. In this respect, she is identified as Māyāḥ who abides in Brahman. However, as Kinsley (1986:135) correcty points out, 'The emphasis is not on the binding aspect of matter, or the created world, but on the Devī as the ground of the universe." As Śakti, she is incarnated into various forms which manifest her various powers and functions in the world. Thus Mahādevī as Śakti integrates female deities such as the mother goddess of the Indus valley culture, Uṣas ('dawn'); Sarasvatī ('goddess of Wisdom and Knowledge'), of the Vedas; Sītā, the heroine of the epic Rāmāyaṇa; Rādhā, Kṛṣṇa's beloved cowherd girl (gopi) in Harivaṃśa (one of the purāṇas); Lakṣmī, Viṣṇu's wife; and Śiva's wives, Pārvatī, Durgā, and Kālī; as various manifestations of her powers. These forms are viewed as incarnations of Devī, and through them she encompasses the entire range of divine functions. As mother goddess she is the embodiment of the power of creation and nourishment; as Rādhā and Pārvatī, she expresses the power of love; as Durgā, she is the power of destruction of "evil," which is necesssary for the sustenance of the universe; and as Kālī, she manifests the divine power of destruction of the universe for the purpose of its renewal. Additionally, Devī integrates other goddesses such as Mariyamma (of the Dravidian origin in South India), Manasā (of tribal origin in Bengal), and numerous other village goddesses.

The above vision of God as One and many has played a crucial role in uniting the Āryan and Dravidian cultures. What M.N. Srinivas calls the "Sanskritization" or Āryanization of the Dravidian religion—or what can also be seen as the Dravidization of the Āryan religion—is seen in the process of the integration of the two cultures through the assimilation of their respective gods. The Dravidian (or, more precisely, Tamilian) gods such as Mudalvan (originally 'the god of hills') and Māyon ('the god of prosperity') gradually merged with Śiva and Viṣṇu of the Āryan pantheon. It is also argued that the present Śiva of the Hindu pantheon is a result of the merger of several deities of non-Āryan/Dravidian origin.

Another important vision of God as One and many was proposed by Ramakrishna in the 19th century C.E.. According to Ramakrishna, God is One, but there can be infinitely many visions of God. In his view, many religions differ from one another only in their vision of God .

There are various sects or saṃpradāyas, such as Vārkarīpantha (12th century C.E.) in Maharashtra, and Chaitanya's Vaiṣṇavabhakti sampradāya (16th century C.E.) in

Bengal, among others, where the saints (santa) and mystics are recognized as incarnations of God and their words/teachings are recognized as scriptures. This is another way to explain the relationship between One and many Gods. In this view, saints are viewed as human incarnations of God. Janābāi, a 12th century saint from Maharashtra, makes this explicit:

Water and cloud
Cloud and water
Can we separate the two?
Santa is God
and God is santa.
Janī says,
"The difference is
Only in the name."
—Nāmadeva Gātha 250.

Thus, in Hinduism, there is no dichotomy between gods and God, the former are the manifestation of the formless (nirguṇa) in form (saguṇa), in space, and in time. This has led Hindus to accept deities of other religious traditions as expressions of the divine. Thus, Buddha, who challenged and rejected some of the practices of Hinduism, such as the rituals, is accepted as one of the incarnations of the divine. Similarly, Christ and the prophet Mohammed are also accepted as expressions of the divine. It is believed that different times and social circumstances required different forms of the divine to sustain the world, and therefore the divine expresses itself in diverse forms. All forms of the divine are equally valid. A Hindu deity is not superior to the Christian god and vice versa. The worship of any god, Hindu or otherwise, is the worship of God, which is essentially One. (Bhagavadgītā: 9.23). This is the essence of the conversation in the Brhaḍāraṇyakopaniṣad (3.9.4), where Vidagdha Śakalya asks Yājñavalkya, "How many gods are there, Yājñavalkya?" "Thirty three" is the reply, "Yes," he says, "But how many gods are there Yājñavalkya?" "One," (says Yājñavalkya).

The Transient & The Eternal: Integration of two visions of Reality

If there is indeed only one, all-pervasive, eternal Reality (Brahman or God), then what is the status of this transient world of multiple names (nāma) and forms (rūpa)? Are these forms real? If they are, how do they relate to the One? How did this world come into existence? Is it permanent? These questions are discussed at great length in Hindu mythology, theology, and philosophy (darśanas). What underlies these questions is the Hindu inquiry into the nature of existence (sat) by the knowledge of which one understands the nature of everything, whether transitory or eternal. Chāndogya Upaniṣad (6.1.3) describes this quest as follows: "This is the quest for the knowledge of that Ultimate Reality, by knowing which everything which is unknown will be known." (See Hiriyanna, this volume.)

The basic belief of Hinduism is that the world of multiple forms is limited and transitory. But the world is at the same time founded on the one eternal Brahman; it is sustained in Brahman and it returns to Brahman, only to be recreated again. The cycle of creation, sustenance, and destruction of the world is called saṃsāra (that which moves, the impermanent). The Real, according to Hindu belief, is the eternal One. The Maitrī Upaniṣad (6.32) says, "From Him, indeed who is in the self (Ātman), come forth all living creatures, all worlds, all the Vedas, all gods, all beings." Chāndogya Upaniṣad (6.2.1) reiterates a similar thought: "In the beginning . . . this world was just Being (sat) one only, without a second." Taittirīya Upaniṣad (2.6) attributes desire (kāma), the creative impulse, to the One Being. "He desired, "Would that I were many! Let me procreate myself!"...Having performed austerities, He created the whole world."

Brahman is the one formless Being, but its counterpart among the created forms (humans, animals, plants, trees, and inanimate beings) is called Ātman. There is no distinction between Brahman and Ātman. Ātman is Brahman within forms. The forms are transient, but Ātman is not. Ātman is generally translated as self or soul. Each individual existence has dual dimensions—one the eternal Ātman and the other, the transitory dimension of body (form). While the transitory dimension gives a separate, unique identity to each individual, the other dimension of Ātman represents Brahman in embodied forms. Thus Hinduism does not believe that each person has a separate soul. The relationship between Brahman and Ātman can be analogically understood as the relationship that exists between one indivisible space and the infinite structures or forms that enclose the space—that is, the indivisible space seems to be fragmented superficially.

Since the permanent is called Real (sat), the impermanent world is called unreal (asat), in the sense that it exists only temporarily. It is called māyā (that which is measurable and therefore "limited"). The term māyā is interpreted variously within the philosophy, theology, and practice of Hinduism. It is called "the creative power" of God in Śvetaśvatara Upaniṣad (4.9-10), where it is said that Maheśvara (God/Lord) is māyin (the magician-one who has māyā) who, with his magical powers, creates the illusion of the world with many forms. In Ṛgveda (6.47.18), māyā is viewed as the power of the Vedic gods to hide themselves in different forms. The Upaniṣads emphasize the creative aspect of māyā and point out its power to conceal the true nature of reality. Because of the creation of the transitory forms, the identity of Brahman and Ātman remains concealed. According to Bṛhadāraṇyaka Upaniṣad (2.4.14, 4.5.15), the appearance of separate existences conceals their fundamental unity. This creative and concealing power of māyā is also recognized in the Iśa Upaniṣad (1.16), where it is claimed that the face of Truth is covered with a golden disc (māyā). Because māyā is the impediment in the path of knowledge of the Real (since individuals get attached to their form and other forms and fail to understand Reality), māyā is interpreted negatively as attachment to the unreal, deceptive temptress named "this world." The Upaniṣads, however, do not treat the world as an illusion or non-existent entity.

The dominant view of māyā , typically ascribed to Śankara, the 9th century philosopher, is that the world is a mere dream or illusion and therefore meaningless and inconsequential. In fact, however, for Śankara, the real is that which is eternal, and therefore Brahman; unreal is that which is transitory, and therefore, the world of multitudes of forms. According to him, the world is unreal separated from Brahman and real as the manifestation of Brahman. Radhakrishnan (1927: 583) correctly claims, "Unreal the world is, illusory it is not." (See Hiriyanna and Kesavan, this volume.)

Māyā has raised a great deal of controversy about the goal of Hinduism. Is Hinduism a world-denying religion? The answer is that it is not. What Hinduism emphasizes is the eternal dimension of the world. It treats knowledge of Reality as the prerequisite for a meaningful life in this world. To accept the divinity of all is to accept the ultimate oneness of all existences (to accept the fundamental unity of all apparently diverse entities—whether abstract or concrete). This injunction to go beyond the observable is the foundation of the Hindu ethics of tolerance toward other forms of existence. "Seeing all things equal, the enlightened may look on the Brāhmaṇa, learned and gentle, on the cow, on the elephant, on the dog, the eater of the dogs with the same attitude." (Bhagavadgītā 15:18).

In fact, it is here that we find the seed of the Hindu method of acquiring knowledge. True knowledge is the synthesis of apparently mutually exclusive and/or contradictory entities. In its essence, māyā provides a framework to be transcended so that its true nature may be understood. It is viewed as līlā (play) of God.

> Only when it is seen as divine play is the world of contingencies finally revealed as sacred. This discovery leads to feelings of bliss, not of anguish. . . . Eyes that hitherto saw the profane world as a meaningless cycle of sorrow, once opened to a direct apprehension of reality, perceive that māyā belongs to the realm of awe, rapture and the supernatural. (Lennoy 1971:287).

According to Vivekananda, (cited in Nikhilananda 1984:227), a 19th century mystic-philosopher, māyā is a "statement of facts" that life is full of contradictions. The position of Vedānta (one of the dominent branches of Hindu philosophy), according to Vivekananda,

> is neither pessimism nor optimism. It does not say that the world is all evil or all good. It says that our evil is of no less value than our good, and our good of no more value than our evil. They are bound together. This is the world and knowing this, you work with patience.

The value of māyā as a path to knowledge is beautifully illustrated in Matsya Purāṇa, one of the earliest Purāṇas where Nārada, Viṣṇu's favorite disciple, is desperate to know the nature of māyā. Viṣṇu sends him to a village (a metaphor for the world) to get him a brass pot full of water to drink. Nārada, once in the village, gets increasingly involved with the village affairs, gets married, and has three children. During this time, he forgets his mission of taking back water for Viṣṇu, until one day, torrential rain sweeps away the village. Nārada loses everything—his home, wife, and children—in the floods. Suddenly, the transience of worldly life dawns on him and he realizes the true nature of māyā. The myth makes the point that it is only in living through māyā that one understands its true nature (for a complete version, see Zimmer 1948: 31-35).

Another myth about the sage Mārkaṇḍeya in *Matsya Purana* (167.13-35), beautifully explains the nature of māyā. The sage had been living within the belly of the sleeping god Viṣṇu. but fell out through Viṣṇu's parted lips into the cosmic sea. The world within and the world outside of Viṣnu had nothing in common. In the cosmic sea there was no sun, or moon, not even the earth. Mārkaṇḍeya asks himself, "Was I dreaming then and am awake now, or was I awake then and am dreaming now?" This myth allegorically represents two states of mind—one where the mind is "trapped" into limited, immediate vision and the other where the mind is free of the bond of the immediate. It is only in the second state that one experiences the oneness of all. Taken out of its philosophical context, māyā can be seen as the power of the immediate context which prevents us from envisioning the totality of the existential context. Māyā is like the physicist's encounter with innumerable physical phenomena. In order to understand the true nature of the phenomena, the physicist has to go beyond the observable particularities and fathom the underlying connection (see O' Flaherty 1984).

The Notion of Time: The Substratum of Diversity

Since time is the substratum of all human and cosmic activities, Hinduism has tried to grapple with the nature of time. According to Hinduism, there was no time before the creation of the universe and there will not be any time should this cycle stop sometime (as a conceptual possibility) in the future. Thus, māyā (the creation) and time are inseparable. Nīlakaṇṭha in his commentary on Ganesha Gita says, "The past and the future, the moment as well as the aeon of that which is to come, be it near or removed; the coarse and the minute, all these things are contained in the Self of Reflection; behold, it is māyā unfolding " (Goudriaan 1978:31-31). Time can only be measured in terms of the cycle—the four sequential phases (kṛtayuga, tretāyuga, dvāparayuga, and kaliyuga) through which the universe passes. The universe deteriorates at the physical and ethical levels as it passes through these phases; the first phase marks the peak and the fourth phase marks the lowest point. Seen from this perspective, time is circular. It is constantly "renewed" at the time of the creation of the universe, "grows old" and "dies" only to be revived again. It is as transitory as the universe. (See Pandharipande 1990 and also see Kesavan, this volume.)

This circular vision of time has influenced the Hindu view of death and destruction. Although everything dies in time, everything is also revived in time. Death is not viewed as total annihilation; rather, it is viewed as an inevitable and necessary corollary to creation. Death is as important as creation, for without death and destruction there would not be any creation. Death is merely a pause between two births. Nothing dies forever in the phenomenal reality:

> jātasya hi dhruvo mṛtyuh dhruvo janma mṛtasya ca.
> 'For the born, death is unavoidable, and for the dead, birth is certain.
> —Bhagavadgītā 2:27

The transformation is constant. One form dies, and a new form is born. It is therefore not surprising that in Hinduism the god of destruction, Śiva, occupies the same position as Viṣṇu, the god of sustenance, and Brahmā, the god of creation. Implicit in this cyclical vision of time is the notion of what White (1962: 130) calls "the self-perpetuating nature of all things." Needham (1965: 540) describes this vision when he says that Hindus,

> seek the ultimate origin or predisposition of the Indian conviction in the proformally Indian world view of endless cyclicity; change, kalpas and mahākalpas succeeding one another in self-sufficient and unwearing round. For Hindus as Taoists the universe itself was a perpetual-motion machine.

Another interesting dimension of time in Hinduism is its repetitive nature. Since time is not unidirectional, no moment in itself is really unique. The universe goes through the same phases (of creation, sustenance, and destruction) and so does time, with all its "fractions"—the years, months, days, and moments. The nature of the events which take place in each cycle of the universe may change, but not the nature of time as the underlying substratum, since the "uniqueness" is attributed to events rather than time. The ancient history of India is therefore recorded primarily in terms of the sequence of the events and only secondarily in terms of time. What happened is viewed as more important than when it happened. The term for history is itihāsa ("thus existed"/"happened here"). Viewed from the cosmic perspective, the distinction among past, present, and future is superfluous. As long as one is "trapped" into māyā, or time, one is never going to attain permanence. The goal is to cross-over the barrier of time. While creation is (at least the perceived) separation of many forms from one, Śiva's dance (tāṇḍava) at the time of the dissolution of the world symbolically suggests the merging of "many" back into one—into Brahman. Eternity in Hinduism is not the endless continuation of time; it is timelessness. *Maitri Upanishad* (6.15) supports this view: "There are, verily, two forms of Brahman: time, and timeless ... Time cooks (ripens) all things, indeed, in the great self. He who knows in what time is cooked, he is the knower of the Veda."

The Quest: The Vision of 'One' in Many

According to Hinduism, the need for religion is the need for knowledge of reality—phenomenal and transcendental. True knowledge of the phenomenal world provides not only a glimpse of the transcendental, but also a framework for organizing the social, moral/ethical, and religious behavior of human beings. In the Upaniṣads, this quest is described as follows:

> yena jñātena avijnātaṃ vijñātaṃ bhavati
> [This is the quest for the knowledge of that ultimate reality] by knowing which everything which is not known will be known.
> —Chandōgyōpaniṣad: 6.1.3

True knowledge is the realization of the divinity of all: "All of this is Brahman indeed" (sarvaṃ khalu idaṃ brahma) and also, "I am Brahman" (ahaṃ brahmāsmi) Chandōgyōpaniṣad: 3.14.1.

Individuality acts as a barrier between oneself and Brahman. This false perception of reality prevents human beings from experiencing the oneness of everything. There is a belief in Hinduism that all problems, social, and individual, are rooted in the false perception of the world. All the social evils of the world which cause suffering (murder for power, money, or other material gain, for example) arise due to the false perception of reality. Māyā makes people see only their individual, separate identities and blurs their "real" identity. True understanding of reality leads to a vision of the equality of all, at all levels—spiritual, social, and individual. One cannot hurt others because there are no "others." One cannot aspire to one's own good at the cost of others, because there is no one exclusive of others. Similar to the parts of the body, all parts must function in consonance with all other parts. For example, one cannot think of cutting off the arms to benefit the legs. The Hindu prayer in the Upaniṣad reveals this emphasis on the "real" and the urge for its realization:

> asato mā sad gamaya
> tamaso mā jyotir gamaya
> mṛtyor māmrtaṃ gamaya
> Lead me from unreal to real,
> from darkness to light,
> from death to immortality.
> —Bṛhadāraṇyakopaniṣad: 1.3.28

However, as long as there is rebirth, one is bound to be trapped in the mistaken vision of separatedness. Thus, in order to reach the ultimate state of knowledge, the release from māyā/saṃsāra/rebirth is essential.

Karma and Rebirth: Explaining and Conquering Diversity

The belief in constant cosmic transformation (recycling of matter or energy) is rooted in the belief that everything that exists in the cosmos goes through constant recycling, one form changing into another new form. Thus, similar to the cosmic rebirth, is the concept of the rebirth of individual forms. All forms are interchangeable across births—human, animal, plant and so on.

The totality of cosmic action (Karma) determines the nature and forms of the transformation. At the microlevel, it is the actions (Karma) performed by the individual which determine the nature and form of that individual's rebirth. In other words, actions performed in one birth control the nature of the next birth. This is the Karma theory of universal causation. Creation being the first action, it becomes the cause for the chain of causation to go on forever.

The ethical dimension of the Karma theory lies in the belief that "meritorious" acts (puṇya) performed in life guarantee a glorious birth in heaven (svarga), and "wrong" deeds (pāpa) lead human beings either to hell (naraka) or rebirth in a lower form. Gods, humans, animals, plants, or inanimate objects are one of the possible forms in which one may be reborn. While belief in the cosmic cycle provides an independent, and to some extent predetermined, course, the theory of Karma emphasizes the role and control of human beings over their future birth. While the present birth is the result of one's Karma in the previous birth, the actions in this birth shape the next birth (See Hiriyanna, this volume). This theory had its origin in the Mīmāṇsā philosophy (based on the sacrificial ritual tradition of Hinduism), according to which every action creates a force (apūrva)—a potency which under proper conditions will bring about certain results (For further discussion on apūrva, see Halbfass 1980: 268-302).

The most important aspect of Karma is that it is finite and hence it is different from the Greek *moira* (see Klostermaier 1989:205) which cannot be influenced. The influence of Karma can be counteracted by Karma. Epic mythology is full of the examples of the finite powers of Karma. For example, the Rāmāyaṇa notes that Rāvaṇa's good deeds in past lives made him a powerful king, but his evil deeds in his present birth caused him to die a tragic death. Pilgrimages, tapas (austerities), vratas (vows such as fasting, alms giving, etc.), japa (recitation of god's name), etc., are all viewed as puṇya, "merit," and counteract the effect of the previous Karma. The Yogavāśiṣṭha (2:5.5), a twelfth century text on Hindu philosophy, points out that the "present karma" can overcome the "past karma." In a conversation with Rāma, Vasiṣṭha says, "Know that creativity is twofold, that of the past and that of the present. Through human effort (puruṣārtha), the prior is quickly vanquished by the present." (English translation by C. Chapple, 1986: 71) (See also Kak, this volume.).

The Hindu belief in the theory of Karma explains various things, notably the diversity of forms, experiences, and tendencies; why there are so many kinds of beings, both human and non-human; why one person is rich and another poor; and so on. Each birth brings with it an inherited baggage of tendencies and potential Saṃskāras which makes each existence unique. Thus, no two forms are identical in their makeup (genetic) or experiences (caused by their unique interaction with the surroundings). The major emphasis of the Karma theory is that the disparity of the forms and their experiences are not necessarily explainable on the basis of the external facts, but rather on the basis of the internal conditions of Karma.

Judging Right Action: Hindu Ethics

The question of judging right vs. wrong action has often bewildered the learned, not to mention the common people of the world. Although it is not difficult to define the parameters in an absolute sense (for example, a right action is one which promotes the well being of the individual, society, and the world), it is extremely difficult to decide which is the "right action" when there is a conflict between or among individual, social, or global interests. The Bhagavadgītā, the gospel of Hinduism, epitomizes this human dilemma. Which one should one choose: an action conducive to one's own (individual) well-being or one conducive to the well-being of society?

According to Hinduism, this parameter is called *Dharma* ('duty'—literally, that which holds together, maintains, or upholds). The action which is conducive to upholding three orders of existence—individual, social, and global—is the dharma , duty, of an individual. Dharma encompasses three categories: the principle of harmony in the entire universe (Sanātana Dharma), relativistic caste or class or group duties (Varṇāśrama Dharma), and rules /principles of personal moral conduct (Svadharma). These three must function in harmony. In the event of a conflict of interests among these different orders, social duty prevails over individual duty. The individual must place the interests of society over and above his or her individual interests. Hinduism places enormous emphasis on maintaining the social order.

It is believed that an ideal society is structured in the global context and is naturally in harmony with other existences—the social laws would never violate the universal laws. Such a society also provides full scope for individuals to realize their potential. Just as society must always strive to fit into the global structure (and not erode it), similarly an individual must fit into the social structure (and not destroy it). The epic and purāṇic stories and myths abound with "ideal" heroes and heroines (Rāma, Arjuna, Bharata) who choose to sacrifice their individual interests in favor of their social duty.

The Karma theory has had an enormous impact on the lives of the people of India. On the one hand, it has prompted people to accept their conditions (social, political, economic) as a consequence of their past Karma (See K.L. Seshagiri Rao, this volume, on Gandhi's response to this doctrine.), and on the other hand, it has provided them with a strong sense of control over their future lives. Right action becomes a challenge in the face of disasters (physical, mental, and economic) and a promise for a better future.

It is important to note here that the merit of an action is judged by the intention behind its performance (for selfish or non-selfish reasons) and not by its results, since the outcome of any action depends on various external factors and not only on the performer's intentions. Thus, the only true control the performer of an action has is with regard to his or her motives. For example, when Oppenheimer had to give away the secret knowledge of the atomic bomb, he faced this perennial dilemma—should he worry about the outcome of his actions or not—and called himself Arjuna of the Bhagavadgītā, who was faced with a similar choice. Finally, he realized that one can never be sure of the consequences of one's actions (for further discussion, see Smith 1958: 12). One cannot evaluate actions from the point of view of their results. When Arjuna is reluctant to participate in the war with his own relatives and friends, Kṛṣṇa advises Arjuna,

> karmaṇyevādhikaraste mā phaleṣu kadāčana
> To actions alone are you entitled, not to their fruits
> —Bhagavadgītā 2:47.

This view of action and responsibility releases individuals from the tension and pressure of failure or success, since it is only the action which succeeds or fails. The doer is fully responsible only for his or her intentional actions and not for their results. Since variables which may intervene between that action and the result contribute to the occurrence/non-occurrence of the result, the result cannot be the responsibilty solely of the actor.

For purposes of defining social duty, *Varnashrama Dharma*, Hindu society has been divided into the following four groups (Cāturvarṇa) :

1. Brāhmaṇas - intellectuals
2. Kṣatriyas - warriors and administrators
3. Vaiśyas - traders and merchants
4. Śūdras - laborers

Although the earlier (Vedic) structure of society refers to these classes as "Varṇas" (based on skin color), later they were based on "jatis" (birth). There are duties prescribed for each of the groups: teaching for the Brāhmaṇas, protection of the society for the Kṣatriyas, taking care of the economy for the Vaiśyas, and helping the first three groups for the Śūdras. The origin of the four-fold society is described in the Puruṣa Sūkta (Ṛgveda 10:190) as originating out of the dismembered body of the primeval being, Puruṣa. From his mouth were created the Brāhmaṇas, from his arms came the Kṣatriyas, from his thighs came the Vaiśyas, and from his feet the Śūdras.

This social organization was based on the perceived needs of society and the differences in the potential/tendencies of human beings. (i.e., not all individuals want to or can perform the same jobs). It treats the four classes as interdependent groups whose interaction is based on reciprocity. While a Brāhmaṇa transmits the "spiritual" or the "sacred" to the king and other classes, he is dependent on the rest of the classes for his well-being in the material world. The king and the merchants provide physical protection and economic stability, but depend on the Brāhmaṇas for their spiritual development. The Śūdras,who depend on the other classes for their livelihood, offer their physical labor to the other three classes so that they can perform their duties well. The hierarchy of these four classes is based on the level of physical, intellectual, and spiritual capacity and development of individuals. Thus the Brāhmaṇas, (priests, teachers, and intellectuals in general) are at the top and the Śūdras (laborers) are at the bottom. Viewed from this perspective, the social/religious system assigns not only prestige and privilege but also the responsibility of taking care of different classes.The Brāhmaṇas at the top had maximum prestige and privileges along with maximum responsibility. The entire life of a Brāhmaṇa was, and still is, supposed to be an exemplary model for others. While the Brāhmaṇa's responsibility is to "cleanse" the society of its "spiritual pollution" through the performance of religoius duties, the Śūdras are responsible, for example, for keping the society physically clean by performing jobs such as washing and cleaning the private and public places. The assumption is that both are equally needed for a stable society. Additonally, this social stratification provides a cohesive framework for integrating the secular and spiritual life , '. . .in which mortal actions (karma) simultaneously facilitate the conduct of orderly economic(artha) and secular (kāma) life and the pursuit of salvation (mokṣa)' (Gould 1987:18). Thus, this much-maligned caste system reflects one of the most striking features of Hindu integration.

From approximately 2000 B.C.E. until about 700 B.C.E, it is believed, this social structure emphasized the interdependence of the four groups, along with intergroup mobility (depending upon one's abilities), and equal social prestige for all groups. However, over a period of time, membership in each group came to be determined by birth rather than by individual ability. Since it was believed that the make-up of an individual in terms of the "*Samsakaras*" (tendencies or aptitudes) is determined by the power of Karma (actions) which operates across births, restricting membership to a social group by birth alone was viewed as a natural corollary of the Karma theory. Thus, birth into a Brāhmaṇa family guaranteed, to to speak, Brāhmaṇic Saṃsakāra. This narrow interpretation changed the former open structure of the society based on ability to a structure with closed classes based on birth.

Once intergroup mobility was prohibited, the social structure developed into a hierarchical structure with an undeniable advantage being enjoyed by the first three classes, while the fourth class lost all prestige, privilege, and personal dignity; and the lowest of that class were reduced to the status of "untouchables." Gandhi, one of the leaders of the Hindu reformist movement in the early twentieth century, re-interpreted the system in favor of its original interpretation. He argued that it was not that the system was faulty; it was its interpretation which was wrong. Needless to say, this social structure is gradually losing its relevance in the face of the modernization and urbanization of the Hindu world.

As Parsons says categorically in *The Structure of Social Action*, "Hinduism as a religion is but an aspect of this social system, with no independent status apart from it."(P. 557). It is true that the caste-based structure uniquely differentiates Hinduism from other religions, and it has been most influential in determining the dynamics of social and political life in India for thousands of years. Though the function of the castes has changed in different periods in history, it has remained a powerful force in the society. Since it is occupationally determined, it allows outsiders such as ādivāsis (indigenous people) to be included in the system based upon their occupation. Today, there are thousands of subcastes in India. Also, the caste system has impacted other religions in India such as Islam, Sikhism, and Christianity, each of which developed a complex system of castes within their own religious structures. (See Srinivas, Kesavan, and Hardgrave, this volume.)

The crucial aspect of the caste system was its dual function—one social and the other spiritual. At the social level, it provided a structure to match the potential (guṇa) of individuals with the needs of the society. At the spiritual level, it provided an opportunity to prepare oneself to be worthy of liberation from māyā by performing caste duties (svadharma) without selfish desires (niṣkāma karma). Additionally, freedom from one's caste was possible across births. At the spiritual level, all castes were equal. This dimension of caste was forgotten in the later pre-Buddhist period. It is important to note here that the ultimate spiritual goal of transcending the cycle of rebirth was never believed to be attainable within the social structure. It was not the power of the knowledge of the Vedas and rituals which established the superiority of the Brāhmaṇas over other castes; rather, it was their power to detach themselves from worldly desires which placed them at the top of the hierarchy. The caste system, devoid of its spiritual base, created havoc in the Hindu society in the periods starting from the sixth century B.C.E.

Ashramas: The Four Stages of Life

The four stages of life present a second parameter for determining the duties of individuals. The four stages (*Ashramas*) together provide a synthesis of the life of an individual. These stages are in sequence: 1) Brahmačarya, the stage of learning or studenthood, where a 12 year old from the first three castes is initiated into education through the ritual of Upanayana (literally, to bring to the teacher); 2) Gṛhasthāśrama, the stage of living a householder's life, where one is supposed to enjoy family life; 3) Vānaprasthāśrama, the stage of living a forest dweller's life, where one is expected to mentally and physically move away from māyā and focus on mokṣa 'liberation' from it; and 4) Sanyāsāśrama, the stage where the elderly are expected to renounce their worldly possessions and desires completely and gradually proceed towards mokṣa. The concept of Āśramas treats an individual's life as a whole and each stage marks the growth of the individual into successively larger ties (family, society, and the universe). Therefore, for most Hindus, this structure provides a relatively simple path towards achievement of the spiritual goal, mokṣa, without giving up the other three goals: *dharma* (duty), *artha* (wealth), and *kama* (love/pleasure). What is implied in this scheme of sequential stages is that physical growth must be complemented by mental/spiritual growth and that this growth is essential for leading a happy life in this world.

The Hindu Samskaras: 'Sanctifying' the Individual Life

The Hindu community across the world is unified on the basis of the Hindu *Samskara*, the sacraments which initiate an individual into the Hindu socio-religious community. A Hindu is accepted as Saṃskrt (cultured/cultivated) when he or she follows these sacraments. *Manusmruti* (2.26), one of the major 'law books,' describes the function of the sacraments as that of purifying and sanctifying the body and mind. They are the bridges between this 'phenomenal' reality and the 'absolute' reality. They are firmly anchored in the primary Hindu beliefs of the divine, Karma, rebirth, and most importantly, the oneness of all. On the one hand, they provide cohesiveness and meaning to the individual's life-cycle (thereby making it 'meaningful' at a very personal level), and, on the other hand, they symbolically represent an individual life-cycle as a replica of the cosmic cycle. Thus, they perform the dual function of individuation and universalization of an individual's life and thereby emphasize the primary Hindu belief that the individual receives meaning through connection with, and not separation from, the cosmic reality.

Some of the major saṃskāras are jātakarma (the ritual performed at the birth of a child), upanayana (the initiation), vivāha (marraige), and antyeṣṭi (the rituals performed at the end of life—the funeral rituals). There is a great deal of variation in the actual observance of these sacraments across India, and there are additional rituals deemed important in various parts of the country. However, the above are the most commonly observed saṃskāras across diverse Hindu communities. These saṃskāras invariably involve *homa*, a fire ritual sacrifice, offered to the gods (a clear continuation of the Vedic sacrifice), a priest who reads scriptural passages either in Sanskrit, or at times, from the other Śaivite or Vaiṣṇavite or local scriptures, and mediates between the host and the gods. Hinduism continues to celebrate its Indo-European heritage, which involves worship of the forces of nature—mainly fire and water. The creative, sustaining, and all-cosuming power of fire (tapas) is revered at the birth-ritual, marriage-ritual and, finally, at the funeral ritual. The primary connection of the individual with the larger reality (family, society, the divine) is constantly repeated in these sacraments. For example, a child's first name should be that of a god and the second should indicate its caste (e.g., Śarman for Brāhaṃana, Varman for Kśatriya, Gupta for Vaiśya, and Dāsa for Śūdra; *Vishnu Purana* 3.10). In Maharasthra, Tamil Nadu, Andhra Pradesh, and Karnataka, the father's name generally intervenes between the first name and the family name. In the marriage-rituals, the bride and the bridegroom circumambulate the fire three or five times saying, "I am heaven, you are earth, I am sāma (chant), you are ṛk (hymn).". The prayers from the Vedas which are recited at the funeral ritual clearly suggest the merging of the phenomenal body into "the five elements" (Pañcamahābhūtas) and the departure of Ātman from the body: "Now my breath and spirit goes to the Eternal, and this body ends in ashes; Oṃ, O mind! remember, remember the deeds, remember the actions!...I am he. Oṃ, the supreme Brahaman." (Yajurveda, 40.15,17). Thus, the sacraments continually remind individuals that they are anchored in the cosmic reality.

A Synthesis of Different Approaches: The Yogas

Athough the perfect state of being is that of oneness with the Divine and thereby with the entire creation, it is believed that this state is not easy to reach. The process of "perfecting" oneself is life-long and, at times, continues across births. A Hindu is believed to be constantly perfecting himself or herself through actions, emotions, and thoughts—constantly striving to go beyond, outgrowing the trap of individuality, constantly enlarging one's identity by identifying with the family, society, and the cosmos (in that order). This is why family duty constitutes religious duty in Hinduism. In fact, as Hiriyanna (1952: 35) correctly points out,

> the question whether the highest value is attainable is not of much consequence. We may grant that it is not finally attained, and that man's reach will always exceed his grasp. What really matters is the deliberate choosing of it as the ideal to be pursued, and thereafter making a persistent and continued advance towards it.

Hinduism is intolerant and quite dogmatic regarding its foundational belief: namely, that the root of suffering is in the individuation and separation of identities and the solution lies in the perception of unity. However, its dogma ends here. It does not prescribe one single path (to the exclusion of others) to achieve the goal. Any path (of any religion or other belief system, such as science) which leads to the realizaton of the unity is viewed as the right path. Prescribing one path for all human beings is an inconceivable fallacy according to Hinduism. Thus Śrī Kṛṣṇa declares: "Whatever form any devotee with faith wishes to worship, I make that faith of his steady." (Bhagavadgītā, 7:21), " Whatever path men travel is my path. No matter where they walk, it leads to me." (Bhagavadgītā, 4:11). However, it is important to note here that the equality of paths is justified in Hinduism on the basis of the common goal of attaining the knowledge of Reality. This goal must be the motivating force behind a path which in practice is realized in unselfish thought, feeling, and action. Thus, in the Bhagavadgītā, the apparently noble action of withdrawing from war is censured by Kṛṣṇa because it betrays Arjuna's selfish concerns, while an apparently evil action (i.e., a war) is sanctioned as legitimate on the basis of an unselfish goal.

At any given point in time, within a lifespan or across different births, human personality is believed to be the sum total and the result of all earlier tendencies (saṃskāras). Thus, since human beings vary in their dispositions, it is expected that they will choose different paths. Three major personality types are recognized (although others may exist): intellectually driven, emotionally driven, and activity driven (doers). The Bhagavadgītā outlines a different path for each of the three different types: the path of Knowledge (Jñāna Yoga), the path of devotion (Bhakti Yoga), and the path of action (Karma Yoga). The term 'Yoga' literally means union (union with Brahman). The path which leads to this union is also called Yoga. By focusing one's intellect (buddhi) inward on one's global identity, an intellectual can transcend his or her narrow identity. This can be done by following the method of Jñāna Yoga, which, through mental and physical exercises brings the senses and the mind under control (not letting them dictate their cravings) and thus makes one look inward on the one's true identity. Those who follow the second path, the path of devotion, direct their emotions toward a diety in millions of different forms: an image/statue of a god or goddess, a rock, a tree, a human being in whom they envision the "divine" or the ultimate reality. They worship these symbols by becoming intensely attached, and in so doing they connect themselves to the divine. They identify themselves with the deity by constantly thinking that they are doing, thinking, and feeling everything for the deity and not for themselves. Thus they gradually grow out of their narrow identity and see themselves rooted in the deity. When the devotee's mind is fully absorbed in the form (saguṇa) of a deity (for example, Kṛṣṇa), it is inconceivable for him or her to give up Kṛṣṇa for the formless Brahman. When Uddhava, Kṛṣṇa's friend, asks Kṛṣṇa's beloved cowherd girls (gopis) to forget Kṛṣṇa and concentrate on his formless, unqualified Being, their answer succintly portrays their intense, unwavering love for Kṛṣṇa. They say,

> Udho! We do not have ten or twenty hearts! Only one (heart) that we had, has gone to Kṛṣṇa. How can we even worship your (formless) God? Don't we need a heart to worship God?" (Sūrdas Bhramargīt-sār 1966: 278).

This identification with their deity leads them to the realization of their deity's identification with the entire universe, and thus their intense love for their own deity gradually results in their identification with and love for the entire universe. True devotees of God thus experience the cosmicization of their emotions of love, their love for the entire universe, and they see their god in every existence of the universe.

The third path, of action that assumes that "selfless" actions (i.e., actions performed without the desire for selfish gains) can lead toward enlarging one's identity. By performing such actions for others—for example for the family or society—one grows out of oneself. This is the reason why social duty is valued over individual duty. Social duty, according to Hinduism, is not intended to suppress individual identity; rather, it is the process through which it may be enlarged. The implications of the belief in diverse paths are as follows:

Hinduism accepts all ways of approaching the divine (which by definition transcends individual existence) as valid. There may be various methods of worship, various deities, various religious systems, but they are all equally valid systems since they all lead individuals toward the awareness of a larger identity. No one system or method, or god, is inherently superior to others.

The belief in many paths explains why literally millions of deities in various forms and shapes are worshipped in Hinduism. Each deity is a unique expression of the infinite. As mentioned before, there are an enormous variety of deities : male and female, live (prophets) and lifeless (rocks), concrete (the sun) and abstract (knowledge), Śiva (destruction) and Viṣṇu (sustenance). Daily worship of these deties, pilgrimages to the temples, and the writing of hymns and prayers have contributed over the last two millinnea toward the apparently heterogeneous composition of Hinduism. The coexistence of diverse social groups defined by their allegiance to certain forms of deities (Śiva, Viṣṇu, etc.) has from time to time led Hinduism into sectarianism. However, it is important to note here that the basic belief in the infinite expressions of and paths to the divine has never been abandoned in any sect of Hinduism. The evidence to support this assumption comes from the fact that never in its history has Hinduism (in any form) accepted "conversion," which is viewed as the violation of the principle of intrinsic/inherent equality and inherent multiplicity. Moreover, the worship of a deity has never prompted Hindus to assume that the infinite divinity is exclusively expressed in the limited form of that single deity (its images or statues). It is believed that in the beginning it is very difficult for the mind to conceive of formless infinity. Just as a bucket cannot hold an ocean, so also the conditioned mind cannot experience or even conceptualize the all-pervasive ultimate reality. So worship of a deity is merely a first step which, when taken sincerely, leads to successively higher steps toward the experience of God.

Despite their doctrinal differences, all systems of Indian philosophy and theology (such as Advaita Vedānta, Viśiṣṭādvaita, and Sāmkhya, among others) converge on one belief, namely, the way to permanent happiness or peace cannot be found in the phenomenal world, so one must therefore go beyond it. This conviction regarding the essential inconsequentiality of the phenomenal world is expressed in the code of behavior prescribed by the Hindu tradition for common people with average desires and average stamina, as opposed to the truly virtuous person who has no attachment to the material world. For a common person tradition prescribes four goals: dharma (duty), artha (wealth), kāma (love), and mokṣa (liberation from the cycle of rebirths). After one has enjoyed material prosperity and love (having earned both according to the established laws of a particular society), an individual is encouraged to abandon the worldly life and ties in order to find true knowledge of the self. The duties or dharmas prescribed for an individual through his or her different stages of life amply demonstrate this world view.

Once again, the diversity of paths is justified by the unity of their goal—the knowledge (not analytical or objective, but intuitive and experiential) of the divinity and oneness of all. Additionally, what unifies the paths is their direction toward the goal. But the ultimate status of the means/paths is unambiguously described in Tripuratapinyupaniṣad (5:19-21) (Shaurie 1979:133).

> The sharp mind, after study of texts,
> On knowledge and wisdom intent
> Must forsake all, as one who seeks grain
> Forsakes the husk perforce.

The paths are never identified with the goal, for it is believed that the goal—the Ultimate—cannot be known merely by rituals, actions, or knowledge; one has to experience it with one's whole being. Kenopaniṣad (1.3) says,

> There the eye goes not, speech goes not, nor the mind. We know not, we understand not . . . .Thus we have heard from the ancients who explained it to us.

Contextualization and Integration: Dynamic Nature of Hinduism

In the preceding sections, the dominant Hindu beliefs have been discussed. This is not to say that these beliefs emerged and existed together throughout the history of Hinduism. Far from it. Many beliefs and practices emerged as responses to the socio-political and religious contexts at different points in time. Emergence of the diverse versions of Hinduism with what appear to be mutually exclusive beliefs (for example, belief in one God but worship of many gods, Śaivism and Vaiṣṇavism, the path of knowledge of the formless God and the ritual worship of innumerable forms of God) and their gradual integration within the system are two fascinating processes which must be understood in order to trace and explain the course of the river named Hinduism. These two processes can be described as contextualization and integration. Contextualization involves defining beliefs and/or practices according to the need or demand of the context. This involves a relatively narrow definition of Hinduism (for example, performing rituals as the only way to achieve the ultimate goal of life or performance of the caste duties as the only true duty of a Hindu). This process gave rise to various sects and/or strands of Hinduism. On the other hand, the process of synthesis or integration presents a contextual and broad intepretation of Hinduism, treating the mutually exclusive systems of beliefs as part of the broad framework of Hinduism, which is based on the fundamental unity of all forms of thought, action, and existence. Although in principle, it is possible to contextualize a system without giving up its acontextual basic principles, the history of India shows that the contextualization of the Hindu faith, disconnected from its unified vision of reality, has resulted in the dissimilation of various Hindu systems, while the a contextual synthesis has produced an assimilation of the diverse patterns of the system. By means of the former, Hinduism has grown into a system of complex and heterogeneous patterns, while by the latter it has maintained its continuity through diverse periods.

To analyze Hinduism meaningfully requires an exploration and identification of those forces which were instrumental in the contextualization and decontextualization of the system at various points in time. In the following discussion, we will take a very brief look at the major periods in the history of Hinduism.

In the Vedic period (2000 B.C.E. to 500 C.E.), the threefold scriptures dominated the Hindu system. There were the Mantras (the four Vedas), the Brāhmaṇas (the manuals of the Vedic rituals), and the Upaniṣads and the Āraṇyakas (the philosophical treatises on the Mantras). These three scriptures did not contradict eact other; rather, they focused on three different dimensions of the Hindu system. While the Mantras described the phenomenal world and the elements which governed it (devas and rta), the Brāhmaṇas provided guidelines for living a good and prosperous life in "this world" through the worship of the Vedic gods by performing sacrificial rituals. The Upaniṣads focused on the explorations into the Eternal One foundation (Brahman) of this constantly changing phenomenal world.

In the post-Vedic period (up to 1000 C.E.), we can observe three major developments in Hinduism whose origin can be traced to either the sacrificial rituals of the Brahmaṇas or to the philosophical speculations of the Upaniṣads. These three developments have contributed significantly to the contextualization of the Hindu system.

The first development is marked by the emergence of ritual literature (Kalpa sūtras) during the period 500 B.C.E.-200 B.C.E. which are the manuals of rituals based on the karma theory of the Brahmaṇas. These consist of Śraūtasūtras, the texts on the public (Vedic) sacrificial rituals, Grhya Sūtras, the treatises of domestical rituals, and Dharma Sūtras, the manuals of social/individual duties for human beings. It was believed that through the performance of the "right actions" (ritualistic) the Vedic ideal might be attained. Thus, the Kalpasūtras defined the pattern of "religious behavior" for the common people.

The second, and perhaps one of the most significant developments in Hinduism took place around the period 200 B.C.E. to 300 C.E., where we see the emergence of theism elaborated in the two epics—the Mahābhārata and the Rāmāyaṇa. These two epics brought the Upaniṣadic teachings to the common people through the depiction of the human life in its various facets. The abstract metaphysics of the Upaniṣads were incomprehensible to the common people; the epics made them linguistically and theoretically accessible. The Rāmāyaṇa and the Mahābhārata illustrate the ideal of dharma and the consequences of its observance (specially the Rāmāyṇa) and non-observance (specially the Mahābhārata). The epics provided guidelines for "ideal behavior" (e.g., the role model is to be Rāma, not Rāvaṇa).

The third, and perhaps the major, development in Hinduism was during the Purāṇic period (300 C.E.-750 C.E.). Purāṇas (stories of ancient gods) portray the god's response to the needs of the common people. The Vedic religion did not have temples or images of God, and during that period sacrificial ritual was the dominant method of relating to God. This religion was too abstract for the common people. The eighteen mahāpurāṇas (the great Purāṇas) do not claim to present new material but rather reformulate the Upaniṣadic teaching in a new genre and in new symbols. The concretization of the abstract Brahman into various gods (Śiva, Viṣṇu, and particularly the most prominent, Kṛṣṇa), projects the divine into time (kāla) and space (deśa). The creation (sarga) and dissolution (pratisarga) of the world, the ages or aeons (manvantara), and the genealagies (vaṃśa) of gods are the major themes which are elaborated with numerous myths.

The Purāṇas introduce temples (mandira) as abode of God and image (mūrti) as God's presence in time and space. They also introduce the ritual worship (pujā) of images of the deities as a substitute for the Vedic sacrifices. The Bhāgavata Purāṇa is perhaps the most revered Purāṇa, and in it lies the origin of the later Bhakti (devotion) traditions. This Purāṇa illustrates nine steps of bhakti (devotion): listening to the songs of the deity (Śravaṇa); the repetition of god's name (japa or nāmasaṃkīrana); remembrance (smaraṇa); veneration of feet (pādasevaṇa); worship (pūjā); prostrating before the image (vandanā); service (dāsya); friendship (sakhyā); and self-surrender (ātmanivedana).

The notion of prasāda (God's grace) finds its free expression in the Purāṇas. The Purāṇas integrated the karma action of the Brahmaṇas (in the form of pūjā), a well-defined way to relate to god, and the all-encompassing and compassionate nature of God. Additionally, the notion of the Avatāras (descents of Viṣṇu) strongly supported the value of maintaining the Varṇāśrama Dharma (the system of fourfold division of society and the four phases of life). The Purāṇas also promoted the worship of devī (the feminine divine), the mother goddess, who finds full expression in the Śakta and Tāntra literature in the later periods.

The above developments in the post-Vedic period illustrate the process of contextualization of Vedic beliefs in their respective contemporary social contexts, where there was a need to make religion "realistic" and comprehensible to the common people. This need within the system was further emphasized by the rise of Buddhism and Jainism and the influence of the Greeks, Huṇas, Scithians, and others, who used concrete images for worship (for further discussion on the impact of the Greek religion on Hinduism, see Hopkins1971:59-62). This contextualization became instrumental in the later sectarian developments in Hinduism, where the mutually exclusive systems of Śaiva, Vaiṣnava, and Tantra became dogmatic and exclusive of other systems. Additionally, the Varṇāśrama dharma, which had defined social and individual duties based on belief in karma and punar-janma (rebirth), created a highly hierarchical structure of unequal rights given to the members of particular social groups within society.

The rituals, which were supposed to allow flexibility and simplification of the Vedic sacrifice, yielded a rigid ritualism which lost sight of the need to go beyond the rituals to the knowledge of God: the vision of diversity at the social and spiritual level became divorced from vision of their basic unity.

The two major forces in Hinduism which reinterpreted Hinduism and brought synthesis and integration are the Bhagavadgītā and the Advaita Vedānta philosophy of Śankara (ninth century C.E.). Neither of these challenged the authority of the Vedas. The Bhagavadgītā convincingly argued for the spiritual identity of all existence and the multiplicity of the manifestations of God. Based on the difference in the qualities or potentials had (guṇas) of human beings, diversity of the paths to attain the goal of life was explicitly accepted by the Bhagavadgītā. It presented a framework for a society where people with different potentials had opportunities to fit in. This vision of the "unity" among apparent diversities held Hinduism together in the face of potential disintegration caused by internal dogmatism and external threat.

While the Bhagavadgītā integrated multiple systems including rituals by treating them as different paths to the same goal, Śankara, the ninth century philosopher, brought about unity by emphasizing the inconsequentiality of the world from the standpoint of the knowledge of the absolute or ultimate reality, "This is all indeed Brahman." He accepted the religious actions necessary for maintaining the worldly order. However, he argued that actions based on the false notion of one's independent identity cannot in themselves lead to the Truth. The false perception of the identity of the world as separate from Brahman is, according to him, similar to the perception of a rope as a snake (rajjusarpa). From a distance, a rope may look like a snake, but, as one gets closer to it, one understands the true reality of the rope. The world is like the snake—a false perception of Brahman; as the knowledge of the one absolute reality dawns, the perception of multiplicity of the world disappears. Actions which reinforce separation (doer and the deed) cannot lead to the knowledge of unity. Śankara on the one hand pulled Hinduism out of the conflicts between diverse, complex, and mutually exclusive, ritually-based sects, and, on the other hand, he provided an antithesis to Buddhism and Jainism which had attacked Hinduism for its ritualism.

The phase of medieval Hinduism (1000 C.E. to 1400 C.E.) marks the arrival of the Muslims in India. While describing the sociopolitical situation in India at that time Morgan (1953:39) points out,

There is no doubt that the Hindus suffered terribly on account of the religious fanaticism of the Muslim conquerors. There the forcible conversions, destruction of temples, and desecration of holy places.

Hinduism was forced to defend itself against agressive Islam. Since confrontation with Islam was impossible due to the political power which Islam wielded, Hinduism withdrew from contact with Islam and became introverted. It tried to preserve its identity by accentuating the particulars which separated it from Islam. This served to consolidate the Hindus and, more importantly, separate them from the Muslims. Hinduism came to be narrowly defined in terms of the caste and rituals and other social practices. This was required by the sociopolitical context of the time. Emphasizing the "universal" character of Hinduism would have been detrimental to the goal of preserving the Hindu identity. As a result, the atrocities committed by Brāhmaṇāḍ and (the upper castes) toward the Śūdras increased, and women were shut off from public life under the guise of "preserving their chastity." Cut off from its "universal" aspect, Hinduism disintergrated into mutually-exclusive communities trying to preserve their individual identity. Caste became the only link among them. Retrogressive practices surfaced.

This contextualization of Hinduism was counteracted by strong groups of devotees, sampradāyas , in various parts of India. The Vārkarī Pantha, supported by the worshippers of Viṭthal in Mahārāshtra (1200 C.E.-1800 C.E.); Rāmānanda(14th century C.E.), the ardent worshipper of Rāma; the mystic Kabīr (15th century C.E.), who treated Hinduism and Islamic beliefs as identical; Sūfis in the north India; Alvāras (10th century C.E.); Nāyanmārs (700 C.E. to tenth century C.E.); the Haridāsa and the Viraśaiva saints (Vaiṣnava and Śaiva respectively) in south India; the Rādhā-Krishna cult based on the philosophical teachings of Niṃbārka (12th century C.E.); Mīrābai in Rajasthan (16th century C.E.); Vallabha (15th century C.E.); and Chaitanya (16th century C.E.) in Bengal were some of the prominent landmarks during the Muslim period. These sects and saints continued to draw the impetus for their movements from the traditional devotional sects (Bhakti-marga) of Hinduism. Each had a particular deity (Rāma, Kṛṣṇa, Śiva) whom they worshipped; however, their worship bypassed restrictions on language, caste, rituals, and gender. The only qualification needed for a devotee was faith in God. Pilgrimages to holy places (tīrtha), repetition of God's name (japa), and singing prayers (bhajan and kīrtan) were all viewed as legitimate ways to worship. These devotional movements were based on the universal character of

Hinduism as experienced by the saints and mystics. Once again we see the integration of Hinduism on the basis of its universal principles. Nānak, a 15th century mystic, brought about a fusion of Hinduism and Islam into a new system of beliefs—Sikhism. The mystics and saints of this period on the one hand consolidated diverse castes, beliefs, and practices and maintained the Hindu identity in the face of Muslim expansionist rule. The teachings of these "integrators" are illuminating. They either emphasize the equality of all deities worshipped in various forms, rituals, languages, and other practices by accepting them as incarnations of One God, or they point out that all of the deities are equally worthless toward understanding the true nature of God, if they restrict the vision of God exclusively to that deity. Kabir says:

> The Hindu dies saying 'Ram',
> the Muslim 'Khuda'.
> Says Kabir : one lives
> When one goes to neither.
> — Schomer (1987:71)

> Gorakhṉath, a major mystic, says:
> The Hindu call on Ram
> The Muslim on Khuda
> The Yogi calls on the Invisible one,
> In whom there is neither Ram nor Khuda.
> — Schomer (1987:70)

Following Muslim rule, India came under British rule, which brought with it a Western empirical view of the world, a new language (English), a new system of education, modern technolgy, and most of all, a vision of material success. Hinduism, which was already ailing often discriminatory and punitive Muslim rule, poverty, age-old oppressive social and ritualistic practices, and a dearth of interest in political power and nationalism, confronted a new oppresive rule. While Muslims were committed to religious expansionism, the British were determined to enlarge the domain of their political power. If Hinduism were to be reformed, the British (and a number of Hindus too) believed that "reformed Hinduism should be neither polytheistic nor pantheistic, but monotheistic. All intelligent people now believe in existence of only one true God. There are no such beings as Śiva, Saraswati, Durga, or three hundred and thirty million of the Hindu pantheon. . . .The blasphemous assertion aham brahmāsmi, I am Brahma, would no longer be made. . . . All idols would be destroyed. . . .The Vedas, the Code of Manu, the Rāmāyana, Mahābhārata, the Purāṇas, etc., seen as teaching polytheism, pantheism, containing debasing representations of God, unjust laws, false history, false science, false morals, would no longer be considered sacred books. Hindu worship in temples would cease. . . . Castes would no longer be recognized. Take away sweetness from sugar and it is no longer sugar, deprive a man of reason, and he is no longer a human being. Hinduism without its gods, its sacred books, its temples, its worship, its caste, would be no longer Hinduism, but an entirely different religion, like the Sādharana Brahmo Samaj. It would be simply theistic." ("India Hindu and India Christian or, What Hinduism has done for India and what Christianity would do for it. An appeal to thoughtful Hindus," 1900;40; Quoted in Klostermaier 1989:386).

History did not oblige the British prediction. Hinduism not only recovered, but bounced back with more vitality than ever before, without giving up its traditional beliefs. Four major movements were launched in response to the sociopolitical context. Ram Mohan Roy's (1772-1833) movement, based on social and religious reform, was called Brāhma Samāj (the society of the believers in Brahmā). Harmful practices such as child-marriage and satī were eradicated because of the constant efforts of Roy. He accepted the Vedas not as flawless but as being full of error. He promoted the worship of only one god (Brahma), as opposed to many gods. In general, he promoted a compromise between Hinduism and Christianity. This contextualization of Hinduism was an attempt to abolish the diversity in Hinduism at the cost of its basic belief in the multiple manifestations of one god.

In contrast, Dayānanda Saraswatī (1824-1883) contextualized Hinduism in the orthodox mold of Sanātana dharma. In his work Satyārtha Prakāśa, he presented the principles of Sanātana dharma. He revived the system of gurukulas (literally guru's abode—training/teaching institutions). He introduced Śuddhi-ceremony (similar to conversion in Christianity) to allow Hindus who had converted to Islam and Christianity to return to Hinduism. He created Ārya Samaj (society of the Āryans). Dayananda's Ārya Samaj, though rooted in orthodox Hindu system, did not take into account the contemporary developments in Hinduism. His was the contextualization of Hinduism within the Vedic orthodoxy without any reference to the changing sociopolitical situation under the British rule. The above two movements presented a somewhat narrow and reductionist view of Hinduism.

There were two other movements which had an enormous impact on Hinduism as well as on Hindu society: The first was the Ramakrishna Mission founded by Swami Vivekananda during the late 19th century and the second was Gandhi's movement in the 1930s. What these movements shared was that they revived the "universal" character of Hinduism and provided solutions to contemporary problems within the framework of universal beliefs. They did not reform Hinduism; they re-interpreted it. While Gandhi's movement was predominantly responsible for national freedom, the Ramakrishna Mission played a key role in preserving Hinduism without excluding any other religion.

Both Ramakrishna and Gandhi interpreted Hinduism in their sociocultural context within its universal framework of the unity of all Hindus and non-Hindus. At the same time, they consolidated and empowered the Hindu system of faith. They both promoted non-sectarian Hinduism. Ramakrishna did not defend Hinduism as a system to be protected against the threat of other religions; rather, he promoted eclecticism and the all-inclusiveness of Hinduism. Islam and Christianity were not to be feared but rather accepted as legitimate paths toward the realization of the Truth. As Ramakrishna says,

> It is not good to feel that one's own religion alone is true and all others are false. God is one only, and not two. Different people call on Him by different names: some as Allāh, some as God, and others as Krishna, Śiva, and Brahman. It is like the water in a lake. Some drink it at one place and call it 'jal', others at another place and call it 'pāni', and still others at a third place and call it 'water'. The Hindus call it 'jal', the Christians 'water', and the Mussalmāns 'pāni'. But it is one and the same thing. Opinions are but paths. Each religion is but a path leading to God, as rivers come from different directions and ultimately become one in the one ocean.
>
> —Ramakrishna (1942: 264-265).

Ramakrishna's integration of all faiths was based on his vision of Hinduism as a universal religion. Ramakrishna's disciple, Swami Vivekananda emphasized the importance of the equality of religions and further promoted the need to acknowledge the diversity of religious faiths. In his well-known talk at the Parlaiment of World's Religions in Chicago in 1890, Swami Vivekananda said,

> The Christian is not to become a Hindu or Buddhist, nor a Hindu or a Buddhist to become a Christian. But each must assimilate the spirit of others and yet preserve its individuality and grow according to his own law of growth. A river flows a thousand miles down the circuitous mountain side to where it joins the seas, and a man standing there to tell it to go back and start anew and assume a more direct course! That man is a fool. You are a river that flows from the heights of Zion. I flow from the lofty peaks of the Himalayas. I don't say to you, go back and come down as I did, you're wrong. This is more wrong than foolish. Stick to your beliefs. The truth is never lost. Books may perish, nations may go down in a crash, but the truth is preserved and is taken up by some man and handed back to society which proves a grand and continuous revelation of God.
>
> —Vivekananda (1973: 428)

Both the guru Ramakrishna and the disciple Vivekananda based their mission on the basic belief of the oneness of all in Advaita Vedānta. They have clearly shown the relevance of Hinduism to the modern world of constantly interacting faiths, societies, and traditions. Further, Vivekananda promoted the mission of "service to mankind," which was derived from the Hindu doctrine of divinity of all. "Seeing God in man" and, thereby, helping the underpreviledged (e.g., through hospitals and schools) thus became a crucial aspect of his religious mission.

Gandhi made Hinduism relevant to the movement for national freedom from British rule. He claimed to be a Hindu first and a political leader second. Gandhi treated the Bhagavadgītā as his scripture. Self rule or self-governance for him was spiritual freedom, which is the basic right of every human being. Freedom of thought requires social and political freedom, and thus, the political movement for national freedom was spiritually and religiously justified. Moreover, the path to achieve freedom had to be one of non-violence (ahiṃsā). Gandhi pointed out that the Hindu belief in the underlying oneness of all phenomena forbids violence of any kind on three grounds. First, since there is no "other" in the absolute sense of the term, any violence directed toward another consequently hurts the violent person or society. Second, if one is convinced (on intellectual, moral, and ethical grounds) of the "truth" of one's conviction (of the right to the spiritual, social, and political freedom of all human beings), then one should be able to convince others, including one's enemies, of its validity. If it is the same soul which abides in all human beings, then the opponent must have the capacity to realize the validity of one's views. The third rationale against violence is that one's method of convincing an opponent must be of satyāgraha (holding on to the truth even in the face of death) and following the non-violent path of constant discussions, persuasions, and accomodations to one's opponent's views. Non-violence for Gandhi is the expression of the truth, the unity of all. It is a constant adaptation to the environment, constant accomodation of different views (including those of one's opponents), and the development of one's position in the context of another's views. Non-violence, he believed, has spiritual and moral power which violence does not or cannot ever have. The question does arise time and again: what if Gandhi had failed in his efforts to convince his opponents (the British) of the validity of his proposal? Gandhi believed that non-violence could never fail in any walk of life—domestic, institutional, economic, or political. "Where it has seemed sometimes to have failed, I have ascribed it to my imperfections. I claim no perfection for myself but I claim to be a passionate seeker after truth." (quoted in Bondurant, 1958: 113). Additionally, Gandhi removed the amnesia about the spiritual equality of the social classes from the minds of Hindus and proclaimed that the Sudras (lower castes) were Harijan (God's people) and thereby actively fought the social discrimination against them.

While Ramakrishna rejuvinated Hinduism, Gandhi made it politically and socially powerful. Similarly, Ramana Maharshi, Aurobindo Ghosh, and Sai Baba, among others, vehemently promoted Hinduism based on its universal character. In general, it was the interpretation of the particular context within universal principles. Once again, it was the integrative rather than the segragationist nature of Hinduism which had prevailed.

Conclusion

In the preceding discussion, we have seen that at various periods in its history, Hinduism has resolved a number of socio-political and religious issues within the framework of its all-inclusive worldview. What needs to be stressed in this context is that this integration, at the existential as well as conceptual levels, was not identical in its purpose or methods at different points in time. It is difficult, though not impossible, to establish a correlation between the goal and the method of integration. However, what we can say beyond doubt is that integration did take place and that the methods used for this process had their origin in the all-inclusive worldview of Hinduism. A brief recapitulation of the discussion will succinctly illuminate the variety of the processes which led to various types of integration.

The integration of many gods and goddesses of the Hindu and non-Hindu pantheon was possible because of the basic Hindu belief in the existence of One God with its many manifestations. The processes of Sanskritization or Āryanization of non-Āryan gods and Dravidization or Indiginization of the Āryan gods were justified and/or sanctioned within the Hindu belief system. Similarly, the synthesis of many gods within the Hindu system during and before the Purāṇic period was facilitated by the notion of Āvatāra (the incarnation of God).

The Bhagavadgītā marks one of the grandest theories of integration at all levels—existential, social, and spiritual. It presents a theory which consists of diverse processes of integration. What is important to note here is that all of the processes were rooted in the primary Hindu belief in the oneness and divinity of all. The Bhagavadgītā focused on the ontological unity of all existences (based on the belief that everything is created from the One and is rooted in the One). Through the acceptance of gods of different sects and religions as many incarnations of the One God, the Bhagavadgītā brought about the integration of various belief systems. By treating rituals, selfless actions, and meditation as three of the many possible paths to reach the single goal of oneness with God and other existences, the Bhagavadgītā sanctioned various apparently mutually exclusive religious practices as legitimate. This integration was based on the unity of the goal. And finally, the integration of the four castes was based on the intergroup mobility across births, the cohesiveness of the social structure, and, most importantly, the variation in the potential of individuals. Moreover, the social position was not a barrier to the accomplishment of the spiritual goal.

The great "integrators" of the medieval period broke down the dichotomies in Hinduism at conceptual as well as at practical levels. They liberated the Hindu system from the restrictions of language, rituals, scriptures, and castes, and emphasized the experiential dimension of Truth. The mystics and saints sanctioned the use of a variety of languages (Āryan as well as Dravidian), rituals, scriptures, and other practices as legitimate. It was their experience of the Truth (and not mere knowledge of the scriptures) which allowed them to integrate the Hindu system. The saints appealed to the universal dimension of Hinduism—the faith in One God and the experience of it within themselves. Bhakti, devotion to the personal deity, was sanctioned as the path.

Ramakrishna consolidated various belief-systems (Islam, Hinduism, Sikhism, and Christianity, among others) by claiming that they merely different visions of the same divine. Gandhi integrated Hindu society by considering the social, political, and religious problems as interconnected, thereby breaking down the walls between "this worldly" and "other worldly" concerns. Thus, he justified the freedom movement as the movement toward the "freedom of the soul."

In order to understand the integrative vision of Hinduism, it is crucial to recognize that the Hindu integration of diverse forms is not based on destroying or curtailing individual identities, whether they be existential, conceptual, concrete, or abstract. Rather, the goal of integration in Hinduism is to explain apparently mutually exclusive opposites on the basis of a larger underlying framework, which should be able to justify opposites as logical possibilities. In this approach to integration, the competing realities are treated as manifestations of that one underlying framework/rationale. They present a challenge, an avenue which leads to higher knowledge.

The issue of the identity of Hinduism is once again raised within the context of its interaction with Islam and Sikhism. After about a thousand years, Hinduism is defining itself as a majority religion in India vis-a-vis the minority religions. There is a tension between narrowly contextualizing Hinduism as a religion different from others and emphasizing its universal character. The outcome remains to be seen. Another context where Hinduism needs to adapt and change is in the diaspora (to the US, the UK, Canada, Trinidad, Fiji, and others) where it is a minority religion. Will Hinduism define itself narrowly or will its universal dimension take over? We will have to wait and see. If history is any indication, Hinduism will not give up its universal character. For if it does, it will not be Hinduism.

Works Cited

Bondurant, J.V. 1958. *Conquest of violence : the Gandhian philosophy of conflict.* Berkeley: University of California Press.

Bose, A.C. 1966. *Hymns from the Vedas.* Bombay : Asia Publishing House.

Chapple, C. 1986. *Karma and creativity.* Albany : State University of New York Press.

Dandekar, R.N. 1967. *Some aspects of the history of Hinduism.* Poona : University of Poona.

Dumont, L. 1970. "Religion/Politics and History of India." In L. Dumont, *Collected papers in Indian sociology.* The Hague : Mouton.

Gatewood, L.E. 1985. *Devi and the spouse goddess.* Riverdale : The Riverdale Company Inc. Publishers.

Goudriaan, T. 1978. *Māyā divine and human. Delhi* : Motilal Banarsidass.

Gould, H.A. 1987. *The Hindu caste system: the sacralization of a social order.* Delhi: Chanakya Publications.

Halbfass. 1980. "Karma, Apūrva, and 'Natural' Causes : Observations on the Growth and Limits of the theory of Śāstras. In *Karma and rebirth in classical Indian traditions.* Berkeley : University of California Press.

Hiriyanna, M. 1952. *The quest for perfection.* Mysore : Kavyalaya Publishers.

Hopkins, T.J. 1971. *The Hindu religious tradition.*Belmont, California : Wadsworth Publishing Company.

Kinsley, D. 1986. *Hindu Goddesses : visions of the divine feminine in the Hindu Religious tradition.* Berkeley : University of California Press.

Klostermair, K.K. 1989. *A survey of Hinduism.* Albany : State University of New York Press.

Lapierre, D. 1985. *The city of joy.* New York : Warner Books.

Lennoy, R. 1971. *The speaking tree: A study of Indian culture and society.* London : Oxford University Press.

The complete works of Swami Vivekanada. 1973. Māyavati Memorial Edition (14th Edition).Calcutta : Advaita Ashrama.

Morgan, K. 1953. *The religion of the Hindus.* 1953. Delhi : Motilal Banarsidass.

Nāmdev Gatha. 1970. Bombay: Shasakiya Mudran va lekhan samagri.

Needham, J. 1965 *Science and civilizations in China.* Cambridge.

Nikhilanda, Swami. 1984. *Vivekananda: The Yogas and other works.* New York: Ramakrishna-Vivekananda Center.

_____________. 1942. *The gospel of Sri Ramakrishna.* New York: Ramakrishna-Vivekananda Center.

O'Flaherty, W.D. 1984. *Dreams, illusion and other realities.* Chicago : The University of Chicago Press.

Pandharipande, R.V. 1990. *The eternal Self and cycle of Saṟs!ra : an introduction to Asian mythology and religion.* Massachusetts : Ginn Press.

Radhakrishnan, S. 1927. *Indian philosophy.* London : George Allen Unwin.

Schomer, K. 1987. "The Dohā as a Vehicle of Sant Teachings". In *The Sants.* edited by Schomer, K. and McLeod, W. H. Delhi : Motilal Banarsidass.

Shaurie, A. 1979. *Hinduism: essence and consequence.* Sahibabad : Vikas Publishing House.

Smith, H. 1958. *The world's religions.* San Fransisco : Harper.

Srinivas, M.N. 1956. A note on Sanskritization and Westernization. *Far Eastern Quarterly.*15: 481-496

Shairi, G.P. 1966. (translated and edited). *Surdas: Bhramargit-sār.* Agra: Vinod Pustak Mandir.

Wadley, S.S. 1992. "Women and the Hindu Tradition." In *Women in India : Two Perspectives.* Jacobson, D. and S. Wadley (ed.). Delhi : Manohar.

White, L. Jr. 1962. *Medieval technology and social change.* Oxford: Oxford University Press.

Yadav, B.S. 1980. "V*aiṣṇavism on Hans Kung: a Hindu theology religious pluralism.*" *Religion and Society* (Bangalore) Vol. 27 no.2.

Zimmer, H. 1948. *Myths and symbols in Indian art and civilization.* (1995 Edition) edited by Campbell, J. Princeton: Princeton University Press.

Chapter 13

Contemporary Hinduism

Arvind Sharma

"Eternity is in love with the productions of time." If this statement is true, then how much more would the eternal be in love with the contemporary and, more specifically how much more would the Sanātana Dharma (eternal religion) be in love with contemporary Hinduism or Yugadharma? This chapter will explore the manifestations of contemporary Hinduism.

If one may use a geometric metaphor to represent a tradition, each religion can be likened to a charmed circle. When we draw a circle, circumference and center spring simultaneously into existence. For our purposes, however, it may be more useful to consider one as coming into existence after the other, the circumference after the center or the center after the circumference. If that be the case, then, with certain religions, the center precedes the drawing of the circumference. Christianity and Islam are pre-eminent examples of this type of religion. Their center is provided by a given body of doctrines and practices, and the religious community grows around such a nucleus. The defining doctrines and practices come first, and the community forms around them. In the case of certain other religions, the circumference comes first and then the center is identified. Today's Judaism is a religion of this type. To put it succinctly, there are Christians because there is Christianity, and there are Muslims because there is Islam, but there is Judaism because there are Jews.

We can designate the religions of the first type as "Religions of the Center" and the second type as "Religions of Circumference," then Christianity and Islam could be described to as "Religions of the Center" and Judaism as a "Religion of Circumference." In this classification, Hinduism is a religion of circumference. There is Hinduism because there are Hindus. Hinduism may now and then lack foci but it cannot lack loci; one does not have to become a Hindu to be a Hindu, although it is now possible to be a Hindu by "converting" to Hinduism.

This metaphor, although helpful, is not very accurate. For instance, the conventions of mathematics encourage us to look upon the concepts of circle or square as static, but religions constitute a dynamic reality. That is to say, the circumference, while still a circumference, could well constitute a shifting, undulating, or moving circumference, as well as a contracting or expanding one. A religion, as a circle, may exhibit both these forms of dynamism. Additionally, the center could also be reconfigured, though this is more true of religions of circumference. Thus, Judaism has not only contracted in terms of the circle, but also the Holocaust has led to a change in the nature of its center. It is perhaps less theocentric now than it was before that event.

If Hinduism is a religion of circumference, then contemporary Hinduism is characterized by some changes in its circumference. In a geographic sense, it has undergone extension, with the emigration of the Hindus to other parts of the world from their homeland in India. The process started in the last century, with the movement of indentured laborers to Fiji , the Mauritius and Caribbean Islands and the movement of Indian trading communities to East Africa, for example. Sometimes, the two movements overlapped, as in South Africa. But it is in the second half of the present century that Indian emigration, especially to the West, has assumed major proportions (see Helweg, this volume). And if Indians migrate, can Hinduism be far behind? Soon one million of the USA's three hundred million people will be Hindu. The Hindus of the Indian diaspora now constitute an increasingly powerful voice in defining Hinduism, perhaps exercising a clout out of proportion to their numbers on account of the resources they command. Add to this the fact that some in the West have embraced Hinduism ardently and voluntarily and the clout of Hindus outside India becomes even more of a factor to reckon with. The popular monthly, *Hinduism Today*, is published by one such group of Hindus.

From the beginning of the eighteenth century, the universalizing element within Hinduism has also become increasingly significant. In modern Hinduism, the path of knowledge was exemplified by Ramana Maharshi (1879-1950); that of devotion by

Ramakrishna (1836-1886); that of action by Mahatma Gandhi (1869-1948); and "no-path" by Jiddu Krishnamurti (1895-1986). These examples of the spirit of Hinduism possess universal appeal. Hinduism continues to embody the paradox of a religion primarily ethnic in composition but potentially universal in appeal; a paradox softened by the fact that people outside India are also turning to it without having to abandon their native faith. We may be witnessing once more the redefinition of Hinduism.

This contrasts with the position of Hindus in India, where they have declined from eighty-five percent to eighty-three percent of India's population in the second half of this century and have repeatedly failed to convert their statistical majority into a political one. At the moment, Hindu identity in India is under siege politically, socially and rhetorically: politically, through the obfuscation of Hindu self-assertion with its communal perversion; socially, through the affirmation of competing identities along caste, regional, and linguistic fault-lines, and rhetorically, by it marginalization in elite discourse. (See Hardgrave, and Srinivas in this volume.)

The problem of defining Hinduism boils down to one of defining a Hindu, and this has been problematized in India in terms of contemporary Hinduism. There is, at one extreme, the view that Hinduism is a culture rather than a religion and that therefore every Indian is a Hindu, as it were. This seems to be the significance of Hindutva, when it is differentiated from Hinduism. At the other extreme lies the view that only a caste Hindu can be properly so called and that the former "untouchables," now known as Dalits and the tribal population of India as well, are either only nominally Hindu or fall outside its pale. There is also an intermediate position, with legal backing, which regards all Indians who are not "Muslim, Christian, Zoroastrian, or Jew" as Hindus. A somewhat less inclusive intermediate position is also possible. It would exclude Buddhists, Sikhs, and Jainas form the category of Hindus but continue to include Dalits and Tribals. These definitional options reflect the state of ferment that Hinduism—and India—is in. Just as medieval Hinduism was characterized by the Bhakti movement, contemporary Hinduism is characterized by what may be called the Śakti movement or the empowerment of various classes as well as the masses, thereby generating a politics of identity at several levels because such empowerment is proceeding at several levels. In modern Hinduism, the political was personal during the struggle for Independence; in post-independent, that is, contemporary Hinduism, the personal has become political.

Independence from British rule empowered Indians as a whole; Indian secularism empowered minorities a long time ago, while recent political movements have empowered Hindus as a whole, as well as other distinct entities within Hinduism, such as the Backward Classes and former Untouchables. The designation of this movement as a Śakti movement is further justified by the fact that empowerment along gender lines is now on the horizon. Too many genies are out of the bottle to be able to fulfill the wishes of their masters. In fact, one might well wonder who or where the master is. What has been uncaged, however, can only be tamed. It cannot be returned to the cage, and this imparts a tumultuous dimension to contemporary Hinduism.

What Is Contemporary?

When does the modern become contemporary? The decision must be arbitrary, though not whimsical. In the case of the Hindu tradition, it may even be fixed with some precision—midnight of August 14, 1947 when India experienced the bittersweet moment of both being partitioned and becoming independent. After Independence, it should have emerged into a free world like a lion emerging from a cage. Instead, because of Partition, it entered the comity of nations somewhat subdued. There can be little doubt that contemporary Hinduism would have followed a different course if India had not been partitioned. The point was made in blood when Mahatma Gandhi was assassinated on January 30, 1948; this was symbolic of the blood-letting which accompanied partition. Time seemed to be suspended when one witnessed the immersion of his remaining ashes, forty-nine years later to the very day, by his great grandson at Allahabad. How many recall that the immersion of his ashes in the Indus river was denied by the Pakistani government in 1948, a country he had given his life to keep afloat. There need be no symmetry in virtue, but there is virtue in symmetry.

Mahatma Gandhi was the coping stone of modern Hinduism, the blood bath in which he drowned was the concrete in which the foundations of contemporary Hinduism were laid. The Indian state virtually ignored the belated immersion of Mahatma Gandhi's ashes on January 30, 1997 but accorded belated recognition to Netaji Subhas Chandra Bose as a national hero, on the centennial of his birth on January 23, 1997 (Burns 1997: A12). Bose, a patriot, who, as opposed to Gandhi, advocated the violent overthrow of the British, is a fitting metaphor for our times. The parabolic quality of the metaphor in the context of contemporary Hinduism is enhanced if it is contrastively suggested that while the unheard word from Gandhi's lips may have been Rahīm after he had uttered Rām□as he fell (Lavan, 1996, 3), the Babari Mosque was razed to the ground on December 6, 1992 also in the name of Rama. The turning point in Mahatma Gandhi's life came when he was unceremoniously ejected from a railway compartment to accommodate the whim of a white passenger, an incident which drove him to campaign against racism non-violently, while that of Subhas Chandra Bose came when he slapped his British teacher at his college for talking insultingly about Indians and was rusticated for it. These represent two responses from within the Hindu tradition to racism and imperialism.

The pulsating reality of Hinduism in contemporary India seems to be undergoing an alteration. This is an indication of how far contemporary Hinduism has come, or how far it has strayed, depending on our point of view. Or perhaps we don't have to choose. The Buddha performed a miracle in which he would turn one half of his body into a blaze of fire and the other into a torrent of water. This could serve as a metaphor for the miracle contemporary Hinduism is being called upon to perform. Its universalism may have to undergo a baptism of fire within India, even as it refreshes the world with its cooling and healing waters

Contemporary Hinduism and Hindu Scriptures

The Bhagavadgītā remains as popular as ever, but in contemporary Hinduism, the Vedas have received a new lease of life for reasons as powerful as they are unlikely. This statement might raise a few eyebrows. Have not the Vedas always been acknowledged as the fountainhead of Hinduism? Yes, that has always been true, but in the past, although less so in modern Hinduism, its adherents used to slake their religious thirst more downstream. Two highly divergent factors, as divergent as the scholarly is from the popular, seem to be responsible for the new development. Moreover, in the scholarly realm itself, two distinct factors have been operating in two distinct theaters, India and the West. In India, the revival of interest in the Vedas has, curiously, come about because an increasingly larger proportion of women are pursuing Vedic studies and thus carrying it back home. In the West, although this also applies to India, the question of the so-called invasion of India by the Aryans is being contested so strongly by Indians that even Western mainstream scholarship has had to offer renewed justification for this basic thesis of Western Indology. The idea is being dismissed as an imperial fantasy by the scholars at one end of one spectrum (Feuerstein 1995), while at the other, the idea of a cataclysmic invasion has been toned down to that of gradual immigration (Erdosy 1995). This scholarly dispute has had the side effect of raising interest in the Vedas to a higher level.

In the popular realm, however, curiously once again, it is the Ayurveda which has contributed to this revival, as alternative medicine extends its toehold to a foothold in the Western medical establishment and then becomes the beneficiary of a pizza effect of sorts, a term used by anthropologists to refer to a rise in status of an item in the original culture after a higher value is attached to it in a host culture. This is specially noteworthy for two reasons. Within Hinduism, there has been a subterranean division of opinion as to whether the Vedas are the source of only spiritual knowledge or of both sacred and secular knowledge. The Vedānta tradition illustrates the former position, while the evolution of Gandharvaveda, Sthapatyaveda, Dhanurveda, and Āyurveda attest to the latter. Swami Dayānanda (1824-1883) opted for the latter view and extended it by attempting to discover modern science in the Vedas. However, interestingly, now it is the traditional system of Hindu medicine which has become associated with the Vedas. This aspect of the Veda (as distinguished from other similar texts) was not only open to the Śūdras but welcomed them as students (Murty 1991: 20)—uninhibited as they were by ritualistic scruples in the pursuit of medical knowledge. This point will subsequently connect with the role of castes in contemporary Hinduism. (See M.N. Srinivas in this volume.)

Thus, there are ample indications that the Vedas are beginning to occupy more space in the Hindu imagination now than was the case in the period immediately preceding it. The Vedas are, after all, as much symbolic as literal in their significance, which explains in part the difficulties scholars sometime have in figuring out their implication (Krishna 1996: 63-109).

Religious Tolerance in Contemporary Hinduism

Some, if not many, have argued that the entire edifice of Hindu tolerance collapsed like a house of cards with the razing of the mosque in Ayodhya. Sober reflection, however, points to a different conclusion. According to surveys conducted a week after the incident, approval of the demolition among the Hindus hovered around twenty-five percent. At the end of the second week, it rose to forty-eight percent after four BJP state governments were dismissed by the central government, three of them illegally, according to a subsequent judgment of the Supreme Court. This could easily have bumped the figure up. Years after the event, the approval rate remains the same. Nevertheless, Hindu tolerance is being tested and tried in contemporary India. One factor at work here is internal to Hinduism. Many Hindu leaders have criticized

Hinduism even in the past for being tolerant to the point of being morally lax. Rabindranath Tagore told Romain Roland, when Roland began to praise the spirit of religious toleration in India:

> Perhaps that has also been our weakness, and it is due to an indiscriminate spirit of toleration that all forms of religious creed and crudities have run riot in India, making it difficult for us to realize the true foundation of our spiritual faith. The practice of animal sacrifice, for instance, has nothing to do with our religion, yet many people sanction it on the ground of tradition. Similar aberrations of religion can be found in every country. Our concern in India today is to remove them and intensify the larger beliefs which are our true spiritual language. We should stress always the "larger sense." Truth cannot afford to be tolerant where it faces positive evil, it is like sunlight, which makes the existence of evil germs impossible. As a matter of fact, Indian religious life suffers today from the lack of a wholesome spirit of intolerance, which is characteristic of creative religion . . .
>
> —Chakravarty (1961:104, 105).

Hinduism then is what you can get away with! In this dubious respect, Hinduism continues to be "tolerant." The rise in crime and religion-related violence, rampant consumerism, ecological neglect—all point to the need for strengthening the moral tone of Hinduism. Moreover, the response-threshold of the Hindus in the face of perceived insults has been steadily decreasing over the past two decades, and in some circles, this is interpreted as decline in its level of tolerance. The fact that the internationally acclaimed painter M.F. Hussain had to apologize, in 1996, for nude paintings of a Hindu goddess and a Hindu heroine, he drew fifteen years ago clearly points in that direction, whatever our individual sentiments about it may be.

The explanations of Hindu tolerance range from Hindu hubris to Hindu hospitality, but at its heart lies the insight that if you reduce truth to a particular form of it, you lose it. The charge that Hinduism includes all the religions within itself is misleading because Hinduism includes all of them and itself. There is no standard line in contemporary Hinduism, only standard deviation.

One factor which has problematized Hindu tolerance is the continuing Hindu ambivalence towards two religions of non-Indian origin in India, namely, Islam and Christianity. Hinduism continues to look askance toward conversion, while these religions are proselytizing religions which claim to have the truth. According to contemporary Hinduism, only the Truth has the truth; we can only have a truth. Although it is not so much opposed to "calm conversion," for spiritual reasons, it remains passionately opposed to "alarm conversion"—when people are either coerced or tempted into it. Moreover, contemporary Hinduism is also overcoming its amnesia regarding how it has been oppressed in the past by these religions and interprets the increasing clamor for "minority rights" (read: freedom to aggressively proselytize) as continuing forms of it. If we place alongside this, the perception that Indian secularism is anti-Hindu in nature, the erosion of Hindu tolerance does not appear that mysterious. The fact that such a representative movement of modern Hinduism as the Ramakrishna Mission should have had to declare itself as a non-Hindu body in order to function freely and protect itself against interference by the state is an invidious and egregious example of the prevailing state of affairs. Anecdotal evidence in support can also be adduced. A newspaper in Madras refused to carry the news of the appointment of Professor K. Sivaraman to the first-ever chair in Hindu studies in North America instituted at Concordia Univ., on grounds that printing such news would impugn its "secular" credentials. Hinduism has long worked under the assumption that the surest way to find an enemy is to look for one. Its predicament arises from not knowing what to do if forced to confront the fact that enemies may be looking at it with obvious intolerance, when it itself is not programmed to look with such intolerance.

Tolerance remains the signature of Hinduism, amidst protests that it is becoming almost illegible. It would be premature to conclude, however, that contemporary Hinduism has given up on it. On the contrary, it seems to achieve an unprecedented extension in the remark with which the Hindu Swami Muktananda greeted the Jewish Rabbi Richard Rubenstein: "I hope you do not believe in your religion, I don't believe in mine," which culminated in a burst of Hinjew hilarity.

Karma and Caste

In classical Hinduism, the concepts of Karma and rebirth, and the institutes of varṇa, jāti and untouchability all fit snugly together. In modern Hinduism, they were deconstructed. Mahatma Gandhi disconnected untouchability from varṇa and jāti or the caste system as we know it, although the two together are perhaps more accurately translated as the claste system [(class: varṇa) + (caste: jāti)]. Dr. B.R. Ambedkar detached the doctrines of Karma and rebirth from both the caste system as well as "untouchability" and going a step further, became a Buddhist. Contemporary

Hinduism also disconnects all of them and could conceptually detach even Karma from rebirth. Thus, contemporary Hinduism has accepted the Jaina, Buddhist, Sikh, and Hindu materialist critiques of the traditional caste system. Many Hindus even now maintain, without necessarily abandoning belief in rebirth, that the results of one's action manifest themselves even in the course of a single life, given the steadily rising life-expectancy. Similarly, contemporary Hinduism accepts birth as a basis of positive discrimination through affirmative action policies, while rejecting negative discrimination on that basis thus extending the doctrine of Karma to include not merely individual but social justice as well.

The two main forces operating in contemporary Hinduism are those of historical and social justice. Hindus as a whole seem to feel that their historical struggle for political recognition is being unfairly frustrated; groups within Hinduism feel that their claims to compensation for past wrongs have not been addressed. These two forces are symbolized by the kamandala (holy water-gourd) and Mandal (a moniker for a commission by that name: Government of India, 1980) which recommended extension of reservations beyond the former Untouchables to include the Backward Classes as well. These two forces, which have alternatively also been dubbed Mandal and Mandir (a reference to the movement of build a Rāma Temple in Ayodhya), paradoxically represent competing as well as reinforcing claims on contemporary Hindu awareness, if the behavior of the political parties can serve as a weather-bell. Each party, claiming to espouse one wing of opinion, has been forced to accommodate the aspirations of the other wing to a certain extent, thereby recognizing and validating both. It might be worth bearing in mind here that while politics may favor mobilization through polarization, statesmanship consists in mobilization without polarization. The self-assertion of the Dalits and Backward Castes, however, is a distinct feature of contemporary Hinduism. In this context, those who treat the introduction and extension of reservations purely as a numbers game overlook its symbolic value. Manu is in many ways a false reference point for contemporary Hinduism but to the extent that Manu has been identified with formulating an unjust caste system, the reversing of Manu through positive discrimination is a very powerful signal of one's intentions. Intentions, however, may not be enough. Every year, an average of 15,000 annual openings of government jobs will have to be shared by about 5,000 Backward Classes. But intentions do count—both in and of themselves and as a prelude to action. After all, one can be equally skeptical of the extent to which Manu's infamous discriminatory provisions reflect reality (Spear 1994:70).

Contemporary Hinduism and the Position of Women

Contemporary Hinduism has witnessed the beginning of a drastic transformation in the position of women in the field of religion, just as modern Hinduism witnessed it in the field of politics, of which the Salt March provided sensational evidence. The best indication of the revolutionary nature of the transition, on whose threshold we seem to be standing, is provided by the admission of women to priesthood—long a male bastion of Hinduism and many other religious traditions as well. Even here the fact that women priests have begun to perform the obsequies (antyeṣṭī)—and in Kāsī (Varanasi, the holiest city for Hindus) too—another bastion of orthodoxy (*India Today* 1994, 13)—amounts to a revolution within a revolution. Not only are women becoming priests, they are also being trained as such (*Hinduism Today* 1997, 40).

This empowerment of women is a broad-based phenomenon. In the political sphere, women are rising to positions of power and influence, and many of them are drawn from the lower castes. Mayawati, a Dalit leader, has already served as the Chief Minister of Uttar Pradesh, India's most populous state; Uma Bharati, who is not a high caste Hindu woman, is a powerful voice within the BJP, while the low-caste, illiterate, and former dacoit Phoolan Devi has attained national and even international recognition. Her conversation with a corespondent is revealing:

> "But were you the leader? And if so, how did you get to the top?" I persisted, adding that there were some, including Mohar Singh, who claimed that not unlike a host of women leaders across what was once British India, including Prime Ministers in Sri Lanka, Bangladesh, and Pakistan, she had simply inherited dynastic power from a man. She looked somewhat startled , and then she said, "Of course I was the leader! And don't ever question me about that again. And let me ask you something: What's so strange about that? Wasn't Indira Gandhi the Prime Minister of India? Yes, if she had not been Nehru's daughter, she might not have been, but she lasted in office far longer than he did. And if Mohar Singh doesn't think that women should lead gangs, why doesn't he rise up against those who have raped? If all these gang leaders, who happen to be men, would fight against these atrocities, then they would end. It's not to earn money

> that a woman becomes a dacoit; it's for retribution and revenge. And you tell Mohar Singh that I had absolutely no problem in being the leader of men. Instead of calling me Phoolan, they often called me Phool Singh -which was a testament to my strength. They cleaned my guns, cooked my food, and every morning and every evening they bowed before me, and paid homage to me..." She paused, apparently considering her next words carefully, and then she said: "For centuries every dacoit has honored the goddess Durga. And she is what sustained me: what ever she has, I have; whatever she wants, I want. And all of the men in my gang considered me to be a reincarnation of Durga."
>
> —Weaver (1996: 104).

The career of Phoolan Devi, who hails from the low-caste Mallah (boatmen) community, bears a striking resemblance in some ways to the story of Satyavatī in the Mahābhārata (Ghosh 1996:51-76).

The traditional preference for male offspring, abetted by the misuse of modern science through prenatal sex determination is skewing the sex ratio in favor of the male to such a degree that statisticians are predicting a demographic disaster, or worse. Thus the ambiguity which has characterized the position of women in traditional Hinduism persists in contemporary Hinduism.

Hindusim and Human Rights

Contemporary Hinduism is reacting to contemporary trends, such as the movement for Human Rights. In fact, a tentative declaration of human rights from a Hindu perspective already exists and extends the concepts of human rights in at least four directions: (1) it adds to the right to life, the right to longevity; (2) it asserts the right of every human being as an heir to the entire religious heritage of humanity and not just one religion; (3) it asserts the right to compensation for the violation of human rights and (4) it affirms the global right to immigration (see the Appendix).

Contemporary Hinduism, Ecology, and Consumerism

In terms of ecology, contemporary India needs contemporary Hinduism. In its haste to industrialize, India is heading towards an ecological crisis, if it is not already in it, and contemporary Hinduism can help head it off. It has been identifying various resources within the tradition available in this respect. One resource which in its traditional form seemed to intuit the concept of sustainable development (Dwivedi 1990), may no longer be available in the caste system. But other resources can still be deployed. Prominent among these are a sense of reverence for nature, a belief in a natural and moral order (ṛta and karma), vegetarianism, veneration of the cow, and a commitment to nonviolence combined with an absence of predatory anthro-pocentrism (Young 1995: 126). It is interesting how some features of Hinduism, such as vegetarianism, which had hitherto been considered regressive from a modernistic perspective, take on a progressive character in the context of contemporary developments, such as the ecological crisis. There is no humorist like history.

The ecological crisis is aggravated by population growth and consumerism. The former leads to increased consumption regardless of consumerism. As India's population approaches the figure of one billion, the strain on the resources is bound to increase. If we add to this, the increasing population of the masses and the increasing levels of consumption of the classes, one has a recipe for a serious crisis which will sorely test Hindu spiritual values of self-restraint and its renunciation ethic. However, in this quest, not only Hindu philosophy but Hindu mythology could lend a hand. The following story, narrated here in its generic form, is found in many Purāṇas and hagiographic literature: A childless couple is told by a God that they will conceive and bear a son. The couple is then given a choice—either they can have a son who will live long but not have good character, or have a son who is a paragon of virtue but dies young. The couple opt for the latter. As the time of death approaches, they are grief-stricken. The son is then saved by a miracle or the grace of a deity. A contemporary Hindu scholar offers the following ecological interpretation:

> The story highlights the quality of his life in terms of his dharmic behavior and virtue. I think it is possible to reinterpret the story in a different way one may either have many children with an inferior quality of life and no health or food resources to go around or, one may have one or two children, and make available the best resources for them. A higher quality of life for one or two children, rather than spreading the poverty around to more should be stressed. By the miracle achieved in the steadying of the population rates, humanity may be saved (Narayanan 1997:33-34).

Conclusion

The place of contemporary Hinduism in the context of globalization must also be addressed. As consumerism pulls humanity down to the lowest common denominator, contemporary Hinduism will have to engage in the endeavor of raising it to the highest common factor. It is almost like another episode in the endless mythical struggle between the gods and the demons. Once again, the gods have their back to the wall and the demons are on the point of prevailing. It is usually at this point that an incarnation occurs.

Who can prophesy? Not we who only teach it and not practice it, and certainly not I who does not even preach it but merely teaches it. But I will, at this point, draw support from an illustrious namesake Aurobindo Ghose (1872-1950) who has been hailed as the prophet of modern India. At one stage of his life, he maintained, more or less, that God ceased to incarnate Himself as a human being, that He was now incarnating Himself as the Indian nation to spiritualize the world. As academics, we may bemoan this vision which perpetuates the worst stereotype of spiritual India and the material West, but as Hindus, as contemporary Hindus, can we afford to remain unmoved by it? For the verdict whether Aurobindo Ghose was a genuine prophet or not now lies in our hands!

APPENDIX:

Toward a Hindu Declaration of Universal Human Rights

Preamble

A Hindu is like any other human being, only more so, wherefore all human beings possess the following rights as they are all children of the earth and descended from Manu and possess rationality and morality in common.

Rights as Ends

All human beings possess the natural right to pursue virtuous, material, sensuous, and spiritual ends (dharma-artha-kāma-mokṣa).

Rights as Means

Dharma Rights

All humans are free to choose their own spiritual path and pursue their religion freely and fairly. As the observance of religion is rooted in right knowledge, all have the right to such knowledge.

All human beings are always entitled to simultaneously participate in all the religions of the world as their own by the mere fact of their humanity.

Artha Rights

All have the right to life, property and a proper standard of living. And all have the right to self-government and good government, to secure the good of one and all. At the very minimum good government is characterized by adequate provision of food, clothing, shelter, medicare, and education. These have no maximum.

Kama Rights

All have the right to enjoy all kinds of pleasures subject to morality.

Moksha Rightds

It is the supreme right of all to seek their salvation or emancipation through a path of their choice in accordance with their nature.

Rights Pertaining to the State

I. *Rights based on Non-Violence (ahiṃsa):*

The right to protection of person, of life, of longevity; of due process against arbitrary detention; provision of free legal defense, and only thereafter the liability to due punishment; equality before law and in punishment and adequate compensation for false imprisonment and punishment.

II. *Rights based on Truth (satya):*

The right to presumption of innocence until proven guilty.

III. *Rights based on Non-Appropriation (asteya):*

The right to property.

IV. *Rights based on Purity (śauca):*

The right to freedom from pollution.

V. *Rights based on Self-Restraint (indriyanigrahah):*

The right that the organs of the State do not trespass on the privacy and dignity of the individual.

Additional Rights

As the entire earth constitutes one extended family, all human beings have the unrestricted right to freedom of movement across all countries; nations and states all over the world. Human beings possess the right to due compensation should aforesaid rights be violated, irrespective of whether the violation occurs in the past, present or future.

Works Cited

Burns, John F. 1997. India Rehabilitates Wartime Leader who Fought for Japan. *New York Times,* 24 January.

Chakravarty, Amiya (ed.) 1961. *A Tagore Reader.* Boston: Beacon Press.

Dwivedi, O.P. 1990. *Satyagraha* for Conservation: Awakening the Spirit of Hinduism. In *Ethics of Environment and Development*, edited by J. Engel, Ronald, and Joan Gibb. New York: John Wiley and Sons.

Erdosy, George (ed.) 1995. *The Indo-Aryans of Ancient South Asia.* Berlin & New York: Walter de Gruyter.

Feuerstein, Georg, Subhash Kak, and David Frawley. 1995. *In Search of the Cradle of Civilization: New Light on Ancient India.* Wheaton, IL: Quest Books.

Ghosh, Jayatri 1996. Satyavati: The Matriarch of the *Mahabharata.* In *Visions of Virtue: Women In the Hindu Tradition*, edited by Mandakranta Bose. Vancouver, B.C.

Government of India. n.d. *Reservations for Backward Classes: Mandal Commission Report on the Backward Classes Commission, 1980.* Delhi: Akalanka Publications.

Krishna, Daya. [1991]1996. *Indian Philosophy: A Counter Perspective.* Delhi: Oxford University Press.

Lavanam. 1996. Mahatma Gandhi's Last Words. *Vigil* 12.5:3-4.

Murty, K. Satchidananda. 1993. *Vedic Hermeneutics.* Delhi: Motilal Banarsidass.

Narayanan, Vasudha. One Tree is Equal to Ten Sons. *Journal of the American Academy of Religion.*

Spear, Percival (ed.) 1994. *The Oxford History of India.* Delhi: Oxford University Press.

Weaver, Mary Anne. 1996. India's Bandit Queen. *The Atlantic Monthly* 278.5:89-104.

Young, William A. 1995. *The World's Religions: Worldviews and Contemporary Issues.* Englewood Cliffs, NJ: Prentice Hall.

IV | Society & Politics

Chapter 14

Caste: A Systemic Change

M. N. Srinivas

The 1950's were indeed heady years, with a newly independent India busy laying the foundations for a progressive republic pursuing a policy of planned development, and making its voice heard in international forums under the leadership of Jawaharlal Nehru[1]. The horrors of Partition were beginning to fade, and six hundred and odd princely states had been absorbed into the Union. Perhaps most important of all, the Constitution of India (1950), the blueprint for the country's parliamentary democracy based on adult franchise, was adopted by the Constituent Assembly with the goal of establishing an egalitarian social and economic order. The decision to give a vote to every citizen aged twenty-one and above came as a surprise to thoughtful people, considering the fact that at that timeonly 18.33 percent of the population was literate (male: 27.16 and female: 8.86), and that 82.71 percent of them lived in isolated villages lacking essential facilities of civilized existence. However, in spite of such adverse conditions, democracy has struck roots in India.

Subsequent to the partition of the country in 1947, unsettled conditions prevailed in some parts in the years following the end of the War. Perhaps in reaction to these conditions, the Constitution provided for a strong Center. Some administrative measures following the adoption of the Constitution further strengthened the Center at the expense of the States. For example, the establishment of a Planning Commission, charged with producing five-year plans for the development of the entire country and monitoring its progress everywhere, was a major step in strengthening the Center. Economic centralization was given clear expression in the doctrine that the Government of India would control "the commanding heights of the economy", the private sector being allotted a secondary role. It was also required to obtain permission for starting an industry and for the amount it could produce, any increase requiring permission from the bureaucracy. Permits and licenses were required for importing machinery, raw materials etc. The entire system came to be known later as the "license-permit raj" and it conferred enormous powers on the bureaucracy. (See Srinivasan, this volume.) In the course of three decades or so, the system resulted in corruption penetrating every nook and corner of the administration, both at the Center and in the States. Several other measures such as the introduction of prohibition, failure to introduce electoral reforms and pervasive controls favored the corruption of public life and the rise of smugglers, blackmarketeers, and other anti-social elements.

However, on the positive side, the Government was able to build huge factories for producing iron and steel, fertilizers, coal, lignite etc., and to construct huge dams across rivers for producing electricity and increasing the area under irrigation. Jawaharlal Nehru described these dams and factories as "the temples of modern India". He firmly believed that in modern science and technology lay the solution for India's myriad ills such as mass poverty, illiteracy, ignorance, and superstition. (See Narasimhaiah and Pai, this volume.) A number of national laboratories were set up in different parts of the country to promote scientific and technological research. The University Grants Commission, the Council for Scientific and Industrial Research, and a host of other institutions were created to improve the quality of higher education and to promote research. The infrastructure for a modern and progressive state was being created. These measures introduced a sense of euphoria among the urban middle classes who felt that their country was firmly set on the course of democracy, development and modernization, even though the country's oft-proclaimed aim of building "a casteless and classless society" seemed to many a hyperbole.

Caste in Post-Independence India

It was against this background, and in this atmosphere of elite self-hypnosis, that my Presidential Address, "Caste in Modern India", was read before the Anthropology and Archeology Section of the Indian Science Congress which met in Calcutta in January 1957. I had brought together in my Address evidence to highlight the fact that with the prospect of the transfer of power, even a small amount of it, to the

Indian people from the British rulers in the 1920s, castes had become increasingly active in politico-economic contexts, in order to benefit from access to power. I cited by way of illustration, the non-Brahmin movement in Madras which was active since 1916, and which attempted to unite all "non-Brahmins", including Muslims and Christians, in order to demand reservation in the new legislatures to come into existence under the Government of India Act, 1919. I referred to the part played by caste associations in articulating the needs and demands of castes, and the entry of castes into politics. I mentioned also the gradual weakening of the ideas of purity and impurity which were central to traditional caste.

My address provoked *The Times of India* to remark in an editorial (21 January 1957) that I was "exaggerating" the role of caste in Indian public life and politics. But the general elections which followed a few weeks later demonstrated clearly the fact that politicians had appealed successfully to caste loyalties in order to win votes. The Congress Working Committee, meeting soon after the elections, took formal note of the fact that caste considerations had played a large part in influencing votes. (But it did not mention that its candidates were among those who had benefited greatly by appealing to caste loyalties.) Mr. Jaya Prakash Narayan, the well-known leader from Bihar, commented that irrespective of the party from which a candidate contested the elections, he really stood from his caste (Srinivas 1962: 2).

There is no doubt, however, about the success of democracy in India, which has conducted eleven general elections and dozens of elections to State legislatures. Indian democracy is one of the secular miracles of the modern world when it is remembered that the size of the electorate at the last elections was about four-hundred million, and that forty-eight percent voters were illiterate and most of them lived in over six-hundred thousand villages. Further, the seventy-third and seventy-fourth amendments to the Constitution came into effect in 1993, making it mandatory for state governments to introduce self-government at the district and lower levels, and also in towns and cities (Pančayat Act 1992 and Nagarpalika Act 1992).

It must be pointed out that adult franchise has been crucial in bringing about a revolution, a revolution which was non-violent to begin with but is becoming increasingly violent as the idea of equality of all citizens gets translated into reality.

Article 14 of the Constitution proclaims the equality of citizens before law: "The State shall not deny to any person equality before the law or the equal protection of the laws within the territory of India". Further, "While the principle [of equality] is generally stated in Article 14 which extends to all persons, citizens or aliens, Articles 15 and 16 deal with particular aspects of that equality. Thus, (a) Article 15 is available to citizens only and it prohibits discrimination against any citizen on any matter at the disposal of the State on any of the specified grounds, namely, religion, race, caste, sex or place of birth. (b) Article 16 is also confined to citizens, but it is restricted to one aspect of public discrimination, namely employment under State" (Basu 1994:90).

The banning of Untouchability may be looked at as a logical consequence of the application of Article 15. But Article 17 specifically bans the practice of Untouchability, stating "`Untouchability' is abolished and its practice in any form is forbidden. The enforcement of any disability arising out of `Untouchability' shall be an offence punishable in accordance with the law". Further, "Parliament is authorised to make a law prescribing the punishment for this offence (Article 35), and in exercise of this power, Parliament has enacted the Untouchability (Offences) Act, 1955, which has been amended and renamed (in 1976) as the Protection of Civil Rights Act, 1955" (Basu 1994:93).

But the success of Indian democracy, paradoxical as it may seem, also owes something to caste. At the village level, caste consists of a network of people linked to each other by kinship, and these in turn have links with their castefolk in other villages and towns, and also with the members of other castes living in their own and neighboring villages. This kind of tightly knit society acted as a network which politicians articulated to get elected. Briefly then, the social order of India in the early 1950's, where caste and village were basic elements, made possible bloc-voting, and I referred to the rich and influential leaders of the dominant caste as "vote banks" (Srinivas 1955: 31). The phrase caught on, and has become part of the political lexicon of democratic India.

While the articulation of primordial institutions for mobilizing people facilitated democratic politics, it also led to the need to route political messages through them. No leader or party saw the contradiction involved in asking the leaders of dominant castes in villages to spread the message of equality to their traditional dependents and oppressees. Referring to the socialist rhetoric of the Congress leaders, a young Okkaliga in Rampura asked me, way back in 1948, "How can all people be equal? Are the five fingers of the hand equal?" Besides, leaders of the dominant castes in villages sensed new political and economic opportunities in democracy: they saw their castemen and local leaders becoming legislators and ministers, people approachable for favors. Published lists of state ministers were scrutinized to find out their caste affiliations.

Another factor which favored mobilization was group-based protective discrimination, or "reservation," as it is popularly known. Reservation for the Scheduled Castes and Tribes not only helped mobilize the weakest sections of the society but worked, at least initially, for their integration with other groups. Not only did political parties put up candidates from these sections in designated constituencies, but tried to attract all the voters living in that area to vote for the party candidates. Candidates had to be acceptable to voters from castes and ethnic groups other than their own.

To recapitulate: the main thrust of my address, "Caste in Modern India", went against the dominant rhetoric of the day, that caste was on its way out. On the contrary, adult franchise strengthened caste in politico-economic contexts, and conflict between castes for access to political power, government employment and higher education became a fact of Indian public life. Such conflict has only increased over the years, while politicians who come to power through caste, and stay in power through manipulating caste combinations, speak in public about establishing a caste-free society.

Historical Background

In order to grasp the significance of the changes which are occurring in caste, it is necessary to go back to the beginnings of the nineteenth century. Briefly, British rule was qualitatively different from previous regimes in that it brought with it modern knowledge and ideas, and new technology. Steam-powered ships, railways, printing, post and telegraph, roads and bridges, modern armaments, and bureaucracy, all had the effect of integrating the Indian economy with the British imperial economy. New ideas and values such as democracy, the rule of law and the rights of citizens, also came in, although slowly. Christian missionaries came in, determined to convert the natives to Christianity. (For a detailed discussion of the changes during British rule see Srinivas 1996, Chapters 2, 3, and 4, and Bhattacharya, this volume.)

As far back as 1670, when John Fryer visited South India, he noted that the artisan castes "have always maintained a struggle for a higher place than that allowed to them by Brahminical authority. There is no doubt as to the fact that the members of this great caste (Kammalans) dispute the supremacy of the Brahmin, and that they hold themselves to be equal in rank with them" (Ghurye 1994: 6). But it appears as though the artisans' assertion of equality with the Brahmins, their wearing the sacred thread, and calling themselves Vishwa Karma Brahmins, resulted in rousing the antagonism of all the other castes, not only Brahmins. In the villages of southern Karnataka, for instance, artisan castes were subjected to several disabilities in spite of the fact that agriculture could not be carried on without their aid. The point to note, however, is that medieval South India was home to several strong movements to reject caste, the most powerful of them being the Veerashaiva movement in Karnataka in the twelfth century. Perhaps the backward classes movement of the nineteenth and twentieth centuries should be viewed against the background of the peninsular Bhakti movement.

An anti-Brahmin element seems to have been part of the social and cultural life of India for millennia, but it found powerful expression in the Bhakti movement of medieval South India, encompassing the region now covered by Tamil Nadu, Karnataka, Andhra Pradesh and Maharashtra. It was a movement for equality, cutting across not only caste but gender. It was a revolt of the common people against the elitism of the Brahmin and Sanskrit. It asserted that neither elaborate ritual nor esoteric knowledge was necessary for salvation. Real love of god and simple prayers were enough. The movement surfaced in parts of South India in different times, and it attracted large numbers of men and women from all castes. But it failed to make a dent on caste because it did not touch the caste-based system of production at the local level.

In talking about changes in caste in recent times, reference must be made, however briefly, to the Backward Classes Movement of South India, originating formally in Madras in 1916. But in a sense, signs of the backward classes' awakening were already there in the nineteenth century: The non-Brahmin movement of peninsular India was a response of a downtrodden section of Hindu society to the challenge of caste in the new context of British rule and Western liberal-rationalist ideology. One of the founders of the movement was Jyotirao Phule of Poona, a man of the Gardener caste, who founded the Satya Shodhak Samaj in 1873 with the object of asserting the worth of a human being irrespective of his birth in a particular caste. In certain respects, Phule's reforms anticipated the program of the non-Brahmins, not to engage Brahmin priests to conduct their rituals. He saw the need for the education of the non-Brahmins, and in 1848 he started a school for the Untouchables in Poona. He demanded adequate representation for members of all castes in the services and local bodies (Srinivas 1962: 20).

When at the end of World War I the British Government in England planned the transfer of a modest amount of power to Indians, non-Brahmin leaders in Bombay and Madras demanded reservation of seats in the legislatures to be introduced under

Government of India Act 1919. Ghurye has the following comments on the results of such demands in Bombay: In the Reformed Constitution framed by Montague and Lord Chelmsford; special representation through mixed electorates was conceded to the non-Brahmins. Under these provisions the whole Hindu populace was divided into three sections: (a) Brahmins and allied castes; (b) intermediate classes formed by Marathas and others; and (c) the backward classes, including the so-called Untouchables. This classification, with the classification of other Indians like the Parsis in the appropriate section, was also followed in recruiting the various services (Ghurye 1994: 277).

The representations of non-Brahmin leaders yielded similar results in Madras: 'The backward classes movement', as it is now referred to, had its origins in the 'non-Brahmin Conference' held in Madras in 1916 by the leaders of non-Brahmin castes. The term 'non-Brahmin' was interpreted widely. It included not only Hindus, but Muslims and Christians as well. The leaders were from the elite sections of their communities. All of them were united in their resentment of the dominance of Brahmins—a three percent minority—in higher education, in the new professions, and in the bureaucracy. Brahmin dominance in these new areas was attributed to their being the highest caste and to their using that position to exploit the others and keep them ignorant. Reservations were demanded to offset the advantages suffered by the 97 percent non-Brahmins. This was necessary, they believed, for rendering justice to the lower castes, and the party formed by these non-Brahmin leaders called itself the 'Justice Party'. It demanded reservation of seats in the legislature constituted under the reforms introduced by the Government of India Act 1919. Subsequently the party was able to obtain 28 out of the 98 elected seats in the legislature, declared as 'reserved'. It scored another victory in November 1927 when what came to be known as the 'Communal Government Order' was passed by the Government of Madras, earmarking the share of each caste category in government jobs. Thus in a unit of twelve jobs, five were allocated to the non-Brahmin Hindus, two each to Brahmins, Anglo-Indians and Christians, and Muslims, and one to 'others'(Srinivas 1996: xv, xvi).

However, it is not widely known that the princely state of Mysore was the first to introduce reservation in government jobs for non-Brahmins. According to G. Thimmaiah,

> During the period between 1874 and 1895, the Government of Mysore reserved twenty percent of the middle and lower level jobs in the police department for

> Brahmins, and 80 percent for other Hindus and Muslims and Indian Christians. Again, from 1914, the Government of Mysore introduced a system of nomination for reasonably qualified candidates from non-Brahmin castes/ communities to the post of Assistant Commissioner. Not satisfied with these measures, non-Brahmin leaders started demanding adequate representation in government service, and an increase in public expenditure on education. (Thimmaiah 1993:53).

Caste associations of the dominant Okkaligas and Lingayats were founded as far back as 1906 and 1907 respectively, with the aim of promoting education (Thimmaiah 1993: 56). A committee was appointed in 1918 under the Chief Justice, Sir Leslie Miller, to increase the representation of backward communities in government service, and to provide special facilities for promoting higher and professional education among the backwards, The Miller Committee classified all castes into (a) Brahmins, (b) other caste Hindus, (c) Muhammadans, (d) Europeans and Indian Christians and (e) depressed castes. The Committee recommended that while distributing government jobs according to the reservation policy, the first preference should be given to the depressed castes [the present Scheduled Castes (SCs)]. Accordingly, the extent of benefits recommended were to be implemented in reverse order, that is, first to the depressed castes, then to the other caste Hindus, then Muslims and Indian Christians, and finally, Brahmins (Thimmaiah 1993:64).

The Miller Committee recommended the award of scholarships (including foreign scholarships) to backward class candidates to help them complete their university education. In addition to setting up government hostels, the Committee recommended that grants-in-aid should be given to provide hostels run by private parties to increase hostel facilities for students of the backward classes (Thimmaiah 1993: 65).

Reservation of jobs did also obtain in Hyderabad State during the 1930s: eighty percent of jobs in the government were reserved for Muslims who constituted approximately twenty percent of the population.

The heterogeneity inherent in the "non-Brahmin" category surfaced soon and created conflicts among the constituents. For instance, in Madras, groups located in the lower strata of non-Brahmins felt that they were not getting their share of benefits and demanded a revision of the Communal G.O. of 1927. The demands made by the Vanniya Kula Kshatriyas (also called Vanniyars, and earlier, Padayachis) provide an example of the kind of situation which arose in the 1930s: "In a memorial in July 1938, the Vanniyakula Maha Sangam of Madras (founded in 1888) informed the Chief Minister that Vanniyars were far behind other communities in education and employment; and despite having more than 200 graduates, had only six of the 1713 gazetted officers. The Vanniyars' main requests were for communal representation, relaxation of age limit for entry into services, and preference in appointments to local bodies" (Radhakrishnan 1996:117).

> "The persistent demands by various organizations of the poorer sections of non-Brahmins, including the Scheduled Castes, led to the revision of the Communal G.O. in 1947, twenty years after it was first promulgated. According to the latter, in a unit of 14 appointments, the G.O. allotted six (42.9 percent) to forward non-Brahmin Hindus, Brahmins and SCs, and one (7.1 percent) each to Anglo-Indians/Christians, and Muslims (see G.O. 3437 Public, 21 November 1947)" (Radhakrishnan 1996: 121).

The net result of the change was the "non-Brahmin Hindu" category was divided into "forward" and "backward", resulting in the latter being allotted two out of a total of eight. The total number of units was raised from twelve to fourteen and the section that lost was the "other", a residual category even in the original allotment.

The above instance highlights a striking feature of reservation or "protective discrimination" as practiced in India. It is widely known that the benefits and concessions allotted to the "backward" are highjacked by the more influential and better-off sections depriving the poorer in each category or group. One of the ways in which the administration has tried to meet this situation is by breaking up the "backward classes" into several sub-divisions, and allotting to each sub-division a proportion of the benefits. One of the names used for this is "compartmental reservation".

Another device for meeting the demands of the innumerable backward castes is to raise the quantum of reservation. Thus in Karnataka, over seventy percent of jobs and education seats are allotted to backward classes (including SC and ST), while in Tamil Nadu sixty-nine percent of the jobs and seats have been reserved for the backwards. And the Tamil Nadu reservation has been placed in the "Ninth Schedule" of the Constitution, a Schedule meant initially for land reform legislation, in order to put it beyond the purview of the courts. (However, this decision runs contrary to the November 1992 judgement of the Supreme Court which has decreed that reservation should not exceed 50 percent of the total.)

But, however ingenious the classification of the backward classes, it has not been able to prevent the more influential in each category from securing the benefits and depriving the poor. Further, since stratification occurs not only in categories such as "backward", "more backward", "Scheduled Caste" and "Scheduled Tribe" but in each unit of these categories, the lower groups have a feeling that they are being done out of their legitimate share by their more influential rivals. Thus, even among the Scheduled Castes, the more advanced sub-castes tend to get more than their share as compared to the poorer ones. At least, that is the complaint. Finally, a caste once classified as backward will fight determinedly to retain the label as it ensures easier access to scarce resources like higher education and government jobs. The classic example of such reluctance is provided by Lingayats and Okkaligas in Karnataka, the two dominant castes of the state, who each own a considerable amount of local land, who also have a large number of highly-educated and skilled professionals, and finally, wield considerable political power at every level of the system, from village to Parliament. In this context, the decision of the Supreme Court in its famous Mandal judgement (November 1992) that "creamy layer" in each backward class should be identified and declared ineligible for benefits, has been met with the strong and unanimous opposition of the leaders of backward classes all over the country. Kerala legislature has even passed a resolution stating that there is no "creamy layer" among the backward classes of Kerala, and this has led to the Supreme Court ordering the appointment of a Committee to go into the truth of the resolution. No account of reservation can omit a reference to the Constitutional provision of reservation of seats in legislatures for the Scheduled Castes and Scheduled Tribes, in proportion to their numbers to the total population. Thus, eighteen percent of seats in Parliament are reserved for Scheduled Castes and five percent for Scheduled Tribes. Such reservation also applies to State legislatures, and now to Panchayati Raj institutions. The Constitution also displayed a special concern for the promotion of the educational and economic interests of the SCs and STs, and for their protection from exploitation by the others. According to Article 4.6, "the State shall promote, with special care, the educational and economic interests of the weaker sections of the people and, in particular, of the Scheduled Castes and Scheduled Tribes, and shall protect them from social injustice and all forms of exploitation", and Article 335 provides for the employment of these sections in the government. It is clear that the Constitution accorded to the Scheduled Castes and Scheduled Tribes, protection of a higher order than that for the "socially and educationally backward classes" (also referred to as the "Other Backward Classes" (OBC)). Further, lists of Scheduled Castes and Scheduled Tribes are maintained by the Government of India, whereas lists of the "socially and educationally backward classes (SEBC)" are prepared by the state governments, and until very recently, West Bengal and Orissa had not prepared such lists. Again, as far as SEBC (OBC) were concerned, reservation of jobs and seats in educational institutions were available only at the state level until August 1990, when the then Prime Minister, V.P. Singh, declared that 27 percent of jobs in the Government of India would be reserved for the backward classes. In taking such a decision, V.P. Singh was giving effect to a main recommendation of the Mandal Commission whose report was submitted to the government as far back as 1980. The Mandal Commission listed as many as 3743 backward castes among Hindus alone. V.P. Singh's decision met with opposition from principally the higher castes in the Hindi region, and it was also the subject of litigation in the Supreme Court which gave its verdict in November 1992. (See in this connection Srinivas 1996, Chapters 10 and 11).

Caste and Competition

In brief, it would not be inaccurate to state that intercaste relations, at least at the middle and higher levels, are turning out to be essentially a struggle for obtaining secular benefits such as education, government employment and entry into the learned professions, and for access to political power which in turn opens the door to all sorts of benefits. Such a struggle is common in the urban areas but it encompasses also the richer sections of rural society. The rural rich are both a model and an obstacle to the upward mobility of the poor from the lower castes. But reservation has opened the door, albeit largely symbolic and even often deceptive, to the world outside the village, and to upward mobility. Here kinship, caste, and local links are articulated by everyone including the rural poor to move into the urban areas, and to obtain salaried jobs.

As already mentioned, a concomitant of the intense conflict for secular benefits is weakening of purity-impurity ideas, and the increasing "enclaving" of ritual and religion. Sanskritization is becoming secondary in the sense that it seems to be a mere appendage to secular mobility. But it continues to be necessary as the symbolic trumpeting of higher secular status. But Sanskritization, unaccompanied by economic betterment, is a symbol of backwardness. With the Scheduled, and other so-called lower castes, however, it has become a flag of revolt: "We are getting Sanskritized, we dare you to prevent us", seems to be the message to the higher castes. The oppressed know that the police, law courts and legislatures are there to prevent the dominant and upper castes from intervening as in the pre-Independence years.

As I have explained earlier, caste provided ready-made local networks which were used by politicians, either acting on their own, or on behalf of a political party, to mobilize people for a variety of purposes. This was easier when castes had formed associations. Their earlier role was putting forward claims to high status in the hierarchy, but this receded in importance as getting included in the official "backward classes" list opened the doors to education, entry into the professions, and employment in the government.

Numerical strength added to the political clout of a caste, and one way to increase numerical strength was to lower sub-caste barriers and form new caste-categories. To cite an example: In the 1930's, the Okkaligas were divided into four or five named endogamous groups in the princely state of Mysore, and each stressed its distinctiveness. But now with increased competitiveness between castes, not only have all Okkaliga groups come together, but culturally and socially distinct sub-castes such as the Telugu-speaking Reddys and Tulu-speaking Bunts, are all included in a single caste category taking on the name of Gowda which meant 'headman'. (Gowda now means prestige and power in the political lexicon of Karnataka.) But the old castes have not become defunct: The majority of a sub-caste still continue to marry within it, in contrast to the educated elite who marry ignoring the old sub-caste lines. The resilience of sub-caste boundaries not only enable people to move up and increase their political strength but provide for new identities better able to survive in an atmosphere of ruthless competition between caste-combinations.

However, the caution needs to be uttered that competition between castes was not totally absent in the traditional system, especially at the supra-local levels. The pre-British political system was fluid at the lower levels, and provided opportunities for able and ambitious leaders of dominant castes to become chieftains (Naik, Palegar) or even minor rajas. The varna rank of Kṣatriya has been occupied from very early times by a variety of castes which were lucky to capture power: "The historian Panikkar has maintained that there has been no such caste as the Kṣatriya during the last two thousand years. According to him, the Nandas were the last 'true' Kṣatriyas, and they disappeared from history in the fifth century B.C. Since then, every known royal family has come from a non-Kṣatriya caste, including the famous Rajput dynasties of medieval India" (Panikkar quoted in Srinivas 1966:9). But according to Romila

Thapar, even the Nandas were not Kshatriyass, let alone "true" ones: "The Nandas .... were of low origin. Some sources state that the founder, Mahapadma, was the son of a Shudra mother, others that he was born of the union of a barber with a courtesan. Curiously enough, the Nandas were the first of a number of non-Kshatriya dynasties" (Thapar 1966:57).

The point to note is that competition and conflict between castes did exist even in traditional caste but was confined to the supra-local level, and perhaps in politico-economic matters. What is different in the new situation, however, is that competition and conflict are the order of the day. When different castes come together, it is usually to oppose a third, as when upper castes unite to put down the Scheduled Castes.

More than a quarter of India's 920 million people live in towns and cities, and the latter are polyglot, multi-ethnic, multi-religious and multi-caste. It is impossible to place them all in a hierarchy. (It is possible, however, that many of them carry pictures of local hierarchies in their minds even when they are rejecting a hierarchical order at the conscious level.) What strikes the observer is the difference between the myriad groups, each with its traditions, rituals and customs.

While caste as a hierarchical social order is breaking down, individual castes continue to exist, reconstituted and redefined by ingesting former sub-castes, to become bigger, fight more effectively for access to political power, for economic opportunities and for education. Castes continue to help their members by providing networks which they articulate for a variety of purposes. Castes also provide a sense of identity to their members, a sense of belonging. Citizenship alone does not seem to be enough. People seem to need to identify themselves with groups and categories which they are familiar with, and which they can look to for help and succor in times of need.

Village caste is also beginning to change, and change profoundly. Traditionally, the different sections of castes living in a village came together to produce foodgrains and other essentials of life. Edmund Leach regarded village caste as true caste and regarded competition between castes as acting in "defiance of caste principles." According to Leach, "the caste society as a whole is, in Durkheim's sense, an organic system with each particular caste and sub-caste filling a distinctive functional role. It is a system of labor division from which the element of competition among the workers has been largely excluded (Leach 1960: 5).

Land reform legislation, the legal banning of bonded labor, the opening of new opportunities to the weaker sections of the society, and in particular, the Scheduled Castes, the increasing popularity of commercial crops, mechanization, and increasing monetization of the rural economy, have all contributed further to the weakening of the traditional economic and social ties between different caste groups in villages. It is only in the poor and backward parts of rural India that jajmani (traditional system of caste-based division of labor) continues to function. The jajmani system is an endangered phenomenon destined to disappear from the face of rural India.

Another major source of change in rural India is the increasing tendency on the part of the Scheduled Castes to challenge the authority of the higher castes, in particular the dominant castes. The fact that there was a significant overlap between the Scheduled Castes and landless laborers on the one hand, and dominant castes and land ownership on the other, has only sharpened the conflict between the two. When the Scheduled Castes refuse to perform the services which they traditionally performed, or defy the dominant castes in some way, the latter take revenge on the former, sometimes by resorting to violence. In some parts of the country, the Scheduled Castes are getting organized to assert themselves and confront the upper castes if necessary. More and more, villages are likely to become battlegrounds in which the upper castes, mainly the dominants, will be fighting the Dalits (as the Scheduled Castes like to call themselves). The struggle will be bloody, and perhaps long-drawn-out. The taming of the dominant castes is going to be a major problem for Indian democracy, and Panchayati Raj, which places considerable resources with the local bodies, is likely to sharpen inter-caste conflict at the village, *tehsil* and district levels.

It needs to be pointed out in this connection that right from the sixth century B.C., when Jainism and Buddhism appeared on the scene, continuous attacks have been made on Brahminical claims to supremacy in the caste hierarchy, on the excessive ritualism which Brahmins had developed, and the elitism of Sanskrit. (See Chapple, this volume.) The medieval Bhakti movement which was a feature of most parts of the country at varying points of time, also carried the banner of revolt against caste and its inequalities. They gave self-respect and the hope of salvation, to millions of low-status groups and to women. The Brahmin was ridiculed for his preoccupation with purity-impurity, his addiction to elaborate and complicated ritual, and his claims to supremacy. The Bhakti saints proclaimed that love of god alone mattered and all else was irrelevant.

But powerful as these movements were, they failed to make a dent on caste hierarchy for, at the village level, the system of production of foodgrains and other necessities, was inextricably bound up with caste-based division of labor. It was only with the establishment of British rule and the many forces which it let loose, that the idea of an alternative system of production not based on caste emerged, and this acquired salience in the first few decades of the twentieth century, and the post-Independence years have brought the country closer to a system of local production freed from caste-based division of labor. The jajmani system is beginning to disintegrate. In its total disappearance lie the true seeds of equality.

The situation may be summed up by saying that a variety of forces are resulting in the certain destruction of the caste-based system of production at the village or local level. This system served India for over two millennia but it is giving way. On the other hand, individual castes are competing with each other for access to secular benefits. This conflict is only likely to become sharper in the near future. India's revolution seems destined to be a slow, bleeding one, unrecognized by its middle classes in urban areas.

A discussion of the future of caste must take note of the increasing salience of the middle classes. The urge to become part of the middle classes is now widespread, cutting across religion, language and caste. One way of describing the situation is to state that upwardly mobile families or sections of castes, want very much to become part of the middle classes, and once this happens, education, profession and lifestyle become the determinants of status, pushing caste to the background. And it is among the middle classes that marriages are crossing traditional barriers of all sorts. Young people are found announcing with pride, that their parents belong to different castes, or even different ethnic or religious groups. Membership of the middle classes seems to provide a solvent to caste-based divisiveness. In the large-scale embourgeoisement of its people seems to lie the prospect of dissolution of caste identities, even as politicians are busy trying to preserve every kind of division in order to keep themselves in power.

Endnote

[1] Earlier versions of this paper were presented at The National Institute of Advanced Studies, Bangalore, and the Department of Philosophy, Jadavpur University, Calcutta. My thanks are due to Ms Dhanu Nayak for critically reading the manuscript and preparing it for publication.

Works Cited

Basu, D.D. 1994. *Introduction to the Constitution of India.* New Delhi: Prentice-Hall.

Ghurye, G.S. 1994. *Caste and Race in India.* Bombay: Popular Prakashan, 5th Edition.

Leach, E.R. (ed.) 1960. *Aspects of Caste in South India, Ceylon and North-West Pakistan.* Cambridge: Cambridge University Press.

Radhakrishnan, P. 1996. "The Backward Classes Movement in Tamil Nadu." *Caste: Its Twentieth Century Avatar* ed. by M.N. Srinivas. New Delhi: Viking.

Srinivas, M. N. 1955. "The Social System of a Mysore Village". *Village India* ed. by Marriott, M. Chicago: University of Chicago Press.

________________. 1962. *Caste in Modern India.* Bombay: Asia Publishing House.

________________. 1966. *Social Change in Modern India.* Berkeley & Los Angeles: University of California Press.

______________. (ed.) 1996. *Caste: Its Twentieth Century Avatar.* New Delhi: Viking.

Thapar, R. 1966. *A History of India,* Volume 1. Harmondsworth: Penguin.

Thimmaiah. 1993. *Power Politics and Social Justice: The Backward Classes in Karnataka.* New Delhi: Sage Publications.

Chapter 15 | Affirmative Action Programs in India

H.K. Kesavan

In almost all countries, the formulation of public policies directed towards eliminating the differences between the advantaged and disadvantaged sections of society has received special attention. Affirmative action programs take on a different complexion depending on the nature of the problems. In the United States, for instance, the problems of social and economic inequity stem from the long neglect of acknowledging African-Americans in mainstream society. Although slavery is a thing of the past and segregation is virtually eliminated due to the combination of a strong civil rights movement and the exercise of judicial statesmanship on the part of the Supreme Court, there is still a wide gap between income levels between blacks and whites. Since African Americans constitute twelve percent of the population, it becomes an economic imperative to improve their standard of living in order to ensure a modicum of distributive justice. Although social justice does not automatically follow economic justice, it is certainly a major step in the right direction. The current affirmative action programs in America have staunch advocates as well as determined detractors; furthermore, the views held by the opposite camps have undergone a transformation just as society itself has.

In the case of India, the rationale for introducing affirmative action programs has arisen from the gross neglect of the interests of the backward class (BC), which belong to the lower rungs of the rigid caste hierarchy of the Hindu religion and also those of the scheduled castes and scheduled tribes (SC and ST). The latter groups put together have a combined strength of nearly 120 million people, and their abysmally low standard of living has remained a blight on society as a whole. Gandhiji made the telling point that the injustice faced by the lower castes in the caste hierarchy, grievous as it is, pales into insignificance compared to the injustice meted out to the so-called outcastes. Apart from considerations of social justice and compassion to our fellow citizens, enlightened self-interest alone should inform us that we cannot afford to perpetuate the grotesque inequities of life if we have to ensure a higher level of productivity for the country as a whole.

In addition to the disadvantaged sections of the Hindu society, there is also a sizable number of Muslims who have been left behind for a variety of reasons. It is pointless to argue that some of the reasons for their economic backwardness are of their own making. Influenced by their orthodox clergy, the bulk of Muslims have denied themselves educational opportunities provided by secular India, however meager they may be in terms of fulfilling their real needs. Although the problems of the disadvantaged sections in the U.S. and India have entirely different origins, there are, however, some similarities in the arguments advanced for and against affirmative action programs in the two countries. It would be of interest first to outline some of these arguments as they apply to America since the public debate has been vigorously carried on for quite some time in newspapers, television, and scholarly publications, followed by a discussion of some corrective measures undertaken by the Supreme Court in favor of civil rights. Undoubtedly, the American experience will provide additional insights for an exploration of affirmative action programs in India.

Affirmative Action in the U.S.

In the America of the 1960's, there was universal acceptance of the criterion of merit for deciding on promotions in the work place. In a country that is driven by fanatical faith in the opportunities provided by the free market, the successful group of people argued that the golden principle of competition should be equally applicable to the spheres of education and work. At the other end of the spectrum, the egalitarians also had tacitly agreed that merit should be the main criterion in opening up opportunities for nudging upwards in the social hierarchy. The African-American leadership of the day was proud to assert that African-Americans would prefer to be judged by their internal strength rather than the pigment of their skin.

But as the country has moved to the post-industrial era, propelled mainly by information technology, the faith in merit as the sole criterion has been questioned.

As a result of tumultuous change in the economy, the gap between the rich and the poor has widened considerably; furthermore, the security of the large middle class which was traditionally considered the engine for economic growth has been shaken. Those with higher education working at the cutting edge of technology in all walks of life earn disproportionately more than other educated people. As for the less educated, their living standards have dropped precipitously in relation to the former group because of a variety of economic and social reasons. Perhaps the principal reason is that productivity is now dependent on the combined man-machine intelligence that is characteristic of the post-industrial era. This hybrid intelligence is mainly due to the revolution that has taken place in a wide range of technologies which are dependent on computers, communication, and control for accomplishing increased levels of production. Contrast this situation with the notion of productivity associated with the era ushered in by the first industrial revolution where machines did not have the capabilities of intelligence that we now associate with computers.

One can clearly observe that the notion of work itself has changed in the post-industrial era and along with it our criteria for separating blue collar and white collar workers has also changed. The classification is no more the simple difference that lies between human intelligence and physical labor, but it is now the difference that lies between man-machine intelligence and human labor. The differences in income between the white and blue collar workers are inevitably accentuated by the different levels of education they receive. The gap between the two groups has widened more than ever before. As a result of the uneven distribution of income, even those who traditionally belonged to the successful group have now begun to question the blind faith placed in meritocracy as the sole criterion for economic advancement. Since members of this group belong to the intelligentsia, they are also able to marshal any number of seemingly convincing reasons to downplay the criterion strictly based on merit in the modern economy. For instance, they question the enormous faith that is placed on examinations where a quantitative measure is assigned to measure the degree of merit. IQ tests are outright ridiculed for their notorious unreliability to measure intelligence in a comprehensive manner. The intelligentsia points out that it is utterly foolish to hold the principle of competition in such reverence in a society that is already competitive. When the intelligentsia is cornered into the disadvantaged group because of intangible forces unleashed by improved methods of production, one can safely assume that it can clearly articulate reasons in support of affirmative action directed to its advantage, thus dethroning consideration of merit from its high pedestal. In contrast, when the poor and uneducated constitute the disadvantaged group of the society, they find themselves unable to advance coherent reasons as to why they deserve special attention, except to scream when it really hurts. It is interesting to go over some of the main arguments made by the intelligentsia against meritocracy. Those from the left argue that extolling the virtues of meritocracy is hypocritical since it is at best only a thinly-veiled disguise to preserve one's own class interests afforded by higher education. They think that it is akin to the case advanced by the bourgeoisie of the previous generations in defense of preserving their property rights. In fact, those who derive advantages through education and access to information are considered worse than the bourgeoisie because they think that they owe their success entirely to themselves. This is the sum and substance of the arguments advanced by the left-wing historian Christopher Lasch in his book, *The Revolt of the Elites*, published in 1995.

From the opposite end of the spectrum, right-wing members of the intelligentsia also argue against affirmative action programs, making use of the argument of meritocracy. They point out that these programs have a tendency to freeze the differences between the races by institutionalizing them. They implicitly suggest that African-Americans cannot make headway without the active assistance of the whites which, to say the least, is completely counterproductive.

We shall now briefly dwell on the two rival theories about affirmative action which strangely enough have one thing in common: they both point to the futility of elevating merit as a primary criterion for professional and social advancement. We will first take up the argument against affirmative action then follow it up with the argument in support of it and point out their commonality as far as meritocracy is concerned.

One of the thought-provoking books arguing against affirmative action programs is a widely-read book called *The Bell Curve* that appeared in 1994 by social scientist Charles Murray and the late Harvard psychologist Richard Herrnstein. Their principal thesis is that America is advancing the cause for social mobility through affirmative action programs at a dangerously high cost. They lament over the decline in that has occurred in social cohesion and frown over the steep decline in ordinary civic virtues that society is drifting towards. Those who have succeeded on the basis of higher education have preferred to stay in prim isolation from mainstream problems. As for the disadvantaged sections of society, their lives in the core of the inner cities have deteriorated to unacceptably low standards because of the schism that exists between them and those who have moved away to the suburbia.

Central to Murray and Herrnstein's thesis is the assumption that brain counts for more than brawn in today's society and that it is nature more than nurture that is responsible for differences in brain power. What made their thesis highly controversial is their assertion that the fact that African-Americans scored almost fifteen percent less, on average, than whites in IQ tests is to be attributed to their genes. If the authors are right about this conclusion, it would only mean that African-Americans are inhibited by factors of biological inheritance and, consequently, condemned to lead substandard lives compared to the whites. Implicitly, this is also an argument against using the criterion of merit since it assumes that merit is related to basic biological factors and therefore cannot be used as a vehicle for bringing about social advancement.

Subsequent to the publication of the controversial book, the authors have advanced reasons as to why the main thesis of *The Bell Curve* is fundamentally flawed. Their arguments place more importance on nurture than nature, and on environmental conditions rather than on factors of inheritance. They assert that human intelligence can most definitely be improved by providing greater facilities to individuals. They vigorously defend the importance of social policies directed towards removing basic inequalities between groups of individuals based on their faith that such differences do not evolve genetically. Many support this viewpoint on the basis of their personal experiences. They believe that the deficiencies in performance can most certainly be remedied if steps are taken to raise the level of expectations of the individuals who are suffering from a variety of handicaps by providing them with proper opportunities for advancement and, in addition, providing them with role models that they can emulate. Since this argument is mainly concerned with a crying need for implementing enlightened social policies, it also steers clear of placing importance on meritocracy.

Affirmative Action in India

In India, the differences in social and economic status between groups of individuals have arisen from religious rather than racial considerations, unlike in America. Both the Aryans of the north and the Dravidians of the south belong to the Caucasian race as modern geneticists would readily confirm in unambiguous terms. This fact needs special mention since a misconception persists in the country about supposed racial differences on the basis of some differences in physical features of the peoples of the two regions. Fortunately, these misperceptions have not given rise to any tension on this score. Between race and religion, racial differences are indubitably more divisive than those arising from differences in religion. But it does not follow from this broad observation that the religious problems of India are relatively easier to solve on this account.

There are two sets of problems faced by Indian policy makers in the field of affirmative action. The first set of problems is endemic to Hinduism arising from caste differences; the second set of problems relates to the clash of cultures between the Hindus and Muslims.[1]

Caste Differences

There are four main castes amongst the Hindus arranged in a hierarchical order: these are the Brahmins, Kshatriyas, Vaishyas, and Shudras. In addition, there are also the so-called outcastes who belong to the lowest echelons of the society and are grouped separately outside the rigid caste hierarchy. Within each main caste, there is a proliferation of subcastes which vary from one region to another. Historically speaking, the four categories were described as varnas which had more to do with division of labor that should prevail within a society dedicated to spiritual ideals. Each varna was prescribed its own special cannons of conduct.

The Brahmins, for instance, constituted the small section of the society whose ideal role was to interpret the scriptures and lead lives of exemplary character dedicated to the realization of the highest eternal truths governing man and the universe. Similarly, the expectations of the other three varnas were also clearly defined. The most important thing to note is that no inequality amongst the varnas was suggested in the four-way classification. They were all assigned equal status, and their complementary nature was emphasized for the good of the society as a whole. Furthermore, these varnas were considered dynamic in character which meant that a varna of an individual did not automatically come as a birth right. It was something that had to be earned through work and dedication making use of one's natural talents. In fact, it has been suggested that the classification of a society into the four varnas is present in every country whether one recognizes it or not.

But the caste system is a ghastly misrepresentation of the classification of the society based on varnas. It is static in character with the result that a caste is determined by birth rather than intrinsic individual merit. The caste system is therefore completely devoid of any notion of complementarity between its four castes. Not only is the notion of equality between castes denied, but it is substituted by a vicious hierarchy amongst them. It is no wonder that any reference to the historical idea of varnas does not provide solace to those who suffer from the man-made pernicious divisions introduced by the caste system. Furthermore, living in an era of the economic man, where almost everyone is obsessed with the idea of economic advancement as the sole aim in life, it is senseless to draw comparisons from a system of classification which was meant to uphold a spiritual goal as the be-all and end-all of life.

One has to deal with the systems as they are and not as they ought to be. In terms of meritocracy, while the varna system of a utopian society, dedicated to purely spiritual values, loftily upholds the criterion of merit, the caste system discards it altogether since it does not provide any mobility between castes. It is useful to remind ourselves that while the spiritual message is addressed at the level of the individual, the corresponding religion, on the other hand, does not ask for a discriminating understanding of the message on the part of a member belonging to it. This may be one of the reasons why misunderstandings and misrepresentations easily occur when the ideals of the spiritual realm are projected on to the religious sphere. The precepts and practices of a religion are bound to vary because of this difficulty, but nowhere is this schism more perilous than between the benign precept of varna and the malignant practice of caste system.

The scheduled castes and scheduled tribes have long been neglected by upper caste Hindus. The subhuman conditions that they have been subjected to in the long history of the country are undoubtedly a matter of disgrace to upper-caste Hindus. Added to the abject misery resulting from the most inhumane treatment of untouchability, they also had to suffer from the problem of "unseeability" from members of their superior castes which included almost everyone else. Even the majority of the intelligentsia either pretended not to see their problems or was blissfully ignorant of them. It is into this social setting that Gandhiji arrived and made it his mission to increase the social awareness of the nation towards the problems of the SC and ST. Problems of deep divisions based on ignorance and prejudice cannot be solved merely through enlightened legislation without educating the public as to its need. It is to the eternal credit of Gandhiji that he prepared the ground for a concerted attack on improving the conditions of the downtrodden through the intervention of the new state of independent India.

The socio-economic problems of the disadvantaged sections of the society can be visualized on the basis of a coordinate system where the horizontal axis represents the ascending order of the caste hierarchy, and the vertical axis denotes the ascending order of income levels, the origin of the coordinate system corresponding to the lowest caste and income level. Since incomes are not directly related to castes, a poor Brahmin, for instance, while placed farthermost on the horizontal axis, is placed on the vertical axis close to the origin. Alternatively, there could be a rich member belonging to a lower caste who is placed high on the vertical axis but low on the horizontal one. Thus, a poor Brahmin, or for that matter a poor upper-caste Hindu, will never be placed at the origin unlike his or her counterpart belonging to the backward classes, which is the essence of the argument in favor of affirmative action to bring about social justice.

In this matrix of stupidity, someone who has a low income and who also, say, belongs to the group of SC and ST, only has the option of moving vertically to improve income, since any horizontal movement to improve caste status is denied to him or her. However, there will always be a deep psychological urge in that person to mimic the outward manners of the upper castes in order to be socially accepted. The person may, for instance, change his or her name to a more Brahmin or Kshatriya sounding name as has increasingly been done in recent years. This latter phenomenon, peculiar to the Hindu society, has been a subject of intensive study by Indian sociologists.

There is another route, however, to escape from the fetters of the caste hierarchy altogether and that is to bolt away from the Hindu religion. In fact, some SC and ST members have embraced Christianity and Buddhism in order to escape from the tyranny of the caste system of Hinduism. They are also very vulnerable to receive evangelical messages of other religions.

Muslims

The problem posed by the relative economic backwardness of the Muslims has entirely different roots. Ever since Islam came to India, the religion has coexisted with Hinduism without interacting at the deeper spiritual levels. In fact, Hindus have never shown any interest in such discussions with Christians either, which is the other great world religion that came to India.

This is because Hindus have always felt that their religion has provided answers to the fundamental issues concerning man and the universe through the insights of their seers and the authority of their scriptural texts. Furthermore, they are proud of the fact that they had this knowledge long before the religions of the invaders to the subcontinent came on the scene. There is also another important reason for their sincere belief in the need for peaceful coexistence of all religions.

Hindus are not anxious to impose their views on members of other religions since they accept that there may be other equally valid paths for the realization of God. Because of this mindset, Hindus do not take kindly to the idea of evangelism by religionists in their midst. The manner in which Islam came to India through violence, plunder, and forcible conversions has also left a deep scar on the Hindu psyche. Hindus feel that five centuries of Muslim rule was only a short blip on the long panorama of Indian history which was quintessentially Hindu in nature. At the time of the transfer of power from the British in 1947, the Muslim League led by Mohamed Ali Jinnah successfully argued for the partition of the subcontinent on the basis of religion. But India now has more Muslims than Pakistan, and Indian Muslims enjoy the status of first class citizens in secular India, as indeed it is their right to do so. Consequently, the economic and social problems of Indian Muslims have to be resolved squarely within the framework of a democratic society devoted to secular ideals. The country cannot afford to have a theocratic model applicable to Muslims only within a secular India.

Muslims have traditionally denied themselves opportunities for better education that are available to all Indians irrespective of their religious affiliations. It is true that the promise made in the Indian constitution about free and compulsory education to all children who come within the age group of six to fourteen years has not been fulfilled because of financial reasons, but this lapse does not differentiate between children belonging to different religions. The first and foremost step that has to be taken to improve the lot of the Muslims is to convince them to adopt secular attitudes by minimizing the influence of the Islamic clergy on matters of education and economic well-being. The spectacular success of the family planning program in neighboring Bangladesh, where its Muslim citizens have clearly understood the relationship between smaller families and better living conditions, offers hope that Indian Muslims are also capable of determining for themselves the path for their economic betterment without the guidance of their clergy.

Fortunately, the Muslims do not have the caste problem of the Hindus, and so their upward mobility is entirely possible by improving economic conditions through better education and a concerted effort to make them stakeholders in the future of the country. These changes will not only alleviate their immediate problems but will also serve as concrete steps for achieving a rapprochement with the majority Hindus.

In the meantime, Muslims should also be the recipients of affirmative action programs that are meant for the disadvantaged sections of the society. Also, every effort should be made to provide visible representation to Muslims in all spheres of life.

Other Backward Classes

The most publicized effort on the part of the government to provide better opportunities for the backward classes and to members of SC and ST was during the brief tenure of the V. P. Singh government (December 2, 1989 to November 10, 1990) when it decided to implement the Mandal Commission Report which was gathering dust until then. The main purpose of the Commission was to establish social justice rather than tackle the more general problem of eradication of poverty. Towards this end, the Commission recommended allotment of generous quotas for admission to educational institutions and provision of job openings under the purview of government and public sector enterprises.

The Reservation Policy was construed as a courageous act of social engineering to restore justice to nearly fifty-two percent of the population who were reckoned as belonging to the backward classes. Since this is an affirmative action program based on quotas, the immediate casualty of this public policy was the criterion of merit in education and the work place. The well-qualified people, who were denied opportunities in order to accommodate a high proportion of applicants entering on the basis of quotas reserved for their castes, were totally frustrated by the unjust limits placed on the realization of their full potential. When the policy was brought into force, there were huge public protests organized by the students; intellectuals also spoke out against it, pointing out its retrogressive effects. But the government did not yield ground; it had anticipated such a reaction and knew very well that it was the beneficiaries of the policy that had the political power to vote it into office rather than those opposing it. Once reservation of seats based on a formula devised on the basis of caste considerations proved to be a populist cause, subsequent governments formed by different political parties only improved on its reach without questioning the validity of the solution that was offered to solve a longstanding problem that had troubled the conscience of the nation. They witnessed the ridiculous competition on the part of several subcastes to declare themselves as belonging to the backward classes in order to qualify for the entitlement of the affirmative action program. The impact of the affirmative action program has been far-reaching and has taken on ramifications that were entirely unexpected by the major political parties. As the popular saying goes, the politics of India has been thoroughly Mandalised ever since the Mandal Commission Report was implemented. What is meant by that phrase is that new political parties have sprung up in different regions of the country purely on caste lines in order to ensure a fair share in the exercise of political power in the country. The rise of these regional parties has altered the political equation to such an extent that the new political arithmetic makes it very difficult for a national party to form a majority government at the center.

India might very well have entered an era of relative political instability because of the need for national parties to forge alliances with caste-based regional ones in order to form a government. There are those who say that the rise of regional parties represents the true diversity of India, and a government formed by factoring this reality into its political equation is likely to be more stable than otherwise. Time alone will tell which viewpoint is correct.

Problems of a Developing Nation

The problems of India are mind-boggling compared to those of developed nations. We shall mention only a few not necessarily in their order of importance. First is the population problem. The developed countries have attained more or less zero-population growth so that a planning exercise can be carried on in a controlled fashion with very predictable results. In the case of India, the annual increase in population is comparable to the population of Australia, although the rate of growth is slowing down. When we refer to India at the time of independence in 1947, we sometimes forget we are referring to an India of only about 350 million people. If only the population had stayed under 500 million, Indians would, on average, be much richer now, and the problems of the disadvantaged would not be as severe as at present. Economic prosperity would certainly have muted the social injustice intrinsic to the caste system.

The second problem that needs to be mentioned is that during the course of the last fifty years, in its Herculean efforts to make up for lost time, India has had to face problems posed by the rapid changes in technology that are taking place in all sectors of the economy on a highly compressed time-scale. The country did not have the luxury of going from one phase to the next in an orderly and leisurely way. It had to face problems simultaneously posed by a pre-industrial and an industrial society where the time for new innovations is getting shorter and shorter. One cliche that one hears in this regard is that India is forced to live in all centuries at the same time.

A third problem is that the country has had to come to terms with ecological constraints placed on development even before an acceptable level of development had taken place to ensure basic living standards for its huge population. In the best of circumstances, the balance between economic development and concern for environment is a delicate one. In the case of India, it takes on the proportion of an ethical and moral dilemma because of the necessity for more development in order to ensure at least a minimum standard of living for all its people.

Another problem is that, unlike democratic governments of developed countries, Indian democracy had to embark on its schemes for modernization in an atmosphere where, right from the beginning, its populace was very much aware of its fundamental rights. It also had to contend with strong labor unions which had links to political parties even before the country had achieved acceptable levels of productivity. While an individual or a union in a vibrant democracy must have recourse to seek remedial measures whenever legitimate rights are transgressed, excessive claims resulting in the need for judicial arbitration can act as deterrents to rapid progress at least in the initial stages of development. The dilemma posed by the need for preserving individual rights as against the necessity for abridging these rights in order to ensure the common good is a complex one faced by many democratic countries, and the problem becomes more acute in the case of a young democracy. (See Hardgrave, this volume.)

Finally, India, after more than four decades of experimentation with a planned economy, has just recently accepted the new paradigm of globalization and liberalization which was ushered in after the termination of the Cold War. This new trend necessitates the need for cultivating an international perspective on many of the national problems. (See Srinivasan and Tandon, this volume.)

Merit Based Affirmative Action in India

We shall now return to our main theme of examining the criterion of merit for ensuring social mobility and economic advancement in India which is beset with many complex economic and social problems. The discussion of merit in American society was not intended to compare the problems of that society with those of India regarding affirmative action programs, but to glean some of the essential arguments being advanced for and against meritocracy in America with the expectation that they may provide some fresh insights in the study of the Indian problem.

Now that we have presented a brief survey of the nature of the problems of inequity as they arise in the Indian society, we shall conclude our discussion by examining the importance of the role of merit as a criterion in the affirmative action programs.

Unlike America, India had never placed a premium on the value of competition in an all-pervasive way. The type of economy that prevailed until 1992 had almost crippled the spirit of entrepreneurship in people working in the economic sector. Except in isolated spheres like recruitment to the administrative service, entry into higher institutes of science and technology and for certain jobs advertised by the public service commission, the ideal of competition was not given exclusive importance. At the other end of the spectrum, the leadership of the backward classes was vehemently opposed to the principle of free competition because they did not want to indulge in an unequal contest resulting from opportunities that were long denied to them due to caste discrimination. Furthermore, poverty and unemployment take on a different meaning in India where the government has not yet been able to provide a safety net for people suffering from those disadvantages. Since the poor and unemployed cannot expect to become wards of the state, they cannot afford to indulge in such pious virtues as relying on their pride instead of claiming what is legitimately due to them through affirmative action programs.

The debate about genetic differences in intellectual capabilities between races, which has engendered some interest in America, is totally inapplicable to the Indian scene because of the absence of a racial problem. The foolhardy could argue that the backward classes and those belonging to SC and ST are genetically inferior in levels of intelligence compared to the upper castes, but there is absolutely no scientific evidence to support this view. Nor can this prejudicial view be supported on the basis of experience. As for the argument that competition as a criterion for advancement is upheld by those privileged few who are educated in order to preserve their class interests, we find an echo of this in the Indian scene also. For instance, apparently there is a strong desire on the part of the top civil servants to preserve the status quo in the Indian Institutes of Technology (IITs), which is widely regarded as elitist, in order to ensure that their children have better opportunities to go abroad after receiving a solid education. From the foregoing discussion, it is clear that the central problem can never be resolved if it is cast in terms of elitism versus egalitarianism. Affirmative action programs which abrogate the principle of merit and competition constitute one extreme solution. The opposite solution is to put competition on a high pedestal to the exclusion of any consideration for those who are left behind for no fault of their own. In reality, one needs a balanced approach where due consideration is given to both points of view. We have to recognize the need for meritocracy even to advance the cause of egalitarianism, just as we recognize that it is the general acceptance of egalitarian causes that can admit the healthy growth of pockets of elitism.

Conclusion

In summary, the need for affirmative action to advance the interests of the backward classes and those belonging to SC and ST can not be denied. But the quota system for admissions to educational institutions and for jobs and promotions as implemented on the basis of the Mandal Commission Report does constitute an extreme solution skewed in favor of egalitarianism at the cost of undermining the necessity for giving weighted consideration to merit and the principle of competition. Based on the demographic profile of India, one can easily visualize that real societal change can come about only when large sections of disadvantaged groups are given plentiful opportunities for basic education and economic advancement. Since a great number of such people inhabit rural India, policies directed towards improvement of villages in a comprehensive way will go a long way toward alleviating the problem. The main thrust of such affirmative action programs should be to provide equal opportunities to people who were long denied their legitimate rights for social advancement. Concurrently, the pernicious quota system for admissions, jobs, and promotions should be scrapped in favor of a system which shifts its focus to the background of the individual; those in need should be identified and aided without compromising the criterion of merit.

Interestingly, the enigma posed by elitism versus egalitarianism also finds an important place in the spiritual realm. According to Hindus, the message of spiritual advancement is directed towards an individual and not towards a group of people. The scriptures uphold the view that every individual is invested with the natural ability for spiritual advancement irrespective of race, religion, level of education, or economic status. The ability to attain a transcendental level of consciousness is the prerogative of every human being. Accordingly, it is a perfectly egalitarian principle. Some have called it a truly socialistic principle. However, the scriptures also inform us that each individual starts from his or her own unique level of spiritual assets on the path of self-realization. Furthermore, we are informed that these assets are a result of the individual soul's merits accrued over a series of lives as a result of conscious and deliberate actions which are governed by the karma principle. (See Hiriyanna, Kesavan, and Pandharipande, this volume.)

This is patently an elitist principle, which can also be called a capitalistic principle. We can see from this brief description that the two contending principles coexist in harmony because of the assurance that it is the destiny of every individual to attain self-realization sooner or later. The enigma posed by the opposing views of elitism and egalitarianism on the conscious plane of mind admit a synthesis only on the transcendental level of consciousness. As a matter of practical guidance for leading one's day-to-day life, emphasis is placed on the fact that life should be effectively used to advance spiritually, then in a manner consistent with one's natural endowments.

Discussion of the problem as it appears in the spiritual realm is not of immediate help if life's main goal is considered to be economic in nature as is the prevailing philosophy of the world we live in. The discussion can, at best, point towards the scenario in which the irreconcilable differences in our society arising from differences in endowments and opportunities between individuals and groups admit the possibility of a harmonious solution. However, the light it sheds clearly points to the utter futility of upholding extreme solutions in favor of either elitism or egalitarianism.

As mentioned earlier on, the problems of India are manifold. At one end of the spectrum, the country has to live with the new economic paradigm of globalization and economic reforms, and the pragmatic choice of political democracy in a country consisting of a huge population beset by so many diversities. This implies that we need people with the kind of intelligence and technological expertise demanded by the twenty-first century in order to survive as a nation and compete with the rest of the world. At the other end of the spectrum, the country has to pay special attention to the advancement of large sections of people who are still struggling with the problems of an earlier century. These have to be addressed by intelligent affirmative action programs which do not mitigate the efficacy of the former group. The two problems are clearly interdependent in nature, and the future of the country lies in our ability to devise successful public policies which can achieve a balance between the two. The political leadership of the country should revisit the solution proffered by the Mandal Commission before long-standing damage is done to the general well-being of the country.

ENDNOTE

[1]There is a third problem, of course, which pertains to women in the work force but we have not addressed that issue separately because it is subsumed in our discussion of meritocracy in the work place. (See Raman, this volume.)

Works Cited

Murray, Charles and Herrnstein, Richard. 1994. *The Bell Curve.* New York & Toronto: Free Press.

Lasch, Christopher. 1995. *The Revolt of the Elites and the betrayal of democracy.* New York: W. W. Norton.

Kesavan, Hiremaglur K. 1997. Political Diary of a NRI. Unpublished manuscript.

Chapter 16

Dilemmas of Democracy in India

Robert L. Hardgrave, Jr.

On August 15, 1947, ending its long struggle for freedom, India secured independence, and the leadership of the new nation made its "tryst with destiny" in commitment to the establishment of a secular and democratic state. Their trust in the people of India was embodied in the grant of universal suffrage--the right of every adult, male and female, to exercise the power of the vote. It was a trust that was not misplaced, for with each election, democracy has taken deeper root. Turnout at the ballot box has been impressively high, and the Indian voter, attuned to the interests involved and with often shrewd judgment, has demonstrated remarkable political literacy. The strength of India's democracy is reflected in the periodic and peaceful transfer of power from one party to another. But democracy in India, as in other culturally diverse societies such as the United States, confronts fundamental dilemmas in the relationship of majority rule and minority rights. The challenge is to secure the "right" balance, but that is never easy nor is it readily clear what that balance should be or how it can be fairly attained.

India came to independence in 1947 in the trauma of partition[1]. The Indian nationalist movement, led by Mohandas Gandhi and Jawaharlal Nehru, had struggled for a free India that would unite what was then British India and the 562 princely states under British paramountcy in a secular and democratic state. But to Mohammad Ali Jinnah, leader of the Muslim League, such an India would relegate Muslims, who made up twenty-four percent of the population, to the position of a permanent minority in what he envisaged as a Hindu-dominated state. For Jinnah, India was "two nations," Hindu and Muslim, and he was determined that Muslims secure protection in an Islamic state of Pakistan, made up of the Muslim-majority areas of India. In the violence that accompanied the partition, some half million people were killed and upwards of eleven million Hindus and Muslims crossed the newly-created borders as refugees. But Jinnah's Pakistan was partial even as a Muslim homeland, for it left nearly half of the subcontinent's Muslims in India.

Today, Muslims are India's largest religious minority, with eleven percent of the total population. Among other religious groups, the Sikhs, some of whom had sought an independent Sikhistan in 1947, are concentrated in the Punjab and number less than two percent of the population. Christians, Buddhists, Jains, Parsees, and Jews give further richness to India's religious diversity, but their comparatively small numbers only accentuate the overwhelming proportion of Hindus, with some eighty-three percent of the population.

The Hindus, even though they share a Great Tradition, are themselves divided into a myriad of sects and are socially segmented by thousands of castes and subcastes, hierarchically ranked in traditional terms and regionally organized. The geographic regions of India are linguistically and culturally distinct. There are more than a dozen major languages, grouped into those of the Dravidian South India and Indo-European (or Aryan) North India, of which Hindi, spoken by thirty percent of all Indians, is recognized by the Constitution as the official language of India. In addition to the many Indo-European and Dravidian languages and dialects, there are various tribal languages spoken by peoples across India, most notably in southern Bihar and in the seven states of the Northeast. (See Chapters by B. Kachru, Y. Kachru, and K. Sridhar in this volume).

Constitutional Protection of Minorities

In confronting this potentially overwhelming diversity, the framers of India's Constitution sought to shape an overarching Indian identity even as they gave recognition to the pluralism of a multicultural society through guarantees of fundamental rights, as in specific provisions for the protection of minorities. These include freedom of religion (Articles 25-28); the right of any section of citizens to use and conserve their "distinct language, script or culture" (Article 29); and the right of "all minorities, whether based on religion or language," to establish and administer educational institutions of their choice (Article 30). With respect to caste, the Constitution declared the practice of "untouchability" unlawful (Article 17), but as to compensatory justice and open opportunity, a certain percentage of admissions to colleges and universities and to government employment were to be "reserved" for Scheduled Castes (untouchables) and aboriginal Scheduled Tribes (Article 335). Similarly, to ensure adequate political representation, Scheduled Castes and Tribes were allotted reserved seats in the Lok Sabha, the lower house of parliament, and in the state assemblies in proportion to their population (Article 330). These reservations were to have ended in 1960, but by constitutional amendment, they have been extended at ten-year intervals. (See Chapters by Srinivas and Kesavan in this volume).

Federalism and the Party System

Despite enormous pressures, India has been remarkably successful in accommodating cultural diversity and managing ethnic conflict through democratic institutions. This has been, in significant part, the product of that diversity itself, for at the national level—the Center, as it is termed—no single ethnic group can dominate. At the state level in India's federal system, each of the twenty-five states reflects a dominant ethnolinguistic group, but these groups are in turn divided by caste, sect, religion, and a host of socioeconomic interests. Federalism provides, albeit imperfectly, a venue for the expression of cultural distinctiveness within the Indian union, but it also serves to compartmentalize conflict. The cultural conflicts of one state rarely spill over into another, and the Center can thus more effectively manage and contain them. Even as India reflects a multitude of cross-cutting identities, religion has the potential to shape a national majority. Hindus—eighty-three percent of India's population—are divided by caste, sect, and language, but political appeals on the basis of pan-Hindu identity, facilitated by modern communication, have begun to forge an increasingly self-conscious religious community that transcends its heterogeneous character and, in its expression as Hindu nationalism, poses a challenge to India as a secular state.

India's party system, like the constitutional framework, has served to sustain democratic politics and national unity, providing access to rapidly expanding political participation and newly mobilized groups. For all but some six years since 1947, India has been governed at the Center by the Congress party, the nationalist party that had led India to independence. For the first two decades after independence, the main arena of political competition at both national and state levels was within the Congress party, but beginning in the mid-1960s, with increasing frequency, regional parties successfully challenged Congress power in various states, and in 1977, opposition parties for the first time defeated the Congress to bring a change in the ruling party at the Center.

Today, in India's multi-party system, there are at the Center three major forces, represented by various parties that at least claim to be "national" in character. The Congress, long the dominant party in Indian politics, traditionally drew its support widely from across the country, from all classes and groups, but a critical margin of support come from religious minorities, notably Muslims, and from untouchables. Over the 1980s and accelerating during the period of Congress rule under Prime Minister P. V. Narasimha Rao, 1991 to 1996, the Congress base of support deeply eroded, and the 1996 elections gave the party a stunning defeat.

The Bharatiya Janata Party (BJP), the party of Hindu nationalism, emerged as the largest single party in Parliament, with 160 seats. From its base in the Hindi heartland of North India, it has dramatically expanded its support by direct appeals to a pan-Hindu religious sentiment, and though its strength is still concentrated in the North, the BJP has made inroads, especially among the urban middle classes, into other parts of India. The 1996 elections gave the BJP an opportunity to form a government, but unable to secure the requisite majority support in Parliament, the new Prime Minister, Atal Behari Vajpayee, resigned after thirteen days in power[2].

The third force at the Center is made up of the various Janata Dal factions that draw support principally from the rural peasant classes, mainly in North India, and the Left Front, led by the Communist Party (Marxist), the ruling party of West Bengal. Together with several regional parties, these parties (with the CPM extending its support but remaining outside the coalition) came together to form a United Front government under Prime Minister H. D. Deve Gowda, former Janata Dal chief minister of Karnataka state. The 13-party UF coalition constituted a minority government and was sustained only by outside support from the Congress. In late March 1997, the Congress, under the leadership of party president Sitaram Kesri, withdrew its support in a bid to form a new Congress-led government. The Congress effort failed, and the Congress agreed to support, again from the outside, a reconstituted United Front under the prime ministership of Inder Kumar Gujral.

The Congress remains the only genuinely all-India party, for the other claimants for power at the Center have bases of support that are largely confined to particular regions. Any party or coalition that is to rule at the national level, however, must necessarily be multicultural in its social base, representing a range of cultural identities. Even the BJP, in seeking to forge a Hindu nation, must cast its net broadly.

At the state level, national parties compete with those that are wholly regional in their base of support, and in a number of states, regional parties, identified with particular ethnic, linguistic, or religious groups, are the major political forces. In Tamil Nadu, Tamil nationalist parties—the DMK and AIADMK—have ruled since 1967; in Andhra Pradesh, the Telugu Desam is the major rival to the Congress; in the Punjab, it is the Sikh party, the Akali Dal; and in the Northeast, ethnically-based regional parties compete with Congress for state rule. Ethnically or religiously based parties, while expressing regional identity within a united India, pose a potential threat to cultural minorities within the state, for many of these parties have sought to advance their cause by nativist appeals to the "sons of the soil" directed against migrants from other parts of India or against indigenous religious and linguistic minorities. Such appeals dramatically expose the tensions and the dilemmas inherent in multicultural democracy.

Liberal democracy rests on a dual commitment to majority rule and minority rights. The legitimacy of a majority at any given time depends on the maintenance of an open marketplace of ideas, free and periodic elections through which the majority can be challenged, and the guarantee of basic human rights for all persons. But how and in what form are minority rights to be protected? Liberal democracy is classically expressed in terms of individual rights, and the Preamble to the Indian Constitution embodies a commitment to justice, liberty, equality, and fraternity in terms of the individual. Yet minority interests are typically expressed in terms of group identity, and political demands may call for the protection or promotion of language, religion, and culture, or of the "group" more generally, in ways that conflict not only with "the will of the majority," but with the constitutional guarantees of individual rights and equal protection. This tension, and the inherent dilemmas therein, can be seen in India in the contexts of (1) linguistic/ethnic regionalism and separatism; (2) caste reservations; and (3) secularism and Hindu-Muslim communal relations[3].

Regionalism and Separatism

With independence, the princely states were integrated into the Indian union, but these newly created states were linguistically and culturally heterogeneous. Long before independence, the Congress party had organized its provincial branches along linguistic lines and demands for the reorganization of states on a linguistic basis brought the issue before the Constituent Assembly. Nehru and the Congress leadership feared that linguistic states would have a "subnational bias" that would retard national integration and unleash "fissiparous tendencies," threatening the unity of India. Moreover, they argued, most states, however the boundaries might be drawn, would still have linguistic minorities. But the logic in democratic terms for linguistic states—that state administration and judicial processes be conducted in the language of the local majority—was compelling, and political pressure for the reorganization of states ultimately proved irresistible. Beginning in 1953, with the creation of Andhra Pradesh as a Telugu-speaking state, and then in 1956, with more general reorganization on a linguistic basis, the principle of language as the basis for state boundaries was broadly accepted.

States Reorganization in 1956, however, neither completed the process nor quelled demands for the creation of new states. In 1960, following widespread agitation and violence, Bombay was bifurcated to form the linguistic states of Maharashtra and Gujarat; in 1966, the Sikhs secured Punjab, and in the following years, several tribal states were carved out of the northeast. In 1987, India's twenty-fifth state was created as the former Portuguese colony of Goa was elevated to statehood. The pressures continue today. In the late 1980s, Nepalis in West Bengal's Darjeeling District raised the demand for a separate "Gurkhaland" state within India. After two years of violence, in which more than 300 people were killed, the Gurkha National Liberation Front accepted a proposal for what would be, in effect, an autonomous region within the state of West Bengal, only to renew the demand in 1993 for a separate Gurkha state. The Bodo tribals of Assam have pursued a violent struggle—thus far unsuccessfully—for the creation of a separate Bodoland. More formidable is the demand by tribals of mineral-rich southern Bihar and contiguous districts of neighboring states for a Jharkhand state. The demand has been voiced with varying intensity since 1947, but in 1992, it reemerged with new militancy, as strikes and bombings were directed to an economic blockade of the region. Most recently, in 1996, the United Front government of Prime Minister Deve Gowda gave its support for the creation of Uttarakhand, a new state to be carved out of northwestern hill districts of Uttar Pradesh. The proposal gave impetus to demands from various groups throughout India for the creation of separate states.

The organization of states on a linguistic basis provides the framework for expanded political participation. It permits people more effective access to government for the articulation of demands—but demands that often reflect the parochialism of language and region. The creation of linguistic states reinforced regionalism and has stirred demands for increased state autonomy. Although India guarantees the free movement of people[4], almost every state outside the Hindi heartland of central India has spawned a militant nativist movement directed at outsiders. The fundamental issue has been employment for local people, and many state governments, either officially or unofficially, have supported the protection of jobs for the "sons of the soil." Among the most virulent is the Shiv Sena, a regional party in Maharashtra that came to power in the 1996 state assembly elections. Exploiting grievances and economic frustration, the Shiv Sena, under the banner "Maharashtra for the Maharashtrians," directed its attack, both verbal and physical, initially at South Indian immigrants and in recent years at Muslims. In the Northeast, the issue for the Assamese is not only jobs, but the preservation of the Assamese language and culture in the face of a demographic shift that threatens to make the Assamese a minority in their own state. Bengalis have migrated into Assam for more than a century, but since 1971, the influx of "foreigners," illegal aliens (Bengali Muslims from Bangladesh), has deepened ethnic insecurity and served as the catalyst for a movement that engulfed Assam in violence. In the six-year long agitation, more than 5000 people were killed in ethnic conflict. In 1986, the government of Prime Minister Rajiv Gandhi reached a settlement with the movement leaders, and by the terms of the accord, in addition to commitments for the deportation of illegal immigrants and enhanced economic development, the central government promised to provide "legislative and administrative safeguards to protect the cultural, social, and linguistic identity and heritage" of the Assamese people.

Assam's agony did not end with the accord—as yet largely unfulfilled—and, like other states in the ethnically turbulent Northeast, Assam continues to be episodically in turmoil. In the tribal states of Nagaland and Mizoram, India has fought insurgency movements since 1947, and among the tribal peoples of the Northeast more generally, the aspiration for independence from India has been met by a determined Indian response to secure the territorial integrity of the union.

India is a federal system with a strong constitutional bias toward the Center. The Constitution allocates powers according to three lists: Center, State, and Concurrent, but, through various articles, it provides the Center with a capacity to intervene and even to dismiss elected state governments and impose direct central authority through "President's Rule." Under Prime Minister Indira Gandhi (1966-1977; 1980-1984), centralization of power increased dramatically, both in administration of government and in the structure and operation of the ruling Congress party. The result was an increasing, imbalance in the federal relationship of the Center and the states and, concomitantly, a growing regionalization of politics, with heightened demands from the non-Hindi states of "the periphery" for greater state autonomy. It is seen in Tamil Nadu, where the issue of Hindi as the national language was the catalyst for the rise of the regional DMK and its offshoot, AIADMK to power; in Andhra Pradesh, with the victory of the Telugu Desam party, and in West Bengal, where the Communist Party (Marxist) functions essentially as a regional party. Most notable, however, is the Punjab, where in 1982, the Akali Dal, the Sikh political party, pushed demands for greater state autonomy and strident Sikh militants launched a campaign of terrorism for an independent nation of Khalistan.

Punjab and Kashmir

No "ethnic" conflict in India has been more traumatic politically and emotionally than that of the Punjab, "homeland" of the Sikhs, who make up some fifty-five to sixty percent of the population there. At least 20,000 people have died in the violence. The state had been under President's Rule for extended periods marked by draconian instruments of law and order[5]. This has nurtured mutual distrust between Hindu and Sikh and, in such official actions as the army's entry in June 1984 into the Golden Temple at Amritsar, has alienated much of the Sikh community from the government, if not from India itself. It was in vengeance for the violation of the Sikh temple that two Sikh members of her own bodyguard murdered Prime Minister Indira Gandhi in October 1984. While tensions originally developed over nonsectarian demands behind which all Punjabis, Hindu and Sikh could rally, the Akali Dal set the issues in the context of various demands for the protection of Sikh religious interests that excluded Hindus and to which the government, affirming its commitment to secularism, would not yield. For the militants, challenging the Akali Dal for Sikh leadership, this was proof positive that the Sikh religion could be protected only by an independent theocratic Sikh state. For the Akalis, the issue was political power; for the militants, it was (or so they claimed) Sikh identity itself and the fear of absorption into the Hindu mass. Aggrieved though they were, most Sikhs in the Punjab opposed the idea of Khalistan, and by the late 1980s, for many terrorist gangs, political and religious goals had been displaced by extortion, robbery, and murder as a way of life. The people, sickened by both terrorism and police repression, were ready for a return of the political process. After fifty-six months of direct rule from New Delhi, state assembly elections were held in February 1992. Under terrorist threat and an Akali boycott, a low voter turnout brought a Sikh-led Congress government to power.

Initially, with little credibility, the government won increasing popular confidence, and in the village council elections held in January 1993, with no attempt by terrorists to influence the vote, 82 percent of the electorate turned out to vote. With the restoration of self-government and the continued application of police forces against the militants, the Punjab crisis eased—though the specter of episodic terrorism remains a backdrop to any return to normalcy. In February 1997, in state assembly elections, the Akali Dal came to power in coalition with the BJP.

In the far-northern state of Kashmir, India faces an even more serious problem because of its international dimension and the extent of alienation among the population. India and Pakistan have fought two wars over what was once the princely state of Jammu and Kashmir, and it remains the principal source of antagonism between the two nations. For India, the state—now divided by a "line of control"—is fully a part of the Indian union; with its sixty-five percent Muslim majority, it stands as a symbolic rebuttal to the "two nation" theory that underlays the founding of Pakistan. Moreover, India asserts that Kashmir's inclusion in India serves as a guarantor of the secular state. Pakistan demands that the people of Kashmir decide by plebiscite whether to be a part of India or Pakistan—a demand that rests on the assumption that the decision would be for Pakistan. However, the largest number of the state's Muslims would likely choose an independent Kashmir, and this has been the goal of the Jammu and Kashmir Liberation Front (JKLF), albeit, until 1988, with comparatively little political support.

The state is itself ethnically divided, with Hindus predominant in Jammu and Tibetan Buddhists in the sparsely populated region of Ladakh. It is in Kashmir proper that Muslims make up the overwhelming majority, but their numbers, some four million, are a small portion of India's more than 100 million Muslim population. Under the rule of the National Conference, the regional Muslim party of Jammu and Kashmir, the state had been comparatively quiet, but in the late 1980s more and more Kashmiri Muslims increasingly alienated by fraudulent elections, widespread corruption, and the failure of the Center to develop the state economically—responded to the nationalist call for the liberation of Kashmir from "Hindu India." In 1988, the JKLF and an assortment of separatist and fundamentalist groups initiated a wave of strikes, bombings, and assassinations. Imposing President's Rule, the Center responded with what was decried as an indiscriminate use of force, deepening the alienation of the people of Kashmir.

The principal groups involved in the Kashmir insurgency are the Jammu and Kashmir Liberation Front, supporting an independent and secular Kashmir, and the fundamentalist Hezb-ul-Mujahideen, with close links to Pakistan's Jammiat-i-Islami party and the presumed recipient of Pakistani largess. Both are affiliated politically with the All-Party Hurriyat Conference, an aggregate of some thirty militant groups.

The sources of the separatist movement are internal to Kashmir and owe their origin to years of maladministration at home and political interference from New Delhi, but the agitation has been supported and exacerbated by elements within Pakistan[6]. Some 250,000 to 400,000 troops of the Indian Army and paramilitary forces are deployed in Kashmir, but their inability to suppress the uprising underscores the limits of force when it is unaccompanied by a political process that effectively engages at least those few prepared to enter into dialogue. But as the death toll of more than 15,000 since 1989 continued to mount, more and more Kashmiris yearned for an end to the violence. In September 1996, long-promised state elections returned Kashmir to civilian rule under a National Conference government headed by former chief minister Farooq Abdullah. Voter turnout was some 30 percent, and observers deemed the elections generally free, but the parties of the Hurriyat Conference boycotted the elections and a substantial number of people—for whatever reason—did not participate. If the new government is to gain credibility and legitimacy, it must extend the political process and widen participation through local elections, and it must draw those who remain outside the political process into negotiation. And integral to any resolution of the conflict, the Center must grant substantial and meaningful autonomy to the state, just as the state itself must recognize its internal diversity by granting substantial autonomy to the regions of Ladakh, Jammu, and Kashmir proper.

Kashmir underscores a dilemma inherent in any demand for regional autonomy when based on ethnic, religious, and cultural claims. Within the State of Jammu and Kashmir, not only does Ladakh have a Buddhist majority and Jammu a Hindu majority, but each region has important, culturally distinct minorities, and any grant of autonomy must recognize their rights both in individual and group terms. In Kashmir proper, the Hindu Pandit minority is no less Kashmiri than the Muslim majority, but in the decade of insurgency, victim to acts of terrorism, most Pandits have been compelled to flee their homes as refugees. Any resolution of the Kashmir crisis must insure their return and secure their rigthts under the terms of agreement that may be reached.

India's federal system provides a structure that once compartmentalized social unrest, and political crises could often be contained within the boundaries of a state or region. But the centralization of power also centralized problems, bringing to the desk of the Prime Minister issues once resolved at the state level. A federal balance must be restored, with a meaningful devolution of power to the states—indeed, perhaps to an increased number of states and possibly "autonomous regions" within states—but a devolution accompanied by the constitutional guarantee of civil rights and liberties to ensure the equal protection of each person before the law. Among the many measures for redressing the balance between the Center and the states that have been considered, the most compelling include an end to the arbitrary dismissal of state governments and imposition of President's Rule; a more equitable sharing of revenues; and a respect by the Center for spheres of public policy that are properly state concerns[7].

Caste Reservations

Hindu society in India is divided by caste and subcaste in a complex hierarchy from the Brahmin to the untouchable. The Constitution of India abolished untouchability and specified that no citizen be subject to any disability or restriction with regard to places of public use or accommodation on the basis of caste. Political representation was guaranteed for Scheduled Castes (untouchables) and Tribes through the reservation of seats in elected legislative bodies, from Parliament to village councils, in proportion to their population. But despite these various provisions and the extended protections of the Untouchability (Offenses) Act, untouchables—today numbering more than 130 million—continue to suffer discrimination and deprivation. To address this situation and to overcome the cumulative results of past discrimination, the government instituted a program of "protective discrimination", an Indian version of affirmative action, that reserved 22.5 percent of all central government jobs for Scheduled Castes and Tribes. Comparable reservations were provided for state employment, and reservations were extended to college and university admissions. The system has been controversial, and many caste Hindus, particularly Brahmins, who have been denied government employment or entrance into universities, feel that they have been victims of reverse discrimination. Far more controversial, however, has been the extension of reservations to "other backward classes," specific castes identified by their low level of social and educational advancement. Predominantly rural, they account for a substantial portion of India's population and in many states command significant political power. In response to that power, a number of states have extended reservations in university admissions and government employment to the "backward" castes.

In 1980, the Backward Classes Commission, chaired by former Bihar state chief minister B. P. Mandal (himself a member of a backward caste), recommended the reservation of 27 percent of all central government jobs for the backward classes, in addition to the 22.5 percent already reserved for the Scheduled Castes and Tribes. The 3,743 castes and subcastes identified as beneficiaries make up 52 percent of the Indian population. The report gathered dust for a decade, but in 1990, Prime Minister V.P. Singh announced that his Janata Dal government would implement the Mandal recommendations. The decision brought widespread criticism from the press and strong opposition from higher castes, especially students. In New Delhi and other urban areas in North India, violent protests, acts of self-immolation, and shootings by the police raised the specter of "caste war." Singh declared the reservations a matter of social justice, but to his political opponents it was seen as a cynical political move to shore up his threatened base of support among the backward peasant castes. Given the numbers involved, however, no political party could oppose the reservations outright, although the left argued for reservations based on income and educational criteria rather than upon caste. Implementation was stayed by the Supreme Court, pending a ruling on the constitutionality of the measure. Returned to power in 1991, the Congress party government, headed by P.V. Narasimha Rao, sought to mollify opposition to the reservations by adding a 10 percent reservation for the poor of the higher castes. In November 1992, the Supreme Court upheld the reservation for backward castes, with the provision that it be need-based, but struck down the additional 10 percent as constitutionally impermissible. The complexities of the court decision effectively preclude implementation of the reservation, but the controversy has sharpened caste enmities.

Rather than leading India toward a casteless society, reservations on the basis of caste have reinforced caste identities. Reservations for untouchables may indeed be compelling, because it is their caste identity that has been the source of stigma and discrimination, but in using caste rather than individual need as the criterion for benefits, their identity as untouchables is officially sanctioned. Moreover, the dilemma is manifest in that all untouchables do not benefit equally. Reservations go disproportionately to the more "advanced" among the untouchables, while those most in need remain effectively excluded.

The backward castes share with the untouchables a comparatively low level of educational and social advancement, but their position is not the result of discrimination based on caste, nor do they suffer the stigma and disabilities associated with untouchability. And for all their "backwardness" as a group, they command considerable political power, and, as peasants, many among them enjoy increasing prosperity. If, arguably, to overcome caste-based discrimination against untouchables, caste-based benefits are required, the same contention cannot justify caste-based reservations for the backward castes. Against the image of the poor Brahmin passed over in favor of the advantaged member of a backward caste, the appropriate response is to individual need and merit, not group identity.

Hindu-Muslim Conflict

India is a secular state but a society defined by religious identities and riven by communal mistrust and hatreds. In India, the term "communal" refers principally to Hindu-Muslim conflict, and with memories of partition still bitterly nurtured, Hindu-Muslim tensions are sustained by jealousy and fear. Each year several hundred incidents of communal violence and rioting are officially reported, and their number and intensity have grown in the past two decades. In December 1992, following the destruction of the mosque at Ayodhya by Hindu fanatics, rioting across India left some 1,200 persons dead. In January 1993, Bombay witnessed a nine-day orgy of Hindu-Muslim violence with more than 600 people killed.

Since the early 1980s, the rise of Muslim fundamentalism in India has spurred a heightened Hindu consciousness and led Hindu nationalists to project India's eighty-three percent Hindu majority as threatened. Hindu nationalism is rooted in the late nineteenth century and is today represented by an increasingly formidable range of organizations and parties—the powerful paramilitary Rashtriya Swayamsevak Sangh (RSS); its revivalist affiliate, Vishwa Hindu Parishad (VHP); and the Bharatiya Janata Party (BJP), the leading opposition political party that seeks to take control of the central government. With visions of a revitalized Hindu India, they portray India's secularism as no more than a guise for pampering religious minorities.

Secularism in India does not erect a wall of separation between church and state, but rather seeks to recognize and foster all religious communities. The Constitution guarantees freedom of worship and the right of each religious group to establish and administer its own schools and to maintain its distinct traditions. But in India, as in the United States, the form and degree of state accommodation of religious practices have been matters of controversy. The appropriate democratic balance between majority preference and minority protection is fundamentally at issue.

In the wake of partition and the heightened insecurity of India's remaining Muslim population, the Congress government under Nehru permitted Muslims to retain their personal law, governing such matters as marriage, divorce, and inheritance, while amalgamating other Indians under a uniform civil code. For Hindu nationalists, who would recognize no exceptions, this smacked of a pseudo-secularism that privileged Muslims over Hindus. The issue was dramatically confronted in the 1985 Shah Bano case. The Supreme Court had ruled in favor of a seventy-three-year-old woman, Shah Bano—divorced after forty-three years of marriage by her husband in the traditional Muslim manner—and awarded her a monthly maintenance from her husband, where Muslim personal law would have required none. Muslim clerics, with the cry of "Islam in danger," rallied Muslims to the cause and warned that imposition of a uniform civil code would deny them the right to follow the injunctions of their faith. In an attempt to stem the loss of Muslim support from the Congress party, Prime Minister Rajiv Gandhi (initially favorable to the judgment) announced support for the Muslim Women (Protection of Rights on Divorce) Bill that would remove Muslim divorce from provisions of law and, in effect, scuttle the Supreme Court decision. Though welcomed by traditional Muslims, the bill came under immediate attack by progressive Muslims, women, secularists, and Hindu chauvinists. Hindus are not disadvantaged by the application of Muslim personal law, although Muslim women may surely enjoy fewer rights than their Hindu sisters. But this was not a human rights issue for Hindu nationalists; rather, the government's response to the Shah Bano case simply demonstrated the appeasement of minorities they had long denounced. In pandering to Muslims, Hindu nationalists declared that the Congress party had sold out India's Hindu majority.

Hindu nationalists project a mythic Hindu majority that denies the diversity that makes Hinduism—and India—what it is. They have reinvented a muscular Hinduism that would, through the state, impose a conformity as oppressive to the individual Hindu as to the recalcitrant minority. Religion, for Hindu nationalists, is the vehicle by which they seek to achieve political power and restore, Ram-rajya, the ideal rule of the mythic age of Lord Ram. The conceptual catalyst is Hindutva, "Hindu-ness," a term that embodies the notion that all Indians, including Muslims, are culturally part of a Hindu nation.

The god Ram is the potent symbol that Hindu nationalists have chosen to weld Hindus, disparate in their profusion of sects and traditions, into a self-conscious community. Ayodhya, in the state of Uttar Pradesh, is the presumed birthplace of Lord Ram, and devotees assert that in the sixteenth century, the Mughal emperor, Babur, destroyed the temple marking the birthplace and, in its place, constructed a mosque, the Babri Masjid. In 1989, efforts by the Vishwa Hindu Parishad and other Hindu revivalist groups to demolish the Babri Masjid and to "recapture injured Hindu pride" through the construction of a new Ram Janmabhoomi temple precipitated what was to that time probably the most serious Hindu-Muslim rioting since partition in 1947. In 1990, to galvanize Hindu sentiment behind the BJP, party president L.K. Advani launched his *rath yatra* (chariot pilgrimage), a 10,000-kilometer journey, in a van fashioned to look like a mythological chariot, across the heart of North India to Ayodhya, to launch the construction of the new temple. Prime Minister V.P. Singh, invoking the principles of secularism, warned that the mosque would be protected "at all costs." As Advani and other BJP leaders approached Ayodhya, they were arrested. The BJP, in turn, withdrew its parliamentary support from the minority Singh government, and on a vote of no-confidence, the Prime Minister submitted his resignation. In the fall of 1992, the VHP and BJP vowed that on December 6 they would begin construction of the new temple to Ram at the sacred site. More than 200,000 Hindu militants converged on Ayodhya and, at the appointed hour, stormed through the police barricades and demolished the Muslim shrine. The police and paramilitary guarding the mosque offered little resistance. In face of the action and subsequent rioting, the Congress government of Narasimha Rao seemed paralyzed, but when the Prime Minister did act, he ordered the dismissal of the BJP government of Uttar Pradesh, India's most populous state, and the imposition of President's rule, that is, direct rule by the central government. A week later, the governments of the remaining three BJP-ruled states were dismissed. Advani and other Hindu nationalist leaders were arrested and charged with inciting the militants, and the government banned, for two years, three Hindu communal organizations (the RSS, the VHP, and the Bajrang Dal) and two Muslim fundamentalist groups. The president of the VHP vowed that any government efforts to impede the construction of the new Ram temple would result in "a confrontation of unimaginable magnitude."

As Hindu-Muslim tensions have deepened, India's secularism has been increasingly challenged at every level of society, from the drawing rooms of New Delhi intellectuals and the rising urban "consumer" middle class to the saffron-clad militants of the VHP and the armed zealots of the Bajrang Dal and the Shiv Sena. The challenge is to India as a secular state and to its capacity to secure democracy, justice, and equality in a multicultural society.

Majority Rule and Minority Rights

Indian experience enables us to draw a range of conclusions with respect to the democratic management of ethnic and religious conflict. Democratic management of ethnic conflict requires a substantive distribution of power between the center and the periphery and among the different conflict groups within the country. A balance must be maintained between checking the over-centralizing tendencies of political power and containing the centrifugal, "fissiparous" tendencies in a multicultural state. There is tension as well between the liberal emphasis on individual rights and the assertion of group rights and identity, and the democratic polity must find its way toward balance here as well. The base in any balance, however, must be a recognition and guarantee of fundamental human rights.

Historically in India, problems of ethnic and religious conflict have eased when political and group leaders have sought to deal with them through accommodation, bargaining, and the political process, and particularly when the Center has sought accommodation with minority groups. Problems have intensified when the Center has sought to intervene directly to impose an outcome on a group or region asserting its distinct interests and identity. Force alone has been unable to overcome separatist tendencies, but if successfully applied, it must be accompanied by political dialogue and accommodation.

In every democracy, there is inherent tension between majority rule and minority rights, but the two are inextricably bound together. Indeed, democracy is sustained because there is no single, monolithic, and permanent majority, but rather a shifting pattern of "minorities rule". The "minorities" may reflect the cross-cutting social cleavages and overlapping memberships that characterize the idealized model of democratic pluralism or the mosaic of distinct groups that define their identity in terms of one or a combination of cultural attributes such as religion, language, or caste. But in each case, there must be an underlying political culture of mutual respect and trust or, at minimum, a basic agreement on the rules of the political game among the various groups themselves. Lacking such a consensus, one group, or perhaps a coalition, may seek power and domination over others; but it may be that the center cannot hold and that the society itself is torn apart by war and secession.

In India, in a political culture of mutual distrust, the dangers are legion. India's democracy is challenged by communalism, casteism, and separatism. But for all the pressures and dilemmas that India faces as a multi-cultural state, Indian democracy, sustained through eleven elections, shows remarkable strength and resilience. India's democracy is grounded in the power of the people, and the faith of those who led India to freedom is confirmed by the vitality of political life in India today. In its struggle to find the "right" balance in securing majority rule with minority rights, India--facing enormous challenge--has made substantial achievement.

Endnotes

1. This chapter is an updated and revised version of Hardgrave 1993. This revision is published with the permission of John Hopkins University Press.
2. The growth of the BJP is reflected in its increase in seats in the Lok Sabha, India's lower house of Parliament-- from two seats won in 1984 (7.4% of the vote) to eighty-five seats (11.4%) in 1989, and, contesting twice as many seats as in the earlier election, 119 (21%) in 1991. In 1996, with roughly twenty-two percent of the popular vote, the BJP won 160 seats.
3. For an extended discussion of these issue areas, with extensive bibliographical references, see Hardgrave & Kochanek 1993: 125-66; 167-215.
4. This subject is temporary, transitional, and special provisions, such as restrictions on the transfer of land to non-tribal areas and, reflecting the terms of Kashmir's accession to the Union and its unique constitutional status, the sale of property to non-resident in the state of Jammu and Kashmir.
5. Provisions for designated "disturbed areas" permit arrest and detention without trial for as long as two years; secret trials by special tribunals, and wide powers of censorship. For a discussion of the array of such laws, see Hardgrave & Kochanek 1993: 209-12.
6. See Ganguly 1997.
7. The 1988 Sarkaria Commission Report on Center-State Relations made a number of recommendations that would enhance "co-operative federalism," but its measured proposals have been largely ignored.

Works Cited

Ganguly, Sumit. 1997. *The Crisis in Kashmir: Portents of War, Hope of Peace.* Cambridge: Woodrow Wilson Center Press & Cambridge University Press.

Hardgrave, Robert L., Jr. 1993. India: Dilemmas of Diversity. *Journal of Democracy* 4:54-68.

Hardgrave, Robert L., Jr. and Stanley A. Kochanek. 1993. *India: Government and Politics in a Developing Nation.* 5th ed. Forth Worth: Harcourt Brace Jovanovich.

Chapter 17

The Spiritual Self in Indian Psychology

Alan Roland

Without positing the realization of an inner spiritual self (*Atman*)—a self considered to be one with the godhead (*Brahman*)—as the basic and ultimate goal of life (*moksha*), it is virtually impossible to comprehend Indian psychological makeup, society, and culture.[1] The assumption of an inner spiritual reality within everyone and the possibility of spiritual realization through many paths are fundamental to the consciousness and preconsciousness of Indians. Within an Indian context, these assumptions have to be explicitly denied when they are not implicitly adhered to, in contrast to the dominant "rational-scientific" culture of the contemporary secular West, where they are usually ignored or denigrated.[2]

This is not to say that all Indians are actively engaged or even interested in spiritual pursuits and disciplines. Nor is this meant to minimize the increasing numbers of Americans seriously involved in one or another form of Eastern disciplines. I am simply emphasizing the prevailing views of reality in contemporary Indian and American consciousness.

To give an idea of how deeply these assumptions are ingrained: One woman patient, Rashi, with two very young children bemusedly commented during one session, "I know if I get up at 4 a.m. every morning and meditate and pray, sooner or later I shall experience God. But I am just too tired to get up so early." Or on a more serious note, some highly respected social scientists with doctorates from major American and

English universities commented, "No matter what position you are in life, it [the spiritual self] kind of tugs at your coattails."[3] I have not yet heard anything close to these kinds of comments from patients, colleagues, or friends in America, regardless of ethnic or religious background, unless they are themselves seriously involved in a spiritual quest.

With three of my eighteen Indian patients, unless I took their spiritual aspirations seriously, psychoanalytic therapy would have been adversely affected. To have ignored or denigrated Ashis's frequent associations around his involvements with spiritual persons and his own practices as regressive or psychopathological would have resulted in serious problems in working together. Even more to the point, when Shakuntala sensed the unreceptiveness of her former therapist to her spiritual life, she simply left her inner struggles around this major dimension out of her free associations. Yet psychoanalytic therapy was highly relevant in both cases in helping these patients toward some partial resolution of inner conflicts and deficits that were having a stultifying effect on their spiritual pursuits; Ashis's inner conflicts with his father needed to be ameliorated for him to pursue his writing as *sādhanā*; whereas Shakuntala had to resolve her lack of discipline resulting from paternal indulgence, which interfered with the assiduous practice of daily meditation.

The spiritual dimension was even more central in the psychoanalytic therapy of Rashmi, a Hindu woman artist who had arranged her own marriage in the modernized circles of Bombay. Rashmi experienced intense anxiety that her strong spiritual strivings involving her painting had no place whatsoever in this marriage, as her husband, though a substantial man, was not at all oriented in this direction. Through dream analysis, the roots of Rashmi's intense anxiety became clarified. A maternal uncle, a highly venerated holy man, had greatly encouraged Rashmi during her childhood in spiritual pursuits and painting but unfortunately had died when she was eleven. When her family then spent time with her father's family, Rashmi felt deeply stultified by them, as they seemed to lack any genuine spiritual presence. Later, she was able to resume the cultivation of her inner life through art with a couple of unusual teachers. By interpreting an unconscious displacement wherein she unwittingly perceived her husband as being as threatening to her inner development as her father's family, her anxiety subsided appreciably, and she was able to continue reasonably comfortably with both her painting and her marriage.

It is further assumed in the Indian cultural context that everyone is at different stages along the road, inwardly evolved and involved to varying degrees and that only the extremely rare person has attained a high degree of self-realization. In the Indian cultural context it is that person, or one actively engaged in the search, who is profoundly respected at all levels of society. As an instance, a highly respected Indian psychologist related that as she got off her train in Delhi in the early hours of the morning, the taxi drivers were rather sour over the prospect of getting up and driving her home—until she said, "Oh, come on, I've just returned from a pilgrimage and I'm exhausted." One immediately took her home.

To discuss the spiritual self meaningfully, one must immediately confront two major issues. First, it is impossible to write about the spiritual self perceptively unless one has undergone various practices for extended periods of time. Haas (1956) has cogently asserted that there is nothing mystical in mysticism: one simply has to be intensely involved—and have both talent and inclination in this direction—in various disciplines such as breathing and meditation, prayer and worship, and to be so involved over extended periods of time under the tutelage of an instructor to have some idea of what it is all about. (The same, of course, is true for psychoanalysis, where it is extremely difficult to have any real sense of unconscious motivation, defenses and conflict, as well as transference, resistances, and dream analysis without going through one's own psychoanalysis.) What various writers and others have described is that these spiritual practices are generally geared toward a calming and concentrating of the mind and emotions, so as to permit an inner transformation, allowing the emergence of other levels of consciousness and being.

The second major difficulty resides in the issue of terminology: there are no truly accurate concepts for what are ineffable inner experiences. Thus myths and metaphors, parables, and other imagery have inevitably been used by those who have realized the spiritual self to convey some sense of their experiences. I am fully aware that my concept of the spiritual self is no better than other concepts traditionally used. From a psychological standpoint, what I am trying to convey is that, phenomenologically, there is a different inner experiential ego state or kind of consciousness separate from everyday waking and dream consciousness, with a different sense of inner being. Perhaps aesthetic experiences are experientially closest to the kinds of inner ego states present in various centering and meditative practices. The spiritual self is also immanent in that these inner states of consciousness and being are actually experienced and are not transcendent in the way spoken of by Kant and other Western philosophers.[4] Further, there are inner psychological structures and inclinations of a very different kind from what we encounter in psychoanalytic work that may be actualized through various spiritual disciplines or allowed to remain nascent and quiescent. There is the still further difficulty in addressing a Western psychoanalytic audience on various aspects of the spiritual self. It is certainly a topic that has never received any welcome reception within the psychoanalytic community, with important exceptions in the Jungian group and certain segments of neo-Freudian psychoanalysis. Although Freud (1927: 1930) was somewhat wary of making definitive valuations in this area, instead directing his attention to the role of religion within the psyche of the Western common man, he and other psychoanalysts have approached any spiritual search as being essentially reducible to some form of compensation or psychopathology. In our more sophisticated psychoanalysis of today, the spiritual self is usually relegated to an unconscious effort to reassert symbiotic union with the mother—a newer version of the oceanic feeling. In its place, Freud and psychoanalysis have posited the ideal of the rational, scientific man (Meltzer 1978).

Reductionism of the Spiritual Self in Psychoanalytic Theory

This reductionistic strategy of psychoanalysis, which the literary critic Leon Edel (1966) referred to as leaving muddied footprints in other discipline, has been taken over by other psychoanalytic writers about Indian personality. Carstairs (1957), coming from a Kleinian viewpoint, has rendered the spiritual path as motivated by unconscious infantile fantasies of trying to regain infantile omnipotence, repossession of the early gratifying mother and intense gratification of infantile sexuality, and the symbiotic togetherness of prenatal existence. More recently, J. Moussaieff Masson (1976, 1980), a Sanskrit scholar later trained in psychoanalysis, has asserted reductionistic strategies *ad absurdum* in the area of Indian studies by drawing upon the full psychoanalytic armamentarium of psychopathology. His seemingly meticulous Sanskrit and psychoanalytic scholarship is unfortunately flawed by his wild methodology of speculating loosely on ancient Indian texts as well as modern Indian biography without any effort whatsoever to ground his speculations in any actual clinical data of Indian patients who are involved in spiritual disciplines.[5] Finally, Edward Shils (1961), a sociologist, simply agrees with the standard psychoanalytic formulation that the striving for mōkṣa is for symbiotic reunion or merger with the mother. One can thus be Kleinian or classical or even contemporary Freudian in outlook, but the overwhelming reductionism on the spiritual self in Indian personality remains.

In more recent years, two Catholic psychoanalysts, William Meissner (1984) and Anna Marie Rizzuto (1979), have used Winnicott's object relations theory to update the relationship between psychoanalysis and religion. By emphasizing Winnicott's positive views on illusion as central to early childhood development, and to symbolization in all of the realms of culture, including religion, they have developed a new psychoanalytic slant on religion, thus critiquing the Cartesian dualism inherent in Freud's pitting reality over illusion. Similar to Freud, both have generally steered away from any detailed consideration of spiritual experiences. Kakar (1991) has used their Winnicotian spin on illusion to justify viewing the "oceanic feeling" of great Indian mystics such as Ramakrishna as being regressive but in a positive way. Kakar thus continues the psychoanalytic tradition of reductionism on spiritual experiences but in a more sophisticated way.

However, there are occasional psychoanalysts who indicate a different position. The English psychoanalyst and artist, Marion Milner (1973), cites her personal meditation experiences while also reviewing the more explicit mystic positions of Bion (1977)—the latter being one of the only psychoanalysts besides Jung and his followers to introduce this dimension explicitly into psychoanalytic thinking. R. D. Laing, involved in Buddhism, also belongs to this group, though he was omitted from Milner's paper. More forthright involvement in American psychoanalytic circles has come mainly from the Karen Horney group, Erich Fromm, and Erik Erikson. Karen Horney, Harold Kelman, David Shainberg, Antonio Wenkert, and others of this group, originally inclined in this direction from their interest in Hassidic Judaism and Martin Buber; later they became involved in Zen Buddhism through Dr. Akihisa Kondo, who was in training with them. Kondo introduced Horney and Fromm to D. T. Suzuki, the renowned teacher of Zen Buddhism; Fromm then influenced a number of members of the William Alanson White Institute in New York City. Erikson (1958, 1969) has, of course, a long-standing interest in *homo religiosus* through his work on Martin Luther and Gandhi. In recent years, other American Freudian psychoanalysts have become deeply interested in the spiritual self: Margaret Brenman-Gibson, an associate of Erikson;[6] Harmon Ephron, co-founder of the Flower Fifth Avenue Psychoanalytic Institute, with his wife, Pat Carrington, and a few other associates;[7] and Elsa First, trained at Hampstead in London, and currently practicing and writing in New York City.[8] Morris Carstairs himself has, in the 1980s, become involved in Tibetan Buddhism.

Much more recently, there has been a resurgence of interest in the interface between psychoanalysis and spirituality, mainly through psychoanalysts and/or psychoanalysts in training, who are seriously involved in Zen Buddhist or Burmese

Vipassana Buddhist or Tibetan Buddhist meditation. Analysts or analysts-in-training, such as Nina Coltart (1992), Paul Cooper (1995), Mark Finn (1992), Jeffrey Rubin (1996), and John Suler (1993), are all actively writing on the interface between the process and theory of psychoanalysis and Buddhist meditation and theory. Other analysts such as Eigen and Leavy (1995) write in the broad area of psychoanalysis and mysticism. There have also been a few large conferences on Buddhism and psychotherapy, at which the Dalai Lama has occasionally spoken, and a literature on the subject by psychologists and psychiatrists involved in both such as Brown (1986), Engler (1986), Epstein (1995), Goleman (1977), Kornfield (1997), and Wilbur (1986).

The Familial and Spiritual Selves: Continuity

The interrelationship between the Indian familial self and the spiritual self is psychologically far more complex and paradoxical than meets the eye. The spiritual self simultaneously encompasses both continuity with and counterpoint to various aspects of the familial self. Hindu thought recognizes the psychological phenomenon or experiential duality of the phenomenological self (*jiva-ātman*), particularly in the everyday consciousness of "I-ness" (*ahamkāra*) versus the inner experience of spirit or ātman. Simultaneously, Hindu philosophy is profoundly monistic—in contrast to Western thought, which emphasizes dualities between spirit and matter, sacred and secular—in its positing various aspects of the phenomenological world, including the phenomenological self, as essentially manifestations of spirit (Brahman).[9] Experientially, a person may not be aware of this. Further, the fundamental goal of all relationships and living is the gradual self-transformation toward finer and subtler qualities and refined aspects of power in the quest for self-realization.[10] Thus, my paradoxical assertion that the spiritual self is simultaneously on a continuum with the familial self and in counterpoint to it spells out psychologically both the Hindu monistic position and the dualistic, experiential one.

Continuity is present in a variety of ways that are quite different from what has been imagined and implied by psychological writers, particularly those in the reductionistic stance of psychoanalysis (Carstairs 1957; Masson 1976, 1980; Shils 1961), while the strong counterpoint between the two is completely overlooked. There appear to be five major categories of continuity, all interrelated in a variety of ways. Broadly speaking, these bridges between the two selves are: the presence and utilization of certain psychosocial dimensions of hierarchical relationships in realizing the spiritual self, a Hindu cultural world view giving spiritual meaning to interpersonal transactions and the various goals and stages of life, a mythic orientation to everyday relationships, a personal-cosmic involvement with destiny, and the practice of a wide variety of rituals frequently associated with both myths and personal-cosmic correspondences.

Hierarchical Relationships

One can readily observe that certain central structures of the familial self, ones especially oriented around hierarchical relationships by quality and the qualitative mode of hierarchical relationships, are frequently intensely involved in ongoing efforts to realize the spiritual self. In hierarchical relationships governed by the quality of the person, there is a marked veneration of the superior, with strong efforts to subordinate oneself, to be as close as possible, to have *darshan*, in order to incorporate, identify with, and share in the superior qualities of the other for inner self-transformations. These focal attitudes of hierarchy by quality, originating in childhood, are later extended to more and more venerated beings—from highly respected familial and community members to gurus and to the worship of various gods, goddesses, and *avatars* or incarnations—in a continuity between the familial self and spiritual self. As an example, Ashis, in his devoted readings of Tagore, Gandhi, and Coomaraswamy, was trying to associate himself as closely as possible to share in their superior qualities, as he did even more with two outstanding benefactors at work.

In *bhakti* devotional worship, various facets of symbiosis-reciprocity involved in hierarchical intimacy relationships become clearly accentuated. Intense emotional connectedness and reciprocal affective exchanges, a sense of "we-ness," and permeable ego boundaries are all intensely involved in bhakti worship. The devotee seeks, through intense emotionality, to be merged with the god, goddess, or incarnation—whether Shiva, Durga, Krishna, or whomever—and in turn through the merger expects the reciprocity of divine bliss. Sensuality becomes intensely heightened and becomes an important facet of bhakti religious experience (Miller 1977). In the worship of Krishna, the most frequent form of the bhakti cults, men draw upon their early identification with the maternal feminine to identify consciously with Radha in her divine passion for Krishna.

It is not difficult to see why psychologically these modes of religious worship, which so stress longings for and experiences of merging with the god, are overwhelmingly reduced in psychological writing to a regressive pull to the elation and omnipotent union in the early mother-infant symbiotic tie (Carstairs 1957; Kakar 1983, 151-190;

Masson 1976, 1980; Shils 1961). The psychological reality is, however, not that the path of *bhakti* is a regression to more symbiotic modes of relating but that the aspirants use their internalized symbiotic modes in the service of their spiritual practices. Further, the imagery of a symbiotic, familial mode of relating becomes a metaphor for another level of union or, at minimum, a complex interplay of different levels of a monistic reality in intentional ambiguity.[11]

What has been profoundly overlooked is that however much these religious modes of worship and experience are related to the intense mother-child symbiotic relationship, the actual religious experience enables the person to become increasingly individuated, differentiated, and separated from intensely emotional, familial involvements. This experience thus becomes an essential counterpoint to the familial self.

Transactions and Transformations

Another major category of continuity between the familial self and the spiritual self is the Hindu world view that gives meaning to the reciprocal exchanges so fundamental to hierarchical relationships as self-transformations. As Marriott (1976) and other ethnosociologists have increasingly spelled out, all kinds of transactions and exchanges, as well as the directionality of how much and what one gives and receives, are utilized or avoided to enable the person to move toward the more subtle and purer substances and qualities and more refined power, and away from the grosser ones in their inner transformations. There are profound cultural assumptions that everything transacted and exchanged between people from food to words are substances of grosser or finer nature, that through permeable boundaries they enter and help transform a person's nature, and that anyone's nature is a particular composite of a variety of substances and qualities, and is therefore different from another's. Those persons and/or groups who deal in subtler substances (such as teachers) have traditionally been accorded greater respect and hierarchical rank socially.

Another part of this internalized Hindu world view involving self-transformation are basic orienting concepts around dharma, karma, and samskara. These give meaning to various aspects of the familial self in its multiple relationships and experiences in a monistic continuum with the spiritual self and are really concerned with a soul in pilgrimage to its ultimate spiritual realization throughout a multitude of lives. Thus, by living correctly according to one's dharma, a person also moves along his or her spiritual path. How one life is lived affects the circumstances in another (karma), which in turn will affect the future life. And the kinds of relationships, experiences, and deeds constantly leave imprints (samskāras) that effect inner transformations. Not only is meaning given, but all kinds of practices are attended to that will, it is hoped, further inner transformation such as eating certain foods and avoiding others.

The life cycle is seen in a similar light. If the first two stages—that of student and householder, examples par excellence of the familial self—are lived properly according to one's dharma, which also encompasses the proper fulfillment of desire (*kama*) and wealth and power (*artha*), then there are inner transformations that help the person toward realization of the spiritual self in the third and fourth stages of life. To whatever extent these cultural orientations are implemented, they lend symbolic significance for interconnecting the familial and spiritual selves in a monistic cultural style.

Mythic Orientation

One of the strongest lynchpins linking the familial and spiritual selves in Hindus is their mythic orientation, an essential part of their conscience. Women, especially, traditionally experience everyday relationships within the framework of myths, which are a guide to the complex familial hierarchical relationships and situations.

Simultaneously, the myth also conveys the presence in everyday relationships of the divine and the demonic through metonymic thinking (Ramanujan 1980) that links these relationships with mythic images in a monistic view of reality. Thus, aspects of another reality may manifest themselves through relative, friend, or stranger. The myth always allows for the interplay of a spiritual level of reality and self in what is seemingly the most mundane and prosaic of persons and relationships. In the myths themselves, although some are much more oriented towards varied aspects of hierarchical relationships and the familial self and others stress more the spiritual self and reality, the two levels are almost always intertwined (O'Flaherty 1980). The myth therefore constantly orients the person toward the continuity of the familial and spiritual selves in everyday life, while at times it is a strong counterpoint to both the familial self and hierarchical relationships. Hanchette (1982) and Wadley (1975) report that mothers aspire to embody characteristics of one or another mother goddess in their everyday mothering relationships, thus using mythic models to integrate aspects of a familial with a spiritual self.

A strikingly moving personal example of this mythic orientation was related to me by an Indian psychologist. She was visiting her family at a time when her sister had just undergone an operation, when life-threatening postoperative complications set in. I suddenly awakened after midnight and felt I just must go to the hospital. My parents didn't stop me though it was very late. When I got there, I found a few nurses in her room. She seemed in a terrible state. I could just sense the vibrations that the nurses expected her to die and that she soon could. I immediately sent them all out and said I would take care of her. I began to pace up and down the room, always looking at my sister and keeping in mind images of the Himalayas from my recent pilgrimage. I was absolutely determined not to let her die. I had become Sāvitri to wrest her from the hands of death. A couple of hours later I somehow knew there was a turning point and she would be all right. The next morning after she awakened, my sister told me that she had a dream that night of slowly and uncontrollably sinking into a morass, when suddenly a hand reached out and pulled her out. She now felt much better, and soon recovered. It became evident how this woman drew upon a lifelong childhood identification with the mythic figure, Sāvitri—a clever and determined woman who tricked Yama, the god of death, from taking her husband as was fated—to help rescue her sister.

From this perspective, there is no opposition in Indian culture between myth as social charter (Malinowski 1954:108)—that is, as guideline to extended family and communal hierarchical relationships—and myth as indicative of a spiritual reality and self.[12] Both are always implicitly present. Very little study has been made, however, of the everyday psychological use of myths in this dual perspective.[13] Western psychoanalysts of whatever persuasion are faced with the situation that their patients simply do not have an everyday mythic orientation to life because there is no vitally alive mythic culture, except perhaps in isolated pockets. Jungians, by the use of dreams and various products of the imagination, do dredge up mythic and archetypal themes that they then relate to the person's life. But even here, Western persons are not psychologically functioning with the myth as a pervasive part of their mental space from childhood. Since there is almost nothing written on an everyday mythic orientation in Western psychoanalysis and psychology, and since these are the theoretical models for Indian therapists and psychologists, the latter are rarely oriented toward research in this area—even when some of them are personally highly involved in a mythic orientation. Instead they take for granted their own mythic functioning, or, as Kakar (1978) does, follow the traditional path of psychoanalysis in simply using myths to elucidate psychological makeup.

Personal-Cosmic Involvement with Destiny

Profoundly linking the familial and spiritual selves is the fourth category of a personal-cosmic involvement with destiny.[14] Indians are deeply concerned with the unfolding of destiny, not only of persons, but also of families, *jatis*, and now political parties and leaders. Implicit are the gradual inner transformations of the familial self as they take place through destiny in the vicissitudes of everyday relationships. Indians tend to be constantly on the look-out for signs and predictors, relying a great deal on the personal-cosmic to arrange and manage their practical affairs and relationships—marriage, education, career, children, health, wealth, and power—as auspiciously as possible. This everyday conscious and preconscious awareness of the personal-cosmic involvement with destiny is profoundly ingrained as a major dimension in the Hindu psyche in a way that it simply is not in the overwhelming majority of contemporary Westerners.

Culturally speaking, destiny is essentially linked to the unfolding of a person's and/or group's moral actions and experiences and attachments from past lives and to the influence of celestial bodies in the present—all of these influences being played out in everyday relationships and situations metonymically and varying considerably with the particular person and situation (Pugh 1977, 1978). This unfolding of human destiny can be revealed through astrology and palmistry, clairvoyant and telepathic dreams, premonitions, contact with the spirit world, and such. It is evident that the personal-cosmic world is by no means a unitary one; rather, it encompasses a variety of dimensions and methods.

The personal-cosmic world was referred to at one point or another by all of my Indian patients, and seemed to constitute an important area of their cognitive map of reality, particularly for my Hindu patients. Ashis, more than any of the others, was constantly using readings from the personal-cosmic world in the form of palmistry consultations with Professor Mukerjee to gain direction in his career. But the directions suggested by Professor Mukerjee were not simply to achieve some kind of career success; they were much more to develop and utilize Ashis's literary-meditative or spiritual side of himself in his work—something Ashis could only do to a limited extent because of inner conflicts with his father's values. His mode of working with Professor Mukerjee seems analogous to what was reported in an anthropological investigation into astrological advisory sessions.[15]

Shakuntala and Meena, like most women, used predictions from astrology and/or palmistry regarding their prospects for marriage—the latter maintaining hope from them in her thirties that she would finally be married. Shakuntala also had premonitions a family member would die. Rustum and Ashis, like most men, used readings from astrology and palmistry for direction and advancement in career. The former's engineering education in the United States was arranged solely on the basis of an astrological consultation, although his family are highly Westernized Parsees.

Clairvoyant dreams were reported in detail by Shakuntala and Laxmi, as well as by others on social occasions. The openness toward having clairvoyant dreams is not only infinitely beyond what I have encountered in New York City, but Hindus also have a decided penchant to act on a dream they believe to be clairvoyant—thus fulfilling their destiny. As an example, a psychoanalyst offhandedly related the following dream and its sequel:

> I dreamt of a holy man or *sadhu* staying in a room on the third floor of a building on Grant Road (Bombay). The next morning after having the dream, I got in my car and drove over to Grant Road. There was a building just like the one in my dream. I got out of the car, went to that room on the third floor, knocked on the door, and went in. There was the *sadhu*. I said to him, "You appeared in my dream, so I thought I would come over to meet you."

Still another dimension of the personal-cosmic world related to the unfolding of destiny is the spirit world. In counseling sessions with three different groups of female college students, there was a recurrent theme: they were all involved in trying to contact the spirit world for advice and predictions as to what would happen to them. Both a social worker and a psychoanalyst gave the following psychodynamic explanation: These sixteen and seventeen-year-old adolescent girls would have arranged marriages in only a few years with absolutely no say on their part as to who the husband or the husband's family would be and would carry the whole burden of adjustment on their shoulders. They were therefore trying to contact the spirits as a common adolescent way of trying to assert control over their lives and destiny. But what was even more striking is that both of my colleagues, in voicing their psychological insight, did not in the least deny the existence of the spirit world—that is, souls between reincarnations—or the possibility that the spirits could shed light on these girls' destiny.

It also emerged from the case data that there is an active stance toward altering or shaping destiny through counteracting adverse influences and maximizing good ones. This sharply contrasts with the usual Western stereotype of Indian passive resignation and acceptance of fate. Thus, Ashis asserted himself in a number of directions to try to fulfill Professor Mukerjee's guidance to develop the more literary-meditative side of his talents, as did Meena in trying to arrange her own marriage through putting marital ads in newspapers and contacting her social network for potential spouses. Viewed from one angle, their actions were in many respects similar to what many Americans would do. But from another angle, their inner sense of themselves was much more connected to larger forces and influences than is that of Americans; they feel connected to a much longer time perspective, to a sense of inner evolution through life events and relationships, and to an ultimate sense that their efforts would only prove fruitful if they were in accord with their destiny.

For Shakuntala, a ritual was used to maximize an auspicious time and offset adverse planetary influences, the assumption being that through the self-transformations involved in performing the ritual, her marital destiny might be partially altered. Anthropological studies report other methods that are used, ranging from alms-giving, taking vows, and going on pilgrimages, to using appropriate gems, charms, and concoctions, to observing auspicious or inauspicious times and cycles for undertaking various ventures, to associating with persons of counteracting influences. All of these methods are to aid in inner transformations that will reverse or mitigate adverse celestial influences and/or karma. This integral connection between remedial measures and astrology was matter-of-factly expressed by a woman educated in a British-style boarding school, who related that she had little use for astrology because she was away from home so much that she could not learn the necessary rituals to counteract adverse celestial influences as revealed through astrological readings (Mehta 1970).

As psychologically important as the personal-cosmic involvement with destiny is to the Hindu, it is anathema to the scientifically educated Western mind. Westerners, with but rare exceptions, respond to the personal-cosmic in Indians as superstition and ignorance. It is simply too much for the Western mind, grounded in well over a century and a half of rationalism, science, empiricism, and positivism to take very seriously, nor are American South Asian specialists necessarily exempt from these reactions.

According to Haas (1956), the objectivization of phenomena and the fundamental split between subject and object in the Western mind has all but obliterated the personal-cosmic world from Western consciousness; it has survived only in rare pockets, and has been resurrected in certain artistic and philosophical circles over the last hundred years or so by Theosophy and Anthroposophy (Washton-Long 1980), and now in the "counterculture" by a host of Eastern teachers. But since the personal-cosmic world is still perceived so negatively by the dominant world view of modern Western culture, many of its current manifestations are shadow reactions occurring in highly commercialized, degenerative forms (pers. com. Manisha Roy). In an interview, Professor Mukerjee commented,

> The West has investigated issues of causality and time, place and person, but not of destiny. In the sense of destiny, time becomes extremely complicated; it is not a linear sense of time at all. There are issues of premonitions as to what will happen in the future, what part one will have and what part one can play. This concern with human destiny is deeply tied in with the ultimate goal of spiritual realization. The ability to see destiny and cosmic influences is related to yogic practices and a person's spiritual development.

The personal-cosmic involvement with destiny and self-transformation is as much present among highly educated, scientifically trained Indians as it is with the uneducated. Scientists generally experience little if any conflict between objectivization and analysis of phenomena in the scientific approach and their concern with destiny. They simply view these two endeavors as related to different layers of reality, each valid on its own level; they have a wide toleration of the ambiguity involving different levels of reality, as is central to Hindu culture (Egnor 1980; Nandy 1980).

How are we to understand Indian involvement in the personal-cosmic world from a psychological standpoint? It is apparent that Indians, from illiterate villagers to educated urbanites, live in a highly peopled world, not only the social world of kinsmen and other groups, but with a whole inner host of more invisible powers, influences, and spirits that can affect them through permeable ego boundaries. In turn, the person can exert influence on this invisible world through rituals and other means.

Can a psychoanalyst comment meaningfully on the personal-cosmic including psychic phenomena and the spirit world? Freud (1922) gradually recognized the validity of phenomena like telepathy, but he focused primarily on telepathic occurrences as relating to patients' unconscious motivations and processes of distortion, rather than on the nature of psychic phenomena themselves. Since Freud, there has been remarkable indifference and resistance on the part of Freudian psychoanalysts to examine psychic phenomena. As an exception, Eisenbud (1953) perceptively noted that telepathy in the psychoanalytic relationship invariably involves the unconscious of the analyst as well as the patient.

Kakar sees a strong tendency toward magical and animistic thinking just beneath the surface in most Indians. He asserts that reality for Indians emanates from the deeper and phylogenetically much older structural layer of personality—the id, the mental representative of the organism's instinctual drives. Reality, according to Hindu belief, can be apprehended or known only through those archaic, unconscious, preverbal processes of sensing and feeling (like intuition, or what is known as extrasensory perception) which are thought to be in touch with the fundamental rhythms and harmonies of the universe (Kakar 1978:20).

After noting that Hindu culture relies a great deal on primary process thinking involving representational and affective visual and sensual images to convey abstract points, he writes,

> The projection of one's own emotions onto others, the tendency to see neutral and human "objects" predominantly as extensions of oneself, the belief in spirits animating the world outside and the shuttling back and forth between secondary and primary process modes are common features of daily intercourse. The emphasis on primary thought processes finds cultural expression in innumerable Hindu folk-tales in which trees speak and birds and animals are all too human, in the widespread Hindu belief in astrology and planetary influence on individual lives, and in the attribution of benign or baleful emanations to certain precious and semiprecious stones (1978:105).

Then Kakar continues,

> The widespread (conscious and preconscious) conviction that knowledge gained through ordering, categorizing, logical reasoning, is *avidya*, the not knowledge, and real knowledge is only attainable through direct, primary process thinking and perception; the imperative that inspires the yogi's meditation and the artist's sādhana, namely that to reach their avowed goals they must enlarge the inner world rather than act on the outer one; . . . the indifferent respect given to eminent scientists and professionals, compared

> with the unequivocal reverence for . . . spiritual preceptors . . . are a few of the indicators of the emphasis on the primary processes of mental life (1978:107).

Kakar then relates this mode of thinking to the ego configurations generated through the prolonged mother-child symbiotic relationship.

I have quoted Kakar at length because of the fundamental question as to whether the striving for the realization of the spiritual self and the orientation to the personal-cosmic preoccupation with destiny can be basically subsumed under the primary process, as he apparently does. There is no question that primary process thinking is overwhelmingly present in Indian culture and in the Indian mind and is quite adaptive in a society that is so oriented toward relationships and inner feelings. There is also no question that a major component of the thinking involved in the mass of Indians' relationship to all kinds of psychic and personal-cosmic phenomena is replete with fantasy, externalization, and wish-fulfillment, which is constitutive of the primary process.

However, unless one totally rejects any validity to the striving for the realization of the spiritual self, to the powers (*siddhis*) that sometimes accrue in the process, and to the varied facets of the personal-cosmic involvement with destiny, as related in the case data reported above (including Kakar's own first-hand observation of a group of persons carrying burning hot coals with no ill effects as a religious ritual in a village festival), then these phenomena simply cannot be subsumed under the primary process. The primary process works by *symbolic* expressions of displacements, condensations, and symbolism, not by actual influences over external phenomena, extrasensory perception, or emanations and correspondences.

Perhaps we can take a cue from some of the recent work on cognitive modes involved in artistic creativity. There has never been any question of the strong presence of the primary process in artistic creativity, later elaborated in the more sophisticated theories of Ehrenzweig (1967), Kris (1952), and Noy (1968), to involve an integration of primary and secondary process thinking. However, the more recent research of Rothenberg (1979) with outstanding writers and artists indicates that there are essential translogical modes of thinking in artistic creativity involving antithetical conceptualizations and metaphor formation, which are not present either in the primary process or in the usual rational, conceptual secondary processes. In my own work (Roland 1972, 1981), I have demonstrated how primary process thinking is integrated within the artist's work and governed by these translogical modes of thought, the former giving emotional power to the artistic vision of the latter.

I think other modes of thinking and being must inevitably be present in those genuine instances of clairvoyant dreams, contacts with the spirit world, and accurate predictions from astrology, palmistry, and such. I do not think these can be subsumed under the guise of the usual psychoanalytic definitions of primary and secondary process thinking, in whatever combinations. I suspect that they must be related more to yogic observations that, through various forms of breathing exercises, rituals, prayer, meditation, and such, there is some kind of inner transformation of energies, qualities, perception, knowledge, and control. Certainly, some of this has already been documented by certain medical experiments at the Menninger Foundation on Swami Rama (Rama et al. 1976), who has control of certain bodily processes that are usually considered involuntary. There are also the experiments involving beta, alpha, and theta EEG waves, cited by Kakar (1978, 18), but also conducted in Japan on states of consciousness. At the very least, Freudian psychoanalysts would do well to be modest with regard to understanding these phenomena. The contemporary culture of science, which they have profoundly internalized into their own ego-ideal, could well be examined critically, and they might expand their horizons to investigate some of these phenomena. Jungian psychology, in contrast, is far more receptive to the personal-cosmic psychic phenomena and issues of self-transformation (Jung 1968). There is no question that through their concept of synchronicity, originally gleaned from Chinese Taoist philosophy and practices, Jungians are attuned to a noncausal concatenation of inner psychological and outer social and physical events; some Jungian analysts are seriously involved in astrology and palmistry.

Rituals

The fifth and final category mediating the familial and spiritual selves is the extensive use of rituals, frequently interrelated with the Hindu mythic orientation and sometimes the magic-cosmic continuity in human affairs. While these three cultural categories are often closely interwoven in actual practice, I think it heuristically valuable from a psychological perspective to treat them as relatively separate, since they mediate the continuity between the familial and spiritual selves in recognizably different ways. Rituals are frequently performed around extended family concerns and needs, such as the occurrence of illness, the wish for a child, the concern for a good marriage, or the reasonable prosperity of the family (Hanchette 1988; Srinivas 1978).

The efficacy of the ritual in attaining these family-related goals is through subtle mutual actions and attitudes that help transform the performer and others closely associated (Raheja 1976). Self-transformation is thus central to the psychology of ritualistic performance (Marriott 1976; Wadley 1975). As the ritual is properly performed and the person becomes transformed from *tamasic* and *rajasic* to more *sattvic* qualities,[16] these more subtle and refined qualities then effect changes in grosser substance, thus fulfilling the needs of the familial-social world.

Cognitively, rituals express the constant interchange and interpenetration of the divine with the mundane (pers. com. Kapila Vatsyayan). Hindus, Vatsyayan observes, are particularly oriented toward the symbolic transformation of everyday household and other objects into sacred items for ritual and worship; the items then regain their more prosaic meaning after the *puja* or ritual worship is over. She cites as an example a rectangular eyeglass case that one may put on the ground and draw certain geometric shapes around; then by reciting certain mantras, one uses the eyeglass case as an object of worship. When the worship is finished, one will pick it up and relate to it once again simply as an eyeglass case. Thus, all kinds of objects can be utilized for ritual worship in the service of self-transformation.

Indian scientists who have this monistic view of reality, emphasizing continuity from subtle to gross substance, experience no conflict in both being involved in scientific investigation and in the performance of various rituals.[17] Thus, at the time of this writing, an internationally noted Indian chemist performs daily rituals to aid his teenage grandson abroad afflicted with childhood diabetes.

The Familial and Spiritual Selves: Counterpoint

It is a profound paradox that the realization of the spiritual self by Hindus is in experiential counterpoint to their familial self, even while the spiritual self is in continuity with the familial self as elaborated above. Counterpoint is nowhere more clearly seen psychologically than around the issues of detachment and *maya* (illusion). In the intense emotional involvement in familial hierarchical intimacy relationships, while there are considerable gratifications of dependency and esteem needs, there are equally potent possibilities and actualities for disappointment, frustration, hurt, and anger. In Hindu religious philosophy, these intense emotional attachments with their disappointments and hurt can only be loosened through efforts to realize the spiritual self, through effecting a new bonding on a spiritual level of reality. *Maya* can be viewed from this perspective not simply as illusion, as it usually is, but rather as the strong emotional attachments of the familial self that profoundly distract the person from his or her real nature or the spiritual self. As the person becomes increasingly involved in the realization of the spiritual self, he or she still relates to others and fulfills responsibilities, but without the intense looking to the other for the fulfillment of wishes and esteem and to be needed. What is termed detachment can be viewed psychologically as increasing involvement in the spiritual self and a loosening of the powerful emotional bonds in familial-social relationships (pers. com. B. K. Ramanujam).

This theme of detachment is beautifully expressed in R. K. Narayan's novel, *The Vendor of Sweets*.[18] The father, Jagan, is intensely attached to and easily manipulated by his increasingly Westernized son until he finally becomes involved in the mythological figure of the goddess. Turning more to this spiritual reality, he then fulfills his responsibilities to his son, but handles him in a firmer, more appropriate way, since his attachment and wish to be needed by the son have been loosened. The novel thus humorously revels in the traditional Hindu theme of self-realization and detachment—not escapism, as V. S. Naipaul (1977) would have it.

The simultaneity of continuity and counterpoint by detachment clearly emerges in the biography of Justice Ranade by his wife (Sakala 1981). Continuity is present in his bhakti worship, while counterpoint and detachment are strikingly present as his wife experiences his being far less emotionally involved with her as he becomes increasingly involved in the spiritual self.

Still another aspect of counterpoint by detachment involves the pervasively intense sensuality and sexuality of Indians. In the West, sexuality is increasingly associated with personal autonomy and separation from the parents as a child grows older; whereas in India, sexuality connotes greatly increased familial obligations and enmeshments (Grey 1973). Thus, the striving for brahmacharya or sexual abstinence and renunciation in adulthood in the service of spiritual disciplines (in adolescence, it is considered appropriate for the preparation for becoming a householder) can also be viewed as a step in the loosening of the intense personal attachments and obligations in extended family-communal relationships and a reaching toward personal autonomy in the spiritual sphere. In the case of Gandhi's striving Sarya, Grey (1973) is appropriately critical of Erikson's (1969) emphasis on defensive motivation rather than a striving for competency and autonomy.

Viewing the counterpoint of the spiritual self to the familial self from still another angle is A. K. Ramanujan's (1980) grammatical perspective of context-sensitive and context-free cultural ideals. Citing the overwhelming contextual emphasis of Indian culture and social patterns, he then emphasizes the strong context-free counterpoints involving the four goals of life, the four stages (*ashramas*) of the life cycle, and religious movements, particularly bhakti:

Where *kama*, *artha*, and *dharma* are all relational in their values, tied to place, time, personal character and social role, *moksa* is the release from all relations. If *brahmacharya* (celibate studentship) is preparation for a fully relational life, *grhasthashrama* (householder stage) is a full realization of it .... *Vanaprastha* (the retiring forest-dweller stage) loosens the bonds, and *sanyasa* (renunciation) cremates all one's past and present relationships . . . . In each of these the pattern is the same: a necessary sequence in time with strict rules of phase and context, ending in a free state . . . . Bhakti defies all contextual structures: every pigeonhole of caste, ritual, gender, appropriate clothing and custom, stage of life, the whole system of *homo hierarchicus* ("everything in its place") is the target of its irony (p.26).

Similarly, pilgrimage institutionalizes a strong counterpoint to the familial self, as the pilgrim, like the renouncer, becomes dead to the contextual enmeshments, responsibilities, and obligations of family and *jati* in the quest for the spiritual self. From a more psychological perspective, through a series of rituals and inner disciplines, the pilgrim strives to transcend the intense emotional involvements of the familial self to attain more illumined qualities and powers (Daniel 1976).

In a still further variation of counterpoint, there is far more room for individuation, individualized instruction, privacy, and separation in the spiritual quest than in the rest of the culture, and greatly enhanced individuality (Dhairyam 1961). The cultural particularistic view of one's personal nature is given only limited accord in the social sphere, since the expectations of the etiquette of hierarchical relationships are given equal if not considerably more weight. On the other hand, considerably more choice and differentiation is accorded for a person's spiritual practices and beliefs, including choosing a guru, of whom there are a great variety. The practice of one or another kind of yoga is based to a considerable extent on individual cognitive style, temperament, emotional makeup, inclinations, motivation and aspiration, talent and capacity, and level of attainment.[19] There is a basic supposition of inborn spiritual-psychic structures. Thus, when I asked a recognized guru how she decided on the mantra she would assign to a disciple, she answered that through her own meditation she could perceive the spiritual makeup of that disciple and so assign the suitable mantra (pers. com. Mattarji). The mantra is thus chosen on a highly individualized basis and may differ from that of other family members or even the guru.

There is also considerable privacy and often secrecy involved in individual spiritual practices, key ingredients in the separation process. As one long-term Western observer put it, "They will far more readily discuss all kinds of sexual practices and personal problems with you than their spiritual practices. Only upon the closest intimacy will anyone tell you what they are doing" (pers. com. Arthur Eisenberg). This is corroborated by social scientists who, upon being asked how many educated persons still practice meditation, answered that you will frequently not know who is or isn't involved even if you may know the person quite well. Moreover, many gurus may not be very visible, in contrast to the better known ones who give lectures, hold classes, have ashrams, or even fly around the world. The point is that Indians are extremely reticent on the subject unless they perceive the other to be readily receptive and noncondescending.

Congruence and counterpoint coexist in the context of daily life. Efforts to realize the spiritual self are not simply confined to the renouncer, as Dumont (1970) implies (thus counterpointing the renouncer with the caste-bound man).[20] The effort to realize the spiritual self is present at various stages in the life cycle in any number of Indians I met, so that I must posit it as the central theme of Indian individuation throughout life. That it tends to become much stronger at later stages of life, from the time one's children have grown up and married according to the traditional schema of the life cycle, does not negate its central psychological position throughout life.

Conclusion

I would like to ascend once more to my imaginary platform in psychological space and see if we can make out the major contours of the ultimate ideals of Indian and American civilizations that give a spoken or unspoken shape to the self in each society. In this perspective, I see the holy man and the artist as the contrasting ideals, not Dumont's (1970) collective man and renouncer or Marriott's (1976) dividual versus individual. I am using the artist in the Rankian and Eriksonian sense of a person analogous to the hero who creates his or her own personality and identity out of different components of the self, who is motivated by the actualization of his own potentialities, and creates in order to change the identity of his audience and ultimately society (Erikson 1950, 1968; Brenman-Gibson 1981; Menaker 1982; Rank 1932). The holy man, on the other hand—and I use this word advisedly instead of the renouncer, as the holy man may be within society or may renounce it—realizes a state of profound consciousness and being, becomes transformed into a different kind of social being who is a model for others, without ties to anyone, and helps others to effect this same inner transformation. This is without necessarily attempting to make any fundamental change in society.[21]

What about the Indian artist? Traditionally, the artist in India has aspired to states similar to those of the holy man in his striving to depict them and is therefore far more in the vein of the holy man than the Western self-creating artist. Today, however, the Indian artist frequently mediates between the more traditional familial-spiritual self and strong individualizing changes (pers. com. Meena Alexander).

End Notes

1. This particular way of expressing the spiritual self is that of Advaita Vedanta philosophy.
2. There are, of course, numerous exceptions to the dominant positivistic, scientific worldview in the West, ranging from groups mystically oriented within Catholicism, Protestantism, and Judaism to others in the arts.
3. Comments made at the Centre for the Study of Developing Societies in Delhi.
4. Kant used the concept of the transcendent self as a reality that transcends human cognition and the categories of the mind, but is essentially unknowable and beyond experience. The first part of his conception is similar to the Indian notion of Atman, but the last part is definitely not.
5. There is also criticism of Masson's scholarship and methodological approach by Sanskritists. See Wilhelm Halbfass's (1982) review of The Oceanic Feeling.
6. Dr. Brenmen-Gibson's interest has mainly centered in Transcendental Meditation.
7. Patricia Carrington's (1977) book summarizes the results of numerous research projects in America on various forms of simple meditation or centering techniques. In one chapter she recounts the interesting results of a small group of psychoanalytic therapists who have used simple meditation techniques themselves and with their patients.
8. Elsa First, like Morris Carstairs, follows Tibetan Buddhism. I know of at least three therapists who have become interested in various aspects of meditation through being introduced to it by their children.
9. Again, this is the position of the Advait! Vedant! school of philosophy.
10. This cultural view is formalized in Sankya philosophy, particularly in its emphasis on the different qualities (gunas).
11. Margaret Egnor (1980) elaborates the notion of intentional ambiguity as central to

Hindu culture, particularly in its playfulness with different levels of reality. Ambiguity is emphasized and embraced in the subtle, multiple levels of communication, in the acceptance of opposing models of the universe, in the double nature of many Indian deities, in the social position of women, and in many other aspects of Indian culture and society.

12. This opposition has been posited by O'Flaherty (1980).

13 Exception to this are Roy 1979, B.K. Ramanujam 1980, and Obeysekere 1981, 1984.

14. Haas (1956) uses the term magic-cosmos, not in its pejorative sense within the current Western rationalist-scientific world view, but rather as a nonrational, noncausal, monistic relationship between planetary and other celestial bodies with past lives on the one hand, and with everyday relationships and events on the other, through correspondences, identities, and emanations that arc metonymically understood. Philosophically, this is based on the idea that human beings constitute a microcosm with a number of inner correspondences and identities with the forces of the macrocosm or cosmos.

15. Through mutual collaboration, astrologer and client establish a contextual framework for celestial readings and influences in everyday problems and relationships, which are then understood metonymically in terms of correspondences and identities between the two-with advice then being given as to how to handle these problems through certain actions and rituals (Perinbanayagam 1981).

16. The philosophical suppositions of ritual efficacy are based on S!nkhyvan philosophy.

17. This seems similar to certain Catholic scientists in the West, although the philosophical premises are different.

18. This analysis of The Vendor of sweets emerged from the astute comments of Bharati Mukeherjee and B.K. Ramanujam at a seminar on "The Indian Self in Its Social and Cultural Contexts," Southern Asian Institute, Columbia University, Much 1980.

19. The four basic categories of yoga are generally acknowledged as devotional (bhakti yoga), work and service to others (karma yoga), inner discrimination and knowledge (jnana yoga), and the various postures, breathing exercises, and meditative practices of raja yoga (Vivekananda 1949) (See Feuerstein, this volume). These yogas, suitable to different temperaments, are seemingly related to Freud's (1931) concept of libidinal types.

20. Veena Das (1977) questions the soundness of this structural opposition, instead seeing the Brahmin as mediator between the caste-bound man and the renouncer.
21. Obviously, some spiritual leaders did who were involved in the Indian struggle with British colonialism, including Gandhi, Tagore, Aurobindo, and Vivekanada.

Works Cited

Bion, W. 1977. *Seven servants.* New York: Jason Aronson.

Brenman-Gibson, M. 1981. *Clifford Odets: American playwright.* New York: Atheneum.

Brown, D. 1986. The stages of meditation in cross-cultural perspective. In *Transformations of consciousness: Conventional and contemplative perspectives on development,* edited by Wilbur, K., J. Engler, and D. Brown. Boston & London: Shambala.

Carrington, P. 1977. *Freedom in meditation.* Garden City, New York: Anchor Press/ Doubleday.

Carstairs, M. 1957. *The twice-born, a study of high-caste Hindus.* London: Hogarth Press.

Coltart, N. 1992. The practice of psychoanalysis and Buddhism. In *Slouching towards Bethlehem.* New York & London: Guilford Press.

Cooper, P. 1995. Affects and affect states: A case study on the integration of Buddhist analytic meditation and psychoanalysis. Unpublished paper.

Daniel, E.V. 1976. A pilgrim's progress: A Peircean point of view. Unpublished paper presented at the National Conference on Women's Studies, SNDT College, Bombay.

Das, V. 1977. *Structure and cognition: Aspects of Hindu caste and ritual.* Delhi: Oxford University Press.

Dhairyam, D. 1961. Research need for development of psychotherapy. In *Recent trends in psychotherapy,* edited by T.K. Menon. Bombay: Orient Longmans.

Dumont, L. 1970. *Homo hierarchicus.* Chicago: University of Chicago Press.

Edel, L. 1966. Hawthorne's symbolism and psychoanalysis. In *Hidden patterns: Studies in psychoanalytic literary criticism,* edited by L. Manheim and E. Manheim. New York: Macmillan.

Egnor, M. 1980. Ambiguity in the oral exegesis of a sacred text, *Tirukkovaiyar.* Unpublished paper.

Ehrenzweig, A. 1967. *The hidden order of art.* Berkeley & Los Angeles: University of California Press.

Eigen, M. 1995. Stones in a stream. In *Psychoanalytic Review* 82:371-90.

Eisenbud, J. 1953. Telepathy and problems of psychoanalysis. In *Psychoanalysis and the occult*, edited by G. Devereux. New York: International Universities Press.

Engler, J. 1986. Therapeutic aims in psychotherapy and meditation. In *Transformations of consciousness: Conventional and contemplative perspectives on development*, edited by Wilbur, K., J. Engler, and D. Brown. Boston & London: Shambala.

Epstein, M. 1995. *Thoughts without a thinker: Psychotherapy from a Buddhist perspective.* New York: Basic Books.

Erikson. 1950. *Childhood and society*. New York: W.W. Norton.

______. 1958. *Young man Luther.* New York: W.W. Norton.

______. 1968. *Identity, youth and crisis.* New York: W.W. Norton.

______. 1969. *Gandhi's truth.* New York: W.W. Norton.

Finn, M. 1992. Transitional space and Tibetan Buddhism: The object relations of meditation. In *Object relations theory and religious experience,* edited by M. Finn and J. Gartner. New York: Praeger.

Freud, S. 1922. Dreams and telepathy. *Standard edition* 18:195-220. London: Hogarth Press, 1953.

______. 1927. Future of an illusion. *Standard edition* 21:5-58. London: Hogarth Press, 1953.

______. 1930. Civilization and its discontents. *Standard edition* 21:64-148. London: Hogarth Press, 1953.

______. 1931. Libidinal types. *Standard edition* 21:215-20. London: Hogarth Press, 1953.

Goleman, D. 1977. *The varieties of meditative experience.* New York: Dutton.

Grey, A. 1973. Oedipus in Hindu dreams. *Contemporary Psychoanalysis* 9:327-55.

Haas, W. 1956. *Destiny of the mind, East and West.* New York: Doubleday.

Halbfass, W. 1982. Book review: *The oceanic feeling* by J.M. Masson. *Journal of Asian Studies* 41:387-88.

Hanchette, S. 1988. *Coloured rice: Symbolic structure in Hindu family festivals.* Delhi: Hindustan Publishing Corporation.

Jung, C.G. (ed.) 1968. *Man and his symbols.* New York: Dell.

Kakar, S. 1978. *The inner world: A psychoanalytic study of childhood and society in India.* Delhi: Oxford University Press.

______. 1991. *The analyst and the mystic.* New Delhi: Viking by Penguin Books India.

Kornfield, J. 1977. *Living Buddhist masters.* Santa Cruz: Unity Press.

Kris, E. 1952. *Psychoanalytic explorations in art.* New York: International Universities Press.

Malinowski, B. 1954. Myth in primitive psychology. In *Magic, science and religion.* New York: Doubleday.

Marriott, M. 1976. Hindu transactions: Diversity without dualism. In *Transaction and meaning, directions in the anthropology of exchange and symbolic behavior*, edited by B. Kapferer. Philadelphia: ISHI Publishing.

Masson, J.M. 1976. The psychology of the ascetic. *Journal of Asian Studies* 35:611-25.

________. 1980. *The oceanic feeling: The origins of religious sentiment in ancient India.* Dordrecht, Holland: D. Reidel.

Mehta, R. 1970. *The Western educated Hindu woman.* Bombay: Asia Publishing House.

Meissner, W. W. 1984. *Psychoanalysis and religious experience.* New York & London: Yale University Press.

Meltzer, D. 1978. Part I, Freud's clinical development. In *The Kleinian development.* Perthshire: Clunie Press.

Menaker, E. 1982. *Otto Rank: A rediscovered legacy.* New York: Columbia University Press.

Miller, B.S. (trans. and ed.) 1977. *Love song of the dark lord, Jayadeva's Gitagovinda.* New York: Columbia University Press.

Milner, M. 1973. Some notes on psychoanalytic ideas on mysticism. In *The suppressed madness of sane men.* 1987. London: Tavistock Publications.

Naipaul, V.S. 1977. *India: A wounded civilization.* New York: Alfred A. Knopf.

Nandy, A. 1980. *Alternative sciences.* New Delhi: Allied Publishers.

Noy, P. 1968. A theory of art and aesthetic experience. *Psychoanalytic Review* 55:623-45.

Obeysekere, G. 1981. *Medusa's hair.* Chicago: University of Chicago Press.

_____. 1984. *The cult of the goddess Pattini.* Chicago: University of Chicago Press.

O'Flaherty, W. 1980. Inside and outside the mouth of God: The boundary between myth and reality. *Daedalus* 109:93-126.

Perinbanayagam, R.S. 1981. Self, other, and astrology: Esoteric therapy in Sri Lanka. *Journal of Psychiatry* 44:69-79.

Pugh, J. 1977. Fate and experience in the Hindu and Moslem cultures of North India: An astrological view, part I. Unpublished paper presented at the Annual Meeting of the American Anthropological Association, Houston, December.

_____. 1978. The astrological advisory session. Unpublished paper presented at the A.C.L.S./S.S.R.C. Workshop on the Person and Interpersonal Relationships in South Asia: An Exploration of Indigenous Conceptual Systems, Chicago, January.

Raheja, G.G. 1976. Transformational processes in Hindu ritual: Concepts of "per son" and "action" in the performance of a *vrat.* Unpublished paper presented at the A.C.L.S./S.S.R.C. Workshop on the Person and Interpersonal Relationships in South Asia: An Exploration of Indigenous Conceptual Systems, Chicago, May.

Rama, S., R. Ballentine, and S. Ajaya. 1976. *Yoga and psychotherapy, the evolution of consciousness.* Glenview, IL: Himalayan Institute.

Ramanujam, B.K. 1980. Odyssey of an Indian villager: Mythic orientations in psychotherapy. Unpublished paper presented at the A.C.L.S./S.S.R.C. Workshop on Hierarchy and Mythology in South Asia, Chicago, September.

Ramanujan, A.K. 1980. Is there an Indian way of thinking? Unpublished paper presented at the A.C.L.S./S.S.R.C. Workshop on Mythology and Hierarchy, Chicago, September.

Rank, O. 1932. *Art and the artist.* New York: Alfred A. Knopf.

Rizzuto, A. 1979. *The birth of the living God: A psychoanalytic study.* Chicago & London: University of Chicago Press.

Roland, A. 1972. Imagery and symbolic expression in dreams and art. *International Journal of Psycho-Analysis* 52:531-39.

_____. 1981. Imagery and the self in artistic creativity and psychoanalytic criticism. *Psychoanalytic Review* 68:409-20.

Rothenberg, A. 1979. *Creativity, the emerging goddess.* Chicago: University of Chicago Press.

Roy, M. 1979. Animus and Indian women. *Harvest* 25:70-79.

Rubin, J. 1996. *Psychotherapy and Buddhism: Toward an Integration.* New York: Plenum Press.

Sakala, C. 1981. The stream of our lives: Self and interpersonal relationship in Chitpavan Brahmin personal narratives. University of Chicago Master's thesis.

Shils, E. 1961. *The intellectual between tradition and modernity: The Indian situation. Comparative Studies in Society and History*, Supplement I. The Hague: Mouton.

Srinivas, M. N. 1978. *The changing position of Indian women.* Delhi: Oxford University Press.

Vivekananda, S. 1949. *Collected papers.* New York: Ramakrishna-Vivekanada Center.

Wadley, S. 1975. *Shakti, power in the conceptual structure of Karimpur religion.* Chicago: Department of Anthropology, University of Chicago.

Washton-Long, R.C. 1980. *Kandinsky: The advent of an abstract style.* London: Oxford University Press.

Wilbur, K., J. Engler, and D. Brown. 1986. *Transformations of consciousness: conventional and contemplative perspectives on development.* Boston & London: Shambala.

Chapter 18 | Walking Two Paces Behind: Women's Education in India

Sita Anantha Raman

> [Tamil] Sisters! Although you have so many qualities and capabilities, you cannot know what is happening in the outside world because you are uneducated. So much has occurred elsewhere that you need to know! Only an education can make clear to women what is imortant in family and in national life. There is no other discipline that can do this. Until then neither husband, brother, nor son will respect you, that is certain. You will be eternally denigrated ... The essence of equality that is at the heart of Hinduism is unmatched, but Western society has made its truth a reality in its institutions. We need to demonstrate the same truth about Hinduism. Only you, our women, have the gifts to stimulate us in this endeavor (Bharati 1935:58-59).

It is a profound irony that while many Indians worship knowledge in its pristine form as the goddess Saraswati, Indian women have long been kept in educational subservience. Education is the acquisition of skills valued by the community, and as it is commensurate with some form of power, which often had religious undertones during most eras of Indian history, it has frequently been the domain of the (predominantly male) elite. Despite nationalist rhetoric about a remote but rosy past when Indian society evenly distributed educational opportunities to both sexes and to all its members, India has been, and still is, deeply stratified on various caste and class lines and by gender biases, which have often intensified under the processes of Sanskritization and Westernization. In some primordial indigenous communities like the Birhor tribe in the Jharkhand region, there is some degree of gender parity in the division of labor and the access to valuable skills like tool-making (Kelkar & Nathan 1991:34-41). Other pre-Aryan vestigeal matrilineal rights in other groups have frequently been superceded in the ancient and modern eras by mainstream Sanskritic and Western patriarchal norms, based on the rationale that such "civilizing" changes promote cultural, colonial, and national uniformity as well as aiding tribal integration into a commercialized economy.

This chapter will begin with a summary of gender relations in India, and then proceed to a descriptive analysis of classical notions of knowledge and sacral space, the systems of informal and formal learning that thrived under royal and elite patronage until the eighteenth century, and of women's access to such avenues of power. Under missionary and then colonial educational domination, fundamental institutional changes took place as literacy and Western secular schools became the normative models. In their eagerness to proselytize to large numbers of Indians, missionaries espoused the rights of women and the lower castes to education, thus challenging both traditional Indian attitudes to sacral knowledge and social power, and elite male assumptions of caste and gender superiority. However, European educationists also brought their own notions of patriarchy, sexual prudery, and cultural superiority that denigrated indigenous institutions and overlooked the informal learning patterns available to women for some centuries. As nineteenth-century elite Indian reformers were often the products of missionary schools and in awe of colonial officialdom, they were indoctrinated by their documentary distortions on the state of Indian education. However, as they also profoundly distrusted missionary motives for educating girls and feared the dilution of domestic cultural transmission, they sought to teach them at home and in schools through a curriculum based on Indian literature and selected secular subjects. Such schools, which often reified patriarchal norms even as they evoked national pride, catered to a new breed of elite women who struggled to overcome male intellectual domination, while accepting the inevitability of walking two social steps behind the male.

The gap between female and male educational opportunities was evident to reformers like Gopal Krishna Gokhale and Subramania Bharati, but there was a difference of opinion about women's abilities and their right to equal education. Gokhale addressed the issue of poor standards in government schools at an 1897 Educational

Congress in England, but he also succumbed to Victorian rhetoric about Indian women's "refined sensibilities" and religious bent of mind, their basic inferiority and need for uplift by males (Raman 1996:196-97). In his 1910 Elementary Education Bill to the Imperial Legislative Council, Gokhale asked for mandatory free education, comparing the two percent literacy rate in British India unfavorably with that in the independent princely states. He also cautiously added that at first "compulsion should be only for boys and not for girls" (Natesan1920:599). Although Gokhale intended to request an extension of that right to girls after it had been guaranteed to boys, one wonders that he did not do this simultaneously. He clearly had access to that year's statistics, which stated that for every 100 boys, a mere 15 girls were currently enrolled in school. This discriminatory attitude by one of India's respected reformers reflects a deep seated malaise that still haunts women fifty years after Independence.

However, other more pressing feminist pleas fell upon receptive ears after World War I as India awoke from sleepy acquiescence of colonial rule to national awareness and social tumult. Subramania Bharati, the fiery patriot-feminist, used his literary genius to exhort men to educate girls, and women to boldly demand education as a right (Raman 1996:151-57). Female education formed an integral plank of the nationalist agenda for social change, and reformers also felt they had to validate themselves as a civilized nation. A growing number now perceived the logical connection between the theoretical ideal of freedom and its practical extension to women and the underclass through vigorous educational programs. Between 1911 and 1921, literacy rates rose noticeably from 1.1 percent to 1.8 percent (female) and 11.3 percent to 13 percent (male), plodding majestically in a stately, but painstaking, ascent to 6 percent (female) and 22.6 percent (male) on the eve of independence. Since then, each decade has revealed an escalation in literacy so that by 1961 the female and male rates were 15.34 percent and 27.16 percent respectively (Kanwar & Jagannathan 1995). The 1991 census results show that the rate stands at 39.19 percent (female) and 64.20 percent (male). However, women trail considerably nationwide eighty years after Bharati made his moving appeal. There is, therefore, no room for complacency in the coming century until Indians discard the notion that gender and other biases as inevitable or acceptable, and until they demand equitable schooling for all. Moreover, keeping girls in school must be a primary objective not solely because educated women make better wives and mothers, but because they are a crucial resource for a nation to waste haphazardly. India's survival may depend upon the respect it gives to female talent and its social commitment.

Knowledge, Spiritual Space and Cultural Transmission

While India's veneration of goddesses and of the sexual forces operative in the world appear in early Indus Valley sites, there is hardly any historical information about gender relations in this civilization. Females were represented as matronly goddesses or nurturing figures, in the form of a *yoni*, in seals possibly as priestesses with long braids performing ritual sacrifice around a tree, and as the ubiquitous copper dancing girl. If we make a giant assumption that the figures on the seals were indeed female and not male priests with braids, we can venture to speak of some esoteric or mystical knowledge possessed by women and thus empowering them. The proximity to trees argues in favor of female figures since women have been closely associated with arboreal worship in early Indian statuary, but the evidence is still too obscure to make a firm conclusion about gender relations in India around 3000 B.C.E.

With the arrival of Aryan tribes around 1500 B.C.E., we note textual references to the social position of women. While early Vedic hymns indicate that females had some rights in a patriarchal society, the Rig Vedic pantheon was predominantly male, and the few goddesses like Ushas or Aditi, although lauded in exquisite poetry, appear in their sexual guise as mothers, wives, and seductive beings. Thus, the poems were largely the creative enterprise of male bards, and there appear to have been no females to perform the ritual sacrifices that Aryans considered to be integral to the maintenance of cosmic order (ṛta). For a society which placed so high a value upon progeny, women were clearly seen primarily as reproductive agents. References indicate that females had the right to wear the upper caste sacred thread, and that they performed various mundane jobs. However, there is no evidence that women were allowed routinely to chant the mystical Sanskrit sacrificial hymns or mantras, or that there was even gender or caste distribution of this knowledge. If there were any women who did routinely chant mantras after 1000 B.C.E., they were textually dissuaded from doing so by referring to their birth as unwelcome (Atharva Veda 6:2.3) and the cause of misery (Aitaraya Brāhmaṇa 8:31.1). However, the illuminating dialogues in the Brihadāraṇyaka Upaniṣad (3:6, 3:8, 4:5.5) between Gargi and Maitreyi and the sage Yajñavalkya reveal that women occasionally challenged patriarchal norms, probably wore the sacred thread, and debated on the nature of Brahman with male intellects on an equal plane.

Through subsequent centuries, this tradition was nurtured domestically by intelligent mothers even as patriarchy appeared to triumph socially. This is revealed in the Sanskrit and Tamil epics which depict women as both subject and object. Examples of various female characters are the redoutable Kunti whose virtue was rewarded with the knowledge of secret but secondary mantras which bestowed motherhood upon her; the gentle Sita whose life was shadowed by male love and male lust, but who was finally emboldened to shed husband for chaste motherhood; the loyal Kannagi who lost her husband to a learned courtesan, but whose virtue empowered her to destroy an unrighteous city. The message was that women could overcome barriers to a fair access to knowledge as power by the superior spiritual power of chastity.

Traditionally, knowledge and its transmission both in the oral and written form was considered sacred by Indians who equated it with mystical enlightenment. The body of sacred books in Sanskrit included Vedic revelations (śruti), which were prohibited to women and śudras by 1000 B.C.E., and numerous secondary texts or smṛti. The earliest examples of smṛti were the Sanskrit epics, the Rāmāyaṇa and the Mahābhārata, into which the sacred Bhagavad Gītā was included after 200 B.C.E. After this date, women had access to a growing corpus of smṛti literature, expositions like the Dharma Sūtra, books on secular knowledge like the Mānavadharma Śastra (Manu's Law Books), and numerous works on lore collectively known as the Puranas, notable examples of which are the Viṣṇu Purāna, Shiva Purāna, Bhāgavatam, and Dēvi Māhātmyam composed in the classical era.

Of the smṛtis, the Bhagavad Gītā is especially noteworthy for its impact on Hindu society as it gave scriptural validation to devotional prayer (bhakti pūjā) as a legitimate path to salvation. In a few short but specific verses it opened the floodgates of religious knowledge to women and the lower castes, and enabled them to challenge the power of male priests through domestic ritual (Bhagavad Gītā 9:26-29, 32). During times of social stress from the Huna invasions of the fourth and fifth centuries to the eighteenth century European intrusions and conquests, whenever religious and academic centers were either destroyed or decayed, women transmitted their knowledge of the smṛtis in the safety of their homes. This important fact was underestimated by colonial observers who overlooked this arena of intellectual activity since it lay outside the geographical space of public schools. Since after the late classical era few girls probably sat in open attendance in verandahs where such schools operated, their apparent absence from academic participation led European observers in the eighteenth and nineteenth centuries to conclude that Indian women were universally uneducated. This stigma persisted due to colonial documentary misinformation, a subject which will be discussed later.

If Hindu women had access to a spiritual space and some texts, which they either read or learnt by rote, so too did the earliest Buddhist and Jain women. Dissent was common in Indian tradition from the sixth century with major examples of such radical departure from mainstream social and intellectual conservatism being the "heterodox" philosophies of the Jains, Buddhists, and the Ājīvikas. Such departures were also primarily male expressions of discontent and that patriarchal exclusiveness dominated within the inner circle of arhants, monks, and other enlightened beings. However, after having discarded caste hierarchies and widened the spectrum of debate, elite male Buddhists and Jains were compelled to accept the new challenge from women by granting them a spiritual, intellectual, and social space within their sects. The Buddha is recorded as having hesitated to accept female monastics as they would disrupt Sangha discipline, but the first aspirant nuns led by his foster mother stood their ground and won the concession from him. Their writings are compiled in the *Therigatha*, (Teachings of the Elder Women), while the third and fourth century Mahayana Buddhist text, *Srimala Sutra*, expounds the philsophy of a female saint (Tharu & Lalitha 1989; Wayman & Wayman 1974). Other texts like the Jātakas performed a similar function to the Hindu Purānas, and were in all likelihood sustained as much by Buddhist women as by monks since Indic society operated with cross-sectarian similarity in some fundamental aspects of family life (see Chapple in this volume).

Apart from these Sanskrit works, there is the corpus of Tamil literature from the early Christian era between the first and third centuries when poetic assemblies or Sangams were held in Madurai. Some poets were women, like the legendary Auvaiyar, whose terse aphorisms are taught to children. The epic Silappadikaram describes the poetic and musical skill of a courtesan, Madhavi, while its sequel, Manimekhalai, narrates the travails of her daughter who is a nun (see Partha sarathy, this volume). If in the Dravidian region female scholarship was fairly acceptable, other groups in the region had a few matriarchal rights. As early as the second century C.E., there is evidence of royal matriliny in south India since Ptolemy made reference to a Pandyan queen. Female rulers from the Chalukya and Chola dynasties appear on the pages of South Indian history from the early medieval centuries. Matrilineal succession amongst the rulers of Kerala and amongst the Nayar community in that state has resulted in considerable female autonomy, and in the dynamic regencies of gifted queens like Lakshmibai and Parvatibai in the beginning of the nineteenth century. That women's rights are more readily recognized is proven by the 1991 Census records which show that some southern states like modern Kerala and Tamil Nadu have female literacy rates higher than the national average, the former being the highest at 86.1 percent, while the latter stands at 51.33 percent ranking seventh (Government of India 1991:57).

Indigenous Schools, Royal Philanthropy and Women Students

There are some early seventeenth century Jesuit references to indigenous schooling systems which flourished in India prior to the Protestants who began to proselytize through missions around 1700. It is now well established that medieval Hindu and Muslim kings routinely promoted religious education either in pyal schools, thus named since they were located on verandahs adjacent to temples or private homes, or in Muslim maktabs, which were schools situated near mosques. The primary impetus for giving alms in Indian tradition was the notion that karmic merit would accrue to those who promoted the learning of sacred and semi-sacred literature amongst brāhmins, monks, and saintly nuns. As Muslims consider knowledge of the Qur'an to be integral to understanding Islamic precepts, boys were taught the suras or verses in public classes, while girls were expected to be instructed at home. Thus, religious endowments by rulers constituted an important element of their political commitment.

A study of medieval educational philanthropy in south India gives an indication of the extent of female attendance in local schools before Christian missionaries started Bible classes. From the eleventh to the eighteenth centuries Chola, Vijayanagar, and Nayaka rulers routinely established temple schools, made grants of cash, land, or buildings, subsidized teachers (pandits), or paid fees for students, who were largely boys from the elite castes. Private philanthropy was rarer, and it usually consisted of paying a student's fees, feeding on ritual occasions, or occasionally gifting a building. The Vijayanagar emperors, especially, set the precedent for subsequent Hindu kings by establishing large scale charitable institutions called *chattrams*, one of the main features of which was education. After the empire's debacle at Talikota in 1565, the emergent smaller kingdoms of Madurai, Thanjavur, Vellore, and Jinji pursued this model of royal philanthropy. Between the sixteenth and eighteenth centuries the former overlords, the Nayaka rajas, funded a number of schools through gifts of cash, land, coconuts, rice, and other produce. The earliest European reference to such patronage was by the Jesuit Roberto de Nobili who described the Madurai Nayaka rulers as supporting ten thousand brahmins, who were instructed in Sanskrit theology rituals and philosopy. Between 1749 and 1837 Thanjavur rajas also established several substantial endowments at various sites, which were located on the pilgrimage road to Rameswaram. The ten largest chattrams were named after their favorite queens, and in 1799 when Raja Serfoji signed over power to the East India Company, he described his charities as "descended from the elder to the younger queen," in what seems to have been a form of female inheritance. The chattrams included hospitals, rest houses, hospitals, and asylums for the destitute regardless of caste. They also held free Tamil primary schools with some boarding facilities, which were open to all, and conducted Sanskrit classes, which were not open to the untouchables. Eventually between 1871 and 1873, many *pyal* schools were absorbed into the colonial municipal school system run by local boards. One *chattram* site in Nidamangalam became the locus of a government girls school. It is tantalizing to speculate whether the earlier pyal school at Nidamangalam, which is mentioned in eighteenth century *chattram* records, had also been originally intended to be largely for girls in eighteenth-century Thanjavur (see Raman 1994:11-13).

Apart from karmic merit, philanthropists also sought earthly benefits for circulating wealth in the community, and educational gifting formed an important aspect of social redistribution. There are several references to cross-sectarian benefactions by royalty to worthy merchant communities. For example, Nayaka kings near the river Tambraparani and the rajas of Pudukkottai made grateful contributions to prominent Muslim merchants and artisans. These gifts consisted of revenue lands (inams) to shrines and mosques where Qur'anic classes are traditionally held (Bayly 1989:88-91).

Cross sectarian support to education by both Hindu and Muslim kings continued till the 20th century. Thanjavur's Raja Tulsaji (1763-1787) and his successor, Serfoji (1798-1824) apparently had a whole-hearted admiration for the work of Reverand C.F. Swartz of the Society for the Propagation of the Gospel (SPCK). They thus donated large sums to start a Christian school in the city fort, the village of Kannanthangudi, for "the education and support of fifty poor Christian children," and gave the SPCK the right to start other village schools for Hindu children to be taught by missionaries (Hickey 1872:101-2). When Swartz died in 1798, he bequeathed a fortune of Rs.85,000, largely the gifts of Indian royalty, to the SPCK. In a similar fashion, in 1786 the Nawab of Arcot also donated the large sum of Rs.80,000 and some buildings to Lady Campbell's Female Orphan Asylum which sheltered the offspring of soldiers who died in the Anglo-French conflicts. Although the children were from various backgrounds and sects, they were taught by SPCK teachers and eventually converted to Christianity.

In 1822, Governor Thomas Munro of the Madras Presidency ordered his districtc ollectors to gather evidence of the state of education in South India. These men then began the first detailed surveys of pyal schools and colleges, the castes of students and teachers, the curriculum, the funding, and the expenditures. They appear to have been impressed by the number and scale of local schools where subjects like astronomy, astrology, mathematics, law texts (*Sastrapottam of Hindoo law*), and Sanskrit, Tamil, Telegu, Hindi, and Persian texts were taught in several Indian scripts (Raman 1996). They present a few misconceptions based on their insufficient knowledge of indigenous social nuances, and their conclusions on the extent of female education were erroneous since they did not investigate the possibility of girls being taught in the inner rooms adjacent to the verandahs where boys were taught. However, it is important to note that they tried to present a fair description of what they observed, and quickly noted that while they as rulers had thus far done little to encourage education, the former princely Indian kingdoms, had promoted learning generously through considerable land grants so that South India had an extensive system of indigenous schools and colleges. Teaching involved reading and oral recitation of Hindu texts, some writing, computation especially useful for vaiṣhya and śūdra boys of the merchant and artisanal communities, and sometimes some astronomy and astrology to boys. Besides instruction in the Vedas to a select few, many schools taught a wide range of Sanskrit smṛtis, sūtras, and śāstras on customary law, as well as Persian, and regional language texts of social importance. Thus in Tamil regions, the Jain saint Tiruvalluvar's book of aphorisms, Tirukkural (third century), formed an important subject of study, while the rich array of bhakti literature in Tamil, Telegu, and Kannada was integral to the curriculum in schools in other linguistic regions of the Madras Presidency.

While most *pyal* schools largely catered to village boys, they were theoretically coeducational with the girls probably sitting separately. Male students came from the four castes, but there were also some shudra girls from the weaving (keykeler) and dancing castes. South Indian girls from the class of temple dancers known as devadasis, who maintained the classical traditions of Karnatak music and Bharata Natyam dance, attended these schools in order to learn the epics, Puraṇas, and Tamil poetry integral for their performances in temples or in royal courts. Governor Munro's collectors noted that devadasis were in open attendance at these schools. That they were technically śūdras is an interesting commentary on the availability of education to girls and some members of the lower castes at this time (Raman 1996:xii). In Sanskritic schools catering to the elite castes in south India, there is also evidence that upper caste girls were sometimes taught all but the Vedas in inner rooms adjacent to the verandahs where boys were instructed. Thus, one woman would proudly recall that her maternal ancestor was as well versed in Hindu law from the *Manusmriti* as were the boys (Raman 1996:104).

There are historical references to pre-modern and early modern era queens and princesses in the Tamil, Telegu, and Kerala regions who either wrote music, composed poetry and plays, or played instruments. For example, Kundavai, sister and co-ruler with Raja Raja Chola (tenth century), is reputed to have been musically gifted. In the seventeenth century, the court of Raghunatha Nayaka of Thanjavur accorded high praise to the poet and princess Ramachandramba for her erudition and compostions (Raman 1994:8). One eighteenth century princess of Travancore is recorded as being as gifted a musical composer as her brother and king, Swati Tirunal (Menon nd). Obviously, such women were carefully instructed at home in the arts and in some aspects of statecraft.

Other upper caste girls were taught to read semi-sacred texts, chant verses, and write accounts and simple letters in the privacy of their homes. One caste woman described her first day of instruction as a visit to the temple where she was taught her first mantra. However, this informal education also hinged upon the family tradtion of female education, the girl's own inclination, and the family sense of honor which urgently sought her marriage just before or after puberty. Thus, in many instances, by the nineteenth century women were habitually cloistered in the kitchen regions of their husband's homes and often admonished if they read too long, sang too loudly or in mixed company, or neglected their housework. Moreover, although middle class girls were economically dependent upon benign male family members, they were discouraged from learning skills other than cookery or midwifery that would entice them from home. Similarly, middle class Muslim girls would receive a rudimentary education in the zenana, in needlework, and in Qur'anic verses taught by an aged *ustad* or a female *ustad bi.* They were, however, often dissuaded from writing since it would encourage them to pen love letters to men forbidden into the domestic circle. Moreover these girls were not taught other skills that would enable them to leave home for work. Thus, although there are tantalizing references to upper class female ability and to their recognition by men, the majority of girls and boys, particularly from the artisanal and laboring castes, were left fairly unlettered. In a society divided on the lines of hereditary occupations, education was deemed unnecessary for the majority. Literate caste males held the key to this avenue of power, education for most middle class girls was haphazard and brief, and for poorer girls it has remained non-existent.

Missionary Education

With the arrival of the Portuguese into Goa in 1498, indigenous systems of education were destined to be revamped. The Jesuits, in particular, were the earliest Catholic order to be involved in education since this had been their initial thrust from the time of their formation under Ignatius Loyola. Besides Portuguese conversion of the people of the Konkan and Malabar and their marriage with local women, by the sixteenth century they had attracted the intense religious curiosity of the Mughal emperor Akbar. He invited several Jesuits to court to debate with scholars from other sects, and being pleased with them, granted them land and funds in Agra to start a school for children from some thirty Indian families (Mukherji 1951:15-16). Catholic missionary activity progressed apace especially in Goa, the region around Bombay, and in South India. Except for their colleges, primary classes must have included girls as this would have been essential to their primary goal of proselytizing.

Early missionary endeavor often followed the traditional pattern of coeducational schools, especially since students attended only for a short time during the primary years, and since they were short of staff. Mission schools in this era also did not separate the sexes during instruction except when the subjects were practical in nature. The Protestants, however, were the first to seriously promote female education by beginning specific classes for them, the earliest being the Danes who started SPCK schools in Serampore in Bengal and in Tranquebar where they were generously helped by the Thanjavur rajas in 1647. Between 1707 and 1712 the reverend Zeiganbalg started a few schools open to all castes, with one expressly for girls. In 1715, the English East India Company started the St. Mary's Charity School with board and lodging for thirty Anglo-Indian orphan boys and girls in Fort St. George. This school, however, clearly had gender specific education, with the boys being instructed to "read, write, cast accounts, or what they may be further capable of," while the girls were to be "instructed in reading and the necessary parts of housewifery" (Law 1915: 14-25). The East India Company soon began to encourage other Protestant ministers to start schools in south, east, and west India, so that by the end of the eighteenth century there was a network of Christian schools, many coeducational, teaching often in the regional languages.

In 1813, the British Parliament granted the East India Company Rs.100,000 to promote education in India, and by 1833 had opened the door to an avalanche of Protestant missionaries accompanied by their wives. Many female missionaries accompanied their mates to climatically inhospitable places and began the first classes for girls in sheds and huts. Thus, we hear of groups like the Baptists in Serampore, the London Missionary Society, the Christian Missionary Society, the Scottish Protestant Mission, and the American Madura Mission actively engaged in teaching girls in various parts of the country. While their curriculum emphasized Biblical knowledge, as was the case with most schools in early modern Europe, the work of the Protestants in spreading literacy through the regional languages is particularly noteworthy. Since they deemed it integral for salvation to teach the convert the written word of the Gospel, they learnt the vernaculars into which they translated and printed the Bible. Their use of the printing press spread literacy and they proudly distinguished their methods from those of Hindus and Muslims, whom they scorned for pursuing rote learning. The earliest English ministers like, Dr. Bell and his successor, Dr. Cordiner, borrowed from pyal schools the tactile method of tracing the alphabet upon sand and the use of student monitors since they were low cost and highly effective in inculcating primary literacy. These came to be known, in fact, as the Bell System and the Madras System, and they were introduced into primary schools even in England (Law 1915:49-56). However, few of the later missionaries actually visited indigenous schools, and their exaggerations were an integral facet of their conviction of intellectual superiority. This they assiduously cultivated in their manner to their students, campaigning unceasingly against the "evils" and "follies" of Hinduism, whether religious, intellectual, or social. They sought to tap into the discontent amongst the lower castes and women whom they knew were underprivileged, partly out of genuine compassion for their inferior status, but also because initially higher caste males saw mission schools as a religious and social threat. Moreover, the missionaries knew that if they could covert the females in a household they would bring in more family members to the church's teachings. Orphans from the lower castes and higher caste widows became eager Bible women, drawn by the possibility of being literate in a society which had largely reserved this for higher caste men. Some female converts would change their names to English ones, and write abject letters of admiration to European teachers or sponsors in Leeds or Manchester, thus betraying their sense of cultural anomie and loss. Some like Pandita Ramabai fought for women to be free from male subordination on the domestic and intellectual fronts, but as her moorings remained firmly Indian she inspired others to do the same.

After 1830, when the promotion of English opened the door to job opportunities, the quality of missionary teaching and the inclusion of more secular subjects into the curriculum drew upper caste males to Christian schools. However, it was only later in the century that evangelicals toned down their overtly aggressive indoctrination and started schools expressly for upper caste girls. Their sense of triumph was great at this juncture, but many had come a long way from the earnest seekers of souls in the early nineteenth century, having now a deeper sense of educational commitment almost above their goal of conversion. Moreover, as their experience in the field of education grew, they began teacher-training colleges such as the Sarah Tucker Institute for Teachers in the Tamil region; their graduates became the staff of schools without missionary agenda, and their reputation as educators of women grew. By 1885, with the growth of nationalism, elite males began to establish their own model secular schools with an indigenous cultural emphasis, but they frequently had teachers who emulated the European teaching methods.

As far as women were concerned, the missionary success was noticeable in the general improvement in education amongst converts. In the Madras Presidency, for instance, their extensive work in teaching and converting tribals, lower castes, and women resulted in a higher rate of literacy, putting some of the higher castes to shame. In the first detailed census taken in 1871 under British rule, while Christians formed less than 1 percent of the population, 32 percent of the girls in school were Christians. The first female college graduate in the Madras Presidency was Kamala Sattianadhan, a high caste Christian, and such women continued to educate others. The Christian contribution in promoting female literacy cannot be gainsaid. Even today the highest female and male literacy rates are to be found in Kerala, Mizoram, and Goa which have the highest concentration of Christians.

Women's Education Under Colonial Rule

The 1813 Parliamentary grant to the East India Company to further education had induced missionaries to sail to India, and this was followed by a spurt of Indian royal philanthropy to Protestant efforts in practical and academic education. In Travancore the regent *ranis*, Lakshmibai (1810-1815) and Parvatibai (1815-1829), donated substantial amounts to the Christian Missionary Society through the mediation of the Resident, Colonel Munro. The main mission in Nagercoil was at that time led by Charles and Mrs. Mault, who taught widowed and lower caste women the skill of lace making while instructing them in the Bible. This attracted the notice of Lakshmibai, who gave fertile paddy and coconut fields in 1814, while in the coming years Parvatibai first donated the sum of Rs. 5000, a school building, lands and their produce, and a further sum of Rs. 20,000 directly to the Maults to promote their work with girls and the low caste. Their other donations included cash and land to start a girls' boarding school and a college for men, in a manner similar to that of the Rajas of Cochin and Thanjavur (Cheriyan 1935: 180-190; Yesudas 1980:45-46, 53-54).

Thus far, the East India Company's policy was ambiguous since it did little in an official capacity to further education directly but did so through individuals who encouraged missionaries. In England at this time, there was a growing belief in the philosophy of Utilitarianism, which advocated both individualism and efficient government through bureaucracies to dispense social welfare. The ideas became extremely popular in bourgeois and aristocratic circles of power, as the new liberals were convinced of their moral obligation to improve the condition of the subject peoples of India. One such person was the Madras Governor Thomas Munro, who envisaged a grand program to educate India for her eventual self-rule, but his demise put an end to his plans. In Calcutta, in 1820, a private philanthropist named David Hare started and maintained a school for girls out of personal funds. This was later emulated by J.E.D. Bethune in 1849 with the help of similarly enlightened Bengalis like Ram Gopal Ghosh and Babu Jaikissen Mookherjee (Das 1959). In Ahmedabad, a Rao Bahadur Maghabhai Kharamchand began two girls schools, while in Madras a T.Gopalakistnah Pillay did the same. Such consciousness was probably stimulated by the fact that women's education had broadened considerably in industrializing Britain.

In India, between 1828 and 1832 Governor General Bentinck and his law minister, T.B. Macaulay, spearheaded the new liberal policy by proclaiming Britain's responsibility to rule benevolently through Western secular law, which basically stemmed from Christian ethics, to spread Western ideas through English education, and to alleviate social constraints on women by legal enactment against sati. Their colleague in England was Charles Wood whose 1854 Dispatch is a major landmark in Indian educational history. With this document, the government committed itself to furthering education in India through grants to private schools and the formation of educational departments in each presidency, but it was to be contingent upon the active cooperation of the Indian elite since self help and government charity were the key features of the new regime. Although its reference to women was a brief statement about "not underrating" female education and praise for private Indian interest in starting schools, the government's program to give grants to boys schools was eventually legally extended to girls institutions. Immediately after this, records show that a T. Gopalakistnah Pillay, applied for such a grant for his school for girls, which he had begun two years earlier with some upper caste Madras colleagues on the Western model. It was known as the Royapettah Hindu Female School. While the governor's approval of the school is recorded in its official logs, there appears to be no more information on the fate of this local endeavor (Raman 1996:13-14). Missionaries also jumped on the grant bandwagon, and they applied for aid for their coeducational schools. Although such grants were small, financial aid often kept these primary schools alive and infused much enthusiasm for government's declaration of interest.

The next decades proceeded much more favorably for boys than it did for girls until about 1860 when a renewed vigor in British involvement was visible after the visit of Mary Carpenter, a noted secular educationist. The friend of Ram Mohan Roy and several elite Indian males who favored women's education in Bombay, Madras, and Calcutta, Carpenter was to spearhead the formation of purely government girls schools. Convinced that Indian girls needed more stimulation and that many were kept at home due to fear of conversion in Christian institutions, she favored instruction in an non-sectarian environment in which Western curricular models and methods were used. She believed that Indians would educate their daughters if there were women teachers, she conceived the design of starting of teachers training school in the presidencies. She then approached the Calcutta government to grant an annual sum to create the post of a female inspector of girls schools, begin primary girls schools in the three main provinces, hire the first batch of non-missionary teachers, and start a training school, which she hoped would eventually provide Indian girls with a legitimate and respectable occupation. Her project was based on the example of the maharaja of Vijayanagaram, who had begun a school for elite girls in Madras city. It was approved; the schools began in earnest with the financial support of leading men in the region. In 1877, she made a notable statement in Parliament on the improvement in women's education from the plan. The Madras government did not always appreciate her persistence, and actively connived to prevent her from serving as the inspector of schools, but she must have been immune to misogyny for she disregarded it. Although she was over-optimistic about the training of widow teachers and the grand improvement in women's lives that would result from these schools, she must be given credit for beginning a venture that would eventually expand women's education in India. Many feminist leaders of the Madras Presidency were graduates of the teachers training school which was her brainchild (Carpenter 1868:142-65).

Over the coming years, secular girls schools struggled to attract students since the idea of formal female education was disregarded by a society that severely inhibited the participation of middle and upper class women in non-domestic affairs. Early marriage precluded the education of Hindu girls for more than a few years, and Muslim girls were subject to the restrictions of *pardah* so that few of them would be sent away from home unless they could afford the luxury of a covered carriage. Enrolment statistics until the twentieth century reveal that schools were an indulgence for those brave enough to expose their daughters to the gaze of outsiders and resist social ostracism by delaying their daughters' marriages for an education. Many, however, began to perceive the value of literacy on principle, and to employ western teachers with newer methods to give their girls secular instruction within the home. By 1880 there was a growing consciousness among elite male Indians that contemporary norms on marriage and widowhood needed to be revamped since they stemmed either from a misreading of Hindu texts, or from sources whose current relevance was debatable. The valiant spread the word of reform through associations and journals, and attempted to guarantee girls a longer childhood, a protracted period of study, a carefree youth unburdened by frequent childbirth and domestic drudgery, and to innocent young widows, a naturally full sexual life.

Social reform was primarily intended for elite women by elite men who wished to validate themselves in the eyes of the colonial masters. Despite this possible motive, their work cannot be ignored. Many took their cause seriously, understood that women's education was really at the heart of all social change. Morever, although one cannot ignore Indian male paternalism and their inculcation of lofty female ideals predicated upon domestic responsibility and sacrifice for the primary advancement of males, social reformers opened the door to women's education and released both men and women from the thralldom of sexually unjust customs.

Meanwhile, late nineteenth-century official documents downplayed the importance of this indigenous movement to overturn deeply ingrained customs, and failed at times to commend Indians for the growing numbers of small local efforts, chastising them in imperial rhetoric for not doing enough in practical terms. Change, they said, had to come from inside Indian society, and could not be imposed from above solely through government actions. While this argument is not entirely invalid, colonial policy itself practiced a form of gender discrimination since expended far less on girls education than it did on that of boys. In the Madras Presidency, fifty years after Wood's Despatch between the years 1893 and 1896, government secondary-school expenditure on girls was about one third of the amount spent on boys; in the field of primary education government spent less than half on girls that it did on boys, with the major part of the funds coming from the higher provincial treasury rather than from municipal and local bodies (Raman 1996:93-94). Thus, if conservative Indian patriarchy was largely loath to educate its girls, Western patriarchy in the late industrial era domesticated its women by attributing to them greater sensitivity but lower intelligence. This had been brought home earlier by the 1881 Education Commission headed by the liberal educationist, W.W. Hunter, who was ably guided by a greater number of elite Indian officials than in former surveys. The report was realistic and provided a genuine challenge to both colonial and Indian patriarchs since it concluded that women's education was in a woeful condition. It laid the blame on poor funding and willful misrepresentation by provincial governments which were primarily responsible for promoting girls education, on inadequate textbooks, socially irrelevant curricula, and inadequate spatial arrangements. Moreover, the Hunter Commission's sympathetic approach to Indians was a skillful piece of diplomacy since it indicated that they too needed to promote actively women's education and not merely accuse the western government of neglecting its duty. This commission also gave indigenous schools recognition for having inculcated literacy in the primary classes by using texts that were culturally meaningful to the population, and advised government to give grants to these private ventures if they abided by official standards. The voice in favor of female and lower class democratic education had been voiced openly by liberal officials.

With rising national consciousness in the new century, many more Indians took up the social challenge through reform associations which promoted female literacy. The ḍrya Samaj in Punjab and Gujarat, the Brahmo Samaj and the Ramakrishna Mission in Bengal, the Prarthana Samaj in western India, Viresalingam Pantulu and the Brahmo Samaj in the Telegu and northern Tamil regions, and the Theosophical Society all now emphasized the need for a changed educational system for both girls and boys. This national system was to be based on Western models of instruction and a curriculum which included Indian and English texts and secular subjects like history and hygiene. Annie Besant's work is most notable since she was a moving force in starting girls schools on such a model first in Benares and later in the south. She and others like her resurrected the ideals of Sita, Savitri, Gargi, and Maitreyi as models for modern Indian women who were urged to become more self-sacrificing and brilliant than the ancients. Indian women were told that they were not inferior, but that they had "a deep spiritual culture," and that they required a "sound practical training" as well as knowledge of their ancient female traditions. Besant argued passionately using elevated, sometimes inaccurate, symbolism about the great educational ideals of ancient India, which had been destroyed by the baser commercialized ideals of the West, and urged women to consider it their duty to save the nation from decay (Besant 1899). In her plan to create a national scheme of education for Indian women she urged them to aspire to the highest intellectual rewards, pursue a practical domestic curriculum, and also become the spiritual light of the home. She also urged them never to compete with men as this was artificial and had misled Western women. Besant (1904:1-11) issued a stern warning to those men who "thwarted them in their upward climbing, or to place unnecessary obstacles in their path." Besant and her supporters like P.S. Sivaswamy Ayyar were instrumental in beginning a number of National Schools for girls and boys under the auspices of the Theosophical Educational Trust, and were also influential in shaping the educational philosophies of twentieth-century reformers who started smaller schools based upon the Besant curriculum for girls. However, enrolment still remained abysmal since lower caste women found such education to be largely irrelevant until educated women themselves organized to promote the education of their sisters. In 1917, the Women's Indian Association was established, and under the leadership of Irish women like Margaret Cousins and Dorothy Jinarajadasa, and Indian women like Dr. Muthulakshmi Reddi, Sarojini Naidu, Saralabai Naik, and Begam Hasrat Mohani, started schools to raise female literacy, to teach hygiene and childcare, and promote practical skills amongst women. It also began to the fight to get the female franchise, and eventually argue their case in legislative bodies. It is noteworthy that the first Indian woman legislator was Muthulakshmi Reddi. By 1921 middle class Indian society finally recognized the importance of women's education and the possibility of women in the skilled workforce, especially as teachers, doctors, and nurses. The demand for girls schools rose in these post-war years, but while government began a noticeable number of institutions for girls between 1921 and 1927, there was still a considerable gender discrepancy in expenditure, hiring, pay, and facilities.

Conclusion

Women's education in India has moved at a snail's pace for most of the last one hundred years due both to Indian and Western patriarchal assumptions about women's ability and responsibilities. In a society with a deep core of domestic expectations about women's roles, women have attempted to explore their other talents as a valid right. It is a matter of considerable importance to note that women have struggled long and hard to overcome such suppression, and that male reformers attempted to move in that direction and further women's educational opportunities by starting schools, personally teaching their girls, and in advocating this cause in associations and journals, and on the legislative floor in the late nineteenth and early twentieth centuries. With the burgeoning struggle for independence and the shift from social to political issues , programs for women were subsumed under those for the general populace. While the importance of general social amelioration cannot be easily dismissed from a solely feminist perspective, societal improvement is often predicated based on the value that is placed upon women's intellectual, emotional, and sexual wellbeing.

After independence, Indian government schemes both on the state and provincial levels have increased, and attempts have been made to draw girls to school through mid-day meal schemes, and free books and uniforms. Due to the welfare thrust of this program in the first two decades (Agarwal 1995:14-16) primary enrolment jumped substantially for both girls and boys from sixty-four girls every hundred boys in 1951, to three hundred and eighty-nine girls to seven hundred and twenty boys in 1981(Chaudhary 1995:57-64). The National Literacy Mission in the 1980s and 1990s brought about a significant surge in general literacy through the use of female tutors in the rural cells, thus indicating that one educated woman could result in the education of a whole village.

However, the fact remains that statistics point to continued gender discrepancies in overall literacy and in enrolment at primary, secondary, and higher educational levels. Some of these stem from demands placed on girls to remain at home as caretakers of smaller children, the use of female children as domestic labor, and early marriage which continues to have a girl married before she completes her schooling. Such traditions haunt Indian women, while newer demands crush their rights in additional ways. Thus, while women's lives have certainly shed some of the educational and occupational constraints imposed upon them earlier and many men accept women professionals as both inevitable and creditable, in some rural and urban sections, new forms of gender oppression have surfaced based upon a pseudo-religious and commercial disregard for female dignity. In other circles, the search for individual fulfillment has ended in the arid satisfaction of lost domestic happiness, yet this must be a choice made by women, and not by males who would decide the extent or content of female education and the quality of their lives. Until such conservatism is shed, Indian women will wait long for gender parity in India.

Works Cited

Agarwal, Usha. 1995. *Indian woman, education and development.* Ambala: The Indian Publication.

Bayly, Susan. 1989. *Saints, goddesses and kings: Muslims and Christians in South Indian History 1700-1900.* Cambridge: Cambridge University Press.

Besant, Annie. 1899. An interview in *Arya Bala Bodhini*, July 1899. Theosophical Society Archives.

__________. 1904. *The education of Indian girls*, pamphlet no. 25. Benaras: Theosophical Society.

Bharti, Subramaniam. 1935. *Katturaikal: Mather* [Essays on women]. Triplicane: Bharati Publishing House.

Carpenter, Mary. 1868. *Six months in India*, vol. 2. London: Longmans Green.

Chaudhary, Pratima. 1995. *Women's education in India.* New Delhi: Har Anand Publications.

Cheriyan, P. 1935. *Malabar Christians and the Church Missionary Society, 1816-1856.* Kottayam: Christian Missionary Society.

Das, M. N. 1959. *Studies in the economic and social development of India, 1848-1956.* Calcutta: Firma KLM.

Hickey, William. 1872. *Tanjore Maratha principality in South India.* Madras.

Kanwar, Asha and Neela Jagannathan. 1995. *Speaking for ourselves.* New Delhi: Manohar.

Kelkar, Govind and Dev Nathan. 1991. *Gender and tribe.* New Delhi: Kali for Women.

Law, Narendranath. 1915. *Promotion of learning in India by Early European settlers upto 1800 A.D.* London: Longmans Green.

Menon, Shungoony. 1984 [1878]. *History of Travancore.* Trivandrum: Cosmos.

Mukherji, S. N. 1951. *History of education in India.* Baroda: Acharya.

Natesan, G. A. (ed.) 1920. *Speeches of Gopal Krishna Gokhale.* Madras: G. A. Natesan.

Raman, Sita. 1994. From Chattrams to National Schools: Educational philanthropy in South India, 18th-20th centuries. In *Selected papers in Asian Studies*, 52. Proceedings of the Western Conference of the Association for Asian Studies held at Utah.

________. 1996. *Getting girls to school: Social reform in Tamil districts, 1870-1930*. Calcutta: Stree.

Tharu, Susie and K. Lalitha. 1989. *Women writing in India*. New Delhi: Feminist Press.

Wayman, Alex and Hideko Wayman (tr.). 1974. *The lion's roar of Srimala*. New York: Columbia University Press.

Yesudas, R. N. 1980. *The history of the London Missionary Society in Travancore, 1806-1908*. Travancore: Kerela Historical Society.

V | Science & Technology

Chapter 19 | Aspects of Science in Ancient India

Subhash C. Kak

Veda means knowledge. We call our earliest period *Vedic*, which is suggestive of the importance of acquiring knowledge, to that period of Indian history. For quite some time, scholars believed that this knowledge amounted to no more than speculations regarding the self; this is what we are still told in some schoolbooks. New insights, however, in archaeology, astronomy, history of science, and Vedic scholarship have shown that such a view is wrong. We now know that Vedic knowledge embraced physics, mathematics, astronomy, logic, cognition, and other disciplines. This has significant implications for our understanding of the history of ideas and the evolution of early civilizations.

Reconstructions of the earliest science are based not only on the Vedas but also on their appendices called the Vedāngas. The six Vedangas deal with: kalpa (performance of ritual with its basis of geometry, mathematics and calendrics); śikṣā (phonetics); chhandas (metrical structures); nirukta, (etymology); vyakarana (grammar); and jyotisha (astronomy and other cyclical phenomena). (See Keshavan in this volume for details). Then, there are naturalistic descriptions in the various Vedic books that tell us a lot about scientific ideas of those times.

Vedic World View

Briefly, Vedic texts present a tripartite and recursive world view. The universe is viewed as three regions of earth, space, and sky with the corresponding entities of

Vişve Devah (all gods), Indra, and Agni. Counting the joining regions leads to a total of five categories where, as we see in Figure 1, water separates earth and fire, and air separates fire and ether. In Vedic ritual, the three regions are assigned different fire altars. Furthermore, the five categories are represented in terms of altars of five layers. The great altars are built of a thousand bricks of a variety of dimensions. That the details of the altar constructions code astronomical knowledge is a fascinating chapter in the history of astronomy (Kak 1994a; 1995a,b).

In the Vedic world view, processes in the sky, on earth, and within the mind are connected. The Vedic ṛṣis were aware that all descriptions of the universe lead to logical paradoxes. The one category transcending all oppositions was termed brahman. Understanding the nature of consciousness was of paramount importance in this view, but this did not mean that other sciences were ignored. Vedic ritual was a sym bolic retelling of this world view. (See Diagram 1 below.)

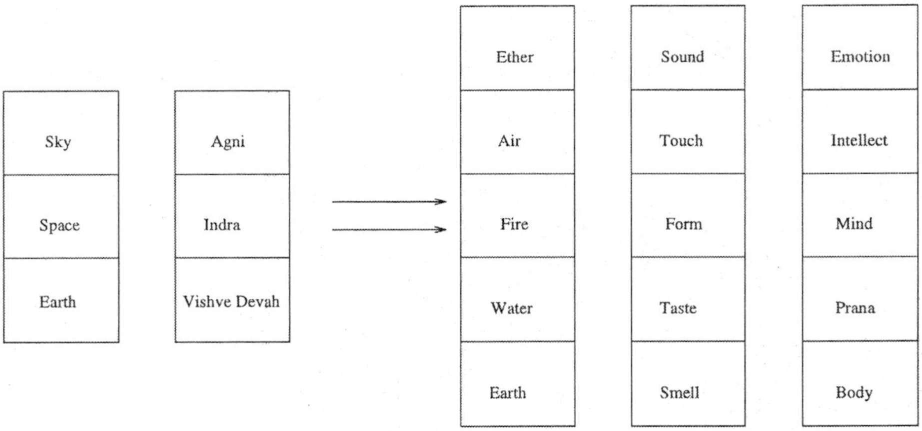

Diagram 1: From the Tripartic Model to Five Categories of Analysis.

Chronology

To place Vedic science in its context it is necessary to have an understanding of the chronology of Vedic literature. There are astronomical references in the Vedas that recall events in the third or fourth millennium B.C.E. and earlier. The recent discovery (e.g., Feuerstein et al. 1995) that Sarasvati, the preeminent river of the Rig Vedic times, went dry around 1900 B.C.E. due to tectonic upheavals implies that the Rig Veda is to be dated prior to this epoch, perhaps prior to 2000 B.C.E. since the literature that immediately follows the Rig Veda does not speak of any geological catastrophe. But we cannot be very precise. There exist traditional accounts in the Purāṇas that assign greater antiquity to the Rig Veda: for example, the Kaliyuga tradition speaks of 3100 B.C.E. and the Varāhamihira tradition mentions 2400 B.C.E. According to Henri-Paul Francfort (1992) of the Indo-French team that surveyed this area, the Sarasvati river had ceased to be a perennial river by the third millennium B.C.E.; this supports those who argue for the older dates. But in the absence of conclusive evidence, it is prudent to take the most conservative of these dates, namely 2000 B.C.E. as the latest period to be associated with the Rig Veda.

In the past century or so, textbook accounts were based on the now disproved supposition that the Rig Veda is to be dated about 1500-1000 B.C.E. and, therefore, the question of the dates assigned to the Brāhmaṇas, Sūtras, and other literature remains open. A detailed chronology of the literature that followed Rig Veda has not yet been worked out. A chronology was attempted based solely on the internal astronomical evidence in the book *Ancient Indian Chronology* by the science historian P.C. Sengupta in 1947. Although Sengupta's dates have the virtue of inner consistency, they have neither been examined carefully by other scholars nor checked against archaeological evidence. This means that we can only speak in the greatest of generalities regarding the chronology of the texts: assign the Rig Veda to the third millennium B.C.E. and earlier, and the Brahmanas to the second millennium. This also implies that the archaeological finds of the Indus-Sarasvati period, which are coeval with Rig Veda literature, can be used to cross-check textual evidence.

Similarly, no comprehensive studies of ancient Indian science exist. Textbook accounts like the one to be found in Basham's *The Wonder That Was India* are hopelessly out of date. But there are some excellent surveys of selected material. The task of putting it all together into a comprehensive whole will be a major task for historians of science.

This essay presents an assortment of topics from ancient Indian science. We begin with an outline of the models used in the Vedic cognitive science; these models parallel those used in ancient Indian physics. We also review mathematics, astronomy, grammar, logic and medicine.

Vedic Cognitive Science

The Rig Veda speaks of cosmic order. It is assumed that there exist equivalencies of various kinds between the outer and the inner worlds. It is these connections that make it possible for our minds to comprehend the universe. It is noteworthy that the analytical methods are used both in the examination of the outer world as well as the inner world. This allowed the Vedic rishis to place in sharp focus paradoxical aspects of analytical knowledge. Such paradoxes have become only too familiar to the contemporary scientist in all branches of inquiry (Kak 1986).

In the Vedic view, the complementary nature of the mind and the outer world is of fundamental significance. Knowledge is classified in two ways: the lower or dual and the higher or unified. What this means is that knowledge is superficially dual and paradoxical but at a deeper level it has unity. The Vedic view claims that the material and the conscious are aspects of the same transcendental reality.

The idea of complementarity is at the basis of the systematization of Indian philosophic traditions as well, so that complementary approaches are paired together. We have the groups of logic (nyāya) and physics (vaiśhēṣhika), cosmology (sānkhya) and psychology (yoga), and language (mīmamsa) and reality (vedanta). Although these philosophical schools were formalized in the post-Vedic age, we find an anticipation of these ideas in the Vedic texts as well.

In the Rig Veda, there is reference to the yoking of the horses to the chariot of Indra, Ashvins, or Agni, and we are told elsewhere that these gods represent the essential mind. The same metaphor of the chariot for a person is encountered in *Katha Upanishad* and the *Bhagavadgita*; this chariot is pulled in different directions by the horses, representing senses, which are yoked to it. The mind is the driver who holds the reins to these horses, but next to the mind sits the true observer, the self, who represents a universal unity. Without this self, no coherent behavior is possible. (See Pandharipande, and Hiriyanna in this volume for details.)

The Five Levels

In the *Taittiriya Upanishad*, the individual is represented in terms of five different sheaths or levels that enclose the individual's self. These levels, shown in an ascending order, are:

The physical body (annamaya koṣa)
Energy sheath (pranamaya koṣa)
Mental sheath (manomaya koṣa)
Intellect sheath (vijnanamaya koṣa)
Emotion sheath (anandamaya koṣa)

These sheaths are defined at increasingly finer levels. At the highest level, above the emotion sheath, is the self. It is significant that emotion is placed higher than the intellect. This is a recognition of the fact that eventually meaning is communicated by associations which are influenced by the emotional state.

The energy that underlies physical and mental processes is called *prana.* One may look at an individual in three different levels. At the lowest level is the physical body, at the next level are the energy systems at work, and at the highest level are thoughts. Since the three levels are interrelated, the energy situation may be changed by inputs either at the physical or mental level. When the energy state is agitated and restless, it is characterized by *rajas*; when it is dull and lethargic, it is characterized by *tamas*; the state of equilibrium and balance is termed *sattva.* The key notion is that each level represents characteristics that are emergent on the ground of the previous level. In this theory, the mind is an emergent entity, but this emergence requires the presence of the self.

The Structure of the Mind

The Sānkhya system takes the mind as consisting of five components: manas, ahankāra, chitta, buddhi, and ātman. Again these categories parallel those of Figure 1. Manas is the lower mind which collects sense impressions. Its perceptions shift from moment to moment. This sensory-motor mind obtains its inputs from the senses of hearing, touch, sight, taste, and smell. Each of these senses may be governed by a separate agent.

Ahankāra is the sense of "I-ness" that associates some perceptions to a subjective and personal experience. Once sensory impressions have been related to I-ness by ahankāra, their evaluation and resulting decisions are arrived at by buddhi, the intellect. Manas, ahankāra, and buddhi are collectively called the internal instruments of the mind.

Chitta, is the memory bank of the mind. These memories constitute the foundation on which the rest of the mind operates. But chitta is not merely a passive instrument. The organization of the new impressions throws up instinctual or primitive urges that creates different emotional states. This mental complex surrounds the innermost aspect of consciousness which is called ātman, (the self), *brahman*, or jīva. Ātman is considered to be beyond a finite enumeration of categories.

All this amounts to a brilliant analysis of the individual. The traditions of yoga and tantra emerged out of it. No wonder, this model has continued to inspire people around the world to this day.

Mathematical and Physical Sciences

Here we review some new findings related to the early period of Indian science which show that the outer world was not ignored.

Geometry and Mathematics

Seidenberg, by examining the evidence in the *Shatapatha Brahmana*, showed that Indian geometry predates Greek geometry by centuries. Seidenberg argues that the birth of geometry and mathematics had a ritual origin. For example, the earth was represented by a circular altar and the heavens were represented by a square altar, and the ritual consisted of converting the circle into a square of an identical area. Here we see the beginnings of geometry. In his paper on the origin of mathematics, Seidenberg (1978) concluded:

> Old-Babylonia (1700 B.C.E.)got the theorem of Pythagoras from India or that both Old-Babylonia and India got it from a third source. Now the Sanskrit scholars do not give me a date so far back as 1700 B.C.E. Therefore I postulate a pre-Old-Babylonian, i.e., pre-1700 B.C.E., source of the kind of geometric rituals we see preserved in the Sulvasutras, or at least for the mathematics involved in these rituals.

This was before archaeological finds disproved the earlier assumption of a break in Indian civilization in the second millennium B.C.E.; it was this assumption of the Sanskritists that led Seidenberg to postulate a third earlier source. Now with this new knowledge, Seidenberg's conclusion of India being the source of the geometric and mathematical knowledge of the ancient world fits in with the chronology of the texts.

Barend van Nooten (1993) shows that binary numbers were known at the time of Pingala's *Chhandahshastra.* Pingala, who lived around the early first century B.C.E., used binary numbers to classify Vedic meters. Such binary numbers were used to classify meters. The knowledge of binary numbers indicates a deep understanding of arithmatic. A binary representation requires the use of only two symbols, rather than the ten required in the usual decimal representation and has now become the basis of information storage in terms of sequences of zeros and ones in modern-day computers.

Astronomy

Using hitherto neglected texts related to ritual and the Vedic indices, an astronomy of the third millennium B.C.E. has been discovered (Kak 1994a; 1995a,b). Here altars symbolize different parts of the year. In one ritual, pebbles were placed around altars for the earth, atmosphere, and sky. The number of pebbles were twenty-one, seventy-eight, and two-hundred-sixty-one, respectively which add up to the 360 days of the year.

The organization of the Vedic books was according to an astronomical code. The Vedic ritual followed the seasons hence the importance of astronomy. We also know that the second millennium text *Vedanga Jyotisha* went beyond the earlier calendrical astronomy to develop a theory for the mean motions of the sun and the moon. This marked the beginnings of the application of mathematics to the motions of the heavenly bodies. (See Diagram 2 below.)

The Vedic planetary model is given in Figure 2. The sun was taken to be midway in the skies. A considerable amount of Vedic mythology regarding the struggle between the demons and the gods is a metaphorical retelling of the motions of Venus and Mars (Frawley 1994). The myth of Vishnu's three strides codes information about

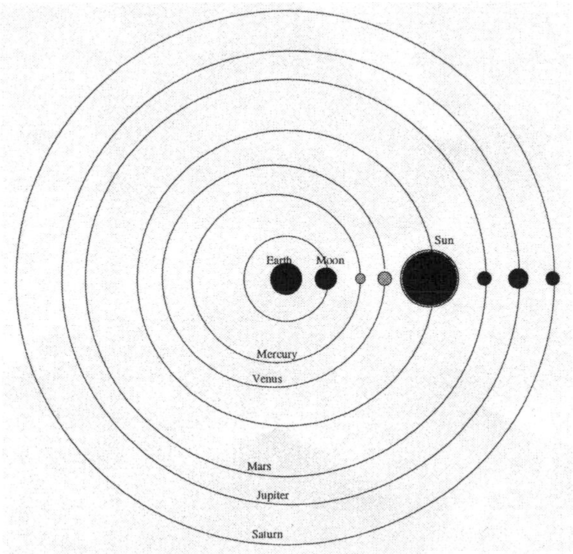

Diagram 2: The Vedic Planetary Model.

the synodic period of Mercury (Kak 1996a). Probabilistic arguments suggest that the Vedic people knew the periods of the five classical planets.

Writing and Grammar

Cryptological analysis has revealed that the Brahmī script of the Mauryan times evolved out of the third millennium Sarasvati (Indus) script. It also appears that the symbol for zero was derived from the fish sign that stood for "ten" in Brahmī; this occurred around 50 B.C.E.- C.E. 50 (Kak 1994b).

Panini's grammar (sixth century B.C.E. or earlier) provides 4,000 rules that describe the Sanskrit of his day completely. This grammar is acknowledged to be one of the greatest intellectual achievements of all time. The great variety of language mirrors, in many ways, the complexity of nature. What is remarkable is that Panini set out to describe the entire grammar in terms of a finite number of rules. Frits Staal (1988) shows that the grammar of Panini represents a universal grammatical and computing system. From this perspective, it anticipates the logical framework of modern computers (Kak 1987).

Music

Ernest McClain (1978) describes the tonal basis of early myth. McClain argues that the connections between music and myth are even deeper than astronomy and myth. The invariance at the basis of tones could very well have served as the ideal for the development of the earliest astronomy. The *Sama Veda*, where the hymns were supposed to be sung, was compared to the sky. Apparently, this comparison was to emphasize the musical basis of astronomy. The Vedic hymns are according to a variety of meters, but what purpose, if any, lay behind a specific choice is unknown. Peter Raster has found also astonishing phonetic structure in a hymn of the Rig Veda that he has analyzed.

Medicine

There is a close parallel between Indian and Greek medicine. For example, the idea of breath (prāṇa in Sanskrit, and *pneuma* in Greek)is central to both. Jean Filliozat (1970) argues that the idea of the correct association between the three elements of the wind, the gall, and the phlegm, which was described first by Plato in Greek medicine, appears to be derived from the earlier tridoṣa theory of āyurveda. Filliozat suggests that the transmission occurred via the Persian empire. These discoveries not only call for a revision of the textbook accounts of Indian science but also call for new research to assess the impact on other civilizations of these ideas.

Rhythms of Life

We have spoken of how the Vedas speak of the connections between the external and the internal worlds. The hymns speak often of the stars and the planets. These are sometimes the luminaries in the sky or those in the firmament of our inner landscapes or both. To the question of how the motions of an object, millions of miles away, have any influence on the life of a human being, one can only say that the universe is interconnected. In this ecological perspective, the physical planets do not influence the individual directly. Rather, the intricate clockwork of the universe runs on forces that are reflected in the periodicities of the astral bodies as do the cycles of behaviors of all terrestrial beings and plants.

It is not the gravitational pull of the planet that causes a certain response, but an internal clock governed by genes. We know this because in some mutant organisms, the internal clock works according to periods that have no apparent astronomical basis. So these cycles can be considered to be a manifestation of the motions of the body's inner "planets." In the language of evolution theory, one would argue that these periods get reflected in the genetic inheritance of the biological system as a result of the advantage over millions of years that provided for survival.

The most fundamental rhythms are matched to the periods of the sun or the moon. It is reasonable to assume that with their emphasis on time-bound rituals and the calendar, the ancients discovered many biological periods. This would include the 24-hour -50-minute circadian rhythm, the connection of the menstrual cycle with the motions of the moon, the life cycles of various plants, the semimonthly estrus cycle of sheep, the three-week cycles of cattle and pigs, and the six-month cycle of dogs.

The moon (Soma) is called the Vāčaspati (lord of speech) in the Rig Veda. It is also taken to awaken eager thoughts. Other many references suggest that in the Rig Vedic times, the moon was taken to be connected with the mind. This is stated most directly in the famous Puruṣasūkta (Cosmic Man Hymn) of the Rig Veda where it is stated that the mind is born of the moon and in Śatapatha Brāhmaṇa where "the mind is the moon". Considering the fact that the relationships between the astronomical and the terrestrial were taken in terms of periodicities, doubtless, this slogan indicates that the mind is governed by the period of the moon.

Fire, having become speech, entered the mouth Air,
becoming scent, entered the nostrils
The sun, becoming sight, entered the eyes
The regions becoming hearing, entered the ears
The plants, becoming hairs, entered the skin
The moon, having become mind, entered the heart.
(Aitareya Āraṇyaka 2.4.2.4)

This verse from the Upaniṣadic period speaks at many levels. At the literal level, there is an association of the elements with various cognitive centers. At another level, the verse connects the time evolution of the external object to the cognitive center. Fire represents consciousness and this ebbs and flows with a daily rhythm. Air represents seasons, so here the rhythm is longer. The sun and sight have a 24-hour cycle. The regions denote other motions in the skies, so hearing manifests cycles that are connected to the planets. The plants have daily and annual periods; the hairs of the body have an annual period. The mind has a period of 24 hours and 50 minutes like that of the moon.

What are the seats of these cycles? According to tantra, the čakras of the body are the centers of the different elements as well as cognitive capacities and rhythms related to "internal planets". The knowledge of these rhythms appears to have led to astrology.

Cosmology

We have seen how the logical apparatus that was brought to bear on the outer world was applied to the analysis of the mind. But the question remains: How does inanimate matter come to have awareness? This metaphysical question is answered by postulating entities for smell, taste, form, touch, and sound as in Figure 1. In the Sānkhya system, a total of twenty-four such categories are assumed. These categories are supposed to emerge at the end of a long chain of evolution and they may be considered to be material. The breath of life into the instruments of sight, touch, hearing and so on is provided by the twenty-fifth category, which is puruṣa, the soul.

The recursive Vedic world-view requires that the universe itself go through cycles of creation and destruction. This view became a part of the astronomical framework and ultimately very long cycles of billions of years were assumed. The Sānkhya evolution takes the life forms to evolve into an increasingly complex system until the end of the cycle. The categories of Sāṅkhya operate at the level of the individual as well. Life mirrors the entire creation cycle and cognition mirrors a life-history. Surprisingly similar is the modern phrase: ontogeny is phylogeny, and microgeny (the cognitive process) is a speeded-up ontogeny (Brown 1994).

Implications

We are in the midst of a paradigm shift in our understanding of Vedic science and cosmology. We now know that measurement astronomy is to be dated to at least the third millennium B.C.E. which is more than a thousand years earlier than was believed only a decade ago, and mathematics and geometry are dated at least to the beginning of the second millennium B.C.E. Indian mythology is being interpreted in terms of its underlying astronomy and/or cognitive science.

What does it all mean for our understanding of Indian civilization and its interactions with Mesopotamia, Egypt, China, and Greece? Contemporary science has begun to examine Vedic theories on the nature of the "self" to see if they might be of value in the search for a science of consciousness (e.g., Kak 1996b). Man has mastered the outer world and Vedic science formed the basis for that enterprise; it is now possible that the exploration of the inner world, which is the heart of modern science, will also be along paths long heralded by Vedic ṛṣis.

Indian Science after Aryabhata

In the earliest period of Indian science, it is exceptional when we know the authorship of a text or an idea. For example, although Lagadha (c. 1400 B.C.E.) is the author of Vedāṅga Jyotiṣa, we do not know if its astronomy was developed by him or if he merely summarized what was then well known. Likewise, we are not sure of the individual contributions in the śulba Sūtras of Baudhayana, Āpastamba, and other authors, which describe geometry, or Pingala's *Chandasutra* discussed above. The major exception to the anonymous nature of early Indian science is the grammatical tradition starting with Panini.

With Āryabhaṭa of Kusumapura (born 476 C.E.), we enter a new phase in which it becomes easier to trace the authorship of specific ideas. But even here there remain other aspects which are not so well understood. For example, the evolution of Indian medicine is not as well documented as that of Indian mathematics. Moreover, the manner in which the philosophical basis underlying Indian science evolved is not entirely clear. Thus, many texts speak of the relativity of time and space—abstract concepts that developed in the scientific context just a hundred years ago. The Purāṇas speak of countless universes, time flowing at different rates for different observers, and so on. Thus, many texts speak of the relativity of time and space—abstract concepts that developed in the scientific context just a hundred years ago. The Mahābhārata speaks of an embryo being divided into one hundred parts each becoming, after maturation in a separate pot, a healthy baby; this is how the Kaurava brothers are born. There is also mention of an embryo, conceived in one womb, being transferred to the womb of another woman from where it is born; the transferred embryo is Balarama, and this is how he is a brother to Krishna although he was born to Rohini and not Devaki.

There is an ancient mention of "space travelers" wearing airtight suits in the Mahābhārata which may be classified as an early form of science fiction. According to the well-known Sanskritist J.A.B. van Buitenen, in the accounts in Book 3 called *The Razing of Saubha* and *The War of the Yakshas*:

> the aerial city is nothing but an armed camp with flame-throwers and thundering cannon, no doubt a spaceship. The name of the demons is also revealing: they were *Nivatakavacas*, "clad in airtight armor," which can hardly be anything but space suits. (van Buitenen 1975: 202)

Universes defined recursively are described in the famous episode of Indra and the ants in *Brahmavaivarta Purana*. Here Viṣhnu, in the guise of a boy, explains to Indra that the ants he sees walking on the ground have all been Indras in their own solar systems in different times. These flights of imagination are to be traced to more than a straightforward generalization of the motions of the planets into a cyclic universe. They must be viewed in the background of an amazingly sophisticated tradition of cognitive and analytical thought (see e.g. Staal 1988; Kak 1994).

Mathematics and Astronomy

One would expect that the development of early Indian mathematics and astronomy went through several phases but we don't have sufficient data to reconstruct these phases. A certain astronomy has been inferred from the Vedic books, but there existed additional sources which have not survived. For example, there were early astronomical siddhāntas of which we know now only from late commentaries written during the Gupta period (320-600); this period provided a long period of stability and prosperity that saw a great flowering of art, literature, and the sciences.(See chapters by S.R.Rao, R.C.Sharma, and Krishnamoorthy, this volume.)

Of the eighteen early siddhāntas the summaries of only five are available now. Perhaps one reason that the earlier texts were lost is because their theories were superseded by the more accurate later works. In addition to these siddhāntas, practical manuals, astronomical tables, description of instruments, and other miscellaneous writings have also come down to us (Sarma 1985). The Purāṇas also have some material on astronomy.

Aryabhata

Āryabhata is the author of the first of the later siddhāntas called *Aryabhatiyam* which sketches his mathematical, planetary, and cosmic theories. This book is divided into four chapters: (i) the astronomical constants and the sine table, (ii) mathematics required for computations, (iii) division of time and rules for computing the longitudes of planets using eccentrics and epicycles, (iv) the armillary sphere, rules relating to problems of trigonometry and the computation of eclipses.

The parameters of *Aryabhatiyam* have as their origin, the commencement of Kaliyuga on Friday, February 18, 3102 B.C.E. He wrote another book where the epoch is a bit different.(See also Keshvan, this volume, on the Vedas)

Āryabhata took the earth to spin on its axis; this idea appears to have been his innovation. He also considered the heavenly motions to go through a cycle of 4.32 billion years; here he went with an older tradition, but he introduced a new scheme of subdivisions within this great cycle. According to the historian Hugh Thurston, "Not only did Āryabhata believe that the earth rotates, but there are glimmerings in his system (and other similar systems) of a possible underlying theory in which the earth (and the planets) orbits the sun, rather than the sun orbiting the earth. The evidence is that the basic planetary periods are relative to the sun."

That Āryabhata was aware of the relativity of motion is clear from this passage in his book: "Just as a man in a boat sees the trees on the bank move in the opposite direction, so an observer on the equator sees the stationary stars as moving precisely toward the west."

Varahamihira

Varāhamihira (died 587) lived in Ujjain and he wrote three important books: *Panchasiddhantika*, *Brihat Samhita*, and *Brihat Jataka*. The first is a summary of five early astronomical systems including the *Surya Siddhanta*. (The modern *Surya Siddhanta* is different in many details from this ancient one.) Another system described by him, the *Paitamaha Siddhānta*, appears to have many similarities with the ancient *Vedanga Jyotisha* of Lagadha.

Brihat Samhita is a compilation of an assortment of topics that provides interesting details of the beliefs of those times. *Brihat Jataka* is a book on astrology which appears to be considerably influenced by Greek astrology.

Brahmagupta

Brahmagupta of Bhilamala in Rajasthan, who was born in 598, wrote his masterpiece, *Brahmasphuta Siddhanta*, in 628. His school, which was a rival to that of Āryabhata, has been very influential in western and northern India. Brahmagupta's work was translated into Arabic in 771 or 773 at Baghdad and it became famous in the Arabic world as *Sindhind.*

One of Brahmagupta's chief contributions is the solution of a certain second order indeterminate equation which is of great significance in number theory.

Another of his books, the *Khandakhadyaka*, remained a popular handbook for astronomical computations for centuries.

Bhaskara

Bhāskara (born 1114), who was from the Karnataka region, was an outstanding mathematician and astronomer. Amongst his mathematical contributions is the concept of differentials. He was the author of *Siddhanta Shiromani*, a book in four parts: (i) *Lilavati* on arithmetic, (ii) *Bijaganita* on algebra, (iii) *Ganitadhyaya*, and (iv) *Goladhyaya* on astronomy. He epicyclic-eccentric theories of planetary motions are more developed than in the earlier siddhantas.

Subsequent to Bhāskara we see a flourishing tradition of mathematics and astronomy in Kerala which saw itself as a successor to the school of Āryabhata. We know of the contributions of very many scholars in this tradition, of whom we will speak only of two below.

Madhava

Mādhava (c. 1340-1425) developed a procedure to determine the positions of the moon every thirty-six minutes. He also provided methods to estimate the motions of the planets. He gave power series expansions for trigonometric functions, and for *pi* correct to eleven decimal places.

Nilakantha Somayaji

Nilakantha (c. 1444-1545) was a very prolific scholar who wrote several works on astronomy. It appears that Nilakantha found the correct formulation for the equation of the center of the planets and his model must be considered a true heliocentric model of the solar system. He also improved upon the power series techniques of Mādhava.

The methods developed by the Kerala mathematicians were far ahead of the European mathematics of the day.

Concepts of Space, Time, and Matter

Yoga Vashishta is an ancient Indian text, over 29,000 verses long, traditionally attributed to Valmiki, author of the epic Rāmāyaṇa which is over two thousand years old. But the internal evidence of the text indicates that it was authored or compiled later. It has been dated variously as early as the sixth century or as late as the thirteenth or the fourteenth century (Chapple 1984). Dasgupta (1975) dated it about the sixth century on the basis that one of its verses appears to be copied from one of Kālidāsa's plays considering Kālidāsa to have lived around the fifth century. The traditional date of of Kālidāsa is 50 BC and new arguments (Kak 1990) support this earlier date so that the estimates regarding the age of *Yoga Vashishta* are further muddled.

Yoga Vashishta may be viewed as a book of philosophy or as a philosophical novel. It describes the instruction given by Vaśiṣṭha to Rāma, the hero of the epic Rāmāyana. Its premise may be termed radical idealism and it is couched in a fashion that has many parallels with the notion of a participatory universe argued by modern philosophers. Its most interesting passages from the scientific point of view relate to the description of the nature of space, time, matter, and consciousness. It should be emphasized that the ideas in *Yoga Vashishta* do not stand in isolation. Similar ideas are to be found in the Vedic texts. At its deepest level the Vedic conception is to view reality in a monist manner; at the next level one may speak of the dichotomy of mind and matter. Ideas similar to those found in *Yoga Vashishta* are also encountered in Purāṇas and Tantric literature.

I provide a random selection of these passages taken from the abridged translation of the book done by Venkatesananda (1984). The page numbers given at the end of each passage are from the Venkatesananda translation.

Time

Time cannot be analyzed... Time uses two balls known as the sun and the moon for its pastime. (page 16) The world is like a potter's wheel: the wheel looks as if it stands still, though it revolves at a terrific speed. (18) Just as space does not have a fixed span, time does not have a fixed span either. Just as the world and its creation are mere appearances, a moment and an epoch are also imaginary. (55) Infinite consciousness held in itself the notion of a unit of time equal to one-millionth of the twinkling of an eye; and from this evolved the time-scale right upto an epoch consisting of several revolutions of the four ages, which is the life-span of one cosmic creation. Infinite consciousness itself is uninvolved in these, for it is devoid of rising and setting (which are essential to all time-scales), and it is devoid of a beginning, middle and end. (72)

Space

There are three types of space—the psychological space, the physical space and the infinite space of consciousness. (52) The infinite space of undivided consciousness is that which exists in all, inside and outside... The finite space of divided consciousness is that which created divisions of time, which pervades all beings... The physical space is that in which the elements exist. The latter two are not independent of the first. (96)

Other Universes

On the slopes of a far-distant mountain range there is a solid rock within which I dwell. The world within this rock is just like yours: it has its own inhabitants, ...the sun and the moon and all the rest of it. I have been in it for countless aeons. (402) The entire universe is contained in a subatomic particle, and the three worlds exist within one strand of hair. (404)

Matter

(There are) countless universes, diverse in composition and space-time structure... In every one of them there are continents and mountains, villages and cities inhabited by people who have their time-space and life-span. (401-2) In every atom there are worlds within worlds. (55)

Experience

Direct experience alone is the basis for all proofs...That substratum is the experiencing intelligence which itself becomes the experiencer, the act of experiencing, and the experience. (36) Everyone has two bodies, the one physical and the other mental. The physical body is insentient and seeks its own destruction; the mind is finite but orderly. (124) I have carefully investigated, I have observed everything from the tips of my toes to the top of my head, and I have not found anything of which I could say, 'This I am.' Who is 'I'? I am the all-pervading consciousness which is itself not an object of knowledge or knowing and is free from self-hood. I am that which is indivisible, which has no name, which does not undergo change, which is beyond all concepts of unity and diversity, which is beyond measure. (214) I remember that once upon a time there was nothing on this earth, neither trees and plants, nor even mountains. For a period of eleven thousand years the earth was covered by lava. In those days there was neither day nor night below the polar region: for in the rest of the earth neither the sun nor the moon shone. Only one half of the polar region was illumined. Then demons ruled the earth. They were deluded, powerful and prosperous, and the earth was their playground. Apart from the polar region the rest of the earth was covered with water. And then for a very long time the whole earth was covered with forests, except the polar region. Then there arose great mountains, but without any human inhabitants. For a period of ten thousand years the earth was covered with the corpses of the demons. (280)

Mind

The same infinite self conceives within itself the duality of oneself and the other. (39) Thought is mind, there is no distinction between the two. (41) The body can neither enjoy nor suffer. It is the mind alone that experiences. (109-110) The mind has no body, no support and no form; yet by this mind is everything consumed in this world. This is indeed a great mystery. He who says that he is destroyed by the mind which has no substantiality at all, says in effect that his head was smashed by the lotus petal... The hero who is able to destroy a real enemy standing in front of him is himself destroyed by this mind which is non-material. The intelligence which is other than self-knowledge is what constitutes the mind. (175)

Complementarity

The absolute alone exists now and for ever. When one thinks of it as a void, it is because of the feeling one has that it is not void; when one thinks of it as not-void, it is because there is a feeling that it is void. (46) All fundamental elements continued to act on one another—as experiencer and experience—and the entire creation came into being like ripples on the surface of the ocean. And, they are interwoven and mixed up so effectively that they cannot be extricated from one another till the cosmic dissolution. (48)

Consciousness

The entire universe is forever the same as the consciousness that dwells in every atom. (41) The five elements are the seed of which the world is the tree; and the eternal consciousness is the seed of the elements. (48) Cosmic consciousness alone exists now and ever; in it are no worlds, no created beings. That consciousness reflected in itself appears to be creation. (49) This consciousness is not knowable: when it wishes to become the knowable, it is known as the universe. Mind, intellect, egotism, the five great elements, and the world— all these innumerable names and forms are all consciousness alone. (50) The world exists because consciousness is, and the world is the body of consciousness. There is no division, no difference, no distinction. Hence the universe can be said to be both real and unreal: real because of the reality of consciousness which is its own reality, and unreal because the universe does not exist as universe, independent of consciousness. (50) Consciousness is pure, eternal and infinite: it does not arise nor cease to be. It is ever there in the moving and unmoving creatures, in the sky, on the mountain and in fire and air. (67) Millions of universes appear in the infinite consciousness like specks of dust in a beam of light. In one small atom all the three worlds appear to be, with all their components like space, time, action, substance, day and night. (120) The universe exists in infinite consciousness. Infinite consciousness is unmanifest, though omnipresent, even as space, though existing everywhere, is manifest. (141) The manifestation of the omnipotence of infinite consciousness enters into an alliance with time, space and causation. Thence arise infinite names and forms. (145) The Lord who is infinite consciousness is the silent but alert witness of this cosmic dance. He is not different from the dancer (the cosmic natural order) and the dance (the happenings). (296)

The Yoga Vasishtha Model of Knowledge

Yoga Vasishtha is not written as a systematic text. But the above descriptions may be used to reconstruct its system of knowledge. *Yoga Vasishtha* appears to accept the idea that laws are intrinsic to the universe. In other words, the laws of nature in an unfolding universe will also evolve. According to *Yoga Vasishtha*, new information does not emerge out of the inanimate world but it is a result of the exchange between mind and matter. It also appears to accept consciousness as a kind of fundamental field that pervades the whole universe. One might speculate that the parallels between *Yoga Vasishtha* and some recent ideas of physics are a result of the inherent structure of the mind.

The Shri Yantra

Although our immediate information on the Śri Yantra comes from medieval sources, some scholars have seen the antecedents of the yantra in Book 10 of the *Atharvaveda*. The Śri Yantra consists of nine triangles inscribed within a circle which leads to the formation of forty-three little triangles (Figure 1) (Kulaichev 1984). Whatever the antiquity of the idea of this design, it is certain that the yantra was made both on flat and curved surfaces during the middle ages. The drawing of the triangles on the curved surface implies the knowledge that the sum of the angles of such triangles exceeds hundred and eighty degrees.

The question that the physicist and historian of science John Barrow (1992) has asked is whether these shapes intimate a knowledge of non-Euclidean geometry in India centuries before its systematic study in Europe. It is possible that the yantras were made by craftsmen who had no appreciation of its mathematical properties. But scholars have argued that the intricacies of the construction of this yantra requires mathematical knowledge. (See Diagram 3 on the following page.)

Conclusion

This has been a survey of selected topics that are of potential interest to an understanding of the development of science in India. If the revisions in our understanding required for these topics are indicative of other subjects also then we are in for a most radical rewriting of the history of science in India.

My survey of these topics did not stress enough one aspect of Indian thought that sets it apart from that of most other nations, namely the belief that thought by itself can lead to objective knowledge. Being counter to the reductionist program of mainstream science, this aspect of Indian thought has been bitterly condemned by most historians of science as being irrational and mystical. Now that reductionism is in retreat in mainstream science itself one would expect a less emotional assessment of Indian ideas. We can hope to address issues such as how do some ideas in India happen to be ages ahead of their times.

Students of scientific creativity increasingly accept that conceptual advances do not appear in any rational manner. Might then one accept the claim of Srinivasa Ramanujan that his theorems were revealed to him in his dreams by the goddess Nāmagiri? This claim, so persistently made by Ramanujan, has generally been dismissed by his biographers (see, for example, Kanigel, 1991). Were Ramanujan's astonishing discoveries instrumented by the autonomously creative potential of consciousness, represented by him by the image of Nāmagiri? If that be the case then the marvellous imagination shown in *Yoga-Vasishtha* and other Indian texts becomes easier to comprehend.

Diagram 3: The Basic Shri Yantra and its Variants.

Works Cited

Barrow, J. 1992. *Pi in the Sky*. Oxford: Oxford University Press.

Basham, A.L. 1967. *The Wonder that was India.* New York: Grove Press

Brown, J.W. 1994. Morphogenesis and mental process. *Development and Psychopathology.* 6:551-63.

Chapple, C. 1984. Introduction and bibliography in Venkatesananda (1984).

Dasgupta, S. 1975 (1932). *A History of Indian Philosophy*. Delhi: Motilal Banarsidass.

Feuerstein, G., S. Kak and D. Frawley. 1995. *In Search of the Cradle of Civilization.* Wheaton: Quest Books.

Filliozat, J. 1970. The expansion of Indian medicine abroad. *India's Contributions to World Thought and Culture*, edited by Lokesh Chandra. Madras: Vivekananda Memorial Committee. 67-70.

Francfort, H.P. 1992. Evidence for Harappan irrigation system in Haryana and Rajasthan. *Eastern Anthropologist.* 45:87-103.

Frawley, D. 1994. Planets in the Vedic literature. *Indian Journal of History of Science.* 29:495-506.

Kak, S. 1986. *The Nature of Physical Reality*. New York: Peter Lang.

_____. 1987. The Paninian approach to natural language processing. *International Journal of Approximate Reasoning.* 1:117-30.

_____. 1990. Kalidasa and the Agnimitra problem. *Journal of the Oriental Institute* 40.51-54.

_____. 1994. *India at Century's End.* New Delhi: VOI.

_____. 1994a. *The Astronomical Code of the Rgveda.* New Delhi: Aditya.

_____. 1994b. The evolution of writing in India. *Indian Journal of History of Science.* 28:375-88.

_____. 1995a. The astronomy of the age of geometric altars. *Quarterly Journal of the Royal Astronomical Society*. 36:385-96.

_____. 1995b. From Vedic science to Vedanta. *The Adyar Library Bulletin.* 59:1-36.

_____. 1996a. Knowledge of planets in the third millennium B.C.E. *Quarterly Journal of the Royal Astronomical Society*. 37:709-15.

_____. 1996b. Reflections in clouded mirrors: selfhood in animals and machines. *Learning as Self-Organization*, edited by K.H. Pribram and J. King Mahwah. NJ: Lawrence Erlbaum.

Kanigel, R. 1991. *The Man Who Knew Infinity: A Life of the Mathematical Genius, Ramanujan.* New York: C. Scribner's.

Kulaichev, A.P. 1984. Sriyantra and its mathematical properties. *Indian Journal of History of Science* 19.279-92.

McClain, E.G. 1978. *The Myth of Invariance.* Boulder: Shambhala.

Sarma, K.V. 1985. A survey of source materials. *Indian Journal of History of Science* 20. 1-20.

Seidenberg, A. 1978. The origin of mathematics. *Archive for History of Exact Sciences.* 18:301-342.

Sengupta, P.C. 1947. *Ancient Indian Chronology*. Calcutta: University of Calcutta Press.

Staal, F. 1988. *Universals.* Chicago: University of Chicago Press.

van Buitenen, J.A.B. 1975. *The Mahabharata*, vol. 2 Chicago: University of Chicago Press.

van Nooten, B. 1993. Binary numbers in Indian antiquity. *Journal of Indian Philosophy.* 21:31-50.

Venkatesananda, S. (tr.), 1984. *The Concise Yoga Vasishtha* Albany: State University of New York Press.

Chapter 20

Science & Technology in India A Critical Look

M.A. Pai

The development of Science and Technology in India can be looked at in three different time frames: the first includes the period from Vedic times until 1800 C.E.; the second covers the colonial period until 1947; and the third is the period since independence. There are, unfortunately, not many resources to fall back upon to get an overall perspective. Perhaps the best one is a succinct publication by the Indian National Science Academy, *Science in India*, (Mukerji & Subbarayappa 1984) which gives an overview of Indian science from Vedic times up to the eighties. (For a discussion of Vedic science, see Kak, this volume.) My goal, in writing this chapter, is twofold: first, I would like to review the developments in science and technology in India; secondly, I would like to examine the extent to which these developments have been successful in improving the life of the common individual, and then, to analyze the reasons for their success or failure.

One could argue, perhaps justifiably so, that very few countries of the size of India have accomplished comparable results in this century given the fact that India has done this within the framework of a democratic system similar to that of many Western countries. There are certain sectors in the economy which have performed much better than others. For any visitor to India, the gradual worsening of the infra structure, in terms of roads, electric power, water, sanitation, and so on, stands in stark contrast with the achievements in atomic energy, space, defense, agriculture, and to a certain extent, the computer software sector. In the course of my discussion here, I will attempt to provide insights into some possible corrective strategies for improving the infrastructure.

This chapter is organized as follows: Following the distinction of the three periods of Indian science and technology in India, I will first touch upon the traditions of Indian science from 1000 B.C.E. until the advent of British colonial rule; I will then review the impact of the British rule in creating certain scientific institutions and a scientific temper, which, in retrospect, seems critical to what India has done since 1947. My outline of the third period will highlight the creation of the science and technology infrastructure, thanks, largely, to Jawaharlal Nehru who perceived that science alone could liberate India from its economic and social ills. The work of his successors will also be discussed. Finally, I will touch upon the impact of economic liberalization since 1991 on science and technology. There are different perceptions of economic liberalization. One has to view it as the continuation of the other three periods of science in India. It is difficult to be judgmental at this point, but any serious student of economic development cannot simply look at foreign investments as the panacea for a nation's problems. In Western countries, foreign investments have been accompanied by competition within the country, such as that within the automobile industry in the USA. Only future events will tell whether such forces will be unleashed in India and if true market forces will emerge.

Science in India Until 1800

The existence of Indus Valley Civilization and elsewhere in the Indian subcontinent is the earliest evidence that science had its early beginnings in the Indian subcontinent. Perhaps the only concrete conclusion one can come to from the excavations is that people at that time had a good concept of geometry and of town planning. Then in the eighth century, there was good interaction between Arabic and Indian scholars. Brahmagupta's works were translated into Arabic and it was during that period that the Hindu system of decimal enumeration was explained by the Arabic scholars, thus giving the popular perception in the West that the concept of zero is an Arabic invention. In the ninth and tenth century, the Indian medical knowledge and surgical practices such as those of the great medical scholar Susruta were also well known in the Arabic world.

Mathematics flourished from the fifth century onwards from the works of Āryabhata who gave the value of *pi* as 3.1416 to Brahmagupta (seventh century C.E.) whose contribution lies in the solution of equations. Trigonometry also flourished in this period and much of this knowledge made its way to the West through the Arabic scholars.

Astronomy was another science in which Indian mathematicians excelled during those years. In the early centuries of the Christian era, astronomers like Varāhamira (sixth century C.E.) who dealt with planetary motions, Aryabhaṭa I who postulated the concept of the rotation of earth on its own axis, and Brahmagupta who wrote voluminous works on mathematics and astronomy were some of the leading people of science.

In the field of medicine the two great classics, *SuḍŪruta Samhita* and *Charaka Samhita* contain an extensive body of knowledge about various aspects of medicine and surgery. Between the thirteenth and fourteenth century, the Unani medicine flourished under the Mughal rule and co-existed with Ayurvedic medicine. In the area of technology, metallurgy constitutes an achievement of high profile as witnessed through the iron pillars in Delhi, the temples of South India and the cave temples of Ajanta and Ellora.

The advent of paper in the twelfth and thirteenth centuries possibly imported from Central Asia enabled many manuscripts to be written mostly in Sanskrit. Some of the interesting and fascinating acoustical monuments such as the "musical pillars" of the temple at Hampi, the whispering gallery in Gol Gumbaz in Bijapur can be placed roughly in the time period between the thirteenth and fourteenth century. Man and the environment co-existed in a harmonious fashion. This helped the assimilation of Western science beginning in 1800. However it is also clear that innovation seemed to have tapered off due to a variety of factors ranging from lack of interaction between craftsmen, lack of teamwork, casteism and successive invasions from the Northwest. It is during this period that Western influence started in the form of trade initially in 1600 and then in the form of conquest in 1757 and colonial rule for nearly 200 years.

Science During Colonial Rule

The first Western colony in India was established by the Portuguese in Goa in 1510. They had no substantial impact on science in India. Beginning in 1608, when the East India company was first formed in Surat, there was a slow but steady impact of Western science on India in several stages. Initially confined to trade, after consolidating political power in 1757, the British began creating a number of scientific organizations in India. According to Nehru, India was a highly developed manufacturing country exporting her manufactured goods to Europe and other countries. The ship building industry was flourishing and was as advanced industrially as any other country prior to the industrial revolution. When the machine age began in England, Indian goods continued to pour into England and had to be stopped by very heavy duties and in some cases by outright prohibitions (1946). Further, Nehru asserts that the arrival and subsequent domination of the East India company could not have happened at a worse time for India (1946: 285). It was during the Company's ascension when the West began to benefit from the fruits of the industrial revolution which somehow bypassed India, either intentionally because of the supremacy of the trading class or due to the inherent social structure of India. Again to quote Nehru,

> It is clear that however highly organized its pre-industrial economy was, it (India) could not compete for long with products of industrialized countries. It had to industrialize itself or submit to foreign economic penetration which would have led to political interference. As it happened, foreign political domination came first and this led to a rapid destruction of the economy India had built up, without anything positive or constructive taking place (1946).

Nehru, who shaped India's science and technology policy after independence, was deeply aware of this historic confluence of events which influenced his view about science in India.

Colonial rule, as we shall see later, carefully nurtured several basic scientific areas in India such as Botany, Zoology, Geology, Meteorology, and Astronomy—mainly for the benefit of the ruling class; but in the process, the spirit of scientific inquiry also permeated the Indian mind. *Science in India* contains details of these scientific pursuits and their impact on the West.

The Royal Botanic Garden of Sibpur (W. Bengal) was started in 1787 by the British, and with its 15,000 trees, provided a rich resource for research in the West. The Botanic Survey of India (1890) was responsible for making it possible for several exotic plants of commercial importance such as rubber, tea, potato, coffee, cinchona, and spices to take firm root on the Indian soil.

In the field of agriculture, there was little effort by the British to encourage farmers to produce, leading to the notorious Zamindari system which is still prevalent in some of the poorest parts of India. In 1943, the famine in Bengal, which was similar to the 1770 famine in Bengal and Bihar, wiped out a third of the population. Lack of a proper food policy led to the stagnation of food grain production between 1900 to 1930 (Nehru 1946). There were a number of other factors such as lack of proper social structure, World War II and the consequent disruption, and unfavorable weather which contributed to the 1943 famine. This again led Nehru, after 1947, to enact both land reforms and inject science into the agricultural sphere.

After 1857, when the British consolidated their political position in India, a systematic effort was made to develop several areas of science and technology education as well as the infrastructure. In 1857, the first three universities were established in Calcutta, Bombay, and Madras. In 1816, the noted social reformer, Raja Ram Mohan Roy, started a school in Calcutta to teach English to the Indians, initially called the Hindu College and later the Presidency College. Roy was one of the first Indians to imbibe the best in Western culture, as well as Christianity and other religions, and above all, a faith in science. He wrote to the Governor General emphasizing the need for education in "Mathematics, Natural Philosophy, Chemistry, Anatomy and other useful Sciences". He founded the Indian Press and was a proponent of a free press along with several other Englishmen. It also helped the other languages in India to disseminate their rich literature. Moreover, the early Christian missionaries in Bengal helped in the task. This progressive spread of education in English together with contact with English literature broadened the horizons of Indian intellectuals. All these eventually led, ironically, to the establishment of the Indian National Congress in 1885, which later was at the forefront of the Indian Independence movement.

In 1847, the first College of Engineering, named after James Thomson, Lt. Gov. of Northwest Provinces, was established at Roorkee; today it is known as the University of Roorkee. The first medical college was set up in Calcutta in 1835. The railway system, introduced after 1857, enabled, in some sense, the British to effect greater communication between the regions of the far-flung colony while it also ushered in the industrial age in India. The railway system, introduced by the British, served to integrate the country with its diverse cultures in different regions, especially after independence. Indian men of vision urged Indians to learn English and through it science, which in retrospect contributed greatly to India catching up with the West in the field of scientific and technical education. There were eminent scientists before the turn of the nineteenth century such as M. L. Sircar, Asuthosh Mookerjee, P. C. Ray, and J. C. Bose. M. L. Sircar founded the Indian Association for the Cultivation of Science which was to produce in the twentieth century the first Nobel Laureate of India, C. V. Raman. J. C. Bose's contribution to plant physiology was the forerunner for today's research in photo-chemistry and photosynthesis. These men of vision laid the foundations for later researchers. C. V. Raman's discovery of what is now known as the "Raman effect" awarded him the Nobel Prize in physics in 1930, and his later work on the nature of light is at the core of modern day work in lasers. Other prominent scientific researchers of pre-independence days were people like M. N. Saha (Astrophysics) and S. N. Bose (Bose-Einstein statistics).

The great mathematical gift that India gave to the rest of the world in recent times was Srinivasa Ramanujam, who unlike others mentioned earlier, had no formal university training. His genius was recognized by Professor Hardy of Cambridge who went out of his way to nurture his brilliance and got him to come to Cambridge to do some original work in number theory. Ramanujam became a Fellow of the Royal Society in 1918. He died at the young age of 33.

During the early part of the twentieth century, the British government recognized the brilliance of individuals in science and took practical steps to promote institutional growth. A number of institutes were created which were to become focal points of economic development in the post-independence era. Some of these were the Imperial Agricultural Research Institute at Pusa in Bihar (1903)(shifted to New Delhi in 1935), the Forest Research Institute in Dehradun (1906), the Indian Statistical Institute (1931) and the Bose Institute (1917) both in Calcutta, the Haffkine Institute at Bombay (1899), and the Indian Association for the Cultivation of Science in Calcutta (1876). In the private sector, J. N. Tata established the Indian Institute of Science in Bangalore (1911). While the focus was mainly on science, Karnataka (then Mysore) produced a visionary engineer, M. Visveswarayya, who through his commitment to excellence, transformed the state of Mysore into a showcase for all-around industrial development including multi-purpose dams for irrigation and power. It is interesting to note that these activities in science ran parallel with the nationalistic movements of Tilak, Gandhi, and Nehru. Hence, a transition to systematic development of science and technology in the post independence era became an easier task.

Following the creation of scientific institutions, it was also felt that to better disseminate research findings, it was important to have professional societies as well. As a result, the first Indian Science Congress was held on January 15-17, 1914 in Calcutta under the auspices of the Asiatic Society of Bengal. The Indian Mathematical Society (1907), the Institution of Engineers (India) (1920), and the Indian Botanical Society (1921), to name a few, were established in quick succession. In 1935, the Indian Science Congress Association established the National Institute of Sciences of India

(NISI) in Calcutta. This was to become later the premier science association in India, namely the Indian National Science Academy (1939) in New Delhi.

What we have seen so far are largely unplanned and even sporadic achievements in science in India prior to independence, mainly accomplished by individuals with a passion for research. Nevertheless, they contained the essential ingredients for planned development. Then 1947 saw the partition of the Indian subcontinent into India and Pakistan.

Science and Technology after Independence

The achievements in science and technology prior to 1947 were largely at the individual level, but nevertheless attained international recognition; the achievements after 1947 were directed more towards institution building and, on a planned basis, geared toward the economic well-being of a large country. Even before independence, the Indian National Congress had a National Planning Committee under Nehru in 1939. It was clear in the late 1930s and early 1940s that independence was inevitable for India. Hence people like Nehru had clear ideas as to how they would harness Indian science for fueling economic development. When independence was ushered in and Nehru became the first Prime Minister, there was a smooth transition into planned development for the country. Looking at the vast amount of backwardness, along with the social and religious divide, Nehru came to the obvious conclusion that a firm underpinning of science and technology was essential for India to move forward. India had chosen the Western model of a free, democratic, and secular society. The private sector in India was largely feudal in nature except for a few leading industrial houses. In the early years of planning, Nehru was influenced by the giants of Indian science like P. C. Mahalanobis, Homi Bhabha, and Shanti Swarup Bhatnagar. Mahalnobis helped Nehru with the drawing up of the first five year plan, setting up of the Indian Statistical Institute and started the internationally respected journal *Sankhya*. Nehru turned to Homi Bhabha for help in developing atomic energy for peaceful purposes which resulted in the creation of the Department of Atomic Energy. Bhabha's vision also foresaw the coming of the electronic revolution, and his report on electronics helped set up the Electronics Corporation of India Ltd. (ECIL), which was to play a key role in the development of low cost television sets in the country. As a policy, only when the Indian television industry was able to generate the required expertise, could collaborative ventures with foreign firms start. In the field of atomic energy, the Bhabha Atomic Research Center is the premier institute under the Department of Atomic Energy (DAE) and has various subsidiary units elsewhere in the country. A significant achievement has been the capability of the Indian industry to build an atomic power plant almost entirely on its own. Beginning with the Boiling Water Reactor (BWR) at Tarapur Power Plant, near Bombay, using technology from the U.S., and the Pressurized Water Reactor (PWR) using Canadian technology, at the Rajasthan Power Plant, the country has become completely self-sufficienct in the research and development of advanced technologies, as can be seen in such projects as the Fast Breeder Reactor (FBR) being developed at Kalpakkam in Madras. The systematic method in which expertise was developed in atomic energy was unfortunately not followed in the conventional energy sector. The result is that power blackouts have now become the norm rather than the exception. It is interesting to compare these two sectors and draw appropriate lessons for the future. One could argue that after the development of the Tarapur Power Plant and the Rajasthan Power Plant, the West imposed a virtual embargo on technology related to the atomic energy sector. The result was that the country looked inward for expertise and found it there in terms of manpower and innovation.

In the conventional energy sector, India started very well, with Bharat Heavy Electricals (BHEL) occupying a visible position. But under some pretext or the other, both the State Electricity Boards and the private sector went for virtual turn-key projects from abroad. The result was that though the projects came, knowledge acquisition did not. Also, when plants were being built with foreign loans such as those from the IMF or the World Bank, there were always technical clauses which prevented firms like BHEL from competitive bidding. With the exponential increase in demand for power in a rapidly industrialized economy with poor maintenance of the power grid, the power crisis today has become unmanageable.

It is argued by many that only foreign investments can turn the tide. This will solve the immediate short-term problem. However, in a sector like power, it is not merely the establishment of power plants but the whole process of the networking of the grid to maintain frequency and voltage within limits that is the key issue. It is here that the country has failed. One can only hope that the right lessons have been learned—long term planning and knowledge building.

In 1947, Nehru also relied on Shanti Swarup Bhatnagar, who helped set up the Council of Scientific and Industrial Research (CSIR), which has a chain of nearly forty laboratories spread across the country to do research and development in a wide range of disciplines. In many of these laboratories, both frontier type, and relevant research and development for the nation's needs are being carried out. Government laboratories all over the world have a tendency to become unwieldy and slow to transfer technology to the production stage. Since 1990, when the country entered the economic liberalization era, these laboratories have been mandated to become self-sufficient through industry support instead of assured government support. Recently, it has come up with a document called "CSIR 2001: Vision and Strategies" which has as its goal impressing the need to "emerge from the comforts of satisfactory under-performance into the demanding world of stretching objectives and high achievements". The building of the infrastructure, such as CSIR suggests, is an eloquent way to pay tribute to the vision of Nehru and Bhatnagar just as atomic energy development is a fitting memorial to Nehru and Bhabha.

There are many who will criticize Indian science and technology for its poor performance over the last five decades. But along with that, one should also praise the efforts of its numerous scientists who have worked under conditions far removed from the comforts of developed societies in the West, and yet have done credible research and development. It is this infrastructure that is the legacy of Nehru and which the nation can tap given the necessary mandate and support from the highest level.

Another person who made a qualitative change in the Indian science and technology scenario was Vikram Sarabhai. After the untimely death of Bhabha in 1966 in an airplane crash, Vikram Sarabhai took over AEC and then, because of his interest in cosmic rays, started the Space Science and Technology program. Today, the success of the Indian Space Research Organization (ISRO), with its many proud achievements in the space sector, is a matter of pride for the country. Its impact in the improvement of global communication, remote sensing, and weather forecasting has been phenomenal. As in the atomic energy sector, space technology is also a sensitive field with respect to interacting with advanced countries. The fact that ISRO succeeded, with most of its engineers drawn from engineering colleges and not the IITs, speaks volumes for the basically high quality of scientific manpower in India. The same comment applies to the even more sensitive area of missile development in the defense sector, where under the leadership of Dr. A. P. J. Abdul Kalam, the country has acquired great sophistication.

Nehru believed that the mainstays of the economy such as power, steel, heavy machinery, banking, and insurance must be reserved for the public sector, leaving other sectors such as the consumer and service industries to the private sector. He has been criticized by many for this policy of "mixed economy." Looking back, one can say that with efficient management skills, consistent with the democratic structure, India could have done as well as China with its rigid dictatorial style. The question then arises as to why India excelled in atomic energy, manpower development, space, and the defense sector while the results were mixed and even disappointing in other sectors. In the steel and power sectors for example, there is enough expertise in the country for design and production. But every time a big project comes up, the electricity boards and the private sector go abroad for expertise. This points to a failure in the mechanism of allocation of expertise that exists in India, and our bureaucratic structure. Not to address these lapses will only result in more foreign dominance of the private sector through collaborative efforts. These collaborations, as we shall see in the computer software area, do not add to knowledge acquisition which is essential for a country aiming at self-reliance.

It is a well known fact that the science and technology manpower build-up received a big boost after 1947. Basic science in India has had a tradition of research since the nineteenth century. But engineering and technology have lacked that tradition. With this in view, the five IITs were set up starting in the late 50s at Kharagpur, Bombay; Delhi, Kanpur; and Madras to complement the existing institutions such as the Indian Institute of Service, University of Roorke, and Banaras Hindu University. Each of the IITs profited vastly from their interaction with the advanced countries in the world and through this collaboration produced excellent graduates and maintained high standards. Of these IITs, Kanpur made the greatest impact on the country's engineering curricula in two major respects: the introduction of the semester system and the course-wise promotion system which now has become the norm in the country, and the writing of high quality inexpensive textbooks subsidized by the National Book Trust of India. Another area where IIT Kanpur made a lasting impact was in the field of computer science education in India. Starting in the early 1960s with a series of short courses on computer programming using the IBM 1620 computer a computer science culture slowly developed in the country, and in 1978 IIT Kanpur formally started the Bachelor's degree program in computer science. In the 1970s, when IBM pulled out of India due to the government's restriction on foreign equity participation, many predicted a collapse of the computer industry. Curiously what happened was just the reverse. The Department of Electronics saw the big potential for India's participation in the software market. The country saw a phenomenal growth in the number of persons getting trained in computer programming. One could draw a parallel between this and the self sufficiency which has been achieved in the atomic energy and the space industries, where the country has been forced to look inward.

The expectations that the IITs would be the Cal-Techs or the MITs of India did not materialize because most of the graduates went to do their higher studies at schools like MIT, Berkeley, Stanford, Illinois, and other leading schools in the USA and Europe. In a democratic framework, this phenomena could not be checked, and it would not have been the proper move either. The country failed by not raising the level of the other technical institutions to the level of the IITs. Today, nearly 100,000 people take the IIT entrance exam for a mere 2,000 seats, i.e., about 2 percent of the students. By any standard 10 percent of the students are qualified to attend the IITs. Here again, one requires the vision to pull the country out of a slump. The same thing is true of primary education.

Since liberalization, there has been a tendency on the part of foreign trained Indians to return and set up high-tech entrepreneurial industries. But this is insignificant compared to similar efforts by expatriates of the Pacific rim countries. The political structures are different no doubt, but what one perceives within the country today is the lack of the vision of a Nehru or the past giants of science. A brief effort in the telecommunications field by Sam Pitroda at the Center for Development of Telematics (CDoT) in the mid 1980s showed what could be done with local talent. If foreign collaborations are allowed to proceed indiscriminately, then competition on a level playing field is impossible. The government must, with the help of carefully committed people in S & T, make proper decisions. The example of the U.S. Auto Industry is a classic one of how, through the use of carefully nurtured initiatives and measures, a country can rejuvenate an indigenous industry. Japan, Korea and China guard their own technological enterprises with great pride and concern. India has to learn the proper lessons from these examples.

Conclusion

In this chapter, I have attempted to take a critical look at science and technology in order to discuss where we have succeeded and where we have failed. While the science and technology infrastructure is in place thanks to the efforts during the first two or three decades following independence, it is not yielding the dividends that it should. One would hope that liberalization would unleash creative forces and make it possible for this infrastructure to be fully utilized whether through state means or through privatization. Privatization, with strict regulatory controls and oversight by a government free of corruption and bureaucracy, seems to be the best option at the moment. India is fortunate, compared to other developing societies, in terms of having free, democratic institutions with proper legal mechanisms in place. India also has the second largest English speaking population in the world. Moreover, the quality of manpower and talent are excellent. It will take vision, commitment, and self-confidence on the part of India to take a leading role in science and technology. There is certainly no dearth of expertise.

WORKS CITED

Mukerji, S.K., and B.V. Subbarayappa (eds.) 1984. *Science In India: A changing profile* New Delhi: Indian National Science Academy.

Nehru, Jawaharlal. 1946. *Discovery of India.* New York: John Day.

VI | Business & Economics

Chapter 21

India's Economy Over Five Millennia 3000 B.C.E. to 2000 C.E.

T.N. Srinivasan

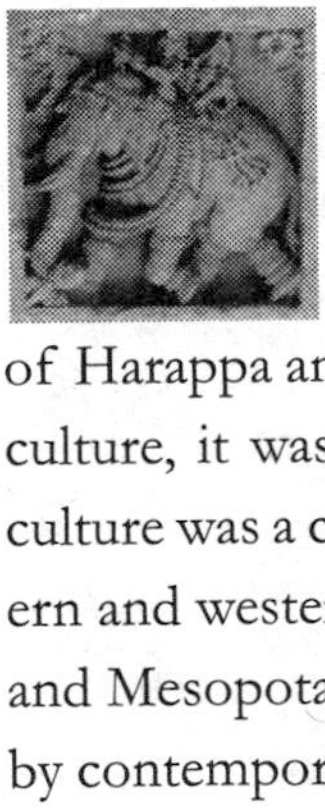

According to Thapar (1966), the earliest traces of human activity in India go back to the period between 400,000 to 200,000 B.C.E. A slow evolution culminated in the Indus Valley Civilization around 2500 B.C.E, which was revealed by excavations between 1921 and 1922 in the cities of Harappa and Mohenjedaro (now in Pakistan). Currently referred to as the Harappa culture, it was the most extensive of the ancient civilizations in area The Harappa culture was a city culture whose people engaged in a flourishing trade within the northern and western areas of the subcontinent, and also with peoples of the Persian Gulf and Mesopotamia (Thapar 1966: 24). Their level of living appears to have been high by contemporary standards (Lal 1988:16) (See S.R. Rao, this volume, for details).

The Harappa culture had declined and almost completely disintegrated by 1500 B.C.E. when the Indo-Aryans, with a pre-urban and less advanced culture, migrated in. The Aryans were initially divided into three social classes: the warriors, the priests, and the common people. For the Aryans:

> There was no consciousness of caste, professions were not hereditary, nor were there any rules limiting marriages within these classes, or taboos on whom one could eat with. The three divisions merely facilitated social and economic organization. The first step in the direction of caste (as distinct from class) was

taken when the Aryans treated Dasas [the indigenous people of Northern India, whom Aryans conquered and of whom they were contemptuous] as beyond the social pale (Thapar 1966: 37).

By the late Vedic period, Brahmans established religious sanctions to caste division. A brief digression on the caste system is in order because of its extraordinary stability. Lal's (1988) is the latest, and perhaps the most ambitious attempt to provide an economic interpretation of the caste system. In his view:

> Amongst human institutions, the caste system has been both unique and one of the most enduring...[It] was probably a second-best optimal response to the problems faced by the ancient Indians concerning (1) endemic political instability, (2) obtaining a secure labor supply for labor-intensive settled agriculture in the Indo-Gangetic plains, and (3) uncertainty concerning the outputs and inputs of the major form of economic activity—tropical agriculture—arising from the vagaries of the monsoon...[This] socio-economic system established by the ancient Hindus provided them with a standard of living which, though low by modern standards, remained high by the standards of bygone years for many centuries (Lal 1988: 72-73).

While abhorring the social and economic inequalities perpetuated by the caste system, Lal rightly focuses on the stability of the system despite attempts to change it. His analysis leads him to conclude that neither the Muslims, who failed to make any fundamental changes in the polity, society, or economy, nor the British who, "by the end of the nineteenth century...increasingly became an upper caste, on the traditional Indian form, endogamous, occupationally specialized, pollution-conscious (though its polluting objects were different), and with hierarchically arranged subcastes" (Lal 1988: 232), succeeded in reforming the caste system. Even the democratic leaders of independent India have failed in this respect as caste considerations continue to dominate contemporary politics (see Srinivas, this volume).

The epics Mahābhārata and Rāmāyaṇa are presumed to be concerned with events which took place between c.1000 and 700 B.C.E., but as the versions which survive date from the first half of the first millennium C.E. they can hardly be regarded as authentic sources for the study of the period to which they pertain (Thapar 1996:31).

> The evidence from these epics (to the extent borne out by other supporting information), taken together with the Vedas and Puranas, suggests a patriarchal society with an extended family as the basic unit and a simple standard of living. Houses were made of wood with thatched roofs and the staple diet was milk and *ghi* (clarified butter), vegetables, fruit and barley in various forms. On cer emonial occasions...a more elaborate meal was customary, including flesh of ox, goat and sheep, washed down with *sura* or *madhu*, both highly intoxicating...clothes were simple, most people wearing only a lower garment or cloak, but ornaments were more elaborate and clearly a source of pleasure to their owners. Leisure hours were spent mainly in playing music, singing, dancing, gambling, and chariot-racing for the more energetic (Thapar 1966: 41-42).

MAURYAN EMPIRE

Moving forward to the period of the Mauryas, from the accession of Chandragupta in 321 B.C.E., through Ashoka's reign [268-31 B.C.E.], to the decline and the ascendancy of the Sungas in 185 B.C.E., sources of information become more plentiful and reliable. First of all, following Alexander's invasion of India during 327-25 B.C.E., there were continuing political and commercial contacts with Greeks. Greek sources of this era provide significant, but not necessarily entirely reliable information. Second, we have the *Arthaśāstra*, attributed to Kautilya (also known as Chanakya or Vishnugupta). According to tradition, in order to avenge an insult by the then ruling dynasty of the Nandas, Kautilya "destroyed the power of the Nandas and placed Chandragupta Maurya on the throne of Magadha" (Kangle 1965: 59). As such, the date of *Arthaśāstra* is assumed to be the end of fourth century B.C.E.

"Arthaśāstra" means "the science of statecraft or of politics and administration" (Kangle 1965:2). Written long before Machiavelli's *The Prince,* which it is usually compared to, *Arthaśāstra* contains fifteen chapters dealing with the internal administration of the state, its relation with neighboring states, and several miscellaneous issues (Kangle 1965:19).

Space limitations preclude anything but a brief summary of the fascinating description in the Arthaśāstra of the economy, society, and state. The population of the sub-continent around this period is estimated to have been in the range of 100-181 million (Thapar 1966: 27). Three principal vocations of the population are recognized: agriculture (considered to be the most important), cattle-tending, and trade. All unoccupied land belongs to the state, while agricultural land is to be given to those farmers willing to pay lifetime taxes. If they fail to till the fields, land may be taken away from them and given to others, or even farmed by the state with the help of farm servants and traders. For farmers bringing land under cultivation for the first time, the state is to help with seeds, cattle, concessions and tax remissions and even cash. But this assistance is a loan to be recovered at the farmers convenience. While scholars debate whether all land belonged to the state, the text recognizes private ownership of land besides state owned land. Gifts of land to priests, preceptors and others are recommended as grants to Brahmins (*brahmadeyani*). This recommendation was followed in the Pallava and Chola empires of South India during 600-1200 C.E.

Building irrigation works is an important state activity, though privately owned irrigation tanks are also discussed. Udakabhāga or the irrigation rate of state provided water, is a fifth or a third of crop yield depending on whether water is lifted by hand or with the aid of bullocks or mechanical contrivance. The main tax on farmers is bhāga (portion or share) at the rate of one-sixth of the produce. The state is required to maintain a full record of all agricultural holdings with details about the different types of fields and crops raised in them. It is also expected to keep a strict watch over the sowing and the harvesting of crops to avoid being cheated of its legitimate dues.

All trade is under state control, with the panyādhyaksa "the superintendent of trade" in charge. He is to fix prices of various commodities after taking into consideration such factors as the investment of capital, interest charges, duties paid, rent, etc. A profit of five percent (presumably over costs) on indigenous goods and ten percent on foreign goods is allowed, with heavy fines prescribed for exceeding these limits. Apart from the private trader, the state itself is to engage in trade on a fairly extensive scale. All imported goods, normally are liable to a duty called ṣulka. But ṣulka also refers to excise duties on indigenous goods in addition to referring to customs duties on exports and imports. Besides engaging in trade, the state is expected to be active in mining, manufacturing industries, and above all in the textile industry. Interest rate on borrowing and lending is set by the state at one and half percent per month. (Interestingly this is the rate credit card companies charge currently in the United States!) A salary structure for ministers and other state functionaries is laid down, which, interestingly, recognizes that payment of an adequate salary was essential to prevent corruption and ensure loyalty.

It is hard to tell whether the precepts of the *Arthaśāstra* were in fact followed in practice. It describes a bureaucratic police state which has rigid control over the entire economy. That it presupposes economic planning by the state, as a few scholars have suggested, seems far fetched. Similar rigid controls appear in many ancient societies, including that of Egypt under the Ptolemys. It cannot be denied that in post-independence India, the state control over the economy was progressively extended in ways that bear an uncanny resemblance to those advocated in the Arthaṣastra.

End of Mauryas to the Delhi Sultanate

The period from the decline of the Maurya's to the establishment of the first Muslim Turkish sultanate in 1206 C.E. in North India, includes that of the classical Gupta dynasty (320-420 C.E.) and the reign of Harshavardhana during the seventh century C.E. in the North. Furthermore, there are several kingdoms such as the Chalukyas, the Rashtrakutas, and the Palas in the western and eastern parts of the peninsula as well as the Pallava, Pandya and Chola kingdoms of the extreme South. Several visitors (Fa-Hsien and Hsuan Tsang from China and Marco Polo from Italy, to mention just three) have left accounts of the life of the courts and the people of this period. Also, evidence from several inscriptions on copper plates, coins, and artifacts is available. Many battles and wars were fought and kingdoms rose and fell. The influence of Buddhism and Jainism waxed and eventually waned, while that of Hinduism was revived by popular (e.g. Bhakti) as well as philosophical (Advaita, Dvaita, Viśishtadvaita) movements originating from the South and spreading to the rest of the country. Also, the economy seems to have survived all these vicissitudes.

> The princely courts existed in states of great splendour, as did the great religious establishment. Considerable labor was employed in construction of great temples of medieval India, and we find in some areas the construction of vast tanks for irrigation...Foodstuffs, particularly grain, were transported over great distances... under the Pallava and early Chola dynasties...Coromandel, and under the Pala dynasty of Bengal, overseas trade was responsible for a great expansion of Hindu cultural influence in South-east Asia and Indonesia... (Digby 1982:47).

The Mughals

The period, starting from the first sultanate in 1206 C.E., through the rise and fall of the great Mughals, to the ascendancy of the British in the late eighteenth century, includes the rule of the sultanates in Delhi followed by the Mughals, the Vijayanagara kingdom in the South and the Maratha empire in the West and Central India. Lal summarizes the economic conditions of this period as follows:

> ...during times of peace and law and order the population was probably stagnant around 100 million, and levels of living during Akbar's time [1556-1605 C.E.] were probably not much lower than those of India at the time of independence in 1947. But over this long period there were obviously periods of famine, war, and disease...The most prosperous periods were the centuries of stability, the fourteenth and sixteenth...the sixteenth century probably returned India to the same levels of living that existed in the fourteenth... (Lal 1988: 86)

Following the historian T.G.P. Spear, Lal suggests that "the standard of living of the masses of the Indian people at height of the Moghul empire was probably comparable with that in Elizabethan England" (ibid: 85).

The British Period

The British period could be deemed to begin from Robert Clive's victory in 1757 at Plassey to end of India's independence in 1947. Many nationalists have argued that British imperialism destroyed the economy, prevented industrialization as well as rapid development. Others have claimed that without the British there would not have been a state nor a sub-continental common market called India or Pakistan. Clearly the legacy of British rule in terms of legal, administrative, as well as political institutions (albeit limited in their decision-making power and in their representativeness) was very important for post-independence India. The functioning of these institutions in terms of integrity, efficiency, and equity, regrettably has deteriorated since independence.

The economic achievements of the British era were decidedly mixed (see Bhattacharya, this volume). The population of the Indian sub-continent was estimated by the demographer Kingsley Davis to have been 125 million in 1750, which doubled to 255 million in 1871, the year of the first population census, and to 389 million in 1941, the year of the last census under the British (Visaria & Visaria 1983). Real per capita income (index, 1920=100) grew from 73 in 1868-69 to 104 in 1930, and fell to 101 by 1945 (Heston 1983). Heston reports that in terms of purchasing power parities, India's per capita income was almost twenty-five percent of that of the USA in 1869, only to *fall* to about seven percent a century later, suggesting that Indian income grew at a considerably slower rate relative to the growth of US incomes. Morris points out that "between the 1850's, when the first major industries started, and 1914, India had created the world's largest jute manufacturing industry, the fourth or fifth largest cotton textile industry...and the third-largest railway network" (Morris 1983: 553). Even after 1914, Indian industrial growth was rapid—the index of manufacturing production (1913=100) in 1938 was 239.7 in India. Only Japan's production index at 552.0 exceeded that of India. Others such as Canada, Chile, Italy, Germany, USA and the world as a whole had a lower index of production (Lal 1988, Table 8.5(B): 188).

Yet modern industrial processes did not spread easily from sector to sector, and the total effect was not cumulative. At the time of independence, India was still largely non-industrial and one of the world's poorest areas (Morris 1983:553).

Furthermore, Lal suggests that although the relative speed with which indigenous entrepreneurship and capital were organized to establish a modern textile industry under a regime of free trade and laissez-faire suggests that neither, in itself, held back Indian industrialization—there were areas, such as industrial training for the social promotion of industry which were neglected by the colonial authorities (Lal 1988: 218). He concludes that laissez-faire industrial policy was not socially justifiable...equally harmful...was the slow and inadequate provision of social overhead facilities (ibid: 218). Lal points out that there was a consensus among nationalist leaders, intellectuals, and businessmen "that laissez-faire was the root of all evil and central planning the new panacea" (ibid: 229). I turn next to this consensus and the roots of the post-independence development strateg

Origins of Post-Independence Economic Development Strategy

The very first attempt at formulating a plan for India's development was made by Sir M. Visveswaraya in 1934. He proposed *doubling national income within ten years* and argued that:

> The Indian problem is fundamentally industrial and should be solved by the same methods have proved efficacious in countries like the United States of America, Japan, and Canada, and latterly also with startling success in Soviet Russia ... India cannot prosper except through rapid industrialization... industrialization has to be organized, planned and worked for." He strongly advocated import substitution

in manufactured goods, particularly in staple products such as clothing, steel, sugar, and salt, arguing that "India may be an industrially developed country or it may be a market for manufactured goods from outside and not both" (Visveswaraya 1934: 351-353).

The National Planning Committee of the Indian National Congress, constituted in 1938 under the chairmanship of Jawaharlal Nehru, completed its work before Nehru and several of its members were arrested in October 1940. It declared that:

(1) The overarching objective of planning was to insure an adequate standard of living for the masses; in other words, to get rid of the appalling poverty of the people. The irreducible minimum, in terms of money, had been estimated by economists at figures varying from Rs. 15 to Rs. 25 per capita per month (at prewar prices) ... [To] insure an irreducible minimum standard for everybody, the national income had to be greatly increased, and in addition to this increased production there had to be a more equitable distribution of wealth.

A ten-year period was to be fixed for the plan, with control figures for different periods and different sectors of economic life. Certain objective tests were also suggested: (1). The improvement of nutrition—a balanced diet having a calorific value of 2400 to 2800 units for an adult worker. (2). Improvement in clothing from the then consumption of about 15 yards to at least 30 yards per capita per annum. (3). Housing standards to reach at least 100 square feet per capita. Further, certain indices of progress had to be kept in mind: (a) Increase in agricultural production, (b) Increase in industrial production, (c) Diminution of unemployment, (d) Increase in per capita income, (e) Liquidation of illiteracy, (f) Increase in public utility services, (g) Provision of medical aid on the basis of one unit for 100 population, (h) Increase in the average expectation of life (402-403).

(2) Industrialization was deemed to be the primary instrument for achieving the overarching objective: "the problems of poverty and unemployment, of national defense and of economic regeneration in general cannot be solved without industrialization" (401).

(3) Promotion of heavy industries and industries providing capital goods and universal intermediates was deemed vital.

(4) On large- versus small-scale industries also, the committee was clear in its emphasis on large-scale industry:... An attempt to build up a country's economy largely on the basis of cottage and small-scale industries is doomed to failure. It will not solve the basic problems of the country or maintain freedom, nor will it fit in with the world framework, except as a colonial appendage (413).

(5) The dominant role of the state and the public sector in industrial development was also spelled out in clear terms, "while free enterprise was not ruled out as such, its scope was severely restricted... defense industries... must be owned and controlled by the state". Regarding other key industries, state control would be sufficient. Such control of these industries, however, had to be rigid. Public utilities should be owned by some organ of the state (403).

(6) The committee also laid down the principles governing land and credit: Agricultural land, mines, quarries, rivers and forests are forms of national wealth, ownership of which must vest absolutely in the people of India collectively. The co-operative principle should be applied to the exploitation of land by developing collective and co-operative farms. If banks, insurance, etc. were not to be nationalized, they should at least be under the control of the state, thus leading to a state regulation of capital and credit. It was also desirable to control the export and import trade. By these various means a considerable measure of state control would be established in regard to land as well as in industry as a whole [while] allowing private initiative to continue in a restricted sphere (404).

(7) National self-sufficiency was declared to be a very important objective: The objective for the country as a whole was the attainment, as far as possible, of national self-sufficiency. International trade was certainly not excluded, but we were anxious to avoid being drawn into the whirlpool of economic imperialism (403).

The People's Plan of the Indian Federation of Labor also identified poverty as the central problem of the Indian economy (Banerjee et al. 1944). Its authors argued that lack of large-scale industrial development in India was due to the all-too-meager purchasing power of a large majority of its people and advocated for the development of agriculture and the provision of basic needs of the people within ten years. They also stressed the need for state control of banks and foreign trade.

The so-called *Bombay Plan*, put together by a group of businessmen, proposed doubling per capita income within a period of fifteen years with "the modest aim of securing a general standard of living which would leave a reasonable margin over the minimum requirements of human life." The minimum requirements of their plan included a balanced daily diet, modest amounts of clothing and housing per person, and some provision for education and health. The authors maintained "that every person above the age of 10 should be able to read and write and to take intelligent interest in private and social life is yet another of the constituents of a minimum standard of living" (emphasis added). They opted for a "more balanced economy" in which the predominance of agriculture would be reduced, while clearly recognizing its importance from the point of view of employment (Thakurdas et al. 1944: 9, 12-13, 22, 26 and 31).

The Bombay Plan also emphasized large scale basic or heavy industries, while at the same time recognizing that,

> consumption goods industries should be developed so as to meet at least our essential requirements...as far as possible, our industrial units [should be] on a scale which is not larger than is strictly necessary for economical working so that they can come into production within a short time and lend themselves more easily to regional distribution (Thakurdas et al. 1944:58).

A disciple of Mahatma Gandhi, Principal Shriman Narayan Agarwal, published *The Gandhian Plan of Economic Development for India* in 1944. He describes it in a later work (Agarwal 1960), as quite different in its conception and organizational framework from the others in that it advocated the least amount of state control and emphasized that without economic equality democracy cannot survive. As a Gandhian, Agarwal was for cottage industrialism and against large scale industrialization and mechanization. Some of these Gandhian ideas later manifested themselves in post-independence era planning in the form of subsidization of small scale and cottage industries, and restrictions on the expansion of large scale industries that competed with small scale industries.

Post-Independence Plans: Objectives and Policy Framework

The objectives of planning for national development as articulated in all pre-independence plans were incorporated in the sections of the Constitution of India adopted in 1950 dealing with the Directive Principles for State Policy. Furthermore, the resolution that established, the Planning Commission in 1950 also set for the Commission to "translate... the goals of social and economic policy prescribed in the Directive Principles of the Constitution... into a national program based upon the assessment of needs and resources" (Srinivasan 1992:116-117).

The First Five-Year Plan (1951-56) reiterated many of these objectives and policies. For instance, "the central objective of planning in India at the present stage is to initiate a process of development which will raise living standards and open out to the people new opportunities for a richer and more varied life" (7). Adoption of modern technology and rapid capital accumulation were deemed the key factors in promoting development. The dominant role of the state and the public sector in development was also reiterated with the argument that "a rapid expansion of the economic and social responsibilities of the State will alone be capable of satisfying the legitimate expectations of the people" (31-32).

Controls over production, prices, investment, and foreign trade were deemed essential:

> Viewed in the proper perspective, controls are but another aspect of the problem of incentives, for to the extent that controls limit the freedom of action on the part of certain classes, they provide correspondingly an incentive to certain others and the practical problem is always to balance the loss of satisfaction in one case against the gain in the other. For one to ask for fuller employment and more rapid development and at the same time to object to controls is obviously to support two contradictory objectives (42-43, emphasis added).

Although the First Five-Year Plan set the overall interventionist framework of policy, it was the second plan, authored by Professor P. C. Mahalanobis, that provided the analytical foundation for the development strategy that was pursued for the subsequent thirty-five years. It emphasized the development of heavy industries, import substitution across the board, and vast expansion of the public sector. The massive investment (relative to resources available for its financing) proposed in the Second Plan precipitated "a balance of payments" crisis. In response, an elaborate system of controls (that was expanded in subsequent decades) was put in place to enforce the plans and their underlying development strategy.

At its most expansive and inclusive, the system involved: *industrial licensing* under which the scale, technology, and location of any investment project other than relatively small ones were regulated and permission was needed to expand, relocate, and change the output or input mixes of operating plants; the *exchange control system* which required exporters to surrender their foreign exchange earnings to the Central Bank at the official exchange rate, and allocated the exchange earnings to users through *import licensing*; *capital issues control*, under which access to domestic equity markets and debt finance was controlled; *price controls* (complete or partial) on some vital consumption goods (for example, foodgrains, sugar, vegetable oils) and critical inputs (for example, fertilizer, irrigation water, fuel); *made-to-measure protection* from import competition, granted to domestic producers in many "priority" industries, including in particular the equipment producers. The agricultural sector was insulated from world markets, subject to land ceiling and tenancy legislation, and forced to sell part of the output at fixed prices; but it was also provided subsidies on irrigation, fertilizer and electricity. Large commercial banks, which were nationalized in 1969, were subject to directed and selective credit controls, controls on deposit and lending rates, and in effect had to lend nearly two-thirds of their loanable funds to government through the operation of reserve requirements of various kinds.

The crucial feature of all these regulations is that they were essentially *discretionary* rather than *rule-based* and *automatic*. Although some principles and priorities were to govern the exercise of these regulatory powers, they were largely non-operational for two reasons: first, it was impossible, even in theory, to devise a set of principles or rules for a large number of regulations, ostensibly meant to serve the multiple, and not mutually consistent, goals of the industrial policy; second, the problem of translating whatever rules there were into operational decisions was nearly impossible. The allocative mechanism was largely in the form of quantitative restrictions unrelated to market realities. Furthermore, chaotic incentive structure and the unleashing of rapacious rent-seeking and political corruption were the inevitable outcomes. Indeed, the discretionary regulatory system instituted in the name of planning for national development, instead became a cancer in the body politic. The indictments, for personal and political corruption, of former Prime Minister Rao, other ministers, civil servants, and politicians is ample testimony to this.

Another dimension to the exercise of regulatory power was that it was *anticipatory* in nature—that is, the regulations were meant to prevent any prospective deviation from the objectives of policy from ever occurring rather than to punish or cure any deviant behavior that actually occurred. While preventive, rather than curative, medicine is often preferable in health care systems, it is clearly not appropriate in industrial regulations. Yet in India, a system of *curative* health care and *preventive* industrial regulations has been in existence since the fifties!

Achievements and Failures Since Independence

It is sobering to review the achievements (see Table 1 at the end of this chapter) under four decades of planning for and extensive controls on economic activity.

First, the extent of poverty, that is, the proportion of the population with monthly per capita private consumption expenditure below a very modest poverty line has indeed gone down, from over half the population in the mid fifties to about a third in the late eighties and further to less than a fifth in 1993-94 according to official estimates. Most of the reduction occurred in the eighties during which period GDP grew over five percent per year as compared to around 3.5 percent per year in the previous three decades. Unfortunately, this spurt of growth was achieved by unsustainable fiscal expansion financed by domestic credit and external borrowing.

Second, in contrast to the targets for income growth of 5.5 percent to 7.5 percent per year in the various five year plans since the Mahalanobis second plan, national income only grew at an average rate of less than four percent per year in the forty-year period (1950-51 to 1990-91).

Third, self-sufficiency, at very modest levels of consumption, was achieved in a number of commodities including, notably, foodgrains.

Fourth, life expectancy increased from thirty-two years in the mid-forties to about fifty-nine years in the late eighties. The rate of infant mortality fell from over one hundred and seventy-five per one thousand live births in 1950 to under one hundred in 1990. Literacy rate rose from eighteen percent in 1951 to fifty-two in 1991. These achievements are modest in comparison to the achievements of other developing countries in South Asia (e.g. Sri Lanka) and elsewhere.

Fifth, industrial production, as measured by the general index, rose twelve-fold between 1950 and 1991. Although the share of manufacturing industry in the GDP rose modestly from about a sixth to a fifth between 1950-51 and 1990-91, its share in gainful employment changed much more slowly, with agriculture continuing to be dominant, and still accounting for over two-thirds of the labor force in the late eighties as compared to about three-fourths in the early fifties.

Sixth, the share of gross domestic capital formation in GDP almost doubled from 14.7 percent in 1950-51 to 23.6 percent in 1990-91. However, there was no commensurate increase in the rate of growth of the GDP, due to of the capital-intensive character of the investment.

Seventh, the public sector became dominant, with a share of the public sector (administration and enterprises) in the GDP exceeding twenty-five percent, and in the economy's capital stock exceeding about forty-five percent at the end of the eighties. All major banks and insurance companies were nationalized in 1969, and these banks accounted for over ninety percent of the financial sector's assets in the early nineties. While the public-sector banks have succeeded in mobilizing savings, extending banking to rural areas, and directing credit to "priority" sectors, the subsidies and defaults have become so large that the policy of subsidized and directed credit has become unsustainable, and the net worth of the banking sector has been eroded.

Eighth, with the emphasis on import-substituting industrialization, implemented through controls on foreign trade, India's share in world exports fell from its level which was above 2 percent at independence to about 0.5 percent in 1990.

The concern that the poor might not be sharing in whatever growth that was occurring emerged early on and led to the appointment, in 1960, of the Mahalanobis Committee on Distribution of Income and Levels of Living. Even more significant, in 1962 Pitambar Pant of the Planning Commission prepared a study for providing the basic needs of the entire Indian population in fifteen years (Srinivasan and Bardhan 1974, Chapter 1). Unfortunately, these laudable efforts did not lead to any rethinking of the development strategy.

Rao-Manmohan Singh Reforms: Origins and Rationale

Bhagwati (1992) has succinctly summarized the factors that explain Indian economic failure. He divides tham into three major groups:

> ... extensive bureaucratic controls over production, investment and trade; inward-looking trade and foreign investment policies; and a substantial public sector, going well beyond the conventional confines of public utilities and infrastructure.

The former two adversely affected the private sector's efficiency. The last, with the inefficient functioning of public sector enterprises, impaired additionally the public sector enterprises contribution to the economy. Together, the three sets of policy decisions broadly set strict limits to what India could get out of its investment (48). In Bhagwati's view, none of the rationales for the control system were "compelling in logic and all of them misguided, [their] costs were certainly considerable" (Bhagwati 1992:58).

These systemic failures were well known even prior to the initiation of the Rao-Manmohan Singh reforms. Indeed, Prime Ministers Indira Gandhi and Rajiv Gandhi had initiated hesitant and limited reforms. These in effect removed egregious distortions here and there, but left the basic control system intact. It is unlikely that coherent and systemic reforms would have come about, but for the acute crisis faced by the Indian economy in early 1991.

This crisis was brought about by several factors. First, was the unsustainable fiscal profligacy of the eighties that resulted in a large fiscal deficit of 8.3% of the GDP by 1990-91 for the central government alone, which doesn't include the deficit of state governments and the losses of public sector enterprises. Second, the Gulf War of 1991 raised the cost of imported crude oil, it substantially reduced exports to the Gulf area, eliminated remittances from emigrant Indian workers and resulted in expenditures on bringing them home. Third, with an unstable coalition government at the center, political uncertainties adversely affected the confidence of external creditors, including non-resident Indians (NRI). Therefore the rate of inflation rose to double digits; and the outflow of NRI deposits, the lengthening (shortening) of the lag between exports (imports), and corresponding foreign exchange receipts (payments), in anticipation of a devaluation, resulted in a steep fall in foreign exchange reserves to the equivalent of the cost of just two weeks of imports.

The government in power during the severe crisis attempted to abate through a series of draconian measures. As the Ministry of Finance (1992:10) put it, "by June 1991, the balance of payments crisis had become overwhelmingly a crisis of confidence in the Government's ability to manage the balance of payments. The loss of confidence had itself undermined the Government"'s capability to deal with the crisis by closing off all recourse to external credit. A default on payments, for the first time in our history, had become a serious possibility in June 1991."

Although it took immediate policy measures to avoid defaulting on external debt, the Rao government that came to power on June 26, 1991 recognized the long-term problems with India's economic management that underpinned development strategy of India's the previous decades. In July 1991, the government announced a series of far-reaching reforms which included: an initial devaluation of the rupee and subsequent market determination of its exchange rate; abolition of import licensing and quantitative restrictions (QR's) except on imports of manufactured consumer goods and some agricultural commodities; convertibility (with some notable exceptions) of the rupee on the *current account*; reduction in the number of tariff lines as well as tariff rates; reduction in excise duties on a number of commodities; some limited reforms of direct taxes; abolition of industrial licensing, except for investment in a few industries for locational reasons or for environmental considerations; relaxation of restrictions on large industrial houses under the Monopolies and Restrictive Trade Practices (MRTP) Act; easing of entry requirements (including equity participation) for direct foreign investment; and allowing private investment in some industries hitherto reserved for public sector investment. A National Renewal Fund for assisting workers currently employed in enterprises that would have to be scaled down or closed altogether was established. Reform of the financial sector included simplification of the interest rate structure with the elimination of interest rate floors on large loans, replacement of fixed term deposit rates by an interest rate ceiling, reductions in government preemption of loanable funds and monetization, and improving the capital position of the banks.

These reforms are systemic and conceived as a package of coordinated action in several areas. They go beyond liberalizing the more irksome controls at the margin, and are based on the realization that the benefits from reforming one sector could be limited if other related sectors are not also reformed.

Achievements of Reforms

A meaningful evaluation of policy reform is possible only by comparing the economy after the reforms are completed and have had their full and intended effect, to a counterfactual state in which the economy would have been, given the same economic environment exogenous to policy, if had there been no reforms. Such an evaluation is a daunting analytical task and is beyond the scope of this paper. The Indian reform process has been in place for only six years and is still incomplete. As such, while it is too soon to see the medium to longer term beneficial effects of reforms, recent economic performance will surely reflect, in part, the inevitable and unavoidable short-term costs. Over-interpreting recent trends is thus a danger. With these caveats, I proceed.

The Ministry of Finance (1996a, 1996b, 1997) provides ample evidence that the achievements, (See Table 2 at the end of this chapter) thus far, of economic reforms have been remarkable. The reforms have "led to a revival of strong economic growth, rapid expansion of productive employment, a reduction of poverty and a marked decline in inflation" (Ministry of Finance 1996b:1). Further, "the growth achieved in the post-crisis period was a noteworthy achievement by international standards and was more sustainable than the growth in the immediate pre-crisis period."
In brief,

• growth of GDP at factor cost, which had fallen to a mere 0.8% in 1992-93, accelerated significantly to 6.0% in 1993-94, 7.2% in 1994-95, 7.1% in 1995-96 and is estimated at 6.8% in 1996-97.

• industrial growth, after attaining 9.4% in 1994-95, accelerated to 11.7% during 1995-96. What is even more remarkable, is that the production of capital goods, which had been heavily protected in the pre-liberalization era, and had fallen for three years in a row after liberalization, grew by 24.8% in 1994-95, and by 18.2% during1995-1996. Unfortunately, because of a significant slow down in the growth of electricity generation, both industrial production and capital goods production slowed to 9.8% and 16.6% respectively during April-October 1996.

• wholesale price inflation, which exceeded 10% in 1993-94 and 1994-95, has slowed to 4.4% in 1995-96. It has since risen to over 7% at the end of 1996-97.

• growth in the value of exports in US dollar terms has ranged between 18.4% `and 20.8% in the three years 1993-1996. It has slowed considerably to 6.4% during the first 10 months of 1996-97.

• current account deficit as a proportion of GDP has remained below 2% consistently ever since as compared to 3.2% in the crisis year of 1990-91.

• foreign currency assets, which had fallen to less than a billion dollars at the height of the crisis, rose to $20.8 billion at the end of 1994-95 and has since declined to $17 billion at the end of 1995-96. It recovered to $19.8 billion at the middle of Jan. 1997.

• gross domestic savings as a proportion of the GDP, after falling by about 1.5% to 2.5% during 1991-94 from a peak level of 24.3 in 1990-91, has recovered to 24.9% in 1994-95 and 25.6% in 1995-96. However, gross domestic capital formation at 27.4% of the GDP in 1995-96 is slightly below the level of 27.7% in 1990-91.

These achievements are impressive. Yet there are some disquieting features in important areas and as yet unfinished tasks.

Remaining Tasks

Foreign Trade

Quantitative restrictions (QR's) on most imports have been abolished. But tariffs, despite recent reductions, are still high and non-uniform across goods. The budget for 1997-98 has set the maximum tariff rate at 40%. The weighted average import for is likely to be about 25%. These are high in comparison to most other developing countries in Asia.

Customs revenue has fallen from 3.9% of GDP in 1990-91 to 3.2% in 1995-96, which leads to fears that any significant further reductions in tariff rates will exacerbate the problem of bringing down the fiscal deficit. However, as the industrial sector grows rapidly, imports will *increase* and so will revenues, even at lower tariff rates. This would be the case, especially in consumer goods if quotas were to be removed. Thus such fears of a revenue loss seem exaggerated.

It is time to reconsider the rationale for restricting consumer goods imports. First, it makes no economic sense to restrict its imports of a good and deeming it a luxury, while at the same time raising the incentives for the production of its domestic substitute. Second, private demand prevented from being satisfied by luxury imports will be diverted to the purchase of domestic substitutes, thus exacerbating inflationary tendencies. Third, characterizing refrigerators, air conditioners, and consumer electronics as "luxury" goods, reflects prejudices and not any deep economic reasoning. It also ignores their dual use, i.e. use in production as well as in consumption and hence, disregards the positive productivity implications of their use in production.

Some fear that liberalizing imports in general, and consumer goods imports in particular, will lead to a surge of imports and create a balance of payments crisis which could abort economic liberalization. As long as the government observes fiscal and monetary restraint the pressure on the balance of payments will be contained.

Also the substantial real depreciation of the rupee since 1991 should restrain the demand for imports, even with the reduction of tariffs and elimination of QR's.

Imports of almost all agricultural commodities are subject to quantitative restrictions or canalisation. Only sugar, pulses, and some edible oils are allowed to be imported under a low tariff. Exports of rice and hard wheat are no longer restricted, while exports of coarse grains, pulses, coffee, oilseeds, edible oils, and sugar are. The trade regime, on the whole, still seems biased against agriculture. However inputs into agriculture, such as fertilizer, irrigation water and electricity are heavily subsidized and agricultural income is not subject to tax. Within agriculture the incentives delivered by the system vary across commodities, with some being significantly unprotected, while others are conferred high protection.

While protection of manufactures and the overvaluation of the rupee and its implicit tax on agriculture have been reduced, it is imperative that all *quantitative restrictions* (QR''s) on agricultural exports and imports are phased out. There are some commodities (fertilizers, jute, rice, sugar, tea) in which India's trade could conceivably affect world prices. While this calls for some flexibility in eliminating, altogether, government interventions in agricultural imports and exports, it does not argue for an indefinite continuation of QR's.

Finally, as trade policy is liberalized, with imports of all types of goods being freed, and international competition becoming an increasing reality on the Indian scene, there arises a need for making institutional changes to accompany and support the new regime.

Anti-dumping measures (ADM's) and practices are currently being used for protectionist purposes in the European Union (EU) and in the United States (US). While India must retain, or create, appropriate ADM's and institutions to implement them, purely as defensive and bargaining tools, she should join other developing countries in limiting the protectionist use of ADM's by strengthening the ADM discipline in the WTO [World Trade Organization]. Also, India will have to put in place safe guard procedures to handle the market disruption problems that can arise when imports are freed from restraints.

The recent changes regarding direct foreign investment (DFI) should be viewed in the context of global competition to attract DFI. Since India's past attitude towards DFI was hostile, until foreign investors begin to view the new welcoming attitude as credible and irreversible, DFI flows into India will continue to be modest, as compared to the flows into China, Malaysia, and Thailand, for example. In contrast to the goal of attracting $10 billion per year, the actual flows were about $2.1 billion in 1995-96, and $1.7 billion during April-December 1996. Portfolio flows were also of the same order. Credibility can not be achieved sooner if the draconian laws that controlled foreign exchange transactions in the past are repealed. As long as they remain on the statute books, investors could not reasonably preclude the possibility that the government might revert to their use at the slightest sign of a balance of payments problem arising again. The Finance Minister in his budget speech on February 28, 1997 has promised a new law consistent with full current account convertibility, and the objective of progressively liberalizing capital account transactions.

Once India makes a successful transition from an essentially inward-looking posture to an outward-oriented economy, India also has to ensure that global trading and investment opportunities remain maximally available. It is, therefore, in India's interest to support multilateral disciplines that could contain the outbreak of unilateralism by the stronger trading nations. Multilateralism is the best defense of the weak. But the fact that the tendency to create preferential trading arrangements, euphemistically called "free trade" areas (FTA), has gathered momentum since the conclusion of the Uruguay Round has to be recognized. After all, India itself is actively promoting a South Asian Preferential Trading Arrangement. Whether India's diplomacy, which in the past was cold to joining a grouping such as the Association of South East Asian Nations (ASEAN), should now be geared to seeking membership in larger regional blocs, such as Asian Pacific Economic Cooperation (APEC) forum, needs to be examined.

Industrial Sector

With the abolition of capacity licensing for most industries and the reform of import policies, by and large, most of the constraints on industry, imposed by the central government, have been relaxed considerably with the exception of the regulations under the Monopolies and Restrictive Trade Practices Act (MRTP). Since vigorous import competition and the threat of punishment for any proven restrictive practice should be more than adequate to prevent oligopolistic behavior, the MRTP regulations are largely unnecessary.

Privatization of public sector enterprises has made some progress with sales of their equity to the general public. However, selling only fractions of total equity to the private sector may not elicit the efficiency improvements in the management of such enterprises. While there are many relevant issues that ought to be examined, including whether a public enterprise should be restructured before privatization (see Seabright

1993), it is essential to announce a policy fully renouncing the creation of any new public sector enterprises in areas where the private sector will invest and where "security" or other social considerations do not require governmental ownership.

Without a change in labor laws and the creation of institutions to ease the adjustment problems of labor when retrenched, privatisation efforts will not make rapid progress. As Professor Mahalanobis (1969) pointed out long ago:

> in India... labor laws... are probably the most highly protective of labor interests in the narrowest sense, in the whole world. There is practically no link between output and remuneration; hiring and firing are highly restricted (Mahalanobis 1969: 442).

He suggested allowing enterprises freedom of hiring and firing, while setting up a Labor Reserve to absorb laid-off surplus workers, and to train them for other jobs while being productively used in the meantime (Mahalanobis (1961:157-158).

The operation of the National Renewal Fund, established to ease the adjustment problems of labor could, benefit from seriously considering the proposal of Mahalanobis. The policies and performance of state governments with respect to the provision of land, water, electricity, etc. to industry could, and do, inhibit industrial investment and output growth. Finally reforms of policies of state governments are sorely needed.

Agriculture

Four broad areas, other than foreign trade and agriculture, in which policy reforms are worth considering, are: (1) the public distribution system; (2) subsidization of agricultural inputs; fertilizer, irrigation and electricity; (3) agricultural credit.

Public Distribution System (PDS)

The PDS supplies specified quantities of foodgrains, edible oils, sugar, and kerosene at subsidized prices to holders of ration cards. The supplies for the PDS are procured through domestic purchases and imports by the Food Corporation of India (FCI), and state governments. Besides purchasing for the PDS, government also buys raw cotton and natural rubber, as well, under its price support program. The pressure for increasing procurement prices, year after year, have proved politically irresistible.

The direct budgetary costs of PDS have been growing. The central government alone has spent about 4%-5% of its total revenue expenditure on food subsidies during 1994-97. The inefficiency of FCI (its excessive staffing, inefficiencies in its purchase, storage and transport operations) is reflected in the budgetary subsidy. There are also implicit subsidies such as the cost of the preference given by railways to FCI, in the transportation of agricultural commodities, and concessions to FCI, in the interest rate charged on credit to FCI by the banks.

Ostensibly, the PDS is meant to be a "safety net" for the poor. Yet according to some unpublished estimates of Subbarao (1989), four Northern states in which 50% of India's poor live, accounted for only 10% of PDS supplies in 1990. Minhas (1990) finds that in 1986-87, over 60 percent of the population (rural and urban) did not avail themselves of the PDS in rice and wheat. Over 80% (resp. 70%) of the urban (resp. rural) population did not buy edible oils from the PDS. Only with respect to sugar and kerosene, did a large majority of the population use the PDS. Parikh (1993) reports that in the major states of North India more than 90% of the population do not purchase *any* cereals from the PDS. Further, the PDS was not particularly well targeted. Except in Andhra Pradesh and Kerala, the subsidy from PDS purchases was a very small proportion of the expenditure of the poor on cereals. The PDS was not cost effective in reaching the poorest 20% of the households, with less than 30% of the amount spent on subsidies reaching the poor.

The PDS, while not being cost-effective in reaching the poorest, supplied the same commodities to the non-poor, also at subsidized prices. Effective targeting of the PDS to the poor, through some open and transparent procedure, could be entrusted to local bodies (at the village or block level). Kerala seems to have reduced, if not eliminated, the non-poor from access to the PDS through such targeting. Some other states have followed Kerala's example. Apart from poor targeting, the PDS also suffers from leakage of supplies to the open market from fair price shops. Some estimates put such leakages to a third of rice, wheat, and sugar offtake from the PDS and over a half of edible oil. In effect, these leakages are unintended transfers to the shopkeepers.

A well functioning PDS system will provide a safety net for the poor at the least cost to the state. If a perfect and cheap means test were available, providing income support to those identified as poor would, at once, relieve the government of intervening in any market, and would let the poor choose what they wish to do with their incomes. Of course the incentive aspect of such a scheme, inducing a smaller labor supply, could be serious.

If providing income support is ruled out, commodity based targeting through self-selection might still be feasible. For example, a PDS confined only to the distribution of coarse cereals is most likely to be used only by the poor. In any case sugar, and edible oils should be excluded from PDS altogether since the case for supplying them is extremely weak.

The cost of operation of the PDS should be minimized. A system of food stamps under which stamps are used to pay for part of the cost of commodity purchases from the open market should be considered. With the poor buying from the market, the government would not be involved in the purchase, transport, and storage of commodities. Thus, the FCI could be dismantled. If there is significant inflation in food prices, food stamps of fixed nominal face value would progressively lose part of their real value. But, with flexibility in the design of the scheme (for example, one could consider indexing the value of stamps by the prices of coarse grains or other such commodities bought only by the poor) such problems could be tackled. A move to food stamps, away from the present PDS, seems to be the most attractive approach. Even if it is deemed infeasible, it is still desirable to do away with the inefficient FCI by letting the private sector supply the quantity of grains needed for the PDS at the place and time needed and at a cost determined by competitive bids. By making the entire process of the call, receipt, opening, and acceptance of bids, as transparent and open as possible, and associating local representatives of the poor with it, possible abuses of the system could be minimized.

Apart from the PDS, the government has stood ready to intervene in markets to maintain a price floor (i.e., support price) and to stabilize prices. These interventions necessitated the operation of buffer stocks in some cereals, oil seeds, cotton, and natural rubber. Price stabilization is not necessarily desirable and, in any case, integration of India into the and world markets could stabilize prices. Even if it is deemed necessary to maintain domestic buffer stocks, such stocks could be acquired without direct public sector involvement in the purchase and storage, contracting out the acquisition and storage through a bidding scheme similar to the one suggested for the PDS.

Subsidies on Agricultural Inputs

The three major subsidies are with respect to fertilizers, irrigation, and electricity. In 1994-95, fertilizer subsidies amounted to 4% to the Central Government's total revenue expenditure! There is considerable evidence that even with an increase in fertilizer price to import parity levels, the marginal returns on fertilizer use would be attractive to farmers. Canalization of fertilizer imports should be eliminated and replaced with imports by traders. A modest tariff should be set which could be reduced in a phased manner or maintained, if India continues to import a significant part of world trade in the long run. Rationalization of the domestic fertilizer industry should also be considered in order to phase out high cost producers.

Even without providing for capital costs, current expenditures on irrigation system continue to exceed water charges. Given high returns to irrigation, raising water charges proportionately would not significantly reduce income to farmers from the cultivation of irrigated crops. Irrigation, which is the responsibility of state governments, is run by overstaffed and inefficient departments with no interest in recovering irrigation costs, since they have no access to the use of irrigation revenues. Since the capacity (administrative and political) of state governments to reform the irrigation system management is limited, not much can be expected in the short to medium run by way of major reforms. This is no reason, however, for not raising irrigation charges, significantly, while awaiting reforms.

Electricity use in agriculture has grown very rapidly. According to the World Bank, farmers have been heavily subsidized at a price that is less than half of the long-term marginal cost of supply. Electricity generation and distribution are largely the responsibilities of State Electricity Boards (SEB's). The SEB's vary in the efficiency of their operations and maintenance of generation and transmission facilities. Electricity is supplied, free of charge, to farmers in states such as Tamil Nadu or at a very low price, in almost all others. Although there are a number of difficult issues involved in reforming the power sector while awaiting the resolution of those issues, the price paid by agriculturists for electricity could be raised in a phased manner.

Agricultural Credit

The major objective of agricultural credit policy, according to the Ministry of Finance (1996a), is to "enable farmers, especially small and marginal farmers, to adopt modern technology and improved agricultural practices" (p. 139). This same publication states that "though there is an overall increase in agricultural credit, yet there is a grave problem of overdues which has been inhibiting credit expansion and viability of the lending institution" (p. 139). Overdues, as a proportion of total agricultural advances of commercial banks, amounted to over 40% in 1994.

The share of institutional credit in total rural credit has increased, but still, informal credit continues to be very significant in rural areas. In the mid-eighties an average of only 27% of India's farmers were reported to have used cooperative credit, and only 4% of farmers used credit from commercial banks, while two-thirds of term credit went to large farms. Thus, it is clear that the objectives of agricultural credit policy are not being achieved.

Interference in the operation of the agricultural credit system is ubiquitous, with politically motivated periodic loan *melas* (festivals) and loan *mafis* (forgiveness)! "Cheap" credit is not an ideal instrument for rural poverty alleviation. Given that the lion's share of term credit and the interest subsidies accrue to the non-poor thus, pending reform of the financial sector, eliminating interest subsidies should be considered.

Infrastructure

The basic infrastructure (leaving aside irrigation and social sectors of education and health) consists of transport, power, telecommunications, urban water, and sewerage. All of these sectors produce goods and services that are not internationally traded. Scale economies, network externalities, long gestation lags in investment, non-rivalry and public goods aspects are involved as well. These facts raise difficult analytical and policy issues.

Power

Lack of reliable, relatively inexpensive power could significantly reduce beneficial output effects of economic liberalization. The entire gamut of issues relating to power generation, transmission, distribution, and pricing, and, above all, the extent of state involvement in the power sector need to be thoroughly reviewed. Power generation has been opened for private investors, domestic and foreign investors, and a package of incentives have been announced. Yet, as long as the price which private generators receive is controlled by the state, and issues relating to administered prices of fuels (such as coal and natural gas) and to controls on prices are charged to various classes of users of electricity are resolved, the response of private investors is likely to be constrained. While awaiting the results of a well designed study of the sector for instituting long term reforms, some of the subsidies, such as those relating to agricultural and household users of electricity, could and should be eliminated.

Transport

Railways and airlines (until recently) have been state monopolies. Goods transportation by road is almost entirely private, while public and private operations coexist in passenger transportation. Railway passenger fares and freight rates are administered prices, and cross-subsidization of passenger fares through freight rates could be significant. Railways are also required to favor the freight of the public sector over that of the private sector in the allocation of wagons. The phenomenal growth of freight movement over long distances in lorries, reflects to a considerable extent the cost, uncertainties, and other impediments associated with such movement on the railways.

In India, there is only a system of motor vehicle tax, and no tolls are levied on the use of the highway system. There is no link between the revenue from these taxes and the cost of the investment and maintenance of the highway network. The recognition that to meet the projected growth in road traffic, a massive investment in expanding and upgrading the National Highway network would be needed and that such an investment is beyond the capacity of the public sector, has led the government to seek private sector (domestic and foreign) participation in highway development on a build-operate-transfer basis for a period of thirty years. A National Highway Authority of India has been established. But a number of institutional and regulatory issues, particularly those relating to acquisition of land, are yet to be resolved.

A well-designed and forward-looking study of the social costs and benefits of the entire transport system should be undertaken immediately. Also, the administered prices of energy and policies, regarding energy inputs, have to be reconsidered. Also obvious irrationalities in rate structures and taxes should be eliminated. All the transportation subsidies should be made transparent rather than left implicit.

The state-owned Indian Airlines Corporation (IAC) is no longer a monopoly and faces competition from a few privately owned airlines. There are no compelling social arguments for not privatizing the IAC and Air India. Greater competition will come about if the domestic air transport sector is opened to foreign airlines, a step few countries are yet to take.

India's major ports are congested and the bureaucratic procedures for clearance of cargo are archaic. Limited privatization of ports has been initiated. But there is a long way to go before Indian ports are comparable to Singapore or Hong Kong in its efficiency of handling.

Telecommunication

Efficient telecommunications are vital for rapid and flexible response to changing economic environments. Indian telecommunications are far from being efficient and adequate. Network externalities are likely to be significant in this sector. Some steps have already been taken to allow private (domestic and foreign) investment in this sector. A National Telecom Policy announced in May 1994 provides for the participation of companies registered in India in basic telecom services. Guidelines for the entry of private companies into this sector have been announced, and licenses for the provision of services of various types have been awarded based on competitive bids. A Telecom Regulatory Authority has been established.

Fiscal and Monetary Reforms

The public sector consists of central, state, and local governments, as well as enterprises (departmental and non-departmental, financial and non-financial). Excluding local authorities and non-departmental undertakings of state governments, which together are not significant, the rest of the public sector spent more than they received so that the overall gap between outlays and current revenues was 11% of the GDP in 1994-95. As part of the stabilization program, the central government's fiscal deficit was to be brought down from 8.3% in 1990-91 to around 5% in 1992-93. The actual fiscal deficit for 1995-96 was 5.8%. It is estimated at 5% for 1996-97, and budgeted at 4.5% for 1997-98.

While the *overall developmental* expenditure of governments at all levels, as a proportion of GDP, came down from 19.8% in 1990-91 to 18.3% for 1994-95, non-developmental outlays, in fact, went up from 13.2% in 1990-91 to 13.9% in 1994-95. Besides, gross capital formation by the central government has remained virtually unchanged at 1.6% of the GDP. The Gowda government has accorded high priority to reducing the fiscal deficit. Hopefully any proposed reduction in government expenditure in *real terms* would not be targeted largely at *developmental expenditure.*

Reductions in real public investment expenditure, if uncompensated by such efficiency improvements or offset by increases in private investment, could seriously affect future growth. Avenues for reducing non-developmental expenditures should be explored before further reductions in developmental expenditures are envisaged. For example, there is room for examining the compensation and fringe benefits enjoyed by government and public sector employees. In an economy in which an overwhelming majority of workers in the agriculture and the unorganized sectors have no job protection or access to fringe benefits, India's provision to a microscopic minority is questionable. At the very least, the value of benefits enjoyed by government and public sector employees, as of now could be merged into their current salaries and such benefits could be abolished from now on until a scheme for social insurance (old age, health unemployment) for *all* workers could be instituted. Indeed the resources thus saved, if efficiently utilized in providing health and schooling to the poor, could result in benefits accruing to the poor, and not only to the not so poor. The report of the Pay Commission on wages and salaries of the central government employees, published in February 1997, has made several recommendations for reform.

Reduction in budgetary support to public enterprises is possible, though it would depend on the pace of privatization of some, and on efficiency improvements from rationalization in others. Articulation and effective implementation of what has come to be called "Exit Policy" is essential for accelerating the pace. With a thorough reform of the public distribution system, an exchange rate that is not overvalued, and reductions in the quantitative restrictions on foreign trade in agricultural outputs and inputs, food and fertilizer subsidies could be gradually phased out.

The Indian fiscal base is very narrow. The share of direct taxes in the total tax revenue of the central government was only 29% in 1994-95. While it may be administratively difficult to bring into the tax net several millions who would be potentially taxable, if the exemption limit were to be set very low, it could be argued that, even in India, widening the base and lowering the rate would be desirable. In the case of states, one of the direct taxes, namely land revenue, is no longer a major source of revenue. Given the fact the returns to land (net cost of cultivation) have risen substantially in the last four decades, and given that the implicit subsidies to irrigation, electricity, credit, and fertilizers received by farmers are likely to be phased out, if at all, only over an extended period of time. A strong case could be made for raising land taxes or reintroducing them where they have been abolished.

Nearly a third of the gross fiscal deficit of the central government in 1990-91 was monetized. Indeed through instruments such as the mandatory incremental cash reserve ratio (ICRR) and statutory liquidity ratio (SLR), the government has forced the commercial banks to hold a larger share of relatively low yielding government liabilities in their asset portfolio than they would otherwise have held.

Unlike in some developed countries such as the USA, the Reserve Bank of India is not free to formulate monetary policies on its own without being dictated by the central government. Thus, the central government has not been forced to trim its fiscal sails for fear of being unable to finance its deficits, at a low cost. The reform of the financial sector should not be viewed independently of the attempts to reduce the fiscal deficits and the reform of the fiscal system, but as an integral part of the reform of the public sector.

Future Prospects

Six years have elapsed since the systemic reforms were initiated by the Rao government. The achievements thus far with reforms have been encouraging. Growth has resumed on a sounder basis in the last three years. Above all, no political party of any consequence is advocating a return to pre-reform system of economic management. At the same time, it is also evident that there is no political consensus for accelerating and deepening the reforms.

The United Front (UF) government of Prime Minister, Deve Gowda, had committed itself to promoting faster growth and has categorically stated in its common minimum program that "there is no substitute for growth. It is growth which creates jobs and generates incomes...The country needs to grow at over 7% per year in the next 10 years in order to abolish endemic poverty and unemployment" (Business Standard, June 10, 1996). The UF is also "committed to bringing the fiscal deficit below 4% of GNP. The management of fiscal deficit will therefore enjoy the highest priority" (ibid).

There is a welcome recognition that the "economy cannot grow and the needs of the people cannot be met without more capacity in power: oil, telecom, railways, roads and ports" (ibid). However, instead than saying that the cumulative investment needs, at $200 billion, over the next five years is so large that "there is ample room for all modes of investment, public and private, domestic and foreign" and that "transparent rules and regulations will be drawn up to attract foreign investment and the award of contracts if any," (ibid) the UF program is silent on reforms in the provision of the needed infrastructure. In particular, it does not address the very serious problems of State Electricity Boards.

On the public sector, the program repeats the well-worn cliche that "the public sector will continue to be an important component of Indian industry." While acknowledging that "the public sector requires to be reformed and restructured" (ibid), it does not ask whether there is any social rationale for the public sector to be engaged in any given activity, and if there is, to see how it can be organized efficiently. Instead, the UF proposes to "identify public sector companies that have comparative advantage and will support them in their drive to become global giants. Other profit making companies will be strengthened" (ibid).

With respect to labor laws, the UF program seems also to put the interests of the labor aristocracy in the organized manufacturing and public sectors, before that of the overwhelming majority of the labor force. With respect to foreign trade and foreign investment policies, the UF program blows hot and cold: on the one hand, it recognizes the need for and welcomes, foreign investment but, on the otherhand, it tries to restrict sectors into which such investment would be allowed. Protection of small scale and cottage industries from import competition is also being promised. Unspecified reforms of the financial sector are proposed. Regarding the agricultural sector, poverty alleviation, public distribution of foodgrains, etc., the program does not reflect any deep understanding of the structural failures of the past.

The Finance Minister of the UF government, Mr. P. Chidambaram, acting as the Commerce Minister of the previous Rao government, was an active participant in the formulation and implementation of market-oriented reforms. In presenting the first budget of the UF government, he expressed his strong commitment to Common Minimum Program and asserted that the UF government has no usfor:

jobless growth; nor for growth that leaves untouched large sections of the people. We will remove controls and regulations over agriculture and industry. We will keep our economy open and competitive in order to encourage more foreign trade and attract more foreign investment. We will reform the tax system. We will broaden and deepen reforms of the financial and capital markets even while strengthening independent regulators like the Reserve Bank of India (RBI) and the Securities and Exchange Board of India (SEBI). Above all, we will observe fiscal and monetary prudence which is the key to low inflation and rapid growth.

The Minister claimed that two of the budget objectives were "to remain steadfast on the course of economic reforms and liberalization aimed at accelerating economic growth" and "to ensure fiscal prudence and macro-economic stability." But his budget in fact increased the subsidies on phosphatic and potassic fertilizers and extended those on tractors and power tillers to a larger proportion of farmers. The total outlay of subsidies on grain sold through the public distribution system and those on all the major subsidies (fertilizers, food and exports) together are to go up by 16% in 1996-97, compared to 1995-96. The minister has, however, promised a discussion paper, which lists all the subsidies, visible and hidden, so that the parliament can have an informal debate on subsidies. Although some import tariffs are to be reduced, a special across-the-board import duty of 2% has been imposed to raise resources for investment in infrastructure. The overall fiscal deficit is set to come down 5% of GDP in 1996-97, with a promise by the Finance Minister to "move along the path of reducing the fiscal deficit to 4%" in his next budget. The Minister also proposed the appointment of a high level Expenditure Management and Reform Commission to recommend steps for public expenditure management and control by the central government. It has yet to be appointed.

A number of incentives for foreign direct investment and foreign institutional investors have been included in the budget. Prime Minister Gowda, in his address at the meeting of world business leaders at Davos Switzerland in February 1997, assured business leaders that India needed, and welcomed, foreign capital and would do whatever was possible to remove obstacles to foreign investors. While the reduction in the surcharge on corporation tax and in capital gains tax should promote investment, the new "minimum alternative tax (MAT)" at about 12% on companies that would have paid no tax after availing of all the eligible deductions is certainly a dampener. Prices on the Bombay Stock Exchange have, in fact, responded negatively to MAT. The Finance Minister announced the initiation of steps to set up an independent Tariff Commission and the approval of a proposal, to establish a Disinvestment Commission to provide transparency to disinvestment procedures in public enterprises. Both have since been set up. The budgets for 1996-97 and 1997-98 do not advance trade liberalization and privatization to the necessary extent, other than to include any actions on the recommendations of the committee that enquired into the reforms of the public sector insurance monopoly.

To be fair, a common minimum program, being by definition the lowest common denominator of the political perspectives of a very diverse group of parties in a coalition, cannot be nothing more than a compromise lacking in coherence. Hopefully, in practice, common sense rather than ideology will prevail. The reality of the contemporary global economy is that without a considerable acceleration and deepening reforms, particularly in the areas of privatization, labor, and bankruptcy laws, infrastructural investment, India cannot hope to achieve the rapid and sustained growth needed to eliminate abject poverty, and will be left behind by other Asian countries. Fortunately the Finance Minister is clearly aware of this as evidenced by his budget speech of February 28, 1997:

> Our goal must be to achieve rapid and broad-based growth which alone can ensure higher employment, better living standards and a humane and just society. The challenges that we face today are not unique to India. Other countries, including our friends in Asia, have faced similar challenges. Japan showed the way. Other Asian countries are surging ahead. And, finally, there is the example of China, powering its way to becoming the second largest economy in the world. These countries have shown that with courage, wisdom and pragmatism they can find their rightful places in the world (Speech of the Finance Minister, Part B, February 28, 1997).

He concluded his speech with an apt quote from poet Rabindranath Tagore:

> Thy call has sped over all countries of the world. And men have gathered around thy seat. The day is come; but where is India? Does she still remain hidden, lagging behind? Let her take up her burden and march with all (ibid).

Table 1: Indian Economy 1950-1996

	1950-51	*1995-96*
GDP at Factor Cost (1980-82 Prices Rs. Crore)	42,871	274,209 [1]
Per Capita Net National Product (1980-81 Prices, Rupees)	1,127	2,573 [1]
Index of Industrial Production (1980-81=100)	18.3	283.3 [2]
Index of Agricultural Production (triennium ending 1981-82=100)	46.2	164.3
Gross Domestic Capital Formation (as percent of GDP)	10.2	27.4 [1]
Gross Domestic Savings (as percent of GDP)	10.4	25.6 [1]
Foodgrains Production (millions tonnes)	50.8	185.1 [2]
Wholesale price index (1981-82=100)	17	313
Exports (US $ millions)	1,269	31,797
Imports (US $ millions)	1,273	36,678
Population (millions)	362	916 [3]
Birth Rate (per thousand)	40	28
Death Rate (per thousand)	27	9
Male Life Expectancy	32.4 [4]	60.4 [5]
Female Life Expectancy	31.7 [4]	61.2 [5]
Total Life Expectancy	32.1 [4]	60.8 [5]
Male Literacy Rate	27 [6]	64 [7]
Female Literacy Rate (percent)	9 [6]	39 [7]
Total Literacy Rate	18 [6]	52 [7]

Notes:

[1] Quick Estimates.

[2] Provisional Estimates.

[3] Projection for 1995.

[4] Midpoint of 1941-50.

[5] Projection for June 1992.

[6] 1951 (for population age 5 and above)

[7] 1991 (for population age 7 and above)

Table 2A: Key Indicators in Absolute Values

	1990-91	1991-92	1992-93	1993-94	1994-95	1995-96	1996-97
Gross Domestic Product (Rs. thousand crore)							
At Current Prices	477.8	552.0	627.6	719.5	843.3	967.8 Q	NA
At 1980-1981 Prices	212.3	214.1	223.4	233.8	249.9	267.3 Q	285.3 E
Gross National Product (Rs. thousand crore)							
At Current Prices	478.2	542.0	615.8	731.9	858.3	985.8 Q	NA
At 1980-1981 Prices	208.6	209.8	218.7	238.9	256.1	274.2 Q	292.9 E
Agricultural Production	192.2	188.5	151.5	157.3	165.0	164.3	169.2 A
Foodgrain production (million tonnes)	176.4	168.4	179.5	184.3	191.5	185.0	191.2 A
Industrial production (1980-1981 = 100)	212.6	212.5	218.9	232.0	253.7	283.3	291.2
Electricity generated (TWH)	264.6	287.0	301.1	323.5	351.0	380.1	291.5
Wholesale price index (1981-1982 = 100)	191.8	217.8	233.1	258.3	286.8	299.5	319.8
Consumer price index for industrial workers (1982 = 100)	201.0	229.0	243.0	267.0	293.0	319.0	349.0
Money Supply (M3) (Rs. thousand crore)	265.8	317.5	366.8	434.4	531.4	601.8	655.5
Imports at Current Prices (Rs. Crore)	43198.0	47851.0	63375.0	73101.0	89971.0	122678.0	97111.0
(US $ million)	24075.0	19411.0	21882.0	23306.0	28654.0	36678.0	27453.0
Exports at Current Prices (Rs. Crore)	32553.0	44041.0	53688.0	69751.0	82674.0	106353.0	85623.0
(US $ million)	18143.0	17865.0	18537.0	22238.0	26330.0	31797.0	24205.0
Foreign current assets (Rs. Crore)	4388.0	14578.0	20140.0	47287.0	66006.0	58446.0	71210.0
(US $ million)	2236.0	5631.0	6434.0	15068.0	20809.0	17044.0	19847.0
Exchange rate (Rs. /US$) (Period Average)	17.9	24.7	28.9	31.3	31.4	33.4	35.4

Table 2B: Key Indicators in Percent Change Over Previous Year

	1990-91	*1991-92*	*1992-93*	*1993-94*	*1994-95*	*1995-96*	*1996-97*
Gross Domestic Product (Rs. thousand crore)							
At Current Prices	16.9	15.5	13.7	16.2	17.2	14.8 Q	NA
At 1980-1981 Prices	5.3	0.08	4.3	6.0	6.9	7.0 Q	6.7 E
Gross National Product (Rs. thousand crore)							
At Current Prices	11.9	13.3	13.6	16.0	17.3	14.8 Q	NA
At 1980-1981 Prices	4.9	0.6	4.2	6.0	7.2	7.1 Q	6.8 E
Agricultural Production	3.0	-1.9	4.1	3.8	4.9	-0.4	3.0 A
Foodgrain production (million tonnes)	3.2	-4.5	6.6	2.7	3.9	-3.4	3.3 A
Industrial production (1980-1981 = 100)	8.3	0.0	2.3	6.0	9.4	11.7	9.8
Electricity generated (TWH)	7.8	8.5	5.0	7.4	8.5	8.3	3.5
Wholesale price index (1981-1982 = 100)	12.1	13.6	7.0	10.8	10.2	4.4	7.6
Consumer price index for industrial workers (1982 = 100)	13.6	13.9	6.1	9.9	9.7	8.9	8.7
Money Supply (M3) (Rs. thousand crore)	15.1	19.4	15.7	18.4	22.3	13.2	10.6
Imports at Current Prices (Rs. Crore)	22.3	10.8	32.4	15.3	23.1	36.4	12.8
(US $ million)	13.5	-19.4	12.7	6.5	22.9	28.0	4.4
Exports at Current Prices (Rs. Crore)	17.7	35.3	21.9	29.9	18.5	28.6	14.9
(US $ million)	9.2	-1.5	3.8	20.0	18.4	20.8	6.4
Foreign current assets (Rs. Crore)	-24.2	232.2	38.2	134.8	39.6	-11.5	21.8
(US $ million)	-33.6	151.8	14.3	134.2	38.1	-18.1	16.4
Exchange rate (Rs/US$) (Period Average)	7.20	27.20	14.90	7.70	0.10	6.10	5.60

Works Cited

Agarwal, S. N. 1960. *Principles of Gandhian planning.* Bombay: Kitab Mahal.

Banerjee, B. N., G. D. Parikh and V. M. Tarkunde. 1944. *People's plan for economic development of India.* Bombay: Indian Federation of Labor.

Bhagwati, J. 1992. *India's economy: The shackled giant.* Oxford: Clarendon Press.

Bhagwati, J. and T. N. Srinivasan. 1993. *India's economic reforms.* New Delhi: Ministry of Finance, Department of Economic Affairs.

Central Statistical Organisation. 1995. *National accounts statistics 1995.* New Delhi: Government of India Press.

Chopra, A., C. Collyns, R. Hemming and K. Parker. 1995. *India: Economic reform and growth.* Occasional Paper 134. Washington, D.C.: International Monetary Fund.

Digby, Simon. 1982. *Economic conditions before 1200.* In T. Raychaudhuri and I. Habib (eds.) *Cambridge economic history of India. Volume 1.*Cambridge: Cambridge University Press. 45-47.

Heston, A. 1983. *National income.* In D. Kumar (ed.) *The Cambridge economic history of India. Volume 2.* Cambridge: Cambridge University Press. 376-462.

Kangle, R. P. 1965. The Kautilya Arthaśāstra. Part III. Bombay: University of Bombay.

Lal, D. 1988. *The Hindu equilibrium. Volume 1.* Oxford: Clarendon Press.

Mahalanobis, P.C. 1961. *Talks on planning.* Indian Statistical Series No. 14. Calcutta: Statistical Publishing Society.

_____. 1969. "The Asian Drama": An Indian view. Sankhyā: *The Indian Journal of Statistics.* Series B. 31.3-4.

Minhas, B. S. 1990. *Brief notes on access to subsidized food and social services in India.* Washington, D.C.: World Bank (processed).

Ministry of Finance. Government of India. 1992. *Economic Survey 1991-92.* New Delhi: Government of India Press.

______________. 1993. *Economic Survey 1992-93.* New Delhi: Government of India Press.

______________. 1996a. *Economic Survey 1995-96.* New Delhi: Government of India Press.

______________. 1996b. *Economic Survey 1995-96*: An Update. New Delhi, Government of India Press.

______________. 1997. *Economic Survey 1996-97.* New Delhi: Government of India Press.

Morris, M. D. 1983. *The growth of large-scale industry to 1947.* In D. Kumar (ed.) *The Cambridge economic history of India. Vol. 2.* Cambridge: Cambridge University Press. 553-676.

Naoroji, D. 1901. *Poverty and un-British rule in India.* New York: Swan Sonnenschein and Company.

Nehru, J. 1946. *The discovery of India.* New York: The John Day Company.

Parikh, K. S. 1993. *Who Gets How Much From PDS: How Effectively Does it Reach the Poor.* Bombay: Indira Gandhi Institute of Development Research (processed).

Planning Commission. 1951. *The first five year plan.* New Delhi: Government Printing Office.

_____ 1964. *Report of the committee on distribution of income and levels of living. Part 1.* New Delhi: Government of India Press.

Seabright, P. 1993. *Infrastructure and industrial policy in South Asia: Achieving the transition to a new regulatory environment.* Washington, D.C.: World Bank (processed).

Srinivasan, T. N. and P. K. Bardhan. 1974. *Poverty and income distribution in India.* Calcutta: Statistical Publishing Society.

Srinivasan, T. N. 1992. Planning and foreign trade reconsidered. In S. Roy and W. James (ed.) *Foundations of India's political economy.* New Delhi: Sage Publications.

_____________. 1996. Indian economic reforms: Background, rationale, achievements, and future prospects. Forthcoming in G. Rosen et al. *India's new economic policy: Liberalization and regionalization.* JAI Press.

Subbarao, K. 1989. Improving nutrition in India. World Bank Discussion Paper 49. Thakurdas, P., J. Tata, G. Birla, A. Dalal, S. Ram, K. Lalbhai, A. Shroff and J. Matthai.

__________. 1944. *A plan of economic development of India.* London: Penquin Books.

Thapar, R. 1966. *A history of India, Vol. 1.* Baltimore Maryland: Penquin Books.

Visaria, L. and P. Visaria. 1983. Population (1757-1947). In D. Kumar (ed.) *The Cambridge economic history of India. Vol. 2.* Cambridge: Cambridge University Press. 463-532.

Visveswaraya, M. 1934. *Planned economy for India.* Bangalore: Bangalore Press.

Chapter 22 | Indian Trade and Finance: A Historical Perspective

Prakash Tandon

Celebrating India's fiftieth year of Independence is a good occasion to look back and forward. Paul Valery said: he who looks deepest into the past looks farthest into the future; Kirkegard said: the past is to be understood but the future is to be lived in.

Of added interest to us is that after four decades of economic vacillation, in the 1990's we decided to go into the future with a policy of liberalization. When Rajiv Gandhi first announced economic liberalization in 1989, the *London Economist* said that it was a good and timely step forward, but he should consider giving the Indian economy freedom. Historically, whenever Indians have gone abroad, they have prospered because they have been able to exercise their initiative in an environment of freedom; give the same freedom in India they will be just as prosperous.

First, let us go back into the deep past of India's trade, finance, and economy. The early Indus Valley civilization goes back to Mohenjodaro and Harappa, mainly a city culture, 3000-1500 B.C.E, spreading over half a million square miles, from the Indus plain to Delhi, Kalibangan in Rajasthan and the Lothal port in Kathiawar. It did a flourishing inland and maritime trade with the Persian Gulf and beyond, areas north and west of the Indus river, and Hindukush mountains, forming a large cultural-trading complex. Its undeciphered inscribed seals numbering about two thousand, small, flat, square or rectangular in shape, with a human or animal pictorial motif, appear to have been the tokens of merchants, and were possibly used for trading in country produce in the cities.

About 600 B.C.E, the early tribal organizations gave way to kingdoms and monarchies. The Nandas, sometimes described as the first empire builders of India, inherited the large kingdom of Magadha and extended it to distant frontiers. In 321 B.C.E, they were succeeded by the Mauryas, who raised the Aryans to imperial heights. The Mauryans developed a fiscal and administrative structure based on a treatise on government and the economy ascribed to Kautilya's (also known as Chanakya) *Arthashastra*. Kautilya was the chief adviser of Chandragupta, and helped him evolve a strategy for both defeating the Nandas and establishing his empire and consolidating its economy and wealth.

The empire ultimately spread beyond the sub-continent to the north and northwest. Ashoka is supposed to have founded Srinagar in Kashmir, while Khotan in Central Asia is said to have been a part of the Mauryan Empire. The Mauryan economy, based on agriculture and its surpluses, acquired strength and sophistication. Trade was helped by efficiency in administration, while the crafts gradually grew into small industries. The sale of merchandise was strictly supervised: the manufacture date was stamped on all articles and prices were controlled for consumers' protection; the toll was one-fifth of the value of the commodity and the trade tax one-fifth of the toll, a total of 24 percent. Moreover, tax evasion was heavily punished.

In the subsequent period of fragmentation and disunity, until the Imperial Guptas in 320 C.E., India enjoyed a greatly expanded export trade and a flow of wealth due to the increasing demand for its products from the Roman and Chinese empires; it was a period too of intellectual and artistic growth. According to Romila Thapar,

> Through all the political vicissitudes of the Shungas, Satavahanas, Indo-Greeks, Shakas, Kushanas, Cheras and Cholas, the merchant continued to grow from strength to strength. The Mauryan Empire had opened up the subcontinent by building roads and attempting to develop a uniform system of administration. The occupation of northwestern India by non-Indian peoples was advantageous to the merchant, since it led to trade with regions which had as yet been untapped. The Indo-Greek kings encouraged contact with Western Asia and the Mediterranean world. The Shakas, Parhians and Kushanas brought central Asia into the orbit of the Indian merchant and this in turn led to trade with China. The Roman demand for spices and similar luxuries took Indian traders to South-East Asia and bought Roman traders to southern and western India. Through all of

> India the merchant community prospered, as is evident from inscriptions, from their donations to charities, and from the literature of the time. Not surprisingly, the religions supported by the merchants, Buddhism and Jainism, saw their heyday during these centuries. However, this is not to suggest that economic activity was limited to trade, or that agriculture had decreased; the latter continued to yield revenue. But the boom in mercantile activity had brought those associated with commerce to the fore.

Dikshitar, in his *Indian Congress History*, summed up well the function of guilds:

> Just as village panchayats preserved self-government in the villages, the guilds preserved self-government in trade; but of course they learned to exercise their power well beyond their trading activities. After the Mauryan Empire, the guilds became an even more important factor in urban life, both in organizing production and in shaping public opinion. The vast majority of artisans joined the guilds, since it was difficult for them to compete as individuals against the guilds, which in addition offered social status and a degree of general security. With the increasing demand for particular commodities and the consequent necessity to raise their output, some guilds began to employ hired labor and slaves. The guilds had to be registered in the locality where they functioned and had to obtain permission from the local authorities to change their location. Artisans of no matter what craft could constitute a guild, and most crafts had their guilds, since these offered great advantages. Leading guilds were those of the potters, metal-workers, and carpenters. Their size can be gauged from the fact that even at an earlier period one wealthy potter, named Saddalaputta, had owned five hundred potters workshops; in addition, he had organized his own distribution and owned a large number of boats which took the pottery from the workshops to the various ports on the Ganges. With an increase in commerce, the major guilds were even larger.

The guilds fixed rules of work, the quality of the finished product, and its price to safeguard both the artisan and the customer. The guilds also controlled the prices of manufactured articles, and these either depended on the quality of the work or were calculated according to a fixed scale. The behavior of guild members was controlled through a guild court. Customary usage of the guild (*Srenidharma*) had the force of law. That the guild also intervened in the private lives of its members is clear from the regulation that if a married woman wished to join the Buddhist Order as a nun, she had to obtain not only permission from her husband but also from the guild to which he belonged.

Apart from the guild, there were other workers' bodies, such as workers' co-operatives. These generally included artisans and various crafts associated with a particular enterprise, for example, architecture—city building or temple building—was entrusted to cooperatives which had as their members specialized workers such as architects, engineers, brick-layers, and the like.

Trade Routes

The main axis of Mauryan trade was the Royal Road from Patna to Gandhara, connecting Charsadda, Kabul, Taxila, Hastinapur, Kannauj, Prayag, and Patna. It was always rebuilt fairly close to its original alignment, notably by Sher Shah Suri, 1540-45, who built *saris* providing amenities, and by the British from Calcutta to the legendary Khyber Pass, the road of Kipling's *Kim*. Today we call it Sher Shah Suri Marg, National Highway 1. From Taxila, routes connected it with central Asia, while the roads from Patala in Sind and Baryagaza (Bharoch) met at Ujjain and joined it at Mathura. It was connected with the south, and through Tamluk, a port in the Ganges delta, with Burma, the Coromandel coast, and Ceylon. Patna, Patliputra, the focal point at its height, was a city with so many foreigners that, according to Megasthenes, a municipal board was set up for proper care of the foreigners: "Among Indian officers are appointed even officers whose duty is to see that no foreigner is wronged." This is reminiscent of posters in Nehru's time reminding people that "Tourists are Our Guests."

The Indian rivers, Ganga, Yamuna, and Indus in the north, Narmada in the center, and Krishna, Godavari, and Kaveri in the south, were great navigable waterways. Capitals of kingdoms and cultures were founded on their banks, around which agriculture, trade, arts, and crafts flourished. Many well known peninsula ports connected inland centers in overseas trade: there are Satavahana coins, second century B.C. E-second century C.E., with four rigged sea going vessels. The Buddha says,

> Long ago ocean going merchants were to plunge forth upon the sea on board a ship, taking with them a shore-sighting bird. When the ship was out of sight of land, they would set this shore-sighting bird free, and it would go to the east, south, west and north and to their intermediate points and rise aloft. If on the

horizon, it caught sight of land, thither it would go, but if not, it would come back to the ship again.

The *Rg Veda* too mentions that "'Varuna, who knows the path of the bird flying through the air, he abiding in the ocean, knows also the cause of the ships." There is also a remarkable Vedic prayer for safe conduct at sea.

The Indian vessels, starting with coastal craft, gradually expanded trade with Malaya, the Persian Gulf, East Africa, and with the Mediterranean through the Red Sea, while the Persian Gulf was connected with Selucia and Babylon. According to Pliny, the largest Indian ship weighed seventy five tons, but there are accounts of even bigger ships carrying up to 700 passengers. The Arabs made use of the monsoon winds for sailing to western Indian ports, which was much faster than the coastal route and less hazardous as well.

By the end of the first century B.C.E, India had a network of trade routes: the highways and river valleys, river navigation with ferries, oxen, mules, and asses, camels in the deserts, coastal shipping, and sea travel. Externally, the overland routes connected India with central and western Asia, and with Indian trading stations and merchant colonies in Kashgar, Yarkand, Khotan, Turban, and others, and through the sea and land routes to the Mediterranean. In the east, trading connections extended to Malaya, Java, Sumatra, and Bali, especially to meet the Roman demand for spices and similar luxuries.

Exports

Ancient India had a more interesting and colorful variety of exports than today; it was a great source of exotic luxuries for the West. About 2000 B.C.E., the Indus Valley people had begun to spin and weave cotton and export it. A dyed fragment of cloth has been found at Mohenjodaro. India's diverse exports included slaves, animals, birds, tigers, lions, leopards, peacocks, monkeys, hides, leather, leather goods, precious wood products, fine cotton and silk textiles, jewels, pearls, furs, horns and tails, especially of the rhinoceros, tortoise shell, ivory, and clarified butter (*ghee*).

There was also re-export of imported products. Roman merchants used Indian middlemen for importing Chinese luxuries and spices through Assam and Burma and the sea route via Java, Sumatra, Bali, and Malaya, products that were greatly valued for their quality and elegance, especially as the Indian elephant's tusks were of better quality than the norm. Pearls came from the fisheries in the Indian ocean. Silk and yarn were imported from China, the yarn woven into very fine cloth, and re-exported. Indian merchants had established themselves in central Asia and the Old Silk Route, with establishments in Kashgar, Yarkand, Khotan, and so on.

Pepper, then used as a drug and digestive, and cinnamon were exported to Egypt, Greece, Rome, China, Arabia, and Persia. Other exports included plants and herbs from the Himalayas: aloes, nerd, costus, bdellium, reminiscent of serpina plant that provided the first heart medicine in the 1950s, and others for drugs, incense, ointments and medicines, dyes, indigo and sesame oil; rice to East Africa; wheat and cane sugar; a variety of timbers; ebony, teak for ship-building, black wood (*shisham*, rosewood) from Punjab, sandalwood, the Himalayan birch bark for writing paper, wrapping and wall covering bamboo.

Moreover, India was rich in minerals. Megasthenes said, "It has also underground numerous veins of all sorts of metals, for it contains much gold and silver, copper, iron in no small quantity, and even tin and other metals." Copper, iron and steel, the mineral fiber of asbestos, an incombustible material used in the sepulchers of rich Romans, precious stones and gems, diamonds, agate, carnelian, sapphire, quartz, rock crystals, beryl, lapis lazuli, garnets, and turquoise were exported.

India's trading partners through the ages had a balance of trade problem. Pliny complained that Indian trade was a serious drain on the national income of Rome. The trade was largely in luxury articles---spices, jewels, textiles, amusing animals, parrots, apes, and peacocks. Sir Thomas Roe's epigram that "Europe bleedeth to enrich Asia" represented a contemporary Western view of a much older phenomenon that had also disturbed the Roman Empire. The international drain of specie flowed from the West to the East, and hordes of Roman coins found in the ports of South and West India attest this. William Hawkins, who set up the first factory for the East India Company at Surat in 1608, said that "India is rich in silver, for all nations bring coins, and carry away commodities for the same; and this coin is buried in India, and goeth not out." The complaint was heard again in British Parliament two hundred years later when it was said that even an English housemaid wants to wear calico.

Imports

Horses (especially the Arabian), were an important import from the West, as were also silk, sesame, flax, linen, parchment, and exotic papers. Though liquor was distilled in India from a variety of sources—vine grapes, molasses, rice and sugarcane, wine, made from grapes and dates, was also imported from the West. Gold and gold coins were imported in large quantities from the gold fields and mines in Egypt and Siberia; silver too, especially from the Romans who had advanced the art and science of metallurgy; as well as rubies, topaz, and coral from Upper Burma. India did not have lead and brass and imported these for making coins. Copper, tin and lead were imported through Baryagaza. Other minerals that were imported were antimony and red and yellow sulfides of arsenic.

Early Money and Coins

The Harappans of the Indus Valley used agricultural products as their media of exchange as early as in 3000 B.C.E. The large granaries of Harappa and Mohenjodaro were replenished by a system of state tribute and served as a bank or treasury in the state economy. Their seals were regarded as tokens of merchants.

The later, pastoral, Vedic people used cows as the medium of transaction, and passages in the *Rg Veda* refer to the price of ten cows for an image of Indra , which a sage is said to have refused for even a hundred, a thousand, or even ten thousand cows. The fine for murder was a hundred cows; the Bharat army went to war to collect cows, and Indra sent his messenger to recover his stolen treasure of cows. Gavishta, literally the search for cows, came to mean "to fight." There is a story about Sunahsepa, a boy, being offered for sacrifice to Harishchandra by his father for a hundred cows; the grisly part of the story is that when no one came forward to fasten the boy to the stake, the father offered himself for another hundred cows and to sacrifice his son for yet another hundred. Fines for theft, the price of a bride, and *dakshina* (honorarium) paid to priests were in cows. The cow remained a medium of exchange till the middle of the fifth century B.C.E. when Pinion refers to the purchase of a cow by its tail—*go puchchka*--a custom whereby the tail of the cow was put in the hands of the purchaser or the *dan*, remnants of the practice of *go-dan* that is not yet dead. Stanley Wolpert's comments on the cow in his book, *A New History of India*:

Cows were so highly valued by Aryans that they came to be treated as currency and were paid to brahmans for performing religious services. The Vedic Aryans were, however, beef eaters and wine drinkers, as well as warriors. It is not clear exactly when the Indians began to consider the cow divine; it must have been a later development, or perhaps a pre-Aryan concept resurrected in transmuted from, since we can assume that the pre-Aryans worshiped the bull. Indians may thus have been the earliest people, though they would not remain the only ones, to worship their money, wealth, object of worship, provider of food, and of food, and perhaps its sanctity came from the rise in its economic value.

The Vedic people, looking for an alternative medium of exchange, began using an ornament called *nishka*, a form of necklace and a work of art. The *Rg Veda* refers to Ushas, dawn, as fashioning a *nishka*, wearing a garland. A distinguished scholar, Idyllic Aruni of Kuru-Panchala, is referred to in the *Gopatha-Brahmana* as travelling throughout the country with a challenge for a debate and an offer of *nishka* attached to his banner to the one who could defeat him. Even today in Varanasi during the month of Shravana, in Kajali (a seasonal song) competitions, parties of singers carry flags with paper money attached and challenge others, with the victor taking the winnings from the flags. In the *Atharva Veda,* a poet praises the generosity of his patrons who gave him one hundred *nishkas*, ten necklaces, three hundred horses, and ten thousand cows.

Gold in ingot form too acquired currency value according to the *Rig Veda.* it came from the sands of the rivers of South India and central Asia. Round metallic pieces called *satamana*, meaning a hundred units, are mentioned in the later Samhitas and the Brahmanas, between 1500-800 B.C.E. Two such pieces attached to a royal chariot at a coronation sacrifice ceremony were later given to the priest. There was another piece, *pada*, meaning one-fourth. In the *Brihadaranyaka Upanishad*, on the occasion of a philosophy conference, the most outstanding scholar received the prize of one thousand cows, each with ten *padas* attached to its horn.

While it is difficult to date the stages of the evolution of coinage from barter of produce, cattle, implements, seeds, shells, and others to ingots and pieces of metals of inherent value to coins, there is evidence that India, through Harappan and Vedic times, went through these stages of evolution both independently and perhaps earlier than elsewhere.

Early Banking

Money lending in India can be traced back to the Vedic period, although the details of money lending and remittance of money in cash or by credit instruments is available only from the fifth century B.C.E. onwards. The *Jataka* mention the existence of *seths* or bankers, and the *Smrithi* refer to certain legal rates of interest .

Usury was practiced, but was held in contempt. *Vashistha*, the law-giver, prohibited brahmins and ksatriyas from practicing it. Some form of credit machinery must have existed to finance the ancient maritime trade, which is mentioned in the *Jataka*, but all that is known is that money lending and trade operations were conducted by the *vanias*, the modern *banias*, derived from the Sanskrit *vanijya* or trade.

From the laws of Manu, recorded in the second and third centuries C.E., it appears that money lending and allied activities had assumed considerable importance and deposit banking in some form had come into existence. Manu laid down that A sensible man should make a deposit only with a person of [good] family, of good conduct and acquainted with the law, veracious, having many relatives, wealthy and honorable [Aryan]. . . . In money transactions interest paid at one time [not by installments] shall never exceed the double of the principle; on grain, fruit, wool or hair, [and] beasts of burden, it must not exceed five times [the original amount]. . . . Stipulated interest beyond the legal rate being against the law, cannot be recovered.

Before the indigenous banker came into existence, the custom seems to have been to hoard capital wealth or deposit it with a friend. Gradually, bankers and guilds began to receive deposits and hold them as trust properties. No definite information is available whether they received deposits on payment of interest or for safe custody only. The *Arthashastra* lays down definite rules for the hoarding and utilization of wealth on interest, but is silent on the subject of deposit banking. Most early bankers were, however, traders who combined trade with banking.

There is evidence to show that in all important trade centers of the Buddhist period, there lived many *sresthis* or bankers of great influence, who occupied prominent positions in guilds of commercial and industrial activities. Their main function was to finance traders, merchant adventurers, or explorers in search of valuable materials, and kings in times of war and financial stress. Lending money on interest was common, the loans being secured by mortgage, by pledge of movable, or by surety. The *Arthashastra* prescribed the maximum legal rate of interest on secured loans at 15 percent and that on unsecured loans at 60 percent without any discrimination as to caste; the rate might go up to 120 percent or 240 percent according to the risk involved, in special circumstances. The Dharma Shastras, though in general agreement with the *Arthashastra*, introduced caste as an important factor in money lending, expectedly to the advantage of the higher castes. Buddha's own attitude towards merchants was interesting: A merchant is like a honey bee who, sucks the honey from the flower but does not harm it.

Credit Instruments

Reference to the earliest known credit instruments is found in the *Jataka*, seventh to second Century B.C.E., of signet rings used as deposit or security, of wives and children pledged or sold for debt, and of IOU's or debt sheets. *Hundis*, the oldest surviving form of credit instrument, were widely in use as early as the twelfth century C.E. Indian bankers usually worked independent of one another, and the important among them had branches in different parts of their province and even outside, managed by *munims* or agents, whose honesty and integrity was proverbial. They readily helped members of their fraternity. Their establishments were small, efficient, and economical, their accounting procedures simple but accurate, with no auditing or balance sheets, and they were personally available to clients at all times of the day and night. Their borrowers were intimately known to them which made it easier to gauge their credit worthiness and keep a watch. They rarely failed to lend whenever there was a demand, and their readiness to meet any emergency gave confidence to the traders and the public. Deposits from the public, on current account or for fixed terms, were paid interest at rates varying between 3 percent and 9 percent, depending on such factors as the season, amount, duration, relations with depositors, and their own standing. Deposits were accepted under the *khatapata* system, but receipts given were only by the banker or the depositor when the money was deposited or withdrawn through a bearer (other than the depositor), who was of course known to the banker.

Hundis are of two types: demand, *darshani* or *dekhanhar*; and usance, *muddati*. *Darshan hundis* are payable on demand while *muddati hundis* are payable after expiry of the stipulated period. Both types may be *Shahjog*, payable to a shah or respectable person, or *Dhanjog*, payable to a *dhani* or the holder of the instrument. According to the law, *Shahjog hundis* must bear an endorsement in favor of the payee, but in practice, payment is made to a person of credit, and endorsement is immaterial.

Farmanjog and *jokhami* are two other forms of *hundis*. *Farman jog hundis* are payable on demand while *jokhami hundis*, which are drawn against goods dispatched, more or less resemble documentary bills of exchange and contain certain conditions in accordance with which if goods are lost or destroyed in transit, the drawer or the holder of the *hundi* has to suffer the loss. Payment of such *hundis* is made on safe receipt of the goods and their purchaser acts as a sort of insurance agent. With the growing service of insurance companies *Jokhami hundis* went out of use.

A *hundi* is usually followed by an advice which contains all the details of the *hundi*, including the date, the amount, and the payee's name. If the advice or *nakal* (meaning a copy or duplicate) is not received, the drawee may may keep the payment of the *hundi* in abeyance until such advice confirming it is received.

Though the dishonor of *Marwari hundis* has been a rare occurrence, the *sahukars* sometimes did take care of non-payment of *hundis* drawn by them upon persons of not a very high credit in the market, from whom they had to receive money. In fact, the dishonor of a *hundi* did more harm to the credit of the endorser than that of the drawer or drawee. Hence, at the time of selling their *hundi*, the endorser would mention the name of a party (residing at the place of payment of the *hundi*) on the face of the instrument, to whom it should be shown before it was treated as finally dishonored. The seller of the *hundi* generally mentioned the name of his agent or branch as *Sira Karna* or *Zikri*. The general form of the *Zikri* is *Hundi nikarne par Seth Juharmal Gambhirmal ne bata di o* (On dishonor show the *hundi* to *Seth Juharmal Gambhirmal*). The *Zikri chitthi* may be written on a separate slip of paper attached to the *hundi*.

Sometimes *hundis* were drawn between the merchants and their agents or *arahatiyas*: *Hamare Gharu* (on our own house) *hundis* were those drawn by a firm on its agents to cover transactions. Inversely, *hundis* drawn to cover transactions undertaken or any other work done on the advice of the agents were called *Tumhare Gharu* (on your house) *hundis*.

Later Banking

During the early dynasties of the Muslim period, *Multanis* and *shroffs* financed internal trade and commerce between different centers and acted as bankers to the Muslim rulers. It appears from the writings of a few Muslim historians, European travelers, state records, and the *Ain-e-Akbari*, that both under the early Muslim and Mughal rulers in India, indigenous bankers played a prominent part in lending money, financing internal and foreign trade with cash or bills, and giving financial assistance to rulers. Military contingents in the tenth and eleventh centuries were invariably accompanied by a banker or *gumashta* who disbursed salaries and pay of officers and *sepoys*. Exact information is not available about the rates of interest charged but it appears from available evidence that they were higher than those prescribed in Kautilya's *Arthashastra*. The Imperial Gazetteer records that Feroz Shah (1351-86) borrowed large sums of money from the banker Sasoti of Delhi for payment to his army. The soldiers of Delhi were paid by cash orders, *italaq*, in outlying places. These were discounted at Delhi by financiers who made a regular business of it and earned a good income.

"Indigenous" Bankers

The British commonly applied the term "indigenous bankers" or "indigenous" to all kinds of private bankers: money lenders, banking or money lending firms, with the distinction that the banker, be it an individual or a private firm, in addition to making loans, received deposits and dealt in *hundis*, clearly both banking functions; while the money lender, also an individual or a private firm, made only loans, and did not usually receive deposits or deal in *hundis*. The investors deposited their savings in a bank or lent it out, not as regular business, but merely to add to their principal income, while the money lenders lent their funds as regular business to earn interest.

Indigenous banking remained confined to certain known banking castes, principally the Vaishyas, then the Jains, both spread all over; the Chettis of Madras and Burma; the Marwaris of Rajputana and central India; the Shikarpuris and Multanis of Sind and Bombay; the Rathis or Bohras of Gujarat and the north-western part of the United Provinces; and the Khatris, who claim to be Kshatriyas of Punjab. The number of Mohammedan indigenous bankers gradually increased in the nineteenth and twentieth centuries, as more and more ignored the religious prohibition on receiving interest. In fact, a new class of Pathan petty moneylenders spread all over India, specializing in lending to factory workers. They stood outside the factory gates on payday and with their brawn and menacing looks managed to keep bad debts low and trade lucrative. They preferred to collect interest on a continuing basis rather than receive back the principal. But on the whole, Muslims did not go beyond money lending and that only in a limited manner.

The British Period

The early English traders in India in the seventeenth century could not make much use of the indigenous bankers because they did not understand their language, and the Indian bankers had no experience in the finances of the former's trade. Therefore, although the East India Company established connections with the bankers, borrowed funds from them, and for the first few years, collected a portion of the land revenue through them, the English agency houses in Calcutta and Bombay began to conduct their own banking business, besides commerce. The East India Company prevented the establishment in India of banking on Western lines, on the ground that agency houses and indigenous bankers were more suited to the needs of the country. As trade passed from the hands of private merchants to agency houses, the *baniya* became more than a mere factotum of private European gentlemen; he increasingly functioned as a guarantee broker and a financier. Subsequently, when the banking functions of the agency houses came to be performed by bankers themselves, the guarantee business of the *baniya* passed into the hands of *shroffs* or bill brokers, performing essentially the same functions in spite of a new name.

As the European servants of the Company were encouraged to do private business, many of them set up businesses independently after leaving the Company and amassed fortunes with both their own savings and borrowed funds. An early example was Captain Grindlay. Another was Richard Cox, who in 1858 was appointed army agent to the regiment of Foot Guards and soon became a recognized leading army agent and joined Henry S. King. Cox and Kings was acquired by Lloyds Bank in 1923 and thus entered the field of banking. Later, Lloyds and National Bank merged and this led to the National and Grindlay's Bank; even later, it became a part of the Australia and New Zealand (ANZ) Group of Australia.

Parkinson was critical of the banking activities of the agency houses:

> The British businessmen brought to their affairs neither capital and energy nor ability. They were not in a position to teach anything to the natives and introduced nothing that was novel in banking. They survived as long as they did only because they were able to inspire confidence in other white men. They borrowed from one part of the civil and military services of government at a high rate of interest, the portion of the salary they saved, and lent it at a still higher rate to others of the same establishment for a time, who required or wished to spend more than they earned; or they employed it at a higher rate of profit for great commercial or manufacturing establishments scattered over India. Those which continued to transact the business of banking, while carrying on trading activities at the same time, exposed themselves and their depositors to immense and unanticipated risks.

While Parkinson's opinion has much truth, the pioneering contribution of the British European agency houses and the Indian houses that followed, their contribution to the development of Indian industry, especially the entry of Indian houses into textiles and jute, infrastructure, plantations, and overseas trade, was significant. Admittedly, the English agency houses, as they entered banking, had little capital of their own, and they did not possess knowledge of modern European or conventional Indian banking so that the vicissitudes and trade crises that visited their agency businesses were wholly transmitted to their banking activities. Whenever an agency house failed, so did its bank. Yet, due to the Company's opposition to starting a bank, it was left to the managing agencies to take the initiative and fill the growing void.

The first bank was started by Alexander and Company, the *Bank of Hindostan*, as a department and counting house to finance foreign trade; it had no up-country branches nor made arrangements with indigenous banks, so that it was unable to transmit government revenue. While it successfully withstood three severe runs on it in 1791, 1819, and 1829, it failed when Alexander and Company itself failed in 1832. The Calcutta Bank, similarly established by Palmer and Company in 1824, failed in 1829 upon the failure of Palmer. A number of other banks of other agency houses shared the same fate. To relieve the distress caused by the crisis of the 1830s, Lord William Bentinck created a government agency to receive deposits at no interest. Its business was transferred to the Bank of Bengal in 1856.

Central banking as an idea emerged in India even earlier than the formation of the Bank of England in 1694. The idea was first mooted in 1683, but it took till 1935 to form the Reserve Bank of India. In 1773, Warren Hastings revived the idea when he proposed the establishment of the General Bank of Bengal and Bihar, the main features of which were elaborately worked out, even employing the serviCEs of Indian bankers. Warren Hastings, however, was in a minority on his own council, and in April 1774, the Court of Directors in London wrote to the Governor-General-in-Council, recommending CErtain changes with respect to the bank. While Hastings and Barwell opposed the changes, they were overruled by their own colleagues Francis, Monson, and Clavering, who succeeded in getting the resolution passed on February 15, 1775, providing for the closure of the bank. During its existence of about twenty months, it had realized a net profit of Rs 2 lakh, half of which had gone to the Treasury.

Sometimes opposed by the Court of Directors, at other times by the Council in Calcutta, and later by the managing agents and their banks in India, the idea of a central bank was thwarted right through the eighteenth century and beyond. In fact, in 1787, the Court even prohibited the authorities in India from lending their support to any banking institution in Calcutta.

In 1913-14, the Chamberlain Commission, in the absencof a consensus on the question of central banking functions as an integral part of currency and exchange, entrusted J.M. Keynes with drawing up a plan for the Commission's consideration. In his lengthy treatise, Keynes too suggested establishing a state bank by merging the three Presidency banks. The Commission felt that the matter deserved early consideration, but expressed its inability to comment favorably or otherwise on the proposal itself. The outbreak of World War I shelved the proposal.

Attempts to form a central bank continued to be as regularly made as they were defeated, but the inherent compulsion of the need for a central bank continued. In 1867, a similar proposal had been opposed by the government out of fear that it may itself be overshadowed by a strong financial institution, while in 1899, the merger proposed by the government had been opposed by the three Presidency banks. In 1919, the proposal was accepted by all concerned and the Imperial Bank of India was born in 1921, entrusted with the discharge of commercial and central banking functions. The concept of an apex central bank, an entity apart and by itself, remained unclear until the Royal Commission on Indian Currency and Finance, the Hilton Young Commission, recommended in 1926 that a central bank should be set up, called the Reserve Bank of India, to provide a unity of policy in the control of credit, as an entirely new institution, quite apart from the Imperial Bank. Like other central banks of the world, it would have the usual four rights: to issue notes, to hold reserves of the commercial banks, to buy and sell securities, and to discount bills. Like the Bank of England, the Reserve Bank was to be a shareholders' bank with a fully paid up capital of Rs 5 crore, but unlike it, with a view to ensuring for it beyond any manner of doubt freedom from political pressure and conduct of business on lines of prudent finance, a Director of the bank was not to be a member of the provincial or central legislative or a representative of any commercial bank. The Bank was to enjoy an assured life of twenty-five years, in the first instance, as compared with twelve years in the case of Bank of England at its inception in 1694. Finally, like the Bank of England, it was to work through two departments -- the issue department and the banking department.

When bill to form the Reserve Bank was finally introduced in the Indian legislature in the 1930's, it was the Indian members who opposed it, but in 1935, the proposal, stalled for 252 years, was finally adopted. Its history is worth recalling because the Reserve Bank is the hub of the nationalized banking system today.

Conclusion

In retrospect, there were three great periods of state permissiveness and encouragement of trade and the economy: the Mauryan, Akbar's Mughal, and the British. India's share of world trade must have been quite large in the centuries B.C.E., when with the exception of Indo-Roman, there was hardly any international trade elsewhere. Rome traded with India on behalf of Europe, and India for South-East Asia, including China, before the famous China Silk Route was developed. Much later, it was described in the typical superlatives of Marco Polo. Even during the British period, in 1938, the last year before the war, India's share of world trade was 3.8 percent which dropped 50 years later to 0.4 percent despite active state planning and regulation or perhaps because of it. Today, India's share is even less than that of some neighboring cities states.

India is ready to take a U-turn, and the leading world economies are waiting encouragingly for the Sleeping Tiger to wake up and again actively contribute to world trade and join the new process of globalization. Unfortunately, many among the political leadership and even the intelligentsia, have still not recovered from the trauma of a millenium of foreign domination; they are still afraid of the two and half centuries of the British period being replaced by American "neo-colonialism." Fortunately, they also realize that change is inexorable; it can only take India one way—forward.

Today, Indians may look into the future with the confidence that with a good endowment of natural resources of raw-materials, human talent, and finances, they are well equipped to advance. They have a remarkable assortment of excellent universities and institutions of higher learning —graduate, post graduate, research in the sciences and humanities, whose members are invited abroad. This has often been called the "brain drain," a misnomer because India has enough capability to meet her needs and that from abroad. Financially, Indians have a large spread of competent banking and financial institutions. Adding to these advantages is that despite its frailties, we have a democracy that has survived half a century with its legislative and elections processes well intact. Some of the world's leaders are coming to India to tap the potential of large demand backed by a high national savings rate, which, at nearly 25 percent is second only to Japan's. Interestingly, these organizations are looking for Indian talent that they can develop for their Indian as well as overseas needs.

Correspondingly, the Indian Americans in the United States are doing very well, with a per capita income at $26,000 (a few years ago), exceeding the national average of $21,000, and surpassing even the larger and older immigrant groups. More interesting, American-born Indians, about half a million strong, had a graduation percentage of approximately 70 percent compared with the American national average of about 28 percent.

India should, therefore, while remembering her past with its endowments and achievements, and learning from our half century of experimentation with democracy, planning, and socialism, go into the future with a confidence that she has great contributions to make. In the new global world, as Nobel Laureate Tinbergen said: there might well soon be a world ministry of finance and a world ministry of world health, today's World Bank and WHO. There will also be global enterprises. In this scenario, Indians should prepare themselves with a Global Indian Community.

Works Cited

Thapar, R.V. 1966. *A History of India.* Vol. 1. Harmondsworth: Penguin.

VII | Fine Arts & Architecture

Chapter 23

The Quest for Divinity in Indian Art

R.C. Sharma

Indian philosophy, literature, and art reflect, in different ways, the view that the search for the Divine is the goal of life. True success lies in their ability to lead us to a higher plane and awaken our consciousness after appreciating and realizing the significance of an object. Art has been described as the expression of thought in visual form. But the expression must be a result of the happy blend of beauty and spirit. Indian aesthetics does not confine itself to the outer form; the inward vision is more significant. It is this aspect which makes an art divine, Divya.

The Gītā reveals that all beautiful and glorious things are offshoots of Divine Splendor. Very often a divine aspect, like the soul, remains concealed and can be visualized by gifted eyes only. The vision to appreciate a creation of art is as necessary as the object itself. It is for this reason that Arjuna was graciously given the divine eye by the Lord Kṛśṇa to be able to see him in His cosmic form. Modern medical science, being based on matter, does not accept the spirit or soul which is beyond matter and which cannot be grasped by an instrument, howsoever advanced it may be, as the instrument itself is made of matter. To realize the soul or to listen to its message, we have to place ourselves on a pedestal of higher consciousness or a supermundane plane. If this is not done we are bound to confine ourselves only to the surface of beauty. We will miss the ocean of nectar, content only with a few drops of water.

There is Divinity in every object but we have to discover it. Sri Aurobindo's revelations faithfully unfold the characteristic of Indian art when he says:

> Indian art's highest business is to disclose something of the Self, the Infinite, the Divine to the regard of the soul, the Self through its expressions, the Infinite through its living finite symbols, the Divine through his powers. Or the Godheads are to be revealed, luminously interpreted or in some way suggested to the soul's understanding.... when this hieratic art comes down from these altitudes to the intermediate worlds behind ours, to the lesser godheads or genii, it still carries into them some power or some hint from above. And when it comes quite down to the material world and the life of man and the things of external Nature, it does not altogether get rid of the greater vision.... there is always something more in which the seeing presentation of life floats as in an immaterial atmosphere.
>
> (Aurobindo 1971:17)

The moods, modes, and movements of society are reflected in the mirror of art and architecture. The art of a country cannot be studied in isolation, it is interwoven with architecture. In art we view a single object, but in architecture we examine piece by piece. Stūpas, čaityas, temples, memorials, palaces are not just construction alone but are celestial specimens of art as well. They are richly engraved or decorated with sculptures, motifs, and flora and fauna providing an aesthetic feast to the onlooker. Here also the same principle of the quest for divinity applies. Enumerating the distinguishing features of architecture of different countries, Percy Brown rightly assesses that the Greeks were known for refined perfection, the Romans for scientific construction, the French for energy through Gothic style, the Italians during the Renaissance for scholarship of the age, but the Indians were known for spiritual content. "It is evident that the fundamental purpose of the building art was to represent in concrete form the prevailing religious consciousness of the people" (Brown 1956:1).

Agrawala (1965:4-5) elaborately dealing with this aspect is of the view that although art is a human creation (mānuṣī śilpa), it remains very close to divine creation (daivī silpa) because it is through divine inspiration that an artist creates a piece of art and it is adorned with divine beauty in its form (rūpa) and meaning (artha). Manifestation of and dedication to the Divine has been the main function of Indian art and architecture. In early India common people or even kings did not bother to put up a monumental building for residential purposes, hence such remains are extremely rare.

However, we have a large number of religious edifices either rock-cut or plain. To make them stronger and long-lasting a non-perishable medium was used replacing timber. This was the case with engravers, carvers, artisans, painters, and craftsmen too whose names remain unknown.

They considered their works as offering (naivedya) to the Divine. The convention continues from a hoary past, as the Vedic seer, after pouring each oblation into the fire ended with a hymn by saying idaṃ na mama meaning "it is not for me." Perfect devotion and a sense of self-sacrifice has been the foundation of religious and spiritual attainment. This is nicely explained in our scriptures. Do your work and never crave the fruit of your labor. One should care neither for name (nāma) nor for figure (rūpa) or their merits and demerits. Even when the concept of God and Soul remained subdued due to Buddhist and Jaina philosophical thoughts, the divine element continued and devotion was focused on the Buddha/Bodhisattva, Jinas, and other folk deities. Canonic literature and archaeological evidence supports this idea.

Merit earned by the installation of an image did not go to the self but to the Ācharyas, monks or parents. Sometimes it was for the welfare of the common people: the pedestal inscription of a Buddha image records that its purpose was the welfare of all beings by Yaśa, daughter of Grahadina (Mathura Museum No. 78.34). Similarly, a Jaina Āyāgapaṭṭa (tablet of homage) was set up in honour of the Tirthankaras by courtesan Vasu, the daughter of courtesan Lonasobhika (see Sharma 1994a:80-81). These are a few citations among the numerous sculptures unearthed from Mathura. Subsequently, the image was termed deyadharma (pious gift) to a religious place and it aimed at achieving supreme knowledge (lōkōttara jāña) by all (Sharma 1994:139). Thus even though God and Soul are not recorded, the divine aspect in the form of religious merit and supermundane bliss remained intact.

Basic Elements of Art

There are four basic elements behind the formation of an art object: rasa (aggregate form of human emotions or sentiments), artha (meaning), chanda (rhythm), and rūpa (form). These are common to literature and to a great extent to music also. Rūpa represents śabda (words) in the case of literature. Rasa is the most vital of these and very often it is expected to be the ultimate goal of art and literature. The Divine has often been called rasa (raso vai sah). The number of rasas is not certain. These differ in view of the impact generated through a work of art. Bharata in his famous treatise Nāṭyaśāstra (11-5, 17) lists eight *rasas*: śṛngāra (amorous), hāsya (comic), karuṇā (pathetic), raudra (furious), vīra (heroic), bhayānaka (terrible), bībhatsa (odious), and adbhḷta (marvelous). The impact on the viewers is respectively noticed in the following emotions: rati (love), hāsya (mirth), śoka (sorrow), krodha (anger), utsāha (energy), bhaya (fear), jugupsā (disgust), and vismaya (astonishment) (see Chatham 1981:24). Later, śānta (quiescent) was added and its impact was experienced in the form of tranquillity. The Vaiśṇnavas were keen to add two more rasas: mādhurya (sweet), vātsalya (fondness) (see Goswami 1997). In addition to these, dāsya (service) has also been suggested. Goswami Tulsīdāsa seems to suggest another rasa, captioning it sarala (natural).

All these emotions are represented in sculptures and paintings. If a piece of art is not able to generate at least one of these emotions, the very purpose of its creation is defeated. The element of rasa is undoubtedly very important; although it is not the ultimate aim. The *rasa* or the state of ecstasy may be a short lived joy or a feeling of fear, disgust, or surprise depending on the object of art. We may be charged with different consequents (anubhāva) while viewing the combat between Durgā and the buffalo demon Mahiśa but the message on top of all is the victory of the Divine over Evil. This manifestation of divinity is the real goal of art in India. The second important element is *artha* which is the meaning or message of an art product. Through the message, the viewer is filled with a particular emotion. Without meaning, art is pointless. In literature, speech and meaning are inseparable as both are essential in literary work. These have been conceived as Ardhanārīśvara, the combined aspect of male and female energy complementing each other and always united as expressed by the great poet Kālidāsa. The message of an icon or painting is conveyed through posture (mudrā), attribute (āyudha), color (varṇa), and expression (bhāva) etc. The third aspect, *chanda*, is an outcome of proper composition, symmetry and harmony of the figure. Finally, (*rūpa)* imparts the visual shape to the vision and action of an artist through a medium like clay, stone, metal, cloth, paper etc. The medium is transformed into an image, architecture, painting, or a decorative motif (see Agrawala 1965:4).

The expression daivāsuram, which one often encounters in Indian scriptures beginning from the Vedic period, suggests an eternal duel between the Divine and the demonic forces. But it is Divinity which emerges victorious even if it has to wage a fierce battle against evil. The fight is sometimes seen but often remains concealed. In the battlefield it is fought with arms and ammunitions, but the invisible war is fought by the self against its own vices. Only a righteous person is able to win by the grace of the Divine. Indian art is full of such renderings where the deity is shown crushing the demons: the Rāmayaṇa, the Mahābhārata, the Bhāgavata, and the Purāṇic narrations repeatedly present such episodes. Durgā's fight against Mahiṣa, Niśumbha and other demons is well known and has been a popular subject of artists for centuries.

The Buddha, before attaining Enlightenment, faced the attack of Māra comprising damsels and won not with the help of the sword but through strength of character. It was a big test of life which the Buddha passed with firm determination. In his previous births (jātakas) he was also put through various tortures and sufferings but remained unshaken and sacrificed everything to remove the sufferings of others. Piety, compassion, and non-violence, the divine virtues, were the weapons of the Bodhisattva, and these were used by him against hatred, anger, and violence. The Jātaka narrations were widely displayed on the early Indian Stūpa architecture. The aim behind carving such episodes was not to display the merit of the artist or to analyze the anatomical details but to spread the message of values and virtues of life in society. If we ignore that inner meaning, we fail to understand the real spirit of Indian art where form or matter does not dominate.

Coomaraswamy (1994:26) observes, "The life of pleasure only, one of which the end is pleasure, is subhuman, every animal knows what it likes and seeks for …" He elaborates,

> The Indian actor prepares for his performance by prayer. The Indian architect is often spoken of as visiting heaven and there making notes of the prevailing focus of architecture which he imitates here below. All traditional architecture, in fact, follows a cosmic pattern. Those who think of their house as only a "machine to live in" should judge their point of view by that of a Neolithic man, who also lived in a house, but a house that embodied a cosmology… (p.32)

Thus Oriental and particularly the Indian traditions have much more to offer to make art an offering to and a manifestation of the Divine when an artist feels that he is an instrument (nimitta) and not a creator. This attitude changes the entire concept of art and elevates us from the lower level to the higher level of divine consciousness. This must be the aim of our artistic zeal in any medium.

Sculptural Art in India: A Classification

The seed of art sprouted with the dawn of civilization as we come across the evidence for it right from pre-historic times. A reasonable representation of the development of sculptural art in India in various periods is as follows:

Table 3: Indian Art: Periods of Development

Period	*Date*
Pre or Proto-historic	c. 3rd - 2nd millennium B.C.E.
Vedic	c. 2000-1000 B.C.E.
Copper Hoard	c. 12th - 11th century B.C.E.
Mahajanapada	c. 1000-400 B.C.E.
Mauryan	c. 325-184 B.C.E.
Sunga	c. 184-72 B.C.E.
Indo Greek	c. 3rd century - 1st century B.C.E.
Satavahana[1]	c. 2nd century B.C.E. - 2nd century C.E.
Saka-Kushana[2]	c. 1st century B.C.E. - 2nd century C.E.
Ikshvakus[3]	c. late 2nd - 3rd century C.E.
Chalukyan[4]	c. 550-642 C.E.
Rashtrakuta	c. 753-973 C.E.
Pandya	c. 1251-1310 C.E.
Hoysala	c. 12th - 13th century C.E.
Vijayanagara[5]	c. 1336-1564 C.E.
Palas and Senas[6]	c. 10th - 13th century C.E.
Gurjara Pratihara[7]	c. 900-1000 C.E.
Gahadavalas	c. 1085-1200 C.E.
Sultan	c. 11th - 15th century C.E.
Mughal	c. 1526-1800 C.E.
British	c. 1800-1947
Indian Republic	c. 1947-Present

[1]Central and Western India, [2]Northern India, [3, 4]Deccan, [5]Southern India, [6]Eastern India, and [7]Central India.

Unlike sculptures, the classification of paintings has more of a regional bias than a dynastic sequence. Pre-historic rock shelter paintings are followed by the wall paintings in Ajanta, Bagh, Sittanavasal etc. The tradition of miniature paintings in palm leaf folios presenting Buddhist figures began in the 8th century C.E. in eastern India. After about five centuries, paper was used for writing manuscripts and their illustrations. The lead was taken by regions such as Gujarat and Rajasthan, where Jaina and Vaiśṇava themes found favor. The Mughals gave much impetus to paintings; besides book illustrations, independent miniatures and portraits were also produced. The courts of kings and chiefs encouraged this art and a number of regional styles and their sub-schools came into existence, such as, Rajasthani, Pahari,and Deccani to name just a few.

Figure 12: Lion Capitol from Ashoka column in Sarnath,
c. 274-237 B.C.E., Museum of Archaeology

Figure 13: Yakshi from Didarganj, Late Mauryan, c. 200 B.C.E, Patna Museum.

Figure 14: Gateway and Railing of Stupa from Bharhut, Shunga Period, 1st Century B.C.E., Indian Museum, Calcutta.

Figure 15: Nave of Chaitya Hall, Karle, 2nd Century C.E.

Figure 16: Chaitya Hall, Bhaja, exterior view, Shunga Period, 1st Century B.C.E.

Figure 17: Standing Buddha, Mathura, Gupta Period, 4th Century C.E., National Museum, Delhi

Figure 18: Shiva Maheshvara, from Elephanta, 8th Century C.E.

Figure 19: Kandarya Mahadeva Temple, Khajuraho, 10th Century C.E.

Figure 20: Celestial Beauty, Khajuraho, 10th Century C.E.

Figure 21: Natya Sarasvati, Hoysala, Belur, 11th Century C.E.

Figure 22: Dilwarra Temple, interior, Mt. Abu, 11th Century C.E.

Artists have been using various media to express their ideas: clay, wood, leaves, leather, skin, cloth, paper, glass, ivory, metal, and several precious, semiprecious, and ordinary stones. The use of stone can be a guiding factor for ascertaining the performance, style, and sometimes the period of the art. Spotted red sand stone is typically used in Mathurā art, and the Gandhara school is known for the use of grayish-bluish schist stone. The Kushana artists of Mathura, owing to heavy demand, could not afford to be choosy and their sculptures bear patches or spots but in the Gupta period Mathura sculptor opted for better stuff which was usually devoid of spots. Similarly, while in Chunar and Sarnath buff stone was commonly used, in eastern India, black basalt was preferred. In the early centuries of the Common Era, a local variety of off-white lime stone, which is an inferior variety of marble, was used in Amaravati and Nagarjunakonda in southern India (see Sharma 1994b:10-11).

Sculpural Art up to the Seventh Century

While it is not possible to analyze each medium of art, a brief survey of sculptural art up to the seventh century is presented. The earliest remains are in the form of stone tools (palaeoliths) used for hunting and self-defense but these do not convey any artistic sensibility. The late stone age culture does bear the imprint of the aesthetic urge of the cave dwellers through drawings in Madhya Pradesh and Uttar Pradesh. No sculptural remains of the period have, however, come to light. The Indus or Harappan objects belonging to the third and second millennium B.C.E. are known for their realism, imagination, and depiction of nature. The small nude torso from Harappa shows a high perfection of sculptural art through its fine curves and contours. Its nudity remains a controversial issue, and it is not possible to determine whether the figure represents a divine being or a Yogi. The male bust probably representing a priest wears a trefoil pattern scarf and a ribbon tied round the head. The large half open eyes bespeak a serene contemplation and inward vision befitting a man of higher consciousness. Thus from the very beginning of sculptural activity a feeling of divinity has been conveyed.

Art and Architecture in the Vedic Period

The Vedic people lead a forest (āśramā) and pastoral (gochara) life, and used mainly wood, bamboo, leaves, and straw for domestic and religious purposes. These, being of perishable nature, have not withstood climatic adversities. But Vedic literature is stocked with references to the rich aesthetic conventions of the age. A good form has been appreciated by the sage of the Ṛgveda (1.163.7) and art has been conceived as the manifestation of a number of pleasant forms (4.47.17, 6.47.18). Indra has been addressed as Surūpaktnu (maker of beautiful forms) and Viśvarūpa (Universal form) (1.4.1, 3.38.4). Similarly, Viśvakarma has been called Sādhukarmā (creator of beautiful forms) (10.81.7). We also come across words like pratimā, rūpa, pratirupa, and suśilpa. It would be interesting to note that the word vāmā occurs for beauty in the Ṛgveda (5.82.6) and probably it is for this reason that the fair sex was called Vāmā (beauty personified) but later a different sense was connoted, such as occupying the left side, opposite, or diverse.

We find a detailed description of architecture in the Vedic literature. The names recorded for "house" are dama, śālā, gṛha, pastya sadana, durona, harmya. The components of a house were dvāra (door), sadas (sitting room), patnī sadana (ladies apartment), agniśālā (fire place). Houses of large dimensions (bṛihatmāna), sometimes had one thousand pillars (sahasra-sthūṇa), and were sometimes inlaid with gold (hiraṇya rūpa) or copper plate (aya sthūṇa). These were the audience halls of kings for meetings of sabhā and samiti councils (2.41.5). It must, however, be pointed out that even large and beautiful architectural complexes were made of timber; this fact is well recorded in the Śālasūkta of Atharvaveda. Houses were so richly decorated with carvings and auspicious motifs that they were often compared to a good looking bride (vadhūmiva te śale). Vedic life on the whole was pious and divine and the fireplace formed an important part of house planning. Offering to gods through fire (yajña) was an expression of gratitude to the Divine.

Mauryan Art: Ashoka Pillars

The Vedic tradition of using wood for art and architecture continued until the Mauryan age when the use of stone commenced. It was a landmark in the history of Indian art, and Aśoka the Great must be given credit for it. Beside spreading the message of piety and good moral conduct, the emperor must have longed to be remembered forever for his valor and deeds of public welfare. He, therefore, selected stone as the medium for inscribing his edicts. Extracting huge stone blocks from quarries, shaping them as pillars with surmounting animals or wheels, imparting lustrous polish, carefully packing and transporting them to distant quarters for installation were huge and commendable tasks which were accomplished with utmost perfection. By doing this, Aśoka wanted to impress upon his subjects and his neighbors that his empire was no more a tribal or rural entity but it was an advanced and mighty nation capable of undertaking formidable tasks (Ray 1975:36).

The tall, heavy columns stand on their own and did not require a platform or any additional support. The dimension and weight of each piece was so well calculated that it was fixed in the earth with stone pieces has and remained stable in its position weathering all climatic hazards. Their unique way of installation and sudden dominant position in the topography of the region indicates the will power and authority of the monarch and his ability to create wonder. Each column has four important components: (a) a rough portion pierced into the earth, (b) a tapering round shaft culminating in an inverted lotus or bell, (c) a round abacus with beautiful reliefs, and (d) a surmounting animal or wheel.

The art of the age suggests a happy blend of Indian, Iranian, and Greek conventions. No doubt much inspiration was derived from the Achamenian sculptural art which was at its zenith in the time of Darius but remained confined mainly to the technique of carving and polishing. The installation of pillars was an ancient practice as a yūpa was set up at the time of sacrifice. Indrayadṣṭī was put up and a fair was held as *Indramaha*. Some scholars believe that some of the columns used by Aśoka were already in existence before him (see Gupta 1980:44-45). The animals on top like the lion, bull, horse, and elephant are known as auspicious or noble, hence called Mahā Ājaneya (Agrawala 1965:100). These may well be associated with Buddhism or Buddha's life: the elephant for birth, the lion for his clan, the bull for dharma, and the horse for renunciation on horseback. Aśoka's inclination towards Buddhism after the Kalinga war is well known. It would be more appropriate to call some of his columns, like the famous lion capital at Sarnath with a wheel on the top, *cakradhvaja* (capital with wheel) instead of *simhadhvaja* (lion capital).

Aesthetically, these columns are superb specimens of art, but the excellence was achieved gradually: Basrikha, for its archaic nature, may be the first or even pre-Aśokan; Rumindei was put up in the twentieth regnal year; the Rampurva and Lauria Nandan lion pillars belong to the twenty-sixth and twenty-seventh year, respectively; the Sarnath pillar appears to be the last to be set up although there is no date given on it. The pillars showed a marked improvement as the years rolled on. Balance, harmony, and integration of shaft, abacus, and crowning animals was the main problem facing the Mauryan court artist, and it was finally met with success in the Sarnath pillar. From the point of view of calligraphy too, these columns are outstanding as every letter is sharply, carefully and nicely chiseled and flaws remain a rarity. Brāhmī script and local dialects were used for mass communication. In the frontier regions Kharoshti and Aramaic scripts were preferred.

Mauryan court art was a sudden appearance and was extinguished with the fall of the dynasty. It actually served a distinct purpose: to propagate a code of conduct and royal command and to warn those who intended to disturb peace. It did not have a lasting impact, however, and the people remained busy following the cult practices. Their art is represented by yakṣa statues which were installed as guardian deities outside villages. The image of Yakṣī from Didarganj (now in Patna Museum) is a magnificent product. The ring or disc stones belonging to the period between the third and second centuries B.C.E. are good examples of peoples' art. Nature is dominant and the almost nude mother goddess may represent the fertility cult. These have been found in different places between Taxila in the Northwest and Patna in the East. In architecture timber traditions were followed. Of course, some caves were excavated in the hills of Barabar and Nagarjuni for the use of monks.

Sunga Art

The art of the Śunga period (2nd-1st century B.C.E.) is known for low relief, flat appearance, simple treatment, and double knotted turbans worn by males. The rendering looks like line drawing in stone and the three dimensional effect is wanting. Here, art and architecture become inseparable, and the real artistic grandeur is seen in the stūpas of the age. The depiction of symbols, auspicious motifs, and flora and fauna are the hallmarks of the period. Some new divinities emerged and Gajalakṣmī (goddess of prosperity anointed by two elephants) is quite conspicuous. Yakṣas and yakṣīs appear as tree and water deities. The worship of Nāga (serpent deities) was also in vogue and they were sometimes depicted in the human form with a snake hood. The Buddha is represented through symbols like a begging bowl, wheel, elephant, horse, tree, lion, relic casket, or halo; these were all associated with his life in one way or another. The Jātaka (previous births of the Buddha) stories were a favorite theme. These inspire devotees to lead a pious life following good conduct and to be prepared to suffer miseries for the welfare of others. Women appear both as deities and devotees in simple form. Śunga art, depicting almost all movements of the society of that age, functioned as the vehicle for religious communication (Saraswati 1975:36).

Ananya: A Portrait of India

Arts of India

Plate 1. Tidal dock for berthing ships at Lothal.

Plate 2. Protection wall of ancient Dwarka submerged in sea.

Plate 3. Dwarkadhish Temple, Dwarka.

Plate 4. Long fortification wall submerged in the sea.

Plate 5. Bodhisattva Padmapani, Ajanta.

Plate 6. Durga killing Buffalo demon, Mahishasuramardini Cave, Mamallapuram.

Plate 7. Siva and Parvati, Kejriwala Collection, Bangalore.

Plate 8. Nataraja. On loan from Dr. William T and Jimmie Dell Price, Amarillo Museum of Art, Texas.

Plate 9. Tara from Kurkihar, 9th Century C.E., Patna Museum.

Plate 10. Achyuta Raya, Achyuta Raya Temple, Hampi.

Plate 11. Reliefs on the Rama Temple, Hampi.

Plate 12. Lintel from a Naga temple, 1st Century C.E., Mathura Museum.

Plate 13. Yaksha from Parbhan, 3rd-2nd B.C.E, Mathura Museum.

Plate 14. Dream of Queen Maya, 2nd Century B.C.E., Bharhut.

Plate 15. Arjuna's Penance or Descent of Ganga, Mamallapuram.

Plate 16. Sanchi Stupa, North Gate, 1st Century B.C.E.

Plate 17. Seated Buddha, Gandhara.

Plate 18. Buddha from Sarnath, Gupta Period.

Plate 19. Seated Buddha, Gandhara,
2nd Century C.E., Edinburgh, Royal Scottish Museum.

Plate 20. Kandariya Mahadeva Temple, Chandella, 11th Century C.E.

Plate 21. Marble Bracket Figure,
Western Rajasthan, 13th Century C.E.

Photo: Bharat Ramamrutham

Plate 22. Nataraja Temple, Chidambaram. 12th Century C.E.

Photo: George Mitchelle

Plate 23. Sun Temple, Konarak. 13th Century C.E.

Plate 24. Prasadhisa, 1st Century C.E., Bharat Kala Bhavan.

Plate 25. Karttikeya, 2nd Century C.E., Mathura Museum.

Plate 26. Bust of Buddha (fasting), Lahore Museum.

Plate 27. Ardhanarishvara, Gupta Period, Mathura Museum.

Plate 28. Rishabhanatha, 6th Century C.E., Mathura Museum.

Plate 29. Female bust, Gupta Period, 6th Century C.E., Gwalior.

Plate 30. Karttikeya, Gupta Period.

Plate 31. Buddha, Gupta Period, Sarnath Style, 4th Century C.E.

Plate 32. Charminar, Hyderabad, 16th Century C.E.

Plate 33. Taj Mahal, Agra, 17th Century C.E.

Plate 34. Golgumbaz Mausoleum, Bijapur, 17th Century C.E.

Plate 35. Aiyanar on an Elephant, Thogur, 16th Century C.E., Government Museum, Madras.

THE STUPAS

The Stūpa was the focal point of art and architecture during the śunga period. The bodily remains or "wearings" of great kings, sages, or pontiffs were deposited in a casket which was covered with mud. Subsequently, depending on its importance, the spot was further encased by bricks from time to time and was transformed into an oval shaped mound. To protect it from wild animals a railing was provided with one, two, or four entrances. The railing (vedikā) and its gates (toraṇas) were richly decorated with figures and motifs in addition to the Jātakas and scenes from the life of the Buddha. It had four members: the ālambana pindikā (basement stone), stambha (upright pillar), sūcīs (crossbars), and uśnīśa (coping). No mortar was used and the entire complex was erected through sockets and tenons: either the tenon of the pillar was set into the sockets of the coping, or the vertical sockets on the sides of the railing posts received the cross bar. The gates allowed indirect entry to restrict the passage of animals into the stūpa. Its top was also provided with a small railing and a crowning umbrella (chatrayaṣṭi) but it was not accessible to people, only the celestials and divinities were supposed to descend from heaven to pay homage.

There were two important stūpas: the one at Bharhut near Satna (Madhya Pradesh), being in ruins, was removed by A. Cunningham to the Indian Museum, Calcutta; a few remains were later brought to the Allahabad Museum. The Stūpa at Sanchi, near Bhopal in Madhya Pradesh, still exists on the spot. It was built slightly later than the Bharhut Stūpa. Unlike the Bharhut Stūpa whose entire rail and gates were carved on both sides, the railings of the Sanchi Stūpa are plain. The southern gate of the Sanchi Stūpa bears an inscription saying that the gate was carved by the guild of ivory carvers of Vidisha. The place was dear to Aśoka when he administered this region as Governor. He had, therefore, installed a lion pillar to cherish his sweet memory. The Bharhut Stūpa served as an open air exhibition as a good number of the episodes depicted bear inscription for identification. From the names of donors, we are informed that people from distant quarters came and contributed to the construction of the Stūpa.

It should also be pointed out that besides conveying a philosophical message, the Stūpas showed all sorts of social functions, processions, worship, music, dance, and sports. Sometimes humorous scenes were illustrated. This indicates that despite containing relics of the great man, the edifice did not symbolize death, but a joyful event when he received salvation after attaining enlightenment. It therefore, represented light, knowledge, and happiness. At times, it was lit with a row of lamps and was seen as a tower of light from a distance. Beside Bharhut and Sanchi, Stūpas were also put up at Bodhgaya, Amaravati, and Mathura before the Common Era.

Mathura and Gandhara Schools

Two great schools of sculptural art evolved and developed almost simultaneously in Mathura and Gandhara under the patronage of the Kushana kings. While the Mathura school was confined to a small region with several workshops in the capital town, the Gandhara school was spread in a large area in present day Pakistan and Afghanistan.

Mathura art is known for the use of spotted red sand stone, replacement of symbols by anthropomorphic forms, origin and development of the Buddha and Jaina images, continuation of earlier art traditions of Central India (particularly of Bharhut), assimilation of foreign elements, fusion of the primitive yakṣa cult with the pantheon of other sects, development of new art forms, introduction of portrait figures, delineation of female figures with special care and charm, and overall faithful depiction of different modes of life (Sharma 1994a:39). The products of Mathura were installed at distant places like Sārnath, Kausambi, and Kuśinagar. Small pieces have been recovered from Chandraketugarh (West Bengal), Mahāsthan (Bangladesh), Taxila (Pakistan) and Begram (Afghanistan). In 1985, The Stūpa railing unearthed at Sanghol between Chandigarh and Ludhiana in Punjab was of the Mathura school.

Vogel states the significance of the Mathura School when he observes, "The vast amount of the sculptural remains discovered at Mathura would suffice to show the importance of this place in the history of Indian art" (Vogel 1906-7:142-43). General Cunningham made the same assessment when he remarked, "Everywhere in the North-West, I found the old Buddhist statues are made of Sikri's sandstone from which it would appear that Mathura must have been the great manufactory for the supply of Buddhist sculpture in Northern India" (Cunningham, p.35).

The School had its origin several centuries before the Kushana rule as evidenced by several yakṣa statues of the third and second centuries B.C.E. recovered from the region. The epigraph between the feet of the gigantic yakṣa image from Parkham belonging to the period between the third and the second centuries B.C.E. (Mathura Museum No. C.1) suggests that sculptural art at Mathura was handed down from teacher to student. Kuṇika was the master artist and his disciple Gomitaka carved these yakṣa statues. Fortunately, we find several other names of sculptors in the sculpture inscriptions: Rāma, Joṭisa, Dāsa, Śivamitra, Simharakṣita, Simha, Deyahn, Viṣṇu, and Jayakula (Sharma 1984;139). Dinna was the master artist who shaped a good number of excellent Buddha images in the Gupta period.

The symbols and decorative motifs are of vital importance in early Mathura art and architecture. These are common in Buddhism, Jainism, and Brāhmanism and represent purity, prosperity, and auspiciousness. Some important motifs are Svastika, Mangalakalaśa, Pūrṇaghaṭa, Phalapātra, Śrivatsa, Dharmačakra, Śankhanidhi, Padmanidhi, Garuḍa, Kalpalatā, Talavṛkṣa, Triratna, Bodhivṛkṣa, and Caityavṛkśa. The animals and birds which found favor for depiction are the elephant, bull, lion, deer, snake, goose, peacock, and fabulous or composite figures. Some of these motifs are not merely decoration but convey a deep metaphysical meaning which place them on a high pedestal. Proper understanding of such illustrations is the basic requisite for the appreciation of art.

Mathura has been the stronghold of three major religions in ancient India. Hence, images and shrines of these sects were put up simultaneously from c. 2nd century B.C.E. to the 7th century C.E. The Buddhist and Jaina pantheons emerged from symbols and culminated in superb life size images in the Gupta period. Brāhmanism or Hinduism had already started image worship through yakṣa images, and later, a large number of beautiful statues of Viṣṇu, Vāsudeva, Balarāma, Śiva, Pārvatī, Gaṇeśa, Kārttikeya, Durgā, Kubera, and Nāgas were carved. The Jaina images evolved from Āyāgapaṭas (tablets of homage) which are carved with several auspicious motifs (aṣṭamangalas). Later, independent images of Jinas either seated in meditation (dhyānastha) or standing in penance (daṇḍa or kāyotsarga) appeared. The portrait figures of the Kushana kings were made and set up in a Devakula at Māṭ near Mathura. The epithet often used by the dynasty was Devaputra (God's children) as rulers considered themselves superhuman. The complex housing their statues was, therefore, Devakula. Some scholars believe that foreign artists were also at work and they were responsible for carving such statues as those of Vima, Kanishka, Huvishka, Chashtana. This is not unlikely as there was a good deal of exchange between Mathura and Gandhara.

The earlier icons bear impact of Yakṣa with volume, heaviness, and corpulence, but gradually the quality improves: the mass is desiccated, suppleness appears, and the figure looks lively. Images of the Gupta period represent perfect harmony of physical beauty and a serene facial expression portraying the deity in a state of divine bliss; this was the most notable contribution of the Mathura artist. The Jina statues are sky clad, the Buddha wears a Sanghāṭī with rippling folds (as Chinese silk was imported) and the Hindu deities wear garments and ornaments as required.

The Gandhara style of sculptural art is typified by the use of gray or bluish stone, subsequently stucco and sometimes metal. Fusion of different alien features like Greek, Roman, Bactrian, Iranian, and Indian, anatomical details and muscular treatment, heavy and coarse drapery are some notable characteristics. The essential theme is Buddhist and rarely have other deities been shown. The life scenes of the Buddha were very popular and the Master was visualized in Gandhara art as a great man and not as a deity, hence he is often shown with moustaches or in an emaciated form when fasting. The new deities emerging in this art are Vajrapāṇī (escort of the Buddha armed with thunderbolt), Pančika, and Hārīti. The Buddha himself appears in different gestures and postures like abhaya (protection), dhyāna (meditation), bhūmisparśa (earth touching), and upadeśa or vyākhyāna (preaching).

The interaction between Gandhara and Mathura began in the second century. For instance, the drape covering the left shoulder, the abhaya pose, the Jātaka narration, auspicious motifs, dhoti, sari, shawl, Śālbhañjikā, elephants, the garuḍa, peacock, lotus, and the wheel went from Mathura to Gandhara. On the other hand, drapery covering both shoulders, stitched dress, shoes and sandals, Bachas or Sileners drinking wine, the Vajrap!1i, Pañcika, and H!rīti postures, and royal portraiture were the Gandhara features adopted by the Mathura school. Some Gandhara specimens have been discovered in the Mathura region and Mathura figures have been picked up from the Gandhara area.

A good number of Mathura sculptures are inscribed and record the year of installation, hence it is easy to frame a chronological development of the school. The Gandhara images are rarely inscribed and only eight record a year but the era to which the year belongs remains obscure. Consequently, it is very difficult to analyze the production sequence of the Gandhara School.

By the end of the second century C.E. the Kushana rule weakened, and the following century in Northern India was an era of turmoil, uncertainty, and confusion. Art in the third century, (which was the period of transition between the Kushana and Gupta rule) is notable for several new trends: The heavy folds of garments were gradually replaced by the thin and transparent treatment; ears became elongated and eyes changed shape from almond to lotus; the hair developed curls; the body became thin; smiles on faces started giving way to serenity; and finally nimbus decorations began. At this time, several alien features disappeared. The Gandhara and alien influences lessened to a great extent.

Gupta Art

With the advent of Gupta rule in 319 C.E., the political scenario changed. A firm grip over administration brought back normalcy and peace; prosperity and stability provided an atmosphere conducive to the furtherance of art. The intellectual resurgence of the age and the high ideals conceived and followed by the reigning kings made a deep impact on society, and artists were busy translating them into products. Quantity was excelled by quality. Although the Gupta style had started functioning in the fourth century C.E., and continued until the end of the sixth century, the fifth century was the blooming phase of Gupta art. During this period, the concept of beauty and its appreciation changed. Passionate addiction to worldly pleasures through the exposure of physical charm was restricted. Sensuous overtures were now outdated and replaced by spiritual ecstasy. The wearing of too many ornaments became outmoded as the figures were lit with divine grace and bliss. Beauty now aspired to higher aims rather than limiting itself to worldly pleasure. This phenomenon has been described by Kalidāsa, the preeminent poet of the age (*Kumarsambhava* 5.36). Some of the Buddha images of the Mathura School created in the Gupta period are among the finest examples of Indian art. The indelible efforts and dedication of Mathura artists during the preceding five centuries resulted in shaping beautiful icons which represent sculpture at its best.

The standing Buddha images (two in Mathura Museum A.5, 76.25, one in the Indian Museum, Calcutta, and another at the Rashtrapati Bhavan, New Delhi) are remarkable innovations, probably of one sculptor (Dinna). The aesthetic novelties of the age include: a sublime expression on the face; rich nimbus beginning from the full-blown lotus followed by a number of concentric bands like twisted wreath issuing from crocodile heads; a rosette; stylized peacocks or geese intertwined with lotuses and entwined wreath rosettes; a beaded circle; and finally the retaining of the earlier scalloped border of curly hair, large ears, louts bud shaped half open eyes, and three lines on the neck (trivalaya). The chief objective behind installing these images, which has been well achieved, was the attainment of supreme knowledge (annuttarajñānāṣāpti) as recorded in the inscription on the pedestal.

Sarnath

The other great center of art was Sarnath near Varanasi, the place of the First Sermon of the Buddha. Aśoka had bestowed his favor on the place by installing the most magnificent lion pillar. The workshop of the Mauryan product at Chunar was not far from here, but it had not yet come into eminence as a school of art. Much inspiration was derived from Mathura which enjoyed the continuity of sculptural art several centuries before the Sarnath School. As Kramrisch observes, "the Sarnath version of the Mathura prototype is subtler than the original" (Kramrisch 1935:63). The use of buff sand stone quarried from Chunar, foldless or diaphanous garments, fewer number of bands in the halo, and overall graceful treatment are the special characteristics of Sarnath. While a good number of Brāhmanical images were also fashioned, the school is known for its excellent Buddhist images. Signifying the importance of the place, the first teaching of the Buddha was the most sought after theme. The worship of the wheel was already in vogue, and a shrine for that purpose also existed (Williams 1982:78).

There was a gradual development of the Buddha/Bodhisattva images produced at Sarnath. The earlier ones show a somewhat heavy, folksy touch with less sublimity, but gradually, the quality ascended and outstanding figures were chiseled out. The heaviness and toughness of the body was transformed into full and delicate roundness, and the face reflected complete serenity under brooding eyelids. As N. R. Ray remarks,

> with the passage of time, the physiognomical type grows longer, the head slightly smaller and lighter, plastic sculptural treatment more delicate and sensitive and altogether a supra-sensuous, extra-mundane soaring elegance results, till finally the modelling and outline seem to throb with an almost uncanny sensitiveness...
>
> (Ray 1954:524).

Both Mathura and Sarnath studios presented stone steles illustrating the life scenes of the Buddha in different compartments: the birth at Lumbini, penance and Enlightenment at Bodhgaya, his first sermon at Sarnath, and demise at Kusinagar were repeatedly shown. Although the number is less, the Bodhisattva sculptures have been shaped with the same grace and elegance. The Buddha is in monk's robe but the Bodhisattva wears princely garments and ornaments and sometimes holds a lotus, hence identified as Avalokiteśvara Padmapāṇi.

Innumerable Śaivite and Vaiṣṇava images have also been recovered at Sarnath as well as in Mathura. These bespeak the same high quality of treatment as the Buddhist figures. The Ardhanārī śvara heads, Umā Maheśvara, Kārttikeya, Māhāviṣṇu, Viśvarūpa, Viṣṇu are some of the remarkable specimens. The classical Gupta idiom was occasionally practiced in Allahabad, Bodhgaya, and some parts of Madhya Pradesh but nowhere did a dynamic school flourish as in Mathura and Sarnath. The matrimonial alliance of the Gupta rulers with the Vākāṭakas in Maharashtra resulted in turning out several beautiful specimens of Gupta-Vākāṭaka art. Śiva Vāmana" (now in the National Museum, New Delhi), from Mansor in Nagpur, Maharashtra, is an excellent example.

The Hindu Temple

The Hindu temple evolved in the Gupta period and was not only the abode of God but also a repository of art. The kings of the dynasty followed a policy of religious eclecticism and encouraged artistic activities. But basically they were Bhāgavatas or Vaiṣṇavas, and the Brāhmaṇic shrines developed from primitive platforms to a temple which comprised a sanctum (garbhgṛiha) and a vestibule. Gradually, the flat roof cella rose into a tower (śikhara). As the stūpa in the Śunga-Kushana period evolved from the Vedic yajña with fire and railing, similarly, the temple evolved from a stūpa whose dhātumañjuṣā was transformed into dhātugarbha and the railing adjusted into the high terrace (pīṭha).

The Daśāvatāra temple at Devagarh in the Lalitpur district of Uttar Pradesh is a fine example. The doorway is richly carved with rosettes, creeper, couples (pramathas) and two sacred river goddesses Gangā and Yamunā on their crocodile and tortoise mounts, respectively. Their depiction aimed to convey the feeling of purification to devotees while entering the shrine. The niches of the three other sides display three important Bhāgavata scenes through beautiful sculptures. These are: (1) Gajendramokṣa: Viṣṇu's descent to earth to rescue the lord of elephants from the deadly clutches of the Nagā; (2) Nara Nārāyaṇa tapahścaryā: the performance of penance of sages Nara and Nārāyaṇa at Badrinātha in the Himalaya; and (3) Śeṣaśayī Viṣṇu: Viṣṇu sleeping on the cosmic serpent. Apart from depicting Puranic legends, these are imbibed with metaphysical messages such as the attainment of salvation through the grace of the Lord, ordeal to achieve higher goals, and to enjoy peace and tranquility even in the trying circumstances. The plinth contains scenes from Rāmāyaṇa, such as the episode of Ahalyā, Rāma uprooting the Dundubhi tree, and Rāma, Lakṣmaṇa, and Sītā proceeding to the forest. The scenes associated with Kṛṣṇa are: the birth of Kṛṣṇa, Nanda, and Yaśodā; the child Kṛṣṇa kicking the cart; and Kṛṣṇa with Sudāmā. The inscription records that the temple was "the gift of Bhāgavata Govinda at the holy feet of the Lord of Keshavapura" (Mathura). Aesthetically, the sculptures are excellent examples of Gupta art (Agrawala 1965:220-25). The other Gupta period temples were situated at Sanchi Nachna, Bhurma, and Dara, all in Madhya Pradesh.

In the Gupta period seers and poets longed to create heaven on earth and this coveted aim was to be achieved by providing abodes for the deities. Heavenly prosperity is suggested by the abundance of gold coins which themselves are beautiful specimens of art and represent a variety of deities. Manifestation of Divine Glory through His beautiful and charming figures and His attractive abode was well depicted by the Gupta artists. The conduct and ideals of kings were also highly inspiring as portrayed in Kālidāsa's *Raghuvaṃśa* (1.5-9).

Towards the end of the sixth century C.E., Northern India suffered a terrible blow at the demonic hands of the barbarian Hūṇas who not only plundered the prosperity of the Golden Age but also mercilessly destroyed almost all noble artistic and architectural creations. For about a century, efforts were made to imitate the Gupta trends. We do occasionally come across some beautiful pieces, but the original grace could not be revived. The ascending graph of infusing divinity in art fell sharply with the disintegration of the Gupta Empire, and regional styles developed from the eighth century. As time passed, emphasis was laid on stylization, ornamentation, attributes, and postures. A number of new and complex pantheons emerged, and amorous and erotic scenes found their place on the religious shrines. Art was dominated by iconography for the purpose of ritualistic meditation and worship, but the divinity did not return.

Works Cited

Agrawala. V.S. 1965. *Studies in Indian Art*. Varanasi: Vishwavidyalaya Prakashan.

Brown, Percy. 1965-68. *Indian Architecture*, 5th edn. Bombay: Taraporewala.

Chatham, Doris Clark. 1981. *Rasa and Sculpture in Kala Dar'sana*. Delhi: American Institute of Indian Studies.

Coomaraswamy, A.K. 1994. *Christian and Oriental Philosophy of Art*, 1941. New York: Dover.

Cunningham, A. Archaeological Survey Report, XI. Delhi: Indological Book House.

Goswami, Shrivatsa. 1997. Paper presented at a seminar organized by Bharat Kala Bhavan, Banaras Hindu Universisty.

Gupta S.P. 1980. *The Roots of Indian Art.* Delhi:

Kramrisch, S. 1935. *Indian Sculpture.* The Heritage of India Series. Calcutta: YMCA Publishing House; London: Oxford University Press, 1933.

Ray, N.R. 1954. *Classical Age.* Bombay:

______. 1975. *Maurya and Post Maurya Art.* Delhi:

Saraswati, S.K. 1975. *A Survey of Indian Sculpture.* Calcutta: Firma KL. Mukhopadhyay (1957).

Sharma, R.C. 1994. A Glimpse of Indian Art, *Alamkara:* Indian Art Exhibition

_________. 1994. *The Splendour of Mathura Art and Museum.* Singapore: National Heritage Board.

Sri Aurobindo.1971. *India and her Future.* Pondichery: Sri Aurobindo Ashram.

Vogel, J. Ph. 1906-7. *Archaeological Survey Report*

Williams, J.G. 1982. *The Art of Gupta India.* Princeton: Princeton University Press.

Chapter 24 | The Heroic Tradition in South Indian Art: Ascetics, Gods & Kings

Nalini Rao

Although South India has always had a distinctive and a well-established artistic tradition of its own, it has not received the attention it deserves. Encompassing the broadest range of monuments in the form of innumerable temples, gateways, shrines, monasteries, mosques and churches, it includes a large variety of stone and metal sculptures and paintings. The evidence that remains, however, is only a scattered fragment of what must have been a widespread and flourishing activity, destroyed by inclement weather, vandalism and invading armies. The dispersal of such a vibrant tradition was possible due to the quick assimilation and transmission of ideas, techniques, and styles brought in from various regions, and by different dynasties that ruled between the fifth and fifteenth centuries C.E. The period of building activity and the accompanying sculptural art shifted to the south after the marvelous efflorescence of Gupta art in North India. South of the Vindhyas, the three great empires—the Chalukyas in the Deccan, Pallavas of Kanchi on the coast, and Pandyas in the far south rose to power and invented new, ambitious modes of architecture. Later, the Rashtrakutas who supplanted the Chalukyas of Badami as the power in the Deccan, and the imperial Cholas of Tanjore, with the Chalukyas of Vengi wedged in between them, formed two dominants and further developed the technique of temple forms with their stylistic and regional variations. The stone tradition continued and reached unprecedented heights under the Vijayanagara rulers whose empire extended over much of the entire south.

This chapter is a brief description of the heroic tradition in the sculptural art of South India. The focus is on the visual imagery of ascetic, divine, and kingly heroes. The lives, myths, and spiritual power of ascetics and divinities was a dominant factor and a unifying theme in the figural tradition. In this chapter, I will discuss the nature and visual qualities of the heroes, modes of narrative representation, depiction of mythology and philosophy, and finally, heroes as part of a wider traditional belief system. The figural repertoire that decorates official architecture is almost entirely religious, with the largest number being Hindu heroes articulated on temple walls, and fewer Buddhist and Jain representations (Figure 23).

Figure 23: Entrance, Channakesava Temple (Hoysala), Belur

Ascetic Heroes

The earliest artistic evidence of the heroic tradition is in the form of representations of the ascetic teacher, Buddha, who was venerated for his spiritual attainments and Enlightenment. This heroic achievement, together with events from his life and his teachings, were immortalized in stone, narrative, and iconic forms. Buddhist art was to develop an elaborate iconography to include Buddhas and Bodhisattvas (the essence of the Buddha) that became canonical in Asian Buddhist art. The focus of this art was the symbolic reliquary architecture (stūpa) (See R.C. Sharma, this volume) and the functional monastic establishments (saṇgha) with elaborate decorations, for the propagation of Buddhist teachings. Buddhist architectural development in the Deccan paralleled contemporary artistic developments in the Gandhara and Mathura regions. A salient feature of this tradition was the building of monasteries, some of which were simple while others were large and complex like those at Karli (Figure 24).

Figure 24: Couples, Buddha Image, Facade, Buddhist Cave, Karli

A remarkable feature of the Buddhist tradition was cave architecture which flowered spectacularly in Ajanta. Here, about twenty-nine Buddhist caves were excavated exemplifying major achievements in architecture, sculpture, and painting. The caves constitute complete monastic entities including living quarters, devotional areas, and assembly halls which provide important insights into Buddhist theology, mythology, and religion. Apart from portraying the events from the life of Buddha, such as the

Birth of Buddha, the Enlightenment, the First Sermon, and the Great Departure in narrative form, these moments were immortalized in a figural form through the use of lakṣanas (cognizable or iconographic marks), gestures, and poses which transform them into icons of veneration and worship. Buddha's towering spiritual personality dominates the facade of Cave No. 19 at Ajanta where a number of seated and standing Buddhas are represented. His moral teachings were represented in the form of jātaka stories (stories of Buddha's past life) which indirectly expressed the values of the tradition. The continuous narrative scheme can be seen in the mural paintings at Ajanta, such as the Vessantara Jātaka in Cave No. 17, where the hero appears successively in the varied combination scenes. Also portrayed are the Bodhisattvas, who are personifications of Buddha's virtues and powers, such as the Bodhisattva Avalokitesvara, the picture of compassion and sacrifice, and Bodhisattva Padmapani (holding a lotus in hand) (Plate 5). Schematic compositions interwoven with popular and contemporary scenes make a powerful impact as observed over the door of Cave No.17, where a row of seven past Buddhas and Maitreya are portrayed above yakṣa couples. When the qualities of narrative content were modified by program ideology and philosophical speculation, iconic forms expanded to include past and future Buddhas seen in numerous Deccan caves, such as the Ellora and Aurangabad caves (Figure 25). In Amrāvati and Nāgārjunakoṇḍa under the Śatavāhanas and Ikṣvākus, large monastic establishments and their associated art styles were distinctly related to those in Karli, Nasik, and Kanheri in the Deccan. The second century art in Amaravati illustrates Buddhist legends and events on the veneer of sculpted stone slabs and an ornate vedika (railing). These in turn influenced the canons in later South Indian art, particularly in regard to the grouping of figures, character types, and costumes (Zwalf 1985: 17). Among other scenes of the hero, images of Buddhist jātaka stories on the doorframe of a double-storied Buddhist cave above the Meguti hill in Aihole are depicted in concise monoscenic narration, while a colossal image of the Buddha is in the shrine. The Amaravati tradition continued under the Ikṣvāku kings in the Buddhist monasteries in Nāgārjunakonda where the great Āčarya Nāgārajuna, the founder of the Mādhyamika school of Buddhism and a proponent of the Mahāyāna doctrine, is believed to have lived. Here, the figural compositions of the stone reliefs are more animated, with a sophisticated spatial arrangement. Buddhist art, while developing the symbolic function, also maintained the narrative content of visual heroes.

Figure 25: Kailasanatha Temple, Ellora

Mahāvīra, founder of Jainism, is another widely known and admired ascetic hero. Images of twenty-four Tīrthānkaras and associated figures found in elaborately decorated Jain temples, especially in Karnataka, vividly illustrate the rigor of monastic and lay ascetic practices in Jainism. A Jina or "conqueror" is one who has achieved complete victory over attachment and aversions. A Jina is also called Tīrthankara or "one who establishes a tīrtha (ford or crossing place), across what is often called "the ocean of existence." He is believed to have been an extraordinary human being who conquered the attachments and aversions that stand in the way of liberation from worldly bondage. By either name—Jina or Tīrthankara—these great personages are Jainism's principal objects of veneration found in the innumerable Jain temples, especially in Karnataka. The colossal figure of Gommaṭēśvara (Bāhubali) in Śravaṇabeḷagoḷa, standing amidst creepers, is a spiritual king, reflecting the religion's highest aspirations and adherence to the ethics of nonviolence and asceticism (Babb 1996: 9) (Figure 26). The Image of Mahavira, in Badami Cave number 4, is symbolic and transposes the avenue of war from the outer field of battle to an inner zone of liberation.

Gurus

Another category of ascetic heroes that is of special importance is the Hindu guru whose image is found in South Indian Hindu monasteries called maṭhas or maṭams. These are religious institutions peculiar to South India and serve as schools which perform the functions of feeding, boarding, as well as worship. Specializing in different religious and philosophical systems of thought, their growth may be traced to the period of Shankara (See Kesavan on the Vedas, this volume) with continuous and spectacular developments occurring in imagery, ritual, and worship till the present time. The maṭhas, in contrast to temples, are simple in architecture and less decorated. The focus of worship is not in the figural form, but in the form of an aniconic symbol (vrindāvana); the principal figure is the guru (either living or dead) whose role extends into the wider community. Although the image of the gurus is not as conspicuously depicted as that of gods in a temple, their importance in the community is unquestionable. In the religious architecture of the maṭha, such as those in Sringeri, Mantrālaya, and Kānchipuram, the visual importance and the darśan of the aniconic symbol of the guru is of special significance. The maṭha may be said to be the institutionalization of the guru, the earnest and sincere spiritual hero, historical or living.

Figure 26: Gommateshwara, Sravanabelagola

Divine Heroes

The second and more popular form of the hero is the one who is transcendent, idealized and divine—the god or gods whose mode of representation was not very different from the iconographic formulas of Buddhist iconography. The Hindu legacy of divinities which were abstract concepts during Vedic times (Organ 1970: 4) were now articulated in figural form and depicted prolifically on temples which grew into ostentatious structures with a grandiose display of diverse mythical heroes.

The tradition of sculptural representation of gods in South India emerged during the time of the Pallavas and Chalukyas, who kept alive the narrative myths of the gods. Myths may be said to reflect those events in the history of a community which it considers its central fact and its spiritual foundation (Klostermaier 1984: 2). In visually perceptible symbols and signs the heroes retold the story of the myth by enacting the dramatic moment of the story. Many of the deities are fashioned with multiple arms, each hand bearing an emblem or a weapon, or posed in a gesture called a mudrā. The emblems and mudrās indicate the various powers that belong to the deity (Eck 1981: 28). The Hindu semiotic system of elaborate iconography used gestures, objects held in the hand, subsidiary and attendant figures, sometimes facial expression, and even the personal experience of the poet-saints. In fact, the Bhakti cults of Tamil saints played a major role in providing an impetus to artistic developments. The divine heroes expressed that all power is moral; they stood for the power of good over evil, as well as abstract ideas of unity over multiplicity (Klostermaier 1989: 144). For instance, the formidable goddess Mahiṣāsuramardini is the symbol of the power of good. Her primary mythological function is to combat the demons who threaten the stability of the cosmos. In this role, she is depicted as a great battle queen with many arms, each of which wields a weapon and rides a fierce lion (Kingsley 1986: 95). In the Mahiṣāsuramardini cave at Māmallāpuram (Plate 6), the intervention of the goddess is dramatized. An element of surprise hangs over with a similarity of scale and rhythmic spatial arrangement, and a diagonal movement acts as an instrument of effective narrative transmission. In the figure of the goddess in the Durga temple at Aihole (Figure 27), the conflict is resolved and her triumph is complete. With the focus on the principal figure, the diagonal movements of the arms however serve to extend the narrative beyond the primary visual field.

Figure 27: Durga, Durga Temple, Aihole

Another popular hero is Śiva, the god of paradoxes. In his innumerable forms, all opposites are resolved (Figure 28). He is the universal progenitor; he is the wild huntsman of the forests and the teacher of the arts and sciences in the mountains; the supreme dancer, creator and also the destroyer who leads man to salvation; the naked wanderer in the wilderness carrying a skull, frightener of man and lover of women. The iconographic representation of Maheśamūrti, at Gharapuri (Elephanta), is a product of yogic vision. The Yogeśvara Śiva at Ellora serves as a vehicle for the realization of a state higher than the physical state, in the manner of an ascetic tradition. The Ardhanarīśwara in Bādāmi Cave No. 3 is the androgynous image, half Man-half Woman God form, which is half Śiva and half Śakti, or the male and female principles in one (Figure 29). With his wife, Uma, he is the loving husband (Plate7) and as Rāvaṇānugrahamūrti, he is the giver of grace (Figure 30). He is the supreme dancer, Naṭarāja, (Plate8) who leads man to salvation. The lord who dances in the circle of flames of this changing world holds the drum of creation and the fire of destruction, demonstrates the triumph of of knowledge over ignorance, by subduing the demon. Simultaneously, he shows his mercy by a raised hand, signifying his palm to the worshipper, and with another hand, is physically pointing to his upraised foot, where his worshipper may take refuge. The image of the Tāṇḍava dance of Śiva in Bādāmi Cave No. 1 (Figure 31) is the combination and juxtaposition of simple gestures through which he expresses the ambiguities, the tensions and the paradoxes of creation and destruction, time and eternity, grace and illusion. In the beauty of his innumerable forms, we see terror; in their horror is divine grace. But within its varying nature, the supreme being is uninvolved, calm and blissful, transcendent, beyond the duality of good and evil, unaffected by any happening in the material universe. This is also depicted in the figure of Viṣṇu, the preserver, in the Durga Temple at Aihole. However, the aniconic symbols, such as the Liṇga have the same power of figural compositions, as the Hindu world recognizes that the two approaches of discriminating form and formlessness are inseparable. (See Hiriyanna's chapter on the Upaniṣads in this volume.) As Betty Heimann put it,

> Whenever the uninitiated outsider is surprised, embarrassed, or repulsed by the exuberant paraphernalia of materialistic display in Hindu cult, he must keep in mind that side by side with these stands the utmost abstraction in religious feeling and thought, the search for the Neti-Neti Brahman, the "not this, not that," which denies itself to all representations, higher or lower (Heimann 1964:33).

Figure 28: Śiva on Bull,
Durga Temple, Aihole

Figure 29: Ardhanarishwara,
(Androgynous form of Śiva),
Cave No. 3, Badami

Figure 30: Ravana Shaking Mount Kailasa, Ellora

Epic Heroes

The repertoire of the Indian image world also includes epic heroes carved in living stone. The narrative reliefs from the epic, Rāmāyaṇa are chiselled in the Virūpākṣa temple at Paṭṭadakal and the Hazara Rāma temple at Hampi. In addition scenes from the Mahābhārata potray the kingly aspect of heroes as in the Virūpākṣa temple at Paṭṭadakal while stories from the life of Lord Kṛṣṇa are visually depicted on numerous monuments, one of the earliest being in the rock cut caves at Badami. Even minor heroes from the Rāmāyaṇa, Mahābhārata have been visualized and worshipped, such as Hanumān, the monkey God, who is the chief ally of Rāma, and Arjuna. The most impressive sculptural composition is at Māmallapuram—the famous relief that has been identified as the Descent of the Ganges River or Arjuna's Penance (Plate 15). Measuring about thirty meters in height, it contains a large number of life size figures.

A major cleft of the rock is a natural feature skillfully incorporated into the design and subject matter of the carving. Here the narrative, which has peculiar properties, and the written literature need analysis which will provide theoretical models for the art historian. Even the five epic heroes, the Pāndava brothers, are immortalized in the rock-cut monolithic temples. It does not matter whether the heroes have a historical or mythological existence. Whether there actually was a fight between the Pāndavas and Kauravas on the Kurukṣetra battleground is of no consequence when one recognizes that conflict between good and evil, or more particularly the conflict between happiness and unhappiness, is a constant in human nature.

Figure 31: Tandava Dance of Siva, Facade of Cave No. 1, Badami

Kings

Although religious and ascetic heroes were important determinants affecting art, they were not the sole factors affecting art production. Kings exerted a major influence on the creation of art; art patronage by kings came from wealth, often gained through military conquest. A victorious king legitimized the wealth and position he had acquired and every king built a bigger religious edifice in his name. The Kailāsanātha temple at Kānchīpuram was called the Rājasimheśvara temple after Rājasimha, who named the deity enshrined in it and the temple after himself, calling it Rājasimha Pallavēśvara, in keeping with a practice that was to become very popular in South India (Huntington 1985: 314). A return after military campaigns led the king to emulate and compete with the building achievement he had seen during military adventures in enemy territory. This resulted in such famous monuments as the Virūpākṣa temple at Paṭṭadakal and the Kailasanātha temple at Ellora.

The form of heroism which we call kingly does not figure prominently in the form of portraiture, yet it was not nonexistent. Royal representations of Pallava kings of Māmalla and Mahendravarman are found in the Ādivarāha Cave in Māmallāpuram, a potrait of Narasimhavarman Māmalla I in the Dharmarāja Ratha and those of Rājarāja Chōola and his queen Lōkamahādevi in the Brihadēṣwara Temple at Tanjore. Kings were also lovers of art, and since they were knowledgeable about it-- they were often depicted in official stone sculpture. The Kalyani Chalukyan king, Bhūlōkamalla Somēṣvara refers to the sabhā or assembly of lovers of art in his famous work Abhilāṣatīrtha Chintāmani or *Raja Manasollasa* while the *Shivatattvaratnakara* of Basava Bhupala of Keladi mentions royal patronage of potrait sculpture. Sometimes religious figures of gods had political meanings, such as in the Varāha and Trivikrama panels. These figures were deliberately chosen to refer to specific achievements of the king Māmalla— presumably his defeat of the Chalukyan king, Pulakēṣin. Securely identifiable portraits of the Vijayanagara king Krishandēvarāya and his two queens in the Tirumalai temple at Tirupati, small portraits of the same king at Hampi, and those of Ačutarāya have been identified (Plate 10). However, the criteria for the identification of uninscribed portraits were usually lakṣaṇas (cognizable or iconographical marks) such as number of arms, lacking attributes, architectural context, and particularly the idiosyncratic features, by which is meant an attribute or a physical characteristic that identifies the figure in a specific way. These may be incidents from the life of the individual or specific royal emblems which had political influence. About fifteen free standing royal portraits have been unearthed by the excavations at

Hampi. From the placement of the royal portraits in the palace area, and in the premises of the temple, the scale, and the manner of portrayal, they reveal important aspects such as the heroic, devotional, religious, liberal and dharmic aspects of South Indian medieval kingship (Rao 1991: 80).

Figure 32: Head of a Royal Personage, Archaeological Museum, Hampi

Secular Heroes

Another type of royal narrative scenes found largely on temple walls are very significant from the point of view of secular heroes. Among those are royal heroes, on the Rāma temple (Plate 11), and the secular monument of Mahānavami Dibba in Hampi (Vijayanagara), where images of the kings witnessing processions and royal festivals give an insight into the ritual and religious aspects of kingship (Figure 32). They were often associated with the rejuvenation of powers connected with the king and his religious, military, and social roles. Ritual celebrations had a political purpose and a social function, in the maintenance of their rule and exaltation of the sovereign. Royal imagery, although not large in size or number, was a visual form of power which expressed the internal dynamics of imperial authority.

While queens are occasionally represented as wives of the king, women are largely depicted as relaxed, gorgeously adorned, and imbued with an atmosphere of sensuous pleasure. They are handled with tender expressiveness such as we find in the female figure at Kuravatti (Figure 33), where she is within coiled serpents and birds; the madanika figure in the Kesava temple at Belur (Figure 34); and in sensual paradise in the mithuna figure in the Badami Cave No. 3 (Figure 35). The female figures, represented on brackets, are a visual translation of perhaps literary or idealized heroines, full-fledged, gorgeous, ideal, and court beauties, but they do not offer sufficient detailed information to interpret a specific story successfully.

It may be surmised that the heroes help establish a distinctive sculptural tradition and visual imagery. Ascetic and divine heroes transcended their limits and were embodiments of spiritual qualities. The amazing diversity of deities connected with extensive mythology, theology, and philosophy were effective visual narratives which could persuade an audience without the use of words. The veneration by the devotee, poet-saint, religious artist, patron, and the public were sufficient proof of the effectiveness of artistic expression of visual heroes. All the heroes—ascetic, divine and kingly, had one similar content in that they were created for adoration. The heroic tradition asserted the importance of a value system according to which all men can attain full dimension of a spiritual life. Although, due to hierarchical and social issues, people differ in their attainments of full human potential, it is possible for everyone. The heroes are not dead in India, for they still have implications for the artistic tradition which presents the nobility of the perfecting human being; the perfected human being is to be approximated.

Figure 33: Bracket figure, Mallikārjunaswamy Temple, Kuruvatti, Bellary District.

Figure 34: Woman with Parrot, Bracket figure, Channakesava Temple, Belur

Figure 35: Mithuna (couple), Cave No. 3, Badami, Karnataka

Figure 36: Bronze figure of Sambhandar, Vijaynagara, 15-16th Century

Works Cited

Appadurai, A. 1977. Kings, Sects and Temples in South India, 1359-1700 A.D. *Indian Economic and Social History Review* 14:42-73.Babb, L. A. 1996. *Absent Lord: ascetics and kings in the Jain ritual culture.* Berkeley: University of California Press.

Barnett, L. D.1977. *Hindu gods and heroes.* Delhi: Ess Ess Publications.

Dallapiccola, A. L. (ed.) 1985. *Vijayanagara city and empire: new currents of research*, 2 vols. Stuttgart: Franz Steiner Verlag Wiesbaden.

Eck, Diana L. 1981. *Darshan: seeing the divine image in India.* 2nd revised edition. Pennsylvania: Anima Books.

Heimann, B. 1964. *Facets of Indian thought.* London: George Allen and Unwin.

Hinks, R. P. 1976. *Greek and Roman portrait sculpture.* London: Trustees of the British Museum.

Huntington, S. 1985. *The art of ancient India: Buddhist, Hindu, Jain.* New York: Weatherhill.

Kingsley, D. 1986. *Hindu Goddesses: visions of the divine feminine in the Hindu religious tradition.* Berkeley: University of California Press.

Klostermaier, K. K. 1984. *Mythologies and philosophies of salvation in the theistic traditions of India.* Waterloo: Wilfrid Laurier University Press.

_______________1989. *A survey of Hinduism.* Albany: State University of New York Press.

Michell, G.1995. *The new Cambridge history of India 1:6 Architecture and art of Southern India.* Cambridge: Cambridge University Press.

Organ, T.W. 1970. *The Hindu quest for the perfection of man.* Athens: Ohio University Press.

Pal, P. 1994. *The peaceful liberators: Jain art from India.* Los Angeles: Los Angeles Museum of Art.

Rao, N. (forthcoming) *Royal artistic imagery at Vijayanagara.* New Delhi: Aditya Prakashan.

Zwalf, W. (ed.) 1985. *Buddhism: art and faith.* London: British Museums Publications

Chapter 25

The Architecture of Freedom

Satish Grover

It may come as a surprise to many that Indian architects of modern times have been honored with International Awards. Architects like Charles Correa, Balakrishna Doshi, Raj Rewal have won many a laurel in the world of architecture awarded by the various Institutes of Architecture. Indian architects have received, and frequently been part of the master jury of, the prestigious Aga Khan Award in architecture. And in 1990, Charles Correa won the UIA Gold medal, which is recognized as equivalent of the Nobel Prize in architecture. Books have been written about Indian architects and the state of contemporary architecture in India has been critically discussed and acclaimed, abroad and at home. At the time of Independence there was not a single journal on the Indian architectural scene; today there are at least half a dozen journals with a fairly sustained international and local readership and recognition. These include *Architectural Design, The Indian Architect, Indian Builder, Inside-Outside, Architecture Plus Design* and many other specialist professional journals. Some of these have won merit awards too. In 1947 there were only three fledgling Departments of Architecture, as part of the technical institute imparting architectural education and awarding diplomas and degrees. Today there are more than 91 such teaching institutes and departments in universities. There is even a university devoted entirely to architecture and planning. Starting from a handful of draftsmen and architects to serve their imperial rulers, today, a half century later, there are as many as 21,500 registered architects in the country and many of them are running independent professional practices. They areemployed in both the public and private sectors, practicing independently or teaching, and researching in schools. These are raw statistics, no doubt, but nevertheless an impressive testimony to the phenomenal growth of the profession in just half a century. Let us now look at the immediate past and also of beyond statistics.

Freedom

On the fateful night of 15th August 1947, things changed dramatically in the capital city. New and Old Delhi became the repositories of refugees from across the new borders of India and Pakistan. The formality of Lutyens'New Delhi was upturned by the haphazard commercial and residential settlements of the refugees—some temporary, and many others which, irrespective of planning, wedged themselves permanently into the new urban scene. To deflect some of this largely Punjabi and Multani population to a new, viable urban alternative, Jawaharlal Nehru, the first Prime Minister of free India, decided to build a brand new capital for the state of Punjab. Christened Chandigarh—after an ancient temple to the goddess Chandi in the region—this new city was destined to become the fountainhead of architecture and urban planning of independent India. And thus begins the story of the resurgence of Indian architecture.

The City of Chandigarh

Le Corbusier was appointed as architect for the city. Sixty two years old at the time, he had acquired the reputation of being the *enfant terrible* of the architectural scene in the West. He was enormously talented, and besides designing a vast repertoire of buildings in many countries including the erstwhile Soviet union, he had also written books and pamphlets to promote his visions of a 'universal modern architecture.' However, perhaps because of a rather pugnacious nature, no nation had yet given him the opportunity of designing a completely new city, though he had, on his own initiative, drawn up, with visionary zeal, detailed plans for many communities and cities.

After his first visit to India and to the proposed site for Chandigarh he stated, " It is the hour that I have been waiting for—for India, the humane and profound civilization—to construct a capital." In India he experienced the "bright blue sky, the relentless sun, the hot winds, the cool moon, the fury of the monsoon," and after ten days of intensive work a draft plan for a 6,000 hectare Chandigarh that was to accommodate a population of half a million emerged. The outcome was a plan that was a composition of 'sectors,' 1,200m x 800m, defined by high speed traffic roads, a distant industrial complex, a main shopping-cum-office complex in the center, and a Capital Complex at the Northern head of the city, immediately below the Shivalik hills. To Le Corbusier this arrangement was reflective of the human body. The 'head' was the administrative part of the 'body' and the university, located to the west, formed the 'thinking' center. The business district, placed centrally, was the 'heart,' where energy was produced to fuel the machines for living and working. The matrix of streets and residential blocks formed the 'body' proper of the city, and at its 'feet,' at a suitable distance, lay the industrial sectors.

Sure, the creation of Chandigarh left many people bewildered or even horrified. Nehru justified the city as a representation of an India "unfettered by the past." And the forces unleashed were too powerful and energetic to be deterred either by the new brown sahibs lamenting the departure of the British or the conventionalists looking back blindly to India's glorious past. When the notions of modernism were adopted by schools teaching architecture, the train of modernism, for good or worse, was moving full speed ahead.

No doubt, as in every revolutionary movement (and this really was one), there is the good and the bad. The modern movement in India was no exception to this rule. The saving grace was that the good was very good and the bad at its worst was plebeian but not entirely devoid of purpose. It was a matter of which drawer the architect took his leaves from, out of the top, the middle, or the bottom. Of course the bottom drawer provided the "quickies" which rapidly sprouted all over India even in the countryside. They were absolutely plain—quickly and cheaply constructed mere boxes with holes punched in them for doors and windows, devoid of any purpose or message beyond providing the most basic of shelters. But we should keep in mind that these, too, were badly needed in a country where even a permanent roof over one's head was a great boon. The middle drawer was readily adopted by the middle class. This consisted of a shelter with proper doors and windows and a few pasted artifacts to establish pretensions of 'status.'

The New Urban Scene

These structures undoubtedly had the most widespread impact on the Indian scene. They were also to be seen in the new landscapes of the rural, the semi-urban (or semi-rural) and the urban areas. To these the Central and the State Public Works Departments (P.W.D.) made a most generous contribution. Totally regardless of context, the same Type A's, B's and C's were built all over the country, just like the P.W.D. building the same culvert over all the *nallahs* in the country. Fortunately, there were enough who opted for the top drawer, and have carried the beacon to date. It is with their achievement that we should be more concerned. And why not? We judge the state of Indian music by talking of Ravi Shankars and Ali Akbars and the like, not by the atrocious Hindi pop which is all prevalent. Don't we say that Indian cinema is healthy by alluding to Satyajit Ray and not to the typical productsof Bollywood? One could discern this fact in almost any artistic endeavor. In the same strain, I would say that modern Indian architecture is today near its peak.

Different from the earlier post-independence years—which saw Indian designers grappling with the problems of establishing a new architecture for a nation in need of modernization today, architects across the subcontinent reveal a maturity in their work which is both sophisticated in its understanding of the modern idiom and reverent in its mindfulness of India's living past. The opening of the economy in 1991 has once more positioned the country at the edge of a new building boom, bringing with it the promise of many new opportunities for Indian architects here to show their talents.

The Heroic Age

Charles Correa, one of India's—and indeed the world's--most prominent architects, recently designed and completed the Inter-University Center for Astrophysics and Astronomy in Pune. This modern building complex in shades of mauve complemented by stone transforms the traditional elements of design, such as the open-to-sky courtyard pergolas and the entrance gateway, into a modern idiom. Similarity, his vibrantly colored Jawahar Kala Kendra museum in Jaipur, gained its inspiration from the traditional nine square *mandala*, or ancient geometric cosmic energy diagram that provided the blueprint for the Hindu temple design, but in expression it is very much a twentieth century building. Deeply interested in traditional Indian architecture is also Balkrishna Doshi, a contemporary of Correa's (and a student of Le Corbusier's) who broke new ground when he designed the Indian Institute of Management in Bangalore. Enwrapped in a modernist sheath of brick, it features several elements of traditional Indian city planning, including *chowks* (squares), gateways, and connecting streets. On the other side of the subcontinent stands this author's Oberoi Hotel in Bhubaneshwar, a contemporary hotel whose plan borrows from Indian temple architecture a sequence of *mandapams* or public spaces progressing to the *garbha griha*, or the heart, where one finds the pool.

All of these contemporary buildings carry a common theme. The architect today recognizes the wisdom in the building forms of the past, and yet realizes the need to evolve a contemporary idiom that reflects the changing world he or she lives in. "Indian architecture," a term generally thought to apply to historic buildings on the subcontinent, has now broadened its scope to include a whole new category of buildings, and like the banyan tree, its roots are many. Into these virgin and challenging arenas entered the first generation of Indian architects. Habib Rahman, Achyut Kanvinde, and the late Durga Bajpai were among the first group to be schooled in America. Influenced by the aesthetics of the revolutionary Bauhaus School, the cradle of Modernism in the West, they advocated functionalism, simplicity, structural clarity and use of modern materials like steel and glass—far cry from the decorative, stylistic designs of the past. These young novitiates were impatient to contribute their Western learning to the buoyant mood of a free India, " unfettered by the past." Rahman, trained both as a mechanical engineer and an architect, was a pioneer in setting the pace for modern trends in government buildings. The new Secretariat for West Bengal in Calcutta, completed in the early fifties, was the first high rise building in India. His housing scheme for government employees; the familiar Rabindra Bhawan in Delhi; and three poetic memorials to national leaders including Maulana Azad are representative of this early phase. Bajpai and Mody's Oberoi Hotel in New Delhi and Kanvinde's Indian Institute of Technology in Kanpur are other landmarks.

The City of Ahmedabad

In Ahmedabad, Gujarat, a parallel center of activity has developed, inspired by the visionary outlook of the prosperous mill-owner families. Taking advantage of Le Corbusier's presence in the country, they had invited him to Ahmedabad as well. Doshi, then a young architect who had worked in Le Corbusier's studio in Paris was commissioned as the architect for building in the city, and became a major designer exploiting the plasticity of concrete. From early on, bolder forms of his work matured to the subtler vaulted composition of his own office and research center, *Sangath*, and later the Gandhi Labor Institute, both completed in the eighties. Both these buildings have an external part finished with broken white glazed tiles--an example of recycled waste material that reflects indirect sunlight, thus minimizing heat absorption. They reflect Doshi's concern with the fine and technological arts even then. On a deeper level, his architecture continues to imbibe the philosophical and traditional elements of his own culture in the search for a regional identity. Ahmedabad has always been a major nerve center for architectural practice and theory, the latter a result of the Ahmedabad School for which Doshi was largely responsible. Charles Correa's deep understanding, even at that time, of the paradox of tradition in a modern environment is clearly seen in one of his earliest and most seminal works, the Gandhi Sanghrahalya in the Sabarmati Ashram in Ahmedabad. The cluster of familiar pyramidal tile-roofed huts, open from the sides, is infused with a modernist vocabulary in a serene and almost hypnotic manner. The theme of traditional spaces, the open-to-sky courtyards, the hierarchy of location, as articulated in cosmic beliefs and mandalas remain central to Correa's work. "We will have to learn how to absorb the mythic images and values," he says, and "re-invent them in terms of new inspirations. We must enlarge our perspective so as to take cognizance of not only the public and private issues involved in our decisions, but the sacred ones as well."

The Building Boom

The sixties heralded an unprecedented burst of building activity for the entire country, setting in motion a momentum which hasn't flagged since. So much so that blueprints for city planning became as necessary as they were for architecture. The British system of two cities—the cantonment, orderly and planned for the elite, and the 'other,' haphazard half for the rest--was now archaic under the democratic system. Master plans were drawn in detail laying down building controls and regulations for different land uses. Thousands of opportunities were created for architects; thousands of offices, large and small, opened up; and buildings mushroomed in a plethora of shapes and visual expressions. It was a period of intense experimentation and invention. Sure of a strong foundation, architects experienced a liberation to wander into hitherto uncharted territories; new building types emerged — institutional buildings for all kinds of training and development requirements, exhibition architecture, sports complexes, five-star hotels, museums and commercial complexes.

Above all, architects had been recognized as class of professionals the country needed. The buildings of this period established new genres in the expanding vocabulary of contemporary Indian architecture. There was a growing consciousness, in the public mind as much as in the agenda of sponsoring authorities, that form was as important as function; that centers for learning, for trade, for art and culture needed visibility and identity; that the persona of buildings was an essential part of their being.

Doshi took the lead. The India International Center, brainchild of Dr. C.D. Deshmukh, was conceived as a center for research and intellectual interaction. Situated alongside the beautiful Lodi Gardens, it was designed by Joseph Allen Stein, an American architect who adopted India as his homeland. It is a lyrical complex of buildings which recognizes the importance of landscape and environment. A complete antithesis to this was Raj Rowal's Pragati Maidan pavilion complex planned for trade and industrial fairs. A gigantic program originally designed for steel but finally executed in concrete, the permanent exhibition halls set new standards for exhibition architecture, and recognized the role of the engineer as a design partner.

Building Alternatives

In the vibrant Indian democracy, the reactions to the modern movement led to a very wide range of alternatives for development. A new vernacular idiom was also emerging, exploiting the potential of local materials and styles. The Kalakshetra Theatre in Madras, for instance, is a reflection of the traditional vernacular architecture of South India, in the same way as a "modern" house in mountainous Kulu. The necessity for cost effective and alternative building technologies inspired by time-tested methods had given birth to various building research institutions that have promoted building with reinforced mud blocks, bamboo and thatch, local stone, etc. The mortality rate of these alternate idioms has been high, because sometimes they were based on the romantic but economically inviable notions of revivalism of untenable crafts and traditions; in others, because of their very limited applicability in terms of undue dependence on very local conditions. But ultimately, those died at the altar of 'durability' due to a very strong preference for the '*pucca*,' which modern architecture, with its built in notions of long term economy, was eminently capable of delivering.

The Local and the Universal

However, these were experiments; some of them may have failed but there is no doubting the good intentions that prompted them. But lately, a more dangerous trend has affected, unfortunately, even top drawer architects. This is the glamor of the 'international style,' 'post modernism,' 'neo-modernism,' and so on. Many an Indian architect has mistaken these styles for movements instead of the fads that they are. Popular Indian architects, perhaps in their innocence, enjoy the freedom that this 'no rules' provided. The "anything goes" notions have produced bizarre results. Fortunately, the fountain-head from where these concepts emanated is itself running out of steam, and one can only hope that sanity returns to these architects. Let us instead be guided by the advice of an American of yore, Lewis Mumford, and aim to create "a genuine universalism in which the warmth, the intimate, the personal attribute of a local culture would mingle with ideas and forms that are common to all men in all times." Ingredients for fulfilling both notions are amply available in the country today.

VIII | Language & Literature

Chapter 26 Language in Indian Society

Braj B. Kachru

The Indian subcontinent is perceived as a 'Tower of Babel,' a sociolinguistic 'problem area' and a region of linguistic anarchy. This perception of India has traditionally been emphasized by those, both in India in the West, who consider diversity to be a marker of non-cohesiveness and a hurtful strain on social and political harmony. However, as we shall see, such analysis ignores the many important functions performed by the diverse languages, well as the strong networks of convergence that unify communication patterns in India.[1]

At one level, India does present a daunting profile of complexities. The indicators of such complexities, repeated as mantras, include India's population (now close to the billion mark), the diversity of its language families, and the enormous number of languages and dialects spoken in this vast region. The ethnic and religious pluralism of the country is represented by the followers of over half a dozen principal religions of the world who have lived together for centuries. These religions include Hinduism (82 percent), Islam (12.1 percent), Christianity (2.34 percent), Sikhism (1.94 percent), Buddhism (0.76 percent), and Jainism (0.4 percent). The two religions, Christianity and Islam, are not native to India (as are Hinduism, Sikhism, Buddhism, and Jainism), but these, too, have been Indianized in many interesting ways. India is also home to over 120,000 Zoroastrians and a dwindling number of followers of Judaism. All of these religions have a long history of contact, convergence, and also of various types of tensions which occasionally flare up. This religious pluralism, and the age-old caste hierarchy, naturally has relevance to our understanding of the profile of India's languages, and resultant language attitudes and language conflicts. There has also been the ongoing conflict and controversy on language in India's education policies.

It must be mentioned, however, that social scientists, including language specialists, have traditionally focused attention on the diversity of India, but very few attempts have been made to present the deep strands of civilizational unity that provide ideological, cultural, and linguistic cohesiveness to the country (cf. Harrison 1960). There are just a handful of scholarly attempts that explain the bonds that have evolved, sustained, and often strengthened, what has been called the underlying idea of India and the manifestations of this unifying vision of Indianness in the arts, literature, philosophy, languages and communication across the subcontinent. This vision of India is presented, for example, by independent India's first Prime Minister, Jawaharlal Nehru, when he says that India "... is a myth and an idea, a dream and a vision, and yet very real and present and pervasive" (Nehru 1967). Nehru further explains:

> India is not a mere geographical identity. It is something much more and deeper. It is an idea which has influenced the people who have lived here and who have come from other countries and found a home here since the beginnings of civilization. (Nehru 1967)

This chapter, then, is an attempt to present a linguistic profile of India and its communication networks, and to discuss the various dimensions of not only India's linguistic complexities but also the unity in the function of languages in multilingual Indian society. In other words, it presents the strands of Indianness in India's linguistic diversity.

A Linguistic Profile of India

The four genetically unrelated language families represented in India are Indo-Aryan, Dravidian, Sino-Tibetan, and Austro-Asiatic. The estimated total number of languages and their dialects, however, is substantially larger—the census report estimates about 1,652. This figure makes India the repository of the largest number of languages and dialects in the world.

This, of course, is a daunting profile of India's national languages. But in reality, it is less complex than it appears. The majority of Indians use languages that belong to only two large language groups, Indo-Aryan (estimated 59 percent of the population) and Dravidian (estimated 20 percent). These two language families, then, comprise almost 80 percent of the Indian population and represent over 680 languages and dialects spoken in the country. Furthermore, speakers of a set of 18 languages (see below) account for the overwhelming majority of India's population. In a sense that makes communication less daunting and more manageable.

The Indian Constitution, after a prolonged and agonizing debate, recognized fifteen languages as India's "national" languages. The latest figure, however, is eighteen, after-three languages, Konkani, Manipuri, and Nepali were added to the list. (See Table 4 below.) [2]

Table 4: Principal Languages and Speakers

Language	*Speakers*
Assamese	14.8 M
Bengali	68.3 M
Gujarati	44.0 M
Hindi	350.3 M
Kannada	35.7 M
Kashmiri	0.44 M
Konkani	15.7 M
Malayalam	34.4 M
Manipuri	9.01 M
Marathi	65.8 M
Nepali	13.6 M
Oriya	30.3 M
Punjabi	24.7 M
Sanskrit	2,946
Sindhi	31.0 M
Tamil	59.3 M
Telugu	71.9 M
Urdu	46.8 M

After the reorganization of state boundaries on linguistic lines in 1956, several languages were associated with well-defined linguistic regions, and in many cases, the name of a state and the name of a language is identical (e.g., in Punjab state, the language is Punjabi; in Bengal state, the language is Bengali; in Orissa, it is Oriya; in Tamil Nadu, it is Tamil; and in Gujarat, it is Gujarati). This is, however, not true of all the states—the language of Andhra Pradesh is Telugu and that of Kerala is Malayalam.

India's Constitution, however, recognizes only Hindi (in Devanāgarī ("Divine City's Writing") script) as the "official" language of the Republic. This was actually the first official attempt to give Hindi the position of a pan-Indian language. It has developed since the twelfth century as a mixture of many dialects of *madhya desa* (Central India) including those bordering Bengal. In its structure Hindi is not much different from Urdu, which is the national language of Pakistan and the state language of India's Kashmir. The status of English is that of an "associate" official language. Originally, this status was given to English only for a period of fifteen years, until 1965. The Official Languages Act of 1963, however, removed that time constraint for an indefinite period.

Why fifteen, now eighteen, "national" languages? What was the motivation for this number and the selection process? The reasons for selection of the languages in the Eighth Schedule of India's Constitution are varied, but include:

- the numerical strength of the speakers of a language
- the literary traditions associated with the language
- the regional representation of the speakers of the major languages, and
- the power of political pressure groups

The selection of just eighteen out of estimated 1,652 languages and dialects was not easy, nor was it necessarily logical. A variety of political, emotional, and other considerations determined the choice. Sanskrit ("The Perfected Language") was chosen as it is the language of India's cultural, literary, and historical past. And it continues to be used by Hindus all over India and elsewhere in major rituals and in religious contexts--Hindus also call it devavāṇī ("Gods' language"). A majority of Indian languages with significant numbers of speakers and well-defined boundaries were included, e.g., Assamese, Bengali, Marathi, and Tamil. Languages such as Kashmiri, Sindhi, and Nepali, with smaller numbers of speakers, were recognized due to various political and other pressures. A linguistic mosaic was created to represent India's pluralistic cultural, communicative, and ethnic networks. On the whole, what the architects of the Constitution had in mind seems to have worked, certainly during the critical and decisive period of post-Independence stress and the competing demands for regional identities. But that is only a part of the story (cf. Gupta, Abbi, and Aggarwal 1995).

Languages and Identities: Repertoires and Functions

On the basis of this linguistic profile of India, a person from what is perceived as a monolingual society, for example, the United States, might ask: What is it like to function in a linguistically pluralistic society such as India? The answer is that in coun-

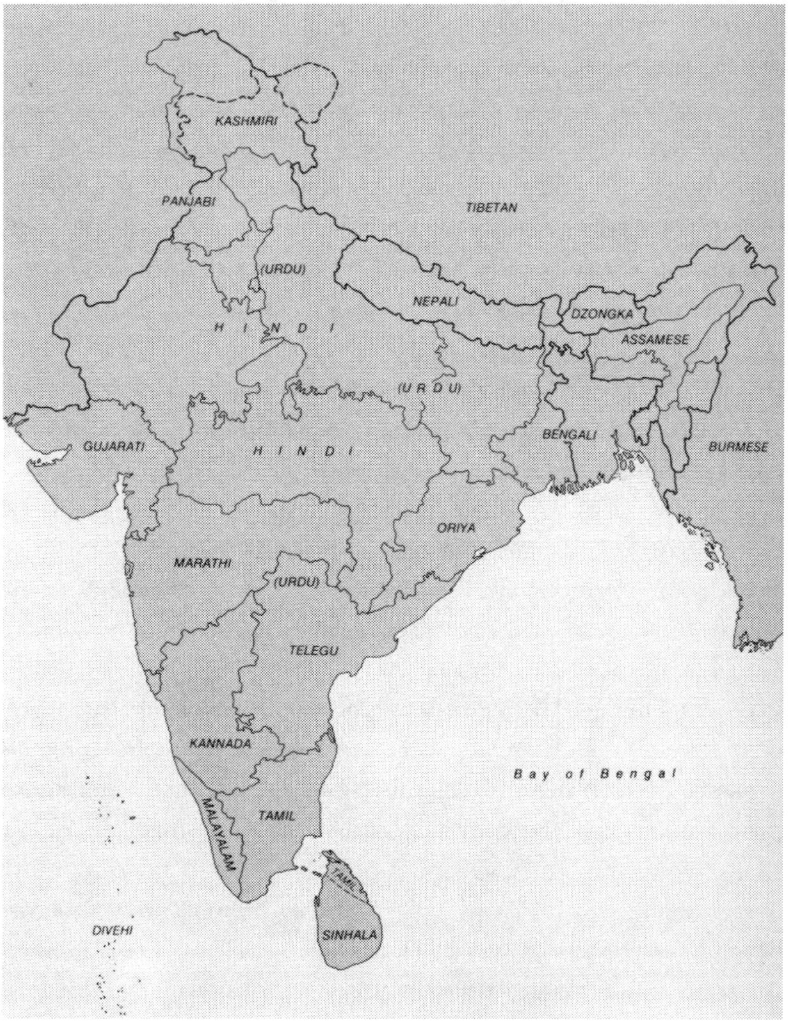

Figure 37: Prinicipal Languages of India, Based on *The Cambridge Encyclopedia of India, Pakistan, Bangladesh, Sri Lanka.* (1989)

tries like India, Singapore, and Nigeria—to give just three examples—a multilingual individual sets up a language hierarchy, makes linguistic choices, and establishes linguistic spaces in which a particular language or dialect is used. The choices are made according to the roles a person envisages for oneself and for one's children in society.

In India, as in other multilingual societies, one is, therefore, always aware of various types of linguistic identities. These identities are maintained and strengthened by the use of appropriate codes of communication. Thus, one may use a village dialect, which may or may not also be a caste dialect (e.g., Brahmin or Non-Brahmin), a regional language (e.g., Bengali, Kashmiri), and a wider link-language such as Hindi and/or English. The choice of language ultimately depends on what linguistic space one desires to acquire in terms of communication and types of function. It is through strategic use of these linguistic resources that one establishes and expresses various identities and functions in the power structure: social, educational, administrative, legal, professional, and so on. It is also for this reason that choices of language loyalty, maintenance, and shift /change evolve. We see evidence of such shifts in the census reports and in language-related conflicts in India and in other parts of the world.

In multilingual societies the language choice mostly depends on answers to questions such as: Does a particular language, for example, Kashmiri or Gujarati, provide mobility in terms of function? What roles can one perform with a particular language or dialect when one moves out of that language or dialect speaking area? What is the "economic value" of a particular language in terms of access to a profession (e.g., becoming a medical doctor, car mechanic, lawyer, merchant, or engineer)? What are the groups in which the language or dialect provides membership in terms of ethnicity, religion, status, or region?

In India, as in other multilingual societies, people generally have a linguistic repertoire that equips them for various functions in society. The linguistic repertoire represents the total range of languages and dialects that members of a language community have at their command for interaction and communication with other members of the community. The range of the repertoire depends on the contexts of interaction and the geographical range of linguistic functions (village, district, region, and state, across the states, and beyond the borders of India). Thus, depending on these important variables, the repertoire may include dialects or styles of a language, a variety of distinct languages from a closely related language family; or a language which is unrelated to the language family (e.g., Sanskrit in the Dravidian region, Tamil in the Indo-Aryan region, and Persian in North India). It is not unusual to find in India persons using three or four languages not only in everyday social interaction, but also in literary creativity.

It is useful to describe language function with reference to two types of linguistic repertoires: individual and societal. This functional multilingualism is evident in several language-related policies of post-Imperial India. I will discuss here four cases of national policy based on linguistic pluralism: the use of languages in education, the recognition of national literatures, and languages in broadcasting and in print media.

The first example of such pluralism is the use of the *Three Language Formula* in the national educational system. This formula, proposed in the 1960's, was meant to introduce an integrative approach to language in education. In a nutshell, the formula entails the study of three languages during the school years: the regional language, Hindi, and English. In the so-called *madhya deśa* (central India), the students are expected to learn a Dravidian language (Kannada, Malayalam, Telugu, or Tamil). This formula, ideally speaking, is a linguistic balancing act, so that the language load of learners is nationally equal, regardless of the language and the region in which the students live. It also makes sense in what one can accomplish in functional terms with these three linguistic tools. The success in implementation of this proposal is, however, very uneven, and cynicism about its usefulness is abundant (cf. Kachru 1994b: 542-8; for the history of education in India, Nurullah and Naik 1951; for a discussion on English in Indian education, see Singh 1979, and Ram 1983.)

The second example of the national policy based on functional multilingualism is the recognition of *multiple national literatures* by the Sahitya Akademi (the National Academy of Letters) founded by the Government of India in 1954 to promote literary activity in India's major languages and also by state-sponsored language academies in each state. The Sahitya Akademi considers many more languages and literatures for its annual awards than the eighteen languages recognized in the Constitution.

The third example is the multiplicity of languages used by the government-operated electronic media, *Akashvani* (All India Radio: literally 'voice from space') and the *Doordarshan* (Indian Television: literally 'distant vision'). In both radio and television, the multilingual character of India is aggressively represented by including a string of 'major' and 'minor' languages in the programs.

The fourth example is the *use of languages by the print media.* The Republic of India has a vibrant free press, using over 92 languages. The print media includes 14,531 newspapers and periodicals, comprising 929 dailies, 4,225 weeklies, and 9,299 others. In this multiplicity of voices and multi-tongued media, the English language press has a vital role—second only to Hindi. There are now seven daily newspapers with continuous publication for over a century—four of these are in English: *The Times of India*, Bombay (estd.1850); *The Pioneer*, Lucknow (1865); *The Mail*, Madras (1867); and *Amrita Bazar Patrika*, Calcutta (1868). The first English newspaper in India, *The Bengal Gazette* or *Calcutta General Advertiser*, was owned by an Englishman named James Augustus Hicky. The first Indian-owned English newspaper, with an identical name, *The Bengal Gazette*, was published by Gangadhar Bhatachargee (1816). In the 19th century, the first Indian language newspaper were started by Christian missionaries who were also instrumental in cutting type for Indian languages. This had far-reaching effects in introducing literacy in India.

The father of Indian journalism was the social revolutionary and thinker Rammohan Roy (1772?-1833). Roy started journals in three languages, English, Bengali, and Persian: *Brahman Sambādh* (1821), *Sambādh Kaumudi* (1821), and *Mirat-ul-Akhbār* (1921). His aim was to counter the work of the missionaries. Roy's activities upset the government and resulted in the suppressive Vernacular Press Act (1823), which curtailed the Indian voice. A pan-Indian political dialogue was initiated by three English magazines, which contributed toward consciousness raising and social awareness: G. A. Natesan's *Indian Review* (Madras, now Chennai), Ramanand Chatterjee's *Modern Review* (Calcutta), and Tej Bahadur Sapru's *Twentieth Century* (Allahabad).

We see the same multilingual tradition in India's *book publishing*. In this again, Hindi and English language publishers top the list. Publishing houses number 15,000; of these 75 percent are small presses, with 45 percent of the book titles published in English. The National Book Trust (established in 1957) and Children's Book Trust are two government-sponsored agencies for the promotion of books in India's languages. Each state in India has a regional academy for encouraging and supporting book publication in regional languages.

Contact Languages and Languages for Wider Communication

In this extensive linguistic diversity, considerable communication, administration, and business is transacted in what are called contact languages or languages of wider communication. Such languages, ideally speaking, have currency across regional, ethnic, caste, and linguistic boundaries.

Sanskrit

India's chief classical language, which had elevated, pan-Indian functions in religious, philosophical, and metaphysical discourse, and in rituals and literary creativity, is Sanskrit. The social penetration of the language and its creative uses were originally essentially restricted to the Brahmins. All the major languages and regions of India clearly demonstrate the major impact of Sanskrit, resulting in a process known as Sanskritization.

Kashmir is an example of such impact from one state of India. Due to the recent history of turmoil in the state, one may forget that, in the past, Kashmir had been the citadel of Sanskrit culture and learning. Before the Islamic impact, the language of literary creativity and intellectual discourse in Kashmir was Sanskrit. Sanskrit fulfilled most of the formal and elite roles of discourse, including philosophy (e.g., trika darśana), poetics (e.g., Ānandavardhana, c. 850 C.E., who expounded *dhvani* and *rasa* poetic theories), historical narrative (e.g., Kalhana's *Rajatarangin*ī), and satire (e.g., Kśemendra). All these Sanskrit manuscripts in Kashmir were preserved in Śaradā script (see section on writing systems below).

Persian

These roles of Sanskrit continued until the penetration of Islam. In Kashmir, as in several other regions of North India, Persian ultimately replaced Sanskrit. The induction of Persian in India was primarily due to the efforts of, as Stanley Wolpert observes, the Sultans of Delhi, and later, Mughal Emperors. They "spread Perso-Arabic poetry and prose with their swords of Islamic conquest and conversion."(Wolpert 1991: 185). Persian was used particularly as a language of the courts, administration, and also of literary creativity. The hegemony of Persian lasted for over four centuries, resulting in the Persianization of Kashmiri literary and intellectual culture. The ancestral Sanskrit language was reduced to essentially ritualistic roles. The Pandits of Kashmir gradually turned to Persian and used it as a language of access, even to study their own Hindu religious and cultural texts such as the Mahabhārata, Bhāgavata, Rāmayaṇa, Ṣivapurāṇa, and the BhagavadGītā. Pushp, a Kashmiri Sanskrit scholar, tells us that the Hindus enjoyed reading Persian classics like the *Mathanvi* of Moulana Rumi, the *Shahnama* of Firdusi and the *Sikandarnama* of Nizami. These used to be taught in the *maktabs* often run by Kashmiri Pandit *akhuns*. (Pushp 1992: 22)

The Pandits of Kashmir established close identity with the Perso-Arabic script and produced religious texts in this script so that literate Hindus could read them without depending on the Devanāgāri script. This was particularly true of those texts that covered Hindu rituals (karmakāṇḍa), astrology (jyotiṣāstra), and the indigenous medical system (Āyurveda). The Pandits of Kashmir, as Cook observes:

> ...composed a new Shaiva literature in Persian verse. The classical Persian gazal became the ode to Shiva, Lord of the La Makan, Spaceless Space. The technical vocabulary of Erfan suited their purposes perfectly, and morning prayers were

> conducted in a Persian which listening neighbours could not distinguish from songs of the "Orafa." Whatever position they [the Pandits] won for themselves in India when forced out of Kashmir by Persian-speaking invaders, the Pandit emigrés continued to compose their Persian Shaiva odes.(Cook 1958: 28)

This identity with the language continued until Urdu, and later English, were introduced in the state. The Kashmir situation is just an example of what actually happened in several other northern and central Indian regions when Persian acquired important roles.

Sanskrit, Again

The debate on the status of Sanskrit in ancient and modern India has occupied scholars—both Indian and Western—for a long time. In the past, as Fleet reminds us, Sanskrit was used, as a spoken language, by pandits for instruction, as well as conversation, as the most readily used tool of communication and still is, in many contexts.[3]

The question whether Sanskrit was used in busy market places, and in interaction with one's neighbors, is not easy to answer. There is, however, no doubt that Sanskrit has a long history as an elite language of high religious and cultivated literary traditions. It has been the pan-Indian language that articulated various visions and philosophies of Hinduism and its diverse traditions, and that of life and living in general.

And now experiments are afoot—though modest—to revive the language for day-to-day communication. One should not be surprised if one is asked, "katham asti bhavān?" (How are you?) in the 1990's in Sanskrit. This is actually what happens now in a small village, Mathuru, in Karnataka's Shimoga district. This village is only a couple of hundred miles away from the Silicon capital of India, Bangalore. The expected response to the above question asked in Sanskrit is supposed to be but, "sammyak asmi, twām katham asi?," meaning "I'm fine. How are you?"

In this little village of about 1,200 inhabitants on the banks of river Tunga, Sanskrit is not dead. It is not exclusively the language of the elite: It is also the language of the mailman who greets you and says, "idam bhavataye patram" (This is your mail.). This experiment in the use of Sanskrit was started in 1987 and is being watched with interest. Whatever the ultimate result of this experiment in "living in the Vedic era but with 20th-century comforts like radio and TV," as one housewife puts it, one thing is certain: Sanskrit continues to be secure in its rich traditional philosophy, literary creativity, and its place in the ritual texts of Hindus.[4]

Indian English

It is, however, Indian English, yet another initially imposed language, which gradually, but definitely, acquired the status of a pan-Indian language. The year 1997 marks Independent India's 50th anniversary. It also marks the 162nd anniversary of the institutionalization of English in India. English acquired this position by the much-discussed and much-maligned *Minute* of Thomas Babington Macaulay (1800-1859), which was introduced in the Parliament on February 2, 1835. The implications of this Minute have indeed been far-reaching: It became a blueprint for India's educational policy. It also started an on-going debate on the success of Macaulay's mission of creating "a class of persons, Indians in blood and colour, but English in taste, in opinions, in morals and in intellect." One view is that as English was introduced in India's communication network, the native Indian languages suffered and the brown sahibs who controlled the elitist imperial language developed into a power bloc, certainly more important than the Persian-knowing Indians of that time.

In Macaulay's view, India's native languages were "poor and rude" and the learning of the East was "a little hocus-pocus about the cusa-grass and the modes of absorption into the Deity" (Bryant 1932: 56-7). And his knowledge of the subcontinent's languages and literatures was not all that profound. He himself confesses that:

> I have no knowledge of either Sanskrit or Arabic. But I have done what I could to form a correct estimate of their value . . . I am quite ready to take the oriental learning at the valuation of the orientalists themselves. I have never found one amongst them who could deny that a single shelf of a good European library was worth the whole native literature of India and Arabia.

Macaulay was adamant that his *Minute* be approved, and when it was presented to the Supreme Council of India, he was unambiguous about his position. He indicated to the Council "his intention of resigning if they were not accepted"(Bryant 1932: 56). The *Minute* received a Seal of Approval from Lord William Bentick (1774-1839) on March 7, 1835. Almost a century later a British educator and linguist, J. R. Firth (1890-1960), held "superficial Lord Macaulay" responsible for "the superficiality characteristic of Indian education" (Firth 1930: 210-1). Yet another view is that of Rammohan

Roy and some of his Indian contemporaries, who were,

> filled with sanguine hopes [that] European gentlemen of talents and education would instruct the natives of India in mathematics, natural philosophy, chemistry, anatomy and other useful sciences which the natives of Europe have carried to a degree of perfection that has raised them above the inhabitants of other parts of the world. (Roy 1823: 99-101)

The products of English education—a significant number of them—indeed remained "Indian in blood and colour," but formed opinions, values, and visions which were not consistent with the belief of the architect of the *Minute*. The English language was used by the Indian National Congress (founded in 1885) as the medium to spread a message across India that mobilized national opinion among the English-educated for a cultural renaissance and political consciousness-raising. The cultural Englishness of the language gradually diminished as it was used to study India's past, and to contrast two types of India: one, that of Max Müller and the other, for example, of Katherine Mayo. Mayo's book, mischievously titled *Mother India* (1927), was characterized by Gandhi as a "drain inspector's report." While Mayo's book upset educated Indians, it was used by imperial Britain for its political advantage. English-educated Indians used the English language to "write back" to the Katherine Mayos of that time. This writing developed into a genre of its own in works such as, *Unhappy India* (1928) by Lala Lajpat Rai, and *Uncle Sam* (1929) by K.L. Gauba. This genre later acquired other dimensions—political, historical, and nationalistic -- in the hands of nationalist leaders who wrote in English and in their mother tongues, including G. K. Gokhale, B. G. Tilak, M. K. Gandhi, V. Savarkar, J. L. Nehru, and others. India was slowly rediscovering herself and one important medium was the English language. This is what Bankim Chandra Chatterji meant when he said that,

> there is no hope for India until the Bengali and the Panjabi understand and influence each other, and can bring their influence to bear upon the Englishman. This can be done only through the medium of English (cited in Wolpert 1991:187).

Macaulay's Minute certainly changed India, but in a direction different from what was on the imperialist's agenda.

Indianization of English

The perceptions of English in India and its penetration into the life of the country suggests that it has become a sort of a linguistic elephant being felt and described by various blind people--the perceptions about the users and uses of English vary from one to another depending on what aspect of India's English elephant they are touching. There is significant variation in the uses of English. The varieties are marked by the region and the dominant language of its users (e.g., *Punjabi* English, *Bengali* English, *Tamil* English), and profession (e.g., office babu, mufussil district officers, officers of the Indian Administrative Service, and the senior network of the Indian Defense forces). Then there is the *Masala English* of magazines, such as *Stardust,* the *Zee* Channel of Indian television, and a variety of pidginized varieties, such as, *Babu English, Butler English* and *Boxwallah English*[5]. These varieties and functions demonstrate how vibrant and Indianized the English language has become and specifically how deeply it has penetrated into various layers of Indian society.

The colonial context of the language has also been defied and transformed by a long and impressive list of writers of Indian English. Thus, the language of the Colonizer was not only institutionalized and acculturated, but also became a medium of pan-Indian elite interaction, of national introspection, and gradually, developed into what may be called Caliban's weapon of revenge—a medium for "talking back" and "writing back" to the Imperial masters. English went on to become an additional language of the "intellectual make up" of Western educated Indians.[6]

All these major and minor varieties—pidginized and non-pidginized—have contributed to the making of the Indian English elephant and each creativity further adds to the "elephantness." There is, however, no denying the fact that English has now become part of India's linguistic and literary traditions. It has been, for example, Sanskritized, as in Raja Rao's metaphysical novel, *The Serpent and the Rope*) and Punjabiized, as in Mulk Raj Anand's social novels, *Coolie* and *Untouchable.*

The multilingual competence of Indians and their cultural diversity is reflected in Indian uses of the English language, for example, in newspaper headlines, such as,

JNU karamcharis begin dharna (*The Statesman*, May 1981),
Marathwada band over pandal fire (*The Indian Express*, May 1981), and
Lakhpati swindler held (*The Hindustan Times,* May 1981).

In these three captions, words such as *karamcharis* (workers), *dharna* (sit in), *band* (strike), *pandal* (podium), and *lakhpati* (one who is rich and possesses money in "lakhs," or hundreds of thousand rupees) are from Indian languages, and the newspapers take it for granted that a reader has bi- or multilingual competence. In this sense, then, these newspapers are not necessarily meant for the non-Indian "native speaker" reader of English (that is, for example, from the U.K., or U.S.A.) but for a "native user" of Indian English. The text is not Indianized by the use of Indian words only. Consider, for example, the following English words used with typical Indian meanings:

batch-mate: a class-mate or fellow student
body-bath: an ordinary bath, as opposed to a head-bath (particularly used in South India)
break/crack one's head: to rack one's brains
co-daughter-in-law: any one of several daughters-in-law like oneself in a family
cousin-brother: a male cousin
cousin-sister: a female cousin
cut one's own hands: to be in a weak position
dearness allowance: a cost-of-living allowance
eat someone's head: to be a nuisance
Eve-teasing: harrassing young women
four-twenty: a swindler (from the number of a section of the Indian Penal Code)
issueless: childless
outstation: a check issued on a non-local bank
stand on someone's head: to supervise carefully

The Indianization is also reflected in the complete acculturation of the text, for example, in the following passage by Raja Rao (1963: 10).

> 'Today,' he says, 'it will be the story of Siva and Parvati.' And Parvati in penance becomes the country and Siva becomes heaven knows what! 'Siva is the three-eyed,' he says 'and Swaraj too is three-eyed: Self-purification, Hindu-Moslem unity, Khaddar.' And then he talks of Damayanthi and Sakunthala and Yashodha and everywhere there is something about our country and something about Swaraj. Never had we heard Harikathas like this. And he can sing too, can Jayamarchar. He can keep us in tears for hours together. But the Harikahta he did, which I can

> never forget in this life and in all lives to come, is about the birth of Gandhiji. 'What a title for Harikatha!' cried out old Venkatalakshamma, the mother of the Postmaster. 'It is neither about Rama nor Krishna.' 'but,' said her son, who too has been to the city, 'but, Mother, the Mahatma is a saint, a holy man.' 'Holy man or lover of a widow, what does it matter to me? When I go to the temple I want to hear about Rama and Krishna and Mahadeva and not all this city non sense,' said she. And being an obedient son, he was silent. But the old woman came along that evening. She could never stay away from a Harikatha. And sitting beside us, how she wept!

In this passage the underlying cultural and historical presuppositions are different from what have traditionally been associated with the literary canon of English. One has to understand Śiva and Pārvati with reference to the multitude of the pantheon of Hindu gods. It is in that mythological context that three-eyed (Sanskrit *trinetra*) makes sense: It refers to Lord Śiva's manifestation when he opens his 'third eye', located on his forehead, spitting fire and destroying the creation. The three names Damayanthi, Śakuntalā, and Yaśodā refer to India's great classics: Damayanti, the wife of Nala; Śakuntalā, who was later immortalized in Kālidāsa's (5th century) play of the same name; and Yaśoda, the mother of Krishna, the major character of the epic Mahābhārata. The passage then relates to contemporary India and to Gandhi's India, and the political implications of Hindu-Muslim unity and the symbolic role of *khaddar* (hand spun cloth) in India's independence movement. The Harikathā man is the traditional narrator of religious and mythological stories who embeds all this culture and history in the fabric of the story. In this passage, then, English, is a mādhyam (medium) and the mantra (message) relates to India's traditional culture and contemporary political struggle.

We see this process aggressively continued in the 'liberated' English of the new generation of Indian English writers, for example, in Shashi Tharoor's *The Great Indian Novel.* These culture-specific functions of Indian English are understandably evident in the news media, in matrimonial advertisements, in obituaries, and so on. The matrimonial columns reflect Indian sensitivity to color, caste hierarchy, regional attitudes, and family structure. These advertisements, for example, ask for "graduate, Bhardwaja gotram, Astasastram girl, subset no bar, preferably convent-educated," "average complexion," and sometimes prefer "mutual alliance." Indians invite a "cousin-brother," or a "cousin-sister" to a "military hotel" with a "compound wall" situated on "kutcha road" where they do not eat on a "dining-leaf." A Brahmin in South India normally has "forehead-marking" or a "caste mark" and a "nine-stranded thread". Indians have "England-returned" or "America-returned" relatives, such as a "co-brother-in-law" who has an "issueless" sister. They also have strong feelings about "intermarriage" or "interdining" due to various "communal" considerations. Indians use their "tiffin-carriers" to carry lunch, which may include "coconut paysam," when they go "out of station." And when an Indian—particularly in the South—is not ready to take a "head bath," they may just take a "body bath." And finally, death is announced as "leaving for heavenly abode," or just "sad demise," and arrangements are made for "kirtan and ardasa" for the "peace of departed soul." These are just a few examples from the socially appropriate and culturally conditioned lexicon of Indian English. [7]

There are also other, less elitist, language varieties which are used for communication in India. These are termed *bazaar* languages (market codes). The bazaar languages have regional roles, but some of them also have roles across regions. Bazaar Hindi (Hindustani), for example, has attained the status of a major contact language, both as a national variety, and in its regional varieties, such as, Bombaiya Hindi (used in Bombay, now called Mumbai); Kalkatiya Hindi (Calcutta Hindi); and Madrasi Hindi (Madras, now renamed Chennai). At another level, Hindustani also has national currency. It is used in various parts of India and refers to a variety of language which does not use an excess of Persianized or Sanskritized vocabulary, as is the case in Urdu and Hindi, respectively. Gandhi was a great supporter of Hindustani. He tried to use it in his publications and also proposed its use as independent India's national language. That proposal, however, did not receive much support.

Persian and English are not the only languages with colonial associations. There are some other colonial languages that have left their mark on the subcontinent. These include French in the former French settlement of Pondicherry, in South India, and Portuguese in the former Portuguese colony, Goa, on the West coast. In its depth of societal penetration, extended range of functions, and impact, English, however, has surpassed all other colonial languages in India.

Language Variation

The Indian subcontinent is a paradigm example of a sociolinguistic gold mine: it has a multiplicity of languages and a wide range of variation within single languages. A North Indian saying captures this aspect: pānč kos par pānī badle, bīs kos par bhāṣā ("the water changes after every ten miles, and the language after every forty miles").

A variety of political and ideological reasons have motivated language specialists in the past to emphasize the caste- and region-based variation in languages (e.g., Brahmin and non-Brahmin dialects, or Dharwar Kannada as opposed to Bangalore Kannada). Such selective focus has resulted in an almost total neglect of other types of language differences. The result is that language variation has been perceived essentially as static and not as a dynamic, interactive communicative phenomenon. We see that dynamic nature in the impact of English and Persian on India's languages, and in the influence of Dravidian (e.g., Kannada and Telugu) languages on Indo-Aryan languages (e.g., Marathi and Hindi).

In post-Imperial, two aspects of language have received considerable attention: One is *diglossia* and *triglossia*—that is, the coexistence of two or three varieties of a language, each with its own specific functions. The other is *mixing*, in which two or more languages are used in a stream of discourse, for example, mixing of Hindi and English, or Telugu and English, or Kashmiri and Persian. This is a very common process in India and elsewhere. Consider the italicized words in the first example below, which shows the use of Persian words in a legal text:

> *mukadme* ke liye is ek purāne *phaisle* kī *nakal* cāhiye. Uske liye pahle *tahsil* men *darkhāst* dī thī.

The next example has extensive use of English words in what is intended to be a Hindi text:

> "*We are very good friends, Sir,* lekin, *you know* . . . mai *official work* ko dosti se zyādā mahatva deta hun . . .agar āp manlen to main Batra ko khud is *point* par *agree* kara lunga." Aur vah Batra se ja kar kahegā—"*You were wrong my dear—boss* mere *point* par *agree* karte hain."

This kind of mixing is prevalent in other languages too. S.N. Sridhar, discussing the mixing of English and Urdu (Perso-Arabic) in Kannada says:

> . . . the more educated a person, the more he tends to mix elements from English

in his Kannada, and the more earthy and 'physical' a person, the greater the mixture of Perso-Arabic elements in his Kannada. (Sridhar 1978: 113)

Diglossia or the distinction between "high" and "low," or "classical" and "popular" varieties is again all-pervasive in India. All major Indian languages have at least two distinct varieties— "high" and "low"—and the difference can clearly be identified in the vocabulary, the grammar, the sound system, and in the styles. The well-known example, discussed in detail in the literature on the subject, is that of Telugu (a Dravidian language), which has a literary variety (grānthika) and the colloquial variety (vyāvhārika). This distinction is also present in other literary Dravidian languages, such as, Tamil, Malayalam, and Kannada, and in Indo-Aryan languages, for example, Bengali. In Bengali, the literary variety is called *sādhubhāṣā* and the colloquial variety *čalitbhāṣā*. These distinctions are not only of theoretical interest but have significant educational, communicative, and other implications for use of language in the media, in teaching literacy, and in the empowerment of the people. The "high" or elevated variety of language, often taught in schools and advocated by the pundits, is not necessarily intelligible to those who speak and easily understand only the "low" (colloquial) variety of the language.

Writing Systems (Scripts)

In communication, writing systems are vital linguistic tools, and India is a repository of many distinct writing systems. All scripts current in India, except for the Perso-Arabic and Roman scripts, are derived from the ancient Brahmī script. This script was used for Indian orthography around the 3rd century B.C.E. and may be derived from either an ancient Semitic (Aramaic) script or from symbols found on Harappan seals (see the chapter by S.R. Rao in this volume). There are eight writing systems current in India in addition to Roman and Perso-Arabic: Bengali-Assamese-Manipuri, Devanagari, Gujarati, Gurumukhi, Kannada-Telugu, Malayalam, Oriya, and Tamil.

The profile of the scripts becomes somewhat complex when we consider the minority languages of India in general and the tribal languages in particular. The non-tribal minority language Kashmiri provides a good example of this complexity. The Kashmiri is written in four scripts: Devanagari, Perso-Arabic, Roman, and for some very restricted functions—by the Pandits of Kashmir—in the ṣāradā script. Another minority language, Konkani, is written in Devanagari, Kannada, Malayalam, and

Roman scripts. The total number of speakers of Konkani, used primarily in the former Portuguese colony of Goa, is 1,570,108. The Sindhi language, transplanted to India after the partition, is written both in the Arabic and Devanagari scripts. The situation of the tribal languages is more complicated. For example, Santhali, spoken by 4,332,511 persons (1981 census), is written in five scripts. The multiplicity of scripts is clearly due to historical, political, and religious factors. The use of a particular script out of the available choices is often related to issues of ideology and the identities which users of a script desire to articulate. That is one major reason why the state of Kashmir adopted Urdu as the state language and recommended Perso-Arabic script for writing Kashmiri, even though it is ill-suited to the language.

In the long literary history of India, some scripts have remained static while the languages have undergone invariable change. A script may represent the idealized linguistic "norm" with which the current spoken language may not necessarily match. This has been well-illustrated in the case of the Sanskritic alphabet. In Oriya script, for example, a distinction is made between /s/, /ś/, and /ṣ/; but in the spoken language, that distinction is not maintained. We see the identical problem of non-matching grids in written Kashmiri. In this language, the Devanagari and Śāradā scripts make distinctions between g and gh, d and dh, and dḍ and dḍh. These distinctions are, however, not made in the spoken language.

Figure 38: Various Indian Scripts as Seen on Indian Currency

One might ask a pragmatic question about India's multiplicity of scripts: Why not adopt a unified script for all Indian languages? There has been, in fact, no lack of effort in this direction. In fact, arguments supporting such a move were presented well before India's independence. A variety of proposals and recommendations have been made. The major rationales for a unified script include fostering the cultural unity of India, administrative convenience, economy in printing, and ease in introducing literacy. And having said this, it should be noted that these proposals have not received enthusiastic support and have never advanced beyond the blueprint stage. The main reason for the indifference to such proposals is that most of India's major languages have rich literary and religious traditions, and there is almost a mystical identification with the script. Some of the scripts have even acquired a religious sanctity and a close emotional identity with the language: Devanagari for the Hindus, Perso-Arabic for the Muslims, Gurumukhi for the Sikhs, and Roman for some Indian Christians.

Linguistic Minorities

It may sound like a paradox to claim that India is essentially a country of linguistic minorities. It certainly depends on how one defines the term "linguistic minority." Such minorities comprise a significant part of even those states that were carved out after great political turmoil on the basis of what has been termed majority languages. This step was taken, as mentioned earlier, on the recommendation of the States Reorganization Commission in 1956. These states include among the Indo-Aryan language speaking states.

Assamese-speaking Assam;
Bengali-speaking West Bengal;
Punjabi-speaking Punjab;
Gujarati-speaking Gujarat;
Marathi-speaking Maharashtra, and so on.

Among the Dravidian language speaking states, we have
Telugu-speaking Andhra Pradesh
Tamil-speaking Tamil Nadu
Kannada-speaking Karnataka
Malayalam-speaking Kerala.

In the above contexts, the term "majority" refers to a linguistic group which has numerical strength over other language or dialect groups. As an aside, I might add here that the labels (e.g., majority) are misleading, since the largest single majority language, Hindi-Urdu, is understood in various degrees by just 45 percent of India's population. The paradox of this situation is that in several states the number of minority language speakers is substantially larger than the total number of what are termed the majority language speakers. Table 4 shows distribution of regional and minority languages in various states of India (based on census of India 1981).

In several such states, the minority language speakers are, linguistically speaking, in a precarious position. They are generally at the linguistic mercy of the so-called majority language users. Their linguistic rights have been compromised by a linguistic formula in which they have hardly any representation. This dependence on the majority group shows in language, particularly, in education, in the status of the literature of the minority community, and in the attitude toward the language of the minority communities.

There are the following major types of minority languages in India. First, those who speak minor languages (that is, languages not included in the Eighth Schedule of the Constitution); second, those who speak major languages, but have migrated to other language areas where their language has no status (e.g., Telugu migrants in Karnataka); and third, those who belong to scheduled castes and tribes (e.g., Gondi, Santhali) and religious minorities (cf. K. Sridhar 1996: 331-2).

India's Consitution provides various types of protections to linguistic minorities. For example, consider the following articles:

> Article 350-A. It should be the endeavour of every State and of every local authority within the state to provide adequate facilities for instruction in the mother tongue in the primary stage of education to children belonging to linguistic minority groups; and the President may issue such directions to any State as he considers necessary or proper for securing the provision of such facilities.
>
> Article 350-B. There shall be a special officer to investigate all matters relating to the safeguards provided for linguistic minorities under this Constitution and report to the President upon those matters at such intervals as the President may direct, and the President shall cause all such reports to be laid before each house of Parliament, and sent to the Governments of the States concerned...

The central government has also established the Office of the Commissioner for Linguistic Minorities to safeguard and protect the educational rights of such communities.(cf. Sridhar, K. 1996: 333-4)

Table 5: Distribution of Regional and Minority Languages

State/Union Territory	*Single largest language and the total to household population (%)*	*Percentage of population speaking other minority languages*
Andhra Pradesh	Telugu (85.13)	14.87
Assam	[No Census]	-
Bihar	Hindi (80.17)	19.83
Gujarat	Gujarati (90.73)	9.27
Haryana	Hindi (88.77)	11.23
Himachal Pradesh	Hindi (88.95)	11.05
Jammu and Kashmir	Kashmiri (52.73)	47.27
Karnataka	Kannada (65.69)	34.31
Kerala	Malayalam (95.99)	4.01
Madhya Pradesh	Hindi (84.37)	15.63
Maharashtra	Marathi (73.62)	26.38
Manipur	Manipuri (62.36)	37.64
Meghalaya	Khasi (47.46)	52.34
Negaland	Ao (13.94)	86.06
Orissa	Oriya (82.83)	17.17
Punjab	Punjabi (84.88)	15.12
Rajasthan	Hindi (89.89)	10.11
Sikkim	Nepali (62.57)	37.43
Tamil Nadu	Tamil (85.35)	14.65
Tripura	Bengali (69.59)	30.41
Uttar Pradesh	Hindi (89.68)	10.32
West Bengal	Bengali (86.34)	13.66
Andaman and Nicobar	Bengali (24.68)	75.32
Arunachal Pradesh	Nissi/Dafla (23.59)	76.41
Chandigarh	Hindi (55.11)	44.89
Dadra and Nagar Havoli	Bhili/Bhilodi (68.69)	31.31
Delhi	Hindi (76.29)	23.71
Goa, Daman, and Diu	Konkani (56.65)	43.35
Lakshadweep	Malayalam (84.51)	15.49
Mizoram	Lushai/Mizo (77.59)	22.41
Pondicherry	Tamil (89.18)	10.82

Language Standardization

What does one mean by language standardization when the languages of India have been used for centuries with effectiveness and success? What does the standardization process entail and accomplish? The term refers to more than one process. One major process involves equipping a language so that functionally it can be used effectively and appropriately in changing social, educational, scientific, and technological contexts. In that sense, one main issue of standardization involves developing specialized languages (technically called registers) for use in the areas of science, technology, and law, for example: devising ways of simplifying the writing systems so that a language may be adapted to the technological needs of the media (e.g., teleprinters, typesetting, typewriters, computers etc.); introducing terminological uniformity in the formation of new terms for the use of Indian languages in the domains of science and technology; and developing suitable writing systems and pedagogical and other reference materials (e.g., dictionaries) for languages which have traditionally been just oral and have no writing systems.

The above issues have generated ongoing debates and controversies related to the underlying approaches to these issues and their methodologies. There is also a serious conflict between the approaches of the "purists" and the "non-purists" to the processes of standardization. The "purists" essentially maintain traditionalist positions, and the "non-purists" challenge such positions in favor of meeting the new challenges with non-traditional answers. A number of issues concerning standardization of India's languages and their implications on communication relate to what is called language planning.

Language Planning and Language Policies

In India there has been considerable debate on planning the status and use of various languages and initiating language policies. The most articulate earlier national debate with far-reaching, all-India implications was the Occidentalist/Orientalist controversy, which I have discussed earlier in the connection with Macaulay's Minute (cf. Kachru 1986, 1994b and Ram 1983). The heated debate represented two positions on the use of languages and educational philosophy in Indian education. Macaulay and other Occidentalists supported transplanting English in India, while another group, the Orientalists, favored local (native) languages. In this debate, as we have seen, Macaulay emerged victorious. His *Minute* eventually laid the foundations for India's language policy and the use of language in education and, in its various reincarnations, this policy has been with us for over 160 years. The controversies that this policy initiated have as yet not abated.

The language issue has dominated India's national and regional political scene during the post-Independence period, as it did during the Imperial period. The debate has often taken a violent form. It was after a prolonged and very acrimonious national debate that the Three Language Formula was proposed in the 1960's. This formula was not endorsed with equal excitement by all the states and Union Territories. The reactions ranged from enthusiastic and cynical. Tamil Nadu and Manipur did not endorse it. The madhya deśa (the Hindi belt) initiated teachings of Dravidian languages in a superficial way just to pay lip-service to the formula so that Hindi could be brought in through the back door in South India, West Bengal, and other non-Hindi areas.

Language Conflicts

All these frustrations and assertions for identities ultimately lead to language conflicts. The Indian subcontinent has had more than its share of violent language riots, resulting in the destruction of property, death, and extreme acts of exhibition of language loyalties, including cases of self-immolation in protest. The underlying motivations for language conflicts are primarily of three types. The first major motivation is to seek recognition of a language not already listed in the national—or regional-language policy. The second motivation is seeking status and recognition as a "language" instead of a "dialect."[7] This motive, for example, existed in the cases of Rajasthani in the state of Rajasthan, and that of Maithili in the state of Bihar. The third motivation is a belief in the religious association of a language with a particular religious group. In this case the important point is the symbolic significance of a language to a religious group. This attitude is unrelated to the pragmatic way in which a language is used. In spite of contradictory empirical evidence and actual language use, the Punjabi-speaking Hindus identify themselves with the Hindi-speakers as opposed to the Punjabi-speakers. The attitude toward Urdu and its increasing association with the Muslims and Islam also reminds one of this situation. The fourth motivation for language conflict shows in the resistance to accept what is believed to be an imposed language from India's Central government. This resistance has been expressed at various times, and with varying degrees of vehemence, against the imposition of Hindi, for example, in Bengal, Tamil Nadu, and Karnataka and against English, primarily in

Bihar, Uttar Pradesh, and Rajasthan. At the regional level, violent demonstrations have occurred against Urdu in Uttar Pradesh and Karnataka.

Language conflicts become more visible and violent particularly during the periods of India's elections: one aim of such conflicts seems to be to destabilize political power groups either at the national or regional levels. These linguistic conflicts thus are closely related to the agendas of the politicians.

Paradigms and Realities: Language Diversity as Problem and as Resource

Multilingual and multicultural societies have paid an immense price for their diversity, particularly in how such societies are perceived by those who erroneously consider themselves linguistically homogeneous. The West has traditionally been suspicious of diversity—linguistic or otherwise; it has viewed diversity as a potential source of anarchy, confusion, and conflict. There is abundant material—both scholarly and not-so-scholarly—that reflects this Western attitude. This attitude was, of course, most articulate during the Imperial past. And even now, during the post-Imperial period, this attitude has not been quite abandoned.

India's diversity, and the resultant issues that the country has had to confront, continue to be viewed in a negative sense. There are two major reasons for this negative attitude. First, there is the lingering belief that linguistically and culturally homogeneous societies are intrinsically more cohesive, more stable, and less prone to internal conflicts. It is, therefore, believed that multilingual societies are confrontational and noncohesive. Second, there is a theoretical and methodological compulsion to view Indian society as static and as a composite of dichotomies. The language researchers have, therefore, attempted to capture India's linguistic pluralism with reference to such dichotomies: lower caste vs. upper caste; Hindu vs. Muslim; mother tongue vs. non-mother tongue. The problem with such dichotomies is that when applied to multilingual societies, they are not necessarily insightful. In fact, these often provide only a partial account of multilinguals' linguistic behavior and communicative strategies.

In the post-1960's period, gradually researchers have initiated different ways of looking at India's—and other multilingual societies'—communicative behavior. The emphasis is increasingly on the dynamic nature and integrative motives of these societies' linguistic repertoires and language interactions. From this new perspective, languages and dialects are viewed as repertoires of resources in which mixing and switching of languages have functional appropriateness and symbolize various types of identities. That is actually how languages function in India—in a pragmatic context.

Unifying Patterns in Indian Languages

What has been characterized as the "Tower of Babel," as the functional linguistic deficiency of India, does not appear as chaotic, if viewed and discussed within the broad historical and linguistic contexts of this vast region. There have been several such theoretically and functionally insightful attempts. One such attempt is the conceptualization of India as a "linguistic area"(cf. Emeneau 1956 and Masica 1976). This concept is based on the empirically sustained theory that languages belonging to India—actually, the whole of South Asia—have a long tradition of contact and convergence. A language or a language family gradually, influenced by another language or language family. For example, Kannada shows influences from Marathi, Tamil and Telugu from other neighboring languages, and Sanskrit and Indo-Aryan languages from some Dravidian languages. The "convergence" reflects in the development of shared features due to prolonged contact. This convergence has been termed the Indo-Aryanization of the Dravidian languages and the Dravidinization of Indo-Aryan languages (cf. Sridhar 1981 and Abbi 1992). And this linguistic "look-alikeness" is not restricted to simply the borrowing of words, but goes much deeper. We find such interface in many features of grammar, in discourse strategies, and in development of literary genres and traditions.

The next step in such investigations has been to go beyond linguistic convergence and to investigate India as a "sociolinguistic area"(cf. D'Souza 1987, Pandit 1972, and Dimock, Jr., Kachru, and Krishnamurti 1992) In this area, research has provided insights into evidence of shared characteristics across India's various language families in terms of "speech acts" and style-ranges; discourse and literary strategies; "mixing" of two or more languages and the rules for such mixing; speech functions of politeness, abuse, curses, and flattery; processes used for Englishization, Persianization and Sanskritization, and their impact; regularities in personal names and other aspects of naming, technically called onomnastics; the use of sound symbolism in oral or literary traditions; characteristics of "secret" codes (for example the language of thieves); and, development of restricted languages at all-India centers of cross-linguistic get-togethers, for example, at the centers of pilgrimmage such as Prayag, Varanasi, Hardwar in North India, and Tirupati in South India.

This approach to India's diversity and the use of languages in Indian society, helps us to find patterns and meaningful cross-currents of unity in the diversity. India's assimilative forces reveal themselves in interesting patterns of three dimensions: linguistic, sociolinguistic, and literary. There is thus a triad of language interaction in Indian society(cf. Chatterji 1963; Mukherji 1975, 1981; and Kachru 1992).

Let me provide here an example of the last dimension of the various strands of the shared canons of cultural and literary traditions. These shared features have resulted in what eminent Indian linguist Suniti Kumar Chatterji (1963;118) considers: "the real integration of India into one single entity, in spite of some basic and fundamental racial, linguistic and cultural diversities"(1963: 118). And this integration manifests itself, as Chatterji further reminds us,

> through the world of the epics and the puranas and the philosophical literature of Sanskrit (especially Vedanta as supplemented by Islamic Tasawwuf), in the ancient and medieval times. . .(133)

From the earliest to contemporary times,various secular and religious movements have crossed one language area to another, "by study and adaptation of the original works in a particular language rather than regular translation". (See Parthasarathy in this volume.) For example, one strand of bhakti (devotional) poetry flourished in different regions, in the east in Bengal, in the north in Punjab, and in the south in the Dravidian language areas. The impact of the siddhas extended to central India and Rajasthan. The diffusion of the Sant Sahitya (literature of the "Saints") shows identical trends. We see this in the sant poet Kabir (1440-1518), in Tulsidas (1532-1623), and in Mirabai (1503-1573). The Sufi tradition cut across several language and literary boundaries and flourished in Sindhi, Punjabi, Hindi, Urdu, and Kashmiri.

Third, we must take into account the layer after layer of varied internal (laukik) and external (videśī) impacts in syncretism in India's languages and cultures. One example is the Sufi tradition mentioned above. The other example is that of the Vaiṣṇava tradition, the devotees of the god Vishnu or one of his avatāras (incarnations), particularly Rāma and Kṛishna. Sufism provides an example of external (or foreign) impact, and the spread of Vaiṣṇnavism an example of internal (or native) impact. The Sufi tradition brought together several strands of Shiaism of Islam and sects of Hinduism and resulted in a unique synthesis—both ideological and literary. We see this again particularly in literatures in Hindi, Urdu, Kashmiri, Punjabi, and Sindhi.

The two major external impacts on languages and communication in Indian society have been the Muslim and Anglo-Saxon. These influences to various degrees reflect in India's religious and literary and philosophical traditions. The Islamic impact brought major changes in the north and parts of central India. The Anglo-Saxon impact overwhelmed the whole subcontinent.

The process of Persianization and Englishization initiated, directly and indirectly, self-awareness, self-introspection, and cultural-awareness in Indian literatures. Persianization came with an aggressive and, in some parts of India, a proselytizing face of Islam and Islamization, as did Englishization with Western faces, ideologies, and agendas. But Indians turned these linguistic "weapons" around and Indianized them to articulate Indian identities. They did this indeed with considerable success and dexterity.

What we see, then, is that issues related to language in Indian society will be better understood if we study these issues within the context of the enormous size of the country, its linguistically and ethnically pluralistic populations, its extensive and varied colonial history, its long tradition of language assimilation, and its immense power of acculturation.

End Notes

[1] I am grateful to Amita Kachru for her useful comments on an earlier version of this paper and to Kyutae Jung for assistance in library research.

[2] This is the number of respondents who identified Sanskrit as their first language in one of the earlier census reports.

[3] See Fleet 1904 cited in Hock 1992: 248.

[4] See an interesting piece entitled, "The living word: Who said Sanskrit is a dead language? Not the people of this Karnataka village" by Stephen David in India Today, March 15, 1997, p.7. See also Hock (1992) for a contemporary profile of Sanskrit in Uttar Pradesh, and for references on this topic.

[5] The term 'Babu English' (baboo) was originally used for English-using clerks in Bengali-speaking parts of India. But it later characterized the Indian style of English with ornamental flourish and extreme politeness.

[6] This term was used by Indian English writer Raja Rao in "The Author's Foreword" in Kanthapura (1938).

[7]The meaning of some of the Indian English expressions used in the examples is given below:

Bharadwaja gotram 'family lineage stemming from the Bharadwaja;' Astasastram 'eight branches of learning;' subset 'subcaste;' convent-educated 'educated in an English medium school, traditionally run by Christian missionaries;' average complexion 'not dark;' mutual alliance 'a son and a daughter of one family married to a daughter and son of the other family, respectively;' military hotel 'a non-vegetarian restaurant in South India;' compound-wall 'a boundary wall;' kutcha road 'a dirt road;' dining leaf 'a banana, lotus, or other leaf on which food is served;' forehead-marking 'a religious mark, indicative of a caste mark;' America-returned 'one who has been to the USA' cf. 'England-returned;' co-brother-in-law 'a man married to one's wife's sister;' issueless 'without progeny.'

[8] The term "dialect" is often used in a pejorative sense and implies a status lower than what is implied by the term "language."

Works Cited

Abbi, A. 1992. Contact, conflict, and compromise: The genesis of reduplicated structures in South Asian languages. In *Dimensions of Sociolinguistics in South Asia: Papers in Memory of Gerald Kelley.* Edited by Edward C. Dimock Jr., Braj B. Kachru, and B. Krishnamurti. New Delhi: Oxford and IBH Publishing Company, Pvt. Ltd.

Bhatia, T. K., and W. Ritchie, eds. 1989. *Code-mixing: English across languages.* In *World Englishes* 8 (3).

Brass, P. 1974. *Language, Religion and Politics in North India.* London: Cambridge University Press.

Bryant, A. 1932. *Macaulay.* Edinburgh: Edinburgh University Press.

Chatterji, S. K. 1963. The Literary Unity of India. In *Languages and Literatures of Modern India.* Calcutta: Bengal Publishers. Also in Mukherji ed. 1981.

Dimock, Edward C. Jr., Braj B. Kachru,and B. Krishnamurti. eds. 1992. *Dimensions of Sociolinguistics in South Asia: Papers in Memory of Gerald Kelley.* New Delhi: Oxford and IBH Publishing Company, Pvt. Ltd.

D'souza, J. 1987. *South Asia as a sociolinguistic area.* Doctoral dissertation, University of Illinois at Urbana-Champaign.

Emeneau, M. B. 1956. India as a linguistic area. *Language* 32:3-16.

Firth, J.R. 1930. *Speech.* London: Sixpenny Library. No. 121 reprinted by London: Oxford University Press, 1966.

Gupta, R.S., A. Abbi and K. S. Aggarwal, eds. 1995. *Language and the State: Perspectives on the Eighth Schedule*. New Delhi: Creative Books.

Harrison, S. S. 1960. *India: the most dangerous decades*. Princeton: Princeton University Press.

Hock, H. H. 1992. Spoken Sanskrit in Uttar Pradesh: Profile of a dying prestige language. In Dimock, Jr., Kachru, and Krishnamurti, eds. 1992.

Kachru, B. B. 1986. *The Indianization of English: The English language in India*. New Delhi: Oxford University Press.

Kachru, B. B. 1992. Cultural contact and literary creativity in a multilingual society. In Dimock, Jr. Kachru, and Krishnamurti, eds. 1992.

Kachru, B. B. 1994a. Englishization and contact linguistics. *World Englishes* 13 (2): 135-154.

Kachru, B. B. 1994b. English in South Asia. In *The Cambridge History of the English Language*. Vol. V. Edited by Robert Burchfield. Cambridge: Cambridge University Press.

Kachru, Y. 1997. Culture and communication in India. In this volume.

Masica, C. P. 1976. *Defining a linguistic area: South Asia*. Chicago: University of Chicago Press.

Mukherji, S. 1975. *Towards a literary history of India*. Simla: Indian Institute of Advanced Study.

Mukherji, S. ed. 1981. *The idea of an Indian literature*. Mysore: Central Institute of Indian Languages.

Nehru, J. 1941 [1967]. The *discovery of India*. Delhi: Oxford University Press.

Nurullah, S. and J. P. Naik, eds. 1951. *A history of education in India*. Bombay: Macmillan.

Pandit, P. B. 1972. *India as a sociolinguistic area*. Poona: University of Poona

Pushp, P. N. 1996. Kashmir and the linguistic predicament of the state. In *Jammu, Kashmir and Ladakh: Linguistic Predicament*. Edited by P.N. Pushp and K. Warikoo. Delhi: Har-Anand Publications.

Ram, T. 1983. *Trading in Language: The Story of English in India*. Delhi: GDK.

Shapiro, M. C. and H. Schiffman. 1975. *Language and society in South Asia*. Seattle: University of Washington, Department of Asian Languages and Literatures.

Singh, K. and S. Manoharan. 1993. *Languages and Scripts* (People of India, National Series volume IX). Delhi: Oxford University Press.

Sridhar, K. K. 1996. Language in education: Minorities and multilingualism in India. In *International Review of Education*. 42 (4): 327-347.

Sridhar, S.N. 1978. On the functions of code-mixing in Kannada. In *Aspects of sociolinguistics in South Asia.* Edited by Braj B. Kachru and S.N. Sridhar. Special issue of *International Journal of Sociology of Language*16: 109-117.

Sridhar, S. N. 1981. Linguistic convergence: Indo-Aryanization of Dravidian languages. *Lingua* 53, 199-220.

Wolpert, S. 1991. *India.* Berkley: University of California Press

Chapter 27

Sanskrit Literature

K. Krishnamoorthy

The earliest and most glorious chapter, not only in the history of Sanskrit literature but in the history of world literature and culture, is the vast body of writing known as Veda (wisdom). It is the most ancient record left by hoary sages holding a mirror to all human interests—literary, socio-political, religious, mythological, cultural, and philosophical. While the first composition, called the Ṛgveda (hymns), may be as old as 2000 B.C.E., the collections themselves of this as well as of the other three Vedas—Yajus (prose formulae), Sāman (songs set to music), and Atharvan (magical spells and incantations)—are considered by scholars to be not later than 1500 B.C.E.

The Sanskrit language of the Vedas is so archaic that it is closer to Avestan than to that of the later epics, plays, and poems. It admits of a wide variety of verbal forms, prepositions, pronouns, and noun inflections unknown to Sanskrit standardized by the great grammarian, Pāṇini (circa 500 B.C.E.). It has accent, which not only conditions recitation but also controls the meaning of the words, a phenomenon obsolete already by the time of Panini. The Vedic quantitative measures are comparatively simple and lax without any complicated metrics, the only regularity observed is limited to the cadence (or last four or five syllables) of a hemistich. It is a singular feat of Indian learning which has preserved these texts by oral transmission for so many centuries without any change either in accent or punctuation. Tradition regards these texts as divine revelations (śruti) and sacred scriptures. They are revered authority in all matters concerning human beings in their life here on earth as well as hereafter.

Vedic Poetry

Western Orientalists like F. Max Muller were fascinated by the Ṛgveda not so much by its religion, which is centered in sacrifice—the offering of simple oblations like ghee (melted and clarified butter) into the holy domestic fire—but by other features. These include the poetic fervor of the hymns, which make us visualize the various aspects of cosmic natural forces as divine manifestations; the linguistic affinities transparent in Indo-European word forms in such diverse languages as Greek, Latin, German, English, Finnish, Latvian, Russian, and Old Avestan, which led to the foundation of a new field of study known as "comparative philology" (linguistics); and also the striking parallels between Vedic mythology and the mythology of the Greeks and other ancient peoples. If during the past 150 years Western scholarship has added new branches of antiquarian studies like comparative religion, comparative linguistics, comparative mythology, and comparative social institutions, it is entirely because of the "discovery" of Sanskrit in the late eighteenth century by the West.

Though some Indologists are wont to regard the entire Ṛgveda as a hieratic handiwork of greedy priests, a student of literature will find therein several gems of pure poetry, where the creative afflatus finds a free and spontaneous expression. The hymns to Uṣas, the goddess of the dawn, and to Savitṛ, the sun-god who animates birds and beasts alike with joyful activity, are but two examples. The simple joys and sorrows of the Aryans settled in India on the banks of the seven rivers (in the Northwest), bubbling with a zest for life and adventure, are beautifully reflected in the Ṛgvedic hymns. They offer their oblations in the sacred fire, invoking the blessings of gods like Agni, Indra, and Varuna, and the hymns are primarily religious. Yet the homely similes and metaphors in their prayers reveal a consummate poetic art. Their pastoral life, rich in cows and offspring, also had moments of exaltation and exhilaration. They were oppressed by fears of divine wrath and devilish dark forces at the same time. Their loves and hates, too, had heart-warming and heart-rending aspects. Occasionally, we find them speculating on cosmological problems and attempting philosophical explanations. Their love of wine and women, sports like chariot-racing, and gambling also inspired some lovely lines. Thus Ṛgvedic poetry is the most ancient record available today, not only of the Vedic Indian but also of human beings in general. Though steeped in religion, it is not blind to the profane joys of life.

Like all branches of learning in India, poetry, too, has its first beginnings in the Ṛgveda itself. Some of the dialogue (ākhyāna) hymns in the Ṛgveda might have provided the seeds for the later pantomimes and plays in Sanskrit. These very hymns were, for the most part, reset with prose formulae to constitute what is known as the Yajurveda to help the sacrificial priest. When they were further redacted and set to music, they came to be called the Sāmaveda or the Veda of musical songs, and several schools came into vogue specializing in the three Vedas, since all these were assigned a due place in the performance of sacrifice, an institution which tended to become more and more complex by adding details of ritual, each of which was sacrosanct. Yet the Yajurveda and Sāmaveda have no literary value of their own.

Not so the Atharvaveda, which came to be ranked as a Veda only after some initial opposition, though it is chronologically as old as the Ṛgveda. The opposition of the orthodox camp was occasioned by the preponderance of witchcraft and black magic in the hymns and spells of the Atharvaveda. While the other three Vedas contained adorations of exalted and virtuous divinities, the Atharvaveda gave room for imprecations, love-charms, and magic cures as well, which were popular in that ancient society. Nevertheless, we find in some of these hymns the higher reaches of philosophy on the one hand, and the most charming adorations of Mother Earth on the other.

Vedic Legends in Prose

Apart from the vast body of Vedic verse, we have an equally large library of ritualistic prose known as Brāhmaṇa (circa 1000 B.C.E.) on the minutiae of sacrificial ritual. From the literary perspective, it is insipid and usually dismissed as "theological twaddle." But like oases in an arid desert, we do come across upākhyānas or literary episodes such as that of Śunahśepa in the Aitareya Brāhmaṇa (associated with the Ṛgveda) and that of Purūravas and Urvaśi in Śatapatha Brāhmaṇa (coming under the Yajurveda). The stories are full of dramatic suspense and literary interest. Though they are dovetailed in these theological texts into the fabric of ritual, one can see that, taken in themselves, they can be reckoned as the earliest specimens of literary prose in Sanskrit.

This trend becomes more and more pronounced in the still later works of the Vedic age, as in the Āraṇyakas "forest texts" and the Upaniṣads "esoteric teachings", that mostly belong to the period from 800 to 600 B.C.E. Some of these latter, e.g.,

Kaṭha and Muṇḍaka, are in verse. But others like the Bṛhadāraṇyaka contain philosophical dialogues reminiscent of Plato. Hence this Upaniṣad, expounding Yājñyavalkya's philosophy of Ātman, as Deussen remarks, "for richness and warmth of expression surely stands alone in Indian literature, and perhaps in the literature of nations." The verse Upaniṣads also set the pattern for the later Bhagavadgītā, celebrated as the cream of the later epic, Mahābhārata. While the locale of the Ṛgveda is mostly the Punjab, that of the other works is as wide as the whole of Northern India.

Epics

The two premiere epics in Sanskrit are the Rāmāyana of Vālmīki and the Mahābhārata of Vyāsa. Unlike the sages of the Vedic hymns, who are only called *rsis* (seers) of divinely revealed hymns, Vālmīki and Vyāsa are regarded by tradition as personal authors of the two epics, respectively. Yet modern scholarship has succeeded in showing that these two are more or less eponymous, and they were no more than individual redactors of pre-existing popular ballads and folktales, in verse more refined than those of the Vedic chants, but yet not as classical as those of succeeding kāvya or art-epic poets. Though chronologically the encyclopedic Mahābhārata in its final shape is undoubtedly posterior to the Rāmāyana, it is not impossible that its nucleus contains material much older than that of the sister-epic Rāmāyana. From the purely literary standpoint, however, the Rāmāyana is far more unified and artistic, and the age-old tradition of regarding Vālmīki as the Ādi-kavi or father of Sanskrit poetry is thus justified. Out of its seven books (with 24,000 verses in all), only the first and last appear to be later additions, whereas the voluminous Mahābhārata (with more than one hundred thousand verses) seems to have undergone a series of interpolations from about 500 B.C.E. up to 400 C.E. But the present Rāmāyana was already complete by 200 C.E., along with its additions. The story of Rāma is found in an abridged form in the present Mahābhārata, yet the latter is more archaic than the former and belongs to the region of Kuru-Pančāla, the heartland of North India, whereas the former is more refined in style and replete with poetic conventions, besides arising in the more eastern region of Kosala-Magadha. The critical editions of these two major epics have revealed how they enjoyed unbroken popularity in the whole of India down the centuries and also in Greater India—i.e., Indonesia, Vietnam, and other areas—since there are numerous recensions and versions well preserved in hundreds of manuscripts throughout India. Indeed, the bulk of all later Sanskrit literature is directly or indirectly influenced by the two major epics.

Almost every classical Sanskrit poet or playwright pays homage to these two author-sages, Vyāsa and Vālmīki, as the pathmakers of the poetic tradition. It should be noted, however, that only the Rāmāyana is out-and-out a poem, whereas the Mahābhārata is not only a poem but a historico-political narrative, a theological law-book, a textbook of ethics, a treatise on philosophy, and many other texts, all in one. Both these epics have exercised a deep influence on the life and thought of Indians down the centuries. They have also served as sourcebooks for later authors of plays, poems, and other literary genres.

Vālmīki's great epic is outstanding and unique in the history of world poetry. The hero of the poem, Rāma, is a paragon of all the noble ideals prized by the Indian people. He is at once a dutiful son, an affectionate brother, a loving husband, a stern and relentless hero, and an ideal king. Daśaratha, his father, is depicted as an old king who invites disaster on himself and misery on others because of his weakness for one of his queens, Kaikeyi. Lakṣmana and Bharata compete with each other in their readiness for the sacrifice demanded by fraternal love, and Sitā is the beau ideal of a faithful wife in the midst of a hundred trials. On the other side, Rāvana, the arch-villain, is a demon and is depicted as a foil to Rāma. Blinded by his power and might, he breaks every code of dharma, but his success is short-lived; his titanic strength fails him in his battle with the righteous Rāma. He dies miserably, illustrating how the wages of sin are death and desolation.

Although the didactic element is evident throughout, Vālmīki's poetry is steeped in the *rasas* of tender pathos (karuṇa) and heroism (vīra) which overwhelm the reader with their afflatus. Vālmīki is equally at home in the depiction of the whole gamut of emotions and feelings that surge in a human heart, and he uses the supernatural element very sparingly. His communion with nature in all her moods is indeed masterly. The interest of the poem is thus a result of a deft handling of all the elements: narrative, character, and life message. To crown it all, Vālmīki has perfected a style at once limpid and sprightly, and his best effects are so deftly achieved that they appear uncontrived. We have in him an abundance of artful turns of expression that become cliches in the hands of later poets.

But we move to a different world altogether when we enter the maze of the Mahābhārata. The Pāndava heroes and their half brothers, the Kauravas, are all victims of ambition and avarice, with varying degrees of dharma and adharma in their thought and action. Intrigue, rivalry, and divine strength drive them to an internecine battle, which rages furiously until everyone is slain or laid low. Not even Kṛṣṇa, the avatar, can change this pre-ordained course of events. This main story is interspersed with innumerable lengthy disquisitions on law, ethical values, philosophy, socio-political norms, myths and legends, and so forth, that try the reader's patience. But a literary student will find that the epic has within itself a number of smaller epics, each with a unified interest of its own. Thus, the episodes of Nala and Damayantī, Sāvitrī and Satyavān, and others may be deemed as epic poems in their own right. Poetic graces are but few and the ruling sentiment vague, but as a sourcebook for later writers, it is indeed unique. Indeed, the Mahābhārata should be looked upon as a thesaurus of everything Indians valued and created in the realm of thought in the course of several centuries (44 B.C.E. to 100 C.E.), and the poetry therein is only of marginal interest.

Classical Sanskrit Kavya Before Kalidasa

From the spontaneous abundance of the epics to the cultivated artistry of classical kāvya in Sanskrit, we see a transition but dimly, since the bulk of pre-Kālidāsā literature is lost. The detailed rules of versification, the large variety of meters experimented upon, and even their enchanting names, found in early authors of metrics like Pingala (circa 200 C.E.), point to a many-sided activity of court poets in lyrical as well as dramatic forms. Bharata's rules of dramaturgy, music, and dance in his Nātyaśāstra (about the same time) confirm this. Stray references to individual works in embellished prose and lyrical verse are found in Patānjali (circa 150 B.C.E.). The detailed account of a nāgaraka (man-about-town) furnished by Vātsyāyana, a celebrated author on erotics (circa 200 C.E.), presents a society given to sensual pleasures and cultivating as many as sixty-four arts (kalās). Courtesans provided saloons where these arts could flourish. In this new culture, many a sophistication and fashion arose, heralding a new movement in poetry. Several deviant ways of expression, especially for eulogizing kings and describing the charms of women, were devised by ingenious poets, and these were codified as alankāras or figures of speech in books on rhetoric, the earliest of which, again, are lost. Yet how the simple Sanskrit of the epics had been chiseled into a scintillating conventional and ornate medium brimming with alliteration, chime, hyperbole, paradox, and so forth is illustrated by a few epigraphs on the one hand, and by the works of the Buddhist poet, Aśvaghoṣa, on the other. This spans the period of about six centuries, three before and three after the Common Era.

Epigraphs

Epigraphs represent the genre of kāvya called praśasti or eulogy, which is most popular in Sanskrit. Rudradaman's Junagadh Inscription (150 C.E.) has already the profusion of long compounds and alliterative effects in prose and actually names some literary qualities like "sweetness," "strikingness," and "brilliance." Samudragupta's Allahabad Pillar Inscription (350 C.E.) describes at length the all-Indian conquests of King Samudragupta in ornate prose and verse. The king is compared to epic heroes and styled a kavirāja or emperor among poets, whom the other poets tried to imitate. The highly conventional and artificial kavya style was thus an established fact long before Kālidāsa, the master-poet in Sanskrit.

The same conclusion is strengthened by the two art epics which have come down to us from the pen of the Buddhist poet Aśvaghoṣa, the mentor of Kaniṣka (second century C.E.). The Buddhačarita describes the life of Buddha in twenty-eight cantos (only thirteen are extant) with all the conventional imagery and descriptions like that of the city, the harem, the sporting women, sunrise, and so forth. Yet the poet succeeds in underscoring the wave of renunciation that overwhelms the prince, Siddhārtha, and his sense of *welt-schmerz* ("world pain," or sorrow that one feels and accepts as one's necessary portion in life). His other mahākāvya or ornate epic is Saundarananda, depicting the sensuous attachment of Nanda to his charming wife Sundarī and his ultimate disenchantment thanks to the labors of his half brother, the Buddha. The didactic and religious elements in the poems are unmistakable. Yet they are noteworthy as embodying full-bodied developments of self-consciously constructed Sanskrit kāvya, striking out a new path distinct from the popular ballad-poetry of the epics and choosing the line of ascetic-poetry, already illustrated in the Mahābhārata.

Secular drama, too, had already progressed, shaking off the shackles of sacrificial religion in which it might have first arisen, to judge from Bhāsa's plays (circa 200 C.E.), since quite a few of them are based on folktales, though the majority depict epic themes. His magnum opus is the Svapnavāsavadattā, a play based on the story of King Udayana's love for Vāsavadattā, celebrated in Guṇāḍhya's Bṛhatkathā (a vast treasurehold of fables and romantic tales) written in Paiśāčī, a kind of Prākṛt, now unfortunately lost. The verses in these plays are often highly lyrical. Similarly, we know from Patanjali's Mahābhāsya (150 B.C.E.) that there were Sanskrit romantic tales of heroines in love, like Bhaimarathe, Vāsavadattā, and Sumanettarā.

Kalidasa

Kālidāsa, by the universal judgment of critics, ancient and modern, represents the high watermark of Sanskrit poetry and drama. Here we might say a word only about his poems, since his plays will be surveyed later under drama. He is expressly alluded to by Ravikīrti in an epigraph (634 C.E.) and imitated by Vatsabhaṭṭi in another epigraph (472 C.E.). The poems so imitated by him are the two lyrics of Kālidāsa, Ṛtusamhāra (The Cycle of Seasons) and Meghadūta (The Cloud-Messenger). These facts and the widespread tradition that Kālidāsa was a poet laureate of King Vikramāditya point to Chandragupta II (380-413 C.E.) as the patron of this celebrated poet, who had also Ujjain as one of his subcapitals—a city for which Kālidāsa exhibits special fondness.

The Ṛtusamhāra is a short lyrical collection, each of the six Indian seasons being described in a separate canto from the eyes of a lover to his newlywed. It is a "lover's calendar," wherein each change of weather, each flower and creeper, each bird and beast contributes in a new way to the enhancement of their connubial bliss. The poet's communion with nature at its most delicate aspects is complete, and his song as sweet as it is simple.

The poet's lyrical genius takes wings in the next poem, Meghadūta, which is a gem in Sanskrit lyrical poetry. The hero is a demigod suffering separation from his divine beloved, cursed as he is to be a human on earth for one full year. The advent of the rains makes him lose his head, and he crazily imagines the moving cloud high above to be a friend who might carry his love-message to his pining beloved in Alakā, a city high up in the Himalayas. The poet endows life to mountains and clouds, turning them into friends, and talks of rivers as beloveds eagerly awaiting union with him. With masterly strokes he describes the landscape and the important cities and temples en route, and especially the fairyland of Alakā, where the denizens know nothing but sensual bliss, day in and day out. This celebration of love-in-separation is indeed a unique achievement in Sanskrit poetry, so much so that scores of such messenger-poems were attempted by later writers, though none could come anywhere near the original either in grace or in expression of feeling.

The first Mahākāvya or ornate epic from Kālidāsa is Raghuvaṃśa, in ten cantos recounting the glories of the solar race of kings according to legendary lore. We have here a pageant of heroes, representing diverse ideals of kingship. Dilipa, the childless but pious king, is advised by his guru to serve the cow, Nandini; Dilipa does his duty well and is even ready to lay down his life to save that of the cow. Seeing this devotion, he is blessed with a child by the cow. Raghu is a great war hero whose arms defeat even Indra and who conquers the entire earth, only to spend all his earnings in sacrificial gifts to the deserving and the needy. His son is Aja, who wins the hand of the beautiful princess Indumatī in *Svayamvara* or open choice of the bride. He is so shaken by her untimely death that he laments disconsolately and follows her soon by giving up his body in the holy confluence of the Ganges and the Jumna, after crowning his son, Daśaratha. Then the story of the Rāmāyana is summed up with remarkable originality in poetic treatment. Sītā's disappearance in the bowels of the earth is tragic to a degree, and the lives of Lava and Kuṣa are marked with interesting episodes until Agnivarṇa comes, the last in the line, who throws ideals to the winds and leads a licentious life, inviting upon himself a premature end. The touch of a master is evident throughout, and Kalidasa's genius has never been surpassed. His skill in the use of telling similes and suggestive imagery, his delineation of tender sentiments, and his perfect style, at once simple and appealing, have won for him universal acclaim. These make him a national poet of India, entitled to a place among the world's best poets.

Kālidāsa's second mahākāvya is *Kumarasambhava*, in eight cantos, which describes the divine love of Pārvati and Śiva, designed to beget a son capable of destroying Tāraka, the redoubtable demon who had defeated all the gods, including Brahma, Viṣṇu, and Indra. The poet's love of the sublime and the beautiful is happily blended here with the nature of divine love, where sensuality is burnt to ashes in the fire of asceticism.

Though widely read in all the studies of his time, Kālidāsa wears the mantle of his learning lightly and never allows his scholarship to outrun his poetic judgment. He imbibes the values of epic religion and gives them a universality unknown before or ever after. He plumbs the depths of the most profound and subtlest emotions and shows his acute discernment in the choice of meters and expressions to depict them in their finest shades. He is a high priest of Nature, combining care with grace, and scores his success effortlessly. He remains for all time the apogee of Sanskrit poetry.

Post-Kalidasa Poets

The achievement of Kālidāsa was so great and inimitable that later poets had to use all their ingenuity in devising newer modes of refinement to the kāvya, while retaining the pattern of Kālidāsa. Among mahākāvya writers, Bhāravi (circa 550 C.E.), from the South, took up the epic theme of the single contact of Śiva with Arjuna in his poem, Kiratārjunīya. The story loses importance; filigree work with diverse turns and tropes becomes more valuable. Yet in parts he can depict characters like Draupadī with power and dignity. The style is heavy and often unintelligible, and without training—especially in rare grammatical forms, figurative turns, varied meters, and stylistic tricks—it grows even further, resulting in difficult poems such as Magha's Śiṣupālavadha (circa 650 C.E.), Bhaṭṭi's Rāvaṇavadha (circa 600 C.E.), Ratnākara's Haravijaya (circa 850 C.E.), and Sriharsa's Maiṣadhīyačarita (circa 1170 C.E.). There is no novelty or interest in the story of these and hundreds of other imitative poems that were written after Kālidāsa. Their purpose is just to startle the scholar with their ingenuity in the use of difficult imagery, hyperbolic fancy, and artificial diction. They parade their learning in different disciplines under the guise of poetry. Most of them are no more than curios today, though they are sometimes held high in the judgment of traditional pundits.

In the medieval period, religious sects began utilizing this genre for the glorification of their ideologies or pontiffs. Among the former, Vedānta Deśika's Yādavābhyudaya (circa 1350 C.E.) is still popular. Śaṃkara-digvijaya of Mādhava, during the same period, is a biography of the great Āčarya of Advaita, replete with several miracles, so dear to popular taste. Sumādhva-vijaya of Nārāyana, also of the same period, portrays in similar terms the supernatural glory of Mādhvāčarya. Rukminīśa-vijaya of Vādirāja (sixteenth century) is modeled after Magha's poem and introduces covertly the philosophical tenets of the Mādhva school of Vaiṣṇavism. Śivalīlārṇava of Nīlakaṇṭha Dīkṣita (seventeenth century) depicts the sixty-four lilas or sports of Śiva and is a highly readable work, combining dignity of diction and fervent devotion. Another equally interesting poem of his is Gaṇgāvataraṇa, describing the legend of the descent of Ganges to earth from heaven in a memorable manner. Nārāyaṇa Bhattatiri's Nārāyaṇīya is a recast of the Bhāgavata, brimming with devotional fervor. All these long poems hail from South India, indicating how the Kāvya tradition was well preserved there when the North was reeling under the impact of Muslim invasions.

A noteworthy improvisation of mahākāvya for historical chronicle saw the rise of historical kāvya or čarita. Padmagupta's *Navasahasankacharita* (circa 1000 C.E.) eulogizes King Munja of Dhāra. Bilhana's *Vikramankadevacharita* glorifies King Vikramāditya VI of Kalyāna in Karnatak (1076-1127 C.E.) as a hero of many battles. Kalhana, the Kashmiri poet (circa 1100 C.E.) is the greatest in this genre, since his *Rājatarangiṇī* covers the history of Kashmir from earliest times down to 1000 C.E. and contains as many as 7,826 verses. Hemačandra, of the same period, wrote a eulogy of the Gujarat king, Kumārapala, under the name Kumārapālačarita. None of these is history in the modern sense; they contain a lot of legendary material and descriptions.

A curious offshoot of the artificial pedantry which the later-day decadents valued is čitra-kāvya or pictorial verse, abounding in verbal acrostics. Verses which read alike both forwards and backwards that read alike in Sanskrit and Prākṛt, and which can be written in geometrical patterns all come under this category. They revel in puns and rhymes and contain at times just one, two, or three consonants recurring through a whole verse. *Kicakavadha* of Nītivarman (circa 850 C.E.), Nalodaya ascribed to Kālidāsa (date and authorship are uncertain), Rakshasa-kāvya attributed to Vararuči and Kālidāsa, Vidagdhamukhamanēana of Dharmadāsa (fifteenth century) are some examples. Some poets like Dhanañjaya (circa 900 C.E.) and Kavirāja (circa 1300 C.E.) wrote *Dvisandhāna-kavyas* or poems that telescope the stories of both the premier epics into a single poem by breaking up words in different ways.

Drama

Unlike Greek drama, tragedy is conspicuous by its absence in Sanskrit. This might have been due partly to its religious origin and partly to the Indian dramatic theory which insisted on a happy ending for plays, with a touch of the supernatural, to enhance popular interest and to serve a didactic purpose by showing good being rewarded and vice punished. There were religious pantomimes and popular shows of legendary gods, kings, and demons in the Vedic and epic times. But full-fledged plays with close-knit plots, rounded characters, and lyrical verse, played by a dramatic troupe headed by a stage manager with paraphernalia of stage conventions, could not have been earlier than 400 B.C.E. This also marks the date of the earliest portions of Bharata's Nāṭyaśāstra, which already knows of ten types of plays, the foremost of which is nāṭaka or serious tragicomedy. Alongside nāṭaka we find prakaraṇa or social comedy, prahasana or farce, and bhana or monologue, minor types which were few and far between. All dramas are conventional; they begin and end with prayers to God.

Among nāṭakas or plays par excellence, the plot is taken from celebrated epics and mythological-legendary lore; the characters are divine, semi-divine, or princely; and they always appear with their entourage. Women, though high-stationed, and low characters talk varieties of Prākṛt, Sanskrit being the privilege only of the lofty hero.

The vidūṣaka or court jester talks Prākṛt, and his sallies promote the love affairs of his king-friend. The supernatural freely operates in shaping the denouement.

Bhasa

The earliest playwright whose plays are extant today, at least in a modified version if not in original form, is Bhāsa (circa 200 C.E.), referred to by Kālidāsa. The most celebrated among his galaxy of plays is the Svapnanāṭaka, which portrays the abiding love of King Udayana for his first queen, Vāsavadattā (though she is supposed to have died), even after his marriage with Padmāvatī. He is dreaming of his first love lying on the couch of Padamāvatī. The theme, taken from Guṇādhya's Bṛhatkathā, is given a very dramatic new turn in this dream scene. In the sister play, Pratijñā-Yaugandharāyaṇa, the ingenious skill of Udayana's minister is portrayed vividly in securing the release of his master from the prison of Mahāsena, father of Vāsavadattā. In the former play, again, the extent of self-sacrifice that Queen Vāsavadattā invites on herself for the eventual welfare of her spouse is well brought out. Among the other plays, the Pratimā-nāṭaka, in which the character of Kaikeyi is absolved from blame by the bold invention of the statue scene, is significant. These plays are stageworthy and have directness of action so rare among later closet plays. The verses also are few and effective. The style is at once direct and forceful, if not brilliant. The other plays ascribed to Bhāsa are either trivial or tedious, with the exception of čārudatta, which might perhaps be only a stage abridgement of the Mṛččhakaṭika.

Kalidasa

As in poetry, so in drama too, the highest place is Kālidāsa's, by universal consent of critics, Eastern and Western alike. The sentiment of love is his forte, and all three of his plays are concerned only with that sentiment in its various aspects. Mālavikāgnimitra is a light play with a much-married king as hero, and his intrigues to win the hand of Mālavikā, an attendant of his first queen, are often bungled by his jester's landing him in strange capers and providing scope for hilarious mirth. The first two suspicious queens confide in a nun at court only to be fooled at last, since she is a secret agent of the servant-maid. In due time, the servant-maid is proved to be a princess betrothed to Agnimitra, and the obstacles for the union of lovers is thus dramatically removed as in the New Attic Comedy.

Vikramorvaśīya is a more serious play wherein the celestial nymph, Urvaśī, falls in love with Purūravas, the earthly king, because of his valor in rescuing her from the clutches of a demon. Her romantic whims bring in a train of unexpected woes as well as ecstasies to the king, who eventually goes mad. His lovelorn frenzy forms one of the most touching scenes in the play, and by a supernatural magic gem he is cured of his madness, and the lovers unite in the end. The poet has skillfully infused melodramatic elements in this play.

Yet the magnum opus of Kālidāsa the playwright is Abhijñāna-Śākuntalā, whose theme, again, is love subjected to severe testing by destiny. Śākuntalā, the heroine, is a semidivine foster-daughter of a hermit, while the hero-king is a friend on earth of Indra, the lord of heaven. A hunting incident brings the two together. They fall in love at first sight, and Śākuntalā conceives the king's child. The absent ascetic, Kaṇva, returns and sends Śākuntalā to the palace. By a sudden curse of the irate sage, Durvāsas, the king cannot recognize Śākuntalā as his wife and rejects her. As she had lost the signet ring he had given her earlier, she has no way of reminding him of the past. The heroine is frisked away to heaven. But the ring finds its way back to the king through a fisherman who gets the ring in the belly of a fish. The king's memory returns, and, sonless as he is, he mourns his stupidity in rejecting his lawful wife. At last, a chance journey to heaven brings him upon her, on his way back to the divine hermitage where Śākuntalā is staying with her son. The boy at play is, by degrees, recognized by the king as his son, and the once-parted lovers unite. Though dramatic incidents are few and the action slow, the depiction of the gamut of love is consummate. Kālidāsa has ably presented the holy hermitage as a foil to the luxuries of the palace. It is the success of innocence against machinations of sophisticated life as well as fate. The token ring and the sage's curse are symbolic inventions not found in the original epic source. India's contribution to world drama presents the cream of Indian culture and life-values in a most appealing style.

Post-Kalidasa Plays

The best romantic comedy in Sanskrit is the Mṛččhakaṭika by Śūdraka, who is most probably the immediate successor of Kālidāsa in time (circa fifth century). It is not a nāṭaka but a prakaraṇa, allowing room for all kinds of low and middling characters. Chārudatta, a merchant youth, is wooed by the courtesan, Vasantasenā, spurning the advances of the king's brother-in-law, the Śakāra who is a villain. The seamy side of life in a city, with gamblers, thieves, rogues, mendicants, and so forth jostling one another, is vividly shown in the background of this love whose course zigzags. Śūdraka's sense of humor has no parallel elsewhere. An element of satire also adds spice to the rich fare of packed action and fast-moving spectacle. The underplot of a political revolution is dramatically devised to bring about the happy ending to the play, which should otherwise have been a tragedy. Realism in the portrayal of a wide variety of ordinary men and women, with all their virtues and vices, makes this play unique. Emperor Harṣa (590-647 C.E.) is the author of three short plays, Ratnāvali, Priyadarsikā, and Nāgānandā. The first two are but variations of Kālidāsa's Mālavikāgnimitrā. The third is indeed a remarkable play, holding out the Buddhist ideal of "self-sacrifice above personal pleasure," illustrated in the hero. He offers himself up to be eaten by the vulture to save a serpent, without even a thought of his beloved and his aged parents in the forest. This indeed adds new dimension to Sanskrit drama.

Viśākhadatta's Mudrārākṣasa (circa 600 C.E.) has a very well knit plot conforming to Aristotelian rules. It is singular in keeping out love and depicting only political intrigue. Kauṭilya, the minister of Chandragupta, sets a wide net in which his rival, Rākṣasa, ultimately gets caught. The sworn enemy of the new king with unshakable loyalty to his dead masters is humbled and made by circumstances to accept service under Chandragupta. The playwright is at his best in presenting the success of human endeavor as against destiny. The almost inevitable tragedy of Rākṣasa is averted by a new turn of events—Rākṣasa has to choose between avoiding a friend's death on his account and his loyalty to dead masters. The play is powerful and the style forceful.

Bhavabhūti (circa 700 C.E.) is held by Indian literary theorists to be a compeer of Kālidāsa in the dramatic art. But his plays are more wordy and long-winded, more poetic than dramatic. His Uttararāmačarita is the best of his three works. With some bold innovations, he shows how the hero, Rāma, was forced by circumstances beyond his control into deserting his dear queen, Sītā, and how he pined for her and how, by the contrivance of Vālmīki and some goddesses, he was finally united with her. While the depth of Rāma's love is portrayed in the famous picture-gallery scene, the final reunion is accomplished with the device of a play within a play. Bhavabhūti is a good stylist but prolix. The plays can be read but not staged successfully. These defects are all the more glaring in his Mahāvīračarita, where the incidents are far too many and descriptions of valor far too lengthy. Even his prakaraṇa, Mālatimādhava, suffers in comparison with Śūdraka's play. There are too many bizarre elements and tedious lucubrations that spoil the dramatic action.

The Venīsamhāra of Bhaṭṭa Nārāyaṇa (circa 800 C.E.), which compresses the details of the bloody Mahābhārata War in a bombastic style, is similar. The author ingeniously introduces incidents of love and mistaken identity into an otherwise grim theme, but they are neither credible nor dramatically apt.

The decadence of Sanskrit drama is complete by the time we come to Rajaśekhara (circa 900 C.E.), who has given us abridged plays of the two epics, Bālarāmāyana and Bālabhārata, and a romantic comedy, Karpūramanjari, closely modeled on the Ratnāvali. Stories, of course, are remodeled; changes are introduced. Yet the dramatic effect is poor.

Kṛṣṇamiśra's Prabodhačandrodaya is an allegorical play. It is a conflict between knowledge and ignorance. This presentation of philosophical concepts as characters reminds us of English Morality Plays.

Dramas of various types continued to be written as literary exercises in all the subsequent centuries. Yet they are mostly coins from the same mould, meant more to be read than staged. The staging of Sanskrit dramas had long become obsolete.

Minor Poems

While the major genres of mahākāvya and nataka conformed to the meticulous standards of the learned, the more popular forms of Sanskrit literature belong to the general class of "minor poems." This class includes lyrics on love, renunciation, and religious devotion as well as self-contained verses—didactic, satirical, humorous, epigrammatic, and allegorical. Their tradition is as old as the epic age. The best known are the following.

Love Poems

By far the most outstanding poet in this category is Bhartṛhari (circa 600 C.E.), whose "centuries" (cycles of one hundred self-contained stanzas or śatakas) on love, renunciation, and morality are universally popular. Amaru (circa 650 C.E.) is indeed the more sensitive poet. His "love-century" gives pen-pictures of all types of women in love in their diverse moods. It richly illustrates the various types of men and women in love, which were classified by theorists. Bilhaṇa's Chorapañčāśikā is a collection of fifty verses singing a lover's reminisces of his sweetheart's charms. A highly erotic octet is Mayūrāśṭaka. The poet is said to be a friend of Bāṇa (circa 650 C.E.). Govardhana's Āryā-saptaśati (circa 1200 C.E.) contains seven hundred stanzas depicting love among rustic folk with a wealth of suggestive imagery. The Gītā-Govinda of Jayadeva (circa 1200 C.E.) is a unique and popular poetic opera-cum-melodrama. Here the lilt of song, melody, and dance combine to glorify the stolen loves of the divine Rādhā and Kṛṣṇa. Jagannātha (seventeenth century) in the Moghul Court wrote Bhāminī-vilāsa, whose mastery of melodious diction and artistic imagery is indeed astounding. The themes of this century of verses are morals, love, and the values of life.

Gnomic Poems

Chāṇakyanīti is a collection of pedagogic maxims (about 350). It might have arisen in early times, since it had already spread to Indonesia by the seventh century. Sundara-Pāṇḍya (circa 450 C.E.) of the South is the author of sixty-two didactic verses called Nīti-dviṣaṣtikā. Bhallaṭa's (circa 870 C.E.) Śataka or century is mostly satirical, symbolic, and euphemistic. This last literary form is called Anyokti. Śilhaṇa's Śantiśataka (circa 1200 C.E.) is in the manner of Bhartṛhari but adds more details about the ways of attaining final emancipation in a wave of breathless yearning. The great Śaṇkarāčārya's (circa 750 C.E.) minor poems like Mōhamudgāra and Charpaṭa-pañjarikā vividly bring out the vanity of material joys and sound a clarion-call to cultivate wisdom leading to liberation.

Satirical Poems

Damodaragupta's (circa 760 C.E.) Kuṭṭanīmata is a satire on the love of courtesans and their snares leading one to destitution. The prolific writer, Kṣemendra (circa 1050 C.E.), has satirized priests, clerks, administrators, doctors, merchants, goldsmiths, and others in Kalāvilāsa. His Darpadalana brings out powerfully the vanity of pride, learning, beauty, valor, and even asceticism. His other satires are Samayamātṛkā, Deśopadeśa, and Narmamālā. Nīlakaṇṭha Dīkṣita (seventeenth century) wrote Kāli-viḍambana after the manner of Kṣemendra. These poems are very popular.

Devotional Poems

Almost all mahākāvyas and purāṇas contain sections of devotional praise to gods and sages. But they also came to be written as independent works from early times as they were invested with religious value. Not all these stotras are of poetic value. To make them poetically artistic, classical figures of sound and sense came to be lavishly employed. The most representative of these is Chaṇḍīśataka of Mayūra. It is rich in praise of the mother-goddess, and in alliterative effects. Soon religious teachers also made this form their own. Thus we have Yāmunačārya's Stotra-ratna (tenth century) recited religiously even today in South Indian temples. Similarly, Puṣpadanta's

Mahimnastava of the same period is still recited in the north. Kulaśekhara's (tenth century) Mukundamālā is famous among Vaiṣṇavites as is the Bhaktāmarastotra of Mānatunga (circa 850 C.E.) among the Jains. Venkaṭādhvarin's (seventeenth century) Lakṣmī-sahasra is a collection of one thousand verses, full of rhyme and chime. Varadarājastava of Appayya Dīkṣita (1554-1626 C.E.) is more sincere in feeling and less artificial. But the finest flowers in this form are the five laharīs or waves composed by Jagannātha (seventeenth century), addressed, respectively, to Gaṇgā, Yamunā, Lakṣmī, Divine Grace (karuṇā), and to the ambrosial rays of the Sun-God. The Stutikusumāñjali of Jagaddhara (fifteenth century) is a vast body of devotional verses, breathing the fervor of ardent devotion to Śiva.

Prose Narrative, Fable, and Romantic Tale

The development of literary prose in Sanskrit presents a curious phenomenon. Prose composition was considered the touchstone of masterminds. The two recognized literary forms in prose from early days were the romantic tale (kathā) and the historico-legendary chronicle (ākhyāyika). What was lost by the absence of meter had to be made up by the profusion of long alliterative compounds, puns, paradoxes, and a host of other figures of speech with an eye on rhythm. The first available work in the kathā form is Vāsavadattā of Subandhu (circa 550 C.E.), which bristles with all these tricks and conventional conceits. More readable is Bāṇabhaṭṭa's Kādambarī, though it is also richly embellished in Subandhu's manner, since its story interest is not inconspicuous. Mostly these works derive their themes from Guṇādhya's Bṛhatkathā, whose late Sanskrit version is Somadeva's verse Kathāsaritsāgara (circa 1050 C.E.). Subandhu's romance deals with the fairytale of the hero who sees his would-be queen in a dream, falls in love with her, and after many adventures ultimately marries her. Similarly, Bāṇabhaṭṭa's masterpiece, Kādambarī, deals with demigods and nymphs and their constant love in several births. The Indian art of emboxing a tale within a tale is effectively utilized here. Bāṇabhaṭṭa's style is at once gorgeous and lively and becomes tender and delicate while depicting the delicate shades of love. His Harṣačarita gives in legendary fashion an autobiography of the author and a biography of the hero-king, interspersed with telling epigrams. Daṇḍin's Daśakumāračarita (circa 700 C.E.) is less artificial and more racy. It contains the adventures of ten princes, lost in the forest, each of whom secures a throne and a queen for himself by his own efforts. The other later works in this form are poor imitations of the three works noticed above.

However, the Pañčatantra (available in many versions) is a most significant collection of fables which was written by Viṣṇuśarman around 300 C.E., selecting stories of pedagogical interest from the Bṛhatkathā. These bird-and-beast fables have migrated all over the world in the course of centuries, undergoing several modifications. The fables are grouped under stratagems, e.g., how to divide friends, how to win them, how to achieve peace, and how to win war. In narration, one story leads on incidentally to another in a chain in such a way that the original story is almost forgotten. This is the artificial unity which binds the fables together. Here birds and beasts become expert politicians and talk of diplomacy and polity. A later popular recast of it is Narayana's Hitopadeśa (circa 1300 C.E.).

Some of the other popular tales are Siṃhāsanadvātriṃśika, containing thirty-two stories related by statuettes of Vikrama's throne, illustrating the emperor's cleverness in the most difficult straits; Śukasaptati, or seventy stories related by a parrot to its mistress, illustrating the dangers that lie in wait for unchaste women; and Vetālapañčavimśati, or twenty-five stories related by a vampire to King Vikramāditya. Most of these are available in several versions, and the original authors are unknown. The stories are indeed popular and have been translated into almost all modern Indian languages.

Mixed Prose and Verse

The name Champū refers to a form combining prose and verse. This literary form came into vogue only after the sixth century and was attempted by learned poets whose goal was to combine the dignity of prose with the appeal of poetry in style, all the while retaining the classical mould of the mahākāvya or art-epic. The first available čampū is Trivikrama's Nalačampū (915 C.E.). The Jaina Somadeva's Yaśastilakačampū (959 C.E.) not only narrates the story of Yaśodhara, but also provides incidentally a vast body of knowledge known at the time. Champū-Rāmāyana, ascribed to Bhoja (eleventh century), and Champū-Bhārata of Anantabhaṭṭa (eleventh century) are artificial recasts of the epics catering to the new taste of pandits. So is the Champū-Bhāgavata of Abhinava Kālidāsa about the same period. All these are works from South India. But in the North, writers of the Chaitanya school, such as Paramānandadāsa and Jīvagosvāmin in the sixteenth century, produced luminous and voluminous čampūs, such as Ānandavṛndāvana—čampū and Gopālačampū, respectively. Nīlakaṇṭhavijaya of Nīlakaṇṭha Dīkṣita is a remarkable composition, breathing new life into an old legend. But the most remarkable work in this genre is the Viśvaguṇādarśa of Venkaṭādhvarin. In this work, two celestial observer-narrators in their space vehicle comment on the merits and demerits of people of the South, their religious customs and manners, dress, and professions.

Anthologies

Important anthologies of gnomic, erotic, and anyokti verses are Subhāṣita-ratnākosa of Vidyakara (circa 1150 C.E.), Sadukti-karṇāmrta of Śrīdharadasa (circa 1200 C.E.), Subhāṣita-Sudhānidhi of Sāyaṇa (circa 1350 C.E.), Śārngadhara-paddhati of Śārngadhara (circa 1350 C.E.), and Subhāḍitāvalī of Vallabhadeva (circa 1450 C.E.).

Translations

Almost all the major works noticed above have been translated into virtually every modern Indian language and also most of the European languages. The Ṛgveda, the Rāmāyana, the Mahābhārata, Śākuntala, Meghadūta, Bhartṛhari-śatakas, Pañčatantra, Mṛččhakaṭika, and the Bhagavadgītā are some works in Sanskrit which have found more than one translator in recent times and have become world classics.

Works Cited

De, S.K. 1947. *History of Sanskrit Literature*. Calcutta: University of Calcutta.

Deussen, Paul. 1966. *The philosophy of the Upanishads*, trans. by A.S. Geden (1966). New York: Dover.

Keith, A.B. 1993 [1925]. *History of Classical Sanskrit Literature*. Delhi Motilal Banarasidass.

Krishnamachariar, M. 1970. *History of Classical Sanskrit Literature*. Delhi: Motilal.

Macdonell, A.A. 1968 [1900]. *A History of Sanskrit Literature*. Reprint, New York: Haskell House.

Muller, Friederich Max. 1926. *A History of Ancient Sanskrit Literature*. Allahabad.

Warder, A.K. 1972-77. *Indian Kavya Literature*, 3 vols. Delhi: Motilal Banarasidass.

Winternitz, M. 1927-77. *A History of Indian Literature*, 3 vols. (Vols. 1 and 2 translated by S. Ketkar and H. Kohn. Vol. 3 translated by S. Jha.) Calcutta: University of Calcutta.

Chapter 28

Translation as an Afterlife: Making Dead Poets Speak

R. Parthasarathy

In order to understand the history of translation in India, we need to understand what the Hindus thought about the nature of language. The *locus classicus* is the following hymn from the Rig Veda:

> uta tvah paśyan na dadarśa vācan,
> uta tvah śṛṇvan na śrnotyēnaṃ.
> One who looked did not see the word,
> One who listened did not hear it (Rig Veda 10.71.4).

The hymn emphasizes the fact that the Word is not revealed to everyone. The uninitiated have no access to it. It was a closely guarded secret by the Brahman priesthood. The Word was never written down; it was communicated only orally. For once it was written down, it was no more than a dead letter. It lost its sacred power and ceased to be a mantra. Under the circumstances, translation was an abomination. For how could the language of the gods, *deva-vani*, as Sanskrit was regarded, be translated into any human tongue? It was simply inconceivable. And so the Rig Veda was not written down until much later. In fact, for over 2,000 years it was orally transmitted—all of its 1028 hymns comprising about 21,200 lines—from one generation to another by priestly families, a process that has continued to this day. It is a phenomenon that has no parallel anywhere else. This explains why the Rig Veda had not been translated in its entirety into any Indian language until recently (I believe there are translations in Hindi and Kannada), although complete translations began appearing in the nineteenth century in French (1848-51), English (1850-88) , and German (1876-77)—a monument to Europe's fascination with Sanskrit.

Translators of the Vedas were regarded as traitors (*traduttori traditori*, as the Italians say), who exposed the Word to unworthy ears. But the European Indologists changed all that, even though Sir William Jones in the late eighteenth century found it almost impossible to find a Brahman to teach him Sanskrit. Jones was an Untouchable in the eyes of the Brahmans. I experienced no such problems from the English, Irish, and Scottish priests of the Salesians of Don Bosco who were more than eager to teach me English. They even arranged for me to study Sanskrit, even though the language was not taught at the school. I am grateful to them for this gift of tongues. Before enrolling in Don Bosco, I went to an elementary school where the medium of instruction was Hindi. To this day, I do my multiplications in Hindi. Therefore, with four languages to speak of Tamil, Sanskrit, Hindi, and English what else could I be except a translator? To make available in English a few of the masterpieces of Indian literature—that has always been my objective. And I am glad to report that the Tamil *Tale of an Anklet* now stands shoulder to shoulder with the major epics of the world.

Drawing upon my translations from the Tamil, Sanskrit, and Pali, I would like to present my thoughts on "Translation as an Afterlife." In the process, I will be talking briefly about these languages and about the problems I encountered in making poets from these languages speak in English. Though it takes a poet to translate a poet, I must confess that at my back I often hear Shelley's despair about translation expressed memorably in his *Defence of Poetry* (1840: 484) "It were as wise to cast a violet into a crucible that you might discover the formal principles of its colour and odour, as seek to transfuse from one language to another the creations of a poet"(Shelley 1942: 484). The word "translate," as we know, comes from the Latin *trans*, "across," "beyond," and *latus*, "to bear" or "carry," therefore "a carrying across." And the Greek for translation is *metaphor*: *meta*, "beyond," and *phero*, "to carry," therefore "a carrying beyond."

Translation is the most intimate act of reading. To interpret his text to his audience, the translator must study the culture that has produced the text, and study it diligently and for a long time, so that he knows what the Sanskrit word *moksha* or the Tamil word aṉanku means (both words lack English equivalents) or what a *Bo* tree, under which the Buddha attained enlightenment, looks like.

The texts that the chapter will discuss are the Tamil Cilappatikāram ["The Tale of an Anklet", fifth century C.E.], the Sanskrit Subhāśitaratnakōṣa ["A Classic Anthology of Fine Verses", 11th century C.E.], and the Pali Therīgīthā [The Songs of the Elder Nuns, sixth century B.C.E.]. Specific problems of idiom, syntax, imagery, meter, and tone will be examined in the course of making English poems from the Indian languages. The chapter will also talk about the differences in the poetics of the Indian languages on the one hand and English on the other, and examine the implications those differences have for the translations.

Tamil

Tamil, the oldest of the four major Dravidian languages, is spoken mainly in Tamil Nadu in south-eastern India. The language was regularized around 250 B.C.E.. However, the earliest Tamil poetry goes back to a period between 100 B.C.E. and 250 C.E., and is found in numerous anthologies that were later gathered together in two great collections: the Eṃṃutokai [The Eight Anthologies] and the Pattuppāṃṃu [The Ten Long Poems].

Throughout its history, Tamil Nadu was relatively isolated and free from the invasions that swamped the rest of the country, except for a brief Muslim interlude (1324-70 C.E.) in Maturai [Madurai]. Though the Aryanization of South India had been going on since the first millennium B.C.E., Tamil Nadu (and Kerala) were not united with the rest of India till the British period. Again, Tamil, among all the Indian languages, has resisted Sanskritization by preserving archaic features of phonology and morphology. As a result, the spoken and written forms are different from each other. Also, unlike other Dravidian scripts, Tamil orthography has resisted the inclusion of special characters for writing down Sanskrit sounds. The only exception is the grantha script that the Tamils used in writing Sanskrit.

For nearly two thousand years, the Tamil country in southern India has had a distinct culture of its own. Early Tamil literature speaks of the country as bounded by the Vēnkaṭam Hills (Tirupati) in the North, by the ocean in the East and West, and by the Kumari Hill (Cape Comorin) in the South. It consisted of the three Tamil kingdoms of the Cōla, the Pāntiya, and the Cēral. Two Greek works, *The Periplus of the Erythrean Sea* (first century C.E.) and Ptolemy's *Geography* (second century C.E.), mention the flourishing Roman trade with southern India, which the Tamil kings encouraged. Poets from Kapilar (first century C.E.) to Subramania Bharati (1882-1921) have sung the praise of the Tamil country. Iḷānko the author of *The Tale of an Anklet,* is no exception. *The Tale of an Anklet* speaks for all Tamils as no other work of Tamil literature does: it presents them with an expansive vision of the Tamil imperium, and embodies at the same time a concern for spiritual knowledge represented by the heroine Kaṇṇaki's apotheosis. No other work has endeared itself more to the Tamils than the unhappy tale of Kōvalaṉ and Kaṇṇaki. *The Tale of an Anklet* is the quintessential Tamil poem that in the words of Subramania Bharati "rends the hearts" ("neñcai aḷḷum cilappatikāram") of all Tamils. This is another reason why it has possessed their imagination for over fifteen hundred years as a staple in both its oral and written traditions, crossing generic boundaries, to be retold in verse, prose, fiction, drama, and film.

The Tale of an Anklet is one of the literary masterpieces of the world: it is to the Tamils what the *Iliad* is to the Greeks—the story of their civilization. Anyone interested in comparative religion will find it especially useful since it abounds in Jaina, Buddhist, and Hindu traditions. It spells out the problems that humanity has been wrestling with for a long time: love, war, the inevitability of death, evil, and God's justice. It unequivocally admonishes us to "Seek the best help to reach heaven" (30.196-97), since life is unstable, and we cannot escape from our fate. Iḷankō is, after all, a Jaina monk who renounces the world, and his perspective on the events in the epic strongly reflects his own spiritual bias. Epics from *Gilgamesh* (c. 2000 B.C.E.) onwards have reflected on these problems.

The translation of *The Tale of an Anklet* into modern English verse is one way of acknowledging the debt I owe Tamil, my mother tongue. My assimilation of the eponymous author Iḷankō is another form of translation—rewriting a poem in English that I could not myself write in Tamil. I envied Iḷankō his great epic, and the only way I could possess the poem, make it my own, was to rewrite it in English. By making Iḷankō speak in the accents of English, I hope, I have breathed life into the poem, and awakened it from its enforced sleep in Tamil. For a poem is firmly rooted in a language. When translated into another language, it is exiled from its own, but is no less a poem for the experience.

Let us look at an example from *The Tale of an Anklet* (*Cilappatikaram*, 1968: 506-7; Parthasarathy 1993: 27-8). Whatever its origins, Iḷankō's Tamil was a not a spoken language. He appears to have embalmed the speech of the bards or pāṇaṉs, who orally kept alive the tradition of the story of Kōvalaṉ and Kaṇṇaki. The diction is elitist and courtly, which is perhaps understandable, as the realm of the epic's passage are the three kingdoms: the Cōḷa, the Pāṇṭiya, and the Cēral.

I. karuttur̲u kaṇavar kaṇṭapi n̲alla
tiruttalu millē n̲ir̲r̲alu milan̲en̲ak
kor̲r̲āvai vāyir por̲r̲oṭi takarttuk
kīḻtticai vāyir kaṇavanoṭu pukuntēn̲
mēr̲r̲icai vāyil var̲iyēn̲ peyarken̲a .(Cillapatikāram 23.179-83)

Let us separate the constituent elements in each line, and translate them. The virgules indicate phrase/clause boundaries which are marked by raised numerals.

II. karuttu-ur̲u kaṇavar kaṇṭa-pin̲ allatu
iruttalum illēn̲ n̲ir̲r̲alum ilan-ena-k
kor̲r̲avai vāy-ir̲ poṇ-toṭi takarttu-k
kiḻ-t-ticai vāy-ir kanavan̲-oṭu pukuntēn̲
mēl-ticai vāy-il var̲iyēn̲ peyark(u)-en̲a

III. /[my] heart-has known [the] husband I have seen-after till/[2]
/sitting there is no standing there is no/[3]-/thus [Kaṇṇaki] vowed/[1]
/[of] Kor̲r̲avai temple-in [the] [her] golden-bracelets breaking/[4]
/[the] East Gate-through [my] husband-with I entered [this city]/[6]
/[the] West Gate-by/[7b]/[and] grieved/[5] /I leave [now alone]/[7a]

This is how the lines appear in my English version (Parthasarathy 1993:205-6).

IV. Kaṇṇaki vowed:
"Till I have seen the husband
My heart has known, I will neither sit nor stand."

Her golden bracelets she then broke in the temple
Of Kor̲r̲avai, and wept:
"With my husband
I entered this city through the East Gate:
I now leave by the West Gate, alone" (23:185-90).

English has blurred the focus of the Tamil original as the latter's phonetic template has all but vanished. Despite all the erosion that has occurred in translation, I have firmly held on to Iḷankō's voice, and anchored my English version to it. The voice often peaks as it does in the famous scene above where Kaṇṇaki leaves Maturai after burning it down. Translation is a necessary rite of passage. Exiled from its own langauge, the poem puts down roots in the host language to begin its life as an immigrant in hopes of eventually becoming a native.

A language and nation remember themselves best in a poem. *The Tale of an Anklet* is the well of Tamil undefiled to which the Tamils return to witness their language and identity most vigorously asserted. In translating a poem, one translates nothing less than an entire culture with all its idiosyncrasies. Here is one. Traditionally, an Indian woman's life ended with the death of her husband. She removed the ornaments on her person, stopped putting the tilaka on her forehead, and shaved her head to indicate her unholy status as a widow. Kaṇṇaki finds herself in this limbo when she vows in the temple of Ko<u>rr</u>avai, that she will not rest till she has seen her husband, and ceremoniously breaks her golden bracelets. Iḷankō turns this gesture, dictated by tradition, into a resonant symbol: earlier, in canto 20, Kaṇṇaki confronts the king with his injustice, and in his presence breaks her anklet to establish her husband's innocence. The king collapses from the shock. So does his queen. And Maturai itself goes up in flames. Only then is Kaṇṇaki's wrath appeased. A woman's ornaments function metonymically as extensions of her power that even kings may not trifle with. The king rules only at the pleasure of his subjects. Such gestures as Kaṇṇaki's are culture-specific. There is no way a translator, short of erecting a babel of footnotes, can alert his English readers to them. But I want the poem to speak without choking itself on too many footnotes, though I appreciate the fondness some translators have for them.

Sanskrit

The word Samskṛta ("Sanskrit") means "perfected" or "refined." The language was standardized from the spoken language by about 500 B.C.E.. It is an inflected language like Greek and Latin. This inflection, by clearly signalling the relations of words with one another in a sentence, allows endless variations of word order. Unaccented functional words in English, such as "the," "a," "with," and "at," are indicated in Sanskrit by a change in the inflectional syllable. Thus, for the three English words "of the book," Sanskrit has only one, *pustakasya*. Thus the inflected nature of Sanskrit makes possible an unusual tightness of construction. Also, the analysis of tropes or figures of speech in Sanskrit is based on poetry; in Greek and Latin, it was originally based on oratory. While Greco-Roman rhetoric focuses on the manner of presentation, Sanskrit poetics emphasized imagery and tone. Nothing is explicitly stated. It is always suggested. Indirect suggestion (*dhvani*) is a fundamental aesthetic principle. (See discussion in Krishnamoorthy, and Satyanarayana, in this volume.) The poems are impersonal. No names are mentioned, as any public acknowledgement would be socially disapproved and in bad taste.

Let us look at an example, 'The Riverbank,' from Vidyākara's *A Classic Anthology of Fine Verses* [*Subhashita Ratnakosha*, 11th century C.E.]. This is one of the few poems on infidelity, and it is by the incomparable Vidya, the foremost woman poet in Sanskrit (Kosambi and Gokhale 1957: 148).

dṛṣtiṃ he prativeśini ksaṇamihāpyasmadgṛhe dāsyasi
prāyo naiva śiśoh pitādya virasāh kaupīrapah pāsyati
ekākinyapi yāmi tadvaramitah srotastamālākulaṃ
nīrāndhrāh stanamālikhantu jaṭharacchedā nalagranthayah
Vidyā, Subhāṣitaratnakoṣa 807

He can't stand well water, the child's father.
Refuses to touch it.
Would you, neighbor, keep an eye on the house
While I slip out for a moment, alone as I am,
To the riverbank overhanging with tamalas
And spiked with bamboos that may prick my breasts
With their sharp, broken stems?

A wife is expected to be faithful to her husband. The poem subverts that expectation by referring to the wife's infidelity obliquely through the use of innuendo (vyañjanā). The poet does not explicitly spell it out as it would offend social conventions. Indian erotic texts, such as the *Kamasutra* of Vātsyāyana [4th century C.E.], recommend the practice of scratching the body with nails during lovemaking. The woman anticipates the marks on her breasts as she sets out to meet her lover under the pretext of fetching water from the river for her husband. Eight kinds of nailmarks are identified: the knife stroke, the half- moon, the circle, the dash, the tiger's claw, the peacock's claw, the hare's jump, and the lotus leaf. Nailmarks are a prelude to lovemaking, and are therefore treasured as souvenirs. "If there are no nailmarks to recall the lover's presence," reminds Vātsyāyana, "it means that passion has long since disappeared, and love has been overcome" (Daniélou 1994: 136).

The task of the translator from Sanskrit into English is to try to bring across the intention of the poet. In Sanskrit poetics, the intention is a *rasa*, a transcendent emotion or state of being induced in the hearer, but inherent in the poem. The emotion is of course the transforming experience of love that knows no boundaries. It is in marked contrast to the restrictions that patriarchy imposes on women to conform to the social proprieties in writing. The line "And spiked with bamboos that may prick my breasts" is the only clue we are offered about the intention. A translator unfamiliar with ancient Hindu erotic practices will be unable to make sense of the poem.

Again, the translator must bear in mind that Tamil and Sanskrit were written to be heard. The ancient Hindus did not read with their eyes only but aloud, and it follows that the sound of a classical text is supremely important and ought not to be disregarded in translating.

It is precisely the imaginative universe of Vidyā's Sanskrit poem that I have tried to bring across in English in all its breathtaking sophistication. I have not been able to resolve the problem with the "tamāla" (*Xanthochymus pictorious Roxb*), a black-barked tree that grows on riverbanks, as I could not find an equivalent tree in English that grows along with the bamboo. So I have left the word untranslated.

Pali

In contrast to Sanskrit, the "perfected" or "refined" language, there were many vernaculars known as Prakrits, the "original" or "natural" languages. One such Prakrit is Pali, the language of the earliest Buddhist scriptures, the *Tipitaka.* Pali means "holy scripture," as opposed to commentary. Pali is a form of the ancient Paiśāchi language spoken in Western India. In the first centuries after his death, the Buddha's sermons in Māgadhī were translated into Paiśāchi, which later developed into Pali. Unlike Hindus, Buddhists had no qualms about translation. The Buddha encouraged his disciples to spread his teachings in their own dialects. Pali is still the religious language of the Theravāda Buddhists of Sri Lanka, Myanmar, and Southeast Asia.

Let us look at an example(Oldenberg and Pischel 1966:106), "Song of a Former Courtesan" by Vimalā, from the *Songs of the Elder Nuns* [Therīgātha, 6th century B.C.E.], said to have been composed during the lifetime of the Buddha (c. 563-483 B.C.E.).

mattā vaṇṇena rūpena sobhaggena yasena ča
yobbanena č' upatthaddhā aññā samatimaññi 'haṃ [72]
vibhusetvā imaṃ kāyaṃ sucittaṃ bālālapanaṃ
aṭṭhāsim vesidvaramhi luddo pāsam iv' oḍḍiya. [73]
pilandhanaṃ vidaṃsenti guyhaṃ pakāsikaṃ bahuṃ
akāsiṃ vividhaṃ māyaṃ ujjagghanti bahuṃ janaṃ [74]
sājja piṇḍaṃ caritvāna muṇḍā sāṃghāṭipārutā
nisinnā rukkhamūlamhi avitakkassa lābhinī [75]
sabbe yogā samucchinnā ye dibbā ye ca mānusā
khepetvā āsave sabbe sītibhuta mhi nibbutā [76]

Vimalā Purāṇagaṇikā, Therīgāthā

Young and overbearing—
Drunk with fame, beauty,
With my figure, its flawless appearance—
I despised other women.

Heavily made-up, I leaned
Against the brothel door
And flashed my wares. Like a hunter,
I laid my snares to surprise fools.

I even taught them a trick or two
As I slipped my clothes off
And bared my secret places.
O how I despised them!

Today, head shaved, wrapped
In a single robe, an almswoman,
I move about, or sit at the foot
Of a tree, empty of all thoughts.

All ties to heaven and earth
I have cut loose forever.
Uprooting every obsession,
I have put out the fires.

The songs were chanted. Each stanza (ślōka) of the *Songs* comprises four verses (*padas*) of eight syllables each. The first two verses, divided by a caesura, form one line; the next two verses, again divided by a caesura, form the second line. Unlike the secular poets of Tamil and Sanskrit, the Pali Buddhist poets attempted to raise the language of their religious songs above that of the profane model. They deliberately shifted the emphasis of their songs away from the love poetry of the secular poets to the attainment of liberation (mokṣa), the true joy which, according to early Buddhist teachings, was granted only to the monk or nun meditating in a world of his or her own. The first of the Buddha's *Four Noble Truths is* suffering (dukkha), and the cause of suffering is desire (taṇhā), including sexual desire. One description of *nirvana* is the dying out of the fires of lust (t̠ār̠ā), greed (lobha), hatred (dveṣha), and illusion (moha).

Vimalā, the former courtesan of Vesāli, after her initiation into the Buddhist order of nuns realizes the impermanence of all things and is on her way to enlightenment. A contemporary of Sappho, her poem is an extraordinary spiritual testament unlike anything in the Lesbian poet. The song is a chant, and there is no way I could reproduce the prosody of the Pali original. So I settled for a vigorous, colloquial idiom spoken simply but passionately in five quatrains. The Pali word for "obsessions" in the last stanza is ā*savas*, "the obsessions of the mind." Buddhism distinguishes four types: 1. the obsession with sensuality (kāmāsava); 2. the obsession with life (bhavāsava); 3. the obsession with ideologies (diṭṭhasāsava); and 4. the obsession of ignorance (avijjāsava). The struggle for the extinction of these *asava*s is one of our primary duties. In his commentary on the *Therigatha,* Dhammapāla of Kañcīpuram (fifth century C.E.) tells the story of Vimalā's initiation into the order.

One day Vimalā saw Moggallāna, one of the Buddha's foremost disciples, in the streets of Vesāli. Infatuated with him, she followed him to his house. There she turned on her charm and tried to seduce him, but was repulsed. Moggallanā lashed out at her: "You bag of dung, tied up with skin. You demoness with lumps on your breast. The nine streams in your body flow all the time, are vile-smelling, and full of dung. A monk desiring purity avoids your body as one avoids dung"(Norman 1966: 106). Vimalā was speechless. The encounter was a turning-point in her life. She renounced her life as a courtesan, and became a Buddhist nun. Vimala's spiritual conversion can be explained in terms of the interdependence of the ascetic and the whore in Indian culture, which considers sexual desire an obstacle to enlightenment.

Vimalā flaunts her sexuality, and is proud of it. Her very identity depends on it. It empowers her to make fools of men for whom she has nothing but contempt. And yet she cannot do without them. Her survival as a courtesan depends on her ability to dispense sexual favors. In the end, she is filled with self-loathing and turns her life around to become a renouncer who has cut loose "All ties to heaven and earth." Free at last, she becomes an *arahant*, the "holy one," the highest stage reached by a Theravāda Buddhist.

Translation is a way of reading a poem, of interpreting it in a second language. Given the differences between languages, not every feature of one language can be imitated by another. Yet it is possible to establish a family resemblance. Eventually, the differences are only of secondary importance. For as Max Picard said: "Languages seem like so many expeditions to find the absolute word"(Picard 1952: 43). Often a single poem may aspire to the status of the absolute word. Such a poem is the *Ramayana*.

A translation must first abolish the word in one language before it attempts, with the word, to restore it in another language. Languages orbit by themselves in splendid isolation. Occasionally, they come into close proximity with one another, thanks to the daring of a translator. Translation ensures the survival of a language, even if its speakers have vanished from the face of the planet.

Works Cited

Caminataiyar, U.V. (Ed.) 1968. *Cilappatikāram* of Ilankovatikal, with the commentry of Atiyarkkunallar. 8th printing. Madras: Sri Tiyakarca viaca veliyitu.

Daniélou, Alain. Trans. 1994. *The Complete Kama Sutra* of Vatsyayana. Rochester, VT: Park Street Press.

Hart, George L, III. 1975. *The Poems of Ancient Tamil: Their Milieu and Their Sanskrit Counterparts*. Berkeley: University of California Press.

Caminataiyar U.Ve. (Ed.) 1962. *Kuruntokai* with a commentary. 4th printing. Madras: Sri Tiyakaraca vilaca veliyitu.

Norman, K. R. 1966. Trans. *The Elders Verses II* [*Theragatha*]. Palit Text Society. London: Luzac.

Parati Cuppiramaniya. 1958. *Kannan pattu* [Kannan's Song]. In *Makakavi Paratiyar kavitaikal* [The Poems of Mahakavi Bharati]. Madurai: Aruna patippakam.

Parthasarathy, R. Trans. 1993. *The Tale of an Anklet* [*Cilappatikaram* of Ilankovatikal]. Translations from the Asian Classics. New York: Columbia University Press.

Picard, Max.1952. *The World of Silence.* Trans. by Stanley Godman. London: Harvill Press.

Shelley, Percy Bysshe. 1977. *Defence of Poetry.* In *Shelley's Poetry and Prose.* Ed. Donald H. Reiman and Sharon B. Powers. Norton Critical Edition. New York: Norton.

Kosambi D.D. and V.V. Gokhale. *1957. Subhasitaratnakosa* of Vidyakara. Ed. Harvard Oriental Series, vol. 42. Cambridge, MA: Harvard University Press.

Tennyson, Alfred Lord. *The Princess: A Medly.* In *The Poetic and Dramatic Works of Alfred Lord Tennyson.* Ed. W. J. Rolfe. Cambridge Poets Series. Boston: Houghton Mifflin, 1898.

Oldenberg, Herman and Pischel.(Ed.) 1966. *Thera- and Theri-Gatha: Stanzas Ascribed to Elders of the Buddhist Order of Recluses.* 2d ed. Pali Text Society. London: Luzac.

Wood, Clement. 1942. *Poet's Handbook.* Garden City, NY: Garden City.

Poetry from India in Tamil, Sanskrit, and Hindi

Translated by R. Parthasarathy

The Tamil poets, Kalporu Ciṟunuraiyār, Naṉṉakaiyār, Palāipāṭiya Perunkaṭunko, Kāvaīpeṇṭu, and Kaṇiyaṉ Pūṇkuṉṟaṉ, were active between 100 B.C.E. and 250 C.E.. The Sanskrit poems are from anthologies compiled between the seventh and eleventh centuries C.E..

Kalporu Ciṟunuraiyār

A Trail of Foam

What do they know about love—
These folks that tell me
To endure its torments?
Is it their strength
That makes them speak so?
It would break my heart
Not to be able to lay eyes upon my lover.
Like floodwaters leaving behind
A trail of foam
As they spend themselves on the rocks,
Minute by minute I too waste away.

Tamil / Kuṟuntokai 290

Nanṉakaiyār

The Heron

He said, *I am leaving. Going away.*
And I knew that once again
He was playing games with me.
Get lost. And don't bother coming back,
I snapped at him.
But where is he, my lord?
For only he can comfort me.
Tears fill the space between my breasts—
Now a vast pond where white heron
With black legs stalk their prey.

Tamil / Kuṟuntokai 325

Pālaipāṭiya Perunkaṭuākō

The Arrow

Though he lives in the same town
He avoids our street.
Should he visit us,
He won't take me, lovingly, in his arms.
Unseeing, he walks past me
As if I were the cremation ground of strangers.
Once I was unashamed—
Passion had robbed me of my senses—
But now, like an arrow sent flying from a bow,
It has landed far off.

Tamil / Kuṟuntokai 231

Kāvar̲peṇṭu

Tiger

Where is your son? you ask,
Leaning against the pillar of my house.
I don't really know where he is.
This womb, that bore him, is now a desolate cave
A tiger once prowled about.
Go, look for him on the battlefield.

Tamil / Pur̲ān̲an̲ūmu 86

Kaṇiyan̲ Pūnkun̲ran̲

Wise Men

Every land is home to us, every man one of our own.
Good and evil don't flow from others.
Pain and help for pain appear by themselves.

Even death isn't new. We don't rejoice
That life is sweet, nor are we distraught with grief.
As a raft swirling in the waters of a deep river

That roars and crashes upon rocks
In a thunderstorm under skies bruised by lightning—
Our life, dear as it is, takes its usual course.

Wise men know this, who foresee all things.
And so we don't stand in awe of the great,
Much less do we hold the small in contempt.

Tamil / Pur̲ān̲an̲ūr̲u 192

Vidyā

Complaint

How fortunate you are, my friends!
You can speak openly about the goings-on
With your lovers: the idle talk, the laughter
And fun, the endless rounds of pleasure.
As for me, once my lover undid the knot of my skirt,
I swear, I remember nothing.

Sanskrit / Subhāṣitaratnakoṣa 574

Anon

The Sheets

Smudged here with betel juice, burnished there
With aloe paste, a splash of powder
In one corner, and lacquer from footprints
Embroidered in another, with flowers
From her hair strewn all over its winding, crumpled folds,
The sheets made no secret of the fact
That the woman was had in every position.

Sanskrit / Amaruśataka 107

Anon

The Pledge

He's broken the pledge,
Banished me from his heart.
No more in love,
He now walks in front of me
Like any other man.
I spend my days thinking of this.
Why my heart doesn't go to pieces, dear friend,
I don't know.

Sanskrit / Subhāṣitaratnakoṣa 697

Māgha

Ars Poetica

Did grammar ever feed the hungry?
Did the nectar of poetry ever quench
Anybody's thirst? There is no way
You can raise a family on book learning.
Make your pile and screw the arts.

Sanskrit

Mīrābaī [1498-1546]

How Can I Sleep Without Krishna?

How can I sleep without Krishna?
Wrenched from his arms how can I survive?
I am driven back by the flames of love.
Without him my house is dark and unwelcome.
Of what use are lamps in his absence?
Not for me the pleasures of the bed:
I spend my nights sleepless.
Does any one know when my love will return?

The lightning thrashes about in the net of black clouds:
Frogs and waterbirds, cuckoos and peacocks
Call out to one another.
In vain I fight back the tears.
Tell me, friends, what shall I do? Where shall I go?
How uproot this pain?

Like a venomous snake, his absence has bitten me:
I feel death in my bones.
Go, bring the herb at once.
Who among my friends will return with my love?

You stole her heart, Lord. When will you meet her?
When will you come to talk and laugh with Mira?

Hindi / Padāvalī 2.72

Chapter 29 | Why Not Worship in the Nude? Reflections of a Novelist in His Time

U.R. Anantha Murthy

The reality for a novelist in India, I am speaking from my Kannada experience, is so complex as to disallow the comforts of either the acceptance of the status-quo or of revolutionary ruthlessness[1]. R.K. Narayan can afford to say 'India will go on' only as a comic realist, in his inimitable low mimetic mode. But when his insightful Indian experience is translated into ideas in a polemical context, it is difficult to defend them. The same is true of Naipaul's indictment of Indian reality. He can afford to speak angrily and ruthlessly and plead for a thoroughgoing modernization in India only in a polemical context. I wonder if he can maintain his position unambiguously in a novel where his imaginative sympathies are fully engaged.

All of us share this dilemma. What we feel and what we think are often in conflict. Even while I am writing this I am engaged in a bewilderingly confusing discussion with my radical friends about an incident in Chandragutti, a village of my district 85 Kms from Shimoga where every year, in March, men and women of all ages offer naked worship to a Goddess in fullfilment of a vow. Early morning they take a dip in the river Varada, wait in the water to get possessed, and then run four or five kilometres and go up a picturesque hill, 800 metres abouve sea level to worship Renukamba. Last month, many young men and women belonging to radical and rationalist organisations went there, with the encouragement of the Social Welfare Department of the Government, to plead with these "backward caste" worshippers that nude worship was 'wrong' and 'inhuman'. This attracted wide media attention and journalists went there too, with their cameras. Earlier, two weeklies run by rationalists and scheduled caste activists had also carried pictures of nude worshippers on their colorful cover pages. These weeklies published articles attacking what, for them, seemed an inhuman "superstitious" practice, while they also aimed at increasing their circulation with the nude pictures.

The encounter between the illiterate believers and the educated middle-class rationalists was both fierce and unexpected. The worshippers broke through the physical barricade of the rationalists who stood on the bank of the river pleading with them to wear clothes. And then they ran to the hill in frenzied possession. Some worshippers even turned violent. The deputy superintendent of police was stripped forcibly of his khaki uniform and forced to go naked in procession with the worshippers. The women-police were also mercilessly stripped by the dancing priestesses, called *Jogithis*. A policewoman, it was reported, felt so humiliated and helpless that she wanted to kill herself. The *Jogithis* with their matted hair and red-and-yellow-powder-smeared faces danced gleefully waving police trousers, helmets, and iron *trishulas* (tridents). The clothed devotees and pilgrims who had gathered in Chandragutti from far and near, by foot, on bullock carts, buses and lorries, ascribed the mass hysteria to the fury of the Goddess Renukamba, even while they felt sympathy for the victims. Nobody seemed to have any sympathy for the photographers whose expensive cameras were smashed like the coconut offerings to the Goddess.

I must not offer myself as typical but my personal feelings and my stance as a novelist—which are related of course, but in a complex manner— have always reacted in an ambivalent manner to conflicts of this kind in my culture. Twenty years ago when I wrote my first novel, *Samskara*, my conscious motivation was more rationalist than what it is today, and I acted culturally and politically from that standpoint. But, even then, I was still moved by the mystical elements in my religious world, which entered into my writing despite myself.

In my second novel, *Bharathipura*, I set out with a conscious rationalist purpose. My Western-educated hero, Jagannath, returns to his temple-town in search of his identity. He wants to authenticate his existence through action in the world of his childhood, the temple-town. He feels that this can be done only by destroying his relation to the God of the temple-town who controls not only the emotional life of the inhabitants but the economic realities of the place also. The God, *Manjunatha*, had been installed some centuries ago in the temple as the over-lord of an indigenous deity, *Bhootharaya*, whom the original inhabitants—now the untouchables—had once worshipped. Jagannath wants this cultural colonization to end and he sets out to demythify the power of the temple. On the *Jatra* day he wants to take the untouchables, to whom the indigenous God, *Bhootharaya,* belongs, into the temple and prove to the devotees that the belief that the untouchables would vomit blood if they enter the sanctum is unfounded. As he prepares the untouchables for the event he passes through agonizing conflicts, personally, in the process of "de-casting" himself. Before taking them into the temple, a symbol of the collective belief, he wants to destroy the myth surrounding the stone Sāligrām of his family, the personal deity for which the sacred lamp has burned ceaselessly for generations. He takes the Sāligrām on his palm and walks out of the house to the untouchables standing outside the gate of his compound. His blood relations and servants of the house look on bewildered and frightened, for the Sāligrām had never been taken out of the ancient house and desecrated like this.

The whole situation becomes charged. Jagannath wants to prove that it is a mere rounded piece of stone, and not a sacred object. But the intensity of the gaze of his relations and his servants—belonging to several castes—turns the stone into a Sāligrām. The very attempt to destroy the myth, paradoxically, enhances the sacredness of the stone. The still unawakened untouchables are mesmerized by the intensity of the situation. The hero stretches out his hand and asks them to touch it and thus make it what it truly is—a mere stone. But they dare not touch it and hence the stone is transformed into a Sāligrām, more potent than what it was, untested. Jagannath feels so disgusted and angry with the untouchables that for a moment he feels like killing them. His fury, which for the hapless untouchables is after all the wrath of a landlord,—for he still stands to them in that economic relation—cows them down and then they touch the Sāligrām passively! The hero suddenly realizes that his old aunt whom he loves, and who is superstitious and doesn't touch the pariah, is humanly kinder to them than he is.

I shall not go into the details of what happens in the novel. Suffice it to say, the myth triumphs in the end. There is also a hint that with education and unavoidable social processes the untouchables will become touchables some time in the future, and they will also become respectable like the other middle class peoples. In the meanwhile, *Manjunatha* the God is reinstalled in the temple. The priest's son who throws the idol into the river for personal vengeance against his domineering father gets deified in an absurd series of events. Does any change take place in Bharathipura?

'Yes' and 'No' is the answer of the novel, *Bharathipura.* Of course I pleased no one, neither my radical friends nor the reactionary status-quoists, by this. I was putting my own rationalism and political radicalism to test in the novel. The form and content of the novel, with its blend of allegory and realism, didn't seem to work as satisfactorily as in *Samskara.* I was biting more than I could chew, but I don't regret it.

In my political action — whatever little a full time teacher like me can do — I have not wavered all these thirty years; I remain a democratic socialist. But with regard to cultural questions I am increasingly and agonizingly growing ambivalent. *Bharathipura* was written about a decade ago, at a time which also saw the rise of activism among the scheduled caste radicals and rationalists in Karnataka. Some of my intimate friends whom I respect, and with whom, politically, I have a lot in common are among these activist groups and therefore my dilemmas cause me and also my friends bafflement and pain. They often feel very angry and also, naturally, intolerant of my dilemmas.

The papers are full of the Chandragutti episode and we meet in a committee room of the Central Institute of Indian Languages in Mysore, under the auspices of a journal that I edit, to discuss the happenings. Our small group consists of two anthropologists, liberals of different persuasions, and a woman activist of great courage and commitment who has luckily come back unscathed from Chandragutti. We are eager to hear the anthropologists and the woman activist. We already have some anthropological data regarding the Chandragutti worship. *The Hindu*, a solidly middle class, even conservative, South Indian newspaper with a Marxist on its editorial board, has published a report with the headline, "Were the volunteers over-enthusiastic?" (The Hindu, Monday, March 24, 1986). The report tells us that we have records of Chandragutti dating back to 1336 A.D. It was an early stronghold of the *Kadamba* kings of Banavasi. The mythological references of Chandragutti date back to the pre-*Kruta Yuga* (*Satya Yuga*) days. This was Sage Jamadagni's hermitage, according to legend. His wife Renuka went to bring water from the river as she did daily, but one day she failed to repeat the miracle of carrying water in a basket as she had lost her purity. She had seen a Kṣatriya king bathing in the river and she was for a moment attracted by him. Her husband Jamadagni perceived what had happened and he ordered his son Parasurama to kill his mother. There are several stories about this. He obeyed his father, and from the pleased father earned the boon of getting his mother back to life, but had to wander round the world in expiation, vainly trying to wash the axe clean of his mother's blood. He also killed all the Kṣatriyas and spared only Rama, who, like him, is an avatar of Vishnu. But the legend in Chandragutti is vivid and dramatic. As the son pursued Renuka to behead her, she ran recklessly and in the process lost all her clothes. She hid herself in the Shiva temple, naked. There is still a cave in Chandragutti below which is a rock shaped like two giant hips, believed to be those of Renuka. There is another legend linking Renuka with Mātangi, who was Renuka's maid servant. Parasurama, before leaving on his mission of killing Kṣatriyas entrusted his mother to the care of Mātangi's son, Beerappa. But he grows into a sex maniac and Mātangi, moved by the plight of helpless women, provided them with clothes.

Even today as the naked women come to the temple of Mātangi they are provided with new clothes. Many of these worshippers are also devotees of Yellamma of Saundatti in Belgaum District. Renukamba and Yellamma are believed to be sisters. There is also a legend that Renuka of KrutaYuga (Satya Yuga) took the form of Yellamma in Kaliyuga. The radical activists are up against practices observed to propitiate Yellamma of Saundatti. Young girls offer themselves as prostitutes in observation of a vow and many of them now-a-days find their ways into Bombay's flesh market owing to commercial exploitation. There are *jogithis* and *khojas* in the Yellamma temple, too. Some activists who went to Chandragutti associate the nude worship with the likely enticement into prostitution.

In our meeting, the anthropologists offer proper technical explanations: for the way in which Dravidian culture has interacted with the Aryan in Chandragutti, and for the unique survival of age-old practices like possession-worship, owing to the inaccessibility of the hilly regions of the Sahyadri range of mountains. And, of course, they ask what is the cultural significance of mother-worship in general, and what it may mean to the lower castes in Chandragutti. And they offer guesses regarding the private psychological problems of the devotees and the therapeutic nature of the nude worship. They speculate on how some women offer their hair, some others their nudity—whatever is held to be most valuable to themselves, to the Goddess. And so on. And finally the anthropologists add: It is futile to attempt to stop a practice until you study in depth what the practice means to the actual believers. But change they must, some day—and their quarrel is only with the tactics employed by the over-enthusiastic activists. They concur with the first sentence of the Hindu report: "Can a deep-seated superstition handed down the centuries be eradicated overnight?"

The woman activist is impatient. We should make a beginning somewhere, shouldn't we? In the name of culture and belief do we tolerate untouchability and the Sati? Have we not legislated against such evil practices? She is also angry with the Government that they did not take enough precautions by way of extra police force. Although she didn't actually say so in the meeting, many of the activists are attacking the Government that the police didn't even burst tear gas shells, and that they had rifles in vain. Some activists suspect the hand of Hindu revivalists in the attack, but one of them also acknowledges that the Vishwa Hindu Parishad, a militant revivalist organization had published pamphlets calling upon the devotees to give up nude worship.

The woman activist is still under shock from what she has seen and one of the anthropologists tries to persuade her that the practice of untouchablility which is a social evil should not be equated with nude worship. Yet he agrees with her that it must go, and that it will go with education and civilization spreading into the area. Another anthropologist speaks of the practice of hooking oneself up in the air on the back and being turned round in the observation of a vow and how the worshipper doesn't even bleed with the hook pierced into the flesh. Such is the intensity of faith in some lower castes and such is the power of possession.

The woman activist looks on bewildered as he goes on to narrate a famous Kannada story by Ananda, "The girl I killed." In the story the girl, who is a prostitute from a respectable and rich landlord family, is given over to the temple as a Basavi in fulfillment of a vow. The story is narrated by a traveller—that he is an uppercaste 'outsider' and a city person is important—collecting historical information on a temple in the vicinity. (Also note that his interest in the temple is aesthetic and historical—not religious.) He stays as a guest in her father's house. The girl in her innocence and gratitude for the affection shown by the sophisticated guest from the city, offers herself to him. He doesn't know what to make of the situation. Being a stranger to such practices and a rationalist-moralist, he is shocked by the inhumanity of the practice. He convinces her how despicable the superstition was, and how she had degraded herself by practicing it, only to find her drowned in a well the next morning. The anthropologist implies by his story that we don't have any right to interfere with the belief-patterns of others. But the story also implies a point I feel that the anthropologist has missed—that one cannot help interacting—even though the result may end up being tragic.

The woman activist is so possessed by her conviction in the rational approach to life that she is too impatient to pay attention to the subtleties of the story's message. I understand how she feels, and why the cool distance and objectivity that the anthropologist enjoys by virtue of his discipline sounds somewhat inauthentic to her.

We have in our midst a linguist belonging to the Sikh faith. Only a week earlier he had spoken with great feeling how his people were driven to fundamentalism because of the desecration of the Golden temple of Amristsar. Today he surprises me with his argument. How can we in India afford to have the objectivity of the anthropologists? The terrorists strike in Punjab because of their faith. Do we merely look on? The *Jogithis* in Chandragutti defend nudity with the tridents. Can we merely look on? The anthropologist doesn't answer him but argues: don't we tolerate the nude sages of the Digambara Jain cult? When thousands of them congregated in Sravanabelagola, didn't our late prime minister, Indira Gandhi pay them a visit and get blessed by them? What about the great twelfth century saint poet, Mahādevi who wandered about naked, and when questioned by her guru, Allama—how could her nudity be genuine when she still covered her genitals with her long hair?—she answered: "Lest its sight embarrass you, Sir!" Why do we tolerate practices of pan-Indian communities, and attack only those of small groups of low castes? Why this double standard? Moreover, do we sell today anything—a soap, a toothbrush, a screwdriver, a shampoo or even a plastic bucket without the help of a nude? What about striptease clubs? We get heated up in cross-talk and the weary woman activist answers that her group has also protested against commercial exploitations of nudity.

As the anthropologists shift from the position that we should preserve what is unique in a culture, to the other position that we must try to change them slowly through sympathetic understanding and education, and as the Sikh linguist argues passionately for a firm position by us who form the national mainstream—which I suspect he will not hold on to firmly, as the situation in Punjab changes—I am reminded of a story by A.K. Ramanujan.

The story is entitled "Annaiah's Anthropology[2]" and had I narrated it in the meeting it could have perhaps induced a deeper self-reflection on the part of the anthropologists present there. Or merely confirmed their own sophisticated skepticism – I don't know. The tone of the narration, as is often the case in Ramanujan's Kannada poetry too, is cool, witty and low-keyed, and, therefore, its end becomes all the more terrifying. Annaiah who had never taken much interest in India while he lived there begins to devour books on Indian anthropology when he comes to Chicago as an economist. He reads with admiration the American academics who write books on Indian rituals with such eye for detail and such interest. A recent book by one Ferguson, fascinates him. Annaiah's orthodox parents live in Mysore and he has also a cousin, Sundara Rao who owns a photo studio in Hunsur. He is piqued to read that Ferguson got much of his material on funeral rites from his cousin. Annainah reads on, with an uneasy curiosity and finds photographs of houses and streets that are familiar to him. Could the picture of the burning corpse be of his own father whose death must have been kept a secret from the son, as he lives far away for his studies? Yes, that was a picture taken by his cousin Sundara Rao who owned a studio. Annaiah is frightened. The book falls down. He picks it up and opens it to read about 'widowhood' and he sees the picture of his shaven mother in red saree as a gratefully acknowledged illustration of widowhood. Annaiah is aghast.

The story works at many levels and symbolizes much more than Annaiah's particular predicament. Annaiah is the modern Indian, fascinated by the west, ignorant of his own culture, yet attached to it emotionally. He dislikes India while he lives there, but loves the country when he goes abroad as is the case with most of us, and there is desecration and corruption deep down in the encounter of East and West. He recovers through anthropology what he has lost in reality, but the anthropology itself is the result of a profound betrayal and also a product of an inauthentic relation with the self. You can't have an anthropological sympathy or curiosity for your own culture, when it hurts you.

I came out of the meeting feeling that the woman activist's position was more authentic than the tolerance and curiosity of an anthropologist. "But don't you see," I had yet asked the woman activist, "something positive in those nude worshippers, a feeling of religious awe that you and I have unfortunately lost? A woman's naked body is an erotic object for us; or exceptionally, an aesthetic experience only if it is handled by a great painter or sculptor. It is neither aesthetic nor erotic for the worshippers. Isn't that profoundly moving? —And can that happen anywhere else in the world? A naked body is sacred for them." One of my friends whose old aunt lives in a village had told me what the old woman had said after witnessing the procession. For her the beautiful and healthy young women who overcome their shame and walk naked had seemed like Goddesses with flower-garlands round their necks. Moreover the processionists were old and young of both sexes including children, and they walked naked not anywhere and not any time, but only in Chandragutti on a particular day—rehearsing an event of the timeless past of India—reverentially.

My feelings must seem like poetic romanticism to the woman activist, naturally. I seek to find out how my friend Devanuru Mahadeva feels about the whole episode. Mahadeva is an activist himself of the scheduled caste group. He is perhaps the best fiction writer among Kannada writers in their thirties. He has written two novelettes and a collection of stories. He writes about the actual condition and the slow awakening of the untouchables with a depth of poetic feeling and objectivity that is all the more remarkable considering his passionate political engagement with the day-to-day struggle of the untouchable castes for equality and self-respect. His stories abound in rituals and intimate description of the everyday life of his characters in their misery as well as their ecstasy. The success of his daring is largely due to the low mimetic mode he employs. The novelette, Oḍālāḷa, where a hungry family eats up a whole bagful of peanuts sitting around a fire without leaving a trace of their theft to the police who search their poor cottage in the morning, is a moving story of the revolutionary potentiality of the untouchable castes even in the midst of their misery. The old woman in Oḍālāḷa who goes in search of a lost rooster she has lovingly reared grows in the story into the proportions of the mythological mother symbolizing the elemental urge of caring. She quarrels, weeps loudly, admonishes her children, tells mythical stories, curses heartily and yet what is remarkable about this earthy woman is that she cares. A young girl in the family draws the picture of a peacock on the wall, a school-going child marvels at his sister's creation, the old woman who has no time for nonsense like a peacock dancing on the mud wall still tells him a mythical story, where the child becomes a potential prince—and at night they all sit and eat the stolen peanuts around a fire forgetting the lacerating quarrels and frustrations of the day. The peanut-eating is as intense a creative act, almost a yajna, as the peacock drawing in the story. In this world of simple ritualistic folk-life is also heard of rumblings of the coming change. One of the peanut eaters, who wears a wrist watch, entertains the family crowd with his story of defying a hotelier and demanding respectful service along with others.

Mahadeva can't afford to look on the nude worshippers, many of whom belong to his caste, with anthropological curiosity. Nor can he want them to stay put in a magical world. He wants them to become conscious of their rights in the modern democratic society. Yet I feel he ought to be able, the kind of poetic novelist that he is, to see the grandeur of the souls of the nude worshippers—however necessary and inevitable it is for them to come out of their magical universe—a universe that Blake and Lawrence and Yeats had longed for in the analytical and scientific western civilization. Mahadeva tells me it would have been all right for them to worship in the nude, if the onlookers were also nude, and if some of the girls were not forced or dragged out to go nude. I understand what he means, I add, sadly, it can't remain the same, particularly after what had happened and the nude worshippers displayed on cover pages.

I ask myself another question—which is very important for me. How would the *Vacanakaras* of the 12th century, particularly the great mystic poets, Basava and Allama, who protested against the 'little' as well as 'great' traditions have reacted to the nude worshippers? I can only speculate. They would have perhaps pleaded with them for a less magical and more spiritual God-awareness. And that could have been a more meaningful encounter in our tradition than between our modernizers and the magical worshippers.

I dare to say "yes" in a young poet's ear alone when he accosts me with the question: "Is Renuka true? Is Yellamma true?" I am alone with him and so I say, "yes". I am surprised at the leap I have taken, but I have hopes of striking a chord in his heart for he is a poet. He looks uncomprehendingly at my flushed face. Have I betrayed a part of me, the ever vigilant sceptic in me whom the Baconian-Cartesian epistemology of the scientific west has nourished with a good salary and comfortable working conditions? Haven't I become what I am by demythifying, even desecrating the world of my childhood? As a boy growing up in my village didn't I urinate stealthily and secretly on sacred stones under trees to prove to myself that they have no power over me? I remember the terror I had overcoming spending sleepless nights, and hence the ambivalence that enters into my youthful stories and novels. No, I can't be an absolutist, for I am a novelist and not a poet. My dream of combining Marxism with mysticism in actual praxis will never come true. In a literary work, perhaps, but not in actual life. Only as a poet Wordsworth cried in weary despair, "Great God! I would rather be a pagan suckled in a creed outworn." Nor can one be indifferent, or merely curious, or patronizingly tolerant. Chandragutti is no longer inaccessible. There are buses plying from Shimoga and the once thick forests surrounding the village are now thin, thanks to the greedy contractors and corrupt timber merchants and forest officials. The quick growing, inhospitable eucalyptus are planted everywhere with world bank aid for the multi-millionaire Birla's factories. The *Jogithis* — the matted haired, fierce priestesses of Yellamma of Saundatti—are under suspicion of recruiting girls for the flourishing flesh trade in Bombay. And Bombay attracts fun-seeking tourists from all over the world.

Yet I dared to write a long story a couple of years ago into which I have put, I hope, all my agonizing perplexities. I was prompted to write it. When a grasshopper accidentally hopped into my sunlit room and I told my daughter that the dear thing is called in Kannada "Sūryana Kudure" (The Sun-horse[3]). And that started the story. Wasn't Marx wrong to say that the rural calm can only produce idiocy? Hasn't the rural culture dared to connect the Sun with an otherwise insignificant and vulnerable insect? The joy and reverence for life and the daring imagination seen in the naming of an insect profoundly moved me and I wrote "Suryana Kudure". The story took me back into the magical universe of my childhood. The restless son of my hero is willing even to commit patricide, such is the threat to my hero's way of life, and a sensibility that has become comically impractical. Yet I am temporarily won over by him after a ritualistic magical oil bath and the serenity with which he overcomes the violent encounter between him and his son who wants to get away from the idiocy of the limited village life. His son, after all, is on the path I have myself walked, yet the father makes me see, by his own ecstatic absorption, the wonder of the Surya's horse perched on a hedge. The story has moved many of my critics, only as momentarily as myself under the charm of my hero, but the next moment the implicit ideas in the story makes way for angry polemics. As my other novel Awasthe too did, where my political hero wearied by the corruptions of parliamentary democracy wants to return to the glowing quotidian way of his boyhood days in the village. He wants to organize the unorganized poor of the village for revolutionary change rather than reformistic modernization, perhaps a weak resolve — but no critic recognizes it even. Such is the hold of modernization on us that we feel there is no other viable path. Look at what is happening in China, they say.

Purnachandra Tejasvi, an important novelist of my generation, has his own version of the encounter between age old beliefs and modern civilization. In his recent novel, *Chidambara Rahasya*, the clash between the two is only apparent, but together they contribute to the stagnation and final destruction of a moffusil town, Kesrur. A greedy and heartless merchant denudes the surrounding forest of its trees and slowly the lantana weed pervades. The novel begins like a detective story and effortlessly gathers significance as it progresses. The young immature boys of Kesrur college yearn for the friendship of girls. This gets expressed in their boyish pranks, and also in their boredom and hunger for adventure, and in the rationalist movement against the superstition of the elders of the town. The town is peopled by a scientist experimenting on improved varieties of cardamom, an intelligence-man investigating into the suspected murder of an agricultural scientist believed to be killed in an international conspiracy, a poet guiding the young in the rationalist movement, a free thinking college lecturer, rival communalists trying to build temples and mosques, insensitive pleasure-loving estate owners, black-marketeers, Muslim timber merchants and drug peddlars. The fate of all these is linked with that of the once thick jungle which is growing into a tangle of lantana weeds. The whole narrative is in a low mimetic mode, but the novel ends in a disaster. The conspiracies of the corrupt timber merchant, and of local politicians who build up vote banks for selfish gains result in a forest fire which destroys indiscriminately the good, the bad and the indifferent inhabitants of the town. The novel ends with a Hindu girl and a Muslim boy belonging to the rival communities of the accursed town, escaping through the burning lantana weeds to the summit of a rock. This is the most poetic and symbolic passage of the novel, counterbalancing the senseless fury of the fire. Otherwise the novel moves in a relaxed low-mimetic mode.

Mahatma Gandhi, back from South Africa, entered Indian Politics not with a religious book, but with a political tract, *Hind Swaraj*. This is in the form of a dialogue with a terrorist. Mahatma Gandhi asks the question why the British are in India and answers himself -- because we Indians are in love with modern civilization. If modern civilization is bad for us it is bad for the British, too. Like all great visionaries, Mahatma Gandhi is also an extremist. No one in India has paid any heed to the Mahatma about what he thinks are the evils of modern civilization and its unimportance to human happiness or search for truth. Not even his dearest disciple, Nehru, paid any heed to him. We are all in love with modern civilization in India whether we are capitalists, communists or liberals. But the masses of the Indian sub-continent, with their innumerable children, poverty, superstitious practices and caste-bound loyalties are quite content in their lives. Because of them 'India will go on' as she is, the immemorial past just repeated in the present, for they expect nothing more from life than the bare necessities that a backward subsistence economy can give them. Gods are still propitiated by these masses of people, and their humdrum life glows at such moments.

No wonder this inertia enrages the energetic modernizers. The 'Emergency' that Mrs. Gandhi proclaimed in 1975 gave full expression to this rage in some of Sanjay Gandhi's programs. People were operated upon forcibly to bring population down and roads were broadened removing hutment dwellers mercilessly beyond the city limits. These words of a Delhi University sociologist quoted by Shiva Naipaul ("The Emergency and the Meteor", *The Observer*, 11th January, 1981) express what many felt at that time:

> Sanjay did express a certain dark side of the Indian personality. I recognize that darkness in myself. 'Sometimes', he said slowly, deliberately, 'when you look around you, when you see the decay and pointlessness, when you see, year after year, this grotesque beggarly mass ceaselessly reproducing itself like some...like some kind of vegetable gone out of control... suddenly there comes an overwhelming hatred. Crush the brutes! Stamp them out! It's a racial self-disgust some of us develop towards ourselves...that is the darkness I speak about'...

Tejasvi's Kesurur also burns — although Tejasvi is not a Sanjayite — giving us a feeling that it is fit only to die. Many of us feel that way sometimes, surrounded as we are by squalor and apathy and the corruption of political life in the country. But the democratic system also works in strange ways to our utter bafflement. It can remove an all powerful Mrs. Gandhi and bring her back to power also. Rajiv Gandhi's party wins the parliament seats in my state of Karnataka, but loses within three months the State Assembly election. Modernizers, impatient with the pace of change, can't give up hope altogether. Shri Rajiv Gandhi tries to usher in the age of computers preparing the country for the 21st century. We, the modernizers, send our children to English medium schools and look for a day when the English translated wisdom of the Upaniṣads, the imported computers, and sitar music on video cassettes coexist peacefully and enrich our temporal as well as spiritual existence. In the meanwhile, there are going to be too many mouths to feed in the country, and some of them defiantly walk naked to worship a Goddess on a hill. And they fight back with tridents. Some political activists who have always been critical of police brutality ask angrily: What were the police doing with their rifles? Alas, they do not examine self-critically the implications of what they ask.

Yes—all of us are modernizers in one way or the other, but with an uneasy conscience, if we are sensitive. The great writers among us see it as inevitable and search for ways to preserve what is best and unique in Indian Civilization. Some of the novelists of the pre-independence idealism who had begun to write before I was born are still with us. Masti Venkatesha Iyengar is 95 years old. He has a gentle and profound insight into what lasts in India, and what elements inherent in human nature threaten it. Shakespeare, Wordsworth, Leslie Stephen, Arnold and Valmiki — the best in the traditions of the East and the West -- have gone into the making of his liberal humanist sensibility. His novel, *Chikaveera Rajendra* is about colonization (like Chinua Achebe's *Things Fall Apart*) — how a decadent kingdom is manipulated into submission by the British. Some of its passages of inhuman cruelty juxtaposed against divine tolerance of love have Dostoeveskian intensity about them. A large number of his better stories deal with cultural amnesia, and how it is overcome, thanks to the positively beneficial result of our encounter with the West. Masti, still orthodox in his ways, reminds us that tradition and modernization need not be always antagonistic. He has read Valmiki and Shakespeare as if they were his contemporaries. The crisis of modern life confirms his faith in tradition. But there is only one Masti in my language, and his simple faith and certainty is impossible for any of us.

Kuvempu [K.V. Puttappa], 82 years old now, is nearer to us in his conflicts with the past of India. He is a rationalist so far as religious rituals and caste systems are concerned. Being himself the first great non-brahmin writer of our century, he has always remained a non-conformist. Born in the hilly regions of Sahyadri he grew up in Ramakrishna Ashram and became, in later life, an admirer of Aurobindo. His diction is highly Sanskritised and he has recreated Rāmāyaṇa in blank verse, where Shakespearean, Miltonic and Indian spiritual influences coalesce. His vision is a curious combination of scientific rationalism and transcendental other-worldliness. The integration achieved in his writing, of East and West, of scientific rationality and miracle of avatar and rebirth can't remain intact once he begins to theorize. He is still an angry man. Although he is a great votary for Kannada as medium of instruction, he said, recently, that without a knowledge of the English language he would have been a serf in a Brahmin's house clearing cowdung in his cattle-shed. This took many by surprise coming as it did from Kuvempu, but the aging poet infuriated the Brahmins. He advocates now an "unhoused" consciousness, of the world citizen who owes allegiance to neither country nor religion.

I am not much of an admirer of the impressive absolutism and the egotistical sublime of his highly Sanskritized verse, but the two novels he has written are great works in Kannada. The first novel *Kanuru Subbamma Heggadathi* is dense in details of life lived in the hilly regions of Sahyadri, and so is the second novel, *Malegalalli Madumagalu* but set in remoter time. The second novel has the dimensions of an epic, and only in Joyce have I come across a similar range and depth of the quotidian. "Trust the tale and not the artist," is certainly true of Kuvempu's novels. They reveal more than he intends.

In his first novel, which is important for the purpose of this paper, we see his hero in conflict with his environment. After a university education in Mysore he returns to his village, almost inaccessibly surrounded by forests and hills. He is an outsider there to the beliefs and practices of his people and he can achieve oneness only with nature. There is a scene in the novel, almost absurd but significant, where we find the hero reading English classics of the Romantic Age sitting upstairs in his faction-ridden, unhappy, joint-family house. Alienation as a theme enters into Kannada fiction for the first time here in this novel, published in 1936. Manik Bandopadhyaya's *A Puppet's Tale* was also first published in 1936. The Indian versions of the *Return of the Native* theme have much to tell us of the interactions of the East and the West, of the encounters between city and village, of the alienated hero who is happy in neither place. The theme continues to haunt us even today. Shanthinatha Desai, a novelist of my generation, wrote mostly urban novels but now he has surprised his readers by his new novel, *Beeja* ("Seed") where the hero living in Bombay returns to his village to perform the funeral rites of his father and feels compelled to live in his native place. This isn't mere nostalgia, for he comes back to his family house to meet the political and economic challenges of the world he thought he had left behind. It is also necessary for him to come to terms with his own life. Another important novelist of my generation, Yashwant Chittal writes about the Kafkaesque city, Bombay. In *Shikari* ("The Hunt") the hero carries with him wherever he moves, the past of his village childhood. In Chittal again, the traditional values and the values of modern scientific civilization come into conflict without any simple resolution. His city characters are easily psychologized by the author, but not so his full blooded, enigmatic village characters. The traditional family ties haunt Chittal. It is in a way the reversal of the theme of the *Return of the Native* – the native can't return, he is stuck in Bombay and has to find a solution to his tangled life in his fierce monologues. The comforts of an air-conditioned modern civilization turn into a nightmare. The West is as much with us as the East is, already, for Chittal. All of us, as I said before, are reluctant modernizers. The superstitious village life haunts us as much as it repels us. But then the Kannada in which we write is wholesome and vigorous only in the childhood of our village days. The period in which most of us are writing is intellectually lived in English. There is a problem, too, in this schizophrenic situation.

One of the early novels written in Kannada, M.S. Puttanna's *Madiddunno Maharaya* ("Reap what you sow"), which saw publication in 1915, has a curious combination of myth and reality – the impulse to modernize as well as to mythify. In a preface written in English, significantly, Puttanna declares:

> Most of the works in Kannada ... are either expansions or contractions of our two great epics, Rāmāyaṇa and Mahābhāratha ... while this repetition is laudable on the one hand, it has, on the other, all the shortcomings of mere imitation without originality, dryness without curiosity, and a mental cramp without intellectual liberty.

If this expresses an impulse to demythify and modernize—an intention to explore reality through realistic narration—Puttanna hastens to add:

> The question is whether such pitfalls cannot be avoided by transferring the attention from those ideal heroes and heroines to a conception of characters of our daily life, which in their nature and in their deeds, more or less approach the ideal Rama and Seetha, Yudhisthira and Draupadi.

The impulse expressed here is to absorb reality into myth again. What he wants to write is both allegory and novel, on the surface a realistic story which deeply is also a fable. Puttanna could have led to Garcia Marquez—there are already elements of magical realism in his novel. A woman believed to be dead magically rises again, reenacting the travails and the triumph of Seetha. The novel itself is a disguised Rāmāyaṇa, with a wicked sorcerer as Ravana. Yet what gives life to the work are the realistic descriptions, where the modern in Puttanna sees with a skeptical and critical eye the world around him. To affirm you may need myth, but to discover you need realism—that is how you feel as you read Puttanna. The believers—like the naked worshippers of Chandragutti—say 'yes' either ignorantly or in mystic illumination. They wait in the river until they get possessed by the goddess and then they walk naked unaware of the eyes around them. But the novelist is essentially a sceptic, a 'nay' sayer much of the time, and yet not always, and not finally. His glory and triumph lie in the fact that his art is the bastard child of journalism and poetry. The ambivalent state of the sceptic who needs to believe, and of the believer who can't but doubt—the predicament of most of us, aggravated further by the impact of the scientific West on a traditional society—are already seen in Puttanna. The novel deals with matters that have dominated the creative imagination of most of our writers, the most impressive being Puttanna's knowledge of caste system and of official corruption. The dual impulses—to mythify and to modernize—jostle together in an unexpected combination of allegory and realism—creative modes necessary for grasping the entire reality of Indian life. As Puttanna can lead to a Garcia Marquez, he can lead to the writing of a novel like *Samskara*, too. And also, in an opposite direction, to the impressive achievement of Bhyrappa's *Parva* ("Canto") where the entire Mahābhārata is anthropoligized and demythified.

Not only Puttanna, whom I had not read until recently, but Shivaram Karanth, an important influence on my thinking and writing leads to a writer like me. Karanth is a confirmed agnostic and rationalist, and remains one in his late 80s, which in itself is a remarkable thing in India. He is not only a novelist; his achievement in popularizing scientific outlook is profoundly impressive. His interest in the past of Indian culture is essentially anthropological. *Mookajjiya Kanasugalu* ("Dreams of a Grandmother"), interestingly, mediates anthropological insights through the person of a visionary old woman who has extra-sensory perception. Karanth is a great literary figure for us in his relentless non-conformism and love of truth and justice. I sometimes feel that his admiration of Western Civilization almost borders on blindness, but he is so profoundly rooted in the life of his rural people that his personal preferences and prejudices can't mar his creativity. Not only Karanth, but other writers like Chaduranga become real again when they begin to write about the rural world they know. In Chaduranga's case he began to write under the influence of the progressive movement of the 40's which declared a war against the stranglehold of the traditional past on India. But his novel *Vaishakha* abounds in the celebration of rural life despite the threat it faces from its own inequities and unconscious cruelties.

Srikrishna Alanahalli, an impressive writer in his thirties, has also his rationalist quarrels with the traditional India rooted in the village. Yet, for him, the uprooting brought about by the impact of the city on the village, however inevitable, is still cruel and wicked (for instance in *Parasangada Gendethimma*). Another writer, Lankesh, one of the most influential of our times, deserves greater attention than I can give him here. His *Mussanjeya Kathaprasanga* ("Narrative of a Gathering Dusk") as a novel is seemingly formless, relaxed and buoyant in style, and also ruthless in its depiction of the injustices of rural life. Yet the progressive desire for change animating the whole novel, particularly when it affects the rich landowner in the story is tinged with sadness.

Returning to Karanth, what destroys the serenity of his pastoral world in *Marali Mannige* ("Back to the Soil"), whose moral values are derived from the struggle for existence in a subsistence economy is the threat that comes from within the pastoral calm itself. In the novel, it is the orthodox father himself who wants his son to become an officer with English education. He doesn't want him to be a priest. Consequently, the son is spoilt by the idleness of town life and he takes to evil ways. Only the idealist of the third generation makes a conscious decision to return to the village — with the determination to relate to and reform his people. There is thus the theme of the Return of the Native in this novel, too, as in many of us writing today. What to me is interesting in Karanth is the enigma that, while Karanth himself is a modernizer, he derives his values from people who are outside the pale of modern civilization. His simple, god-believing old women whose struggle for self-respect is profoundly moving in the midst of their poverty carry the quintessence of Karanth's values. Karanth's Laxminarayana, the wicked useless man, is a product of modernization, which paradoxically was longed for by his unsuspecting orthodox father himself. This process is unconvincingly reversed by the idealist, a product of the Indian struggle for Independence. Laxminaryana, the English educated wicked man must have haunted many of us in our own growing up under the influence of the West. But Karanth doesn't ask the question: Why does Laxminarayana become what he is? Why does his own father want to break the serenity of the pastoral world? Karanth is essentially ethical and moral, but not metaphysical. Once you put the question metaphysically, Karanth's realism seems inadequate. This realization must have unconsciously led me to the form of Samskara, and also the characterization of Naranappa.

Mistah Kurtz went with his great idealism and empty rhetoric to bring the sanity of modern Christian civilization to Africa, but ended up crying, "Exterminate the Brutes". In our times, the Chinese have invaded Tibet, the Russians Afghanistan, and the Americans are everywhere except where the Russians are, and the elite in India are no exception in their relation to the masses. And the novel, significantly, has one of its beginnings in Robinson Crusoe meeting Friday in the jungle.

If I write further I may begin to say more than I mean. I wouldn't have been a fiction writer if it were not for the impact of the scepticism of the modern civilization on me. And also, I must add, the kind of fiction writer I am is due to my quarrel with modern civilization.

Endnotes

[Editors' Note: The events referred to here pre-date 1986. The annual Nude Worship at Chandragutti has been subsequently stopped by a State Government order. The writers Masti, Kuvempu, and Alanahalli Krishna are no longer living. However, the issues and concerns which are addressed are still relevant in contemporary India.]

[1] This is the text of the paper presented at a conference on Indian Literature, University of Chicago, at the Festival of India, April 17-20, 1986.

[2, 3] See English translations by Narayan Hegde, "Stallion of the Sun" and "Annayya's Anthropology" in *From Kauveri to Godavari : Modern Kannada Short Stories*, Ramachandra Sharma, ed. New Delhi: Penguin India, 1992.

Chapter 30

Culture & Communication in India

Yamuna Kachru

The relationship between language as a means of communication and culture as realized through language has always been controversial. Whether language defines culture or culture determines language has been debated in the literature for decades. We find cultures and languages differing from each other across the world since people in different geographical locations and sociocultural contexts over time experience life differently. It is fascinating to study the patterns of variation in language use for communication in differing sociocultural contexts. This study, however, is only analogous to a few brush strokes on a huge canvas representing culture and communication in India.

In this chapter I first define, for my purposes, what we mean by terms such as "culture," "society," "communication," and "communicative style" before discussing the interface of culture and communicative style. Subsequently, the interaction of culture with styles of verbal interaction is illustrated by drawing upon the data of speech acts and conventions of writing, especially argumentative writing, in the Indian context. The data and discussion, I hope, clearly demonstrate how Indian cultural values of intimacy with family and friends, respect toward elders and mentors, acknowledgement of one's predecessors' scholarship and creative achievements, and reconciling the need for individual freedom with the necessity for social harmony are reflected in Indian communicative styles.

Culture and Society

There are many definitions of culture in the social sciences and they lead to the conclusion that culture is manifest in symbolic forms, including language, and it is both historic and immediate. It enables humans to make sense of their experiences, and it shapes actions—verbal as well as a variety of others, and in turn is shaped by them. The relationship between culture and human cognition and activities is dynamic rather than static.

Actions include not only the making of artifacts, conducting rituals, etc., but also behaving in culturally appropriate ways. Behavior in turn includes verbal interaction in socially defined contexts using appropriate dialects or languages. The use of language varieties, in turn, has to conform to notions of appropriateness held in the community. For example, in multilingual India, it is common to use mixed codes incorporating several dialects and/or languages. For instance, it is common to use a mixtue of Hindi, Panjabi and English in every day language in Delhi. The same is true of Kannada and English in Bangalore, and Tamil and English in Chennai (Madras). In a remote village in Uttar Pradesh, where few would be proficient in English, depending upon the region, a mixing of Braj or Awadhi with Hindi is more likely to occur. Greetings in India are likely to be "namaste" or "namaskāra" or "adāb arz" or "sat srī akāl"; the Western mode of greeting, shaking hands, is restricted to certain official and formal contexts.

The shared conventions evident in the above examples lead us to the notion of society. The definitions found in social scientific literature make it clear that a society signifies an organic group of individuals. The whole is characterized by internal relations of dependency among groups, e.g., groups of parents and children have relations with other groups, such as teachers, educational adminstrators, and health care authorities. It is also characterized by a relation of external differentiation among various such wholes, e.g., Japanese society in some sense is different from Indian society. Additionally, within a society there are norms of behavior that all groups of individuals constituting the whole must follow, e.g., greeting elders, friends, and acquaintances. The manifestations of such behavior may vary among the subgroups within a group, but the behavior itself will follow certain norms common to the group as a whole.[1]

Communication and Communicative Styles

In this chapter I will use the term communication to mean the information that is exchanged between participants in conversation, that is, communication as verbal interaction. In both the spoken and the written modes, participants exchange three types of information. The first is factual, i.e., the meaning of words and expressions. "Factual" here does not mean "true;" The sentence, *The monkey told the crocodile that he had left his heart up on the branch of a tree* has a conceptual content, although it is not "true" in the real world. The second type of information is information about the speaker's or writer's identity, attributes, attitudes, and mood. The third type of information enables participants to start or end an interaction, signal transitions, control time-sharing, etc., in an acceptable way in the spoken mode, or signal the topic, shift of topic, cohesion, coherence, etc., in the written mode. Each speech community has its characteristic ways of structuring these different types of information, which define its range of communicative styles.

Interaction of Cultural Meaning and Communicative Style

The study of language use in communication has been studied profitably by many disciplines. The linguistic-philosophic-semantic discussions of *speech acts, cooperative principles,* and *conversational implicature* provide a great deal of insight into language use in general.[2] The theory of speech acts proposes that uttering a string of meaningful sounds is not only performing the act of speaking, but also performing a variety of acts such as informing, questioning, ordering, etc., through that very act of speaking. It does not make sense to ask of many such acts if they are true or false; what is of interest is to determine if they are appropriate or inappropriate in a given context. For instance, if one says, "Bring me a glass of water!", depending upon a number of conditions, the request may be judged appropriate or inappropriate, but not true or false. The request is appropriate if a parent says that to a child, for instance, but ill-chosen if it is directed by a young adult toward his/her father or mother. Similarly, there is no truth value in questions such as "Did you see my umbrella?" It may be appropriate or inappropriate to ask such a question under certain conditions.

Speech acts may be direct and literal, as in the two examples above, or indirect and non-literal, as in the next example. The notions of cooperative principle and conversational implicature (Grice 1975) are helpful in studying indirect speech acts as in the following exchange:

A: What did you think of Mr. Neta's lecture?
B: He is certainly eloquent.

Most people listening to this would agree that speaker B does not think much of the content of the lecture, because (s)he mentions only the manner of delivery. Assuming B is being cooperative in this piece of conversation and not perverse, B's indirect reply invites A to infer that in B's opinion, the content of Mr. Neta's lecture was not terribly impressive. Such indirect and non-literal speech acts are not always easy to interpret; each culture has its own conventions for their use.

Each sociocultural group has its own norms that determine which speech acts are appropriate in which context, involving which participants, using which utterances in which language(s) or dialect(s). For example, in the Hindi-speaking region of India, a greeting directed to an elder may elicit a reciprocal greeting or blessing. Consider the example below, cited from a short story by Mrinal Pande, in which a young woman visits her class mate, Ratti, in her absence and the following exchange takes place between the young woman and Ratti's mother..[3]

"rattī..." pardā haṭā kar kamre me kuč̌h-kuč̌h dohre badan kī mahilā ne praveś kiyā... mãĩ haṛbaṛā kar uṭh khaṛī huī - "*namaste.*"
"khuś raho. baiṭho. mãĩ ne samjhā rattī lauṭ āyī hai."

"Ratti..." A rather stout lady pushed the drapes aside and entered the room. I rose in a hurry - "*namaste.*"
"May you be happy. Be seated. I thought Ratti has come back."

Note that the young woman's greeting gets a response "May you be happy," which is a typical blessing. This is the traditional pattern of greeting-response in most languages of India. However, the contact with English has introduced changes in language use and increasingly, the following pattern is also becoming common.[4]

tab tak nītū bhī skūl se ā gayī thī aur salāmī kā vahī daur śuru ho gayā thā.
"*namaste,* ankalji."
"*namaste*. kahiye nītūjī, tumhāre kyā hāl-č̌āl hãĩ?"

By then, Nitu had also come back from school and the same cycle of greetings had begun again.
"namaste Uncle+honorific"
"namaste. Tell+honorific Neetu+honorific, How are you+familiar?"

The little girl greets her parents' friend and addresses him as "uncle" and adds a honorific particle to show respect. The man in turn uses the same greeting and adds the same honorific particle and uses the polite form with the verb "tell", but switches to the familiar second person pronoun to ask how she is. The use of honorific is to create a light mood; but the absence of the blessing in response to the greeting is typical of Englishized Hindi.

Typical domains for indirect speech acts in India range from talking about health to death. That is to say, no direct inquiry as to someone's health, or direct reference to one's possible or impending death is appropriate in the Indian socio-cultural context. For instance, in the Hindi-speaking region, it is customary to inquire after one's health by making a statement such as the following:

suna hai, dushmanō kī tabīyat ājkal kuč̌h vaisī hī rahtī hai.
(I) have heard that (your) enemies are in rather indifferent health these days.

It is considered quite inappropriate to refer directly to the addressee's health by saying "your health." Similarly, it would be highly infelicitous of an insurance agent to begin his pitch for selling insurance to a customer in India by saying, for instance, "Should you die next year,...." The customary way of referring to such an unfortunate event is by saying, "May God not will this, but should something happen..."

Sociological studies on face-to-face interaction look at conversation as ritualistic behavior. They discuss *face* as an important concept in characterizing the image that people attempt to project, negotiate, and maintain in such interactions. The concept of "face" is inextricably linked with the concept of "politeness" as well as the concept of "cooperation" discussed above. Consider how a dinner invitation is made and accepted or rejected in India. Normally one does not accept an invitation to dinner immediately. There may be exchanges such as the following (rendered into English from an Indian language, such as Hindi):

A: We will be delighted if you could share a meal with us on Saturday evening.
B: Why go to so much trouble? After all, everyone is so busy during the week. The weekend is the only time when one can relax. We will drop by to see you some time during the weekend.
A: It will be no trouble at all. It will be a simple meal, nothing elaborate.
B: Shall we bring some thing?
A: Just yourselves, and a good appetite. See you at 7.
B: We will meet then.

What is going on here? Presumably, both participants are conscious of each other's "face" and the image of themselves that they want to project. To accept A's invitation immediately would either imply that A is obliged to invite B, or that B has to accommodate A's wishes for some reason. The first alternative would damage A's image, the second B's. Also, B has to be sure that A is sincere in inviting him/her before accepting the invitation. Thus, the initial reluctance saves both participants' images. A's subsequent insistence in his/her second turn ("It will be no trouble . . .") indicates the sincerity of the invitation, so B hints at his/her willingness to accept the invitation by offering to bring something. The eventual acceptance of the invitation restores social harmony and enhances the image of each participant. Note that no thanks are given—that is not socially appropriate among friends.

Sociolinguistics and ethnography of communication provide the framework for analyzing the social context of interaction. In the above example, the social context consists of the nature of the social event (i.e., invitation to dinner); the details of the relationship between participants (friendship); the setting, i.e., place and time of interaction (possiblly the place of work); and the code or codes used by the participants.

Researchers in anthropology, sociolinguistics, artificial intelligence and psychology use concepts such as *schema*, *frame*, and *script* to describe the nature of background sociocultural knowledge essential for successful conversation and for organizing and interpreting texts. In the above example, both participants know that invitation-response is a matter of negotiation, not of immediate acceptance or refusal. They also are aware of each other's roles, i.e., each knows that the other and his/her spouse have jobs which keep them busy during the week. Also, A knows that B knows where (s)he lives, since the time for the dinner is mentioned, but not the place. A and B both tacitly agree what kind of dinner would be appropriate, because no mention is made of any dietary restriction (e.g., vegetarian). Obviously, no successful interaction is possible without shared background knowledge.

I will draw upon these concepts in discussing communication in the Indian context.

Speech Acts

As mentioned above, cultural conventions for performing speech acts differ among communities. Strategies for performing speech acts are different in various communities, and the range of appropriateness of particular speech acts differ from community to community. The first may be illustrated by the conventions of expressing gratitude in India. There is no set expression such as "thank you" that directly signals the speech act of thanking. Hindi employs the speech acts of blessing, complimenting, or thanking to express gratitude:[5]

Informal situations:
Blessing (if expressing gratitude to a younger person)
Appreciation of inherent qualities or effort or help rendered (if equal)
Expression of one's helplessness and grateful acceptance of favor (if superior in status);

Formal situations:
Thanks.

An example of the situation where appreciation of the other's help in view of one's own predicament is used to thank someone is the following excerpt from Premchand's famous novel, *Godan* (1961:65).

> sahsā unhōne dekhā, ek yuvatī kināre kī ek jhopṛī se niklī, čiṛiya ko bahte dekh kar sāṛī ko janghō tak čaṛhāyā aur panī mē ghus paṛī. Ek kṣaṇ mē usne čiṛiya pakaṛ lī aur mehtā ko dikhāte hue bolī—panī se nikal ao bābūjī, tumhārī čiṛiyā yah hai . . .
> mehtā ne use dhanyavād dete hue kahā—tum baṛe mauke se pahūnč gayī, nahī mujhe jāne kitnī dūr tairnā paṛtā.

> All of a sudden he saw a young woman coming out of a hut, hitching up her saree to her thighs as soon as she spotted the bird floating away, and entering the water. Within a minute she caught the bird and showed it to Mehta and said: "Come out of the water, Sir, here is your bird." Mehta said, thanking her - "You arrived just in time, otherwise, who knows how far I would have had to swim."

There is no specific expression such as "thanks" in the dialog; Mehta praises the young woman for her promptness, which, according to the narrator, expresses his gratitude for her timely help. The word dhanyavād "thanks" occurs in the narrator's description of the character's action, not in the character's speech.

The second type of variation, i.e., the differing range of appropriateness of particular speech acts, may be exemplified by the speech act labeled "saugandh khānā" in Hindi, "āṇe iḍuvudu" in Kannada, "śapath ghene" in Marathi, "qasam khānā" in Urdu, and similar expressions in other Indian languages. It roughly translates as "to swear." It is, however, different from the English "swear;" it only shares the following meanings with it— to assert, promise, agree to, or confirm on oath. The other, more negative meanings of the English item (such as curse, abuse) are not shared by the Hindi item. Another difference is that one can "swear" by anything dear or valuable to one, e.g. one's own self, one's eyes or head, one's kin, and, of course, the sacred text, *Bhagavadgita*, one's mother, or God. It conveys the meanings of strong assertion, persuasion, challenge, promise, or entreaty, depending upon the context. Two examples of how it is used in Indian English with the forces of strong assertion and persuasion, respectively, are given below (excerpts from Raja Rao's. *The Policeman and The Rose.*):

> "Hey, brother, what is it all about?"
> "Nothing. I think it's about the quarrel between Ramaji and Subbaji.
> "You know about the Cornerstone?"
> "But, on my mother's soul, I thought they were going to the court?" (p. 17)

In this example, one villager is trying to find out from another villager what the bailiff's drum meant. The first villager "swears" in order to convince the second that what he is saying is really true.

In the next example, an older sister is scolding a younger brother for arguing with her:

"...And Ramu," she cried desperately, 'I have enough of quarreling all the time. In the name of our holy mother can't you leave me alone!" (p. 88)

The expression "holy mother" in the above example does not refer to any deity; it refers to the siblings' biological mother. The sister is trying to persuade her brother to drop the topic they have been arguing about.

These examples make it clear that the cultural meanings of "saugandh khānā" is very different from "to swear" in the Anglo-American English-speaking context. And the range of use of such "swearing" is also different from that of the Anglo-American cultural context.

The norms of politeness in the Indian context are different. Just one factor in politeness, the age factor, may be taken as an illustration. The second person singular pronoun (e.g., tū in Hindi, Marathi, and Urdu; tūi in Bengali) is not used for the elderly, no matter what the status difference. For example, parents reprimand children for using this form for the elderly maids and servants in the family. Relatives, and friends of one's parents or older siblings must be addressed by proper kinship terms, hence the multiplicity of uncles, aunts, older brothers and sisters in every social gathering in India.

The same considerations of cultural values govern conventions of writing in the Indian context.

Conventions of Writing

Writing effectively involves instruction and, usually, many years of practice. Unlike speech, which is universal, literacy is not universal, and was not wide-spread until very recently. Even now there are societies and cultures where literacy plays no role (or a minimal role) in the life of the community. Literacy practices vary a great deal across cultures and require careful study, as has been shown by anthropological and ethnographic research. I will concentrate here on one domain of literacy practice, that of academic writing, and within that, one genre, argumentative and/or persuasive writing in the Indian context.

Argumentation

In most literate societies text types are classified into various categories. For example, texts in English are said to be of four types, depending on whether they emphasize the writer, the reader, the message, or the language. These are expressive, persuasive, reference, and literary texts, respectively. According to their communicative function, however, text types are labeled descriptive, narrative and argumentative. Yet another way of classifying texts is discussed in Youga 1989, which classifies texts according to their purpose and mentions three major ones: sharing experiences with the audience, changing audience behavior or attitudes, and explaining the subject matter to the audience. These are called expressive, persuasive, and informative, respectively.[6]

In spite of such attempts at classifying texts into types in the literature, it has been recognized that text types are not exclusive. For instance, the overlap between argumentation and narration has been noted and it has been recognized that texts are multifunctional, normally displaying features of more than one type, and constantly shifting from one type to another. In view of the difficulty of identifying text types, it has been suggested that they be seen as abstractions. The conclusion is unavoidable that although the abstract notion of text type is useful in research, the types usually overlap in real life (Kachru 1997).

Cultural Values in Argumentation

In contrasting argumentation across cultures, I will focus on cultural factors as they define argumentation within cultures, and not on the linguistic realization of argumentation in the distinct languages. In terms of the culture-specific definitions of text types, it is not clear that all languages and cultures share all text types identified and discussed in various literate traditions. For instance, there is a text type in Hindi labeled "deliberative" (vičārātmak), which is not necessarily equivalent to the Anglo-American "argumentative" essay. In an argumentative text, the goal is to convince the audience that the view put forward in the text is right and superior to all competing opinions. In the deliberative text, on the other hand, the points in favor and those against a particular position are put forward so that the audience is informed on all facets of an issue, and the decision as to which one of the positions presented is right or wrong is left to the members of the audience. The writers' task is to present the competing views in such a way that their readers come to accept the shared view, i.e., arrive at a consensus to preserve social harmony. This will be discussed more fully with reference to the Indian tradition of argumentation/persuasion.

The Indian Tradition

The notion of argumentation is well-developed in the Indian tradition (Datta 1978 [1967]: 118). According to Matilal (1990: 156-166), there was a tradition of

Vādavidyā, a discipline dealing with the categories of debate over various philosophical, religious, moral and doctrinal issues, and there were several vāda manuals available around the beginning of the Christian era. An honest debate, or vāda, was said to be characterized by the employment of logical arguments, and the use of rational means and proper evidence to establish the truth.

In the Indian logico-philosophical discussions, the word for cognition in general is prajnā, the word for valid cognition is pramā, and that for the source of valid knowledge is pramāṇa. Perception (pratyakṣa), inference (anumāna), authority (śabda) and postulation (arthāpatti) are all recognized as valid sources of knowledge. An important distinction is made between the psychological process of inference that takes place in one's own mind and the demonstrative form of inference used for convincing others. The demonstrative form has five steps (Datta 1978 [1967]: 126):

(A) clear enunciation of the proposition to be proved;
(B) statement of reason;
(C) statement of universal relation, supported by concrete instances;
(D) application of the universal relation to the present case;
(E) conclusion.

The validity of a theory is also indirectly established by indirect hypothetical argument (tarka), which consists of showing that the supposition of its contradictory leads to undesirable consequences. This is the logico-philosophical notion of argumentation, which is not necessarily reflected in all academic writing. In fact, Indian writing, like its Chinese and Japanese counterparts, has been characterized by some Western academics as "non-linear", which means that the writing does not necessarily start with a thesis statement and end with a conclusion based upon direct elaboration supporting the thesis. Indian argumentative/persuasive writing may start with some background information, go through various positions that can be taken with regard to the topic, and contain a direct statement of the writer's purpose toward the very end. Thus, there may be no linear development exemplified by a topic treatment schema such as introduction-elaboration-conclusion.

A piece of Indian argumentative writing in English may illustrate this point. The piece in question was written by a candidate for the Bachelor of Arts degree in an Indian university. Since the text is lengthy, only its outline and analysis are presented below; the text is reproduced in the Appendix.

Non-linear Structure:
Paragraph 1: Global Introduction
Paragraph 2: Problem [Sentence 6]; Elaboration [S's 7-9]; Comment [S 10]
Paragraph 3: Introduction [S's 11-15]; Comment [S 16]; Introduction [S 17]; Comment [S's 18-19]
Paragraph 4: Problem [S's 20-21]; Comment [S 22]; Solution [S 23 (1st clause)]; Problem [S 23]; Comment [S's 24-25]
Paragraph 5: Solution [S's 26-30]; Comment [S's 31-32]

The introductory part of the essay talks globally about growing up and about the world being both good and evil, without mentioning the major topic of the essay—the dowry system. The statement of the problem in the second paragraph is not kept distinct from the elaboration of the problem, or comment indicating the writer's opinions or stance toward the dowry system. The three middle paragraphs go back and forth between introduction, problem, elaboration, and comment. Only the first paragraph maintains the sort of unity of paragraph prescribed in the American rhetoric courses.

I have also analyzed papers written by established scholars and shown that Indian academic writing does not conform to the direct linear writing conventions prescribed in contemporary American academic writing. For example, I examined the scholarly papers in a volume on South Asian linguistics edited and published in India (Lakshmi Bai and Reddy 1991). Fourteen of the fifteen papers written by Indian scholars have the type of non-linear structure illustrated above. What is more interesting is that two of the papers written by American authors for the same volume also have a non-linear structure. Thus, it seems that no matter what the idealized notion of an argumentative text may be, individual writers may or may not follow the generic type closely in every detail. It is, however, undeniable that by and large, variation from the idealized norm of argumentation resulting in indirectness is tolerated more often in the Indian tradition than in the contemporary American tradition.

Note that it is the domain of use of indirectness rather than indirectness itself which is under comparison here. In face-to-face interactions, direct criticism, disagreement, disapproval, etc., are felt to be aggressive, imposing, and crude in American culture also. Extending the tactful behavior of indirect criticism and disagreement to academic writing, however, is perceived to cause problems in the Anglo-American academic setting and has resulted in a new field of research—contrastive rhetoric—devoted to a comparison of conventions of writing across languages and cultures.

Indian and American Conventions of Writing

In earlier research, the following points have been emphasized in comparing American and Asian, including Indian, writing: The Asian tradition privileges societal harmony and unity over individual interests (Oliver 1971: 261-65).

The cultural values of the Chinese, Indians, and Japanese stress harmony and tolerance and try to minimize both practical and intellectual cleavages and confrontation (Moore 1981 [1967b]: 294). In the Western tradition, too, some feminist scholars have started emphasizing this aspect of academic discourse. The aggressive exchanges that characterize differing "theories" in a given discipline are said to result from the need to exercise control and dominate typical of male social behavior. Feminist scholars feel that a non-confrontational, cooperative, female style of discussion may be more suitable for increasing the knowledge base of the world.

The Asian traditions value a "high" style in writing, i.e., stylistic embellishments, quotations, idioms and metaphors, which are considered distracting by American teachers of rhetoric.

Individual writers choose their own styles. Readers, writers, and editors have to decide how much individual creativity in style is to be tolerated. Compare the constructed text in (A), which is similar to many story problems school children are expected to solve, with the 12th century Indian text in algebra in (B) below (Monier Wiliams 1963 [1893]: 193):

> (A) Nina spent one-fifth of her weekly allowance on snacks, one third on magazines, three times the difference of those numbers on school. She was left with five rupees. What was the amount of her allowance?

> (B) Eight rubies, ten emeralds and a hundred pearls, which are in thy earring, my beloved, were purchased by me for thee at an equal amount, and the sum of the prices of a set of the three sorts of gems was less than half a hundred; tell me the price of each, auspicious woman (Monier-Williams 1963 [1983]: 193).

As compared to the text in (B), the problem in (A) is boring and colorless. There is something to be said for a text that is more colorful and may hold the learners' attention more successfully than a prosaic piece of text. Great scientists, after all, are known for invoking very powerful images for scientific discoveries they speak and write about. Notions of creativity differ among individuals and among traditions.

The strategies of privileging rhetorical modes of the past at the expense of individual originality and creativity and of uncritically invoking the tradition of scholarship in order to justify one's position is less highly valued in the Western tradition.

Eastern traditions value the author who can display knowledge of earlier scholarship and who acknowledges the authority of preceding scholars. In reality, earlier scholarship is of value in both the Eastern and Western traditions, the use one makes of earlier scholarship in the context of one's own research is different. In the Western tradition, earlier literature is cited to locate one's work within a certain domain and to point out the inadequacies of earlier research. In the Eastern tradition, on the other hand, literature is not cited only to locate one's work within the field or to disagree with or point out the shortcomings of earlier treatment of some phenomenon. It is considered good manners to acknowledge one's gratitude and display one's respect for predecessors while establishing links between the current work and previous scholarship. It is also considered polite to bring in one's own individuality and creativity in commentaries on, rather than refutations of, earlier works.

Originality

This brings in the related issue of originality. It is a misconception to think that originality necessarily lies in novelty. Some of the most original works in the Chinese and Indian philosophical and literary traditions have been commentaries (vyākhyā or tīkā. In medieval Hindi literature there is a whole genre of what are known as Sākhi, which echo the sayings of earlier poets. Sākhī is said to be the New Indo-Aryan form of Sanskrit sākṣī, which means "witness." In its metrical form, it is a couplet. The couplets are usually moral and ethical aphorisms. Very similar couplets have been composed by several medieval poets in various dialects of Hindi; they are original in the sense that the metaphor, the imagery, and the linguistic devices are different in each case, not the substance. For instance, one poet may say that tormenting the poor is self-destrucative and evoke an image of lifeless skin, i.e., the bellows (made of goat skin), turning even iron to ashes. Another poet may express the same idea by bringing in the imagery of the dust we trample under our feet and pointing out that even a speck of the same dust is capable of causing endless pain if it gets into our eyes. Indian literary creativity does not see originality in claiming novelty, or believe that originality lies exclusively in disavowing an earlier tradition which forms the necessary backdrop for any work of art.

Allusions and appeals to earlier works in literary genres is valued in the Western tradition, too. Again, it is an issue of genre-specificity, domains, and particularity of treatment, rather than the strategy itself.

In the Indian tradition samvāda (dialogue) rather than vivāda (dispute, argumentation) is the method of seeking and imparting knowledge, as illustrated in the Upaniṣads, and the Bhagavadgītā. Consider the following dialogue between King Janaka and Sage Yajñavalkya in Bṛhadāraṇyaka Upaniṣad (IV.3.2-6: 596-601).[7]

> "Yajñavalkya, what serves as the light for a man?"
> "The light of the sun, O Emperor. It is through the light of the sun that he sits, goes out, works and returns."
> "It is just so, Yajñavalkya."
> "When the sun has set, Yajñavalkya, what exactly serves as the light for a man?"
> "The moon serves as his light. It is through the light of the moon that he sits,"[8]
> "It is just so, Yajñavalkya."
> "When the sun and the moon have both set, Yajñavalkya, what exactly serves as the light for a man?"
> "The fire serves as his light. It is through the fire that he sits,..."
> "It is just so, Yajñavalkya."
> "When the sun and the moon have both set, and the fire has gone out, Yajñavalkya, what exactly serves as the light for a man?"
> "Speech (sound) serves as his light. Therefore, O Emperor, even when one's own hand is not clearly visible, if a sound is uttered, one manages to go there."
> "It is just so, Yajñavalkya." (IV.3.5)
> "When the sun and the moon have both set, the fire has gone out, and speech has stopped, Yajñavalkya, what exactly serves as the light for a man?"
> "The self serves as his light. It is through the light of the self that he sits, ..."
> "It is just so, Yajñavalkya."

(See chapters by Hiriyana and Pandharipande in this volume.)

Finally comes the question: "Which is the self?" in IV.3.7 and the answer comprises the rest of Section IV of the Upaniṣad. The discussion thus proceeds from the known, the familiar, the concrete, to the unknown, the unfamiliar, the abstract. This may seem a round about way of presenting arguments for the existence of self distinct from body, but the method privileges explicit step by step logical development. This is different from the method of direct linear argumentation which consists of first proposing the existence of self as the point to be proved, proceeding to present arguments to prove it, and finally showing that the claim has been justified.

Conclusion

I would like to conclude this discussion by emphasizing the interrelationship of culture and language use. It is evident from the examples discussed above that Indian cultural values are reflected in particular conventions of conversational interaction and writing in India. These values include considerations of intimacy with members of one's family and friends; deference and respect toward scholars, teachers, and elders; acknowledgment of the debt to one's predecessors in creativity and scholarship; and resolution of conflicting demands of individual and privileges on the one hand, and maintenance of social harmony and well-being on the other. And it is these cultural values that give shape to the distinctly Indian ways of using language(s) for communication.

Endnotes

[1] For example, the exact manner (bowing, touching the feet, giving a hug) and verbal expressions involved (pranam, namaskāra, adāb arz, sat srī akāl) for greeting elders may vary across social and religious groups, but elders will be greeted with the same high degree of respect regardless of the regional, caste, or religious groups in India.

[2] The theory of speech acts is discussed in *How to do things with words* by J. L. Austin, Clarendon Press, Oxford, 1962; and *Speech acts: an essay in the philosophy of language* by J.R. Searle, Cambridge University Press, Cambridge, 1969. Non-literal and indirect speech acts are discussed by J.R. Searle in a chapter entitled "Indirect speech acts" in *Syntax and semantics 3: speech acts*, edited by P. Cole and J.L. Morgan, Academic Press, New York, 59-82. The concepts of cooperative paricnciple and conversational implicature are discussed in a chapter entitled "Logic and conversation" by H.P. Grice in the same volume, 41-58.

[3] The excerpt is from a collection of short stories, *bachuli chaukidarin ki karhi* by Mrinal Pande, Radhakrishna Prakashan Pvt. Ltd., New Delhi, 1990.
[4] The excerpt is from a collection of short stories, *man na bhaye das bīs* by Malti Joshi, Saraswati Vihar, Delhi,1982: 107.
[5] Although I am limiting my observations to the Hindi speech community, in my experience, the same is true, more or less, of other communities in India, too. I am not aware of any Indian language community where patterns of expressing gratitude involve explicit expressions such as "thank you." Of course, I am aware that the "English-knowing educated" Indians are increasingly using the Anglo-American patterns of saying "thank you" and " I am sorry"(Apte 1974, Kachru 1995).
[6]. The sources of these classifications are identified in Kachru (1997). For more discussion on conventions of writing in India, see Kachru (1983, 1987, 1988, and 1996).
[7] The material quoted here is from the Bṛhadāraṇyaka Upaniṣad with the commentary of Śankarāčārya, translated by Svami Madhavananda, Advaita Ashrama, Calcutta, 1965 (4th edition), section 111, pp. 593-699.
[8] The "..." represents the repetition of the material as in the previous reply by the sage. Repetition made memorization of lengthy texts possible, and memorization was important in the Indian tradition as it relied upon oral transmission of knowledge. There is no evidence that written texts played a major role in the everyday life of scholars in ancient India.

Works Cited

Apte, Mahadeo L. 1974. 'Thank you' and South Asian languages: A comparative sociolinguistic study. *International Journal of the Sociology of Languge,* 3. 67-89

Datta, Dhirendra Mohan. 1967. *Epistemological methods in Indian philosophy.* In Moore 1967b] 1978. 118-35.

Kachru, Yamuna 1983 Linguistics and written discourse in particular languages: constrastive studies: English and Hindi. *Annual Review of Applied Liguistics,* (1982) 3. 50-77

______1987. Cross-cultural texts, dicourse strategies and discourse interpretation. In Larry E. Smith (ed.) *Discourse across cultures: Strategies in world Englishes.* London: Prentice Hall International. 87-100

______1988. Writers in Hindi and English. In Purves, Alan (ed.) *Writing across languages and cultures: issues in contrastive rhetoric.* Newbury Park, CA: Sage. 109-137

______1995. Lexical exponents of cultural contact: Speech act verbs in Hindi-English dictionaries. In *Cultures, ideologies, and the dictionary: Studies in honor of Ladislav Zgusta.* B. Kachru and Henry Kahane (eds.). Tubingen: Max Niemeyer Verlag. 261-274.

______1996. Language and cultural meaning: Expository writing in South Asian English. In *South Asian English: Structure, Use and Users.* Robert J. Baumgardner (ed.), Urbana, Illinois: University of Illinois Press, 127-140

______1997. Culture and argumentative writing in world Englishes. In Larry E. Smith et.al. (eds.) *World Englishes 2000.* Honolulu, HI: University of Hawaii Press. (In Press)

Lakshmi Bai, B. and B. Ramakrishna Reddy (eds.) 1991. *Studies in Dravidian and general linguistics: A festschrift for Bh. Krishnamurti.* Hyderabad: Osmania University Publications in Linguistics.

Matilal, Bimal Krishna. 1990. *The word and the world: India's contribution to the study of language.* Oxford: Oxford University Press.

Monier-Williams, Monier. 1893. *Indian wisdom* (2nd edition). Chowkhamba Sanskrit Series Office, Varanasi, 1963.

Moore, Charles A. (ed.) 1967a. *The Indian Mind.* Honolulu, HI: The University of Hawaii Press.

Moore, Charles A. (ed.) 1967b. *The Japanese Mind.* Honolulu, HI: The University of Hawaii Press. [1981 edition]

Oliver, Robert T. 1971. *Communication and culture in ancient India and China.* Syracuse, NY: Syracuse University Press.

Premchand, Dhanpat Rai. 1961 edition. *Godan.* Allahabad, Saraswati Press.

Appendix

"Dowry System" in India

1.Growing up is a discarding of dreams and a realisation of the various facts of life A general awareness creeps in. 3. It is a process of drinking deep the spring of knowledge and perceiving the different facets of life. 4. Life is panorama of events, moments of joys and sorrows. 5. The world around us is manifested by both, good and evil. 6. Dowry system is one of the prevalent evils of today. 7. Like a diabolic adder it stings the life of many innocent people and is the burning topic of discussion. 8. Looking down the vista of years, we find that it has permeated gradually into the fabrics of our customs and has acquired a prodigious form lately. 9. Marriage which is supposed to be a sacred ceremony is made sour and becomes like any other business transaction. 10. The extracting of money from the bride's family is ridiculous, attrocious [sic] and above all sacrilegeous. 11. It is truly said that making somebody happy is a question of give and take. 12. Human beings by instinct show their concern and love by giving gifts. 13. This even holds true for a bride's father. 14. All fathers have a penchant to give something to their daughters. 15. It is a propensity of human nature to see their daughters well settled. 16. But this exchange of gift should be a willing gesture and not an imposed cannon. 17. The money and affluence becomes an asset to start a settlement in life. 18. But it should be considered a crime if the money is taken from someone who is left financially crippled. 19. Each one should learn to lay the bricks of her own house herself. 20. Dowry system is biting into the very vitals of the Indian society. 21. There are many evidences of burning of the bride, and disparages in matches because of this root cause. 22. To eradicate this will be to clear the weeds of our society. 23. There are many laws passesd on this issue but still it needs to be dealt by delving deeper. 24. It is said that "Eclipses stain both moon and sun". 25. The custom of dowry is the biggest flaw and a scar which mars the beauty of a sacred union. 26. Various endeavours are being made to eradicate this. 27. But what is necessary, that it should be the loudest cry of each person! 28. Someone has to take a firm stand and the first step so that it benefits mankind. 29. Everything can be cured and all evils can be purged. 30. After all Raja Ram Mohan Roy did succeed in abolishing Sati system, Lord William Bentick worked to elevate the positionof women. 31. To wipe out this will be like a rise from a stagnant, putrid pool to the greatest height of perfection. 32. Living will be a bliss!

IX Film, Music and Theatre

Chapter 31

Theatre in India

Girish Karnad

Performed in urban, glitzy movie houses and on rural, well-worn ground, theatre in India is expansive and experimental. Theatre can simultaneously be entertainment, political commentary, and artistic statement, and can be composed in traditional, realistic, and postmodern forms. Indian playwrights and directors have had years of changing influences. Theatre often gropes toward the past, looking for meaning, with the tools of the present: video, lighting, shifting audiences. But to have impact on the heart of society, drama must attempt honesty—not merely by using a mythical Indian history, but by engaging actively with possibilities in the present. Like masks worn by actors that allow them to express otherwise hushed truths, Indian theatre enables immediate, manipulative representations of reality.

I belong to the first generation of playwrights to come of age after India became independent. Perhaps the best way for me to give you an idea of the state of Indian theatre is to present a mosaic of impressions, ideas, feelings, and anecdotes from my experience. As in the case of the protagonist in Salman Rushdie's *Midnight's Children*, autobiography can sometimes become a metaphor for history.

Every theatre is rooted in the culture of its own language, so there are as many theatre situations as there are languages. India has oral traditions, riddles, proverbs, songs, ballads, tales, and epics in more than 3,000 mother-tongues. These forms are potentially or partially theatrical. As one moves from the kitchen in the village (for that is where tales are told) to the electronically equipped movie hall in the big city, one encounters theatre in different guises. To make any sense of the subject at all, I shall stick to a narrow definition of theatre and its purpose, which I hope will become clearer as I go along.

In my childhood, in a small town in Karnaṭaka, I was exposed to two theatre forms that seemed to represent irreconcilably different worlds. Father took the entire family to see plays staged by troupes of professional actors called *natak* companies, which toured the countryside throughout the year. The plays were staged in semi-permanent structures on proscenium stages, with wings and drop curtains, and were illuminated by petromax lamps.

Once the harvest was over, I went with the servants to sit up nights watching the more traditional Yakṣagāna performances. The stage, a platform with a canopy and a back curtain, was erected in the open air and lit by torches.

By the time I was in my early teens, the *natak* companies had ceased to function and yakṣagāna had begun to seem quaint, even silly, to me. Soon we moved to a big city. This city had a college and electricity but no professional theatre.

I saw theatre again only when I went to Bombay for my postgraduate studies. One of the first things I did in Bombay was to go and see a play, which happened to be Strindberg's *Miss Julie* directed by the brilliant young Ebrahim Alkazi.

I have been told since then that it was one of Alkazi's less successful productions. The papers tore it to shreds the next day. But when I walked out of the theatre that evening, I felt as though I had been put through an emotionally or even a physically painful rite of passage. I had read some Western playwrights in college, but nothing had prepared me for the power and violence I experienced that day. By the norms I had been brought up on, the very notion of laying bare the inner recesses of the human psyche like this for public consumption seemed obscene. What impressed me as much as the psychological cannibalism of the play was the way lights faded in and out on stage. Until we moved to the city, we had lived in houses lit by hurricane lamps. Even in the city, electricity was something we switched on and off. The realization that there were instruments called dimmers that could gently fade the lights in or out opened up a whole new world of magical possibilities.

Most of my contemporaries went through some similar experience at some point in their lives. We stepped out of mythological plays lit by torches or petromax lamps straight into Strindberg and dimmers. The new technology could not be divorced from the new psychology. The two together defined a stage that was like nothing we had known or suspected. I have often wondered whether it wasn't that evening that, without being actually aware of it, I decided I wanted to be a playwright.

At the end of my stay in Bombay, I received a scholarship to go abroad for further studies. It is difficult to describe to an American audience, or even to the younger generation of Indians, the kind of tensions that this award created. My family was of course delighted, but it was close-knit and I was the first of its members to go abroad. My family wanted me to return home after my studies, marry within the caste, and settle down to a safe job; I was keen to launch out into the world and go where adventure led me. What made the situation suffocating was that in the manner of the Brahmin middle class, nothing was discussed or even expressed openly.

In the midst of these tensions, a few weeks before leaving for England, I suddenly found myself writing a play. The play, *Yayati*, surprised me in several ways. First, because it was a play and I had always imagined I was a poet. Second, because it appeared in Kannada, the language of my childhood, rather than in English, in which I had trained myself to write. Lastly, it was a story from the Mahābhārata, from which I considered myself alienated. In fact, I hadn't been aware I remembered the myth until I started writing the play. It was the myth of King Yayāti.

While still in the prime of his life, King Yayāti was cursed to old age for a moral lapse on his part. Distraught at the thought of impending decrepitude, Yayāti searched for a young man who would be willing to give him his youth in exchange for the curse and found him in his own son. Thus, the son became old; the father became young, younger than his son. The myth ends on a note of self-realization and tranquility. But, befitting a young Indian who had just discovered Strindberg and Anouilh, my play had a tragic end.

At the time of writing, I had seen the play only as an escape from my tensions. But, looking back, I am surprised how accurately the myth reflected my anxieties, my resentment at the elders who seemed to be demanding that I sacrifice my future for their peace of mind. By the time I had finished writing the play, it was not my parents but this myth that had appeared out of nowhere to come to my aid that seemed to pose the real challenge. It had nailed me to my past.

Alkazi was fond of Anouilh, and my admiration for his production of *Antigone* and *Eurydice* had probably much to do with my turning back to my own mythology. The point is that the mythology was there, ready, waiting for me when I turned. Admiration, however, cannot explain the close modeling of *Yayāti* on *Antigone* for form and style. I had no theatrical form to turn to. This is a problem many Indian playwrights face today, particularly those from North India, where there is little exposure to theatre. A playwright needs a tradition he can call his own, even if it is only to reject it. Anouilh could refer to Greek tragedy and its neoclassical reincarnation as well as to the theatre of occupied France. I could only imitate Anouilh, for there was nothing to refer to: the *natak* companies and Yakṣagāna seemed to belong to another world altogether. Nothing filled the void they had left.

It is extraordinary how little professional theatre is to be seen in most Indian cities, and even in places that show some evidence of theatrical activity, how little is moderately good. In Bombay, one can see scores of Marathi and Gujarati plays advertised in daily papers. Calcutta has a few plays staged in Bengali. No other cities in India have regular professional theatre.

To understand why urban Indian theatre is in this state today, one has to go back to the nineteenth century, when what is called modern Indian theatre first made its appearance, independently in Bombay and Calcutta. It is no coincidence that these cities were both creations of the British maritime trade with no pre-British Indian history. The populations of these cities had benefited from British education and had prospered financially under British rule. It was inevitable, then, that the entertainment they sought for themselves should also be modeled on English theatre. Two features of the new theatre borrowed from the West were to set it totally apart from anything that preceded it and to qualify it for the adjective modern.

The first feature was the proscenium stage, which radically altered the traditional player-audience relationship. The audience was separated from the stage, which discouraged active participation and response. The wings and drop curtains led to an emphasis on illusionism and other stage tricks. The second innovation, far more important in its impact, was the sale of tickets, which changed the relationship of the theatregoers to the theatre itself. Until then, acting groups in India had depended on patronage of temples, princes, and high officials (as even the new theatre initially did in Calcutta). Since it had no financial stake in the show, the audience was willing to take a risk where the performance itself was concerned. Its attitude was similar to that still found in the performance of Hindustani music, in which the artist is judged by his ability to improvise within strictly laid-down limits and hence has the right to occasionally not come up to the mark. In folk theatres, actors today still train for particular roles rather than rehearse for particular shows. It is not unusual for an actor to meet the rest of a cast for the first time during a performance. The actors' training helps them to determine the shape of the whole show by improvising responses to one another on stage.

Once an audience has to pay to see a show, it begins to demand its money's worth. Performances become prepackaged goods sold in endless replications. The run of the play in the competitive market decides its worth and freezes it in a shape it cannot change without affecting its saleability. How closely this new kind of theatre was wedded to the ethos of the colonial city can be seen from the fact that when this model of theatre succeeded in Bombay and Calcutta, its first imitations appeared in Madras, another city created by British trade and administration with no pre-British Indian history of its own.

Of the two cities that gave birth to modern Indian theatre, Calcutta had a more homogeneous audience with a language that unified it. Exposure to the West had actually led to a flowering of new literature in Bengali. The language situation in Bombay was more complex. The new theatre groups had been started by Parsi entrepreneurs who spoke Gujarati at home. After starting with productions in English, they switched to Gujarati, then to Urdu, and finally, in search of wider audiences around the turn of the century, to Hindi. The expanding audience was mainly Hindu, while many of the writers for the Parsi companies were Muslim, since Urdu literature had flowered in Muslim courts. The Parsi entrepreneur had to ensure that the fare pleased all tastes and communities and developed a style that was essentially neutral with regard to communal differences and preferences. The plays dealt with subjects ranging from Middle Eastern romances to Hindu myths and adaptations of Shakespeare, but the treatment avoided all religious and ethical nuances. Secularism was a fashionable concept, and, in the hands of the Parsi entrepreneurs, became another name for its escapist fare. The word *entertainment* came to mean submergence in spectacle or stage tricks—and continues to mean that today for the film-going and television-watching middle class.

There was another reason why the drama produced by this theatre remained entirely trivial. Ashis Nandy has drawn our attention to, and brilliantly analyzed, the double set of values by which the urban bourgeoisie seemed to live—professing faith in Western values of equality, individualism, secularism, or free competition in public while sticking to caste and family loyalties at home. Whatever the sociological justification for this division, its effects on drama were disastrous. To have any value at all, drama must at some level engage honestly with the contradictions that lie at the heart of the society it talks to and about. The Parsi theatre society refused to acknowledge the existence of any problem. As a result, although it ruled supreme for almost seventy-five years, the theatre and its many reincarnations in the regional languages produced no drama of any consequence.

Its greatest contribution, in fact, was in the field of music, for although its Victorian model had no songs or dances, this theatre was Indian enough to realize that here entertainment by definition demands music. In India, the mere gathering of people leads to music, at family get-togethers, tea parties, political meetings, and friends' circles. The Parsi drew music from any available source—folk songs, religious songs of Hindus and Muslims, and classical music and created a unique style immediately recognizable as theatre music. Some of the great stars of this theatre were great singers. A play became so identified with songs that it was not unusual for most of the audience to walk out of the hall en masse as soon as a song was over, to return later only when the next song began. If film music today is a separate institution by itself, healthier than the film industry, which provides film music with the vehicles in which to situate songs—often quite arbitrarily—the credit must go to the use of songs in the Parsi theatre.

Naturally, once Indian movies started to include talking—or singing—the Parsi theatre edifice collapsed without a fight. In the West, theatre survived the onslaught of movies, for it had produced a body of plays whose pleasure could be fully savored only when staged. No film, no television version can fully communicate what Shakespeare, Ibsen, or Chekhov can give on stage. The Parsi theatre family had only a repertoire of songs, dances, spectacles, and romantic escapades to justify its existence--and all these could be supplied more cheaply on a much vaster scale by the film industry.

It is interesting that the new film industry developed in the very cities that had given birth to the urban Indian theatre—Bombay, Calcutta, and Madras. Commercial films also borrowed the basic principles of entertainment from the theatre and explored the film form only to the extent to which these principles could be accommodated within it. Not surprisingly, the contribution of half a century of commercial filmmaking lies in the extraordinary range and richness of its music.

This relationship between the film industry and the urban theatre has continued since then, mainly because films, like theatre, have remained an essentially urban medium. There are less than 15,000 cinema halls in India, including traveling tent theatres. When one allows for the fact that a city like Bangalore has nearly 100 cinema halls, the urban bias in the distribution of these halls becomes apparent. The distribution exactly duplicates the density distribution of nāṭak companies. More than half the cinema halls in the country are situated in the four southern states, all of which have a history of flourishing *natak* companies. Maharashtra, Bengal, and Gujarat repeat the same pattern.

Again, since the 1930's, which saw the collapse of the Parsi theatre system, revival in theatre activity has been witnessed only in those cities where the local language film industry has collapsed. In Bombay, the aggressive Hindi film industry pushed the Marathi film industry into the background in its own state, which in turn led to a revival of Marathi theatre to fill the vacuum. The loss of the East Bengal market after partition, and postwar competition from Hindi films, debilitated the movie industry in Calcutta and thus led to a revival of Bengali theatre in the 1950's. In the 1970's a long-ignored folk theatre form called jātrā was reorganized by entrepreneurs to meet the need for entertainment in rural Bengal. The success of the jātrās has been so phenomenal that many have now invaded Calcutta, taking away urban actors and actresses from theatre by offering fabulous fees. Theatre in Calcutta is in trouble again. (See Gokhale in this volume.)

The fact that theatre does not exist in isolation but is a link in a long chain of reflexive relationships connecting different entertainment media, and that each one of these forms defines itself in terms of or in relation to the form immediately next to it spatially or temporally, may seem too obvious to require further insistence. It needs to be stressed only because any efforts to preserve, encourage, and develop traditional art forms in danger of extinction need to bear this principle of the substitution of forms in mind and also because this important relationship is entirely missing from most discussions of the history of Indian art forms.

Standard, official art history is based on the assumption that there is such thing as a homogeneous "Indian culture," within which Indian theatre, Indian dance, Indian music, and so on find their own homogeneous identities without conflict. According to this theory, when applied to the field of performing arts, all traditional forms are merely expressions of a basic philosophy, an attitude toward life and the arts, which is common to all Indians and which has remained unchanged through the centuries, so that no history needs to be taken into account. It is further asserted that the *Natya Shastra*, an ancient (though probably not the most ancient) treatise on drama attributed to a mythical poet called Bharata Muni, gives the earliest statement of this philosophy. Actually, what this philosophy is, is never spelled out. But that precisely is the point: the *Natya Shastra* plays the same role in this school of aesthetics that the

Vedas play in the orthodox schools of Indian philosophy. It is the principle of their acceptance, rather than their actual content, which is of the essence.

The enormous diversity of performing arts in India is too obvious to be denied. What is explicitly denied is that conflicting philosophies, historical situations, and cultural attitudes may have shaped these different forms and may motivate them still today. "Diversity," it is insisted, only points to "an underlying unity." Most of these theorists are Brahmins who, while theorizing, identify Brahminism with Hinduism and then proceed to assume that every Indian is Hindu in thought and spirit. In view of the Sanskrit bias of Brahminism, it is not surprising that even folk and tribal material—if studied at all—is studied in the light of Sanskrit texts. For instance, while discussing the first few chapters of the *Natya Shastra*, Dr. Kapila Vatsyayan says:

> Many regional dance drama forms which are still performed today in India, particularly the three different forms of Chhāu [masked drama], rigorously observe these preliminary rites before a performance... the worship... performed on both the Sanskrit stage and in its living continuations-regional theater forms like Kuṭiyārṭam and Mayurbhaul (a form of Chhāu).

The phrases "still performed today" and "living continuations" are surely disingenuous. They conceal the fact that Chhāu as a theatrical form is only 100 years old, that it was initially a hunting ritual dance that was blended with the defunct martial arts to create a balletlike form. Later, local princes employed Brahmin gurus to polish this tribal form into a vehicle for nontribal, Hindu myths. The principles of the *Natya Shastra* were thus a later injection into a non-Hindu art form to gain respectability for it. Though there is little justification—apart of course from political necessity—for such deliberate obfuscation in the late 1980s, it hardly needs to be pointed out that the myth of an all-Indian cultural unity had a valid role to play in the colonial as well as the immediate post-Independence period.

In 1961, a seminar was organized in New Delhi by the Sangeet Nāṭak Akademi (academy in charge of the performing arts) on the future of Indian theatre. From the very start, participants fell into opposing camps: those who thought traditional Indian theatre had relevance to contemporary work and those who considered this attitude regressive and antimodern. Neither side examined what forms they were actually talking about and whether different traditional forms might have different kinds of relevance. Both sides in effect agreed on the concept of a traditional Indian theatre.

For a practitioner, however, such generalizations were hardly helpful. If the concept of tradition is to be of any use at all, one must try to understand it in all its complexity, even illogicality, and with as little mystification as possible.

Before I go on to talk of my experiments with traditional theatre forms, I must deal with another major Western influence: realism. A study of the reasons that realism has failed to produce any worthwhile drama in India may help explain the sense of urgency with which one approached native forms.

Realism made its appearance in the thirties, in reaction to the vacuity of the nāṭak companies as well as in response to the challenge thrown by the leaders of the national Independence movement that we had to prove ourselves worthy of independence by cleansing our society of its many ills. This was essentially the playwright's theatre. The productions were often directed by the playwrights themselves. Unlike the Parsi theatre, where every move was controlled by budgetary considerations, the realistic theatre was motivated by genuine idealism. The writer, the actors, and the audience were all united by a common concern for social reform and national independence and in their optimism believed changing history possible. Often the groups consisted entirely of university teachers, their students, and white-collar workers, who saw this kind of theatre as a mission rather than as a profession. They remained amateurs. But their involvement and brilliance gave many of these plays an immediacy, a sharp edge, unseen before in the company natak plays. It must be stated right here that if in the West the need of a person to be seen as an individual, as a being unique in himself, has remained the central concern of the realistic theatre, in India realism never went beyond social problems. As has often been pointed out, in India individualism has never been accepted as a value in itself and every Indian defines himself in relational terms, in terms of his relationship to the other members of his family, clan, and caste. Issues too are perceived in the same relational terms. I have often noticed that even Western plays concerned with the problem of the individual tend to be perceived by Indian audiences as dealing with social relations. When Arthur Miller's A *View from the Bridge* was staged in Madras a few years ago, the audience could not accept or understand the need for the incest motif in the story. If Eddie Carbone insisted on breaking up the love affair of his orphan niece (who is also his ward) with an illegal immigrant, the audience found nothing objectionable in his behavior. It was an uncle's duty to make sure that his niece was not duped by unscrupulous young men in search of the American nationality. At another seminar, only lip service was paid to the standard American interpretation of Miller's *Death of a Salesman* as a play about a man's pursuit of the

American dream. The participants obviously saw the breakup of a close-knit family as the real theme of the play.

Indian realistic drama was an improvement over its predecessor, the company nāṭak play, in that it took itself seriously as art and also as an instrument of social change. Yet its inability to shake off the overpowering influence of the European model was to stunt its development: Bernard Shaw was the new inspiration, along with Ibsen (as interpreted by Shaw). The proscenium stage continued, only the grand sets were replaced by the three walled living room. And this literal borrowing of the Western parlor for description of the Indian home pinpoints the basic weakness in the analytical method of the playwrights.

In the West, the living room has come to represent the last refuge of the individual, the safe and sure center from which he can confront the sociopolitical processes of the outside world. The living room in an Indian home serves exactly the opposite purpose: it is the deliberately neutral space in which, in a show of formal cordiality, the family keeps at bay people from the outside world. Nothing is meant to happen in an Indian living room. Most people, given tea in the living room, know that they are not to venture further into the house. For it is in the kitchen and the god's room—beyond the living room—that issues close to the heart of the family are debated, resolved, or left to fester. Nor could anything be less Indian than the behavior of the Shavian characters, lucid in expounding their points of view, uninhibited by who they are, whom they are addressing, who is listening and where. Hierarchies decide the nature and direction of communication in India. In many land-owning families, fathers and sons do not address each other directly but only through the women of the house or the servants. In Brahmin families, women express opinions on family matters only when the men have sat down for their meals. And so on. It is not uncommon to see in Indian realistic plays, women of the house sitting alongside the menfolk, openly discussing the most private family matters in front of total strangers, a situation unthinkable in traditional Indian homes.

One inevitably comes to the conclusion that these playwrights were so conditioned by the tools of analysis they borrowed from their Western models that they were incapable of seeing even the true geography of their own houses. Of course, it is also possible to argue that these playwrights, many of whom came from the upper castes, were never really serious about getting to the heart of the problem they had started out to analyze.

The three-walled living room continues to provide the setting for most social plays in Bombay and Calcutta today, announcing at the very first sight their total lack of connection with the actuality of social life outside. Only occasionally has a play like Vijay Tendulkar's *Sakharam Binder* made meaningful use of the layout of an Indian home to give precise expression to his theme.

My three years in England had convinced me Western theatre had nothing to offer us. The newly fashionable experiments—like absurdist theatre—had already started to repeat themselves. I had to find my own way, and in desperation I turned to what was most easily available: the nāṭak companies of my childhood.

For my second play, *Tughlaq,* I took my subject matter from medieval history and tried to fit it into the ready-made structure perfected by the orginal Parsi theatre and perpetuated without the slightest modification by the nāṭak companies. A company play consisted of a mechanical alternation of "shallow" and "deep" scenes. The shallow scenes were played in the foreground of the proscenium stage, against a drop curtain, which usually showed a street scene. These scenes were devoted to low comedy, whose ancestry could be traced back both to Shakespeare and to the folk theatre, and kept the audience occupied while the set was being changed in the deep scene behind the curtain. In the deep scene the entire stage space was used to present elaborate palaces and gardens in which heroic characters emoted in lofty rhetoric.

The first half of *Tughlaq* follows this model quite comfortably, but the second half began to rebel against the straight jacket I was putting it in. The most striking aspect of the political scene in the 1960s was the way the newly enfranchised electorate was slowly becoming aware of the power placed in its hands for the first time in history. The other equally visible movement was the gradual displacement of pre-Independence idealism by hard-nosed political cynicism. My shallow scenes refused to remain subsidiary to the deep scenes and in the last scene, the lowly comic entered the deep scene on a par with the king. The form I had borrowed from the company nāṭak was, I felt, too fragile for anything more serious than its repertoire of melodramas. With my very first experience in that style, its possibilities seemed exhausted.

But I had used no songs. My exposure to the Western theatre had made me shy of music in a serious play. And I had to ask myself whether one could in fairness claim, while forswearing its main feature, that one had explored the possibilities of a tradition. *Tughlaq* convinced me of the centrality music had in Indian communication. Not just music but other theatrical conventions too, which we have not looked at: dance, verse, monologues, puppets.

Where was one to begin? The logical starting point should have been the classical Sanskrit theatre. Apart from being the earliest known form of theatre in India, it is the only one in our history which qualifies for the description *Indian theatre.* Sanskrit "the perfected"—was the pan-Indian language which was no one's mother tongue but everyone's medium for intellectual communication, a language of courtly, philosophical, legal, technical, and literary discourse. By 600 C.E., it was widely accepted as a court language, even in South India. Female and lower-class characters in Sanskrit plays did not use Sanskrit, but spoke in Prakrit—"the natural." Prakrits must have been close to mother tongues at some point in history, for by the time Sanskrit drama had come into its own, they too had become formal and inflexible. Given the neutrality of these languages with reference to geographical and cultural variations, playwrights from all over India contributed to Sanskrit drama, and some plays like *Ratnavali* seem to have been staged and proved popular in different parts of India (See chapters by Krishnamoorthy and B. Kachru, in this volume.). In this sense the theatre was Indian. It was also genuine theatre. Its precise objective was to entertain. The *Natya Shastra* states that Brahma created theatre as the fifth Veda in response to a demand for a pastime *(kridaniyakam)* accessible to all layers of the society. Bharata Muni, to whom the *Natya Shastra* is attributed, lists the following among the goals of drama:

> occasionally piety, occasionally sport, occasionally wealth, occasionally peace of mind, occasionally laughter, occasionally fighting, occasionally sexual passion, occasionally slaughter .... [Theatre] will produce wholesome instruction, create courage, pastime (entertainment) and pleasure.

Given the importance of Sanskrit theatre in the history of Indian stage, one could have expected the drama to inspire at least some of the playwrights investigating the "Indian" identity of their theatre. But no playwright of this century—not even Tagore, who tried hard—has shown any genuine influence of Sanskrit drama. Modern writers find it hard to respond to the well-ordered universe taken for granted in these plays, in which everyone from the gods to the lowest mortals finds an allotted slot and in which few of the basic values are open to question. Besides, a lot of misunderstanding has been caused by sheer ignorance. Because unhappy endings are forbidden, it is assumed the plays have no sense of the tragic. Because patronage came from the courts, which probably deliberately limited the audience to a few courtiers, it is assumed that these plays were elitist—an impression strengthened by bad translations and careless reading.

There is, however, a more practical reason that Sanskrit drama has rarely struck a responsive chord in the most sympathetic of viewers: most productions of Sanskrit plays are so consistently bad that it is easy after a while to attribute the failure to the texts themselves rather than to the well-meaning and hardworking group of actors.

To do justice to a Sanskrit play, a producer needs a fully worked out style that is complex and subtle and a cast of actors who have been thoroughly trained in that style. One cannot cast any set of actors nurtured in company *natak* notions or in the realist school and make the plays work.

Only in the last decade have two theatre directors—Kavalan Narayana Panikkar in Kerala and Ratan Thiyam in Manipur (notice the geographical spread)—staged Sanskrit plays with actors specifically trained for that purpose. The results have been spectacular. They have shown that, when properly staged, there is nothing otherworldly or quaint about Sanskrit drama.

Sanskrit drama flourished between 200 B.C.E. and about 700 C.E. No other theatre in the world has had as long and continuous a history. Parallel with it there must have been performances in the languages of the common people, though we have no evidence of the exact nature of these performances. It has been conjectured that some of the ten dramatic forms listed in the Natya Shastra probably refer to the more popular varieties. By 1000 C.E., Sanskrit theatres had long been dead, and regional languages, mother tongues, unlike Sanskrit, had begun to emerge as vehicles of artistic and philosophical expression.

It is interesting that while the new regional language literatures on the whole followed Sanskrit models, they did not produce written drama. Theatre as it developed in the postclassical period depended on improvised dialogue, with only the musical parts of the performance handed down. Its aesthetic too differed, since many of these forms probably originated in folk ritual. Chandrashekhar Kambar has described how many elements of the possession ritual in honor of Goddess Mariamma are in fact theatrical, involving as they do, putting on makeup, dressing up, miming the myth of the goddess, and being possessed. The resemblance between theatre forms like kathakali and Yakṣagāna and the spirit cults in the neighboring areas is too close to be missed. The fact that many of these forms indulge unashamedly in scenes of terror, violence, and death—forbidden in Sanskrit theatre—is surely attributable to their origins in folk ritual.

Another major influence on the postclassical period was *bhakti* which literally means devotion or faith. Starting in a corner of South India, the bhakti movement swept right across India, spreading the message of total surrender to the Lord's love, of complete immersion in religious rapture. Bhakti turned theatre into a handmaiden of religion, against the secular assumptions of Sanskrit and folk theatre. While bhakti created new ritual forms like rāslīlā and rāmlīlā (theatrical games by which devotees participate in the ecstatic play of Rāma and Kṛṣṇa) to spread their word, its missionary zeal is probably responsible for the contempt with which many secular theatre forms are treated in India today,

During the 1960s the central question facing every serious playwright was how to draw on these various strands in the traditional theatre—some of which had lost contact with urban civilization during the course of the last 200 years and many of which seemed deeply rooted in religious sensibility—so as to revitalize our own work. Immediately after Independence, the government of India founded three autonomous academies—Sahitya for literature, Sangeet Nāṭak for the performing arts, and Lalit Kalā for the fine arts—whose main function was the discovery, retrieval, and rejuvenation of arts on the brink of extinction. Parallel with these three central academies were bodies the state governments set up. Though most of the reasons for the criticism leveled against these bodies—red tape, ignorance, insensitivity, waste—were justifiable, these state organizations did valuable work in bringing the richness of our own forgotten past to our attention again. The question was, could this paraphernalia of masks, half curtains, mime, dance, and music become meaningful outside its own context?

It was when I was focusing on the question of the use of masks and their relationship to theatre music that my play *Hayavadana* suddenly began to take shape in my head. The play is based on Thomas Mann's *The Transposed Heads,* which in turn is based on one of the riddles in the anthology Vetālapancavimśatikathā.

A young bride finds herself in the unenviable position of discovering that both her husband and his best friend have committed suicide by beheading themselves for her sake. When the bride, despairing of her own future, also tries to commit suicide, Goddess Kālī appears in front of her and tells her that if she will only rejoin the heads to the bodies, the men will come back to life again. The woman does as told. The men come back to life, only to find she has mixed up the heads. The story ends with a question: Who is the real husband, the one with the husband's head or the one with his body?

The Vetālapancavimśatikathā answers: since the essence of a man is represented by his head, the husband's head will identify the husband even in the new situation.

Mann carries this logic to its ultimate conclusion. Since the head is the man, the body should alter to fit the head. At the end of Mann's story, the bodies have transformed themselves to fit the heads so perfectly that the men are physically exactly as they were at the start of the story. The problem is unresolved.

The basic equation in the tale of the head with the man's person seemed to me to provide perfect justification for the use of masks. For if in modern Western theatre the mask is used in contrast to the face, the persona as against the real person, as Peter Brook points out in *The Empty Space,* in Indian traditional theatre, as in the Greek, the mask is only the face writ large. The mask is a method of projecting the personality of the character to a vast audience. (It is interesting that Sanskrit theatre, playing to a small audience of 200 to 400, did not use masks for normal, human characters.) The mask is the face, is the man, in fact is more, for in folk rituals, the mask represents the spirit by whom the dancer seeks to be possessed. Putting on the mask or mask-like makeup is the first step to being possessed.

This brought me face to face with the fact that in many traditional forms, certainly in the Yakṣagāna I had seen in my childhood—performances begin with the worship of Lord Ganesh, a god with an elephant's head who very often is represented on stage only by the mask of the elephant head.

Ganesh's head says nothing about his personality. In fact, according to the myth, Ganesh was beheaded by his father, and when the original head could not be found, the head of an elephant that was conveniently at hand was substituted. Whatever the sexual symbolism of the head, the choice of the animal itself was accidental to the god's personality.

As I was struggling with these implications of the mask, I sensed a third being in the space between the divine (Ganesh) and the human (the main story). The play is named after this character. *Hayavadana* means the one with the horse's head: the story of a man who wants to shed his horse's head and become human provides the outer panel within which the main story is framed. Hayavadana's attempts to become a complete man end ironically. The head is the man. He becomes a complete horse. The central logic of the tale "The Head Is the Man" remains intact, while its basic premise (that the head represents the thinking part of man and is therefore the supreme limb) is subverted.

The energy of folk theatre comes from the fact that while it seems to support traditional values, it is also capable of subverting them, looking at them from various points of view. The conventions of the chorus, the mask, and the comic episode permit the simultaneous presentation of widely divergent points of view, some of them even irreconcilable with each other. The form can give rise to a genuine dialectic. In Yakṣagāna, the dialogue is improvised and the characters are permitted to justify their actions directly to the audience. Often, a capable actor playing the evil protagonist Duryodhana will convince the audience that his character has acted nobly throughout the Mahabharata while someone like the god Krishna has been the villain of the piece. The audience applauds to show its appreciation of the actor's arguments. The performance then continues according to the accepted story line, in which Krishna is divine and Duryodhana is wicked. Such debates give each performance a new perspective, make each show a fresh exploration.

If I had to grope my way to the final form of *Hayavadana,* Chandrashekhar Kambar, who also writes in Kannada, arrived at it much more naturally in his play *Jokumaraswamy.* Born and brought up in a village, he was a member of a *bayalata* (an open-air theatre) troupe and thus had a professional's detailed acquaintance with the bayalata form.

Jokumāraswāmy deals with a rite in honor of Jokumāra, a phallic deity who in the form of a snake gourd is worshipped, and ritually eaten by those who desire children. The plot situations are all stock: the impotent chieftain's virgin wife feeds the snake gourd by mistake to the village rake and has a child by him. The chieftain takes revenge by killing the rake but cannot disclaim the baby, which seems like public proof of his virility.

The explicit message of the play is the same as in Brecht's prologue to *The Caucasian Chalk Circle* and, as a political statement, carries as little conviction: land should belong to the peasant who plows it rather than to the landlord who owns it only legally. The strength of the play and its political implications lie in Kambar's analysis of political power as a mode of compensating for sexual inadequacy and of philandering as a psychosexual equivalent of anarchism. A fertility ritual provides the framework for the action; it also provides a basis from which to question notions of virility and power.

The last fifteen years have seen many other plays that have come from the inspiration and form of traditional Indian theatre. Jabhar Patel's production of Vijay Tendulkar's *Ghashiram Kotwal,* certainly a milestone in the history of modern Indian theatre, used a human curtain of ten singers, which alternately concealed and opened up to reveal the corrupt politics of decadent eighteenth-century Pune. The play is about political leaders who create demons to destroy their political enemies, but the demons get out of hand and turn on their own creators. It is a recurrent theme in Indian mythology. Its contemporary relevance was conclusively proved—ten years after the first showing of the play—by Indira Gandhi and Sant Bhindranwale in the Punjab.

It must be admitted that the popularity of traditional forms on the urban stage has much to do with the technical freedom they offer the director. Music, mime, and exotic imagery open up vast opportunities for colorful improvisation, which nevertheless can and alas all to often does degenerate into self-indulgence. While there are productions today which combine traditional theatre techniques with modern choreography and visual design to an effect unimaginable in the 60's, most such efforts tend to be imitative and soulless. It is as though now that the problem has found a technical solution, the spirit of the quest has been lost.

Naga-Mandala is based on two oral tales I heard from A.K. Ramanujan. These tales are narrated by women, normally the older women in the family, while the children are being fed in the evenings, in the kitchen or being put to bed. The other adults present on these occasions are also women. Therefore these tales, though directed at the children, often serve as a parallel system of communication among the women in the family.

They also express a distinctly woman's understanding of reality around her, a lived counterpoint to the patriarchal structures of classical text and institutions. The position of Rani in the story of *Naga-Mandala*, for instance, can be seen as a metaphor for the situation of a young girl in the bosom of a joint family where she sees her husband only in two unconnected roles as a stranger during the day and as a lover at night. Inevitably, the pattern of relationships she is forced to weave from these disjointed encounters must be something of a fiction. The empty house Rani is locked in could be the family she is married into.

Many of these tales also talk about the nature of tales. The story of the flames comments on the paradoxical nature of oral tales in general: they have an existence of their own, independent of the teller and yet live only when they are passed on from the possessor of the tale to the listener. Seen thus, the status of a tale becomes akin to that of a daughter, for traditionally a daughter too is not meant to be kept at home too long but has to be passed on. This identity adds poignant and ironic undertones to the relationship of the teller to the tales.

It needs to be stressed here that these tales are not leftovers from the past. In the words of Ramanujan, "Even in a large modern city like Madras, Bombay or Calcutta, even in western-style nuclear families with their well planned 2.2 children, folklore... is only a suburb away, a cousin or a grandmother away."

It has not been easy for me to talk about Indian theatre. The major concern of the Indian theatre in the post-Independence period has been to try to define its "Indianness" and to relate itself to the past from which it was cut off. The awful part is that most of these explorations have been done by enthusiastic amateurs, who find it extremely difficult to continue to work in theatre. Most of them have to go into film or television, thus perpetuating the amateur status of the theatre they have helped to keep alive. I see myself as a playwright, but I make a living in film and television. There is a very high elasticity of substitution between the different performing media in India: the participant too gets tossed about violently. We can talk of the excellent work of playwrights like Tendulkar, Kambar, and Eikunchavar, of actors like Vijaya Mehra, Shambhumitra, and Naseeruddin Shah, of directors like Thiyam, Panikkar, B. V. Karantha, and Satyadev Dubey and yet have no continuing professional theatre to point to.

Where does one go from here? Since I began on an autobiographical note, let me say I shall go on writing plays, theatre or no theatre, as at least some of my contemporaries will, I know, too. One writes because one has to: the pleasure one has derived from the theatre drives one on. One writes in the hope that one day there will be more of a professional theatre on which to stage one's work. Meanwhile, one makes a living.

Beyond that, the question of what lies in store for the Indian theatre should be rephrased to include the four media--theatre, cinema, television, and video--for their futures are inextricably intertwined. (I should ideally also include radio, which can reach nearly 95 percent of the population of the country. But I know of no detailed study of its impact.) I have already commented on the reflexive relationship between urban theatre and film. Television was introduced in the mid-1960's in major Indian cities but came into its own only in 1983, when the Ministry of Information and Broadcasting opened its doors to private advertising and started telecasting soap operas produced and sponsored by private, nongovernmental companies.

The very first Hindi soap opera became a national hit. Television, until then watched only for the commercial films telecast weekly as well as for other programs like *Chitrahaar,* a collage of film songs, suddenly developed a viewership of its own. In 1985 alone, the total number of television sets in India leapt from 5.2 million to 7.2 million. Each set, it is estimated, had an average audience of ten people. Cinema attendance slumped and critics started pointing out that the American and European television experience should have prepared our film industry for mass desertion by its audience in favor of the new toy.

But then something unexpected happened. Within six months, cinema attendance started booming again. The last several years have shown that the big budget films at least do not seem to have been affected by television, except of course on Sundays, when a Hindi feature film is televised.

The most plausible explanation for this about-face of the new audience is that television let it down. The main viewership for commercial films in cities is the industrial working class and other low-income groups as well as women from all strata of society. Television controlled by educated middle-class bureaucrats, programmed by educated middle-class bureaucrats, sensitive to comments by educated middle-class critics, and geared to urban white-collar tastes has nothing to offer these classes, whose expectations of entertainment are still "traditional": they believe a performance should last at least two to two and a half hours and that it should tell an emotionally charged story using songs, dances, or music. The Chekhovian fare handed out by television in twenty-three-minute slots just does not meet the needs of this audience. There is the additional attraction that cinema offers a chance for some kind of privacy, an escape from the overcrowded slums in which most of this audience lives.

Television thus has not materially affected commercial cinema. What it has destroyed—at least temporarily—is "parallel cinema," a movement inspired by the success of Satyajit Ray's films, essentially neoclassical in style, committed to an analysis of contemporary social and political problems. The films of parallel cinema—which, interestingly, usually do not use songs and dances—have been supported by the educated urban middle class. This class has now switched its patronage to television and video. Angry radical filmmakers of the parallel cinema now depend on the patronage of television to make a living.

Soon more than 80 percent of the population of the country will come within the beaming range of television. The cultural and social impact of the very introduction of television into the countryside could be enormous. There is the inevitable impact of the medium itself. The flow of information in rural families is meant to be hierarchically controlled: men and elders process the information that comes into the house. They decide whether it is good for women and children. (I say *meant* because certain kinds of information must flow from woman to woman, bypassing men.) With television, the whole family, indeed the whole village, receives information together, flattening out age and sex hierarchies. In fact, children grasp television messages much faster than adults, whose visual grammar is more elementary. This situation could entirely alter the nature of relationships within the family.

Limiting one's attention to the impact of the new medium on other performing arts, one may conjecture that traditional performing arts, lacking the stamina and capital of commercial cinema, will vanish entirely from the scene; expectations regarding entertainment could alter totally, but only if television becomes a genuine medium of entertainment for the rural population. If the present urban middle-class notions of entertainment continue to shape its policies, television is likely to remain ineffective, even if cheap sets put it within the reach of every family.

Video is the real joker in the pack. Today it is almost impossible to forecast in which direction it is likely to grow and what place it will have in the daily life of the people. Already it is the video, and not television, that has affected the fortunes of the film industry. Fifteen years ago, commercial Indian films had markets spreading from Southeast Asia through the Middle East to Greece and Turkey, as well as in the immigrant congeries in England, in East, West, and South Africa, in Canada and the United States. Within five years of the arrival of video, most of these markets disappeared. Almost all movie houses specializing in the exhibition of Hindi films in these areas closed down. Whereas in 1975 a major film producer in Bombay could cover a substantial portion of his budget from advances made by distributors abroad, now he hopes to sell his video rights for what price he can get before pirated copies appear in the market. Many producers have been known to pirate their own films in an effort to flood the black market before others do so.

Video parlors dot the landscape. Video films play in long-distance buses, in wayside tea shops, in hair-cutting salons. In Bombay I have seen special sheds in which fisher women slice and clean their fish or get ready for the market while they watch illegally exhibited video films. Video will soon invade the remotest corner, as films and theatre have not, and without the supercilious attitudes of television. Since most of the operations are illegal, the fare shown is likely to consist of brutal violence and the hard-core pornography of pirated Indian films. Most questions about the future of theatre pale before the spectre of uncontrollable expansion of the video network across the country. Yet I cannot help worrying about theatre.

The media occupy a shifting landscape in which the next electronic gadget could turn a mass medium into a traditional art form. Perhaps quite unrealistically, I dream of the day when a similar ripple will reestablish theatre—flesh and blood actors enacting a well-written text to a gathering of people who have come to witness the performance—where it belongs, at the center of the daily life of the people.

Endnotes

1. Reprinted by permission of *Daedalus*, Journal of American Academy of Arts and Sciences, from the issue entitled, "Another India," Fall 1989, Vol. 118, No. 4.

2. I am grateful to Dr. A. K. Ramanujan for many of the concepts used in this paper.

Works Cited

Bhat, G.K. 1985. *Bharata-Natya-Manjari.* Poona: Bhandarkar Oriental Institute.

Brook, Peter. 1968. *The Empty Space.* New York: Penguin.

Kambar, Chandrashekhar . 1972. "Ritual in Kannada Folk Theatre," *Sangeet Natak* 25: 5-22.

Nandy, Asish. 1983. *The Intimate Enemy.* New York: Oxford University Press.

Ramanujan, A. K. 1986. Two Realms of Kannada Folklore. In *Another Harmony: New Essays on the Folklore of India,* edited by Stuart H. Blackburn and A. K. Ramanujan. Berkeley: University of California Press.

____________. 1989. Telling Tales. *Dedalus* 118.4: 239-61.

Vatsayan, Kapila. 1981. Dance and Movement Techniques of Sanskrit Theater. In *Sanskrit Drama in Performance* edited by Rachel Van M. Baumer and James R. Brandon, Honolulu: University Press of Hawaii.

Chapter 32 | Contemporary Indian TheRatre

Shanta Gokhale

The cultural renaissance of the post-Independence years gave a fillip to theatre all over India and saw the birth of a new tradition in Indian theatre. Folk, traditional, and classical theatre forms already had their own seasonal, ritual, or entertainment bases in their respective regions. They took their narratives from mythology and fell broadly into a song-dance-prose format. Costumes and make-up were wildly vivid, acting styles declamatory, and performance spaces informal, having their place within the community's public spaces. The new theatre which came into being with the country's thrust towards modernity was powered by the dream of building a nation founded on democratic and secular principles.

India's first acquaintance with formal dramatic literature came in the middle of the nineteenth century with the opening of universities in Bombay, Calcutta, Madras, and Pune. The youth in universities were introduced, on the one hand, to the works of Shakespeare, and on the other, to the their own Sanskrit dramatists: Kālidāsa, Bhavabhgti, Śudraka, Nārayanabhaṭṭa, and others. Aspiring dramatists in the regional languages received apprenticeship by translating, adapting, and emulating Shakespeare and Sanskrit dramatists.

By the 1930's, social and political history had made both classical and modern models irrelevant. Symbolic of this time was perhaps the fact that while on the one hand, Le Corbusier was invited to design and create the modernist city of Chandigarh, on the other, the Central Academies of the arts endorsed a so-called return to roots by encouraging the folk and the classical traditions with their patronage. A society setting out to re-mint itself as a coin with two heads facing opposite sides, one looking forward towards modernity, the other turned backward towards indigenous cultural identity, found itself trapped between two dramatic modes: While the realism of Ibsen allowed dramatists to deal with the social and moral problems of an emergent society, the folk and traditional theatre appeared to offer the only cultural roots which the largely urban dramatists and directors saw.

Those who made theatre for State patronage with an eye on the foreign market, chose the color, song, and dance of folk traditions. European theatre too was turning to the East for its rich theatrical resources, branding its products with the highly valorized epithet "intercultural." In regions like Bengal and Maharashtra, however, where a strong, unbroken theatre tradition had been in place for over a hundred years by the time the country won its independence, the people had the decisive voice on what kind of theatre would be done: for they, not the State, were the patrons of the theatre.

The Growth of Contemporary Theatre: The Giants

It is impossible to capture the history of contemporary Indian theatre in a single frame for the simple reason that there is no single history. Each region has evolved its own way of moving forward while looking back. One can only hope to indicate the whys and hows of these moves, by looking at the philosophies and work of some of the most significant practitioners of theatre in the country since Independence.

The history of modern theatre in India begins with Shombhu Mitra (b.1915) who has achieved legendary status during his lifetime. Fascinated with theatre from his boyhood years, he entered the professional stage in Calcutta at the age of twenty-four. Disenchanted with the profit-motivated selection of plays, ornate props, and painted scenery, Mitra quit the scene.

By the thirties, the professional theatre had begun to decline. It made very little sense at a time of global and local upheavals: World War II, the birth of the Azad Hind Force, the bombing of Calcutta, the manmade Bengal famine of 1943, the Naval Mutiny of 1945, and the communal riots of 1946, followed by the brutal killings during the partition of the country in which Bengal suffered a gash straight through the heart. These were the horrors which were drastically changing people's perception of human life.

It was in response to this that Mitra joined the *Indian People's Theatre Association (*IPTA*)* in the early forties and directed Bijon Bhattacharya's *Nabanna* about the Bengal famine in 1944. This play was a radical departure from any that had been written and staged until then. The use of space and lighting, the style of speech and acting, even the use of a dialect in stage speech were all new, breaking and re-forming the known language of theatre. With *Nabanna*, Mitra became the father of modern Indian theatre. Though this immensely significant and successful play had been produced by IPTA, Mitra was not a Communist and would not submit to the Party line which IPTA imposed on its members. In 1948, he set up his own group, *Bohurupee*, launching Bengal's group theatre movement.

Of all the plays he directed and acted in until his retirement from theatre in the mid-eighties, the one that was hailed throughout the country was Tagore's *Raktakarabi* (1954). In a tribute to Mitra on his 77th birth anniversary (*Probe India*, August 1992), senior director Habib Tanvir said, "I have had the chance to see many different productions of Tagore's plays, but I feel that no other director has been able to give form to their 'feelings' except Mitra. . . . [T]his play has had a profound impact on the theatre of the entire country."

Unlike Shombhu Mitra, Utpal Dutt (1929-1993) declared himself a leftist political playwright. He too joined IPTA in the middle of his career which had begun with English plays, but was charged with being a Trotskyite and was thrown out. Whereas Mitra was committed to new theatre which concerned itself with the aesthetics of theatre, its verbal, acting, and production language, Dutt was committed to "people's theatre", and was concerned with using every theatrical means to awaken people to their condition.

Dutt's *Angar* (1939), about a recent coal-mine disaster, was the first play he wrote, directed, and produced. His earlier plays had been either translations/adaptations of Western classics or modern works, or Bengali plays written largely by earlier writers like Rabindranath Tagore and Michael Madhusudan Dutt. *Angar* was also the first play to be staged at Minerva, a professional theatre, which for the first time was filled to capacity without the enticement of song and dance. What Dutt had given the audience, instead, was spectacle—the coal-mine setting, the struggle of the miners, and the deliberate flooding of the mines by the authorities.

Dutt continued to stage his political plays on the professional stage until the end of the sixties, when political exigencies forced other choices on him. The upsurge of the *Naxalbari* movement, supported by China, brought daily violence to Bengal. During that decade, Dutt wrote and directed nearly twenty plays for the popular *Jatra* theatre. With these plays, he accelerated the hesitant entry of politics into the *Jatra* repertoire.

The *Little Theatre Group* which Dutt formed after parting ways with IPTA, succumbed to internal ideological differences and betrayals. As resilient as ever, Dutt formed the *People's Little Theatre.* Dutt's first major production for the new group was *Tiner Talwar* (1971). Hailed countrywide by critics and theatre lovers alike for its intelligent use of melodrama, the rich nuances of its verbal text, and its bold use of theatre machinery which had been cast aside by the realists of the new theatre, *Tiner Talwar* was theatre speaking about itself. Accounting for the extraordinary power of this non-political play, Dutt said in an interview with theatre scholar Samik Bandopadhyay, "*Tiner Talwar*... was a statement with which all our actors and actresses had identified themselves. That is how the teamwork and the sincerity of the actors came through so powerfully" (Jacob 1989).

If an exact contrast is to be sought for Utpal Dutt, one finds it in Badal Sircar, (b.1925). He forms the third point of the Calcutta theatre triangle of the sixties and seventies. A civil engineer and town planner by training, Sircar went to the USA with a Jawaharlal Nehru Research Fellowship in 1972 to work on a theatre of synthesis as a rural-urban link.

Sircar's *Evam Indrajit* (1962) became one of the most widely translated and performed plays of the late sixties. At the very time, however, when he was being hailed as the new voice of the middle-class, he was questioning himself about whether he wanted to be just that. This self-questioning finally led to his giving up the proscenium theatre altogether and committing himself to what he called the *Third Theatre*; the first two being the middle-class urban and the folk. Since its inception, Sircar's *Third Theatre* has been an inspiration for many theatre movements all over the country.

Whereas Dutt had proclaimed that political theatre should be performed on every platform available, including the proscenium and the *Jatra* stage, Badal Sircar was convinced that the nature of the performing space was implicated in the language of theatre and must be chosen to help create that language. In the seventies, Badal Sircar and his group, *Shatabdi*, stepped out of the proscenium frame and into an ordinary assembly hall to play to an audience sitting on benches on three sides of the performing space. This enabled an intimate dialogue to be conducted between the players and the played-to, allowing the latter to become participants in the "reality" of the performance. This was different from their normal role of passively accepting the fabrication of reality that was offered to them on the proscenium stage. The *Third Theatre*, minus auditorium, costumes, lights, make-up, freed Sircar from the need for media support and from the need to sell his "product". His audience was free to walk in and pay a donation if they so desired.

Sircar's best-known and most widely staged play, *Michhil*, was first performed in April 1974 in village Ramchadrapur in West Bengal; his second play, *Bhoma* was first performed in March 1976 in village Rangabelia in West Bengal; his third play, *Basi Itihas* was first performed in July 1979 at the Calcutta Theosophical Society Hall.

Contemporary Theatre in Bengal

The time of the giants is over. Some theatre practitioners who continue to redefine theatre in Bengal and have been acknowledged on the national level are Rudraprasad Sengupta, Shyamanand Jalan, Probir Guha, and Usha Ganguli. I shall briefly describe here the work of Guha and Ganguli..

Probir Guha's *Living Alternative Theatre* is, in a sense, an offshoot of Badal Sircar's movement. Based in the industrial town of Khardah, 20 km from Calcutta, the group puts itself directly in touch with the audience through plays that reflect the daily impact of social, economic, and political forces on the people. His actors and actresses are socially-committed volunteers. Guha believes in fostering positive violence in the bodies of his actors. Towards this end, they are trained in various Indian martial arts systems. In a paper presented at the international seminar, *Actor at Work*, organized at the National Center for the Performing Arts (NCPA), Mumbai, in November 1991, Guha said of his theatre,

> I find my themes from happenings and encounters that occur only too often on the streets, in the slums, in train compartments, in village hutments, in workplaces and worksites. . . . I pick these situations up, re-mold them to a point of shock and present them to the public. There is a desire to create a violent effect on the audience so that their complaisance cracks and they discover themselves.

Despite doing plays in Hindi, Usha Ganguli has managed, over the last twenty-one years of work with her group *Rangkarmee*, to acquire a large following in Calcutta and elsewhere in Bengal and the rest of the country. A trained Bharat Natyam dancer, she began her career with a group that performed for the richer section of the Hindi-speaking population of Calcutta. This did not satisfy her either ideologically or aesthetically. She realized she wanted to do more consciously committed plays that would reach out to students, clerks, housewives—anybody.

Rangkarmee was formed in January 1976. Its members came from all walks of life, but their continuance with the group depended on whether they were willing to be theatre workers as the group name demanded or whether they were there only for the limelight. Those who stayed dedicated themselves to doing socially-relevant plays. They were given rigorous training in acting, management, and back-stage work. Over the two decades and more of the group's existence, each of its present repertoire of half-a-dozen plays has had at least a hundred shows.

The most celebrated *Rangkarmee* production is *Rudali* (1993), based on Mahashweta Devi's short story about professional women mourners in Bihar. The script for the stage evolved through workshops which included well-known writers, Ganguli herself, and one of the members of *Rangkarmee.* Ascetically mounted, without set, lights or music, and performed in the naturalistic style with Usha Ganguli playing the main role, the play has traveled all over India and brought acclaim from critics and audiences alike.

Theatre in Maharashtra

In Bengal, there is a tradition of writer-directors; indeed, of directors who have written in order to do the kind of theatre they want to do. In Maharashtra, there is a strong playwriting tradition in which the playwright is not necessarily directly associated with the brass tacks of theatre. Therefore, when we come to theatre in Maharashtra, it is only right that we should begin with playwrights who have been responsible for changing the language of modern Marathi theatre.

When Vijay Tendulkar (b. 1928) began writing, the new theatre movement in Mumbai was just gaining popularity. Young people, mostly collegians, were raring to put an end to the earlier song-and-declamation and later sentiment-and-diluted social commentaries and to replace them with theatrical expressions relevant to their own times. Tendulkar was in the vanguard of this movement which included later stars like Vijaya Mehta and Shreeram Lagoo. Unlike most playwrights, Tendulkar was in close touch with the directors, designers, and actors of the stage and was thus able to hone his playwriting craft with their practical comments.

The first Tendulkar play to cross the language barrier was *Shantata! Court Chalu Ahe* (1968) which was staged in Bengali and Hindi. In quick succession thereafter came *Gidhade*, (1971), *Sakharam Binder* (1972) and *Ghashiram Kotwal* (1973). The latter three plays ran into problems with the censors and/or the public. *Gidhade* offended the sensibilities of the middle-class audience with its portrayal of its protagonists, a middle-class family, as vultures. The censors objected to its abusive language and, amongst other scenes, to one in which the pregnant sister enters in a blood-stained sari after being kicked by her brother causing a miscarriage. The censors objected to the abusive language in *Sakharam Binder* too, while the audience protested against the protagonist Sakharam's being beaten up by his mistress. *Ghashiram Kotwal* angered historians by its portrayal of Nana Phadnavis, Chancellor to the Peshwa, which they said was historically wrong, while it offended the Pune Brahmins because it depicted the Brahmins in that era as lecherous, greedy, and corrupt. Lust for power, greed, corruption and the consequent violence are the themes which Tendulkar explores through the story of *Ghashiram Kotwal*, the North Indian Brahmin who came to Pune to make his fortune. He was given unlimited power by the Chancellor, who had his eyes on Ghashiram's daughter. Once he tired of her, he cut Ghashiram down brutally.

Ghashiram Kotwal became a cause célèbre in 1980 when it was scheduled to tour Europe. The Shiv Sena, which today rules the Maharashtra State, went to court demanding an injunction on the tour on the plea that it would create a "wrong impression" of the country. The court's decision allowing the play to go came just two days before the troup was due to leave. They were allowed to go on condition that they would make a declaration before the curtain went up on every show that Nana Phadnavis was a great statesman who fought the British tooth and nail during his Chancellorship. Everybody connected with the play lived in terror during those days.

Tendulkar chose to cast his play in the *Dashavatar* folk form because he was fascinated by the multiple theatrical uses its idea of a human curtain could be put to. In the *Dashavatar*, the chorus stands in a semi-circle swaying rhythmically and singing its comments on the action. In *Ghashiram*, the chorus was used both to hide and reveal the action in tantalizing, often bitingly ironic ways. Mime, song and dance from folk tradition, and the *sutradhar* from classical theatre were used to give the play fluidity and create possibilities to take the work beyond the particular into the universal. *Ghashiram Kotwal* was and is a brilliant piece of theatre perfectly amalgamating a modern theme, a contemporary sensibility and the folk theatre form, but it has been held responsible for spawning a progeny which uses folk elements to decorate their work in a spurious attempt to make it indigenous.

Mahesh Elkunchwar (b. 1939) began writing plays in 1968, after he saw a Tendulkar play which demonstrated how much power the senior playwright's terse, economic, more-left-unsaid-than-said style of dialogue writing held. A lecturer in a Nagpur college, Elkunchwar made his mark with *Holi* (1970) which Vijaya Mehta directed for her group *Rangayan*, bringing out the brutality of its depiction of campus violence through ragging.

Several of Elkunchwar's plays including *Holi, Pratibimb* (1987), and *Atmakatha* (1988) have been translated into Hindi, English, and Bengali. His most ambitious work to date has been his trilogy which traces, through the fortunes of a small town family of Brahmin landlords, the crumbling of the feudal order, the plundering of the countryside by greedy jungle contractors, and a metaphorical reduction of the region to drought and barrenness. The first part of the trilogy, *Wada Chirebandi* (1982), was directed for the mainstream stage by Vijaya Mehta in 1985. Part two, *Magna Talyakathi*, and part three, *Yuganta*, were written in quick succession ten years later. The entire trilogy was directed for Awishkar by Chandrakant Kulkarni in 1994 to mark the hundred and fiftieth anniversary of Marathi theatre.

Elkunchwar is a confirmed realist. He does not see his roots in folk theatre and would consider it a betrayal of his urban individualism and his Western-oriented sensibility to use folk elements in his plays. Wada Chirebandi is one of the finest examples of consummate realism in contemporary Marathi dramatic literature.

Satish Alekar (b. 1949) is a bio-chemist by training and has recently been appointed Director of the Performing Arts Department of Pune University. He was one of the young members of the *Progressive Dramatic Association* who split from the parent group over the decision to stop performing *Ghashiram Kotwal* after the public furor against it. The young members including Alekar, Dr. Jabbar Patel, and Dr. Mohan Agash formed a new group, *Theatre Academy,* and made *Ghashiram* their first production. Satish Alekar wrote and directed several plays for the *Theatre Academy*, the most successful being *Mahanirvan* (1974). He wrote the play in the *kirtan* form. Having grown up in the heart of Pune, this form of musical religious sermon was very close to him. His acute sense of irony found in this form a perfect vehicle for its own subversion. The play is an irreverent look at Hindu death rituals, written with the spontaneous zest and quirky humor that marks all Alekar's works.

Mahanirvan, although a highly successful play, is flawed. It has been translated and produced in Hindi and Bengali. Alekar's finest play to date remains the more difficult and therefore less popular *Begum Barve* (1979). It delves into the real and fantasy worlds of two sets of people—a pair of government clerks, and a female impersonator of the old music theatre days and his employer, a ruthless cripple. *Begum Barve* has been published in English translation but performed, apart from the original Marathi, only in Hindi.

Vijaya Mehta (b. 1934) was one of the pioneers of the new theatre in Mumbai, both as a director and an actress. The first plays she directed were realistic. In those days in the context of the dominant theatre which was melodramatic, musical, declamatory or sentimental and mushy, realism was seen as a bold experiment. The group of young collegians who collected around her looked up to her for leadership. Together they formed *Rangayan* in 1954. They saw themselves as a theatre laboratory and study group. Every new play they produced was preceded and followed by discussions designed to develop the understanding of theatre by its members and cultivate the taste of the audience for this new realistic theatre. In 1971, the group split. The actor-couple Arvind and Sulabha Deshpande and a few others from the old group, notably organizer Arun Kakade, formed a new group, *Awishkar*. Their first play was a spectacular production of Karnad's *Tughlaq*, translated into Marathi by Vijay Tendulkar, directed by Arvind Deshpande and designed with a stunning set comprising multiple levels by Damu Kenkre.

Mehta, hurt and disillusioned, joined the mainstream stage, where, along with Shreeram Lagoo she was responsible for introducing a new understated acting style. Although she directed many excellent productions for the mainstream stage, including Jaywant Dalvi's *Barrister* which she later made into a film, she could not endure the pressures of touring and the aesthetic compromises of working in the mainstream for too long. After quitting the mainstream, Mehta did some visually stunning productions of the classics *Mudrarakshasa* and *Shakuntala.* The music was composed by Bhaskar Chandavarkar and the sets were designed by the artist D. G. Godse. She also directed Girish Karnad's *Hayavadan* and *Nagmandal* in the mid-eighties. (See Karnad, this volume.)

Although Vijaya Mehta has attempted many forms of theatre including Brecht, and has always produced impeccable productions, her forte is still the meticulously planned realistic play where biographies of characters are constructed and the acting graph plotted accordingly. She has been a great team leader and organizer and has been wholly responsible for bringing rigorous professionalism and a serious concern for developing the aesthetics of theatre to the non-professional stage.

Dr. Jabbar Patel is a practicing gynecologist who lives and works in Daund, halfway between Pune and Sholapur. The three plays he has directed for *Theatre Academy* have all involved large casts, ensemble work, and music. *Ghashiram Kotwal*, under his direction, is by far the most traveled Marathi production of all times. During the twenty-five years that *Theatre Academy* ran the production, it saw two generations of actors being inducted and trained, although the main role continued to be played by the inimitable Dr. Mohan Agashe as Nana Phadnavis till the production was wound up. Fifty boys were trained to dance and sing and were put through a regimen of exercises to prepare them for *Ghashiram*. The music, a major contribution to the success of the play, was composed by Bhaskar Chandavarkar. So integrated was music, dance, and the prose text that the director had to interact very closely with the composer and the choreographer. The result was a theatrical tour de force very different in character from the naturalistic plays Marathi theatre excelled in. The success of *Ghashiram Kotwal* at the box-office also served to subsidize the Academy's less popular productions like *Begum Barve*.

Patel's next production, *Teen Pashacha Tamasha*, (1977) was P. L. Deshpande's adaptation of Brecht's *Threepenny Opera*. This production, while excellently performed and sung by Madhuri Purandare as Rangu (Jenny), Nandu Bhende as Ankush (Macheath), and Chandrakant Kale as Peachum, did not enjoy the same popularity as *Ghashiram*. Dr. Jabbar Patel has been making films for the last twenty years, his latest being a *magnum opus* on the life and work of Dr. Babasaheb Ambedkar.

Satyadev Dubey has been one of the most influential directors in Maharashtra. It is not uncommon to hear theatre enthusiasts from small towns in the state say that some chance viewing of some play, such as Shyam Manohar's strangely quirky play, *Yakrut* (1986), changed their perception of theatre and its possibilities completely.

Satyadev Dubey is the only director from the sixties' generation to have stayed in touch with every succeeding generation of writers-directors on the non-professional stage. The playwrights' workshop which he organized in Pune in 1973 was crucial in bringing together the emergent generation of playwrights. Fifteen years later, he held Sunday workshops for the new playwrights. As a subjective selection from amongst the dozens of plays he has directed, *Andha Yug* (1962), *Hayavadan* (1972) and *Aranya* (1984) have been his most outstanding Hindi productions and Elkunchwar's *Raktapushp* (1981), his most sensitive Marathi production.

Figure 39: *Impressions of Bheema* by Adishakti

Figure 40: *Ghasiram Kotwal* by Theatre Academy

Figure 41: A Scene from Usha Ganguli's *Rudali*. Photo Kushal Gangopadhyay

Figure 42: *Khel Guru Ka* Directed by Bansi Kaul

Figure 43: *Wada Chirebandi* by Kala Vaibhav

Figure 44: *Karnabharam* by Sopanam (K.N. Panikkar)

The Chhabildas Movement

Something unique happened to non-professional theatre in Mumbai in 1974. Arvind and Sulabha Deshpande managed to persuade the Chhabildas School in Dadar to rent out its assembly hall to their group *Awishkar* at concessional rates for experimental plays. This school hall soon became a buzzing center of theatre activity, making the name Chhabildas synonymous with the experimental movement in Maharashtra. As the eighties came to an end, theatre activity dwindled and the movement became moribund. The school soon withdrew the concessions it had once offered to young theatre people. Today, the hall is available at the normal rental and, while off-beat plays are still performed there, Chhabildas is no longer a meeting place where things "happen."

Kannada Theater

Like Bengal and Maharashtra, the itinerant company theatre tradition in Karnataka also declined in the thirties, but unlike the other two States, it was not replaced immediately by a new theatre movement. In a speech given at the Meet the Author program organized by the *Sahitya Akademi* and the India International Centre in Delhi in November 1988, Girish Karnad (b. 1938), the most well-known of the modern Kannada playwrights, said about the time he started writing plays: "Why do you write plays in the first place? There is no theatre and not only is there no theatre but there is no really meaningful tradition of theatre within which I have grown up."

Karnad had to set about creating a new tradition. He rejected the realistic play which Maharashtra had made its own because it falsified the social reality in India. His perception was that the drawing room in which realistic plays were more often than not set, was not the private space in India as it was in Europe where the most intimate family discussions could take place. If anything, the drawing room was a facade and Indian life played itself out in the darker rooms within.

In his paper "In search of a new theatre" read at a Berlin theatre seminar in 1992, Karnad sees himself influenced by Western playwrights in his first play, *Yayati* (1961), based on the well-known father-son myth: "That is, at the most intense moment of self-expression, while my past had come to my aid with a ready-made narrative within which I could contain and explore my insecurities, there had been no dramatic structure in my own tradition to which I could relate myself."

In Tughlaq (1964), Karnad turned to the old Parsi theatre for a model, constructing the play with alternating "deep" and "shallow" scenes. *Hayavadan* (1971) was written as a masked play posing the philosophical question of whether the head governs the body or the body, the head. The answer, or lack of it, was presented through well-known Indian folk tales and Thomas Mann's German short story, *Transposed Heads*. *Naga-Mandala* (1988), also based on two folk-tales from Karnataka, was written during the year Karnad spent at the University of Chicago as visiting professor and Fullbright-scholar-in-residence. (See Karnad, this volume, for a detailed discussion.)

If Girish Karnad had no models to look to when he began writing plays, Chandrasekhar Kambar, who was born and brought up in a region where the folk theatre form *Bayalata* was still alive and practiced had no such problem. He cast his most well-known play, *Jokumaraswamy* (1972), translated into Hindi, Marathi, Punjabi, Gujarati, and Tamil, in the *Bayalata* form. It retells a traditional fertility myth using traditional music while raising the contemporary issue of peasants' rights to the land they till.

"The stage, in order to represent the world, must not become the world itself." This epigrammatic remark, made by B. V. Karanth in his interview with Kiritnatha Kurtukoti in the *Sangeet Natak Akademi's* publication *Contemporary Indian Theatre*, is the tenet by which he has directed his productions over the last thirty years or more. During this period, he has been at the head of three institutions—the National School of Drama, Delhi, *Rangmandal*, the repertory of the Bharat Bhavan in Bhopal, and *Rangayana*, the actors' training school and repertory in Mysore. His production of Karnad's *Hayavadan* has been highly acclaimed. He has also directed children's plays and is perhaps the most influential and highly regarded director in Karnataka and outside.

One of the most interesting theatre stories of post-Independence India is K. V. Subanna's *Ninasam*. Subanna and his friends formed this amateur group in 1949, fired with the idea of contributing to the making of a new India through theatre. Located in their remote village Hegoddu, 350 km from Bangalore, they worked enthusiastically for ten years with the encouragement of family and the community. Then with the general post-Independence disillusionment that set in throughout the country, *Ninasam* grew apathetic and crumbled.

In the sixties, a literary movement, *Navya*, was born in Bangalore. Sensing an all-Karnataka cultural renaissance, *Ninasam* woke up in 1967 and has never closed its eyes since. Over the years, the repertory expanded its activities to include a training center for actors and an itinerant repertory, *Tirugata*, which caters to all nineteen districts of the State. *Ninasam* also has a film society and its own annual film festival.

K. V. Subanna stands for community-specific theatre. In the paper he read at the *Actor at Work* seminar at the National Center for the Performing Arts (NCPA) in 1991, he confessed that he was partial to the new literature and realistic plays which confronted social issues, but his associates and the local community preferred company-style plays with a loud gesture language and voice projection. A middle road was found in the selection of plays through confrontation and discussion. Even the politics or the lack thereof of the *Ninasam* repertoire and "also the style of our productions . . . evolved through this kind of confrontation, quarrel and resolution or synthesis." Distinguishing between *prekshaka* (audience) and *samajika* (community), he went on to say, "You can speak to an audience, but your intimacies can be shared only with a community through a homogeneity of culture." Given this belief, he finds concepts like pan-Indian, national, international and cross-cultural extremely naive.

Malayalam Theatre

K. N. Panikkar (b. 1928), is a poet who lives and works in Thiruvananthapuram, Kerala. His theatre started as an extension of his poetry and even today, draws its strength from his poetic imagination. He writes and directs his own plays for his group, Sopanam, which he established in 1974. He also trains his actors using the innumerable theatre forms and martial arts disciplines that abound in the tiny state of Kerala. The martial art called *kalaripayattu* is used as the basic system in the training of the actor's body; simultaneously, the actor is also trained in acquiring the inner state of being that is required for the theatre.

Pannikar's most well-known and widely performed productions are Bhasa's *Urubhangam* and his own *Karim Kutty* (1982) and *Ottayan* (1985). His plays work as parables, allowing their traditional folklore content and indigenous theatre language to be imbued with contemporary significance. His answer to the charge of revivalism that critics have leveled against him for using rituals in his work is, "This type of criticism is commonly raised by people committed to a political philosophy. I don't have such a commitment. Also, I have placed no restriction on entering any region of human endeavor for my work. I use ritual as one of the most powerful forms of theatrical expression." (Interview with K. S. Narayana Pillai in *Contemporary Indian Theatre*, Sangeet Natak Akademi.)

Manipuri Theatre

Like Kerala in the South, Manipur in the North-east also has its own traditional dance, drama, and story-telling traditions on which Ratan Thiyam draws. Trained in theatre at the National School of Drama (1971-1974), he returned to Imphal to set up his own theatre group, the *Chorus Repertory Theatre*, in 1976. His most well-known works are the *Mahabharata* trilogy *Urubhangam* (1981), *Chakravyuha* (1984), and *Karnabharam* (1989). Of these, his most widely traveled, admired and written about production is *Chakravyuha*, which deals with the death of Abhimanyu, son of Arjun. Like other writers-directors working in post-colonial times, Thiyam too uses theatre to straddle the divide between indigenous theatre traditions and contemporary issues. On the one hand, he sees *Chakaravyuha* as a symbol of the conflict between two generations—callow youth pitted against experienced warriors; on the other hand it symbolizes the conflict between the individual and society—Abhimanyu against the seven charioteers. Ultimately, he sees it as a protest against violence and the threat of World War III which the younger generation faces.

Heisnam Kanhailal expresses the feelings of anger and despair of a neglected people through his work. Manipur's cultural history is dominated by the imposition of Vaishṇavism on the local people and its post-Independence political history, by its marginalization on account of its remote geographical position and its people's racial difference from the national mainstream. Kanhailal's strong sense of ethnicity first drove him to steep himself in tradition. Then, under the influence of Badal Sircar, he moved out of the ethnic enclosure into a wider perspective. Finally, he arrived at what he terms the "theatre of transcendence", which goes beyond verbal language and expresses itself through movement, song, and dance.

Kanhailal's wife, Sabitri, is one of the finest actresses in India. Nobody who has seen her performance in Kanhailal's most celebrated production, *Pebet*, in which she plays the mother bird anxious for one of her seven babies captured by a cat who teaches it to speak and behave like itself, can ever forget her expressive body movements and her extraordinary voice.

Hindi Theatre

Habib Tanvi is one of the Hindi theatre directors who started using folk artists in his plays very early on, in an effort to make them more relevant to himself. Returning from his training in England, he found that most of what he had learned made no sense in his native environment. He therefore began working with tribals from the

Chhatisgarh region of Madhya Pradesh using their theatre language and some of their folklore in his productions. His group, *Naya Theatre*, formed in 1959, has been doing plays regularly since, struggling for survival every bit of the way. His most celebrated plays have been *Agra Bazaar* (1970) on the bazaar poet Nazir and *Charandas Chor* (1976) about a thief who inadvertently makes a pledge to his guru never to lie.

Although Tanvir himself has been working in the folk idiom, or rather because he has chosen to do so out of individual commitment, he is severely critical of the folksy trend that started in the seventies in a bid to appear "rooted".

Bansi Kaul came to theatre from a richly varied background which included painting road signs and the backs of trucks. Kaul has been fascinated with the idea of the *vidushak*. His group, *Rang-Vidushak*, is comprised of members who have outside jobs and come mostly from the lower middle-class. In training them for his proposed theatre of the *vidushak*, he needed to find sources of body language that were immediately accessible to them. He found them on the streets, e.g., street entertainers and gymnasts. Observation and documentation of their gestures and body language is Kaul's training methodology. His plays tell simple tales energetically and humorously, while exploring that eternal character of Indian theatre, the *vidushak*.

English Theatre

Ebrahim Alkazi was trained at the Royal Academy of Dramatic Arts, London. Returning to Mumbai, he set up the city's first amateur theatre group, the Theatre Group in the early fifties. His sensibility was Western, his language English, his audience elitist. Yet, Alkazi's influence penetrated the local Marathi theatre through Vijaya Mehta's apprenticeship on the advice of her counselors when she began doing serious theatre. He gave her the methodology of rehearsal, time, resources, and team management. He also gave her the visual and performative aesthetics of realistic theatre.

Alkazi's Stanislavskian naturalism, set designs using levels articulated by occasional architectural elements like a pillar or a doorway, the orchestration of costume, lighting, music, and verbal text to arrive at a totality of theatrical effect, came as a radical departure for an audience grown used to star performers, the supremacy of the verbal text, and melodramatic delivery of lines. During his fourteen years in Mumbai, Alkazi staged many of the best-known plays of the West, from the Greeks, Shakespeare, and Moliere, to Ibsen, Chekhov, and Strindberg, and on to Anouillh, Osborne, and Beckett. His first Hindi production came after he moved to Delhi in 1961 as the first director of the National School of Drama (NSD). Two of his most well-known productions during his sixteen-year tenure at the NSD were of Dharmavir Bharati's *Andha Yug*, dealing with the aftermath of the Kurukshetra war between the Pandavas and the Kauravas, and Girish Karnad's Kannada play *Tughlaq* in Hindi translation. The latter was performed in the Old Fort in Delhi, giving the production a grand, spectacular scale.

Whether he staged his productions in an indoor auditorium or out in an open environment, Alkazi adhered to the Stanislavkian style of acting, and it was this tradition that he bequeathed to the National School of Drama. Although successors like B. V. Karanth broke this mold by introducing the folk elements of music and dance, the strength of the NSD repertory continues to be realism.

Mahesh Dattani is a playwright from Bangalore. He writes in English and has had five plays published, almost all of them performed in Bangalore, most in Mumbai and a couple in Delhi and Calcutta. Dattani has no hang-ups about using the language of India's ex-rulers. He uses it because it is his to write on themes which are also specifically his. His protagonists are not only Gujaratis like himself, but Gujaratis from Bangalore. The very specificity of his characters, however, carries his plays beyond those confines to become universally relevant. Realistic in form, complex in structure, many of them are shot through with an unforced humor that makes them generally appealing.

Veenapani Chawla has been steadily working towards creating an indigenous language of theatre although she works in English. Indeed, she is the only theatre practitioner who has succeeded in indigenizing the verbal language through classical and traditional body language. She trained in the *Chhau* dance form of the Northeast and the martial art, *Kalaripayattu*, from Kerala. Vinay Kumar, the actor she has been working with for the last five years, is a graduate of the drama school in Trissur, Kerala, where he received some training in Kerala's traditional theatre and martial arts forms. Their most impressive production to date has been a one-hour one-actor play, *Impressions of Bheema* in which Vinay Kumar plays Bheema from boyhood to old age. The reading time of the script, written by Chawla, is no more than ten minutes, but its performance time is one hour. Vinay Kumar's body, a perfectly trained and tuned instrument, makes even the tiniest muscular ripple expressive. He speaks a heavily accented and Malayali-inflected English which at once frees him from artificiality and brings the play closer to the audience.

Indian theatre today is as richly varied as its languages and its terrain. What is common to all the theatres described here is their perpetual struggle to survive.

Theatre practitioners like to console themselves with the thought that always being on the edge is what theatre is all about. Yet, a wider patronage would do Indian theatre no harm.

Works Cited

Actor at work: 1991 Report of an International Seminar, National Center for the Performing Arts.

Jacob, P. (ed.) 1989. *Contemporary Indian Theatre -- Interviews with Playwrights and Directors.* Delhi: Sangeet Natak Akademi.

No Title. [Compilation of papers presented at the Berlin theatre seminar, March 1992]

Chapter 33 | The Distinctiveness of Indian Cinema

Wimal Dissanayake

As we celebrate the fiftieth anniversary of Indian independence and take stock of the achievements of the past five decades, an area that merits close attention is the art of cinema. As an art form, film is not indigenous to India the way poetry, dance, or drama is. It is imported from the West. Before long, however, film became an indigenized art form, taking root in the consciousness of the people, appealing to millions of film-goers. Today, it is the dominant form of entertainment in India, despite the increasing attraction of television. It is said that about ten million movie-goers buy tickets daily to see films. India is also the largest film-producing country in the world, with over 900 films each year. Indian films are seen avidly not only in South and Southeast Asia, but also in East Africa, Mauritius, the Caribbean, the Middle East, Britain, Canada, Australia, the United States, and countries associated with the former Soviet Union. Raj Kapoor, one of the most popular actors and directors in the fifties, was regarded as a kind of folk hero in certain parts of the former Soviet Union.

Indian cinema opens a most interesting window on Indian culture. It brings us face to face with various facets of Indian culture with an intimacy unavailable to many other media. According to the British culture critic Raymond Williams, culture is a "whole way of life." In the opinion of the eminent American anthropologist, Clifford Geertz, culture can be regarded as the "webs of significance that human beings spin around themselves." Therefore, in studying culture, we acquire a deeper understanding of the ways, patterns of behavior, values, arts and crafts, and the practices of everyday life of the people inhabiting a given culture. By examining the evolution of Indian cinema, we can attain a deeper understanding of Indian culture as well as the complex ways in which it has transformed itself over the years.

Indian cinema, like most other cinemas in the world, has evolved in response to various social, cultural, and political contexts and challenges. In order to deepen our understanding of the distinctiveness of Indian cinema, its characteristic features and privileged concepts, we need to pay close attention to the forces that have shaped Indian films and the transformations in theme and style that have taken place during the eight decades of its existence.

The honor of making the first Indian feature film by an Indian goes to Dhundiraj Govind Phalke. His *Raja Harischandra*, released on May 3, 1913, is generally regarded as the first Indian feature film. It was totally Indian in production and was shown as an independent and self-contained work in its own right. Phalke, from his early days, evinced a great interest in poetry, drama, and magic. One day, he happened to see a film titled, *The Life of Christ*, and was immediately inspired to make a similar film based on the life of Lord Krishna. As he watched the film, he said that images were flowing into his mind connected to various incidents in Lord Krishna's life. *Raja Harischandra* is a fifty-minute film that became instantly popular. It laid the foundation for a thriving film industry in India as well as for a vastly popular genre of mythological films. One can say that the mythological film narrating the actions of gods and goddesses is a unique product of Indian cinema in the way that the Western is of Hollywood. Apart from its own characteristic heroes and villains, gods and demons, immediately recognizable costumes and settings, this genre is informed by a powerful moral imagination in which good triumphs over evil, thereby reinforcing the moral order. This mythological genre maintains its broad appeal to this day.

The success of Phalke served to fortify the foundations of the film industry in India in that mass entertainment and moral edification were amalgamated in a way that ensured mass appeal. Once film as a popular mode of entertainment achieved a firm footing, film-makers began to make their presence felt in many other parts of the country. In 1918, the first feature film was made in the south. Based on the *Mahabharata*, it was called *Keechaka Vadham*. By 1920, that is, seven years after the first feature film was produced, Indian cinema was established on secure foundations. Eighteen films were produced in 1920, forty films in 1921, and eighty in 1925. As cinema began to grow more and more popular among the masses and the consequent establishment of a lucrative industry, several highly gifted film-makers made their debut—Suchat Singh, Dinesh Ganguli, Himansu Rai, and V. Shantaram are perhaps the most important among them.

A substantial number of films made during this early period were inspired by the two celebrated epics, the *Ramayana* and the *Mahabharata*. Many of the directors sought to invest their mythological narratives with a recognizable social message that had a deep relevance to contemporary society. The film-makers associated with this phase in the development of Indian cinema were Janus-faced; they looked back to the past admiringly and sought to reconnect with tradition at the same time they strove to draw on the resources and innovations of Hollywood. This simultaneous gaze on the Indian past and Hollywood continues to be a major preoccupation of popular Indian cinema.

Until the 1930s, all films that were produced in India were silent films. In 1931, the first Indian talkie, *Alam Ara*, was made. It was a costume drama dealing with fantasy and contained many melodious songs. *Alam Ara* was a stunning success. In that year, twenty-seven films were made in four languages: Hindi, Bengali, Tamil, and Telugu. The introduction of sound resulted in the ever-increasing emphasis on music and song. Indeed, music came to be regarded as a defining element in Indian cinema, and even to this day many movie-goers repeatedly go to see the same film because of its music. The phenomenal success of *Alam Ara* encouraged many other directors to follow in its footsteps. Music and fantasy came to be seen as indispensable elements of the filmic experience, and at times the emphasis on music was clearly overdone. For example, it is said by film historians that a film made in 1932 contained as many as seventy songs.

With the increasing popularity of this new medium of mass entertainment, film directors became more ambitious and aimed to reclaim newer territories for cinematic exploration. The 1930s saw the emergence of a deep interest in the investigation of social themes that had a vital bearing on everyday lives and practices. V. Shantaram, for example, in his film *Amritmanthan* (1934), held up for scrutiny the theological absolutions and ritualistic excesses that were gathering momentum at the time. *Devdas*, made in 1935 and which became a landmark in popular Indian cinema, sought to depict the self-defeating nature of rigid social conventionalism. *Jeevan Nataka* (1942), another important film produced during this period, had as its theme the harmful effects of modernization.

By about the 1940s, several interesting phenomena related to the development of Indian cinema could be observed. The art of cinematography had clearly established itself as a significant domain of pleasure and mass entertainment. Although cinema as an art form was undoubtedly an importation from the West, it had been indigenized very quickly and was successful in portraying characteristic Indian experiences and modes of feeling. Even in the very early stages of Indian film-making, this fact was uppermost in the minds of Indian film-makers. Phalke's writings on cinema and culture clearly tend to reinforce this view. By the 1940s, Indian film-makers had succeeded in forging a winning formula for success at the box office. This formula consisted of song, dance, spectacle, rhetoric, and fantasy. A very close and significant relationship between epic consciousness and the art of cinema had been established. Moreover, film was increasingly being recognized as a vital instrument of social criticism. It was against this background that film directors like V. Shantaram, Raj Kapoor, Mehboob Khan, and Bimal Roy had chosen to make their films that were to engender national as well as international interest. For example, Raj Kapoor became a celebrity not only in India but also in other parts of South Asia, Southeast Asia, East Africa, the Middle East and, as we noted above, the former Soviet Union. During the year that followed, a number of indubitably talented film directors like Bimal Roy, Guru Dutt, and Raj Kapoor were successful in winning increasing recognition for Indian cinema in many parts of the world.

This was also a period of great social change and trauma for the country. Even as India was moving rapidly towards capitalism and modernization, it was also coping with issues of nationalism, independence, and ethnic and religious tensions. The popular films produced during this period offer an interesting perspective on these changes. The 1950s are generally regarded by film historians as the *Golden Age* of popular Indian cinema, for by now cinema was firmly established as art, entertainment, and industry. However, cinema was still an urban art, and under the influence of cinema, a rapid urbanization of consciousness was taking place as never before. This, in turn, of course, facilitated the development of Indian cinema. Interestingly, some of the most well-known films produced during this period, such as *Awaara* (1951), *Pyaasa* (1957), *Kaagaz Ke Phool* (1959), and *Shree 420* (1955), dealt with aspects of urbanization.

While the popular tradition of Indian film-making was developing with undiminished vigor, by the mid-1950s, a distinctively artistic cinema took shape thanks to the pioneering efforts of the Bengali film-maker, Satyajit Ray. His *Pather Panchali* (Song of the Road), made in 1955, won for him and Indian cinema great international recognition and critical acclaim. It was given the "best human document" award at the 1966 Cannes film festival and went on to win prestigious awards at San Fransisco, Vancouver, Ontario, Stratford, and other film festivals. This film, based on a well-known Bengali novel, chronicles very realistically and sensitively the privations and hardships encountered by a Brahmin family living during the opening years of the present century. If popular Indian filmmakers looked towards Hollywood musicals for inspiration, Satyajit Ray's cinematic imagination was stirred by the work of Renoir and the neo-realists. *Pather Panchali*, along with *Aparajito* (Unvanquished), *Apur Sansar* (The World of Apu)—generally referred to as the Apu Trilogy—are regarded as masterpieces of world cinema. After making the trilogy, Ray went on to create such outstanding works of cinema as *Charulatha* (1964), *Devi* (1960) and *Jalsaghar* (Music Room) (1958). Satyajit Ray's cinema—with its emphasis on realism, psychological analysis, visual poetry, outdoor shooting as opposed to shooting in studios, and the use of non-professional actors and actresses—was in sharp contrast to the popular Indian cinema.

Ray, who a few years ago before his death was given the lifetime award by Hollywood, was primarily responsible for the creation of an internationally recognized artistic cinema in India. Very quickly, a number of very sensitive and gifted filmmakers—such as Mrinal Sen, Adoor Gopalakrishnan, G. Aravindan, Mani Kaul, Kumar Sahani, Buddhadeb Dasgupta, Gautam Ghose, Ketan Mehta, Aparna Sen, Govind Nihalani, Shyam Benegal, Vijaya Mehta, Shaji Karun, and others—emerged as able proponents of the strengths and potentialities of artistic cinema. This body of work is generally referred to as "New Cinema" as opposed to mainstream popular cinema. Another filmmaker—a contemporary of Ray—Ritwik Ghatak, has belatedly won national and international recognition as a film director who boldly sought to explore political themes using the strengths of the Indian artistic traditions.

Formative Forces

It is against this background that I wish to examine in more detail the forces that shaped Indian cinema and gave it its distinctiveness. In this regard, I feel that six forces that have had a profound impact on the growth of Indian cinema deserve closer analysis. They are:

- The two celebrated epics—the *Ramayana* and the *Mahabharata*.
- Classical Indian theater.
- The folk theater.
- The Parsi theater of the nineteenth century.
- Hollywood.
- Musical television.

Let us consider each of them in a little more detail in order to obtain a clearer picture of the forces that shaped and continue to shape Indian cinema and make it what it is.

The Epics

From the very earliest times, the two epics, the *Ramayana* and the *Mahabharata* have exercised a profound influence on the thought, the imagination, the outlook of the vast majority of Indian people. They were at the heart of classical Indian poetry, drama, art, and sculpture, feeding the imagination of various types of artists and informing the consciousness of the people. Therefore, it is wholly understandable that these two epics have had a profound impact on the growth of Indian cinema and invested it with a unique identity. This influence can be analyzed at four levels: themes, narratives, ideology, and communication. From the very beginning up until modern times, the two epics have continued to provide Indian filmmakers with plots and themes. The very first Indian film, *Raja Harishchandra*, was based on the *Ramayana*, and since then scores of filmmakers have mined these two epics for plots and themes. In addition, certain topics linked to notions of motherhood, patrimony, and revenge—as, for example, articulated in such films as *Mother India* (1957), *Awaara* (1951), and *Zanzeer* (1974)—are directly traceable to the two epics.

What is distinctive about Indian cinema can be best understood by examining its narrative structure. Despite the fact that Indian cinema was greatly influenced by Hollywood, the art of narration, with its endless digressions, detours, and plots within plots, remains unmistakably Indian. Here again, the impact of the two epics is very clear. Instead of the linear and direct narratives realistically conceived that we find in Hollywood films, Indian popular cinema offers us a different structure of narrative, which can most productively be understood in terms of the story-telling characteristic of the two epics.

We must consider next the question of ideology. Despite various attempts at social analysis, highlighting the disparities between the rich and the poor, emphasizing social justice, it can legitimately be said that Indian cinema, especially the popular variety, is committed to the maintenance of the status quo. The nature of the economics of film production and the distribution system being what they are, this is hardly surprising. For example, if we take a filmmaker like Raj Kapoor, who was extremely popular in the 1950s and 1960s, we see how he created a cinema of security that did not fundamentally challenge the status quo, by skilfully deploying melodrama, music and spectacle. This observation is equally valid with regard to most other filmmakers, past and present, in India. The central ideology underpinning the two epics is one of preserving the existing social order and its privileged values. As some commentators have pointed out, as a result of the *Ramayana* and the *Mahabharata* being ideological instruments employed for the expansion of values and beliefs endorsed by the ruling classes, there is also a significant way in which the Indian popular cinema legitimizes its own existence through a reinscription of its values onto those of the two epics.

The vital link that exists between the two epics and the mainstream Indian cinema can be usefully understood in terms of the idea of communication as well. The epics, which were transmitted orally, were closely related to ritual and folk performance. Being at the center of Indian culture, the two epics found articulation in a variety of ways and forms in local narratives. This promoted the proliferation of different narratives and performances within the solidly established matrix of the two epics. Similarly, the Indian popular cinema can be understood in relation to this analogy between the two epics and their endless performances. The discourse of the Indian popular cinema, as with the epics, has its basic text, and the different movies that are made can be likened to the diverse epic performances and narratives. Therefore, to discuss the interconnections between the two epics and popular Indian cinema in terms of themes, narrative, ideology, and communication is to open up an important dimension of the discourse of Indian cinema.

Classical Indian Theater and Folk Theater

Sanskrit theater constitutes one of the richest and most sophisticated expressions of classical Indian culture. It was highly stylized, and its mode of presentation was episodic, laying the utmost emphasis on spectacle. In it, music and mime intermingled creatively to fashion a distinct theatrical experience. It was highly conventional with specific rules governing the portrayal of character. We can identify a number of features of classical Indian drama that have an interesting bearing on the structure of popular Indian cinema. Owing to a number of causes, Sanskrit drama began to decline after the tenth century. Concurrently, numerous dramatic forms sprang up or matured in the various regions of India which, albeit of an unrefined nature, preserved and embodied the essence of the classical Indian theatrical tradition. The *Yatra* of Bengal, *Ram Lila* and *Krishna Lila* of Uttar Pradesh, *Tamasha* of Maharashtra, *Nautanki* of Rajasthan, *Bhavai* of Gujarat, *Terukkuttu* of Tamilnadu, *Vithinatakam* of Andhra, and *Yakshagana* of Karnataka are perhaps the most prominent among them. These various folk dramas, which are the work of untutored peasants, have one important feature in common, namely, that in varying degrees of competence and authenticity they embody in a living form the characteristic features of the classical Indian theater. The classical Indian theater, as well as these folk dramas, has played a formative role in the creation of the distinctiveness of Indian cinema. In the use of song and dance, humor, the structure of narrative, and the informing melodramatic imagination, these folk plays have had a far-reaching impact on the sensibility of Indian popular filmmakers.

The Parsi Theater

In exploring the different cultural forces that gave Indian cinema its distinctiveness, we need to consider next the influence of the Parsi theater that came into existence in the nineteenth century. The Parsis, who were rich, talented, and versatile, took up drama both in Hindustani and Gujarati. During the nineteenth century, the Parsis, who had gained a wide reputation as talented playwrights and skilful technicians, influenced theater in both North and South India. There were several Parsi theatrical companies that toured the country and performed before huge audiences. These dramatists possessed a practical cast of mind and were primarily motivated by commercial success. Stylistically, these plays displayed a curious mixture of realism and fantasy, music and realistic dialogue, narrative and spectacle, and stage ingenuity, all combined within the framework of melodrama. The Parsi theater, with its lilting songs, bawdy humor, bons mots, sensationalism, and dazzling stagecraft, was designed to appeal to the broad mass of people, and it did. Sophisticated, elitist critics used epithets such as "hybrid," "coarse," "vulgar," "melodramatic," and "sensational" to characterize these plays. The Parsi theater, which drew upon both Western and Indian forms of entertainment, constituted an effort to appeal to the lowest common denominator. These plays, of course, bear an uncanny resemblance to the generality of Indian films of the popular type. If the folk dramas were based in rural areas and presented the vocabulary of traditionally inherited theatrical expression, the Parsi theater signified an urban theater exposed to Western modes of entertainment and the production of pleasure. A close study of the Parsi theater and Indian popular films would bring to light the remarkable similarities in terms of theme, emotion, and styles of presentation.

Hollywood

Next I wish to call attention to the impact of Hollywood which is unmistakably present in most Asian cinemas. As I stated earlier, cinema is not an indigenous art form in the sense that it had its origin in the West; it is an importation from the West, and the impact of Hollywood has been deep and far-reaching. Asian audiences were enthralled by the magic of Hollywood cinema. This is certainly the case in India, where filmmakers were quick to adapt the ethos, resources, and inventiveness of Hollywood to suit local tastes, sensibilities, and outlook. Indian filmmakers were fascinated by the technical inventiveness of their Hollywood counterparts and sought to emulate them in creating colorful worlds of fantasy. The glamour linked to the star system and the commercial advantageousness of the studio system were also quickly adopted. Very often, story lines, characters and sequences were bodily lifted from Hollywood films and reshaped to suit indigenous sensibilities. Moreover, different film directors were attracted by different aspects and artists associated with Hollywood cinema. For example, Raj Kapoor was a great admirer of the work of Charlie Chaplin, Harold Lloyd, Laurel and Hardy, the Marx Brothers, and Buster Keaton. It was Chaplin, however, who engaged his deepest comic imagination. Raj Kapoor succeeded in very large measure in indigenizing Chaplin in a way that would appeal to the vast body of moviegoers.

Indian filmmakers were greatly fascinated by the Hollywood musicals. These musicals connected in some interesting ways to some of the characteristic features of theater and stage performance. The hey day of Hollywood musicals was from the 1930s to the 1950s, and many of the musicals made during these two decades had as their theme the world of entertainment itself. The plots of these films were to a large extent conventional. The music and spectacle facilitated the characters in the story, as well as the spectators, to indulge in flights of fancy. This aspect appealed greatly to the Indian filmmakers. While drawing upon Hollywood musicals, the Indian commercial cinema adopted a different strategy in that the plot was not employed to heal the split between narrative and spectacle. Instead, song and dance sequences were and are used as natural expressions of emotions and situations emerging from everyday life. The Indian filmmakers, while seeking to enhance the element of fantasy through music and dance and spectacle, created the impression that songs and dances are the natural and logical mode of articulation of emotion in the given situation.

Music Television

The sixth cultural force shaping the evolution of Indian cinema is modern musical television. This is a relatively newer force making its presence somewhere in the 1980s. Indian popular films produced in the late 1980s and 1990s show a remarkable impact of music television disseminated through international channels. The pace, quick cutting, dance sequences, and camera angles that one associates with modem musical television are increasingly impacting Indian cinema. One has only to examine the work of a film director like Mani Ratnam to realize the truth of this statement. As modern Indian audiences become more and more exposed to music television programs, with their innovative techniques of presentation, their sensibilities are obviously being shaped by them. Hence, it is hardly surprising that modern Indian commercial filmmakers, in order to retain their mass appeal, have chosen to draw more and more on the techniques of MTV. These, then, are some of the cultural forces that have shaped Indian cinema and given it its distinctive character.

Here we need to draw a distinction between "popular" and "artistic" Indian cinema. Popular films are seen and appreciated by the vast mass of Indian moviegoers; they are melodramatic, often musicals, with simple and clear moral messages. They represent a distinctively Indian approach to filmmaking. The artistic films, which constitute only about 10 percent of the total output, are realistic, often inspired by neo-realism, and seek to capture a segment of Indian reality. These are the films that get shown at international film festivals in London, Paris, Berlin, Venice, Tokyo, and Toronto. Internationally acclaimed filmmakers like Satyajit Ray, Mrinal Sen, Ritwik Ghatak, and Adoor Gopalakrishnan represent the artistic tradition. There are very clear differences in terms of theme, style, and technique between these two traditions of filmmaking.

Genres

The question of genres in Indian cinema is a fascinating one, and hence merits closer analysis. There are a number of genres associated with Indian popular cinema: mythological films which narrate fantasies associated with ancient times, devotional films that foreground the various forms of communication with divinity, romantic films dealing with erotic passions as they confront social convention, action films that focus on physicality, historical films with colorful costumes and settings, social films that highlight important social issues, and family melodramas that examine tensions within the matrix of the family are perhaps the most important among them. There is nothing particularly distinctive about these gems. What is distinctive are the ways in which these genres have been handled by Indian filmmakers, investing them with a characteristically Indian cultural imprint. These popular films have played a significant role in the construction of popular consciousness; they are the most dominant and pervasive force responsible for creating in the mind of the public the nature and significance of such notions as heroism, duty, courage, modernity, consumerism, and fashions. The relationship between Indian popular cinema and modernity is extremely close. Whatever the genre may be in which the filmic experience is communicated, all popular films display a culturally grounded engagement with modernity.

Mythological Films

The mythological films constitute a very significant segment of Indian popular cinema. They have their roots in the ancient past in the sense that they deal with characters and events taken from the distant past, very often as found in the epics and scriptures. The interactions among gods, demons, and other supramundane powers form the core of these mythological films. But they are, of course, not merely historical; they display the interplay between past and present. The very fact that these traditional stories are presented in a modern technologized medium like film underlines this fact. What is interesting about this mythological imagination is that it informs in interesting ways films based on modern experiences as well. The idea of purity and femininity as symbolized by Sita and the image of villainy emblematized by Ravana are not confined to stories depicting episodes from the *Ramayana*. They also can be seen in films dealing with contemporary experiences, like *Kartavya* (1985), as well.

Devotional Films

Let us consider next the genre of devotional films that bear a distinctly Indian imprint. One of the best films of this genre is *Sant Tukaram*, directed by V. Damle and S. Fathelal. *Sant Tukaram* was the first Indian film to win an award at the prestigious Venice film festival. The film deals with a poet-saint who lived in the seventeenth century. He holds the villagers enthralled by his songs of devotion. His wife is somewhat perturbed by his behavior and urges him to become more practical and attend to his family duties. Tukaram has also to contend with an envious priest and aspiring saint, Salomalo, who hatches various plots against him. Divine intervention results in the saving of Tukaram and the villagers from various catastrophes. As time passes, great leaders come from long distances to sit at the feet of the poet-saint. He is offered wealth and other material blandishments, but he rejects them. When the time comes for Sant Tukaram to leave, a divine vehicle is sent for him, and he invites his wife to join him. She says that she is quite happy with her home and children and decides to stay on earth. The story is converted into a memorable musical with devotionality at the center. A film like *Sant Tukaram* manifests the distinctiveness of Indian religious films.

Social Drama

Let us consider another genre, the social drama. This genre figured very prominently from the early stages of Indian cinema. What is interesting about the social dramas is the way in which social issues are portrayed cinematically with a distinct Indian flavor. *Achut Kanya*, made in 1936, is a popular early film that deals with a significant social issue that had been highlighted by national leaders such as Gandhi and Nehru. This film explores the relationship between a Brahmin boy and an untouchable girl. They cannot unite, as caste and religious barriers stand in their way. The Brahmin boy is compelled to marry someone he does not love, and the girl similarly is forced into a marriage she dislikes. They happen to meet at a village fair. The girl's husband, livid with anger, misconstrues this meeting and a fight ensues between him and his wife's former friend. This takes place on a level-crossing. A train comes down the track. The girl tries to separate the two combatants and is tragically run over and killed. Through the tragedy, the filmmaker highlights the problem of untouchability. Many of the early social dramas combine melodrama, spectacle and social commentary.

These traits are clearly discernible in more modern films as well. For example, Mani Ratnam's film, *Bombay*, made in 1995, generated a great deal of interest as well as controversy both within and outside India. It is a film that explores a highly sensitive issue: the relationship between Hindus and Muslims in India. The film narrates the love relationship between a young Hindu man and a young Muslim woman. The Hindu is a journalist. Their respective families are at first strongly against their union. They run away to Bombay and get married secretly. They have two children. Later their families come to accept them. Just as things were beginning to look bright for the couple, the fierce and bloody clashes between the Hindus and Muslims erupt in the city of Bombay. In this film, director Mani Ratnam has aimed to point out the self-defeating nature and futility of extremist thinking and xenophobia and the dire need to take a more rational approach to the question of religious loyalties and ethnic bonds in the context of a multiracial, multi-religious India. Once again the story unfolds within the framework of melodrama.

Romance

Romance and eroticism have always been vital ingredients in poplar Indian cinema. As with most other traditions of cinema in the East and the West, romantic films are extremely popular in India. This has been the case from the very inception of Indian cinema. Here again, one sees very clearly the shaping hand of culture. In comparison with Western films, for example, overt sexuality is prohibited in Indian films. Hence much of the sexuality is conveyed through suggestion, innuendo, culturally coded signs, and symbols. Here songs and dances play a very crucial role. In these romantic films, the sentiments expressed and the ways of expression are rooted in traditional culture. Indian film historians have remarked that in order to understand the real meaning of Indian romantic films, we need to reconnect them with traditional lore and cultural practices. In this regard, the *Laila-Majnu* tradition and *Radha-Krishna* tradition are highly relevant. In the *Laila-Majnu* tradition, love is seen as the essential desire of God; earthly love is regarded as a preparation for divine love. The absolute devotion of the woman to the man, marital fidelity, and loving secretly but without guilt are some of the important aspects of this tradition. The *Radha-Krishna* tradition, on the other hand, places emphasis on the here and now. The desire to capture the joy of each moment as it passes, and love seen not as something tragic, but tender and joyous, are some of the interesting ingredients of this tradition. At times, in popular films like, *Barsaat* and *Andaaz*, both traditions are present. What this brief discussion of the different genres that go to form popular Indian cinema points to is the importance of reading the cultural inscriptions and coded signs found in these different genres. It is indeed these cultural inscriptions that give Indian popular cinema its distinctive flavor.

Melodramas

Popular Indian films are, by and large, morality plays in which good triumphs over evil, and the social order, disrupted by the actions of immoral and villainous people, is restored through the power of goodness. Entertainment and moral edification are combined in a way that has a direct appeal to the vast masses of moviegoers. Hence, the idea of evil is central in the popular Indian filmic discourse. As was stated earlier, Indian popular films are basically melodramas. As commentators on melodrama have pointed out, the polarization between good and bad, the clash between moral and immoral, the antagonism between what is wholesome and evil, is an indispensable element of melodrama. The presence of evil is crucial to melodrama because melodramas seek to establish the authority of a moral universe. By vanquishing the villain and the evil he or she incarnates, melodramas seek to reassert the moral authority of a world that for an anxious moment looked as if it would fall prey to the dark forces of evil. When we examine popular Indian cinema this fact becomes very clear.

Style and Technique

I have discussed so far some outstanding features of the content of Indian films. Next, I wish to focus on style and technique that are as important as the content. Indian popular films are largely melodramatic musicals which, in a western sense, are non-naturalistic. The story does not progress in a linear fashion, but meanders with detours and stories embedded within stories. This circular form of narration is commonly found in classical Indian literature as well as folk literature. Song, music, and dance play a very important role in conveying the meaning of the story as well as generating preferred emotions. For example, songs fulfill a number of important functions within the filmic experience. They generate emotion; they underline moral messages; they convey eroticism and sexuality whose overt expression is disallowed on the screen; they create the mental framework for the reception of certain sequences. Similarly, dance sequences are important and fulfill several functions. Indian popular films are, at times, contemptuously referred to as *masalas* (spices). Just as one makes use of different spices in cooking, the filmmaker, it is contended, uses the standard elements associated with the given formula for success. Therefore, song, dance, melodrama, stunts, fights, cabaret sequences, exaggerated humor, are seen as vital ingredients. While there is much substance to this charge, and some of the worst films are nothing but that, it is important to bear in mind that the more talented and more successful popular filmmakers all have deployed these elements with remarkable ingenuity to create a cinema that bears the distinct stamp of Indian culture, in the way that Hong Kong filmmakers have used the styles and techniques and choreography of traditional martial arts to create a distinctively Chinese style of filmmaking.

Until recent times, when we talked about popular Indian cinema we generally referred to the Hindi films produced in Bombay. Hence, popular Indian films are referred to as "Bombay Films" or even "Bollywood." But this is no longer the case. A substantial number of popular films are now being produced in the South, as well in languages such as Tamil and Telugu. Despite the diversity of origin and the preferred language, it can fairly be said that popular Indian films display a body of readily identifiable characteristics in terms of theme, character, narrative, and style. Very little of these characteristic traits have changed over time.

Art Films

The artistic films differ sharply from the popular films. They are realistic, often ethnographic in nature, and seek to capture important aspects of Indian reality. By and large, they avoid glamour and glitz and concentrate on the use of cinema as an artistic medium capable of exploring important segments of Indian experience. They are usually, though not always, low-budget films and get shown at international film festivals. The artistic films, understandably, do not enjoy the kind of popularity that the popular films do. Very often, they are made in regional languages like Bengali, Kannada, and Malayalam and do not receive pan-Indian exposure. In terms of the commitment to serious cinema, to fashion cinema into a significant medium of artistic communication, to eschew the vulgarities and crudities one often associates with popular Indian cinema, film directors associated with the artistic tradition differ significantly from their counterparts in popular cinema.

Satyajit Ray

When we talk of artistic cinema in India, the name that immediately comes up is that of the late Satyajit Ray. This is because he was primarily responsible for fashioning this genre and winning international recognition for it. His film, *Pather Panchali* made in 1955, inaugurated this genre. In 1992, in a poll conducted by the magazine *Sight and Sound*, this film was voted one of the ten greatest films of all time. Ray is undoubtedly one of the great masters of international cinema. "The Song of the Road" portrays the childhood world of Apu, the little boy whose growth, triumphs, and defeats are recounted in the other two films that go to form the Apu trilogy. The second film in this highly acclaimed trilogy, *Aparajito* (Unvanquished), explores the world of Apu from the age of ten to seventeen, and the third film, *Apur Sansar* (The World of Apu), narrates the grown-up Apu's life, dealing with his marriage and fatherhood against the backdrop of urban life in Calcutta. These films offer contrasts in terms of theme, style, and technique to the popular films.

Satyajit Ray, who is generally regarded as India's greatest filmmaker, is considered, along with Renoir and de Sica, one of the greatest masters of humanist cinema. His film, *The Music Room* (1958), deals with an arrogant member of the declining aristocracy who displays both his refined taste and ruinous self-indulgence. *The Big City*, made in 1963, focuses on the impact of urbanization on consciousness and ways of living. Arati, a young girl, decides to take up a job, much against the wishes of some of the elders of the family, and this has a disruptive effect on the fictional household. The film, *Goddess*, made in 1960, is a study of religiosity and sexuality as they are curiously integrated. This film narrates, with great sensitivity and control of the medium of cinema, the life of a young woman as she strives to come to terms with her enforced upper-class idleness, suppressed artistic abilities, and an illicit love for her cousin. And similarly, his film, *The Home and the World*, made in 1984, based on a novel by Rabindranath Tagore, explores the question of female subjectivity against a political backdrop. These artistic films employ understatement and controlled emotion effectively, something totally absent in the popular tradition. There is a visual lyricism and a deep humanism that sophisticated audiences, the world over, find wholly satisfying. Satyajit Ray made a number of other equally significant films in the same mold that have won for him and Indian cinema great international acclaim.

Apart from Satyajit Ray, there are many other distinguished film directors associated with the artistic cinema. Among them, Ritwik Ghatak, Mrinal Sen, Adoor Gopalakrishnan, G. Aravindan, Kumar Sahani, Mani Kaul, Ketan Mehta, Aparna Sen, Shyam Benegal, Govind Nihalani, Shaji Karun, Vijaya Mehta, Buddhadeb Dasgupta, Gautam Ghose, and Aribam Sharma deserve special mention. All of them seek to capture on the screen a segment of Indian reality avoiding the glamour and the exuberance linked to popular cinema. Let us, for example, consider Adoor Gopalakrishnan's film, *Rat Trap*, which has won many prestigious awards. Unni is the pitiable protagonist of this film. He is a middle-aged man, unmarried, set in traditional ways, who is unable to come to terms with social change and make the necessary adjustments. He is demanding and authoritarian and is emblematic of the decaying feudal class. This film narrates his inability to adapt to social change and the catastrophic consequences that follow. As in Ray's films, in Gopalakrishnan's films, too, we find a remarkable use of understatement, the slow meditative camera that carefully weighs the meaning of the most mundane event, and the avoidance of flashy exuberance that one normally associates with popular cinema. Similarly, Gopalakrishnan, in his film *Face to Face*, examines the theme of self and modernization, this time from a different angle of vision. The protagonist of the film is Sreedharan. He is a leader of a trade union, a devoted Communist, and party worker, who is deeply respected by his colleagues. Suddenly, an unexpected change comes over his life. He begins to shun politics. The film deals with the love and death of Sreedharan. Once again the style of the film is reminiscent of the neo-realist tradition.

The two main branches of Indian cinema, the popular and the artistic, both relate to Indian reality and Indian consciousness, but in two recognizably different ways. In the case of popular cinema, the techniques are largely shaped by traditional narrative, while those of the artistic cinema are Western in nature and largely neo-realistic. However, in terms of the experiences explored, the artistic films are much closer to Indian reality than the popular films, which are largely fantasies. Themes like self and modernization, alienation, the clash of tradition and modernity and the ensuing confusion of values, Westernization, the problems besetting the institution of the family, the role of the artist in an increasingly consumer society, and the subjectivity of women—themes that are crucial to a proper understanding of contemporary Indian society—find expression in artistic cinema.

The styles of presentation and techniques associated with popular cinema merit our closest attention. In the case of artistic films, most often, all aspects of filmmaking are considered ancillary to the presentation of a realistic narrative. Hence, camera angles are largely at eye-level; lighting is unobtrusive; framing concentrates on the main action of a given scene; cuts are effected at logical junctures in the flow of action. Popular cinema, which grows out of different roots, never felt the need to follow this pattern of filmmaking. Indian popular filmmakers, with their inordinate love for dramatic camera movements, extravagant use of color, flashy editing, and self-conscious use of sound, depart significantly from the "invisible" style associated with artistic cinema. Indian popular film directors seek to create a different type of film and narrative discourse. The narrative closure, unobtrusive editing, continuity of image, shot centering, frame balance, and sequential editing adopted by the artistic filmmakers, aimed to create in the minds of the spectator the impression that what is being shown on the screen is an objective reporting of reality rather than a created sequence of events. On the other hand, the Indian popular film directors do not shy away from the fact that what is being shown on the screen is a creation, a fabrication, by the makers of the film.

Religion and Cinema

From the very beginning, religion has been a formative influence on Indian cinema, serving to invest it with a clear indigenous cultural imprint. India is a multi-religious society. There are many religions in India, such as Hinduism, Islam, Christianity, Buddhism, Jainism, Sikhism, and Zoroastrianism. However, the vast majority of Indian films that bear a religious imprint are Hindu in substance and outlook. Recall that D.G. Phalke, the originator of Indian cinema, was moved to make his first feature film, *Raja Harishchandra*, based on a Hindu religious story, after having seen a film on the life of Christ. I also pointed out how, from the very beginning, Indian filmmakers were drawn to the two highly venerated epics, the *Ramayana* and the *Mahabharata,* for stories and episodes, characters, themes, and values to be communicated through cinema. And this practice continues up to the present day: religion and cinema are inseparably linked in Indian culture. An exploration of this relationship will further clarify the distinct ways in which Indian cinema has evolved.

In order to understand the subtle nuances of meaning in Indian film texts that deal directly or indirectly with Hinduism, we need to pay attention to a number of different concepts linked to Indian cinema. These concepts, as they find articulation in Indian films, are somewhat different from the ways in which they have been formulated in the original classical texts; they have been reborn in the popular imagination. Among these concepts, those of *karma*, *dharma*, *maya*, *rebirth*, and renunciation are perhaps the most significant. Let us consider each of them very briefly(see Pandharipande and A. Sharma in this volume). The concept of karma states that every action has its inevitable consequences. A person's life is determined by the good deeds and the bad deeds that he or she has performed in previous lives. And the concept of karma is closely linked to the idea of dharma, or the moral code according to which good and bad deeds are assessed. The concept of karma is closely connected to the idea of rebirth and seeks to explain the sufferings and hardships that one has to encounter in day-to-day living. Although the concept of karma, as enunciated in classical Indian texts, is a very complex one touching on philosophical and moral issues, in the popular mind and in the popular cinema, it has been simplified to mean that some people are rich and others are poor, some people are healthy and others are not, because of the karma, the past deeds. Similarly, the concept of dharma, as formulated in traditional Indian texts, is a very complex one dealing with issues of social order, law, religious sanctions, morality, duties and obligations, and so on. However, in the popular imagination and popular cinema it has been simplified to mean the maintenance of the social order and the acceptance of one's prescribed status in life. The notion of maya, as understood by the public and as portrayed in cinema, is that the world in point of fact is illusory. There is a veil drawn between human beings and reality, and that veil is that of maya. This is tied to the concept of *moksha* (liberation). So long as human beings fail to realize that the phenomenal world is illusory and that there is a deeper and real world of the inner self, they will be caught in the never-ending cycle of rebirth and fail to achieve liberation. The idea of rebirth is central to the Hindu view of life. Human beings are born again and again until they realize the deeper actuality of life. The human soul remains the same; but it takes on and discards many bodily shapes. As the famous Hindu text, the *Bhagavadgita*, states:

> As a man casts off his worn-out clothes
> And takes on other new ones in their place,
> So does the embodied soul cast off his worn-out bodies
> And enters others new.

The idea of renunciation is also vital to the Hindu view of life and finds expression in many films. According to the Hindus, there are four stages in a person's life: First a student, second a householder, third a hermit, fourth a holy man or one who has renounced worldly life in order to search out the truth of existence. Hence the idea of renunciation is a highly prized virtue. In Indian films, then, mostly of the popular variety, these concepts appear and reappear in watered-down forms. In order to understand the distinctiveness of Indian cinema, we need to pay close attention to the ways in which these concepts inform Indian films.

The relationship between religion and cinema is best analyzed in terms of five significant categories. The first category includes those films that deal directly with religious stories mostly of a mythological nature. Here the two epics have proved to be a veritable treasure trove. For example, the ever-popular story of Rama and Sita, and the abduction of Sita by the cruel demon king Ravana, and the eventual defeat of Ravana and the establishment of the purity of Sita, finds repeated expression in Indian cinema. The second category includes films that deal with the lives of saints. A number of films have been made whose express purpose has been the portrayal of the lives of saints. *Sant Tukaram* (1936), a film to which I alluded to earlier, is a classic film that deals with the life of a saint. *Sant Tulsidas* (1939) also illustrates well the nature and significance of this form of filmmaking. Tulsidas is well known as the author who rewrote the original Valmiki *Ramayana.* To the utter dismay of his teacher, the poet spends his time with his beloved, Ratnavali. However, quite suddenly, and happily for everyone concerned, Tulsidas discovers his life's vocation amidst a storm. He becomes an ascetic, settles down in Benares, and starts to work on his translation. The film recounts these events within an established religious framework.

Films dealing with the lives of saints are made even today. In this regard, the film *Adi Shankaracharya*, made by G.V. Iyer, is most interesting. It is the first film made in Sanskrit. The film is set in Kerala in the eighth century and tells the story of Shankara, the best known Advaita Vedanta philosopher. The film opens with Shankara as a young boy living in a village and being introduced to the various Brahmanical rituals. After the death of his father, the boy is drawn toward philosophy. He wishes to explore the mysteries of existence. He leads the life of a mendicant and spends his time studying religious texts. He has little interest in marriage and in leading a household life. He tells his mother that he would remain a devoted son while leading the life of a mendicant scholar. His teacher entrusts him with the task of writing new commentaries to ancient religious texts. He excels at it. He becomes an ascetic and goes up to the Himalayas. He by now had acquired a widespread reputation as a man of learning. The film shows how, at the young age of thirty, he is successful in transcending all earthly illusions and becoming one with the Ultimate. G.V. Iyer made two other saint films, one dealing with Madhavacharya and the other with Shri Ramanujacharya.

Some of the saint films have had a profound influence on the thought and imagination of large numbers of people. For example, the film *Jai Santoshi Ma*, made in 1985 by Vijay Sharma, was instrumental in transforming a little-known goddess into one of the most popular icons. She attained a wide acceptance among modern working-class women toiling in the cities. Satyavati is the foremost disciple of the goddess, Santoshi, on earth. When Satyavati marries Birju, the wives of the three deities, Brahma,

Vishnu, and Shiva, feel terribly jealous and so create a string of problems and crises to test her faith and devotion. She emerges triumphantly from these tests, and with her faith shining as ever before. Consequently, Santoshi is admitted to the godly pantheon.

In the third category are all those films in which religious symbols, concepts, and images play a central role. As we look back on the evolution of Indian poetry, drama, sculpture, painting, and so on, we see that religious concepts and images have been at the heart of the communicated experience. Therefore it comes as no surprise that even in films that do not display any overt connection to religion, either in terms of plot or character, one observes the imprint of religious ideas and images. Let us consider a few examples. The unarguably popular film director Raj Kapoor can not be described as a maker of religious films. He was primarily interested in producing popular romantic musicals that were secular in outlook. But even in his films one observes the use of religious concepts. In his film, *Satyam, Shivam, Sundaram* (1978), there is a clear focus on the three virtues of love, truth, and beauty. Although this film, like his other films, deals with romantic love through song and dance, there is a conscious attempt here to make use of religious ideas to give more focus to the story.

Another example is Girish Kasaravalli's film, *Ritual*, which has as its structuring device a Brahmanic ritual called *ghatashraddha*. It is a ritual through which Brahmin widows were excommunicated. The film narrates the story of Yamuna, a young widowed daughter of a Brahmin scholar who is seduced by a school teacher and becomes pregnant. The close-knit Brahmin community is outraged. Yamuna's father decides to perform the ritual of *ghatashraddha* himself. She is abandoned by the community and her head is shaved. To be cast into widowhood is tantamount to falling from divine grace. To enjoy life as a widow is an irredeemable act. Hence, one who is guilty of such an act is excommunicated through this ritual, which simulates the rituals of death on a living person. As we survey Indian cinema, we are likely to find many films that are not overtly religious, but that contain religious concepts as a way of organizing the narrative.

In the fourth category I would like to include films that deal with specific religious cults. Like *Jai Santoshi Ma*, discussed earlier, another film that illustrates this point is *Ishanou*, made by Aribam Syam Sharma. This film portrays the Meitei cult prevalent in Manipuri in India. This cult, as depicted in the film, incites female adherents to join it by mystical powers that send clear signals to them that cannot be ignored. *Ishanou* deals with a family that lives peacefully and happily in the Manipuri valley under the protection and care of an old woman. All of a sudden, the young wife, Tampha, becomes possessed by the deity Maibi. She leaves her home to be an active participant in the Maibi sect. The film contains exotic dances and rituals that illustrate the power of this religious cult.

Finally, we have films that seek to offer critiques of religious institutions, practices, and understandings. There have been such films from the very early times. For example, films that aim to demonstrate the inequities of untouchability, from the perspective of an enlightened humanism, belong in this category. Here I would like to refer to two films that were made in more recent times: the film *Devi* (Goddess), by Satyajit Ray, and *Samskara* in Kannada. "Goddess" narrates the story of a young woman, Dayamoyee, and her recently widowed father-in-law, who comes to believe that she is Goddess Kali incarnate. His son, a university student, tries to persuade him through rational arguments that it is not so, but the old man is not persuaded. He transforms her into an icon for prayer in the village. Before long she acquires a reputation for curing people through miracles. Dayamoyee is herself now so flattered by all this attention and miraculous powers that she is reluctant to go to the city with her husband. However, things take an unexpected turn, for her own son dies of illness and totally disillusioned, she goes mad. The film deals with the Durga/Kali legend that is so widespread in Bengal. Satyajit Ray has sought to examine critically the over-zealousness associated with religiosity. *Samskara* in Kannada, which also offers a critique of this nature, has as its theme the dilemmas faced by an orthodox Brahmanic community.

These five categories of religious films are all related to Hinduism. There have been, of course, films made in India that deal with other religions as well. The film *Angulimal* (1964) directed by Vijay Bhatt, deals with a Buddhist theme. The film is based on a well-known Buddhist story about a ruthless robber. He is called Angulimal because he wears a garland of human fingers that he has cut off from his victims. He engages in bloody and cruel rituals with the misplaced hope of acquiring divine powers. He happens to encounter the Buddha and sees the futility of his actions. He repents his past deeds and decides to follow the compassionate teachings of the Buddha. Similarly, the film *Nanak Nam Jahaz Hai* (1968) deals with a Sikh religious experience. The film captures the teachings of Guru Nanak. Films exploring concepts and images associated with Islam and other religions, too, have been made.

Religion, of course, is a theme that is found in most cinemas of the world. However, the concepts as well as styles of presentation that characterize Indian religious films bear the distinct cultural imprint of India.

Film in India, as indeed in many other countries, has been both a reflector and a promoter of modernization. India, like most other countries, is caught up in the process of modernization. Some parts of the country are modernizing at a faster pace than others, but no part of the country is unaffected by it. Questions of rationality, secularism, individuality, science, and technology are foregrounded as never before. At the same time, rationality and the scientific outlook are not divorced from culture; in fact, they are products of culture. We find, then, not a uniform and universal modernity but rather a series of cultural modernities. This fact is important in understanding Indian society as well as Indian films. One sees in Indian films—certainly in those belonging to the artistic tradition, but increasingly in the popular tradition as well—a conflict between religious values and modernizing values. The clash between these values, as seen, for example, in the films of directors like Satyajit Ray and Ritwik Ghatak, displays a characteristically Indian form and configuration

It is useful to think of cinema as a cultural practice and to locate the films in that larger universe of discourse, exploring the complex ways in which the economic, cultural, political, technological, and ideological aspects are interconnected. India is not only the largest film-producing country in the world but also one that possesses a most distinct cinema. That distinctiveness can most usefully be understood both in relation to the cultural past and modern social transformations. Indian cinema opens a remarkable window onto Indian society and culture. It continues to shape values, belief systems, styles of living, and understandings of reality even as it provides large numbers of moviegoers with pathways to fantasy. Hence, as we celebrate the fiftieth anniversary of Indian independence, the achievements of both the artistic and popular filmmakers in creating a distinctly Indian cinema needs to be explored more fully.

Works Cited

Bamouw, Erik and S. Krishnaswamy. 1980. *Sholay—A Cultural Reading.* New Delhi: Wiley Press.

Dissanayake, Wimal. et.al. 1992. Toward a Theoretical Critique of Bombay Cinema. In *Cinema* vol. 6.

Miller, Barbara Stoler Tr. 1986. *The Bhagavad-Gita.* New York: Bantam Books.

Rangoonwalia, F. 1983. Indian Cinema: Past and Present in *Indian Film.* New York: Oxford University Press.

Chapter 34

Karnataka Music: A Synoptic Survey

R. Sathyanarayana

The art music practiced in Karnāṭaka, Andhra, Tamil Nadu and Kerala is occasionally called South Indian music and, frequently, Karnāṭaka music. Karnāṭaka has comprised large parts of South India at different times. This is especially true of the Vijayanagara empire which extended over large portions of the present Karnāṭaka, Andhra, Tamil Nadu and Kerala and was, in fact, called the Karnāṭaka empire. This coincided with a period which witnessed the development of the principles and practices crucial to the evolution of Karnāṭaka music. It is also a historical coincidence that these principles and practices were influenced by musicians, composers and musicologists who hailed from Karnāṭaka or migrated from Karnāṭaka. This is by no means to depreciate the great and immortal contributions of Andhra, Tamil Nadu and Kerala, which have made Karnāṭaka music what it is today.

Indeed, the name 'Karnāṭaka music' (as the name 'Hindustani music') is very recent in origin. The first available textual mention of the names Hindustani music and Karnāṭaka music dates from only 1917.

Origins of Dichotomy Between Hindustani and Karnataka Music

It is generally contended that Indian music was one integral art, being uniformly the same all over India untill about a thousand years ago. It does not seem plausible. However, similarity or identity in cultural values must have conferred some degree of internal logical and formal coherence on the practice of this art throughout the country. This was further promoted by the fact that the distinguishing feature of Indian music is the quadrology of rāga, tāla, prabandha, and vādya. This naturally admitted a uniform methodology, technique, and theory. However, every major treatise of Indian music contains indication of provincial contribution and variation. Sanskrit language has served as an instrument of integration in India from the earliest times. It has done so again in Indian musicology.

The emergence of Indian music in the northern and southern streams may be traced to both external and internal stresses. During the Sultānate regime in Delhi, the rulers patronized brilliant musicians from Persia and Arabia. Later, the Mughal emperors attracted musical talent from such distant seats of musical excellence as Iran, Turkey, Transoxania, Oxus, Mongolia, etc. (See chapters by Gopal and Habib, in this volume.) In consequence of such royal patronage and preference, influence of exotic cultures, and interaction and admixture of musical styles, there emerged a new shape of music forged on the anvils of the royal courts of Delhi and of the Bahmani rulers of Bijapur. Such inter-diffusion proceeded at three levels: creative material, theoretical core, and empirical usage.

Internal stress constituted the strongest reason for such decisive change. Dual tonality, permutability of the lowest degree of the scale, omissibility of the first and fifth degrees of the octave, inflexibility of classificatory schemes and prescriptions regarding the performance of ancient music because of ascribed Vedic origin, inability of the grāma-mūrchhanā-tāna-jāti apparatus—foundational to ancient Indian music —to accommodate the new creative and theoretical impact of exotic and folk sources, etc., brought about a morphic change in theory. It was during this period that basic transformations were taking place in the basic scale. The entirety of music came to be based on the lowest degree of the scale instead of on two tonics; intervals were flattened or sharpened to accord with contemporary usage; inevitability or nonomissibility of madhyama yielded to the invariance of pañčama as a result of which pratimadhyama (tritone) could be accommodated logically within the tonal organization of a single archetypal scale.

Karnāṭaka music commenced its emergence as a distinct entity from about the middle of the 14th century. By this time, Indian music was ripe to shed the burden of what was archaic or redundant and respond to contemporary needs. The North and the South achieved this each in its characteristic way. The reemergence of Indian music as Hindustani music took the form of absorption and assimilation of alien and invasive influences, that is, due to external logic. Renascence in the South flowed along the line of internal logic, as a reaction to internal stresses and the need to resolve self-generated tensions and reactionary trends. As a consequence, Hindustani music retains traces of exotic impress even today while Karnāṭaka music still retains an authentic and traditional descent. The overall result for both systems was a new lease on life. Both streams flowed in different directions, with occasional confluences and sometimes on conceptually parallel beds. A notable difference is that in Hindustani music evolution has occurred in more or less discontinuous conceptual changes and by individual genius and its schools, while, in Karnāṭaka music, conceptual changes in both theory and practice were gradual, and coherent in space and time, i.e. individual genius and enterprise became a logical extension or commentary on traditional heritage and were woven into a continuous pattern.

Transition

The sage Vidyāranya who inspired the founding of the Karnāṭaka (Vijayanagara) empire also probably founded Karnāṭaka music in this empire. The 13th and 14th centuries C.E. reveal a state of instability in the cultural history of South India. This is reflected in the political, social, religious, and cultural life of the people of this period, especially in music.

Sri Vidyaranya was the spearhead of this renascence and brought order into chaos in South India. The melodic aspect of our music was in chaos, torn between archaic, rigid prescription and permissive usage. Alien and exotic influences were also invading and inundating the hinterland of musical practice. In his *Sangitasara* he created the meḷa concept to replace the archaic grāma and its paraphernalia. This ushered in a new era through reorganization of the tonic, scalic temperament, synonymization of the trilogy, namely, key, tonality and modulation. This indeed heralded the evolution of Scalic reorganization and soon paved the way for temperament of intervals, the standardization of the corpus of intervals in contemporary usage into twelve semitones, and their exact representation on four forms of scalic organization (meḷa) on the Vīṇā. This led to the concept of grouping of rāgas. Thus the seeds were sown for the development of the trilogy—svarameḷa, vīṇāmeḷa and rāgameḷa—in terms of which Karnāṭaka music was to evolve in the following centuries. Similar chaos had resulted in tāla by proliferation, same names with different structures, same structures with different names, use of the indeterminate pause (virāma), variable size of the laghu, etc. This problem was solved by the Haridāsas of Karnāṭaka, who developed a simple, comprehensive and compact system of tālas in the 15th-16th centuries. The compositional forms, prolific in their 76 major structures and over 3000 subvarieties, were also replaced by their present analogues by the Haridāsas, the great musical trinity, and a host of other composers.

Evolution

Karnāṭaka music maybe said to have emerged as a distinct entity when it developed an independent form and content. This was achieved through innovation, by aligning practice with the already existing framework of theory as its extension or modification. This technique is native to the genius of Indian culture and is found applied in every aspect of its civilization.

Thus a differentiating conceptual frame was developed with a supporting structure of technique for its expression; differentiating content was developed, on the other hand, a corpus of compositional forms. Thus the origins of Karnāṭaka music are analyzable in terms of the quadrology, namely rāga, tāla, prabandha, and vādya. The first three are included in the principle of čaturdanḍī (literally, four pillars,) namely Gīta, ālāpa, thāya, and prabandha. This principle was first enunciated by Gopalanayaka in the 14th century; it is a distinguishing feature of Karnāṭaka music and remained its guiding principle till about the 18th century.

Raga

All melodic content of Indian music, comprising the above čaturdanḍī, stems from rāga. Rāga is a melodic situation which has a specific or characteristic (musical) expressiveness; it arises out of melodic movement. The specificity of its expressiveness accrues from the way its tonal material is employed. The tonal material may be analyzed into ten vital characteristics (prāṇas) such as, the notes of attack, rest, initial and medial pauses, recurrence and nonrecurrence, range in the upper and lower registers, specified note-affinities, gamaka, and so forth.

The earliest available definition of rāga is found in Mātanga's Brchaddeshi (281):

yosau dhvani viśeṣastu svara varṇa vibhuṣitah
rañjako janačittānām sa rāgah kathito budhaih

The following elements in the definition are of special interest: The rāga has aesthetic appeal (rañjaka) for (common) people (jana) and not the elite. It is a special kind of sound (dhvani-viśeṣa), i.e. sound other than one employed for transactional or communicative purpose; sound which is not normally found (organized) in the referential world, but is abstracted, idealized or refined into a musical symbol. Thus the singing voice is different from the speaking voice or voice used for communication or nonaesthetic expression; sounds of musical instruments are different from those of the phenomenal world. Dhvani means suggestiveness in poetry. Similarly, dhvani in rāga is expressiveness rather than expression. It suggests meanings (autonomous to music) which transcend those which are revealed by the mere sound sequence. Indeed, the rāga begins (because of dhvani) where the melodic structure and dynamics end. The specific aesthetic experience characteristic of a given rāga is generated by dhvani. It is the total experience of the rāga, not an ingredient or component. In respect of the interaction between musician and rāga listener, an interesting parallel may be noticed in a passage from Mātanga which also defines rāga thus:

> svara varṇa viśeṣeṇa dhvani bhedena vā punah
> rajyate ena saččittam sa rāgah sammatah satām.

The terms 'sat' and 'satām' are synonymous with 'sahṛdaya' i.e. an aesthetically susceptible listener.

When nonverbal, the expression of its meaning through dhvani may be regarded as rāga. The use of such sounds in varying durations such as druta and vilambita is essential to rāga because, other things being equal, it is this variability which bestows multiplicity of possible expressions, each of them conferring specificity or individuality. The concept of sphōṭa from language can be readily extended to rāga because, although the meaningful elements (svaras in music, words in languages) occur in a sequence, the meaning of the whole may be perceived in a "burst" (sphōṭa) only at the end of the final symbol: in other words, dhvani conveys the whole sense of the rāga, in a burst and not in stages or phases.

Again, the phrase 'svara-varṇa-vibhuṣitah' in the above definition merits attention. There is an apparent redundancy in this passage because the act of singing melodic phrases includes 'svara'. It is not so; for svara here indicates the primary aesthetic appeal which it affords in its own autonomy. This includes those selements of a musical note which contribute to its ranjakatva, e.g. snigdhatā, anuraṇana, śrutyanantarabhāvitva, gamaka, dūraśrāvyatā, etc., which constitute its psychoacoustic attributes. I designate these with the term 'sonemes' on analogy with the linguistic symbol, phoneme. Next, varṇa signifies melodic kinematics, i.e., the continuous locus of a moving sound. It is this sound which assumes the character and role of the ten vital characteristics, such as raha, amśa, nyāsa etc., and elucidates the rāgatva of a rāga. This is why the svara per se and its movement, varṇa, are both included in the definition. Both have the power of beautification. 'Vibhuṣitah' thus suggests this power of suggested meaning, i.e. beauty, and is thus a semantic dimension of dhvani.

The foregoing is relevant because three of the caturdanḍī, namely, ālāpa, thāya and prabandha, rest on the foundation of the first danḍi, namely, rāga, in Karnāṭaka music.

Melodic apparatus: Intervals

Rāga inheres the scale. The scale is divided into seven primary steps or degrees called svaras: sadja, ṛṣabha, gāndhāra, madhyama, pañčama, dhaivata and niṣāda. These are regarded in theory as having intervals which are made up of a fixed number of subdivisions called śrutis. Thus the seven notes have 22 śrutis, allocated thus: sadja (sa) (4), ṛṣabha (ri) (3), gāndhāra (ga) (2), madhyama (ma) (4), pañčama (pa) (4), dhaivata (dha) (3) and niṣāda (2). These notes are defined as śuddha when they manifest on the 4th, 7th, 9th, 13th, 17th, 20th and 22nd śruti respectively. These become vikṛta (modified) in two ways: (1) by assuming an interval measured by a different number of śrutis; (2) by occupying a different śruti than the one of its śuddha position. Thus sa became čyuta when it manifested on the third śruti instead of the fourth; in this case, ni became kaiśiki by manifesting on the first instead of the 22nd śruti. Similarly sa was 'ačyuta', another modified form, when it manifested on the fourth śruti itself but niṣāda occupied the second śruti to become kākāli. Thus in the first sa becomes vikṛta both because it occupied a different śruti and has a different interval, i.e., two śrutis. In the second, it becomes vikṛta even though it is still on the fourth śruti because it has only two śrutis. It may be noticed that the sa is allowed an interval of two or four śrutis, but not of three. Further, the first and second śrutis become common, or sādhārana, by this technique of modification. Hence this was called sadja-sādhārana. Madhyama sādhārana operated similarly. In the first technique, ga progressed (from the 9th) to the 10th śruti while ma regressed (from the 13th) to the 12th śruti. In the second, ma remained on the 13th śruti but ga occupied the 11th (i.e., the second śruti of ma), to become 'antara'. Thus again the interval ga-ma could be only of two or four śrutis but never of three and the 10th and llth śrutis were 'common' to both notes. Ri was śuddha if it was on the seventh śruti and sadja occupied the fourth śruti. It was vikṛta if it was (still) on the seventh śruti but sadja regressed to the third śruti (in sadja sadharaṇa) and thus had an interval of four, instead of three, śrutis. Similarly, dhaivata was reckoned śuddha if it occupied the 20th śruti and if pañčama was on the 17th śruti; it became vikṛta even if it as still on the 20th śruti but pañčama had regressed (as in madhyama grāma) to the 16th śruti and had thus itself become vikṛta pañčama.

It may be noted in the foregoing that svara-vikṛti is reckoned in two alternative ways, reckoning its position or distance from the lowest degree (sa) of the scale and reckoning it relative to the just precedent svara. This was scientific and committed to the grāma-mūrchhanā system but cumbersome. As will be seen presently this was thoroughly revised and reformed in the 15th-16th centuries. The svaras were regarded as generated by or from the śrutis which fulfilled two important theoretical purposes—they provided depth or interval, i.e., extensivity, to the svara. Secondly, each note was regarded as the manifested māturity of a locus of a moving point of sound, cumulatively gathering musical expressiveness progressively as it proceeded spirally upward through its śrutis and in doing so acquired different degrees and color, thus acquiring the individual (musical) personality symbolized by the particular svara.

Melodic Apparatus: Grama-Murchhana-Tana

The seven svaras were sequentially organized into a parents scale called grāma which epitomized all scalic concomitants such as mūrchhanā, tāna, etc., elements of melodic movement such as varṇa and alamkāra, and expressive potential such as vādi, etc. Three such parent exemplars or archetypal scales were postulated in ancient Indian music, namely, sadja grāma, madhyama grāma and gāndhāra grāma. They were so named because the respective notes determined the character of the entire melody body comprised by them; they constituted the initial, terminal and most frequent notes and served as nuclear centres to which the respective melody corpus naturally gravitated. The gāndhāra grāma became obsolete ('went to heaven') because its intervals became very much at variance with those of usage. Sadja grāma was defined as the ordered intervallic arrangement in which the svaras occupied the above mentioned śuddha positions; the madhyama grāma differed from it in only one respect, viz. its pañčama occupied the 16th, not 17th śruti. This differentiating śruti was called pramana śruti. By modal shift of tonic, that is, by rotating the same scale around each of the seven notes separately in ascent and descent, maintaining the same mutual intervallic relations, seven derived scales called mūrchhanās were obtained in each grāma, thus totalling fourteen. By omitting one of a few prescribed notes in each mūrchhanā, hexatonic scales called ādāva-tānas were derived. By omitting the note causing ādavatva and its consonant note, pentatonic scales called auduva-tānas were obtained. Eighty four tinas were thus derived. The mūrchhanā, sadava-tāna, and auduva-tāna were employed as theoretical apparatus to compare, derive or create sampūrna (heptatonic) sādva and auduva rāgas which were in vogue in contemporary music. Besides these śuddha tānas, other permutations and combinations of different numbers of notes were also systematically derived. They were called kūta-tānas. These served as devices in theory to compare melodic phrases in musical practice.

Raga Scalic Revolution

The beginning of Karnāṭaka music are found in a conceptual metamorphosis in rāga. This may be traced to the obsolescence of grāma. The 14th century witnessed trends which culminated in the 15th century in which both grāmas fused into one parental archetype which retained the name of sadja grāma but not its paraphernalia. This merger was a fait accompli by the 16th century. The sadja grāma became the standard for definition, comparison and creation of melodic material. This also resulted in the gravitation of the entire corpus of melody uniformly to a unicentric focus, namely, the lowest note of the scale. This conferred an upward tendency on melodic movement.

Several changes inevitably followed from this. The choice of a single note—the lowest note—as the reference pitch (dhara śruti) greatly modified the contours of melody. Madhyama was no longer indestructible (avināaśi) i.e., nonomissible, in melodic structures; its nonomissibility arose from its determination and differentiation of the grāma in which the music was composed. Since there was no longer such a need, it yielded place to pañčama which now became prakṛti or invariable (i.e., without modification). These and other changes were followed by scalic temperament; musical intervals were realigned: vikṛta pañčama of madhyama grāma was incorporated as prati(nidhi) madhyama into sadja grāma by regressing to the 15th śruti, ṛṣabha and dhaivata became vikṛta by assuming four śrutis each. Antara gāndhāra and kākali niṣāda now possessed each an interval of five, not four, śrutis and occupied respectively the 12th and 3rd śrutis instead of the tenth and second. The tritone, now called pratinidhi madhyama had an interval of six śrutis. Similarly, sādhārana gāndhāra occupied the tenth śruti (with three śrutis and with no regression of madhyama to the 12th śruti); kaiśiki niṣāda was similarly an interval of three, not two, śrutis occupying the first śruti and no longer required sadja to occupy the third śruti, so that sadja and madhyama could now have an interval of three śrutis each, which was previously proscribed. The maximum size of an interval was raised from four to six śrutis, and the minimum reduced from two śrutis to one.

A major breakthrough in the development of the melodic structure in Karnāṭaka music occurred in the full exploitation of the denominational potential of a musical note in terms of contextual extension. This was achieved through two principles, namely, alternative denomination (paryāya tattva) and representative expression (pratinidhi tattva). According to the former, the same given degree of pitch (svara sthāna) could assume the character of a precedent or subsequent note depending on the context. For example, the note on the ninth śruti functions as (pañčaśruti) ṛṣabha if the next lower degree is sadja and the next higher degree is gāndhāra. But the same would function as śuddha gāndhāra if the immediately precedent note is ṛṣabha (seventh śruti) and the immediately following note is madhyama (13th or 15th śruti). Thus the vocabulary of melodic expression is thus considerably enlarged, namely, 16 denominations for 12 svarasthānas. According to the latter, a given degree of pitch in the scale could substitute for a theoretically or conventionally prescribed but empirically obsolete note, e.g., ancient antara gāndhāra was replaced by a note newly named čyuta-madhyama-gāndhāra (12th śruti), so named because it acquired the denomination of gāndhāra at the position of the (ancient) čyuta-madhyama. The latter represented the former. This principle ingeniously replaced the deadwood of the ancient antara gāndhāra and kākali niṣāda which were prescribed to be used very sparingly.

Raga Classification

Another revolutionary change which helped to crystallize Karnāṭaka music into its modern form is innovation in rāga classification. But by far the most productive scheme of rāga classification was derived from Vidyāraṇya's meḷa concept. He divided all extant rāgas into groups (meḷa), such that the members of any given group bore physically similar (i.e. intervallic) structures and materials and each group differed from the rest. The most typical, representative or leading rāga from each meḷa was chosen so that it had all the seven notes (in ascent, descent or both or in toto) and was designated the meḷakartā (group maker) and the respective group was defined as being contained in this meḷa: the meḷa was defined as the ordered arrangement of the seven notes. The meḷa possessed no character of the rāga, but could, when the ten vital characteristics were judiciously bestowed, become a rāga also. (This scheme directly inspired into existence the samsthāna or thāta scheme of classification inaugurated by Hṛdayanārāyana in his *Hrdayakautuka* and *Hrdayaprakasa* and followed by Ločana in his *Ragataramgini* in Hindustani music). Vidyāranya's meḷa concept was worked out in detail in the 16th and 17th centuries. In Rāmāmātya's and Poluri Govinda's time this was firmly engendered in both theory and practice. In fact, Punḍarīka Viṭṭhala proposes a highly logical, practicable and adequate mathematical scheme of deriving 90 meḷas, while Somanātha derives a comprehensive scheme of 960 meḷas based on the permutation of svarasthānas. Both schemes employ the principles of paryāya and pratinidhi explained above. Venkatamākhin employed the same principles and derived the scheme of 72 meḷas. Owing to the purely historical accident that Pundarīka Viṭṭhala and Sāmanātha expounded their schemes in places in which not Karnāṭaka music but Hindustani music prevailed and the Venkatamakhin scheme was adopted by the Musical Trinity and their schools, the latter became enduring and is now firmly established as an indivisible and indispensable part of Karnāṭaka music.

An interesting attempt was made in ancient Indian music to establish theoretical, comparative standards in the form of generalized melodic frames called jātis. A jāti was defined in terms of the physical concomitants of melodic expression such as the vital characteristics of rāga mentioned above. Seven pure and 11 modified jātis were described by Bharata and Dattila for this purpose. By manipulating the elements of melodic expression by permutation, the frames were generalized and it was possible to comprehend several rāgas at once in a single jāti. The meḷa concept was augmented by other associated concepts and slowly, but inexorably, evolved into its present status. It originated as an organization of all the seven notes in a regular sequence; this was realized in the form of rāga (the meḷakarta) such that it was sufficient if the ārōha (ascent) plus the avarōha (descent) together had all the seven notes; but it was not necessary to have all seven notes in ascent and in descent separately. The second significant development came in the 18th century when consensus of musicological thought required that rāga forming the meḷa should be both avakrasampūrṇa and rāgānga. Meḷakarta and its derivative rāgas are at present related as progenitor (janaka) and progeny (janya). This was inaugurated in the 16th century by Punḍarīka Viṭṭhala and was revived by a group of musicological treatises, e.g. *Ragalakshanam* (anonymous), *Sangitaratnakara* (anonymous, Kannada), *Samgrahacudamani* (Govindacarya), *Sangitasara samgrahamu* (Tiruvenkatakavi) and others in the 18th century. All rāgas are derived today from the respective meḷakartas in terms of the intervallic material employed; according to the number of notes employed, a rāga is classified as pentatonic (auduva), hexatonic (ṣāḍava), and heptatonic (ḍāṟpūṭnā). A rāga is classified as avakra if it does not have prescribed curved phrases in its melodic movement and as vakra if it has. Rāgas are further classified on the criterion of their intervallic affiliation with the exemplar meḷakarta. A janya rāga is defined as upānga if it does not employ any note which is not found in its parent meḷakarta. If it does, it is bhāsānga, thus seeking to incorporate a shade of expressiveness which is not native to its meḷa. Kriyānga rāga possesses an action-evoking affective content.

Karnāṭaka music has several rāgas of which two or more bear a close similarity, or even identity, in their scales. The differences in their musical personalities arise because of differences in the treatment, amśa (or jīva) svaras, special sañčāras (melodic phrases), same notes treated to different gamakas, peculiar phraseology, limitation to particular registers, special affinities between two or more notes, difference in nyāsa svara, difference in the degree of strength or weakness of the same or corresponding notes, etc. There are few — if any, miśra rāgas in Karnāṭaka music. They are formed by inserting several bhāṣānga (accidental) svaras and specific curvatures, e.g. Ahiri. They differ from miśra rāgas of Hindustani music in one important respect: specificity of phrase, curvature or bhāsānga svara in such rāgas is not associated with this or that rāga as a component as is done in their Hindustani analogues. That is, they are not regarded as composed of avayava-rāgas but as single wholes. Perhaps they should be called samkīrṇa rāgas.

Mutual Influence: Family Classification

The two streams of Indian music confluence again and again, draw mutual succour and flow in augmented vigour again in their own separate courses. Three such instances may be noted in the context of rāga: family classification, deification or iconification, and rāgavelā (appropriate times for rendering rāgas). Some of the earliest mentions or applications of these are found anterior to the dichotomization of Indian music and some in the environment of Karnāṭaka music; these were operative in the practice of Karnāṭaka music for a comparatively short time but migrated to the North and entrenched themselves firmly in Hindustani music from about the 16th century till the beginnings of the 20th century. Rāgavelā is still a strong force in today's Hindustani music. Because of the influence they exerted on Hindustani music, their emergence and history in Karnāṭaka music will be briefly examined here.

Ragavela

The system of classifying rāga on the criterion of similarity or proximity of aesthetic import (bhāva) is as ancient as grāma-rāgas and is coeval with them. This means that the intervallic content of rāgas derived from, or otherwise related to, an archetypal rāga often differed from one another. Besides, ancient authorities of the pre-Mātanga era such as Śardula, Yastika, Durgaśakti and Kaśyapa have named rāga in both masculine and feminine gender. Such usage continues uninterrupted in both Hindustani and Karnāṭaka music.

However, an explicit division of rāga into male and female appears in Indian music as late as the 14th century. These references are found in poetry written in Kannada and Telugu. Such family classification, based on nonintervallic affiliations, such as affective or aesthetic, was adopted in Hindustani music with gusto from the 16th century and was a strong musicological force till the beginning of the present century when it was completely replaced by thala classification.

Mutual Influence: Raga Iconification

In a sense, the gender classification into male, female or neuter rāgas or family classification into husband, wife, son, daughter-in-law, and servant-maid rāgas is natural, logical, and suitable to an art form like music. Abstraction of the concrete and concretization of the qualitative and quantification of the qualitative are fundamental traits of the human mind. Rāga iconification may be therefore regarded as an endeavour to translate, transpose or transform an experience lying in one sensory (aural) area into another (visual) through conceptual and imagery association in a creative context.

These two branches of rāga classification are basic facets of the musician's creative mind. Of these, the one based on physical, e.g. intervallic, similarity or affiliation is critical, analytical, and extrovert. The other, based on similitude of aesthetic import, is imaginative, contemplative, synthesizing, and introvert in endeavour. The first is a discipline or śāstric approach and the second a creative one. Most authors choose one or the other in describing ragas; there is no dearth, however, of authors who employ both schemes.

Concretization and iconification have been used extensively in Indian music. Deification of svaras is elaborately treated in many treatises. The principle of iconification was extended to rāgas. Thus both rāgamālā paintings and contemplative texts seeking to iconify rāgas are available in both Karnāṭaka music and Hindustānī music from before the 16th century. It must be remembered that this is not merely a pictorial model of an aural experience but an instrument of personification, or of creating or expressing personality. Rāga is here regarded as a definite person. The chief objective of an iconifying contemplative verse (dhyānaśloka) or rāgamālā painting is to evoke a central mood of a person who is in complete harmony with nature and his/her environment. Every person may be characterized with an underlying, enduring, dominant mental state (sthāyī bhāva) which differentiates him/her from all others and confers specificity and speciality.

Depending on time, environment, and internal stimulatory factors, his/her mental state is in a continuous flux against the background of the above-mentioned enduring state. This flux maybe designated sanĉārī bhāva. Likewise every rāga maybe considered to have a distinct personality characterized by its intervallic content, gamaka, etc. as also its above-mentioned vital characteristics. The technique underlying rāga iconification is to build up an imagery on an anthropomorphic model. Therefore, it employs such apparatus, method, etc. of delineation and limning as are best suited to depict this central, enduring, dominant mental state (sthāyī bhāva). The image is then built up from symbolic material such as natural setting and environment, train of attendants, associates and their acts of service, posture, movement, vehicle, weapons, pet animals, colour, line, shading, costumery, jewellery and such other beautifying, emphasizing, or enhancing agents, etc. These may be regarded as vibhāvas (determinants, referential concomitants). Bhāvas (general mental states) and anubhāvas (consequent states) endow the sthāyī bhāva with emotivity. This frame is sufficiently capacious to be filled with sanĉāri bhāvas (dynamic, fluctuating mental states). Contemplation of, and implict involvement with, the iconifying description or of the rāgamālā picture can induce inspiration or stimulate perception of the tributaries of bhāvas and anubhāvas as well as the mainstream of sthāyī bhāva at the sensory level in the expressive flow of rāga during its performance. For such aural and visual descriptions constitute the symbols of the primary and secondary components of the aesthetic personality of a rāga. When aural experience transcends to the contemplative or spiritual stratum, it is extrapolated on to another medium imaged as an emotive or aesthetic situation personalized and expressed as such with the aid of appropriate symbols, apparatus, and techniques. When colour, line, light and shade and perspective are employed, the end product is a visual presentation called rāgamālā painting. In course of time this kind of painting acquired a distinct tradition and lineage; it then branched out into Rajputāna, Mughal, Kāngra, Bengali, and other styles. Rāgamālā paintings have secured a permanent niche in Indian painting and recognition in the comity of international painting.

Rāga iconification and deification originated of course as a cultural endeavour based on an aesthetic urge or psychological need. But it also developed religious or theological dimensions with spiritual overtones. In fact, Sōmanātha states explicitly that iconified rāgas also partake of divinity. Srikanṭha elevates rāga iconification to dogma: howsoever skilled a musician may be, he shall not obtain the direct and oblique fruits promised in sangitsastra unless he/she contemplates these deities or icons; this is why the sages have composed the dhyānaślokas. I have discussed rāga-family classification and rāga inconification in Indian music at some length elsewhere.

Mutual Influence: Ragavela

In India, implicit in musical practice is a theory from very early times that a rāga is optimally effective when performed at a particular time of day or night or in a particular season. The following assumptions seem to be implicit in such rāga-time theory:

> (i) Human mental states bear a rhythmic correspondence, i.e., they recur periodically with biorhythm and with diurnal cycles and seasonal cycles. (ii) Such correspondence is general; it extends over a range of mental states and a range of time. (iii) A rāga is stimulated by a mental state in the listener. Such rāga-induced states bear a one-to-one correspondence with or approximate to the states mentioned in (i). (iv) The mental state experienced by a performer or listener as mentioned in (iii) in a range mentioned in (ii) becomes individuated by a process of personal emotive/affective association. (v) The quality of mental state mentioned in (iii) is related to the physical parameters of the rāga such as intervals, gamaka, the ten vital characteristics. etc. (vi) By manipulating the physical parameters of the rāga, it is possible to simulate or emphasize the semblance or shade of an emotive state (rāga) such as vīra, karunā, sṛngāra, etc.

In accordance with this (rāgavelā) theory the period between two successive dawns is divided into eight watches (yāma) of three hours each, more broadly into forenoon (pūrvāhna), noon or midday (madhyāhna), afternoon (aparāhna); or the time may be simply indicated as dawn (prabhāta), evening (sāyam), night (niśā/rātri); rāga performance may be prescribed in respect of one of these; there are also rāgas which are fit to be performed at any time, i.e. at all times. Besides these narrow widths of time, longer periods such as particular season are also prescribed for performance of rāgas. Rāgamālā paintings conform to such time prescriptions, if any. Today there is a more or less rigorous conformity to this in Hindustani music, largely by conventional sanction; for the theory still remains to be tested with systematic experiment and observation. This convention inheres a serious disadvantage, viz. rāgas which are prescribed to be performed late at night or very early morning are eroded from usage for lack of exposure. An elaborate rāgavelā theory relating performance time of rāgas to svaravikṛti (śuddha/komal) has been formulated by Bhatkhande and Karnad.

The theory of rāgavelā is a survival from the predichotomy period in Indian music for such time prescriptions are found in many major treatises of this period. It prevailed widely in Karnāṭaka music also till relatively recently. This is supported by numerous literary references in Kannada.

Tala: Ancient Practice

Tāla is the substrate of sangīta, i.e. singing, instrumentation and dancing. Any music or dance event may be precisely located within defined time limits with the help of tāla. It performs two functions; it measures out a composition in time; it establishes correspondences in various events occurring at a given moment. The first is accomplished through consecutivity and the second through simultaneity.

Tāla is defined as kāla (time); it operates through a fixed span of time which is neither too long nor too short and which progresses continuously in a spiral. Each cycle is called āvarta. This is formed of a number of component structural units, each called anga, literally, organ. Each anga commences with an accent (beat, ghāta.) The number of each anga and the order in which the angas occur are fixed in a tāla. The sum of the durations of all the angas is the avarta. Each tāla differs from others in its angas in the āvarta.

In ancient India sangīta (gīta, vādya and nṛtta) was classified into mārga and desī. The marga variety was discovered by the gods (and therefore flowed in a beginningless tradition), to be employed for spiritual or religious edification. The desī form of these arts, on the other hand, was inspired by popular taste and changed from place to place and time to time.

Tala Revolution

As in rāga and prabandha, the 15th-16th centuries were critical to the evolution of tāla. System and organization were brought into tāla theory at this time with the enunciation of praṇa by Ačyutarāya, who was probably inspired by Aṣṭāvadhāna Somanārya. The essential elements of this theory were already present but widely scattered and diffuse. These were collimated into ten vital characteristics (daśa prāṇas) in analogy with rāga; these not only described the tāla in all its aspects, but differentiated one from another. They were kāla, kalā, mārga, kriyā, anga, graha, jāti, laya, yati, and prastāra. Kalā is the speed of performance, The first, second, third, etc., speeds are double the just precedent one. Kalā is the progressive expansion of the āvarta cycle by a factor of two, useful in accommodating given melody structures into magnified time frames. Kriyā is the act of performing an anga. There are eight sounded (saśabda) and silent (niśabda) kriyās which are again divided into mārga and desī. Graha is the position in the āvarta cycle at which the song or a part of it commences. It is sama if both āvarta and melody line commence together; it is visama if they do not. Visama is again of two kinds; in anāgata, the āvarta commences first and the melody line commences after this; in atīta, the melody line precedes the beginning of the āvarta. Mārga is a tāla praṇa which connotes difference in relative sizes of the steps which are needed to traverse the āvarta span and is of five kinds, namely, čitrātma, čitratāra, čitra, vartikā, and dakśinā, each of which is double the just precedent mārga. Anga is explained above. Jāti refers to the size of the laghu; it is triṣra, čaturaṣra, khanda, miśra, and sankīrna if has 3,4,5,7, or 9 units of time respectively. Laya is tempo, i.e., the time interval between any two successive kriyās; it is druta if fast, madhya if middle, and vilamba if slow. This element has also suffered from overclassification into druta, madhya, etc. Yati is the arrangement of angas into a regular or discernible pattern; it is sama, visama, srotovaha, gopuččha, mṛdanga, damaru, pipīlika, kharjūra, etc. Just like laghu, guru, and pluta, prastāra is a borrowing from prosody. It is one of six mathematical devices (Ṣat pratyaya) for schematic tabulation of various aspects of tāla.

The Haridāsas of Karnāṭaka brought order and system into the wilderness of tāla practice. They organized a compact and logically coherent tāla system in Karnāṭaka music. Among the revolutionary ideas and practices they initiated were: transformation of virāma into anu (anu) druta, an anga with the fixed duration of one unit of time (i.e., one half of druta); extension of the jāti concept to the laghu; restriction of the use of anudruta (only in jhampa tāla) to only one, of druta to a minimum of one and a maximum of two, of laghu to a miminum of one and maximum of three;

exclusive use of only three angas, namely, anudruta, druta and laghu; transforming druta virāma into tisrajāti laghu, decomposing a laghu virāma into a laghu and druta, etc.

The revolution of tāla took the shape of reformation and restructuring rather than replacement or recreation. The Haridāsas selected tāla structures which were time-honored but had specific and restricted usage. They transformed them into a compact and comprehensive system with consummate skill and with laudable parsimony in athetization, adaptation, and generalization. These tālas were prescibed to be employed in a set of ancient musical forms, collectively called sālagasgda prabandha. There were eight songs in it and each employed a different, prescribed tāla, each had many varieties. The Haridāsas reduced it to a single tālamalikā composition and renamed it suḷādi. They modified both the structure and the tāla; they stabilized this transformed composition in musical practice by composing it in large numbers and propagating them through a variety of word themes such as orthodoxy, suḷādi dogma, social, moral, ethical, spiritual, and other values, to such effect that the suḷādi has rightly come to be regarded as one of their special contribution to Karnāṭaka music.

The suḷādi tālas were originally nine: dhruva, mathya, rūpaka, jhampā, triputa, adda, eka, jhombada, and ragana mathya. These were invariably associated each with a laghu of particular jāti, e.g., jhampā had a miśra jāti laghu; adda (atta) had a khanda jāti laghu. These were eka kāla tālas, i.e., the time unit in each anga was telescoped into a single syllable, so that the āvarta could be shown by proximately placed ghatas (accent, beat). They are known as chapū tālas. Only two of these, triśra triputa and triśra rūpaka, have today survived as miśra chapū and khanda chapū tālas respectively, the adjectival terms indicating the total number of units in the āvarta. Musical exigency required the āvarta, and hence the angas to magnify into various sizes; this was accomplished through such devices as kalā and mārga. Further, when the laghu jāti was uniformly applied to all tālas, two events resulted: ragana mathya tāla merged into čaturaśra jāti mathya tāla; the jhombada merged into čaturaśa triputa tāla, popularly called ādī tāla by inverting the order of the angas in its āvarta; secondly, a total of 35 tāla varieties became available. A further device was developed, namely, each tāla unit in the angas of the āvarta was subdivided into 3,4,5,7 or 9 equal parts; these were respectively called triśra, čaturaśa, khanda, miśra and sankīrna gatis, which determined the gait of the melodic structures. Thus the subvarities multiplied into 175. Sometimes an assertion that there are 175 tālas in Karnāṭaka music is encountered. It is incorrect to say so; there are only seven tālas. One other change also occurred in the suḷādi tālas: in order to accommodate temporal values in music and dance, dhruva and jhampa tālas had evolved into vīṇādandi and nātyadandi forms: the laghuśekhara (laghuvirāma) in the latter was decomposed into a laghu and a druta so that it became identical with the former.

The use of suḷādi tālas became so exclusive that not only were the newly evolved musical forms set only in them, but even the ancient forms such as śrivardhana, harṣavardhana, pañčahangi, umātilaka kaivāda, svarānka, etc. also were composed in them from the 16th century.

Chaturdandi

A major concept which distinguished Karnāṭaka music is that of danḍi (literally, pillar.) The entirety of musical practice was regarded as resting on four genres: ālāpa, thāya, gīta, and prabandha. These are the čaturdanḍī. The triology or rāga, tāla, and prabandha, differences in treatment of which distinguish Karnāṭaka music from Hindustani music, rests on čaturdanḍī. These will be briefly described here with cursory indication of their present state.

Alapa

Ālāpa is the extempore creation of a melodic personality in terms of tonal situations (svarasandarbha) which are comprehended in the scale and ten vital characteristics of a rāga. This is the acme of both Karnāṭaka music and of its creative genuis. This personality is delineated and limited on a canvas of broad and fairly elastic structural rules, grammar, and idiom. It has been adequately systematized in early treatises.

Thus, an ālāpa is performed in six broad physical phases; āksiptikā (vulg. āyitta) manifests the emergence of tile rāga in brief, introductory melodic passages, rāgavardhani (vulg. karaṇa, edupu, yadupu) elaborates or develops the rāga motifs; the rāga grows or increases in this phase. In other words, the rāgavardhani develops and sustains the body of the rāga. Vidārī is the next phase in which the rāgavardhani is gradually and properly phased out. That is, it separates by suitable techniques the various paragraphs (rāgavardhanis) in the essay (ālāpa). Two rāgavardhanis are prescribed with their respective vidari while a third is optionally employed (with its vidārī.) Sthāyī is the next phase. Clusters of tānas blooming around a given note of the rāga are unfolded in sthāyī, both in ascent and descent, in the scheme of establishing the personality of the rāga. Sthāyī is performed on all svaras which are vital to the individuality of the rāga. In vartani (vulg. makarini), clusters of tānas are built around other notes bringing it to a penultimate phase. Muktāyi is the final phase in which the ālāpa is brought to a close. It is the cadential part of the melodic structure of rāga and finally rests on the nyāsa svara.

Attempts were made early in Indian music in structuring ālāpa around tonal nuclei. Four such areas were recognized and designated svasthānas. The first was sthāyī which was also the graha svara or amśa svara. Melodic movement was executed around it and the notes preceding it in the lower register as also two notes above it in the scale, gravitating to the sthāyī. The second svasthāna was the fourth note from the sthāyī called dvyardha. The rāga moved around this note, gravitated to it and paused on it (or on the sthāyī). The third svasthāna was around the fifth, sixth and seventh notes from the sthāyī. They were called ardhasthita or ardhasvaras. The rāga was executed around these individually and collectively in a stepwise manner and paused on them (or on the sthāyī). The final stage of the melodic dynamics was the eighth note (dviguna svara) i.e., the sthāyī note itself in the higher register. Rāga moved around it and the notes above it and finally rested on the sthāyī. Then the rāga was established again (rāgasthāpanā) in short characteristic phrases, thus concluding the rāgālāpa on the nyāsa svara. Melodic movement was qualified with appropriate gamakas and with notes which were appropriate to the rāga; occasionally a note or notes which were omitted in the rāga normally were also permitted to be used if they helped in enhancing the beauty of ālāpa and emphasizing the melodic personality of the rāga. Melodic movement was also qualified with phrases which were special to the rāga (viśeṣa sañčāras) and vital or essential (jīvasvara sañčāras).

As in many cultural values, south India has retained historical continuity in ālāpa also. The above methods of rāgālāpa are still traceable in Karnāṭaka music, albeit with some minor modifications. On the other hand, the method of developing a rāga in terms of vādi and samvādi notes is fully retained and zealously guarded in Hindustani music rather than in Karnāṭaka music. Rāgālapti is met with, but rarely, in Hindustani music in which rūpakālapti dominates.

Thaya

Thāya is the second member of the čaturdanḍī and has no parallel in Hindustani music. It is a phonetic deterioration of the Samskṛta sthāya in vernacular usage. The term originally cannoted merely the organ or segment (sañčāra) of a rāga but acquired a special restricted meaning in the 16th-17th centuries, when it was frozen into a separate musical form. The method of singing this is described for the first time by

Venkatamakhin. He devotes a separate chapter for its description. A sthāyī is sung on any note appropriate to a rāga, and a tāna is sung on each of the next four notes in conformity with the nature of the rāga, first in ascent and then in descent. Thus eight tānas are performed; next, any note in these eight tānas is made sthāyī and the melodic movement is executed in and around it and is finally rested on mandrasadja. This is called makarini; it is followed by muktāyi, i.e., the finale of the rāga.

From the foregoing description the thāya appears to be a fragment of ālāpa involving vartanī and muktāyi such that the vatanī was rendered in a special way, namely, the tānas which were prescribed to be performed on various notes during the sthāyī phase are performed here and a sthāyī is executed on any note and the mandrasadja is made nyasa. Karnāṭaka music does not today have this form, which needs to be restored. It seems to be replaced with another cognate form called tāna, called also madhyamakāla. This is called kataka by Tulaja and is thus some 250 years old. Like sthāya (thāya) which acquired a restricted, technical meaning during the 17th century, tāna also acquired a similar, restricted, technical meaning to connote segments or organs of a rāga performed in rhythmic or prosodial patterns after ālāpa on the vīṇā or before the rendering of pallavi composition.

Gita

Gīta is the third danḍi. It means generally anything which is sung, but acquired a special, restricted meaning in the 17th century to denote a suḷādi. In modern parlance it denotes a simple—the simplest—song type to which the fresher student of Karnāṭaka music is introduced. In both senses, gīta is a distinct contribution of the Haridāsas of Karnāṭaka.

Prabandha

Prabandha is the fourth and final danḍi. Prabandha (literally, construction) is any musical composition; it may be set to tāla (nibaddha) or not (anibaddha). It may have specific prescription in respect of rāga, tāla, čhandas (metre), rasa, etc. (niryukta) or not (aniryukta). Its six organs are solmization (svara), word content (pada), onomatopeic instrumental sounds (pāta), laudatory address to the hero/patron/deity of the song (biruda), the auspicious (and ālāpa carrier) syllables tāna, and tāla. A prabandha is classified tārāvali bhāvanī, dīpanī, ānandinī or medini if it employs 2, 3, 4, 5 or all 6 of these angas (no prabandha is possible with only one anga). Its musical structure may be analyzed thus: its introductory or beginning passage is udgrāha; the body of the song or its refrain is dhruva; a passage spanning these two is melāpaka; the concluding passage is called ābhoga. An optional passage bridging the dhruva and ābhoga is employed only in sālāgasūda prabandhas.

A major difference between Hindustani music and Karnāṭaka music is the historical discontinuity of the song forms in the former; the foregoing prabandhas were almost completely lost sight of from about the 15th-16th centuries in north India while many of them continued to be composed and performed in south India till about the 18th century. The old and new forms coexisted in Karnāṭaka music during the above transition period: some of the new forms were logical evolutions from the old forms; some were entirely new; but the forms in vogue contemporarily were left undescribed in musical treatises of the 16-18th centuries. The exemplar of the kṛti, kīrtana, pada and jāvali was the form created and proliferated by the Haridāsas from the 14th century. This was called dāsara pada or devaranāma. The tillāna has undoubtedly evolved from kaivāda prabandha. The varṇa was inaugurated by Govindasamayya and his brother Kuvanasamayya, but its enduring influence came from Ādi-appaya in the 18th century. Devaranāma, ugābhoga, suḷādi, vrttanāma, nāmāvali, the opera and many such forms were contributions of the Haridāsas.

Most of these forms received experimentation and impetus equally from Karnāṭaka, Andhra, Tamil Nadu and Kerala. The prototype of kṛti is found in the songs of Narahari Tirtha in the 14th century, proliferated by the Ādya saints, Śrīpādarāja,.Vyāsarāja, Purandaradāsa, Kanakadāsa, Vijayadāsa etc. from Karnāṭaka; the Tāllapakam family, Vīrabhadrayya, Rāmadāsa, Sesha Ayyangar, Kṛṣṇasvāmayya etc. from Andhra; the great musical trinity (Tyāgarāja, Mudduswāmi Dīkṣita and Śyāmāśāstri) and their schools in Tamil Nadu, Svāti Tirunāl and his band of composers in Kerala. The varṇa grew into present state largely in Tamil Nadu and Kerala.

While the age of Purandaradāsa, who is honoured as the Karnāṭakasangītapitāmaha, witnessed the culmination of Karnāṭaka music in form and content, the age of the musical trinity marked its renaissance and emphasized its spiritual, ethical, and social values.

Telugu is the medium of word expression in Karnāṭaka music today. Samskṛta has the second place of honour. The songs of Arunagirināthār, Kotiśvara Ayyar, Subrahmanya Bhārati and such other great composers have given an important status to Tamil besides ancient tevārams, tiruvāymoli and the pans in which they were composed. Varṇa, tillāna, and pada are composed almost exclusively in Telugu even now.

Jāvali is available in Kannada, Telugu and Tamil. The compositions of Svāti Tirunāl and others have elevated Malayālam to a considerable position in musical expression.

Musical Forms

Musical forms in vogue in modern Karnāṭaka music will now be briefly described.

Svarajati

All songs in Karnāṭaka music are segmented, with only a few exceptions. The svarajāti, set to a single rāga and single tāla, has many stanzas, the first of which serves as refrain, pallavi. Each segment consists of solfa passages arranged in prosodial groupings called jātis. Occassionally words are set to the music such that note duration and syllabic duration coincide with each other (yathākṣara). The words, if any, have devotional theme.

This form entered Karnāṭaka music in the first or second quarter of the 18th century. Hundreds of svarajātis composed by Śyāmāśāstri, Ādi-appaya, Svāti Tirunāl, Ponnayya, Vadivel, Cinnikṛsnadāsa, Vīṇā Śeśanna, Mysore Sadāśiva Rao, etc. are available. These are largely introductory in scope, but the three svarajātis composed by Śyamaśāstri are excellent songs and have high performance potential as first song of a concert. A reciprocal song type called jātisvara is popular in Bharatanātyam.

Varna

The varṇa may be regarded as structurally bridging svarajāti and kṛti, for its second half resembles the former and the first half resembles the latter. Its first half consists of three (or four) elements: the first is pallavi composed in two āvarta lengths; the anupallavi follows it and is of equal length. The third is optional and has an equal length and is called upapallavi. These are set to words of an erotic, laudatory or devotional theme. The melody lines are in slow tempo, replete with gamakas, such that the rāga personality is adequately brought out. In fact, varṇa is esteemed for the intimate familiarity with rāga it brings to its practitioner. The final line of words carries the composer's signature (ankita.) The final element of the first half is a two or four āvarta-line solfa passage phased out into jātis. This half rests on the first line of the pallavi.

The second half commences with a single melodic line set to words. This is called čaraṇa or eṭṭugade. The first half together with the čaraṇa completes its resemblance to kṛti. The čaraṇa is followed by three or four solfa passages called eṭṭugade svaras. The density, phraseology, and complexity of the svaras increase progressively to a climax in the final passage. The second half rests on čaraṇa. The čaraṇa is repeated after each eṭṭugade svara. Occasionally, the čittasvara and eṭṭugade svaras are also set to words. There are two kinds of varaṇas: čaukavarṇa or padavarṇa is in slow tempo, the čittasvara and eṭṭugade svaras are set to words and the entire literary theme is erotic. The tāna varṇa is in a somewhat faster tempo, has a devotional or laudatory theme, and is usually set to āditāla.

Kriti

The kṛti, kīrtana, pada, jāvali, and devaranāma are all derived from the same dhātu examplar, namely, pallavi, anupallavi, čaraṇas, sometimes the anupallavi is absent; čaraṇas are odd numbered, usually three. The final čaraṇa carries the composer's signature. The čaraṇas are all set to the same music, except in a few instances, e.g., pañčaratna kṛtis of Tyāgarāja. The kṛtis of Muddusvāmi Dīksita do not have anupallavi, and have only one čaraṇa; on the other hand, they contain mātu-dhātu passages in madhyamakāla inserted after the pallavi and čaraṇa. In most other kṛtis e.g., of Tyāgarāja if the dhātus of pallavi, anupallavi and first half of the čaraṇa are designated A, B and C, then the music of the kṛti may be shown as ABCB; occasionally it is ABAB; when anupallavi is absent, as in divyanāma sankīrtana, it is even A A A. The kṛti may be in slow (vilambita), middle (madhya) and, rarely, fast (druta) tempo. The mātu (word theme) of the kṛti or devaranāma may be praise of God, spiritual quest, moral or ethical exhortation, social reformation etc. The pada has the same musical structure and segmentation but always set in slow tempo and generally to chāpu tāla; the mātu is invariably an erotic theme consisting of the yearning of the lovelorn heroine nāyikā for the hero nāyaka and vice versa. The pada is often interpreted in spiritual symbolism as representing the yearning of the individual soul for union with the universal soul. The jāvali has physical love of the hero for the heroine or vice versa for its word theme and is set to light, attractive rāgas (rakti rāgas) in contrast with padas which are set to rāgas evoking serious and deep moods. The jāvalis are also set to simple tālas. The composers of kṛti, devaranāma, pada and jāvali are too numerous to warrant separate mention. It is sufficient to say that they constitute the bulk of the compositional wealth of Karnāṭaka music and that the kṛti accounts for more than half of the content of an average concert.

Tillana, Astapadi

The tillāna is composed in patas set to a rāga and a tāla with brief solfa passages and word passages carrying the composer's signature at the end. The mātu is adulation, prayer, supplication of love, dedication to God or the hero or the patron. The aṣtapadi is a song from the *Gitagovinda* of Jayadeva Sarasvati. It has a pallavi and anupallavi which is also the refrain and called dhruvapada. It has eight-couplet čaraṇas (hence the name aṣtapadi), the last of which bears the composer's signature. It has been adapted to the rāgas and tālas of Karnāṭaka music from about the early 18th century. It is usually prefaced with a preceding śloka which sets forth in a narration the context and background for the word theme in the aśtapadi. Rana Khumbhakarna (15th century) standardized aśtapadi performance in north India; Tirumalapattanam Ramudu Bhagavata (18th century) inaugurated the performance of its modern version in Karnāṭaka music.

Daru, Pallavi, Sloka

Daru is derived from the Samskṛata word dhruvā which is described by Bharatamuni as a song performed in a play to carry forward the story by narration and abhinaya by various dramatis personae on various occasions. It was still used so until about 200 years ago. It is set to a single rāga and tāla; it is divided into pallavi, anupallavi (which is often absent), and three or five čaraṇas. Sometimes there are eight čaraṇas, when the daru is appropriately called aṣtaka. Darus are performed for entry of a character, monologue, aside, dialogue, description, kolāta (stick-dance), dance, etc. If the dance is inserted at the beginning of a daru, it is called mukhajāti; it is called makutajāti and antyajāti if dance is performed at the end of a section or at the end of the daru respectively.

Pallavi is a single-line melody set to one or more short word phrases or a brief sentence such that the syllables are rigidly fixed in span of one (rarely, two or more) āvarta of a (the same, or rarely different) tāla which is elaborated in terms of the expressive potential of rāga and tāla, as also the affective content, if any. It is the highest form of scholarship and spontaneous, creative imagination in Karnāṭaka music. It is prefaced by an elaborate and detailed ālāpana of the rāga to which the pallavi is set; this followed by tāna. The tāna consists of clusters of musical phrases arranged in beautiful prosodial combinations. It is usually performed in a garland of rāgas, notably in a time-honored set of five rāgas, namely, Nāta, Gaula, Arabhi, Varāli, and Śri (collectively called ghana-rāga-pañčaka). When performed on the vīṇā (to which it is specially appropriate,) it may be followed by a kṛti in slow tempo instead of pallavi. The pallavi line is extended by neravalu and kalpanā svara (see next section) in rāgamalikā. The tāna and pallavi are about 250 years old.

A śloka (verse) from Rāmakarnāmṛtram Kṛṣṇakarnāmṛtam, Mukundamālā stōtra, Saundaryalaharī, Amaruśataka, etc. is usually performed at the end of a recital of Karnātaka music, usually in a garland of rāgas, but not set to a tāla. Mangala (literally, auspicious) is a song usually from Purandaradāsa (in Karnātaka) or Tyāgarāja (in south India, including Karnāṭaka) which is performed at the conclusion of a recital in a spirit of benediction. All the forms described in this section are also used in Bharatanātyam.

Creative and Decorative Elements

In Karnāṭaka music the performer not only interprets a song of the composer, but also enlarges its scope with his own composition, sometimes predetermined, and sometimes spontaneous. All this creation is extempore, a secondary creative imagination superimposed upon the primary creativity of the composer, its quality a measure of the mood, receptivity, and susceptibility to the composer's suggestion and ability of the performer.

Thus rāgālāpana prefaces the rendering of a song, and consists of purely spontaneous elaboration and development of melodic motifs as well as its affective and aesthetic content withhin the scope of a scale. It also provides an introduction to the song, a canvas on which to paint it, or a frame to contain it, a background on which it may be mounted and emphasized. Tāna, as already mentioned, consists of ālāpana of a rāga set to groupings of notes in various rhythmic patterns; it combines both rāga and rhytlun in a manner which is unique in the world of music. Kapanā svara is the weaving of svara patterns in different tempos, rhythms and gaits (gatis) in the given tāla āvarta so as to dovetail exactly into the point of commencement (graha. edupu) of the mātu in the tāla āvarta. Neravalu is the exposition of both mātu and dhātu occuring in a given segment of the song in different but logically coherent, developed variations, moods and aesthetic forms. Sangati is the variation of a melodic theme in a given verbal context, developed progressively from simplicity to complexity; it involves increasing embellishment, svara density and melodic dynamics gradually. The foregoing elements are collectively designated manodharma sangīta.

Decorative elements are designed by the composer or performer to enhance the beauty of a composition by techniques and extensioiisjudiciously applied. Sangati may be classified as both manodharma sangīta and decorative element. Madhyamkala sāhitya is a mātu segment set in double speed, in taut cross-rhythms with dense syllabic population, unevenly distributed and inserted after the anupallavi, if any, or after the pallavi in its absence and after the čaraṇa. This was effectively employed by Muddusvāmi Dīksita and Śyamaśāstri, probably for the first time. The citiasvara is a well balanced solfa passage added after the čaraṇa and is sometimes set to words also. The mātu may display segments in which a series of new words is formed by the progressive addition of a syllable. The former is called gopuččha yati and the latter srotovaha yati. Often, the mātu syllables coincide with the syllable symbolizing the svara. This is called svaraksara. The name of the rāga is sometimes (especially by Muddusvāmi Dīksita) ingeniously woven into the fabric of the mātu to form a natural and integral part of a larger word or phrase. This is called rāgankita. The čittasvara or the mātu of a song may be composed to include clusters of pataksvaras. The cittasvara is sometimes so composed that it reads the same when reversed. This is called anuloma-viloma svara (e.g. 'SadāVīṇātasādare' of Muddusvāmi Dīksita in Revagupti rāga.) The mātu may be composed in a mixture of languages, especially Samskṛta, Malayālam, Tamil and Telugu. It is called manipravāla (e.g. some songs of Svāti Tirunāl). The mātu may be densely decorated with alliteration and with the recurrence of similar or same phonetic community.

Most of the foregoing creative and decorative elements commenced their career in Karnātaka music about 250 years ago.

Instrumentation

The musical instruments used in a recital of Karnātaka music are chiefly the tambūra (ri),vīṇā, gottuvādya, violin and mandolin among chordophones (tata), flute, nāgasvaram, saxophone and clarinet among aerophones (susira), mṛdanga, khañjira, dhōlak. and tavil among the membranophones (avanaddlha, ānaddha, vitata), the triangle, morsing, tāla, jalatarang and ghaṭa among idiophones (ghana). The more important of these will be briefly described here.

Chordophones

Tambura

The Tambūra (also called Tamburi, and, in Hindustani music, Tanpura) is the drone instrument in both Karnātaka music and Hindustani music. It provides the reference pitch to which all the music is oriented and is therefore a prime instrument. It crystallized into a definite form and structure in the 14th-15th century and is mentioned for the first time by Srīpādarāja (1404-1502), then by Vyāsarāja (1447-1539) and Purandaradāsa (1484-1564). This instrument is referred to as danḍige by Kannada poets and Haridāsas. It consists of a hemispherical resonator of jackwood (or other wood) to which a long neck of the same wood is fixed. Four strings pass over a bridge placed on the plate of the resonator and over the neck and are fixed to pegs which are attached to a short tube shaped like, and placed beyond, the neck. They are tuned to mandra *pa*, madhya *sa*, madhya *sa* and (brass string) to mandra *sa*. Occasionally, there are additional strings tuned to other notes which emphasize the tonal structure of the rāga being performed. The first string is tuned to mandra *ma* in case of female voices or to obtain a higher reference pitch, or the latter Tambūra is made shorter to accommodate the same tuning but higher pitch.

Vina

The vīṇā is one of the most ancient keyboard instrument of India. Its present form emerged from about the 18th century. Prior to this period, its keyboard was of two varieties; one in which the frets could be moved to different positions to give the notes of a desired rāga, another which had fixed frets for all the svarasthanas so that it could accommodate any and every rāga. Each was tuned in three different ways (accordatura) to give different ranges in the tonal continuum. As many as 33 kinds of vīṇā were known even as late as the 16th century. The one now in exclusive use in Karnātaka music is called Sarasvati vīṇā. It was inaugurated by Tulaja (c.1730) under the name Tulajendramela vīṇā. It consists of a hemispherical resonator of jackwood (or other suitable wood) to which is attached a neck bearing a keyboard carrying 24 brass or bronze (recently, even steel) frets. The neck has a gourd to serve as a prop near the end of the keyboard. A bridge made of ebony or jackwood is fixed at the center of the plate on the resonator. The upper surface of the bridge has a steel and/ or brass or bronze piece fixed to it with lac. Seven strings are looped into a small extension of the resonator plate. Four of these are passed over the bridge and across the frets and are fixed to four pegs fixed to a 'head' which is attached to tile neck. The first two are of brass and are tuned respectively to anumandra *pa* and mandra *sa*. The other two are of steel and are tuned to mandra *pa* and madhya *sa*. The three other strings are of steel and pass over a side bridge (attached to the main bridge on the side of the performer) and on the side of the neck and are fixed to pegs provided on the side of the neck (nearest the performer). These are tuned to madhya *sa*, madhya *pa* and tara *sa* from top to bottom. They are called śruti strings or tipi strings. Up to about 1900 C.E. the performing posture of the vīṇā corresponded to the resonator resting on the crossed legs of the squatting performer and the neck slanting along the left side of the chest and the prop gourd positioned at the left shoulder. The left fingers of the performer slid over the keyboard up and down while the right fingers plucked the strings near the bridge. But now the vīṇā is positioned horizontally, the resonator resting on the ground near the right knee of crossed legs while the prop gourd rests on the left lap. The left forearm passes under the neck and the left fingers slide horizontally over the keyboard, stopping the strings at the desired fret by pressing it behind it with the tips of the forefinger and middle finger, and deflecting it away from him along the fret to generate any desired note or its shade. The right forefinger and miiddle finger pluck the strings, while the little finger (and rarely also the ring finger) pluck the śruti strings to mark the angas of the tāla āvarta and to mark rhythmic groupings or phraseology while performing tāna.

Gottuvadya

Goṭṭuvādya is known since about 1620 since it is mentioned in Raghunatha Nayaka's Śringārasāvitri as gotivādya. The instrument is also known as mahānātaka Vīṇā. Sambamoorthy claims a Tamil origin for its name Goṭṭuvādya, deriving it from kodu (stick). It may be noticed, however, that a more plausible and probable derivation is available in Kannada: goṭṭu means hard, completely dry. The instrument is not played with a stick, but with a hard, dry piece of wood called goṭṭu. Alternatively, gōtu refers in Kannada to a technique of playing on the vīṇā where the desired gamaka is obtained by horizontal movement of the finger along the string rather than deflecting the string. It may be noticed that this is exactly the way the instrument is played. The gottuvādya is identical with the vīṇā in every way except that it has no keyboard and that the svara positions are obtained by stopping the plucked string at the appropriate position by pressing the gottu with the left hand. The gottu is made of a hard, dry wood such as rosewood or ebony.

Violin

In the form in which it is employed today in Indian music the violin is undoubtedly an importation from Europe. But it is not improbable that the European violin evolved from a form which was imported from India and entered Indian music in the 18th century. The earliest introduction of the violin into Indian music was at least about 1760 C.E. This was in Śrīrangapaṭṭaṇa, the then capital of Mysore in the royal court of Tippu Sultan. A mural painting on the eastern wall of his palace Darya Daulat, dated 1784 C.E., contains a panel (fourth in the fourth row) of young women, one of whom is a dancer and others are musicians; one musician is playing on the violin in a form and posture which are modern.

Mandolin

The mandolin is a very recent addition to the instrumentarium of Karnātaka music. Only its accordatura and techniques are adapted to this music without any structural or acoustical modification. So, it need not be discussed here.

Aerophones

Flute

The flute employed in classical Indian music is the single, transverse-blown type. It is a cylindrical tube of uniform bore closed at one end. It is made of various materials such as seasoned bamboo (Samskṛta vēṇu, hence the name), ebony, sandal, red sandal, ivory, iron, steel, copper, bronze, silver, gold, and even synthetic plastic. It is called bānsuri in Hindustani music (vāmśa svarī-bāns surī-bānsurī.) The difference between the North Indian and South Indian varieties is of size and range. The former tend to be longer and bigger. The tone range, described in terms of low scale and high scale, is measured by the ratio of the diameter: length. The flute may be considered in three parts: the head in which the mukharandhra (embouchure, blowing hole) is situated about 0.75 inch from the stop; the middle in which there are no holes; the foot in which there are usually six, but sometimes seven to nine holes, depending on the range required. All these and the embouchure occur in straight line, and the holes other than the embouchure are equally spaced out and are of the same approximate width. The first hole nearest the mukhararandhra is called tararandhra since this gives the highest note. The overall tone range of the flute depends on, and is usually expressed in terms of, the distance between the mkharandhra and the tārandhra. Based on this, 14 types of flute have been described in ancient Indian musical treatises. The pressure and volume of air blown is a contributory factor in determining the pitch of the note produced. Overblowing produces the corresponding octave note. The flute covers ordinarily a range of 2-5 registers and corresponds in quality and range nearest to the human singing voice. By completely opening, partly opening and completely closing the holes, different notes may be obtained. Gamakas and different subtle shades of notes such as the illusory note, implied note, transient note, etc., may be produced by the appropriate movements of the fingers on and above the holes. The embouchure is placed on the chin so that half of it is covered by the underlip. The jet of air produced by the flutist must strike the other edge of the embouchure at its central point to produce a tone of optimum quality. Otherwise the tone quality will be bad and apaśruti (note/s displaced from their true positions) will result. The embouchure may be fractionally covered with bee's wax for correction and minor adjustments of fundamental pitch. Besides the above, the flute also has one or two vent holes on the side and/or underside to assist in fingering techniques and gamakas.

Nagasvaram

Nāgasvaram is also called nādasvara wrongly, nayanam in Tamil and valaga in Kannada. It consists of a wooden tube of conical bore between 2 to 2.5 feet filled with a small metal bell at the bottom and a metal cap at the top. The bell also may be of the same wood. The cap is in the form of a staple and is fitted with a double reed. Spare reeds and an ivory bodkin to clean the reeds with are attached on a string to the instrument. The number of finger holes vary, but are generally seven or eight. Several vent holes are also provided at the rear or the side to control the pitch and for gamaka manipulation. The nāgasvaram is named variously, depending on its size. The largest of the family is Bāri (bhāri=big or large, in Dravidian languages), and the smaller is called Timiri. The ensembles employing these are respectively called periya (big) meḷa in Tamil and doḍḍa meḷa in Kannada and činna or čikka (small) meḷa. Smaller ones are called Mauri (Samskṛta madhukari). A very small variety is called mukhavīṇā. The blowing is different from other aerophones. Since the reed is completely held in the mouth, no air is wasted, but the pitch variations are brought out also by variation in the volume of air intensity of blowing. The fingering techniques correspond to those obtaining in the flute. Rarely, a nāgasvaram made of stone may also be found. The drone for nāgasvaram is provided by the ottu, which is similar to, but longer than, the nāgasvaram but without the finger holes. It therefore gives a monotone which serves as the reference pitch. However, it is provided with a few vent holes at the bottom which may be fully or partially closed with wax to adjust the drone pitch exactly to the required value.

The saxophone and clarinet being exact borrowings from Western music, and retained without adaptation or modification in structure or acoustics need not be described here.

Jalataranga

The Jalataranga is an idiophone but may be conveniently described here (since it is a svaravādya rather than layavādya.) It is said to have flourished in ancient times under the name Udaka-vādya (literally, water-instrument) but is a relatively recent addition to Karnātaka music, dating probably from about 150 years. The jalataranga consists of 18 porcelain cups of progressively increasing volume. They are specially prepared to give a sonorous tone. The note is produced when the cup is struck with a light bamboo stick. The pitch produced is inversely proportional to the volume of water in (and size of) the cup and depends on the volume of air resonating over it. The cups are arranged in a semicircle before the performer who operates with both hands. The cups are filled with varying amounts of water. The water also helps in stabilizing the cup and in conferring continuity on the note. Further, various gamakas may be manipulated by bringing the stick into contact with the water surface. It also offers an easy and ready method of making slight adjustments in tuning. For the pitch may be diminished by adding water or raised by removing it. This also provides for tuning the same set of cups for different rāgas by adjusting the amount of water. That the instrument is not more popular than it is, is understandable because its tuning is both tedious and time-consuming. Further, the notes are largely discrete, thus, resulting in lack of coherence and intelligibility. Also, the drastic limitation on gamakas is a serious handicap.

MEMBRANOPHONES

Mrdanga

The leader of percussive instruments used for rhythm accompaniment is undoubtedly the mṛdanga. It is one of the most ancient of Indian musical instruments whose origin is buried deep in myth and legend. Mṛdanga means a body of clay; this indicates that it used to be made of clay in early times, as it is, occasionally, even now. The tone quality, the perfection in material and method of construction, the augmentation of rhythmic structure of song, and the variety of sounds it can generate, are peculiar only to this instrument; these are an impressive contribution to the world of music by Karnātaka music.

The mṛdanga is a double-head drum. It is made of clay, jackwood, neem, acacia, red sandal, or redwood. It is hollow, broadest at about the middle, and tapers towards both ends. It is hollowed out of a single piece of wood and looks as if two unequal flower pots are attached face to face. It has, as already mentioned, two heads:

the right head has three superimposed, concentric, tightly stretched skins. The outermost is a ring of calf skin. This is called reppe (eyelid) in Kannada and Telugu. It is also called mītu. The intermediate membrane, called chāpu (beat, stroke) is made of sheep skin or goatskin. A mixture of manganese dust, boiled rice and tamarind paste or fine iron dust and boiled rice is ground intimately layer after layer and fixed parmanently to the central circular region of the chāpu and allowed to form a homogeneous dry fixture, thickest at the centre and thinning out towards the edge. This mixture is called karaṇi in Kannada and Telugu; it is called sōru or marundu in Tamil. This acoustically loads the membrane and is mostly responsible for the unique tone quality of the instrument, producing a radial overtone spectrum in the Baeyer Series. The paste of the above mixture is applied in small grains and is then rubbed and polished with a smooth, hard stone. The innermost membrane is of buffalo skin.

The left head consists of an outer ring of buffalo skin and an inner membrane of sheepskin. The central region of this is loaded with a thick aqueous paste orrine soji or of boiled rice and ashes. This is applied temporarily to the desired thickness (determined by the desired pitch) just before the performance and is scraped off after it. It should not be allowed to dry out during the performance. The pitch of the membrane is inversely proportional to the amount of the loading. The right head is tuned to the reference pitch and the left head to its octave note in the lower register. Each head has a leather hoop to which the membranes are fastened in 16 eyelets, with a thong of buffalo hide which tighten the hoops. The thong (bāru) is a single, continuous ribbon and is threaded into the eyelets of the left and right heads alternately and is tightly stretched across the body of the mṛdanga. Small, cylindrical, solid, wooden pieces (gaṭṭas) are wedged between the thong and the body in order to raise or lower the pitch. If they are driven towards the head, tension in the thong and hence in the membrane rises; the pitch is consequently raised and vice versa. Minor adjustments in tuning are made by hitting the rim of eyelets in the hoop at the appropriate place downwards with calculated force with a round, polished stone or small hammer to raise the pitch and upwards to lower it.

The mṛdanga is made in three sizes to accomodate different reference pitch ranges. Thus for male voices and low reference pitch, the belly or drum is 24 inches, 0.5 inch thick and is divided into 11 inches of left segment and 13 inches of right segment—36 inches wide where they meet. The right head is 6.75 inches in diameter, the left head is 7.75 inches. For low female voices (and śruti "4-1/2") the above dimensions are retained except that each of the heads is shorter by one and a half inch in diameter.

For low male voices and high fernale voices śruti "5-1/2 - 6-1/2") the above dimensions are modified thus: the drum is 1/2 inch thick and 22-1/2 inches long, divided into 10-1/3 inches and 12 inches for the left and right heads respectively, 34 inches round where they meet. The right head is 6.25 inches in diameter and the left is 7.5 inches.

Dolak and Tavil

The Dōlak and Tavil resemble the mṛdanga in that they are both double-headed percussives. The dōlak, also called dhōlak, has come into use in Karnātaka music recitals only in recent years as an auxiliary accompaniment and is thus elevated to the status of an art music instrument from that of a folk music instrument. It is a wooden cylindrical shell with hoops on both extremes which stretch buffalo skin or sheepskin membranes; these are tightened by cotton cords or ropes passing through circular metal rings on the middle of the shelf. These rings are used in tuning. The heads are unloaded and are plain. The right head is played with the right fingers covered with calico, plaster cloth, etc. to protect them from damage and to give a brittle, discrete quality to the sound. The left head is played with a stick. The overall effect is a loud, guttural, brittle sound which offers an attractive contrast to the mellow sounds of the mṛdanga.

The tavil is used exclusively as sole percussive accompaniment to the nāgasvaram. Its loud, commanding tone is very appropriate to the nāgasvaram. A big ensemble may have two main nāgasvaram performers, one oṭṭu, two tavils, one triangle player and one (hand) cymbal player. The unison, variation, and eager, gapless repartee of the nāgasvaram players and the extraordinary sophistication, technique and scholarship as well as the dialogue between the tavil players has no parallel in any other musical system of the world.

The tavil is made of a single block of wood hollowed out into a cylinder 0.10 to 0.125 inch thick, tapering at both ends. Both ends have thick hoops of hemp over which the parchment is tautly stretched. The hoops are attached with leather thongs to the shell. Leather straps are also passed round the middle, interlaced with braces which may be tightened or loosened to tune the head to the desired pitch. The right head is played with the right fingers covered suitably as with the dolak and the left head is played with a drumstick. Both heads are unloaded.

Khañjira

The Khañjira is undoubtedly a borrowal from Islam and is popular all over India as a folk music instrument. It has acquired a unique status and much popularity in Karnātaka music for nearly 150 years. It is a single-head percussive consisting of a circular wooden frame. A lizard skin is tautly stretched on the frame. Its pitch may be slightly lowered by dampening the under surface of the skin with traces of water and may be slightly raised by warming the head. The frame is provided with three or four slits carrying jingle-plates or small dance bells which produce a pleasant jingle or tinkle with the rhythm. The khañjira is held with the left hand and played with the right fingers. The instrument is also used as auxilary accompaniment with mṛdanga in Karnātaka music concerts.

IDIOPHONES

The other instruments, Ghaṭa, Morsing (Egyptian harp), Tāla (cymbals) and triangle are idiophones and are all rhythm instruments.

Ghaṭa (literally, pot) is a baked clay pot with an open mouth which is narrow, considering the size of the ghaṭa. Rarely, the mouth is tautly covered with a leather membrane. It is a very ancient instrument. The mouth is pressed against or towards the stomach of the performer, to add to the resonance. Both hands are employed in playing it on most of the surface using discrete, simultaneous, successive strokes, thumping, etc. resulting in a large variety of sounds. The brittle, discrete, dry, resounding, bright sounds of the instrument offer a good foil to the mṛdanga with which it is used as an auxiliary accompaniment in a concert or as an accompaniment to the Vīṇā. It can be tuned only within very narrow limits; its sounds have no acoustical character.

Morsing is the Egyptian harp and is a very common folk music instrument. It also is an auxiliary accompaniment with the mṛdanga.

The Tāla is a pair of small cymbals of bell metal. They are struck against each other to mark the angas in the tāla āvarta. The Trivali is a steel triangle described in our music treatises since about a thousand years as an idiophone. It is suspended from the left band and struck with a steel rod to mark the angas in the tāla āvarta. Both Tāla and Trivali are used in a nāgasvaram recital to mark time.

Unlike Hindustani music, Karnātaka instrumental music is modelled, influenced by vocal music and is therefore largely dependent on words and word-bound forms. It has yet to develop musical forms which exploit the resources and techniques which characterize each instrument. The instrumental techniques developed nearly a thousand years ago and described by Saṛngadēva, Sōmanātha, and others in respect of various musical instruments await reconstruction and restoration to the contemporary concert platform.

Concert Conventions

A concert of Karnāṭaka music is called kačēri. Formerly a concert was called kēḷike or vinike. When arranged by a concert-arranging organization (sangītasabha), the concert is called sabhākačēri, when it is somewhat more serious and academic. The present form of the concert was probably inaugurated in the royal courts of Tanjore, e.g., Tulaja, Sarabhoji, etc. and gradually diffused through the royal courts of Mysore and Travancore down to the smaller courts of chieftans. Thus, it is about 250 years old.

The organizer informs the accompanying musicians of the reference pitch of the main performer. Both arrive at the concert venue a few minutes before the scheduled commencement of the concert and tune the tambūra and (then) the accompanying instruments in a relatively silent environment, to the reference pitch (adharasruti) of the main performer.

The seating order of musicians on the concert stage follows a conventional sanction. The main performer occupies the fore-midplatform, facing the audience. His disciple, if any, sits to his rear and gives vocal support and performs the tāla; the violinist and mṛdangist are seated near the front corners of the platform, to the left and right of the main performer, and face each other. If the mṛdangist is left handed, their positions are reversed. If the main performer is a vocalist, auxiliary accompaniments are optionally arranged. Thus the khañjira, ghaṭa, dōlak, konegōlu and morsing artists are each seated progressively behind the preceding one, morsing occupying the rear middle of the platform. One or two tambūras are performed incessantly throughout the concert to the rear of the main performer, on one or both sides of the disciple, if any. When this full complement of accompaniments is not used, the order of preference of use is as mentioned above. The minimum is a tambūra, violin and mṛdanga. If it is a vīṇā or goṭṭuvādya concert, the accompaniment may be limited to a mṛdanga or ghaṭa. The main performer is the leader of the group; accompaniments are expected to subserve him. Among the percussives, the mṛdangist is the leader; other percussive accompanists function under his guidance.

The main performer seeks (as a formality and out of respect or politeness) the permission of the chief patron, president, organizer or senior musicians who may be among the audience and commences the concert. A generation ago, the first song of the concert was always the varṇa, rendered briskly or in a slow tempo followed by execution in higher speeds and triśra gati. This practice is now being slowly eroded. The initial phase is in a brisk pace and consists of a series of short kṛtis in attractive (rakti) rāgas in middle tempo, sometimes preceded by a brief rāgālāpana, sometimes interspersed with kalpanā svara, sometimes with both, sometimes with neither. A recent trend in performing kalpanā svrara and/or ālāpana for every composition in this phase robs it of variety and balance and should be discouraged. When there is an alapana introduction it stimulates curiosity in the informed section of the audience as to which kṛti of which composer would follow, and offers a setting for the performer for rendering the kṛti replete with rāgabhāva.

In the middle phase the performer takes up detailed, elaborate ālāpana of such a rāga which is conducive to profound aesthetic experience, to ready elaboration, and susceptible to execution in different paces.

This is followed with a kṛti in slow tempo or if the concert is set up in an atmosphere of scholarship or academic interest or is presented to the cognoscentee, with a pallavi. This is the focal point, the piece de resistance, of the concert. If pallavi is rendered, it is preceded by tāna after rāgalapana. Kṛti or pallavi, the performance includes detailed neravalu and kalpanā svara. The latter usually and the former occasionally in a pallavi is executed in rāgamalikā. It is here that the accompanists have an opportunity to display their excellence in skill, imaginativeness, scholarship, and so forth. The percussionists have the lion's share of this opportunity, for they are offered a spacious opportunity for solo performance. The concert reaches its climax in this phase.

The third phase is oriented to emotive expression. Two or three devaraṇamas, sometimes prefaced with an appropriate ugabhogya are rendered (in Karnātaka, and corresponding compositions forms are performed in Tamil, Telugu or Malayālam).

These are followed by one or more each of pada, jāvali, aṣtapadi, daru and tillāna, in that order. A śloka in Samskṛta is performed in rāgamalikā after this. The concert concludes with a mangaḷa (benedictory song) in the rāga Madhyamāvati, Suruti or Saurastra.

Conclusion

The above concert plan of Karnātaka music reveals a principle which characterizes both Karnātaka music and Indian culture. The concert commences with praise of

God. It develops the creative beauty and nādā and lāyā progressively. It depicts the introspection, insight, self-criticism, surrender, and so on which the devotee and the seeker experiences when caught in the trap which the world of fellow beings and his own prejudices, illusions, weakness, hypocrisy lay for him. Thus the individual passes through a phase of catharsis of jīva-rasa, i.e. emotional crisis of the inner man. Then follows a phase of saundarya-rasa where the fluid formal beauty of nada and laya dominates, lifting the soul to a plane of pure aesthesis, another process of cleansing, elevation, edification. After this climax, the third phase proceeds to rasavīsrānti, a state of rest, freedom from all affective and emotive experience. This auspicious tranquility, repose, restfulness is the destination of all art. The river of art experience meanders amidst dales and forests, ups and downs, subterranean caves, plateaus and plains of human experience of the outer world of reference and the inner world of the individual, and finally reaches the brimful ocean of peace, an ocean of unqualified joy which is kin to the bliss of brahman, where one loses one's self to become oneself, where this mundane, mortal rasa becomes that transcendental, immortal rasa, where this beauty is transmuted into that Beauty which is also Truth and Auspiciousness.

These are the foundations of all Indian art; this is their goal. These are the foundations of Karnāṭaka music; this is its goal.

Works Cited

Abhinavagupta. 1891. Dhvanyaloka-locana. Commentary on Anandavardhana's *Dhvanyaloka*, Ed by Durgaprasad, Kashinath Panduranga Parab. Bombay: Nirnayasagar Press.

Acyutaraya. Tala kalabdhi, extr. Ramakrishna Kavi, M., Bharatakosha, q.v.

Bathkande, V.N. 1925. *The modern Hindustani Raga system and the simplest method of studying the same.* Lucknow: Report of the Fourth All-India Music Confernce.

Bharata. 1894. Natyashastram. Ed by Shivadatta. Kashinatha Panduranga

Parab. Kavyamala Series 42. Bombay.

Bhimakavi. *Basavapuranam,* Ed. R.C. Hiremath, Dharawada, 1958.

Boyden, D.P. 1961. The Violin. In *Musical instruments through the ages.* London: Pelican Books.

Damodara, C. 1952. *Sangita darpanam,* Ed. Vasudeva Sastri, K. Tanjore: Sarasvati Mahal library.

Govinda, Poluri. 1952 *Raga tala cintamani.* Ed. Subba Row. Madras, Government Oriental manuscrips Library.

Govindacharya 1938. *Samgrahacudamani.* Ed. Subrahmanya Sastri, S. Madras: Adyar Library.

Gunavarma II 1938. *Puspadanta puranam.* Ed. Venkata Rao, A., Sesha Iyengar, H., Madras: Madras University Kannada Series.

Janna 1930. *Anantananthapuranam.* Ed. Srinivasachar, D., Rangaswami Iyenger, H.R. Mysore: Oriental Library.

Karnad, S.N. 1925Time theory. In Report of the Fourth All Indian Music Conference. Lucknow.

Mangarasa 1923. *Samyaktvakaumudi.* Belgaum: Chaugule.

Matanga 1928. *Brihaddeshi.* Ed. Sambashiva Sastri, K., Trivandrum: Trivandrum Samskrita Series.

Mudduvenkatamakhin 1978. *Ragalakshanam.* Ed. & Tr. Sathyanarayana, R. Bangalore: Bangalore University.

Nanyadeva 1976. *Sarasvatihrdayalamkarahara (Bharatabhasya).* Ed. Chaitanya Desai, Vol. 2. Khairagarh, Madhya Pradesh, Indira Kala Sangita Viswavidyalaya.

Narada 1920. *Sangitamakaranda.* Ed. by M. R. Telang, Gaekwad Oriental Series 16, Baroda: Oriental Institute.

Padmananka 1909. *Padmarajapuranam.* Ed. Mallaradhya, B. Bangalore.

Paralikar, K. A. 1917. *Sangitasudhakara.* Ed. by Vishnu Sharma. Poona: Aryabhushana Press.

Pundarika Vitthala 1986. *Ragamala, Sadragacandrodaya, Ragamanjari, Nartana Nirnaya (Pundarikamala)* Ed. & Tr. Sathyanarayana, R. Bangalore, Karnataka Sangeetha Nritya Academy and Direcorate of Kannada & Culture, Government of Karnataka.

Ramamatya 1932. *Svaramelakalanidhi.* Ed. Ramaswami Aiyer, M.S. Chidambaram: Annamalai University.

Ratnakara Varni 1923. *Bharatesha vaibhavam. Ed.* Mangesha Rao. Mangalore: Jaina Yuvaka Sangha.

Sambamoorthy, P. 1952, 1959, 1971. *A Dictionary of South Indian music and musicians.* Madras: Indian Music Publishing House.

___________ 1960. *History of Indian Music.* Madras: Indian Music Publishing House.

Sathyanarayna, R. 1968. *Bharatanatya: A critical study*. Mysore: Sri Varalakshmi Academies of Fine Arts.

__________1980. *Karnataka sangitavahini*. Mysore: University of Mysore.

__________1984. *Raga-Iconification in Indian music*. Madras: Vivekananda Kendra Patrika.

__________1972. *Shruti: The scalic foundation*. Mysore: Sri Varalakshmi Academies of Fine Arts.

Somanatha. 1945. *Ragavibodha* Ed. Subrahmanya Sastri, S. Madras: Adyar Library.

Somanatha, Palkuriki. 1942 *Basavapuranamu* Ed. Thammaya, Bandaru. Madras: Vavilla Ramaswami Sastrulu and Sons.

Srikantha 1963. *Rasakaumudi*. Ed. Jani, A. N. Baroda: Oriental Institute.

Sundaram Iyer, P.A. 1968. *Supremacy of the violin*. In sourvenir. Kanchana, D.K. (Karnataka) Tyagaraja Mahotsava. Sri Lakshminarayana Sangitakalashala Samsthe.

Tiruvenkatakavi. 1940. *Sangitasarasangrahamu*. Ed. Subbaramayya, G. Madras: Music Academy.

Tulaja. 1942. *Sangitasaramtratam*. Ed. Subrahmanya Sastri, S. Madras: Music Academi.

Venkatamakhin 1978. *Caturdandi Prakashika* Ed & Tr. Sathyanarayana, R. Bangalore: Bangalore University.

Figure 45: Frieze of Musicians and Dancers
from the Purana Mahadeva Temple, Sikar.

Figure 46: Asavari ragini, perhaps from Malwa.

X | Makers of Modern India

Chapter 35 Mahatma Gandhi: My Life is My Message

K.L. Seshagiri Rao

A political drawing done in 1968 showed Gandhi seated in a lotus posture, with a quietly respectful Martin Luther King, Jr., standing before him. In the caption, Gandhi says to the recent martyr, "The odd thing about assassins, Dr. King, is that they think they have killed you." And just as Gandhi lived on enough to inspire King to make a "pilgrimage to nonviolence," so King and his triumphant non-violent campaign for civil rights enkindled interest and faith in non-violent resistance widely. King gladly acknowledges his debt to Gandhi, saying that he found his message "profound and electrifying." In the non-violent technique, he saw a moral way to win over the oppressed people of the world in their fight against injustice.

No thinker in modern times has, perhaps, experienced so keen a struggle within himself regarding the momentous issues of religious faith as has Mahatma Gandhi. His whole life was one unceasing quest for anchorage of faith in a "living God." His was a personality in which the deepest strand was the religious. It was the religious motivation that made his life a compelling example and the center of attention of people throughout the world. For him, the best kind of life was the life of good deeds and selfless service to humanity. Though he did not yield himself to the persistent efforts made to convert him to a religion other than his own, he could incorporate the insights of other religions into his in an endeavor to realize the inner truths of all religions. Faith and reason, the spiritual and the ethical, had so blended in him that he was able to steer clear of the irrational superstitions that smother what is of inestimable value in religion.

Further, though he opened his mind to the powerful influences of modern thought currents, he never gave up his roots in his religious faith and held on to them valiantly in his life-long pilgrimage toward the realization of Truth. He focused his attention on the necessity of living religiously. His religious consciousness was both mystical and prophetic; he made social life his field of research. He insisted on truth and nonviolence in every sphere of life. For him, religion and truth were so coequal that his religion may be said to be the religion of truth, and the way to it was ahimsā, nonviolence. Thus, in Horace Alexander's words, truth and nonviolence constituted "the essence of his faith—twin suns around which all the lesser planets of his faith revolved" (1949: 4). It is therefore not by accident that Gandhi called his autobiography *The Story of My Experiments with Truth.*

Early Influences

The environment into which the child Mohandas Karamchand Gandhi was born had certain elements that molded and shaped his life and mind. He belonged to a highly respected vaisya family; he was a Vaisnava by faith. The members of his family were noted more for piety and honest living than for wealth or scholarship. Karamchand Gandhi, the father of Mohandas, had no education save that of experience; he was "truthful, brave and generous, but short-tempered (Gandhi 1966: 4). He rose to be Dewan of Rajkot and later of Vankaner in Kathiawar.

Mohandas' mother was a deeply religious woman who went to the temple daily, never took a meal before prayer, and frequently undertook fasts. Gandhi had a deep and steadfast love for his mother. The gentleness of her character and her deep piety made a profound impression on him from his earliest years. Throughout his life, he was concerned with the cultivation and appreciation of at least three virtues of the Hindu faith in which he was brought up by his mother: ahimsā, brahmačarya (celibacy), and aparigraha (non-acquisition). It was in such a background that his early years were spent. The roots of his emotional makeup and intellectual creativity lay in Hindu religious texts like the Rāmāyana and Mahābhārata, the Bhagavadgītā, the Upaniṣads, and the Vaiṣṇava lyrics. C. F. Andrews observes:

> The more we study Mahatma Gandhi's own life and teaching, the more certain it becomes that the Hindu religion has been the greatest of all influences in shaping his ideas and actions. He is in no sense a literalist or a fundamentalist in his adher ence to the Hindu scriptures. His extraordinary tolerance and sympathy with other faiths colors his whole outlook on human life, and makes him at times seem nearer to the acceptance of an indeterminate position than he really is. But his mother's influence as a devout and gentle Hindu saint perpetually returns to his mind and conscience... (1949:60).

At school, he was shy and kept himself aloof from his classmates. He liked to go to plays. The play Hariśčandra, based on a story from the epic Mahabharata, had aroused his imagination in his early years. The ordeals undergone by Hariśčandra for his devotion to truth made a deep impression on him. He asked himself, why should not all be truthful like Hariśčandra? (Gandhi 1966:7).

Religion played a vital part in the life of the Gandhi family. In Kathiawar, Jainism exercised an enduring influence along with Vaiṣṇavism. Gandhi's nonviolence, vegetarianism, and many other traits of his religious personality date from his very early years. His father had friends of all faiths, who visited him frequently for religious discussions. Young Mohandas, while attending on his father, listened to these discussions with Hindus, Muslims, Parsis, Jains, and adherents of other religions. During this period, he also read the Rāmāyaṇa, the Bhāgavata, and the Manusmṛti from his father's library. All these made him very tolerant in his religious ideas and unsectarian in nature. He later wrote, "In Rajkot, however, I got an early grounding in toleration for all branches of Hinduism and sister religions. For my father and mother would visit the Haveli (Vaiśnava place of congregation) as also Shiva's and Rama's temples, and would take or send us youngsters there.

In his teens, Gandhi was for some time drawn towards atheism. He had regard for morality as the basis of all things and for truth as the substance of morality.

> "Truth became my sole objective," he wrote. "It began to grow in magnitude every day, and my definition of it also has been ever widening" (Gandhi 1966: 34).

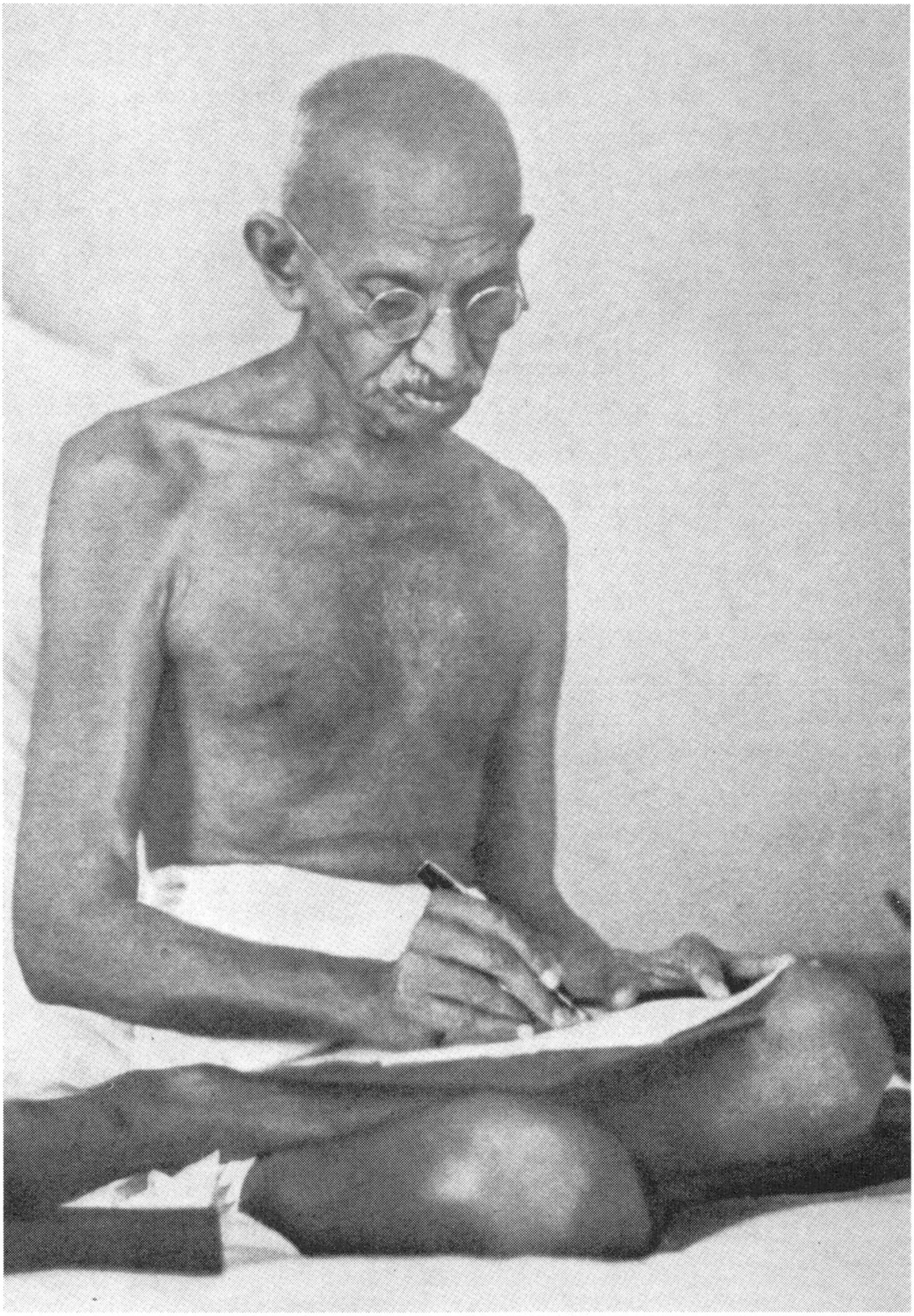

Figure 47: Mahatma Gandhi

In studying the early years of Gandhi's life, one can easily see in them the seeds that later flowered into full bloom (Williams).

> His innate love of truth, desire for the freedom of his Motherland, love of simple things and simple people, passion for purity, even to austerity, tried cour age and quiet moral strength—all these qualities were struggling within him to find suitable expression in a field of labor big enough to call them to play.

In England, he spent a large part of his time cultivating the personal acquaintance of several men who had made their mark in the fields of religion and ethics—Theosophists, Christians, even atheists. He joined the Vegetarian Society of England and started a Vegetarian Club in his locality (Bayswater), became its secretary, and was an ardent propagandist for vegetarianism. The literature of the theosophists introduced him to the religious movement for the unity of religions. Edwin Arnold's *The Light of Asia,* about the life of the Buddha, made a lasting impression on him, and his English version of the Bhagavadgītā, *The Song Celestial*, stirred him so deeply that for the rest of his life it became his constant guide. He was also much moved by the teachings of the New Testament and, especially, the Sermon on the Mount. The verses, "But I say unto you, that ye resist not evil; but whosoever shall smite thee on thy right cheek, turn to him the other also," went straight to his heart. Gandhi wrote later about this experience, "My young mind tried to unify the teaching of the Gītā, the Light of Asia, and the Sermon on the Mount. That renunciation was the highest form of religion appealed to me greatly" (Gandhi 1966: 69). Further, from Carlyle's *Heroes and Hero Worship* he learned of Mohammed's "greatness, brave and austere living" (69). He also read Washington Irving's *Life of Mohammed and His Successors.* He also gained knowledge of different religious traditions. From them, he received some of the basic principles of his life, and he became inclined towards a life in which East and West could meet.

South Africa

Gandhi's life in South Africa presented to him direct experience of the distorted as well as the good aspects of religion. He had hardly set foot in South Africa, in the spring of 1891, when he became involved in the racial and color conflict. One experience in South Africa changed the course of his life. He was traveling in a train with a first-class ticket and was turned out of his compartment to make way for a white passenger. In the midnight cold of Maritzburg, he was not allowed even to enter a waiting room, because of the color of his skin. Then the moment of decision came: should he go back to India or stay in South Africa and start a life-long struggle for human justice? He decided to stay and fight injustice, and not to flee. Once, when he was kicked by a policeman off a footpath near President Kruger's house without the slightest warning, he said to himself, "The hardship to which I am subjected is superficial—only a symptom of the deep disease of color prejudice. I should try, if possible, to root out the disease and suffer hardships in the process (Gandhi 1966: 163). Very soon, he organized a permanent organization to look after the interests of the Indian community called the "Natal Indian Congress." He developed a passion for serving the poor. He wrote:

> If I found myself entirely absorbed in the service of the community, the reason behind it was my desire for self-realization. I had made the religion of service my own as I felt that God could be realized only through service. . . I had gone to South Africa for travel, for finding an escape from Kathiawad intrigues and for gaining my livelihood. But, as I have said, I found myself in search of God and striving for self-realization. I began to realize more and more the infinite possibilities of universal love. (Gandhi 1966: 158-160)

When the Boer War began in 1899, Gandhi organized an Indian Ambulance corps and offered its services to the authorities. In 1904, when plague broke out in Johannesburg, he closed his law office and devoted himself to sanitary work and the evacuation and nursing of the victims. In 1906, when the Zulu rebellion occurred in Natal, he organized, from among the Indian community, a stretcher-bearer company and offered its services to the government, which accepted it with Gandhi as the sergeant major.

At Johannesburg, Gandhi had a flourishing law practice. He gained increasing influence. His words were heeded by a large portion of Indians in South Africa. There was a deep hunger in him that could not be satisfied by worldly success. He could find no abiding satisfaction in material gain. John Ruskin's *Unto This Last* (which Gandhi summarized later in Gujarati under the title Sarvōdaya) makes a critical study of modern civilization and pleads passionately for new social values. It made a decisive impression on him. He read it during one of his journeys from Johannesburg to Durban:

> The book was impossible to lay aside; once I had begun it, it gripped me. I could not get any sleep that night. I determined to change my life in accordance with the ideals of that book... I believe that I discovered some of my deepest convictions reflected in this great book of Ruskin, and that is why it so captured me and made me transform my life. (Gandhi 1966:288-9)

He realized "that a life of labor, i.e., the life of the tiller of the soil and the handicraftsman is the life worth living" (Gandhi 1966: 299). It was an important event in Gandhi's life. He got up at dawn that morning and resolved to give up his career as a successful lawyer in order to become an Indian peasant; he decided to transform his whole mode of existence, his profession, and even his private life. To realize the new way of life, he founded an ashram, the Phoenix Settlement, near Durban in Natal, South Africa. It was a little colony consisting of Indian and European friends and colleagues who lived and worked happily together in public service. He established the International Printing Press and published a journal named *Indian Opinion.* This periodical contributed immensely to the molding of political awareness of Indians in South Africa.

While carrying on his public work, he was slowly revolutionizing his private life. A passion for simplicity and service took hold of him. He cut down the expenditure of his household, became his own barber and washerman, and taught his children at home without sending them to any school. He volunteered to become a compounder and a nurse in a charitable hospital and gave two hours of his time in the morning to this work. It was at this time that Gandhi took his vow of brahmačarya (celibacy) for life, to be able to devote himself solely to the love and service of his fellow men.

One of the persons who exercised a most decisive influence on Gandhi during this period was Tolstoy. During his first year in Africa, while he lived in Pretoria, Gandhi read *The Kingdom of God Is Within You.* The teaching of the book that the Sermon on the Mount was a sufficient guide to life—along with its profound sorrow concerning war, conscription, injustice, and oppression—was as if written for Gandhi. In answering an American correspondent, he later referred to this and some other influences,

> You have given me a teacher in Thoreau, who furnished me through his essay on the 'Duty of Civil Disobedience' scientific confirmation of what I was doing in South Africa; Great Britain gave me Ruskin, whose *Unto This Last* transformed

> me overnight from a lawyer and city dweller into a rustic living away from Durban on a farm, three miles from the nearest railway station; and Russia gave me in Tolstoy a teacher who furnished a reasoned basis for my nonviolence. Tolstoy blessed my movement in South Africa when it was still in its infancy and of whose wonderful possibilities I had yet to learn. It was he who prophesied in his letter to me that I was leading a movement which was destined to bring a message of hope to the downtrodden people of the earth (Tendulkar 1953, 177).

Gandhi shaped a new political tool for the masses, satyāgraha. He started, in 1906, his first large scale civil disobedience movement. He refused to abide by a newly enacted repressive and humiliating South African law, which required all Indians to obtain certificates of registration by giving fingerprints. The South African Indians, under Gandhi's leadership, launched a nonviolent struggle against the blatant discrimination to which the Transvaal Government was subjecting them. A great number of Indians refused to register, submitting to imprisonment rather than accepting discrimination. Gandhi was arrested on the orders of General Smuts. This was his first experience of prison life (1908). Soon jails became filled, and the government was extremely embarrassed with the entire situation. After a protracted struggle for the rights of the Indians in South Africa, Gandhi achieved his first great victory. The law requiring registration was abolished and several other concessions were granted to Indians. It is during this eventful period of his life that the basic outline of his religious and moral philosophy was drawn in the light of his spiritual and practical experience.

Removal of Untouchability

On returning to India, he founded another ashram at Sabarmati, Satyāgraha Ashram, with some of his fellow workers from Phoenix. All the members of the ashram were pledged to nonviolence, vegetarianism, and non-possession.

Gandhi had no place for untouchability. He denounced it as a travesty of religion and a blot on Hinduism. He was never able to reconcile himself to untouchability. He regarded it as an "excrescence." Gandhi invited an untouchable family to live with him in Sabarmati ashram upon his return from South Africa. The members of the ashram accepted them as equals. However, this admission of untouchables to the ashram caused a good deal of opposition to Gandhi in the country. But in all these things he was undaunted, because he was prompted by religious longing. He wrote:

> What I want to achieve—what I have been striving and pining to achieve these thirty years—is self-realization, to see God face to face, to attain Mokṣa. I live and move and have my being in pursuit of this goal. All that I do by way of speaking and writing, and all my ventures in the political field are directed to this same end. (Gandhi 1966: xii)

Within a lifetime, Gandhi, by his teachings, personal example, and reforming zeal, transformed the untouchables into a fearless, progressive, and vital element of the Indian nation. In the history of Hinduism, at no other time was there a man who staked his all for the uplift of the depressed of India. And in so far as this reformation was in relation to the so-called lowest strata in the Hindu community, its effect touched every strata of the Hindu society, thus setting into motion one of the most powerful liberalizing forces in human religious history. He wrote in the *Harijan* of January 30, 1937:

> Untouchability is repugnant to reason and to the instinct of mercy, pity and love... And I should be content to be torn into pieces rather than to disown the suppressed classes. Hindus will certainly never deserve freedom, nor get it, if they allow this noble religion to be disgraced by the retention of the taint of untouchability. And as I love Hinduism dearer than life itself, the taint has become for me an intolerable burden. Let us not deny God by denying a fifth of our race the right of association on equal footing.

Gandhi also waged relentless battle against the terrible abuses that had crept into the caste system. His very insistence on truth led him to focus its revealing light on the cruelties of the prevalent caste-system. The caste-system was, he believed, opposed to the basic concept of love and sought to break loose from the shackles of the past. But in all this zeal for reform, he remained convinced of the basic truths of his own tradition.

Even while Gandhi was engaged in struggles that were not apparently religious in character (like the "Salt Satyāgraha" or the "Quit India Program"), his dominant motive was a religious one; of doing everything in a spirit of dedication to God. He wrote in Harijan,

Man's ultimate aim is the realization of God, and all his activities, social, religious, have to be guided by the ultimate aim of the vision of God. The immediate service of all human beings becomes a necessary part of the endeavor, simply because the only way to find God is to see Him in His creation and be one with it. This can only be done by service of all. I am part and parcel of the whole and I cannot find Him apart from the rest of humanity. My countrymen are my nearest neighbors. They have become so helpless, so resourceless, so inert that I must concentrate myself on serving them. If I could persuade myself that I could find Him in a Himalayan cave I would proceed there immediately, but I know that I cannot find Him apart from humanity (August 29, 1936).

In 1919, Mahatma Gandhi led the first national Satyāgraha movement in protest of the Rowlatt Acts, a war-time legislation which enabled British authorities to imprison Indians without trial, when accused of sedition. Gandhi felt the bills curtailed the civil liberties of Indians and began his Satyāgraha campaign on April 6th by launching a nationwide *hartal*, calling for all businesses to shut down. Seven days later, Gandhi was placed under arrest, leading to violent demonstrations. In retribution, British troops literally massacred 379 Indians in Jalianwalabagh, Amritsar. Gandhi was appalled at the horrible outcome, and canceled the Satyāgraha campaign of civil disobedience in order to better enlighten his people on the true spirit of Satyāgraha. In remorse for the violence which did occur on the part of the Indians, Gandhi fasted. He set forth the principle of non-violent resistance clearly:

There is no half way between truth and non-violence on the one hand, and untruth and violence on the other. We may never be strong enough to be entirely non-violent in thought, word and deed. But we must keep non-violence as our goal and make steady progress towards it. The attainment of freedom, whether for a man, a nation or the world, must be in exact proportion to the attainment of non-violence by each. Let those, therefore, who believe in non-violence as the only method of achieving real freedom, keep the lamp of non-violence burning bright in the midst of the impenetrable gloom. The truth of a few will count, the untruth of millions will vanish like chaff before a whiff of wind (Gandhi 1963: 178).

In 1930, after ten years of practicing non-violent civil disobedience and non-cooperation in the fight for independence, Gandhi led still another major Satyāgraha campaign. He chose to violate the Salt Act, which adversely affected many of the poorest sections of the communities. He led demonstrators 200 miles from Sabarmati to the seashore at Dandi. There he illegally removed some salt from the sea. Hundreds of thousands of satyagrahi's joined the protest in support of Gandhi across the country, and many were arrested. By 1931, a solution was reached in the form of the Irwin-Gandhi Agreement. The restrictions on salt manufacturing were eased, the making of salt for private use was legalized, and the nearly 100,000 non-violent demonstrators in prison were released.

In 1942, Gandhi was still at work seeking independence for India. On August 8th, the All-India Congress committee, which had introduced the "Quit India" resolution, authorized "mass Satyāgraha" for India, led by Gandhi and the Congress leader, Jawaharlal Nehru. Unfortunately, violence by non-satyāgrahis, hatred and fear, accompanied the campaign, which was to last for the next five years. During this period, Gandhi traveled often, seeking adherence to non-violent means from his people and concessions from the British government. Finally it was announced that the British would leave India by 1948. Gandhi was opposed to the partition of the country but left with no choice he too, reluctantly, agreed to the settlement.

After twenty-seven years of struggle for freedom, India and Gandhi had their victory in 1947. The independence of India marked a monumental feat in world history, for it was the first complete solution of a major conflict between two nations that resulted from non-violent resistance. But more than merely granting freedom for a people, the nonviolent method is what eventually unified all Indians and gave them the necessary self-respect, self-reliance, courage and persistence, and also resulted in mutual respect and good feelings between Britain and India in the end.

In the economic sphere, Gandhi was well "ahead of his time." While his colleagues were obsessed with making India a competitive Western-style manufacturing state, Gandhi had already foreseen the danger of creating that world of "unrelated objects" and "pointless existence." In his opinion, man should not use what he does not really need. Any extra production due to a person's superior talent must belong to the community. Wealth is to be held in common as God's gift to all creatures. He developed, therefore, a theory of Trusteeship and stressed the moral responsibility to one's fellow beings.

Gandhi staunchly believed in the concept of "bread labor," which insists that every person who wants to eat must work. An idler who stuffs his stomach is a thief. Gandhi felt that manual labor built character, virtue, and self reliance. He wanted "production by the masses and for the masses." He wanted machinery where it would be of benefit for all. This meant a refinement and continued emphasis on village industries, because it was in the village that the misery of India would be broken or maintained. Gandhi understood the connection between rapid industrialization, social injustice, loss of identity, and creative satisfaction from life.

Gandhi, all through his life, devoted much time and energy to the promotion of Hindu-Muslim unity. He once fasted for three weeks for this cause. He said, "My penance is the prayer of a bleeding heart ... it is a warning to Hindus and Muslims who have professed to love me." He wrote, " If not during my lifetime, I know after my death both Hindus and Muslims will bear witness that I had never ceased to yearn after communal peace (Gandhi 1963: 178). Earlier, he had supported the Muslims in the Khilafat Movement and agitated for the release of the Ali brothers. C. F. Andrews observes,

> During one period of the Non-Cooperation Movement, he made the nearest approach to Islam that has ever been made by Hinduism in recent times. He found that the devout followers of Islam, who revered the Caliph at Constantinople as the Head of their religion, had been outraged by the ignominious terms of surrender imposed upon the command of the Faithful at the end of the war; for the victorious destroyed much of the Caliph's temporal authority, thus threatening it at its very center...At this point, Mahatma Gandhi, whose one intense longing had always been to unite Hindus and Muslims together, in one common Indian Nation, seized the psychological opportunity of supporting the Muslims in what he held to be a righteous cause. He promised them his entire devotion on behalf of their Caliph and gave himself wholeheartedly to them. Thus, this Kahilafat question, which was agitating Islam in India became for a time the direct means of a cordial reconciliation (Andrews 1949: 55-57).

Thanks to Gandhi's efforts, India became a friend on equal terms with England. A great imperial power surrendered its domain smoothly and peacefully to the people it had governed for nearly two centuries, but Gandhi was then not in Delhi to celebrate the coming of Independence. He was in Noakhali in Bengal giving strength and hope to those who were victims of religious hatred and violence.

In the wake of the partition of the country, hundreds of thousands of Hindus and Muslims were killed in the Punjab, Bengal, and Bihar. Gandhi threw himself into the struggle to heal the breach between the two communities. He toured riot-affected areas preaching the need for peace and good will. A mob attacked Gandhi himself in Calcutta. He had become the symbol of the Hindu intransigence to angry Muslims, while his efforts to protect Muslims infuriated the suffering Hindus. He began a fast in Calcutta and worked a miracle. Lord Mountbatten, then the Governor-General of India, wrote to Gandhi: "In the Punjab, we have 55,000 soldiers and large-scale rioting on our hands. In Bengal our forces consist of one man, and there is no rioting" (Pyarelal 1958: 382).

Then he traveled to Delhi; the capital was ringed with violence and shaken by murders. He spoke to the crowds; he explained that a Hindu, a Muslim, and a Christian were all brothers, sons of the same God. And he started another fast—the eighteenth and the last of his life. At the age of 78 he broke the fast only when he received definite assurances from Hindu and Muslim leaders that they would do their utmost to stop violence, and when India paid over Pakistan's share in the assets of the undivided State (about 40 million pounds).

Gandhi was not unaware of the magnitude of the problem with which he was dealing. He had to face religious fanaticism and bigotry, superstition and ignorance, selfishness and hypocrisy, even atheism and indifference. Many a time, his was a voice crying in the wilderness. His plea for tolerance (non-violence) and reverence towards the faith of other men often fell on deaf ears. It is difficult to say how far Gandhi succeeded in establishing the relationship of love and reverence between Hindus and Muslims in India. Obviously, much more remains to be done. As he often used to say, he was only beginning the experiment with nonviolence. He was just trying to put people on the road.

Gandhi wanted peace to be established not merely between Hindu and Muslims, but among the adherents of all the religions of the world. He once wrote, "Hindu-Muslim unity means not only unity between Hindus and Muslims, but between all those who believe India to be their home—no matter to what faith they belong". In fact, the problem that faced Gandhi in India is a world problem. With the annihilation of distance by modern science and technology, the world has become a single unit. The meeting of religions, therefore, is not confined to India only; it is now a universal encounter. The problem of the mutual relationships of the religions can no more be postponed or sidestepped. In the interests of lasting peace and harmony among the peoples of the world, the problem has to be successfully tackled; this demands a sympathetic study and understanding, on the part of believers of all faiths, of the different religions of the world. In this connection, Gandhi's life and example throw fresh light on the problem and bring a new and sensitive approach to its solution based on mutual understanding.

Gandhi advocated harmony among the world's religions instead of playing down the importance of any of them. The sciences, which study the natural world, do not claim "any monopoly of wisdom for their own particular branch of study nor quarrel about the superiority of one science over the others" (Gandhi 1966: 9). In a similar way, Gandhi held, each religion must bring its individual contribution to humanity's understanding of the spiritual world and not quarrel about the superiority of one religion over another, for God's love embraces the whole world. He believed that all the world religions are God-given and that they serve the people to whom they are revealed. They are allies engaged in the common cause of the moral and spiritual uplift of humanity. In the context of the emerging world community, all the great religions are useful, necessary, and complementary to one another as revealing different facets of the one Truth.

The problems that threaten the world community are not merely political or economic; they arise as well from certain basic religious and spiritual attitudes. If the faith and integrity of others are not respected, genuine communication, and consequently, the world community will be at best a dream. Arnold Toynbee, after surveying the history of the entire human race, has made the following significant observation: At this supremely dangerous moment in human history, the only way of salvation for mankind is the Indian way —Emperor Ashoka's and Mahatma Gandhi's principle of nonviolence and Shri Ramakrishna's testimony to the harmony of all religions. Here we have an attitude and spirit that can make it possible for the human race to grow into a single family—and, in the Atomic Age, this is the only alternative to destroying ourselves.

Works Cited

Alexander, Horace. 1949. Introduction to *Mahatma Gandhi's Ideas* by C. F. Andrews. London: Allen and Unwin.

Andrews, C.F. 1949. *Mahatma Gandhi's Ideas.* London: Allen and Unwin.

Gandhi, M.K. 1966. *An Autobiography.* Boston: Beacon Press.

Williams, Rushbrook. *Great Men of India.* The Home Library Club.

Tendulkar, D.G. 1953. *Mahatma Gandhi.* Vol.6. Bombay: Vitthalbhai K. Jhaveri & Tendulkar.

Gandhi, M.K. *Cooperation.* 1963. Ahmdabad: Navjivan Publishing House.

Pyarelal. 1958, *Mahatama Gandhi - The Last Phase.* Ahmedabad: Navajivan Publishing House. Vol. II.

Young India, April 16 1931

Lal, R. B. *The Gita in the light of Modern Science.* Bombay: Somaiya Publications.

Toynbee, Arnold. Mahatma Gandhi. *Bhavan's Journal,* 28.2.

Chapter 36

Gandhi and the West

C.D. Narasimhaiah

The debt that one great man owes to another is something difficult to assess and it is futile to seek to determine the extent of any such conceptual influence except when curiosity prompts one to trace the origin of an idea or attitude. It is no sign of maturity in a people to dwell on the ownership of ideas too much, for ultimately ideas themselves matter less than what use they are put to.

Throughout her long history, India has always been encountering peoples drawn to her shores by love of her wealth or learning—possibly one of the reasons why Indian culture has a continuity, not in a static, but vital way. She came in contact with Egyptians, Greeks, Chinese, Arabs, Central Asians, and the peoples of the Mediterranean, and during the past three hundred years, Europeans. Only the Europeans stayed apart while others intermingled with us. Precisely because of this encounter of contrasting cultures there has been some unrest but it has also sustained and stimulated Indian life. In any case the encounter hasn't produced a "mestizo culture" that sprang up, in the countries of South America which imitated Europe in ignorance of their own cultures. Much less has the encounter encouraged India to devour other cultures and destroy their identities, as the monolithic American culture has done, apparently in its praise of unity of culture. A composite culture has been India's pride through the ages. This is an acute insight of Gandhi's considering how little, it is believed, Gandhi had known of the American scene.

It is curious, but perhaps true, that while Tagore the internationalist wrote in despair that the English-educated Indian's voice became an echo, his whole life a quotation—he did not feel the impact but was a servile receiver—Gandhi seemed at first to have greater faith despite his apparent horror of Western civilization. He believed that if the mass of English-educated Indian youth are not entirely denationalized it is because their ancient culture is too deeply rooted in them. The leaders of the Indian Renaissance in the nineteenth century, while they admired English education and English institutions, responsed from a strong Indian base indeed. Two of the most outstanding examples are Raja Rammohan Roy and Vivekananda.

For a descendant of these, Gandhi must have, to start with at least, looked quite disappointing. He was just past twenty when he went to England weathering formidable opposition from his own relations. Why did he go? "In a word, ambition ," he said later. But it was not vague, it had a purpose, it was his "cherished goal" to become a barrister, but also to see England "the land of philosophers and poets, the very center of civilization." It was a callow young Indian that affected the "English gentleman ", wore frock coat and top hat, and took lessons in music and dancing. He learnt to take care of his consonants and cultivated the habit of deliberate articulation. This as well as his early meticulousness in dress persisted to the end of his life; whether in the way he used words, the way he resisted "smart expression" and "cultivated" words "carefully and prayerfully," or in the manner he wore his loin cloth and let the elegant folds of his shawl sit on his shoulders.

The "English gentleman" was only destined to be the "springboard" from which to take a leap forward, but first of all to repudiate what he so much sought after. For very soon almost everything Western came under fire, samples of which are contained in expressions such as these:

> "Satanic civilization" of the West, "the glamour of the West," "the Golden Fleece," "to run after (which) is to court certain death," "Europe today is only nominally Christian. In reality it is worshipping Mammon;"

insatiable material ambition at one end, and consequent war at the other; "our geography is different, our history is different, our ways of living are different... where there are millions and millions of units of idle labor it is no use thinking of labor-saving devices." And the consequent "boycott" and burning of "British goods." As with economy so with the art of government—he reacted sharply against "parliamentary democracy." He, an oriental, with standing accusation against the East by the practitioners of allopathic medicine of indulging in occultism, had the courage to hit back on Western medicine as "black magic" which demoralizes man with its "palliatives" instead of "strengthening his character."

From innocent, thoughtless imitation to almost unqualified condemnation! But there were bridges between. After his return from the Round Table Conference he refuted the irreconcilable doctrine of the East and the West and proclaimed to his countrymen: "I have been convinced more than ever that human nature is much the same no matter under what clime it flourishes and that if you approached people with trust and affection you would have ten-fold trust and thousand-fold affection returned to you." Not a particularly well-phrased sentiment—even a banality—however, it does reflect his faith in the irreducible minimum of good that is in all men. He resiled from extreme positions and evinced positive interest in wanting to "profit from the light that came from the West" — "light," "not glamour." He will not bar his doors and windows against the West. "Let all the cultures," he said in an oft-quoted remark, "of all the lands blow about my house, but I shall refuse to be swept off my feet by any." And from this position of tolerance he can move on to firm faith in the West: "Let us engrave on our hearts the motto of a Western philosopher: plain living and high thinking"— again, a trite remark for the aesthetically disposed but such was Gandhi's terrific earnestness that the cliché did not inhibit his full response to the ideals that were held up before him. I must, hasten to add that Gandhi has not progressed chronologically from one position to another, in the way I have enumerated; I have only tried to classify for convenience some of the significant shifts in his complex reaction to the West and I shall have occasion to dwell in detail on his more complex responses to the West presently.

Dr. Oldfield in his book *My Friend Gandhi* speaks of two kinds of Indians that came to England : Some that fail in their encounters with a different mode of life and these "commonplace minds", "drop into the ordinary run of English diet, English habits and general mediocrity. And the other can stand firm in their faith and be prepared to die for it and they prove themselves men indeed ." He adds: "Upon this class of men does the mantle of Gandhi still fall and the future of India depend."

It is well known that Gandhi's vegetarian obsessions in England brought him in contact with some of the finest Englishmen of the day, some of them well-known Socialists and ardent Christians. One of them commended the Bible to Gandhi's attention with "Read the Bible if only for my sake." The Old Testament sent him "to sleep" but he had a profound experience when he came to the New Testament :

> My young mind tried to unify the teaching of the *Gita*, *The Light of Asia* and The Sermon on the Mount. That renunciation was the highest form of religion appealed to me greatly. But I say unto you, that ye resist not evil and if any man take away thy coat let him have thy cloak delighted me beyond measure. It was the New Testament which really awakened me to the rightness and value of Passive Resistance.

But this great admirer of the Sermon on the Mount "refused to set Jesus on a solitary throne—words which echo Vivekananda's ruthless critical analysis of Christianity in his American speeches.

Pyarelal, in his very fine piece of writing on Gandhi remarks that "Socialism in England came under two kinds of leadership—under pioneers like Henry Salt and Edward Carpenter, it hoped that Labor would return to the land and become simple in its needs. But the Webbs, Shaw, and Hyndman representing the other shade of thought preferred an industrial community. The former lost the day." Perhaps true. But Pyarelal likes to believe, and that is what disturbs one, that Gandhi picked up the last thread and applied it to the uplift of the Indian villages. According to him, these, namely, vegetarianism and handicrafts became "the two central planks in India's non-violent struggle for independence under his lead." This, I fear, is a very misleading impression, as both ahimsa (which in any case is very different from the cult of vegetarianism as practised in the West) and handicrafts have had several thousand years of history in India. All one can say is that even the approximation and sophisticated articulation of these very old Indian practices by British intellectuals may have pleasantly surprised Gandhi who apparently had originally associated England with mechanization and meat-eating. In any case the British or even Irish intellectuals could not have brought much conviction either into their own thinking or, to one like Gandhi on vegetarianism, as we can see from Bernard Shaw's remarks. "It is as mean to send the cow to the slaughter house when she becomes old as to send your mother to the gallows when she falls sick or has ceased to give suck." A typically (clever) Shavian statement!

Well, the strongest word Shaw uses is "mean." One hadn't thought that to send a mother to the gallows was just a "mean" act (unless the word is diluted of its meaning) but Shaw's desire for effect must have outrun his sense of precision for words. Besides, Shaw's objection is presumably to sending an "old cow" to the slaughter house. This celebrated vegetarian wouldn't probably have had any objection to the killing of a fat calf or a milking cow. Now compare with this Gandhi's reference to the cow as a "poem of pity" that it is symbol of the entire sub-human world; and to respect this "gentle animal" is for man to be "taken beyond this species and to realize his identity with all that lives."

Ruskin and Gandhi

It is the same with Socialism and handicrafts for which Gandhi is said to be indebted to Ruskin. Let us leave Gandhi for a while and try to understand the Western writers who find themselves in juxtaposition with Gandhi because of his own acknowledged indebtedness. There are whole papers devoted to each of them and I am only trying to comment in passing on the degree of relevance in associating Gandhi with these writers. It is embarrassing to trace influences, enumerate parallels and cite cross-references in the manner of school boys. Far more rewarding is to understand how each of these great men, including Gandhi, is a product of his milieu, to know the challenges his environment posed and to assess his response as a combined expression of his tradition, his milieu, his personal temperament and his unique vision of life. The object of this chapter is to try and offer some sort of concerted, informed corrective to glib generalizations about influences on the basis of superficial resemblances and expressions of indebtedness made in modesty; in any case, to gain a critical appreciation of what Gandhi did with the ideas he took from others, in comparison with what the Western writers themselves did with their own ideas.

Consider John Ruskin, to start with. Towards the end of the eighteenth century England witnessed unprecedented industrial development and all those ills which Dickens describes in moving terms in a succession of novels—insanitary slums, starvation wages, and drunkenness of the poor. Ruskin traces all the ills to the pillage of the laborer: the landlord pillages the peasant, the lawyer pillages the client and the merchant everyone by adultrating foodstuffs. We are told that women and children in mines pulled large wheelless tubs laden with coal. And then, he saw "a wilderness of spinning wheels," yet the people had no clothes; "every leaf of English greenwood" was blackened with coal, and yet the people died of cold; harbors were full of ships laden with wheat, but the people died of hunger.

Eminent thinkers like Malthus wrote: "To prevent recurrence of misery is, alas! beyond the power of man," and *The London Times* we are told, endorsed it and explained it away as the result of "Nature's simplest laws." Even so sensitive an intellectual as John Stuart Mill maintained that political economy had nothing to do with moral judgments. And William Morris, disciple of Ruskin, was convinced that only by violent usurpation of power could the masses free themselves from their masters. How perilously close to the "dictatorship of the proletariat!"

Now, briefly, this was the background against which Ruskin had to operate. Fortunately for him the air was charged with reform: George Eliot preached the Religion of Humanity in novel after novel; Thomas and Carlyle preached the Gospel of Work—he asked if all the financiers of Europe could undertake in one joint-stock company to make one shoeblack happy beyond an hour or two, for the shoeblack has a soul other than his stomach. Ruskin, who admired Carlyle enormously, joined in with his gospel of social justice. Thanks to the religious background at home provided largely by his mother and his study of Plato, Ruskin's "rage against inequality became divine." Like Gandhi, Ruskin too put the emphasis on the personal character of the reformer. "Here I am," said Ruskin, trying to reform the world and "I suppose I ought to begin with myself." One reads of instances in his life, of street-cleaning, road-digging, sinking an enormous fortune in lands and houses for philanthropic purposes, and volunteering services in the working men's college. But primarily "to fill starved people's bellies is the only thing a man can do in this generation," he asserted again and again.

He knew he could not expect the higher classes to initiate reform. Parliament, to him, was "darkness voluble;" it was a "circumlocution office." And neither ballots nor barricades, he believed, would alter man's condition and so he tried to touch their hearts through the ethics of Christ. His artistic predisposition lent strong support to it. As an artist he believed that mindless mechanical perfection is not good for man—it produces a new class of slaves, mindless tools rather than men. The artist who believed in the whole man, in the totality of experience and not in its fragmentariness, opposed the division of labor as the division of man—"learning to make points of pins and heads of nails." He pleaded that "England feed all hungry, not merely the deserving hungry, nor the industrial hungry nor the well-intentioned hungry." Instead of organizing a labor movement he advocated "filial loyalty from the employee and fatherly benevolence from the captains of industry." One is constrained to add that this paternalism did not work—"the laborer's voice was worth a rat's squeak"—it didn't work any more than Gandhi's trusteeship theory did, though the latter met with considerable success in Gandhi's own life-time and at the hands of his disciple Vinoba Bhave. But what interests readers of Ruskin nearly a century after is the way he "mobilized" sentiment by "every telling biblical phrase, every word that had overtones of feeling" to win attention to his views. He was among the first of modern thinkers who brought emotion into what Carlyle called that "dismal science" of economics and "morals into the law of supply and demand." Where a Gandhi would innocently repeat the biblical statement, "Man does not live by bread alone," Ruskin the artist would add, "but also by the desert manna, by every wondrous word and unknowable work of God." It is by such felicity of phrasing, religious fervor, and sincerity of purpose that Ruskin could exert the kind of influence he did: "In no other socialist movement has Christian thought had such a powerful leavening effect," wrote Clement Attlee, the Labor Prime Minister. And one gathers, too, that Ruskin's *Unto This Last* was a potent influence with a considerable number of Labor Members of Parliament in England.

But that was not immediately—it was more than half a century after Ruskin's death. St. George's Guild which Ruskin founded was in a quandary in Ruskin's own life-time. "Those perplexed souls" of the Guild never quite knew what their master wanted. For while they were seeking help in cooperative farming, we are told that their master was purchasing emeralds for the Guild Museum at Sheffield or was off in Venice making studies of "Dream of St. Ursula." He offered grandiose plans to control the flooding of the Rhine, the Rhone, and the Po, and liked others to emulate his example all along the Alps. "If they don't do," all Ruskin could do was to say "it is their fault—not mine." He said very bravely, though, "But if I die, I will die digging like Faust"—this was mere attitudinizing when one recalls the earnestness with which Faust and, equally his creator, Goethe, addressed themselves to social welfare. Now, what could the men do with what a critic of Ruskin calls their "dreary, dilatory, makeshift master who preferred painting flowers to reforming the world?" It is true that the master couldn't help his insanity. He had at least the sense to wind up the affairs of the Guild at once—"so that I may come out of it with clean hands and a pure heart." It is obvious he was not meant to start a movement. There is pathos in the way he described himself as "a reed shaken with the wind." And for others, what remains is fortunately not so much his own example but his exhortation, the impact which the exhortation of a writer has on his readers for generations to come:

> Raise the veil boldly; face the light and if, as yet, the light of the eye can only be through tears, and the light of the body through sack cloth, go thou forth weeping, bearing precious seed, until the time comes.

The time came, not for Ruskin but to one who read him, literally to go about with a sack cloth. A friend of Gandhi puts into his hands a copy of Ruskin's *Unto This Last* to read during his journey from Johannesburg to Durban: "The book was impossible to lay aside, once I had begun it," says Gandhi. "It gripped me. Johannesburg to Durban was a twenty-four hours' journey. The train reached there in the evening. I could not get any sleep that night. I determined to change my life in accordance with the ideals of the book." Not determination only, but he "arose with the dawn ready, to reduce these principles into practice."

The result was the Phoenix Settlement, an impossible ideal, "the beautiful vaporings of an unpractical idealist," rendered into a most practical proposition, "the blueprint" for his reformistic work. Comparison of St. George's Guild with the Phoenix Settlement is superfluous for those who are acquainted with the origin and working of both. Suffice to say that for Gandhi, social obligations had a profound religious sanction as the evocative expression *Daridranarayana* connotes—the reason why he could declare with conviction that even God dare not appear before a hungry man except in the form of food. He was not content to talk about spinning and working with hands but did it all himself and lived on the most frugal diet, and the barest minimum of clothing possible.

To those who preached the Western brand of Socialism in India, Gandhi would say in the characteristic Indian way that he admired their concern and sacrifice but since he could not keep pace with them he would ask them to stop for him in their march, collect him, and take him along with them. Which meant respect for the individual. He feared that Communism was a natural corollary to the Socialism of the West, and he did "not want to rise on the ashes of the blind, the deaf, and the dumb." In that Socialism they will probably have no place. "I want freedom for the full expression of personality. I must be free to build a staircase to Sirius, if I want to." For Gandhi, socialism will not wait till "all were converted" but "starts with the first convert." He illuminates his stand with a vivid image from mathematics: "If there is one such you can add zeros to the one and the first zero will account for ten...If however the beginner is a zero... multiplicity of zeros will also produce zero value." One now appreciates the unusual importance Gandhi attaches to purity of conduct in a leader. He said his socialism is "as pure as crystal... requires crystal—like means to achieve it." To him socialism was a religious creed, not a political ideology.

Tolstoy and Gandhi

The comparison of Gandhi with the writers of the West is all to Gandhi's advantage when we come to Tolstoy. Born a Count, Tolstoy inherited a huge property of several estates covering more than five thousand acres with more than three hundred serfs and their families. His own father's retirement from government service on ideological grounds and the misrule of successive governments especially the beaurocratic regime of Nicholas I fostered in Tolstoy a mistrust of government. Add to it the rise of the self-seeking and corrupt, capitalistic bourgeoisie who were a "parasitic drain" on the peasants. His social conscience was stirred by the contrast between the "godly" life of the peasants and the egotistic life of his own class. He began to renounce pleasures and live for others.

Tolstoy realized that only three types of life are possible: the egoistic, the social, and the Christian. "The history and the destiny of humanity " consisted for Tolstoy in passing from the egoistic to the Christian attitude—surprising how so great a man could only think within the Christian framework while talking of the history and destiny of man as though Christianity was all the religion that mankind professed or practised. That is by the way, but it is interesting how, in contrast to Tolstoy, Gandhi was far more inclusive—he included every religion in his scheme of things and studied everyone of them assiduously. "I do not believe in the exclusive divinity of the Vedas. I believe the Bible, the Koran and the Zend-Avesta to be as divinely inspired as the Vedas." Tolstoy, too, like Gandhi disapproved of the egoistic life totally, but unlike Gandhi, Tolstoy thought, the social was vague "humanity is fiction and it is impossible to love it." And it followed therefore thsat only the last one was man's destiny. Following this Tolstoy insisted on two things; the dissolution of the armed forces; and the ownership of the land by the peasantry. No wonder Lenin recommended in 1910 the widest publicity for Tolstoy's work as an aid to the socialist revolution.

But the revolution that ensued was not the one that Tolstoy worked for. He ruled out violence of all kinds whether of the Church or the State—the violence of the Church has gone, we know, but what of violence of the State? Tolstoy was up against a Church which existed in the name of Christ, but its connivance at violence, he held, "perverts the teaching of Christ." This, perversion of truth by the Church and the exploitation of the peasantry by the State became an obsession with Tolstoy. In his

Kingdom of God is Within You he compiles evidence from Europe, America and Russia to show how everyone subscribed to Christ's teaching of "Resist not evil." In Russia itself, he pointed out how some peasants refused to take up military service on religious conviction. They submitted readily to the most cruel punishments but refused to render military service. Tolstoy comments: They were sent to Georgia and the Commander-in-Chief of the army was asked to "correct them." That was the end of their non-resistance. The argument against Tolstoy's non-resistance is that Christ's teaching is not in harmony with our industrial age; if so, Tolstoy would say, "do away with machines." He saw that mechanization threatened to substitute "the pulsing of the machine for the rhythm of nature."

His view of art after conversion to Christ's teaching must be understood in this context. He pleaded: Art must remove violence, only art can do it ; and only that art which unites people in the same feelings and promotes brotherhood among men is great art—the reason why he rated Dickens higher than Shakespeare. Gandhi was to denounce the Taj Mahal on the same ground—to him it was no work of art, but an embodiment of slave labor. He would, one supposes, have approved of the temples of India and the cathedrals of Europe as works of art because they were built out of the prayers of pilgrims. We know he did prefer the music of the spinning wheel to everything else except perhaps that of the *Gita* and the *Ramayana* of Tulsidas, by the same criterion as Tolstoy's. Now, coming back to Tolstoy, a year before his death Tolstoy spoke—yes, it was all speaking or writing—passionately at the Peace Congress of 1909 in Sweden and asked the Congress to make their choice: "We have to repudiate either Christ and his teachings or the State with its armies and war." His countrymen have kept both, paid lip-service to one and actively fostered the other: teaching good, oh, unteachably after evil! The point I am at pains to make is, Tolstoy renounced all he had, himself lived nobly and simply but could not be the leader of the revolution—that was reserved for Lenin. Tolstoy's work ended with protests, passionate speeches, and addresses to peace conferences. Now Gandhi reads Tolstoy's *The Kingdom of God is within You* when, in his own words, he is passing through a severe crisis of scepticism and doubt. He explains its impact on him: "I was at that time a believer in violence. Its reading cured me of my scepticism and made me a firm believer in non-violence. What has appealed to me most in Tolstoy's life is he practised what he preached and reckoned no cost too great in his pursuit of truth! "What, one asks, was the cost Tolstoy paid for pursuing truth? Renunciation of luxuries in his own life and living a life of truth?" But what is that compared to the cost of making nonviolence the creed of millions involving all of whom in an encounter with a "satanic" government? Within ten years after the commencement of his struggle for independence in India, and three decades before his death, a colonial of the most powerful empire on earth had the courage to say at a public meeting organized by students of the Benares University in 1920, when there was not a ray of hope for India's independence:

> All of us have had many anxious moments while the Viceroy was going through the streets of Benares. There were detectives stationed in many places. We were horrified. We asked ourselves: "Why this distrust? Is it not better that even Lord Hardinge should die than live a living death?" We may fret, we may resent but let us not forget that India of today in her impatience has produced an army of anarchists. I myself am an anarchist, but of another type.

Now where did Gandhi get this courage from? Not from Thoreau or Tolstoy though they may have given him support for what was within him. It came mainly from the deep wells of Hinduism:

> If we trust and fear God, we shall have to fear no one, not Maharajas, not Viceroys, not detectives, not even King George. I honor the anarchist for his love of country. I honor him for his bravery in being willing to die for his country.

The West had heard the language of military strength of the despot and the conqueror, and of assertion of the mob against the tyrant but it had not heard the voice of warning from the man of God after the Renaissance. Note some of the expressions Gandhi used at the time: "Such an empire cannot live if there is a just God ruling the universe." He knew "he was playing with fire," but he had the gumption to tell the Imperial Government on another occasion that if he was set free from prison he would still do the same." Now he spells out the future course: We have "now reached almost the end of our resources in speechmaking, and it is not enough that our ears are feasted, that our eyes are feasted, but it is necessary that our hearts have got to be touched and... our hands and feet have got to be moved."

Every word drips with energy and it is a call to action, for non-violence is truly the weapon of the brave man who cannot shy away from action in the name of thought;

only, in the context in which he found himself in India then, action meant for him "the quiet courage of dying without killing." As Jawaharlal Nehru writes in his *Discovery of India*:

> A bitter sense of humiliation and passionate anger filled our people. All the unending talk of constitutional reform and Indianization of the services was a mockery and an insult when the manhood of our country was being crushed and the inexorable and continuous process of exploitation was deepening our poverty and sapping our vitality. We had become a derelict nation.

And there is the refrain of helplessness in paragraph after paragraph of Nehru's writing: "Yet what could we do, how change this vicious process?" or "How could we pull India out of this quagmire of poverty and defeatism which sucked her in?" It was when the country was in this "quagmire" of despondency that Gandhi came. In Nehru's words, again, for hardly anyone has realized so acutely and critically the significance of Gandhi's emergence on the Indian scene as Nehru has done:

> And then Gandhi came. He was like a powerful current of fresh air that made us stretch ourselves and take deep breath, like a beam of light that pierced the darkness and removed the scales from our eyes, like a whirlwind that upsets many things but most of all the working of people's minds. He did not descend from the top; he seemed to emerge from the millions of India, speaking their language and incessantly drawing attention to them and their appalling condition...Get off the backs of these peasants and workers, he told us, all you who live by their exploitation; get rid of the system that produces this poverty and misery. Political freedom took new shape then and acquired new content.

Thoreau and Gandhi

Now, can we say this of any of the three writers from whom Gandhi has drawn stimulus for his work?: That he did not descend from the top; that he seemed to emerge from the millions of India, speaking their language. Well, precisely, this is the measure of Gandhi's success, as it is the measure of their failure in one sense. Only Thoreau, of all the three writers, seems to come closest to Gandhi though from his own account, what he borrowed from Thoreau is only a name, for *Satyagraha* has been in practice in this country for centuries and Gandhi himself had practised it in

South Africa, both when he was thrown out of the first class railway compartment and when he was beaten in the streets after his arrival there—and both these happened much before he had ever heard of Thoreau's "Civil Disobedience."

Gandhi writes:

> My first introduction to Thoreau was, I think, in 1907 when I was in the thick of the passive resistance struggle. His essay on Civil Disobedience left a deep impression upon me. I translated a portion for the readers of the *Indian Opinion*, which I was then editing. The essay seemed so truthful and convincing that I felt the need of knowing more about Thoreau and I have read his life, his *Walden*, and his shorter essays with great pleasure and equal profit.

But Thoreau, alone, of the three writers, lived in many respects in a manner Gandhi would have most approved of—I have in mind the objective and the urgency with which Thoreau went to live in Walden, preached the abolition of slavery, rallied to John Brown's aid, and himself refused to pay the poll-tax because the money went to a wrong cause—waging of the Mexican war—and for refusing to pay the tax, went to prison though only for a day. Only he, among the three writers of the West may be considered to have lived the most virtuous life; only he showed himself capable of some action. And his passionate desire for action comes out again and again in statements like: "There are nine hundred and ninety nine patrons of virtue to every virtuous man." "There are orators, politicians, eloquent men by the thousand but the speaker has not yet opened his mouth...who is capable of settling the much vexed questions of the day." "Man must reason from the hands and feet to the head, not the other way."

Everyone of these Gandhi would have endorsed unhesitatingly. There are, besides these, many minor but important resemblances in the modes of living of Thoreau and Gandhi and precisely because of their close resemblance, I think it is most fruitful to take a close look at the life and work of Thoreau and Gandhi, more so because Thoreau was the only one of the three who had made a reasonably close study of the Hindu books most of which had also influenced Gandhi so profoundly. He often compared himself with the Hindus, bathed in the pond early morning considering it as sacred as the Ganges water, ate rice, kept away from meat and drink, read the *Gita*, and felt so ecstatic that he thought one line from the *Gita* was worth the whole state of Massachusetts put together, and in comparison with its wisdom "our Shakespeare" was "green" merely.

He did not escape into the Walden forest but went there to transact some private business—to confront the essential facts of life, to drive life to a corner and suck the marrow out of it, to see what it is like to live according to the dictates of one's conscience and then proclaim the results to the world instead of going there in the evening of one's life. Besides, he has many lives to live and cannot give too much time to any one. And then, for him, to live is to live a life of 'simplicity,' independence, magnanimity, and trust. Consider the terrific urgency and impatience with which question follows question to get at the truth of life: "Why do men degenerate ever? What makes families run out? What is the nature of the luxury which enervates and destroys nations? Are we sure there is none of it in our own lives?"

It was evident to him that the mass of mankind live "mean and sneaking lives," "lives of quiet desperation." Thoreau's question was: Is it necessary? Well, he must try it out himself, the way Gandhi made his experiments with Truth. Being a writer Thoreau could well have said with Keats: Axioms of philosophy are not axioms until they are tested on our pulses. For he did test it all. It is an experiment which lasted two years two months and two days. It is interesting that he left Concord for Walden on 4th July when the rest of the country was in jubilation, even as Gandhi was in riot-torn Bengal on the day of India's Independence, rather than in New Delhi. Only, Thoreau was in solitude while Gandhi was in the thick of work. And these two essential attitudes are to me very important in understanding these two men. Thoreau was sick of the incessant activity and insatiable wants of his countrymen—the labors of Hercules are nothing before them, he says, because they are only twelve while those of mankind have no end. Why do people work for six days in the week forged in their "own golden or silver fetters" and keep the seventh day for Sabbath, instead of the other way: Work for one day—it was enough to work for one day—and keep the other six days for the joy and wonder of creation. For all his love of Shakespeare and the values he represented, Thoreau had the audacity to write:

Tell Shakespeare to attend some leisure hour
For now I've business with this drop of dew.

For he thought you will not find health in society, but in nature. Society is always diseased, and the best is most so." Stevenson is reported to have remarked humorously that "Admetus (whose flock Thoreau grazed) never got less work out of any servant since the world began." But Thoreau's defence was: What need is there to "keep farms, houses, barns, cattle, and farming tools" all "more easily acquired than got rid of." He claimed that he himself kept no dog, cat (and what is more interesting in our comparison of Thoreau and Gandhi), cow or spinning wheel. Except for the cow and the spinning wheel, especially the latter, Gandhi himself might have said all that Thoreau did say, but it is in the manner in which experience came and the way the organization of experience showed itself in the corresponding organization of words that the distinction between the two should interest not merely students of literature but those who seek to judge Thoreau and Gandhi—judge them by what they thought or said. And ultimately except for the generation that knew Gandhi first-hand the world, including his own countrymen, will have nothing to go by but their writings and recorded speeches.[1] And so judged, how do they emerge? Consider a few examples of what they said and the responses they evoke in us: Take such simple things as food, clothing, and shelter to which Gandhi made repeated references. Gandhi abstained from meat-eating, and much of what he said or did in this regard simply had a long and hallowed religious sanction and there simply was no questioning it. As for Thoreau, he was "not unusually squeamish." "I could," he says, "sometimes eat a fried rat with a good relish, if it were necessary." And he had his support in the *Veda* from which he quotes: "He who has true faith in the Omnipresent Supreme Being may eat all that exists" and is careful to qualify it with: "Vedanta limits this privilege to the time of distress." But he gave up flesh because it was not "agreeable to my imagination" and anyone who cares to preserve his "poetic faculties" must "abstain from animal food," for even nations are "betrayed" by their "vast abdomens", "such apparently slight cause destroyed Greece and Rome, and may destroy England and America." Lastly, it is his compassion for all that is living that argues against killing animals: "Who hears the fishes cry? " or "The hare in its extremity cries like a child." The remarkably adult yet innocent expression of their (partridges) open and serene eyes is very memorable. All intelligence seems reflected in them. Such an eye was not born when the bird was, but is coeval with the sky it reflects. The woods do not yield another such gem." When man has his passions under control and is pure it marks his "flowering" and he "flows at once to God when the channel of purity is open." It is by placing things in their larger perspective that he invests even the commonplace with a significance—the illumination comes from multiple sources.

This is how he presents—the presentation is an enactment—the necessity for clothes: Clothes, he says, must be a necessity, must be the result of a "crisis in our lives." He seeks support for his stand analogically: "The loon retires to solitary ponds to spend it: Thus also the snake casts its slough, and the caterpillar its wormy coat by an internal industry and expansion." A real compulsion from inside, not vulgar fashion must make way for new clothes. But what is the world's way? He says: "The head-monkey at Paris puts on a traveller's cap, and all the monkeys in America do the same. That is why dressing hasn't risen to the dignity of an art." His sense of humor, though grim, was extraordinary. One remembers what Gandhi said: But for my sense of humor I should have committed suicide.

Now move on to Thoreau: As for clothes, so for shelter. His plea is for spending more time in the open than indoors. Consider how he marshalls arguments in his favors: Children do, poets and philosophers do; so do the peasants. Above all, Thoreau sees in it a cosmic reason: "There shouldn't be obstruction between us and the celestial bodies" then he clinches his point with an illustration from the ways of birds: "Birds do not sing in caves nor doves cherish innocence in dovecots."

From commonplace observation he moves on to human civilization for an argument : "If civilization is a real advance in the condition of man it must be shown that it has produced better dwellings without making them more costly." And there is his own personal example : didn't he build his house singlehanded and complete it according to the needs of the seasons? It cost him only $28.12 1/2 —the way he kept strict accounts! Only Gandhi could surpass him—no other writer, not Ruskin, not Tolstoy in this respect—as is revealed from the scrupulous accounting of every pie spent by him in London as a student and later as a public servant in South Africa and India.

Thoreau has recourse to classical mythology to reinforce his point about cheap dwellings: "Momus objected to the house which Minerva made because she had not made it movable, by which means a bad neighbor might be avoided." Yet another example, this time from history, Egyptian history: "The myriads who built the pyramids to be tombs of the Pharaohs were fed on garlic, and may be, were not decently buried themselves." Thoreau would rather have their bodies drowned in Nile or thrown to the dogs than be buried in pyramids. And one more example from humdrum life, now to rouse the conscience of civilized man: "The mason who finishes the cornice of the palace returns at night perchance to a hut not so good as a wig wam." And so "It certainly is fair to look at that class by whose labor the works which distinguish this generation are accomplished." It is not enough to say that there must not be palaces for the few and huts for the millions; the case has to be worked out. If it is not worked out, as it was not by Gandhi, is that the price the man of action, always pushed around, pays for not nourishing his imagination? But do imagination's mercies accomplish what perpetual nagging may fail to do? Howsoever trivial is the example Thoreau cites, see how he can raise it to a higher plane because of the profound truth that only felt experience can convey: He had, it seems, three pieces of limestone on his desk and he was terrified to find that "they required to be dusted daily when the furniture of my mind was all undusted still, and I threw them out of the window in disgust." An act like this and the pressure behind the words can do more than all the sermons against acquisition of things. He seized upon significant things and actions in the life of man and dramatized them as only an imaginative writer can do, for example, the way he conceived the fewness of things! He said he had only three chairs in his house: one for solitude, two for friendship and three for society. This is not a matter of scholarship only (for Gandhi claimed he could have written Marx better if only he could summon to his aid scholarship) but of imaginative apprehension of the truths of life in commonplace things, when things become images and images in turn assume the status of symbols. Truth seldom dawns on us as effectively as through a symbol. It must therefore be admitted that whatever Gandhi thought of Marx, he could not have presented the case for simple living with the compulsion of a Thoreau, the compulsion being the gift of art. For, despite his protests to the contrary:

> My life has been the one I would have writ
> But I could not both live and utter it.

he did succeed in both, though, in the one, only in a limited way, but certainly in a remarkable way compared to writers like Nathaniel Hawthorne whose grievance against the Brookfarm experiment was: "You cannot idealize manual labor." Besides, Thoreau's justification for not undertaking mass reform was:" It is not important that all should be as good as you but there must be some absolute good somewhere to leaven the lump," as was evident when Gorky remarked on seeing Tolstoy sitting on a boulder near the sea "I am not an orphan on this earth so long as this man is alive;" the same has been said for Thoreau: "There can be little doubt that the spirit of Walden has pervaded the American consciousness, stiffened the American lip, steadied the American nerve, in ponderable degree."

Like Gandhi, Thoreau too was opposed to the technological civilization, but how memorable his reactions have become whether it is against the railroad, or the post and telegraph. It is his unusual ability to bring things into focus and perceive clearly that makes for memorableness. Consider some of these: "We do not ride the railroad, it rides upon us;" or, why do you lay telegraphic wires across continents? Is it to get the first news that Princess Adelaide has whooping cough? As for letters, he doesn't remember receiving or writing more than one or two letters of any worth in all his life.

But, artist that he is, there is freedom from fads and consequently one sees an ambivalence in his attitude. There are times when he can get excited by "the poetry of the railroad," how it brought life to the wilderness or how the railway whistle has electrified the atmosphere and is glad to note that "to do things the railroad fashion is now the word." In the same way the hum of mere telegraphic wire was "aeolian harp" to him and sent him back to Greek poetry. He would distinguish between simplicity as a fad and simplicity born of wisdom, and in support of the latter he would argue, "It is not the tub that makes Diogenes, the Jove-born, but Diogenes the tub." It is here that some of Gandhi's fads inhibited emotional response and simplified thinking. His ear, for example, was so attuned to the music of the spinning wheel that its hum, it seems, drowned every other music; rather, it filtered out all music but that of the spinning wheel, (and, of course, that of the Gita and the Ramayana). He showed very poor understanding of poetry when he wrote to Tagore that the "poet sings for the morrow," and asked him in passionate language to leave his Muse and spin on the charkha. For "India is a house on fire: let the poet bring his bucket of water." And this is the penalty a reformer pays for his passion for reform—it seems to block the channels of sensation and perception, except the few that the reformer wishes to keep open.

Now Thoreau did not claim to reform the world exactly, though he was vexed by the "tragedy of mediocrity." He declared : "The only obligation which I have the right to assume is to do at any time what I think right." What sounds anarchical is somewhat softened by a plea for tolerance for the otherness, as we see in the following: "If a man does not keep pace with his companions, perhaps it is because he hears a different drummer. Let him keep pace to the music he hears." But in the process he is so lost in responding to the drumbeat of his own choice that he begins to believe in the rightness of his own actions and develops self-esteem bordering on narcissism. "The greater part of what my neighbors call good I believe in my soul to be bad, and if I repent of anything it is very likely to be my good behavior. What demon possessed me that I behaved so well." Now this is clearly not merely self-esteem but bad taste born of a supreme sense of one's own infallibility.

But, one has sympathy for Thoreau when he takes the position: "Your fellowman to whom you are apprenticed is ever bolting right the other way;" and so it is futile to waste your time in trying to go along with him. "The man who goes alone can start today... (not) wait till that other is ready." Besides, "you are not drilling soldiers, who may turn out hirelings after all." When provoked, he would go so far as to say "I came into this world, not chiefly to make this a good place to live in but to live in it, be it good or bad"; and as for himself, he would "rather keep a bachelor's hall in hell than go to board in heaven." It is clear that he eschews social obligations from his sphere of obligations—his obligation is primarily to himself, not in a narrow sense, but to the higher law that governs his life; he must go where his genius leads him. In following the call of his own genius he is not ashamed of reconciling himself to the theory of the survival of the fittest:

> I am not responsible for the successful working of the machinery of society. I am not the son of an engineer. I perceive that when an acron and a chestnut fall side by side, the one does not remain inert to make way for the other, but both obey their own laws, and spring and grow and flourish as best they can, till one, perchance, overshadows and destroys the other.

Here, it seems, is naked assertion of the ego which conceals the tone of "For mine own good all causes shall give way," but the sophisticated articulation which has recourse to but, if, and perchance, softens the violence to an extent.

Thoreau's social obligation does not go far; it is negative. First, not to be so unjust as to "wrest the plank" from a drowning man; he would rather drown himself; and then, which is fair, but not particularly noble or magnanimous, that he would simply wish to refuse allegiance to the State, to withdraw and stand aloof from it effectively. Nay, he is even prepared to do something more: "I quickly declare war with the State." That would have been edifying but for the qualifying clause which follows, "though I will still make what use and what advantage of her I can, as is usual in such cases." Here is an instance not of the State exploiting the individual, but vice-versa.

Figure 48: Mahatma Gandhi

Notice here the parallel to Thoreau in Gandhi's earlier public life in South Africa. While he must have known that the Boers had a just cause, Gandhi still advocated co-operation with the British Empire. He considered it his duty as a subject of the Empire to be loyal to the government; and even thought it unjust for every man to think he could criticize the government. It is well-known that he volunteered his services to tend the sick in the British army during the Boer War. Is it because his political sense had not been quickened sufficiently? Or is it because centuries of subjection had made even the best of us in India loyal to the government? Or is it, one is constrained to ask, expediency that prompted him to co-operate with the government and win its goodwill for India and Indians in South Africa? If so, this was reprehensible in one like Gandhi. In this respect, despite what he said, Thoreau emerges nobler in action, for he thought it a "disgrace" to co-operate with a government—his own, here—which was waging an unjust war with Mexico and kept slaves. He denounced Massachusetts for letting her soul "trail in dirt." And he even pleaded passionately, poetically and yet without the remotest suspicion of pathetic fallacy:

> All nature would be affected and the sun's brightness fade, and the winds would sigh humanely, and the clouds rain and the woods shed their tears and put on mourning in midsummer if any man for a just cause grieve.

He could be more business-like, in the manner of Gandhi, a practical idealist:

> I know this well, that if one thousand, one hundred, if ten men whom I could name—if ten honest men only—ay, if one honest man in the State of Massachu setts, ceasing to hold slaves were actually to withdraw from this co-partnership, and be locked up in the country jail therefore, it would be the abolition of slavery in America.

But, if reports be true, what happened is not particularly edifying. He did go to prison for his disobedience, spent one night and came out of it, thanks to the intervention of an aunt who paid the tax for him. Now, here is something which Gandhi would not have let anyone do. For it matters little whether you pay or your aunt pays.

These inconsistencies and contradictions are not infrequent in Thoreau though they are less frequent than in Gandhi, but Thoreau did not have to wage a daily war with authority. However, Gandhi did admit his contradictions and considered them a sign of growth in one who was experimenting with truth, and he clarified to the public that in case of inconsistency his later position on any issue must be taken as final. Thoreau offered no such defence. Indeed he justified it as inevitable when one is acting from principle—"action from principle" "not only divides families away, it divides the individual separating the diabolical in him from the divine."

It is possible that the New England Puritan background made for some sort of self-righteousness and even haughtiness in Thoreau. But largely it was the commercial values which dominated New England thinking that must have made him want to disassociate himself from those values and save at least himself from damnation. The American assertion of the ego which expressed itself on the physical plane in the extension of the frontier, manifested itself in his case as an attempt at acquisition of a new dimension, the extension of the inner frontier, the enrichment of the life of the mind and the soul—which must be considered rare and unique in the American context. Essentially it was a preoccupation with the self, though in rare cases like Thoreau's, the preoccupation was with the transcendental self. The net result however makes for a minimal, not maximal, discharge of one's social obligations as can be seen in his: "I cannot expect like Orpheus to change the nature of the rocks and trees and beasts." He would at best take care to keep himself free from taint. "If a man is thought-free, fancy-free, imagination free, unwise rulers cannot fatally interrupt him."

Alexis de Tocqueville, that classic commentator of the American scene, who is said to have invented the word individualism, observed that "individualism saps the virtues of public life and then is absorbed into the egoistic." He noted that while "egotism is as old as the world, individualism is of democratic origin"—that was Toqueville's fear for the future of American democracy. Recent political thinkers have demonstrated in their own thinking how Toqueville's fears have come true.

It is good to be aware that there is a tradition of duty in Western religious and philosophical thinking. The Calvinists for instance insisted that all that is not duty is sin. The Positivist School of Auguste Comte pointed out that the individual had no rights but only duties—the right to do his duty. But neither of these has entered the mainstream of Western life ; they are not part of the living tradition of the West. Not even Plato, despite the ceaseless academic claim for the impact of Hellenism on Western thinking, for Plato tells us in his *Republic* that the mass of mankind are groping in a dark cave and one man (that is, the creative minority) who sees the light of day goes back to the cave to draw the uncreative mass into the open. My contention is that these scattered religious and philosophical thoughts have not been translated into a "tradition of action." Even when translated into action, the farthest the man of thought has gone is presented in "shall I at least set my lands in order?"

Now the entire life and work of Gandhi is a repudiation of the individualism of the West and simultaneously, a rejection of the Western as well as the Russian kind of Socialism. For, he aspired after the freedom to build, in his own words, "a staircase to Sirius"—he anticipated the American astronauts so long ago. This man of God said so unequivocally that he was "endeavoring to see God through the service of humanity, for "I know." (he said) "that God is neither in heaven nor down below but in everyone." Hence his mission to "wipe every tear from every eye." Even his day of silence was a day of intense activity; and his prayer meetings ended with discourses on social issues. "Anything," he said, "which I cannot share with the masses is taboo to me." Hence also his declaration that he didn't wish to be reborn but if he did he would wish to be born as an untouchable to share their sorrows. Elsewhere he said with a conviction whose sincerity is unmistakable: "Suffering is the mark of the human tribe. It is an eternal law. The mother suffers so that her child may live. . . The condition of wheat growing is that the seed grain should perish." From the natural law Gandhi turns to history for support: "No country has ever risen without being purified through the fire of suffering. . . the purer the suffering the greater the progress."[2]

This profound social concern of Gandhi issues from the immemorial Indian tradition, which has unceasingly advocated self-realization in and through society. Gandhi repeats times without number the ancient Indian doctrine from the Mahabharata, that for the good of the family an individual may be sacrificed, and a family in the interest of the village and a whole village for the good of the country, which calls for narrow loyalties—loyalty to one-self is indisputably a narrow one—to make room for larger ones. "An individual's success," thought Gandhi, "will be like a millionaire's donating free food to millions of starving people." In Gandhi's scheme, and generally in the Indian scheme of things, neither is the society domineering nor does the individual feel the need to assert. Neither, because both individual and society recognize a higher law than both. Neither feels the necessity to push the other to an extremity with the result a spirit of accommodation has become the pervasive principle of life. Without such accommodativeness there clearly could not have been a long line of most distinguished individuals throughout India's history, but their greatness is invariably in proportion to their capacity not to exalt the self, indeed to deny it. Her leaders have invariably been men of the spirit. Here is no Bill of Rights or the Rights of Man. Nor is there the Divine Right of Kingship. But if the king was sometimes looked upon by his people as God's deputy, the *Arthashastra* records that "The king, on receiving the royal authority from the people's hands at the time of coronation, had to take the oath: May I be deprived of heaven, of life, and of offspring if I oppress you." For in the happiness of his subjects lies his happiness; in their welfare his welfare. It is interesting that in a popular version of the *Ramayana*, Kusa and Lava raise the question whether the king had no right of his own when the people indulged in gossip about his wife's character. Apparently not. But by suffering Sita became the mother of the race. There may be hundred Ramas, said Vivekananda in one of his American speeches, but there is only one Sita.

> Yet there the nightingale
> Filled all the desert with inviolable voice.

It is possible to look at the epic as woven round an abducted woman as the *Iliad* is around Helen, but the two are at opposite ends—the one at the giving and the other at the receiving end. Interesting that in our own time Motilal's son, Harrow and Cambridge-educated Jawaharlal Nehru, when still in his twenties on seeing the plight of the kisans in U.P., said to himself: It is better to be accursed with those unfortunate people than be saved alone.

Now what one misses not merely in Thoreau but in all the three writers we are preoccupied with is their desire for action is not incommensurate with the intensity of their thought—there is, if one may look upon W. B. Yeats' distinction as still valid, a dichotomy, certainly a discrepancy between "perfection of the work" and "perfection of the life." Perfection of life is a misnomer according to the Indian tradition without social and metaphysical obligations—and the reason why action, disinterested action, becomes the central sustaining principle of the universe according to the *Bhagavad Gita*. If I cease to act for one split second, the universe goes to pieces, says Krishna to Arjuna. The Indian gods themselves took birth after birth for the good of the world. In myth, legend and epic, exceptional individuals have given their life so that others may live. Curiously, action has invariably accompanied suffering and sacrifice of the self, and since that is disinterested action it has led to vindication of the truth. Is that why Gandhi claimed that "the Rishis who discovered the law of non-violence were greater geniuses than Newton,... greater warriors than Wellington"? Thus Bhagiratha brought the Ganga down the plains, Dadhichi gave his backbone to the gods to smite the relentless clouds with and bring rain to parched earth; thus Dasaratha sent his son to the forest and Rama himself banished Sita in obedience to the people's wishes. Thus Savithri decided to marry Satyavan in the full knowledge he was destined not to last beyond a year after her marriage, and Harischandra sold his wife and child, and himself was in the employ of the lowest of the low ; so did the child Prahlad drink poison. So did Nachiketa and Ekalavya bear suffering at their tender age to come out of the fire purer and stronger for the suffering—suffering is action, action suffering. Not merely in the Upanishads, legends and epics but in history too: the Buddha who spoke not of God, did nevertheless ask Ananda not to cross the threshold of this life even if he saw one human being in distress. He sounds as though he felt the *dukha* [misery] of this world in his entrails. It is for the same reason that H. G. Wells considered the great victors of the Western world mere incendiary schoolboys in comparison with Asoka. Whatever the impact of these myths on the "lost generation" of western educated intellectuals at one time we have now been reassured by psychologists and anthropologists of the West of the value of a national myth as the shaping spirit in the life of a people. All one has to do is to tap the national myth and release the psychic energy.

If a country's myths are the finest expressions of its collective unconscious, their significance is too profound to be minimized—only callow teenagers will do so today after the work Frazer and Jung. One would go so far as to say: if you have no myth you must invent one. This country did not have to invent any, what with its magnificent mythical imagination. What Gandhi did was to invoke that imagination, to tap those hidden reservoirs of psychic energy and make them flow in our veins. Each people must fulfil their destiny in terms of their *swadharma*, an inner principle (would Hopkins's "inscape" be an adequate equivalent?) by which, for example, the oyster receives the rain from above, goes down to the bottom of the sea and diligently shapes the pearl-now, the pearl, is it the gift of the rain? of the sea? of the incessant inner industry of the oyster? The questions answer themselves.

It is not for nothing that on the assassination of Gandhi *The London Times*, not known to be very friendly to Gandhi or Hinduism, brought out a fitting editorial to say that no country but India and no religion but Hinduism could have produced a Gandhi; not for nothing did Arnold Toynbee, distinguished historian, write: Gandhi is not only India's benefactor but England's benefactor too: he civilized us; and Stanley Jones, the American Christian missionary, could say that Gandhi converted him to his own faith. But millions of Indians, educated Indians, have only been at the receiving end in relation to Western thought, while a man like Gandhi, because he could respond from the deep well of India's wisdom, he alone could travel farther than did the millions and enrich mankind's heritage—and enrich even those from whom he received the stimulus. Here is the paradox of an essentially contemplative culture throwing up a saintly leader who could teach action to the action-oriented West.

End Notes

I have tried to discuss Gandhi's views using his own words as much as possible. Because of the numerousness of the citations I have not given the page numbers.

[1]. It is interesting, however, that the Buddha is judged by the mass of mankind, not by his teachings but by his life, his great example and it is as such that he has entered the mainstream of Indian thought and legend. Gandhi believed primarily in action and in support argued that "the rose does not need to write a book or deliver a sermon on the scent it sheds." That is how he himself became an intimate part of the Indian legend. "Where he sat became a temple and where he trod the ground was hallowed," Nehru was to say in Gandhi's own life-time. And Gandhi had to fight against the Mahatmahood himself.

[2]. The Vaishnava tradition which nourished Gandhi has its foundations in legend's like the following, which abound in Tamil literature: Ramaniuja, the great exponent of Vaishnavism, was one day being taken in procession. At the head of the procession were his two great disciples, Dasarathi and Kuresa. On sighting a chandala woman Dasarathi felt perturbed and shouted to her to get away quickly lest her presence should pollute the great Master. And the woman whined: "Where shall I go? To my right is the God Sri Ranganatha, to my left is the river Cauvery, in my front is the Master and behind are the mansions of the great disciples; above is the sky, and the earth below does dot claim me yet." At this Kuresa, the other disciple, felt a sense of shame and bid his companion, as Brahmin, to subject himself to *prayaschitta* (expiation) rather than cause hurt to the unfortunate woman. The essence of this ritual is in the suffering one inflicts on oneself in penitence.

Chapter 37

Jawaharlal Nehru's Sense of History

C. D. Narasimhaiah

In response to a generous gesture by Mrs. Indira Gandhi in the late sixties, because she was "keen" that I should take charge of Jawaharlal Nehru's papers, I assured her that I would walk every mile from Mysore to comply, so precious was his memory. But when she added, "It means, in the first instance, you should come to Delhi for five years," as a teacher rooted in Mysore, I begged to be excused. I suggested, to a dignitary in the Nehru Memorial Foundation, that the person they chose should either be a historian with a pronounced literary sensibility or a literary person who had a sense of history; for, Nehru exemplified in himself a combination of both these gifts, although in his characteristic modesty he protested he was "neither a historian nor a man of letters," and that indeed he "came late to history and not through a mass of facts, but through art and literature."

Jawaharlal Nehru approved of the ancient Indian tradition of treating myth and legend as symbolically true and of considering them as historical in nature. Ancient Indians did not keep myth and history apart. Today, some well-known Western historians have begun to look at "myth as history." While on the one hand, Nehru criticized "the magical and supernatural elements" in the myths, on the other hand, he believed "they were imaginatively true." In his consideration of history, he alluded to *The Arabian Nights*, the *Panchatantra*, Greek mythology or the story of Arthur and his knights because of their cultural significance claiming that he would "hate to throw away all the beauty and imaginative symbolism that those stories and allegories contain." He pointed out the value of myths for the common man who "is pulled up from the drudgery and ugliness of everyday existence to higher realms" which exist by virtue of myths and legends. One cannot fail to admire a mind which was open to the rich imagination of myths as well as scientific facts and processes. Nehru's writings had an expansiveness which fused dream and reality and inspired a feeling of perfection and fulfillment. The following lines are just one example: "Those were the days when life was full and in harmony with Nature, when man's mind gazed with wonder and delight on the mystery of the Universe, when heaven and earth were very near to each other, and gods and goddesses came down from Kailas."

Consider the titles of his two books on history: The word "glimpses" in *Glimpses of World History* suggests, in Trevelyan's words, "the moment of illumination without having actually seen it ," which suited his intention to "awaken" his daughter's curiosity. He chose to do this in the form of letters, because, as he put it, "I want if possible to talk to you as if you were here." In order to make history seem more interesting to his daughter, he added "intimate touches" and wove legend and history together. The lines, "Let us take our seats on Aladdin's Magic Carpet and go round the world of those days visiting places of interest," make the dull atlas, which is the despair of examinees, "an exciting affair." Even as the foremost leader of the Indian National Movement, next only to Gandhi, Nehru considered Nationalism to be an anti-feeling, as he believed that it "feeds and fattens on hatred of other nations." He was convinced, like Trevelyan, Toynbee, and Butterfield, that it was impossible to study the history of any country without being aware of the history of the world as a whole. Indeed, his *Letters* starts with the story of the earth.

The Discovery of India, his other book, may well suggest the determined search of an earnest archaeologist excavating layer after layer. His geological metaphor for India, a"palimpsest," needs to be spelled out and is best done in his own words: "[s]he was like some ancient palimpsest on which layer upon layer of thought and reverie had been inscribed and yet no succeeding layer had completely hidden or erased what had been written previously." These lines are symbolic of how Nehru trained himself to accept tradition and change—"a continuity and vitality," in his own words. The heavily consonanted words, "excrescence", "abortion," "twisted," "petrified," and "stunted" in a later passage reflect a veritable rescue operation, because for him the past did not exhaust all obligations and he could "not write about the present without experiencing it through action." Consider the persistent questioning of this "man of thought" who was also a "man of action"—not thinking in the categories of W.B. Yeats' "perfection of the life" or "perfection of the work," but realizing both, each through the other. What did India represent in the past? What gave her strength then? How did she lose that old strength? And has she lost it completely? Does she represent anything vital now apart from being a home of many millions of people? How does she fit into the modern world? For if the Indian people lacked an inner vitality, then all our political efforts and shouting were all make-believe and would not carry far.

Books and monuments did not satisfy him. He journeyed through India in the company of great travelers of the past from China and Western and Central Asia, for India was to him "this lady with a past," beckoning with her "sphinx-like face" and "elusive and sometimes mocking smile." This "child of the mountains" who had played on the banks of the Ganga could not forget the cries, "*Gangamataki jai*," of that sea of humanity, which despite its poverty and misery, had gathered from all parts of the country at the *Kumbha mela*. Nehru remarked that India "clings" to him "as to all her children." He, who had set out in his obsession with the "temper of science" to remove "the cobwebs of the past" and give India "a garb of modernity," felt inhibited by thoughts of himself being a "link" with the past; and, he asked, "Who am I to break that past?"

Once, he stood on a mound of Mohenjo-Daro, and all round him he saw houses and streets of this ancient civilization of 5000 years ago which was, even then, old and advanced. He pressed forward:

> [a]t Saranath near Banaras I would almost see the Buddha preaching his Fire Sermon and some of his recorded words came like a distant echo. Asoka's pillars of stone with their inscriptions would speak to me in their magnificent language. At Fathepur-Sikri Akbar forgetful of his empire was seated holding converse with the learned of all faiths, curious to learn something new.

There are in *The Discovery* all these things that conventional history books on India contain, accounts of the *Vedas*, the *Upanishads*, and the Epics, the early civilization of the Indus Valley, the teachings of Buddha, Mahavira and Guru Nanak, the successive invasion of India by outsiders, and India's contact with other countries. But his constant effort was to make the past meaningful to the present. With that end in view he dwelt on those aspects which were missed or distorted or not sufficiently stressed by most historians. It was important for his purpose to speak of the "continuity," "vitality," and "staying power" of Indian culture through the ages so he could interpret properly the two dominant trends of thought— "acceptance" and "negation" of life, the former being more pronounced than the latter.

Nehru doesn't miss the opportunity to correct the prevalent Western notion of mistaking Buddha's "Middle Path" for negation. Hence his scintillating portrait of Buddha which must give the lie to it:

> Seated on the lotus flower, calm and impassive above passion and desire, so far away he seems, out of reach, unattainable. His eyes are closed but some power of the spirit looks out of them and a vital energy fills the frame.

This vitality and purity made for the spread of Buddhism all over Asia. So attractive was the portrait, possibly, that *but*, the word for "image" in Persian and Hindustani, came from Ancient Greece to India through Afghanistan. Nehru doesn't miss the irony of history since Buddha was opposed to image worship.

Nehru's mode of vivifying the facts of history through art is seen at its best in his account of the Italian Renaissance. He saw it in terms of the work of artists, sculptors, painters, and poets:

> ...for the shadow of these great sons of hers lies on her still, and as you pass the streets of this beautiful city [Florence] or look at the lovely Arno as it flows by under the medieval bridges, an enchantment comes over you and the past becomes vivid and alive. Dante goes by and Beatrice, the lady he loved, passes leaving faint perfume trailing behind her. And Leonardo seems to march along the narrow streets, lost in thought pondering over the mysteries of Life and Nature. (Despite the evocative details which his writings are full of, he had the humility to say that he had only "skimmed" over the surface and placed merely the skeleton of old happenings.)

As for the Italian Renaissance, so for India of the Middle Ages. Now he referred to Kautilya's *Arthasastra*, for it was "as if a window were opened which enables us to have a peep at India in the 4th century B.C E." Likewise, he used Sukracharya's *Nitisara* to complete his account of tenth-century India. Babar's *Memoirs* for Akbar's time and Kalhana's *Rajatarangini* for Kashmir are two more examples of his effort at reconstructing the history of India.

Figure 49: Jawaharlal Nerhu

But Nehru's accounts continually direct our attention to an expanding future. Take a casual observation like this: "[s]ometimes as I was passing along a country road or through a village, I would start with surprise on seeing a fine type of man or beautiful woman...," where his amalgamating vision connected the past and the present, for they reminded him of some "fresco of ancient times," and he wondered how the type had endured and continued through the ages in spite of all the horror and misery India had gone through.

The historian, being also a responsible leader, saw vistas opening out before him: "What could we not do with these people under better conditions! They are not all 'mute Miltons and silent inglorious Cromwells,'" because he had trained himself to be free from self-deception. Occasionally, if a poor Brahmin, like Ramanujan, fought his way through life's hardships, he was sure to catch Nehru's perceiving eye, and he was sure to bring up this "extraordinary figure" in his account of mathematics in Ancient India. This clerk in the Customs Office was "bubbling over with some irrepressible quality of instinctive genius and played about with numbers and equations in his spare time and by a lucky chance he went to Cambridge and became Fellow of the Royal Society at 31 and died two years later, probably of tuberculosis." The portrait closes with a tribute by Julian Huxley, who referred to him as "the greatest mathematician of the century." Then follows the inescapable reflection: "Ramanujan's brief life and death are symbolic of conditions in India. Of our millions how few get any education at all, and how many live on the verge of starvation, and if life opened its gates to them... how can we hope to build a new India and a new world." Here is the urgency of a true historian, and yet all this would not find a place in history books, for, can aspiring clerks be historical figures?

For Nehru, Ramanujan was more important than Alexander the Great who gets a whole chapter to himself in history books. Nehru conceded that Alexander was a famous conqueror, he didn't fail to observe that the latter was "a conceited young man" who did not even leave good roads behind him in his country. He came like a meteor and disappeared like one. But "history has succeeded in attaching glamour to his name," leaving out of account great Greek thinkers like Plato, Socrates, and the eminent tragedians. Alexander invited further damnation in Nehru's mention of Ghengis Khan. For Ghengis was "the greatest military genius the world has known. Caesar and Alexander are like matchwood before him." Illiterate himself, Ghengis Khan was partial to learning. Similarly, Nehru drew attention to Sankara who, in the eighth century, even before the science of geography was born, added a "sense of national unity and national consciousness" by locating centers of culture in the four corners of India. Learn from him: Nehru seems to rebuke the wrangling intellectuals but nowhere is he given to moralizing. His eye catches another dynamic Indian living a thousand years later: Vivekananda, "a monk who thundered across the American continent. Every word of this monk dripped with energy," as he exhorted people to "be fearless, be strong."

Nehru remarked with wonder at how more than a thousand years ago the mighty caves of Ellora were carved out of solid rock with the stupendous Kailas temple in the center. Again he wondered how the painter-monks of Ajanta had known the moving drama of life and how lovingly they had "painted beautiful women, princesses, singers, and dancers, seated, standing, beautifying themselves or in procession"—which made him ask why this art was more popular on the Continent than in England, and how far it was conditioned by the "unfortunate political relationship," a question which art historians and literary critics have begun to ask today in India and elsewhere. Indians are blamed, too, at Nehru's hands: Indian art, which was at its height in the seventh and eighth centuries and influenced Southeast Asia so much, itself became hopelessly imitative. The original inspiration faded because the mind and the soil became overworked and undernourished without fresh currents and ideas. Now comes a most discriminating observation:

> So long as India kept her mind open to the world and gave of her riches to others and received from them what she lacked, she remained fresh and strong and vital. But the more she withdrew into her shell ... the more she lost. Life became increasingly a dull round of the art of creating beauty, her children lost even the capacity to recognize it.

It is such observations and admonitions which abound in *The Discovery* that mark him out as a unique historian. Literature fares no better at Nehru's hands: "What was a thing of life and joy, so lovely and musical and full of imaginative daring is covered with the dust of the scholar's study and smells of the midnight oil." He frowned on the "sterile approach of the philologist" and recommended a poetic approach. He was distressed that "the glow of the morning had long faded away, high noon was past, the heart seems to petrify, its beats are slower with decay of limbs." "Creative energy has dried up" was his constant refrain. He draws our attention to the irony of a people who built ships, traveled on uncharted seas, and established an Empire,

Sri Vijaya, at the magnificent Angkor in Combodia, larger than Rome of the Caesars, with a million inhabitants, should have come to consider sea voyaging taboo. But there were "frequent bursts of creative energy" which he calls resurgence: one in the time of Akbar in the North and another by Krishnadevaraya at Vijayanagar in the South. He sees, too, that there was more literacy in India in the eighteenth century than in England, and India was technically more advanced than Europe. Our weakness and internal dissension were an invitation to the foreigner. Almost the entire second half of *The Discovery* is devoted to the coming of the British to India, as the beginning of industrialization in England marked the beginning of India's ruralization. While in every country there has been a shift of population from agriculture to industry, from village to town, in India the process was reversed. But why blame the invader? He asks us to read Alberuni's description of Indians as "haughty, foolishly vain, self-centered, and stolid."

An observation of Radhakrishnan's that Indian philosophy lost its vigor with the loss of Indian freedom brings out his strong reaction: "Why did India lose her freedom?" asks Nehru. Something rotten must have crept into the body politic. Similarly he answers the charge that Sanskrit drama declined with the disappearance of royal patronage during the Indo-Afghan and Moghul periods. He thinks that, except in the art of image-making, the Muslim rulers gave excellent encouragement to Indian music, art, and painting. In his view this drama must have "lacked in inner vitality." Well, it is there right before our eyes and bears testimony to his stand. Again his grouse is that we looked upon Hindu Scriptures as Holy Writ. As for himself, he would "analyse and criticize" them and consider them as having been written by the "astonishing mind of man."

It is this kind of disinterestedness in his intellectual make-up that permits him to admit that the Indian National Congress was dominated by the Hindus and had a Hindu outlook—a criticism which could well have come from the mouth of Jinnah. Here is a person who wouldn't turn a blind eye to his much-admired father's failings, observing that he "lacked spirituality" and "if there were a bourgeois democracy my father would be the pillar of its constitution." The tone is the same when he spoke of Gandhi, too. Here is Gandhi's chief lieutenant who could bring himself to say, "Gandhiji did not train the nation to think," for the way of faith was not the right one where a country was concerned. He observes that Gandhiji "spoke in his best dictatorial accent"—one whose own manner of speaking abounded in 'ifs and buts,' 'becauses' and 'althoughs,' and couldn't help saying so. Such a one has earned the right to regret that the "Muslims didn't develop a middle class and have not eliminated the feudal elements." It is such fierce objectivity that inspired his wrath toward British historians who divided Indian history into Hindu India, Muslim India, and British India, for if religion were the basis of an epoch, they should have called the last period Christian India. The British historian stands accused of being biased especially in view of the standing charge against his "Divide and Rule" policy. Nehru's argument is that "Islam did not invade India; it had come to India many centuries earlier. The Afghans and the Moghuls who invaded India were gradually Indianized and they began to look upon India as their homeland. It is well known that Akbar married a Rajput princess and he was on the friendliest terms with the Hindus. The new rulers [British] lived apart. There was an unbridgeable gulf in tradition, outlook, income, and ways of living."

While almost every poet, philosopher, and historian of any country echoes the recorded view that modern Europe and perhaps America are the children of the Hellenic spirit, Nehru takes a different stand. He boldly asserts that there is no organic connection between Hellenic civilization and modern Europe. The modern notion that the really important thing is to be comfortable is entirely foreign to the underlying Greek or any other ancient civilization. Actually it is not modern Europe or America but India that is far nearer in spirit and outlook to that of old Greece.

It is possible Nehru leaves out of account the fact that the West is heir to the empirical approach of Aristotle whom European classicists consider "master of the sapient throng." Nehru probably believed that not Aristotle, but Plato and Platonism were central to Hellenism.

When it comes to ancient Indian supremacy in the science of mathematics, Nehru attributes it to the compelling force behind the mathematical inventions of ancient India. He contends:

> They cannot be the momentary illumination of an erratic genius much in advance of his time but they were essentially the product of the social milieu and they answered some insistent demand of the times. Society had grown complex and large numbers of people were engaged in outside trade. It was impossible to carry on without some simple method of calculation. It must have been this necessity that lay behind invention of the mathematical symbol, zero.

That his consideration was not Indian versus Western is seen best in his fairness even to Christian missionaries who came to convert Indians. It was not for him to ignore or minimize the admirable work they did in the areas of undeveloped languages and the collection of folklore. Similarly, although he is a bitter critic of British imperialism, "he praises England for sending to India the England of Shakespeare and Milton and political revolution and scientific progress." He is sorry that "British imperialism crippled British public life and made her forget the lessons of her own history and literature." This critic of British imperialism doesn't fail to admit the coming of England as the coming of a dynamic society and modern consciousness onto a static society wedded to medieval habits of thought.

But he soon adds that the British themselves were unaware that they were agents of progress. But, Nehru failed to recognize that if British impact was "peripheral" and "only touched a minority," it only means that that is the way culture functions—it affects a tiny minority which in the course of time develops into mass civilization. In our own country, we have seen the Brahmin minority culture become the great Hindu civilization in the course of time. The growth of modern literatures in our languages is largely due to our contact with English literature.

This is evident when we compare it with our contact with Persian and Arabic literatures which left our literatures almost untouched. It was not an unmixed blessing, though, as we went too far in looking up to England as the agent of progress and modernity, having been taken in by its prestige in the world at large. Unfortunately it arrested the development of our own tradition in our literary works. Much that happened wouldn't do credit either to the British or to ourselves. Tags like the "Indian Shelley" for Tagore and "Indian Shakespeare" for Kalidasa were obviously proof of our "cultural cringe." In one sense at least, Gandhi was right when he proclaimed from the housetops, "Let all the cultures of all the lands blow over my house but I shall refuse to be blown off my feet by any." Elsewhere Gandhi also added that if the mass of Indian youth is not entirely denationalized it is because our ancient culture is deeply rooted in them.

With all that, however, no one can ignore Nehru's unsurpassed realization of the impact of Gandhi on Indian society: He compares him to "a current of fresh air," to a "beam of light" that pierces the darkness, and to a "whirlwind that upsets many things but most of all the working of men's minds."

It is uncritical to call it a veritable "Ode to the West Wind," because Shelley's poem is self-centered, not so Nehru's evocation of Gandhi's impact on the Indian scene. As an example of Nehru's fairness it should be added that while Nehru shared the feelings of his countrymen in hoping for little from England under Churchill's leadership, unlike many of his countrymen, Nehru conceded, writing his *Discovery* in Churchill's prison at Ahmadnagar; "he was a big man who could take a big step." It is not generally known in India that Churchill more than reciprocated this sentiment when in 1948 Nehru visited England as India's first Prime Minister. At a banquet held by Attlee in Nehru's honor, after a formal hand-shake, old Churchill walked up to Nehru and stood before him to say, "Mr. Nehru, I hear you are going to the States from here. I wish I could accompany you. If I came with you I would present you to the people of America: "here is a man who is free from fear and hate, two of the besetting sins of man."

One is inclined to ask, after coming to the end of *The Discovery*, whether, if by some misfortune Gandhi had not come upon the Indian scene, Jawaharlal's book would not have fired the imagination of his countrymen. Yes, it would undoubtedly have had an impact, but only among the intellectuals, not the masses, though the masses too listened to his speeches as they would to the "Flute of Sri Krishna." For instance, when as Prime Minister, Nehru goes to address the Irrigation Engineers Conference at Bhakra Nangal Dam in Punjab, he asks the engineers if they have told the workers the story of the Ganga, because it is the story of Indian civilization; it is on her banks that empires were built and when they decayed new ones took their place. He realizes it is not the engineers' business, but if he made an imaginative approach "the stone and the water they work with will acquire a new dimension." The masses could never be out of sight for him.

It is a similar imaginative note that he strikes at the Southeast Asian Air Navigation Conference. He thinks that the human being who walks on two legs on solid earth suddenly acquired a third dimension and leaped into the air. Obviously the history of humanity stands vividly before Nehru.

But the most momentous international occasion, soon after Independence, was when he called the Conference of Asian Nations. It is a great event in the history of Asia and of the world. He lifts his audience from the present and transports them to immemorial antiquity when Asia was the cradle of civilization:

> We stand at the end of an era and on the threshold of a new period of history. Standing on this watershed... we can look back on our long past. Asia, after a long period of quiescence, has suddenly become important again in world affairs. It was here civilization began and man searched unceasingly for truth and the spirit of man stood out like a beacon which lit up the whole world.

He tells his audience how "this mighty continent" became just a field for the rival imperialisms of Europe, and Europe became the center of history and progress in human affairs. "A change is coming over the scene. It is at this great moment that we meet here and it is the pride and privilege of the people of India to welcome their fellow Asians from other countries."

He is careful to add that in this Conference there are no leaders and no followers. He reminds them of the intercourse between India and China, Indonesia and Indo-China, and all the countries of Southeast Asia to make them feel the oneness of Asia in their hearts.

A great occasion was sure to bring forth the best in Nehru. Even in a brief message which he gave to the Buddhist Conference at Sanchi he sees "something of history." "I came to Sanchi, not to give you a message but to search for something myself. In this torn and distorted world, I am a very confused person. I see no light and often stumble. I try to search for what is lacking in me." The utter integrity of the speaker made a profound impact on those present. Because of Buddha's date, namely sixth century B.C.E., Nehru remembers him in *The Glimpses* along with Mahavira, Zoroaster, Confucius, and Pythagoras. Dates do matter to his unifying vision on such an occasion—such is his appreciation for values that he looks around the world to see if a particular time produced men of the same caliber. Yes, they were all great thinkers and were imbued with a sense of mission in life. He brings up a small point to bracket some of them in view of what was common among them—some of them at least were vegetarian.

For instance, the year 1848 was the year of revolutions, but how different each of them was. In some, suppressed nationalism caused uprising, such as Italy, Poland, Bohemia, and Hungary. In France, it was the tyranny and exploitation of the monarch that caused the uprising. And, in England, there wasn't a revolution, but the Chartist movement.

Even the tombs could provide him with an opportunity to talk of the two rivals to the throne, Humayun and Shershah: "the Afghan's tomb is a stern, strong, imperious looking building like the man. Humayun's tomb is a polished and elegant building." And yet, one is in Bihar, the other in Delhi. Nehru could see the striking contrast at once. No one could today miss the prominent Aurangazeb Road in the heart of New Delhi; that, was Nehru's gesture as Prime Minister to a man who "set the hands of the clock back." But Nehru asks, "Is it not possible that Aurangazeb took an adverse view of the Hindus as they became too critical of his rule." A vicious circle, is all that one could say today.

As he looked at the statue of Clive at the India House he was naturally amused that the British should censure him in Parliament (as they impeached Warren Hastings) and yet install his statue outside the India House. Nehru comments: "[i]t is his spirit that dwells inside and shapes British policy in India."

While Machiavelli figures prominently in European political thinking, Nehru puts him in his place with effortless ease. For instance, he writes: "[Machiavelli] was an ordinary politician who wrote a book which became famous... What did he say in it after all? The greater the scoundrel the better the prince." And he adds a perceptive, if shattering and trenchant generalization: "[b]eneath the kidglove of civilization is the red claw of the beast."

But his truly unforgettable speeches changed with a sense of history, and his deeply felt emotions came in quick succession: The first on India's attainment of Independence in 1947, and the next on the assassination of Gandhi, the very next year. He calls, in the first speech, India's independence "a Tryst with Destiny":

> Long years ago we made a tryst with destiny, and now the time comes when we shall redeem the pledge... At the stroke of the midnight hour, when the world sleeps, India will awaken to life and freedom. A moment comes which comes but rarely in history, when we step out from the old to the new when an age ends, when the soul of a nation, long suppressed, finds utterance. It is fitting at this moment we take a pledge of dedication to the service of India and her people and to the still larger cause of humanity.

The only great speech that comes to my mind on a similar occasion is that of Abraham Lincoln at Gettysburg. And, Lincoln was native to English, while Nehru had acquired it. Lincoln begins: "Four score and seven years ago our fathers brought forth upon this continent a new nation conceived in liberty and dedicated to the proposition that all men are created equal."

For me, at least, the speech at once gives the impression of well-wrought solemnity at once: The phrase "four score and seven" lets it fall into a studied pattern. Compare the phrase with Nehru's, "Long years ago we made a tryst with destiny." The note of loftiness is unmistakably there but in "Long years ago" there is a *talking* voice as against the oratorical, and it also makes for a sense of intimate participation—the distance between the speaker and the listeners disappears.

That he should dedicate the country "to the service of humanity" at once makes him heir to the well-known Indian concept of *vasudhaiva kutumbakam*, the Earth Family, which is much in keeping with Nehru's favorite internationalism. The assassination of Gandhi agitated him deeply as he said, "The light has gone out of our lives and there is darkness everywhere." But his profound sense of history helps him to lift himself from the present and comfort himself and others: "the light that has illumined this country...will still be seen" a thousand years later and will bring solace "to innumerable hearts."

It is in the same spirit that he dismisses such sweeping generalizations as the "Materialistic West" and "Spiritual East." He believes that the difference is really between an industrialized West and the East which is largely agricultural. And fifty years later, even Nehru's terms do not hold, because the East is catching up with the West in industry and technology. But largely he was thinking of the burning of scientists as heretics and banishing of philosophers—because they had praised Confucius or slighted Christianity. To which can be added, because Nehru does talk about them, various European missions: "the white man's burden" of England, "the civilizing mission" of France, the "Kultur" of Germany, "Communism" of Russia, the "Fascism" of Italy, and "God's own country" (now "the Great Society") of America.

But luckily Asian countries have no missions except those thrust upon them by the "Orientalism" of the West. What really hurts him are the aggressive and exploitative instincts of European nations, whose aggression and exploitation was in the name of a theoretically superior civilization. He thinks that the British government has to take responsibility, in particular, for "tolerating aggression in Manchuria," "betraying Abyssinia," and "aiding Fascist rebels" in Europe. His "heart is full of the tragedy of Spain." For above all, it is the ancient home of liberty which struggled for freedom even in the days of Ferdinand and Isabella—clearly it is the human value that concerns him, whether in Europe or Asia. His sense of deep distress comes through in the way the crumbling of Europe figures in his work.

The map of Europe has *changed* suddenly and many nations have ceased to be. Poland *went*, Denmark and Norway *succumbed*, France *fell* suddenly and completely." All these went into the German orbit. The Baltic Countries and Bessarabia have more or less been *absorbed* by Soviet Russia."

We must not fail to see the artist's hand in this account. He shows himself to be most resourceful in the handling of verbs to indicate precisely how they lost their identity. The verbs in italics above show the plight of smaller countries as though they were moths in the presence of fire. The term "crumbling world" itself is a vivid image of disintegration.

When he writes about the Russia of Lenin, and Turkey under Kemal Pasha, he feels as though some personal good has come his way, as though he has won his personal salvation, because it is the greater good of humanity. In thinking over the troubles and conflicts of Europe he says, "I forgot to some extent my own personal and national troubles. I would even feel proud occasionally at the fact that I was alive at this great revolutionary period of history."

When he becomes Prime Minister of the newly—awakened India, he who had seen Big Powers "swoop down," in his own words, "like vultures" upon defenseless countries to share the spoils—the Big Two, Big Three, Big Four, and Big Five, and back again to Big Two—naturally he objected to joining either bloc in view of economic consideration:

> I say with a challenge that even if Jawaharlal Nehru went mad, the Congress and the country will not depart from the policy of non-alignment. If some body does not want to give us aid, let him keep his money with him... Frankly speaking I do not care two pence for their great material power. If they want to bomb India, well, let them. Why should I spend sleepless nights over them?

This is probably one of his harshest utterances, but he had to say what he did, driven by self-respect as an individual and as leader of a backward country—"third world" is the tag bestowed upon us by the wealthy West. *The Washington Post,* of all papers, could take a sane and sympathetic view of his stand because, they noted, "Nehru after all did what the founders of the Republic of the United States did—to give his country peace for a few generations by isolating itself from power politics." The remarkable thing which even *The Post* could not notice is that Nehru did not "isolate" himself, he only refused to join military or power blocs but pursued an independent of policy. Only Mr. Attlee among the elder statesmen of the West was able to see that "Nehru is far too civilized a human being to fall for the old doctrines of Marxism-Leninism and far too respectful of human dignity to introduce totalitarian practices." Even so, Mr. Attlee only spoke as a Western statesman and a Russian could have said something similar against imperialistic designs in defense of Nehru's non-alignment.

More than economic aid or military help, to Nehru the artist and man on destiny, the objection to two blocs is intellectual. To think of only two blocs is to place too great a limitation of the power of thinking or action. The Bandung Conference and the part Nehru played in it is the strongest proof of his defiance toward the two blocs and a sure tribute to his sense of history and statesmanship. It brought the emergent nations together and gave them dignity and a sense of purpose. Nasser appreciated Nehru's dynamic neutrality when it did not deter him from taking sides with Egypt, against the British, on the question of the Suez Canal. Nehru's stand was: "If colonialism succeeds in coming back to Egypt, it will reverse the entire course of history and mean the return of the enemy to other countries from which it had been forced to go."

Nasser, who knew where the shoe pinched, paid a handsome tribute to Nehru when he said, "What a quick comprehension of a complicated situation! And with what scintillating and brave words he conveyed it! It gave us courage and stirred us to fight back." Because of the trust and courage he gave to minor powers, and his own championship of justice as against international gangsterism, the oppressed people of the world could say what Vincent Sheean has said of him:

> We are willing to wait for him to make up his mind—a privilege we are reluctant to accord to any other head of a Government on earth, because we know he is struggling honestly, sincerely... to reach the right decision. The others crackle and snap or fizzle down...

Jawaharlal thinks, feels, suffers, finds his way and the whole world is willing to wait until he has done so. During the present century there is nothing at all comparable to this phenomenon. It is in this attitude of fighting against extreme nationalism, formalism, and dogmatism that Nehru made the great decision to stay within the Commonwealth—the first stabilizing decision he made for his country after its independence. Some said it was a great blunder, others called it an outrage against national sentiment. But Nehru knew better, and he assured his countrymen that he had never done anything against the honor and self-respect of India's people. His chief reason for staying in the Commonwealth was that:

> The world is full of strife today and disaster looms on the horizon. Every step therefore which leads to lessening of the tension in the world should be a welcome step. I think it is good any way that the old conflict should be resolved in a friendly way. Old wounds must be healed.

After this assurance there was nothing more his critics could say against him. When a Member of Parliament spoke of the dead concept of a "Greater India" after India became independent, Nehru made fun of him and compared him to Bismark. The thrust went deeper when he added: "But Bismarck is dead and his politics are more dead. And the "Hon'ble Member seems to be living in a remote past."

There were moments when rebuke would not work or he did not care to rebuke. When he was moved by distress anywhere in the world it was as though one of his own limbs was turned and twisted and he underwent an agony of the heart. Consider, for instance, the Korean question.

The Korean situation was being discussed in Parliament and at the end of the debate the Prime Minister stood up to win his country's sympathy and support for the unfortunate Korean people. At this point he makes recourse to first-hand evidence—a letter Nehru received from a Korean woman who writes: "My country is sick and dying of cold, disease and starvation." Nehru remembers it and remarks when his turn comes, "As I am listening to Honourable Members many pictures are floating before my mind—pictures of marching armies and dying people, and statesmen, holding converse in a room in Washington." How shall we escape? asks Nehru. "Ostrich-like, shall we hide our heads? Or play our brave parts in the shaping of events?" "Brave," but not arrogant, for he has said times without number that he felt "very humble before the problems of the world."

That is why when he is discussing a dynasty, a battle, an alliance, an attempt at conquest or rebellion, the questions he invariably asks are moral: "But what good came of it at last? Why was it a famous victory? [etc. etc.]"

He realized more than most historians or statesmen how fate and events had placed him in the center of the Indian stage—and he knew India must play a role in promoting the good of the world, and so at every turn he took, he thought of things in a big way. Nothing can explain his grasp of history, his sense of history, better than the series of questions he asks again and again: "What kind of a world will we have?...Will it be a fairer and happier world where the good things of life will be reserved not for a few but are freely enjoyed by the masses?"

And to such a world we have an obligation, wherever we may live and whatever may happen to any part of it. Nehru thinks "we all have a responsibility for the state of the world," and we must apply the "touch of healing." If this is not to have a sense of history, then I do not know what is.

The Chinese invasion in 1961 brought forth his poignant reaction: "A few hundred miles this way or that on the mountain top does not matter very much," but what hurt him was the "opportunistic mentality" of a trusted neighbor. The great powers were angry, that Nehru did not denounce the invader in strong language. But his stand was: "The language of cold war does not help. What the world needs is the touch of healing."

End Note

All the citations in this chapter are taken from the works of Nehru given below. I have tried to discuss Nehru's views using his own words as much as possible. Because of the numerousness of the citations I have not given the page numbers.

Works Cited

Nehru, Jawaharlal. 1946. *The Discovery of India.* New York: John Day.

______________. 1942. *Glimpses of World History.* New York: John Day.

______________. *Speeches from 1947 to 1964.* 4 vols. Delhi: The Publications Division of Govt. of India.

______________. 1941 [1936]. *Toward Freedom.* New York: John Day. Reprint of 1936 edition, entitled *An Autobiography.* London: John Lane.

XI Cultural Idenity and Diaspora

Chapter 38 | Muslims in India

Sheila McDonough

The Muslim Calendar begins in the year 622 C.E. because in this year the Prophet Muhammad and his followers left their native town of Mecca and emigrated to the city of Medina. Muslims consider this date to be the point at which a new form of religious, political, and social order came into existence. This new order was set up according to principles that members of the new community believed were based on revelations made to the Prophet over a period of twelve years. The revelations continued to come to him until his death ten years later in 632 C.E.

These revelations constitute the scripture called the Qur'an. Muslims believe that this is the last of the direct revelations from God which will come to humanity. According to the Qur'an, the revelations which came to the Prophet Muhammad consisted of the same essential truths which had been coming to other prophets many times before him, but which had been lost because of human corruption and failure. The Qur'an teaches that revelation first came to Adam, after he and his wife disobeyed God's commandments, and later came again through Noah, Abraham, Moses, Jesus, and many other prophets. The Muslim belief is that the message was always the same—to acknowledge the one God who is the creator of everything, and to live morally good lives in preparation for the final Day of Judgment. According to the Qur'an, humans have rebelled against these teachings and become corrupt in their practices.

The Qur'an mentions by name several prophets other than the ones named in the Bible, and says that there have been many other prophets to other peoples. The persons called disbelievers in the Qur'an are the people of Mecca to whom the revelations were addressed during the Prophet's lifetime. Many of them mocked him, and called him a liar. The word *kafir* comes from a root meaning "to deny"; the kafirs were those who denied the truth of the new revelation and refused to reform their practices. These practices included tribal codes of blood revenge inherited from the centuries old customs of the desert Arabs, and the charging of excessive rates of interest as was common among the traders of the relatively new commercial city of Mecca.

The new religion arose among the city dwellers of Mecca, most of whom, including the Prophet Muhammad, made their living as traders. Mecca was on the trade routes overland from South Asia to the Mediterranean. Caravans which made the hazardous trips successfully made their owners very rich, but the business was very risky. Those who made money then used their money to lend it out at high rates of interest to those who had failed. The rich were getting richer and the poor poorer. The revelations of the Qur'an include a strong critique of unjust social practices, including usury, and stress the need for the corporate well-being of all the members of the new community.

The issues at stake between the new religion and the old religion of the Meccans and the desert Arabs included reform of tribal practices, specifically blood revenge, and the killing of female babies, refusal to accept the idols of the polytheistic desert tribes, affirmation of the unity of the one God who created, sustains, and will finally judge all human life, and social change. A new institution of marriage was established which contrasted with the relatively unstructured sexual practices of the desert Arabs, and clear guidelines were established for family life. Finally, new economic policies forbidding usury and insisting on honesty in commercial practices were set forth.

When the new community was established in Medina, the Prophet Muhammad continued to receive revelations. He was also the executive and judicial head of the new community; he settled disputes, made decisions about the welfare of the community and interpreted the revelations. He also consulted with other members of the community on many occasions. The last period of his life in the new city was complicated by an on-going war with the leaders of his native city of Mecca. War broke out three times between Mecca and Medina, and each time the Muslims survived and became stronger. Finally, just two years before the death of the Prophet Muhammad, Mecca was captured by the Muslims. Their former opponents accepted Islam, idols were removed from the Kaaba, the latter became the center for an annual Muslim pilgrimage, and the new religion of Islam became the basis for a new form of social order which extended over most of the Arabian peninsula. The old tribal wars and antagonisms were abolished and replaced by a new form of brotherhood, a new social order based on acceptance of the guidance of the revelation of the Qur'an. This new order was potentially open to any and all who accepted the revelation.

After the death of the Prophet Muhammad, who left no sons, leadership of the community was entrusted to selected individual members of the community, Caliphs, who took on all the functions which the Prophet had held except the receiving of revelation and the authority to interpret the revelation. The first four Caliphs remained in Mecca; the fifth Caliph moved out to Damascus. The community had expanded very rapidly under the leadership of the early Caliphs as the Muslim armies defeated the empires of the Zoroastrian Persians and the Byzantine Christians.

Muslim Expansion

This first rapid expansion stopped within several decades after the death of the Prophet, and was never again to advance so quickly and easily. In the following centuries, Muslims mainly occupied themselves with the governing of their vast new territories and with the economic development of their people. Earlier Christian writing about these Muslim conquests attributed the successes of Muslims in Christian territories to violent, aggressive militarism. The seminal study of the conquests by Thomas Arnold, *The Preaching of Islam*, criticizes those earlier forms of Western historiography, and showed that man of the Muslim successes resulted from dissatisfaction in local populations with the governing styles of earlier Empires.

Once the Muslims had recaptured Mecca, the earlier trading oligarchy of that city became active in the spreading of Islam. The original expansion occurred under the leadership of former members of the trading oligarchy, and was motivated in part by the urge to strengthen trade. The first Muslim dynasty, the Ummayad, consolidated its power by establishing military garrisons outside the conquered cities. Most historians of the Ummayad period now agree that the Arab merchants dominating the regime made little effort to convert the population of the areas they had conquered. They wanted to consolidate their economic dominance of the area and keep the trade in their own hands. Local populations were treated as "people of the book." The Qur'an had indicated that Jews and Christians had received revelation, and were therefore entitled to keep their personal religious rituals and personal law when they were ruled by Muslims. When the expanding armies encountered other religions, Zoroastrianismin the first instance, the original response was to treat these people in the same way as Jews and Christians. The Ummayad procedure was to treat Zoroastrians also as people of the book.

It seems that the original rapid expansion occurred partly as a result of the fatigue of the peoples of the area with the five centuries long continual wars with the Zoroastrians and Christians, and with the campaigns against heresy waged by various Byzantine Christian empires (Arnold 1961). Many of the populations accepted Muslim rule probably as a better alternative than what they had been experiencing.

This rapid historical expansion raises theoretical questions as to whether Muslims necessarily feel an obligation to conquer other peoples, or whether they are ready to co-exist with other cultures. There is no simple yes or no answer to this question, because both attitudes have existed at different times in Muslim history. Perhaps the most realistic way to view the historical record is to acknowledge that when opportunity presented itself, the Muslims took it, and when expansion was not feasible, they accepted the realities of the situation.

The first Muslim community in Medina had war imposed on them by their enemies from Mecca; they learned through battle the necessity of fighting in order for their new social order to survive. The motives of the first Caliphs in strengthening Islam by establishing Muslim dominance over the Arabian peninsula was rooted in this experienced need for security. However, the internal decay of those empires was one of the major reasons for the rapid expansion of the new Muslim society.

The Qur'an clearly says that there shall be no compulsion in religion (Surah 2: 256), a point that has been well understood by all traditional Muslim religious and political thinkers. As indicated, the first Arab conquerors were not interested in converting the conquered peoples. However, the conquered peoples were treated as second class citizens who were not entitled to join the armies, not share in the booty. They were considered protected persons who should pay special taxes for the privelege of being protected by the Arab armies. Non-Muslim persons conquered in battle could be enslaved, a practice common in the ancient Mediterranean world. One possible way to escape slavery was to convert Violence may sometimes have been used on the battlefield to induce conversion, but this was not the normal practice, nor was it justified by the official teaching.

Early Muslim Expansions

This early Muslim expansion included the first Muslims to settle in territories in India. In 7ll C.E. some Muslims under the leadership of the Arab general, Muhammad bin Qasim, conquered some territory in what is now Sind (MacLean 1989). These Muslims lived within a hundred years of the death of the Prophet Muhammad, so that the way of life they set up in Sind would have resembled the patterns of the original Muslim community.

Earlier historical writing about the conquest of Sind tended wither to portray the conquest as motivated by violent aggressiveness, or to go to the other extreme of portraying the Arab conquerors as peaceable and tolerant. A recent study of these events based on analysis of the primary sources, *Religion and Society in Arab Sind,* by Derryl N. Maclean, takes issue with both these earlier approaches. Maclean says the primary sourced indicate that Muslim policy in Sind followed closely the policy of Arab armies elsewhere in the Ummayad Empire. Since Zoroastrians had been treated as people of the book, so the Arab conquerors in Sind treated the conquered Buddhist and Hindu populations as people of the book. They had to pay the taxes of persons in the category of protected peoples, but they were allowed to keep their religious rituals and religious buildings. Temples were allowed to be built and repaired at this time, just as churches were.

This conquest of Sind took place because some widows of Arab traders were returning by sea from Ceylon, and were attacked by pirates near what is modern Karachi. Expeditions were sent to punish the pirates, and this led to the eventual conquest of Sind. Trade had led Muslims to many new territories along the coast of Africa, to Malaysia, Indonesia, and the coast of China among other places. When trade was interfered with, Muslims armies often followed to ensure the effective progress of commerce. Many other traders over the centuries settled on the coast from Gujarat to Kerala. As we indicated earlier, the first adherents of Islam were traders in Mecca, and the impulse to establish commerce has subsequently been the most dominating characteristic of the wandering Muslims who have gone everywhere in the world.

The Muslim community established gradually by the traders in Sind was the first Muslim community to take root in India. The reasons for the success of the Muslim armies in this part of the world were probably similar to the reasons for their successes in Byzantine, Christian, and Zoroastrian territories. In this case, the population was mainly Buddhist. The Muslim armies were efficient and well organized, and the administrative policies of the Muslims also helped solidify their conquests.

Muslim traders were landing in other parts of India as well, much as they were expanding into Africa. In most cases, they settled and took part in life as part of the local communities. Sind was the first place where Muslim rule was established. In this case, the population was mainly Buddhist. After the Muslim conquests, many of the Buddhist monks seem to have left the area, and the Buddhist monasteries decayed and eventually disappeared. The Buddhist merchants may eventually have converted, some going back into Hinduism and others to Islam. Buddhism faded out in the area, as it did in other parts of India.

Umar, the second Caliph of Islam, is credited with having designed most of the administrative policies followed by Muslims when they conquered new territories (Nu'mani 1957). The policies followed by Muhammad bin Qasim in administering the new Muslim territories in Sind followed very closely the policies which other Arab commanders had followed in lands conquered from Christians and Zoroastrians. These policies included permitting other religious communities to keep their personal law.

After subsequent Muslim conquests in India from the eleventh century onwards, the question of treating Hindus and Buddhists as people of the book became more controversial. Many later Muslim thinkers tended to apply the models of the first Islamic experience to all subsequent experience. Christians and Jews were not viewed as intransigent enemies of Islam partly because they had not been part of the original Meccan oligarchy which had opposed and fought the Prophet Muhammad and his followers. Since they had scriptures, they were assumed to be more acceptable. The pre-Islamic Arab rulers of Mecca represented the enemies of Islam. The alter question was whether or not all idolaters were to be equated with pre-Islamic Arabs. The Arab conquerors of Sind, as pragmatic activists, did not make that assumption. Some of the later Muslim religious thinkers did. In reality, Muslim practice towards all other communities has differed over time, and therefore the study has to be contextual. What happens in any one century is necessarily what will happen later.

Muhammad bin Qasim was one of many Arab generals who had taken over the administration of new territory, and who was expected to govern that territory in terms of the patterns established under the Caliphate of Umar. This pattern included settling troops in settlements outside cities, and allowing the local municipal governments to carry on more or less as before. The Arabs used local talent in government wherever they could, not least because their own personnel were stretched very thin over a vast empire.

It seems that the first Muslim conquerors to enter India were more open-minded on this issue than the later invaders who came from the eleventh century onwards. During this early period, the local Hindus were permitted to repair one of their temples. The instructions were that as long as they paid their dues to the Muslim state, they were to be allowed to practice their own religion freely. This was a very different attitude than that of the later Muslim conquerors who destroyed temples. Later, Muslim attitudes and practices in India were often influenced by the changes and developments taking place elsewhere in the Muslim world. The invaders that came from Afghanistan in the eleventh century were motivated largely by desire for loot. Later invaders similarly attacked Indian Muslim centers for a similar motive.

The split between Sunni and Shia Muslims, which occurred after the death of the fourth Caliph Ali, meant that both Sunni and Shia came to India. The death-in-battle of Ali's son, Husain, is commemorated annually by the Shia who consider this event a tragedy on a cosmic scale (Ayoub 1978.) These events entered into Indian history because some Ismaili Muslims, a branch of the Shia, had assumed power in North Africa and subsequently in Egypt in the ninth century. Their emissaries came to Sind in the ninth century, and some of them eventually established Ismaili rule in Multan The Ismailis did have the practice of attempting to convet persons to their cause, since they were a minority in the Muslim world looking for support. Their conversion techniques were based on work with individuals, sometimes permitting the individuals to keep much of their former faith and practice. From that time forward, there have been Ismaili and other Shia in India even though the Multan rulers were eventually replaced by Sunnis.

Another important change took place in the central Muslim areas when the Ummayad rulers were overthrown by the Abbasids in 750 C.E. The Ummayads were Arabs who were directly the heirs of the original Muslims in terms of culture. The very success of the new Islamic civilization had led to discontent among the many other ethnic groups who had become Muslim. A revolution occurred, and the new dynasty, the Abbasid, created a cosmopolitan society of persons from many ethnic backgrounds.

Under the Arab rulers of Sind, Indian knowledge in mathematics and medicine was welcomed by the Muslims. This policy was carried on by the early Abbasids. Muslim scholars were sent from Baghdad to India to study medicine and pharmacology, and Hindu scholars came to Baghdad, where many of them became chief physicians in the hospitals and translated into Arabic Sanskrit books on many scientific subjects.

At least fifteen works in Sanskrit which were translated into Arabic have been preserved. The system of numbers now called Arabic numerals came from India into Abbasid civilization (Ikram 1964.)

The Abbasid civilization expanded into Central Asia which meant that many nomadic Turkish tribes entered into the Muslim culture. The Abbasid civilization centered in Baghdad had translated many Greek materials, including Aristotle, at a time when the Christian world had fallen into disarray and had lost knowledge of the Greek sciences. For the tribes in Central Asia, joining Muslim civilization meant connecting themselves to a much more developed civilization, and beginning to take part in commercial activities which had a vast scope.

Central Asian Invasions

The later movements of Muslims into India came from these Central Asian tribes, most of whom were Persian speaking but of Turkish ethnic background. The later Muslim movements into India came by way of Afghanistan, through the mountain passes. Arabic ceased to be the dominant language of Indian Muslims; it was replaced in North India by Persian, and eventually by the development of the new language, Urdu. Arabic remained dominant in Muslim settlements in South India.

There was not much significant movement of Muslims into India for three centuries after the original settlements in Sind. This changed in the eleventh century. The Muslims from the Central Asian tribes had established a strong center of political power and culture in Ghazni in Afghanistan, which became second only to Baghdad as an important Muslim city. From there, Mahmud of Ghazni entered India and won an important battle in 1001. A confederacy of Hindus was organized against him, but was eventually defeated. It was Mahmud of Ghazni who instigated and carried out a policy of looting Hindu temples for booty (Ikram 19640). This behavior was based much more on the tribal practices of Central Asian tribes for whom looting enemies was not uncommon, than it was on the rules established by the early Muslim Caliphs like Umar on how to behave towards conquered peoples. Umar had insisted on respectful treatment of Christian Churches.

At this time, the scholar al-Biruni wrote a study of what he observed of religious thought and practice in India. He was one of the first Muslim writers to pay serious intellectual attention to Hinduism. His book *Kitab-ul-Hind* is a masterpiece of what today might be considered comparative religion and anthropology. He had learnedSanskrit and translated a number of works from Sanskrit into Arabic. He wrote in praise of Hindu mathematicians, philosophers, and astrologers as representatives of a high mental culture. He also found much to praise in Hindu art. His negative comments on Hindu thinkers referred to what he considered a closed-in mental attitude towards the new, and an unwillingness to share ideas and to open themselves towards the wider world.

Al-Biruni criticized the temple-looting policies of Mahmud of Ghazni as detrimental to the mutual acceptance of Hindus and Muslims. He wrote:

> Mahmud utterly ruined the prosperity of the country, and performed wonderful exploits by which the Hindus became like atoms of dust scattered in all directions, and like a tale of old in the mouth of the people. Their scattered remains cherish, of course, the most inveterate aversion towards all Muslims. This is the reason, too, why Hindu sciences have retired far away from those parts of the country conquered by us, and have fled to places which our hand cannot yet reach, to Kashmir, Benares and other places (Ikram 1964:31-32).

As this comment indicates, not all Muslims approved of the looting activities of Mahmud and other generals like him. One finds the first Muslim poets already speaking against the corruption of the political leaders, and later, the sufis tended to develop attitudes to Hindu religious life quite different from many of the aggressive military leaders. The Muslim community held within itself many diverse points of view, even among the Muslims who had been companions of the Prophet Muhammad.

The sufis, Muslim mystics, developed into more systematically organized religious brotherhoods in the third and fourth islamic centuries. The point of view they typically represented— concentrated on personal religious discipline and self-knowledge— had existed among individuals in the first generations of Muslims, and was usually present in Muslim communities subsequently. In the Indian context, the sufis became significant at the same period in which sufi orders were establishing themselves as an important popular phenomenon among Muslims elsewhere in the Muslim world, that is from the tenth century onwards (Hodgson 1974;vol 2:215). The sufis were particularly interested in techniques of self-mastery and of furthering intuitive religious insights. Many of them were therefore interested in Hindu religious thought and practice. Like al-Biruni, many of them wanted to know what they could learn from Hindus, and to share spiritual experiences. Mujeeb has commented that the sufiswere the only Muslims to take a serious interest in Hinduism (Mujeeb 1967:1670.)

From the tenth century onwards, the Muslim expansion into India became more widespread and effective in terms of the establishment of Muslim rule, and the dissemination of Muslim social and religious practices. Several new dynasties were established, and spread their authority over Northern India. In the international Muslim world, the thirteenth century was characterized by the disastrous defeat of the last Abbasid Caliphs by the Mongol invaders from the remotest corner of Central Asia. Baghdad was destroyed in 1258. This was the effective end of the high culture established by the Abbasids; the next few centuries were characterized by decentralisation among the Muslim powers, internal wars among Muslims, and a retreat from the intellectual dynamism of the earlier period.

The Mongol incursions into India were stopped by the Muslim rulers in India, and the subcontinent was spared some of the destructiveness inflicted by the Mongols elsewhere in the Muslim world, and in Russia and China. One result of the chaos occurring outside India was that many refugees, including many scholars, sufis and Muslim religious leaders, came into India to get away from the Mongols.

Following the defeat of the Mongols in India, one of the most successful of the Muslim rulers was Balban (1265-1287 C.E.) (Ikram 1964.) His policy was to stress the power of the ruler as emperor to design and implement social and political policy. He enhanced royal status by developing rituals of court etiquette, somewhat as the French rulers did later at Versailles. The interest in making sure that trade could flourish, which we indicated was one of the earliest and most basic motives of Muslim policy, was exhibited clearly by the activities of Balban. He did not try to expand the area of Muslim control in India, but he took many measures to ensure external peace and internal security by tackling problems of robbing bands of warriors. He made roads secure for trade.

The next Muslim dynasty, the Khiljis, expanded Muslim control into South India. The Tughluqs followed and consolidated Muslim power. However the fourteenth century was a time of famine, and this, together with the cost of many internal wars, led to widespread rebellions and the disintegration of much of Muslim authority over India. Muhammad Tughluq had tried to conciliate Hindus, and to appoint many of them to high positions. He tried to introduce social reforms, such as the abolition of *sati*. His cousin who followed him, Firuz Tughluq, reverted to a more strict interpretation of Islamic religious law. The *jizya* was imposed on Hindus for the first time. By this time, many more Muslim *ulama*, scholars of religious law, had come into India, and they may have been influential in counselling the ruler to be stricter with the Hindus.

Islamic Orthodoxy

The issue of what constitutes Islamic orthodoxy is not a simple matter, not least because *orthodox* is a Greek term with specific meaning in terms of how Roman Catholics establish doctrine; it is not an Arabic word at all, and has no real roots in traditional Muslim thought. In Greek, *ortho* means straight, and *dox*, teaching. In the middle of the ninth century, that is 200 years after the death of the Prophet Muhammad, various Muslim individuals, unhappy with what must have seemed deviant behavior from their political elite, acted on their own to collect oral memories of what the Prophet had said and done. Once these materials were sorted out and written down, they became known as Hadith, traditions of the Prophet, the second source of authority among Muslims after the Qur'an (Hodgson 1974 vol. 1:386-92.)

The next step was that other individuals, again acting without any kind of official support, used the Hadith and the Qur'an to articulate views as to what correct Muslim behavior ought to be. Those who did this became the founders of the major schools of Islamic law. The four founders of Sunni law were all in jail and in trouble with the authorities at one time or another in their lives. Once the schools of religious-legal thought were articulated in this spontaneous way, those who had trained themselves in this manner gradually became the judges in the courts of religious law, and the teachers of the religious tradition.

A further development which took place under the direction of the political thinker and administrator, Nizam ul Mulk, in the eleventh century, was the establishment throughout the Muslim world of the new institutions of *madrasas* to train the scholar-jurists, the ulama. Fazlur Rahman (1979:181-92) remarks that very little of the intellectual vitality of the earlier Muslim periods was exhibited by those who graduated from the madrasas because the curriculum of the madrasas was designed to produce exponents of adherence to textual materials, rather than to encourage new thinking about the application of basic principles to real life. The ulama were usually trained to give answers in the light of familiarity with the classical texts, but not to exercise original thinking. This madrasa system of training ulama was brought into India and became the chief source of what is sometimes called Islamic orthodoxy. One can understand why a political expert like Nizam ul Mulk would consider uniformity of ideas and practices a source of strength.One result, however, of the curriculum and educational politics that were established in this way, was a downgrading of original thinking on religious and legal matters.

In the fifteenth century, the central Muslim power in India collapsed into anarchy and turmoil, but independent kingdoms arose in different parts of India which meant that in many respects Muslim life became more indigenous. One noteworthy development in the earlier period had been that a Muslim woman, Raziyya, had become the ruler in 1232, even though the ulama had ruled that this could not be done (Ikram 1964:510). This kind of development meant that many of the ulama accepted the position that they would concern themselves with guiding the Muslim populace but would not interfere with the Muslim state.

The fourteenth and fifteenth centuries were a time of a great flowering of personal religious devotion expressed and stimulated by religious poetry among both Muslims and Hindus. Poetry as a vehicle of spontaneous personal religious feeling developed in all the major Indian languages. Great poets such as Nanak and Kabir of this era tended to use symbols from both the Islamic and the Hindu religious traditions, sometimes inter-changeably. There was often criticism in these songs of the sterility of the traditional religious authorities in terms of stimulating fresh inspiration and energy. Many of these poets lived lives of freely chosen poverty, and roamed the country singing verses to any who would listen.

The next Muslim dynasty, the Mughal, exercised power over much of India. (See Gopal, and Habib, this volume for details.) They were gradually challenged by the Europeans. These came, much as the Muslims had done, in search of expanding trade. Just as the Muslims took political power originally in order to protect trade, so did the British. The rebellion of Muslim and Hindu soldiers in the British army in 1857 led to the final abolition of the last vestiges of Muslim political power in India. Queen Victoria was proclaimed Empress of India.

In the century between the British seizure of control over India in 1857 and the independence of the new nations of India and Pakistan in 1947, a great deal happened, not least being the two World Wars, the Russian revolution and the revolution led by Ataturk in Turkey against the last medieval Muslim ruler, the Turkish caliph. This latter point means that the political, social and economic structures of the medieval Islamic empires were collapsing everywhere, and not merely in India.

Figure 50: Muslim reading Koran, early morning, Jami Mosque, Ahmedabad.

Sayyid Ahmed Khan

The Muslim thinker who emerged with the most constructive ideas after the destruction of the last vestiges of the Mughal empire by the British in 1857 was Sayyid Ahmed Khan (1817-1898.) He came from a family of upper class Muslim government officials living in Delhi. He received a traditional education at his home, but he also went to a new school set up by the British in Delhi. At first, he refused to believe that the earth went around the sun, but was finally convinced. This meant that he acknowledged the replacement of traditional Mughal astronomical thought by new ideas, and, in a general sense, his mind was opened to testing of any new ideas that came to him in the light of reason.

He was convinced that the rebellion of 1857 collapsed because Muslim educational practices had failed to keep up with the advances of knowledge that been occurring in western societies since the founding of the western universities in the twelfth century. He said that much of the thought and practice of the Muslims in India would have to change if the Muslims were to become active participants in the processes of the development of the modern world. He therefore raised the money to establish a modern Muslim University in India, Aligarh, and arranged for much translation of western scientific writings into Urdu. He also published a journal, *Tahzib-al-Akhlaq*, in which he urged the Indian Muslims to sort out in their thinking the differences between customs and basic religious principles. For example, eating with the hands instead of knives and forks was just a custom, but alcohol was a religious issue. (McDonough 1984)

It was Sayyid Ahmad Khan who argued most vigorously against the idea that India under the British was *dar-al-harb*, a place where Muslims could not live in peace. Technically, if the ulama say that a place is *dar-al-harb*, Muslims are supposed to fight the government. Sayyid Ahmad Khan maintained that the essential Muslim position was that Muslims must be allowed to practice their religious life freely; if this was permitted, they could be loyal to the state. The opposite view, upheld by some but not all of the ulama, was that Muslims must consider themselves enemies of the non-Muslim state.

This is a complex issue because, as we have seen, in traditional Indian Muslim kingdoms, the kings exercised authority and were not necessarily restricted by the opinions of the ulama. Sayyid Ahmad Khan, as a descendant of generations of Muslim administrators, was inclined to look at issues more from a practical point of view. The fact that a scholar gave an opinion centuries ago does not necessarily bind the present generation. Muslims for centuries accepted slavery as natural and right; they no longer do so.

He knew, however, that the ulama would influence opinion, and he undertook to argue this and other issues on the basis of the same textual sources that the ulama used. The traditional method of debating issues among ulama is by the issuing of opinions, fatwas, on contested matters. It often happens that members of ulama class offer opinions which differ from each other. It also often happens, as one can see from the historical record, that the ulama in one century oppose new practices, like the printing presses, which are taken for granted as acceptable in another age (Berkes 1964:40)

The Indian ulama also developed new educational institutions of their own after the establishment of British rule, the most well known of which was Deoband. The curriculum in these institutions was not radically changed however, and therefore the graduates continued to offer their opinions in the light of the same information that had characterised the thinking of generations before them.

Immediately after World War I, the leaders of the Indian Muslims organized the Khilafat movement to lobby the victorious powers on behalf of the Turkish Caliph. When the Turks abolished the Caliphate, some Indian Muslims, such as Maulana Azad, decided to work with the Congress party, while others decided to work for separate Muslim electorates, and failing that guarantee, to opt for a new country. Many of the Muslims who had supported the non co-operation movement, which Gandhi had led at this time, had become disheartened when he called the movement off after violence broke out (McDonough 1994). Negotiations between the Congress party leadership and the Muslim leaders working through the Muslim League were carried on between the two World Wars. No mutually acceptable agreement was found. Therefore at the end of the war, many Muslims opted to live in the new Muslim nation of Pakistan. East Pakistan broke away and became another new nation, Bangla Desh, in the early seventies.

Presently, about 12% of the population of India is Muslim, and Pakistan and Bangla Desh are on the Western and Eastern borders. Within India, much turmoil has occurred with respect to the questions related to underlying issues of whether Hindus and Muslims can work together constructively in devising new patterns of political, social, religious and economic life. The issues between the diverse religious communities are not finished, not least because the economic development of the area requires that the three nations devise new ways of effective co-existence. Conflict over who should control Kashmir has been one burning issue (see chapter by Hardgrave, this volume.) As with other highly controversial questions in the modern world, solution will require effective diplomacy, since the alternative is on-going mutual distrust and hostility for the foreseeable future.

Current Conflicts

Within India, the major problems have been conflict over questions of religious law, the destruction of the mosque known as the Babri Masjid, and the rise of religious extremism among both Hindus and Muslims. At the time of independence, the constitution devised for India permitted the Muslims to keep their own religious law, while at the same time indicating that eventually a common civil code for all Indian citizens would be desirable. The pattern of allowing separate personal law for different religious communities was the pattern of the early Muslim empires.

Muslims within India, because of their status as a minority community much worried about discrimination against them in jobs and opportunities for development, have tended to allow representatives of the ulama, and even of the more extremist groups like the Jamaat Islami, to become their spokespersons. What the Jamaat Islami represents is a kind of Islamic revivalism which is currently widespread in the Muslim world. In this case, the ideas originated among Indian Muslims and spread elsewhere (Sivan 1985:22.) This kind of revivalism might be characterised as a type of 'separatist modernism'. The revivalists want modern economic development, but they want the power to use this development restricted to persons who share exactly the same understanding of Islam.

In this century, religious extremism exists among all religious communities. In every case, the idea is that only one interpretation of the tradition is acceptable, and that the followers must have political power in order to build their version of a better future (Embree 1990). In almost every other Muslim independent nation, Muslims have acknowledged the necessity to exercise what is called *ijtihad*, fresh new reasoning on matters of religious law. However, in India, representatives of the minority Muslim community have responded to the perceived threats of losing their identity by drawing in on themselves and refusing to adapt their religious codes.

The two major recent issues of conflict with respect to Muslims in India have been the Babri Masjid question, and what is called the Shah Bano affair. These issues came to the fore in 1986. In the first case, a Hindu revivalist movement instigated the destruction of a Mosque which was said to have been built by the first Mughal emperor Babur. Presumably, on a symbolic level, this represented revenge for the destruction of Hindu temples by the invaders like Mahmud of Ghazni. The symbolic reason given was that a temple of the Hindu God Rama belonged on that site.

The Shah Bano affair occurred when a Hindu judge, hearing a case in which a divorced Muslim woman asked for financial support from her former husband, commented in his ruling in her favour that this opinion was more in harmony with Qur'anic principles than the actual practice of traditional Muslim law which did not acknowledge the right to support. The resulting fury arose from anger within the Muslim community at the idea of a non-Muslim daring to interpret the meaning of Islamic principles. (Embree 1990) The fact that other independent Muslim countries were moving to re-interpret traditional Islamic religious law on matters of this kind was considered irrelevant.

In English, there is an expression 'Catch 22,' which means a conflict in which decisions either way are fraught with danger. The question of the role of Islamic personal law in India is one such matter. The designers of the Indian constitution presumably assumed that with time, Indian Muslims would accept willingly their citizenship in India and would be ready to accept a common civil code for the nation. But the Indian Muslims, feeling threatened as a minority, have tended to focus on retaining the personal law unchanged as a guarantee of their identity. One obvious need is for Muslims to feel less threatened. Another is for Muslims themselves to think through and make decisions about their personal law.

A better education in the history of Islamic jurisprudence might enable Muslims to think these issues through with less fear of change. Many Muslim leaders of modern Islamic religious thought, such as Iqbal, have advocated both the freedom to develop new interpretations of the law, and the need for the Muslims to be the ones to do this. In Muslim countries as elsewhere, it has been the organized Muslim women's movements that have advocated changes in the direction of more rights for women.

Under Mahatma Gandhi's leadership, the founders of the Indian nation had evolved an understanding that all religious traditions teach essentially the same truths, namely that the divine source of life is ultimately one, and that serious religious persons can and should respect each other and live together in peace. In Gandhi's lifetime, he experienced close personal friendships with his Muslim friends in South Africa; they worked together tirelessly for more than 20 years against racist policies. He had expected the same close co-operation in the struggle to drive the British out of India. He got such co-operation from the majority of the Muslim leaders in the 1919-1922 period. However, the collapse of the Khilafat and non-cooperation movements in 1923 led to Muslim disillusion and withdrawal. This means that Muslims would work well with Hindus under certain circumstances, and not in others. Gandhi, caught up in the need for unity characteristic of an independence struggle, did not perhaps sufficiently realise or think about the needs of minorities in any democratic system to have ways of protecting themselves against discrimination by the majority.

One of the Muslims who worked most effectively with Gandhi, Zakir Husain, subsequently became the first Muslim President of India. Yet one of Zakir Husain's brothers opted to go to Pakistan and became vice-chancellor of a university there. This indicates that Muslims suffered much genuine perplexity as to how they could best preserve their basic principles while yet working with Hindus in building new civilizations in the South Asian sub-continent. Some took one path; others went another way. The situation at present is that the future is open, and many new paths need to be developed, both for the well-being of all the citizens of India, and for better relations between the three nations that have resulted from this long history of interrelationship between religious communities. When Zakir Husain became President of India, he expressed his hopes for the future as follows:

"I began my public career at the feet of Mahatmaji and he has been my guide and inspirer. I have endeavoured to follow in my life some of Mahatmaji's teachings, and, in this new opportunity of serving our people that I have got, I shall do my utmost to take our people towards what Gandhiji strove restlessly to achieve—a pure life, individual and social, an insistence on the means being as pure as the ends, an active and sustained sympathy for the weak and downtrodden, and a fervent desire to forge unity among the diverse sections of the Indian people as the first condition for helping to establish peace and human brotherhood in the world based on truth and non-violence. This is what he called *Ram Raj*." (Mujeeb 1972: 235,236)

Zakir Husain rightly maintained that the word Ram for Gandhi was a symbol of goodness and justice. Justice between majorities and minorities requires careful diplomatic procedures based on mutual knowledge, and mutual respect. In this regard, Gandhi's legacy of insistence on the importance of mutual respect could be significant for the future of South Asia.

Works Cited

Ahmad, A. 1967. *Islamic modernism in India and Pakistan*. London: Oxford University Press.

Ali, Y. 1975. *The Holy Quran text, translation and commentary*. Muslim Students Association.

Arnold, T. reprinted 1961. *The preaching of Islam*. Lahore: Ashraf.

Ayoub, M. 1978. *Redemptive suffering in Islam: a study of the devotional aspects of Ashura in Twelver Shi'ism*. The Hague: Mouton.

Berkes, N. 1964. *The rise of secularism in Turkey*. Montreal: McGill University Press.

Coulson, N.J. 1969. *Conflicts and tensions in Islamic jurisprudence*. Chicago: University of Chicago Press.

Embree, A. 1990. *Utopias in conflict: religion and nationalism in modern India*. Berkeley: University of California Press.

Ewing, K. 1988. *Shar'iat and ambiguity in South Asian Islam*. Berkeley: University of California Press.

Gandhi, R. 1995. *The good boatman: a portrait of Gandhi*. New Delhi: Viking.

Hardy, P. 1972. *The Muslims of British India*. Cambridge: Cambridge University Press.

Hasan, M. 1981. *Communal and pan-Islamic trends in colonial India*. New Delhi: Manohar.

Hodgson, M. 1974. *The Venture of Islam*. 3 vols. Chicago: University of Chicago Press.

Ikram, S. 1964. *Muslim civilization in India*. New York: Columbia University Press.

Ikram, S. and P. Spear. 1955. *The cultural heritage of Pakistan*. London: Oxford University Press.

Madan, T. 1995. *Muslim Communities of South Asia*. New Delhi: Manohar.

McDonough, S. 1994. *Gandhi's Responses to Islam*. New Delhi: D.K.Printworld.

McDonough, S. 1984. *Muslim ethics and modernity: comparative study of the ethical thought of Sayyid Ahmad Khan and Mawlana Mawdudi*. Waterloo, Ontario: Wilfred Laurier University Press.

MacLean, D. 1989. *Religion and Society in Arab Sind*. Leiden: Brill.

Mujeeb, M. 1967. *The Indian Muslims*. London: Allen & Unwin.

Mujeeb, M. 1972. *Dr. Zakir Husain: A biography*. New Delhi: National Book Trust.

Nasr, S.V. 1996. *Mawdudi & the making of Islamic revivalism*. New York: Oxford University Press.

Nasr, S.V. 1994. *The vanguard of the Islamic revolution: The Jama'at Islami of Pakistan*. Berkeley: University of California Press.

Nu'mani, S. 1947. *Umar the great the second caliph of Islam.* (Trans. Maulana Zafar Ali Khan.) Lahore: Ashraf.

Rahman, Fazlur. 1979. *Islam.* Second edn. Chicago: University of Chicago Press.

Sivan, E. 1985. *Radical Islam, medieval theology and modern politics.* New Haven: Yale University Press.

__________. 1968. Ed. *Dr. Zakir Husain presentation volume.* New Delhi: Maktaba Jamia.

Chapter 39 | Asian Indian Communities in the United States

Kamal K. Sridhar

The Asian Indian immigrants in the U.S. are a group consisting of people who claim several identities, e.g., regional, linguistic, social (caste, occupation, income, and so on.), religious (Hindu, Muslim, Christian, Buddhist, Sikh, Jain, Zoroastrian, and so forth). Coming from a traditionally multilingual and pluricultural country, will this community be successful in maintaining its languages and cultural traditions in the U.S.? To answer this question, this chapter will examine language maintenance patterns of Asian Indians in the U.S., and compare them with situations obtaining in India and elsewhere. It may be useful to provide a brief overview of the linguistic situation in India as a background to the discussion.

The linguistic scene in India is fairly complicated. The 1981 census of India reported 107 mother tongues being spoken in India (Krishnamurti 1989). However, this figure is not reliable because, in the 1961 census, 1,652 mother tongues were reported (Pattanayak 1971, Srivastava 1988). The figures vary for a number of reasons: for example, a given language may be reported under as many as 92 different names reflecting the returnee's ethnic, professional, attitudinal and other affiliations; and several varieties of the same language exist, some are mutually unintelligible, others are not. Counting only the languages reported by more than 1,000 persons and excluding foreign mother tongues, we get approximately 400 languages used in India. These belong to four different language families: Indo-Aryan, Dravidian, Sino-Tibetan, and Austro-

Asiatic. (See B. Kachru, in this volume.) In addition to the vast number of languages, a further complication is the presence and use of more than 40 scripts, religious and caste dialects, diglossic variation (high and low varieties of the same language), and code-mixed varieties (mixing of two languages, K. Sridhar 1989, ch.1). Switching from one language to another (code-mixing and code-switching) is a feature of multilingual communities and is common in India (Sridhar and Sridhar 1980). Most Indians constantly switch from one language to another, although the extent to which they mix languages may vary. While mixing and switching is often viewed as the cause of language loss and sometimes even language death elsewhere in the world, in the case of India, mixing and switching has been a way of life (Sridhar 1997) for thousands of years. Hence, it is significant for our purposes, especially in discussing language maintenance among members of this community.

Historical reasons contributed to the linguistic reorganization of India, with 25 major states and other "union (federal) territories," most of which are identified by a distinct language spoken by the majority of the people in the region. Apart from the dominant regional language, every region is inhabited by several types of minority language speakers, e.g., speakers of tribal languages, migrant language speakers, religious minorities, etc. The density of minority language speakers varies from one state to another, ranging between 5 percent in Kerala to 84.5 percent in Nagaland. The educational system also promotes multilingualism as is evidenced by the protection given to minority languages, and the active promotion of the "Three Language Formula." According to this policy, every school-going child learns to read and write in his or her mother-tongue (or the regional language in the case of languages without scripts and literary traditions), Hindi (the official language of the country), and English (the associate official language of the country). There are regional variations on this basic pattern.

Bilingualism as the Norm in India

As a result of various historical, geographic, and political factors, bilingualism is the norm in India. Some salient features of Asian Indian bilingualism (Sridhar 1989, 1996) are as follows:

1. The fluidity of language identity, leading to the under-reporting and variable reporting of the extent of bilingualism in the area (Khubchandani 1983);

2. The high degree of societal bilingualism, not only in border areas and among the educated population, but also on a very widespread scale among the population in general;

3. The widespread use of "mixed" language varieties;

4. The phenomenon of linguistic convergence (i.e., the tendency for languages in contact to adopt one another's formal features, resulting in the formation of South Asian "linguistic area" (Emeneau 1956, D'Souza 1987);

5. The tendency on the part of minority language speakers to maintain their languages, despite a low level of literacy and inadequate formal language instruction.

As Pandit (1972) explains it, a Gujarati spice merchant settled in Bombay can simultaneously control five or six languages. Such a merchant will speak Gujarati in his family domain, Marathi in a vegetable market, Hindi with the milkman, Kacchi and Konkani in trading circles, and even English on formal occasions. Such a person may be poorly rated in the area of explicit knowledge of linguistic rules of these languages, but in terms of verbal linguistic ability, he can easily be labelled a multilingual, and fairly proficient in controlling different life situations with ease and skill. For this reason, in spite of considerable illiteracy, a societal type of bilingualism/multilingualism (e.g., the case of the Gujarati spice merchant) has become the life blood of India's verbal repertoire. It is this type of bilingualism that has contributed to language maintenance rather than language shift.

Another distinctive feature of Indian bilingualism that needs discussion in the context of language maintenance is its stability, i.e., speakers of Indian languages tend to maintain their languages over generations and centuries, even when they live away from the region where it is spoken (Agnihotri 1979, Bhatia 1981, Gambhir 1981, Mesthrie 1992, Moag 1978, Siegel 1987, to mention just a few). Although this claim has not gone unchallenged, especially with reference to the loss of some tribal and minority languages (Chakledar 1981, Ekka 1979, Mahapatra 1979, Srivastava 1988), there is enough evidence of long range maintenance to warrant a detailed study of this phenomenon. The migrant speech communities continue to speak their own language in the home domain. Through their mother tongues, they endeavor to maintain their ethnic identities (Bhatt 1989, Mukherjee 1980, Rangila 1986, Satyanath 1982). Since diversity in food habits, dress, rituals, and languages is expected, and both the migrant speech community and the host community agree on limited separation, this results in cultural pluralism. Thus, while the migrant speech community retains its native language as an effective device for ethnic separateness and survival, it may acquire the language of the host community as a job-select language. Such cases of partial shift rather than total assimilation are seen all over India (e.g., Tamil-speaking Palghat Iyers settled in Malayalam-speaking Kerala, Saurarashtri-speaking Gujaratis settled in Tamil-speaking Tamil Nadu, three-hundred year old Marathi community settled in Tamil Nadu, Tamil speakers settled in Marathi-speaking Bombay, and the Telugu-speaking merchants and other Andhras from the neighboring Andhra Pradesh in Kannada-speaking Karnataka, to mention just a few.

Several explanations have been offered for this maintenance. "Group internal" factors include the maintenance of social ties and kin relationships which link the out-of-state community and the home-based community. In addition, Gumperz and Wilson (1971) have proposed "ethnic separateness of home life," that is, a strict separation between the public and private (intra-kin) spheres of activity, as the central variable. The crucial question, as Southworth and Apte (1974) rightly point out, is why "ethnic separateness" is so critical in South Asia as compared to other parts of the world. They also offer a partial answer by noting that the groups who have maintained their linguistic separateness are for the most part "rather small groups who could be said to have some particular reason for remaining separate," such as prestige (e.g., Brahmins), particular occupational identification (e.g., goldsmiths, tailors), or enforced separation (e.g., in the case of the so-called untouchables). It would be interesting to see if Asian Indians in the U.S. follow similar patterns of maintenance as in India. But before we do that, a brief note on Asian Indians in the U.S. follows.

Asian Indians in the U.S.: A Historical Perspective

A colonial diary from the year 1790 records the first arrival of an East Indian in North America, a man from Madras (South India) to Salem, Massachusetts. He had come to America with a colonial sea captain and with a desire to expand trade between

New England, Britain, and South Asia (Helweg and Helweg 1990: 45-46). The numbers that followed him are not in any way substantial. Only six Asian Indians participated in Salem's Fourth of July celebrations in the year 1851. Most of the Asian Indians who came during this period were merchants, who travelled to Chicago and San Francisco for trade purposes, but returned to India. A larger number of Asian Indians came to the U.S. through Vancouver, Canada. Hundreds of Asian Indians (mostly Sikhs) were brought by the Canadian Pacific Railway Lines. They were followed by a substantial number of others. From Vancouver they spread south to the U.S., to Washington State, and to California. The first Asian Indians in the U.S., most of whom were farmers from the state of Punjab, probably never exceeded 6,000 during the period 1904-1923. They settled down in California, forming little communities in Yuba City. Due to their distinctive turbans, language, and food habits, they were noticeable and subjected to discrimination. During the same period, a small group of educated Asian Indians also came to the U.S., who faced the same discrimination. Their increasing numbers created a clamor among the local residents. Responding to this public clamor, the U.S. Supreme Court ruled in 1923 that East Asians are not eligible for citizenship because they are not white according to a 1790 naturalization law that restricted citizenship only to "free white" people. This law was successfully challenged by an Asian Indian lawyer, Sakaram Ganesh Pandit, who argued that East Asians are Aryans (hence white) and was allowed to retain his American citizenship. In 1946 the U.S. Congress enacted laws allowing East Indians citizenship in the U.S., and allotted an annual immigration quota of 100 people. The 1965 immigration law that allowed every nationality equal immigration rights and gave preferential treatment to professionals increased immigration of Asian Indians to the U.S. (for a more detailed history of the Asian Indians in the U.S., readers are referred to Saran and Eames 1980, Helweg and Helweg 1990). Thus, almost the entire population of Asian Indians in the U.S. (except for the Sikh communities in Yuba City) are post-1960 arrivals.

Asian Indian Communities in the U.S.

According to the 1990 census, the total population of Asian Indians in the U.S. is 815,447. (The corresponding figure in the 1980 Census was 361,500.) They are spread all over the U.S., with varying degrees of concentration (See Helweg, in this volume.) The largest numbers of Asian Indians are in California (159,973), followed by New York (140,985). See Table 6 at the end of this chapter for the rest of the figures for Asian Indians in the different states in the U.S.

In a recent report, *USA Today* (1993) uses the census data to rank the fifty most common languages spoken in the U.S. It also mentions the state which has the highest concentration of each of these language groups. Hindi is ranked fourteenth, the other Asian Indian languages and their ranks are as follows: Gujarati (twenty-six), Punjabi (thirty-nine), Bengali (forty-four), Malayalam (forty-eight).

Coming from a traditionally multilingual and pluricultural society, and being familiar with English, which serves as the most commonly used second language among the educated speakers at least, what patterns of language maintenance, if any, are being followed by the speakers of Asian Indian languages? The post-1965 immigrants, who are mainly professionals, are sometimes referred to as *New Ethnics*. "The new wave of Indian immigrants, which started in 1965, has brought mostly professional and middle class people from India... Although no surveys are available, it is reasonable to assume that Indians are not considered 'colored' in the United States today as they are in Britain. In England, Indians are a racial category; in the United States they are an ethnic group" (Varma 1987: 30). Compared to the earlier Asian Indian immigrants, the new generation of immigrants occupy mostly professional jobs (engineers, doctors, lawyers, professors, scientists, and so on). They also have the added advantage of an extensive knowledge of and fluency in the English language, unlike many other immigrant groups. This allows them to take up well-paying, white collar jobs and directly enter the American middle-class, economically speaking, without much hardship.

Singh (1991) compares the economic achievements of Asian Indians to Whites, Blacks and Hispanics. He concludes, "Asian Indians appear to outperform their "comparable" white counterparts when it comes to converting their overall resources into economic achievement" (Singh 1991:1). However, due to liberalization of immigration laws (that allow children, parents, and siblings of naturalized citizens to immigrate to the U.S.), the Asian Indian community is no longer made of only professionals. It is now a little more diverse in terms of levels of education and occupation. In a recent bulletin posted on the Internet (February 10, 1997), the following details were highlighted about Asian Indians in the U.S.:

87.5 percent have completed high school degree;
62 percent have an advanced degree, more than any other group in the U.S.;
Their mean family income is $59,777, which makes them one of the highest paid groups.

These figures support our impressions of the Asian Indian community as a highly educated community, with most members fitting into the middle-class American society.

An Empirical Study of Language Maintenance

Given the diversity of the Asian Indian community and the salience of regional languages and cultures as rallying points, it is reasonable to study language maintenance and/or shift with reference to specific regional groups, to arrive at generalizations inductively. I began the study of language maintenance and/or language shift with speakers of Kannada (referred to as Kannadigas), and expanded the scope of the study to include speakers of Gujarati (referred to as Gujaratis), and Malayalam (referred to as Malayalis). The Kannadigas_were chosen for two reasons: (1) my earlier studies of language use by Kannada speakers (Sridhar 1983) might help me to better interpret Kannada-English bilingualism, and (2) the existence of a systematic study of language maintenance and/or shift among Kannadigas in New Delhi (Satyanath 1982) permits a comparison between patterns of language maintenance within and outside India. The Gujarati community was chosen for several reasons, chief among them being: (1) it is one of the largest communities in the U.S. (it is the fourth largest community in New York state with a population of 9,910 speakers); (2) it has pioneered migration both within India, e.g., the Saurashtri's in Tamil Nadu, South India; and outside of India, e.g., Kenya (Neale 1974), Britain (Clark, Peach and Vertovec 1990); and, (3) the members of this community are spread across a wide range of educational and socio-economic status, more so than speakers of other Asian Indian languages. The Malayalis_were chosen for purposes of comparison and contrast. A large percentage of Malayalis follow Christianity. This would allow us to see if religion was an important variable in studies of language maintenance. Both Hindus and Christians were included in the study. The majority, 80 percent, were Syrian Christians, 14.4 percent were Hindus and 4.7 percent were Catholics

All the three language groups speak major regional languages in their respective geographical areas in India, e.g., Kannada in the state of Karnataka, Malayalam in Kerala, and Gujarati in the state of Gujarat. Each of these languages has a rich literary tradition, with Kannada dating back to the ninth century. The state of Kerala, in Southern India, has the highest rate of literacy, followed by Karnataka, also in South India. Gujarat, a state in North Western part of India, is also a state with a relatively high level of literacy.

The three groups were studied as part of a longitudinal project. It is hoped that data from the other Asian Indian language communities will be collected down the road. Part of the problem in studying more populous communities such as the Hindi and Bengali speaking communities is that they do not represent a homogeneous group. For example, in addition to the immigrants from India, a large number of Hindi speakers come from Guyana, Trinidad, Fiji, etc., and a substantial number of Bengali speakers are from Bangladesh. Hence, these communities will be studied at a future date. Since it is impossible to write about all the Asian Indian language groups, I will refer to the three communities I have worked with in the recent past. With slight modifications, it will perhaps be possible to generalize my observations to other language groups within the Asian Indian community living in other parts of the U.S.

The theoretical model adopted in this chapter is that of Fishman (1966), which involves three major topical sub-divisions: (a) habitual language use at more than one point in time or space under conditions of intergroup contact; (b) antecedent, concurrent, or consequent psychological, social, and cultural processes and their relationship to stability or change in habitual language use; and (c) behavior toward language in the contact setting, including directed maintenance or shift efforts. While comparison across time is not possible in the Asian Indian community due to its relatively short span of stay in the U.S., comparison across space has been attempted here with reference to the three communities, e.g., their migrations within India and to other parts of the world (e.g., Kannadigas in New Delhi, Gujaratis in Kenya, etc.). .

Compared to their compatriots, the Kannadigas and the Malayalis who are mostly professionals, the Gujaratis are spread across a wide range of professions and occupations. Keeping this factor in mind, the questionnaire for this group was written in Gujarati. While most of the Kannadiga and the Malayali respondents are from Queens and Manhattan, several of the Gujarati families included in the sample are from New Jersey. The questionnaire elicited the following pieces of information: demographic details, opportunities for use of their respective native language(s), indicators of rootedness in the ethnic tradition, parents' use of languages in different domains, children's proficiency in their respective ethnic tongue, children's use of and attitude toward their ethnic language, parents' efforts toward language maintenance, and parents' attitude toward the future of their ethnic tongue in the U.S. The method adopted for the study included a survey questionnaire administered to willing subjects. Data from the questionnaire was substantiated by (participant) observation in the home setting, in the community setting (during picnics, concerts, meetings, and religious celebrations), and in the school/playground setting.

Findings

The families included in the study represent a fairly young group. Most of them are in the range of 31-50 years. The average length of their stay in the U.S. for the groups ranged from 6.4 years to 16.3 years. The educational qualifications of the men and the women for the three groups showed interesting patterns. See Table 7 at the end of this chapter.

The level of education correlates with types of professions. Most of the males and the females among the Kannadigas and the Malayalis were engaged in some sort of professional job (doctors, lawyers, company and bank executives, etc.). Relatively fewer Gujaratis were employed as professionals. One notices a great deal of variation in the employment pattern of women. Approximately 36 percent of the females in the Gujarati sample with a BA/B.Sc. degree were employed as factory workers, machine operators, filing clerks, etc., while 43 percent of the Malayali women with similar qualifications were employed mostly as nurses in area hospitals, and 62 percent of the Kannadiga women were employed in banks, computer-related fields, etc.

Most of the respondents received their college education through the medium of English. For the Gujaratis there was a substantial difference between the males and the females. Approximately 94 percent of the males and 30 percent of the females were educated through the medium of English at the college level. More than 60 percent of the women in this group reported that the medium for them at the college level was Gujarati. At the high school level, majority of the males and females in the Gujarati group were educated in their mother tongue, while 48 percent of the men and 71 percent of the women in the Malayalam group, and 20 percent of the males and 18 percent of females in the Kannada group had received education through their mother tongues.

Another important variable that we need to consider in addition to the language of instruction is the respondents' patterns of residence before emigrating to the U.S. Most of the respondents in the Malayali and the Kannadiga groups lived in metropolitan cities prior to their immigration. Compared to these groups, only 27 percent of the men and 37 percent of the women in the Gujarati group came from metropolitan cities. These data are significant in that they document the respondents' use of the ethnic language and their familiarity with English. In metropolitan cities, English is often the common medium of communication -- the lingua franca. Living in smaller towns, members of the Gujarati community had more opportunities to use Gujarati.

The next set of questions attempted to solicit data regarding opportunities for the use of the ethnic language in the New York/New Jersey area. It is interesting to note that extensive 'support groups' exist for the three communities. All three groups reported having several friends and relatives in the area, ranging between twelve to thirty-four families per family. Data on the presence of friends and relatives is complemented by information on the frequency of interaction among the families. The communities stay pretty much in touch with other members of their ethnic group. The families get together often on weekends, and during Indian festivals. They attend social events organized by their respective cultural organizations. These data are significant in that they indicate a high degree of social interaction which often results in the use of the ethnic tongue. All the respondents said that they visit India at least once a year. It is not uncommon for the parents to take their children to India for the summer. Also, most of them said that they entertain relatives and friends visiting from India on a regular basis. Given the extended family structure of the Indian society, where all married sons live together, and the rules of hospitality is extended to even distant relatives, these visitors often stay as long as three to six months with them. The native language tends to be used more if the visiting relatives are of the older generation.

Regarding interaction and socialization patterns, the three groups were asked about the frequency of social gatherings, and whether they invited mixed groups of people or mostly members from their own regional language group. Most of the respondents indicated that they got together with friends and relatives at least once in two weeks. As to their patterns of socialization, the results are interesting and are summarized in Table 8 at the end of this chapter.

The table indicates that the groups are very much rooted in their ethnic culture and traditions, with the Gujaratis and the Malayalis being more traditional. There is very little interaction with Americans, which indicates that the groups are self-contained and insular to a certain extent. There are several neighborhoods in the borough of Queens, e.g., Jackson Heights and Flushing, where there are ethnic enclaves of Punjabis, Gujaratis, etc. People tend to interact socially on a regular basis primarily with members of their own language groups. During these get-togethers, the language of conversations is usually the ethnic tongue. Hegde's (1991) study supports these findings. Her study explored the patterns of intra-ethnic (between members of the same language group) and inter-ethnic (between speakers of different Asian Indian languages) interactions of one hundred and thirty-three Asian Indian immigrant families in the New York and New Jersey area. She concludes that the immigrants in her study maintained two distinct interpersonal networks, intra-ethnic and inter-ethnic. Similar findings are reported in Alexander (1990) and Gibson (1988) about earlier settlements of Asian Indians in California.

This pattern of interaction is consistent with other data, e.g., lack of interest in American sports, neighborhood activities, etc. (Note: during the 1992 and 1996 election years there was more Asian Indian involvement at both local and national levels, though still quite marginal). The Asian Indians are still heavily rooted in their home culture, as is evidenced by the set of data indicating their preference for Indian food, especially for dinners and on weekends. Most respondents indicated eating mostly Indian food. The younger generation also eats the same food, though among the younger generation there is some interest in American fast food. Most of the Gujaratis in the study indicated that they were vegetarians, so their children ate mostly Indian vegetarian food.

While most people reported using their mother tongues in social get-togethers, in telephone conversations, a pattern of code-mixing (mixing with English) was reported mostly by Malayalis (60 percent) followed by Kannadigas (57 percent). Among the Gujarati's, only 43 percent reported using a mixed variety in phone conversations. Exclusive use of the ethnic language in telephone conversations was low for the Malayalis (40 percent) and the Kannadigas (43 percent), but comparatively somewhat higher for the Gujarati speakers (57 percent).

Against the data presented so far about the use of the ethnic language by parents, it would be interesting to see the nature and amount of exposure to Indian languages available to the younger generation. It is here, for the first time, that one notices some mismatch. While most parents were categorical in their support for maintaining their languages, the data elicited as regards the exposure to language the children receive tells a different story.

Most parents admitted that in conversing with their friends, they tended to use a somewhat code-mixed variety, i.e., Gujarati mixed with English. The Gujarati community is the only exception, but even here, about 43 percent of the parents report using a code-mixed variety of the language. English is often used along with the native language in order to accommodate the younger generation who are sometimes not as fluent as their parents in the ethnic language. These findings are consistent with studies done with migrant communities within India, e.g., Kannadigas (Satyanath 1982), Kashmiris (Bhatt 1989), Punjabis (Rangila 1986), and Bengalis (Mukherjee (1980) in New Delhi, to mention just a few. This is pretty much the pattern in urban India, with most groups using a code-mixed variety with English slowly moving into the home domain. This is not surprising, as English is the most often used second language among the educated in India. This data is significant in that it indicates the use of English in the home domain for all the three groups. Considering the high level of education and the fact that the parents tend to use mostly English in their job-related conversations, this intrusion of English into the home domain is not surprising.

Efforts Made to Maintain Language

The answers to a number of questions relating to efforts made by parents to maintain the ethnic language at home provided insights into the commitment the parents feel towards the maintenance and use of the ethnic tongue. The efforts ranged from "insisting on children speaking only the native language at home" to "driving children to the local temple(s) and church(es) for native language instruction." These classes, taught in local temples/churches are mostly run by concerned parents. They are usually held during weekends, and are taught by mostly untrained people. Most parents did make an effort to keep the language alive by indicating that they read stories to the children in their native language, and that the children were familiar with nursery rhymes, religious verses/hymns, and popular folk songs from their language area.

Against this background of parental use of the native language and English, it would be interesting to compare the patterns of language use among the children. It is important to keep in mind that the data reported is based on the parents' report rather than actual samples of children's language use. The validity of parents' reports was confirmed by the researcher in informal observations, though a more direct study is certainly needed. A distinctive feature of the present study is the attempt to present a detailed description of the nature and extent of the children's proficiency in the ethnic tongue.

Language Use by the Younger Generation

First of all, the parents were asked whether their children understood the variety of native language spoken in everyday conversations (e.g., when discussing foods, friends, holidays, etc.). The parents were unanimous in pointing out that their children can understand the ethnic tongue where day to day matters are discussed. There were several questions relating to the children's competency in the native tongue. Asked about the language the children chose when responding to the parents, the majority of the parents indicated that a code-mixed variety with English was the preferred language. The only respectable figures for use of the native language is from the Gujarati parents. This could also be due to the fact that the mothers in this language group tended to be less educated than the mothers in the other two groups.

The next set of data dealt with language use during visits to India. As suspected, the children tend to use a mixed variety (i.e., the native language mixed with English). In a subsequent question, when asked if the children seem to be using the ethnic language more with grandparents than with parents, the Kannadiga responses indicate that this is indeed the case with their children. For the Malayali children, it is not an important variable. The responses from the Gujarati parents were surprising. Only 45 percent of the parents claimed this to be the case, while 35 percent claimed that the children use the same amount of Gujarati with the grandparents as they do with the parents. One would have expected more use of the native language with the older generation.

The true measure of maintenance is, of course, the use of the ethnic tongue by younger generation among themselves. There were a few questions that attempted to explore the children's attitude to the ethnic tongue. As a background for this, the parents were asked if the children got together with other children from their language/cultural group on their own. Not surprisingly, the children's pattern of socialization is much more assimilatory than that of their parents. As expected, the children get together with children from various language and cultural backgrounds. Asked about the language used when they get together with children from their native language backgrounds, the Gujarati children tended to use more Gujarati. In the case of the Malayali children, the use of Malayalam was non-existent. English seems to be the preferred language among the second generation. The use of more English by Kannada children is consistent with the findings in Satyanath's study, where Kannada children growing up in New Delhi tend to use the language of the majority (in this case, Hindi). The Gujarati children use more Gujarati, which is supported in the studies on this community by Neale (1974), and others who have looked at the Gujarati community in different parts of the world. The children do have a positive attitude about being spoken to in the native language. Asked how the children feel about being spoken to in the native language, "they don't mind" was opted for by a majority of the parents (Kannadigas 95 percent, Malayalis 48 percent, Gujaratis 66 percent). The observed pattern of children asking their parents to speak to them in English did not receive a high rating among the Kannadigas (5 percent) or the Gujaratis (11 percent), but did so in the case of the Malayalis (78 percent).

Parents' Attitude Towards the Native Language

The last set of questions elicited the attitudes and feelings of the parents toward their native language. Asked about the future of their language in the United States, "it will be maintained by a small number of people" was chosen by 86 percent of Gujarati parents and 100 percent of Kannada parents. The Malayali parents, on the other hand, were more pessimistic and opted strongly in favor of "it will disappear in the next generation."

When probed in a subsequent question about the possibility of their language not surviving after the present generation, few agreed with this fatalistic proposition. They wished that their children would learn the language and use it for inter-ethnic communication. "Children would be better off with English" was opted for by 80 percent of the Malayali parents, 36 percent of the Kannadiga parents, and only 19 percent of the Gujarati parents. The parents are realistic. They realize that complete maintenance is neither necessary nor feasible. The parents were asked to share their thoughts on the topic of language maintenance. Most parents wrote a sentence or two about their efforts and their commitment to maintain their mother tongue. About 70 percent of the Gujarati parents and 64 percent of the Kannada parents pointed out that while they did not expect their children to be fluent in the native language, they hoped that the second generation would be aware of their roots, and make an effort to maintain the culture if not the language. In the case of the Malayali parents, both the children as well as the parents said that speaking the language at home was not enough (Philip 1997). They suggested that classes in Indian languages should be offered at High School and College Levels. All groups were unanimous in their support for maintaining the Indian culture through the maintenance of language.

Conclusion

This study of Asian Indians in the U.S. is in its early stages. As we continue to observe the interaction between the two generations, and the interaction of the second generation Asian Indian children and youths among themselves, there are several differences that we need to keep in mind. First, while the older generation still professes loyalty to their native language, the younger generation does not identify with language groups. The children from all the three groups tended to identify themselves as Indian-Americans, and not as Gujaratis, Kannadigas, or Malayalis. In fact, in the Malayali group, a separate question relating to the children's self-labelling was requested. Forty percent of the Malayali children claimed themselves to be Asian Indians, thirty percent claimed themselves to be Americans, ten percent identified themselves as Malayalis, and twenty percent did not respond to this question.

Second, the children of Asian Indian immigrants may not be *bilingual* in the sense that their parents are; nevertheless, they are not completely monolinguals either. Informal observations also indicate that they are bi-cultural, aware of the cultural norms that have to be observed in the presence of other Asian Indians. They show the same enthusiasm for pop music as their Anglo-American counterparts, but they are equally enthusiastic about attending Asian Indian pop music concerts, especially the Hindi music concerts organized at Madison Square Garden and Nassau Colosseum. The younger generation attends these concerts in large numbers. "Selective adaptation" or "accommodation without assimilation" seem to be more appropriate terms for describing these communities. Gibson's (1988) claims regarding the second and third generation Punjabi-Americans in Valleyside, California, which seems to be appropriate here that "...parents firmly instruct their young to add what is good from majority ways to their own but not to lose what is significant about their [ethnic] heritage. Young people, for their part, adopt more of the majority group's values than their parents would like, but still they resist assimilation..." (1988: 198).

Third, code-mixing and code-switching are a way of life in India. In previous case studies, code-mixing and switching have been used to support claims of language shift, and sometimes even attrition (or language loss). But, in the Indian context, code-mixing with English may account for the survival of not only minority languages in India , but also majority languages, both in India and the U.S. The mixing is so pervasive that one finds code-mixing in newspapers, popular magazines, books of fiction, and sometimes even in published documents from state governments. In oral speech, mixed language is used by everyone, from politicians and film stars to the low-level shopkeepers and household servants (for a detailed discussion, readers are referred to Dubey (1991), Kachru (1990), Sridhar and Sridhar (1980), among others).

Finally, it seems to me that the term *maintenance*, and thereby, by extension, the term *shift*, needs to be redefined in the context of Asian Indians in the U.S. Complete maintenance seems to be an unlikely proposition, since it does not exist even in India.

In the Indian context, most people are neither literate in their languages, nor do they use all the languages in their repertoire in all the domains. Like the case of the Gujarati merchant cited earlier in this chapter, most Asian Indians use different languages for different purposes. They have the required competence in each of the languages in their verbal repertoire. It will be interesting to see if this kind of bilingualism/multilingualism will be maintained or shift to English will occur in the Asian Indian communities in the U.S.

Endnote

I would like to thank Tony Polson and Soma Phillipos for help in collecting the Malayali data and Hema Shah for assistance in collecting the Gujarati data.

Works Cited

Agnihotri, R.K. (1979). Process of assimilation: a sociolinguistic study of Sikh children in Leeds. Unpublished doctoral dissertation, England: York University.

Bhatia, T.K. (1981). Trinidad Hindi: three generations of a transplanted variety. *Studies in the Linguistic Sciences* 11:135-50.

Bhatt, Rakesh M. 1989. Language planning and language conflict: The case of Kashmiri. *International Journal of the Sociology of Language* 75:73-86.

Chakledar, S. 1981. *Linguistic Minority as a Cohesive Force in Indian Federal Process*. Delhi: Associated Publishing House.

Clark, C., Peach, C., and Vertovec, S. (eds.) 1990. *South Asians Overseas: Migration and Ethnicity*. Cambridge: Cambridge University Press.

D'Souza, J. 1987. South Asia as a Scoiolinguistic Area. Unpublished doctoral dissertation, Urbana-Champaign: University of Illinois.

Dubey, V.S. 1991. The lexical style of Indian English newspapers. *World Englishes* 10:19-32.

Ekka, F. 1979. Language loyalty and maintenance among the Kuruxs. In *Language Movements in India*, edited by E. Annamalai. Mysore: Central Institute of Indian Languages. 99-106.

Emeneau, M.B. 1956. India as a linguistic area. *Language* 29:339-53.

Fisher, M. 1980. *The Immigrants of New York City*. Columbia, Missouri: South Asia Books.

Fishman, J.A., V.C. Nahirny, J.E. Hofman, and R.G. Hayde (eds.) 1966. *Language Loyalty in the United States*. The Hague: Mouton.

Gambhir, S. 1981. The East Indian speech community in Guyana: a sociolinguistic study with special reference to Koine formation. Unpublished doctoral dissertation. Philadelphia: University of Pennsylvania.

Gibson, M.A. 1988. *Accomodation without Assimilation: Sikh Immigrants in an American High School.* Ithaca: Cornell University Press.

Gumperz, J.J. and R. Wilson. 1971. Convergence and creolization: A case from Indo-Aryan Dravidian border. In *Pidginization and Creolization of Languages*, edited by D. Hymes. Cambridge University Press. 151-67.

Hegde, R.S. 1991. Adaptation and the Interpersonal Experience: A Study of Asian Indians in the United States. Unpublished doctoral dissertation. Columbus: Ohio State University.

Helweg, A.W. and Helweg, U.M. 1990. *An Immigrant Success Story.* Philadelphia: University of Pennsylvania Press.

Kachru, B.B. 1990. *The Alchemy of English: the Spread, Functions, and Models of Non-Native Englishes.* Urbana: University of Illinois Press.

Khubchandani, L.M. 1983. *Plural languages, plural cultures.* Hawaii: East-West Center.

Krishnamurti, Bh. 1989. A profile of illiteracy in India: problems and prospects. Unpublished manuscript.

Mahapatra, B.P. 1979. Santali language movement in the context of many dominant languages. In *Language Movements in India*, edited by E. Annamalai. Mysore: Central Institute of Indian Languages. 107-17.

Mesthrie, R. 1992. *Language in indenture: A sociolinguistic history of Bhojpuri-Hindi in South Africa.* London and New York: Routledge.

Moag, R. F. 1978. Linguistic adaptations of the Fiji Indians. In *Rama's Banishment: A Centenary Volume on the Fiji Indians*, edited by V. Mishra. Heinemann: Australia.

Mukherjee, A. 1980. Language maintenance and language shift among Panjabis and Bengalis in Delhi: A sociolinguistic perspective. Unpublished doctoral disseration. Delhi: University of Delhi.

Neale, B. 1974. Language use among the Asian communities. In *Language in Kenya*, edited by W.H. Whiteley. Nairobi: Oxford University Press. 263-318.

Pandit, P.B. 1972. *India as a Sociolinguistic Area.* Gune memorial lectures. Ganesh Khind: Poona University Press.

Pattanayak, D.P. 1971. *Distribution of Languages in India, in States and Union Territories.* Mysore: Central Institute of Indian Languages.

Philip, Suby S. 1997. The evolution of Malayalam and its maintenance today among Malayalee immigrants. SUNY-Stony Brook: Center for India Studies. Unpublished Manuscript.

Phillipose, S. 1989. Language maintenance among the Asian Indians in the U.S.: Malayalis in the New York are. SUNY-Stony Brook. Unpublished manuscript.

Rangila, R.S. 1986. *Maintenance of Panjabi Language in Delhi: A Sociolinguistic Study.* Mysore: Central Institute of Indian Languages.

Saran, P. and Eames, E. 1980. *The new ethnics: The Asian Indians in the U.S.* New York: Praeger.

Satyanath, T.S.1982. Kannadigas in Delhi: a sociolinguistic study. Unpublished doctoral dissertation. Delhi: University of Delhi.

Siegel, J. 1987. *Language Contact in a Plantation Environment.* Cambridge: Cambridge University Press.

Singh, G.K. 1991. Immigration, Nativity, and Socioeconomic Assimilation of Asian Indians in the U.S. Unpublished doctoral dissertation. Columbus: Ohio State University.

Southworth, F.C. and Apte, M.L. 1974. Introduction. In_*Contact and convergence in South Asian languages, edited by F.C.Southworth and M.L. Apte.* (Special issue of *International Journal of Dravidian Linguistics.* 3.1). 1-20

Sridhar, K.K. 1997. The languages of India in New York. In *The Multilingual Apple*, edited by O. Garcia and J.A. Fishman. Berlin: Mouton. 257-80.

_______ 1996. Language in education: minorities and multilingualism in India. *International Review of Education* 42.4:327-347. Hamburg: UNESCO Institute of Education. [Speical issue, edited by N. Labrie and S. Churchill].

_______ 1993. Meaning, means, and maintenance. In *Language, Communication, and Social Meaning*, edited by J.E. Alatis. Georgetown: Georgetown University Press. 56-65.

_______ 1989. *English in Indian Bilingualism.* Delhi: Manohar.

Sridhar, S. N. and Sridhar, K.K. 1980. The syntax and psycholinguistics of bilingual code-mixing. *Canadian Journal of Psychology* 34.4:409-18.

Srivastava, R.N. 1988. Societal bilingualism and bilingual education: a study of the Indian situation. In *International Handbook of Bilingualism and Bilingual Education*, edited by C.B. Paulston. Connecticut: Greenwood Press. 247-74. *USA Today.* April 13, 1993. Census: languages not foreign at home.

Table 6: Distribution of Asian Indians in the US

State	*Population*	*State*	*Population*
Alabama	4,848	Montana	248
Alaska	472	Nebraska	1,218
Arizona	5,663	Nevada	1,825
Arkansas	1,329	New Hampshire	1,697
California	159,973	New Jersey	79,440
Colorado	3,836	New Mexico	5,193
Connecticut	11,755	New York	140,985
Delaware	2,183	North Carolina	9,847
Dist. of Columbia	1,601	North Dakota	482
Florida	31,456	Ohio	20,848
Georgia	13,926	Oklahoma	4,546
Hawaii	1,015	Oregon	3,508
Idaho	473	Pennsylvania	28,396
Illinois	64,200	Rhode Island	1,975
Indiana	7,095	South Carolina	3,900
Iowa	3,021	South Dakota	287
Kansas	3,956	Tennessee	5,911
Kentucky	3,922	Texas	55,795
Louisiana	5,083	Utah	1,557
Maine	607	Vermont	529
Maryland	28,330	Virginia	20,494
Massachusetts	19,719	Washington State	8,205
Michigan	23,845	West Virginia	1,981
Minnesota	8,234	Wisconsin	6,914
Mississippi	1,872	Wyoming	240
Missouri	6,111	Wisconsin	6,914

Table 7: Educational Qualifications (In Percentages)

	Kannadigas		*Malayalis*		*Gujaratis*	
	Males	Females	Males	Females	Males	Females
Professional	76	33	76	43	35	17
BA/B.Sc.	24	62	24	43	47	36
High School	--	--	--	14	18	41
Grade School	--	--	--	--	--	6
Total	100	100	100	100	100	100

Table 8: Interaction and Socialization Patterns (in percentages)

	Kannadigas	*Malayalis*	*Gujaratis*
only ethnic group	43	74	77
ethnic+other Indians	67	24	28
mostly Americans	0	0	0
ethnic + Indian + Americans	19	4	4

Note: Some individuals chose more than one response.

Chapter 40 | Asian Indians in the United States: A Socio-Cultural Profile

Arthur W. Helweg

Immigrants have always been a strength in the development of the United States. However, since the implementation of Public Law 89-236 (effective 1968) the United States has benefited from the contributions of the one million strong community whose ethnic origins are from India. They are generally a well-educated, affluent, highly motivated people who, I feel, are a major reason for the U.S. maintaining its current high quality of life and international economic position. Indian immigrants are generally ranked as the ethnic community with the highest income and education in the United States (See Tables 9, 10.) More importantly, their contributions culturally, economically, and politically as individuals have been substantial. As a community, they have enriched American culture, brought technological innovation, appreciably contributed to the intellectual base of the U.S., and increased U.S. economic wealth. At the same time, India has also benefited economically, politically, and socially from her Diaspora.

There is much to learn and analyze about this young but influential community. This chapter is descriptive: it will present a socio-cultural profile of the Asian Indian community of the United States. After providing a historical context, a cultural profile will outline the abstract symbolic system (Kroeber & Parsons 1958) guiding the Asian Indians' orientation to the world around them. Understanding the culture of a people is important because it provides the framework by which they interpret the world) around them as well as their goals and rules of life.

Following the cultural description, I will present a description of Asian Indian society, with its identification of social units and their interrelationships. This is important in order to understand how a people organize themselves to achieve their cultural goals.

Context: Emigration from India

Emigration from South Asia has been a dominant behavioral pattern since the Indus Valley Civilization (2500-1700 B.C.E.), whose merchants frequented distant lands (See Tandon, this volume.) The death of the Buddha (563-483 B.C.E.) resulted in his disciples traveling to other lands to propagate his message—a process that expanded under Emperor Asoka (265-237 B.C.E.; See Gopal, in this volume.) The impact of these forays is still evident today in Central and East Asia where Indian mythology, dance, and theater are still prominent. Movement from Western India to Africa dates back to the second century C.E. Although a flourishing trade existed then, permanent settlements did not develop. Smallscale movement changed to mass emigration as Indians provided cheap labor for Britain's colonies. But it was the indenture system, what Hugh Tinker (1974) termed a "New System of Slavery," where workers signed a contract to work abroad and were supposed to be returned to India when the terms were fulfilled. Unfortunately, abuses toward workers were rampant. They had no recourse to justice and were, in essence, enslaved. The result was the development of the nine million strong Indian Diaspora scattered throughout the former British Empire, concentrating where there were labor intensive economies, especially plantation systems. Notable regions where Indian Diaspora predominates include Mauritius, Fiji, Trinidad and East Africa.

After India obtained independence, destinations for Indian emigrants included the United States, Australia, and the Middle East. Notable movement to the United States started with university students. Wide-scale migration to the United States, the United Kingdom, Australia, and Canada developed in the 1960's, largely due to racial bars being removed by revised immigration regulations. The oil-rich Middle East became a focus for South Asian immigration after 1970.

It must be kept in mind, however, that the Indian migration patterns are not limited to movement to and from the subcontinent. For example, when Indians were expelled from Uganda in 1970, the vast majority went to the United Kingdom, with the United States, Canada, Sweden, Denmark, New Zealand, and the Persian Gulf states taking in sizable numbers (Helweg 1990; 19-25, Tinker 1974, 1976, 1977).

Coming to America

Asian Indians are the most numerous group from South Asia. Before the formation of Pakistan in 1947 (East Pakistan became Bangladesh in 1971), all people from the subcontinent were termed Indian. Presented below is a brief history of Asian Indian immigration to the United States.

Initially, Asian Indians came to the United States as sea captains and traders in the 1790's, actively pursuing trade between India and the North America. Some came as indentured laborers, but unlike the two million indentured in other parts of the British Commonwealth, sufficient records were not kept and the exact number is not know for North America. By 1900, there were about two thousand resident Indians: five hundred merchants and several dozen religious teachers. (See Table 11 for Asian Indian Immigration to the U.S. 1901-1990). After 1905, Asian Indian immigration increased rapidly, and included medical professionals. Six thousand entered the West Coast between 1907 and 1917, while another three thousand were barred entry. Many came down from Canada, where they had faced hostilities, only to have it repeated here. Most were from the region of Punjab, which is now divided between India and Pakistan. The vast majority were adherents of the Sikh faith, although a sizable number were Hindus and Muslims. (For a detailed history of immigration, see K. Sridhar, this volume.)

As Indian immigration increased, anti-Asian violence, which was common on the West Coast spread all over the U.S. Discriminatory laws were passed, prohibiting Indians from owning land and making them permanently ineligible for U.S. citizenship. In fact, the Immigration Act of 1917 is referred to as the "Indian Exclusion Act" (Helweg 1996). In this hostile environment, compounded by the Depression, several thousand chose to return to India. Thus, the 1940 census showed only 2,405 Indians living in the United States, and most of them around Yuba City, California. Since the immigration of Asian Indians was barred and laws prohibited Asian Indians from owning land, some Asian Indians married Mexican women, which gave rise to a new ethnic community, the Punjabi-Mexican community (Leonard 1992).

After the Second World War, legislation gave Asian Indians the right to citizenship, which permitted them to own land. A quota for immigration (one hundred per year) was established, which also allowed family reunification. Between 1948 and 1965, 6,474 Asian Indians entered the United States as immigrants.

Partly due to the national mood during the civil rights movement, the "Immigration and Nationality Act of 1965" removed the national origins clause in the U.S.

immigration legislation. Preference was given to highly educated and skilled individuals. India had a ready pool of such talent and as Table 11 indicates, they took advantage of the new legislation, and the mass movement from India to America began (Helweg 1990, 45-76; Mazumdar 1995, 93-100).

Asian Indian Community: A Profile

It must be kept in mind that the Asian Indian community is not a monolithic whole. For example, early immigrants came because they were well qualified and had no trouble becoming permanent residents. Their qualifications were accepted by American institutions. In fact, 67 percent of the foreign-born Asian Indians had advanced degrees, as opposed to only 25 percent of the American-born. Asian Indians are predominantly engaged in the professional and managerial fields and under-represented in the service, blue-collar categories. (See Table 10.)

The Asian Indians consist of three groups: (1) Initial Immigrants, (2) Second Wave Immigrants, and (3) Sponsored Immigrants. Initial Immigrants are those who came in the 1960's, led by a cohort of very highly educated men. They were doctors, scientists, and academics who migrated for better educational and professional opportunities. They are now in their fifties, many of them earning over $100,000 annually. Generally, their wives have little more than a high school education and do not work outside the home. Their concerns are regarding retirement and their adult children whose successful marriages and education are very important to them.

The Second Wave Immigrants are those who came in the 1970's. Like the initial segment, they too are highly educated professionals. Unlike their earlier compatriots in the initial segment, their wives are highly educated and work outside the home. Their children are college bound teenagers and within this community a high premium is placed upon college education, The third group are those immigrants sponsored by established family members. They are generally less well educated and more likely to be running motels, small grocery stores, gas stations and other ventures. Their concern is to establish themselves in a successful business.

It must also be kept in mind that their country of origin, India, is not monolithic either. It comprises dozens of language groups and four major and several minor religious communities. It can be argued that there is greater cultural diversity within the borders of India than there is within Europe. It must be kept in mind that there is a great deal of variation and that the frameworks set forth here may not be universals.

Asian Indian Society: Demographics

Table 12 sets forth a population profile based on the 1990 U.S. Census. To add, however, the 815,447 Asian Indians are the fourth largest immigrant group. They have increased by 111 percent since 1980 when they numbered 387,223. It is worth noting that the percent of foreign born was up from 70 percent in 1980 to 75 percent in 1990. Also the median age dropped from thirty years to twenty-eight years: the community is, on the average getting younger. Yet, while the median age has dropped, the size of the elderly population has increased. Also, as the gender balance trend is becoming more equitable. In 1966, females comprised 34 percent, in 1993, it was 53 percent. (Rangaswamy 1996: 163-173)

In the 1980's, the trend to sponsor relatives was very strong, thus lowering the education and income levels of the community. The absolute number in poverty doubled, but their percentage to the whole population has remained essentially the same. This challenges the assertion that the Asian Indian community is developing an hour-glass shaped economic profile, that is, there are only rich and poor, with the middle class declining, or being eliminated altogether. The figures do not support that view.

The naturalization rate is lower among Indians than other immigrant groups, including other Asian communities. This was not the case in the past. Earlier Asian Indians led in the naturalization process. However, as Rangaswamy (1996) points out, citizenship is not a sign of assimilation, it is a means for sponsoring relatives under the family reunification clause.

At present, Asian Indians are the fastest growing ethnic community in the United States. That trend is projected to continue.

Residence Pattern

Before 1965, Asian Indians were clustered in the rich agricultural areas of the Sacramento, San Joaquin and Imperial Valleys during the summer and Yuba City, Stockton and El Centro in the winter while a few moved to Arizona, Colorado, New Mexico, Texas, and Utah.

Seventy percent of the Asian Indian population live in eight major industrial-urban states: California, Illinois, Michigan, New Jersey, New York, Ohio, Pennsylvania, and Texas (see Table 13). Yet, like most other recent immigrant groups, Asian Indians tend to live in and around metropolitan areas. New York is home to 106,000 (1.2 percent of the entire city's population), Chicago has 54,000, Los Angeles-Long Beach

44,000, and Washington, D.C. 36,000. In New Jersey, Asian Indians are especially concentrated in the Middlesex-Somerset-Hunterdon region. They account for 2.3 percent of the population—the largest concentration of Asian Indians in the U.S.. They also comprise 2.1 percent of Jersey City's population.

It is common behavior in the U.S. that when an individual enters the professional ranks they move out of ethnic enclaves and into the suburbs, where people are generally more affluent. The professional and affluent among Indians tend to live in suburbs as well. Besides, the vast majority speak English and are familiar with American ways, thus they do not need to rely on their countrymen for help in practical matters. As a result, Asian Indians, for the most part, are usually residentially dispersed (Gall and Gall 1996).

Education

The educational attainment of the Asian Indian population is very high: 73 percent of persons 25 years or older have a high school education or higher (See Table 10). A 1984 study showed a mean high school grade point average 3.8. It is not surprising, therefore, that Asian Indians are found in sizable proportions in the elite colleges in the U.S..

Political Participation

Asian Indian participation is well behind that of other minority communities. A 1986 voter registration study in California found that although there was a 73 percent registration rate among the wider population, only 16.7 percent of Asian Indians had registered. The Asian Indians have used other tactics to gain political influence — they lobby for special interest. For them the issues vary from immigration policy to the U.S.'s role in Pakistan's military buildup. I contend that they have been more successful by taking up the issues and using informal, but effective communication skills. (See Table 14, 16.)

Business

The immigration of business and professional people from South Asia to the United States was minimal before World War II—immigrants at that time were primarily farm laborers. After 1965, most immigrants were salaried professionals. In 1980, only 6.6 percent of South Asian males were self employed.

Reports by the U.S. Department of Commerce charts dramatic growth in the Indian business community. Between 1982 and 1987 the number of Indian businesses doubled and showed a 400% increase in receipts totaling a dollar amount of 6.715 billion. (See Table 15.)

During the five years from 1987 to 1992 Indian-owned businesses grew by 300% more than the national average, totaling 93,340 firms with revenues of 19.3 billion dollars as compared to 6.7 billion just five years earlier.

South Asian restaurants have been a major endeavor since 1965. They are now even in medium-sized communities such as Kalamazoo, Michigan. They have not developed chains or entered into the fast food market yet.

One of the best known areas of South Asian entrepreneurial activity has been the hotel and motel business. It was started by Hindus from the region of Gujarat, most with the surname Patel. They began arriving in California in the late 1940's. They bought dilapidated hotels and motels in deteriorating neighborhoods, where the owners had given up the business as a loss. With hard work and cheap family labor, they turned the entities into a profitable enterprise. Some, like Shashikant Johani, made a fortune in real estate. Using capital from a diamond business and borrowing money from his family, he bought old, run-down real estate, fixed it up, and sold it for profit.

By the mid 1980's, the newsstand business in New York City became practically monopolized by Indian and Pakistani immigrants; they controlled 70 percent of all kiosks. One of the largest operators was Bhawness Kapoor, who in 1983, won a fifteen year license to run all the stands in the city's subway system. By the middle 1990's, immigrants from the Middle East were moving in to the business: the children of newsstand operators were going into different work.

Other enterprises South Asians have been involved with include Laundromats, gift shops and the garment industry. In fact, in the early 1990's, 40 percent of the gas stations in New York City were owned by Punjabi Sikh immigrants.

Asian Indian Attitudes

Attitudes deal with perceptions, not reality. However, it is on perceptions, not reality, that people act and respond to the circumstances. Some things may seem hard for some readers to understand. For example: Why does the highest educated, possibly the most prosperous ethnic community in the United States feel pessimistic about the future of the U.S. economy as well as race relations in general? How come such an affluent community is not more conservative?

Some of the attitudes of Asian Indians in the U.S. are summarized in the Appendix. Given the affluence of the Asian Indian community, it is surprising that they want to be socially responsible, but are not strongly conservative or affiliated with the Republican Party. Being in the high economic and political bracket they are, one would not expect the pessimism about the U.S. economy and ethnic relations, as outlined above.

Asian Indian Culture

When one considers Indian culture, two themes come to mind, the caste system and the emphasis on family honor. Although the concepts will not be dealt with exhaustively here, the reader will gain enough knowledge to better understand Asian Indian behavior in the U.S. (See Table 16.)

As is well known, the caste system is the prevailing cultural institution throughout the subcontinent. It is based on the principles of *dharma*, *karma*, inequality, purity, and reincarnation. In essence, the framework sets forth that the most pure are closest to God, and the less pure farther. One's position is determined by how well one leds one's past life; if one was pious and lived according to the duty (*dharma*) of the caste you were in, you were rewarded (*karma*) with a better position in the next life (Dumont 1966).

One misperception Westerners have about the caste system is that it stifles initiative and entrepreneurial spirit. Anyone acquainted with the people from South Asia knows that nothing could be farther from the truth. In fact, their behavior and comparative success in the United States indicates the opposite. I believe that caste ideology has affected the Asian Indians favorably because most who immigrated were high caste. Thus they were confident that they could do well; failure was not an option. They assumed that if another person could learn and do a task, they could do it also. They were willing to try anything new and were generally successful.

The second concept has to do with *izzat* or honor. In some societies, social evaluation is not an individual endeavor but a group development. In other words, there is a collective identity where the evaluation of your group or family determines your ranking. The evaluation is by communal consensus. There are no formal criteria, but the members of the community or society know what they are. Criteria may vary from community to community, but the point is that honor is bestowed by the community onto the group. Thus, for example, if I do community service, the honor of my whole family is enhanced by communal consensus.

The *izzat* concept has ramifications for the Asian Indians in the United States in at least two ways. They are usually very sensitive and observant as to how people evaluate their behavior. One finds that most Asian Indians in the professional world do very well. There are several reasons for this, many having to do with being especially sensitive to their surroundings. Asian Indians tend to dress impeccably well. They can often talk about baseball and other sports with the most dedicated fan and remain current in news, especially world affairs. All these enhance their sociability, which enables them to have successful careers, for, in most cases, the ability to get along with others is the most important ingredient of success.

I find that for adults, community service or *seva* is highly valued. It is not just a matter of giving money but actually doing work for the community, whether it be serving food in the temple or organizing activities. To get recognition, actual hands-on work must be done.

Benefits to India

The following section will highlight some of the contributions of the non-resident Indians in the U.S. The non-resident Indians' remittances are a tremendous asset. As one travels through the high emigration area of Gujarat, Kerala, and Punjab one is impressed with the prosperity of the regions. Not only have large amounts of capital come from abroad to invest in high technology, but new ideas, originating from abroad, have made their mark.

By the middle 1990's, many Indians had returned from abroad to set up industries or work for international companies establishing a presence in India. The bicultural knowledge and skills of these returnees have contributed to Hyderabad becoming the new Silicon Valley of the world. The impact, however, is not limited to Hyderabad, it can also be seen in Bombay, Calcutta, and Delhi as well as well as Punjab's agriculturally prosperous Doab region.

Asian Indians have also worked hard to promote an understanding of their motherland in the United States. Their efforts are paying off as the relation between India and the United States are improving. But probably the biggest contribution has been the enrichment of countless lives in both the United States and India.

Conclusion

As can be seen from the above, the Asian Indian community not only has an outstandingly rich and interesting story to tell, their contribution to American society has also been rich and varied. As Asian Indians are the fastest growing ethnic community and projections predict this trend will continue, both the United States and India will benefit from this cadre of hard working and entrepreneurial people, whose loyalties are to both the United States and India.

End Notes

[1] These are the results of a 1992 survey of 5,000 Asian American adults in California, only the responses of Asian Indians is recorded here.

Works Cited

Ballard, R.. 1983. The Context and Consequences of Migration: Jullundur and Mirpur Compapred. *New Community*, Vol 11, No.4.

Clark, C., Ceri Peach & Steven Vertovec. 1990. *South Asians Overseas: Migration and Ethnicity*. Cambridge, New York, Port Chester & Sydney: Cambridge University Press.

Dumont, L. 1966. *Homo Hierarchicus: The Caste System and Its Implications*. London: Weidenfeld and Nicolson.

Gall, S. B. and T. Gall, eds. 1993. Statistical Record of Asian Americans. Detroit, Washington, London: Gale Research Inc.

Helweg, A.W. 1984. Emigration and Return—Ramifications for India." *Population Review*, XXVIII, 1 & 2:45-57.

_____________. 1986. "The Indian Diaspora: Influence on International Relations. In *Modern Diasporas in International Politics*. Gabriel Sheffer, ed., London & Sydney: Croom Helm.

_____________. 1986a *Sikhs in England*: Second Edition. Delhi: Oxford University Press.

_____________. 1988. "Emigration and National Security: Ramifications for India." In *Asian Security Issues: National Systems and International Relations*. Lawrence Zeiring and David Dickason, Kalamazoo:An Asian Forum Publication.

_____________. 1989. "Sikh Politics in India: The Emigrant Factor." *In The Sikh Diaspora*. N. Gerald Barrier and Verne Dusenbery, eds., Delhi: Manohar and Columbia: South Asia Publications.

______________. 1996. "The Immigration Act of 1917: The Asian Exclusion Act." In Asian Americans and Congress: A Documentary History. Hyung-Chan Kim. ed., Westport, London: Greenwnood Press.

Helweg, A. W. and U. M. Helweg. 1990. *An Immigrant Success Story*: East Indians in America. Philadelphia: University of Pennsylvania Press.

Kroeber, A. L. and T. Parsons. 1958. The Concepts of Cultural and Social Systems. *American Sociological Review*. XXIII.5:582-583.

La Brack, B. 1987. "Overseas Sikhs and the Economy of Punjab. In Punjab in Perspective: Proceedings of the Research Committee on Punjab Conference, 1987. South Asia Series: Occasional Paper No. 39. Surjit Dulai and Arthur Helweg, eds., East Lansing: Asian Studies Center, Michigan State University.

____________. 1989. "The New Patrons: Sikhs Overseas." In The Sikh Diaspora. N. Gerald Barrier and Verne Dusenbery, eds., Delhi: Manohar and Columbia : South Asia Publications

Leonard, K. I. 1992. *Making Ethnic Choices: California's Punjabi Mexican Americans*. Philadelphia: Temple University Press.

Mazumdar, S. 1995. Asian Indians in the United States. In *The Asian American Encyclopedia*, Vol 1. Franklin Ng, ed., New York, London, Toronto: Marshall Cavendish.

Mogelonsky, M. 1995. Asian-Indians in America. *American Demographics*. August.

Rangaswamy, P. I. 1996. The Imperatives of Choice and Change: Post-1965 Immigrants from India in Metropolitan Chicago. Ph.D. Thesis. Chicago: University of Illinois at Chicago.

Tinker, H. 1974. *A New System of Slavery: The Export of Indian Labour Overseas* 1830-1920. London: Oxford University Press for the Institute of Race Relations.

______________. 1976. *Separate and Unequal*. London: C. Hurst.

______________. 1977. *The Banyan Tree: Overseas Emigrants from India, Pakistan and Bangladesh*. Oxford: Oxford University Press.

US Census Bureau. 1980. *We, the Asian and Pacific Islander Americans.*: Washington, D.C: US Government Printing Office.

US Census Bureau. 1993. *We, the American Asians*. Washsington, D.C.: US Government Printing Office.

Table 9: Median Household Income of Immigrants (By Rank)

Country	*Dollar Amount*
India	$48,320
Philippines	$45,419
Japan	$34,999
United Kingdom	$34,339
Guyana	$34,243
U.S. Born	$30,176
Foreign Born	$28,314

Based on U.S. Census

Table 10: Hold Bachelor's Degrees or Higher (By Rank).

Country	*Percentage*
India	64.9%
Philippines	43.0%
Japan	35.0%
Korea	34.4%
France	31.9%
China	30.9%
Foreign Born	20.4%
U.S. Born	20.3%

Based on U.S. Census

Table 11: Indian Immigrantion to the United States of America.

Year	*Immigrants*
1901-1910	4713
1911-1920	2082
1921-1930	1886
1931-1940	496
1941-1950	1761
1951-1960	1973
1961-1970	30461
1971-1980	172104
1981-1990	267838

Based on U.S. Census

Table 12: Select Characteristics of Asian Indians in the United States.

	1980	*1990*
Total Persons	387,223	815,447
Percent of U.S. total in 1990		.33
Percent increase in population 1980-		95.2
Percent of Asian and Pacific Islander total,		11
Age and Sex	*1980*	*1990*
Percent under 5 years old	11.1	8.5
Percent 18 years old and over	69.9	70.04
Percent 65 years old and over	8.0	2.8
Median age	29.6	28.9
Males per 100 females	99.8	116.0
Type of Family	*1980*	*1990*
Families	97,596	193,379
Married couple families by percent	91.0	89.2
Female householder, no husband	5.7	5.2
Male householder, no wife present	3.4	5.6
Persons per family, average	3.45	3.83
Nativity, Citizenship and Language	*1980*	*1990*
Percent foreign born	70.4	75.4
Percent naturalized citizen	39.6	34.3
Percent of persons 5 years and older who use a language other than English at home	68.9	77.8
Educational Attainment	*1980*	*1990*
Persons 25 years old and over	238,684	464,190
Percent high school graduates	80.1	84.7
Percent 4 or more years of	51.9	58.1
Labor Force Status	*1980*	*1990*
Persons 16 years old and over	278,359	576,157
Labor force	182,137	416,404
Percent in labor force	65.4	72.3
Percent unemployed	5.8	5.6

Table 12: continued.

Occupation	*1980*	*1990*
Employed persons 16 years old and over	139,653	260,532
Managerial and Professional specialty by	48.5	43.6
Technical sales and administrative support	28.0	43.6
Service	7.8	8.1
Farming, forestry and fishing	0.9	0.6
Precision production, craft and repair	5.2	5.2
Operators, fabricators and laborers	9.5	17.8
Workers in Family	*1979*	*1989*
Families	97,596	192,83.6
Number of workers, in percent	6.2	2.8
1 worker	35.6	27.7
2 workers	48.7	51.8
3 or more workers	9.5	17.8
Income	*1979*	*1989*
Median family (U.S. Dollars)	24,993	49,309
Median household (U.S. Dollars)	20,598	44,696
Male 15 years and over (U.S. Dollars)	15,799	
Female, 15 years and over (U.S. Dollars)	6,073	
per capita (U.S. Dollars)	8,667	17,777
Income Below Poverty Level	*1979*	*1989*
Families	7,188	13,964
Percent	7.4	7.4
Persons in poverty	29,339	74,972
Percent	10.6	9.7

Sources: Gall and Gall (1993), U.S. Census Bureau (1980, 1993) and Rangaswamy (1996)

Table 13: Ten U.S. States with Highest Asian Indian Population

Rank	*State*	*Population: 1980*	*Population: 1990*	*Percent change*
1	California	59,774	159,973	167.6
2	New York	67,636	140,985	108.4
3	New Jersey	30,684	79,440	158.9
4	Illinois	37,438	64,200	71.5
5	Texas	23,395	55,795	138.50
6	Florida	11,039	31,457	185.0
7	Pennsylvania	17,230	28,396	64.8
8	Maryland	13,788	28,330	105.5
9	Michigan	15,363	23,845	55.20
10	Ohio	13,602	20,848	53.30
	Total U.S.	387,223	815,447	110.6

Source: Gall and Gall (1993: 689).

Table 14: Political participation of Asian Indians in the U.S.

	Strong Democrat	*Democrat*	*Strong Republican*	*Republican*	*Independent*
Party affiliation	3.8	52.5	--	23.8	20.0
	Most of the time	*Some of the time*	*Now & then*	*Never*	
Follow events in politics and government	62.5	32.5	5.0	--	
	Republican	*Democrat*	*Neither*	*Both*	*Don't Know*
Which political party best organizes & coordinates Asian Americans?	7.5	31.3	36.3	--	--
Which political party cares about Asian Americans?	5.0	56.3	27.5	1.3	10.0
	Very conservative	*Somewhat conservative*	*Middle of the road*	*Somewhat liberal*	*Very liberal*
Liberal or conservative?	--	20.0	47.5	27.5	5.0
	More involved	*About the same*	*Less involved*	*Don't know*	
Should the U.S. be involved with Asia?	66.3	10.0	12.5	11.3	

Source: Gall and Gall (1993).

Table 15: Receipts of Asian Firms in U.S. (1992).

Country	*(Billions of $)*
India	19.3
Chinese	30.5
Japanese	13
Korean	16.8
Filipinos	4.5
Others	8.9

Source: National Bureau of Economic Research.

Table 16: Attitudes of East Indians in the United States

	Better	*Worse*	*Same*	*Don't know*	
Is race relations in U.S. getting better or worse?	2.5	50.0	35	8.6	
	Strongly Agree	*Agree*	*Disagree*	*Strongly Disagree*	*No Opinion*
U.S. is facing long-term economic decline.	36.3	56.3	2.5	0.0	12.9
Should raise taxes.	11.3	13.8	0.3	15	28.8
Should cut taxes	11.3	17.5	32.5	12.5	26.3
Federal government should cut spending	61.3	31.3	1.3	0.0	12.9
Government should not help minorities they should help themselves.	8.8	17.5	36.3	21.3	16.3
Government should help blacks and other minorities to improve their socio-economic position.	20.0	50.0	26.3	0.0	3.8
Asian Americans get their fair share?	0.0	36.3	40.0	13.8	10.0
	Yes	*No*			
Do you care which party wins?	88.8	10.0			
Are you registered voter?	82.5	17.5			

Source: Gall and Gall (1993)

XII | Epilogue

Epilogue

This Time, A Tryst with Technology

V.S. Arunachalam

Even before Independence, India sustained a small and vibrant scientific community with few, but outstanding contributions to its credit. This was managed in spite of abject poverty and widespread illiteracy that discouraged education of any kind, let alone advanced studies in science and technology. Our people might have missed the Industrial Revolution and its economic and social consequences, but not the revolutionary changes that were then taking place in science. Thus, in August 1947, a newly independent India inherited a science community to work with. New laboratories were built, new science departments of the government formed and also commissions to harness the power of atom and space. The government of the day came out with innovations to free science organizations from the rigid and crippling bureaucratic rules and procedures that were then the norm. As though to underline the importance of science further, Prime Minister Nehru kept the portfolio of science with himself and also persuaded the parliament to pass the Science Policy Resolution, a utopian document with few parallels in the history of state and science. Much later, his daughter Srimati Indira Gandhi would also release a similar Technology Policy Statement of her government reiterating the commitment of the state to the pursuance of indigenous technology. With all this support, how have we done in the past fifty years?

Not bad at all, in technology, through our own assessment of success, at least until recently, seemed to be influenced more by the cold war politics and regional geopolitics of the past decades than by achievements that have helped the country to be economically and politically independent, and technologically relevant. India today is largely free of food imports. Thanks to the Green Revolution ushered in by agricultural scientists and farmers, the country has turned the begging bowl into a veritable bread basket. While more needs to be done—our yields are still some of the lowest in the world—the periodic bouts of scarcity and famine have been eliminated forever from the Indian landscape. The country has taken this achievement and similar successes in other areas of agriculture and animal husbandry so much for granted we do not recognize how close India came to becoming a 'failed state, dependent forever on food hand-outs from outside.

There are a few other tales of success, though not of this scale. India today routinely launches remote sensing satellites and will soon be launching on its own, geostationary communications and weather satellites, integrating India into one national village. The villages and towns are successfully connected by more than six million indigenously designed and manufactured C-DOT telephone exchange lines. Indian chemical and pharmaceutical industries now have their own product and process technologies, and are also becoming globally competitive. An Indian battle tank—currently rated as one of the best of its class—is entering into production. India was one of the earliest to build nuclear power reactors and also has indigenously designed successful, surface-to-surface missile.

And in higher technical education, the country has done remarkably well. The Indian institutes of technology are some of the world's best educational institutions of higher learning. Taken together with a few other universities, they provide the Indian youth with the very best engineering education that one could aspire for, and remain mercifully free from political interference and scandals. India, and some would say even the world, stands enriched with a galaxy of outstanding Indian engineers. Very few countries can boast of similar achievements in education.

In spite of this enumeration, there is a lingering feeling of unease among many of us that somehow technology should have served us better. The quality of life of our people should have improved further, the country should have been economically better off, and India should have become an attractive place to live. Strategically, the country should have been seen to be stronger without evoking doubts or concerns from others. This feeling of unease is becoming more frequent when we see on television how better off people are in the West or, for that matter, in East Asia.

Why is this so? How have the people of East Asia done better, in spite of not with a galaxy of scientists and technologists as India did fifty years ago? No two economist would agrees on the origins of inflation or on an ideal policy for taxation, but when it comes to growth through technology, they would all unanimously insist on the necessity for mass education. The technology engine works efficiently only ,when people are better educated, and becomes inefficient and even fails to deliver when people are illiterate. A smaller number of Ph.D.s and B.E.s do not seem to matter as a very large number of high school graduates. Illiteracy is too heavy a burden for the nation to carry.

Only now, with the black-outs and brownouts, choking of roads, fouling of air and jamming of telephones, the country is conscious of its decaying and over-stretched turn. India failed to extend its earlier achievements in building the infrastructure for irrigation to other areas. For many years, building better highways or introducing more telephones were seen as pandering to the needs of the rich that have cars and could afford the costly phones. The government therefore mandated other priorities to the public sector.

Ironically, the United States, the bastion of free enterprise, did exactly the opposite. President Roosevelt, citing a strategic necessity of transporting troops across the American continent initiated a national program of highways that serves that country well. Again, fearing that its Eastern seaports could be blockaded, government laid gas and oil pipelines from the Gulf of Mexico to the industrial areas of the East. More recently, the US defense research establishment and scientific institutions built a technology demonstration network for data communication that has become backbone for interact. Among the other ingredients of Information Technology, this network provides the US its unquestionable lead.

What then should we do? We must make illiteracy eradication as the only major national program. Schools should proliferate, more teachers should be trained and paid better and all new tools of technology for education should be acquired and also developed. If India could eradicate small-pox within eighteen months—much shorter than anticipated by many in the West—there is no reason why the country should not enter the next millennia, all literate.

We must build, using all available resources, a moderm infrastructure for the country. There is also an urgency here. The world is in the midst of a new technological revolution that rivals the industrial revolution of the last two centuries. Information Technology, is fast altering the way people live, learn, work and entertain. The ubiquitous silicon chip and its partner, the optical fiber, is fast transforming the total infrastructural and economic landscape. The power of this technology is doubling every year and the price, continues to fall. Already, the Indian youth is capitalizing on this opportunity writing software, the language of these machines. This trade is worth $1 billion for us, though the world market is huge, over $300 billion, and growing rapidly. With a better infrastructure and support from our government—remember, the Internet would not exist without the American government support— that does not wait for the demand to build, instead provides a network, our business will be worth $20 billion in a few years. India cannot afford to miss, yet once more, another industrial revolution

For a country of our size and history, technology should enable the country to become strong industrially and militarily. The world continues to be a dangerous place and we must be ever vigilant. Security does not mean mere import of weapons from outside. With improving international relations, instead of cutting imports, we seem to be adding more countries to a large list of countries we have for buying weapons! Instead, we must improve our manufacturing and industrial technologies to efficiently produce what our technologists develop. While the former Soviet Union and present day Russia remains a reliable supplier of weapons, they have failed singularly to transfer industrial technologies and help India build an efficient industrial infrastructure. We must correct this debilitating deficiency and strive to develop a state-of-the-art industrial base that will serve us well, both in times of peace and war. Defense and industrial development should be partners and not contestants.

Strategic Strength emanates from a better indent, technological and economic infrastructure than our protestations of imagined capability and anger about systems unavailable to us. Even developed countries have difficulties among themselves in trading military components. One has only to look at the travails of Japan when it started building its indigenous fighter. Our Space organization is showing how one could become self-reliant, in the midst of technology denials, without becoming xenophobic. This is an example worth emulating.

'Second only to life', the physicist Freeman Dyson wrote, 'God's gift to mankind is technology'. In the next fifty years, we should leverage this gift to build the India of our dreams.

Contributors

U. R. Anantha Murthy is a creative writer in Kannaḍa, thinker, critic, and editor. He has published five collections of short stories, four volumes of literary criticism, and four novels. A number of his fictional writings, including his novel *Samskara,* have been made into award-winning films. *Samskara* has been translated into major Indian and European languages, including English. Anantha Murthy has served as a professor of English at Mysore University and as Vice-Chancellor of Bharati University, Kerala. He has taught in several universities in the U. S. A. He was given the Gyanapitha Award, India's most prestigious literary prize, in 1994. He is currently president of the Sahitya Academy, India's National Academy of Letters.

V.S. Arunachalam was Scientific Advisor to the Defense Minister of India for more than ten years, serving five prime ministers and ten defense ministers. He also advised the Indian government on the definition, assessment and review of several major technological and societal programs of the country. Dr. Arunachalam's contribution include both scientific and applied areas. He is the Past President of the Indian National Academy of Engineering and the Indian Institute of Metals and the Aeronautical Society of India. He is also a fellow of the Indian National Science Academy, the Indian Academy of Sciences, and in the Royal Academy of Engineering, U.K. Among Dr. Arunachalam's numerous awards and honors are Padma Vibhushan, the highest civilian honor given by the President of India in 1990, Padma Bhushan in 1985, and the Bhatnagar Prize. Dr. Arunachalam is now a Distinguished Services Professor in the Departments of Engineering and Public Policy, Material Science and Engineering and the Robotics Institute of Carnegie Mellon University, Pittsburgh, Pennsylvania.

Sabyasachi Bhattacharya is former Vice-Chancellor of Vishwa Bharati University (Shanti Niketan) and is currently a professor in the Center for Historical Studies, Jawaharal Nehru University, New Delhi. He has taught at various universities in India and abroad, including Universities of Chicago, Oxford, and the Colegio de Mexico. He has edited several volumes including *Situating Indian history* (with Romila Thapar, 1986), *Essays in modern Indian economic history* (with Pietro Redondi, 1987), *The south Indian economy* (with G.N. Rao et. al., 1991), and *Tagore-Gandhi correspondence* (forthcoming).

Christopher Key Chapple is professor of Theological Studies and the director of Asian and Pacific Studies at Loyola Marymount Unviersity in Los Angeles. Formerly assistant director of Advanced Studies of World Religion at the State University of New York at Stony Brook, he has authored many books and articles on Indic religions. His books include *Nonviolence to animals, earth, and self in Asian traditions* (1993), and *Karma and creativity* (1986).

Georg Feuerstein is founding director of the Yoga Research Center in Lower Lake, California. His publications include twenty-five books and over twenty edited volumes, numerous articles and book reviews. Among his more important works are *The philosophy of classical Yoga (1980), Yoga: The technology of ecstasy (1989)* and *The Shambala encyclopedia of Yoga (1997).*

Shanta Gokhale is arts editor of the *Times of India,* Bombay. She has translated many plays from Marathi into English and her novel *Rita Welinker*, won an Indian national award. Her play *Avinash* has been produced in the original Marathi and in other Indian languages. Gokhale has just completed a major study of Marathi theater, to be published by Seagull Books, Calcutta.

Lallanji Gopal is an editorial fellow on the project of History of Indian Science, Philosophy, and Culture, of the Indian Council for Philosophical Research. He has been rector and acting vice-chancellor of Benares Hindu University, Benares, and director of the Center for Advanced Study of Philosophy. He has authored fifteen books and numerous articles, and has edited twenty volumes.

Satish Grover is professor and head at the School of Planning and Architecture in New Delhi. He has served at universities of Punjab, Ahmedabad, and Bomby, as well as Indian Institutes of Technology at Delhi and Kharagpur. He is one of the founders of Ansal groups' Sushant school of Art and Architecture, Gurgaon, and a member of its governing board. He is also one of the founding members of the magazine *Architecture plus design*. His publications include *Architecture of India: Buddhist and Hindu, and Islamic* are widely usedas basic texts in architecture schools.

Irfan Habib, eduated at Aligarh and Oxford, retired as professor of History from Aligarh Muslim University. He served as the chairman of Indian Council of Historical Research (1986-1993), and as president of Indian History Congress, he has given the Radhakrishnan lectures at Oxford University. He has edited monographs, books, and papers on the history of Indian technology, economic history and historical geography of India. His publications include *Agrarian system of Mughal empire* (1963), *Atlas of the Mughal empire* (1982), and *Essays on Indian history* (1994).

Robert L. Hardgrave, Jr., is Temple professor of Humanities in Government and Asian Studies at the University of Texas at Austin. He received his Ph.D. from the University of Chicago in 1966, and is a specialist on India's domestic politics and international relations. In addition to scholarly papers, he has published books including *The Dravidian movement, The Nadars of Tamilnad, Essays in the political sociology of South India, India: Prospects for political stability,* and *India: Government and politics in a developing nation.* He has served as a consultant on South Asia for the U.S. Department of State and is the senior adviser for South Asia for Political Risk Services, Inc.

Arthur W. Helweg is professor of Anthropology at Western Michigan University, U.S.A. He has done anthropological research regarding development in India and Pakistan. He has also done field research in Australia, England, Romania, and the United States. He has authored over fifty publications including *Sikhs in England* (1986), *Punjab in perspective* (co-edited with Surjit Dulai, 1987), and *East Indians in the US: An immigrant success story* (co-authored with Usha Helweg, 1990). Currently, he is editing a volume on *Ethnic groups in Michigan,* to be published by University of Michigan Press.

Braj B. Kachru is professor of Linguistics in the Center for Advanced Study and Jubilee Professor of Liberal Arts and Sciences at the University of Illinois at Urbana-Champaign, USA. He is founder and coeditor of the journal *World Englishes*, associate editor of *The Oxford companion to the English language*, and series editor of *English in the global context.* He is the past president of the American Association for Applied Linguistics (1984) and president of the International Association for World Englishes (1997-1999). His areas of research include World Englishes, language in society, and South Asian languages and literatures. Among his publications are *The Indianization of English* (1983), *The alchemy of English* (1986), *The other tongue* (1992). Currently, he is director of the Center for Advanced Study at the University of Illinois.

Yamuna Kachru is professor of Linguistics at the University of Illinois at Urbana-Champaign. Her research areas include syntax, semantics, and pragmatics of South Asian languages, especially Hindi; discourse analysis; and the interface of culture and language. She has published scholarly papers, monographs, and edited several books. In addition, she has authored several books including *Aspects of Hindi grammar* and *Hindi ka samsamayik vyakaran.*

Subhash C. Kak is professor of Electrical and Computer Engineering at Lousiana State University, Baton Rouge. He has published several scholarly articles on Vedic science and Indology. His books include *The nature of physical reality* (1986), *Patanjali and cognitive science* (1987), *India at century's end: essays on history and politics* (1994), *The astronomical code of the Rgveda* (1994), and *In search of the cradle of civilization: new light on ancient India* (1995), co-authored with G. Feurestein and D. Frawley.

Girish Karnad is a playwright, director, actor, Rhodes scholar, and a former chairman of the Central Sangeet Natak Akademi. He was also a Homi Bhabha fellow and wrote several plays which were performed in India and the United States. He received the Sangeet Natak Akademi Award and the Natya Sangha Award for his play *Hayavadana* (1971).

Hiremagalur Keshavan is a Distinguished Professor emeritus at the University of Waterloo. He received his Ph.D. in Electrical Engineering from the Universities of Illinois and Michigan State in the U.S.A. During his career he has served as chairman of the department of Electrical Engineering at the University of Waterloo, Ontario, Canada, and later as the founding chairman of the department of Systems Design Engineering at the same university. His recent book, *Science and Mysticism: the Essence of Vedic Philosophy* presents a global view of vedic philosophy from the insights that science provides.

Keralapura Krishnamoorthy (1923-1997) retired as Professor and Head of the department of Sanskrit at Karnatak University, Dharwar. He has published extensively on Sanskrit literature and aesthetics. His publications include critical editions of *Vakroktijivitam* (1977), *Dhvanyaloka* (1982), *Natyasastra* (1982); monographs on *Kalidasa* (1992)and *Bana* (1977); and collections of studies, *Some thoughts on Indian aesthetics (1968)*, *Essays in Sanskrit criticism* (1974) and *Indian literary theories* (1995). His book *Dhvanyaloka and its critics* is widely acclaimed. We are note with sadness that Professor Krishnamoorthy passed away a few days before this volume went to press.

Nirmal K. Mattoo graduated with a degree in Medicine from Delhi and specialized in the field of Nephrology in the United States. He is chief of the Nephrology division in several hospitals in the New York metropolitan area and has published in the field. He has a collection of Gandhara and Kushana sculptures, bronzes from Chola, Vijaynagar, and Kashmir, and Jamawar shawls from Kashmir. He is currently National President of the Association of Indians in America.

Sheila McDonough is professor of Religion at Concordia Univeristy, Montreal, Canada. She is a graduate of the Islamic Studies program at McGill University. She taught for three years at Kinnard College (Pakistan), and has also served as the director of Shastri Foundation for Indo-Canadian Studies (New Delhi). She has published scholarly articles in journals. Her books include *Gandhi's responses to Islam* (1994), and *Muslim ethics and modernity* (1984).

M. A. Pai received his Ph.D. from the University of California at Berkeley in 1961. Prior to coming to the US, he was on the faculty of the Indian Institute of Technology, Kanpur, from 1963-1981, during which time he held several administrative positions including dean of research and development (1976-1978). He has published research papers in the area of power systems and has authored five books. He received the Bhatnagar award for research in Engineering Sciences (1974) from the C.S.I.R. Currently, he is professor of Electrical and Computer Engineering at the University of Illinois at Urbana-Champaign.

Rajeshwari V. Pandharipande is professor of Religious Studies, Linguistics and Comparative Literature at University of Illinois at Urbana-Champaign. Apart from articles on Hindi and Marathi syntax and semantics, she has also authored four books including *The Eternal self and the cycles of samsara: Introduction to Asian mythology and religion* (1990) and *Grammar of Marathi* (1997).

R. Parthasarathy is a poet, translator, critic and editor. He is director of the program in Asian Studies at Skidmore College in New York. He has translated, authored and edited several works and received an award from the Sahitya Akademi and other associations for the translation of the ancient Tamil epic *The tale of an anklet.*

Jose Pereira received his Ph.D. in Ancient Indian History and Culture from the University of Bombay (1959). He was a visiting professor at Higher Institute of Overseas Studies, Lisbon, Portugal (1959-1960), research fellow in the history of Indian art at the University of London (1962-1966), and research associate in the history of Indian art at the American academy of Benaras, Varanasi (1967-69). Currently, he is professor of Theology at Fordham University, New York. His books include *Hindu theology* (1976), *Monolithic Jinas: the iconography of the Jain temples of Ellora* (1979), *Islamic sacred architecture: A stylistic history,* and *Baroque India* (to be published by the Indira Gandhi National Center for the Arts, forthcoming).

Sita Anantha Raman received her Ph.D. from the University of California at Los Angeles. She currently teaches South and Southeast Asian history at Santa Clara University, California. Her doctoral dissertation focuses on women's education and social reform in Tamil Nadu (1870-1930). She has received a Fulbright fellowship (1995) to study the education of Indians in colonial Trinidad. Among her publications is *Getting girls to school* (1996).

Nalini Rao is curator for Asian art at Amarillo museum of art, Texas. She holds a doctorate in ancient history and archaeology from Mysore University and in art history from the University of California at Los Angeles. She specializes in the field of early and medieval Indian and southeast Asian sculpture and architecture, and her interdisciplinary research includes Hindu (especially Vijayanagara) kingship and polity, urban planning, portraiture, monasticism, and ritual.

S.R. Rao has served as superintendent of archaeology of several circles in India, and is an emeritus scientist for marine archeology in the National Institute of Oceanography, Goa. He has discovered fifty ancient Indian sites, including Lothal and the underwater city of Dwarka (Bet-Dwarka). He has published on ancient Indian history, culture, and the Indus script. He was awarded the Jawaharlal Nehru Fellowship and World Ship Award for individual excellence in marine archeology and authored books, including *Lothal and the Indus civilization* and *The decipherment of the Indus script.*

K.L. Sheshagiri Rao is professor of Religious Studies at the University of Virginia (1971-1995), and currently professor emeritus. He received a Fulbright grant and a fellowship of the Center for the Study of World Religions (Harvard University) where he completed his Ph.D. His area of specialization is Indic religions, Gandhian studies, and inter-religious dialog. He is the author of several books, including *The concept of Srddha in early Sanskrit literature, Mahatma Gandhi and C.F. Andrews: A study in Hindu-Christian dialogue, Mahatma Gandhi and comparative religion, The concept of love in world religions, World religions and human responsibility: a Gandhian perspective.*

R. Sathyanarayana specializes in Chemistry and Music. He has worked on several committees and panels for All India Radio and other prominent organizations. He has received numerous awards including the Karnataka State Rajyotsava Award, Rashtrabhooshana, and Sangeeta Kalarathna. He has authored and translated numerous volumes on music. He is currently the president of the Indian Music Congress.

Arvind Sharma is Birks professor of Comparative Religion, faculty of Religious Studies, McGill University, Montreal, Canada. He has taught at several universities, including the University of Sydney. He is author of several books and articles, which include *The philosophy of religion: A Buddhist perspective*, *The Hindu Gita*, and *Hinduism for our times* (Oxford 1996).

R. C. Sharma is the director of Bharat Kala Bhavan and Professor of museology and Art at Benares Hindu University. He has also served as Director General/ Vice-Chancellor, National Museum Institute, New Delhi; president, Museum Association of India; director U.P. State Archeology, and Indian Museum, Calcutta. He has authored several books on Indian art including *Mathura museum and art*, *Gandhara*, *Albums on Mathura*, *Krishna theme in miniatures of Kangra kalam*, and *Buddhist art of Mathura.*

Alan Roland is a practicing psychoanalyst in New York. He is on the faculty of the National Psychological Association for Psychoanalysis and has authored several works including *In search of self in India and Japan* (Princeton, 1989) and *Cross-Cultural Psychoanalysis* (Routledge 1997).

Kamal K. Sridhar, is associate professor of Linguistics and director of the ESL program at the State University of New York at Stony Brook. Her research concerns issues in bilingualism, including non-native varieties of English, language policy and planning, language maintenance, and sociolinguistic patterns of bilingual language use. She has published scholarly papers on these topics. Her book *English in Indian bilingualism* was published in 1989.

S. N. Sridhar is professor of Linguistics and director of Center for India Studies, State Univesity of New York at Stony Brook. His research concerns Indian linguistics, bilingualism, second language acquisition, sociolinguistics and world varieties of English. In addition to many papers and several books, his publications include *Cognition and sentence production: A cross-linguistic study* (Springer, 1989), *Kannada: A descriptive grammar* (Routledge, 1990), and *Indina Kannada: Racane mattu Balake* [Contemporary Kannada: Structure and Functions] (Kannada University 1995). He was twice senior research fellow of the American Institute of Indian Studies. He has also been designated senior/superior Indologist by the National Endowment for the Humanities, USA.

M.N. Srinivas was twice fellow at the Center for Advanced Studies for Behavioral Sciences at Stanford University. He is an honorary member of the American Philosophical Society (Philadelphia), the American. Society of Arts and Sciences (Boston), an Honorary Fellow of Royal Anthropological Society (London), as well as Fellow of the British Academy. He was awarded the Padmabhusan in 1976. He has authored many books, including*Social change in modern India* (Berkeley 1966) and the *Remembered village* (Berkeley 1977). He has taught at Oxford, Manchester, Cornell, Santa Cruise, and Delhi universities and co-founded the Institute for Social and Economic Change in Bangalore. He is currently JRD Tata Visiting Professor at the National Institute of Advanced Studies in Bangalore.

T. N. Srinivasan is Samuel C. Park, Jr., Professor of Economics and director of Economic Growth Center at Yale University. He has taught at the universities of Minnesota, Stanford, and M.I.T., among others. He has worked extensively with the special advisor World Bank as to its Development Research Center. He has published widely on international trade and development, agricultural economics, and microeconomic theory. He has co-edited *The Handbook of Developmental Economics* (3 vols.), and edited numerous books, including *Rural Poverty in South Asia*, *Poverty and Income distribution in India* and *Population, Food, and Rural Development*; he has co-authored *Lectures on International Trade*; *India's Economic Reforms* and other works; he is the Fellow of the Econometric Society of India and the American Academy of Arts and Sciences.

Prakash Tandon has wide experience in industry, banking, management, and economic research. He has been chairman of Hindustan Lever, State Trading Corporation, Punjab National Bank, Indian Institute of Management, (Ahmedabad), and a number of government committees. He was also a director of Reserve bank, IDBI, Hindustan Steel, Food Corporation of India, Hindustan Aeronautics, and Heavy Engineering. He has been director general and president of National Council of Applied Economic Research. He is author of six books on Punjab, banking, and management, including *The Punjabi century*.

INDEX

A

abhaya: 516
Abhimanyu: 707
Abhinava Gupta: 223
academic writing: 654-657
Acosmic Ideal: 166
acosmic view: 171
activism: 187
Actor at Work: 693, 706, 710
adāb arz: 646, 661
Advaita Vedānta: 263, 267, 272
aesthetic: 494, 509, 510
Affirmative Action: 313, 314
Affirmative action programs: 313 , 314
Afghan: 99
Agni: 158, 182
Agra: 88, 99, 100
Agra Bazaar: 708
Agricultural: 76, 88-89, 104, 107, 108, 110, 112, 425, 437, 438, 442-443, 446, 450, 453, 455-460, 462, 464, 479, 635, 834
agricultural sector: 446, 464
ahaṃ-kāra: 172, 176-178
ahimsā: 780
Ahmedabad School: 550
Aihole: 526, 531-533
Air India: 460
Aitareya Āraṇyaka: 165
Ajanta: 61, 423, 498, 525-526, 827
Akali Dal: 333
Akashvani: 561
Akbar: 73-74, 87, 89, 93-94, 96-100, 102, 385, 823, 828
Al-Biruni: 77, 848-849
Ala-ud-din: 70
Alekar, Satish: 696-697
Alexander: 36, 57-58, 60, 486, 792, 826-827
All India Radio: 561
All-India Congress committee: 789
Amaravati: 509, 514, 526
Ambedkar: 214
Andha Yug: 709
Andhra Pradesh: 60, 69, 89, 110, 260, 302, 333-334, 456, 557, 574, 718, 735, 755
Angar: 691
Anglo-American: 653-654, 657, 661
aniconic symbols: 532
annamaya koṣa: 402
anthropology: 650, 849
Anti-dumping measures: 453
aparigraha: 780
apauruṣeya: 249
APEC: 454
apex central bank: 487
apūrva: 276
Arab: 65-66, 477, 835
Arab Invasion: 65
Arabhi: 758
Arabian: 478
Arabic: 48, 141, 214, 412, 422-423, 848-849, 851
Arabic numerals: 848
Aramaic: 512
Archaeological: 495, 520-521
Architects: 545, 548-552
Architecture: 51, 61, 72, 100-101, 199, 476, 491, 494, 496-497, 509-510, 512-513, 515, 520, 523-526, 528-529, 545-551
Ardhanārīśvara: 496
argumentation: 654-655, 657, 659-660
arhant: 617
Arjuna: 62, 187, 189-192, 195, 228, 243, 493, 535, 595, 818
art: 58, 60-61, 68, 70, 74, 76, 87, 101, 139, 143, 159, 164, 172, 234, 277, 348, 411, 479-480, 493-498, 509-521, 523-526, 528, 535, 550, 588, 590, 593, 600, 603-604, 640, 659, 673-674, 676, 706, 709, 711, 714, 716, 719, 725, 735-736, 746, 767, 771, 796, 804, 810-811, 821, 824, 827-828, 849
artha: 257, 259, 263, 494-496
Arthaśāstra: 42-43, 58-59, 61, 437, 439, 470, 474, 481, 483, 818, 826
artisan: 89, 91-92, 495
artisanal industries: 103, 108, 110-111
Aryabhata: 409, 411
Aryan: 49, 330, 376, 378-479, 435-436, 474, 479, 481, 556-557, 560, 571-572, 574, 580, 629, 659, 862, 865
Aryan Invasion: 49
ASEAN: 454
Asian Indian: 861-682, 881, 883-886, 888-891
Asian tradition: 657
Asiatic Society: 35, 101

B

C

D

E

F

G

H

I

J

K

L

M

N

O

P

Q

R

S

T

U

V

W

Y

Z

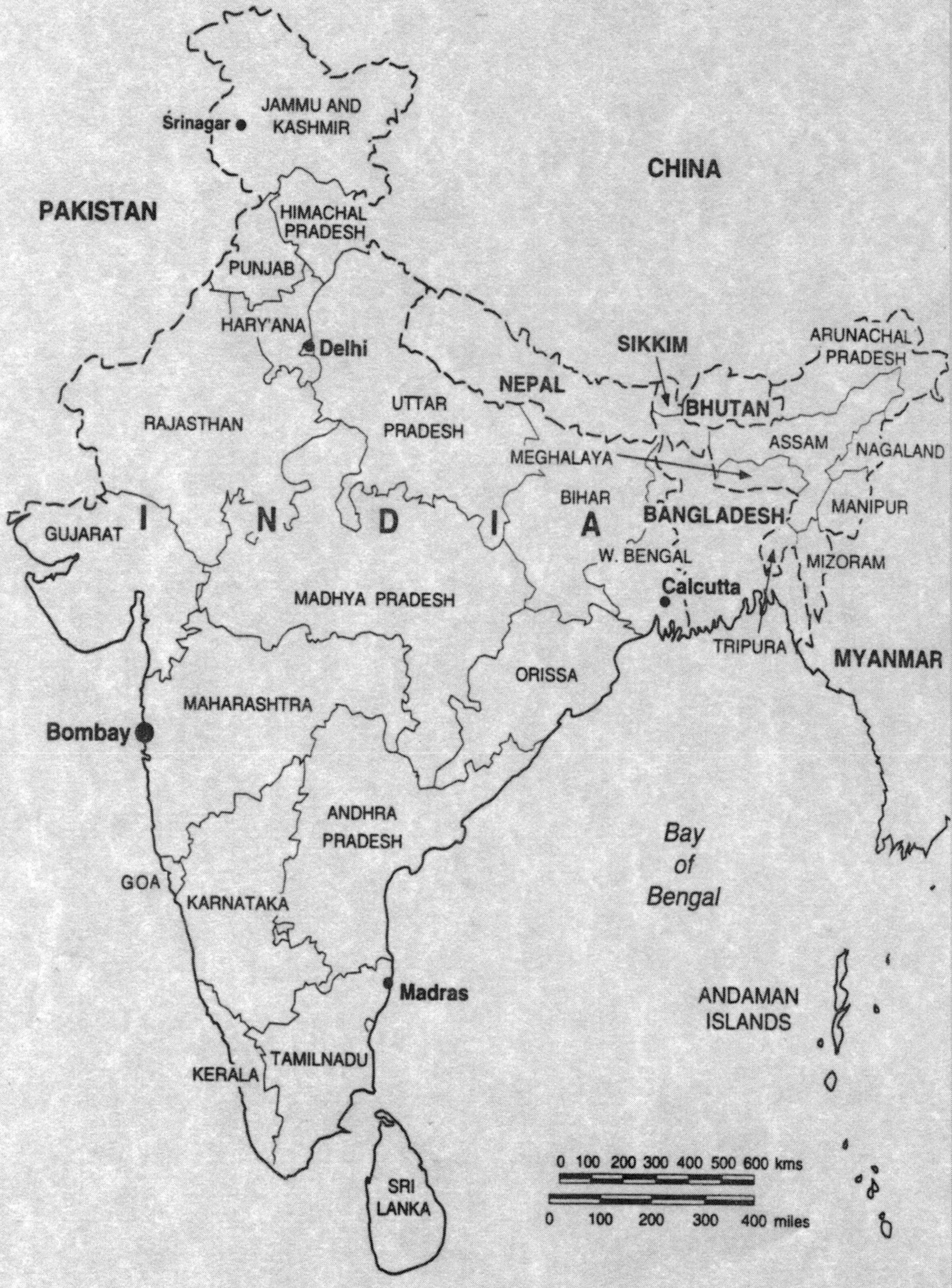

JAMMU AND KASHMIR
Śrinagar
CHINA
PAKISTAN
HIMACHAL PRADESH
PUNJAB
HARY'ANA
Delhi
SIKKIM
ARUNACHAL PRADESH
NEPAL
BHUTAN
RAJASTHAN
UTTAR PRADESH
ASSAM
NAGALAND
MEGHALAYA
BIHAR
MANIPUR
I N D I A
BANGLADESH
GUJARAT
W. BENGAL
MIZORAM
Calcutta
MADHYA PRADESH
TRIPURA
MYANMAR
ORISSA
MAHARASHTRA
Bombay
ANDHRA PRADESH
Bay of Bengal
GOA
KARNATAKA
Madras
ANDAMAN ISLANDS
TAMILNADU
KERALA
0 100 200 300 400 500 600 kms
SRI LANKA
0 100 200 300 400 miles

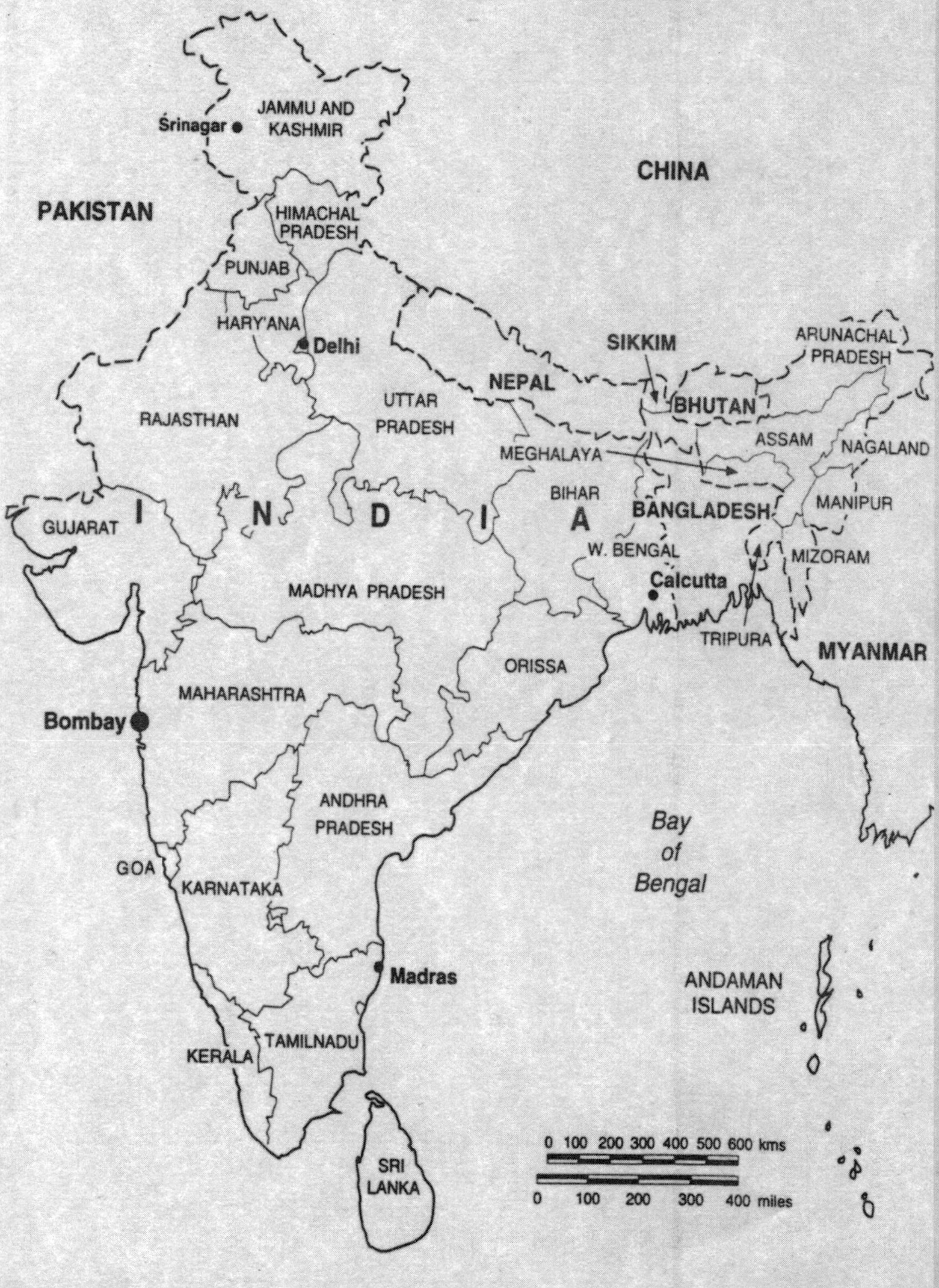

JAMMU AND KASHMIR
Śrinagar
CHINA
PAKISTAN
HIMACHAL PRADESH
PUNJAB
HARY'ANA
Delhi
SIKKIM
ARUNACHAL PRADESH
NEPAL
BHUTAN
RAJASTHAN
UTTAR PRADESH
ASSAM
NAGALAND
MEGHALAYA
BIHAR
MANIPUR
GUJARAT
I N D I A
BANGLADESH
W. BENGAL
MIZORAM
Calcutta
MADHYA PRADESH
TRIPURA
MYANMAR
ORISSA
MAHARASHTRA
Bombay
ANDHRA PRADESH
Bay of Bengal
GOA
KARNATAKA
Madras
ANDAMAN ISLANDS
TAMILNADU
KERALA
SRI LANKA
0 100 200 300 400 500 600 kms
0 100 200 300 400 miles